Blackstone's Statutes
Contract, Tort & Restitution

To Josephine

Blackstone's Statutes

Contract, Tort & Restitution

2006–2007

Seventeenth Edition

Edited by

F. D. Rose

MA, BCL, PhD, MA, of Gray's Inn, Barrister-at-Law
Professor of Commercial Law, University of Bristol

OXFORD
UNIVERSITY PRESS

Contents vii

PART II Proposed Statutes   421

PART III Statutory Instruments   494

ALPHABETICAL CONTENTS

EDITOR'S PREFACE

As in previous editions, this book sets out to present the principal legislative contributions to the law of contract, tort and restitution, together with a selection of specific provisions from more specialist legislation which affects the general law on civil liability and reveals something of its wider context.

It has always been intended that this book should include the core materials to be consulted by students of Contract, Restitution and Torts, a selection of other materials in the area of civil liability, and a few related regulatory and public law provisions. Case law and statute do not exist in isolation, any more than the three main subjects of this book do. They are all part of a dynamic legal architecture, combining elements of old and new, beautiful and ugly, awkward and useful. A citizen may prefer an area of outstanding natural beauty to an industrial estate or a plainly functional new hospital, but the modern landscape cannot be accurately recorded without noting all of its constituents or their different contributions.

When I began this series of statute books, nineteen years ago, this book was less than a third of the size it is now. One must have mixed views about the accretion of legislative material on what is still regarded as an essentially case law subject; but it is inescapable that the area of civil liability is under constant modification by the legislature and that the modern lawyer must be up to date, not only with new developments, but with the persistent revision of familiar legislation. A proper understanding of the law and how it is developing therefore means that an awareness of proposed and impending reforms, and of codes which influence the way in which the law operates in practice, are essential.

As a consequence of a growing number of interests with their own increasingly detailed rules, the law on civil liability inevitably overlaps with many other areas of law and it has been noticeable, on the initial compilation and annual revision of this collection of materials, how far this traditionally case law subject has been affected by a growing amount of specialist legislation. Detailed attention to such enactments is unlikely to be practicable or appropriate in most courses on civil liability and is more likely to occur in other, more public law orientated, courses. But it is a notable feature of the modern law of civil liability that the basic case law principles do not reveal the extent to which, in particular, potentially tortious conduct is legitimated and regulated by legislation. Moreover, modern statutes are increasingly likely to provide for the consequences of transgressions and contract failure; and there is a developing tendency to make criminal wrongdoing the subject of civil procedures. A brief selection of such materials is appropriate in a book of this nature.

The notable feature of this edition is the range and number of amendments to both central and more widespread components of the statutory elements of the law of Contract, Restitution and Torts. The Clean Neighbourhoods and Environmental Act 2005, the Constitutional Reform Act 2005 and the Equality Act 2006 have created ripples throughout this area and the General Product Safety Regulations 1994 have been replaced by new regulations in 2005. Changes have been made to the Damages (Scotland) Act 1976, the Sale of Goods Act 1979, the Supply of Goods and Services Act 1982, the Consumer Protection Act 1987, the Law of Property (Miscellaneous Provisions) Act 1989, the Environmental Protection Act 1990, the Value Added Tax Act 1994, the Damages Act 1996, the Defamation Act 1996, the Noise Act 1986, the Human Rights Act 1988, the Contracts (Rights against Third Parties) Act 1999, the Anti-social Behaviour Act 2003 and the Unfair Terms in Consumer Contracts Regulations 1999. Looking forward, the Compensation Bill 2006, currently before Parliament, is also included.

As in previous editions, in most cases the material is reproduced in its complete, most recent form, all amendments being incorporated within square brackets; occasional omissions are indicated by three dots. Supplementary notes and details of amending provisions, easily available elsewhere, are generally omitted for reasons of space.

As always, I gladly acknowledge the holders' rights in copyright materials. And I continue to be grateful for suggestions as to possible revisions of this collection of materials, whether for additions or deletions.

Francis Rose
7 June 2006

PART I

Statutes

Limitation Act 1623
(21 Jac. I, c. 16)

5 After judgment for defendant, etc., in trespas quare clausum fregit, upon disclaimer of defendant, etc., plaintiff barred of his action

And in all accions of trespas quare clausum fregit hereafter to be brought, wherein the defendant or defendants shall disclaime in his or their plea to make any title or claime to the land in which the trespasse is by the declaracion supposed to be done, and the trespas be by negligence, or involuntary, the defendant or defendants shalbe admitted to pleade a disclaymer, and that the trespas was by negligence, or involuntary, and a tender or offer of sufficient amends for such trespase before the accion brought, whereuppon or uppon some of them, the plaintiffe or plaintiffes shalbe enforced to joyne issue; and if the said issue be found for the defendant or defendants, or the plaintiffe or plaintiffes shalbe nonsuted, the plaintiffe or plaintiffes shalbe clearlie barred from the said accion or accions and all other suite concerning the same.

Statute of Frauds 1677
(29 Chas. II, c. 3)

4 No action against executors, etc. upon a special promise, or upon any agreement, or contract for sale of lands, etc. unless agreement, etc. be in writing and signed

[...] noe action shall be brought [...] whereby to charge the defendant upon any special promise to answere for the debt default or miscarriages of another person [...] unlesse the agreement upon which such action shall be brought or some memorandum or note thereof shall be in writeing and signed by the partie to be charged therewith or some other person thereunto by him lawfully authorised.

Fires Prevention (Metropolis) Act 1774
(14 Geo. III, c. 78)

86 No action to lie against a person where the fire accidentally begins

And [...] no action, suit or process whatever shall be had, maintained or prosecuted against any person in whose house, chamber, stable, barn or other building, or on whose estate any fire shall [...] accidentally begin, nor shall any recompence be made by such person for any damage suffered thereby, any law, usage or custom to the contrary notwithstanding; [...] provided that no contract or agreement made between landlord and tenant shall be hereby defeated or made void.

Libel Act 1792
(32 Geo. III, c. 60)

1   On the trial of an indictment for a libel the jury may give a general verdict upon the whole matter put in issue, and shall not be required by the court to find the defendant guilty merely on proof of the publication, and of the sense ascribed to it in the information

On every such trial the jury sworn to try the issue may give a general verdict of guilty or not guilty upon the whole matter put in issue upon such indictment or information, and shall not be required or directed by the court or judge before whom such indictment or information shall be tried to find the defendant or defendants guilty merely on the proof of the publication by such defendant or defendants of the paper charged to be a libel, and of the sense ascribed to the same in such indictment or information.

2   But the court shall give their opinion and directions on the matter in issue as in other criminal cases

Provided always, that on every such trial the court or judge before whom such indictment or information shall be tried shall, according to their or his discretion, give their or his opinion and directions to the jury on the matter in issue between the King and the defendant or defendants, in like manner as in other criminal cases.

Statute of Frauds Amendment Act 1828
(9 Geo. IV, c. 14)

6   Action not maintainable on representations of character, etc., unless they be in writing signed by the party chargeable

. . No action shall be brought whereby to charge any person upon or by reason of any representation or assurance made or given concerning or relating to the character, conduct, credit, ability, trade, or dealings of any other person, to the intent or purpose that such other person may obtain credit, money, or goods upon, unless such representation or assurance be made in writing, signed by the party to be charged therewith.

Parliamentary Papers Act 1840
(3 & 4 Vict., c. 9)

1   Proceedings, criminal or civil, against persons for publication of papers printed by order of Parliament, to be stayed upon delivery of a certificate and affidavit to the effect that such publication is by order of either House of Parliament

It shall and may be lawful for any person or persons who now is or are, or hereafter shall be, a defendant or defendants in any civil or criminal proceeding commenced or prosecuted in any manner soever, for or on account or in respect of the publication of any such report, paper, votes, or proceedings by such person or persons, or by his, her, or their servant or servants, by or under the authority of either House of Parliament, to bring before the court in which such proceeding shall have been or shall be so commenced or prosecuted, or before any judge of the same (if one of the superior courts at Westminster), first giving twenty-four hours notice of his intention so to do to the prosecutor or plaintiff in such proceeding, a certificate under the hand of [the Speaker of the House of Lords], or of the clerk of the Parliaments, or of the speaker of the House of Commons, or of the clerk of the same house, stating that the report, paper, votes, or proceedings, as the case may be, in respect whereof such civil or criminal proceeding shall have been commenced or prosecuted, was published by such person or persons, or by his, her, or their servant or servants, by order or under the authority of the House of Lords or of the House of Commons, as the case may be, together with an affidavit verifying such certificate; and such court or judge shall thereupon imme- diately stay such civil or criminal proceeding; and the same, and every writ or process issued therein, shall be and shall be deemed and taken to be finally put an end to, determined, and superseded by virtue of this Act.

2   Proceedings to be stayed when commenced in respect of a copy of an authen- ticated report, etc
In case of any civil or criminal proceeding hereafter to be commenced or prosecuted for or on account or in respect of the publication of any copy of such report, paper, votes, or pro- ceedings, it shall be lawful for the defendant or defendants at any stage of the proceedings to lay before the court or judge such report, paper, votes, or proceedings, and such copy, with an affidavit verifying such report, paper, votes, or proceedings, and the correctness of such copy, and the court or judge shall immediately stay such civil or criminal proceedings; and the same, and every writ or process issued therein, shall be and shall be deemed and taken to be finally put an end to, determined, and superseded by virtue of this Act.

3   In proceedings for printing any extract or abstract of a paper, it may be shewn that such extract was bona fide made
It shall be lawful in any civil or criminal proceeding to be commenced or prosecuted for printing any extract from or abstract of such report, paper, votes, or proceedings, to give in evidence [. . .] such report, paper, votes, or proceedings, and to show that such extract or abstract was published bona fide and without malice; and if such shall be the opinion of the jury, a verdict of not guilty shall be entered for the defendant or defendants.

4   Act not to affect the privileges of Parliament
Provided always, that nothing herein contained shall be deemed or taken, or held or con- strued, directly or indirectly, by implication or otherwise, to affect the privileges of Parlia- ment in any manner whatsoever.

Libel Act 1843
(6 & 7 Vict., c. 96)

1   Offer of an apology admissible in evidence of mitigation of damages in action for defamation
[. . .] In any action for defamation it shall be lawful for the defendant (after notice in writing of his intention so to do, duly given to the plaintiff at the time of filing or delivering the plea in such action,) to give in evidence, in mitigation of damages, that he made or offered an apology to the plaintiff for such defamation before the commencement of the action, or as soon afterwards as he had an opportunity of doing so, in case the action shall have been commenced before there was an opportunity of making or offering such apology.

2   In an action against a newspaper for libel, the defendant may plead that it was inserted without malice and without neglect and may pay money into court as amends
[. . .] In an action for libel contained in any public newspaper or other periodical publication it shall be competent to the defendant to plead that such libel was inserted in such newspaper or other periodical publication without actual malice, and without gross negligence, and that before the commencement of the action, or at the earliest opportunity afterwards, he inserted in such newspaper or other periodical publication a full apology for the said libel, or, if the newspaper or periodical publication in which the said libel appeared should be ordin- arily published at intervals exceeding one week, had offered to publish the said apology in

any newspaper or periodical publication to be selected by the plaintiff in such action; [. . .] and to such plea to such action it shall be competent to the plaintiff to reply generally, denying the whole of such plea.

Libel Act 1845
(8 & 9 Vict., c. 75)

2   Defendant not to file such plea without paying money into court by way of amends

[. . .] It shall not be competent to any defendant in such action, whether in England or Ireland, to file any such plea, without at the same time making a payment of money into court by way of amends [. . .], but every such plea so filed without payment of money into court shall be deemed a nullity, and may be treated as such by the plaintiff in the action.

Mercantile Law Amendment Act 1856
(19 & 20 Vict., c. 97)

3   Consideration for guarantee need not appear in writing

No special promise to be made by any person [. . .] to answer for the debt, default, or mis-carriage or another person, being in writing, and signed by the party to be charged therewith, or some other person by him thereunto lawfully authorised, shall be deemed invalid to support an action, suit, or other proceeding to charge the person by whom such promise shall have been made, by reason only that the consideration for such promise does not appear in writing, or by necessary inference from a written document.

5   A surety who discharges the liability to be entitled to assignment of all securities held by the creditor

Every person who, being surety for the debt or duty of another, or being liable with another for any debt or duty, shall pay such debt or perform such duty, shall be entitled to have assigned to him, or to a trustee for him, every judgment, specialty, or other security which shall be held by the creditor in respect of such debt or duty, whether such judgment, specialty, or other security shall or shall not be deemed at law to have been satisfied by the payment of the debt or performance of the duty, and such person shall be entitled to stand in the place of the creditor, and to use all the remedies, and, if need be, and upon a proper indemnity, to use the name of the creditor, in any action or other proceeding, at law or in equity, in order to obtain from the principal debtor, or any co-surety, co-contractor, or co-debtor, as the case may be, indemni-fication for the advances made and loss sustained by the person who shall have so paid such debt or performed such duty, and such payment or performance so made by such surety shall not be pleadable in bar of any such action or other proceeding by him: Provided always, that no co-surety, co-contractor, or co-debtor shall be entitled to recover from any other co-surety, co-contractor, or co-debtor, by the means aforesaid, more than the just proportion to which, as between those parties themselves, such last-mentioned person shall be justly liable.

Offences Against the Person Act 1861
(24 & 25 Vict., c. 100)

44   If the magistrates dismiss the complaint, they shall make out a certificate to that effect

If the Justices, upon the Hearing of any [. . .] Case of Assault or Battery upon the Merits, where the Complaint was preferred by or on the Behalf of the Party aggrieved, [. . .] shall deem the Offence not to be proved, or shall find the Assault or Battery to have been justified, or so trifling as not to merit any Punishment, and shall accordingly dismiss the Complaint, they shall forthwith make out a Certificate [...] stating the Fact of such Dismissal, and shall deliver such Certificate to the Party against whom the Complaint was preferred.

45   Certificate or conviction shall be a bar to any other proceedings

If any Person, against whom any such Complaint as [is mentioned in section 44 of this Act] shall have been preferred by or on the Behalf of the Party aggrieved, shall have obtained such Certificate, or, having been convicted, shall have paid the whole Amount adjudged to be paid, or shall have suffered the Imprisonment or Imprisonment with Hard Labour awarded, in every such Case he shall be released from all further or other Proceedings, Civil or Criminal, for the same Cause.

Apportionment Act 1870

(33 & 34 Vict., c. 35)

2   Rents, &c. to accrue from day to day and be apportionable in respect of time

[...] From and after the passing of this Act all rents, annuities, dividends, and other periodical payments in the nature of income (whether reserved or made payable under an instrument in writing or otherwise) shall, like interest on money lent, be considered as accruing from day to day, and shall be apportionable in respect of time accordingly.

3   Apportioned part of rent, &c. to be payable when the next entire portion shall have become due

The apportioned part of any such rent, annuity, dividend, or other payment shall be payable or recoverable in the case of a continuing rent, annuity, or other such payment when the entire portion of which such apportioned part shall form part shall become due and payable, and not before, and in the case of a rent, annuity, or other such payment determined by reentry, death, or otherwise when the next entire portion of the same would have been payable if the same had not so determined, and not before.

5   Interpretation of terms

In the construction of this Act—

The word "rents" includes rent service, rentcharge, and rent seck, and also tithes and all periodical payments or renderings in lieu of or in the nature of rent or tithe.

The word "annuities" includes salaries and pensions.

The word "dividends" includes (besides dividends strictly so called) all payments made by the name of dividend, bonus, or otherwise out of the revenue of trading or other public companies, divisible between all or any of the members of such respective companies, whether such payments shall be usually made or declared at any fixed times or otherwise; and all such divisible revenue shall, for the purposes of this Act, be deemed to have accrued by equal daily increment during and within the period for or in respect of which the payment of the same revenue shall be declared or expressed to be made, but the said word "dividend" does not include payments in the nature of a return or reimbursement of capital.

6   Act not to apply to policies of assurance

Nothing in this Act contained shall render apportionable any annual sums made payable in policies of assurance of any description.

7   Nor where stipulation made to the contrary

The provisions of this Act shall not extend to any case in which it is or shall be expressly stipulated that no apportionment shall take place.

Law of Libel Amendment Act 1888
(51 & 52 Vict., c. 64)

4 Newspaper reports of proceedings of public meetings and of certain bodies and persons privileged

A fair and accurate report published in any newspaper of the proceedings of a public meeting, or (except where neither the public nor any newspaper reporter is admitted) of any meeting of a vestry, town council, school board, board of guardians, board or local authority formed or constituted under the provisions of any Act of Parliament, or of any committee appointed by any of the above-mentioned bodies, or of any meeting of any commissioners authorised to act by letters patent, Act of Parliament, warrant under the Royal Sign Manual, or other lawful warrant or authority, select committees of either House of Parliament, justices of the peace in quarter sessions assembled for administrative or deliberative purposes, and the publication at the request of any Government office or department, officer of state, commissioner of police, or chief constable of any notice or report issued by them for the information of the public, shall be privileged, unless it shall be proved that such report or publication was published or made maliciously: Provided that nothing in this section shall authorise the publication of any blasphemous or indecent matter: Provided also, that the protection intended to be afforded by this section shall not be available as a defence in any proceedings if it shall be proved that the defendant has been requested to insert in the newspaper in which the report or other publication complained of appeared a reasonable letter or statement by way of contradiction or explanation of such report or other publication, and has refused or neglected to insert the same: Provided further, that nothing in this section contained shall be deemed or construed to limit or abridge any privilege now by law existing, or to protect the publication of any matter not of public concern and the publication of which is not for the public benefit.

For the purposes of this section "public meeting" shall mean any meeting bona fide and lawfully held for a lawful purpose, and for the furtherance or discussion of any matter of public concern, whether the admission thereto be general or restricted.

5 Consolidation of actions

It shall be competent for a judge or the court, upon an application by or on behalf of two or more defendants in actions in respect to the same, or substantially the same, libel brought by one and the same person, to make an order for the consolidation of such actions, so that they shall be tried together; and after such order has been made, and before the trial of the said actions, the defendants in any new actions instituted in respect to the same, or substantially the same, libel shall also be entitled to be joined in a common action upon a joint application being made by such new defendants and the defendants in the actions already consolidated.

In a consolidated action under this section the jury shall assess the whole amount of the damages (if any) in one sum, but a separate verdict shall be taken for or against each defendant in the same way as if the actions consolidated had been tried separately; and if the jury shall have found a verdict against the defendant or defendants in more than one of the actions so consolidated, they shall proceed to apportion the amount of damages which they shall have so found between and against the said last-mentioned defendants; and the judge at the trial, if he awards to the plaintiff the costs of the action, shall thereupon make such order as he shall deem just for the apportionment of such costs between and against such defendants.

Factors Act 1889
(52 & 53 Vict., c. 45)

1 Definitions

For the purposes of this Act—

(1) The expression "mercantile agent" shall mean a mercantile agent having in the customary course of his business as such agent authority either to sell goods or to consign goods for the purpose of sale, or to buy goods, or to raise money on the security of goods:

(2) A person shall be deemed to be in possession of goods or of the documents of title to goods, where the goods or documents are in the actual custody or are held by any other person subject to his control or for him or on his behalf:

(3) The expression "goods" shall include wares and merchandise:

(4) The expression "document of title" shall include any bill of lading, dock warrant, warehouse-keeper's certificate, and warrant or order for the delivery of goods, and any other document used in the ordinary course of business as proof of the possession or control of goods, or authorising or purporting to authorise, either by endorsement or by delivery, the possessor of the document to transfer or receive goods thereby represented:

(5) The expression "pledge" shall include any contract pledging, or giving a lien or security on, goods, whether in consideration of an original advance or of any further or continuing advance or of any pecuniary liability:

(6) The expression "person" shall include any body of persons corporate or unincorporate.

2   Powers of mercantile agent with respect to disposition of goods

(1) Where a mercantile agent is, with the consent of the owner, in possession of goods or of the documents of title to goods, any sale, pledge, or other disposition of the goods, made by him when acting in the ordinary course of business of a mercantile agent, shall, subject to the provisions of this Act, be as valid as if he were expressly authorised by the owner of the goods to make the same; provided that the person taking under the disposition acts in good faith, and has not at the time of the disposition notice that the person making the disposition has not authority to make the same.

(2) Where a mercantile agent has, with the consent of the owner, been in possession of goods or of the documents of title to goods, any sale, pledge, or other disposition, which would have been valid if the consent had continued, shall be valid notwithstanding the determination of the consent; provided that the person taking under the disposition has not at the time thereof notice that the consent has been determined.

(3) Where a mercantile agent has obtained possession of any documents of title to goods by reason of his being or having been, with the consent of the owner, in possession of the goods represented thereby, or of any other documents of title to the goods, his possession of the first-mentioned documents shall, for the purposes of this Act, be deemed to be with the consent of the owner.

(4) For the purposes of this Act the consent of the owner shall be presumed in the absence of evidence to the contrary.

Slander of Women Act 1891
(54 & 55 Vict., c. 51)

1   Amendment of law
Words spoken and published [...] which impute unchastity or adultery to any woman or girl shall not require special damage to render them actionable.

Provided always, that in any action for words spoken and made actionable by this Act, a plaintiff shall not recover more costs than damages, unless the judge shall certify that there was reasonable ground for bringing the action.

Marine Insurance Act 1906
(6 Edw. VII, c. 41)

17   Insurance is uberrimae fidei
A contract of marine insurance is a contract based upon the utmost good faith, and, if the utmost good faith be not observed by either party, the contract may be avoided by the other party.

18   Disclosure by assured

(1) Subject to the provisions of this section, the assured must disclose to the insurer, before the contract is concluded, every material circumstance which is known to the assured, and the assured is deemed to know every circumstance which, in the ordinary course of business, ought to be known by him. If the assured fails to make such disclosure, the insurer may avoid the contract.

(2) Every circumstance is material which would infiuence the judgment of a prudent insurer in fixing the premium, or determining whether he will take the risk.

(3) In the absence of inquiry the following circumstances need not be disclosed, namely:

(a) any circumstance which diminishes the risk;

(b) any circumstance which is known or presumed to be known to the insurer. The insurer is presumed to know matters of common notoriety or knowledge, and matters which an insurer in the ordinary course of his business, as such, ought to know;

(c) any circumstance as to which information is waived by the insurer;

(d) any circumstance which it is superfiuous to disclose by reason of any express or implied warranty.

(4) Whether any particular circumstance, which is not disclosed, be material or not is, in each case, a question of fact.

(5) The term "circumstance" includes any communication made to, or information received by, the assured.

20   Representations pending negotiation of contract

(1) Every material representation made by the assured or his agent to the insurer during the negotiations for the contract, and before the contract is concluded, must be true. If it be untrue the insurer may avoid the contract.

(2) A representation is material which would infiuence the judgment of a prudent insurer in fixing the premium, or determining whether he will take the risk.

(3) A representation may be either a representation as to a matter of fact, or as to a matter of expectation or belief.

(4) A representation as to a matter of fact is true, if it be substantially correct, that is to say, if the difference between what is represented and what is actually correct would not be considered material by a prudent insurer.

(5) A representation as to a matter of expectation or belief is true if it be made in good faith.

(6) A representation may be withdrawn or corrected before the contract is concluded.

(7) Whether a particular representation be material or not is, in each case, a question of fact.

22   Contract must be embodied in policy

Subject to the provisions of any statute, a contract of marine insurance is inadmissible in evidence unless it is embodied in a marine policy in accordance with this Act. The policy may be executed and issued either at the time when the contract is concluded, or afterwards.

33   Nature of warranty

(1) A warranty, in the following sections relating to warranties, means a promissory warranty, that is to say, a warranty by which the assured undertakes that some particular thing shall or shall not be done, or that some condition shall be fulfilled, or whereby he affirms or negatives the existence of a particular state of facts.

(2) A warranty may be express or implied.

(3) A warranty, as above defined, is a condition which must be exactly complied with, whether it be material to the risk or not. If it be not so complied with, then, subject to any express provision in the policy, the insurer is discharged from liability as from the date of the breach of warranty, but without prejudice to any liability incurred by him before that date.

34   When breach of warranty excused

(1) Non-compliance with a warranty is excused when, by reason of a change of circumstances, the warranty ceases to be applicable to the circumstances of the contract, or when compliance with the warranty is rendered unlawful by any subsequent law.

(2) Where a warranty is broken, the assured cannot avail himself of the defence that the breach has been remedied, and the warranty complied with, before loss.

(3) A breach of warranty may be waived by the insurer.

35   Express warranties

(1) An express warranty may be in any form of words from which the intention to warrant is to be inferred.

(2) An express warranty must be included in, or written upon, the policy, or must be contained in some document incorporated by reference into the policy.

(3) An express warranty does not exclude an implied warranty, unless it be inconsistent therewith.

49   Excuses for deviation or delay

(1) Deviation or delay in prosecuting the voyage contemplated by the policy is excused—

(a) where authorised by any special term in the policy; or

(b) where caused by circumstances beyond the control of the master and his employer; or

(c) where reasonably necessary in order to comply with an express or implied warranty; or

(d) where reasonably necessary for the safety of the ship or subject-matter insured; or

(e) for the purpose of saving human life, or aiding a ship in distress where human life may be in danger; or

(f) where reasonably necessary for the purpose of obtaining medical or surgical aid for any person on board the ship; or

(g) where caused by the barratrous conduct of the master or crew, if barratry be one of the perils insured against.

(2) When the cause excusing the deviation or delay ceases to operate, the ship must resume her course, and prosecute her voyage, with reasonable dispatch.

82   Enforcement of return

Where the premium or a proportionate part thereof is, by this Act, declared to be returnable,—

(a) If already paid, it may be recovered by the assured from the insurer; and

(b) If unpaid, it may be retained by the assured or his agent.

83   Return by agreement

Where the policy contains a stipulation for the return of the premium, or a proportionate part thereof, on the happening of a certain event, and that event happens, the premium, or, as the case may be, the proportionate part thereof, is thereupon returnable to the assured.

84   Return for failure of consideration

(1) Where the consideration for the payment of the premium totally fails, and there has been no fraud or illegality on the part of the assured or his agents, the premium is thereupon returnable to the assured.

(2) Where the consideration for the payment of the premium is apportionable and there is a total failure of any apportionable part of the consideration, a proportionate part of the premium is, under the like conditions, thereupon returnable to the assured.

(3) In particular—

(a) Where the policy is void, or is avoided by the insurer as from the commencement of the risk, the premium is returnable, provided that there has been no fraud or illegality on the part of the assured; but if the risk is not apportionable, and has once attached, the premium is not returnable;

(b) Where the subject-matter insured, or part thereof, has never been imperilled, the premium, or, as the case may be, a proportionate part thereof, is returnable: Provided that where the subject-matter has been insured "lost or not lost" and has arrived in safety at the time when the contract is concluded, the premium is not returnable unless, at such time, the insurer knew of the safe arrival;

(c) Where the assured has no insurable interest throughout the currency of the risk, the premium is returnable, provided that this rule does not apply to a policy effected by way of gaming or wagering;

(d) Where the assured has a defeasible interest which is terminated during the currency of the risk, the premium is not returnable;

(e) Where the assured has over-insured under an unvalued policy, a proportionate part of the premium is returnable;

(f) Subject to the foregoing provisions, where the assured has over-insured by double insurance, a proportionate part of the several premiums is returnable: Provided that, if the policies are effected at different times, and any earlier policy has at any time borne the entire risk, or if a claim has been paid on the policy in respect of the full sum insured thereby, no premium is returnable in respect of that policy, and when the double insurance is effected knowingly by the assured no premium is returnable.

87   Implied obligations varied by agreement or usage

(1) Where any right, duty, or liability would arise under a contract of marine insurance by implication of law, it may be negatived or varied by express agreement, or by usage, if the usage be such as to bind both parties to the contract.

Law of Property Act 1925
(15 & 16 Geo. V, c. 20)

41   Stipulations not of the essence of a contract

Stipulations in a contract, as to time or otherwise, which according to rules of equity are not deemed to be or to have become of the essence of the contract, are also construed and have effect at law in accordance with the same rules.

49   Applications to the court by vendor and purchaser

(2) Where the court refuses to grant specific performance of a contract, or in any action for the return of a deposit, the court may, if it thinks fit, order the repayment of any deposit.

(3) This section applies to a contract for the sale or exchange of any interest in land.

56   Persons taking who are not parties and as to indentures

(1) A person may take an immediate or other interest in land or other property, or the benefit of any condition, right of entry, covenant or agreement over or respecting land or other property, although he may not be named as a party to the conveyance or other instrument.

136   Legal assignments of things in action

(1) Any absolute assignment by writing under the hand of the assignor (not purporting to be by way of charge only) of any debt or other legal thing in action, of which express notice in writing has been given to the debtor, trustee or other person from whom the assignor would have been entitled to claim such debt or thing in action, is effectual in law (subject to equities having priority over the right of the assignee) to pass and transfer from the date of such notice—

(a) the legal right to such debt or thing in action;

(b) all legal and other remedies for the same; and

(c) the power to give a good discharge for the same without the concurrence of the assignor:

Provided that, if the debtor, trustee or other person liable in respect of such debt or thing in action has notice—

(a) that the assignment is disputed by the assignor or any person claiming under him; or

(b) of any other opposing or conflicting claims to such debt or thing in action; he may, if he thinks fit, either call upon the persons making claim thereto to interplead concerning the same, or pay the debt or other thing in action into court under the provisions of the Trustee Act 1925.

(2) This section does not affect the provisions of the Policies of Assurance Act 1867.

146 Restrictions on and relief against forfeiture of leases and underleases

(1) A right of re-entry or forfeiture under any proviso or stipulation in a lease for a breach of any covenant or condition in the lease shall not be enforceable, by action or otherwise, unless and until the lessor serves on the lessee a notice—

(a) specifying the particular breach complained of; and

(b) if the breach is capable of remedy, requiring the lessee to remedy the breach;

(c) in any case, requiring the lessee to make compensation in money for the breach; and the lessee fails, within a reasonable time thereafter, to remedy the breach, if it is capable of remedy, and to make reasonable compensation in money, to the satisfaction of the lessor, for the breach.

(2) Where a lessor is proceeding, by action or otherwise, to enforce such a right of reentry or forfeiture, the lessee may, in the lessor's action, if any, or in any action brought by himself, apply to the court for relief; and the court may grant or refuse relief, as the court, having regard to the proceedings and conduct of the parties under the foregoing provisions of this section, and to all the other circumstances, thinks fit; and in case of relief may grant it on such terms, if any, as to costs, expenses, damages, compensation, penalty, or otherwise, including the granting of an injunction to restrain any like breach in the future, as the court, in the circumstances of each case, thinks fit.

(11) This section does not, save as otherwise mentioned, affect the law relating to reentry or forfeiture or relief in case of non-payment of rent.

(12) This section has effect notwithstanding any stipulation to the contrary.

205 General definitions

(1) In this Act unless the context otherwise requires, the following expressions have the meanings hereby assigned to them respectively, that is to say: . . .

(xvii) "Notice" includes constructive notice;

(xx) "Property" includes any thing in action, and any interest in real or personal property;

. . .

Reservoirs (Safety Provisions) Act 1930
(20 & 21 Geo. V, c. 51)

7 Liability for damage and injury

Where damage or injury is caused by the escape of water from a reservoir constructed after the commencement of this Act under statutory powers granted after the passing of this Act, the fact that the reservoir was so constructed shall not exonerate the undertakers from any indictment, action or other proceedings to which they would otherwise have been liable.

Third Parties (Rights Against Insurers) Act 1930
(20 & 21 Geo. V, c. 25)

1   Rights of third parties against insurers on bankruptcy, etc., of the insured

(1) Where under any contract of insurance a person (hereinafter referred to as the insured) is insured against liabilities to third parties which he may incur, then

    (a) in the event of the insured becoming bankrupt or making a composition or arrangement with his creditors; or

    (b) in the case of the insured being a company, in the event of a winding-up order [...] being made, or a resolution for a voluntary winding-up being passed, with respect to the company, [or of the company entering administration] or of a receiver or manager of the company's business or undertaking being duly appointed, or of possession being taken, by or on behalf of the holders of any debentures secured by a floating charge, of any property comprised in or subject to that charge [or of a voluntary arrangement proposed for the purposes of Part I of the Insolvency Act 1986 being approved under that Part];

if, either before or after that event, any such liability as aforesaid is incurred by the insured, his rights against the insurer under the contract in respect of the liability shall, notwithstanding anything in any Act or rule of law to the contrary, be transferred to and vest in the third party to whom the liability was so incurred.

(2) Where [the estate of any person falls to be administered in accordance with an order under section 421 of the Insolvency Act 1986], then, if any debt provable in bankruptcy [(in Scotland, any claim accepted in the sequestration)] is owing by the deceased in respect of a liability against which he was insured under a contract of insurance as being a liability to a third party, the deceased debtor's rights against the insurer under the contract in respect of that liability shall, notwithstanding anything in [any such order][5], be transferred to and vest in the person to whom the debt is owing.

(3) In so far as any contract of insurance made after the commencement of this Act in respect of any liability of the insured to third parties purports, whether directly or indirectly, to avoid the contract or to alter the rights of the parties thereunder upon the happening to the insured of the events specified in paragraph (a) or paragraph (b) of subsection (1) of this section or upon the [estate of any person falling to be administered in accordance with an order under section 421 of the Insolvency Act 1986], the contract shall be of no effect.

(4) Upon a transfer under subsection (1) or subsection (2) of this section, the insurer shall, subject to the provisions of section three of this Act, be under the same liability to the third party as he would have been under to the insured, but—

    (a) if the liability of the insurer to the insured exceeds the liability of the insured to the third party, nothing in this Act shall affect the rights of the insured against the insurer in respect of the excess; and

    (b) if the liability of the insurer to the insured is less than the liability of the insured to the third party, nothing in this Act shall affect the rights of the third party against the insured in respect of the balance.

(5) For the purposes of this Act, the expression "liabilities to third parties", in relation to a person insured under any contract of insurance, shall not include any liability of that person in the capacity of insurer under some other contract of insurance.

(6) This Act shall not apply—

    (a) where a company is wound up voluntarily merely for the purposes of reconstruction or of amalgamation with another company; or

    (b) to any case to which subsections (1) and (2) of section seven of the Workmen's Compensation Act 1925 applies.

2   Duty to give necessary information to third parties

(1) In the event of any person becoming bankrupt or making a composition or arrangement with his creditors, or in the event of [the estate of any person falling to be administered in accordance with an order under section 421 of the Insolvency Act 1986], or in the event of a winding-up order [...] being made, or a resolution for a voluntary winding-up being passed, with respect to any company [or of the company entering administration] or of a receiver or manager of the company's business or undertaking being duly appointed or of possession being taken by or on behalf of the holders of any debentures secured by a floating charge of any property comprised in or subject to the charge it shall be the duty of the bankrupt, debtor, personal representative of the deceased debtor or company, and, as the case may be, of the trustee in bankruptcy, trustee, liquidator, [administator], receiver, or manager, or person in possession of the property to give at the request of any person claiming that the bankrupt, debtor, deceased debtor, or company is under a liability to him such information as may be reasonably required by him for the purpose of ascertaining whether any rights have been transferred to and vested in him by this Act and for the purpose of enforcing such rights, if any, and any contract of insurance, in so far as it purports, whether directly or indirectly, to avoid the contract or to alter the rights of the parties thereunder upon the giving of any such information in the events aforesaid or otherwise to prohibit or prevent the giving thereof in the said events shall be of no effect.

[(1A) The reference in subsection (1) of this section to a trustee includes a reference to the supervisor of a voluntary arrangement proposed for the purposes of, and approved under, Part I or Part VIII of the Insolvency Act 1986.]

(2) If the information given to any person in pursuance of subsection (1) of this section discloses reasonable ground for supposing that there have or may have been transferred to him under this Act rights against any particular insurer, that insurer shall be subject to the same duty as is imposed by the said subsection on the persons therein mentioned.

(3) The duty to give information imposed by this section shall include a duty to allow all contracts of insurance, receipts for premiums, and other relevant documents in the possession or power of the person on whom the duty is so imposed to be inspected and copies thereof to be taken.

3   Settlement between insurers and insured persons

Where the insured has become bankrupt or where in the case of the insured being a company, a winding-up order [or an administration order] has been made or a resolution for a voluntary winding-up has been passed, with respect to the company, no agreement made between the insurer and the insured after liability has been incurred to a third party and after the commencement of the bankruptcy or winding-up [or the day of the administration order], as the case may be, nor any waiver, assignment, or other disposition made by, or payment made to the insured after the commencement [or day] aforesaid shall be effective to defeat or affect the rights transferred to the third party under this Act, but those rights shall be the same as if no such agreement, waiver, assignment, disposition or payment had been made.

[3A   Application to limited liability partnerships

(1) This Act applies to limited liability partnerships as it applies to companies.

(2) In its application to limited liability partnerships, references to a resolution for a voluntary winding-up being passed are references to a determination for a voluntary winding-up being made.]

Law Reform (Miscellaneous Provisions) Act 1934
(24 & 25 Geo. V, c. 41)

1   Effect of death on certain causes of action

(1) Subject to the provisions of this section, on the death of any person after the commencement of this Act all causes of action subsisting against or vested in him shall survive against, or, as the case may be, for the benefit of, his estate. Provided that this subsection shall not apply to causes of action for defamation [...].

[(1A) The right of a person to claim under section 1A of the Fatal Accidents Act 1976 (bereavement) shall not survive for the benefit of his estate on his death.]

(2) Where a cause of action survives as aforesaid for the benefit of the estate of a deceased person, the damages recoverable for the benefit of the estate of that person:—

  [(a) shall not include—

    (i)   any exemplary damages;

    (ii) any damages for loss of income in respect of any period after that person's death;]

  (b) [...]

  (c) where the death of that person has been caused by the act or omission which gives rise to the cause of action, shall be calculated without reference to any loss or gain to his estate consequent on his death, except that a sum in respect of funeral expenses may be included.

(4) Where damage has been suffered by reason of any act or omission in respect of which a cause of action would have subsisted against any person if that person had not died before or at the same time as the damage was suffered, there shall be deemed, for the purposes of this Act, to have been subsisting against him before his death such cause of action in respect of that act or omission as would have subsisted if he had died after the damage was suffered.

(5) The rights conferred by this Act for the benefit of the estates of deceased persons shall be in addition to and not in derogation of any rights conferred on the dependants of deceased persons by [the Fatal Accidents Act 1976 ...] and so much of this Act as relates to causes of action against the estates of deceased persons shall apply in relation to causes of action under the said Act as it applies in relation to other causes of action not expressly excepted from the operation of subsection (1) of this section.

(6) In the event of the insolvency of an estate against which proceedings are maintainable by virtue of this section, any liability in respect of the cause of action in respect of which the proceedings are maintainable shall be deemed to be a debt provable in the administration of the estate, notwithstanding that it is a demand in the nature of unliquidated damages arising otherwise than by a contract, promise or breach of trust.

Law Reform (Married Women and Tortfeasors) Act 1935
(25 & 26 Geo. V, c. 30)

3   Abolition of husband's liability for wife's torts and ante-nuptial contracts, debts and obligations

Subject to the provisions of this Part of this Act, the husband of a married woman shall not, by reason only of his being her husband, be liable—

  (a) in respect of any tort committed by her whether before or after the marriage, or in respect of any contract entered into, or debt or obligation incurred, by her before the marriage; or

  (b) to be sued, or made a party to any legal proceeding brought, in respect of any such tort, contract, debt, or obligation.

4 Savings

(2) For the avoidance of doubt it is hereby declared that nothing in this Part of this Act—

(a) renders the husband of a married woman liable in respect of any contract entered into, or debt or obligation incurred, by her after the marriage in respect of which he would not have been liable if this Act had not been passed;

(b) exempts the husband of a married woman from liability in respect of any contract entered into, or debt or obligation (not being a debt or obligation arising out of a commission of a tort) incurred, by her after the marriage in respect of which he would have been liable if this Act had not been passed;

(c) prevents a husband and wife from acquiring, holding, and disposing of, any property jointly or as tenants in common, or from rendering themselves, or being rendered, jointly liable in respect of any tort, contract, debt or obligation, and of suing and being sued either in tort or in contract or otherwise, in like manner as if they were not married;

(d) prevents the exercise of any joint power given to a husband and wife.

Law Reform (Frustrated Contracts) Act 1943
(6 & 7 Geo. VI, c. 40)

1 Adjustment of rights and liabilities of parties to frustrated contracts

(1) Where a contract governed by English law has become impossible of performance or been otherwise frustrated, and the parties thereto have for that reason been discharged from the further performance of the contract, the following provisions of this section shall, subject to the provisions of section two of this Act, have effect in relation thereto.

(2) All sums paid or payable to any party in pursuance of the contract before the time when the parties were so discharged (in this Act referred to as "the time of discharge") shall, in the case of sums so paid, be recoverable from him as money received by him for the use of the party by whom the sums were paid, and, in the case of sums so payable, cease to be so payable:

Provided that, if the party to whom the sums were so paid or payable incurred expenses before the time of discharge in, or for the purpose of, the performance of the contract, the court may, if it considers it just to do so having regard to all the circumstances of the case, allow him to retain or, as the case may be, recover the whole or any part of the sums so paid or payable, not being an amount in excess of the expenses so incurred.

(3) Where any party to the contract has, by reason of anything done by any other party thereto in, or for the purpose of, the performance of the contract, obtained a valuable benefit (other than a payment of money to which the last foregoing subsection applies) before the time of discharge there shall be recoverable from him by the said other party such sum (if any), not exceeding the value of the said benefit to the party obtaining it, as the court considers just, having regard to all the circumstances of the case and, in particular,—

(a) the amount of any expenses incurred before the time of discharge by the benefited party in, or for the purpose of, the performance of the contract, including any sums paid or payable by him to any other party in pursuance of the contract and retained or recoverable by that party under the last foregoing subsection, and

(b) the effect, in relation to the said benefit, of the circumstances giving rise to the frustration of the contract.

(4) In estimating, for the purposes of the foregoing provisions of this section, the amount of any expenses incurred by any party to the contract, the court may, without prejudice to the generality of the said provisions, include such sum as appears to be reasonable in respect of overhead expenses and in respect of any work or services performed personally by the said party.

(5) In considering whether any sum ought to be recovered or retained under the foregoing provisions of this section by any party to the contract, the court shall not take into account any sums which have, by reason of the circumstances giving rise to the frustration of the contract, become payable to that party under any contract of insurance unless there was an obligation to insure imposed by an express term of the frustrated contract or by or under any enactment.

(6) Where any person has assumed obligations under the contract in consideration of the conferring of a benefit by any other party to the contract upon any other person, whether a party to the contract or not, the court may, if in all the circumstances of the case it considers it just to do so, treat for the purposes of subsection (3) of this section any benefit so conferred as a benefit obtained by the person who has assumed the obligations as aforesaid.

2 Provision as to application of this Act

(1) This Act shall apply to contracts, whether made before or after the commencement of this Act, as respects which the time of discharge is on or after the first day of July, nineteen hundred and forty-three, but not to contracts as respects which the time of discharge is before the said date.

(2) This Act shall apply to contracts to which the Crown is a party in like manner as to contracts between subjects.

(3) Where any contract to which this Act applies contains any provision which, upon the true construction of the contract, is intended to have effect in the event of circumstances arising which operate, or would but for the said provision operate, to frustrate the contract, or is intended to have effect whether such circumstances arise or not, the court shall give effect to the said provision and shall only give effect to the foregoing section of this Act to such extent, if any, as appears to the court to be consistent with the said provision.

(4) Where it appears to the court that a part of any contract to which this Act applies can properly be severed from the remainder of the contract, being a part wholly performed before the time of discharge, or so performed except for the payment in respect of that part of the contract of sums which are or can be ascertained under the contract, the court shall treat that part of the contract as if it were a separate contract and had not been frustrated and shall treat the foregoing section of this Act as only applicable to the remainder of that contract.

(5) This Act shall not apply—

    (a) to any charterparty, except a time charterparty or a charterparty by way of demise, or to any contract (other than a charterparty) for the carriage of goods by sea; or

    (b) to any contract of insurance, save as is provided by subsection (5) of the foregoing section; or

    (c) to any contract to which [section 7 of the Sale of Goods Act 1979] (which avoids contracts for the sale of specific goods which perish before the risk has passed to the buyer) applies, or to any other contract for the sale, or for the sale and delivery, of specific goods, where the contract is frustrated by reason of the fact that the goods have perished.

3 Short title and interpretation

(2) In this Act the expression "court" means, in relation to any matter, the court or arbitrator by or before whom the matter falls to be determined.

Law Reform (Contributory Negligence) Act 1945
(8 & 9 Geo. VI, c. 28)

1 Apportionment of liability in case of contributory negligence

(1) Where any person suffers damage as the result partly of his own fault and partly of the fault of any other person or persons, a claim in respect of that damage shall not be defeated by reason of the fault of the person suffering the damage, but the damages recoverable in

respect thereof shall be reduced to such extent as the court thinks just and equitable having regard to the claimant's share in the responsibility of the damage: Provided that—

  (a) this subsection shall not operate to defeat any defence arising under a contract;
  (b) where any contract or enactment providing for the limitation of liability is applicable to the claim, the amount of damages recoverable by the claimant by virtue of this subsection shall not exceed the maximum limit so applicable.

(2) Where damages are recoverable by any person by virtue of the foregoing subsection subject to such reduction as is therein mentioned, the court shall find and record the total damages which would have been recoverable if the claimant had not been at fault.

(5) Where, in any case to which subsection (1) of this section applies, one of the persons at fault avoids liability to any other such person or his personal representative by pleading the Limitation Act, 1939, or any other enactment limiting the time within which proceedings may be taken, he shall not be entitled to recover any damages [...] from that other person or representative by virtue of the said subsection.

(6) Where any case to which subsection (1) of this section applies is tried with a jury, the jury shall determine the total damages which would have been recoverable if the claimant had not been at fault and the extent to which those damages are to be reduced.

4   Interpretation

The following expressions have the meanings hereby respectively assigned to them, that is to say—

"court" means, in relation to any claim, the court or arbitrator by or before whom the claim falls to be determined;

"damage" includes loss of life and personal injury; [...]

"fault" means negligence, breach of statutory duty or other act or omission which gives rise to liability in tort or would, apart from this Act, give rise to the defence of contributory negligence.

Crown Proceedings Act 1947
(10 & 11 Geo. VI, c. 44)

2   Liability of the Crown in tort

(1) Subject to the provisions of this Act, the Crown shall be subject to all those liabilities in tort to which, if it were a private person of full age and capacity, it would be subject—

  (a) in respect of torts committed by its servants or agents;
  (b) in respect of any breach of those duties which a person owes to his servants or agents at common law by reason of being their employer; and
  (c) in respect of any breach of the duties attaching at common law to the ownership, occupation, possession or control of property:

provided that no proceedings shall lie against the Crown by virtue of paragraph (a) of this subsection in respect of any act or omission of a servant or agent of the Crown unless the act or omission would apart from the provisions of this Act have given rise to a cause of action in tort against that servant or agent or his estate.

(2) Where the Crown is bound by a statutory duty which is binding also upon persons other than the Crown and its officers, then, subject to the provisions of this Act, the Crown shall, in respect of a failure to comply with that duty, be subject to all those liabilities in tort (if any) to which it would be so subject if it were a private person of full age and capacity.

(3) Where any functions are conferred or imposed upon an officer of the Crown as such either by any rule of the common law or by statute, and that officer commits a tort while performing or purporting to perform those functions, the liabilities of the Crown in respect of the tort shall be such as they would have been if those functions had been conferred or imposed solely by virtue of instructions lawfully given by the Crown.

(4) Any enactment which negatives or limits the amount of the liability of any Government department[, part of the Scottish Administration,] or officer of the Crown in respect of any tort committed by that department[, part] or officer shall, in the case of proceedings against the Crown under this section in respect of a tort committed by that department or officer, apply in relation to the Crown as it would have applied in relation to that department or officer if the proceedings against the Crown had been proceedings against that department or officer.

(5) No proceedings shall lie against the Crown by virtue of this section in respect of anything done or omitted to be done by any person while discharging or purporting to discharge any responsibilities of a judicial nature vested in him, or any responsibilities which he has in connection with the execution of judicial process.

(6) No proceedings shall lie against the Crown by virtue of this section in respect of any act, neglect or default of any officer of the Crown, unless that officer has been directly or indirectly appointed by the Crown and was at the material time paid in respect of his duties as an officer of the Crown wholly out of the Consolidated Fund of the United Kingdom, moneys provided by Parliament [...] [the Scottish Consolidated Fund,] or any other Fund certified by the Treasury for the purposes of this subsection or was at the material time holding an office in respect of which the Treasury certify that the holder thereof would normally be so paid.

Law Reform (Personal Injuries) Act 1948
(11 & 12 Geo. VI, c. 41)

1   Common employment
(1) It shall not be a defence to an employer who is sued in respect of personal injuries caused by the negligence of a person employed by him, that that person was at the time the injuries were caused in commonemployment with the person injured.

(3) Any provision contained in a contract of service or apprenticeship, or in an agreement collateral thereto, (including a contract or agreement entered into before the commencement of this Act) shall be void in so far as it would have the effect of excluding or limiting any liability of the employer in respect of personal injuries caused to the person employed or apprenticed by the negligence of persons in common employment with him.

2   Measure of damages
(4) In an action for damages for personal injuries (including any such action arising out of a contract), there shall be disregarded, in determining the reasonableness of any expenses, the possibility of avoiding those expenses or part of them by taking advantage of facilities available under the National Health Service Act, 1977, or the National Health Service (Scotland) Act, 1978, or of any corresponding facilities in Northern Ireland.

3   Definition of "personal injury"
In this Act the expression "personal injury" includes any disease and any impairment of a person's physical or mental condition, and the expression "injured" shall be construed accordingly.

National Parks and Access to the Countryside Act 1949
(12, 13 & 14 Geo. VI, c. 97)

60   Rights of public where access agreement or order in force
(1) Subject to the following provisions of this Part of this Act, where an access agreement or order is in force as respects any land a person who enters upon land comprised in the agreement or order for the purpose of open-air recreation without breaking or damaging any

wall, fence, hedge or gate, or who is on such land for that purpose after having so entered thereon, shall not be treated as a trespasser on that land or incur any other liability by reason only of so entering or being on the land: Provided that this subsection shall not apply to land which for the time being is excepted land as hereinafter defined.

(2) Nothing in the provisions of the last foregoing subsection shall entitle a person to enter or be on any land, or to do anything thereon, in contravention of any prohibition contained in or having effect under any enactment.

(3) An access agreement or order may specify or provide for imposing restrictions subject to which persons may enter or be upon land by virtue of subsection (1) of this section, including in particular, but without prejudice to the generality of this subsection, restrictions excluding the land or any part thereof at particular times from the operation of the said subsection (1); and that subsection shall not apply to any person entering or being on the land in contravention of any such restriction or failing to comply therewith while he is on the land.

66   Effect of access agreement or order on rights and liabilities of owners
(1) A person interested in any land comprised in an access agreement or order, not being excepted land, shall not carry out any work thereon whereby the area to which the public are able to have access by virtue of the agreement or order is substantially reduced: Provided that nothing in this subsection shall affect the doing of anything whereby any land becomes expected land.

(2) The operation of subsection (1) of section sixty of this Act in relation to any land shall not increase the liability, under any enactment not contained in this Act or under any rule of law, of a person interested in that land or adjoining land in respect of the state thereof or of things done or omitted thereon.

Reserve and Auxiliary Forces (Protection of Civil Interests) Act 1951
(14 & 15 Geo. VI, c. 65)

13   Effect of failure to observe restrictions under Part I
(2) In any action for damages for conversion or other proceedings which lie by virtue of any such omission, failure or contravention, the court may take account of the conduct of the defendant with a view, if the court thinks fit, to awarding exemplary damages in respect of the wrong sustained by the plaintiff.

Defamation Act 1952
(15 & 16 Geo. VI & 1 Eliz. II, c. 66)

2   Slander affecting official, professional or business reputation
In an action for slander in respect of words calculated to disparage the plaintiff in an office, profession, calling, trade or business held or carried on by him at the time of the publication, it shall not be necessary to allege or prove special damage, whether or not the words are spoken of the plaintiff in the way of his office, profession, calling, trade or business.

3   Slander of title, etc.
(1) In an action for slander of title, slander of goods or other malicious falsehood, it shall not be necessary to allege or prove special damage—
    (a) if the words upon which the action is founded are calculated to cause pecuniary damage to the plaintiff and are published in writing or other permanent form; or

(b) if the said words are calculated to cause pecuniary damage to the plaintiff in respect of any office, profession, calling, trade or business held or carried on by him at the time of the publication.

(2) Section one of this Act shall apply for the purposes of this section as it applies for the purposes of the law of libel and slander.

5 Justification

In an action for libel or slander in respect of words containing two or more distinct charges against the plaintiff, a defence of justification shall not fail by reason only that the truth of every charge is not proved if the words not proved to be true do not materially injure the plaintiffs reputation having regard to the truth of the remaining charges.

6 Fair comment

In an action for libel or slander in respect of words consisting partly of allegations of fact and partly of expression of opinion, a defence of fair comment shall not fail by reason only that the truth of every allegation or fact is not proved if the expression of opinion is fair comment having regard to such of the facts alleged or referred to in the words complained of as are proved.

9 Extension of certain defences to broadcasting

(1) Section three of the Parliamentary Papers Act, 1840 (which confers protection in respect of proceedings for printing extracts from or abstracts of parliamentary papers) shall have effect as if the reference to printing included a reference to broadcasting by means of wireless telegraphy.

10 Limitation on privilege at elections

A defamatory statement published by or on behalf of a candidate in any election to local government authority [to the Scottish Parliament] or to Parliament shall not be deemed to be published on a privileged occasion on the ground that it is material to a question in issue in the election, whether or not the person by whom it is published is qualified to vote at the election.

11 Agreements for indemnity

An agreement for indemnifying any person against civil liability for libel in respect of the publication of any matter shall not be unlawful unless at the time of the publication that person knows that the matter is defamatory, and does not reasonably believe that there is a good defence to any action brought upon it.

12 Evidence of other damages recovered by plaintiff

In any action for libel or slander the defendant may give evidence in mitigation of damages that the plaintiff has recovered damages, or has brought actions for damages, for libel or slander in respect of the publication of words to the same effect as the words on which the action is founded, or has received or agreed to receive compensation in respect of any such publication.

13 Consolidation of actions for slander etc

Section five of the Law of Libel Amendment Act 1888 (which provides for the consolidation, on the application of the defendants, of two or more actions for libel by the same plaintiff) shall apply to actions for slander of title, slander of goods or other malicious falsehood as it applies to actions for libel; and references in that section to the same, or substantially the same, libel shall be construed accordingly.

16 Interpretation

(1) Any reference in this Act to words shall be construed as including a reference to pictures, visual images, gestures and other methods of signifying meaning.

17 Proceedings affected and savings

(2) Nothing in this Act affects the law relating to criminal libel.

Occupiers' Liability Act 1957
(5 & 6 Eliz. II, c. 31)

1 Preliminary

(1) The rules enacted by the two next following sections shall have effect, in place of the rules of the common law, to regulate the duty which an occupier of premises owes to his visitors in respect of dangers due to the state of the premises or to things done or omitted to be done on them.

(2) The rules so enacted shall regulate the nature of the duty imposed by law in consequence of a person's occupation or control of premises and of any invitation or permission he gives (or is to be treated as giving) to another to enter or use the premises, but they shall not alter the rules of the common law as to the persons on whom a duty is so imposed or to whom it is owed; and accordingly for the purpose of the rules so enacted the persons who are to be treated as an occupier and as his visitors are the same (subject to subsection (4) of this section) as the persons who would at common law be treated as an occupier and as his invitees or licensees.

(3) The rules so enacted in relation to an occupier of premises and his visitors shall also apply, in like manner and to the like extent as the principles applicable at common law to an occupier of premises and his invitees or licensees would apply, to regulate—

    (a) the obligations of a person occupying or having control over any fixed or moveable structure, including any vessel, vehicle or aircraft; and

    (b) the obligations of a person occupying or having control over any premises or structure in respect of damage to property, including the property of persons who are not themselves his visitors.

[(4) A person entering any premises in exercise of rights conferred by virtue of—

    (a) section 2(1) of the Countryside and Rights of Way Act 2000, or

    (b) an access agreement or order under the National Parks and Access to the Countryside Act 1949,

is not, for the purposes of this Act, a visitor of the occupier of those premises.]

2 Extent of occupier's ordinary duty

(1) An occupier of premises owes the same duty, the "common duty of care", to all his visitors, except in so far as he is free to and does extend, restrict, modify or exclude his duty to any visitor or visitors by agreement or otherwise.

(2) The common duty of care is a duty to take such care as in all the circumstances of the case is reasonable to see that the visitor will be reasonably safe in using the premises for the purposes for which he is invited or permitted by the occupier to be there.

(3) The circumstances relevant for the present purposes include the degree of care, and of want of care, which would ordinarily be looked for in such a visitor, so that (for example) in proper cases—

    (a) an occupier must be prepared for children to be less careful than adults; and

    (b) an occupier may expect that a person, in the exercise of his calling, will appreciate and guard against any special risks ordinarily incident to it, so far as the occupier leaves him free to do so.

(4) In determining whether the occupier of premises has discharged the common duty of care to a visitor, regard is to be had to all the circumstances, so that (for example)—

    (a) where damage is caused to a visitor by a danger of which he had been warned by the occupier, the warning is not to be treated without more as absolving the occupier from liability, unless in all the circumstances it was enough to enable the visitor to be reasonably safe; and

    (b) where damage is caused to a visitor by a danger due to the faulty execution of any work of construction, maintenance or repair by an independent contractor employed by the occupier, the occupier is not to be treated without more as answerable for the danger if in all the circumstances he had acted reasonably in entrusting the work to an independent contractor and had taken such steps (if any) as he reasonably ought in order to satisfy himself that the contractor was competent and that the work had been properly done.

(5) The common duty of care does not impose on an occupier any obligation to a visitor in respect of risks willingly accepted as his by the visitor (the question whether a risk was so accepted to be decided on the same principles as in other cases in which one person owes a duty of care to another).

(6) For the purposes of this section, persons who enter premises for any purpose in the exercise of a right conferred by law are to be treated as permitted by the occupier to be there for that purpose, whether they in fact have his permission or not.

3 Effect of contract on occupier's liability to third party

(1) Where an occupier of premises is bound by contract to permit persons who are strangers to the contract to enter or use the premises, the duty of care which he owes to them as his visitors cannot be restricted or excluded by that contract, but (subject to any provision of the contract to the contrary) shall include the duty to perform his obligations under the contract, whether undertaken for their protection or not, in so far as those obligations go beyond the obligations otherwise involved in that duty.

(2) A contract shall not by virtue of this section have the effect, unless it expressly so provides, of making an occupier who has taken all reasonable care answerable to strangers to the contract for dangers due to the faulty execution of any work of construction, main-tenance or repair or other like operation by persons other than himself, his servants and persons acting under his direction and control.

(3) In this section, "stranger to the contract" means a person not for the time being entitled to the benefit of the contract as a party to it or as the successor by assignment or otherwise of a party to it, and accordingly includes a party to the contract who has ceased to be so entitled.

(4) Where by the terms or conditions governing any tenancy (including a statutory tenancy which does not in law amount to a tenancy) either the landlord or the tenant is bound, though not by contract, to permit persons to enter or use premises of which he is the occupier, this section shall apply as if the tenancy were a contract between the landlord and the tenant.

(5) This section, in so far as it prevents the common duty of care from being restricted or excluded, applies to contracts entered into and tenancies created before the commencement of this Act, as well as to those entered into or created after its commencement; but, in so far as it enlarges the duty owed by an occupier beyond the common duty of care, it shall have effect only in relation to obligations which are undertaken after the commencement or which are renewed by agreement (whether express or implied) after that commencement.

5 Implied term in contracts

(1) Where persons enter or use, or bring or send goods to, any premises in exercise of a right conferred by contract with a person occupying or having control of the premises, the duty he owes them in respect of dangers due to the state of the premises or to things done or omitted to be done by them, in so far as the duty depends on a term to be implied in the contract by reason of its conferring that right, shall be the common duty of care.

(2) The foregoing subsection shall apply to fixed and moveable structures as it applies to premises.

(3) This section does not affect the obligations imposed on a person by or by virtue of any contract for the hire of, or for the carriage for reward of persons or goods in, any vehicle, vessel, aircraft or other means of transport, or by virtue of any contract of bailment.

(4) This section does not apply to contracts entered into before the commencement of this Act.

6 General

This Act shall bind the Crown, but as regards the Crown liability in tort shall not bind the Crown further than the Crown is made liable in tort by the Crown Proceedings Act, 1947, and that Act and in particular section two of it shall apply in relation to duties under sections two to four of this Act as statutory duties.

Occupiers' Liability (Scotland) Act 1960
(8 & 9 Eliz. II, c. 30)

1 Variation of rules of common law as to duty of care owed by occupiers

(1) The provisions of the next following section of this Act shall have effect, in place of the rules of the common law, for the purpose of determining the care which a person occupying or having control of land or other premises (in this Act referred to as an "occupier of premises") is required, by reason of such occupation or control, to show towards persons entering on the premises in respect of dangers which are due to the state of the premises or to anything done or omitted to be done on them and for which he is in law responsible.

(2) Nothing in those provisions shall be taken to alter the rules of the common law which determine the person on whom in relation to any premises a duty to show care as aforesaid towards persons entering thereon is incumbent.

(3) Those provisions shall apply, in like manner and to the same extent as they do in relation to an occupier of premises and to persons entering thereon,—

(a) in relation to a person occupying or having control of any fixed or moveable structure, including any vessel, vehicle or aircraft, and to persons entering thereon; and

(b) in relation to an occupier of premises or a person occupying or having control of any such structure and to property thereon, including the property of persons who have not themselves entered on the premises or structure.

2 Extent of occupier's duty to show care

(1) The care which an occupier of premises is required, by reason of his occupation or control of the premises, to show towards a person entering thereon in respect of dangers which are due to the state of the premises or to anything done or omitted to be done on them and for which the occupier is in law responsible shall, except in so far as he is entitled to and does extend, restrict, modify or exclude by agreement his obligations towards that person, be such care as in all the circumstances of the case is reasonable to see that that person will not suffer injury or damage by reason of any such danger.

(2) Nothing in the foregoing subsection shall relieve an occupier of premises of any duty to show in any particular case any higher standard of care which in that case is incumbent on him by virtue of any enactment or rule of law imposing special standards of care on particular classes of persons.

(3) Nothing in the foregoing provisions of this Act shall be held to impose on an occupier any obligation to a person entering on his premises in respect of risks which that person has willingly accepted as his; and any question whether a risk was so accepted shall be decided on the same principles as in other cases in which one person owes to another a duty to show care.

3 Landlord's liability by virtue of responsibility for repairs

(1) Where premises are occupied or used by virtue of a tenancy under which the landlord is responsible for the maintenance or repair of the premises, it shall be the duty of the landlord to show towards any persons who or whose property may from time to time be on the premises the same care in respect of dangers arising from any failure on his part in carrying out his responsibility aforesaid as is required by virtue of the foregoing provisions of this Act to be shown by an occupier of premises towards persons entering on them.

(2) Where premises are occupied or used by virtue of a sub-tenancy, the foregoing sub-section shall apply to any landlord who is responsible for the maintenance or repair of the premises comprised in the sub-tenancy.

(3) Nothing in this section shall relieve a landlord of any duty which he is under apart from this section.

(4) For the purposes of this section, any obligation imposed on a landlord by any enactment by reason of the premises being subject to a tenancy shall be treated as if it were an obligation imposed on him by the tenancy, "tenancy" includes a statutory tenancy which does not in law amount to a tenancy and includes also any contract conferring a right of occupation, and "landlord" shall be construed accordingly.

(5) This section shall apply to tenancies created before the commencement of this Act as well as to tenancies created after its commencement.

4   Application to Crown

This Act shall bind the Crown, but as regards the liability of the Crown for any wrongful or negligent act or omission giving rise to liability in reparation shall not bind the Crown any further than the Crown is made liable in respect of such acts or omissions by the Crown Proceedings Act, 1947, and that Act and in particular section two thereof shall apply in relation to duties under section two or section three of this Act as statutory duties.

Public Bodies (Admission to Meetings) Act 1960
(8 & 9 Eliz. II, c. 67)

1   Admission to public meetings of local authorities and other bodies

(5) Where a meeting of a body is required by this Act to be open to the public during the proceedings or any part of them, and there is supplied to a member of the public attending the meeting, or in pursuance of paragraph (b) of subsection (4) above there is supplied for the benefit of a newspaper, any such copy of the agenda as is mentioned in that paragraph, with or without further statements or particulars for the purpose of indicating the nature of any item included in the agenda, the publication thereby of any defamatory matter contained in the agenda or in the further statements or particulars shall be privileged, unless the publication is proved to be made with malice.

Law Reform (Husband and Wife) Act 1962
(10 & 11 Eliz. II, c. 48)

1   Actions in tort between husband and wife

(1) Subject to the provisions of this section, each of the parties to a marriage shall have the like right of action in tort against the other as if they were not married.

(2) Where an action in tort is brought by one of the parties to a marriage against the other during the subsistence of the marriage, the court may stay the action if it appears—

  (a) that no substantial benefit would accrue to either party from the continuation of the proceedings; or

  (b) that the question or questions in issue could more conveniently be disposed of on an application made under section seventeen of the Married Women's Property Act 1882 (determination of questions between husband and wife as to the title to or possession of property);

and without prejudice to paragraph (b) of this subsection the court may, in such an action, either exercise any power which could be exercised on an application under that said section seventeen, or give such directions as it thinks fit for the disposal under that section of any question arising in the proceedings.

Nuclear Installations Act 1965
(1965, c. 57)

7 Duty of licensee of licensed site

(1) Where a nuclear site licence has been granted in respect of any site, it shall be the duty of the licensee to secure that—

    (a) no such occurrence involving nuclear matter as is mentioned in subsection (2) of this section causes injury to any person or damage to any property of any person other than the licensee, being injury or damage arising out of or resulting from the radioactive properties, or a combination of those and any toxic, explosive or other hazardous properties, of that nuclear matter; and

    (b) no ionising radiations emitted during the period of the licensee's responsibility—

        (i) from anything caused or suffered by the licensee to be on the site which is not nuclear matter; or

        (ii) from any waste discharged (in whatever form) on or from the site, cause injury to any person or damage to any property of any person other than the licensee.

(2) The occurrences referred to in subsection (1)(a) of this section are—

    (a) any occurrence on the licensed site during the period of the licensee's responsibility, being an occurrence involving nuclear matter;

    (b) any occurrence elsewhere than on the licensed site involving nuclear matter which is not excepted matter and which at the time of the occurrence—

        (i) is in the course of carriage on behalf of the licensee as licensee of that site; or

        (ii) is in the course of carriage to that site with the agreement of the licensee from a place outside the relevant territories; and

        (iii) in either case, is not on any other relevant site in the United Kingdom;

    (c) any occurrence elsewhere than on the licensed site involving nuclear matter which is not excepted matter and which—

        (i) having been on the licensed site at any time during the period of the licensee's responsibility; or

        (ii) having been in the course of carriage on behalf of the licensee as licensee of that site,

    has not subsequently been on any relevant site, or in the course of any relevant carriage, or (except in the course of relevant carriage) within the territorial limits of a country which is not a relevant territory.

9 Duty of Crown in respect of certain sites

If a government department uses any site for any purpose which, if section 1 of this Act applied to the Crown, would require the authority of a nuclear site licence in respect of that site, section 7 of this Act shall apply in like manner as if—

    (a) the Crown were the licensee under a nuclear site licence in respect of that site; and

    (b) any reference to the period of the licensee's responsibility were a reference to any period during which the department occupies this site.

12 Right to compensation by virtue of ss. 7 to 10

(1) Where any injury or damage has been caused in breach of a duty imposed by section 7, 8, 9 or 10 of this Act—

    (a) subject to sections 13(1), (3) and (4), 15 and 17(1) of this Act, compensation in respect of that injury or damage shall be payable in accordance with section 16 of this Act wherever the injury or damage was incurred;

    (b) subject to subsections (3) and (4) of this section and to section 21(2) of this Act, no other liability shall be incurred by any person in respect of that injury or damage.

(2) Subject to subsection (3) of this section, any injury or damage which, though not caused in breach of such a duty as aforesaid, is not reasonably separable from injury or damage so caused shall be deemed for the purposes of subsection (1) of this section to have been so caused.

(3) Where any injury or damage is caused partly in breach of such a duty as aforesaid and partly by an emission of ionising radiations which does not constitute such a breach, subsection (2) of this section shall not affect any liability of any person in respect of that emission apart from this Act, but a claimant shall not be entitled to recover compensation in respect of the same injury or damage both under this Act and otherwise than under this Act.

13   Exclusion, extension or reduction of compensation in certain cases

(1) Subject to subsections (2) and (5) of this section, compensation shall not be payable under this Act in respect of injury or damage caused by a breach of a duty imposed by section 7, 8, 9 or 10 thereof if the injury or damage—

    (a) was caused by such an occurrence as is mentioned in section 7(2)(b) or (c) or 10(2)(b) of this Act which is shown to have taken place wholly within the territorial limits of one, and one only, of the relevant territories other than the United Kingdom; or

    (b) was incurred within the territorial limits of a country which is not a relevant territory.

(2) In the case of a breach of a duty imposed by section 7, 8 or 9 of this Act, subsection (1)(b) of this section shall not apply to injury or damage incurred by, or by persons or property on, a ship or aircraft registered in the United Kingdom.

(4) The duty imposed by section 7, 8, 9, 10 or 11 of this Act—

    (a) shall not impose any liability on the person subject to that duty with respect to injury or damage caused by an occurrence which constitutes a breach of that duty if the occurrence, or the causing thereby of the injury or damage, is attributable to hostile action in the course of any armed conflict, including any armed conflict within the United Kingdom; but

    (b) shall impose such a liability where the occurrence, or the causing thereby of the injury or damage, is attributable to a natural disaster, notwithstanding that the disaster is of such an exceptional character that it could not reasonably have been foreseen.

(6) The amount of compensation payable to or in respect of any person under this Act in respect of any injury or damage caused in breach of a duty imposed by section 7, 8, 9 or 10 of this Act may be reduced by reason of the fault of that person if, but only if, and to the extent that, the causing of that injury or damage is attributable to any act of that person committed with the intention of causing harm to any person or property or with reckless disregard for the consequences of his act.

15   Time for bringing claims under ss. 7 to 11

(1) Subject to subsection (2) of this section and to section 16(3) of this Act, but notwithstanding anything in any other enactment, a claim by virtue of any of sections 7 to 11 of this Act may be made at any time before, but shall not be entertained if made at any time after, the expiration of thirty years from the relevant date, that is to say, the date of the occurrence which gave rise to the claim or, where that occurrence was a continuing one, or was one of a succession of occurrences all attributable to a particular happening on a particular relevant site or to the carrying out from time to time on a particular relevant site of a particular operation, the date of the last event in the course of that occurrence or succession of occurrences to which the claim relates.

(2) Notwithstanding anything in subsection (1) of this section, a claim in respect of injury or damage caused by an occurrence involving nuclear matter stolen from, or lost, jettisoned or abandoned by, the person whose breach of a duty imposed by section 7, 8, 9 or 10 of this Act gave rise to the claim shall not be entertained if the occurrence takes place after

the expiration of the period of twenty years beginning with the day when the nuclear matter in question was so stolen, lost, jettisoned or abandoned.

16 Satisfaction of claims by virtue of ss. 7 to 10

(1) The liability of any person to pay compensation under this Act by virtue of a duty imposed on that person by section 7, 8 or 9 thereof shall not require him to make in respect of any one occurrence constituting a breach of that duty payments by way of such compensation exceeding in the aggregate, apart from payments in respect of interest or costs, [£20 million or, in the case of the licensees of such sites as may be prescribed, £5 million.]

[(1A) The Secretary of State may be with the approval of the Treasury by order increase or further increase either or both of the amounts specified in subsection (1) of this section; but an order under this subsection shall not affect liability in respect of any occurrence before (or beginning before) the order comes into force.]

(3) Any claim by virtue of a duty imposed on any person by section 7, 8, 9 or 10 of this Act—

   (a) to the extent to which, by virtue of subsection (1) or (2) of this section, though duly established, it is not or would not be payable by that person; or
   (b) which is made after the expiration of the relevant period; or
   (c) which, being such a claim as is mentioned in section 15(2) of this Act, is made after the expiration of the period of twenty years so mentioned; or
   (d) which is a claim the full satisfaction of which out of funds otherwise required to be, or to be made, available for the purpose is prevented by section 21(1) of this Act, shall be made to the appropriate authority, that is to say—
      (i) in the case of a claim by virtue of the said section 8, the Minister of Technology;
      (ii) in the case of a claim by virtue of the said section 9 (other than a claim in connection with a site used by a department of the Government of Northern Ireland), the Minister in charge of the government department concerned [or where the government department concerned is a part of the Scottish Administration the Scottish Minister];
      (iii) in any other case, the Minister,

and, if established to the satisfaction of the appropriate authority, and to the extent to which it cannot be satisfied out of sums made available for the purpose under section 18 of this Act or by means of a relevant foreign contribution, shall be satisfied by the appropriate authority to such extent and out of funds provided by such means as Parliament may determine.

(4) Where in pursuance of subsection (3) of this section a claim has been made to the appropriate authority, any question affecting the establishment of the claim or as to the amount of any compensation in satisfaction of the claim may, if the authority thinks fit, be referred for decision to the appropriate court, that is to say, to whichever of the High Court, the Court of Session and the High Court of Justice in Northern Ireland would, but for the provisions of this section, have had jurisdiction in accordance with section 17(1) and (2) of this Act to determine the claim; and the claimant may appeal to that court from any decision of the authority on any such question which is not so referred; and on any such reference or appeal—

   (a) the authority shall be entitled to appear and be heard; and
   (b) notwithstanding anything in any Act, the decision of the court shall be final.

(5) In this section, the expression "the relevant period" means the period of ten years beginning with the relevant date within the meaning of section 15(1) of this Act.

18 General cover for compensation by virtue of ss. 7 to 10

(1) In the case of any occurrence in respect of which one or more persons incur liability by virtue of section 7, 8, 9 or 10 of this Act or by virtue of any relevant foreign law made for purposes corresponding to those of any of those sections, but subject to subsections (2) [to (4B)] of this section and to sections 17(3)(b) and 21(1) of this Act, there shall be made available out of moneys provided by Parliament such sums as, when aggregated—

(a) with any funds required by, or by any relevant foreign law made for purposes corresponding to those of, section 19(1) of this Act to be available for the purpose of satisfying claims in respect of that occurrence against any licensee or relevant foreign operator; and

(b) in the case of a claim by virtue of any such foreign law, with any relevant foreign contributions towards the satisfaction of claims in respect of that occurrence, may be necessary to ensure that all claims in respect of that occurrence made within the relevant period and duly established, excluding, but without prejudice to, any claim in respect of interest or costs, are satisfied up to [the aggregate amount specified in subsection (1A) of this section; and

(c) in the case of an occurrence in respect of which the Authority incurs liability, with any amounts payable under a contract of insurance or other arrangements for satisfying claims in respect of that occurrence against the Authority,]

[(1A) The aggregate amount referred to in subsection (1) of this section is the equivalent in sterling of 300 million special drawing rights on—

(a) the day (or first day) of the occurrence in question, or

(b) if the Secretary of State certifies that another day has been fixed in relation to the occurrence in accordance with an international agreement, that other day.]

[*Subsection (1B) provides for subsection (1A) similarly to s. 16(1A)'s provision for s. 16(1).*]

19   Special cover for licensee's liability

(1) Subject to section 3(5) of this Act and to subsection (3) of this section, where a nuclear site licence has been granted in respect of any site, the licensee shall make such provision (either by insurance or by some other means) as the Minister may with the consent of the Treasury approve for sufficient funds to be available at all times to ensure that any claims which have been or may be duly established against the licensee as licensee of that site by virtue of section 7 of this Act or any relevant foreign law made for purposes corresponding to those of section 10 of this Act (excluding, but without prejudice to, any claim in respect of interest or costs) are satisfied up to [the required amount] in respect of each severally of the following periods, that is to say—

(a) the current cover period, if any;

(b) any cover period which ended less than ten years before the time in question;

(c) any earlier cover period in respect of which a claim remains to be disposed of, being a claim made—

(i)   within the relevant period within the meaning of section 16 of this Act; and

(ii) in the case of a claim such as is mentioned in section 15(2) of this Act, also within the period of twenty years so mentioned;

and for the purposes of this section the cover period in respect of which any claim is to be treated as being made shall be that in which the beginning of the relevant period aforesaid fell.

[(1A) In this section "the required amount", in relation to the provision to be made by a licensee in respect of a cover period, means an aggregate amount equal to the amount applicable under section 16(1) of this Act to the licensee, as licensee of the site in question, in respect of an occurrence within that period.]

Criminal Law Act 1967
(1967, c. 58)

3   Use of force in making arrest, etc.

(1) A person may use such force as is reasonable in the circumstances in the prevention of crime, or in effecting or assisting in the lawful arrest of offenders or suspected offenders or of persons unlawfully at large.

14 Civil rights in respect of maintenance and champerty

(1) No person shall, under the law of England and Wales, be liable in tort for any conduct on account of its being maintenance or champerty as known to the common law, except in the case of a cause of action accruing before this section has effect.

(2) The abolition of criminal and civil liability under the law of England and Wales for maintenance and champerty shall not affect any rule of that law as to the cases in which a contract is to be treated as contrary to public policy or otherwise illegal.

Misrepresentation Act 1967
(1967, c. 7)

1 Removal of certain bars to rescission for innocent misrepresentation

Where a person has entered into a contract after a misrepresentation has been made to him, and—

(a) the misrepresentation has become a term of the contract; or

(b) the contract has been performed;

or both, then, if otherwise he would be entitled to rescind the contract without alleging fraud, he shall be so entitled, subject to the provisions of this Act, notwithstanding the matters mentioned in paragraphs (a) and (b) of this section.

2 Damages for misrepresentation

(1) Where a person has entered into a contract after a misrepresentation has been made to him by another party thereto and as a result thereof he has suffered loss, then, if the person making the misrepresentation would be liable to damages in respect thereof had the misrepresentation been made fraudulently, that person shall be so liable notwithstanding that the misrepresentation was not made fraudulently, unless he proves that he had reasonable ground to believe and did believe up to the time the contract was made that the facts represented were true.

(2) Where a person has entered into a contract after a misrepresentation has been made to him otherwise than fraudulently, and he would be entitled, by reason of the misrepresentation, to rescind the contract, then, if it is claimed, in any proceedings arising out of the contract, that the contract ought to be or has been rescinded, the court or arbitrator may declare the contract subsisting and award damages in lieu of rescission, if of opinion that it would be equitable to do so, having regard to the nature of the misrepresentation and the loss that would be caused by it if the contract were upheld, as well as to the loss that rescission would cause to the other party.

(3) Damages may be awarded against a person under subsection (2) of this section whether or not he is liable to damages under subsection (1) thereof, but where he is so liable any award under the said subsection (2) shall be taken into account in assessing his liability under the said subsection (1).

3 Avoidance of provision excluding liability for misrepresentation

[If a contract contains a term which would exclude or restrict—

(a) any liability to which a party to a contract may be subject by reason of any misrepresentation made by him before the contract was made; or

(b) any remedy available to another party to the contract by reason of such a misrepresentation,

that term shall be of no effect except in so far as it satisfies the requirement of reasonableness as stated in section 11(1) of the Unfair Contract Terms Act 1977; and it is for those claiming that the term satisfies that requirement to show that it does.]

Parliamentary Commissioner Act 1967
(1967, c. 13)

10   Reports by Commissioner

(5) For the purposes of the law of defamation, any such publication as is hereinafter mentioned shall be absolutely privileged, that is to say—

(a) the publication of any matter by the Commissioner in making a report to either House of Parliament for the purposes of this Act;

(b) the publication of any matter by a member of the House of Commons in communicating with the Commissioner or his officers for those purposes or by the Commissioner or his officers in communicating with such a member for those purposes;

(c) the publication by such a member to the person by whom a complaint was made under this Act of a report or statement sent to the member in respect of the complaint in pursuance of subsection (1) of this section;

(d) the publication by the Commissioner to such a person as is mentioned in subsection (2) [or (2A)] of this section of a report sent to that person in pursuance of that subsection.

Civil Evidence Act 1968
(1968, c. 64)

11   Convictions as evidence in civil proceedings

(1) In any civil proceedings the fact that a person has been convicted of an offence by or before any court in the United Kingdom or by a court-martial there or elsewhere shall (subject to subsection (3) below) be admissible in evidence for the purpose of proving where to do so is relevant to any issue in those proceedings, that he committed that offence, whether he was so convicted upon a plea of guilty or otherwise and whether or not he is a party to the civil proceedings; but no conviction other than a subsisting one shall be admissible in evidence by virtue of this section.

(2) In any civil proceedings in which by virtue of this section a person is proved to have been convicted of an offence by or before any court in the United Kingdom or by a court-martial there or elsewhere—

(a) he shall be taken to have committed that offence unless the contrary is proved; and

(b) without prejudice to the reception of any other admissible evidence for the purpose of identifying the facts on which the conviction was based, the contents of any documents which is admissible as evidence of the conviction, and the contents of the information, complaint, indictment or charge-sheet on which the person in question was convicted, shall be admissible in evidence for that purpose.

(3) Nothing in this section shall prejudice the operation of section 13 of this Act or any other enactment whereby a conviction or a finding of fact in any criminal proceedings is for the purposes of any other proceedings made conclusive evidence of any fact.

(4) Where in any civil proceedings the contents of any document are admissible in evidence by virtue of subsection (2) above, a copy of that document, or of the material part thereof, purporting to be certified or otherwise authenticated by or on behalf of the court or authority having custody of that document shall be admissible in evidence and shall be taken to be a true copy of that document or part unless the contrary is shown.

13   Conclusiveness of convictions for purposes of defamation actions

(1) In an action for libel or slander in which the question whether [the plaintiff] did or did not commit a criminal offence is relevant to an issue arising in the action, proof that at the time when that issue falls to be determined, [he] stands convicted of that offence shall be

conclusive evidence that he committed that offence; and his conviction thereof shall be admissible in evidence accordingly.

(2) In any such action as aforesaid in which by virtue of this section [the plaintiff] is proved to have been convicted of an offence, the contents of any document which is admissible as evidence of the conviction, and the contents of the information, complaint, indictment or charge-sheet on which [he] was convicted, shall, without prejudice to the reception of any other admissible evidence for the purpose of identifying the facts on which the conviction was based, be admissible in evidence for the purpose of identifying those facts.

[(2A) In the case of an action for libel or slander in which there is more than one plaintiff—

(a) the references in subsections (1) and (2) above to the plaintiff shall be construed as references to any of the plaintiffs, and

(b) proof that any of the plaintiffs stands convicted of an offence shall be conclusive evidence that he committed that offence so far as that fact is relevant to any issue arising in relation to his cause of action or that of any other plaintiff.]

(3) For the purposes of this section a person shall be taken to stand convicted of an offence if but only if there subsists against him a conviction of that offence by or before a court in the United Kingdom or by a court-martial there or elsewhere.

Theatres Act 1968
(1968, c. 54)

4 Amendment of law of defamation

(1) For the purposes of the law of libel and slander (including the law of criminal libel so far as it relates to the publication of defamatory matter) the publication of words in the course of a performance of a play shall, subject to section 7 of this Act, be treated as publication in permanent form.

(2) The foregoing subsection shall apply for the purposes of section 3 (slander of title, etc.) of the Defamation Act 1952 as it applies for the purposes of the law of libel and slander.

(3) In this section "words" includes pictures, visual images, gestures and other methods of signifying meaning.

7 Exceptions for performances given in certain circumstances

(1) Nothing in sections 2 to 4 of this Act shall apply in relation to a performance of a play given on a domestic occasion in a private dwelling.

Trade Descriptions Act 1968
(1968, c. 29)

1 Prohibition of false trade descriptions

(1) Any person who, in the course of a trade or business,—

(a) applies a false trade description to any goods; or

(b) supplies or offers to supply any goods to which a false trade description is applied;

shall, subject to the provisions of this Act, be guilty of an offence.

6 Offer to supply

A person exposing goods for supply or having goods in his possession for supply shall be deemed to offer to supply them.

35 Saving for civil rights

A contract for the supply of any goods shall not be void or unenforceable by reason only of a contravention of any provision of this Act.

Employers' Liability (Compulsory Insurance) Act 1969
(1969, c. 57)

1 Insurance against liability for employees

(1) Except as otherwise provided by this Act, every employer carrying on any business in Great Britain shall insure, and maintain insurance, under one or more approved policies with an authorised insurer or insurers against liability for bodily injury or disease sustained by his employees, and arising out of and in the course of their employment in Great Britain in that business, but except in so far as regulations otherwise provide not including injury or disease suffered or contracted outside Great Britain.

(2) Regulations may provide that the amount for which an employer is required by this Act to insure and maintain insurance shall, either generally or in such cases or classes of case as may be prescribed by the regulations, be limited in such manner as may be so prescribed.

2 Employees to be covered

(1) For the purposes of this Act the term "employee" means an individual who has entered into or works under a contract of service or apprenticeship with an employer whether by way of manual labour, clerical work or otherwise, whether such contract is expressed or implied, oral or in writing.

(2) This Act shall not require an employer to insure—

    (a) in respect of an employee of whom the employer is the husband, wife, [civil partner,] father, mother, grandfather, grandmother, step-father, step-mother, son, daughter, grandson, granddaughter, stepson, stepdaughter, brother, sister, half-brother, half- sister; or

    (b) except as otherwise provided by regulations, in respect of employees not ordinarily resident in Great Britain.

Employers' Liability (Defective Equipment) Act 1969
(1969, c. 37)

1 Extension of employer's liability for defective equipment

(1) Where after the commencement of this Act—

    (a) an employee suffers personal injury in the course of his employment in consequence of a defect in equipment provided by his employer for the purposes of the employer's business; and

    (b) the defect is attributable wholly or partly to the fault of a third party (whether identified or not),

the injury shall be deemed to be also attributable to negligence on the part of the employer (whether or not he is liable in respect of the injury apart from this subsection), but without prejudice to the law relating to contributory negligence and to any remedy by way of contribution or in contract or otherwise which is available to the employer in respect of the injury.

(2) In so far as any agreement purports to exclude or limit any liability of an employer arising under subsection (1) of this section, the agreement shall be void.

(3) In this section—

"business" includes the activities carried on by any public body;

"employee" means a person who is employed by another person under a contract of service or apprenticeship and is so employed for the purposes of a business carried on by that other person, and "employer" shall be construed accordingly;

"equipment" includes any plant and machinery, vehicle, aircraft and clothing;

"fault" means negligence, breach of statutory duty or other act or omission which gives rise to liability in tort in England and Wales or which is wrongful and gives rise to liability in damages in Scotland; and "personal injury" includes loss of life, any impairment of a person's physical or mental condition and any disease.

(4) This section binds the Crown, and persons in the service of the Crown shall accordingly be treated for the purposes of this section as employees of the Crown if they would not be so treated apart from this subsection.

Administration of Justice Act 1970
(1970, c. 31)

40   Punishment for unlawful harassment of debtors

(1) A person commits an offence if, with the object of coercing another person to pay money claimed from the other as a debt due under a contract, he—

(a) harasses the other with demands for payment which, in respect of their frequency or the manner or occasion of making any such demand, or of any threat or publicity by which any demand is accompanied, are calculated to subject him or members of his family or household to alarm, distress or humiliation;

(b) falsely represents, in relation to the money claimed, that criminal proceedings lie for failure to pay it;

(c) falsely represents himself to be authorised in some official capacity to claim or enforce payment; or

(d) utters a document falsely represented by him to have some official character or purporting to have some official character which he knows it has not.

(2) A person may be guilty of an offence by virtue of subsection (1)(a) above if he concerts with others in the taking of such action as is described in that paragraph, notwithstanding that his own course of conduct does not by itself amount to harassment.

(3) Subsection (1)(a) above does not apply to anything done by a person which is reasonable (and otherwise permissible in law) for the purpose—

(a) of securing the discharge of an obligation due, or believed by him to be due, to himself or to persons for whom he acts, or protecting himself or them from future loss; or

(b) of the enforcement of any liability by legal process.

Taxes Management Act 1970
(1970, c. 9)

[30   Recovery of overpayment of tax, etc.

(1) Where an amount of [income tax or capital gains tax] has been repaid to any person which ought not to have been repaid to him, that amount of tax may be assessed and recovered as if it were unpaid tax.

(1A) Subsection (1) above shall not apply where the amount of tax which has been repaid is assessable under section 29 of this Act.

(1B) Subsections (2) to (8) of section 29 of this Act shall apply in relation to an assessment under subsection (1) above as they apply in relation to an assessment under subsection (1) of that section; and subsection (4) of that section as so applied shall have effect as if the reference to the loss of tax were a reference to the repayment of the amount of tax which ought not to have been repaid.

(2) In any case where—

(a) a repayment of tax has been increased in accordance with section 824 [...] of the principal Act or section 283 of the 1992 Act (supplements added to repayments of tax, etc.); and

(b) the whole or any part of that repayment has been paid to any person but ought not to have been paid to him; and

(c) that repayment ought not to have been increased either at all or to any extent; then the amount of the repayment assessed under subsection (1) above may include an amount equal to the amount by which the repayment ought not to have been increased.

(3) In any case where—

(a) a payment, other than a repayment of tax to which subsection (2) above applies, is increased in accordance with section 824 or 825 of the principal Act or section 283 of the 1992 Act; and

(b) that payment ought not to have been increased either at all or to any extent; then an amount equal to the amount by which the payment ought not to have been increased may be assessed and recovered as if it were unpaid income tax [...].

(5) An assessment under this section shall not be out of time under section 34 of this Act if it is made before the end of whichever of the following ends the later, namely—

(a) the [year of assessment] following that in which the amount assessed was repaid or paid as the case may be, or

(b) where a return delivered by the person concerned [...] is enquired into by an officer of the Board, the period ending with the day on which, by virtue of section 28A(5) of this Act, the officer's enquiries are treated as completed.

(6) Subsection (5) above is without prejudice to section 36 of this Act.

(7) In this section any reference to an amount repaid or paid includes a reference to an amount allowed by way of set-off.]

33   Error or mistake

[(1) If any person who has paid income or capital gains tax under an assessment (whether a self-assessment or otherwise) alleges that the assessment was excessive by reason of some error or mistake in a return, he may by notice in writing at any time not later than five years after the 31st January next following the year of assessment to which the return relates, make a claim to the Board for relief.]

(2) On receiving the claim the Board shall inquire into the matter and shall subject to the provisions of this section give by way of repayment such relief [...] in respect of the error or mistake as is reasonable and just:

[(2A) No relief shall be given under this section in respect of—

(a) an error or mistake as to the basis on which the liability of the claimant ought to have been computed where the return was in fact made on the basis or in accordance with the practice generally prevailing at the time when it was made; or

(b) an error or mistake in a claim which is included in the return.]

(3) In determining the claim the Board shall have regard to all the relevant circumstances of the case, and in particular shall consider whether the granting of relief would result in the exclusion from charge to tax of any part of the profits of the claimant, and for this purpose the Board may take into consideration the liability of the claimant and assessment made on him in respect of chargeable periods other than that to which the claim relates.

(4) If any appeal is brought from the decision of the Board on the claim the Special Commissioners shall hear and determine the appeal in accordance with the principles to be followed by the Board in determining claims under this section; and neither the appellant nor the Board shall be entitled to [appeal under section 56A of this Act against the determination of the Special Commissioners except] on a point of law arising in connection with the computation of profits.

(5) In this section "profits"—

(a) in relation to income tax, means income, [, and]

(b) in relation to capital gains tax, means chargeable gains [...].

[33A   Error or mistake in partnership statement

(1) This section applies where, in the case of a trade, profession or business carried on by two or more persons in partnership, those persons allege that the tax charged by self-assessment of theirs [...] was excessive by reason of some error or mistake in a partnership statement.

(2) One of those persons (the representative partner) may, not later than five years after the filing date, by notice in writing make a claim to the Board for relief.

(3) On receiving the claim the Board shall inquire into the matter and shall, subject to subsection (5) below, so amend the partnership statement so as to give such relief in respect of the error or mistake as is reasonable or just.

[(4) Where a partnership statement is amended under subsection (3) above, the Board shall by notice to each of the relevant partners amend—

(a) the partner's self-assessment under section 9 of this Act, or

(b) the partner's company tax return, so as to give effect to the amendments of the partnership statement.]

(5) No relief shall be given under this section in respect of an error or mistake as to the basis on which the liability of the partners ought to have been computed where the partnership statement was in fact made on the basis or in accordance with the practice generally prevailing at the time when it was made.

(6) In determining the claim the Board—

(a) shall have regard to all the relevant circumstances of the case, and

(b) in particular shall consider whether the granting of relief would result in the exclusion from charge to tax of any part of the profits of any of the partners;

and for the purposes of this subsection the Board may take into consideration the liability of the partners and their self-assessments in respect of chargeable periods other than that to which the claim relates.

(7) If any appeal is brought from the decision of the Board on the claim, the Special Commissioners shall hear and determine the appeal in accordance with the principles to be followed by the Board in determining claims under this section.

[(8) Subject to subsection (8A) below, the determination of the Special Commissioners of an appeal under subsection (6) above shall be final and conclusive (notwithstanding any provision having effect by virtue of section 56B of this Act).

(8A) Subsection (8) above does not apply in relation to a point of law arising in connection with the computation of profits.]

Animals Act 1971
(1971, c. 22)

1   New provisions as to strict liability for damage done by animals

(1) The provisions of sections 2 to 5 of this Act replace—

(a) the rules of the common law imposing a strict liability in tort for damage done by an animal on the ground that the animal is regarded as ferae naturae or that its vicious or mischievous propensities are known or presumed to be known;

(b) subsections (1) and (2) of section 1 of the Dogs Act 1906 as amended by the Dogs (Amendment) Act 1928 (injury to cattle or poultry); and

(c) the rules of the common law imposing a liability for cattle trespass.

(2) Expressions used in those sections shall be interpreted in accordance with the provisions of section 6 (as well as those of section 11) of this Act.

2   Liability for damage done by dangerous animals

(1) Where any damage is caused by an animal which belongs to a dangerous species, any person who is a keeper of the animal is liable for the damage, except as otherwise provided by this Act.

(2) Where damage is caused by an animal which does not belong to a dangerous species, a keeper of the animal is liable for the damage, except as otherwise provided by this Act, if—

(a) the damage is of a kind which the animal, unless restrained, was likely to cause or which, if caused by the animal, was likely to be severe; and

(b) the likelihood of the damage or of its being severe was due to characteristics of the animal which are not normally found in animals of the same species or are not normally so found except at particular times or in particular circumstances; and

(c) those characteristics were known to that keeper or were at any time known to a person who at that time had charge of the animal as that keeper's servant or, where that keeper is the head of a household, were known to another keeper of the animal who is a member of that household and under the age of sixteen.

3   Liability for injury done by dogs to livestock

Where a dog causes damage by killing or injuring livestock, any person who is a keeper of the dog is liable for the damage, except as otherwise provided by this Act.

4   Liability for damage and expenses due to trespassing livestock

(1) Where livestock belonging to any person strays on to land in the ownership or occupation of another and—

(a) damage is done by the livestock to the land or to any property on it which is in the ownership or possession of the other person; or

(b) any expenses are reasonably incurred by that other person in keeping the livestock while it cannot be restored to the person to whom it belongs or while it is detained in pursuance of section 7 of this Act, or in ascertaining to whom it belongs; the person to whom the livestock belongs is liable for the damage or expenses, except as otherwise provided by this Act.

(2) For the purposes of this section any livestock belongs to the person in whose possession it is.

5   Exceptions from liability under sections 2 to 4

(1) A person is not liable under sections 2 to 4 of this Act for any damage which is due wholly to the fault of the person suffering it.

(2) A person is not liable under section 2 of this Act for any damage suffered by a person who has voluntarily accepted the risk thereof.

(3) A person is not liable under section 2 of this Act for any damage caused by an animal kept on any premises or structure to a person trespassing there, if it is proved either—

(a) that the animal was not kept there for the protection of persons or property; or

(b) (if the animal was kept there for the protection of persons or property) that keeping it there for that purpose was not unreasonable.

(4) A person is not liable under section 3 of this Act if the livestock was killed or injured on land on to which it had strayed and either the dog belonged to the occupier or its presence on the land was authorised by the occupier.

(5) A person is not liable under section 4 of this Act where the livestock strayed from a highway and its presence there was a lawful use of the highway.

(6) In determining whether any liability for damage under section 4 of this Act is excluded by subsection (1) of this section the damage shall not be treated as due to the fault of the person suffering it by reason only that he could have prevented it by fencing; but a person is not liable under that section where it is proved that the straying of the livestock on to the land would not have occurred but for a breach by any other person, being a person having an interest in the land, of a duty to fence.

6   Interpretation of certain expressions used in sections 2 to 5

(1) The following provisions apply to the interpretation of sections 2 to 5 of this Act.

(2) A dangerous species is a species—

(a) which is not commonly domesticated in the British Islands; and

(b) whose fully grown animals normally have such characteristics that they are likely, unless restrained, to cause severe damage or that any damage they may cause is likely to be severe.

(3) Subject to subsection (4) of this section, a person is a keeper of an animal if—

(a) he owns the animal or has it in his possession; or

(b) he is the head of a household of which a member under the age of sixteen owns the animal or has it in his possession;

and if at any time an animal ceases to be owned by or to be in the possession of a person, any person who immediately before that time was a keeper thereof by virtue of the preceding provisions of this subsection continues to be a keeper of the animal until another person becomes a keeper thereof by virtue of those provisions.

(4) Where an animal is taken into and kept in possession for the purpose of preventing it from causing damage or of restoring it to its owner, a person is not a keeper of it by virtue only of that possession.

(5) Where a person employed as a servant by a keeper of an animal incurs a risk incidental to his employment he shall not be treated as accepting it voluntarily.

7 Detention and sale of trespassing livestock

(1) The right to seize and detain any animal by way of distress damage feasant is hereby abolished.

(2) Where any livestock strays on to any land and is not then under the control of any person the occupier of the land may detain it, subject to subsection (3) of this section, unless ordered to return it by a court.

(3) Where any livestock is detained in pursuance of this section the right to detain it ceases—

(a) at the end of a period of forty-eight hours, unless within that period notice of the detention has been given to the officer in charge of a police station and also, if the person detaining the livestock knows to whom it belongs, to that person; or

(b) when such amount is tendered to the person detaining the livestock as is sufficient to satisfy any claim he may have under section 4 of this Act in respect of the livestock; or,

(c) if he has no such claim, when the livestock is claimed by a person entitled to its possession.

(4) Where livestock has been detained in pursuance of this section for a period of not less than fourteen days the person detaining it may sell it at a market or by public auction, unless proceedings are then pending for the return of the livestock or for any claim under section 4 of this Act in respect of it.

(5) Where any livestock is sold in the exercise of the right conferred by this section and the proceeds of the sale, less the costs thereof and any costs incurred in connection with it, exceed the amount of any claim under section 4 of this Act which the vendor had in respect of the livestock, the excess shall be recoverable from him by the person who would be entitled to the possession of the livestock but for the sale.

(6) A person detaining any livestock in pursuance of this section is liable for any damage caused to it by a failure to treat it with reasonable care and supply it with adequate food and water while it is so detained.

(7) References in this section to a claim under section 4 of this Act in respect of any livestock do not include any claim under that section for damage done by or expenses incurred in respect of the livestock before the straying in connection with which it is detained under this section.

8 Duty to take care to prevent damage from animals straying on to the highway

(1) So much of the rules of the common law relating to liability for negligence as excludes or restricts the duty which a person might owe to others to take such care as is

reasonable to see that damage is not caused by animals straying on to a highway is hereby abolished.

(2) Where damage is caused by animals straying from unfenced land to a highway a person who placed them on the land shall not be regarded as having committed a breach of the duty to take care by reason only of placing them there if—

    (a) the land is common land, or is land situated in an area where fencing is not customary, or is a town or village green; and

    (b) he had a right to place the animals on that land.

9 Killing of or injury to dogs worrying livestock

(1) In any civil proceedings against a person (in this section referred to as the defendant) for killing or causing injury to a dog it shall be a defence to prove—

    (a) that the defendant acted for the protection of any livestock and was a person entitled to act for the protection of that livestock; and

    (b) that within forty-eight hours of the killing or injury notice thereof was given by the defendant to the officer in charge of a police station.

(2) For the purposes of this section a person is entitled to act for the protection of any livestock if, and only if—

    (a) the livestock or the land on which it is belongs to him or to any person under whose express or implied authority he is acting; and

    (b) the circumstances are not such that liability for killing or causing injury to the livestock would be excluded by section 5(4) of this Act.

(3) Subject to subsection (4) of this section, a person killing or causing injury to a dog shall be deemed for the purposes of this section to act for the protection of any livestock if, and only if, either—

    (a) the dog is worrying or is about to worry the livestock and there are no other reasonable means of ending or preventing the worrying; or

    (b) the dog has been worrying livestock, has not left the vicinity and is not under the control of any person and there are no practicable means of ascertaining to whom it belongs.

(4) For the purposes of this section the condition stated in either of the paragraphs of the preceding subsection shall be deemed to have been satisfied if the defendant believed that it was satisfied and had reasonable ground for that belief.

(5) For the purposes of this section—

    (a) an animal belongs to any person if he owns it or has it in his possession; and

    (b) land belongs to any person if he is the occupier thereof.

10 Application of certain enactments to liability under sections 2 to 4

For the purposes of [the Fatal Accidents Act 1976], the Law Reform (Contributory Negligence) Act 1945 and [the Limitation Act 1980] any damage for which a person is liable under sections 2 to 4 of this Act shall be treated as due to his fault.

11 General interpretation

In this Act—

    "common land", and "town or village green" have the same meanings as in the Commons Regulation Act 1965;

    "damage" includes the death of, or injury to, any person (including any disease and any impairment of physical or mental condition);

    "fault" has the same meaning as in the Law Reform (Contributory Negligence) Act 1945;

    "fencing" includes the construction of any obstacle designed to prevent animals from straying;

    "livestock" means cattle, horses, asses, mules, hinnies, sheep, pigs, goats and poultry, and also deer not in the wild state and, in section 3 and 9 also, while in captivity, pheasants, partridges and grouse;

"poultry" means the domestic varieties of the following, that is to say, fowls, turkeys, geese, ducks, guinea-fowls, pigeons, peacocks and quails; and

"species" includes sub-species and variety.

12   Application to Crown

(1) This Act binds the Crown, but nothing in this section shall authorise proceedings to be brought against Her Majesty in her private capacity.

(2) Section 38(3) of the Crown Proceedings Act 1947 (interpretation of references to Her Majesty in her private capacity) shall apply as if this section were contained in that Act.

Carriage of Goods by Sea Act 1971
(1971, c. 19)

1   Application of Hague Rules as amended

(1) In this Act, "the Rules" means the International Convention for the unification of certain rules of law relating to bills of lading signed at Brussels on 25 August 1924, as amended by the Protocol signed at Brussels on 23 February 1968 [and by the Protocol signed at Brussels on 21 December 1979].

(2) The provisions of the Rules, as set out in the Schedule to this Act, shall have the force of law.

(3) Without prejudice to subsection (2) above, the said provisions shall have effect (and have the force of law) in relation to and in connection with the carriage of goods by sea in ships where the port of shipment is a port in the United Kingdom, whether or not the carriage is between ports in two different States within the meaning of Article X of the Rules.

(4) Subject to subsection (6) below, nothing in this section shall be taken as applying anything in the Rules to any contract for the carriage of goods by sea, unless the contract expressly or by implication provides for the issue of a bill of lading or any similar document of title.

(5) [...]

(6) Without prejudice to Article X(c) of the Rules, the Rules shall have the force of law in relation to—

(a) any bill of lading if the contract contained in or evidenced by it expressly provides that the Rules shall govern the contract, and

(b) any receipt which is a non-negotiable document marked as such if the contract contained in or evidenced by it is a contract for the carriage of goods by sea which expressly provides that the Rules are to govern the contract as if the receipt were a bill of lading,

but subject, where paragraph (b) applies, to any necessary modifications and in particular with the omission in Article III of the Rules of the second sentence of paragraph 4 and of paragraph 7.

(7) If and so far as the contract contained in or evidenced by a bill of lading or receipt within paragraph (a) or (b) of subsection (6) above applies to deck cargo or live animals, the Rules as given the force of law by that subsection shall have effect as if Article I(c) did not exclude deck cargo and live animals.

In this subsection "deck cargo" means cargo which by the contract of carriage is stated as being carried on deck and is so carried.

2   Contracting States, etc.

(1) If Her Majesty by Order in council certifies to the following effect, that is to say, that for the purposes of the Rules—

(a) a State specified in the Order is a contracting State, or is a contracting State in respect of any place or territory so specified; or

(b) any place or territory specified in the Order forms part of a State so specified (whether a contracting State or not),

the Order shall, except so far as it has been superseded by a subsequent Order, be conclusive evidence of the matters so certified.

(2) An Order in Council under this section may be varied or revoked by a subsequent Order in Council.

3   Absolute warranty of seaworthiness not to be implied in contracts to which Rules apply

There shall not be implied in any contract for the carriage of goods by sea to which the Rules apply by virtue of this Act any absolute undertaking by the carrier of the goods to provide a seaworthy ship.

4   Application of Act to British possessions, etc.

(1) Her Majesty may by Order in Council direct that this Act shall extend, subject to such exceptions, adaptations and modifications as may be specified in the Order, to all or any of the following territories, that is—

(a) any colony (not being a colony for whose external relations a county other than the United Kingdom is responsible),

(b) any country outside Her Majesty's dominions in which Her Majesty has jurisdiction in right of Her Majesty's Government of the United Kigndom.

(2) An Order in Council under this section may contain such transitional and other consequential and incidental provisions as appear to Her Majesty to be expedient, including provisions amending or repealing any legislation about the carriage of goods by sea forming part of the law of any of the territories mentioned in paragraphs (a) and (b) above.

(3) An Order in Council under this section may be varied or revoked by a subsequent Order in Council.

5   Extension of application of Rules to carriage from ports in British possessions, etc.

(1) Her Majesty may by Order in Council provide that section 1(3) of this Act shall have effect as if the reference therein to the United Kingdom included a reference to all or any of the following territories, that is—

(a) the Isle of Man;

(b) any of the Channel Islands specified in the Order;

(c) any colony specified in the Order (not being a colony for whose external relations a country other than the United Kingdom is responsible);

(d) any associated state (as defined by section 1(3) of the West Indies Act 1967) specified in the Order;

(e) any country specified in the Order, being a country outside Her Majesty's dominions in which Her Majesty has jurisdiction in right of Her Majesty's Government of the United Kingdom.

(2) An Order in Council under this section may be varied or revoked by a subsequent Order in Council.

6   Supplemental

(1) This Act may be cited as the Carriage of Goods by Sea Act 1971.

(2) It is hereby declared that this Act extends to Northern Ireland.

(3) The following enactments shall be repealed, that is—

(a) the Carriage of Goods by Sea Act 1924,

(b) section 12(4)(a) of the Nuclear Installations Act 1965, and without prejudice to section 38(1) of the Interpretation Act 1889, the reference to the said Act of 1924 in section 1(1)(i)(ii) of the Hovercraft Act 1968 shall include a reference to this Act.

(4) It is hereby declared that for the purposes of Article VIII of the Rules [section 18 of the Merchant Shipping Act 1979 (which] entirely exempts shipowners and others in certain

circumstances from liability for loss of, or damage to, goods) is a provision relating to limitation of liability.

(5) This Act shall come into force on such day as Her Majesty may by Order in Council appoint, and, for the purposes of the transition from the law in force immediately before the day appointed under this subsection to the provisions of this Act, the Order appointing the day may provide that those provisions shall have effect subject to such transitional provisions as may be contained in the Order.

SCHEDULE   THE HAGUE RULES AS AMENDED BY THE BRUSSELS PROTOCOL 1968

Article I
In these Rules the following words are employed, with the meanings set out below—
  (a) "Carrier" includes the owner or the charter who enters into a contract of carriage with a shipper.
  (b) "Contract of carriage" applies only to contracts of carriage covered by a bill of lading or any similar document of title, in so far as such document relates to the carriage of goods by sea, including any bill of lading or any similar document as aforesaid issued under or pursuant to a charter party from the moment at which such bill of lading or similar document of title regulates the relations between a carrier and a holder of the same.
  (c) "Goods" includes goods, wares, merchandise, and articles of every kind whatsoever except live animals and cargo which by the contract of carriage is stated as being carried on deck and is so carried.
  (d) "Ship" means any vessel used for the carriage of goods by sea.
  (e) "Carriage of goods" covers the period from the time when the goods are loaded on to the time they are discharged from the ship.

Article II
Subject to the provisions of Article VI, under every contract of carriage of goods by sea the carrier, in relation to the loading, handling, stowage, carriage, custody, care and discharge of such goods, shall be subject to the responsibilities and liabilities, and entitled to the rights and immunities hereinafter set forth.

Article III
(1) The carrier shall be bound before and at the beginning of the voyage to exercise due diligence to—
  (a) Make the ship seaworthy.
  (b) Properly man, equip and supply the ship.
  (c) Make the holds, refrigerating and cool chambers, and all other parts of the ship in which goods are carried, fit and safe for their reception, carriage and preservation.

(2) Subject to the provisions of Article IV, the carrier shall properly and carefully load, handle, stow, carry, keep, care for, and discharge the goods carried.

(3) After receiving the goods into his charge the carrier or the master or agent of the carrier shall, on demand of the shipper, issue to the shipper a bill of lading showing among other things—
  (a) The leading marks necessary for identification of the goods as the same are furnished in writing by the shipper before the loading of such goods starts, provided such marks are stamped or otherwise shown clearly upon the goods if uncovered, or on the cases or coverings in which such goods are contained, in such a manner as should ordinarily remain legible until the end of the voyage.
  (b) Either the number of packages or pieces, or the quantity, or weight, as the case may be, as furnished in writing by the shipper.

(c) The apparent order and condition of the goods. Provided that no carrier, master or agent of the carrier shall be bound to state or show in the bill of lading any marks, number, quantity, or weight which he has reasonable ground for suspecting not accurately to represent the goods actually received, or which he has had no reasonable means of checking.

(4) Such a bill of lading shall be prima facie evidence of the receipt by the carrier of the goods as therein described in accordance with paragraph 3(a), (b) and (c). However, proof to the contrary shall not be admissible when the bill of lading has been transferred to a third party acting in good faith.

(5) The shipper shall be deemed to have guaranteed to the carrier the accuracy at the time of shipment of the marks, number, quantity and weight, as furnished by him, and the shipper shall indemnify the carrier against all loss, damages and expenses arising or resulting from inaccuracies in such particulars. The right of the carrier to such indemnity shall in no way limit his responsibility and liability under the contract of carriage to any person other than the shipper.

(6) Unless notice of loss or damage and the general nature of such loss or damage be given in writing to the carrier or his agent at the port of discharge before or at the time of the removal of the goods into the custody of the person entitled to delivery thereof under the contract of carriage, or, if the loss or damage be not apparent, within three days, such removal shall be prima facie evidence of the delivery by the carrier of the goods as described in the bill of lading.

The notice in writing need not be given if the state of the goods has, at the time of their receipt, been the subject of joint survey or inspection.

Subject to paragraph 6*bis* the carrier and the ship shall in any event be discharged from all liability whatsoever in respect of the goods, unless suit is brought within one year of their delivery or of the date when they should have been delivered. This period may, however, be extended if the parties so agree after the cause of action has arisen.

In the case of any actual or apprehended loss or damage the carrier and the receiver shall give all reasonable facilities to each other for inspecting and tallying the goods.

(6*bis*) An action for indemnity against a third person may be brought even after the expiration of the year provided for in the preceding paragraph if brought within the time allowed by the law of the Court seized of the case. However, the time allowed shall be not less than three months, commencing from the day when the person bringing such action for indemnity has settled the claim or has been served with process in the action against himself.

(7) After the goods are loaded the bill of lading to be issued by the carrier, master, or agent of the carrier, to the shipper shall, if the shipper so demands, be a "shipped" bill of lading, provided that if the shipper shall have previously taken up any document of title to such goods, he shall surrender the same as against the issue of the "shipped" bill of lading, but at the option of the carrier such document of title may be noted at the port of shipment by the carrier, master, or agent with the name or names of the ship or ships upon which the goods have been shipped and the date or dates of shipment, and when so noted if it shows the particulars mentioned in paragraph 3 of Article III, shall for the purpose of this article be deemed to constitute a "shipped" bill of lading.

(8) Any clause, covenant, or agreement in a contract of carriage relieving the carrier or the ship from liability for loss or damage to, or in connection with, goods arising from negligence, fault, or failure in the duties and obligations provided in this article or lessening such liability otherwise than as provided in these Rules, shall be null and void and of no effect. A benefit of insurance in favour of the carrier or similar clause shall be deemed to be a clause relieving the carrier from liability.

Article IV

(1) Neither the carrier nor the ship shall be liable for loss or damage arising or resulting from unseaworthiness unless caused by want of due diligence on the part of the carrier to

make the ship seaworthy, and to secure that the ship is properly manned, equipped and supplied, and to make the holds, refrigerating and cool chambers and all other parts of the ship in which goods are carried fit and safe for their reception, carriage and preservation in accordance with the provisions of paragraph 1 of Article III. Whenever loss or damage has resulted from unseaworthiness the burden of proving the exercise of due diligence shall be on the carrier or other person claiming exemption under this article.

(2) Neither the carrier nor the ship shall be responsible for loss or damage arising or resulting from—

(a) Act, neglect, or default of the master, mariner, pilot, or the servants of the carrier in the navigation or in the management of the ship.

(b) Fire, unless caused by the actual fault or privity of the carrier.

(c) Perils, dangers and accidents of the sea or other navigable waters.

(d) Act of God.

(e) Act of war.

(f) Act of public enemies.

(g) Arrest or restraint of princes, rulers or people, or seizure under legal process.

(h) Quarantine restrictions.

(i) Act or omission of the shipper or owner of the goods, his agent or representative.

(j) Strikes or lockouts or stoppage or restraint of labour from whatever cause, whether partial or general.

(k) Riots and civil commotions.

(l) Saving or attempting to save life or property at sea.

(m) Wastage in bulk or weight or any other loss or damage arising from inherent defect, quality or vice of the goods.

(n) Insufficiency of packing.

(o) Insufficiency or inadequacy of marks.

(p) Latent defects not discoverable by due diligence.

(q) Any other cause arising without the actual fault or privity of the carrier, or without the fault or neglect of the agents or servants of the carrier, but the burden of proof shall be on the person claiming the benefit of this exception to show that neither the actual fault or privity of the carrier nor the fault or neglect of the agents or servants of the carrier contributed to the loss or damage.

(3) The shipper shall not be responsible for the loss or damage sustained by the carrier or the ship arising or resulting from any cause without the act, fault or neglect of the shipper, his agents or his servants.

(4) Any deviation in saving or attempting to save life or property at sea or any reasonable deviation shall not be deemed to be an infringement or breach of these Rules or of the contract of carriage, and the carrier shall not be liable for any loss or damage resulting therefrom.

(5) (a) Unless the nature and value of such goods have been declared by the shipper before shipment and inserted in the bill of lading, neither the carrier nor the ship shall in any event be or become liable for any loss or damage to or in connection with the goods in an amount exceeding [666.67 units of account] per package or unit or [2 units of account per kilogramme] of gross weight of the goods lost or damaged, whichever is the higher.

(b) The total amount recoverable shall be calculated by reference to the value of such goods at the place and time at which the goods are discharged from the ship in accordance with the contract or should have been so discharged.

The value of the goods shall be fixed according to the commodity exchange price, or, if there be no such price, according to the current market price, or, if there be no commodity exchange price or current market price, by reference to the normal value of goods of the same kind and quality.

(c) Where a container, pallet or similar article of transport is used to consolidate goods, the number of packages or units enumerated in the bill of lading as packed in such article of transport shall be deemed the number of packages or units for the purpose of this paragraph as far as these packages or units are concerned. Except as aforesaid such article of transport shall be considered the package or unit.

[(d) The unit of account mentioned in this Article is the special drawing right as defined by the International Monetary Fund. The amounts mentioned in sub-paragraph (a) of this paragraph shall be converted into national currency on the basis of the value of that currency on a date to be determined by the law of the court seized of the case.]

(e) Neither the carrier nor the ship shall be entitled to the benefit of the limitation of liability provided for in this paragraph if it is proved that the damage resulted from an act or omission of the carrier done with intent to cause damage, or recklessly and with knowledge that damage would probably result.

(f) The declaration mentioned in sub-paragraph (a) of this paragraph, if embodied in the bill of lading, shall be prima facie evidence, but shall not be binding or conclusive on the carrier.

(g) By agreement between the carrier, master or agent of the carrier and the shipper other maximum amounts than those mentioned in sub-paragraph (a) of this paragraph may be fixed, provided that no maximum amount so fixed shall be less than the appropriate maximum mentioned in that sub-paragraph.

(h) Neither the carrier nor the ship shall be responsible in any event for loss or damage to, or in connection with, goods if the nature or value thereof has been knowingly mis-stated by the shipper in the bill of lading.

(6) Goods of an inflammable, explosive or dangerous nature to the shipment whereof the carrier, master or agent of the carrier has not consented with knowledge of their nature and character, may at any time before discharge be landed at any place, or destroyed or rendered innocuous by the carrier without compensation and the shipper of such goods shall be liable for all damages and expenses directly or indirectly arising out of or resulting from such shipment. If any such goods shipped with such knowledge and consent shall become a danger to the ship or cargo, they may in like manner be landed at any place, or destroyed or rendered innocuous by the carrier without liability on the part of the carrier except to general average, if any.

Article IV bis

(1) The defences and limits of liability provided for in these Rules shall apply in any action against the carrier in respect of loss or damage to goods covered by a contract of carriage whether the action be founded in contract or in tort.

(2) If such an action is brought against a servant or agent of the carrier (such servant or agent not being an independent contractor), such servant or agent shall be entitled to avail himself of the defences and limits of liability which the carrier is entitled to invoke under these Rules.

(3) The aggregate of the amounts recoverable from the carrier, and such servants and agents, shall in no case exceed the limit provided for in these Rules.

(4) Nevertheless, a servant or agent of the carrier shall not be entitled to avail himself of the provisions of this article, if it is proved that the damage resulted from an act or omission of the servant or agent done with intent to cause damage or recklessly and with knowledge that damage would probably result.

Article V

A carrier shall be at liberty to surrender in whole or in part all or any of his rights and immunities or to increase any of his responsibilities and obligations under these Rules, provided such surrender or increase shall be embodied in the bill of lading issued to the shipper. The provisions of the Rules shall not be applicable to charter parties, but if bills of lading are issued in the case of a ship under a charter party they shall comply with the terms of these Rules. Nothing in these Rules shall be held to prevent the insertion in a bill of lading of any lawful provisions regarding general average.

Article VI

Notwithstanding the provisions of the preceding articles, a carrier, master or agent of the carrier and a shipper shall in regard to any particular goods be at liberty to enter into any agreement in any terms as to the responsibility and liability of the carrier for such goods, andas to the rights and immunitiesof the carrier in respect of such goods, or his obligation as to seaworthiness, so far as this stipulation is not contrary to public policy, or the care or diligence of his servants or agents in regard to the loading, handling, stowage, carriage, custody, care and discharge of the goods carried by sea, provided that in this case no bill of lading has been or shall be issued and that the terms agreed shall be embodied in a receipt which shall be a non-negotiable document and shall be marked as such.

Any agreement so entered into shall have full legal effect. Provided that this article shall not apply to ordinary commercial shipments madein the ordinary course of trade, but only to other shipments where the character or condition of the property to be carried or the circumstances, terms and conditions under which the carriage is to be performed are such as reasonably to justify a special agreement.

Article VII

Nothing herein contained shall prevent a carrier or a shipper from entering into any agreement, stipulation, condition, reservation or exemption as to the responsibility and liability of the carrier or the ship for the loss or damage to, or in connection with, the custody and care and handling of goods prior to the loading on, and subsequent to the discharge from, the ship on which the goods are carried by sea.

Article VIII

The provisions of these Rules shall not affect the rights and obligations of the carrier under any statute for the time being in force relating to the limitation of the liability of owners of sea-going vessels.

Article IX

These rules shall not affect the provisions of any international Convention or national law governing liability for nuclear damage.

Article X

The provisions of these Rules shall apply to every bill of lading relating to the carriage of goods between ports in two different States if:

    (a) the bill of lading is issued in a contracting State,

or

    (b) the carriage is from a port in a contracting State,

or

    (c) the contract contained in or evidenced by the bill of lading provides that these Rules or legislation of any State giving effect to them are to govern the contract, whatever may be the nationality of the ship, the carrier, the shipper, the consignee, or any other interested person.

Unsolicited Goods and Services Act 1971
(1971, c. 30)

2 Demands and threats regarding payment

    (1) A person who, not having reasonable cause to believe there is a right to payment, in the course of any trade or business makes a demand for payment, or asserts a present or

prospective right to payment, for what he knows are unsolicited goods sent (after the commencement of this Act) to another person with a view to his acquiring them [for the purposes of his trade or business], shall be guilty of an offence and on summary conviction shall be liable to a fine not exceeding £200.

(2) A person who, not having reasonable cause to believe there is a right to payment in the course of any trade or business and with a view to obtaining any payment for what he knows are unsolicited goods sent as aforesaid—

(a) threatens to bring any legal proceedings; or
(b) places or causes to be placed the name of any person on a list of defaulters or debtors or threatens to do so; or
(c) invokes or causes to be invoked any other collection procedure or threatens to do so,

shall be guilty of an offence and shall be liable on summary conviction to a fine not exceeding £400.

3   Directory entries

[(1) A person ("the purchaser") shall not be liable to make any payment, and shall be entitled to recover any payment made by him, by way of charge for including or arranging for the inclusion in a directory of an entry relating to that person or his trade or business, unless—

(a) there has been signed by the purchaser or on his behalf an order complying with this section,
(b) there has been signed by the purchaser or on his behalf a note complying with this section of his agreement to the charge and before the note was signed, a copy of it was supplied, for retention by him, to him or a person acting on his behalf, ...
(c) there has been transmitted by the purchaser or a person acting on his behalf an electronic communication which includes a statement that the purchaser agrees to the charge and the relevant condition is satisfied in relation to that communication, or
(d) the charge arises under a contract in relation to which the conditions in section 3B(1) (renewed and extended contracts) are met.]

(2) A person shall be guilty of an offence punishable on summary conviction with a fine not exceeding £400 if, in a case where a payment inrespect of a charge would [...] be recoverable from him in accordance with the terms of subsection (1) above, he demands payment, or asserts a present or prospective right to payment, of the charge or any part of it, without knowing or having reasonable cause to believe [that—

(a) the entry to which the charge relates was ordered in accordance with this section,
(b) a proper note of the agreement has been duly signed, or
(c) the requirements set out in subsection (1)(c) or (d) above have been met.]

(3) For the purposes of [this section—

[(a)] an order for an entry in a directory must be made by means of an order form or other stationery belonging to the [purchaser, which may be sent electronically but which must bear his name and address (or one or more of his addresses);] and
[(b)] the note [of a person's agreement to a charge must—

(i) specify the particulars set out in Part 1 of the Schedule to the Regulatory Reform (Unsolicited Goods and Services Act 1971) (Directory Entries and Demands for Payment) Order 2005, and
(ii) give reasonable particulars of the entry in respect of which the charge would be payable.]

[(3A) In relation to an electronic communication which includes a statement that the purchaser agrees to a charge for including or arranging the inclusion in a directory of any entry, the relevant condition is that—

(a) before the electronic communication was transmitted the information referred to in subsection (3B) below was communicated to the purchaser, and

(b) the electronic communication can readily be produced and retained in a visible and legible form.

(3B) that information is—

(a) the following particulars—

    (i)   the amount of the charge;

    (ii)   the name of the directory or proposed directory;

    (iii) the name of the person producing the directory;

    (iv) the geographic address at which that person is established;

    (v)   if the directory is or is to be available in printed form, the proposed date of publication of the directory or of the issue in which the entry is to be included;

    (vi) if the directory or the issue in which the entry is to be included is to be put on sale, the price at which it is to be offered for sale and the minimum number of copies which are to be available for sale;

    (vii) if the directory or the issue in which the entry is to be included is to be distributed free of charge (whether or not it is also to be put on sale), the minimum number of copies which are to be so distributed;

    (viii) if the directory is or is to be available in a form other than in printed form, adequate details of how it may be accessed; and

(b) reasonable particulars of the entry in respect of which the charge would be payable.

(3C) In this section "electronic communication" has the same meaning as in the Electronic Communications Act 2000.]

(4) Nothing in this section shall apply to a payment due under a contract entered into before the commencement of this Act, or entered into by the acceptance of an offer made before that commencement.

[3B Renewed and extended contracts

(1) The conditions referred to in section 3(1)(d) above are met in relation to a contract ("the new contract") if—

(a) a person ("the purchaser") has entered into an earlier contract ("the earlier contract") for including or arranging for the inclusion in a particular issue or version of a directory ("the earlier directory") of an entry ("the earlier entry") relating to him or his trade or business;

(b) the purchaser was liable to make a payment by way of a charge arising under the earlier contract for including or arranging for the inclusion of the earlier entry in the earlier directory;

(c) the new contract is a contract for including or arranging for the inclusion in a later issue or version of a directory ("the later directory") of an entry ("the later entry") relating to the purchaser or his trade or business;

(d) the form, content and distribution of the later directory is materially the same as the form, content and distribution of the earlier directory;

(e) the form and content of the later entry is materially the same as the form and content of the earlier entry;

(f) if the later directory is published other than in electronic form—

    (i)   the earlier directory was the last, or the last but one, issue or version of the directory to be published before the later directory, and

    (ii) the date of publication of the later directory is not more than 13 months after the date of publication of the earlier directory;

(g) if the later directory is published in electronic form, the first date on which the new contract requires the later entry to be published is not more than the relevant period after the last date on which the earlier contract required the earlier entry to be published;

(h) if it was a term of the earlier contract that the purchaser renew or extend the contract—

   (i) before the start of the new contract the relevant publisher has given notice in writing to the purchaser containing the information set out in Part 3 of the Schedule to the Regulatory Reform (Unsolicited Goods and Services Act 1971) (Directory Entries and Demands for Payment) Order 2005; and

   (ii) the purchaser has not written to the relevant publisher withdrawing his agreement to the renewal or extension of the earlier contract within the period of 21 days starting when he receives the notice referred to in sub-paragraph (i); and

(i) if the parties to the earlier contract and the new contract are different—

   (i) the parties to both contracts have entered into a novation agreement in respect of the earlier contract; or

   (ii) the relevant publisher has given the purchaser the information set out in Part 4 of the Schedule to the Regulatory Reform (Unsolicited Goods and Services Act 1971) (Directory Entries and Demands for Payment) Order 2005.

(2) For the purposes of subsection (1)(d) and (e), the form, content or distribution of the later directory, or the form or content of the later entry, shall be taken to be materially the same as that of the earlier directory or the earlier entry (as the case may be), if a reasonable person in the position of the purchaser would—

(a) view the two as being materially the same; or

(b) view that of the later directory or the later entry as being an improvement on that of the earlier directory or the earlier entry.

(3) For the purposes of subsection (1)(g) "the relevant period" means the period of 13 months or (if shorter) the period of time between the first and last dates on which the earlier contract required the earlier entry to be published.

(4) For the purposes of subsection (1)(h) and (i) "the relevant publisher" is the person with whom the purchaser has entered into the new contract.

(5) The information referred to in subsection (1)(i)(ii) must be given to the purchaser prior to the conclusion of the new contract.]

4   Unsolicited publications

(1) A person shall be guilty of an offence if he sends or causes to be sent to another person any book, magazine or leaflet (or advertising material for any such publication) which he knows or ought reasonably to know is unsolicited and which describes or illustrates human sexual techniques.

(2) A person found guilty of an offence under this section shall be liable on summary conviction to a fine not exceeding £100 for a first offence and to a fine not exceeding £400 for any subsequent offence.

(3) A prosecution for an offence under this section shall not in England and Wales be instituted except by, or with the consent of, the Director of Public Prosecutions.

5   Offences by corporations

(1) Where an offence under this Act which has been committed by a body corporate is proved to have been committed with the consent or connivance of, or to be attributable to any neglect on the part of, any director, manager, secretary, or other similar officer of the body corporate, or of any person who was purporting to act in any such capacity, he as well as the body corporate shall be guilty of that offence and shall be liable to be proceeded against and punished accordingly.

(2) Where the affairs of a body corporate are managed by its members, this section shall apply in relation to the acts or defaults of a member in connection with his functions of management as if he were a director of the body corporate.

6 Interpretation

(1) In this Act, unless the context or subject matter otherwise requires,—

"acquire" includes hire;

"send" includes deliver, and "sender" shall be construed accordingly;

"unsolicited" means, in relation to goods sent to any person, that they are sent without any prior request made by him or on his behalf.

[(2) For the purposes of this Act, any invoice or similar document stating the amount of any payment shall be regarded as asserting a right to the payment unless it complies with the conditions set out in Part 2 of the Schedule to the Regulatory Reform (Unsolicited Goods and Services Act 1971) (Directory Entries and Demands for Payment) Order 2005.]

[(3) Nothing in sections 3 or 3B shall affect the rights of any consumer under the Consumer Protection (Distance Selling) Regulations 2000.]

Defective Premises Act 1972
(1972, c. 35)

1 Duty to build dwellings properly

(1) A person taking on work for or in connection with the provision of a dwelling (whether the dwelling is provided by the erection or by the conversion or enlargement of a building) owes a duty—

    (a) if the dwelling is provided to the order of any person, to that person; and

    (b) without prejudice to paragraph (a) above, to every person who acquires an interest (whether legal or equitable) in the dwelling;

to see that the work which he takes on is done in a workmanlike or, as the case may be, professional manner, with proper materials and so that as regards that work the dwelling will be fit for habitation when completed.

(2) A person who takes on any such work for another on terms that he is to do it in accordance with instructions given by or on behalf of that other shall, to the extent to which he does it properly in accordance with those instructions, be treated for the purposes of this section as discharging the duty imposed on him by subsection (1) above except where he owes a duty to that other to warn him of any defects in the instructions and fails to discharge that duty.

(3) A person shall not be treated for the purposes of subsection (2) above as having given instructions for the doing of work merely because he has agreed to the work being done in a specified manner, with specified materials or to a specified design.

(4) A person who—

    (a) in the course of a business which consists of or includes providing or arranging for the provision of dwellings or installations in dwellings; or

    (b) in the exercise of a power of making such provision or arrangements conferred by or by virtue of any enactment;

arranges for another to take on work for or in connection with the provision of a dwelling shall be treated for the purposes of this section as included among the persons who have taken on the work.

(5) Any cause of action in respect of a breach of the duty imposed by this section shall be deemed, for the purposes of the Limitation Act 1939, the Law Reform (Limitation of Actions, etc.) Act 1954 and the Limitation Act 1963, to have accrued at the time when the dwelling

was completed, but if after that time a person who has done work for or in connection with the provision of the dwelling does further work to rectify the work he has already done, any such cause of action in respect of that further work shall be deemed for those purposes to have accrued at the time when the further work was finished.

[*The references in s. 1(5) should now be read as to the Limitation Act 1980. See the Limitation Act, s. 40(2); the Interpretation Act 1978, s. 17(2).*]

2   Cases excluded from the remedy under section 1

(1)   Where—

(a)   in connection with the provision of a dwelling or its first sale or letting for habitation any rights in respect of defects in the state of the dwelling are conferred by an approved scheme to which this section applies on a person having or acquiring an interest in the dwelling; and

(b)   it is stated in a document of a type approved for the purposes of this section that the requirements as to design or construction imposed by or under the scheme have, or appear to have, been substantially complied with in relation to the dwelling;

no action shall be brought by any person having or acquiring an interest in the dwelling for breach of the duty imposed by section 1 above in relation to the dwelling.

(2)   A scheme to which this section applies—

(a)   may consist of any number of documents and any number of agreements or other transactions between any number of persons; but

(b)   must confer, by virtue of agreements entered into with persons having or acquiring an interest in the dwellings to which the scheme applies, rights on such persons in respect of defects in the state of the dwellings.

(3)   In this section "approved" means approved by the Secretary of State, and the power of the Secretary of State to approve a scheme or document for the purposes of this section shall be exercisable by order, except that any requirements as to construction or design imposed under a scheme to which this section applies may be approved by him without making any order or, if he thinks fit, by order.

(4)   The Secretary of State—

(a)   may approve a scheme or document for the purposes of this section with or without limiting the duration of his approval; and

(b)   may by order revoke or vary a previous order under this section or, without such an order, revoke or vary a previous approval under this section given otherwise than by order.

(5)   The production of a document purporting to be a copy of an approval given by the Secretary of State otherwise than by order and certified by an officer of the Secretary of State to be a true copy of the approval shall be conclusive evidence of the approval, and without proof of the handwriting or official position of the person purporting to sign the certificate.

(6)   The power to make an order under this section shall be exercisable by statutory instrument which shall be subject to annulment in pursuance of a resolution by either House of Parliament.

(7)   Where an interest in a dwelling is compulsorily acquired—

(a)   no action shall be brought by the acquiring authority for breach of the duty imposed by section 1 above in respect of the dwelling; and

(b)   if any work for or in connection with the provision of the dwelling was done otherwise than in the course of a business by the person in occupation of the dwelling at the time of the compulsory acquisition, the acquiring authority and not that person shall be treated as the person who took on the work and accordingly as owing that duty.

3   Duty of care with respect to work done on premises not abated by disposal of premises

(1) Where work of construction, repair, maintenance or demolition or any other work is done on or in relation to premises, any duty of care owed, because of the doing of the work, to persons who might reasonably be expected to be affected by defects in the state of the premises created by the doing of the work shall not be abated by the subsequent disposal of the premises by the person who owed the duty.

(2) This section does not apply—

- (a) in the case of premises which are let, where the relevant tenancy of the premises commenced, or the relevant tenancy agreement of the premises was entered into, before the commencement of this Act;
- (b) in the case of premises disposed of in any other way, when the disposal of the premises was completed, or a contract for their disposal was entered into, before the commencement of this Act; or
- (c) in either case, where the relevant transaction disposing of the premises is entered into in pursuance of an enforceable option by which the consideration for the disposal was fixed before the commencement of this Act.

4   Landlord's duty of care in virtue of obligation or right to repair premises demised

(1) Where premises are let under a tenancy which puts on the landlord an obligation to the tenant for the maintenance or repair of the premises the landlord owes to all persons who might reasonably be expected to be affected by defects in the state of the premises a duty to take such care as is reasonable in all the circumstances to see that they are reasonably safe from personal injury or from damage to their property caused by a relevant defect.

(2) The said duty is owed if the landlord knows (whether as the result of being notified by the tenant or otherwise) or if he ought in all the circumstances to have known of the relevant defect.

(3) In this section "relevant defect" means a defect in the state of the premises existing at or after the material time and arising from, or continuing because of, an act or omission by the landlord which constituted or would if he had had notice of the defect, have constituted a failure by him to carry out his obligation to the tenant for the maintenance or repair of the premises; and for the purposes of the foregoing provision "the material time" means—

- (a) where the tenancy commenced before this Act, the commencement of this Act; and
- (b) in all other cases, the earliest following times, that is to say—
  - (i)   the time when the tenancy commences;
  - (ii) the time when the tenancy agreement is entered into;
  - (iii) the time when possession is taken of the premises in contemplation of the letting.

(4) Where premises are let under a tenancy which expressly or impliedly gives the landlord the right to enter the premises to carry out any description of maintenance or repair of the premises, then, as from the time when he first is, or by notice or otherwise can put himself, in a position to exercise the right and so long as he is or can put himself in that position, he shall be treated for the purposes of subsections (1) to (3) above (but for no other purpose) as if he were under an obligation to the tenant for that description of maintenance or repair of the premises; but the landlord shall not owe the tenant any duty by virtue of this subsection in respect of any defect in the state of the premises arising from, or continuing because of, a failure to carry out an obligation expressly imposed on the tenant by the tenancy.

(5) For the purposes of this section obligations imposed or rights given by any enactment in virtue of a tenancy shall be treated as imposed or given by the tenancy.

(6) This section applies to a right of occupation given by contract or any enactment and not amounting to a tenancy as if the right were a tenancy, and "tenancy" and cognate expressions shall be construed accordingly.

5 Application to Crown

This Act shall bind the Crown, but as regards the Crown's liability in tort shall not bind the Crown further than the Crown is made liable in tort by the Crown Proceedings Act 1947.

6 Supplemental

(1) In this Act: "disposal", in relation to premises, includes a letting, and an assignment or surrender of a tenancy, of the premises and the creation by contract of any other right to occupy the premises, and "dispose" shall be construed accordingly; "personal injury" includes any disease and any impairment of a person's physical or mental condition ...

(2) Any duty imposed by or enforceable by virtue of any provision of this Act is in addition to any duty a person may owe apart from that provision.

(3) Any term of an agreement which purports to exclude or restrict, or has the effect of excluding or restricting, the operation of any of the provisions of this Act, or any liability arising by virtue of any such provision, shall be void.

Supply of Goods (Implied Terms) Act 1973
(1973, c. 13)

8 Implied terms as to title

[(1) In every hire-purchase agreement, other than one to which subsection (2) below applies, there is—

(a) an implied term on the part of the creditor that he will have a right to sell the goods at the time when the property is to pass; and

(b) an implied term that—
  (i)   the goods are free, and will remain free until the time when the property is to pass, from any charge or encumbrance not disclosed or known to the person to whom the goods are bailed or (in Scotland) hired before the agreement is made, and
  (ii) that person will enjoy quiet possession of the goods except so far as it may be disturbed by any person entitled to the benefit of any charge or encumbrance so disclosed or known.

(2) In a hire-purchase agreement, in the case of which there appears from the agreement or is to be inferred from the circumstances of the agreement an intention that the creditor should transfer only such title as he or a third person may have, there is—

(a) an implied term that all charges or encumbrances known to the creditor and not known to the person to whom the goods are bailed or hired have been disclosed to that person before the agreement is made; and

(b) an implied term that neither—
  (i)   the creditor; nor
  (ii) in a case where the parties to the agreement intend that any title which may be transferred shall be only such title as a third person may have, that person; nor
  (iii) anyone claiming through or under the creditor or that third person other-wise than under a charge or encumbrance disclosed or known to the person to whom the goods are bailed or hired, before the agreement is made;

will disturb the quiet possession of the person to whom the goods are bailed or hired.]

[(3) As regards England and Wales and Northern Ireland, the term implied by subsection (1)(a) above is a condition and the terms implied by subsections (1)(b), (2)(a) and (2)(b) above are warranties.]

9   Bailing or hiring by description

[(1) Where under a hire-purchase agreement goods are bailed or (in Scotland) hired by description, there is an implied term that the goods will correspond with the description, and if under the agreement the goods are bailed or hired by reference to a sample as well as a description, it is not sufficient that the bulk of the goods corresponds with the sample if the goods do not also correspond with the description.]

[(1A) As regards England and Wales and Northern Ireland, the term implied by subsection (1) above is a condition.]

[(2) Goods shall not be prevented from being bailed or hired by description by reason only that, being exposed for sale, bailment or hire, they are selected by the person to whom they are bailed or hired.]

10   Implied undertakings as to quality or fitness

[(1) Except as provided by this section and section 11 below and subject to the provisions of any other enactment, including any enactment of the Parliament of Northern Ireland or the Northern Ireland Assembly, there is no implied term as to the quality or fitness for any particular purpose of goods bailed or (in Scotland) hired under a hire-purchase agreement.]

[(2) Where the creditor bails or hires goods under a hire purchase agreement in the course of a business, there is an implied term that the goods supplied under the agreement are of satisfactory quality.

(2A) For the purposes of this Act, goods are of satisfactory quality if they meet the standard that a reasonable person would regard as satisfactory, taking account of any description of the goods, the price (if relevant) and all the other relevant circumstances.

(2B) For the purposes of this Act, the quality of goods includes their state and condition and the following (among others) are in appropriate cases aspects of the quality of goods—

  (a) fitness for all the purposes for which goods of the kind in question are commonly supplied,

  (b) appearance and finish,

  (c) freedom from minor defects,

  (d) safety, and

  (e) durability.

(2C) The term implied by subsection (2) above does not extend to any matter making the quality of goods unsatisfactory—

  (a) which is specifically drawn to the attention of the person to whom the goods are bailed or hired before the agreement is made,

  (b) where that person examines the goods before the agreement is made, which that examination ought to reveal, or

  (c) where the goods are bailed or hired by reference to a sample, which would have been apparent on a reasonable examination of the sample.]

[(2D) If the person to whom the goods are bailed or hired deals as consumer or, in Scotland, if the goods are hired to a person under a consumer contract, the relevant circumstances mentioned in subsection (2A) above include any public statements on the specific characteristics of the goods made about them by the creditor, the producer or his representative, particularly in advertising or on labelling.

(2E) A public statement is not by virtue of subsection (2D) above a relevant circumstance for the purposes of subsection (2A) above in the case of a contract of hire-purchase, if the creditor shows that—

  (a) at the time the contract was made, he was not, and could not reasonably have been, aware of the statement,

  (b) before the contract was made, the statement had been withdrawn in public or, to the extent that it contained anything which was incorrect or misleading, it had been corrected in public, or

  (c) the decision to acquire the goods could not have been influenced by the statement.

(2F) Subsections (2D) and (2E) above do not prevent any public statement from being a relevant circumstance for the purposes of subsection (2A) above (whether or not the person to whom the goods are bailed or hired deals as consumer or, in Scotland, whether or not the goods are hired to a person under a consumer contract) if the statement would have been such a circumstance apart from those subsections.]

[(3) Where the creditor bails or hires goods under a hire-purchase agreement in the course of a business and the person to whom the goods are bailed or hired, expressly or by implication, makes known—

  (a) to the creditor in the course of negotiations conducted by the creditor in relation to the making of the hire-purchase agreement, or

  (b) to a credit-broker in the course of negotiations conducted by that broker in relation to goods sold by him to the creditor before forming the subject matter of the hire-purchase agreement,

any particular purpose for which the goods are being bailed or hired, there is an implied term that the goods supplied under the agreement are reasonably fit for that purpose, whether or not that is a purpose for which such goods are commonly supplied, except where the circumstances show that the person to whom the goods are bailed or hired does not rely, or that it is unreasonable for him to rely, on the skill or judgment of the creditor or credit-broker.

(4) An implied term as to quality or fitness for a particular purpose may be annexed to a hire-purchase agreement by usage.

(5) The preceding provisions of this section apply to a hire-purchase agreement made by a person who in the course of a business is acting as agent for the creditor as they apply to an agreement made by the creditor in the course of a business, except where the creditor is not bailing or hiring in the course of a business and either the person to whom the goods are bailed or hired knows that fact or reasonable steps are taken to bring it to the notice of that person before the agreement is made.

(6) In subsection (3) above and this subsection—

  (a) "credit-broker" means a person acting in the course of a business of credit brokerage;

  (b) "credit brokerage" means the effecting of introductions of individuals desiring to obtain credit—

    (i) to persons carrying on any business so far as it relates to the provision of credit, or

    (ii) to other persons engaged in credit brokerage.]

[(7) As regards England and Wales and Northern Ireland, the terms implied by subsections (2) and (3) above are conditions.]

[(8) In Scotland, "consumer contract" in this section has the same meaning as in section 12A(3) below.]

11 Samples

[(1) Where under a hire-purchase agreement goods are bailed or (in Scotland) hired by reference to a sample, there is an implied term—

  (a) that the bulk will correspond with the sample in quality; and

  (b) that the person to whom the goods are bailed or hired will have a reasonable opportunity of comparing the bulk with the sample; and

  (c) that the goods will be free from any defect, making their quality unsatisfactory, which would not be apparent on reasonable examination of the sample.]

[(2) As regards England and Wales and Northern Ireland, the term implied by subsection (1) above is a condition.]

[11A Modification of remedies for breach of statutory condition in non-consumer cases

(1) Where in the case of a hire purchase agreement—

  (a) the person to whom goods are bailed would, apart from this subsection, have the right to reject them by reason of a breach on the part of the creditor of a term implied by section 9, 10 or 11(1)(a) or (c) above, but

(b) the breach is so slight that it would be unreasonable for him to reject them, then, if the person to whom the goods are bailed does not deal as consumer, the breach is not to be treated as a breach of condition but may be treated as a breach of warranty.

(2) This section applies unless a contrary intention appears in, or is to be implied from, the agreement.

(3) It is for the creditor to show—

(a) that a breach fell within subsection (1)(b) above, and

(b) that the person to whom the goods were bailed did not deal as consumer.

(4) The references in this section to dealing as consumer are to be construed in accordance with Part I of the Unfair Contract Terms Act 1977.

(5) This section does not apply to Scotland.]

[12   Exclusion of implied terms and conditions

(1) An express term does not negative a term implied by this Act unless inconsistent with it.]

[12A   Remedies for breach of hire-purchase agreement as respects Scotland
. . .]

14   Special provisions as to conditional sale agreements

[(1) Section 11(4) of the Sale of Goods Act 1979 (whereby in certain circumstances a breach of a condition in a contract of sale is treated only as a breach of warranty) shall not apply to [a conditional sale agreement where the buyer deals as consumer within Part I of the Unfair Contract Terms Act 1977 . . .

(2) In England and Wales and Northern Ireland a breach of a condition (whether express or implied) to be fulfilled by the seller under any such agreement shall be treated as a breach of warranty, and not as grounds for rejecting the goods and treating the agreement as repudiated, if (but only if) it would have fallen to be so treated had the condition been contained or implied in a corresponding hire-purchase agreement as a condition to be fulfilled by the creditor.]

15   Supplementary

[(1) In sections 8 to 14 above and this section—

"business" includes a profession and the activities of any government department (including a Northern Ireland department), [or local or public authority];

"buyer" and "seller" includes a person to whom rights and duties under a conditional sale agreement have passed by assignment or operation of law;

"conditional sale agreement" means an agreement for the sale of goods under which the purchase price or part of it is payable by instalments, and the property in the goods is to remain in the seller (notwithstanding that the buyer is to be in possession of the goods) until such conditions as to the payment of instalments or otherwise as may be specified in the agreement are fulfilled;

["consumer sale" has the same meaning as in section 55 of the Sale of Goods Act 1979 (as set out in paragraph 11 of Schedule 1 to that Act)];

"creditor" means the person by whom the goods are bailed or (in Scotland) hired under a hire-purchase agreement or the person to whom his rights and duties under the agreement have passed by assignment or operation of law; and

"hire-purchase agreement" means an agreement, other than conditional sale agreement, under which—

(a) goods are bailed or (in Scotland) hired in return for periodical payments by the person to whom they are bailed or hired, and

(b) the property in the goods will pass to that person if the terms of the agreement are complied with and one or more of the following occurs—

(i)   the exercise of an option to purchase by that person,

(ii) the doing of any other specified act by any party to the agreement,

(iii) the happening of any other specified event.

["producer" means the manufacturer of goods, the importer of goods into the European Economic Area or any person purporting to be a producer by placing his name, trade mark or other distinctive sign on the goods;]

(3) In section 14(2) above "corresponding hire-purchase agreement" means, in relation to a conditional sale agreement, a hire-purchase agreement relating to the same goods as the conditional sale agreement and made between the same parties and at the same time and in the same circumstances and, as nearly as may be, in the same terms as the conditional sale agreement.

(4) Nothing in sections 8 to 13 above shall prejudice the operation of any other enactment including any enactment of the Parliament of Northern Ireland or the Northern Ireland Assembly or any rule of law whereby any term, other than one relating to quality or fitness, is to be implied in any hire-purchase agreement.]

Consumer Credit Act 1974
(1974, c. 39)

PART IV

46 False or misleading advertisements

(1) If an advertisement to which this Part applies conveys information which in a material respect is false or misleading the advertiser commits an offence.

(2) Information stating or implying an intention on the advertiser's part which he has not got is false.

PART V

55 Disclosure of information

(1) Regulations may require specified information to be disclosed in the prescribed manner to the debtor or hirer before a regulated agreement is made.

(2) A regulated agreement is not properly executed unless regulations under subsection (1) were complied with before the making of the agreement.

56 Antecedent negotiations

(1) In this Act "antecedent negotiations" means any negotiations with the debtor or hirer—

(a) conducted by the creditor or owner in relation to the making of any regulated agreement, or

(b) conducted by a credit-broker in relation to goods sold or proposed to be sold by the credit-broker to the creditor before forming the subject-matter of a debtor-creditor-supplier agreement within section 12(a), or

(c) conducted by the supplier in relation to a transaction financed or proposed to be financed by a debtor-creditor-supplier agreement within section 12(b) or (c),

and "negotiator" means the person by whom negotiations are so conducted with the debtor or hirer.

(2) Negotiations with the debtor in a case falling within subsection (1)(b) or (c) shall be deemed to be conducted by the negotiator in the capacity of agent of the creditor as well as in his actual capacity.

(3) An agreement is void if, and to the extent that, it purports in relation to an actual or prospective regulated agreement—

(a) to provide that a person acting as, or on behalf of, a negotiator is to be treated as the agent of the debtor or hirer, or

(b) to relieve a person from liability for acts or omissions of any person acting as, or on behalf of, a negotiator.

(4) For the purposes of this Act, antecedent negotiations shall be taken to begin when the negotiator and the debtor or hirer first enter into communication (including communication by advertisement), and to include any representations made by the negotiator to the debtor or hirer and any other dealings between them.

57 Withdrawal from prospective agreement

(1) The withdrawal of a party from a prospective regulated agreement shall operate to apply this Part to the agreement, any linked transaction and any other thing done in anticipation of the making of the agreement as it would apply if the agreement were made and then cancelled under section 69.

60 Form and content of agreements

(1) The Secretary of State shall make regulations as to the form and content of documents embodying regulated agreements, and the regulations shall contain such provisions as appear to him appropriate with a view to ensuring that the debtor or hirer is made aware of—

(a) the rights and duties conferred or imposed on him by the agreement,

(b) the amount and rate of the total charge for credit (in the case of a consumer credit agreement),

(c) the protection and remedies available to him under this Act, and

(d) any other matters which, in the opinion of the Secretary of State, it is desirable for him to know about in connection with the agreement.

65 Consequences of improper execution

(1) An improperly-executed regulated agreement is enforceable against the debtor or hirer on an order of the court only.

67 Cancellable agreements

A regulated agreement may be cancelled by the debtor or hirer in accordance with this Part if the antecedent negotiations included oral representations made when in the presence of the debtor or hirer by an individual acting as, or on behalf of, the negotiator, unless—

(a) the agreement is secured on land, or is a restricted-use credit agreement to finance the purchase of land or is an agreement for a bridging loan in connection with the purchase of land, or

(b) the unexecuted agreement is signed by the debtor or hirer at premises at which any of the following is carrying on any business (whether on a permanent or temporary basis)—

(i)   the creditor or owner;

(ii) any party to a linked transaction (other than the debtor or hirer or a relative of his);

(iii) the negotiator in any antecedent negotiations.

68 Cooling-off period

The debtor or hirer may serve notice of cancellation of a cancellable agreement between his signing of the unexecuted agreement and—

(a) the end of the fifth day following the day on which he received a copy under section 63(2) or a notice under section 64(1)(b), or

(b) if (by virtue of regulations made under section 64(4)) section 64(1)(b) does not apply, the end of the fourteenth day following the day on which he signed the unexecuted agreement.

69   Notice of cancellation

(1) If within the period specified in section 68 the debtor or hirer under a cancellable agreement serves on—

    (a) the creditor or owner, or

    (b) the person specified in the notice under section 64(1), or

    (c) a person who (whether by virtue of subsection (6) or otherwise) is the agent of the creditor or owner,

a notice (a "notice of cancellation") which, however expressed and whether or not conforming to the notice given under section 64(1), indicates the intention of the debtor or hirer to withdraw from the agreement, the notice shall operate—

    (i) to cancel the agreement, and any linked transaction, and

    (ii) to withdraw any offer by the debtor or hirer, or his relative, to enter into a linked transaction.

(4) Except as otherwise provided by or under this Act, an agreement or transaction cancelled under subsection (1) shall be treated as if it had never been entered into.

70   Cancellation: recovery of money paid by debtor or hirer

(1) On the cancellation of a regulated agreement, and of any linked transaction,—

    (a) any sum paid by the debtor or hirer, or his relative, under or in contemplation of the agreement or transaction, including any item in the total charge for credit, shall become repayable, and

    (b) any sum, including any item in the total charge for credit, which but for the cancellation is, or would or might become, payable by the debtor or hirer, or his relative, under the agreement or transaction shall cease to be, or shall not become, so payable, and

    (c) in the case of a debtor-creditor-supplier agreement falling within section 12(b), any sum paid on the debtor's behalf by the creditor to the supplier shall become repayable to the creditor.

(3) A sum repayable under subsection (1) is repayable by the person to whom it was originally paid, but in the case of a debtor-creditor-supplier agreement falling within section 12(b) the creditor and the supplier shall be under a joint and several liability to repay sums paid by the debtor, or his relative, under the agreement or under a linked transaction falling within section 19(1)(b) and accordingly, in such a case, the creditor shall be entitled, in accordance with rules of court, to have the supplier made a party to any proceedings brought against the creditor to recover any such sums.

(4) Subject to any agreement between them, the creditor shall be entitled to be indemnified by the supplier for loss suffered by the creditor in satisfying his liability under subsection (3), including costs reasonably incurred by him in defending proceedings instituted by the debtor.

71   Cancellation: repayment of credit

(1) Notwithstanding the cancellation of a regulated consumer credit agreement, other than a debtor-creditor-supplier agreement for restricted-use credit, the agreement shall continue in force so far as it relates to repayment of credit and payment of interest.

PART VI

75   Liability of creditor for breaches by supplier

(1) If the debtor under a debtor-creditor-supplier agreement falling within section 12(b) or (c) has, in relation to a transaction financed by the agreement, any claim against the supplier in respect of a misrepresentation or breach of contract, he shall have a like claim against the creditor, who, with the supplier, shall accordingly be jointly and severally liable to the debtor.

(2) Subject to any agreement between them, the creditor shall be entitled to be indemnified by the supplier for loss suffered by the creditor in satisfying his liability under subsection (1), including costs reasonably incurred by him in defending proceedings instituted by the debtor.

(3) Subsection (1) does not apply to a claim—

    (a) under a non-commercial agreement, or

    (b) so far as the claim relates to any single item to which the supplier has attached a cash price not exceeding [£100] or more than [£30,000].

(4) This section applies notwithstanding that the debtor, in entering into the transaction, exceeded the credit limit or otherwise contravened any term of the agreement.

(5) In an action brought against the creditor under subsection (1) he shall be entitled, in accordance with rules of court, to have the supplier made a party to the proceedings.

76　Duty to give notice before taking certain action

(1) The creditor or owner is not entitled to enforce a term of a regulated agreement by—

    (a) demanding earlier payment of any sum, or

    (b) recovering possession of any goods or land, or

    (c) treating any right conferred on the debtor or hirer by the agreement as terminated, restricted or deferred,

except by or after giving the debtor or hirer not less than seven days' notice of his intention to do so.

(2) Subsection (1) applies only where—

    (a) a period for the duration of the agreement is specified in the agreement, and

    (b) that period has not ended when the creditor or owner does an act mentioned in subsection (1),

but so applies notwithstanding that, under the agreement, any party is entitled to terminate it before the end of the period so specified.

(6) Subsection (1) does not apply to a right of enforcement arising by reason of any breach by the debtor or hirer of the regulated agreement.

PART VII

87　Need for default notice

(1) Service of a notice on the debtor or hirer in accordance with section 88 (a "default notice") is necessary before the creditor or owner can become entitled, by reason of any breach by the debtor or hirer of a regulated agreement,—

    (a) to terminate the agreement, or

    (b) to demand earlier payment of any sum, or

    (c) to recover possession of any goods or land, or

    (d) to treat any right conferred on the debtor or hirer by the agreement as terminated, restricted or deferred, or

    (e) to enforce any security.

(2) Subsection (1) does not prevent the creditor from treating the right to draw upon any credit as restricted or deferred, and taking such steps as may be necessary to make the restriction or deferment effective.

(4) Regulations may provide that subsection (1) is not to apply to agreements described by the regulations.

88　Contents and effect of default notice

(1) The default notice must be in the prescribed form and specify—

    (a) the nature of the alleged breach;

    (b) if the breach is capable of remedy, what action is required to remedy it and the date before which that action is to be taken;

(c) if the breach is not capable of remedy, the sum (if any) required to be paid as compensation for the breach, and the date before which it is to be paid.

94   Right to complete payments ahead of time

(1) The debtor under a regulated consumer credit agreement is entitled at any time, by notice to the creditor and the payment to the creditor of all amounts payable by the debtor to him under the agreement (less any rebate allowable under section 95), to discharge the debtor's indebtedness under the agreement.

96   Effect on linked transactions

(1) Where for any reason the indebtedness of the debtor under a regulated consumer credit agreement is discharged before the time fixed by the agreement, he, and any relative of his, shall at the same time be discharged from any liability under a linked transaction, other than a debt which has already become payable.

99   Right to terminate hire-purchase etc., agreements

(1) At any time before the final payment by the debtor under a regulated hire-purchase or regulated conditional sale agreement falls due, the debtor shall be entitled to terminate the agreement by giving notice to any person entitled or authorised to receive the sums payable under the agreement.

(2) Termination of an agreement under subsection (1) does not affect any liability under the agreement which has accrued before the termination.

(4) In the case of a conditional sale agreement relating to goods, where the property in the goods, having become vested in the debtor, is transferred to a person who does not become the debtor under the agreement, the debtor shall not thereafter be entitled to terminate the agreement under subsection (1).

100   Liability of debtor on termination of hire-purchase etc., agreement

(1) Where a regulated hire-purchase or regulated conditional sale agreement is terminated under section 99 the debtor shall be liable, unless the agreement provides for a smaller payment, or does not provide for any payment, to pay to the creditor the amount (if any) by which one-half of the total price exceeds the aggregate of the sums paid and the sums due in respect of the total price immediately before the termination.

(3) If in any action the court is satisfied that a sum less than the amount specified in subsection (1) would be equal to the loss sustained by the creditor in consequence of the termination of the agreement by the debtor, the court may make an order for the payment of that sum in lieu of the amount specified in subsection (1).

PART VIII

113   Act not to be evaded by use of security

(1) Where a security is provided in relation to an actual or prospective regulated agreement, the security shall not be enforced so as to benefit the creditor or owner, directly or indirectly, to an extent greater (whether as respects the amount of any payment or the time or manner of its being made) than would be the case if the security were not provided and any obligations of the debtor or hirer, or his relative, under or in relation to the agreement were carried out to the extent (if any) to which they would be enforced under this Act.

(2) In accordance with subsection (1), where a regulated agreement is enforceable on an order of the court or the [OFT] only, any security provided in relation to the agreement is enforceable (so far as provided in relation to the agreement) where such an order has been made in relation to the agreement, but not otherwise.

(7) Where an indemnity [or guarantee] is given in a case where the debtor or hirer is a minor, or [an indemnity is given in a case where he] is otherwise not of full capacity, the reference in subsection (1) to the extent to which his obligations would be enforced shall be

read in relation to the indemnity [or guarantee] as a reference to the extent to which [those obligations] would be enforced if he were of full capacity.

PART IX

127   Enforcement orders in cases of infringement

(1) In the case of an application for an enforcement order under—

    (a) section 65(1) (improperly executed agreements), ... the court shall dismiss the application if, but (subject to subsections (3) and (4)) only if, it considers it just to do so having regard to—

        (i) prejudice caused to any person by the contravention in question, and the degree of culpability for it; and

        (ii) the powers conferred on the court by subsection (2) and sections 135 and 136.

(2) If it appears to the court just to do so, it may in an enforcement order reduce or discharge any sum payable by the debtor or hirer, or any surety, so as to compensate him for prejudice suffered as a result of the contravention in question.

129   Time orders

(1) If it appears to the court just to do so—

    (a) on an application for an enforcement order;

    (b) on an application made by a debtor or hirer under this paragraph after service on him of—

        (i) a default notice, or

        (ii) a notice under section 76(1) or 98(1);

    [(ba) on an application made by a debtor or hirer under this paragraph after he has been given a notice under section 86B or 86C; or]

    (c) in an action brought by a creditor or owner to enforce a regulated agreement or any security, or recover possession of any goods or land to which a regulated agreement relates,

the court may make an order under this section (a "time order").

(2) A time order shall provide for one or both of the following, as the court considers just—

    (a) the payment by the debtor or hirer or any surety of any sum owed under a regulated agreement or a security by such instalments, payable at such times, as the court, having regard to the means of the debtor or hirer and any surety, considers reasonable;

    (b) the remedying by the debtor or hirer of any breach of a regulated agreement (other than non-payment of money) within such period as the court may specify.

132   Financial relief for hirer

(1) Where the owner under a regulated consumer hire agreement recovers possession of goods to which the agreement relates otherwise than by action, the hirer may apply to the court for an order that—

    (a) the whole or part of any sum paid by the hirer to the owner in respect of the goods shall be repaid, and

    (b) the obligation to pay the whole or part of any sum owed by the hirer to the owner in respect of the goods shall cease,

and if it appears to the court just to do so, having regard to the extent of the enjoyment of the goods by the hirer, the court shall grant the application in full or in part.

[140A   Unfair relationships between creditors and debtors

(1) The court may make an order under section 140B in connection with a credit agreement if it determines that the relationship between the creditor and the debtor arising out of the agreement (or the agreement taken with any related agreement) is unfair to the debtor because of one or more of the following—

(a) any of the terms of the agreement or of any related agreement;

(b) the way in which the creditor has exercised or enforced any of his rights under the agreement or any related agreement;

(c) any other thing done (or not done) by, or on behalf of, the creditor (either before or after the making of the agreement or any related agreement).

(2) In deciding whether to make a determination under this section the court shall have regard to all matters it thinks relevant (including matters relating to the creditor and matters relating to the debtor).

(3) For the purposes of this section the court shall (except to the extent that it is not appropriate to do so) treat anything done (or not done) by, or on behalf of, or in relation to, an associate or a former associate of the creditor as if done (or not done) by, or on behalf of, or in relation to, the creditor.

(4) A determination may be made under this section in relation to a relationship notwithstanding that the relationship may have ended.

(5) An order under section 140B shall not be made in connection with a credit agreement which is an exempt agreement by virtue of section 16(6C).]

[140B   Powers of court in relation to unfair relationships

(1) An order under this section in connection with a credit agreement may do one or more of the following—

(a) require the creditor, or any associate or former associate of his, to repay (in whole or in part) any sum paid by the debtor or by a surety by virtue of the agreement or any related agreement (whether paid to the creditor, the associate or the former associate or to any other person);

(b) require the creditor, or any associate or former associate of his, to do or not to do (or to cease doing) anything specified in the order in connection with the agreement or any related agreement;

(c) reduce or discharge any sum payable by the debtor or by a surety by virtue of the agreement or any related agreement;

(d) direct the return to a surety of any property provided by him for the purposes of a security;

(e) otherwise set aside (in whole or in part) any duty imposed on the debtor or on a surety by virtue of the agreement or any related agreement;

(f) alter the terms of the agreement or of any related agreement;

(g) direct accounts to be taken, or (in Scotland) an accounting to be made, between any persons.

(2) An order under this section may be made in connection with a credit agreement only—

(a) on an application made by the debtor or by a surety;

(b) at the instance of the debtor or a surety in any proceedings in any court to which the debtor and the creditor are parties, being proceedings to enforce the agreement or any related agreement; or

(c) at the instance of the debtor or a surety in any other proceedings in any court where the amount paid or payable under the agreement or any related agreement is relevant.

(3) An order under this section may be made notwithstanding that its effect is to place on the creditor, or any associate or former associate of his, a burden in respect of an advantage enjoyed by another person.

(8) A party to any proceedings mentioned in subsection (2) shall be entitled, in accordance with rules of court, to have any person who might be the subject of an order under this section made a party to the proceedings.

(9) If, in any such proceedings, the debtor or a surety alleges that the relationship between the creditor and the debtor is unfair to the debtor, it is for the creditor to prove to the contrary.]

PART XI

162 Powers of entry and inspection

(1) A duly authorised officer of an enforcement authority, at all reasonable hours and on production, if required, of his credentials, may—

(a) in order to ascertain whether a breach of any provision of or under this Act has been committed, inspect any goods and enter any premises (other than premises used only as a dwelling); ...

(c) if he has reasonable cause to believe that a breach of any provision of or under this Act has been committed, seize and detain any goods in order to ascertain (by testing or otherwise) whether such a breach has been committed;

(d) seize and detain any goods, [...] or documents which he has reason to believe may be required as evidence in proceedings for an offence under this Act;

(e) for the purpose of exercising his powers under this subsection to seize goods, [...] or documents, but only if and to the extent that it is reasonably necessary for securing that the provisions of this Act and of any regulations made under it are duly observed, require any person having authority to do so to break open any container and, if that person does not comply, break it open himself.

(2) An officer seizing goods, [...] or documents in exercise of his powers under this section shall not do so without informing the person he seizes them from.

(4) An officer entering premises by virtue of this section may take such other persons and equipment with him as he thinks necessary; and on leaving premises entered by virtue of a warrant under subsection (3) shall, if they are unoccupied or the occupier is temporarily absent, leave them as effectively secured against trespassers as he found them.

(6) A person who is not a duly authorised officer of an enforcement authority, but purports to act as such under this section, commits an offence.

163 Compensation for loss

(1) Where, in exercising his powers under section 162, an officer of an enforcement authority seizes and detains goods and their owner suffers loss by reason of—

(a) that seizure, or

(b) the loss, damage or deterioration of the goods during detention,

then, unless the owner is convicted of an offence under this Act committed in relation to the goods, the authority shall compensate him for the loss so suffered.

165 Obstruction of authorised officers

(1) Any person who—

(a) wilfully obstructs an officer of an enforcement authority acting in pursuance of this Act; or

(b) wilfully fails to comply with any requirement properly made to him by such an officer under section 162; or

(c) without reasonable cause fails to give such an officer (so acting) other assistance or information he may reasonably require in performing his functions under this Act, commits an offence.

170 No further sanctions for breach of Act

(1) A breach of any requirement made (otherwise than by any court) by or under this Act shall incur no civil or criminal sanction as being such a breach, except to the extent (if any) expressly provided by or under this Act.

173 Contracting-out forbidden

(1) A term contained in a regulated agreement or linked transaction, or in any other agreement relating to an actual or prospective regulated agreement or linked transaction, is void if, and to the extent that, it is inconsistent with a provision for the protection of the debtor or hirer or his relative or any surety contained in this Act or in any regulation made under this Act.

(2) Where a provision specifies the duty or liability of the debtor or hirer or his relative or any surety in certain circumstances, a term is inconsistent with that provision if it purports to impose, directly or indirectly, an additional duty or liability on him in those circumstances.

(3) Notwithstanding subsection (1), a provision of this Act under which a thing may be done in relation to any person on an order of the court or the [OFT] only shall not be taken to prevent its being done at any time with that person's consent given at that time, but the refusal of such consent shall not give rise to any liability.

175   Duty of persons deemed to be agents

Where under this Act a person is deemed to receive a notice or payment as agent of the creditor or owner under a regulated agreement, he shall be deemed to be under a contractual duty to the creditor or owner to transmit the notice, or remit the payment, to him forthwith.

181   Power to alter monetary limits etc

(1) The Secretary of State may by order made by statutory instrument amend, or further amend, any of the following provisions of this Act so as to reduce or increase a sum mentioned in that provision, namely, sections ... 75(3)(b) ...

189   Definitions

(1) In this Act, unless the context otherwise requires— ...

"representation" includes any condition or warranty, and any other statement or undertaking, whether oral or in writing; ...

Health and Safety at Work Act 1974
(1974, c. 37)

2   General duties of employers to their employees

(1) It shall be the duty of every employer to ensure, so far as is reasonably practicable, the health, safety and welfare of work of all his employees.

3   General duties of employers and self-employed to persons other than their employees

(1) It shall be the duty of every employer to conduct his undertaking in such a way as to ensure, so far as is reasonably practicable, that persons not in his employment who may be affected thereby are not thereby exposed to risks to their health or safety.

(2) It shall be the duty of every self-employed person to conduct his undertaking in such a way as to ensure, so far as is reasonably practicable, that he and other persons (not being his employees) who may be affected thereby are not thereby exposed to risks to their health or safety.

(3) In such cases as may be prescribed, it shall be the duty of every employer and every self-employed person, in the prescribed circumstances and in the prescribed manner, to give to persons (not being his employees) who may be affected by the way in which he conducts his undertaking the prescribed information about such aspects of the way in which he conducts his undertaking as might affect their health or safety.

4   General duties of persons concerned with premises to persons other than their employees

(1) This section has effect for imposing on persons duties in relation to those who—

(a) are not their employees; but

(b) use non-domestic premises made available to them as a place of work or as a place where they may use plant or substances provided for their use there,

and applies to premises so made available and other non-domestic premises used in connection with them.

(2) It shall be the duty of each person who has, to any extent, control of premises to which this section applies or of the means of access thereto or egress therefrom or of any plant or substance in such premises to take such measures as it is reasonable for a person in his position to take to ensure, so far as is reasonably practicable, that the premises, all means of access thereto or egress therefrom available for use by persons using the premises, and any plant or substance in the premises or, as the case may be, provided for use there, is or are safe and without risks to health.

(3) Where a person has, by virtue of any contract or tenancy, an obligation of any extent in relation to—

(a) the maintenance or repair of any premises to which this section applies or any means of access thereto or egress therefrom; or

(b) the safety of or the absence of risks to health arising from plant or substances in any such premises;

that person shall be treated, for the purposes of subsection (2) above, as being a person who has control of the matters to which his obligation extends.

(4) Any reference in this section to a person having control of any premises or matter is a reference to a person having control of the premises or matter in connection with the carrying on by him of a trade, business or other undertaking (whether for profit or not).

17 Use of approved codes of practice in criminal proceedings

A failure on the part of any person to observe any provision of an approved code of practice shall not of itself render him liable to any civil or criminal proceedings; but where in any criminal proceedings a party is alleged to have committed an offence by reason of a contravention of any requirement or prohibition imposed by or under any such provision as is mentioned in section 16(1) being a provision for which there was an approved code of practice at the time of the alleged contravention, the following subsection shall have effect with respect to that code in relation to those proceedings.

47 Civil liability

(1) Nothing in this Part shall be construed—

(a) as conferring a right of action in any civil proceedings in respect of any failure to comply with any duty imposed by sections 2 to 7 or any contravention of section 8; or

(b) as affecting the extent (if any) to which breach of a duty imposed by any of the existing statutory provisions is actionable; or

(c) as affecting the operation of section 12 of the Nuclear Installations Act 1965 (right to compensation by virtue of certain provisions of that Act).

(2) Breach of a duty imposed by health and safety regulations [...] shall, so far as it causes damages, be actionable except in so far as the regulations provide otherwise.

(3) No provision made by virtue of section 15(6)(b) shall afford a defence in any civil proceedings, whether brought by virtue of subsection (2) above or not; but as regards any duty imposed as mentioned in subsection (2) above health and safety regulations [...] may provide for any defence specified in the regulations to be available in any action for breach of that duty.

(4) Subsections (1)(a) and (2) above are without prejudice to any right of action which exists apart from the provisions of this Act, and subsection (3) above is without prejudice to any defence which may be available apart from the provisions of the regulations there mentioned.

(5) Any term of an agreement which purports to exclude or restrict the operation of subsection (2) above, or any liability arising by virtue of that subsection, shall be void, except in so far as health and safety regulations [...] provide otherwise.

(6) In this section "damage" includes the death of, or injury to, any person (including any disease and any impairment of a person's physical or mental condition).

Rehabilitation of Offenders Act 1974
(1974, c. 53)

4　Effect of rehabilitation

(1) Subject to sections 7 and 8 below, a person who has become a rehabilitated person for the purposes of this Act in respect of a conviction shall be treated for all purposes in law as a person who has not committed or been charged with or prosecuted for or convicted of or sentenced for the offence or offences which were the subject of that conviction; . . .

8　Defamation actions

(1) This section applies to any action for libel or slander begun after the commencement of this Act by a rehabilitated person and founded upon the publication of any matter imputing that the plaintiff has committed or been charged with or prosecuted for or convicted of or sentenced for an offence which was the subject of a spent conviction.

(2) Nothing in section 4(1) above shall affect an action to which this section applies where the publication complained of took place before the conviction in question became spent, and the following provisions of this section shall not apply in any such case.

(3) Subject to subsections (5) and (6) below, nothing in section 4(1) above shall prevent the defendant in an action to which this section applies from relying on any defence of justification or fair comment or of absolute or qualified privilege which is available to him, or restrict the matters he may establish in support of any such defence.

(4) Without prejudice to the generality of subsection (3) above, where in any such action malice is alleged against a defendant who is relying on a defence of qualified privilege, nothing in section 4(1) above shall restrict the matters he may establish in rebuttal of the allegation.

(5) A defendant in any such action shall not by virtue of subsection (3) above be entitled to rely upon the defence of justification if the publication is proved to have been made with malice.

(6) Subject to subsection (7) below a defendant in any such action shall not, by virtue of subsection (3) above, be entitled to rely on any matter or adduce or require any evidence for the purpose of establishing (whether under [section 14 of the Defamation Act 1996] or otherwise) the defence that the matter published constituted a fair and accurate report of judicial proceedings if it is proved that the publication contained a reference to evidence which was ruled to be inadmissible in the proceedings by virtue of section 4(1) above.

(7) Subsection (3) above shall apply without the qualifications imposed by subsection (6) above in relation to—

    (a) any report of judicial proceedings contained in any bona fide series of law reports which does not form part of any other publication and consists solely of reports of proceedings in courts of law, and

    (b) any report or account of judicial proceedings published for bona fide educational, scientific or professional purposes or given in the course of any lecture, class or discussion given or held for any of those purposes.

[(7A) Nothing in section 4(1) above shall restrict the evidence that may be adduced in mitigation of damages under section 13(2) of the Defamation Act 1996.]

Solicitors Act 1974
(1974, c. 47)

37　Professional indemnity

(1) The Council, with the concurrence of the Master of the Rolls, may make rules (in this Act referred to as "indemnity rules") concerning indemnity against loss arising from claims in respect of any description of civil liability incurred—

(a) by a solicitor or former solicitor in connection with his practice or with any trust of which he is or formerly was a trustee;

(b) by an employee or former employee of a solicitor or former solicitor in connection with that solicitor's practice or with any trust of which that solicitor or the employee is or formerly was a trustee.

(2) For the purpose of providing such indemnity, indemnity rules—

(a) may authorise or require the Society to establish and maintain a fund or funds;

(b) may authorise or require the Society to take out and maintain insurance with authorised insurers;

(c) may require solicitors or any specified class of solicitors to take out and maintain insurance with authorised insurers.

[37A   Redress for inadequate professional services

Schedule 1A shall have effect with respect to the provision by solicitors of services which are not of the quality which it is reasonable to expect of them.]

87   Interpretation

(1) In this Act, except where the context otherwise requires,—

"the Council" means the Council of the Society...

"the Society" means the Law Society...

Guard Dogs Act 1975
(1975, c. 50)

1   Control of guard dogs

(1) A person shall not use or permit the use of a guard dog at any premises unless a person ("the handler") who is capable of controlling the dog is present on the premises and the dog is under the control of the handler at all times while it is being so used except while it is secured so that it is not at liberty to go free about the premises.

(3) A person shall not use or permit the use of a guard dog at any premises unless a notice containing a warning that a guard dog is present is clearly exhibited at each entrance to the premises.

2   Restriction on keeping guard dogs without a licence

(1) A person shall not keep a dog at guard dog kennels unless he holds a licence under section 3 of this Act in respect of the kennels.

(2) A person shall not use or permit the use at any premises of a guard dog if he knows or has reasonable cause to suspect that the dog (when not being used as a guard dog) is normally kept at guard dog kennels in breach of subsection (1) of this section.

5   Offences, penalties and civil liability

(1) A person who contravenes section 1 or 2 of this Act shall be guilty of an offence and liable on summary conviction to a fine not exceeding £400.

(2) The provisions of this Act shall not be construed as—

(a) conferring a right of action in any civil proceedings (other than proceedings for the recovery of a fine or any prescribed fee) in respect of any contravention of this Act or of any regulations made under this Act or of any of the terms or conditions of a licence granted under section 3 of this Act; or

(b) derogating from any right of action or other remedy (whether civil or criminal) in proceedings instituted otherwise than by virtue of this Act.

Sex Discrimination Act 1975
(1975, c. 65)

[1   Direct and indirect discrimination against women

(1) In any circumstances relevant for the purposes of any provision of this Act, other than a provision to which subsection (2) applies, a person discriminates against a woman if—

(a) on the ground of her sex he treats her less favourably than he treats or would treat a man, or

(b) he applies to her a requirement or condition which he applies or would apply equally to a man but—

(i) which is such that the proportion of women who can comply with it is considerably smaller than the proportion of men who can comply with it, and

(ii) which he cannot show to be justifiable irrespective of the sex of the person to whom it is applied, and

(iii) which is to her detriment because she cannot comply with it.

(2) In any circumstances relevant for the purposes of a provision to which this subsection applies, a person discriminates against a woman if—

(a) on the ground of her sex, he treats her less favourably than he treats or would treat a man, or

[(b) he applies to her a provision, criterion, or practice which he applies or would apply equally to a man, but—

(i) which puts or would put women at a particular disadvantage when compared with men,

(ii) which puts her at that disadvantage, and

(iii) which he cannot show to be a proportionate means of achieving a legitimate aim.]

(3) Subsection (2) applies to—

(a) any provision of Part 2,

(b) sections 35A and 35B, and

(c) any other provision of Part 3, so far as it applies to vocational training.

2   Sex discrimination against men

(1) Section 1, and the provisions of Parts II and III relating to sex discrimination against women, are to be read as applying equally to the treatment of men, and for that purpose shall have effect with such modifications as are requisite.

(2) In the application of subsection (1) no account shall be taken of special treatment afforded to women in connection with pregnancy or childbirth.

[2A   Discrimination on the grounds of gender reassignment

(1) A person ("A") discriminates against another person ("B") in any circumstances relevant for the purposes of— ...

(c) any other provision of Part III [ss. 22–36], so far as it applies to vocational training if he treats B less favourably than he treats or would treat other persons, and does so on the ground that B intends to undergo, is undergoing or has undergone gender reassignment.]

[4A   Harassment, including sexual harassment

(1) For the purposes of this Act, a person subjects a woman to harassment if—

(a) on the ground of her sex, he engages in unwanted conduct that has the purpose or effect—

(i) of violating her dignity, or

(ii) of creating an intimidating, hostile, degrading, humiliating or offensive environment for her,

(b) he engages in any form of unwanted verbal, non-verbal or physical conduct of a sexual nature that has the purpose or effect—

    (i) of violating her dignity, or

    (ii) of creating an intimidating, hostile, degrading, humiliating or offensive environment for her, or

(c) on the ground of her rejection of or submission to unwanted conduct of a kind mentioned in paragraph (a) or (b), he treats her less favourably than he would treat her had she not rejected, or submitted to, the conduct.

(2) Conduct shall be regarded as having the effect mentioned in sub-paragraph (i) or (ii) of subsection (1)(a) or (b) only if, having regard to all the circumstances, including in particular the perception of the woman, it should reasonably be considered as having that effect.

(3) For the purposes of this Act, a person ("A") subjects another person ("B") to harassment if—

(a) A on the ground that B intends to undergo, is undergoing or has undergone gender reassignment, engages in unwanted conduct that has the purpose or effect—

    (i) of violating B's dignity, or

    (ii) of creating an intimidating, hostile, degrading, humiliating or offensive environment for B, or

(b) A, on the ground of B's rejection of or submission to unwanted conduct of a kind mentioned in paragraph (a), treats B less favourably than A would treat B had B not rejected, or submitted to, the conduct.

(4) Conduct shall be regarded as having the effect mentioned in sub-paragraph (i) or (ii) of subsection (3)(a) only if, having regard to all the circumstances, including in particular the perception of B, it should reasonably be considered as having that effect.

(5) Subsection (1) is to be read as applying equally to the harassment of men, and for that purpose shall have effect with such modifications as are requisite.

(6) For the purposes of subsections (1) and (3), a provision of Part 2 or 3 framed with reference to harassment of women shall be treated as applying equally to the harassment of men, and for that purpose will have effect with such modifications as are requisite.]

29 Discrimination in provision of goods, facilities or services

(1) It is unlawful for any person concerned with the provision (for payment or not) of goods, facilities or services to the public or a section of the public to discriminate against a woman who seeks to obtain or use those goods, facilities or services—

(a) by refusing or deliberately omitting to provide her with any of them, or

(b) by refusing or deliberately omitting to provide her with goods, facilities or services of the like quality, in the like manner and on the like terms as are normal in his case in relation to male members of the public or (where she belongs to a section of the public) to male members of that section.

[(4) In its application in relation to vocational training to discrimination falling within section 2A, subsection (1)(b) shall have effect as if references to male members of the public or of a section of the public, were references to members of the public, or of a section of the public, who do not intend to undergo, are not undergoing and have not undergone gender reassignment.]

41 Liability of employers and principals

(1) Anything done by a person in the course of his employment shall be treated for the purposes of this Act as done by his employer as well as by him, whether or not it was done with the employer's knowledge or approval.

(2) Anything done by a person as agent for another person with the authority (whether express or implied, and whether precedent or subsequent) of that other person shall be treated for the purposes of this Act as done by that other person as well as by him.

(3) In proceedings brought under this Act against any person in respect of an act alleged to have been done by an employee of his it shall be a defence for that person to prove that he

took such steps as were reasonably practicable to prevent the employee from doing that act, or from doing in the course of his employment acts of that description.

66   Claims under Part III [ss. 22–36]

(1) A claim by any person ("the claimant") that another person ("the respondent")—

    (a) has committed an act of discrimination [or harassment] against the claimant which is unlawful by virtue of Part III [other than section 35A or 35B,] ... may be made the subject of civil proceedings in like manner as any other claim in tort or (in Scotland) in reparation for breach of statutory duty.

(3) As respects an unlawful act of discrimination falling within section 1(1)(b) [...] no award of damages shall be made if the respondent proves that the requirement or condition in question was not applied with the intention of treating the claimant unfavourably on the ground of his sex [...].

[(3A) Subsection (3) does not affect the award of damages in respect of an unlawful act of discrimination falling within section 1(2)(b).]

(4) For the avoidance of doubt it is hereby declared that damages in respect of an unlawful act of discrimination [or harassment] may include compensation for injury to feelings whether or not they include compensation under any other head.

77   Validity and revision of contracts

(1) A term of a contract is void where—

    (a) its inclusion renders the making of the contract unlawful by virtue of this Act, or

    (b) it is included in furtherance of an act rendered unlawful by this Act, or

    (c) it provides for the doing of an act which would be rendered unlawful by this Act.

(2) Subsection (1) does not apply to a term the inclusion of which constitutes or is in furtherance of, or provides for, unlawful discrimination against a party to the contract, but the term shall be unenforceable against that party.

(3) A term in a contract which purports to exclude or limit any provision of this Act or the Equal Pay Act 1970 is unenforceable by any person in whose favour the term would operate apart from this subsection.

(4) Subsection (3) does not apply—

    (a) to a contract settling a complaint to which section 63(1) of this Act or section 2 of the Equal Pay Act 1970 applies where the contract is made with the assistance of a conciliation officer;

  [(aa) to a contract settling a complaint to which section 63(1) of this Act or section 2 of the Equal Pay Act 1970 applies if the conditions regulating compromise contracts under this Act are satisfied in relation to the contract;]

    (b) to a contract settling a claim to which section 66 applies.

[(4A) The conditions regulating compromise contracts under this Act are that—

    (a) the contract must be in writing;

    (b) the contract must relate to the particular complaint;

    (c) the complainant must have received [advice from a relevant independent adviser] as to the terms and effect of the proposed contract and in particular its effect on his ability to pursue his complaint before an industrial tribunal;

    (d) there must be in force, when the adviser gives the advice, a [contract of insurance, or an indemnity provided for members of a profession or professional body,] covering the risk of a claim by the complainant in respect of loss arising in consequence of the advice;

    (e) the contract must identify the adviser; and

    (f) the contract must state that the conditions regulating compromise contracts under this Act are satisfied.]

(5) On the application of any person interested in a contract to which subsection (2) applies, a county court or sheriff court may make such order as it thinks just for removing or

modifying any term made unenforceable by that subsection; but such an order shall not be made unless all persons affected have been given notice of the application (except where under rules of court notice may be dispensed with) and have been afforded an opportunity to make representations to the court.

(6) An order under subsection (5) may include provision as respects any period before the making of the order.

Congenital Disabilities (Civil Liability) Act 1976
(1976, c. 28)

1   Civil liability to child born disabled

(1) If a child is born disabled as the result of such an occurrence before its birth as is mentioned in subsection (2) below, and a person (other than the child's own mother) is under this section answerable to the child in respect of the occurrence, the child's disabilities are to be regarded as damage resulting from the wrongful act of that person and actionable accordingly at the suit of the child.

(2) An occurrence to which this section applies is one which—

(a) affected either parent of the child in his or her ability to have a normal, healthy child; or

(b) affected the mother during her pregnancy, or affected her or the child in the course of its birth, so that the child is born with disabilities which would not otherwise have been present.

(3) Subject to the following subsections, a person (here referred to as "the defendant") is answerable to the child if he was liable in tort to the parent or would, if sued in due time, have been so; and it is no answer that there could not have been such liability because the parent suffered no actionable injury, if there was a breach of legal duty which, accompanied by injury, would have given rise to the liability.

(4) In the case of an occurrence preceding the time of conception, the defendant is not answerable to the child if at that time either or both of the parents knew the risk of their child being born disabled (that is to say, the particular risk created by the occurrence); but should it be the child's father who is the defendant, this subsection does not apply if he knew of the risk and the mother did not.

(5) The defendant is not answerable to the child, for anything he did or omitted to do when responsible in a professional capacity for treating or advising the parent, if he took reasonable care having due regard to then received professional opinion applicable to the particular class of case; but this does not mean that he is answerable only because he departed from received opinion.

(6) Liability to the child under this section may be treated as having been excluded or limited by contract made with the parent affected, to the same extent and subject to the same restrictions as liability in the parent's own case; and a contract term which could have been set up by the defendant in an action by the parent, so as to exclude or limit his liability to him or her, operates in the defendant's favour to the same, but no greater, extent in an action under this section by the child.

(7) If in the child's action under this section it is shown that the parent affected shared the responsibility for the child being born disabled, the damages are to be reduced to such extent as the court thinks just and equitable having regard to the extent of the parent's responsibility.

[1A   Extension of section 1 to cover infertility treatments

(1) In any case where—

(a) a child carried by a woman as the result of the placing in her or an embryo or of sperm and eggs or her artificial insemination is born disabled,

(b) the disability results from an act or omission in the course of the selection, or the keeping or use outside the body, of the embryo carried by her or of the gametes used to bring about the creation of the embryo, and

(c) a person is under this section answerable to the child in respect of the act or omission,

the child's disabilities are to be regarded as damage resulting from the wrongful act of that person and actionable accordingly at the suit of the child.

(2) Subject to subsection (3) below and the applied provisions of section 1 of this Act, a person (here referred to as "the defendant") is answerable to the child if he was liable in tort to one or both of the parents (here referred to as "the parent or parents concerned") or would, if sued in due time, have been so; and it is no answer that there could not have been such liability because the parent or parents concerned suffered no actionable injury, if there was a breach of legal duty which, accompanied by injury, would have given rise to the liability.

(3) The defendant is not under this section answerable to the child if at the time the embryo, or the sperm and eggs, are placed in the woman or the time of her insemination (as the case may be) either or both of the parents knew the risk of their child being born disabled (that is to say, the particular risk created by the act or omission).

(4) Subsections (5) to (7) of section 1 of this Act apply for the purposes of this section as they apply for the purposes of that but as if references to the parent or the parent affected were references to the parent or parents concerned.]

2   Liability of woman driving while pregnant

A woman driving a motor vehicle when she knows (or ought reasonably to know) herself to be pregnant is to be regarded as being under the same duty to take care for the safety of her unborn child as the law imposes on her with respect to the safety of other people; and if in consequence of her breach of that duty her child is born with disabilities which would not otherwise have been present, those disabilities are to be regarded as damage resulting from her wrongful act and actionable accordingly at the suit of the child.

3   Disabled birth due to radiation

(1) Section 1 of this Act does not affect the operation of the Nuclear Installations Act 1965 as to liability for, and compensation in respect of, injury or damage caused by occurrences involving nuclear matter or the emission of ionising radiations.

(2) For the avoidance of doubt anything which—

(a) affects a man in his ability to have a normal, healthy child; or

(b) affects a woman in that ability, or so affects her when she is pregnant that her child is born with disabilities which would not otherwise have been present,

is an injury for the purposes of that Act.

(3) If a child is born disabled as the result of an injury to either of its parents caused in breach of a duty imposed by any of sections 7 to 11 of that Act (nuclear site licensees and others to secure that nuclear incidents do not cause injury to persons, etc.), the child's disabilities are to be regarded under the subsequent provisions of that Act (compensation and other matters) as injuries caused on the same occasion, and by the same breach of duty, as was the injury to the parent.

(4) As respects compensation to the child, section 13(6) of that Act (contributory fault of person injured by radiation) is to be applied as if the reference there to fault were to the fault of the parent.

(5) Compensation is not payable in the child's case if the injury to the parent preceded the time of the child's conception and at that time either or both of the parents knew the risk of their child being born disabled (that is to say, the particular risk created by the injury).

4   Interpretation and other supplementary provisions

(1) References in this Act to a child being born disabled or with disabilities are to its being born with any deformity, disease or abnormality, including predisposition (whether or not susceptible or immediate prognosis) to physical or mental defect in the future.

(2) In this Act—

   (a) "born" means born alive (the moment of a child's birth being when it first has a life separate from its mother), and "birth" has a corresponding meaning; and

   (b) "motor vehicle" means a mechanically propelled vehicle intended or adapted for use on roads.

[and references to embryos shall be construed in accordance with section 1 of the Human Fertilisation and Embryology Act 1990].

(3) Liability to a child under section 1 [1A] or 2 of this Act is to be regarded—

   (a) as respects all its incidents and any matters arising or to arise out of it; and

   (b) subject to any contrary context or intention, for the purpose of construing references in enactments and documents to personal or bodily injuries and cognate matters,

as liability for personal injuries sustained by the child immediately after its birth.

(4) No damages shall be recoverable under [any] of those sections in respect of any loss of expectation of life, nor shall any such loss be taken into account in the compensation payable in respect of a child under the Nuclear Installations Act 1965 as extended by section 3, unless (in either case) the child lives for at least 48 hours.

[(4A) In any case where a child carried by a woman as the result of the placing in her of an embryo or of sperm and eggs or her artificial insemination is born disabled, any reference in section 1 of this Act to a parent includes a reference to a person who would be a parent but for sections 27 to 29 of the Human Fertilisation and Embryology Act 1990.]

(5) This Act applies in respect of births after (but not before) its passing, and in respect of any such birth it replaces any law in force before its passing, whereby a person could be liable to a child in respect of disabilities with which it might be born; but in section 1(3) of this Act the expression "liable in tort" does not include any reference to liability by virtue of this Act or to liability by virtue of any such law.

5   Crown application

This Act binds the Crown.

Damages (Scotland) Act 1976
(1976, c. 13)

1   Rights of relatives of a deceased person

(1) Where a person dies in consequence of personal injuries sustained by him as a result of an act or omission of another person, being an act or omission giving rise to liability to pay damages to the injured person or his executor, then, subject to the following provisions of this Act, the person liable to pay those damages (in this section referred to as "the responsible person") shall also be liable to pay damages in accordance with this section to any relative of the deceased, being a relative within the meaning of Schedule 1 to this Act.

(2) No liability shall arise under this section if the liability to the deceased or his executor in respect of the act or omission has been excluded or discharged (whether by antecedent agreement or otherwise) by the deceased before his death, or is excluded by virtue of any enactment.

(3) The damages which the responsible person shall be liable to pay to a relative of a deceased under this section shall (subject to the provisions of this Act) be such as will compensate the relative for any loss of support suffered by him since the date of the deceased's death or likely to be suffered by him as a result of the act or omission in question,

together with any reasonable expense incurred by him in connection with the deceased's funeral.

(4) If the relative is a member of the deceased's immediate family (within the meaning of section 10(2) of this Act) there shall be awarded, without prejudice to any claim under subsection (3) above, such sum of damages, if any, as the court thinks just by way of compensation [all or any of the following—

(a) distress and anxiety endured by the relative in contemplation of the suffering of the deceased before his death;

(b) grief and sorrow of the relative caused by the deceased's death;

(c) the loss of such non-patrimonial benefit as the relative might have been expected to derive from the deceased's society and guidance if the deceased had not died, and the court in making an award under this subsection shall not be required to ascribe specifically any part of the award to any of paragraphs (a), (b) and (c) above.]

(5) [Subject to subsection (5A) below,] In assessing for the purposes of this section the amount of any loss of support suffered by a relative of a deceased no account shall be taken of—

(a) any patrimonial gain or advantage which has accrued or will or may accrue to the relative from the deceased or from any other person by way of succession or settlement;

(b) any insurance money, benefit, pension or gratuity which has been, or will be or may be, paid as a result of the deceased's death;

and in this subsection—

"benefit" means benefit under the Social Security Act 1975 or the Social Security (Northern Ireland) Act 1975, and any payment by a friendly society or trade union for the relief or maintenance of a member's dependants;

"insurance money" includes a return of premiums; and

"pension" includes a return of contributions and any payment of a lump sum in respect of a person's employment.

[(5A) Where a deceased has been awarded a provisional award of damages under section 12(2) of the Administration of Justice Act 1982, the making of that award does not prevent liability from arising under this section but in assessing for the purposes of this section the amount of any loss of support suffered by a relative of the deceased the court shall take into account such part of the provisional award relating to future patrimonial loss as was intended to compensate the deceased for a period beyond the date on which he died.]

(6) In order to establish loss of support for the purposes of this section it shall not be essential for a claimant to show that the deceased was, or might have become, subject to a duty in law to provide or contribute to the support of the claimant; but if any such fact is established it may be taken into account in determining whether, and if so to what extent, the deceased, if he had not died, would have been likely to provide or contribute to such support.

(7) Except as provided in this section [or in Part II of the Administration of Justice Act 1982 or under [regulation 3 of the Railways (Convention on International Carriage by Rail) Regulations 2005] no person shall be entitled by reason of relationship to damages (including damages by way of solatium) in respect of the death of another person.

[1A   Transmissibility to executor of rights of deceased relative

Any right to damages under any provision of section 1 of this Act which is vested in the relative concerned immediately before his death shall be transmitted to the relative's executor; but, in determining the amount of damages payable to an executor by virtue of this section, the court shall have regard only to the period ending immediately before the relative's death.]

[2   Rights transmitted to executor in respect of deceased person's injuries

(1) Subject to the following provisions of this section, there shall be transmitted to the executor of a deceased person the like rights to damages in respect of personal injuries (including a right to damages by way of solatium) sustained by the deceased as were vested in him immediately before his death.

(2) There shall not be transmitted to the executor under this section a right to damages by way of compensation for patrimonial loss attributable to any period after the deceased's death.

(3) In determining the amount of damages by way of solatium payable to an executor by virtue of this section, the court shall have regard only to the period ending immediately before the deceased's death.

(4) In so far as a right to damages vested in the deceased comprised a right to damages (other than for patrimonial loss) in respect of injury resulting from defamation or any other verbal injury or other injury to reputation sustained by the deceased, that right shall be transmitted to the deceased's executor only if an action to enforce that right had been brought by the deceased before his death and had not been concluded by then within the meaning of section 2A(2) of this Act.]

[2A   Enforcement by executor of rights transmitted to him

(1) For the purpose of enforcing any right transmitted to an executor under section 1A or 2 of this Act the executor shall be entitled—

(a) to bring an action; or

(b) if an action for that purpose had been brought by the deceased but had not been concluded before his death, to be sisted as pursuer in that action.

(2) For the purpose of subsection (1) above, an action shall not be taken to be concluded while any appeal is competent or before any appeal taken has been disposed of.]

[4   Executor's claim not to be excluded by relatives' claim: and vice versa

A claim by the executor of a deceased person for damages under section 2 of this Act is not excluded by the making of a claim by a relative of the deceased for damages under section 1 of this Act; [or by a deceased's relative's executor under section 1A of this Act; nor is a claim by a relative of a deceased person or by a deceased relative's executor for damages under the said section 1 or (as the case may be) the said section 1A] excluded by the making of a claim by the deceased's executor for damages under the said section 2; [ ].

6   Limitation of total amount of liability

(1) Where in any action to which [this] section applies, so far as directed against any defender, it is shown that by antecedent agreement, compromise or otherwise, the liability arising in relation to that defender from the personal injuries in question had, before the deceased's death, been limited to damages of a specified or ascertainable amount, or where that liability is so limited by virtue of any enactment nothing in this Act shall make the defender liable to pay damages exceeding that amount; and accordingly where in such an action there are two or more pursuers any damages to which they would respectively be entitled under this Act apart from the said limitation shall, if necessary, be reduced *pro rata*.

(2) Where two or more such actions are conjoined, the conjoined actions shall be treated for the purposes of this section as if they were a single action.

[(3) This section applies to any action in which, following the death of any person from personal injuries, damages are claimed—

(a) by the executor of the deceased, in respect of the injuries from which the deceased died;

(b) in respect of the death of the deceased, by any relative of his or, if the relative has died, by the relative's executor.]

7 Amendment of references in other Acts

In any Act passed before this Act, unless the context otherwise requires, any reference to solatium in respect of the death of any person (however expressed) shall be construed as a reference to a loss of society award within the meaning of section 1 of this Act; and any reference to a dependant of a deceased person, in relation to an action claiming damages in respect of the deceased person's death, shall be construed as including a reference to a relative of the deceased person within the meaning of this Act.

8 Abolition of right to assythment

After the commencement of this Act no person shall in any circumstances have a right to assythment, and accordingly any action claiming that remedy shall (to the extent that it does so) be incompetent.

9 Damages due to injured person for patrimonial loss caused by personal injuries whereby expectation of life is diminished

(1) This section applies to any action for damages in respect of personal injuries sustained by the pursuer where his expected date of death is earlier than it would have been if he had not sustained the injuries.

(2) In assessing, in any action to which this section applies, the amount of any patrimonial loss in respect of the period after the date of decree—

> (a) it shall be assumed that the pursuer will live until the date when he would have been expected to die if he had not sustained the injuries (hereinafter referred to as the "notional date of death");
> (b) the court may have regard to any amount, whether or not it is an amount related to earnings by the pursuer's own labour or other gainful activity, which in its opinion the pursuer, if he had not sustained the injuries in question, would have received in the period up to his notional date of death by way of benefits in money or money's worth, being benefits derived from sources other than the pursuer's own estate;
> (c) the court shall have regard to any diminution of any such amount as aforesaid by virtue of expenses which in the opinion of the court the pursuer, if he had not sustained the injuries in question, would reasonably have incurred in the said period by way of living expenses.

[9A Solatium for loss of expectation of life

(1) In assessing, in an action for damages in respect of personal injuries, the amount of damages by way of solatium, the court shall, if—

> (a) the injured person's expectation of life has been reduced by the injuries; and
> (b) the injured person is, was at any time or is likely to become, aware of that reduction,

have regard to the extent that, in consequence of that awareness, he has suffered or is likely to suffer.

(2) Subject to subsection (1) above, no damages by way of solatium shall be recoverable in respect of loss of expectation of life.

(3) The court in making an award of damages by way of solatium shall not be required to ascribe specifically any part of the award to loss of expectation of life.]

10 Interpretation

(1) In this Act, unless the context otherwise requires—

"personal injuries" includes any disease or any impairment of a person's physical or mental condition [and injury resulting from defamation or any other verbal injury or other injury to reputation];

"relative", in relation to a deceased person, has the meaning assigned to it by Schedule 1 to this Act.

(2) References in this Act to a member of a deceased person's immediate family are references to any relative of his who falls within subparagraph (a), (b) or (c) of paragraph 1 of Schedule 1 to this Act.

(3) References in this Act to any other Act are references to that Act as amended, extended or applied by any other enactment, including this Act.

12 Citation, application to Crown, commencement and extent

(2) This Act binds the Crown.

(5) This Act extends to Scotland only.

SCHEDULES

Section 1   SCHEDULE 1   DEFINITION OF "RELATIVE"

1.   In this Act "relative" in relation to a deceased person includes—
   (a) any person who immediately before the deceased's death was the spouse [or civil partner] of the deceased [or in a relationship which had the characteristics of the relationship between civil partners];
   (b) any person who was a parent or child of the deceased;
   (c) any person not falling within paragraph (b) above who was accepted by the deceased as a child of his family;
   (d) any person who was an ascendant or descendant (other than a parent or child) of the deceased;
   (e) any person who was, or was the issue of, a brother, sister, uncle or aunt of the deceased; [...]
   (f) any person who, having been a spouse of the deceased, had ceased to be so by virtue of a divorce; [and
   (g) any person who, having been a civil partner of the deceased, had ceased to be so by virtue of the dissolution of the civil partnership]
but does not include any other person.
   2. In deducing any relationship for the purposes of the foregoing paragraph—
   (a) any relationship by affinity shall be treated as a relationship by consanguinity; any relationship of the half blood shall be treated as a relationship of the whole blood; and the step-child of any person shall be treated as his child; and
   [(b) Section 1(1) of the Law Reform (Parent and Child) (Scotland) Act 1986 shall apply; and any reference (however expressed) in this Act to a relative shall be construed accordingly.]

Dangerous Wild Animals Act 1976
(1976, c. 38)

1   Licences

(1) Subject to section 5 of this Act, no person shall keep any dangerous wild animal except under the authority of a licence granted in accordance with the provisions of this Act by a local authority.

(3) A local authority shall not grant a licence under this Act unless it is satisfied that—
   (a) it is not contrary to the public interest on the grounds of safety, nuisance or otherwise to grant the licence; ...
   (e) all reasonable precautions will be taken at all such times to prevent and control the spread of infectious diseases; ...

4 Power to seize and to dispose of animals without compensation
(1) Where—
(a) an animal is being kept contrary to section 1(1) of the Act, or
(b) any condition of a licence under this Act is contravened or not complied with, the local authority in whose area any animal concerned is for the time being may seize the animal, and either retain it in the authority's possession or destroy or otherwise dispose of it, and shall not be liable to pay compensation to any person in respect of the exercise of its powers under this subsection.

(2) A local authority which incurs any expenditure in exercising its powers under subsection (1)(a) of this section shall be entitled to recover the amount of the expenditure summarily as a civil debt from any person who was at the time of the seizure a keeper of the animal concerned.

(3) A local authority which incurs any expenditure in exercising its powers under subsection (1)(b) of this section shall be entitled to recover the amount of the expenditure summarily as a civil debt from the person to whom the licence concerned was granted.

Fatal Accidents Act 1976
(1976, c. 30)

1 Right of action for wrongful act causing death
[(1) If death is caused by any wrongful act, neglect or default which is such as would (if death had not ensued) have entitled the person injured to maintain an action and recover damages in respect thereof, the person who would have been liable if death had not ensued shall be liable to an action for damages, notwithstanding the death of the person injured.

(2) Subject to section 1A(2) below, every such action shall be for the benefit of the dependants of the person ("the deceased") whose death has been so caused.

(3) In this Act "dependant" means—
(a) the wife or husband or former wife or husband of the deceased;
[(aa) the civil partner or former civil partner of the deceased;]
(b) any person who—
(i) was living with the deceased in the same household immediately before the date of the death; and
(ii) had been living with the deceased in the same household for at least two years before that date; and
(iii) was living during the whole of that period as the husband or wife [or civil partner] of the deceased;
(c) any parent or other ascendant of the deceased;
(d) any person who was treated by the deceased as his parent;
(e) any child or other descendant of the deceased;
(f) any person (not being a child of the deceased) who, in the case of any marriage to which the deceased was at any time a party, was treated by the deceased as a child of the family in relation to that marriage;
[(fa) any person (not being a child of the deceased) who, in the case of any civil partnership in which the deceased was at any time a civil partner, was treated by the deceased as a child of the family in relation to that civil partnership;]
(g) any person who is, or is the issue of, a brother, sister, uncle or aunt of the deceased.

(4) The reference to the former wife or husband of the deceased in subsection (3)(a) above includes a reference to a person whose marriage to the deceased has been annulled or declared void as well as a person whose marriage to the deceased has been dissolved.

[(4A) The reference to the former civil partner of the deceased in subsection (3)(aa) above includes a reference to a person whose civil partnership with the deceased has been annulled as well as a person whose civil partnership with the deceased has been dissolved.]

(5) In deducing any relationship for the purposes of subsection (3) above—

(a) any relationship [by marriage or civil partnership] shall be treated as a relationship of consanguinity, any relationship of the half blood as a relationship of the whole blood, and the stepchild of any person as his child, and

(b) an illegitimate person shall be treated as the legitimate child of his mother and reputed father.

(6) Any reference in this Act to injury includes any disease and any impairment of a person's physical or mental condition.]

[1A   Bereavement

(1) An action under this Act may consist of or include a claim for damages for bereavement.

(2) A claim for damages for bereavement shall only be for the benefit—

(a) of the wife or husband [or civil partner] of the deceased; and

(b) where the deceased was a minor who was never married [or a civil partner]—

(i)   of his parents, if he was legitimate; and

(ii)   of his mother, if he was illegitimate.

(3) Subject to subsection (5) below, the sum to be awarded as damages under this section shall be [£10,000].

(4) Where there is a claim for damages under this section for the benefit of both the parents of the deceased, the sum awarded shall be divided equally between them (subject to any deduction falling to be made in respect of costs not recovered from the defendant).

(5) The Lord Chancellor may by order made by statutory instrument, subject to annulment in pursuance of a resolution of either House of Parliament, amend this section by varying the sum for the time being specified in subsection (3) above.]

2   Persons entitled to bring the action

(1) The action shall be brought by and in the name of the executor or administrator of the deceased.

(2) If—

(a) there is no executor or administrator of the deceased, or

(b) no action is brought within six months after the death by and in the name of an executor or administrator of the deceased,

the action may be brought by and in the name of all or any of the persons for whose benefit an executor or administrator could have brought it.

(3) Not more than one action shall lie for and in respect of the same subject matter of complaint.

(4) The plaintiff in the action shall be required to deliver to the defendant or his solicitor full particulars of the persons for whom and on whose behalf the action is brought and of the nature of the claim in respect of which damages are sought to be recovered.]

3   Assessment of damages

[(1) In the action such damages, other than damages for bereavement, may be awarded as are proportioned to the injury resulting from the death to the dependants respectively.

(2) After deducting the costs not recovered from the defendant any amount recovered otherwise than as damages for bereavement shall be divided among the dependants in such shares as may be directed.

(3) In an action under this Act where there fall to be assessed damages payable to a widow in respect of the death of her husband there shall not be taken into account the re-marriage of the widow or her prospects of re-marriage.

(4) In an action under this Act where there fall to be assessed damages payable to a person who is a dependant by virtue of section 1(3)(b) above in respect of the death of the person with whom the dependant was living as husband or wife [or civil partner] there shall be taken into account (together with any other matter that appears to the court to be relevant to the action) the fact that the dependant had no enforceable right to financial support by the deceased as a result of their living together.

(5) If the dependants have incurred funeral expenses in respect of the deceased, damages may be awarded in respect of those expenses.

(6) Money paid into court in satisfaction of a cause of action under this Act may be in one sum without specifying any person's share.]

4   Assessment of damages; disregard of benefits
[In assessing damages in respect of a person's death in an action under this Act, benefits which have accrued or will or may accrue to any person from his estate or otherwise as a result of his death shall be disregarded.]

5   Contributory negligence
Where any person dies as the result partly of his own fault and partly of the fault of any other person or persons, and accordingly if an action were brought for the benefit of the estate under the Law Reform (Miscellaneous Provisions) Act 1934 the damages recoverable would be reduced under section 1(1) of the Law Reform (Contributory Negligence) Act 1945, any damages recoverable in an action [...] under this Act shall be reduced to a proportionate extent.

Race Relations Act 1976
(1976, c. 74)

[*The following sections of this Act are similar to the corresponding provisions of the Sex Discrimination Act 1975 (ante) in brackets: RRA, ss 1 (SDA, ss 1, 2), 20 (SDA 29), 32 (SDA 41), 57 (SDA 66), 72 (SDA 77).*]

Protection from Eviction Act 1977
(1977, c. 43)

1   Unlawful eviction and harassment of occupier
(1) In this section "residential occupier", in relation to any premises, means a person occupying the premises as a residence, whether under a contract or by virtue of any enactment or rule of law giving him the right to remain in occupation or restricting the right of any other person to recover possession of the premises.

(2) If any person unlawfully deprives the residential occupier of any premises of his occupation of the premises or any part thereof, or attempts to do so, he shall be guilty of an offence unless he proves that he believed, and had reasonable cause to believe, that the residential occupier had ceased to reside in the premises.

(3) If any person with intent to cause the residential occupier of any premises—
    (a) to give up the occupation of the premises or any part thereof; or
    (b) to refrain from exercising any right or pursuing any remedy in respect of the premises or part thereof;
does acts [likely] to interfere with the peace or comfort of the residential occupier or members of his household, or persistently withdraws or withholds services reasonably required for the occupation of the premises as a residence, he shall be guilty of an offence.

[(3A) Subject to subsection (3B) below, the landlord of a residential occupier or an agent of the landlord shall be guilty of an offence if—

    (a) he does acts likely to interfere with the peace or comfort of the residential occupier or members of his household, or

    (b) he persistently withdraws or withholds services reasonably required for the occupation of the premises in question as a residence,

and (in either case) he knows, or has reasonable cause to believe, that that conduct is likely to cause the residential occupier to give up the occupation of the whole or part of the premises or to refrain from exercising any right or pursuing any remedy in respect of the whole or part of the premises.

(3B) A person shall not be guilty of an offence under subsection (3A) above if he proves that he had reasonable grounds for doing the acts or withdrawing or withholding the services in question.]

(5) Nothing in this section shall be taken to prejudice any liability or remedy to which a person guilty of an offence thereunder may be subject in civil proceedings.

2   Restriction on re-entry without due process of law

Where any premises are let as a dwelling on a lease which is subject to a right of re-entry or forfeiture it shall not be lawful to enforce that right otherwise than by proceedings in the court while any person is lawfully residing in the premises or part of them.

3   Prohibition of eviction without due process of law

(1) Where any premises have been let as a dwelling under a tenancy which is not a statutorily protected tenancy and—

    (a) the tenancy (in this section referred to as the former tenancy) has come to an end, but

    (b) the occupier continues to reside in the premises or part of them, it shall not be lawful for the owner to enforce against the occupier, otherwise than by proceedings in the court, his right to recover possession of the premises.

(2) In this section "the occupier", in relation to any premises, means any person lawfully residing in the premises or part of them at the termination of the former tenancy.

Torts (Interference with Goods) Act 1977
(1977, c. 32)

1   Definition of "wrongful interference with goods"

In this Act "wrongful interference", or "wrongful interference with goods", means—

    (a) conversion of goods (also called trover),

    (b) trespass to goods,

    (c) negligence so far as it results in damage to goods or to an interest in goods,

    (d) subject to section 2, any other tort so far as it results in damage to goods or to an interest in goods.

[and references in this Act (however worded) to proceedings for wrongful interference or to a claim or right to claim for wrongful interference shall include references to proceedings by virtue of Part I of the Consumer Protection Act 1987 or Part II of the Consumer Protection (Northern Ireland) Order 1987 (product liability) in respect of any damage to goods or to an interest in goods or, as the case may be, to a claim or right to claim by virtue of that Part in respect of any such damage.]

2   Abolition of detinue

(1) Detinue is abolished.

(2) An action lies in conversion for loss or destruction of goods which a bailee has allowed to happen in breach of his duty to his bailor (that is to say it lies in a case which is not otherwise conversion, but would have been detinue before detinue was abolished).

3 Forms of judgment where goods are detained

(1) In proceedings for wrongful interference against a person who is in possession or in control of the goods relief may be given in accordance with this section, so far as appropriate.

(2) The relief is—

(a) an order for delivery of the goods, and for payment of any consequential damages, or

(b) an order for delivery of the goods, but giving the defendant the alternative of paying damages by reference to the value of the goods, together in either alternative with payment of any consequential damages, or

(c) damages.

(3) Subject to rules of court—

(a) relief shall be given under only one of paragraphs (a), (b) and (c) of subsection (2),

(b) relief under paragraph (a) of subsection (2) is at the discretion of the court, and the claimant may choose between the others.

(4) If it is shown to the satisfaction of the court that an order under subsection (2)(a) had not been complied with, the court may—

(a) revoke the order, or the relevant part of it, and

(b) make an order for payment of damages by reference to the value of the goods.

(5) Where an order is made under subsection (2)(b) the defendant may satisfy the order by returning the goods at any time before execution of judgment, but without prejudice to liability to pay any consequential damages.

(6) An order for delivery of the goods under subsection (2)(a) or (b) may impose such conditions as may be determined by the court, or pursuant to rules of court, and in particular, where damages by reference to the value of the goods would not be the whole of the value of the goods, may require an allowance to be made by the claimant to reflect the difference.

For example, a bailor's action against the bailee may be one in which the measure of damages is not the full value of the goods, and then the court may order delivery of the goods, but require the bailor to pay the bailee a sum reflecting the difference.

(7) Where under subsection (1) or subsection (2) of section 6 an allowance is to be made in respect of an improvement of the goods, and an order is made under subsection (2)(a) or (b), the court may assess the allowance to be made in respect of the improvement, and by the order require, as a condition for delivery of the goods, that allowance to be made by the claimant.

(8) This section is without prejudice—

(a) to the remedies afforded by section 133 of the Consumer Credit Act, or . . .

(c) to any jurisdiction to afford ancillary or incidental relief.

4 Interlocutory relief where goods are detained

(1) In this section "proceedings" means proceedings for wrongful interference.

(2) On the application of any person in accordance with rules of court, the High Court shall, in such circumstances as may be specified in the rules, have power to make an order providing for the delivery up of any goods which are or may become the subject matter of subsequent proceedings in the court, or as to which any question may arise in proceedings.

(3) Delivery shall be, as the order may provide, to the claimant or to a person appointed by the court for the purpose, and shall be on such terms and conditions as may be specified in the order.

5 Extinction of title on satisfaction of claim for damages

(1) Where damages for wrongful interference are, or would fall to be, assessed on the footing that the claimant is being compensated—

(a) for the whole of his interest in the goods, or

(b) for the whole of his interest in the goods subject to a reduction for contributory negligence, payment of the assessed damages (under all heads), or as the case may be settlement of a claim for damages for the wrong (under all heads), extinguishes the claimant's title to that interest.

(2) In subsection (1) the reference to the settlement of the claim includes—

(a) where the claim is made in court proceedings, and the defendant has paid a sum into court to meet the whole claim, the taking of that sum by the claimant, and

(b) where the claim is made in court proceedings, and the proceedings are settled or compromised, the payment of what is due in accordance with the settlement or compromise, and

(c) where the claim is made out of court and is settled or compromised, the payment of what is due in accordance with the settlement or compromise.

(3) It is hereby declared that subsection (1) does not apply where damages are assessed on the footing that the claimant is being compensated for the whole of his interest in the goods, but the damages paid are limited to some lesser amount by virtue of any enactment or rule of law.

(4) Where under section 7(3) the claimant accounts over to another person (the "third party") so as to compensate (under all heads) the third party for the whole of his interest in the goods, the third party's title to that interest is extinguished.

(5) This section has effect subject to any agreement varying the respective rights of the parties to the agreement, and where the claim is made in court proceedings has effect subject to any order of the court.

6 Allowance for improvement of the goods

(1) If in proceedings for wrongful interference against a person (the "improver") who has improved the goods, it is shown that the improver acted in the mistaken but honest belief that he had a good title to them, an allowance shall be made for the extent to which, at the time as at which the goods fall to be valued in assessing damages, the value of the goods is attributable to the improvement.

(2) If, in proceedings for wrongful interference against a person ("the purchaser") who has purported to purchase the goods—

(a) from the improver, or

(b) where after such a purported sale the goods passed by a further purported sale on one or more occasions, on any such occasion,

it is shown that the purchaser acted in good faith, an allowance shall be made on the principle set out in subsection (1).

For example, where a person in good faith buys a stolen car from the improver and is sued in conversion by the true owner the damages may be reduced to reflect the improvement, but if the person who bought the stolen car from the improver sues the improver for failure of consideration, and the improver acted in good faith, subsection (3) below will ordinarily make a comparable reduction in the damages he recovers from the improver.

(3) If in a case within subsection (2) the person purporting to sell the goods acted in good faith, then in proceedings by the purchaser for recovery of the purchase price because of failure of consideration, or in any other proceedings founded on that failure of consideration, an allowance shall, where appropriate, be made on the principle set out in subsection (1).

(4) This section applies, with the necessary modifications, to a purported bailment or other disposition of goods as it applies to a purported sale of goods.

7 Double liability

(1) In this section "double liability" means the double liability of the wrongdoer which can arise—

(a) where one of two or more rights of action for wrongful interference is founded on a possessory title, or

(b) where the measure of damages in an action for wrongful interference founded on a proprietary title is or includes the entire value of the goods, although the interest is one of two or more interests in the goods.

(2) In proceedings to which any two or more claimants are parties, the relief shall be such as to avoid double liability of the wrongdoer as between those claimants.

(3) On satisfaction, in whole or in part, of any claim for an amount exceeding that recoverable if subsection (2) applied, the claimant is liable to account over to the other person having a right to claim to such extent as will avoid double liability.

(4) Where, as the result of enforcement of a double liability, any claimant is unjustly enriched to an extent, he shall be liable to reimburse the wrongdoer to that extent.

For example, if a converter of goods pays damages first to a finder of the goods, and then to the true owner, the finder is unjustly enriched unless he accounts over to the true owner under subsection (3); and then the true owner is unjustly enriched and becomes liable to reimburse the converter of the goods.

8   Competing rights to the goods

(1) The defendant in an action for wrongful interference shall be entitled to show, in accordance with rules of court, that a third party has a better right than the plaintiff as respects all or any part of the interest claimed by the plaintiff, or in right of which he sues, and any rule of law (sometimes called jus tertii) to the contrary is abolished.

(2) Rules of court relating to proceedings for wrongful interference may—
  (a) require the plaintiff to give particulars of his title,
  (b) require the plaintiff to identify any person who, to his knowledge, has or claims any interest in the goods,
  (c) authorise the defendant to apply for directions as to whether any person should be joined with a view to establishing whether he has a better right than the plaintiff, or has a claim as a result of which the defendant might be doubly liable,
  (d) where a party fails to appear on an application within paragraph (c), or to comply with any direction given by the court on such an application, authorise the court to deprive him of any right of action against the defendant for the wrong either unconditionally, or subject to such terms or conditions as may be specified.

(3) Subsection (2) is without prejudice to any other power of making rules of court.

9   Concurrent actions

(1) This section applies where goods are the subject of two or more claims for wrongful interference (whether or not the claims are founded on the same wrongful act, and whether or not any of the claims relates also to other goods).

(2) Where the goods are the subject of two or more claims under section 6 this section shall apply as if any claim under section 6(3) were a claim for wrongful interference.

(3) If proceedings have been brought in a county court on one of those claims, county court rules may waive, or allow a court to waive, any limit (financial or territorial) on the jurisdiction of county courts in [the County Courts Act 1984] or the County Courts Act [(Northern Ireland) Order 1980] so as to allow another of those claims to be brought in the same county court.

(4) If proceedings are brought on one of the claims in the High Court, and proceedings on any other are brought in a county court, whether prior to the High Court proceedings or not, the High Court may, on the application of the defendant, after notice has been given to the claimant in the county court proceedings—
  (a) order that the county court proceedings be transferred to the High Court, and
  (b) order security for costs or impose such other terms as the court thinks fit.

10   Co-owners

(1) Co-ownership is no defence to an action founded on conversion or trespass to goods where the defendant without the authority of the other co-owner—
  (a) destroys the goods, or disposes of the goods in a way giving a good title to the entire property in the goods, or otherwise does anything equivalent to the destruction of the other's interest in the goods, or

(b) purports to dispose of the goods in a way which would give a good title to the entire property in the goods if he was acting with the authority of all co-owners of the goods.

(2) Subsection (1) shall not affect the law concerning execution or enforcement of judgments, or concerning any form of distress.

(3) Subsection (1)(a) is by way of restatement of existing law so far as it relates to conversion.

11 Minor amendments

(1) Contributory negligence is no defence in proceedings founded on conversion, or on intentional trespass to goods.

(2) Receipt of goods by way of pledge is conversion if the delivery of the goods is conversion.

(3) Denial of title is not of itself conversion.

12 Bailee's power of sale

(1) This section applies to goods in the possession or under the control of a bailee where—

(a) the bailor is in breach of an obligation to take delivery of the goods or, if the terms of the bailment so provide, to give directions as to their delivery, or

(b) the bailee could impose such an obligation by giving notice to the bailor, but is unable to trace or communicate with the bailor, or

(c) the bailee can reasonably expect to be relieved of any duty to safeguard the goods on giving notice to the bailor, but is unable to trace or communicate with the bailor.

(2) In the cases of Part I of Schedule 1 to this Act a bailee may, for the purposes of subsection (1), impose an obligation on the bailor to take delivery of the goods, or as the case may be to give directions as to their delivery, and in those cases the said Part I sets out the method of notification.

(3) If the bailee—

(a) has in accordance with Part II of Schedule 1 to this Act given notice to the bailor of his intention to sell the goods under this subsection, or

(b) has failed to trace or communicate with the bailor with a view to giving him such a notice, after having taken reasonable steps for the purpose,

and is reasonably satisfied that the bailor owns the goods, he shall be entitled, as against the bailor, to sell the goods.

(4) Where subsection (3) applies but the bailor did not in fact own the goods, a sale under this section, or under section 13, shall not give a good title as against the owner, or as against a person claiming under the owner.

(5) A bailee exercising his powers under subsection (3) shall be liable to account to the bailor for the proceeds of sale, less any cost of sale, and—

(a) the account shall be taken on the footing that the bailee should have adopted the best method of sale reasonably available in the circumstances, and

(b) where subsection (3)(a) applies, any sum payable in respect of the goods by the bailor to the bailee which accrued due before the bailee gave notice of intention to sell the goods shall be deductible from the proceeds of sale.

(6) A sale duly made under this section gives a good title to the purchaser as against the bailor.

(7) In this section, section 13, and Schedule 1 to this Act,

(a) "bailor" and "bailee" include their respective successors in title, and

(b) references to what is payable, paid or due to the bailee in respect of the goods include references to what would be payable by the bailor to the bailee as a condition of delivery of the goods at the relevant time.

(8) This section, and Schedule 1 to this Act, have effect subject to the terms of the bailment.

(9) This section shall not apply where the goods were bailed before the commencement of this Act.

13 Sale authorised by the court

(1) If a bailee of the goods to which section 12 applies satisfies the court that he is entitled to sell the goods under section 12, or that he would be so entitled if he had given any notice required in accordance with Schedule 1 to this Act, the court—

    (a) may authorise the sale of the goods subject to such terms and conditions, if any, as may be specified in the order, and

    (b) may authorise the bailee to deduct from the proceeds of sale any costs of sale and any amount due from the bailor to the bailee in respect of the goods, and

    (c) may direct the payment into court of the net proceeds of sale, less any amount deducted under paragraph (b), to be held to the credit of the bailor.

(2) A decision of the court authorising a sale under this section shall, subject to any right of appeal, be conclusive, as against the bailor, of the bailee's entitlement to sell the goods, and gives a good title to the purchaser as against the bailor.

(3) In this section "the court" means the High Court or a county court, [and a county court shall have jurisdiction in the proceedings save that, in Northern Ireland, a county court shall only have jurisdiction in proceedings if the value of the goods does not exceed the county court limit mentioned in Article 10(1) of the County Courts (Northern Ireland) Order 1980.]

14 Interpretation

(1) In this Act, unless the context otherwise requires—

   ...

"goods" includes all chattels personal other than things in action and money....

16 Extent and application to the Crown

(3) This Act shall bind the Crown, but as regards the Crown's liability in tort shall not bind the Crown further than the Crown is made liable in tort by the Crown Proceedings Act 1947.

SCHEDULES

Section 12   SCHEDULE 1   UNCOLLECTED GOODS

PART I   POWER TO IMPOSE OBLIGATION TO COLLECT GOODS

1. (1) For the purposes of section 12(1) a bailee may, in the circumstances specified in this Part of this Schedule, by notice given to the bailor impose on him an obligation to take delivery of the goods.

(2) The notice shall be in writing, and may be given either—

    (a) by delivering it to the bailor, or

    (b) by leaving it at his proper address, or

    (c) by post.

(3) The notice shall—

    (a) specify the name and address of the bailee, and give sufficient particulars of the goods and the address or place where they are held, and

    (b) state that the goods are ready for delivery to the bailor, or where combined with a notice terminating the contract of bailment, will be ready for delivery when the contract is terminated, and

    (c) specify the amount, if any, which is payable by the bailor to the bailee in respect of the goods and which became due before the giving of the notice.

(4) Where the notice is sent by post it may be combined with a notice under Part II of this Schedule if the notice is sent by post in a way complying with paragraph 6(4).

(5) References in this Part of this Schedule to taking delivery of the goods include, where the terms of the bailment admit, references to giving directions as to their delivery.

(6) This Part of this Schedule is without prejudice to the provisions of any contract requiring the bailor to take delivery of the goods.

Goods accepted for repair or other treatment

2. If a bailee has accepted goods for repair or other treatment on the terms (expressed or implied) that they will be re-delivered to the bailor when the repair or other treatment has been carried out, the notice may be given at any time after the repair or other treatment has been carried out.

Goods accepted for valuation or appraisal

3. If a bailee has accepted goods in order to value or appraise them, the notice may be given at any time after the bailee has carried out the valuation or appraisal.

Storage, warehousing, etc.

4. (1) If a bailee is in possession of goods which he has held as custodian, and his obligation as custodian has come to an end, the notice may be given at any time after the ending of the obligation, or may be combined with any notice terminating his obligation as custodian.

(2) This paragraph shall not apply to goods held by a person as mercantile agent, that is to say by a person having in the customary course of his business as a mercantile agent authority either to sell goods or to consign goods for the purpose of sale, or to buy goods, or to raise money on the security of goods.

Supplemental

5. Paragraphs 2, 3 and 4 apply whether or not the bailor has paid any amount due to the bailee in respect of the goods, and whether or not the bailment is for reward, or in the course of business, or gratuitous.

PART II   NOTICE OF INTENTION TO SELL GOODS

6. (1) A notice under section 12(3) shall—
   (a) specify the name and address of the bailee, and give sufficient particulars of the goods and the address or place where they are held, and
   (b) specify the date on or after which the bailee proposes to sell the goods, and
   (c) specify the amount, if any, which is payable by the bailor to the bailee in respect of the goods, and which became due before the giving of the notice.

(2) The period between giving of the notice and the date specified in the notice as that on or after which the bailee proposes to exercise the power of sale shall be such as will afford the bailor a reasonable opportunity of taking delivery of the goods.

(3) If any amount is payable in respect of the goods by the bailor to the bailee, and become due before giving of the notice, the said period shall be not less than three months.

(4) The notice shall be in writing and shall be sent by post in a registered letter, or by the recorded delivery service.

7. (1) The bailee shall not give a notice under section 12(3), or exercise his right to sell the goods pursuant to such a notice, at a time when he has notice that, because of a dispute concerning the goods, the bailor is questioning or refusing to pay all or any part of what the bailee claims to be due to him in respect of the goods.

(2) This paragraph shall be left out of account in determining under section 13(1) whether a bailee of goods is entitled to sell the goods under section 12, or would be so entitled if he had given any notice required in accordance with this Schedule.

Unfair Contract Terms Act 1977
(1977, c. 50)

PART I   AMENDMENT OF THE LAW FOR ENGLAND AND WALES
AND NORTHERN IRELAND

1   Scope of Part I

(1) For the purposes of this Part of this Act, "negligence" means the breach—

    (a) of any obligation, arising from the express or implied terms of a contract, to take reasonable care or exercise reasonable skill in the performance of the contract;

    (b) of any common law duty to take reasonable care or exercise reasonable skill (but not any stricter duty);

    (c) of the common duty of care imposed by the Occupiers' Liability Act 1957 or the Occupier's Liability Act (Northern Ireland) 1957.

(2) This Part of this Act is subject to Part III; and in relation to contracts, the operation of sections 2 to 4 and 7 is subject to the exceptions made by Schedule I.

(3) In the case of both contract and tort, sections 2 to 7 apply (except where the contrary is stated in section 6(4)) only to business liability, that is liability for breach of obligations or duties arising—

    (a) from things done or to be done by a person in the course of a business (whether his own business or another's); or

    (b) from the occupation of premises used for business purposes of the occupier; and references to liability are to be read accordingly [but liability of an occupier of premises for breach of an obligation or duty towards a person obtaining access to the premises for recreational or educational purposes, being liability for loss or damage suffered by reason of the dangerous state of the premises, is not a business liability of the occupier unless granting that person such access for the purposes concerned falls within the business purposes of the occupier].

(4) In relation to any breach of duty or obligation, it is immaterial for any purpose of this Part of this Act whether the breach was inadvertent or intentional, or whether liability for it arises directly or vicariously.

2   Negligence liability

(1) A person cannot by reference to any contract term or to a notice given to persons generally or to particular persons exclude or restrict his liability for death or personal injury resulting from negligence.

(2) In the case of other loss or damage, a person cannot so exclude or restrict his liability for negligence except in so far as the term or notice satisfies the requirement of reasonableness.

(3) Where a contract term or notice purports to exclude or restrict liability for negligence a person's agreement to or awareness of it is not of itself to be taken as indicating his voluntary acceptance of any risk.

3   Liability arising in contract

(1) This section applies as between contracting parties where one of them deals as consumer or on the other's written standard terms of business.

(2) As against that party, the other cannot by reference to any contract term—

    (a) when himself in breach of contract, exclude or restrict any liability of his in respect of the breach; or

    (b) claim to be entitled—

        (i) to render a contractual performance substantially different from that which was reasonably expected of him, or

        (ii) in respect of the whole or any part of his contractual obligation, to render no performance at all,

except in so far as (in any of the cases mentioned above in this subsection) the contra
satisfies the requirement of reasonableness.

4   Unreasonable indemnity clauses

(1) A person dealing as consumer cannot by reference to any contract term be made to indemnify another person (whether a party to the contract or not) in respect of liability that may be incurred by the other for negligence or breach of contract, except in so far as the contract term satisfies the requirement of reasonableness.

(2) This section applies whether the liability in question—

   (a) is directly that of the person to be indemnified or is incurred by him vicariously;

   (b) is to the person dealing as consumer or to someone else.

5   "Guarantee" of consumer goods

(1) In the case of goods of a type ordinarily supplied for private use or consumption, where loss or damage—

   (a) arises from the goods proving defective while in consumer use; and

   (b) results from the negligence of a person concerned in the manufacture or dis-
       tribution of the goods,

liability for the loss or damage cannot be excluded or restricted by reference to any contract term or notice contained in or operating by reference to a guarantee of the goods.

(2) For these purposes—

   (a) goods are to be regarded as "in consumer use" when a person is using them, or has
       them in his possession for use, otherwise than exclusively for the purposes of a
       business; and

   (b) anything in writing is a guarantee if it contains or purports to contain some
       promise or assurance (however worded or presented) that defects will be made
       good by complete or partial replacement, or by repair, monetary compensation or
       otherwise.

(3) This section does not apply as between the parties to a contract under or in pursuance of which possession or ownership of the goods passed.

6   Sale and hire-purchase

(1) Liability for breach of the obligations arising from—

   (a) [section 12 of the Sale of Goods Act 1979] (seller's implied undertakings as to title,
       etc.);

   (b) section 8 of the Supply of Goods (Implied Terms) Act 1973 (the corresponding
       thing in relation to hire-purchase),

cannot be excluded or restricted by reference to any contract term.

(2) As against a person dealing as consumer, liability for breach of the obligations arising from—

   (a) [section 13, 14 or 15 of the [1979] Act] (seller's implied undertakings as to
       conformity of goods with description or sample, or as to their quality or fitness for
       a particular purpose);

   (b) section 9, 10 or 11 of the 1973 Act (the corresponding things in relation to
       hire-purchase),

cannot be excluded or restricted by reference to any contract term.

(3) As against a person dealing otherwise than as consumer, the liability specified in subsection (2) above can be excluded or restricted by reference to a contract term, but only in so far as the term satisfies the requirement of reasonableness.

(4) The liabilities referred to in this section are not only the business liabilities defined by section 1(3), but include those arising under any contract of sale of goods or hire-purchase agreement.

7   Miscellaneous contracts under which goods pass

(1) Where the possession or ownership of goods passes under or in pursuance of a con-tract not governed by the law of sale of goods or hire-purchase, subsections (2) to (4) below apply as regards the effect (if any) to be given to contract terms excluding or restricting liability for breach of obligation arising by implication of law from the nature of the contract.

(2) As against a person dealing as consumer, liability in respect of the goods' corre-spondence with description or sample, or their quality or fitness for any particular purpose, cannot be excluded or restricted by reference to any such term.

(3) As against a person dealing otherwise than as consumer, that liability can be excluded or restricted by reference to such a term, but only in so far as the term satisfies the require-ment of reasonableness.

[(3A) Liability for breach of the obligations arising under section 2 of the Supply of Goods and Services Act 1982 (implied terms about title etc. in certain contracts for the transfer of the property in goods) cannot be excluded or restricted by reference to any such term.]

(4) Liability in respect of—
  (a) the right to transfer ownership of the goods, or give possession; or
  (b) the assurance of quiet possession to a person taking goods in pursuance of the contract,
cannot [(in a case to which subsection (3A) above does not apply)] be excluded or restricted by reference to any such term except in so far as the term satisfies the requirement of reasonableness.

  (c) This section does not apply in the case of goods passing on a redemption of trading stamps within the Trading Stamps Act 1964 or the Trading Stamps Act (Northern Ireland) 1965.

9   Effect of breach

(1) Where for reliance upon it a contract term has to satisfy the requirement of reason-ableness, it may be found to do so and be given effect accordingly notwithstanding that the contract has been terminated either by breach or by a party electing to treat it as repudiated.

(2) Where on a breach the contract is nevertheless affirmed by a party entitled to treat it as repudiated, this does not of itself exclude the requirement of reasonableness in relation to any contract term.

10   Evasion by means of secondary contract

A person is not bound by any contract term prejudicing or taking away rights of his which arise under, or in connection with the performance of, another contract, so far as those rights extend to the enforcement of another's liability which this Part of this Act prevents that other from excluding or restricting.

11   The "reasonableness" test

(1) In relation to a contract term, the requirement of reasonableness for the purposes of this Part of this Act, section 3 of the Misrepresentation Act 1967 and section 3 of the Mis-representation Act (Northern Ireland) 1967 is that the term shall have been a fair and rea-sonable one to be included having regard to the circumstances which were, or ought reasonably to have been, known to or in the contemplation of the parties when the contract was made.

(2) In determining for the purposes of section 6 or 7 above whether a contract term satisfies the requirement of reasonableness, regard shall be had in particular to the matters specified in Schedule 2 to this Act; but this subsection does not prevent the court or arbitrator from holding, in accordance with any rule of law, that a term which purports to exclude or restrict any relevant liability is not a term of the contract.

(3) In relation to a notice (not being a notice having contractual effect), the requirement of reasonableness under this Act is that it should be fair and reasonable to allow reliance on it,

having regard to all the circumstances obtaining when the liability arose or (but for the notice) would have arisen.

(4) Where by reference to a contract term or notice a person seeks to restrict liability to a specified sum of money, and the question arises (under this or any other Act) whether the term or notice satisfies the requirement of reasonableness, regard shall be had in particular (but without prejudice to subsection (2) above in the case of contract terms) to—

(a) the resources which he could expect to be available to him for the purpose of meeting the liability should it arise; and

(b) how far it was open to him to cover himself by insurance.

(5) It is for those claiming that a contract term or notice satisfies the requirement of reasonableness to show that it does.

12 "Dealing as consumer"

(1) A party to a contract "deals as consumer" in relation to another party if—

(a) he neither makes the contract in the course of a business nor holds himself out as doing so; and

(b) the other party does make the contract in the course of a business; and

(c) in the case of a contract governed by the law of sale of goods or hire-purchase, or by section 7 of this Act, the goods passing under or in pursuance of the contract are of a type ordinarily supplied for private use or consumption.

[But if the first party mentioned in subsection (1) is an individual paragraph (c) of that section must be ignored.]

[(2) But the buyer is not in any circumstances to be regarded as dealing as consumer—

(a) if he is an individual and the goods are second hand goods sold at public auction at which individuals have the opportunity of attending the sale in person;

(b) if he is not an individual and the goods are sold by auction or by competitive tender.]

(3) Subject to this, it is for those claiming that a party does not deal as consumer to show that he does not.

13 Varieties of exemption clause

(1) To the extent that this Part of this Act prevents the exclusion or restriction of any liability it also prevents—

(a) making the liability or its enforcement subject to restrictive or onerous conditions;

(b) excluding or restricting any right or remedy in respect of the liability, or subjecting a person to any prejudice in consequence of his pursuing any such right or remedy;

(c) excluding or restricting rules of evidence or procedure;

and (to that extent) sections 2 and 5 to 7 also prevent excluding or restricting liability by reference to terms and notices which exclude or restrict the relevant obligation or duty.

(2) But an agreement in writing to submit present or future differences to arbitration is not to be treated under this Part of this Act as excluding or restricting any liability.

14 Interpretation of Part I

In this Part of the Act—

"business" includes a profession and the activities of any government department or local or public authority;

"goods" has the same meaning as in [the Sale of Goods Act 1979];

"hire-purchase agreement" has the same meaning as in the Consumer Credit Act 1974;

"negligence" has the meaning given by section 1(1);

"notice" includes an announcement, whether or not in writing, and any other communication or pretended communication; and "personal injury" includes any disease and any impairment of physical or mental condition.

PART II   AMENDMENT OF LAW FOR SCOTLAND

15   Scope of Part II

(1) This Part of this Act [...] is subject to Part III of this Act and does not affect the validity of any discharge or indemnity given by a person in consideration of the receipt by him of compensation in settlement of any claim which he has.

(2) Subject to subsection (3) below, sections 16 to 18 of this Act apply to any contract only to the extent that the contract—

    (a) relates to the transfer of the ownership or possession of goods from one person to another (with or without work having been done on them);

    (b) constitutes a contract of service or apprenticeship;

    (c) relates to services of whatever kind, including (without prejudice to the foregoing generality) carriage, deposit and pledge, care and custody, mandate, agency, loan and services relating to the use of land;

    (d) relates to the liability of an occupier of land to persons entering upon or using that land;

    (e) relates to a grant of any right or permission to enter upon or use land not amounting to an estate or interest in the land.

(3) Notwithstanding anything in subsection (2) above, sections 16 to 18—

    (a) do not apply to any contract to the extent that the contract—

        (i)   is a contract of insurance (including a contract to pay an annuity on human life);

        (ii) relates to the formation, constitution or dissolution of any body corporate or unincorporated association or partnership;

    (b) apply to—

    a contract of marine salvage or towage;

    a charter party of a ship or hovercraft;

    a contract for the carriage of goods by ship or hovercraft; or,

    a contract to which subsection (4) below relates,

only to the extent that—

        (i)   both parties deal or hold themselves out as dealing in the course of a business (and then only in so far as the contract purports to exclude or restrict liability for breach of duty in respect of death or personal injury); or

        (ii) the contract is a consumer contract (and then only in favour of the consumer).

(4) This subsection relates to a contract in pursuance of which goods are carried by ship or hovercraft and which either—

    (a) specifies ship or hovercraft as the means of carriage over part of the journey to be covered; or

    (b) makes no provision as to the means of carriage and does not exclude ship or hovercraft as that means,

in so far as the contract operates for and in relation to the carriage of the goods by that means.

16   Liability for breach of duty

(1) [Subject to subsection (1A) below] where a term of a contract [, or a provision of a notice given to persons generally or to particular persons] purports to exclude or restrict liability for breach of duty arising in the course of any business or from the occupation of any premises used for business purposes of the occupier, that term [or provision]—

    (a) shall be void in any case where such exclusion or restriction is in respect of death or personal injury;

(b) shall, in any other case, have no effect if it was not fair and reasonable to incorporate the term in the contract [or, as the case may be, if it is not fair and reasonable to allow reliance on the provision].

[(1A) Nothing in paragraph (b) of subsection (1) above shall be taken as implying that a provision of a notice has effect in circumstances where, apart from that paragraph, it would not have effect.]

(2) Subsection (1)(a) above does not affect the validity of any discharge and indemnity given by a person, on or in connection with an award to him of compensation for pneumoconiosis attributable to employment in the coal industry, in respect of any further claim arising from his contracting that disease.

(3) Where under subsection (1) above a term of a contract [or a provision of a notice] is void or has no effect, the fact that a person has agreed to, or was aware of, the term [or provision] shall not of itself be sufficient evidence that he knowingly and voluntarily assumed any risk.

17 Control of unreasonable exemptions in consumer or standard form contracts

(1) Any term of a contract which is a consumer contract or a standard form contract shall have no effect for the purpose of enabling a party to the contract—

(a) who is in breach of a contractual obligation, to exclude or restrict any liability of his to the consumer in respect of the breach;

(b) in respect of a contractual obligation, to render no performance, or to render a performance substantially different from that which the consumer or customer reasonably expected from the contract;

if it was not fair and reasonable to incorporate the term in the contract.

(2) In this section "customer" means a party to a standard form contract who deals on the basis of written standard terms of business of the other party to the contract who himself deals in the course of a business.

18 Unreasonable indemnity clauses in consumer contracts

(1) Any term of a contract which is a consumer contract shall have no effect for the purpose of making the consumer indemnify another person (whether a party to the contract or not) in respect of liability which that other person may incur as a result of breach of duty or breach of contract, if it was not fair and reasonable to incorporate the term in the contract.

(2) In this section "liability" means liability arising in the course of any business or from the occupation of any premises used for business purposes of the occupier.

19 "Guarantee" of consumer goods

(1) This section applies to a guarantee—

(a) in relation to goods which are of a type ordinarily supplied for private use or consumption; and

(b) which is not a guarantee given by one party to the other party to a contract under or in pursuance of which the ownership or possession of the goods to which the guarantee relates is transferred.

(2) A term of a guarantee to which this section applies shall be void in so far as it purports to exclude or restrict liability for loss or damage (including death or personal injury)—

(a) arising from the goods proving defective while—

(i) in use otherwise than exclusively for the purposes of a business; or

(ii) in the possession of a person for such use; and

(b) resulting from the breach of duty of a person concerned in the manufacture or distribution of the goods.

(3) For the purposes of this section, any document is a guarantee if it contains or purports to contain some promise or assurance (however worded or presented) that defects will be made good by complete or partial replacement, or by repair, monetary compensation or otherwise.

20 Obligations implied by law in sale and hire-purchase contracts

(1) Any term of a contract which purports to exclude or restrict liability for breach of the obligations arising from—

    (a) section 12 of the Sale of Goods Act [1979] (seller's implied undertakings as to title etc.),

    (b) section 8 of the Supply of Goods (Implied Terms) Act 1973 (implied terms as to title in hire-purchase agreements),

shall be void.

(2) Any term of a contract which purports to exclude or restrict liability for breach of the obligations arising from—

    (a) section 13, 14 or 15 of the said Act of [1979] (seller's implied undertakings as to conformity of goods with description or sample, or as to their quality or fitness for a particular purpose);

    (b) section 9, 10 or 11 of the said Act of 1973 (the corresponding provisions in relation to hire-purchase), shall—

        (i) in the case of a consumer contract, be void against the consumer;

        (ii) in any other case, have no effect if it was not fair and reasonable to incorporate the term in the contract.

21 Obligations implied by law in other contracts for the supply of goods

(1) Any term of a contract to which this section applies purporting to exclude or restrict liability for breach of an obligation—

    (a) such as is referred to in subsection (3)(a) below—

        (i) in the case of a consumer contract, shall be void against the consumer, and

        (ii) in any other case, shall have no effect if it was not fair and reasonable to incorporate the term in the contract;

    (b) such as is referred to in subsection (3)(b) below, shall have no effect, if it was not fair and reasonable to incorporate the term in the contract.

(2) This section applies to any contract to the extent that it relates to any such matter as is referred to in section 15(2)(a) of this Act, but does not apply to—

    (a) a contract of sale of goods or a hire-purchase agreement; or

    (b) a charter party of a ship or hovercraft unless it is a consumer contract (and then only in favour of the consumer).

(3) An obligation referred to in this subsection is an obligation incurred under a contract in the course of a business and arising by implication of law from the nature of the contract which relates—

    (a) to the correspondence of goods with description or sample, or to the quality or fitness of the goods for any particular purpose; or

    (b) to any right to transfer ownership or possession of goods, or to the enjoyment of quiet possession of goods.

[(3A) Notwithstanding anything in the foregoing provisions of this section, any term of a contract which purports to exclude or restrict liability for breach of the obligations arising under section 11B of the Supply of Goods and Services Act 1982 (implied terms about title, freedom from encumbrances and quiet possession in certain contracts for the transfer of property in goods) shall be void.]

(4) Nothing in this section applies to the supply of goods on a redemption of trading stamps within the Trading Stamps Act 1964.

22 Consequence of breach

For the avoidance of doubt, where any provision of this Part of this Act requires that the incorporation of a term in a contract must be fair and reasonable for that term to have effect—

    (a) if that requirement is satisfied, the term may be given effect to notwithstanding that the contract has been terminated in consequence of breach of that contract;

(b) for the term to be given effect to, that requirement must be satisfied even where a party who is entitled to rescind the contract elects not to rescind it.

23   Evasion by means of secondary contract

Any term of any contract shall be void which purports to exclude or restrict, or has the effect of excluding or restricting—

(a) the exercise, by a party to any other contract, of any right or remedy which arises in respect of that other contract in consequence of breach of duty, or of obligation, liability for which could not by virtue of the provisions of this Part of this Act be excluded or restricted by a term of that other contract;

(b) the application of the provisions of this Part of this Act in respect of that or any other contract.

24   The "reasonableness" test

(1) In determining for the purposes of this Part of this Act whether it was fair and reasonable to incorporate a term in a contract, regard shall be had only to the circumstances which were, or ought reasonably to have been, known to or in the contemplation of the parties to the contract at the time the contract was made.

(2) In determining for the purposes of section 20 or 21 of this Act whether it was fair and reasonable to incorporate a term in a contract, regard shall be in particular to the matters specified in Schedule 2 to this Act; but this subsection shall not prevent a court or arbiter from holding, in accordance with any rule of law, that a term which purports to exclude or restrict any relevant liability is not a term of the contract.

[(2A) In determining for the purposes of this Part of this Act whether it is fair and reasonable to allow reliance on a provision of a notice (not being a notice having contractual effect), regard shall be had to all the circumstances obtaining when the liability arose or (but for the provision) would have arisen.]

(3) Where a term in a contract [or a provision of a notice] purports to restrict liability to a specified sum of money, and the question arises for the purposes of this Part of this Act whether it was fair and reasonable to incorporate the term in the contract [or whether it is fair and reasonable to allow reliance on the provision], then, without prejudice to subsection (2) above [in the case of a term in a contract,] regard shall be had in particular to—

(a) the resources which the party seeking to rely on that term [or provision] could expect to be available to him for the purposes of meeting the liability should it arise;

(b) how far it was open to that party to cover himself by insurance.

(4) The onus of proving that it was fair and reasonable to incorporate a term in a contract [or that it is fair and reasonable to allow reliance on a provision of a notice] shall lie on the party so contending.

25   Interpretation of Part II

(1) In this part of this Act—

"breach of duty" means [subject to subsections (1A) and (1B) below] the breach—

(a) of any obligation, arising from the express or implied terms of a contract, to take reasonable care or exercise reasonable skill in the performance of the contract;

(b) of any common law duty to take reasonable care or exercise reasonable skill;

(c) of the duty of reasonable care imposed by section 2(1) of the Occupiers' Liability (Scotland) Act 1960;

"business" includes a profession and the activities of any government department or local or public authority;

"consumer" has the meaning assigned to that expression in the definition in this section of "consumer contract";

"consumer contract" means a contract [...] in which—

(a) one party to the contract deals, and the other party to the contract ("the consumer") does not deal or hold himself out as dealing, in the course of a business, and

(b) in the case of a contract such as is mentioned in section 15(2)(a) of this Act, the goods are of a type ordinarily supplied for private use or consumption;

and for the purposes of this Part of this Act the onus of proving that a contract is not to be regarded as a consumer contract shall lie on the party so contending;

"goods" has the same meaning as in [the Sale of Goods Act 1979:]

"hire-purchase agreement" has the same meaning as in section 189(1) of the Consumer Credit Act 1974;

["notice" includes an announcement, whether or not in writing, and any other communication or pretended communication;]

"personal injury" includes any disease and any impairment of physical or mental condition.

[(1A) Where the consumer is an individual, paragraph (b) in the definition of "consumer contract" in subsection (1) must be disregarded.

(1B) The expression "consumer contract" does not include a contract in which—
(a) the buyer is an individual and the goods are second hand goods sold by public auction at which individuals have the opportunity of attending in person; or
(b) the buyer is not an individual and the goods are sold by auction or competitive tender.]¹

(2) In relation to any breach of duty or obligation, it is immaterial for any purpose of this Part of this Act whether the act or omission giving rise to that breach was inadvertent or intentional, or whether liability for it arises directly or vicariously.

(3) In this Part of this Act, any reference to excluding or restricting any liability includes—
(a) making the liability or its enforcement subject to any restrictive or onerous conditions;
(b) excluding or restricting any right or remedy in respect of the liability, or subjecting a person to any prejudice in consequence of his pursuing any such right or remedy;
(c) excluding or restricting any rule of evidence or procedure;
[...]

but does not include an agreement to submit any question to arbitration.

[...]

(5) In sections 15 and 16 and 19 to 21 of this Act, any reference to excluding or restricting liability for breach of an obligation or duty shall include a reference to excluding or restricting the obligation or duty itself.

PART III   PROVISIONS APPLYING TO WHOLE OF UNITED KINGDOM

26 International supply contracts

(1) The limits imposed by this Act on the extent to which a person may exclude or restrict liability by reference to a contract term do not apply to liability arising under such a contract as is described in subsection (3) below.

(2) The terms of such a contract are not subject to any requirement of reasonableness under section 3 or 4: and nothing in Part II of this Act shall require the incorporation of the terms of such a contract to be fair and reasonable for them to have effect.

(3) Subject to subsection (4), that description of contract is one whose characteristics are the following—
(a) either it is a contract of sale of goods or it is one under or in pursuance of which the possession or ownership of goods passes; and
(b) it is made by parties whose places of business (or, if they have none, habitual residences) are in the territories of different States (the Channel Islands and the Isle of Man being treated for this purpose as different States from the United Kingdom).

(4) A contract falls within subsection (3) above only if either—

    (a) the goods in question are, at the time of the conclusion of the contract, in the course of carriage, or will be carried, from the territory of one State to the territory of another; or

    (b) the acts constituting the offer and acceptance have been done in the territories of different States; or

    (c) the contract provides for the goods to be delivered to the territory of a State other than that within whose territory those acts were done.

27 Choice of law clauses

(1) Where the [law applicable to] a contract is the law of any part of the United Kingdom only by choice of the parties (and apart from that choice would be the law of some country outside the United Kingdom) sections 2 to 7 and 16 to 21 of this Act do not operate as part [of the law applicable to the contract].

(2) This Act has effect notwithstanding any contract term which applies or purports to apply the law of some country outside the United Kingdom, where (either or both)—

    (a) the term appears to the court, or arbitrator or arbiter to have been imposed wholly or mainly for the purpose of enabling the party imposing it to evade the operation of this Act; or

    (b) in the making of the contract one of the parties dealt as consumer, and he was then habitually resident in the United Kingdom, and the essential steps necessary for the making of the contract were taken there, whether by him or by others on his behalf.

28 Temporary provision for sea carriage of passengers

(1) This section applies to a contract for carriage by sea of a passenger or of a passenger and his luggage where the provisions of the Athens Convention (with or without modification) do not have, in relation to the contract, the force of law in the United Kingdom.

(2) In a case where—

    (a) the contract is not made in the United Kingdom, and

    (b) neither the place of departure nor the place of destination under it is in the United Kingdom,

a person is not precluded by this Act from excluding or restricting liability for loss or damage, being loss or damage for which the provisions of the Convention would, if they had the force of law in relation to the contract, impose liability on him.

(3) In any other case, a person is not precluded by this Act from excluding or restricting liability for that loss or damage—

    (a) in so far as the exclusion or restriction would have been effective in that case had the provisions of the Convention had the force of law in relation to the contract; or

    (b) in such circumstances and to such extent as may be prescribed, by reference to a prescribed term of the contract.

(4) For the purposes of subsection (3)(a), the values which shall be taken to be the official values in the United Kingdom of the amounts (expressed in gold francs) by reference to which liability under the provisions of the Convention is limited shall be such amounts in sterling as the Secretary of State may from time to time by order made by statutory instrument specify.

(5) In this section,—

    (a) the references to excluding or restricting liability include doing any of those things in relation to the liability which are mentioned in section 13 or section 25(3) and (5); and

    (b) "the Athens Convention" means the Athens Convention relating to the Carriage of Passengers and their Luggage by Sea, 1974; and

    (c) "prescribed" means prescribed by the Secretary of State by regulations made by statutory instrument;

and a statutory instrument containing the regulations shall be subject to annulment in pursuance of a resolution of either House of Parliament.

29 Saving for other relevant legislation

(1) Nothing in this Act removes or restricts the effect of, or prevents reliance upon, any contractual provision which—

> (a) is authorised or required by the express terms or necessary implication of an enactment; or
>
> (b) being made with a view to compliance with an international agreement to which the United Kingdom is a party, does not operate more restrictively than is contemplated by the agreement.

(2) A contract term is to be taken—

> (a) for the purposes of Part I of this Act, as satisfying the requirement of reasonableness...

if it is incorporated or approved by, or incorporated pursuant to a decision or ruling of, a competent authority acting in the exercise of any statutory jurisdiction or function and is not a term in a contract to which the competent authority is itself a party.

(3) In this section—

"competent authority" means any court, arbitrator or arbiter, government department or public authority;

"enactment" means any legislation (including subordinate legislation) of the United Kingdom or Northern Ireland and any instrument having effect by virtue of such legislation; and

"statutory" means conferred by an enactment.

SCHEDULES

Section 1(2)   ## SCHEDULE 1

SCOPE OF SECTIONS 2 TO 4 AND 7

1. Sections 2 to 4 of this Act do not extend to—

> (a) any contract of insurance (including a contract to pay an annuity on human life);
>
> (b) any contract so far as it relates to the creation or transfer of an interest in land, or to the termination of such an interest, whether by extinction, merger, surrender, forfeiture or otherwise;
>
> (c) any contract so far as it relates to the creation or transfer of a right or interest in any patent, trade mark, copyright, registered design, technical or commercial information or other intellectual property, or relates to the termination of any such right or interest;
>
> (d) any contract so far as it relates—
>
>> (i) to the formation or dissolution of a company (which means any body corporate or unincorporated association and includes a partnership), or
>>
>> (ii) to its constitution or the rights or obligations of its corporators or members;
>
> (e) any contract so far as it relates to the creation or transfer of securities or of any right or interest in securities.

2. Section 2(1) extends to—

> (a) any contract of marine salvage or towage;
>
> (b) any charterparty of a ship or hovercraft; and
>
> (c) any contract for the carriage of goods by ship or hovercraft;

but subject to this sections 2 to 4 and 7 do not extend to any such contract except in favour of a person dealing as consumer.

3. Where goods are carried by ship or hovercraft in pursuance of a contract which either—

(a) specifies that as the means of carriage over part of the journey to be covered, or

(b) makes no provision as to the means of carriage and does not exclude that means,

then sections 2(2), 3 and 4 do not, except in favour of a person dealing as consumer, extend to the contract as it operates for and in relation to the carriage of the goods by that means.

4. Section 2(1) and (2) do not extend to a contract of employment, except in favour of the employee.

5. Section 2(1) does not affect the validity of any discharge and indemnity given by a person, on or in connection with an award to him of compensation for pneumoconiosis attributable to employment in the coal industry, in respect of any further claim arising from his contracting that disease.

Sections 11(2) and 24(2)   SCHEDULE 2

"GUIDELINES" FOR APPLICATION OF REASONABLENESS TEST

The matters to which regard is to be had in particular for the purposes of sections 6(3), 7(3) and (4), 20 and 21 are any of the following which appear to be relevant—

(a) the strength of the bargaining positions of the parties relative to each other, taking into account (among other things) alternative means by which the customer's requirements could have been met;

(b) Whether the customer received an inducement to agree to the term, or in accepting it had an opportunity of entering into a similar contract with other persons, but without having to accept a similar term;

(c) whether the customer knew or ought reasonably to have known of the existence and extent of the term (having regard, among other things, to any custom of the trade and any previous course of dealing between the parties);

(d) where the term excludes or restricts any relevant liability if some condition is not complied with, whether it was reasonable at the time of the contract to expect that compliance with that condition would be practicable;

(e) whether the goods were manufactured, processed or adapted to the special order of the customer.

Civil Liability (Contribution) Act 1978
(1978, c. 47)

1   Entitlement to contribution

(1) Subject to the following provisions of this section, any person liable in respect of any damage suffered by another person may recover contribution from any other person liable in respect of the same damage (whether jointly with him or otherwise).

(2) A person shall be entitled to recover contribution by virtue of subsection (1) above notwithstanding that he has ceased to be liable in respect of the damage in question since the time when the damage occurred, provided that he was so liable immediately before he made or was ordered or agreed to make the payment in respect of which the contribution is sought.

(3) A person shall be liable to make contribution by virtue of subsection (1) above notwithstanding that he has ceased to be liable in respect of the damage in question since the time when the damage occurred, unless he ceased to be liable by virtue of the expiry of a period of limitation or prescription which extinguished the right on which the claim against him in respect of the damage was based.

(4) A person who has made or agreed to make any payment in bona fide settlement or compromise of any claim made against him in respect of any damage (including a payment into court which has been accepted) shall be entitled to recover contribution in accordance

with this section without regard to whether or not he himself is or ever was liable in respect of the damage, provided, however, that he would have been liable assuming that the factual basis of the claim against him could be established.

(5) A judgment given in any action brought in any part of the United Kingdom by or on behalf of the person who suffered the damage in question against any person from whom contribution is sought under this section shall be conclusive in the proceedings for contribution as to any issue determined by that judgment in favour of the person from whom the contribution is sought.

(6) References in this section to a person's liability in respect of any damage are references to any such liability which has been or could be established in an action brought against him in England and Wales by or on behalf of the person who suffered the damage; but it is immaterial whether any issue arising in any such action was or would be determined (in accordance with the rules of private international law) by reference to the law of a country outside England and Wales.

2   Assessment of contribution

(1) Subject to subsection (3) below, in any proceedings for contribution under section 1 above the amount of the contribution recoverable from any person shall be such as may be found by the court to be just and equitable having regard to the extent of that person's responsibility for the damage in question.

(2) Subject to subsection (3) below, the court shall have power in any such proceedings to exempt any person from liability to make contribution or to direct that the contribution to be recovered from any person shall amount to a complete indemnity.

(3) Where the amount of the damages which have or might have been awarded in respect of the damage in question in any action brought in England and Wales by or on behalf of the person who suffered it against the person from whom the contribution is sought was or would have been subject to—

(a) any limit imposed by or under any enactment or by any agreement made before the damage occurred;

(b) any reduction by virtue of section 1 of the Law Reform (Contributory Negligence) Act 1945 or section 5 of the Fatal Accidents Act 1976; or

(c) any corresponding limit or reduction under the law of a country outside England and Wales;

the person from whom the contribution is sought shall not by virtue of any contribution awarded under section 1 above be required to pay in respect of the damage a greater amount than the amount of those damages as so limited or reduced.

3   Proceedings against persons jointly liable for the same debt or damage

Judgment recovered against any person liable in respect of any debt or damage shall not be a bar to an action, or to the continuance of an action, against any other person who is (apart from any such bar) jointly liable with him in respect of the same debt or damage.

4   Successive actions against persons liable (jointly or otherwise) for the same damage

If more than one action is brought in respect of any damage by or on behalf of the person by whom it was suffered against persons liable in respect of the damage (whether jointly or otherwise) the plaintiff shall not be entitled to costs in any of those actions, other than that in which judgment is first given, unless the court is of the opinion that there was reasonable ground for bringing the action.

5   Application to the Crown

Without prejudice to section 4(1) of the Crown Proceedings Act 1947 (indemnity and contribution), this Act shall bind the Crown, but nothing in this Act shall be construed as in any way affecting Her Majesty in Her private capacity (including in right of Her Duchy of Lancaster) or the Duchy of Cornwall.

6   Interpretation

(1) A person is liable in respect of any damage for the purposes of this Act if the person who suffered it (or anyone representing his estate or dependants) is entitled to recover compensation from him in respect of that damage (whatever the legal basis of his liability, whether tort, breach of contract, breach of trust or otherwise).

(2) References in this Act to an action brought by or on behalf of the person who suffered any damage include references to an action brought for the benefit of his estate or dependants.

(3) In this Act "dependants" has the same meaning as in the Fatal Accidents Act 1976.

(4) In this Act, except in section 1(5) above, "action" means an action brought in England and Wales.

7   Savings

(3) The right to recover contribution in accordance with section 1 above supersedes any right, other than an express contractual right, to recover contribution (as distinct from indemnity) otherwise than under this Act in corresponding circumstances; but nothing in this Act shall affect—

(a) any express or implied contractual or other right to indemnity; or

(b) any express contractual provision regulating or excluding contribution; which would be enforceable apart from this Act (or render enforceable any agreement for indemnity or contribution which would not be enforceable apart from this Act).

State Immunity Act 1978
(1978, c. 33)

1   General immunity from jurisdiction

(1) A State is immune from the jurisdiction of the courts of the United Kingdom except as provided in the following provisions of this Part of this Act.

(2) A court shall give effect to the immunity conferred by this section even though the State does not appear in the proceedings in question.

3   Commercial transactions and contracts to be performed in United Kingdom

(1) A State is not immune as respects proceedings relating to—

(a) a commercial transaction entered into by the State; or

(b) an obligation of the State which by virtue of a contract (whether a commercial transaction or not) falls to be performed wholly or partly in the United Kingdom.

(2) This section does not apply if the parties to the dispute are States or have otherwise agreed in writing; and subsection (1)(b) above does not apply if the contract (not being a commercial transaction) was made in the territory of the State concerned and the obligation in question is governed by its administrative law.

5   Personal injuries and damage to property

A State is not immune as respects proceedings in respect of—

(a) death or personal injury; or

(b) damage to or loss of tangible property,

caused by an act or omission in the United Kingdom.

Customs and Excise Management Act 1979
(1979, c. 2)

[137A   Recovery of overpaid excise duty

(1) Where a person pays to the Commissioners an amount by way of excise duty which is not due to them, the Commissioners are liable to repay that amount.

(2) The Commissioners shall not be required to make any such repayment unless a claim is made to them in such form, and supported by such documentary evidence, as may be

prescribed by them by regulations; and regulations may make different provision for different cases.

(3) It is a defence to a claim for repayment that the repayment would unjustly enrich the claimant.]

[(4) The Commissioners shall not be liable, on a claim made under this section, to repay any amount paid to them more than three years before the making of the claim.]

[(5) Except as provided by this section the Commissioners are not liable to repay an amount paid to them by way of excise duty by reason of the fact that it was not duty due to them.]

Pneumoconiosis etc. (Workers' Compensation) Act 1979
(1979, c. 41)

1 Lump sum payments

(1) If, on a claim by a person who is disabled by a disease to which this Act applies, the Secretary of State is satisfied that the conditions of entitlement mentioned in section 2(1) below are fulfilled, he shall in accordance with this Act make to that person a payment of such amount as may be prescribed by regulations.

(2) If, on a claim by the dependant of a person who, immediately before he died, was disabled by a disease to which this Act applies, the Secretary of State is satisfied that the conditions of entitlement mentioned in section 2(2) below are fulfilled, he shall in accordance with this Act make to that dependant a payment of such amount as may be so prescribed.

(3) The diseases to which this Act applies are pneumoconiosis, byssinosis and diffuse mesothelioma.

2 Conditions of entitlement

(1) In the case of a person who is disabled by a disease to which this Act applies, the conditions of entitlement are—

(a) that disablement benefit is payable to him in respect of the disease;

(b) that every relevant employer of his has ceased to carry on business; and

(c) that he has not brought any action, or compromised any claim, for damages in repect of the disablement.

(2) In the case of the dependant of a person who, immediately before he died, was disabled by a disease to which this Act applies, the conditions of entitlement are—

(a) that no payment under this Act has been made to the deceased in respect of the disease;

(b) that death benefit is payable to or in respect of the dependant by reason of the deceased's death as a result of the disease, or that disablement benefit was payable to the deceased in respect of the disease immediately before he died;

(c) that every relevant employer of the deceased has ceased to carry on business; and

(d) that neither the deceased nor his personal representatives nor any relative of his has brought any action, or compromised any claim, for damages in respect of the disablement or death.

(4) For the purposes of this section any action which has been dismissed otherwise than on the merits (as for example for want of prosecution or under any enactment relating to the limitation of actions) shall be disregarded.

5 Reconsideration of determinations

(1) Subject to subsection (2) below, the Secretary of State may reconsider a determination that a payment should not be made under this Act on the ground—

(a) that there has been a material change of circumstances since the determination was made; or

(b) that the determination was made in ignorance of, or was based on a mistak
some material fact;

and the Secretary of State may, on the ground set out in paragraph (b) above, reconsider a
determination that such a payment should be made.

(4) If, whether fraudulently or otherwise, any person misrepresents or fails to disclose
any material fact and in consequence of the misrepresentation or failure a payment is made
under this Act, the person to whom the payment was made shall be liable to repay the
amount of that payment to the Secretary of State unless he can show that the misrepresentation or failure occurred without his connivance or consent.

9 Financial provisions

(1) There shall be paid out of moneys provided by Parliament—

(a) any expenditure incurred by the Secretary of State in making payments under this
Act . . .

Sale of Goods Act 1979
(1979, c. 54)

PART I   CONTRACTS TO WHICH ACT APPLIES

1 Contracts to which Act applies

(1) This Act applies to contracts of sale of goods made on or after (but not to those made
before) 1 January 1894.

(2) In relation to contracts made on certain dates, this Act applies subject to the modification of certain of its sections as mentioned in Schedule 1 below.

(3) Any such modification is indicated in the section concerned by a reference to Schedule 1 below.

(4) Accordingly, where a section does not contain such a reference, this Act applies in
relation to the contract concerned without such modification of the section.

PART II   FORMATION OF THE CONTRACT

Contract of sale

2 Contract of sale

(1) A contract of sale of goods is a contract by which the seller transfers or agrees to
transfer the property in goods to the buyer for a money consideration, called the price.

(2) There may be a contract of sale between one part owner and another.

(3) A contract of sale may be absolute or conditional.

(4) Where under a contract of sale the property in the goods is transferred from the seller
to the buyer the contract is called a sale.

(5) Where under a contract of sale the transfer of the property in the goods is to take
place at a future time or subject to some condition later to be fulfilled the contract is called an
agreement to sell.

(6) An agreement to sell becomes a sale when the time elapses or the conditions are
fulfilled subject to which the property in the goods is to be transferred.

3 Capacity to buy and sell

(1) Capacity to buy and sell is regulated by the general law concerning capacity to
contract and to transfer and acquire property.

(2) Where necessaries are sold and delivered [to a minor or][1] to a person who by reason of
[*mental incapacity or*][2] drunkenness is incompetent to contract, he must pay a reasonable
price for them.

(3) In subsection (2) above "necessaries" means goods suitable to the condition in life of the [minor or other][1] person concerned and to his actual requirements at the time of the sale and delivery.

[*1. The words "to a minor or" in s. 3(2) and "minor or other" in s. 3(3) were repealed, for Scotland only, by the Age of Legal Capacity (Scotland) Act 1991, s. 10, Sched. 2.*]

[*2. The words "mental capacity or" no longer have effect in England and Wales: Mental Capacity Act 2005, s. 67(1), Sched. 6, para. 24.*]

4 How contract of sale is made

(1) Subject to this and any other Act, a contract of sale may be made in writing (either with or without seal), or by word of mouth, or partly in writing and partly by word of mouth, or may be implied from the conduct of the parties.

(2) Nothing in this section affects the law relating to corporations.

5 Existing or future goods

(1) The goods which form the subject of a contract of sale may be either existing goods, owned or possessed by the seller, or goods to be manufactured or acquired by him after the making of the contract of sale, in this Act called future goods.

(2) There may be a contract for the sale of goods the acquisition of which by the seller depends on a contingency which may or may not happen.

(3) Where by a contract of sale the seller purports to effect a present sale of future goods, the contract operates as an agreement to sell the goods.

6 Goods which have perished

Where there is a contract for the sale of specific goods, and the goods without the knowledge of the seller have perished at the time when the contract is made, the contract is void.

7 Goods perishing before sale but after agreement to sell

Where there is an agreement to sell specific goods and subsequently the goods, without any fault on the part of the seller or buyer, perish before the risk passes to the buyer, the agreement is avoided.

8 Ascertainment of price

(1) The price in a contract of sale may be fixed by the contract, or may be left to be fixed in a manner agreed by the contract, or may be determined by the course of dealing between the parties.

(2) Where the price is not determined as mentioned in subsection (1) above the buyer must pay a reasonable price.

(3) What is a reasonable price is a question of fact dependent on the circumstances of each particular case.

9 Agreement to sell at valuation

(1) Where there is an agreement to sell goods on the terms that the price is to be fixed by the valuation of a third party, and he cannot or does not make the valuation, the agreement is avoided; but if the goods or any part of them have been delivered to and appropriated by the buyer he must pay a reasonable price for them.

(2) Where the third party is prevented from making the valuation by the fault of the seller or buyer, the party not at fault may maintain an action for damages against the party at fault.

[*Implied terms etc.*]

10 Stipulations about time

(1) Unless a different intention appears from the terms of the contract, stipulations as to time of payment are not of the essence of a contract of sale.

(2) Whether any other stipulation as to time is or is not of the essence of the contract depends on the terms of the contract.

(3) In a contract of sale "month" prima facie means calendar month.

11   When condition to be treated as warranty

[(1) This section does not apply to Scotland.]

(2) Where a contract of sale is subject to a condition to be fulfilled by the seller, the buyer may waive the condition, or may elect to treat the breach of the condition as a breach of warranty and not as a ground for treating the contract as repudiated.

(3) Whether a stipulation in a contract of sale is a condition, the breach of which may give rise to a right to treat the contract as repudiated, or a warranty, the breach of which may give rise to a claim for damages but not to a right to reject the goods and treat the contract as repudiated, depends in each case on the construction of the contract; and a stipulation may be a condition, though called a warranty in the contract.

(4) [Subject to section 35A below] Where a contract of sale is not severable and the buyer has accepted the goods or part of them, the breach of a condition to be fulfilled by the seller can only be treated as a breach of warranty, and not as a ground for rejecting the goods and treating the contract as repudiated, unless there is an express or implied term of the contract to that effect.

(6) Nothing in this section affects a condition or warranty whose fulfilment is excused by law by reason of impossibility or otherwise.

(7) Paragraph 2 of Schedule 1 below applies in relation to a contract made before 22 April 1967 or (in the application of this Act to Northern Ireland) 28 July 1967.

12   Implied terms about title, etc.

(1) In a contract of sale, other than one to which subsection (3) below applies, there is an implied [term] on the part of the seller that in the case of a sale he has a right to sell the goods, and in the case of an agreement to sell he will have such a right at the time when the property is to pass.

(2) In a contract of sale, other than one to which subsection (3) below applies, there is also an implied [term] that—

(a) the goods are free, and will remain free until the time when the property is to pass, from any charge or encumbrance not disclosed or known to the buyer before the contract is made, and

(b) the buyer will enjoy quiet possession of the goods except so far as it may be disturbed by the owner or other person entitled to the benefit of any charge or encumbrance so disclosed or known.

(3) This subsection applies to a contract of sale in the case of which there appears from the contract or is to be inferred from its circumstances an intention that the seller should transfer only such title as he or a third person may have.

(4) In a contract to which subsection (3) above applies there is an implied [term] that all charges or encumbrances known to the seller and not known to the buyer have been disclosed to the buyer before the contract is made.

(5) In a contract to which subsection (3) above applies there is also an implied [term] that none of the following will disturb the buyer's quiet possession of the goods, namely—

(a) the seller;

(b) in a case where the parties to the contract intend that the seller should transfer only such title as a third person may have, that person;

(c) anyone claiming through or under the seller or that third person otherwise than under a charge or encumbrance disclosed or known to the buyer before the contract is made.

[(5A) As regards England and Wales and Northern Ireland, the term implied by subsection (1) above is a condition and the terms implied by subsections (2), (4) and (5) above are warranties.]

(6) Paragraph 3 of Schedule 1 below applies in relation to a contract made before 18 May 1973.

13 Sale by description

(1) Where there is a contract for the sale of goods by description, there is an implied [term] that the goods will correspond with the description.

[(1A) As regards England and Wales and Northern Ireland, the term implied by subsection (1) above is a condition.]

(2) If the sale is by sample as well as by description it is not sufficient that the bulk of the goods corresponds with the sample if the goods do not also correspond with the description.

(3) A sale of goods is not prevented from being a sale by description by reason only that, being exposed for sale or hire, they are selected by the buyer.

(4) Paragraph 4 of Schedule 1 below applies in relation to a contract made before 18 May 1973.

14 Implied terms about quality or fitness

(1) Except as provided by this section and section 15 below and subject to any other enactment, there is no implied [term] about the quality or fitness for any particular purpose of goods supplied under a contract of sale.

[(2) Where the seller sells goods in the course of a business, there is an implied term that the goods supplied under the contract are of satisfactory quality.

(2A) For the purposes of this Act, goods are of satisfactory quality if they meet the standard that a reasonable person would regard as satisfactory, taking account of any description of the goods, the price (if relevant) and all the other relevant circumstances.

(2B) For the purposes of this Act, the quality of goods includes their state and condition and the following (among others) are in appropriate cases aspects of the quality of goods—

(a) fitness for all the purposes for which goods of the kind in question are commonly supplied,
(b) appearance and finish,
(c) freedom from minor defects,
(d) safety, and
(e) durability.

(2C) The term implied by subsection (2) above does not extend to any matter making the quality of goods unsatisfactory—

(a) which is specifically drawn to the buyer's attention before the contract is made,
(b) where the buyer examines the goods before the contract is made, which that examination ought to reveal, or
(c) in the case of a contract for sale by sample, which would have been apparent on a reasonable examination of the sample.]

[(2D) If the buyer deals as consumer or, in Scotland, if a contract of sale is a consumer contract, the relevant circumstances mentioned in subsection (2A) above include any public statements on the specific characteristics of the goods made about them by the seller, the producer or his representative, particularly in advertising or on labelling.

(2E) A public statement is not by virtue of subsection (2D) above a relevant circumstance for the purposes of subsection (2A) above in the case of a contract of sale, if the seller shows that—

(a) at the time the contract was made, he was not, and could not reasonably have been, aware of the statement,
(b) before the contract was made, the statement had been withdrawn in public or, to the extent that it contained anything which was incorrect or misleading, it had been corrected in public, or
(c) the decision to buy the goods could not have been influenced by the statement.

(2F) Subsections (2D) and (2E) above do not prevent any public statement from being a relevant circumstance for the purposes of subsection (2A) above (whether or not the buyer deals as consumer or, in Scotland, whether or not the contract of sale is a consumer contract) if the statement would have been such a circumstance apart from those subsections.]

(3) Where the seller sells goods in the course of a business and the buyer, expressly or by implication, makes known—

(a) to the seller, or

(b) where the purchase price or part of it is payable by instalments and the goods were previously sold by a credit-broker to the seller, to that credit-broker,

any particular purpose for which the goods are being bought, there is an implied [term] that the goods supplied under the contract are reasonably fit for that purpose, whether or not that is a purpose for which such goods are commonly supplied, except where the circumstances show that the buyer does not rely, or that it is unreasonable for him to rely, on the skill or judgment of the seller or credit-broker.

(4) An implied [term] about quality or fitness for a particular purpose may be annexed to a contract of sale by usage.

(5) The preceding provisions of this section apply to a sale by a person who in the course of a business is acting as agent for another as they apply to a sale by a principal in the course of a business, except where that other is not selling in the course of a business and either the buyer knows that fact or reasonable steps are taken to bring it to the notice of the buyer before the contract is made.

[(6) As regards England and Wales and Northern Ireland, the terms implied by subsections (2) and (3) above are conditions.]

(7) Paragraph 5 of Schedule 1 below applies in relation to a contract made on or after 18 May 1973 and before the appointed day, and paragraph 6 in relation to one made before 18 May 1973.

(8) In subsection (7) above and paragraph 5 of Schedule 1 below references to the appointed day are to the day appointed for the purposes of those provisions by an order of the Secretary of State made by statutory instrument.

Sale by sample

15   Sale by sample

(1) A contract of sale is a contract for sale by sample where there is an express or implied term to that effect in the contract.

(2) In the case of a contract for sale by sample there is an implied [term]—

(a) that the bulk will correspond with the sample in quality;

[...]

(b) that the goods will be free from any defect, making their quality unsatisfactory which would not be apparent on reasonable examination of the sample.

[(3) As regards England and Wales and Northern Ireland, the term implied by subsection (2) above is a condition.]

(4) Paragraph 7 of Schedule 1 below applies in relation to a contract made before 18 May 1973.

Miscellaneous

[15A   Modification of remedies for breach of condition in non-consumer cases[1]

(1) Where in the case of a contract of sale—

(a) the buyer would, apart from this subsection, have the right to reject goods by reason of a breach on the part of the seller of a term implied by section 13, 14 or 15 above, but

(b) the breach is so slight that it would be unreasonable for him to reject them, then, if the buyer does not deal as consumer, the breach is not to be treated as a breach of condition but may be treated as a breach of warranty.

(2) This section applies unless a contrary intention appears in, or is to be implied from, the contract.

(3) It is for the seller to show that a breach fell within subsection (1)(b) above.

(4) This section does not apply to Scotland.]

[15B   Remedies for breach of contract as respects Scotland

(1) Where in a contract of sale the seller is in breach of any term of the contract (express or implied), the buyer shall be entitled—

(a) to claim damages, and

(b) if the breach is material, to reject any goods delivered under the contract and treat it as repudiated.

(2) Where a contract of sale is a consumer contract, then, for the purposes of subsection (1)(b) above, breach by the seller of any term (express or implied)—

(a) as to the quality of the goods or their fitness for a purpose,

(b) if the goods are, or are to be, sold by description, that the goods will correspond with the description,

(c) if the goods are, or are to be, sold by reference to a sample, that the bulk will correspond with the sample in quality,

shall be deemed to be a material breach.

(3) This section applies to Scotland only.]

PART III   EFFECTS OF THE CONTRACT

Transfer of property as between seller and buyer

16   Goods must be ascertained

[Subject to section (20A) below] Where there is a contract for the sale of unascertained goods no property in the goods is transferred to the buyer unless and until the goods are ascertained.

17   Property passes when intended to pass

(1) Where there is a contract for the sale of specific or ascertained goods the property in them is transferred to the buyer at such time as the parties to the contract intend it to be transferred.

(2) For the purpose of ascertaining the intention of the parties regard shall be had to the terms of the contract, the conduct of the parties and the circumstances of the case.

18   Rules for ascertaining intention

Unless a different intention appears, the following are rules for ascertaining the intention of the parties as to the time at which the property in the goods is to pass to the buyer.

Rule 1.—Where there is an unconditional contract for the sale of specific goods in a deliverable state the property in the goods passes to the buyer when the contract is made, and it is immaterial whether the time of payment or the time of delivery, or both, be postponed.

Rule 2.—Where there is a contract for the sale of specific goods and the seller is bound to do something to the goods for the purpose of putting them into a deliverable state, the property does not pass until the thing is done and the buyer has notice that it has been done.

Rule 3.—Where there is a contract for the sale of specific goods in a deliverable state but the seller is bound to weigh, measure, test, or do some other act or thing with reference to the goods for the purpose of ascertaining the price, the property does not pass until the act or thing is done and the buyer has notice that it has been done.

Rule 4.—When goods are delivered to the buyer on approval or on sale or return or other similar terms the property in the goods passes to the buyer—

(a) when he signifies his approval or acceptance to the seller or does any other act adopting the transaction;

(b) if he does not signify his approval or acceptance to the seller but retains the goods without giving notice of rejection, then, if a time has been fixed for the return of the goods, on the expiration of that time, and, if no time has been fixed, on the expiration of a reasonable time.

Rule 5.—(1) Where there is a contract for the sale of unascertained or future goods by description, and goods of that description and in a deliverable state are unconditionally appropriated to the contract, either by the seller with the assent of the buyer or by the buyer with the assent of the seller, the property in the goods then passes to the buyer; and the assent may be express or implied, and may be given either before or after the appropriation is made.

(2) Where, in pursuance of the contract, the seller delivers the goods to the buyer or to a carrier or other bailee or custodier (whether named by the buyer or not) for the purpose of transmission to the buyer, and does not reserve the right of disposal, he is to be taken to have unconditionally appropriated the goods to the contract.

[(3) Where there is a contract for the sale of a specified quantity of unascertained goods in a deliverable state forming part of a bulk which is identified either in the contract or by subsequent agreement between the parties and the bulk is reduced to (or to less than) that quantity, then, if the buyer under that contract is the only buyer to whom goods are then due out of the bulk—

(a) the remaining goods are to be taken as appropriated to that contract at the time when the bulk is so reduced; and

(b) the property in those goods then passes to that buyer.

(4) Paragraph (3) above applies also (with the necessary modifications) where a bulk is reduced to (or to less than) the aggregate of the quantities due to a single buyer under separate contracts relating to that bulk and he is the only buyer to whom goods are then due out of that bulk.]

19 Reservation of right of disposal

(1) Where there is a contract for the sale of specific goods or where goods are subsequently appropriated to the contract, the seller may, by the terms of the contract or appropriation, reserve the right of disposal of the goods until certain conditions are fulfilled; and in such a case, notwithstanding the delivery of the goods to the buyer, or to a carrier or other bailee or custodier for the purpose of transmission to the buyer, the property in the goods does not pass to the buyer until the conditions imposed by the seller are fulfilled.

(2) Where goods are shipped, and by the bill of lading the goods are deliverable to the order of the seller or his agent, the seller is prima facie to be taken to reserve the right of disposal.

(3) Where the seller of goods draws on the buyer for the price, and transmits the bill of exchange and bill of lading to the buyer together to secure acceptance or payment of the bill of exchange, the buyer is bound to return the bill of lading if he does not honour the bill of exchange, and if he wrongfully retains the bill of lading the property in the goods does not pass to him.

20 [Passing of risk]

(1) Unless otherwise agreed, the goods remain at the sellers's risk until the property in them is transferred to the buyer, but when the property in them is transferred to the buyer the goods are at the buyer's risk whether delivery has been made or not.

(2) But where delivery has been delayed through the fault of either buyer or seller the goods are at the risk of the party at fault as regards any loss which might not have occurred but for such fault.

(3) Nothing in this section affects the duties or liabilities of either seller or buyer as a bailee or custodier of the goods of the other party.

[(4) In a case where the buyer deals as consumer or, in Scotland, where there is a consumer contract in which the buyer is a consumer, subsections (1) to (3) above must be ignored and the goods remain at the seller's risk until they are delivered to the consumer.]

[20A   Undivided shares in goods forming part of a bulk

(1) This section applies to a contract for the sale of a specified quantity of unascertained goods if the following conditions are met—

    (a) the goods or some of them form part of a bulk which is identified either in the contract or by subsequent agreement between the parties; and

    (b) the buyer has paid the price for some or all of the goods which are the subject of the contract and which form part of the bulk.

(2) Where this section applies, then (unless the parties agree otherwise), as soon as the conditions specified in paragraphs (a) and (b) of subsection (1) above are met or at such later time as the parties may agree—

    (a) property in an undivided share in the bulk is transferred to the buyer; and

    (b) the buyer becomes an owner in common of the bulk.

(3) Subject to subsection (4) below, for the purposes of this section, the undivided share of a buyer in a bulk at any time shall be such share as the quantity of goods paid for and due to the buyer out of the bulk bears to the quantity of goods in the bulk at that time.

(4) Where the aggregate of the undivided shares of buyers in a bulk determined under subsection (3) above would at any time exceed the whole of the bulk at that time, the undivided share in the bulk of each buyer shall be reduced proportionately so that the aggregate of the undivided shares is equal to the whole bulk.

(5) Where a buyer has paid the price for only some of the goods due to him out of a bulk, any delivery to the buyer out of the bulk shall, for the purposes of this section, be ascribed in the first place to the goods in respect of which payment has been made.

(6) For the purpose of this section payment of part of the price for any goods shall be treated as payment for a corresponding part of the goods.]

[20B   Deemed consent by co-owner to dealings in bulk goods

(1) A person who has become an owner in common of a bulk by virtue of section 20A above shall be deemed to have consented to—

    (a) any delivery of goods out of the bulk to any other owner in common of the bulk, being goods which are due to him under his contract;

    (b) any removal, dealing with, delivery or disposal of goods in the bulk by any other person who is an owner in common of the bulk in so far as the goods fall within that co-owner's undivided share in the bulk at the time of the removal, dealing, delivery or disposal.

(2) No cause of action shall accrue to anyone against a person by reason of that person having acted in accordance with paragraph (a) or (b) of subsection (1) above in reliance on any consent deemed to have been given under that subsection.

(3) Nothing in this section or section 20A above shall—

    (a) impose an obligation on a buyer of goods out of a bulk to compensate any other buyer of goods out of that bulk for any shortfall in the goods received by that other buyer;

    (b) affect any contractual arrangement between buyers of goods out of a bulk for adjustments between themselves; or

    (c) affect the rights of any buyer under his contract.]

Transfer of title

21   Sale by person not the owner

(1) Subject to this Act, where goods are sold by a person who is not their owner, and who does not sell them under the authority or with the consent of the owner, the buyer acquires no better title to the goods than the seller had, unless the owner of the goods is by his conduct precluded from denying the seller's authority to sell.

(2) Nothing in this Act affects—

    (a) the provisions of the Factors Acts or any enactment enabling the apparent owner of goods to dispose of them as if he were their true owner;

    (b) the validity of any contract of sale under any special common law or statutory power of sale or under the order of a court of competent jurisdiction.

22 Market overt

[...]

(2) This section does not apply to Scotland.

(3) Paragraph 8 of Schedule 1 below applies in relation to a contract under which goods were sold before 1 January 1968 or (in the application of this Act to Northern Ireland) 29 August 1967.

23 Sale under voidable title

When the seller of goods has a voidable title to them, but his title has not been avoided at the time of the sale, the buyer acquires a good title to the goods, provided he buys them in good faith and without notice of the seller's defect of title.

24 Seller in possession after sale

Where a person having sold goods continues or is in possession of the goods, or of the documents of title to the goods, the delivery or transfer by that person, or by a mercantile agent acting for him, of the goods or documents of title under any sale, pledge, or other disposition thereof, to any person receiving the same in good faith and without notice of the previous sale, has the same effect as if the person making the delivery or transfer were expressly authorised by the owner of the goods to make the same.

25 Buyer in possession after sale

(1) Where a person having bought or agreed to buy goods obtains, with the consent of the seller, possession of the goods or the documents of title to the goods, the delivery or transfer by that person, or by a mercantile agent acting for him, of the goods or documents of title, under any sale, pledge, or other disposition thereof, to any person receiving the same in good faith and without notice of any lien or other right of the original seller in respect of the goods, has the same effect as if the person making the delivery or transfer were a mercantile agent in possession of the goods or documents of title with the consent of the owner.

(2) For the purposes of subsection (1) above—

    (a) the buyer under a conditional sale agreement is to be taken not to be a person who has bought or agreed to buy goods, and

    (b) "conditional sale agreement" means an agreement for the sale of goods which is a consumer credit agreement within the meaning of the Consumer Credit Act 1974 under which the purchase price or part of it is payable by instalments, and the property in the goods is to remain in the seller (notwithstanding that the buyer is to be in possession of the goods) until such conditions as to the payment of instalments or otherwise as may be specified in the agreement are fulfilled.

(3) Paragraph 9 of Schedule 1 below applies in relation to a contract under which a person buys or agrees to buy goods and which is made before the appointed day.

(4) In subsection (3) above and paragraph 9 of Schedule 1 below references to the appointed day are to the day appointed for the purposes of those provisions by an order of the Secretary of State made by statutory instrument.

26 Supplementary to sections 24 and 25

In sections 24 and 25 above "mercantile agent" means a mercantile agent having in the customary course of his business as such agent authority either—

    (a) to sell goods, or

    (b) to consign goods for the purpose of sale, or

    (c) to buy goods, or

    (d) to raise money on the security of goods.

PART IV   PERFORMANCE OF THE CONTRACT

27   Duties of seller and buyer
It is the duty of the seller to deliver the goods, and of the buyer to accept and pay for them, in accordance with the terms of the contract of sale.

28   Payment and delivery are concurrent conditions
Unless otherwise agreed, delivery of the goods and payment of the price are concurrent conditions, that is to say, the seller must be ready and willing to give possession of the goods to the buyer in exchange for the price and the buyer must be ready and willing to pay the price in exchange for possession of the goods.

29   Rules about delivery
(1) Whether it is for the buyer to take possession of the goods or for the seller to send them to the buyer is a question depending in each case on the contract, express or implied, between the parties.

(2) Apart from any such contract, express or implied, the place of delivery is the seller's place of business if he has one, and if not, his residence; except that, if the contract is for the sale of specific goods, which to the knowledge of the parties when the contract is made are in some other place, then that place is the place of delivery.

(3) Where under the contract of sale the seller is bound to send the goods to the buyer, but no time for sending them is fixed, the seller is bound to send them within a reasonable time.

(4) Where the goods at the time of sale are in the possession of a third person, there is no delivery by seller to buyer unless and until the third person acknowledges to the buyer that he holds the goods on his behalf; but nothing in this section affects the operation of the issue or transfer of any document of title to goods.

(5) Demand or tender of delivery may be treated as ineffectual unless made at a reasonable hour; and what is a reasonable hour is a question of fact.

(6) Unless otherwise agreed, the expenses of and incidental to putting the goods into a deliverable state must be borne by the seller.

30   Delivery of wrong quantity
(1) Where the seller delivers to the buyer a quantity of goods less than he contracted to sell, the buyer may reject them, but if the buyer accepts the goods so delivered he must pay for them at the contract rate.

(2) Where the seller delivers to the buyer a quantity of goods larger than he contracted to sell, the buyer may accept the goods included in the contract and reject the rest, or he may reject the whole.

[(2A) A buyer who does not deal as consumer may not—
   (a) where the seller delivers a quantity of goods less than he contracted to sell, reject the goods under subsection (1) above, or
   (b) where the seller delivers a quantity of goods larger than he contracted to sell, reject the whole under subsection (2) above,
if the shortfall or, as the case may be, excess is so slight that it would be unreasonable for him to do so.

(2B) It is for the seller to show that a shortfall or excess fell within subsection (2A) above.

(2C) Subsections (2A) and (2B) above do not apply to Scotland.]

[(2D) Where the seller delivers a quantity of goods—
   (a) less than he contracted to sell, the buyer shall not be entitled to reject the goods under subsection (1) above,
   (b) larger than he contracted to sell, the buyer shall not be entitled to reject the whole under subsection (2) above,
unless the shortfall or excess is material.

(2E) Subsection (2D) above applies to Scotland only.]

(3) Where the seller delivers to the buyer a quantity of goods larger than he contracted to sell and the buyer accepts the whole of the goods so delivered he must pay for them at the contract rate.

(5) This section is subject to any usage of trade, special agreement, or course of dealing between the parties.

31 Instalment deliveries

(1) Unless otherwise agreed, the buyer of goods is not bound to accept delivery of them by instalments.

(2) Where there is a contract for the sale of goods to be delivered by stated instalments, which are to be separately paid for, and the seller makes defective deliveries in respect of one or more instalments, or the buyer neglects or refuses to take delivery of or pay for one or more instalments, it is a question in each case depending on the terms of the contract and the circumstances of the case whether the breach of contract is a repudiation of the whole contract or whether it is a severable breach giving rise to a claim for compensation but not to a right to treat the whole contract as repudiated.

32 Delivery to carrier

(1) Where, in pursuance of a contract of sale, the seller is authorised or required to send the goods to the buyer, delivery of the goods to a carrier (whether named by the buyer or not) for the purpose of transmission to the buyer is prima facie deemed to be delivery of the goods to the buyer.

(2) Unless otherwise authorised by the buyer, the seller must make such contact with the carrier on behalf of the buyer as may be reasonable having regard to the nature of the goods and the other circumstances of the case; and if the seller omits to do so, and the goods are lost or damaged in course of transit, the buyer may decline to treat the delivery to the carrier as a delivery to himself or may hold the seller responsible in damages.

(3) Unless otherwise agreed, where goods are sent by the seller to the buyer by a route involving sea transit, under circumstances in which it is usual to insure, the seller must give such notice to the buyer as may enable him to insure them during their sea transit, and if the seller fails to do so, the goods are at his risk during such sea transit.

[(4) In a case where the buyer deals as consumer or, in Scotland, where there is a consumer contract in which the buyer is a consumer, subsections (1) to (3) above must be ignored, but if in pursuance of a contract of sale the seller is authorised or required to send the goods to the buyer, delivery of the goods to the carrier is not delivery of the goods to the buyer.]

33 Risk where goods are delivered at distant place

Where the seller of goods agrees to deliver them at his own risk at a place other than that where they are when sold, the buyer must nevertheless (unless otherwise agreed) take any risk of deterioration in the goods necessarily incident to the course of transit.

34 Buyer's right of examining the goods

Unless otherwise agreed, when the seller tenders delivery of goods to the buyer, he is bound on request to afford the buyer a reasonable opportunity of examining the goods for the purpose of ascertaining whether they are in conformity with the contract [and, in the case of a contract for sale by sample, of comparing the bulk with the sample].

35 Acceptance

(1) The buyer is deemed to have accepted the goods [subject to subsection (2) below—
    (a) when he intimates to the seller that he has accepted them, or
    (b) when the goods have been delivered to him and he does any act in relation to them which is inconsistent with the ownership of the seller.

(2) Where goods are delivered to the buyer, and he has not previously examined them, he is not deemed to have accepted them under subsection (1) above until he has had a reasonable opportunity of examining them for the purpose—

(a) of ascertaining whether they are in conformity with the contract, and

(b) in the case of a contract for sale by sample, of comparing the bulk with the sample.

(3) Where the buyer deals as consumer or (in Scotland) the contract of sale is a consumer contract, the buyer cannot lose his right to rely on subsection (2) above by agreement, waiver or otherwise.

(4) The buyer is also deemed to have accepted the goods when after the lapse of a reasonable time he retains the goods without intimating to the seller that he has rejected them.

(5) The questions that are material in determining for the purposes of subsection (4) above whether a reasonable time has elapsed include whether the buyer has had a reasonable opportunity of examining the goods for the purpose mentioned in subsection (2) above.

(6) The buyer is not by virtue of this section deemed to have accepted the goods merely because—

(a) he asks for, or agrees to, their repair by or under an arrangement with the seller, or

(b) the goods are delivered to another under a sub-sale or other disposition.

(7) Where the contract is for the sale of goods making one or more commercial units, a buyer accepting any goods included in a unit is deemed to have accepted all the goods making the unit; and in this subsection "commercial unit" means a unit division of which would materially impair the value of the goods or the character of the unit.

(8) Paragraph 10 of Schedule 1 below applies in relation to a contract made before 22 April 1967 or (in the application of this Act to Northern Ireland) 28 July 1967.

[35A   Right of partial rejection

(1) If the buyer—

(a) has the right to reject the goods by reason of a breach on the part of the seller that affects some or all of them, but

(b) accepts some of the goods, including, where there are any goods unaffected by the breach, all such goods,

he does not by accepting them lose his right to reject the rest.

(2) In the case of a buyer having the right to reject an instalment of goods, subsection (1) above applies as if references to the goods were references to the goods comprised in the instalment.

(3) For the purposes of subsection (1) above, goods are affected by a breach if by reason of the breach they are not in conformity with the contract.

(4) This section applies unless a contrary intention appears in, or is to be implied from, the contract.]

36   Buyer not bound to return rejected goods

Unless otherwise agreed, where goods are delivered to the buyer, and he refuses to accept them, having the right to do so, he is not bound to return them to the seller, but it is sufficient if he intimates to the seller that he refuses to accept them.

37   Buyer's liability for not taking delivery of goods

(1) When the seller is ready and willing to deliver the goods, and requests the buyer to take delivery, and the buyer does not within a reasonable time after such request take delivery of the goods, he is liable to the seller for any loss occasioned by his neglect or refusal to take delivery, and also for a reasonable charge for the care and custody of the goods.

(2) Nothing in this section affects the rights of the seller where the neglect or refusal of the buyer to take delivery amounts to a repudiation of the contract.

PART V   RIGHTS OF UNPAID SELLER AGAINST THE GOODS

Preliminary

38   Unpaid seller defined

(1) The seller of goods is an unpaid seller within the meaning of this Act—

(a) when the whole of the price has not been paid or tendered;

(b) when a bill of exchange or other negotiable instrument has been received as conditional payment, and the condition on which it was received has not been fulfilled by reason of the dishonour of the instrument or otherwise.

(2) In this Part of this Act "seller" includes any person who is in the position of a seller, as, for instance, an agent of the seller to whom the bill of lading has been indorsed, or a consignor or agent who has himself paid (or is directly responsible for) the price.

39   Unpaid seller's rights

(1) Subject to this and any other Act, notwithstanding that the property in the goods may have passed to the buyer, the unpaid seller of goods, as such, has by implication of law—

(a) a lien on the goods or right to retain them for the price while he is in possession of them;

(b) in the case of the insolvency of the buyer, a right of stopping the goods in transit after he has parted with the possesion of them;

(c) a right of re-sale as limited by this Act.

(2) Where the property in goods has not passed to the buyer, the unpaid seller has (in addition to his other remedies) a right of withholding delivery similar to and coextensive with his rights of lien or retention and stoppage in transit where the property has passed to the buyer.

Unpaid seller's lien

41   Seller's lien

(1) Subject to this Act, the unpaid seller of goods who is in possession of them is entitled to retain possession of them until payment or tender of the price in the following cases:—

(a) where the goods have been sold without any stipulation as to credit;

(b) where the goods have been sold on credit but the term of credit has expired;

(c) where the buyer becomes insolvent.

(2) The seller may exercise his lien or right of retention notwithstanding that he is in possession of the goods as agent or bailee or custodier for the buyer.

42   Part delivery

Where an unpaid seller has made part delivery of the goods, he may exercise his lien or right of retention on the remainder, unless such part delivery has been made under such circumstances as to show an agreement to waive the lien or right of retention.

43   Termination of lien

(1) The unpaid seller of goods loses his lien or right of retention in respect of them—

(a) when he delivers the goods to a carrier or other bailee or custodier for the purpose of transmission to the buyer without reserving the right of disposal of the goods;

(b) when the buyer or his agent lawfully obtains possession of the goods;

(c) by waiver of the lien or right of retention.

(2) An unpaid seller of goods who has a lien or right of retention in respect of them does not lose his lien or right of retention by reason only that he has obtained judgment or decree for the price of the goods.

Stoppage in transit

44   Right of stoppage in transit

Subject to this Act, when the buyer of goods becomes insolvent the unpaid seller who has parted with the possession of the goods has the right of stopping them in transit, that is to say, he may resume possession of the goods as long as they are in course of transit, and may retain them until payment or tender of the price.

45   Duration of transit

(1) Goods are deemed to be in course of transit from the time when they are delivered to a carrier or other bailee or custodier for the purpose of transmission to the buyer, until the buyer or his agent in that behalf takes delivery of them from the carrier or other bailee or custodier.

(2) If the buyer or his agent in that behalf obtains delivery of the goods before their arrival at the appointed destination, the transit is at an end.

(3) If, after the arrival of the goods at the appointed destination, the carrier or other bailee or custodier acknowledges to the buyer or his agent that he holds the goods on his behalf and continues in possession of them as bailee or custodier for the buyer or his agent, the transit is at an end, and it is immaterial that a further destination for the goods may have been indicated by the buyer.

(4) If the goods are rejected by the buyer, and the carrier or other bailee or custodier continues in possession of them, the transit is not deemed to be at an end, even if the seller has refused to receive them back.

(5) When goods are delivered to a ship chartered by the buyer it is a question depending on the circumstances of the particular case whether they are in the possession of the master as a carrier or as agent to the buyer.

(6) Where the carrier or other bailee or custodier wrongfully refuses to deliver the goods to the buyer or his agent in that behalf, the transit is deemed to be at an end.

(7) Where part delivery of the goods has been made to the buyer or his agent in that behalf, the remainder of the goods may be stopped in transit, unless such part delivery has been made under such circumstances as to show an agreement to give up possession of the whole of the goods.

46   How stoppage in transit is effected

(1) The unpaid seller may exercise his right of stoppage in transit either by taking actual possession of the goods or by giving notice of his claim to the carrier or other bailee or custodier in whose possession the goods are.

(2) The notice may be given either to the person in actual possession of the goods or to his principal.

(3) If given to the principal, the notice is ineffective unless given at such time and under such circumstances that the principal, by the exercise of reasonable diligence, may communicate it to his servant or agent in time to prevent a delivery to the buyer.

(4) When notice of stoppage in transit is given by the seller to the carrier or other bailee or custodier in possession of the goods, he must re-deliver the goods to, or according to the directions of, the seller; and the expenses of the re-delivery must be borne by the seller.

Resale etc. by buyer

47   Effect of sub-sale etc. by buyer

(1) Subject to this Act, the unpaid seller's right of lien or retention or stoppage in transit is not affected by any sale or other disposition of the goods which the buyer may have made, unless the seller has assented to it.

(2) Where a document of title to goods has been lawfully transferred to any person as buyer or owner of the goods, and that person transfers the document to a person who takes it in good faith and for valuable consideration, then—

    (a) if the last-mentioned transfer was by way of sale the unpaid seller's right of lien or retention or stoppage in transit is defeated; and

    (b) if the last-mentioned transfer was made by way of pledge or other disposition for value, the unpaid seller's right of lien or retention of stoppage in transit can only be exercised subject to the rights of the transferee.

Rescission: and re-sale by seller

48   Rescission: and re-sale by seller

(1) Subject to this section, a contract of sale is not rescinded by the mere exercise by an unpaid seller of his right of lien or retention or stoppage in transit.

(2) Where an unpaid seller who has exercised his right of lien or retention or stoppage in transit re-sells the goods, the buyer acquires a good title to them as against the original buyer.

(3) Where the goods are of a perishable nature, or where the unpaid seller gives notice to the buyer of his intention to re-sell, and the buyer does not within a reasonable time pay or tender the price, the unpaid seller may re-sell the goods and recover from the original buyer damages for any loss occasioned by his breach of contract.

(4) Where the seller expressly reserves the right of re-sale in case the buyer should make default, and on the buyer making default re-sells the goods, the original contract of sale is rescinded but without prejudice to any claim the seller may have for damages.

[PART 5A   ADDITIONAL RIGHTS OF BUYER IN CONSUMER CASES

48A   Introductory

(1) This section applies if—
    (a) the buyer deals as consumer or, in Scotland, there is a consumer contract in which the buyer is a consumer, and
    (b) the goods do not conform to the contract of sale at the time of delivery.

(2) If this section applies, the buyer has the right—
    (a) under and in accordance with section 48B below, to require the seller to repair or replace the goods, or
    (b) under and in accordance with section 48C below—
        (i) to require the seller to reduce the purchase price of the goods to the buyer by an appropriate amount, or
        (ii) to rescind the contract with regard to the goods in question.

(3) For the purposes of subsection (1)(b) above goods which do not conform to the contract of sale at any time within the period of six months starting with the date on which the goods were delivered to the buyer must be taken not to have so conformed at that date.

(4) Subsection (3) above does not apply if—
    (a) it is established that the goods did so conform at that date;
    (b) its application is incompatible with the nature of the goods or the nature of the lack of conformity.

48B   Repair or replacement of the goods

(1) If section 48A above applies, the buyer may require the seller—
    (a) to repair the goods, or
    (b) to replace the goods.

(2) If the buyer requires the seller to repair or replace the goods, the seller must—
    (a) repair or, as the case may be, replace the goods within a reasonable time but without causing significant inconvenience to the buyer;
    (b) bear any necessary costs incurred in doing so (including in particular the cost of any labour, materials or postage).

(3) The buyer must not require the seller to repair or, as the case may be, replace the goods if that remedy is—
    (a) impossible, or
    (b) disproportionate in comparison to the other of those remedies, or
    (c) disproportionate in comparison to an appropriate reduction in the purchase price under paragraph (a), or rescission under paragraph (b), of section 48C(1) below.

(4) One remedy is disproportionate in comparison to the other if the one imposes costs on the seller which, in comparison to those imposed on him by the other, are unreasonable, taking into account—
    (a) the value which the goods would have if they conformed to the contract of sale,
    (b) the significance of the lack of conformity, and

    (c) whether the other remedy could be effected without significant inconvenience to the buyer.

    (5) Any question as to what is a reasonable time or significant inconvenience is to be determined by reference to—

        (a) the nature of the goods, and

        (b) the purpose for which the goods were acquired.

48C Reduction of purchase price or rescission of contract

    (1) If section 48A above applies, the buyer may—

        (a) require the seller to reduce the purchase price of the goods in question to the buyer by an appropriate amount, or

        (b) rescind the contract with regard to those goods, if the condition in subsection (2) below is satisfied.

    (2) The condition is that—

        (a) by virtue of section 48B(3) above the buyer may require neither repair nor replacement of the goods; or

        (b) the buyer has required the seller to repair or replace the goods, but the seller is in breach of the requirement of section 48B(2)(a) above to do so within a reasonable time and without significant inconvenience to the buyer.

    (3) For the purposes of this Part, if the buyer rescinds the contract, any reimbursement to the buyer may be reduced to take account of the use he has had of the goods since they were delivered to him.

48D Relation to other remedies etc.

    (1) If the buyer requires the seller to repair or replace the goods the buyer must not act under subsection (2) until he has given the seller a reasonable time in which to repair or replace (as the case may be) the goods.

    (2) The buyer acts under this subsection if—

        (a) in England and Wales or Northern Ireland he rejects the goods and terminates the contract for breach of condition;

        (b) in Scotland he rejects any goods delivered under the contract and treats it as repudiated;

        (c) he requires the goods to be replaced or repaired (as the case may be).

48E Powers of the court

    (1) In any proceedings in which a remedy is sought by virtue of this Part the court, in addition to any other power it has, may act under this section.

    (2) On the application of the buyer the court may make an order requiring specific performance or, in Scotland, specific implement by the seller of any obligation imposed on him by virtue of section 48B above.

    (3) Subsection (4) applies if—

        (a) the buyer requires the seller to give effect to a remedy under section 48B or 48C above or has claims to rescind under section 48C, but

        (b) the court decides that another remedy under section 48B or 48C is appropriate.

    (4) The court may proceed—

        (a) as if the buyer had required the seller to give effect to the other remedy, or if the other remedy is rescission under section 48C

        (b) as if the buyer had claimed to rescind the contract under that section.

    (5) If the buyer has claimed to rescind the contract the court may order that any reimbursement to the buyer is reduced to take account of the use he has had of the goods since they were delivered to him.

    (6) The court may make an order under this section unconditionally or on such terms and conditions as to damages, payment of the price and otherwise as it thinks just.

48F Conformity with the contract

For the purposes of this Part, goods do not conform to a contract of sale if there is, in r
to the goods, a breach of an express term of the contract or a term implied by section 1
15 above.]

PART VI   ACTIONS FOR BREACH OF THE CONTRACT

Seller's remedies

49   Action for price

(1) Where, under a contract of sale, the property in the goods has passed to the buyer and
he wrongfully neglects or refuses to pay for the goods according to the terms of the contract,
the seller may maintain an action against him for the price of the goods.

50   Damages for non-acceptance

(1) Where the buyer wrongfully neglects or refuses to accept and pay for the goods, the
seller may maintain an action against him for damages for non-acceptance.

(2) The measure of damages is the estimated loss directly and naturally resulting, in the
ordinary course of events, from the buyer's breach of contract.

(3) Where there is an available market for the goods in question the measure of damages
is prima facie to be ascertained by the difference between the contract price and the market or
current price at the time or times when the goods ought to have been accepted or (if no time
was fixed for acceptance) at the time of the refusal to accept.

Buyer's remedies

51   Damages for non-delivery

(1) Where the seller wrongfully neglects or refuses to deliver the goods to the buyer, the
buyer may maintain an action against the seller for damages for non-delivery.

(2) The measure of damages is the estimated loss directly and naturally resulting, in the
ordinary course of events, from the seller's breach of contract.

(3) Where there is an available market for the goods in question the measure of damages
is prima facie to be ascertained by the difference between the contract price and the market or
current price of the goods at the time or times when they ought to have been delivered or (if
no time was fixed) at the time of the refusal to deliver.

52   Specific performance

(1) In any action for breach of contract to deliver specific or ascertained goods the court
may, if it thinks fit, on the plaintiff's application, by its judgment or decree direct that the
contract shall be performed specifically, without giving the defendant the option of retaining
the goods on payment of damages.

(3) The judgment or decree may be unconditional, or on such terms and conditions as to
damages, payment of the price and otherwise as seem just to the court.

53   Remedy for breach of warranty

(1) Where there is a breach of warranty by the seller, or where the buyer elects (or is
compelled) to treat any breach of a condition on the part of the seller as a breach of warranty,
the buyer is not by reason only of such breach of warranty entitled to reject the goods; but
he may—

  (a) set up against the seller the breach of warranty in diminution or extinction of the
     price, or

  (b) maintain an action against the seller for damages for the breach of warranty.

(2) The measure of damages for breach of warranty is the estimated loss directly and
naturally resulting, in the ordinary course of events, from the breach of warranty.

(3) In the case of breach of warranty of quality such loss is prima facie the difference between the value of the goods at the time of delivery to the buyer and the value they would have had if they had fulfilled the warranty.

(4) The fact that the buyer has set up the breach of warranty in diminution or extinction of the price does not prevent him from maintaining an action for the same breach of warranty if he has suffered further damage.

[(5) This section does not apply to Scotland.]

[53A   Measure of damages as respects Scotland

(1) The measure of damages for the seller's breach of contract is the estimated loss directly and naturally resulting, in the ordinary course of events, from the breach.

(2) Where the seller's breach consists of the delivery of goods which are not of the quality required by the contract and the buyer retains the goods, such loss as aforesaid is prima facie the difference between the value of the goods at the time of delivery to the buyer and the value they would have had if they had fulfilled the contract.

(3) This section applies to Scotland only.]

Interest etc.

54   Interest, etc.

Nothing in this Act affects the right of the buyer or the seller to recover interest or special damages in any case where by law interest or special damages may be recoverable, or to recover money paid where the consideration for the payment of it has failed.

PART VII   SUPPLEMENTARY

55   Exclusion of implied terms

(1) Where a right, duty or liability would arise under a contract of sale of goods by implication of law, it may (subject to the Unfair Contract Terms Act 1977) be negatived or varied by express agreement, or by the course of dealing between the parties, or by such usage as binds both parties to the contract.

(2) An express [term] does not negative a [term] implied by this Act unless inconsistent with it.

(3) Paragraph 11 of Schedule 1 below applies in relation to a contract made on or after 18 May 1973 and before 1 February 1978, and paragraph 12 in relation to one made before 18 May 1973.

56   Conflict of laws

Paragraph 13 of Schedule 1 below applies in relation to a contract made on or after 18 May 1973 and before 1 February 1978, so as to make provision about conflict of laws in relation to such a contract.

57   Auction sales

(1) Where goods are put up for sale by auction in lots, each lot is prima facie deemed to be the subject of a separate contract of sale.

(2) A sale by auction is complete when the auctioneer announces its completion by the fall of the hammer, or in other customary manner; and until the announcement is made any bidder may retract his bid.

(3) A sale by auction may be notified to be subject to a reserve or upset price, and a right to bid may also be reserved expressly by or on behalf of the seller.

(4) Where a sale by auction is not notified to be subject to a right to bid by or on behalf of the seller, it is not lawful for the seller to bid himself or to employ any person to bid at the sale, or for the auctioneer knowingly to take any bid from the seller or any such person.

(5) A sale contravening subsection (4) above may be treated as fraudulent by the buyer.

(6) Where, in respect of a sale by auction, a right to bid is expressly reserved (but not otherwise) the seller or any one person on his behalf may bid at the auction.

58   Payment into court in Scotland

In Scotland where a buyer has elected to accept goods which he might have rejected, and to treat a breach of contract as only giving rise to a claim for damages, he may, in an action by the seller for the price, be required, in the discretion of the court before which the action depends, to consign or pay into court the price of the goods, or part of the price, or to give other reasonable security for its due payment.

59   Reasonable time a question of fact

Where a reference is made in this Act to a reasonable time the question what is a reasonable time is a question of fact.

60   Rights etc. enforceable by action

Where a right, duty or liability is declared by this Act, it may (unless otherwise provided by this Act) be enforced by action.

61   Interpretation

(1) In this Act, unless the context or subject matter otherwise requires,—

"action" includes counterclaim and set-off, and in Scotland condescendence and claim and compensation;

["bulk" means a mass or collection of goods of the same kind which—

(a) is contained in a defined space or area; and

(b) is such that any goods in the bulk are interchangeable with any other goods therein of the same number or quantity;]

"business" includes a profession and the activities of any government department (including a Northern Ireland department) or local or public authority;

"buyer" means a person who buys or agrees to buy goods;

["consumer contract" has the same meaning as in section 25(1) of the Unfair Contract Terms Act 1977; and for the purposes of this Act the onus of proving that a contract is not to be regarded as a consumer contract shall lie on the seller]

"contract of sale" includes an agreement to sell as well as a sale;

"credit-broker" means a person acting in the course of a business of credit brokerage carried on by him, that is a business of effecting introductions of individuals desiring to obtain credit—

(a) to persons carrying on any business so far as it relates to the provision of credit, or

(b) to other persons engaged in credit brokerage;

"defendant" includes in Scotland defender, respondent, and claimant in a multiple-poinding;

"delivery" means voluntary transfer of possession from one person to another; [except that in relation to sections 20A and 20B above it includes such appropriation of goods to the contract as results in property in the goods being transferred to the buyer;]

"document of title to goods" has the same meaning as it has in the Factors Acts;

"Factors Acts" means the Factors Act 1889, the Factors (Scotland) Act 1890, and any enactment amending or substituted for the same;

"fault" means wrongful act or default;

"future goods" means goods to be manufactured or acquired by the seller after the making of the contract of sale;

"goods" includes all personal chattels other than things in action and money, and in Scotland all corporeal moveables except money; and in particular "goods" includes emblements, industrial growing crops, and things attached to or forming part of the land which are agreed to be severed before sale or under the contract of sale; [and includes an undivided share in goods;]

"plaintiff" includes pursuer, complainer, claimant in a multiplepoinding and defendant or defender counter-claiming;

["producer" means the manufacturer of goods, the importer of goods into the European Economic Area or any person purporting to be a producer by placing his name, trade mark or other distinctive sign on the goods;]

"property" means the general property in goods, and not merely a special property;

["repair" means, in cases where there is a lack of conformity in goods for the purposes of section 48F of this Act, to bring the goods into conformity with the contract;][1]

"sale" includes a bargain and sale as well as a sale and delivery;

"seller" means a person who sells or agrees to sell goods;

"specific goods" means goods identified and agreed on at the time a contract of sale is made; [and includes an undivided share, specified as a fraction or percentage, of goods identified and agreed on as aforesaid]

"warranty" (as regards England and Wales and Northern Ireland) means an agreement with reference to goods which are the subject of a contract of sale, but collateral to the main purpose of such contract, the breach of which gives rise to a claim for damages, but not to a right to reject the goods and treat the contract as repudiated.

(3) A thing is deemed to be done in good faith within the meaning of this Act when it is in fact done honestly, whether it is done negligently or not.

(4) A person is deemed to be insolvent within the meaning of this Act if he has either ceased to pay his debts in the ordinary course of business or he cannot pay his debts as they become due, [...]

(5) Goods are in a deliverable state within the meaning of this Act when they are in such a state that the buyer would under the contract be bound to take delivery of them.

[(5A) References in this Act to dealing as consumer are to be construed in accordance with Part I of the Unfair Contract Terms Act 1977; and, for the purposes of this Act, it is for a seller claiming that the buyer does not deal as consumer to show that he does not.]

(6) As regards the definition of "business" in subsection (1) above, paragraph 14 of Schedule 1 below applies in relation to a contract made on or after 18 May 1973 and before 1 February 1978, and paragraph 15 in relation to one made before 18 May 1973.

62   Savings: rule of law etc.

(1) The rules in bankruptcy relating to contracts of sale apply to those contracts, notwithstanding anything in this Act.

(2) The rules of the common law, including the law merchant, except in so far as they are inconsistent with the provisions of this Act, and in particular the rules relating to the law of principal and agent and the effect of fraud, misrepresentation, duress or coercion, mistake, or other invalidating cause, apply to contracts for the sale of goods.

(3) Nothing in this Act or the Sale of Goods Act 1893 affects the enactments relating to bills of sale, or any enactment relating to the sale of goods which is not expressly repealed or amended by this Act or that.

(4) The provisions of this Act about contracts of sale do not apply to a transaction in the form of a contract of sale which is intended to operate by way of mortgage, pledge, charge, or other security.

(5) Nothing in this Act prejudices or affects the landlord's right of hypothec or sequestration for rent in Scotland.

63   Consequential amendments, repeals and savings

. . .

64   Short title and commencement

(1) This Act may be cited as the Sale of Goods Act 1979.

(2) This act comes into force on 1 January 1980.

Vaccine Damage Payments Act 1979
(1979, c. 17)

1 Payments to persons severely disabled by vaccination

(1) If, on consideration of a claim, the Secretary of State is satisfied—

(a) that a person is, or was immediately before his death, severely disabled as a result of vaccination against any of the diseases to which this Act applies; and

(b) that the conditions of entitlement which are applicable in accordance with section 2 below are fulfilled,

he shall in accordance with this Act make a payment of [the relevant statutory sum] to or for the benefit of that person or to his personal representatives.

[(1A) In subsection (1) above "statutory sum" means [£30,000] or such other sum as is specified by the Secretary of State for the purposes of this Act by order made by statutory instrument with the consent of the Treasury; and the relevant statutory sum for the purposes of that subsection is the statutory sum at the time when a claim for payment is first made.]

(2) The diseases to which this Act applies are—

(a) diphtheria,

(b) tetanus,

(c) whooping cough,

(d) poliomyelitis,

(e) measles,

(f) rubella,

(g) tuberculosis,

(h) smallpox, and

(i) any other disease which is specified by the Secretary of State for the purposes of this Act by order made by statutory instrument.

(3) Subject to section 2(3) below, this Act has effect with respect to a person who is severely disabled as a result of a vaccination given to his mother before he was born as if the vaccination had been given directly to him and, in such circumstances as may be prescribed by regulations under this Act, this Act has effect with respect to a person who is severely disabled as a result of contracting a disease through contact with a third person who was vaccinated against it as if the vaccination had been given to him and the disablement resulted from it.

For the purposes of this Act, a person is severely disabled if he suffers disablement to the extent of [60 per cent] or more, assessed as for the purposes of [section 103 of the Social Security Contributions and Benefits Act 1992 or section 103 of the Social Security Contributions and Benefits (Northern Ireland) Act 1992] (disablement gratuity and pension).

2 Conditions of entitlement

(1) Subject to the provisions of this section, the conditions of entitlement referred to in section 1(1)(b) above are—

(a) that the vaccination in question was carried out—

(i) in the United Kingdom or the Isle of Man, and

(ii) on or after 5 July 1948, and

(iii) in the case of vaccination against smallpox, before 1st August 1971;

(b) except in the case of vaccination against poliomyelitis or rubella, that the vaccination was carried out either at a time when the person to whom it was given was under the age of eighteen or at the time of an outbreak within the United Kingdom or the Isle of Man of the disease against which the vaccination was given; and

(c) that the disabled person was over the age of two on the date when the claim was made or, if he died before that date, that he died after 9th May 1978 and was over the age of two when he died.

3 Determination of claims

(1) Any reference in this Act, other than section 7, to a claim is a reference to a claim for a payment under section 1(1) above which is made—

(a) by or on behalf of the disabled person concerned or, as the case may be, by his personal representatives; and

(b) in the manner prescribed by regulations under this Act; and

[(c) on or before whichever is the later of—

(i) the date on which the disabled person attains the age of 21, or where he has died, the date on which he would have attained the age of 21; and

(ii) the end of the period of six years beginning with the date of the vaccination to which the claim relates;] . . .

6 Payments to or for the benefit of disabled persons

(1) Where a payment under section 1(1) above falls to be made in respect of a disabled person who is over eighteen and capable of managing his own affairs, the payment shall be made to him.

(2) Where such a payment falls to be made in respect of a disabled person who has died, the payment shall be made to his personal representatives.

(3) Where such a payment falls to be made in respect of any other disabled person, the payment shall be made for his benefit by paying it to such trustees as the Secretary of State may appoint to be held by them upon such trusts or, in Scotland, for such purposes and upon such conditions as may be declared by the Secretary of State.

(4) The making of a claim for, or the receipt of, a payment under section 1(1) above does not prejudice the right of any person to institute or carry on proceedings in respect of disablement suffered as a result of vaccination against any disease to which this Act applies; but in any civil proceedings brought in respect of disablement resulting from vaccination against such a disease, the court shall treat a payment made to or in respect of the disabled person concerned under section 1(1) above as paid on account of any damages which the court awards in respect of such disablement.

12 Financial provisions

(4) There shall be paid out of moneys provided by Parliament—

(a) any expenditure incurred by the Secretary of State in making payments under section 1(1) above . . .

Highways Act 1980
(1980, c. 66)

41 Duty to maintain highways maintainable at public expense

(1) The authority who are for the time being the highway authority for a highway maintainable at the public expense are under a duty, subject to subsections (2) and (4) below, to maintain the highway.

[(1A) In particular, a highway authority are under a duty to ensure, so far as is reasonably practicable, that safe passage along a highway is not endangered by snow or ice.]

58 Special defence in action against a highway authority for damages for non-repair of highway

(1) In an action against a highway authority in respect of damage resulting from their failure to maintain a highway maintainable at the public expense it is a defence (without prejudice to any other defence or the application of the law relating to contributory negligence) to prove that the authority had taken such care as in all the circumstances was

reasonably required to secure that the part of the highway to which the action relates was not dangerous for traffic.

102   Provision of works for protecting highways against hazards of nature

(1) The highway authority for a highway maintainable at the public expense may provide and maintain such barriers or other works as they consider necessary for the purpose of affording to the highway protection against snow, flood, landslide or other hazards of nature; and those works may be provided on the highway or on land which, or rights over which, has or have been acquired by the highway authority in the exercise of highway land acquisition powers for that purpose.

(3) A highway authority shall pay compensation to any person who suffers damage by reason of the execution by them under this section of any works on a highway.

[PART 8A   RESTRICTION OF RIGHTS OVER HIGHWAY]

[129A   Gating orders

(1) A council may in accordance with this Part make an order under this section in relation to any relevant highway for which they are the highway authority.

(2) An order under this section is to be known as a "gating order".

(3) Before making a gating order in relation to a relevant highway the council must be satisfied that—

(a) premises adjoining or adjacent to the highway are affected by crime or anti-social behaviour;

(b) the existence of the highway is facilitating the persistent commission of criminal offences or anti-social behaviour; and

(c) it is in all the circumstances expedient to make the order for the purposes of reducing crime or anti-social behaviour.

(4) The circumstances referred to in subsection (3)(c) include—

(a) the likely effect of making the order on the occupiers of premises adjoining or adjacent to the highway;

(b) the likely effect of making the order on other persons in the locality; and

(c) in a case where the highway constitutes a through route, the availability of a reasonably convenient alternative route.]

[129B   Effect of gating orders

(1) A gating order restricts, to the extent specified in the order, the public right of way over the highway to which it relates.

(2) A gating order may in particular—

(a) restrict the public right of way at all times, or in respect of such times, days or periods as may be specified in the order;

(b) exclude persons of a description specified in the order from the effect of the restriction.

(3) A gating order may not be made so as to restrict the public right of way over a highway for the occupiers of premises adjoining or adjacent to the highway.

(4) A gating order may not be made so as to restrict the public right of way over a highway which is the only or principal means of access to any dwelling.

(5) In relation to a highway which is the only or principal means of access to any premises used for business or recreational purposes, a gating order may not be made so as to restrict the public right of way over the highway during periods when those premises are normally used for those purposes.

(6) A gating order may authorise the installation, operation and maintenance of a barrier or barriers for the purpose of enforcing the restriction provided for in the order.]

Interpretation

purposes of this Part—

anti-social behaviour" means behaviour by a person which causes or is likely to cause harassment, alarm or distress to one or more other persons not of the same household as himself;]

165 Dangerous land adjoining street

(1) If, in or on any land adjoining a street, there is an unfenced or inadequately fenced source of danger to persons using the street, the local authority in whose area the street is situated may, by notice to the owner or occupier of that land, require him within such time as may be specified in the notice to execute such works of repair, protection, removal or enclosure as will obviate the danger.

(3) Subject to any order made on appeal, if a person on whom a notice is served under this section fails to comply with the notice within the time specified in it, the authority by whom the notice was served may execute such works as are necessary to comply with the notice and may recover the expenses reasonably incurred by them in so doing from that person.

Limitation Act 1980
(1980, c. 58)

PART I

1 Time limits under Part I subject to exclusion under Part II

(1) This Part of this Act gives the ordinary time limits for bringing actions of the various classes mentioned in the following provisions of this Part.

(2) The ordinary time limits given in this Part of this Act are subject to extension or exclusion in accordance with the provisions of Part II of this Act.

2 Time limit for actions founded on tort

An action founded on tort shall not be brought after the expiration of six years from the date on which the cause of action accrued.

3 Time limit in case of successive conversions and extinction of title of owner of converted goods

(1) Where any cause of action in respect of the conversion of a chattel has accrued to any person and, before he recovers possession of the chattel, a further conversion takes place, no action shall be brought in respect of the further conversion after the expiration of six years from the accrual of the cause of action in respect of the original conversion.

(2) Where any such cause of action has accrued to any person and the period prescribed for bringing that action has expired and he has not during that period recovered possession of the chattel, the title of that person to the chattel shall be extinguished.

4 Special time limit in case of theft

(1) The right of any person from whom a chattel is stolen to bring an action in respect of the theft shall not be subject to the time limits under sections 2 and 3(1) of this Act, but if his title to the chattel is extinguished under section 3(2) of this Act he may not bring an action in respect of a theft preceding the loss of his title, unless the theft in question preceded the conversion from which time began to run for the purposes of section 3(2).

(2) Subsection (1) above shall apply to any conversion related to the theft of a chattel as it applies to the theft of a chattel; and, except as provided below, every conversion following the theft of a chattel before the person from whom it is stolen recovers possession of it shall be regarded for the purposes of this section as related to the theft.

If anyone purchases the stolen chattel in good faith neither the purchase nor any conversion following it shall be regarded as related to the theft.

(3) Any cause of action accruing in respect of the theft or any conversion related to the theft of a chattel to any person from whom the chattel is stolen shall be disregarded for the purpose of applying section 3(1) or (2) of this Act to his case.

(4) Where in any action brought in respect of the conversion of a chattel it is proved that the chattel was stolen from the plaintiff or anyone through whom he claims it shall be presumed that any conversion following the theft is related to the theft unless the contrary is shown.

(5) In this section "theft" includes—

    (a) any conduct outside England and Wales which would be theft if committed in England and Wales; and

    (b) obtaining any chattel (in England and Wales or elsewhere) in the circumstances described in section 15(1) of the Theft Act 1968 (obtaining by deception) or by blackmail within the meaning of section 21 of that Act;

and references in this section to a chattel being "stolen" shall be construed accordingly.

[4A   Time limit for actions for defamation or malicious falsehood

The time limit under section 2 of this Act shall not apply to an action for—

    (a) libel or slander, or

    (b) slander of title, slander of goods or other malicious falsehood,

but no such action shall be brought after the expiration of one year from the date on which the cause of action accrued.]

5   Time limit for actions founded on simple contract

An action founded on simple contract shall not be brought after the expiration of six years from the date on which the cause of action accrued.

6   Special time limit for actions in respect of certain loans

(1) Subject to subsection (3) below, section 5 of this Act shall not bar the right of action on a contract of loan to which this section applies.

(2) This section applies to any contract of loan which—

    (a) does not provide for repayment of the debt on or before a fixed or determinable date; and

    (b) does not effectively (whether or not it purports to do so) make the obligation to repay the debt conditional on a demand for repayment made by or on behalf of the creditor or on any other matter;

except where in connection with taking the loan the debtor enters into any collateral obligation to pay the amount of the debt or any part of it (as, for example, by delivering a promissory note as security for the debt) on terms which would exclude the application of this section to the contract of loan if they applied directly to repayment of the debt.

(3) Where a demand in writing for repayment of the debt under a contract of loan to which this section applies is made by or on behalf of the creditor (or, where there are joint creditors, by or on behalf of any one of them) section 5 of this Act shall thereupon apply as if the cause of action to recover the debt had accrued on the date on which the demand was made.

(4) In this section "promissory note" has the same meaning as in the Bills of Exchange Act 1882.

8   Time limit for actions on a specialty

(1) An action upon a specialty shall not be brought after the expiration of twelve years from the date on which the cause of action accrued.

(2) Subsection (1) above shall not affect any action for which a shorter period of limitation is prescribed by any other provision of this Act.

9   Time limit for actions for sums recoverable by statute

(1) An action to recover any sum recoverable by virtue of any enactment shall not be brought after the expiration of six years from the date on which the cause of action accrued.

(2) Subsection (1) above shall not affect any action to which section 10 of this Act applies.

10 Special time limit for claiming contribution

(1) Where under section 1 of the Civil Liability (Contribution) Act 1978 any person becomes entitled to a right to recover contribution in respect of any damage from any other person, no action to recover contribution by virtue of that right shall be brought after the expiration of two years from the date on which that right accrued.

(2) For the purposes of this section the date on which a right to recover contribution in respect of any damage accrues to any person (referred to below in this section as "the relevant date") shall be ascertained as provided in subsections (3) and (4) below.

(3) If the person in question is held liable in respect of that damage—

(a) by a judgment given in any civil proceedings; or

(b) by an award made on any arbitration;

the relevant date shall be the date on which the judgment is given, or the date of the award (as the case may be).

For the purposes of this subsection no account shall be taken of any judgment or award given or made on appeal in so far as it varies the amount of damages awarded against the person in question.

(4) If, in any case not within subsection (3) above, the person in question makes or agrees to make any payment to one or more persons in compensation for that damage (whether he admits any liability in repect of the damage or not), the relevant date shall be the earliest date on which the amount to be paid by him is agreed between him (or his representative) and the person (or each of the persons, as the case may be) to whom the payment is to be made.

(5) An action to recover contribution shall be one to which sections 28, 32 and 35 of this Act apply, but otherwise Parts II and III of this Act (except sections 34, 37 and 38) shall not apply for the purposes of this section.

11 Special time limit for actions in respect of personal injuries

(1) This section applies to any action for damages for negligence, nuisance or breach of duty (whether the duty exists by virtue of a contract or of provision made by or under a statute or independently of any contract or any such provision) where the damages claimed by the plaintiff for the negligence, nuisance or breach of duty consist of or include damages in respect of personal injuries to the plaintiff or any other person.

[(1A) This section does not apply to any action brought for damages under section 3 of the Protection from Harassment Act 1997.]

(3) An action to which this section applies shall not be brought after the expiration of the period applicable in accordance with subsection (4) or (5) below.

(4) Except where subsection (5) below applies, the period applicable is three years from—

(a) the date on which the cause of action accrued; or

(b) the date of knowledge (if later) of the person injured.

(5) If the injured person dies before the expiration of the period mentioned in subsection (4) above, the period applicable as respects the cause of action surviving for the benefit of his estate by virtue of section 1 of the Law Reform (Miscellaneous Provisions) Act 1934 shall be three years from—

(a) the date of death; or

(b) the date of the personal representative's knowledge; whichever is the later.

[11A Actions in respect of defective products

(1) This section shall apply to an action for damages by virtue of any provision of Part I of the Consumer Protection Act 1987.

(2) None of the time limits given in the preceding provisions of this Act shall apply to an action to which this section applies.

(3) An action to which this section applies shall not be brought after the expiration of the period of ten years from the relevant time, within the meaning of section 4 of the said Act of 1987; and this subsection shall operate to extinguish a right of action and shall do so whether or not that right of action had accrued, or time under the following provisions of this Act had begun to run, at the end of the said period of ten years.

(4) Subject to subsection (5) below, an action to which this section applies in which the damages claimed by the plaintiff consist of or include damages in respect of personal injuries to the plaintiff or any other person or loss of or damage to any property, shall not be brought after the expiration of the period of three years from whichever is the later of—

    (a) the date on which the cause of action accrued; and

    (b) the date of knowledge of the injured person or, in the case of loss of or damage to property, the date of knowledge of the plaintiff or (if earlier) of any person in whom his cause of action was previously vested.

(5) If in a case where the damages claimed by the plaintiff consist of or include damages in respect of personal injuries to the plaintiff or any other person the injured person died before the expiration of the period mentioned in subsection (4) above, the subsection shall have effect as respects the cause of action surviving for the benefit of his estate by virtue of section I of the Law Reform (Miscellaneous Provisions) Act 1934 as if for the reference to that period there were substituted a reference to the period of three years from whichever is the later of—

    (a) the date of death; and

    (b) the date of the personal representative's knowledge.

(6) For the purposes of this section "personal representative" includes any person who is or has been a personal representative of the deceased, including an executor who has not proved the will (whether or not he has renounced probate) but not anyone appointed only as a special personal representative in relation to settled land; and regard shall be had to any knowledge acquired by any such person while a personal representative or previously.

(7) If there is more than one personal representative and their dates of knowledge are different, subsection (5)(b) above shall be read as referring to the earliest of those dates.

(8) Expressions used in this section or section 14 of this Act and in Part I of the Consumer Protection Act 1987 have the same meanings in this section or that section as in that Part; and section 1(1) of that Act (Part I to be construed as enacted for the purpose of complying with the product liability Directive) shall apply for the purpose of construing this section and the following provisions of this Act so far as they relate to an action by virtue of any provision of that Part as it applies for the purpose of construing that Part.]

12   Special time limit for actions under Fatal Accidents legislation

(1) An action under the Fatal Accidents Act 1976 shall not be brought if the death occurred when the person injured could no longer maintain an action and recover damages in respect of the injury (whether because of a time limit in this Act or in any other Act, or for any other reason).

Where any such action by the injured person would have been barred by the time limit in section 11 [or 11A] of this Act, no account shall be taken of the possibility of that time limit being overridden under section 33 of this Act.

(2) None of the time limits given in the preceding provisions of this Act shall apply to an action under the Fatal Accidents Act 1976, but no such action shall be brought after the expiration of three years from—

    (a) the date of death; or

    (b) the date of knowledge of the person for whose benefit the action is brought; whichever is the later.

(3) An action under the Fatal Accidents Act 1976 shall be one to which sections 28, 33 and 35 of this Act apply, and the application to any such action of the time limit under subsection (2) above shall be subject to section 39; but otherwise Parts II and III of this Act shall not apply to any such action.

13 Operation of time limit under section 12 in relation to different dependants

(1) Where there is more than one person for whose benefit an action under the Fatal Accidents Act 1976 is brought, section 12(2)(b) of this Act shall be applied separately to each of them.

(2) Subject to subsection (3) below, if by virtue of subsection (1) above the action would be outside the time limit given by section 12(2) as regards one or more, but not all, of the persons for whose benefit it is brought, the court shall direct that any person as regards whom the action would be outside that limit shall be excluded from those for whom the action is brought.

(3) The court shall not give such a direction if it is shown that if the action were brought exclusively for the benefit of the person in question it would not be defeated by a defence of limitation (whether in consequence of section 28 of this Act or an agreement between the parties not to raise the defence, or otherwise).

14 Definition of date of knowledge for purposes of sections 11 and 12

(1) [Subject to subsection (1A) below,] In sections 11 and 12 of this Act references to a person's date of knowledge are references to the date on which he first had knowledge of the following facts—
(a) that the injury in question was significant; and
(b) that the injury was attributable in whole or in part to the act or omission which is alleged to constitute negligence, nuisance or breach of duty; and
(c) the identity of the defendant; and
(d) if it is alleged that the act or omission was that of a person other than the defendant, the identity of that person and the additional facts supporting the bringing of an action against the defendant;

and knowledge that any acts or omissions did or did not, as a matter of law, involve negligence, nuisance or breach of duty is irrelevant.

[(1A) In section 11A of this Act and in section 12 of this Act so far as that section applies to an action by virtue of section 6(1)(a) of the Consumer Protection Act 1987 (death caused by defective product) references to a person's date of knowledge are references to the date on which he first had knowledge of the following facts—
(a) such facts about the damage caused by the defect as would lead a reasonable person who had suffered such damage to consider it sufficiently serious to justify his instituting proceedings for damages against a defendant who did not dispute liability and was able to satisfy a judgment; and
(b) that the damage was wholly or partly attributable to the facts and circumstances alleged to constitute the defect; and
(c) the identity of the defendant;

but, in determining the date on which a person first had such knowledge there shall be disregarded both the extent (if any) of that person's knowledge on any date of whether particular facts or circumstances would or would not, as a matter of law, constitute a defect and, in a case relating to loss of or damage to property, any knowledge which that person had on a date on which he had no right of action by virtue of Part of I of that Act in respect of the loss or damage.]

(2) For the purposes of this section an injury is significant if the person whose date of knowledge is in question would reasonably have considered it sufficiently serious to justify his instituting proceedings for damages against a defendant who did not dispute liability and was able to satisfy a judgment.

(3) For the purposes of this section a person's knowledge includes knowledge which he might reasonably have been expected to acquire—
(a) from facts observable or ascertainable by him; or
(b) from facts ascertainable by him with the help of medical or other appropriate expert advice which it is reasonable for him to seek;

but a person shall not be fixed under this subsection with knowledge of a fact ascertainable only with the help of expert advice so long as he has taken all reasonable steps to obtain (and, where appropriate, to act on) that advice.

[14A Special time limit for negligence actions where facts relevant to cause of action are not known at date of accrual

(1) This section applies to any action for damages for negligence, other than one to which section 11 of this Act applies, where the starting date for reckoning the period of limitation under subsection (4)(b) below falls after the date on which the cause of action accrued.

(2) Section 2 of this Act shall not apply to an action to which this section applies.

(3) An action to which this section applies shall not be brought after the expiration of the period applicable in accordance with subsection (4) below.

(4) That period is either—

(a) six years from the date on which the cause of action accrued; or

(b) three years from the starting date as defined by subsection (5) below, if that period expires later than the period mentioned in paragraph (a) above.

(5) For the purposes of this section, the starting date for reckoning the period of limitation under subsection (4)(b) above is the earliest date on which the plaintiff or any person in whom the cause of action was vested before him first had both the knowledge required for bringing an action for damages in respect of the relevant damage and a right to bring such an action.

(6) In subsection (5) above "the knowledge required for bringing an action for damages in respect of the relevant damage" means knowledge both—

(a) of the material facts about the damage in respect of which damages are claimed; and

(b) of the other facts relevant to the current action mentioned in subsection (8) below.

(7) For the purposes of subsection (6)(a) above, the material facts about the damage are such facts about the damage as would lead a reasonable person who had suffered such damage to consider it sufficiently serious to justify his instituting proceedings for damages against a defendant who did not dispute liability and was able to satisfy a judgment.

(8) The other facts referred to in subsection (6)(b) above are—

(a) that the damage was attributable in whole or in part to the act or omission which is alleged to constitute negligence; and

(b) the identity of the defendant; and

(c) if it is alleged that the act or omission was that of a person other than the defendant, the identity of that person and the additional facts supporting the bringing of an action against the defendant.

(9) Knowledge that any acts or omissions did or did not, as a matter of law, involve negligence is irrelevant for the purposes of subsection (5) above.

(10) For the purposes of this section a person's knowledge includes knowledge which he might reasonably have been expected to acquire—

(a) from facts observable or ascertainable by him; or

(b) from facts ascertainable by him with the help of appropriate expert advice which it is reasonable for him to seek;

but a person shall not be taken by virtue of this subsection to have knowledge of a fact ascertainable only with the help of expert advice so long as he has taken all reasonable steps to obtain (and, where appropriate, to act on) that advice.]

[14B Overriding time limit for negligence actions not involving personal injuries

(1) An action for damages for negligence, other than one to which section 11 of this Act applies, shall not be brought after the expiration of fifteen years from the date (or, if more than one, from the last of the dates) on which there occurred any act or omission—

(a) which is alleged to constitute negligence; and

(b) to which the damage in respect of which damages are claimed is alleged to be attributable (in whole or in part).

(2) This section bars the right of action in a case to which subsection (1) above applies notwithstanding that—

(a) the cause of action has not yet accrued; or

(b) where section 14A of this Act applies to the action, the date which is for the purposes of that section the starting date for reckoning the period mentioned in subsection (4)(b) of that section has not yet occurred;

before the end of the period of limitation prescribed by this section.]

15   Time limit for actions to recover land

(1) No action shall be brought by any person to recover any land after the expiration of twelve years from the date on which the right of action accrued to him or, if it first accrued to some person through whom he claims, to that person.

(2) Subject to the following provisions of this section, where—

(a) the estate or interest claimed was an estate or interest in reversion or remainder or any other future estate or interest and the right of action to recover the land accrued on the date on which the estate or interest fell into possession by the determination of the preceding estate or interest; and

(b) the person entitled to the preceding estate or interest (not being a term of years absolute) was not in possession of the land on that date;

no action shall be brought by the person entitled to the succeeding estate or interest after the expiration of twelve years from the date on which the right of action accrued to the person entitled to the preceding estate or interest or six years from the date on which the right of action accrued to the person entitled to the succeeding estate or interest, whichever period last expires.

(3) Subsection (2) above shall not apply to any estate or interest which falls into possession on the determination of an entailed interest and which might have been barred by the person entitled to the entailed interest.

(4) No person shall bring an action to recover any estate or interest in land under an assurance taking effect after the right of action to recover the land had accrued to the person by whom the assurance was made or some person through whom he claimed or some person entitled to a preceding estate or interest, unless the action is brought within the period during which the person by whom the assurance was made could have brought such an action.

(5) Where any person is entitled to any estate or interest in land in possession and, while so entitled, is also entitled to any future estate or interest in that land, and his right to recover the estate or interest in possession is barred under this Act, no action shall be brought by that person, or by any person claiming through him, in respect of the future estate or interest, unless in the meantime possession of the land has been recovered by a person entitled to an intermediate estate or interest.

(6) Part I of Schedule 1 to this Act contains provisions for determining the date of accrual of rights of action to recover land in the cases there mentioned.

(7) Part II of that Schedule contains provisions modifying the provisions of this section in their application to actions brought by, or by a person claiming through, the Crown or any spiritual or eleemosynary corporation sole.

16   Time limit for redemption actions

When a mortgagee of land has been in possession of any of the mortgaged land for a period of twelve years, no action to redeem the land of which the mortgagee has been so in possession shall be brought after the end of that period by the mortgagor or any person claiming through him.

17 Extinction of title to land after expiration of time limit
Subject to—
>   (a) section 18 of this Act; [. . .]

at the expiration of the period prescribed by this Act for any person to bring an action to recover land (including a redemption action) the title of that person to the land shall be extinguished.

18 Settled land and land held on trust
(1) Subject to section 21(1) and (2) of this Act, the provisions of this Act shall apply to equitable interests in land, [. . .] as they apply to legal estates. Accordingly a right of action to recover the land shall, for the purposes of this Act but not otherwise, be treated as accruing to a person entitled in possession to such an equitable interest in the like manner and circumstances, and on the same date, as it would accrue if his interest were a legal estate in the land (and any relevant provision of Part I of Schedule 1 to this Act shall apply in any such case accordingly).

(2) Where the period prescribed by this Act has expired for the briging of an action to recover land by a tenant for life or a statutory owner of settled land—
>   (a) his legal estate shall not be extinguished if and so long as the right of action to recover the land of any person entitled to a beneficial interest in the land either has not accrued or has not been barred by this Act; and
>   (b) the legal estate shall accordingly remain vested in the tenant for life or statutory owner and shall devolve in accordance with the Settled Land Act 1925;

but if and when every such right of action has been barred by this Act, his legal estate shall be extinguished.

(3) Where any land is held upon trust [. . .] and the period prescribed by this Act has expired for the bringing of an action to recover the land by the trustees, the estate of the trustees shall not be extinguished if and so long as the right of action to recover the land of any person entitled to a beneficial interest in the land [. . .] either has not accrued or has not been barred by this Act; but if and when every such right of action has been so barred the estate of the trustees shall be extinguished.

(4) Where—
>   (a) any settled land is vested in a statutory owner; or
>   (b) any land is held upon trust [. . .];

an action to recover the land may be brought by the statutory owner or trustees on behalf of any person entitled to a beneficial interest in possession in the land [. . .] whose right of action has not been barred by this Act, notwithstanding that the right of action of the statutory owner or trustees would apart from this provision have been barred by this Act.

19 Time limit for actions to recover rent
No action shall be brought, or distress made, to recover arrears of rent, or damages in respect of arrears of rent, after the expiration of six years from the date on which the arrears became due.

20 Time limit for actions to recover money secured by a mortgage or charge or to recover proceeds of the sale of land
(1) No action shall be brought to recover—
>   (a) any principal sum of money secured by a mortgage or other charge on property (whether real or personal); or
>   (b) proceeds of the sale of land;

after the expiration of twelve years from the date on which the right to receive the money accrued.

(2) No foreclosure action in respect of mortgaged personal property shall be brought after the expiration of twelve years from the date on which the right to foreclose accrued.
But if the mortgagee was in possession of the mortgaged property after that date, the right to foreclose on the property which was in his possession shall not be treated as having accrued for the purposes of this subsection until the date on which his possession discontinued.

(3) The right to receive any principal sum of money secured by a mortgage or other charge and the right to foreclose on the property subject to the mortgage or charge shall not be treated as accruing so long as that property comprises any future interest or any life insurance policy which has not matured or been determined.

(4) Nothing in this section shall apply to a foreclosure action in respect of mortgaged land, but the provisions of this Act relating to actions to recover land shall apply to such an action.

(5) Subject to subsections (6) and (7) below, no action to recover arrears of interest payable in respect of any sum of money secured by a mortgage or other charge or payable in respect of proceeds of the sale of land, or to recover damages in respect of such arrears shall be brought after the expiration of six years from the date on which the interest became due.

(6) Where—

  (a) a prior mortgagee or other incumbrancer has been in possession of the property charged; and
  (b) an action is brought within one year of the discontinuance of that possession by the subsequent incumbrancer;

the subsequent incumbrancer may recover by that action all the arrears of interest which fell due during the period of possession by the prior incumbrancer or damages in respect of those arrears, notwithstanding that the period exceeded six years.

(7) Where—

  (a) the property subject to the mortgage or charge comprises any future interest or life insurance policy; and
  (b) it is a term of the mortgage or charge that arrears of interest shall be treated as part of the principal sum of money secured by the mortgage or charge;

interest shall not be treated as becoming due before the right to recover the principal sum of money has accrued or is treated as having accrued.

21 Time limit for actions in respect of trust property

(1) No period of limitation prescribed by this Act shall apply to an action by a beneficiary under a trust, being an action—

  (a) in respect of any fraud or fraudulent breach of trust to which the trustee was a party or privy; or
  (b) to recover from the trustee trust property or the proceeds of trust property in the possession of the trustee, or previously received by the trustee and converted to his use.

(2) Where a trustee who is also a beneficiary under the trust receives or retains trust property or its proceeds as his share on a distribution of trust property under the trust, his liability in any action brought by virtue of subsection (1)(b) above to recover that property or its proceeds after the expiration of the period of limitation prescribed by this Act for bringing an action to recover trust property shall be limited to the excess over his proper share.

This subsection only applies if the trustee acted honestly and reasonably in making the distribution.

(3) Subject to the preceding provisions of this section, an action by a beneficiary to recover trust property or in respect of any breach of trust, not being an action for which a period of limitation is prescribed by any other provision of this Act, shall not be brought after the expiration of six years from the date on which the right of action accrued. For the purposes of this subsection, the right of action shall not be treated as having accrued to any beneficiary entitled to a future interest in the trust property until the interest fell into possession.

(4) No beneficiary as against whom there would be a good defence under this Act shall derive any greater or other benefit from a judgment or order obtained by any other beneficiary than he could have obtained if he had brought the action and this Act had been pleaded in defence.

22   Time limit for actions claiming personal estate of a deceased person
Subject to section 21(1) and (2) of this Act—
> (a) no action in respect of any claim to the personal estate of a deceased person or to any share or interest in any such estate (whether under a will or on intestacy) shall be brought after the expiration of twelve years from the date on which the right to receive the share or interest accrued; and
> (b) no action to recover arrears of interest in respect of any legacy, or damages in respect of such arrears, shall be brought after the expiration of six years from the date on which the interest became due.

23   Time limit in respect of actions for an account
An action for an account shall not be brought after the expiration of any time limit under this Act which is applicable to the claim which is the basis of the duty to account.

24   Time limit for actions to enforce judgments
(1) An action shall not be brought upon any judgment after the expiration of six years from the date on which the judgment became enforceable.

(2) No arrears of interest in respect of any judgment debt shall be recovered after the expiration of six years from the date on which the interest became due.

26   Administration to date back to death
For the purposes of the provisions of this Act relating to actions for the recovery of land and advowsons an administrator of the estate of a deceased person shall be treated as claiming as if there had been no interval of time between the death of the deceased person and the grant of the letters of administration.

[27A   Actions for recovery of property obtained through unlawful conduct etc.
(1) None of the time limits given in the preceding provisions of this Act applies to any proceedings under Chapter 2 of Part 5 of the Proceeds of Crime Act 2002 (civil recovery of proceeds of unlawful conduct).

(2) Proceedings under that Chapter for a recovery order in respect of any recoverable property shall not be brought after the expiration of the period of twelve years from the date on which the Director's cause of action accrued.

(3) Proceedings under that Chapter are brought when—
> (a) a claim form is issued, or
> (b) an application is made for an interim receiving order,

whichever is the earlier.

(4) The Director's cause of action accrues in respect of any recoverable property—
> (a) in the case of proceedings for a recovery order in respect of property obtained through unlawful conduct, when the property is so obtained,
> (b) in the case of proceedings for a recovery order in respect of any other recoverable property, when the property obtained through unlawful conduct which it represents is so obtained.

(5) If—
> (a) a person would (but for the preceding provisions of this Act) have a cause of action in respect of the conversion of a chattel, and
> (b) proceedings are started under that Chapter for a recovery order in respect of the chattel,

section 3(2) of this Act does not prevent his asserting on an application under section 281 of that Act that the property belongs to him, or the court making a declaration in his favour under that section.

(6) If the court makes such a declaration, his title to the chattel is to be treated as not having been extinguished by section 3(2) of this Act.

(7) Expressions used in this section and Part 5 of that Act have the same meaning in this section as in that Part.]

PART II

28   Extension of limitation period in case of disability

(1) Subject to the following provisions of this section, if on the date when any right of action accrued for which a period of limitation is prescribed by this Act, the person to whom it accrued was under a disability, the action may be brought at any time before the expiration of six years from the date when he ceased to be under a disability or died (whichever first occurred) notwithstanding that the period of limitation has expired.

(2) This section shall not affect any case where the right of action first accrued to some person (not under a disability) through whom the person under a disability claims.

(3) When a right of action which has accrued to a person under a disability accrues, on the death of that person while still under a disability, to another person under a disability, no further extension of time shall be allowed by reason of the disability of the second person.

[(4A) If the action is one to which section 4A of this Act applies, subsection (1) above shall have effect—

    (a) in the case of an action for libel or slander, as if for the words from "at any time" to "occurred)" there were substituted the words "by him at any time before the expiration of one year from the date on which he ceased to be under a disability"; and

    (b) in the case of an action for slander of title, slander of goods or other malicious falsehood, as if for the words "six years" there were substituted the words "one year".]

(5) If the action is one to which section 10 of this Act applies, subsection (1) above shall have effect as if for the words "six years" there were substituted the words "two years".

(6) If the action is one to which section 11 or 12(2) of this Act applies, subsection (1) above shall have effect as if for the words "six years" there were substituted the words "three years".

[(7) If the action is one to which section 11A of this Act applies or one by virtue of section 6(1)(a) of the Consumer Protection Act 1987 (death caused by defective product), subsection (1) above—

    (a) shall not apply to the time limit prescribed by subsection (3) of the said section 11A or to that time limit as applied by virtue of section 12(1) of this Act; and

    (b) in relation to any other time limit prescribed by this Act shall have effect as if for the words "six years" there were substituted the words "three years".]

[28A   Extension for cases where the limitation period is the period under section 14A(4)(b)

(1) Subject to subsection (2) below, if in the case of any action for which a period of limitation is prescribed by section 14A of this Act—

    (a) the period applicable in accordance with subsection (4) of that section is the period mentioned in paragraph (b) of that subsection;

    (b) on the date which is for the purposes of that section the starting date for reckoning that period the person by reference to whose knowledge that date fell to be determined under subsection (5) of that section was under a disability; and

    (c) section 28 of this Act does not apply to the action; the action may be brought at any time before the expiration of three years from the date when he ceased to be under a disability or died (whichever first occurred) notwithstanding that the period mentioned above has expired.

(2) An action may not be brought by virtue of subsection (1) above after the end of the period of limitation prescribed by section 14B of this Act.]

29   Fresh accrual of action on acknowledgment or part payment

    (5) Subject to subsection (6) below, where any right of action has accrued to recover—

        (a) any debt or other liquidated pecuniary claim; or

(b) any claim to the personal estate of a deceased person or to any share or interest in any such estate;

and the person liable or accountable for the claim acknowledges the claim or makes any payment in respect of it the right shall be treated as having accrued on and not before the date of the acknowledgment or payment.

(6) A payment of a part of the rent or interest due at any time shall not extend the period for claiming the remainder then due, but any payment of interest shall be treated as a payment in respect of the principal debt.

(7) Subject to subsection (6) above, a current period of limitation may be repeatedly extended under this section by further acknowledgments or payments, but a right of action, once barred by this Act shall not be revived by any subsequent acknowledgment or payment.

30   Formal provisions as to acknowledgments and part payments

(1) To be effective for the purposes of section 29 of this Act, an acknowledgment must be in writing and signed by the person making it.

(2) For the purposes of section 29, any acknowledgment or payment—

(a) may be made by the agent of the person by whom it is required to be made under that section; and

(b) shall be made to the person, or to an agent of the person, whose title or claim is being acknowledged or, as the case may be, in respect of whose claim the payment is being made.

31   Effect of acknowledgment or part payment on persons other than the maker or recipient

(6) An acknowledgment of any debt or other liquidated pecuniary claim shall bind the acknowledgor and his successors but not any other person.

(7) A payment made in respect of any debt or other liquidated pecuniary claim shall bind all persons liable in respect of the debt or claim.

(8) An acknowledgment by one of several personal representatives of any claim to the personal estate of a deceased person or to any share or interest in any such estate, or a payment by one of several personal representatives in respect of any such claim, shall bind the estate of the deceased person.

(9) In this section "successor", in relation to any mortgagee or person liable in respect of any debt or claim, means his personal representatives and any other person on whom the rights under the mortgage or, as the case may be, the liability in respect of the debt or claim devolve (whether on death or bankruptcy or the disposition of property or the determination of a limited estate or interest in settled property or otherwise).

32   Postponement of limitation period in case of fraud, concealment or mistake

(1) Subject to [subsections (3) and (4A)] below, where in the case of any action for which a period of limitation is prescribed by this Act, either—

(a) the action is based upon the fraud of the defendant; or

(b) any fact relevant to the plaintiff 's right of action has been deliberately concealed from him by the defendant; or

(c) the action is for relief from the consequences of a mistake;

the period of limitation shall not begin to run until the plaintiff has discovered the fraud, concealment or mistake (as the case may be) or could with reasonable diligence have discovered it.

References in this subsection to the defendant include references to the defendant's agent and to any person through whom the defendant claims and his agent.

(2) For the purposes of subsection (1) above, deliberate commission of a breach of duty in circumstances in which it is unlikely to be discovered for some time amounts to deliberate concealment of the facts involved in that breach of duty.

(3) Nothing in this section shall enable any action—

(a) to recover, or recover the value of, any property; or

(b) to enforce any charge against, or set aside any transaction affecting, any property;

to be brought against the purchaser of the property or any person claiming through him in any case where the property has been purchased for valuable consideration by an innocent third party since the fraud or concealment or (as the case may be) the transaction in which the mistake was made took place.

(4) A purchaser is an innocent third party for the purposes of this section—

    (a) in the case of fraud or concealment of any fact relevant to the plaintiff's right of action, if he was not a party to the fraud or (as the case may be) to the concealment of that fact and did not at the time of the purchase know or have reason to believe that the fraud or concealment had taken place; and

    (b) in the case of mistake, if he did not at the time of the purchase know or have reason to believe that the mistake had been made.

[(4A) Subsection (1) above shall not apply in relation to the time limit prescribed by section 11A(3) of this Act or in relation to that time limit as applied by virtue of section 12(1) of this Act.]

[(5) Sections 14A and 14B of this Act shall not apply to any action to which subsection (1)(b) above applies (and accordingly the period of limitation referred to in that subsection, in any case to which either of those sections would otherwise apply, is the period applicable under section 23 of this Act).]

[32A Discretionary exclusion of time limit for actions for defamation or malicious falsehood

(1) If it appears to the court that it would be equitable to allow an action to proceed having regard to the degree to which—

    (a) the operation of section 4A of this Act prejudices the plaintiff or any person whom he represents, and

    (b) any decision of the court under this subsection would prejudice the defendant or any person whom he represents,

the court may direct that that section shall not apply to the action or shall not apply to any specified cause of action to which the action relates.

(2) In acting under this section the court shall have regard to all the circumstances of the case and in particular to—

    (a) the length of, and the reasons for, the delay on the part of the plaintiff;

    (b) where the reason or one of the reasons for the delay was that all or any of the facts relevant to the cause of action did not become known to the plaintiff until after the end of the period mentioned in section 4A—

        (i) the date on which any such facts did become known to him, and

        (ii) the extent to which he acted promptly and reasonably once he knew whether or not the facts in question might be capable of giving rise to an action; and

    (c) the extent to which, having regard to the delay, relevant evidence is likely—

        (i) to be unavailable, or

        (ii) to be less cogent than if the action had been brought within the period mentioned in section 4A.

(3) In the case of an action for slander of title, slander of goods or other malicious falsehood brought by a personal representative—

    (a) the references in subsection (2) above to the plaintiff shall be construed as including the deceased person to whom the cause of action accrued and any previous personal representative of that person; and

    (b) nothing in section 28(3) of this Act shall be construed as affecting the court's discretion under this section.

(4) In this section "the court" means the court in which the action has been brought.]

33   Discretionary exclusion of time limit for actions in respect of personal injuries or death

(1) If it appears to the court that it would be equitable to allow an action to proceed having regard to the degree to which—

    (a) the provisions of section 11 [or 11A] or 12 of this Act prejudice the plaintiff or any person whom he represents; and

    (b) any decision of the court under this subsection would prejudice the defendant or any person whom he represents;

the court may direct that those provisions shall not apply to the action, or shall not apply to any specified cause of action to which the action relates.

[(1A) The court shall not under this section disapply—

    (a) subsection (3) of section 11A; or

    (b) where the damages claimed by the plaintiff are confined to damages for loss of or damage to any property, any other provision in its application to an action by virtue of Part I of the Consumer Protection Act 1987.]

(2) The court shall not under this section disapply section 12(1) except where the reason why the person injured could no longer maintain an action was because of the time limit in section 11 [or subsection (4) of section 11A].

If, for example, the person injured could at his death no longer maintain an action under the Fatal Accidents Act 1976 because of the time limit in Article 29 in Schedule 1 to the Carriage by Air Act 1961, the court has no power to direct that section 12(1) shall not apply.

(3) In acting under this section the court shall have regard to all the circumstances of the case and in particular to—

    (a) the length of, and the reasons for, the delay on the part of the plaintiff;

    (b) the extent to which, having regard to the delay, the evidence adduced or likely to be adduced by the plaintiff or the defendant is or is likely to be less cogent than if the action had been brought within the time allowed by section 11 [, by section 11A] or (as the case may be) by section 12;

    (c) the conduct of the defendant after the cause of action arose, including the extent (if any) to which he responded to requests reasonably made by the plaintiff for information or inspection for the purpose of ascertaining facts which were or might be relevant to the plaintiff's cause of action against the defendant;

    (d) the duration of any disability of the plaintiff arising after the date of the accrual of the cause of action;

    (e) the extent to which the plaintiff acted promptly and reasonably once he knew whether or not the act or omission of the defendant, to which the injury was attributable, might be capable at that time of giving rise to an action for damages;

    (f) the steps, if any, taken by the plaintiff to obtain medical, legal or other expert advice and the nature of any such advice he may have received.

(4) In a case where the person injured died when, because of section 11 [or subsection (4) of section 11A], he could no longer maintain an action and recover damages in respect of the injury, the court shall have regard in particular to the length of, and the reasons for, the delay on the part of the deceased.

(5) In a case under subsection (4) above, or any other case where the time limit, or one of the time limits, depends on the date of knowledge of a person other than the plaintiff, subsection (3) above shall have effect with appropriate modifications, and shall have effect in particular as if references to the plaintiff included references to any person whose date of knowledge is or was relevant in determining a time limit.

(6) A direction by the court disapplying the provisions of section 12(1) shall operate to disapply the provisions to the same effect in section 1(1) of the Fatal Accidents Act 1976.

(7) In this section "the court" means the court in which the action has been brought.

(8) References in this section to section 11 [or 11A] include references to that section as extended by any of the preceding provisions of this Part of this Act or by any provision of Part III of this Act.

35   New claims in pending actions; rules of court

(1) For the purposes of this Act, any new claim made in the course of any action shall be deemed to be a separate action and to have been commenced—

(a) in the case of a new claim made in or by way of third party proceedings, on the date on which those proceedings were commenced; and

(b) in the case of any other new claim, on the same date as the original action.

(2) In this section a new claim means any claim by way of set-off or counterclaim, and any claim involving either—

(a) the addition or substitution of a new cause of action; or

(b) the addition or substitution of a new party;

and "third party proceedings" means any proceedings brought in the course of any action by any party to the action against a person not previously a party to the action, other than proceedings brought by joining any such person as defendant to any claim already made in the original action by the party bringing the proceedings.

(3) Except as provided by section 33 of this Act or by rules of court, neither the High Court nor any county court shall allow a new claim within subsection (1) (b) above, other than an original set-off or counterclaim, to be made in the course of any action after the expiry of any time limit under this Act which would affect a new action to enforce that claim.

For the purposes of this subsection, a claim is an original set-off or an original counterclaim if it is a claim made by way of set-off or (as the case may be) by way of counterclaim by a party who has not previously made any claim in the action.

(4) Rules of court may provide for allowing a new claim to which subsection (3) above applies to be made as there mentioned, but only if the conditions specified in subsection (5) below are satisfied, and subject to any further restrictions the rules may impose.

(5) The conditions referred to in subsection (4) above are the following—

(a) in the case of a claim involving a new cause of action, if the new cause of action arises out of the same facts or substantially the same facts as are already in issue on any claim previously made in the original action; and

(b) in the case of a claim involving a new party, if the addition or substitution of the new party is necessary for the determination of the original action.

(6) The addition or substitution of a new party shall not be regarded for the purposes of subsection (5)(b) above as necessary for the determination of the original action unless either—

(a) the new party is substituted for a party whose name was given in any claim made in the original action in mistake for the new party's name; or

(b) any claim already made in the original action cannot be maintained by or against an existing party unless the new party is joined or substituted as plaintiff or defendant in that action.

(7) Subject to subsection (4) above, rules of court may provide for allowing a party to any action to claim relief in a new capacity in respect of a new cause of action notwithstanding that he had no title to make that claim at the date of the commencement of the action.

This subsection shall not be taken as prejudicing the power of rules of court to provide for allowing a party to claim relief in a new capacity without adding or substituting a new cause of action.

(8) Subsections (3) to (7) above shall apply in relation to a new claim made in the course of third party proceedings as if those proceedings were the original action, and subject to such other modifications as maybe prescribed by rules of court in any case or class of case.

PART III

36 Equitable jurisdiction and remedies

(1) The following time limits under this Act, that is to say—

    (a) the time limit under section 2 for actions founded on tort;

    [(aa) the time limit under section 4A for actions for libel or slander;]

    (b) the time limit under section 5 for actions founded on simple contract;

    (c) the time limit under section 7 for actions to enforce awards where the submission is not by an instrument under seal;

    (d) the time limit under section 8 for actions on a specialty;

    (e) the time limit under section 9 for actions to recover a sum recoverable by virtue of any enactment; and

    (f) the time limit under section 24 for actions to enforce a judgment;

shall not apply to any claim for specific performance of a contract or for an injunction or for other equitable relief, except in so far as any such time limit may be applied by the court by analogy in like manner as the corresponding time limit under any enactment repealed by the Limitation Act 1939 was applied before 1st July 1940.

(2) Nothing in this Act shall affect any equitable jurisdiction to refuse relief on the ground of acquiescence or otherwise.

37 Application to the Crown and the Duke of Cornwall

(1) Except as otherwise expressly provided in this Act, and without prejudice to section 39, this Act shall apply to proceedings by or against the Crown in like manner as it applies to proceedings between subjects.

38 Interpretation

(1) In this Act, unless the context otherwise requires— ...

"personal injuries" includes any disease and any impairment of a person's physical or mental condition, and "injury" and cognate expressions shall be construed accordingly;

(2) For the purposes of this Act a person shall be treated as under a disability while he is an infant, or [lacks capacity (within the meaning of the Mental Capacity Act 2005) to conduct legal procedings].

39 Saving for other limitation enactments

This Act shall not apply to any action or arbitration for which a period of limitation is prescribed by or under any other enactment (whether passed before or after the passing of this Act) or to any action or arbitration to which the Crown is a party and for which, if it were between subjects, a period of limitation would be prescribed by or under any such other enactment.

British Telecommunications Act 1981
(1981, c. 38)

23 Exclusion of certain liabilities in tort in relation to telecommunications

(1) No proceedings in tort shall lie against the Corporation in respect of any loss or damage suffered by any person by reason of—

    (a) failure to provide, or delay in providing, a telecommunication service, apparatus associated therewith or a service ancillary thereto;

    (b) failure, interruption, suspension or restriction of a telecommunication service or a service ancillary thereto or delay of, or fault in, communication by means of a telecommunication service; or

    (c) error in, or omission from, a directory for use in connection with a telecommunication service.

[Senior Courts Act 1981]
[*Supreme Court Act 1981*]

(1981, c. 54)

32   Orders for interim payment

(1) As regards proceedings pending in the High Court, provision may be made by rules of court for enabling the court, in such circumstances as may be prescribed, to make an order requiring a party to the proceedings to make an interim payment of such amount as may be specified in the order, with provision for the payment to be made to such other party to the proceedings as may be so specified or, if the order so provides, by paying it into court.

(2) Any rules of court which make provision in accordance with subsection (1) may include provision for enabling a party to any proceedings who, in pursuance of such an order, has made an interim payment to recover the whole or part of the amount of the payment in such circumstances, and from such other party to the proceedings, as may be determined in accordance with the rules.

(3) Any rules made by virtue of this section may include such incidental, supplementary and consequential provisions as the rule-making authority may consider necessary or expedient.

(4) Nothing in this section shall be construed as affecting the exercise of any power relating to costs, including any power to make rules of court relating to costs.

(5) In this section "interim payment", in relation to a party to any proceedings, means a payment on account of any damages, debt or other sum (excluding any costs) which that party may be held liable to pay to or for the benefit of another party to the proceedings if a final judgment or order of the court in the proceedings is given or made in favour of that other party.

[32A   Orders for provisional damages for personal injuries

(1) This section applies to an action for damages for personal injuries in which there is proved or admitted to be a chance that at some definite or indefinite time in the future the injured person will, as a result of the act or omission which gave rise to the cause of action, develop some serious disease or suffer some serious deterioration in his physical or mental condition.

(2) Subject to subsection (4) below, as regards any action for damages to which this section applies in which a judgment is given in the High Court, provision may be made by rules of court for enabling the court, in such circumstances as may be prescribed, to award the injured person—

    (a) damages assessed on the assumption that the injured person will not develop the disease or suffer the deterioration in his condition; and

    (b) further damages at a future date if he develops the disease or suffers the deterioration.

(3) Any rules made by virtue of this section may include such incidental, supplementary and consequential provisions as the rule-making authority may consider necessary or expedient.

(4) Nothing in this section shall be construed—

    (a) as affecting the exercise of any power relating to costs, including any power to make rules of court relating to costs; or

    (b) as prejudicing any duty of the court under any enactment or rule of law to reduce or limit the total damages which would have been recoverable apart from any such duty.]

35   Provisions supplementary to ss. 33 and 34

(5) In sections [32A,] 33 and 34 and this section— ...

"personal injuries" includes any disease and any impairment of a person's physical or mental condition.

[35A   Powers of High Court to award interest on debts and damages

(1) Subject to rules of court, in proceedings (whenever instituted) before the High Court for the recovery of a debt or damages there may be included in any sum for which judgment is given simple interest, at such rate as the court thinks fit or as rules of court may provide, on all or any part of the debt or damages in respect of which judgment is given, or payment is made before judgment, for all or any part of the period between the date when the cause of action arose and—

(a) in the case of any sum paid before judgment, the date of the payment; and

(b) in the case of the sum for which judgment is given, the date of the judgment.

(2) In relation to a judgment given for damages for personal injuries or death which exceed £200 subsection (1) shall have effect—

(a) with the substitution of "shall be included" for "may be included"; and

(b) with the addition of "unless the court is satisfied that there are special reasons to the contrary" after "given", where first occurring.

(3) Subject to rules of court, where—

(a) there are proceedings (whenever instituted) before the High Court for the recovery of a debt; and

(b) the defendant pays the whole debt to the plaintiff (otherwise than in pursuance of a judgment in the proceedings),

the defendant shall be liable to pay the plaintiff simple interest at such rate as the court thinks fit or as rules of court may provide on all or any part of the debt for all or any part of the period between the date when the cause of action arose and the date of the payment.

(4) Interest in respect of a debt shall not be awarded under this section for a period during which, for whatever reason, interest on the debt already runs.

(5) Without prejudice to the generality of section 84, rules of court may provide for a rate of interest by reference to the rate specified in section 17 of the Judgments Act 1838 as that section has effect from time to time or by reference to a rate for which any other enactment provides.

(6) Interest under this section may be calculated at different rates in respect of different periods.

(7) In this section "plaintiff" means the person seeking the debt or damages and "defendant" means the person from whom the plaintiff seeks the debt or damages and "personal injuries" includes any disease and any impairment of a person's physical or mental condition.]

37   Powers of High Court with respect to injunctions and receivers

(1) The High Court may by order (whether interlocutory or final) grant an injunction or appoint a receiver in all cases in which it appears to the court to be just and convenient to do so.

49   Concurrent administration of law and equity

(1) Subject to the provisions of this or any other Act, every court exercising jurisdiction in England and Wales in any civil cause or matter shall continue to administer law and equity on the basis that, wherever there is any conflict or variance between the rules of equity and the rules of the common law with reference to the same matter, the rules of equity shall prevail.

50   Power to award damages as well as, or in substitution for, injunction or specific performance

Where the Court of Appeal or the High Court has jurisdiction to entertain an application for an injunction or specific performance, it may award damages in addition to, or in substitution for, an injunction or specific performance.

69   Trial by jury

(1) Where, on the application of any party to an action to be tried in the Queen's Bench Division, the court is satisfied that there is in issue—

(a) a charge of fraud against that party; or

(b) a claim in respect of libel, slander, malicious prosecution or false imprisonment; or

(c) any question or issue of a kind prescribed for the purposes of this paragraph,

the action shall be tried with a jury, unless the court is of opinion that the trial requires any prolonged examination of documents or accounts or any scientific or local investigation which cannot conveniently be made with a jury.

Administration of Justice Act 1982
(1982, c. 53)

1   Abolition of right to damages for loss of expectation of life

(1) In an action under the law of England and Wales or the law of Northern Ireland for damages for personal injuries—

(a) no damages shall be recoverable in respect of any loss of expectation of life caused to the injured person by the injuries; but

(b) if the injured person's expectation of life has been reduced by the injuries, the court, in assessing damages in respect of pain and suffering caused by the injuries, shall take account of any suffering caused or likely to be caused to him by awareness that his expectation of life has been so reduced.

(2) The reference in subsection (1)(a) above to damages in respect of loss of expectation of life does not include damages in respect of loss of income.

2   Abolition of actions for loss of services, etc.

No person shall be liable in tort under the law of England and Wales or the law of Northern Ireland—

(a) to a husband on the ground only of having deprived him of the services or society of his wife;

(b) to a parent (or person standing in the place of a parent) on the ground only of his having deprived him of the services of a child; or

(c) on the ground only—

(i)   of having deprived another of the services of his menial servant;

(ii) of having deprived another of the services of his female servant by raping or seducing her; or

(iii) of enticement of a servant or harbouring a servant.

5   Maintenance at public expense to be taken into account in assessment of damages

In an action under the law of England and Wales or the law of Northern Ireland for damages for personal injuries (including any such action arising out of a contract) any saving to the injured person which is attributable to his maintenance wholly or partly at public expense in a hospital, nursing home or other institution shall be set off against any income lost by him as a result of his injuries.

Civil Aviation Act 1982
(1982, c. 16)

76   Liability of aircraft in respect of trespass, nuisance and surface damage

(1) No action shall lie in respect of trespass or in respect of nuisance, by reason only of the flight of an aircraft over any property at a height above the ground which, having regard to wind, weather and all the circumstances of the case is reasonable, or the ordinary incidents

of such flight, so long as the provisions of any Air Navigation Order and of any orders under section 62 above have been duly complied with and there has been no breach of section 81 below.

(2) Subject to subsection (3) below, where material loss or damage is caused to any person or property on land or water by, or by a person in, or an article, animal or person falling from, an aircraft while in flight, taking off or landing, then unless the loss or damage was caused or contributed to by the negligence of the person by whom it was suffered, damages in respect of the loss or damage shall be recoverable without proof of negligence or intention or other cause of action, as if the loss or damage had been caused by the wilful act, neglect, or default of the owner of the aircraft.

(3) Where material loss or damage is caused as aforesaid in circumstances in which—

    (a) damages are recoverable in respect of the said loss or damage by virtue only of subsection (2) above, and

    (b) a legal liability is created in some person other than the owner to pay damages in respect of the said loss or damage,

the owner shall be entitled to be indemnified by that other person against any claim in respect of the said loss or damage.

77 Nuisance caused by aircraft on aerodromes

(1) An Air Navigation Order may provide for regulating the conditions under which noise and vibration may be caused by aircraft on aerodromes and may provide that subsection (2) below shall apply to any aerodrome as respects which provision as to noise and vibration caused by aircraft is so made.

(2) No action shall lie in respect of nuisance by reason only of the noise and vibration caused by aircraft on an aerodrome to which this subsection applies by virtue of an Air Navigation Order, as long as the provisions of any such Order are duly complied with.

Forfeiture Act 1982
(1982, c. 34)

1 The "forfeiture rule"

(1) In this Act, the "forfeiture rule" means the rule of public policy which in certain circumstances precludes a person who has unlawfully killed another from acquiring a benefit in consequence of the killing . . .

2 Power to modify the rule

(1) Where a court determines that the forfeiture rule has precluded a person (in this section referred to as "the offender") who has unlawfully killed another from acquiring any interest in property mentioned in subsection (4) below, the court may make an order under this section modifying the effect of that rule.

(2) The court shall not make an order under this section modifying the effect of the forfeiture rule in any case unless it is satisfied that, having regard to the conduct of the offender and of the deceased and to such other circumstances as appear to the court to be material, the justice of the case requires the effect of the rule to be so modified in that case.

(3) In any case where a person stands convicted of an offence of which unlawful killing is an element, the court shall not make an order under this section modifying the effect of the forfeiture rule in that case unless proceedings for the purpose are brought before the expiry of the period of three months beginning with his conviction.

(4) The interests in property referred to in subsection (1) above are—

    (a) any beneficial interest in property which (apart from the forfeiture rule) the offender would have acquired—

(i)   under the deceased's will (including, as respects Scotland, any writing having testamentary effect) or the law relating to intestacy or by way of ius relicti, ius relictae or legitim;

(ii) on the nomination of the deceased in accordance with the provisions of any enactment;

(iii) as a donatio mortis causa made by the deceased; or

(iv) under a special destination (whether relating to heritable or moveable property); or

(b) any beneficial interest in property which (apart from the forfeiture rule) the offender would have acquired in consequence of the death of the deceased, being property which, before the death, was held on trust for any person.

(5) An order under this section may modify the effect of the forfeiture rule in respect of any interest in property to which the determination referred to in subsection (1) above relates and may do so in either or both of the following ways, that is—

(a) where there is more than one such interest, by excluding the application of the rule in respect of any (but not all) of those interests; and

(b) in the case of any such interest in property, by excluding the application of the rule in respect of part of the property.

(6) On the making of an order under this section, the forfeiture rule shall have effect for all purposes (including purposes relating to anything done before the order is made) subject to the modifications made by the order . . . .

5   Exclusion of murderers

Nothing in this Act or in any order made under section 2 or referred to in section 3(1) of this Act shall affect the application of the forfeiture rule in the case of a person who stands convicted of murder.

Supply of Goods and Services Act 1982
(1982, c. 29)

PART I   SUPPLY OF GOODS

Contracts for the transfer of property in goods

1   The contracts concerned

(1) In this Act [in its application to England and Wales and Northern Ireland] "contract for the transfer of goods" means a contract under which one person transfers or agrees to transfer to another the property in goods, other than an excepted contract.

(2) For the purposes of this section an excepted contract means any of the following:—

(a) a contract of sale of goods;

(b) a hire-purchase agreement;

[...]

(d) a transfer or agreement to transfer which is made by deed and for which there is no consideration other than the presumed consideration imported by the deed;

(e) a contract intended to operate by way of mortgage, pledge, charge or other security.

(3) For the purposes of this Act [in its application to England and Wales and Northern Ireland] a contract is a contract for the transfer of goods whether or not services are also provided or to be provided under the contract, and (subject to subsection (2) above) whatever is the nature of the consideration for the transfer or agreement to transfer.

2 Implied terms about title, etc.

(1) In a contract for the transfer of goods, other than one to which subsection (3) below applies, there is an implied condition on the part of the transferor that in the case of a transfer of the property in the goods he has a right to transfer the property and in the case of an agreement to transfer the property in the goods he will have such a right at the time when the property is to be transferred.

(2) In a contract for the transfer of goods, other than one to which subsection (3) below applies, there is also an implied warranty that—

(a) the goods are free, and will remain free until the time when the property is to be transferred, from any charge or encumbrance not disclosed or known to the transferee before the contract is made, and

(b) the transferee will enjoy quiet possession of the goods except so far as it may be disturbed by the owner or other person entitled to the benefit of any charge or encumbrance so disclosed or known.

(3) This subsection applies to a contract for the transfer of goods in the case of which there appears from the contract or is to be inferred from its circumstances an intention that the transferor should transfer only such title as he or a third person may have.

(4) In a contract to which subsection (3) above applies there is an implied warranty that all charges or encumbrances known to the transferor and not known to the transferee have been disclosed to the transferee before the contract is made.

(5) In a contract to which subsection (3) above applies there is also an implied warranty that none of the following will disturb the transferee's quiet possession of the goods, namely—

(a) the transferor;

(b) in a case where the parties to the contract intend that the transferor should transfer only such title as a third person may have, that person;

(c) anyone claiming through or under the transferor or that third person otherwise than under a charge or encumbrance disclosed or known to the transferee before the contract is made.

3 Implied terms where transfer is by description

(1) This section applies where, under a contract for the transfer of goods, the transferor transfers or agrees to transfer the property in the goods by description.

(2) In such case there is an implied condition that the goods will correspond with the description.

(3) If the transferor transfers or agrees to transfer the property in the goods by sample as well as by description it is not sufficient that the bulk of the goods corresponds with the sample if the goods do not also correspond with the description.

(4) A contract is not prevented from falling within subsection (1) above by reason only that, being exposed for supply, the goods are selected by the transferee.

4 Implied terms about quality or fitness

(1) Except as provided by this section and section 5 below and subject to the provision of any other enactment, there is no implied condition or warranty about the quality or fitness for any particular purpose of goods supplied under a contract for the transfer of goods.

[(2) Where, under such a contract, the transferor transfers the property in goods in the course of a business, there is an implied condition that the goods supplied under the contract are of satisfactory quality.

(2A) For the purposes of this section and section 5 below, goods are of satisfactory quality if they meet the standard that a reasonable person would regard as satisfactory, taking account of any description of the goods, the price (if relevant) and all the other relevant circumstances.]

[(2B) If the transferee deals as consumer, the relevant circumstances mentioned in sub-section (2A) above include any public statements on the specific characteristics of the goods made about them by the transferor, the producer or his representative, particularly in advertising or on labelling.

(2C) A public statement is not by virtue of subsection (2B) above a relevant circumstance for the purposes of subsection (2A) above in the case of a contract for the transfer of goods, if the transferor shows that—

(a) at the time the contract was made, he was not, and could not reasonably have been, aware of the statement,

(b) before the contract was made, the statement had been withdrawn in public or, to the extent that it contained anything which was incorrect or misleading, it had been corrected in public, or

(c) the decision to acquire the goods could not have been influenced by the statement.

(2D) Subsections (2B) and (2C) above do not prevent any public statement from being a relevant circumstance for the purposes of subsection (2A) above (whether or not the transferee deals as consumer) if the statement would have been such a circumstance apart from those subsections.]

[(3) The condition implied by subsection (2) above does not extend to any matter making the quality of goods unsatisfactory—

(a) which is specifically drawn to the transferee's attention before the contract is made,

(b) where the transferee examines the goods before the contract is made, which that examination ought to reveal, or

(c) where the property in the goods is transferred by reference to a sample, which would have been apparent on a reasonable examination of the sample.]

(4) Subsection (5) below applies where, under a contract for the transfer of goods, the transferor transfers the property in goods in the course of a business and the transferee, expressly or by implication, makes known—

(a) to the transferor, or

(b) where the consideration or part of the consideration for the transfer is a sum payable by instalments and the goods were previously sold by a credit-broker to the transferor, to that credit-broker,

any particular purpose for which the goods are being acquired.

(5) In that case there is (subject to subsection (6) below) an implied condition that the goods supplied under the contract are reasonably fit for that purpose, whether or not that is a purpose for which such goods are commonly supplied.

(6) Subsection (5) above does not apply where the circumstances show that the transferee does not rely, or that it is unreasonable for him to rely, on the skill or judgment of the transferor or credit-broker.

(7) An implied condition or warranty about quality or fitness for a particular purpose may be annexed by usage to a contract for the transfer of goods.

(8) The preceding provisions of this section apply to a transfer by a person who in the course of a business is acting as agent for another as they apply to a transfer by a principal in the course of a business, except where that other is not transferring in the course of a business and either the transferee knows that fact or reasonable steps are taken to bring it to the transferee's notice before the contract concerned is made.

5 Implied terms where transfer is by sample

(1) This section applies where, under a contract for the transfer of goods, the transferor transfers or agrees to transfer the property in the goods by reference to a sample.

(2) In such a case there is an implied condition—

(a) that the bulk will correspond with the sample in quality; and

(b) that the transferee will have a reasonable opportunity of comparing the bulk with the sample; and

(c) that the goods will be free from any defect, [making their quality unsatisfactory], which would not be apparent on reasonable examination of the sample.

(4) For the purposes of this section a transferor transfers or agrees to transfer the property in goods by reference to a sample where there is an express or implied term to that effect in the contract concerned.

[5A   Modification of remedies for breach of statutory condition in non-consumer cases

(1) Where in the case of a contract for the transfer of goods—

(a) the transferee would, apart from this subsection, have the right to treat the contract as repudiated by reason of a breach on the part of the transferor of a term implied by section 3, 4 or 5(2)(a) or (c) above, but

(b) the breach is so slight that it would be unreasonable for him to do so,

then, if the transferee does not deal as consumer, the breach is not to be treated as a breach of condition but may be treated as a breach of warranty.

(2) This section applies unless a contrary intention appears in, or is to be implied from, the contract.

(3) It is for the transferor to show that a breach fell within subsection (1)(b) above.]

Contracts for the hire of goods

6   The contracts concerned

(1) In this Act [in its application to England and Wales and Northern Ireland] a "contract for the hire of goods" means a contract under which one person bails or agrees to bail goods to another by way of hire, other than [a hire-purchase agreement].

(3) For the purposes of this Act [in its application to England and Wales and Northern Ireland] a contract is a contract for the hire of goods whether or not services are also provided or to be provided under the contract, and [. . .] whatever is the nature of the consideration for the bailment or agreement to bail by way of hire.

7   Implied terms about right to transfer possession, etc

(1) In a contract for the hire of goods there is an implied condition on the part of the bailor that in the case of a bailment he has a right to transfer possession of the goods by way of hire for the period of the bailment and in the case of an agreement to bail he will have such a right at the time of the bailment.

(2) In a contract for the hire of goods there is also an implied warranty that the bailee will enjoy quiet possession of the goods for the period of the bailment except so far as the possession may be disturbed by the owner or other person entitled to the benefit of any charge or encumbrance disclosed or known to the bailee before the contract is made.

(3) The preceding provisions of this section do not affect the right of the bailor to repossess the goods under an express or implied term of the contract.

8   Implied terms where hire is by description

(1) This section applies where, under a contract for the hire of goods, the bailor bails or agrees to bail the goods by description.

(2) In such a case there is an implied condition that the goods will correspond with the description.

(3) If under the contract the bailor bails or agrees to bail the goods by reference to a sample as well as a description it is not sufficient that the bulk of the goods corresponds with the sample if the goods do not also correspond with the description.

(4) A contract is not prevented from falling within subsection (1) above by reason only that, being exposed for supply, the goods are selected by the bailee.

9 Implied terms about quality or fitness

(1) Except as provided by this section and section 10 below and subject to the provisions of any other enactment, there is no implied condition or warranty about the quality or fitness for any particular purpose of goods bailed under a contract for the hire of goods.

[(2) Where, under such a contract, the bailor bails goods in the course of a business, there is an implied condition that the goods supplied under the contract are of satisfactory quality.]

[(2A) For the purposes of this section and section 10 below, goods are of satisfactory quality if they meet the standard that a reasonable person would regard as satisfactory, taking account of any description of the goods, the consideration for the bailment (if relevant) and all the other relevant circumstances.]

[(2B) If the bailee deals as consumer, the relevant circumstances mentioned in subsection (2A) above include any public statements on the specific characteristics of the goods made about them by the bailor, the producer or his representative, particularly in advertising or on labelling.

(2C) A public statement is not by virtue of subsection (2B) above a relevant circumstance for the purposes of subsection (2A) above in the case of a contract for the hire of goods, if the bailor shows that—

(a) at the time the contract was made, he was not, and could not reasonably have been, aware of the statement,

(b) before the contract was made, the statement had been withdrawn in public or, to the extent that it contained anything which was incorrect or misleading, it had been corrected in public, or

(c) the decision to acquire the goods could not have been influenced by the statement.

(2D) Subsections (2B) and (2C) above do not prevent any public statement from being a relevant circumstance for the purposes of subsection (2A) above (whether or not the bailee deals as consumer) if the statement would have been such a circumstance apart from those subsections.]

[(3) The condition implied by subsection (2) above does not extend to any matter making the quality of goods unsatisfactory—

(a) which is specifically drawn to the bailee's attention before the contract is made,

(b) where the bailee examines the goods before the contract is made, which that examination ought to reveal, or

(c) where the goods are bailed by reference to a sample, which would have been apparent on a reasonable examination of the sample.]

(4) Subsection (5) below applies where, under a contract for the hire of goods, the bailor bails goods in the course of a business and the bailee, expressly or by implication, makes known—

(a) to the bailor in the course of negotiations conducted by him in relation to the making of the contract, or

(b) to a credit-broker in the course of negotiations conducted by that broker in relation to goods sold by him to the bailor before forming the subject matter of the contract,

any particular purpose for which the goods are being bailed.

(5) In that case there is (subject to subsection (6) below) an implied condition that the goods supplied under the contract are reasonably fit for that purpose, whether or not that is a purpose for which such goods are commonly supplied.

(6) Subsection (5) above does not apply where the circumstances show that the bailee does not rely, or that it is unreasonable for him to rely, on the skill or judgment of the bailor or credit-broker.

(7) An implied condition or warranty about quality or fitness for a particular purpose may be annexed by usage to a contract for the hire of goods.

(8) The preceding provisions of this section apply to a bailment by a person who in the course of a business is acting as agent for another as they apply to a bailment by a principal in the course of a business, except where that other is not bailing in the course of a business and either the bailee knows that fact or reasonable steps are taken to bring it to the bailee's notice before the contract concerned is made.

10   Implied terms where hire is by sample

(1) This section applies where, under a contract for the hire of goods, the bailor bails or agrees to bail the goods by reference to a sample.

(2) In such a case there is an implied condition—

(a) that the bulk will correspond with the sample in quality; and

(b) that the bailee will have a reasonable opportunity of comparing the bulk with the sample; and

(c) that the goods will be free from any defect, [making their quality unsatisfactory], which would not be apparent on reasonable examination of the sample.

(4) For the purposes of this section a bailor bails or agrees to bail goods by reference to a sample where there is an express or implied term to that effect in the contract concerned.

[10A   Modification of remedies for breach of statutory condition in non-consumer cases

(1) Where in the case of a contract for the hire of goods—

(a) the bailee would, apart from this subsection, have the right to treat the contract as repudiated by reason of a breach on the part of the bailor of a term implied by section 8, 9 or 10(2)(a) or (c) above, but

(b) the breach is so slight that it would be unreasonable for him to do so,

then, if the bailee does not deal as consumer, the breach is not to be treated as a breach of condition but may be treated as a breach of warranty.

(2) This section applies unless a contrary intention appears in, or is to be implied from, the contract.

(3) It is for the bailor to show that a breach fell within subsection (1)(b) above.]

Exclusion of implied terms, etc.

11   Exclusion of implied terms, etc.

(1) Where a right, duty or liability would arise under a contract for the transfer of goods or a contract for the hire of goods by implication of law, it may (subject to subsection (2) below and the 1977 Act) be negatived or varied by express agreement, or by the course of dealing between the parties, or by such usage as binds both parties to the contract.

(2) An express condition or warranty does not negative a condition or warranty implied by the preceding provisions of this Act unless inconsistent with it.

(3) Nothing in the preceding provisions of this Act prejudices the operation of any other enactment or any rule of law whereby any condition or warranty (other than one relating to quality or fitness) is to be implied in a contract for the transfer of goods or a contract for the hire of goods.

[PART IA   SUPPLY OF GOODS AS RESPECTS SCOTLAND . . .]

[PART 1B   ADDITIONAL RIGHTS OF TRANSFEREE IN CONSUMER CASES

[11M   Introductory

(1) This section applies if—

(a) the transferee deals as consumer or, in Scotland, there is a consumer contract in which the transferee is a consumer, and

(b) the goods do not conform to the contract for the transfer of goods at the time of delivery.

(2) If this section applies, the transferee has the right—

(a) under and in accordance with section 11N below, to require the transferor to repair or replace the goods, or

(b) under and in accordance with section 11P below—

(i) to require the transferor to reduce the amount to be paid for the transfer by the transferee by an appropriate amount, or

(ii) to rescind the contract with regard to the goods in question.

(3) For the purposes of subsection (1)(b) above, goods which do not conform to the contract for the transfer of goods at any time within the period of six months starting with the date on which the goods were delivered to the transferee must be taken not to have so conformed at that date.

(4) Subsection (3) above does not apply if—

(a) it is established that the goods did so conform at that date;

(b) its application is incompatible with the nature of the goods or the nature of the lack of conformity.

(5) For the purposes of this section, "consumer contract" has the same meaning as in section 11F(3) above.]

[11N   Repair or replacement of the goods

(1) If section 11M above applies, the transferee may require the transferor—

(a) to repair the goods, or

(b) to replace the goods.

(2) If the transferee requires the transferor to repair or replace the goods, the transferor must—

(a) repair or, as the case may be, replace the goods within a reasonable time but without causing significant inconvenience to the transferee;

(b) bear any necessary costs incurred in doing so (including in particular the cost of any labour, materials or postage).

(3) The transferee must not require the transferor to repair or, as the case may be, replace the goods if that remedy is—

(a) impossible,

(b) disproportionate in comparison to the other of those remedies, or

(c) disproportionate in comparison to an appropriate reduction in the purchase price under paragraph (a), or rescission under paragraph (b), of section 11P(1) below.

(4) One remedy is disproportionate in comparison to the other if the one imposes costs on the transferor which, in comparison to those imposed on him by the other, are unreasonable, taking into account—

(a) the value which the goods would have if they conformed to the contract for the transfer of goods,

(b) the significance of the lack of conformity to the contract for the transfer of goods, and

(c) whether the other remedy could be effected without significant inconvenience to the transferee.

(5) Any question as to what is a reasonable time or significant inconvenience is to be determined by reference to—

(a) the nature of the goods, and

(b) the purpose for which the goods were acquired.]

[11P   Reduction of purchase price or rescission of contract

(1) If section 11M above applies, the transferee may—

(a) require the transferor to reduce the purchase price of the goods in question to the transferee by an appropriate amount, or

    (b) rescind the contract with regard to those goods,
if the condition in subsection (2) below is satisfied.
    (2) The condition is that—
        (a) by virtue of section 11N(3) above the transferee may require neither repair nor replacement of the goods, or
        (b) the transferee has required the transferor to repair or replace the goods, but the transferor is in breach of the requirement of section 11N(2)(a) above to do so within a reasonable time and without significant inconvenience to the transferee.
    (3) If the transferee rescinds the contract, any reimbursement to the transferee may be reduced to take account of the use he has had of the goods since they were delivered to him.]

[11Q Relation to other remedies etc.

    (1) If the transferee requires the transferor to repair or replace the goods the transferee must not act under subsection (2) until he has given the transferor a reasonable time in which to repair or replace (as the case may be) the goods.
    (2) The transferee acts under this subsection if—
        (a) in England and Wales or Northern Ireland he rejects the goods and terminates the contract for breach of condition;
        (b) in Scotland he rejects any goods delivered under the contract and treats it as repudiated; or
        (c) he requires the goods to be replaced or repaired (as the case may be).]

[11R Powers of the court

    (1) In any proceedings in which a remedy is sought by virtue of this Part the court, in addition to any other power it has, may act under this section.
    (2) On the application of the transferee the court may make an order requiring specific performance or, in Scotland, specific implement by the transferor of any obligation imposed on him by virtue of section 11N above.
    (3) Subsection (4) applies if—
        (a) the transferee requires the transferor to give effect to a remedy under section 11N or 11P above or has claims to rescind under section 11P, but
        (b) the court decides that another remedy under section 11N or 11P is appropriate.
    (4) The court may proceed—
        (a) as if the transferee had required the transferor to give effect to the other remedy, or if the other remedy is rescission under section 11P,
        (b) as if the transferee had claimed to rescind the contract under that section.
    (5) If the transferee has claimed to rescind the contract the court may order that any reimbursement to the transferee is reduced to take account of the use he has had of the goods since they were delivered to him.
    (6) The court may make an order under this section unconditionally or on such terms and conditions as to damages, payment of the price and otherwise as it thinks just.]

[11S Conformity with the contract

    (1) Goods do not conform to a contract for the supply or transfer of goods if—
        (a) there is, in relation to the goods, a breach of an express term of the contract or a term implied by section 3, 4 or 5 above or, in Scotland, by section 11C, 11D or 11E above, or
        (b) installation of the goods forms part of the contract for the transfer of goods, and the goods were installed by the transferor, or under his responsibility, in breach of the term implied by section 13 below or (in Scotland) in breach of any term implied by any rule of law as to the manner in which the installation is carried out.]

PART II   SUPPLY OF SERVICES

12   The contracts concerned

(1) In this Act a "contract for the supply of a service" means, subject to subsection (2) below, a contract under which a person ("the supplier") agrees to carry out a service.

(2) For the purposes of this Act, a contract of service or apprenticeship is not a contract for the supply of a service.

(3) Subject to subsection (2) above, a contract is a contract for the supply of a service for the purposes of this Act whether or not goods are also—

(a) transferred or to be transferred, or

(b) bailed or to be bailed by way of hire,

under the contract, and whatever is the nature of the consideration for which the service is to be carried out.

(4) The Secretary of State may by order provide that one or more of sections 13 to 15 below shall not apply to services of a description specified in the order, and such an order may make different provision for different circumstances.

(5) The power to make an order under subsection (4) above shall be exercisable by statutory instrument subject to annulment in pursuance of a resolution of either House of Parliament.

13   Implied term about care and skill

In a contract for the supply of a service where the supplier is acting in the course of a business, there is an implied term that the supplier will carry out the service with reasonable care and skill.

14   Implied term about time of performance

(1) Where, under a contract for the supply of a service by a supplier acting in the course of a business, the time for the service to be carried out is not fixed by the contract, left to be fixed in a manner agreed by the contract or determined by the course of dealing between the parties, there is an implied term that the supplier will carry out the service within a reasonable time.

(2) What is a reasonable time is a question of fact.

15   Implied term about consideration

(1) Where, under a contract for the supply of a service, the consideration for the service is not determined by the contract, left to be determined in a manner agreed by the contract or determined by the course of dealing between the parties, there is an implied term that the party contracting with the supplier will pay a reasonable charge.

(2) What is a reasonable charge is a question of fact.

16   Exclusion of implied terms, etc.

(1) Where a right, duty or liability would arise under a contract for the supply of a service by virtue of this Part of this Act, it may (subject to subsection (2) below and the 1977 Act) be negatived or varied by express agreement, or by the course of dealing between the parties, or by such usage as binds both parties to the contract.

(2) An express term does not negative a term implied by this Part of this Act unless inconsistent with it.

(3) Nothing in this Part of this Act prejudices—

(a) any rule of law which imposes on the supplier a duty stricter than that imposed by section 13 or 14 above; or

(b) subject to paragraph (a) above, any rule of law whereby any term not inconsistent with this Part of this Act is to be implied in a contract for the supply of a service.

(4) This Part of this Act has effect subject to any other enactment which defines or restricts the rights, duties or liabilities arising in connection with a service of any description.

PART III   SUPPLEMENTARY

18   Interpretation: general

(1) In the preceding provisions of this Act and this section—

"bailee", in relation to a contract for the hire of goods means (depending on the context) a person to whom the goods are bailed under the contract, or a person to whom they are to be so bailed, or a person to whom the rights under the contract of either of those persons have passed;

"bailor", in relation to a contract for the hire of goods, means (depending on the context) a person who bails the goods under the contract, or a person who agrees to do so, or a person to whom the duties under the contract of either of those persons have passed;

"business" includes a profession and the activities of any government department or local or public authority;

"credit-broker" means a person acting in the course of a business of credit brokerage carried on by him;

"credit brokerage" means the effecting of introductions—

(a) of individuals desiring to obtain credit to persons carrying on any business so far as it relates to the provision of credit; or

(b) of individuals desiring to obtain goods on hire to persons carrying on a business which comprises or relates to the bailment [or as regards Scotland the hire] of goods under a contract for the hire of goods; or

(c) of individuals desiring to obtain credit, or to obtain goods on hire, to other credit-brokers;

"enactment" means any legislation (including subordinate legislation) of the United Kingdom or Northern Ireland;

"goods" [includes all personal chattels, other than things in action and money, and as regards Scotland all corporeal moveables; and in particular "goods" includes] emblements, industrial growing crops, and things attached to or forming part of the land which are agreed to be severed before the transfer [bailment or hire] concerned or under the contract concerned];

"hire-purchase agreement" has the same meaning as in the 1974 Act;

["producer" means the manufacturer of goods, the importer of goods into the European Economic Area or any person purporting to be a producer by placing his name, trade mark or other distinctive sign on the goods;]

"property", in relation to goods, means the general property in them and not merely a special property;

["repair" means, in cases where there is a lack of conformity in goods for the purposes of this Act, to bring the goods into conformity with the contract.]

"transferee", in relation to a contract for the transfer of goods, means (depending on the context) a person to whom the property in the goods is transferred under the contract, or a person to whom the property is to be so transferred, or a person to whom the rights under the contract of either of those persons have passed;

"transferor", in relation to a contract for the transfer of goods, means (depending on the context) a person who transfers the property in the goods under the contract, or a person who agrees to do so, or a person to whom the duties under the contract of either of those persons have passed.

(2) In subsection (1) above, in the definitions of bailee, bailor, transferee and transferor, a reference to rights or duties passing is to their passing by assignment, [assignation] operation of law or otherwise.

[(3) For the purposes of this Act, the quality of goods includes their state and condition and the following (among others) are in appropriate cases aspects of the quality of goods—

(a) fitness for all the purposes for which goods of the kind in question are commonly supplied,

(b) appearance and finish,

    (c) freedom from minor defects,

    (d) safety, and

    (e) durability.

  (4) References to this Act to dealing as consumer are to be construed in accordance with Part I of the Unfair Contract Terms Act 1977; and, for the purposes of this Act, it is for the transferor or bailor claiming that the transferee or bailee does not deal as consumer to show that he does not.]

19 Interpretation: references to Acts
In this Act—

    "the 1973 Act" means the Supply of Goods (Implied Terms) Act 1973;

    "the 1974 Act" means the Consumer Credit Act 1974;

    "the 1977 Act" means the Unfair Contract Terms Act 1977; and

    "the 1979 Act" means the Sale of Goods Act 1979.

20 Citation, transitional provisions, commencement and extent
  (1) This Act may be cited as the Supply of Goods and Services Act 1982.

  . . .

Building Act 1984
(1984, c. 55)

1 Power to make building regulations
  (1) The Secretary of State may, for any of the purposes of—

    (a) securing the health, safety, welfare and convenience of persons in or about buildings and of others who may be affected by buildings or matters connected with buildings,

    (b) [(b) furthering the conservation of fuel and power,

    (c) preventing waste, undue consumption, misuse or contamination of water,

    (d) furthering the protection or enhancement of the environment,

    (e) facilitating sustainable development, or

    (f) furthering the prevention or detection of crime,]

make regulations with respect to the [matters mentioned in subsection (1A) below] of buildings and the provision of services, fittings and equipment in or in connection with buildings.

  [(1A) Those matters are—

    (a) the design and construction of buildings;

    (b) the demolition of buildings;

    (c) services, fittings and equipment provided in or in connection with buildings.]

38 Civil liability
  (1) Subject to this section—

    (a) breach of a duty imposed by building regulations, so far as it causes damage, is actionable, except in so far as the regulations provide otherwise, and

    (b) as regards such a duty, building regulations may provide for a prescribed defence to be available in an action for breach of that duty brought by virtue of this subsection.

  (2) Subsection (1) above, and any defence provided for in regulations made by virtue of it, do not apply in the case of a breach of such a duty in connection with a building erected before the date on which that subsection comes into force unless the regulations imposing the duty apply to or in connection with the building by virtue of section 2(2) [or 2A] above or paragraph 8 of Schedule 1 to this Act.

  (3) This section does not affect the extent (if any) to which breach of—

    (a) a duty imposed by or arising in connection with this Part of this Act or any other enactment relating to building regulations, or

(b) a duty imposed by building regulations in a case to which subsection (1) above does not apply,

is actionable, or prejudice a right of action that exists apart from the enactments relating to building regulations.

(4) In this section, "damage" includes the death of, or injury to, any person (including any disease and any impairment of a person's physical or mental condition).

Occupiers' Liability Act 1984
(1984, c. 3)

1 Duty of occupier to persons other than his visitors

(1) The rules enacted by this section shall have effect, in place of the rules of the common law, to determine—

    (a) whether any duty is owed by a person as occupier of premises to persons other than his visitors in respect of any risk of their suffering injury on the premises by reason of any danger due to the state of the premises or to things done or omitted to be done on them; and

    (b) if so, what that duty is.

(2) For the purposes of this section, the persons who are to be treated respectively as an occupier of any premises (which, for those purposes, include any fixed or movable structure) and as his visitors are—

    (a) any person who owes in relation to the premises the duty referred to in section 2 of the Occupiers' Liability Act 1957 (the common duty of care), and

    (b) those who are his visitors for the purposes of that duty.

(3) An occupier of premises owes a duty to another (not being his visitor) in respect of any such risk as is referred to in subsection (1) above if—

    (a) he is aware of the danger or has reasonable grounds to believe that it exists;

    (b) he knows or has reasonable grounds to believe that the other is in the vicinity of the danger concerned or that he may come into the vicinity of the danger (in either case, whether the other has lawful authority for being in that vicinity or not); and

    (c) the risk is one against which, in all the circumstances of the case, he may reasonably be expected to offer the other some protection.

(4) Where, by virtue of this section, an occupier of premises owes a duty to another in respect of such a risk, the duty is to take such care as is reasonable in all the circumstances of the case to see that he does not suffer injury on the premises by reason of the danger concerned.

(5) Any duty owed by virtue of this section in respect of a risk may, in an appropriate case, be discharged by taking such steps as are reasonable inall the circumstances of the case to give warning of the danger concerned or to discourage persons from incurring the risk.

(6) No duty is owed by virtue of this section to any person in respect of risks willingly accepted as his by that person (the question whether a risk was so accepted to be decided on the same principles as in other cases in which one person owes a duty of care to another).

[(6A) At any time when the right conferred by section 2(1) of the Countryside and Rights of Way Act 2000 is exercisable in relation to land which is access land for the purposes of Part I of that Act, an occupier of the land owes (subject to subsection (6C) below) no duty by virtue of this section to any person in respect of—

    (a) a risk resulting from the existence of any natural feature of the landscape, or any river, stream, ditch or pond whether or not a natural feature, or

    (b) a risk of that person suffering injury when passing over, under or through any wall, fence or gate, except by proper use of the gate or of a stile.

(6B) For the purposes of subsection (6A) above, any plant, shrub or tree, of whatever origin, is to be regarded as a natural feature of the landscape.

(6C) Subsection (6A) does not prevent an occupier from owing a duty by virtue of this section in respect of any risk where the danger concerned is due to anything done by the occupier—

(a) with the intention of creating that risk, or
(b) being reckless as to whether that risk is created.]

(7) No duty is owed by virtue of this section to persons using the highway, and this section does not affect any duty owed to such persons.

(8) Where a person owes a duty by virtue of this section, he does not, by reason of any breach of the duty, incur any liability in respect of any loss of or damage to property.

(9) In this section—

"highway" means any part of a highway other than a ferry or waterway;

"injury" means anything resulting in death or personal injury, including any disease and any impairment of physical or mental condition; and

"movable structure" includes any vessel, vehicle or aircraft.

[1A   Special considerations relating to access land

In determining whether any, and if so what, duty is owed by virtue of section 1 by an occupier of land at any time when the right conferred by section 2(1) of the Countryside and Rights of Way Act 2000 is exercisable in relation to the land, regard is to be had, in particular, to—

(a) the fact that the existence of that right ought not to place an undue burden (whether financial or otherwise) on the occupier,
(b) the importance of maintaining the character of the countryside, including features of historic, traditional or archaeological interest, and
(c) any relevant guidance given under section 20 of that Act.]

3   Application to Crown

Section 1 of this Act shall bind the Crown, but as regards the Crown's liability in tort shall not bind the Crown further than the Crown is made liable in tort by the Crown Proceedings Act 1947.

Police and Criminal Evidence Act 1984
(1984, c. 60)

17   Entry for purpose of arrest etc.

(1) Subject to the following provisions of this section, and without prejudice to any other enactment, a constable may enter and search any premises for the purpose—

(a) of executing—
    (i) a warrant of arrect issued in connection with or arising out of criminal proceedings; or
    (ii) a warrant of commitment issued under section 76 of the Magistrates' Courts Act 1980;
(b) of arresting a person for an [indictable] offence; ...
(e) of saving life or limb or preventing serious damage to property.

(4) The power of search conferred by this section is only a power to search to the extent that is reasonably required for the purpose for which the power of entry is exercised.

(5) Subject to subsection (6) below, all the rules of common law under which a constable has power to enter premises without a warrant are hereby abolished.

(6) Nothing in subsection (5) above affects any power of entry to deal with or prevent a breach of the peace.

19   General power of seizure etc.

(1) The powers conferred by subsections (2), (3) and (4) below are exercisable by a constable who is lawfully on any premises.

(2) The constable may seize anything which is on the premises if he has reasonable grounds for believing—

> (a) that it has been obtained in consequence of the commission of an offence; and
>
> (b) that it is necessary to seize it in order to prevent it being concealed, lost, damaged, altered or destroyed.

22   Retention

(1) Subject to subsection (4) below, anything which has been seized by a constable or taken away by a constable following a requirement made by virtue of section 19 or 20 above may be retained so long as is necessary in all the circumstances.

(3) Nothing seized on the ground that it may be used—

> (a) to cause physical injury to any person;
>
> (b) to damage property;
>
> (c) to interfere with evidence; or
>
> (d) to assist in escape from police detention or lawful custody,

may be retained when the person from whom it was seized is no longer in police detention or the custody of a court or is in the custody of a court but has been released on bail.

[*1. SI 2003/174, art. 5 provides that, for the purposes of the Proceeds of Crime Act 2002, s. 22(3) is omitted and s. 22(1) is amended thus: "Subject to subsection (4) below, anything which has been seized by [an appropriate person (within the meaning of Part 8 of the Proceeds of Crime Act 2002)] or taken away by [an appropriate person under a search and seizure warrant issued under section 352 of the Proceeds of Crime Act 2002 for the purposes of a confiscation investigation or a money laundering investigation] may be retained [by the appropriate person or an appropriate officer (within the meaning of Part 8 of the Proceeds of Crime Act 2002)] so long as is necessary in all the circumstances."*]

[24   Arrest without warrant: constables

(1) A constable may arrest without a warrant—

> (a) anyone who is about to commit an offence;
>
> (b) anyone who is in the act of committing an offence;
>
> (c) anyone whom he has reasonable grounds for suspecting to be about to commit an offence;
>
> (d) anyone whom he has reasonable grounds for suspecting to be committing an offence.

(2) If a constable has reasonable grounds for suspecting that an offence has been committed, he may arrest without a warrant anyone whom he has reasonable grounds to suspect of being guilty of it.

(3) If an offence has been committed, a constable may arrest without a warrant—

> (a) anyone who is guilty of the offence;
>
> (b) anyone whom he has reasonable grounds for suspecting to be guilty of it.

(4) But the power of summary arrest conferred by subsection (1), (2) or (3) is exercisable only if the constable has reasonable grounds for believing that for any of the reasons mentioned in subsection (5) it is necessary to arrest the person in question.

(5) The reasons are—

> (a) to enable the name of the person in question to be ascertained (in the case where the constable does not know, and cannot readily ascertain, the person's name, or has reasonable grounds for doubting whether a name given by the person as his name is his real name);
>
> (b) correspondingly as regards the person's address;

    (c) to prevent the person in question—
        (i)   causing physical injury to himself or any other person;
        (ii) suffering physical injury;
        (iii) causing loss of or damage to property;
        (iv) committing an offence against public decency (subject to subsection (6)); or
        (v) causing an unlawful obstruction of the highway;
    (d) to protect a child or other vulnerable person from the person in question;
    (e) to allow the prompt and effective investigation of the offence or of the conduct of the person in question;
    (f) to prevent any prosecution for the offence from being hindered by the disappearance of the person in question.

  (6) Subsection (5)(c)(iv) applies only where members of the public going about their normal business cannot reasonably be expected to avoid the person in question.]

[24A   Arrest without warrant: other persons
  . . .]

[Section 24A provides 'A person other than a constable' with similar powers to those in s. 24.]

32   Search upon arrest

  (1) A constable may search an arrested person, in any case where the person to be searched has been arrested at a place other than a police station, if the constable has reasonable grounds for believing that the arrested person may present a danger to himself or others.

34   Limitations on police detention

  (1) A person arrested for an offence shall not be kept in police detention except in accordance with the provisions of this Part of this Act.

  (2) Subject to subsection (3) below, if at any time a custody officer—
    (a) becomes aware, in relation to any person in police detention, that the grounds for the detention of that person have ceased to apply; and
    (b) is not aware of any other grounds on which the continued detention of that person could be justified under the provisions of this Part of this Act,
it shall be the duty of the custody officer, subject to subsection (4) below, to order his immediate release from custody.

55   Intimate searches

  (2) An officer may not authorise an intimate search of a person for anything unless he has reasonable grounds for believing that it cannot be found without his being intimately searched.

62   Intimate samples

  (1) [Subject to section 63B below] An intimate sample may be taken from a person in police detention only—
    (a) if a police officer of at least the rank of [inspector] authorises it to be taken; and
    (b) if the appropriate consent is given.

  [(1A) An intimate sample may be taken from a person who is not in police detention but from whom, in the course of the investigation of an offence, two or more intimate samples suitable for the same means of analysis have been taken which have proved insufficient—
    (a) if a police officer of at least the rank of inspector authorises it to be taken; and
    (b) if the appropriate consent is given.]

65   Part V—supplementary
In this Part of this Act—. . .
  ["intimate sample" means—
    (a) a sample of blood, semen or any other tissue fluid, urine or pubic hair;
    (b) a dental impression;
    (c) a swab taken from any part of a person's genitals (including pubic hair) or from a person's body orifice other than the mouth;]

Administration of Justice Act 1985
(1985, c. 61)

PART II

12 Establishment of the Council

(1) For the purposes of this Part there shall be a body to be known as the Council for Licensed Conveyancers.

21 Professional indemnity and compensation

(1) The Council shall make rules for indemnifying licensed conveyancers and former licensed conveyancers against losses arising from claims in respect of any description of civil liability incurred by them, or by employees or associates or former employees or associates of theirs, in connection with their practices as licensed conveyancers.

(2) The Council shall also make rules for the making of grants or other payments for the purpose of relieving or mitigating losses suffered by persons in consequence of—

> (a) negligence or fraud or other dishonesty on the part of licensed conveyancers, or of employees or associates of theirs, in connection with their practices (or purported practices) as licensed conveyancers; or
> (b) failure on the part of licensed conveyancers to account for money received by them in connection with their practices (or purported practices) as licensed conveyancers.

Companies Act 1985
(1985, c. 6)

[3A Statement of company's objects: general commercial company

Where the company's memorandum states that the object of the company is to carry on business as a general commercial company—

> (a) the object of the company is to carry on any trade or business whatsoever, and
> (b) the company has power to do all such things as are incidental or conducive to the carrying on of any trade or business by it.]

14 Effect of memorandum and articles

(1) Subject to the provisions of this Act, the memorandum and articles, when registered, bind the company and its members to the same extent as if they respectively had been signed and sealed by each member, and contained covenants on the part of each member to observe all the provisions of the memorandum and of the articles.

[35A company's capacity not limited by its memorandum

(1) The validity of an act done by a company shall not be called into question on the ground of lack of capacity by reason of anything in the company's memorandum.

(2) A member of a company may bring proceedings to restrain the doing of an act which but for subsection (1) would be beyond the company's capacity; but no such proceedings shall lie in respect of an act to be done in fulfilment of a legal obligation arising from a previous act of the company.

(3) It remains the duty of the directors to observe any limitations on their powers flowing from the company's memorandum; and action by the directors which but for subsection (1) would be beyond the company's capacity may only be ratified by the company by special resolution.

A resolution ratifying such action shall not affect any liability incurred by the directors or any other person; relief from any such liability must be agreed to separately by special resolution.]

[35A   Power of directors to bind the company

(1) In favour of a person dealing with a company in good faith, the power of the board of directors to bind the company, or authorise others to do so, shall be deemed to be free of any limitation under the company's constitution.

(2) For this purpose—

(a) a person "deals with" a company if he is a party to any transaction or other act to which the company is a party;

(b) a person shall not be regarded as acting in bad faith by reason only of his knowing that an act is beyond the powers of the directors under the company's constitution; and

(c) a person shall be presumed to have acted in good faith unless the contrary is proved.

(3) The references above to limitations on the directors' powers under the company's constitution include limitations deriving—

(a) from a resolution of the company in general meeting or a meeting of any class of shareholders, or

(b) from any agreement between the members of the company or of any class of shareholders.

(4) Subsection (1) does not affect any right of a member of the company to bring proceedings to restrain the doing of an act which is beyond the powers of the directors; but no such proceedings shall lie in respect of an act to be done in fulfilment of a legal obligation arising from a previous act of the company.

(5) Nor does that subsection affect any liability incurred by the directors, or any other person, by reason of the directors' exceeding their powers.]

[35B   No duty to enquire as to capacity of company or authority of directors

A party to a transaction with a company is not bound to enquire as to whether it is permitted by the company's memorandum or as to any limitation on the powers of the board of directors to bind the company or authorise others to do so.]

[36   Company contracts: England and Wales

Under the law of England and Wales a contract may be made—

(a) by a company, by writing under its common seal, or

(b) on behalf of a company, by any person acting under its authority, express or implied;

and any formalities required by law in the case of a contract made by an individual also apply, unless a contrary intention appears, to a contract made by or on behalf of a company.]

[36C   Pre-incorporation contracts, deeds and obligations

(1) A contract which purports to be made by or on behalf of a company at a time when the company has not been formed has effect, subject to any agreement to the contrary, as one made with the person purporting to act for the company or as agent for it, and he is personally liable on the contract accordingly.

(2) Subsection (1) applies—

(a) to the making of a deed under the law of England and Wales ...]

[111A   Right to damages, etc. not affected

A person is not debarred from obtaining damages or other compensation from a company by reason only of his holding or having held shares in the company or any right to apply or subscribe for shares or to be included in the company's register in respect of shares.]

[309A   Provisions protecting directors from liability

(1) This section applies in relation to any liability attaching to a director of a company in connection with any negligence, default, breach of duty or breach of trust by him in relation to the company.

(2) Any provision which purports to exempt (to any extent) a director of a company from any liability within subsection (1) is void.

(3) Any provision by which a company directly or indirectly provides (to any extent) an indemnity for a director of—

(a) the company, or

(b) an associated company,

against any liability within subsection (1) is void.

This is subject to subsections (4) and (5).

(4) Subsection (3) does not apply to a qualifying third party indemnity provision (see section 309B(1)).

(5) Subsection (3) does not prevent a company from purchasing and maintaining for a director of—

(a) the company, or

(b) an associated company,

insurance against any liability within subsection (1).

(6) In this section—

"associated company", in relation to a company ("C"), means a company which is C's subsidiary, or C's holding company or a subsidiary of C's holding company;

"provision" means a provision of any nature whether or not it is contained in a company's articles or in any contract with a company.]

[322A   Invalidity of certain transactions involving directors, etc.

(1) This section applies where a company enters into a transaction to which the parties include—

(a) a director of the company or of its holding company, or

(b) a person connected with such a director or a company with whom such a director is associated,

and the board of directors, in connection with the transaction, exceed any limitation on their powers under the company's constitution.

(2) The transaction is voidable at the instance of the company.

(3) Whether or not it is avoided, any such party to the transaction as is mentioned in subsection (1)(a) or (b), and any director of the company who authorised the transaction, is liable—

(a) to account to the company for any gain which he has made directly or indirectly by the transaction, and

(b) to indemnify the company for any loss or damage resulting from the transaction.

(4) Nothing in the above provisions shall be construed as excluding the operation of any other enactment of rule of law by virtue of which the transaction may be called in question or any liability to the company may arise.

(5) The transaction ceases to be voidable if—

(a) restitution of any money or other asset which was the subject-matter of the transaction is no longer possible, or

(b) the company is indemnified for any loss or damage resulting from the transaction, or

(c) rights acquired bona fide for value and without actual notice of the directors' exceeding their powers by a person who is not party to the transaction would be affected by the avoidance, or

(d) the transaction is ratified by the company in general meeting, by ordinary or special resolution or otherwise as the case may require.

(6) A person other than a director of the company is not liable under subsection (3) if he shows that at the time the transaction was entered into he did not know that the directors were exceeding their powers.

(7) This section does not affect the operation of section 35A in relation to any party to the transaction not within subsection (1)(a) or (b).

But where a transaction is voidable by virtue of this section and valid by virtue of that section in favour of such a person, the court may, on the application of that person or of the company, make such order affirming, severing or setting aside the transaction, on such terms, as appear to the court to be just.]

349   Company's name to appear in its correspondence, etc.

(4) If an officer of a company or a person on its behalf signs or authorises to be signed on behalf of the company any bill of exchange, promissory note, endorsement, cheque or order for money or goods in which the company's name is not mentioned as required by subsection(1), he is liable to a fine; and he is further personally liable to the holder of the bill of exchange, promissory note, cheque or order for money or goods for the amount of it (unless it is duly paid by the company).

395   Certain charges void if not registered

(1) Subject to the provisions of this Chapter, a charge created by a company registered in England and Wales and being a charge to which this section applies is, so far as any security on the company's property or undertaking is conferred by the charge, void against the liquidator [or administrator] and any creditor of the company, unless the prescribed particulars of the charge together with the instrument (if any) by which the charge is created or evidenced, are delivered to or received by the registrar of companies for registration in the manner required by this Chapter within 21 days after the date of the charge's creation.

(2) Subsection (1) is without prejudice to any contract or obligation for repayment of the money secured by the charge; and when a charge becomes void under this section, the money secured by it immediately becomes payable.

396   Charges which have to be registered

(1) Section 395 applies to the following charges
    (a) a charge for the purpose of securing any issue of debentures,
    (b) a charge on uncalled share capital of the company,
    (c) a charge created or evidenced by an instrument which, if executed by an individual, would require registration as a bill of sale,
    (d) a charge on land (wherever situated) or any interest in it, but not including a charge for any rent or other periodical sum issuing out of the land,
    (e) a charge on book debts of the company,
    (f) a floating charge on the company's undertaking or property,
    (g) a charge on calls made but not paid,
    (h) a charge on a ship or aircraft, or any share in a ship,
    (j) a charge on goodwill, [or on any intellectual property].

(2) Where a negotiable instrument has been given to secure the payment of any book debts of a company, the deposit of the instrument for the purpose of securing an advance to the company is not, for purposes of section 395, to be treated as a charge on those book debts.

(3) The holding of debentures entitling the holder to a charge on land is not for purposes of this section deemed to be an interest in land.

[(3A) The following are "intellectual property" for the purposes of this section—
    (a) any patent, trade mark, . . . registered design, copyright or design right;
    (b) any licence under or in respect of any such right.]

(4) In this Chapter, "charge" includes mortgage.

Housing Act 1985
(1985, c. 68)

[118   The right to acquire

(1) A tenant of a registered social landlord who satisfies the conditions in section 16(1)(a) and (b) of the Housing Act 1996 has the right to acquire, that is to say, the right, in the

circumstances and subject to the conditions and exceptions stated in the following provisions of this Part—

    (a) if the dwelling-house is a house and the landlord owns the freehold, to acquire the freehold of the dwelling-house;

    (b) if the landlord does not own the freehold or if the dwelling-house is a flat (whether or not the landlord owns the freehold), to be granted a lease of the dwelling-house.]

[121AA Information to help tenants decide whether to exercise right to buy etc.

    (1) Every body which lets dwelling-houses under secure tenancies shall prepare a document that contains information for its secure tenants about such matters as are specified in an order made by the Secretary of State.

    (2) The matters that may be so specified are matters which the Secretary of State considers that it would be desirable for secure tenants to have information about when considering whether to exercise the right to buy or the right to acquire on rent to mortgage terms.]

[179 Provisions restricting right to acquire etc. of no effect

    (1) A provision of a lease held by the landlord or a superior landlord, or of an agreement (whenever made), is void in so far as it purports to prohibit or restrict—

    (a) the grant of a lease in pursuance of the right to acquire, or

    (b) the subsequent disposal (whether by way of assignment, sub-lease or otherwise) of a lease so granted,

or to authorise a forfeiture, or impose on the landlord or superior landlord a penalty or disability, in the event of such a grant or disposal.]

Landlord and Tenant Act 1985
(1985, c. 70)

8 Implied terms as to fitness for human habitation

    (1) In a contract to which this section applies for the letting of a house for human habitation there is implied, notwithstanding any stipulation to the contrary—

    (a) a condition that the house is fit for human habitation at the commencement of the tenancy, and

    (b) an undertaking that the house will be kept by the landlord fit for human habitation during the tenancy.

    (2) The landlord, or a person authorised by him in writing, may at reasonable times of the day, on giving 24 hours' notice in writing to the tenant or occupier, enter premises to which this section applies for the purpose of viewing their state and condition.

Surrogacy Arrangements Act 1985
(1985, c. 49)

1 Meaning of "surrogate mother", "surrogacy arrangement" and other terms

    (2) "Surrogate mother" means a woman who carries a child in pursuance of an arrangement—

    (a) made before she began to carry the child, and

    (b) made with a view to any child carried in pursuance of it being handed over to, and [parental responsibility being met] (so far as practicable) by, another person or other persons.

(3) An arrangement is a surrogacy arrangement if, were a woman to whom the arrangement relates to carry a child in pursuance of it, she would be a surrogate mother.

(9) This Act applies to arrangements whether or not they are lawful [. . .].

[1A   Surrogacy arrangements unenforceable

No surrogacy arrangement is enforceable by or against any of the persons making it.]

2   Negotiating surrogacy arrangements on a commercial basis, etc

(1) No person shall on a commercial basis do any of the following acts in the United Kingdom, that is—

    (a) initiate or take part in any negotiations with a view to the making of a surrogacy arrangement,

    (b) offer or agree to negotiate the making of a surrogacy arrangement, or

    (c) compile any information with a view to its use in making, or negotiating the making of, surrogacy arrangements;

and no person shall in the United Kingdom knowingly cause another to do any of those acts on a commercial basis.

Agricultural Holdings Act 1986
(1986, c. 5)

24   Restriction of landlord's remedies for breach of contract of tenancy

Notwithstanding any provision in a contract of tenancy of an agricultural holding making the tenant liable to pay a higher rent or other liquidated damages in the event of a breach or non-fulfilment of a term or condition of the contract, the landlord shall not be entitled to recover in consequence of any such breach or non-fulfilment, by distress or otherwise, any sum in excess of the damage actually suffered by him in consequence of the breach or non-fulfilment.

Insolvency Act 1986
(1986, c. 45)

238   Transactions at an undervalue (England and Wales)

(1) This section applies in the case of a company where—

    [(a) the company enters administration,]

    (b) the company goes into liquidation; and "the office-holder" means the administrator or the liquidator, as the case may be.

(2) Where the company has at a relevant time (defined in section 240) entered into a transaction with any person at an undervalue, the office-holder may apply to the court for an order under this section.

(3) Subject as follows, the court shall, on such an application, make such order as it thinks fit for restoring the position to what it would have been if the company had not entered into that transaction.

(4) For the purposes of this section and section 241, a company enters into a transaction with a person at an undervalue if—

    (a) the company makes a gift to that person or otherwise enters into a transaction with that person on terms that provide for the company to receive no consideration, or

    (b) the company enters into a transaction with that person for a consideration the value of which, in money or money's worth, is significantly less than the value, in money or money's worth, of the consideration provided by the company.

(5) The court shall not make an order under this section in respect of a transaction at an undervalue if it is satisfied—

(a) that the company which entered into the transaction did so in good faith and for the purpose of carrying on its business, and

(b) that at the time it did so there were reasonable grounds for believing that the transaction would benefit the company.

Latent Damage Act 1986
(1986, c. 37)

1   Time limits for negligence actions in respect of latent damage not involving personal injuries

The following sections shall be inserted in the Limitation Act 1980 (referred to below in this Act as the 1980 Act)...

2   Provisions consequential on section 1

...

3   Accrual of cause of action to successive owners in respect of latent damage to property

(1) Subject to the following provisions of this section, where—

(a) a cause of action ("the original cause of action") has accrued to any person in respect of any negligence to which damage to any property in which he has an interest is attributable (in whole or in part); and

(b) another person acquires an interest in that property after the date on which the original cause of action accrued but before the material facts about the damage have become known to any person who, at the time when he first has knowledge of those facts, has any interest in the property;

a fresh cause of action in respect of that negligence shall accrue to that other person on the date on which he acquires his interest in the property.

(2) A cause of action accruing to any person by virtue of subsection (1) above—

(a) shall be treated as if based on breach of a duty of care at common law owed to the person to whom it accrues; and

(b) shall be treated for the purposes of section 14A of the 1980 Act (special time limit for negligence actions where facts relevant to cause of action are not known at date of accrual) as having accrued on the date on which the original cause of action accrued.

(3) Section 28 of the 1980 Act (extension of limitation period in case of disability) shall not apply in relation to any such cause of action.

(4) Subsection (1) above shall not apply in any case where the person acquiring an interest in the damaged property is either—

(a) a person in whom the original cause of action vests by operation of law; or

(b) a person in whom the interest in that property vests by virtue of any order made by a court under section 538 of the Companies Act 1985 (vesting of company property in liquidator).

[*The Companies Act 1985, s. 538 has now been replaced by the Insolvency Act 1986, s. 145.*]

(5) For the purposes of subsection (1)(b) above, the material facts about the damage are such facts about the damage as would lead a reasonable person who has an interest in the damaged property at the time when those facts become known to him to consider it sufficiently serious to justify his instituting proceedings for damages against a defendant who did not dispute liability and was able to satisfy a judgment.

(6) For the purposes of this section a person's knowledge includes knowledge which he might reasonably have been expected to acquire—

    (a) from facts observable or ascertainable by him; or

    (b) from facts ascertained by him with the help of appropriate expert advice which it is reasonable for him to seek;

but a person shall not be taken by virtue of this subsection to have knowledge of a fact ascertainable by him only with the help of expert advice so long as he has taken all reasonable steps to obtain (and, where appropriate, to act on) that advice.

(7) This section shall bind the Crown, but as regards the Crown's liability in tort shall not bind the Crown further than the Crown is made liable in tort by the Crown Proceedings Act 1947.

4 Transitional provisions

(1) Nothing in section 1 or 2 of this Act shall—

    (a) enable any action to be brought which was barred by the 1980 Act or (as the case may be) by the Limitation Act 1939 before this Act comes into force; or

    (b) affect any action commenced before this Act comes into force.

(2) Subject to subsection (1) above, sections 1 and 2 of this Act shall have effect in relation to causes of action accruing before, as well as in relation to causes of action accruing after, this Act comes into force.

(3) Section 3 of this Act shall only apply in cases where an interest in damaged property is acquired after this Act comes into force but shall so apply, subject to subsection (4) below, irrespective of whether the original cause of action accrued before or after this Act comes into force.

(4) Where—

    (a) a person acquires an interest in damaged property in circumstances to which section 3 would apart from this subsection apply; but

    (b) the original cause of action accrued more than six years before this Act comes into force;

a cause of action shall not accrue to that person by virtue of subsection (1) of that section unless section 32(1)(b) of the 1980 Act (postponement of limitation period in case of deliberate concealment of relevant facts) would apply to any action founded on the original cause of action.

Consumer Protection Act 1987
(1987, c. 43)

PART I   PRODUCT LIABILITY

1 Purpose and construction of Part I

(1) This Part shall have effect for the purpose of making such provision as is necessary in order to comply with the product liability Directive and shall be construed accordingly.

(2) In this Part, except in so far as the context otherwise requires—

[...]

"dependant" and "relative" have the same meaning as they have in, respectively, the Fatal Accidents Act 1976 and the Damages (Scotland) Act 1976;

"producer", in relation to a product, means—

    (a) the person who manufactured it;

    (b) in the case of a substance which has not been manufactured but has been won or abstracted, the person who won or abstracted it;

    (c) in the case of a product which has not been manufactured, won or abstracted but essential characteristics of which are attributable to an industrial or other process having been carried out (for example, in relation to agricultural produce), the person who carried out that process;

"product" means any goods or electricity and (subject to subsection (3) below) includes a product which is comprised in another product, whether by virtue of being a component part or raw material or otherwise; and

"the product liability Directive" means the Directive of the Council of the European Communities, dated 25th July 1985, (No. 85/374/EEC) on the approximation of the laws, regulations and administrative provisions of the member States concerning liability for defective products.

(3) For the purposes of this Part a person who supplies any product in which products are comprised, whether by virtue of being component parts or raw materials or otherwise, shall not be treated by reason only of his supply of that product as supplying any of the products so comprised.

2 Liability for defective products

(1) Subject to the following provisions of this Part, where any damage is caused wholly or partly by a defect in a product, every person to whom subsection (2) below applies shall be liable for the damage.

(2) This subsection applies to—
    (a) the producer of the product;
    (b) any person who, by putting his name on the product or using a trade mark or other distinguishing mark in relation to the product, has held himself out to be the producer of the product;
    (c) any person who has imported the product into a member State from a place outside the member States in order, in the course of any business of his, to supply it to another.

(3) Subject as aforesaid, where any damage is caused wholly or partly by a defect in a product, any person who supplied the product (whether to the person who suffered the damage, to the producer of any product in which the product in question is comprised or to any other person) shall be liable for the damage if—
    (a) the person who suffered the damage requests the supplier to identify one or more of the persons (whether still in existence or not) to whom subsection (2) above applies in relation to the product;
    (b) that request is made within a reasonable period after the damage occurs and at a time when it is not reasonably practicable for the person making the request to identify all those persons; and
    (c) the supplier fails, within a reasonable period after receiving the request, either to comply with the request or to identify the person who supplied the product to him.

(5) Where two or more persons are liable by virtue of this Part for the same damage, their liability shall be joint and several.

(6) This section shall be without prejudice to any liability arising otherwise than by virtue of this Part.

3 Meaning of "defect"

(1) Subject to the following provisions of this section, there is a defect in a product for the purposes of this Part if the safety of the product is not such as persons generally are entitled to expect; and for those purposes "safety", in relation to a product, shall include safety with respect to products comprised in that product and safety in the context of risks of damage to property, as well as in the context of risks of death or personal injury.

(2) In determining for the purposes of subsection (1) above what persons generally are entitled to expect in relation to a product all the circumstances shall be taken into account, including—
    (a) the manner in which, and purposes for which, the product has been marketed, its get-up, the use of any mark in relation to the product and any instructions for, or warnings with respect to, doing or refraining from doing anything with or in relation to the product;

(b) what might reasonably be expected to be done with or in relation to the product; and

(c) the time when the product was supplied by its producer to another;

and nothing in this section shall require a defect to be inferred from the fact alone that the safety of a product which is supplied after that time is greater than the safety of the product in question.

4   Defences

(1) In any civil proceedings by virtue of this Part against any person ("the person proceeded against") in respect of a defect in a product it shall be a defence for him to show—

(a) that the defect is attributable to compliance with any requirement imposed by or under any enactment or with any Community obligation; or

(b) that the person proceeded against did not at any time supply the product to another; or

(c) that the following conditions are satisfied, that is to say—

(i) that the only supply of the product to another by the person proceeded against was otherwise than in the course of a business of that person's; and

(ii) that section 2(2) above does not apply to that person or applies to him by virtue only of things done otherwise than with a view to profit; or

(d) that the defect did not exist in the product at the relevant time; or

(e) that the state of scientific and technical knowledge at the relevant time was not such that a producer of products of the same description as the product in question might be expected to have discovered the defect if it had existed in his products while they were under his control; or

(f) that the defect—

(i) constituted an defect in a product ("the subsequent product") in which the product in question had been comprised; and

(ii) was wholly attributable to the design of the subsequent product or to compliance by the producer of the product in question with instructions given by the producer of the subsequent product.

(2) In this section "the relevant time", in relation to electricity, means the time at which it was generated, being a time before it was transmitted or distributed, and in relation to any other product, means—

(a) if the person proceeded against is a person to whom subsection (2) of section 2 above applies in relation to the product, the time when he supplied the product to another;

(b) if that subsection does not apply to that person in relation to the product, the time when the product was last supplied by a person to whom that subsection does apply in relation to the product.

5   Damage giving rise to liability

(1) Subject to the following provisions of this section, in this Part "damage" means death or personal injury or any loss of or damage to any property (including land).

(2) A person shall not be liable under section 2 above in respect of any defect in a product for the loss of or any damage to the product itself or for the loss of or any damage to the whole or any part of any product which has been supplied with the product in question comprised in it.

(3) A person shall not be liable under section 2 above for any loss of or damage to any property which, at the time it is lost or damaged, is not—

(a) of a description of property ordinarily intended for private use, occupation or consumption; and

(b) intended by the person suffering the loss or damage mainly for his own private use, occupation or consumption.

(4) No damages shall be awarded to any person by virtue of this Part in respect of any loss of or damage to any property if the amount which would fall to be so awarded to that person, apart from this subsection and any liability for interest, does not exceed £275.

(5) In determining for the purposes of this Part who has suffered any loss of or damage to property and when any such loss or damage occurred, the loss or damage shall be regarded as having occurred at the earliest time at which a person with an interest in the property had knowledge of the material facts about the loss or damage.

(6) For the purposes of subsection (5) above the material facts about any loss of or damage to any property are such facts about the loss or damage as would lead a reasonable person with an interest in the property to consider the loss or damage sufficiently serious to justify his instituting proceedings for damages against a defendant who did not dispute liability and was able to satisfy a judgment.

(7) For the purposes of subsection (5) above a person's knowledge includes knowledge which he might reasonably have been expected to acquire—

> (a) from facts observable or ascertainable by him; or
> (b) from facts ascertainable by him with the help of appropriate expert advice which it is reasonable for him to seek;

but a person shall not be taken by virtue of this subsection to have knowledge of a fact ascertainable by him only with the help of expert advice unless he has failed to take all reasonable steps to obtain (and, where appropriate, to act on) that advice.

6   Application of certain enactments etc.

(1) Any damage for which a person is liable under section 2 above shall be deemed to have been caused—

> (a) for the purposes of the Fatal Accidents Act 1976, by that person's wrongful act, neglect or default; . . .

(2) Where—

> (a) a person's death is caused wholly or partly by a defect in a product, or a person dies after suffering damage which has been so caused;
> (b) a request such as mentioned in paragraph (a) of subsection (3) of section 2 above is made to a supplier of the product by that person's personal representatives or, in the case of a person whose death is caused wholly or partly by the defect, by any dependant or relative of that person; and
> (c) the conditions specified in paragraphs (b) and (c) of that subsection are satisfied in relation to that request,

this Part shall have effect for the purposes of the Law Reform (Miscellaneous Provisions) Act 1934, the Fatal Accidents Act 1976 and the Damages (Scotland) Act 1976 as if liability of the supplier to that person under that subsection did not depend on that person having requested the supplier to identify certain persons or on the said conditions having been satisfied in relation to a request made by that person.

(3) Section 1 of the Congenital Disabilities (Civil Liability) Act 1976 shall have effect for the purposes of this Part as if—

> (a) a person were answerable to a child in respect of an occurrence caused wholly or partly by a defect in a product if he is or has been liable under section 2 above in respect of any effect of the occurrence on a parent of the child, or would be so liable if the occurrence caused a parent of the child to suffer damage;
> (b) the provisions of this Part relating to liability under section 2 above applied in relation to liability by virtue of paragraph (a) above under the said section 1; and
> (c) subsection (6) of the said section 1 (exclusion of liability) were omitted.

(4) Where any damage is caused partly by a defect in a product and partly by the fault of the person suffering the damage, the Law Reform (Contributory Negligence) Act 1945 and section 5 of the Fatal Accidents Act 1976 (contributory negligence) shall have effect as if the defect were the fault of every person liable by virtue of this Part for the damage caused by the defect.

(5) In subsection (4) above "fault" has the same meaning as in the said Act of 1945.

(6) Schedule 1 to this Act shall have effect for the purpose of amending the Limitation Act 1980 and the Prescription and Limitation (Scotland) Act 1973 in their application in relation to the bringing of actions by virtue of this Part.

(7) It is hereby declared that liability by virtue of this Part is to be treated as liability in tort for the purposes of any enactment conferring jurisdiction on any court with respect to any matter.

(8) Nothing in this Part shall prejudice the operation of section 12 of the Nuclear Installations Act 1965 (rights to compensation for certain breaches of duties confined to rights under that Act).

7 Prohibition on exclusions from liability

The liability of a person by virtue of this Part to a person who has suffered damage caused wholly or partly by a defect in a product, or to a dependant or relative of such a person, shall not be limited or excluded by any contract term, by any notice or by any other provision.

8 Power to modify Part I

(1) Her Majesty may by Order in Council make such modifications of this Part and of any other enactment (including an enactment contained in the following Parts of this Act, or in an Act passed after this Act) as appear to Her Majesty in Council to be necessary or expedient in consequence of any modification of the product liability Directive which is made at any time after the passing of this Act.

9 Application of Part I to Crown

(1) Subject to subsection (2) below, this Part shall bind the Crown.

(2) The Crown shall not, as regards the Crown's liability by virtue of this Part, be bound by this Part further than the Crown is made liable in tort or in reparation under the Crown Proceedings Act 1947, as that Act has effect from time to time.

PART II   CONSUMER SAFETY

11 Safety regulations

(1) The Secretary of State may by regulations under this section ("safety regulations") make such provision as he considers appropriate [. . .] for the purpose of securing—

(a) that goods to which this section applies are safe;

(b) that goods to which this section applies which are unsafe, or would be unsafe in the hands of persons of a particular description, are not made available to persons generally or, as the case may be, to persons of that description; and

(c) that appropriate information is, and inappropriate information is not, provided in relation to goods to which this section applies.

(2) Without prejudice to the generality of subsection (1) above, safety regulations may contain provision—

(a) with respect to the composition or contents, design, construction, finish or packing of goods to which this section applies, with respect to standards for such goods and with respect to other matters relating to such goods;

(b) with respects to the giving, refusal, alteration or cancellation of approvals of such goods, of descriptions of such goods or of standards for such goods;

(c) with respect to the conditions that may be attached to any approval given under the regulations;

(d) for requiring such fees as may be determined by or under the regulations to be paid on the giving or alteration of any approval under the regulations and on the making of an application for such an approval or alteration;

(e) with respect to appeals against refusals, alterations and cancellations of approvals given under the regulations and against the conditions contained in such approvals;

(f) for requiring goods to which this section applies to be approved under the regulations or to conform to the requirements of the regulations or to descriptions or standards specified in or approved by or under the regulations;

(g) with respect to the testing or inspection of goods to which this section applies (including provision for determining the standards to be applied in carrying out any test or inspection);

(h) with respect to the ways of dealing with goods of which some or all do not satisfy a test required by or under the regulations or a standard connected with a procedure so required;

(i) for requiring a mark, warning or instruction or any other information relating to goods to be put on or to accompany the goods or to be used or provided in some other manner in relation to the goods, and for securing that inappropriate information is not given in relation to goods either by means of misleading marks or otherwise;

(j) for prohibiting persons from supplying, or from offering to supply, agreeing to supply, exposing for supply or possessing for supply, goods to which this section applies and component parts and raw materials for such goods;

(k) for requiring information to be given to any such person as may be determined by or under the regulations for the purpose of enabling that person to exercise any function conferred on him by the regulations.

(3) Without prejudice as aforesaid, safety regulations may contain provision—

(a) for requiring persons on whom functions are conferred by or under section 27 below to have regard, in exercising their functions so far as relating to any provision of safety regulations, to matters specified in a direction issued by the Secretary of State with respect to that provision;

(b) for securing that a person shall not be guilty of an offence under section 12 below unless it is shown that the goods in question do not conform to a particular standard;

(c) for securing that proceedings for such an offence are not brought in England and Wales except by or with the consent of the Secretary of State or the Director of Public Prosecutions;

. . .

(e) for enabling a magistrates' court in England and Wales or Northern Ireland to try an information or, in Northern Ireland, a complaint in respect of such an offence if the information was laid or the complaint made within twelve months from the time when the offence was committed;

. . .

(g) for determining the persons by whom, and the manner in which, anything required to be done by or under the regulations is to be done.

(4) Safety regulations shall not provide for any contravention of the regulations to be an offence.

(5) Where the Secretary of State proposes to make safety regulations it shall be his duty before he makes them—

(a) to consult such organisations as appear to him to be representative of interests substantially affected by the proposal;

(b) to consult such other persons as he considers appropriate; and

(c) in the case of proposed regulations relating to goods suitable for use at work, to consult the Health and Safety Commission in relation to the application of the proposed regulations to Great Britain;

but the preceding provisions of this subsection shall not apply in the case of regulations which provide for the regulations to cease to have effect at the end of a period of not more than twelve months beginning with the day on which they come into force and which contain a statement that it appears to the Secretary of State that the need to protect the public requires that the regulations should be made without delay.

(6) The power to make safety regulations shall be exercisable by statutory instrument subject to annulment in pursuance of a resolution of either House of Parliament and shall include power—

    (a) to make different provision for different cases; and

    (b) to make such supplemental, consequential and transitional provision as the Secretary of State considers appropriate.

(7) This section applies to any goods other than—

    (a) growing crops and things comprised in land by virtue of being attached to it;

    (b) water, food, feeding stuff and fertiliser;

    (c) gas which is, is to be or has been supplied by a person authorised to supply it by or under [section 7A of the Gas Act 1986 (licensing of gas suppliers and gas shippers)];

    (d) controlled drugs and licensed medicinal products.

12   Offences against the safety regulations

(1) Where safety regulations prohibit a person from supplying or offering or agreeing to supply any goods or from exposing or possessing any goods for supply, that person shall be guilty of an offence if he contravenes the prohibition.

(2) Where safety regulations require a person who makes or processes any goods in the course of carrying on a business—

    (a) to carry out a particular test or use a particular procedure in connection with the making or processing of the goods with a view to ascertaining whether the goods satisfy any requirements of such regulations; or

    (b) to deal or not to deal in a particular way with a quantity of the goods of which the whole or part does not satisfy such a test or does not satisfy standards connected with such a procedure,

that person shall be guilty of an offence if he does not comply with the requirement.

(3) If a person contravenes a provision of safety regulations which prohibits or requires the provision, by means of a mark or otherwise, of information of a particular kind in relation to goods, he shall be guilty of an offence.

(4) Where safety regulations require any person to give information to another for the purpose of enabling that other to exercise any function, that person shall be guilty of an offence if—

    (a) he fails without reasonable cause to comply with the requirement; or

    (b) in giving the information which is required of him—

        (i)   he makes any statement which he knows is false in a material particular; or

        (ii) he recklessly makes any statement which is false in a material particular.

(5) A person guilty of an offence under this section shall be liable on summary conviction to imprisonment for a term not exceeding six months or to a fine not exceeding level 5 on the standard scale or to both.

13   Prohibition notices and notices to warn

(1) The Secretary of State may—

    (a) serve on any person a notice ("a prohibition notice") prohibiting that person, except with the consent of the Secretary of State, from supplying, or from offering to supply, agreeing to supply, exposing for supply or possessing for supply, any relevant goods which the Secretary of State considers are unsafe and which are described in the notice;

    (b) serve on any person a notice ("a notice to warn") requiring that person at his own expense to publish, in a form and manner and on occasions specified in the notice, a warning about any relevant goods which the Secretary of State considers are unsafe, which that person supplies or has supplied and which are described in the notice.

(2) Schedule 2 to this Act shall have effect with respect to prohibition notices and notices to warn; and the Secretary of State may by regulations make provision specifying the manner in which information is to be given to any person under that Schedule.

(3) A consent given by the Secretary of State for the purposes of a prohibition notice may impose such conditions on the doing of anything for which the consent is required as the Secretary of State considers appropriate.

(4) A person who contravenes a prohibition notice or a notice to warn shall be guilty of an offence and liable on summary conviction to imprisonment for a term not exceeding six months or to a fine not exceeding level 5 on the standard scale or to both.

(5) The power to make regulations under subsection (2) above shall be exercisable by statutory instrument subject to annulment in pursuance of a resolution of either House of Parliament and shall include power—

(a) to make different provision for different cases; and

(b) to make such supplemental, consequential and transitional provision as the Secretary of State considers appropriate.

(6) In this section "relevant goods" means—

(a) in relation to a prohibition notice, any goods to which section 11 above applies; and

(b) in relation to a notice to warn, any goods to which that section applies or any growing crops or things comprised in land by virtue of being attached to it.

[(7) A notice may not be given under this section in respect of any aspect of the safety of goods, or any risk or category of risk associated with goods, concerning which provision is contained in the General Product Safety Regulations 2005.]

14 Suspension notices

(1) Where an enforcement authority has reasonable grounds for suspecting that any safety provision has been contravened in relation to any goods, the authority may serve a notice ("a suspension notice") prohibiting the person on whom it is served, for such period ending not more than six months after the date of the notice as is specified therein, from doing any of the following things without the consent of the authority, that is to say, supplying the goods, offering to supply them, agreeing to supply them or exposing them for supply.

(2) A suspension notice served by an enforcement authority in respect of any goods shall—

(a) describe the goods in a manner sufficient to identify them;

(b) set out the grounds on which the authority suspects that a safety provision has been contravened in relation to the goods; and

(c) state that, and the manner in which, the person on whom the notice is served may appeal against the notice under section 15 below.

(3) A suspension notice served by an enforcement authority for the purpose of prohibiting a person for any period from doing the things mentioned in subsection (1) above in relation to any goods may also require that person to keep the authority informed of the whereabouts throughout that period of any of those goods in which he has an interest.

(4) Where a suspension notice has been served on any person in respect of any goods, no further such notice shall be served on that person in respect of the same goods unless—

(a) proceedings against that person for an offence in respect of a contravention in relation to the goods of a safety provision (not being an offence under this section); or

(b) proceedings for the forfeiture of the goods under section 16 or 17 below, are pending at the end of the period specified in the first-mentioned notice.

(5) A consent given by an enforcement authority for the purposes of subsection (1) above may impose such conditions on the doing of anything for which the consent is required as the authority considers appropriate.

(6) Any person who contravenes a suspension notice shall be guilty of an offence and liable on summary conviction to imprisonment for a term not exceeding six months or to a fine not exceeding level 5 on the standard scale or to both.

(7) Where an enforcement authority serves a suspension notice in respect of any goods, the authority shall be liable to pay compensation to any person having an interest in the goods in respect of any loss or damage caused by reason of the service of the notice if—

(a) there has been no contravention in relation to the goods of any safety provision; and

(b) the exercise of the power is not attributable to any neglect or default by that person.

(8) Any disputed question as to the right to or the amount of any compensation payable under this section shall be determined by arbitration ...

15 Appeals against suspension notices

(1) Any person having an interest in any goods in respect of which a suspension notice is for the time being in force may apply for an order setting aside the notice.

(2) An application under this section may be made—

(a) to any magistrates' court in which proceedings have been brought in England and Wales or Northern Ireland—

(i)   for an offence in respect of a contravention in relation to the goods of any safety provision; or

(ii) for the forfeiture of the goods under section 16 below;

(b) where no such proceedings have been so brought, by way of complaint to a magistrates' court; ...

(3) On an application under this section to a magistrates' court in England and Wales or Northern Ireland the court shall make an order setting aside the suspension notice only if the court is satisfied that there has been no contravention in relation to the goods of any safety provision.

(4) On an application under this section to the sheriff he shall make an order setting aside the suspension notice only if he is satisfied that at the date of making the order—

(a) proceedings for an offence in respect of a contravention in relation to the goods of any safety provision; or

(b) proceedings for the forfeiture of the goods under section 17 below,

have not been brought or, having been brought, have been concluded.

(5) Any person aggrieved by an order made under this section by a magistrates' court in England and Wales or Northern Ireland, or by a decision of such a court not to make such an order, may appeal against that order or decision—

(a) in England and Wales, to the Crown Court;

(b) in Northern Ireland, to the county court;

and an order so made may contain such provision as appears to the court to be appropriate for delaying the coming into force of the order pending the making and determination of any appeal (including any application under section 111 of the Magistrates' Courts Act 1980 or Article 146 of the Magistrates' Courts (Northern Ireland) Order 1981 (statement of case)).

16 Forfeiture: England and Wales and Northern Ireland

(1) An enforcement authority in England and Wales or Northern Ireland may apply under this section for an order for the forfeiture of any goods on the grounds that there has been a contravention in relation to the goods of a safety provision.

(2) An application under this section may be made—

(a) where proceedings have been brought in a magistrates' court for an offence in respect of a contravention in relation to some or all of the goods of any safety provision, to that court;

(b) where an application with respect to some or all of the goods has been made to a magistrates' court under section 15 above or section 33 below, to that court; and

(c) where no application for the forfeiture of the goods has been made under paragraph (a) or (b) above, by way of complaint to a magistrates' court.

(3) On an application under this section the court shall make an order for the forfeiture of any goods only if it is satisfied that there has been a contravention in relation to the goods of a safety provision.

(4) For the avoidance of doubt it is declared that a court may infer for the purposes of this section that there has been a contravention in relation to any goods of a safety provision if it is satisfied that any such provision has been contravened in relation to goods which are representative of those goods (whether by reason of being of the same design or part of the same consignment or batch or otherwise).

(5) Any person aggrieved by an order made under this section by a magistrates' court, or by a decision of such a court not to make such an order, may appeal against that order or decision—

(a) in England and Wales, to the Crown Court;

(b) in Northern Ireland, to the county court;

and an order so made may contain such provision as appears to the court to be appropriate for delaying the coming into force of the order pending the making and determination of any appeal (including any application under section 111 of the Magistrates' Courts Act 1980 or Article 146 of the Magistrates' Courts (Northern Ireland) Order 1981(statement of case)).

(6) Subject to subsection (7) below, where any goods are forfeited under this section they shall be destroyed in accordance with such directions as the court may give.

(7) On making an order under this section a magistrates' court may, if it considers it appropriate to do so, direct that the goods to which the order relates shall (instead of being destroyed) be released, to such person as the court may specify, on condition that that person—

(a) does not supply those goods to any person otherwise than as mentioned in section 46(7)(a) or (b) below; and

(b) complies with any order to pay costs or expenses (including any order under section 35 below) which has been made against that person in the proceedings for the order for forfeiture.

18   Power to obtain information

(1) If the Secretary of State considers that, for the purpose of deciding whether—

(a) to make, vary or revoke any safety regulations; or

(b) to serve, vary or revoke a prohibition notice; or

(c) to serve or revoke a notice to warn,

he requires information which another person is likely to be able to furnish, the Secretary of State may serve on the other person a notice under this section.

(2) A notice served on any person under this section may require that person—

(a) to furnish to the Secretary of State, within a period specified in the notice, such information as is so specified;

(b) to produce such records as are specified in the notice at a time and place so specified and to permit a person appointed by the Secretary of State for the purpose to take copies of the records at that time and place.

(3) A person shall be guilty of an offence if he—

(a) fails, without reasonable cause, to comply with a notice served on him under this section; or

(b) in purporting to comply with a requirement which by virtue of paragraph (a) of subsection (2) above is contained in such a notice—

  (i)   furnishes information which he knows is false in a material particular; or

  (ii) recklessly furnishes information which is false in a material particular.

(4) A person guilty of an offence under subsection (3) above shall—

(a) in the case of an offence under paragraph (a) of that subsection, be liable on summary conviction to a fine not exceeding level 5 on the standard scale; and

(b) in the case of an offence under paragraph (b) of that subsection be liable—
    (i) on conviction on indictment, to a fine;
    (ii) on summary conviction, to a fine not exceeding the statutory maximum.

19   Interpretation of Part II

(1) In this Part—

"controlled drug" means a controlled drug within the meaning of the Misuse of Drugs Act 1971;

"feeding stuff" and "fertiliser" have the same meanings as in Part IV of the Agriculture Act 1970;

"food" does not include anything containing tobacco but, subject to that, has the same meaning as in the [Food Safety Act 1990] or, in relation to Northern Ireland, the same meaning as in the Food and Drugs Act (Northern Ireland) 1958;

"licensed medicinal product" means—

(a) any medicinal product within the meaning of the Medicines Act 1968 in respect of which a product licence within the meaning of that Act is for the time being in force;

or

(b) any other article or substance in respect of which any such licence is for the time being in force in pursuance of an order under section 104 or 105 of that Act (application of Act to other articles and substances);

"safe", in relation to any goods, means such that there is no risk, or no risk apart from one reduced to a minimum, that any of the following will (whether immediately or after a definite or indefinite period) cause the death of, or any personal injury to, any person whatsoever, that is to say—

(a) the goods;

(b) the keeping, use or consumption of the goods;

(c) the assembly of any of the goods which are, or are to be, supplied unassembled;

(d) any emission or leakage from the goods or, as a result of the keeping, use or consumption of the goods, from anything else; or

(e) reliance on the accuracy of any measurement, calculation or other reading made by or by means of the goods,

and [...] "unsafe" shall be construed accordingly;

"tobacco" includes any tobacco produce within the meaning of the Tobacco Products Duty Act 1979 and any article or substance containing tobacco and intended for oral or nasal use.

(2) In the definition of "safe" in subsection (1) above, references to the keeping, use or consumption of any goods are references to—

(a) the keeping, use or consumption of the goods by the persons by whom, and in all or any of the ways or circumstances in which, they might reasonably be expected to be kept, used or consumed; and

(b) the keeping, use or consumption of the goods either alone or in conjunction with other goods in conjunction with which they might reasonably be expected to be kept, used or consumed.

PART III   MISLEADING PRICE INDICATIONS

20   Offence of giving misleading indication

(1) Subject to the following provisions of this Part, a person shall be guilty of an offence if, in the course of any business of his, he gives (by any means whatever) to any consumers an indication which is misleading as to the price at which any goods, services, accommodation or facilities are available (whether generally or from particular persons).

(2) Subject as aforesaid, a person shall be guilty of an offence if—

(a) in the course of any business of his, he has given an indication to any consumers which, after it was given, has become misleading as mentioned in subsection (1) above; and

(b) some or all of those consumers might reasonably be expected to rely on the indication at a time after it has become misleading; and

(c) he fails to take all such steps as are reasonable to prevent those consumers from relying on the indication.

(3) For the purposes of this section it shall be immaterial—

(a) whether the person who gives or gave the indication is or was acting on his own behalf or on behalf of another;

(b) whether or not that person is the person, or included among the persons, from whom the goods, services, accommodation or facilities are available; and

(c) whether the indication is or has become misleading in relation to all the consumers to whom it is or was given or only in relation to some of them.

(4) A person guilty of an offence under subsection (1) or (2) above shall be liable—

(a) on conviction on indictment, to a fine;

(b) on summary conviction, to a fine not exceeding the statutory maximum.

(5) No prosecution for an offence under subsection (1) or (2) above shall be brought after whichever is the earlier of the following, that is to say—

(a) the end of the period of three years beginning with the day on which the offence was committed; and

(b) the end of the period of one year beginning with the day on which the person bringing the prosecution discovered that the offence had been committed.

[(5A) A person is not guilty of an offence under subsection (1) or (2) above, if, in giving the misleading indication which would otherwise constitute an offence under either of those subsections, he is guilty of an offence under section 397 of the Financial Services and Markets Act 2000 (misleading statements and practices).]

(6) In this Part—

"consumer"—

(a) in relation to any goods, means any person who might wish to be supplied with the goods for his own private use or consumption;

(b) in relation to any services or facilities, means any person who might wish to be provided with the services or facilities otherwise than for the purposes of any business of his; and

(c) in relation to any accommodation, means any person who might wish to occupy the accommodation otherwise than for the purposes of any business of his;

"price", in relation to any goods, services, accommodation or facilities, means—

(a) the aggregate of the sums required to be paid by a consumer for or otherwise in respect of the supply of the goods or the provision of the services, accommodation or facilities;

(b) except in section 21 below, any method which will be or has been applied for the purpose of determining that aggregate.

21 Meaning of "misleading"

(1) For the purposes of section 20 above an indication given to any consumers is misleading as to a price if what is conveyed by the indication, or what those consumers might reasonably be expected to infer from the indication or any omission from it, includes any of the following, that is to say—

(a) that the price is less than in fact it is;

(b) that the applicability of the price does not depend on facts or circumstances on which its applicability does in fact depend;

(c) that the price covers matters in respect of which an additional charge is in fact made;

    (d) that a person who in fact has no such expectation—
        (i) expects the price to be increased or reduced (whether or not at a particular time or by a particular amount); or
        (ii) expects the price, or the price as increased or reduced, to be maintained (whether or not for a particular period); or
    (e) that the facts or circumstances by reference to which the consumers might reasonably be expected to judge the validity of any relevant comparison made or implied by the indication are not what in fact they are.

  (2) For the purposes of section 20 above, an indication given to any consumers is misleading as to a method of determining a price if what is conveyed by the indication, or what those consumers might reasonably be expected to infer from the indication or any omission from it, includes any of the following, that is to say—
    (a) that the method is not what in fact it is;
    (b) that the applicability of the method does not depend on facts or circumstances on which its applicability does in fact depend;
    (c) that the method takes into account matters in respect of which an additional charge will in fact be made;
    (d) that a person who in fact has no such expectation—
        (i) expects the method to be altered (whether or not at a particular time or in a particular respect); or
        (ii) expects the method, or that method as altered, to remain unaltered (whether or not for a particular period); or
    (e) that the facts or circumstances by reference to which the consumers might reasonably be expected to judge the validity of any relevant comparison made or implied by the indication are not what in fact they are.

  (3) For the purposes of subsections (1)(e) and (2)(e) above a comparison is a relevant comparison in relation to a price or method of determining a price if it is made between that price or that method, or any price which has been or may be determined by that method, and—
    (a) any price or value which is stated or implied to be, to have been or to be likely to be attributed or attributable to the goods, services, accommodation or facilities in question or to any other goods, services, accommodation or facilities; or
    (b) any method, or other method, which is stated or implied to be, to have been or to be likely to be applied or applicable for the determination of the price or value of the goods, services, accommodation or facilities in question or of the price or value of any other goods, services, accommodation or facilities.

22 Application to provision of services and facilities
  (1) Subject to the following provisions of this section, references in this Part to services or facilities are references to any services or facilities whatever including, in particular—
    (a) the provision of credit or of banking or insurance services and the provision of facilities incidental to the provision of such services;
    (b) the purchase or sale of foreign currency;
    (c) the supply of electricity;
    (d) the provision of a place, other than on a highway, for the parking of a motor vehicle;
    (e) the making or arrangements for a person to put or keep a caravan on any land other than arrangements by virtue of which that person may occupy the caravan as his only or main residence.
  (2) References in this Part to services shall not include references to services provided to an employer under a contract of employment. [...]
  (4) In relation to a service consisting in the purchase or sale of foreign currency, references in this Part to the method by which the price of the service is determined shall include

references to the rate of exchange.

(5) In this section—

"caravan" has the same meaning as in the Caravan Sites and Control of Development Act 1960;

"contract of employment" and "employer" have the same meanings as in [the Employment Rights Act 1996];

"credit" has the same meaning as in the Consumer Credit Act 1974.

23 Application to provision of accommodation etc.

(1) Subject to subsection (2) below, references in this Part to accommodation or facilities being available shall not include references to accommodation or facilities being available to be provided by means of the creation or disposal of an interest in land except where—

    (a) the person who is to create or dispose of the interest will do so in the course of any business of his; and

    (b) the interest to be created or disposed of is a relevant interest in a new dwelling and is to be created or disposed of for the purpose of enabling that dwelling to be occupied as a residence, or one of the residences, of the person acquiring the interest.

(2) Subsection (1) above shall not prevent the application of any provision of this Part in relation to—

    (a) the supply of any goods as part of the same transaction as any creation or disposal of an interest in land; or

    (b) the provision of any services or facilities for the purposes of, or in connection with, any transaction for the creation or disposal of such an interest.

(3) In this section—

"new dwelling" means any building or part of a building in Great Britain which—

    (a) has been constructed or adapted to be occupied as a residence; and

    (b) has not previously been so occupied or has been so occupied only with other premises or as more than one residence,

and includes any yard, garden, out-houses or appurtenances which belong to that building or part or are to be enjoyed with it;

"relevant interest"—

    (a) in relation to a new dwelling in England and Wales, means the freehold estate in the dwelling or a leasehold interest in the dwelling for a term of years absolute of more than twenty-one years, not being a term of which twenty-one years or less remains unexpired;

. . .

24 Defences

(1) In any proceedings against a person for an offence under subsection (1) or (2) of section 2 above in respect of any indication it shall be a defence for that person to show that his acts or omissions were authorised for the purposes of this subsection by regulations made under section 26 below.

(2) In proceedings against a person for an offence under subsection (1) or (2) of section 20 above in respect of an indication published in a book, newspaper, magazine [or film or in a programme included in a programme service (within the meaning of the Broadcasting Act 1990),] it shall be a defence for that person to show that the indication was not contained in an advertisement.

(3) In proceedings against a person for an offence under subsection (1) or (2) of section 20 above in respect of an indication published in an advertisement it shall be a defence for that person to show that—

    (a) he is a person who carries on a business of publishing or arranging for the publication of advertisements;

    (b) he received the advertisement for publication in the ordinary course of that business; and

    (c) at the time of publication he did not know and had no grounds for suspecting that the publication would involve the commission of the offence.

  (4) In any proceedings against a person for an offence under subsection (1) of section 20 above in respect of any indication, it shall be a defence for that person to show that—

    (a) the indication did not relate to the availability from him of any goods, services, accommodation or facilities;

    (b) a price had been recommended to every person from whom the goods, services, accommodation or facilities were indicated as being available;

    (c) the indication related to that price and was misleading as to that price only by reason of a failure by any person to follow the recommendation; and

    (d) it was reasonable for the person who gave the indication to assume that the recommendation was for the most part being followed.

  (5) The provisions of this section are without prejudice to the provisions of section 39 below.

  (6) In this section—

"advertisement" includes a catalogue, a circular and a price list; . . .

25   Code of practice

  (1) The Secretary of State may, after consulting [the Office of Fair Trading] and such other persons as the Secretary of State considers it appropriate to consult, by order approve any code of practice issued (whether by the Secretary of State or another person) for the purpose of—

    (a) giving practical guidance with respect to any of the requirements of section 20 above; and

    (b) promoting what appear to the Secretary of State to be desirable practices as to the circumstances and manner in which any person gives an indication as to the price at which any goods, services, accommodation or facilities are available or indicates any other matter in respect of which any such indication may be misleading.

  (2) A contravention of a code of practice approved under this section shall not of itself give rise to any criminal or civil liability, but in any proceedings against any person for an offence under section 20(1) or (2) above—

    (a) any contravention by that person of such a code may be relied on in relation to any matter for the purpose of establishing that that person committed the offence or of negativing any defence;

    (b) compliance by that person with such a code may be relied on in relation to any matter for the purpose of showing that the commission of the offence by that person has not been established or that that person has a defence.

  (3) Where the Secretary of State approves a code of practice under this section he may, after such consultation as is mentioned in subsection (1) above, at any time by order—

    (a) approve any modification of the code; or

    (b) withdraw his approval;

and references in subsection (2) above to a code of practice approved under this section shall be construed accordingly.

  (4) The power to make an order under this section shall be exercisable by statutory instrument subject to annulment in pursuance of a resolution of either House of Parliament.

26   Power to make regulations

  (1) The Secretary of State may, after consulting [the Office of Fair Trading] and such other persons as the Secretary of State considers it appropriate to consult, by regulations make provision—

(a) for the purpose of regulating the circumstances and manner in which any person—
  (i) gives any indication as to the price at which any goods, services, accommodation or facilities will be or are available or have been supplied or provided; or
  (ii) indicates any other matter in respect of which any such indication may be misleading;

(b) for the purpose of facilitating the enforcement of the provisions of section 20 above or of any regulations made under this section.

(2) The Secretary of State shall not make regulations by virtue of subsection (1)(a) above except in relation to—
  (a) indications given by persons in the course of business; and
  (b) such indications given otherwise than in the course of business as—
    (i) are given by or on behalf of persons by whom accommodation is provided to others by means of leases or licences; and
    (ii) relate to goods, services or facilities supplied or provided to those others in connection with the provision of the accommodation.

(3) Without prejudice to the generality of subsection (1) above, regulations under this section may—
  (a) prohibit an indication as to a price from referring to such matters as may be prescribed by the regulations;
  (b) require an indication as to a price or other matter to be accompanied or supplemented by such explanation or such additional information as may be prescribed by the regulations;
  (c) require information or explanations with respect to a price or other matter to be given to an officer of an enforcement authority and to authorise such an officer to require such information or explanations to be given;
  (d) require any information or explanation provided for the purposes of any regulations made by virtue of paragraph (b) or (c) above to be accurate;
  (e) prohibit the inclusion in indications as to a price or other matter of statements that the indications are not to be relied upon;
  (f) provide that expressions used in any indication as to a price or other matter shall be construed in a particular way for the purposes of this Part;
  (g) provide that a contravention of any provision of the regulations shall constitute a criminal offence punishable—
    (i) on conviction on indictment, by a fine;
    (ii) on summary conviction, by a fine not exceeding the statutory maximum;
  (h) apply any provision of this Act which relates to a criminal offence to an offence created by virtue of paragraph (g) above.

(4) The power to make regulations under this section shall be exercisable by statutory instrument . . .

PART IV   ENFORCEMENT OF PARTS II AND III

27 Enforcement
(1) Subject to the following provisions of this section—
  (a) it shall be the duty of every weights and measures authority in Great Britain to enforce within their area the safety provisions and the provisions made by or under Part III of this Act; and
  (b) it shall be the duty of every district council in Northern Ireland to enforce within their area the safety provisions.

(2) The Secretary of State may by regulations—

(a) wholly or partly transfer any duty imposed by subsection (1) above on a weights and measures authority or a district council in Northern Ireland to such other person who has agreed to the transfer as is specified in the regulations;

(b) relieve such an authority or council of any such duty so far as it is exercisable in relation to such goods as may be described in the regulations.

(3) The power to make regulations under subsection (2) above shall be exercisable by statutory instrument . . .

28 Test purchases

(1) An enforcement authority shall have power, for the purpose of ascertaining whether any safety provision or any provision made by or under Part III of this Act has been contravened in relation to any goods, services, accommodation or facilities—

(a) to make, or to authorise an officer of the authority to make, any purchase of any goods; or

(b) to secure, or to authorise an officer of the authority to secure, the provision of any services, accommodation or facilities.

(2) Where—

(a) any goods purchased under this section by or on behalf of an enforcement authority are submitted to a test; and

(b) the test leads to—

(i) the bringing of proceedings for an offence in respect of a contravention in relation to the goods of any safety provision or of any provision made by or under Part III of this Act or for the forfeiture of the goods under section 16 or 17 above; or

(ii) the serving of a suspension notice in respect of any goods; and

(c) the authority is requested to do so and it is practicable for the authority to comply with the request,

the authority shall allow the person from whom the goods were purchased or any person who is a party to the proceedings or has an interest in any goods to which the notice relates to have the goods tested.

(3) The Secretary of State may by regulations provide that any test of goods purchased under this section by or on behalf of an enforcement authority shall—

(a) be carried out at the expense of the authority in a manner and by a person prescribed by or determined under the regulations; or

(b) be carried out either as mentioned in paragraph (a) above or by the authority in a manner prescribed by the regulations.

(4) The power to make regulations under subsection (3) above shall be exercisable by statutory instrument . . .

(5) Nothing in this section shall authorise the acquisition by or on behalf of an enforcement authority of any interest in land.

29 Powers of search etc.

(1) Subject to the following provisions of this Part, a duly authorised officer of an enforcement authority may at any reasonable hour and on production, if required, of his credentials exercise any of the powers conferred by the following provisions of this section.

(2) The officer may, for the purpose of ascertaining whether there has been any contravention of any safety provision or of any provision made by or under Part III of this Act, inspect any goods and enter any premises other than premises occupied only as a person's residence.

(3) The officer may, for the purpose of ascertaining whether there has been any contravention of any safety provision, examine any procedure (including any arrangements for carrying out a test) connected with the production of any goods.

(4) If the officer has reasonable grounds for suspecting that any goods are manufactured or imported goods which have not been supplied in the United Kingdom since they were manufactured or imported he may—

(a) for the purpose of ascertaining whether there has been any contravention of any safety provision in relation to the goods, require any person carrying on a business, or employed in connection with the business, to produce any records relating to the business;

(b) for the purpose of ascertaining (by testing or otherwise) whether there has been any such contravention, seize and detain the goods;

(c) take copies of, or of any entry in, any records produced by virtue of paragraph (a) above.

(5) If the officer has reasonable grounds for suspecting that there has been a contravention in relation to any goods of any safety provision or of any provision made by or under Part III of this Act, he may—

(a) for the purpose of ascertaining whether there has been any such contravention, require any person carrying on a business, or employed in connection with a business, to produce any records relating to the business;

(b) for the purpose of ascertaining (by testing or otherwise) whether there has been any such contravention, seize and detain the goods;

(c) take copies of, or of any entry in, any records produced by virtue of paragraph (a) above.

(6) The officer may seize and detain—

(a) any goods or records which he has reasonable grounds for believing may be required as evidence in proceedings for an offence in respect of a contravention of any safety provision or of any provision made by or under Part III of this Act.

(b) any goods which he has reasonable grounds for suspecting may be liable to be forfeited under section 16 or 17 above.

(7) If and to the extent that it is reasonably necessary to do so to prevent a contravention of any safety provision or of any provision made by or under Part III of this Act, the officer may, for the purpose of exercising his power under subsection (4), (5) or (6) above to seize any goods or records—

(a) require any person having authority to do so to open any container or to open any vending machine; and

(b) himself open or break open any such container or machine where a requirement made under paragraph (a) above in relation to the container or machine has not been complied with.

30   Provisions supplemental to s. 29

(1) An officer seizing any goods or records under section 29 above shall inform the following persons that the goods or records have been so seized, that is to say—

(a) the person from whom they are seized; and

(b) in the case of imported goods seized on any premises under the control of the Commissioners of Customs and Excise, the importer of those goods (within the meaning of the Customs and Excise Management Act 1979).

(2) If a justice of the peace—

(a) is satisfied by any written information on oath that there are reasonable grounds for believing either—

(i) that any goods or records which any officer has power to inspect under section 29 above are on any premises and that their inspection is likely to disclose evidence that there has been a contravention of any safety provision or of any provision made by or under part III of this Act; or

(ii) that such a contravention has taken place, is taking place or is about to take place on any premises; and

(b) is also satisfied by any such information either—

(i) that admission to the premises has been or is likely to be refused and that notice of intention to apply for a warrant under this subsection has been given to the occupier; or

(ii) that an application for admission, or the giving of such a notice, would defeat the object of the entry or that the premises are unoccupied or that the occupier is temporarily absent and it might defeat the object of the entry to await his return,

the justice may by warrant under his hand, which shall continue in force for a period of one month, authorise any officer of an enforcement authority to enter the premises, if need be by force.

(3) An officer entering any premises by virtue of section 29 above or a warrant under subsection (2) above may take with him such other persons and such equipment as may appear to him necessary.

(4) On leaving any premises which a person is authorised to enter by a warrant under subsection (2) above, that person shall, if the premises are unoccupied or the occupier is temporarily absent, leave the premises as effectively secured against trespassers as he found them.

(5) If any person who is not an officer of an enforcement authority purports to act as such under section 29 above or this section he shall be guilty of an offence and liable on summary conviction to a fine not exceeding level 5 on the standard scale.

(6) Where any goods seized by an officer under section 29 above are submitted to a test, the officer shall inform the persons mentioned in subsection (1) above of the result of the test and, if—

(a) proceedings are brought for an offence in respect of a contravention in relation to the goods of any safety provision or of any provision made by or under Part III of this Act or for the forfeiture of the goods under section 16 or 17 above, or a suspension notice is served in respect of any goods; and

(b) the officer is requested to do so and it is practicable to comply with the request,

the officer shall allow any person who is a party to the proceedings or, as the case may be, has an interest in the goods to which the notice relates to have the goods tested.

(7) The Secretary of State may by regulations provide that any test of goods seized under section 29 above by an officer of an enforcement authority shall—

(a) be carried out at the expense of the authority in a manner and by a person prescribed by or determined under the regulations; or

(b) be carried out either as mentioned in paragraph (a) above or by the authority in a manner prescribed by the regulations.

(8) The power to make regulations under subsection (7) above shall be exercisable by statutory instrument...

31   Power of customs officer to detain goods

(1) A customs officer may, for the purpose of facilitating the exercise by an enforcement authority or officer of such an authority of any functions conferred on the authority or officer by or under Part II of this Act, or by or under this Part in its application for the purposes of the safety provisions, seize any imported goods and detain them for not more than two working days.

(2) Anything seized and detained under this section shall be dealt with during the period of its detention in such manner as the Commissioners of Customs and Excise may direct.

32   Obstruction of authorised officer

(1) Any person who—

(a) intentionally obstructs any officer of an enforcement authority who is acting in pursuance of any provision of this Part or any customs officer who is so acting; or

(b) intentionally fails to comply with any requirement made of him by any officer of any enforcement authority under any provision of this Part; or

(c) without reasonable cause fails to give any officer of an enforcement authority who is so acting any other assistance or information which the officer may reasonably require of him for the purposes of the exercise of the officer's functions under any provision of this Part, shall be guilty of an offence and liable on summary conviction to a fine not exceeding level 5 on the standard scale.

(2) A person shall be guilty of an offence if, in giving any information which is required of him by virtue of subsection (1)(c) above—

(a) he makes any statement which he knows is false in a material particular; or

(b) he recklessly makes a statement which is false in a material particular.

(3) A person guilty of an offence under subsection (2) above shall be liable—

(a) on conviction on indictment, to a fine;

(b) on summary conviction, to a fine not exceeding the statutory maximum.

33 Appeals against detention of goods

(1) Any person having an interest in any goods which are for the time being detained under any provision of this Part by an enforcement authority or by an officer of such an authority may apply for an order requiring the goods to be released to him or to another person.

(2) An application under this section may be made—

(a) to any magistrates' court in which proceedings have been brought in England and Wales or Northern Ireland—

(i) for an offence in respect of a contravention in relation to the goods of any safety provision or of any provision made by or under Part III of this Act; or

(ii) for the forfeiture of the goods under section 16 above;

(b) where no such proceedings have been so brought, by way of complaint to a magistrates' court . . .

(3) On an application under this section to a magistrates' court . . ., an order requiring goods to be released shall be made only if the court . . . is satisfied—

(a) that proceedings—

(i) for an offence in respect of a contravention in relation to the goods of any safety provision or of any provision made by or under Part III of this Act; or

(ii) for the forfeiture of the goods under section 16 or 17 above, have not been brought or, having been brought, have been concluded without the goods being forfeited; and

(b) where no such proceedings have been brought, that more than six months have elapsed since the goods were seized.

(4) Any person aggrieved by an order made under this section by a magistrates' court in England and Wales or Northern Ireland, or by a decision of such a court not to make such an order, may appeal against that order or decision—

(a) in England and Wales, to the Crown Court;

(b) in Northern Ireland, to the county court;

and an order so made may contain such provision as appears to the court to be appropriate for delaying the coming into force of the order pending the making and determination of any appeal (including any application under section 111 of the Magistrates' Courts Act 1980 or Article 146 of the Magistrates' Courts (Northern Ireland) Order 1981 (statement of case)).

34 Compensation for seizure and detention

(1) Where an officer of an enforcement authority exercises any power under section 29 above to seize and detain goods, the enforcement authority shall be liable to pay compensation to any person having an interest in the goods in respect of any loss or damage caused by reason of the exercise of the power if—

(a) there has been no contravention in relation to the goods of any safety provision or of any provision made by or under Part III of this Act; and

(b) the exercise of the power is not attributable to any neglect or default by that person.

(2) Any disputed question as to the right to or the amount of any compensation payable under this section shall be determined by arbitration . . .

35   Recovery of expenses of enforcement

    (1) This section shall apply where a court—

        (a) convicts a person of an offence in respect of a contravention in relation to any goods of any safety provision or of any provision made by or under Part III of this Act; or

        (b) makes an order under section 16 or 17 above for the forfeiture of any goods.

    (2) The court may (in addition to any other order it may make as to costs or expenses) order the person convicted or, as the case may be, any person having an interest in the goods to reimburse an enforcement authority for an expenditure which has been or may be incurred by that authority—

        (a) in connection with any seizure or detention of the goods by or on behalf of the authority; or

        (b) in connection with any compliance by the authority with directions given by the court for the purposes of any order for the forfeiture of the goods.

PART V   MISCELLANEOUS AND SUPPLEMENTAL

37   [Power of Commissioners for Revenue and Customs to disclose information]

    (1) If they think it appropriate to do so for the purpose of facilitating the exercise by any person to whom subsection (2) below applies of any functions conferred on that person by or under Part II of this Act, or by or under Part IV of this Act in its application for the purposes of the safety provisions, [the Commissioners for Her Majesty's Revenue and Customs] may authorise the disclosure to that person of any information obtained [or held] for the purposes of the exercise [by Her Majesty's Revenue and Customs] of their functions in relation to imported goods.

    (2) This subsection applies to an enforcement authority and to any officer of an enforcement authority.

    (3) A disclosure of information made to any person under subsection (1) above shall be made in such manner as may be directed by [the Commissioners for Her Majesty's Revenue and Customs] and may be made through such person acting on behalf of that person as may be so directed.

    (4) Information may be disclosed to a person under subsection (1) above whether or not the disclosure of the information has been requested by or on behalf of that person.

39   Defence of due diligence

    (1) Subject to the following provisions of this section, in proceedings against any person for an offence to which this section applies it shall be a defence for that person to show that he took all reasonable steps and exercised all due diligence to avoid committing the offence.

    (2) Where in any proceedings against any person for such an offence the defence provided by subsection (1) above involves an allegation that the commission of the offence was due—

        (a) to the act or default of another; or

        (b) to reliance on information given by another,

that person shall not, without the leave of the court, be entitled to rely on the defence unless, not less than seven clear days before the hearing of the proceedings, he has served a notice under subsection (3) below on the person bringing the proceedings.

    (3) A notice under this subsection shall give such information identifying or assisting in the identification of the person who committed the act or default or gave the information as is in the possession of the person serving the notice at the time he serves it.

    (4) It is hereby declared that a person shall not be entitled to rely on the defence provided by subsection (1) above by reason of his reliance on information supplied by another, unless he shows that it was reasonable in all the circumstances for him to have relied on the information, having regard in particular—

(a) to the steps which he took, and those which might reasonably have been taken, for the purpose of verifying the information; and

(b) to whether he had any reason to disbelieve the information.

(5) This section shall apply to an offence under section [...] 12(1), (2) or (3), 13(4), 14(6) or 20(1) above.

40 Liability of persons other than principal offender

(1) Where the commission by any person of an offence to which section 39 above applies is due to an act or default committed by some other person in the course of any business of his, the other person shall be guilty of the offence and may be proceeded against and punished by virtue of this subsection whether or not proceedings are taken against the first mentioned person.

(2) Where a body corporate is guilty of an offence under this Act (including where it is so guilty by virtue of subsection (1) above) in respect of any act or default which is shown to have been committed with the consent or connivance of, or to be attributable to any neglect on the part of, any director, manager, secretary or other similar office of the body corporate or any person who was purporting to act in any such capacity he, as well as the body corporate, shall be guilty of that offence and shall be liable to be proceeded against and punished accordingly.

(3) Where the affairs of a body corporate are managed by its members, subsection (2) above shall apply in relation to the acts and defaults of a member in connection with his functions of management as if he were a director of the body corporate.

41 Civil proceedings

(1) An obligation imposed by safety regulations shall be a duty owed to any person who may be affected by a contravention of the obligation and, subject to any provision to the contrary in the regulations and to the defences and other incidents applying to actions for breach of statutory duty, a contravention of any such obligation shall be actionable accordingly.

(2) This Act shall not be construed as conferring any other right of action in civil proceedings, apart from the right conferred by virtue of Part I of this Act, in respect of any loss or damage suffered in consequence of a contravention of a safety provision or of a provision made by or under Part III of this Act.

(3) Subject to any provision to the contrary in the agreement itself, an agreement shall not be void or unenforceable by reason only of a contravention of a safety provision or of a provision made by or under Part III of this Act.

(4) Liability by virtue of subsection (1) above shall not be limited or excluded by any contract term, by any notice or (subject to the power contained in subsection (1) above to limit or exclude it in safety regulations) by any other provision.

(5) Nothing in subsection (1) above shall prejudice the operation of section 12 of the Nuclear Installations Act 1965 (rights to compensation for certain breaches of duties confined to rights under that Act).

(6) In this section "damage" includes personal injury and death.

42 Reports etc.

(1) It shall be the duty of the Secretary of State at least once in every five years to lay before each House of Parliament a report on the exercise during the period to which the report relates of the functions which under Part II of this Act, or under Part IV of this Act in its application for the purposes of the safety provisions, are exercisable by the Secretary of State, weights and measures authorities, district councils in Northern Ireland and persons on whom functions are conferred by regulations made under section 27(2) above.

(2) The Secretary of State may from time to time prepare and lay before each House of Parliament such other reports on the exercise of those functions as he considers appropriate.

(3) Every weights and measures authority, every district council in Northern Ireland and every person on whom functions are conferred by regulations under subsection (2) of section 27 above shall, whenever the Secretary of State so directs, make a report to the Secretary of State on the exercise of the functions exercisable by the authority or council under that section or by that person by virtue of any such regulations.

45 Interpretation

(1) In this Act, except in so far as the context otherwise requires—

"aircraft" includes gliders, balloons and hovercraft;

"business" includes a trade or profession and the activities of a professional or trade association or of a local authority or other public authority;

"conditional sale agreement", "credit—sale agreement" and "hire-purchase agreement" have the same meanings as in the Consumer Credit Act 1974 but as if in the definitions in that Act "goods" had the same meaning as in this Act;

"contravention" includes a failure to comply and cognate expressions shall be construed accordingly;

"enforcement authority" means the Secretary of State, any other Minister of the Crown in charge of a Government department, any such department and any authority, council or other person on whom functions under this Act are conferred by or under section 27 above;

"gas" has the same meaning as in Part I of the Gas Act 1986;

"goods" includes substances, growing crops and things comprised in land by virtue of being attached to it and any ship, aircraft or vehicle;

"information" includes accounts, estimates and returns;

"magistrates' court" in relation to Northern Ireland, means a court of summary jurisdiction;

"modifications" includes additions, alterations and omissions, and cognate expressions shall be construed accordingly;

"motor vehicle" has the same meaning as in [the Road Traffic Act 1988];

"notice" means a notice in writing;

"notice to warn" means a notice under section 13(1)(b) above;

"officer", in relation to an enforcement authority, means a person authorised in writing to assist the authority in carrying out its functions under or for the purposes of the enforcement of any of the safety provisions or of any of the provisions made by or under Part III of this Act;

"personal injury" includes any disease and any other impairment of a person's physical or mental condition;

"premises" includes any place and any ship, aircraft or vehicle;

"prohibition notice" means a notice under section 13(1)(a) above;

"records" includes any books or documents and any records in non-documentary form;

"safety provision" means [. . .] any provision of safety regulations, a prohibition notice or a suspension notice;

"safety regulations" means regulations under section 11 above;

"ship" includes any boat and any other description of vessel used in navigation;

"subordinate legislation" has the same meaning as in the Interpretation Act 1978;

"substance" means any natural or artificial substance, whether in solid, liquid or gaseous form or in the form of a vapour, and includes substances that are comprised in or mixed with other goods;

"supply" and cognate expressions shall be construed in accordance with section 46 below;

"suspension notice" means a notice under section 14 above.

(2) Except in so far as the context otherwise requires, references in this Act to a contravention of a safety provision shall, in relation to any goods, include references to anything which would constitute such a contravention if the goods were supplied to any person.

(3) References in this Act to any goods in relation to which any safety provision has been or may have been contravened shall include references to any goods which it is not reasonably practicable to separate from any such goods.

46   Meaning of "supply"

(1) Subject to the following provisions of this section, references in this Act to supplying goods shall be construed as references to doing any of the following, whether as principal or agent, that is to say—

(a) selling, hiring out or lending the goods;

(b) entering into a hire-purchase agreement to furnish the goods;

(c) the performance of any contract for work and materials to furnish the goods;

(d) providing the goods in exchange for any consideration [. . .] other than money;

(e) providing the goods in or in connection with the performance of any statutory function; or

(f) giving the goods as a prize or otherwise making a gift of the goods; and, in relation to gas or water, those references shall be construed as including references to providing the service by which the gas or water is made available for use.

(2) For the purpose of any reference in this Act to supplying goods, where a person ('the ostensible supplier') supplies goods to another person ('the customer') under a hire-purchase agreement, conditional sale agreement or credit-sale agreement or under an agreement for the hiring of goods (other than a hire-purchase agreement) and the ostensible supplier—

(a) carries on the business of financing the provision of goods for others by means of such agreements; and

(b) in the course of that business acquired his interest in the goods supplied to the customer as a means of financing the provision of them for the customer by a further person ('the effective supplier'),

the effective supplier and not the ostensible supplier shall be treated as supplying the goods to the customer.

(3) Subject to subsection (4) below, the performance of any contract by the erection of any building or structure on any land or by the carrying out of any other building works shall be treated for the purposes of this Act as a supply of goods in so far as, but only in so far as, it involves the provision of any goods to any person by means of their incorporation into the building, structure or works.

(4) Except for the purposes of, and in relation to, notices to warn or any provision made by or under Part III of this Act, references in this Act to supplying goods shall not include references to supplying goods comprised in land where the supply is effected by the creation or disposal of an interest in the land.

(5) Except in Part I of this Act references in this Act to a person's supplying goods shall be confined to references to that person's supplying goods in the course of a business of his, but for the purposes of this subsection it shall be immaterial whether the business is a business of dealing in the goods.

(6) For the purposes of subsection (5) above goods shall not be treated as supplied in the course of a business if they are supplied, in pursuance of an obligation arising under or in connection with the insurance of the goods, to the person with whom they were insured.

(7) Except for the purposes of, and in relation to, prohibition notices or suspension notices, references in Parts II to IV of this Act to supplying goods shall not include—

(a) references to supplying goods where the person supplied carries on a business of buying goods of the same description as those goods and repairing or reconditioning them;

(b) references to supplying goods by a sale of articles as scrap (that is to say, for the value of materials included in the articles rather than for the value of the articles themselves).

(8) Where any goods have at any time been supplied by being hired out or lent to any person, neither a continuation or renewal of the hire or loan (whether on the same or different terms) nor any transaction for the transfer after that time of any interest in the goods to the person to whom they were hired or lent shall be treated for the purposes of this Act as a further supply of the goods to that person.

(9) A ship, aircraft or motor vehicle shall not be treated for the purposes of this Act as supplied to any person by reason only that services consisting in the carriage of goods or passengers in that ship, aircraft or vehicle, or in its use for any other purpose, are provided to that person in pursuance of an agreement relating to the use of the ship, aircraft or vehicle for a particular period or for particular voyages, flights or journeys.

Section 13

SCHEDULE 2

PROHIBITION NOTICES AND NOTICES TO WARN

PART I   PROHIBITION NOTICES

1.   A prohibition notice in respect of any goods shall—
(a) state that the Secretary of State considers that the goods are unsafe;
(b) set out the reasons why the Secretary of State considers that the goods are unsafe;
(c) specify the day on which the notice is to come into force; and
(d) state that the trader may at any time make representations in writing to the Secretary of State for the purpose of establishing that the goods are safe.

2.—(1) If representations in writing about a prohibition notice are made by the trader to the Secretary of State, it shall be the duty of the Secretary of State to consider whether to revoke the notice and—
(a) if he decides to revoke it, to do so;
(b) in any other case, to appoint a person to consider those representations, any further representations made (whether in writing or orally) by the trader about the notice and the statements of any witnesses examined under this Part of this Schedule.

(2) Where the Secretary of State has appointed a person to consider representations about a prohibition notice, he shall serve a notification on the trader which—
(a) states that the trader may make oral representations to the appointed person for the purpose of establishing that the goods to which the notice relates are safe; and
(b) specifies the place and time at which the oral representations may be made.

(3) The time specified in a notification served under sub-paragraph (2) above shall not be before the end of the period of twenty-one days beginning with the day on which the notification is served, unless the trader otherwise agrees.

(4) A person on whom a notification has been served for the purposes of sub-paragraph (2)(b) above or his representative may, at the place and time specified in the notification—
(a) make oral representations to the appointed person for the purpose of establishing that the goods in question are safe; and
(b) call and examine witnesses in connection with the representations.

4.—(1) Where a person is appointed to consider representations about a prohibition notice, it shall be his duty to consider—
(a) any written representations made by the trader about the notice, other than those in respect of which a notification is served under paragraph 3(2)(a) above;
(b) any oral representations made under paragraph 2(4) or 3(4) above; and
(c) any statements made by witnesses in connection with the oral representations, and, after considering any matters under this paragraph, to make a report (including recommendations) to the Secretary of State about the matters considered by him and the notice.

(2) It shall be the duty of the Secretary of State to consider any report made to him under sub-paragraph (1) above and, after considering the report, to inform the trader of his decision with respect to the prohibition notice to which the report relates

5.—(1) The Secretary of State may revoke or vary a prohibition notice by serving on the trader a notification stating that the notice is revoked or, as the case may be, is varied as specified in the notification.

(2) The Secretary of State shall not vary a prohibition notice so as to make the effect of the notice more restrictive for the trader.

(3) Without prejudice to the power conferred by section 13(2) of this Act, the service of a notification under sub-paragraph (1) above shall be sufficient to satisfy the requirement of paragraph 4(2) above that the trader shall be informed of the Secretary of State's decision.

PART II   NOTICES TO WARN

6.—(1) If the Secretary of State proposes to serve a notice to warn on any person in respect of any goods, the Secretary of State, before he serves the notice, shall serve on that person a notification which—

(a) contains a draft of the proposed notice;

(b) states that the Secretary of State proposes to serve a notice in the form of the draft on that person;

(c) states that the Secretary of State considers that the goods described in the draft are unsafe;

(d) sets out the reasons why the Secretary of State considers that those goods are unsafe; and

(e) states that that person may make representations to the Secretary of State for the purpose of establishing that the goods are safe if, before the end of the period of fourteen days beginning with the day on which the notification is served, he informs the Secretary of State—

   (i)   of his intention to make representations; and

   (ii) whether the representations will be made only in writing or both in writing and orally.

(2) Where the Secretary of State has served a notification containing a draft of a proposed notice to warn on any person, he shall not serve a notice to warn on that person in respect of the goods to which the proposed notice relates unless—

(a) the period of fourteen days beginning with the day on which the notification was served expires without the Secretary of State being informed as mentioned in sub-paragraph (1)(e) above;

(b) the period of twenty-eight days beginning with that day expires without any written representations being made by that person to the Secretary of State about the proposed notice; or

(c) the Secretary of State has considered a report about the proposed notice by a person appointed under paragraph 7(1) below.

7.—(1) Where a person on whom a notification containing a draft of a proposed notice to warn has been served—

(a) informs the Secretary of State as mentioned in paragraph 6(1)(e) above before the end of the period of fourteen days beginning with the day on which the notification was served; and

(b) makes written representations to the Secretary of State about the proposed notice before the end of the period of twenty-eight days beginning with that day,

the Secretary of State shall appoint a person to consider those representations, any further representations made by that person about the draft notice and the statements of any witnesses examined under this Part of this Schedule.

(2) Where—
  (a) the Secretary of State has appointed a person to consider representations about a proposed notice to warn; and
  (b) the person whose representations are to be considered has informed the Secretary of State for the purposes of paragraph 6(1)(e) above that the representations he intends to make will include oral representations,

the Secretary of State shall inform the person intending to make the representations of the place and time at which oral representations may be made to the appointed person.

(3) Where a person on whom a notification containing a draft of a proposed notice to warn has been served is informed of a time for the purposes of sub-paragraph (2) above, that time shall not be—
  (a) before the end of the period of twenty-eight days beginning with the day on which the notification was served; or
  (b) before the end of the period of seven days beginning with the day on which that person is informed of the time.

(4) A person who has been informed of a place and time for the purposes of subparagraph (2) above or his representative may, at that place and time—
  (a) make oral representations to the appointed person for the purpose of establishing that the goods to which the proposed notice relates are safe; and
  (b) call and examine witnesses in connection with the representations.

8.—(1) Where a person is appointed to consider representations about a proposed notice to warn, it shall be his duty to consider—
  (a) any written representations made by the person on whom it is proposed to serve the notice; and
  (b) in a case where a place and a time has been appointed under paragraph 7(2) above for oral representations to be made by that person or his representative, any representations so made and any statements made by witnesses in connection with those representations,

and, after considering those matters, to make a report (including recommendations) to the Secretary of State about the matters considered by him and the proposal to serve the notice.

(2) It shall be the duty of the Secretary of State to consider any report made to him under sub-paragraph (1) above and, after considering the report, to inform the person on whom it was proposed that a notice to warn should be served of his decision with respect to the proposal.

(3) If at any time after serving a notification on a person under paragraph 6 above the Secretary of State decides not to serve on that person either the proposed notice to warn or that notice with modifications, the Secretary of State shall inform that person of the decision; and nothing done for the purposes of any of the preceding provisions of this Part of this Schedule before that person was so informed shall—
  (a) entitle the Secretary of State subsequently to serve the proposed notice or that notice with modifications; or
  (b) require the Secretary of State, or any person appointed to consider representations about the proposed notice, subsequently to do anything in respect of, or in consequence of, any such representations.

(4) Where a notification containing a draft of a proposed notice to warn is served on a person in respect of any goods, a notice to warn served on him in consequence of a decision made under sub-paragraph (2) above shall either be in the form of the draft or shall be less onerous than the draft.

9. The Secretary of State may revoke a notice to warn by serving on the person on whom the notice was served a notification stating that the notice is revoked.

PART III   GENERAL

10.—(1) Where in a notification served on any person under this Schedule the Secretary of State has appointed a time for the making of oral representations or the examination of witnesses, he may, by giving that person such notification as the Secretary of State considers appropriate, change that time to a later time or appoint further times at which further representations may be made or the examination of witnesses may be continued; and paragraphs 2(4), 3(4) and 7(4) above shall have effect accordingly.

(2) For the purposes of this Schedule the Secretary of State may appoint a person (instead of the appointed person) to consider any representations or statements, if the person originally appointed, or last appointed under this sub-paragraph, to consider those representations or statements has died or appears to the Secretary of State to be otherwise unable to act.

11. In this Schedule—

"the appointed person" in relation to a prohibition notice or a proposal to serve a notice to warn, means the person for the time being appointed under this Schedule to consider representations about the notice or, as the case may be, about the proposed notice;

"notification" means a notification in writing;

"trader", in relation to a prohibition notice, means the person on whom the notice is or was served.

Minors' Contracts Act 1987
(1987, c. 13)

2   Guarantees

Where—

> (a) a guarantee is given in respect of an obligation of a party to a contract made after the commencement of this Act, and
> (b) the obligation is unenforceable against him (or he repudiates the contract)
> (c) because he was a minor when the contract was made,

the guarantee shall not for that reason alone be unenforceable against the guarantor.

3   Restitution

(1) Where—

> (a) a person ("the plaintiff") has after the commencement of this Act entered into a contract with another ("the defendant"), and
> (b) the contract is unenforceable against the defendant (or he repudiates it) because he was a minor when the contract was made,

the court may, if it is just and equitable to do so, require the defendant to transfer to the plaintiff any property acquired by the defendant under the contract, or any property representing it.

(2) Nothing in this section shall be taken to prejudice any other remedy available to the plaintiff.

Copyright, Designs and Patents Act 1988
(1988, c. 48)

96   Infringement actionable by copyright owner

(1) An infringement of copyright is actionable by the copyright owner.

(2) In an action for infringement of copyright all such relief by way of damages, injunctions, accounts or otherwise is available to the plaintiff as is available in respect of the infringement of any other property right.

97   Provisions as to damages in infringement action

(1) Where in an action for infringement of copyright it is shown that at the time of the infringement the defendant did not know, and had no reason to believe, that copyright subsisted in the work to which the action relates, the plaintiff is not entitled to damages against him, but without prejudice to any other remedy.

(2) The court may in an action for infringement of copyright having regard to all the circumstances, and in particular to—

(a) the flagrancy of the infringement, and

(b) any benefit accruing to the defendant by reason of the infringement,

award such additional damages as the justice of the case may require.

229   Rights and remedies of design right owner

(1) An infringement of design right is actionable by the design right owner.

(2) In an action for infringement of design right all such relief by way of damages, injunctions, accounts or otherwise is available to the plaintiff as is available in respect of the infringement of any other property right.

(3) The court may in an action for infringement of design right, having regard to all the circumstances and in particular to—

(a) the flagrancy of the infringement, and

(b) any benefit accruing to the defendant by reason of the infringement,

award such additional damages as the justice of the case may require.

253   Remedy for groundless threats of infringement proceedings.

(1) Where a person threatens another person with proceedings for infringement of design right, a person aggrieved by the threats may bring an action against him claiming—

(a) a declaration to the effect that the threats are unjustifiable;

(b) an injunction against the continuance of the threats;

(c) damages in respect of any loss which he has sustained by the threats.

(2) If the plaintiff proves that the threats were made and that he is a person aggrieved by them, he is entitled to the relief claimed unless the defendant shows that the acts in respect of which proceedings were threatened did constitute, or if done would have constituted, an infringement of the design right concerned.

(3) Proceedings may not be brought under this section in respect of a threat to bring proceedings for an infringement alleged to consist of making or importing anything.

(4) Mere notification that a design is protected by design right does not constitute a threat of proceedings for the purposes of this section.

Housing Act 1988
(1988, c. 50)

16   Access for repairs

It shall be an implied term of every assured tenancy that the tenant shall afford to the landlord access to the dwelling-house let on the tenancy and all reasonable facilities for executing therein any repairs which the landlord is entitled to execute.

27   Damages for unlawful eviction

(1) This section applies if, at any time after 9th June 1988, a landlord (in this section referred to as "the landlord in default") or any person acting on behalf of the landlord in default unlawfully deprives the residential occupier of any premises of his occupation of the whole or part of the premises.

(2) This section also applies if, at any time after 9th June 1988, a landlord (in this section referred to as "the landlord in default") or any person acting on behalf of the landlord in default—

    (a) attempts unlawfully to deprive the residential occupier of any premises of his occupation of the whole or part of the premises, or

    (b) knowing or having reasonable cause to believe that the conduct is likely to cause the residential occupier of any premises—

        (i) to give up his occupation of the premises or any part thereof, or

        (ii) to refrain from exercising any right or pursuing any remedy in respect of the premises or any part thereof,

does acts likely to interfere with the peace or comfort of the residential occupier or members of his household, or persistently withdraws or withholds services reasonably required for the occupation of the premises as a residence, and, as a result, the residential occupier gives up his occupation of the premises as a residence.

    (3) Subject to the following provisions of this section, where this section applies, the landlord in default shall, by virtue of this section, be liable to pay to the former residential occupier, in respect of his loss of the right to occupy the premises in question as his residence, damages assessed on the basis set out in section 28 below.

    (4) Any liability arising by virtue of subsection (3) above—

    (a) shall be in the nature of a liability in tort; and

    (b) subject to subsection (5) below, shall be in addition to any liability arising apart from this section (whether in tort, contract or otherwise).

    (5) Nothing in this section affects the right of a residential occupier to enforce any liability which arises apart from this section in respect of his loss of the right to occupy premises as his residence; but damages shall not be awarded both in respect of such a liability and in respect of a liability arising by virtue of this section on account of the same loss.

    (6) No liability shall arise by virtue of subsection (3) above if—

    (a) before the date on which proceedings to enforce the liability are finally disposed of, the former residential occupier is reinstated in the premises in question in such circumstances that he becomes again the residential occupier of them; or

    (b) at the request of the former residential occupier, a court makes an order (whether in the nature of an injunction or otherwise) as a result of which he is reinstated as mentioned in paragraph (a) above;

and, for the purposes of paragraph (a) above, proceedings to enforce a liability are finally disposed of on the earliest date by which the proceedings (including any proceedings on or in consequence of an appeal) have been determined and any time for appealing or further appealing has expired, except that if any appeal is abandoned, the proceedings shall be taken to be disposed of on the date of the abandonment.

    (7) If, in proceedings to enforce a liability arising by virtue of subsection (3) above, it appears to the court—

    (a) that, prior to the event which gave rise to the liability, the conduct of the former residential occupier or any person living with him in the premises concerned was such that it is reasonable to mitigate the damages for which the landlord in default would otherwise be liable, or

    (b) that, before the proceedings were begun, the landlord in default offered to reinstate the former residential occupier in the premises in question and either it was unreasonable of the former residential occupier to refuse that offer or, if he had obtained alternative accommodation before the offer was made, it would have been unreasonable of him to refuse that offer if he had not obtained that accommodation,

the court may reduce the amount of damages which would otherwise be payable to such amount as it thinks appropriate.

    (8) In proceedings to enforce a liability arising by virtue of subsection (3) above, it shall be a defence for the defendant to prove that he believed, and had reasonable cause to believe—

(a) that the residential occupier had ceased to reside in the premises in question at the time when he was deprived of occupation as mentioned in subsection (1) above or, as the case may be, when the attempt was made or the acts were done as a result of which he gave up his occupation of those premises; or

(b) that, where the liability would otherwise arise by virtue only of the doing of acts or the withdrawal or withholding of services, he had reasonable grounds for doing the acts or withdrawing or withholding the services in question.

28 The measure of damages

(1) The basis for the assessment of damages referred to in section 27(3) above is the difference in value, determined as at the time immediately before the residential occupier ceased to occupy the premises in question as his residence, between—

(a) the value of the interest of the landlord in default determined on the assumption that the residential occupier continues to have the same right to occupy the premises as before that time; and

(b) the value of that interest determined on the assumption that the residential occupier has ceased to have that right.

(2) In relation to any premises, any reference in this section to the interest of the landlord in default is a reference to his interest in the building in which the premises in question are comprised (whether or not that building contains any other premises) together with its curtilage.

(3) For the purposes of the valuations referred to in subsection (1) above, it shall be assumed—

(a) that the landlord in default is selling his interest on the open market to a willing buyer;

(b) that neither the residential occupier nor any member of his family wishes to buy; and

(c) that it is unlawful to carry out any substantial development of any of the land in which the landlord's interest subsists or to demolish the whole or part of any building on that land.

Local Government Act 1988
(1988, c. 9)

17 Local and other public authority contracts: exclusion of non-commercial considerations

(1) It is the duty of every public authority to which this section applies, in exercising, in relation to its public supply or works contracts, any proposed or any subsisting such contract, as the case may be, any function regulated by this section to exercise that function without reference to matters which are non-commercial matters for the purposes of this section.

(2) The public authorities to which this section applies are those specified in Schedule 2 to this Act.

(3) The contracts which are public supply or works contracts for the purposes of this section are contracts for the supply of goods or materials, for the supply of services or for the execution of works; but this section does not apply in relation to contracts entered into before the commencement of this section.

(4) The functions regulated by this section are—

(a) the inclusion of persons in or the exclusion of persons from—

(i) any list of persons approved for the purposes of public supply or works contracts with the authority, or

(ii) any list of persons from whom tenders for such contracts may be invited;

(b) in relation to a proposed public supply or works contract with the authority—
   (i) the inclusion of persons in or the exclusion of persons from the group of persons from whom tenders are invited,
   (ii) the accepting or not accepting the submission of tenders for the contract,
   (iii) the selecting the person with whom to enter into the contract, or
   (iv) the giving or withholding approval for, or the selecting or nominating, persons to be sub-contractors for the purposes of the contract; and
(c) in relation to a subsisting public supply or works contract with the authority—
   (i) the giving or withholding approval for, or the selecting or nominating, persons to be sub-contractors for the purposes of the contract, or
   (ii) the termination of the contract.

(5) The following matters are non-commercial matters as regards the public supply or works contracts of a public authority, any proposed or any subsisting such contract, as the case may be, that is to say—
(a) the terms and conditions of employment by contractors of their workers or the composition of, the arrangements for the promotion, transfer or training of or the other opportunities afforded to, their workforces;
(b) whether the terms on which contractors contract with their sub-contractors constitute, in the case of contracts with individuals, contracts for the provision by them as self-employed persons of their services only;
(c) any involvement of the business activities or interests of contractors with irrelevant fields of Government policy;
(d) the conduct of contractors or workers in industrial disputes between them or any involvement of the business activities of contractors in industrial disputes between other persons;
(e) the country or territory of origin of supplies to, or the location in any country or territory of the business activities or interests of, contractors;
(f) any political, industrial or sectarian affiliations or interests of contractors or their directors, partners or employees;
(g) financial support or lack of financial support by contractors for any institution to or from which the authority gives or withholds support;
(h) use or non-use by contractors of technical or professional services provided by the authority under the Building Act 1984 or the Building (Scotland) Act 1959.

18   Race relations matters
(1) Except to the extent permitted by subsection (2) below, section 71 of the Race Relations Act 1976 (local authorities to have regard to need to eliminate unlawful racial discrimination and promote equality of opportunity, and good relations, between persons of different racial groups) shall not require or authorise a local authority to exercise any function regulated by section 17 above by reference to a non-commercial matter.

19   Provision supplementary to or consequential on section 17
(8) In any action under section 17(1) above by a person who has submitted a tender for a proposed public supply or works contract arising out of the exercise of functions in relation to the proposed contract the damages shall be limited to damages in respect of expenditure reasonably incurred by him for the purpose of submitting the tender.

Road Traffic Act 1988
(1988, c. 52)

38   The Highway Code
(7) A failure on the part of a person to observe a provision of the Highway Code shall not of itself render that person liable to criminal proceedings of any kind but any such failure

may in any proceedings (whether civil or criminal, and including proceedings for an offence under the Traffic Acts, the Public Passenger Vehicles Act 1981 or sections 18 to 23 of the Transport Act 1985) be relied upon by any party to the proceedings as tending to establish or negative any liability which is in question in those proceedings.

143 Users of motor vehicles to be insured or secured against third-party risks

(1) Subject to the provisions of this Part of this Act—

(a) a person must not use a motor vehicle on a road [or other public place] unless there is in force in relation to the use of the vehicle by that person such a policy of insurance or such a security in respect of third party risks as complies with the requirements of this Part of this Act, and

(b) a person must not cause or permit any other person to use a motor vehicle on a road [or other public place] unless there is in force in relation to the use of the vehicle by that other person such a policy of insurance or such a security in respect of third party risks as complies with the requirements of this Part of this Act.

(2) If a person acts in contravention of subsection (1) above he is guilty of an offence.

(3) A person charged with using a motor vehicle in contravention of this section shall not be convicted if he proves—

(a) that the vehicle did not belong to him and was not in his possession under a contract of hiring or of loan,

(b) that he was using the vehicle in the course of his employment, and

(c) that he neither knew nor had reason to believe that there was not in force in relation to the vehicle such a policy of insurance or security as is mentioned in subsection (1) above.

(4) This Part of this Act does not apply to invalid carriages.

144 Exceptions from requirement of third-party insurance or security

(1) Section 143 of this Act does not apply to a vehicle owned by a person who has deposited and keeps deposited with the Accountant General of the [Senior Courts] the sum of [£500,000], at a time when the vehicle is being driven under the owner's control.

[(1A) The Secretary of State may by order made by statutory instrument substitute a greater sum for the sum for the time being specified in subsection (1) above.]

(2) Section 143 does not apply—

(a) to a vehicle owned—

(i) by the council of a county or county district in England and Wales, the Common Council of the City of London, the council of a London borough, the Inner London Education Authority, or a joint authority (other than a police authority) established by Part IV of the Local Government Act 1985,

(ii) by a [council constituted under section 2 of the Local Government etc. (Scotland) Act 1994] in Scotland, or

(iii) by a joint board or committee in England or Wales, or joint committee in Scotland, which is so constituted as to include among its members representatives of any such council,

at a time when the vehicle is being driven under the owner's control,

(b) to a vehicle owned by a police authority or the Receiver for the Metropolitan Police district, at a time when it is being driven under the owner's control, or to a vehicle at a time when it is being driven for police purposes by or under the direction of a constable, or by a person employed by a police authority, or employed by the Receiver,

(c) to a vehicle at a time when it is being driven on a journey to or from any place undertaken for salvage purposes pursuant to [the Merchant Shipping Act 1995],

(d)   to the use of a vehicle for the purpose of its being provided in pursuance of a direction under section 166(2)(b) of the Army Act 1955 or under the corresponding provision of the Air Force Act 1955,

[(da) to a vehicle owned by a health service body, as defined in section 60(7) of the National Health Service and Community Care Act 1990 [by a Primary Care Trust established under section 16A of the National Health Service Act 1977 by a Local Health Board established under section 16BA of that Act], at a time when the vehicle is being driven under the owner's control,

(db)   to an ambulance owned by a National Health Service trust established under Part I of the National Health Service and Community Care Act 1990 or the National Health Service (Scotland) Act 1978, at a time when a vehicle is being driven under the owner's control,]

[(dc) to an ambulance owned by an NHS foundation trust, at a time when the vehicle is being driven under the owner's control,]

(e)   to a vehicle which is made available by the Secretary of State to any person, body or local authority in pursuance of section 23 or 26 of the National Health Service Act 1977 at a time when it is being used in accordance with the terms on which it is so made available.

145   Requirements in respect of policies of insurance

(1) In order to comply with the requirements of this Part of this Act, a policy of insurance must satisfy the following conditions.

(2) The policy must be issued by an authorised insurer.

(3) Subject to subsection (4) below, the policy—

(a)   must insure such person, persons or classes of persons as may be specified in the policy in respect of any liability which may be incurred by him or them in respect of the death of or bodily injury to any person or damage to property caused by, or arising out of, the use of the vehicle on a road [or other public place] in Great Britain, and

[(aa) must, in the case of a vehicle normally based in the territory of another member State, insure him or them in respect of any civil liability which may be incurred by him or them as a result of an event related to the use of the vehicle in Great Britain if,—

(i) according to the law of that territory, he or they would be required to be insured in respect of a civil liability which would arise under that law as a result of that event if the place where the vehicle was used when the event occurred were in that territory, and

(ii) the cover required by that law would be higher than that required by paragraph (a) above, and]

(b)   must [, in the case of a vehicle normally based in Great Britain,] insure him or them in respect of any liability which may be incurred by him or them in respect of the use of the vehicle and of any trailer, whether or not coupled, in the territory other than Great Britain and Gibraltar of each of the member States of the Communities according to

[(i) the law on compulsory insurance against civil liability in respect of the use ofvehicles of the State in whose territory the event giving rise to the liability occurred; or

(ii) if it would give higher cover, the law which would be applicable under this Part of this Act if the place where the vehicle was used when that event occurred were in Great Britain; and]

(c)   must also insure him or them in respect of any liability which may be incurred by him or them under the provisions of this Part of this Act relating to payment for emergency treatment.

(4) The policy shall not, by virtue of subsection (3)(a) above, be required—

    (a) to cover liability in respect of the death, arising out of and in the course of his employment, of a person in the employment of a person insured by the policy or of bodily injury sustained by such a person arising out of and in the course of his employment, or

    (b) to provide insurance of more than £250,000 in respect of all such liabilities as may be incurred in respect of damage to property caused by, or arising out of, any one accident involving the vehicle, or

    (c) to cover liability in respect of damage to the vehicle, or

    (d) to cover liability in respect of damage to goods carried for hire or reward in or on the vehicle or in or on any trailer (whether or not coupled) drawn by the vehicle, or

    (e) to cover any liability of a person in respect of damage to property in his custody or under his control, or

    (f) to cover any contractual liability.

  [(4A) In the case of a person—

    (a) carried in or upon a vehicle, or

    (b) entering or getting on to, or alighting from, a vehicle,

the provisions of paragraph (a) of subsection (4) above do not apply unless cover in respect of the liability referred to in that paragraph is in fact provided pursuant to a requirement of the Employers' Liability (Compulsory Insurance) Act 1969.]

148 Avoidance of certain exceptions to policies or securities

(1) Where a certificate of insurance or certificate of security has been delivered under section 147 of this Act to the person by whom a policy has been effected or to whom a security has been given, so much of the policy or security as purports to restrict—

    (a) the insurance of the persons insured by the policy, or

    (b) the operation of the security,

(as the case may be) by reference to any of the matters mentioned in subsection (2) below shall, as respects such liabilities as are required to be covered by a policy under section 145 of this Act, be of no effect.

(2) Those matters are—

    (a) the age or physical or mental condition of persons driving the vehicle,

    (b) the condition of the vehicle,

    (c) the number of persons that the vehicle carries,

    (d) the weight or physical characteristics of the goods that the vehicle carries,

    (e) the time at which or the areas within which the vehicle is used,

    (f) the horsepower or cylinder capacity or value of the vehicle,

    (g) the carrying on the vehicle of any particular apparatus, or

    (h) the carrying on the vehicle of any particular means of identification other than any means of identification required to be carried by or under [the Vehicles Excise and Registration Act 1994].

(3) Nothing in subsection (1) above requires an insurer or the giver of a security to pay any sum in respect of the liability of any person otherwise than in or towards the discharge of that liability.

(4) Any sum paid by an insurer or the giver of a security in or towards the discharge of any liability of any person which is covered by the policy or security by virtue only of subsection (1) above is recoverable by the insurer or giver of the security from that person.

(5) A condition in a policy or security issued or given for the purposes of this Part of this Act providing—

    (a) that no liability shall arise under the policy or security, or

    (b) that any liability so arising shall cease,

in the event of some specified thing being done or omitted to be done after the happening of the event giving rise to a claim under the policy or security, shall be of no effect in connection with such liabilities as are required to be covered by a policy under section 145 of this Act.

(6) Nothing in subsection (5) above shall be taken to render void any provision in a policy or security requiring the person insured or secured to pay to the insurer or the giver of the security any sums which the latter may have become liable to pay under the policy or security and which have been applied to the satisfaction of the claims of third parties.

(7) Notwithstanding anything in any enactment, a person issuing a policy of insurance under section 145 of this Act shall be liable to indemnify the persons or classes of persons specified in the policy in respect of any liability which the policy purports to cover in the case of those persons or classes of persons.

149   Avoidance of certain agreements as to liability towards passengers
(1) This section applies where a person uses a motor vehicle in circumstances such that under section 143 of this Act there is required to be in force in relation to his use of it such a policy of insurance or such a security in respect of third-party risks as complies with the requirements of this Part of this Act.

(2) If any other person is carried in or upon the vehicle when the user is so using it, any antecedent agreement or understanding between them (whether intended to be legally binding or not) shall be of no effect so far as it purports or might be held—
    (a) to negative or restrict any such liability of the user in respect of persons carried in or upon the vehicle as is required by section 145 of this Act to be covered by a policy of insurance, or
    (b) to impose any conditions with respect to the enforcement of any such liability of the user.

(3) The fact that a person so carried has willingly accepted as his the risk of negligence on the part of the user shall not be treated as negativing any such liability of the user.

(4) For the purposes of this section—
    (a) references to a person being carried in or upon a vehicle include references to a person entering or getting on to, or alighting from, the vehicle, and
    (b) the reference to an antecedent agreement is to one made at any time before the liability arose.

151   Duty of insurers of persons giving security to satisfy judgment against persons insured or secured against third-party risks
(1) This section applies where, after a certificate of insurance or certificate of security has been delivered under section 147 of this Act to the person by whom a policy has been effected or to whom a security has been given, a judgment to which this subsection applies is obtained.

(2) Subsection (1) above applies to judgments relating to a liability with respect to any matter where liability with respect to that matter is required to be covered by a policy of insurance under section 145 of this Act and either—
    (a) it is a liability covered by the terms of the policy or security to which the certificate relates, and the judgment is obtained against any person who is insured by the policy or whose liability is covered by the security, as the case may be, or
    (b) it is a liability, other than an excluded liability, which would be so covered if the policy insured all persons or, as the case may be, the security covered the liability of all persons, and the judgment is obtained against any person other than one who is insured by the policy or, as the case may be, whose liability is covered by the security.

(3) In deciding for the purposes of subsection (2) above whether a liability is or would be covered by the terms of a policy or security, so much of the policy or security as purports to restrict, as the case may be, the insurance of the persons insured by the policy or the operation of the security by reference to the holding by the driver of the vehicle of a licence authorising him to drive it shall be treated as of no effect.

(4) In subsection (2)(b) above "excluded liability" means a liability in respect of the death of, or bodily injury to, or damage to the property of any person who, at the time of the use which gave rise to the liability, was allowing himself to be carried in or upon the vehicle and knew or had reason to believe that the vehicle had been stolen or unlawfully taken, not being a person who—

    (a) did not know and had no reason to believe that the vehicle had been stolen or unlawfully taken until after the commencement of his journey, and

    (b) could not reasonably have been expected to have alighted from the vehicle.

In this subsection the reference to a person being carried in or upon a vehicle includes a reference to a person entering or getting on to, or alighting from, the vehicle.

(5) Notwithstanding that the insurer may be entitled to avoid or cancel, or may have avoided or cancelled, the policy or security, he must, subject to the provisions of this section, pay to the persons entitled to the benefit of the judgment—

    (a) as regards liability in respect of death or bodily injury, any sum payable under the judgment in respect of the liability, together with any sum which, by virtue of any enactment relating to interest on judgments, is payable in respect of interest on that sum,

    (b) as regards liability in respect of damage to property, any sum required to be paid under subsection (6) below, and

    (c) any amount payable in respect of costs.

(6) This subsection requires—

    (a) where the total of any amounts paid, payable or likely to be payable under the policy or security in respect of damage to property caused by, or arising out of, the accident in question does not exceed £250,000, the payment of any sum payable under the judgment in respect of the liability, together with any sum which, by virtue of any enactment relating to interest on judgments, is payable in repect of interest on that sum,

    (b) where that total exceeds £250,000, the payment of either—

        (i) such proportion of any sum payable under the judgment in respect of the liability as £250,000 bears to that total, together with the same proportion of any sum which, by virtue of any enactment relating to interest on judgments, is payable in respect of interest on that sum, or

        (ii) the difference between the total of any amounts already paid under the policy or security in respect of such damage and £250,000, together with such proportion of any sum which, by virtue of any enactment relating to interest on judgments, is payable in respect of interest on any sum payable under the judgment in respect of the liability as the difference bears to that sum,

    whichever is the less, unless not less than £250,000 has already been paid under the policy or security in respect of such damage (in which case nothing is payable).

(7) Where an insurer becomes liable under this section to pay an amount in respect of a liability of a person who is insured by a policy or whose liability is covered by a security, he is entitled to recover from that person—

    (a) that amount, in a case where he became liable to pay it by virtue only of subsection (3) above, or

    (b) in a case where that amount exceeds the amount for which he would, apart from the provisions of this section, be liable under the policy or security in respect of that liability, the excess.

(8) Where an insurer becomes liable under this section to pay an amount in respect of a liability of a person who is not insured by a policy or whose liability is not covered by a security, he is entitled to recover the amount from that person or from any person who—

    (a) is insured by the policy, or whose liability is covered by the security, by the terms of which the liability would be covered if the policy insured all persons or, as the case may be, the security covered the liability of all persons, and

(b) caused or permitted the use of the vehicle which gave rise to the liability.

(9) In this section—

(a) "insurer" includes a person giving a security,

(c) "liability covered by the terms of the policy or security" means a liability which is covered by the policy or security or which would be so covered but for the fact that the insurer is entitled to avoid or cancel, or has avoided or cancelled, the policy or security.

153   Bankruptcy, etc., of insured or secured persons not to affect claims by third parties

(1) Where, after a certificate of insurance or certificate of security has been delivered under section 147 of this Act to the person by whom a policy has been effected or to whom a security as been given, any of the events mentioned in subsection (2) below happens, the happening of that event shall, notwithstanding anything in the Third Parties (Rights Against Insurers) Act 1930, not affect any such liability of that person as is required to be covered by a policy of insurance under section 145 of this Act.

(2) In the case of the person by whom the policy was effected or to whom the security was given, the events referred to in subsection (1) above are—

(a) that he becomes bankrupt or makes a composition or arrangement with his creditors or that his estate is sequestrated or he grants a trust deed for his creditors,

(b) that he dies and—

(i)   his estate falls to be administered in accordance with an order under section 421 of the Insolvency Act 1986,

(ii)   an award of sequestration of his estate is made, or

(iii) a judicial factor is appointed to administer his estate under section 11A of the Judicial Factors (Scotland) Act 1889,

(c) that if that person is a company—

(i)   a winding-up order [. . .] is made with respect of the company [or the company enters administration],

(ii)   a resolution for a voluntary winding-up is passed with respect to the company,

(iii) a receiver or manager of the company's business or undertaking is duly appointed, or

(iv)   possession is taken, by or on behalf of the holders of any debentures secured by a floating charge, of any property comprised in or subject to the charge.

(3) Nothing in subsection (1) above affects any rights conferred by the Third Parties (Rights Against Insurers) Act 1930 on the person to whom the liability was incurred, being rights so conferred against the person by whom the policy was issued or the security was given.

157   Payment for hospital treatment of traffic casualties

(1) Subject to subsection (2) below, where—

(a) a payment, other than a payment under section 158 of this Act, is made (whether or not with an admission of liability) in respect of the death of, or bodily injury to, any person arising out of the use of a motor vehicle on a road or *in a place to which the public have a right of access* [*in some other public place*],[1] and

(b) the payment is made—

(i)   by an authorised insurer, the payment being made under or in consequence of a policy issued under section 145 of this Act, or

(ii)   by the owner of a vehicle in relation to the use of which a security under this Part of this Act is in force, or

(iii) by the owner of a vehicle who has made a deposit under this Part of this Act, and

(c) the person who has so died or been bodily injured has to the knowledge of the insurer or owner, as the case may be, received treatment at a hospital, whether as an in-patient or as an out-patient, in respect of the injury so arising, the insurer or owner must pay the expenses reasonably incurred by the hospital in affording the treatment, after deducting from the expenses any moneys actually received in payment of a specific charge for the treatment, not being moneys received under any contributory scheme.

(2) The amount to be paid shall not exceed [£2,949.00] for each person treated as an inpatient or [£295.00] for each person treated as an out-patient.

(3) For the purposes of this section "expenses reasonably incurred" means—

(a) in relation to a person who receives treatment at a hospital as an in-patient, an amount for each day he is maintained in the hospital representing the average daily cost, for each in-patient, of the maintenance of the hospital and the staff of the hospital and the maintenance and treatment of the in-patients in the hospital, and

(b) in relation to a person who receives treatment at a hospital as an out-patient, reasonable expenses actually incurred.

[*1. Italics added. In s. 157(1)(a) the bracketed italicised words are substituted for the unbracketed italicised words in the paragraph's application to Scotland: Community Care and Health (Scotland) Act 2002 (asp 5), s. 20(1).*]

158   Payment for emergency treatment of traffic casualties

(1) Subsection (2) below applies where—

(a) medical or surgical treatment or examination is immediately required as a result of bodily injury (including fatal injury) to a person caused by, or arising out of, the use of a motor vehicle on a road [*or in some other public place*]¹ and

(b) the treatment or examination so required (in this Part of this Act referred to as "emergency treatment") is effected by a legally qualified medical practitioner.

(2) The person who was using the vehicle at the time of the event out of which the bodily injury arose must, on a claim being made in accordance with the provisions of section 159 of this Act, pay to the practitioner (or, where emergency treatment is effected by more than one practitioner, to the practitioner by whom it is first effected)—

(a) a fee of [£21.30] in respect of each person in whose case the emergency treatment is effected by him, and

(b) a sum, in respect of any distance in excess of two miles which he must cover in order—

(i) to proceed from the place from which he is summoned to the place where the emergency treatment is carried out by him, and

(ii) to return to the first mentioned place,equal to [41 pence] for every complete mile and additional part of a mile of thatdistance.

(3) Where emergency treatment is first effected in a hospital, the provisions of subsections (1) and (2) above with respect to payment of a fee shall, so far as applicable, but subject (as regards the recipient of a payment) to the provisions of section 159 of this Act, have effect with the substitution of references to the hospital for references to a legally qualified medical practitioner.

(4) Liability incurred under this section by the person using a vehicle shall, where the event out of which it arose was caused by the wrongful act of another person, be treated for the purposes of any claim to recover damage by reason of that wrongful act as damage sustained by the person using the vehicle.

[*1. Italics added. The italicised words in s. 158(1)(a) apply to Scotland: Community Care and Health (Scotland) Act 2002 (asp 5), s. 20(2).*]

159   Supplementary provisions as to payments for treatment

(2) A claim for a payment under section 158 of this Act may be made at the time when the emergency treatment is effected, by oral request to the person who was using the vehicle, and if not so made must be made by request in writing served on him within seven days from

the day on which the emergency treatment was effected.

(4) A payment made under section 158 of this Act shall operate as a discharge, to the extent of the amount paid, of any liability of the person who was using the vehicle, or of any other person, to pay any sum in respect of the expenses of remuneration of the practitioner or hospital concerned of or for effecting the emergency treatment.

Road Traffic (Consequential Provisions) Act 1988
(1988, c. 54)

7 Saving for law of nuisance
Nothing in the Road Traffic Acts authorises a person to use on a road a vehicle so constructed or used as to cause a public or private nuisance . . . or affects the liability, whether under statute or common law, of the driver or owner so using a vehicle.

Companies Act 1989
(1989, c. 40)

48 Exemption from liability for damages
(1) Neither a recognised supervisory body, nor any of its officers or employees or members of its governing body, shall be liable in damages for anything done or omitted in the discharge or purported discharge of functions to which this subsection applies, unless the act or omission is shown to have been in bad faith.

(2) Subsection (1) applies to the functions of the body so far as relating to, or to matters arising out of—
    (a) such rules, practices, powers and arrangements of the body to which the requirements of Part II of Schedule 11 apply, or
    (b) the obligations with which paragraph 16 of that Schedule requires the body to comply,
    (c) any guidance issued by the body, or
    (d) the obligations to which the body is subject by virtue of this Part.

Employment Act 1989
(1989, c. 38)

11 Exemption of Sikhs from requirements as to wearing of safety helmets on construction sites
(1) Any requirement to wear a safety helmet which (apart from this section) would, by virtue of any statutory provision or rule of law, be imposed on a Sikh who is on a construction site shall not apply to him at any time when he is wearing a turban.

(2) Accordingly, where—
    (a) a Sikh who is on a construction site is for the time being wearing a turban, and
    (b) (apart from this section) any associated requirement would, by virtue of any statutory provision or rule of law, be imposed—
        (i) on the Sikh, or
        (ii) on the other person,
in connection with the wearing by the Sikh of a safety helmet, that requirement shall not apply to the Sikh or (as the case may be) to that other person.

(4) It is hereby declared that, where a person does not comply with any requirement, being a requirement which for the time being does not apply to him by virtue of subsection (1) or (2)—

    (a) he shall not be liable in tort to any person in respect of any injury, loss or damage caused by his failure to comply with that requirement...

(5) If a Sikh who is on a construction site—

    (a) does not comply with any requirement to wear a safety helmet, being a requirement which for the time being does not apply to him by virtue of subsection (1), and

    (b) in consequence of any act or omission of some other person sustains any injury, loss or damage which is to any extent attributable to the fact that he is not wearing a safety helmet in compliance with the requirement,

that other person shall, if liable to the Sikh in tort (or, in Scotland, in an action for reparation), be so liable only to the extent that injury, loss or damage would have been sustained by the Sikh even if he had been wearing a safety helmet in compliance with the requirement.

(6) Where—

    (a) the act or omission referred to in subsection (5) causes the death of the Sikh, and

    (b) the Sikh would have sustained some injury (other than loss of life) in consequence of the act or omission even if he had been wearing a safety helmet in compliance with the requirement in question,

the amount of any damages which, by virtue of that subsection, are recoverable in tort (or, in Scotland, in an action for reparation) in respect of that injury shall not exceed the amount of any damages which would (apart from that subsection) be so recoverable in respect of the Sikh's death.

(7) In this section—

"injury" includes loss of life, any impairment of a person's physical or mental condition and any disease; ...

Law of Property (Miscellaneous Provisions) Act 1989
(1989, c. 34)

1 Deeds and their execution

(1) Any rule of law which—

    (a) restricts the substances on which a deed may be written;

    (b) requires a seal for the valid execution of an instrument as a deed by an individual; or

    (c) requires authority by one person to another to deliver an instrument as a deed on his behalf to be given by deed,

is abolished.

(2) An instrument shall not be a deed unless—

    (a) it makes it clear on its face that it is intended to be a deed by the person making it or, as the case may be, by the parties to it (whether by describing itself as a deed or expressing itself to be executed or signed as a deed or otherwise); and

    (b) it is validly executed as a deed

      [(i) by that person or a person authorised to execute it in the name or on behalf of that person, or

      (ii) by one or more of those parties or a person authorised to execute it in the name or on behalf of one of more of those parties.]

(3) An instrument is validly executed as a deed by an individual if, and only if—

    (a) it is signed—

      (i) by him in the presence of a witness who attests the signature; of

      (ii) at his direction and in his presence and the presence of two witnesses who each attest the signature; and

    (b) it is delivered as a deed by him or a person authorised to do so on his behalf.

(4) In subsections (2) and (3) above "sign", in relation to an instrument, includes

    [(a) an individual signing the name of the person or party on whose behalf he executes the instrument; and

(b) making one's mark on the instrument,
and "signature" is to be construed accordingly.]

[(4A) Subsection (3) above applies in the case of an instrument executed by an individual in the name or on behalf of another person whether or not that person is also an individual.]

(5) Where a solicitor [, duly certificated notary public] or licensed conveyancer, or an agent or employee of a solicitor [, duly certificated notary public] or licensed conveyancer, in the course of or in connection with a transaction involving the disposition or creation of an interest in land, purports to deliver an instrument as a deed on behalf of a party to the instrument, it shall be conclusively presumed in favour of a purchaser that he is authorised so to deliver the instrument.

(6) In subsection (5) above—

["purchaser" has the same meaning] as in the Law of Property Act 1925];

["duly certificated notary public" has the same meaning as it has in the Solicitors Act 1974 by virtue of section 87 of that Act;]; and

"interest in land" means any estate, interest or charge in or over land [ ].

(7) Where an instrument under seal that constitutes a deed is required for the purposes of an Act passed before this section comes into force, this section shall have effect as to signing, sealing or delivery of an instrument by an individual in place of any provision of that Act as to signing, sealing or delivery.

(10) The references in this section to the execution of a deed by an individual do not include execution by a corporation sole and the reference in subsection (7) above to signing, sealing or delivery by an individual does not include signing, sealing or delivery by such a corporation.

(11) Nothing in this section applies in relation to instruments delivered as deeds before this section comes into force.

2 Contracts for sale etc. of land to be made by signed writing

(1) A contract for the sale or other disposition of an interest in land can only be made in writing and only by incorporating all the terms which the parties have expressly agreed in one document or, where contracts are exchanged, in each.

(2) The terms may be incorporated in a document either by being set out in it or by reference to some other document.

(3) The document incorporating the terms or, where contracts are exchanged, one of the documents incorporating them (but not necessarily the same one) must be signed by or on behalf of each party to the contract.

(4) Where a contract for the sale or other disposition of an interest in land satisfies the conditions of this section by reason only of the rectification of one or more documents in pursuance of an order of a court, the contract shall come into being, or be deemed to have come into being, at such time as may be specified in the order.

(5) This section does not apply in relation to—

(a) a contract to grant such a lease as is mentioned in section 54(2) of the Law of Property Act 1925 (short leases);

(b) a contract made in the course of a public auction; or

[(c) a contract regulated under the Financial Services and Markets Act 2000, other than a regulated mortgage contract;]

and nothing in this section affects the creation or operation of resulting, implied or constructive trusts.

(6) In this section—

"disposition" has the same meaning as in the Law of Property Act 1925;

"interest in land" means any estate, interest or charge in or over land [ ]

["regulated mortgage contract" must be read with—

(a) section 22 of the Financial Services and Markets Act 2000,

(b) any relevant order under that section, and

(c) Schedule 2 to that Act.]

(7) Nothing in this section shall apply in relation to contracts made before this section comes into force.

(8) Section 40 of the Law of Property Act 1925 (which is superseded by this section) shall cease to have effect.

3 Abolition of rule in *Brian* v *Fothergill*
The rule of law known as the rule in *Brian* v *Fothergill* is abolished in relation to contracts made after this section comes into force.

Broadcasting Act 1990
(1990, c. 42)

166 Defamatory material
(1) For the purposes of the law of libel and slander (including the law of criminal libel so far as it relates to the publication of defamatory matter) the publication of words in the course of any programme included in a programme service shall be treated as publication in permanent form.

(2) Subsection (1) above shall apply for the purposes of section 3 of each of the Defamation Acts (slander of title etc.) as it applies for the purposes of the law of libel and slander.

  . . .

(4) In this section "the Defamation Acts" means the Defamation Act 1952 and the Defamation Act (Northern Ireland) 1955.

Section 203(1)   SCHEDULE 20

MINOR AND CONSEQUENTIAL AMENDMENTS

PARLIAMENTARY PAPERS ACT 1840 (c. 9)

1. Section 3 (protection in respect of proceedings for printing extracts from or abstracts of parliamentary papers) shall have effect as if the reference to printing included a reference to including in a programme service.

Contracts (Applicable Law) Act 1990
(1990, c. 36)

1 Meaning of "the Conventions"
In this Act—
    (a) "the Rome Convention" means the Convention on the law applicable to contractual obligations opened for signature in Rome on 19th June 1980 and signed by the United Kingdom on December 7, 1981; . . .
2 Conventions to have force of law
    (1) Subject to subsections (2) and (3) below, the Conventions shall have the force of law in the United Kingdom.

Section 2   SCHEDULE 1

TITLE I   SCOPE OF THE CONVENTION

Article 1 Scope of the Convention
    1. The rules of the Convention shall apply to contractual obligations in any situation involving a choice between the laws of different countries.

TITLE II   UNIFORM RULES

Article 3   **Freedom of choice**

1. A contract shall be governed by the law chosen by the parties. The choice must be express or demonstrated with reasonable certainty by the terms of the contract or the circumstances of the case. By their choice the parties can select the law applicable to the whole or a part only of the contract.

3. The fact that the parties have chosen a foreign law, whether or not accompanied by the choice of a foreign tribunal, shall not, where all the other elements relevant to the situation at the time of the choice are connected with one country only, prejudice the application of rules of the law of that country which cannot be derogated from by contract, hereinafter called "mandatory rules".

Article 5   **Certain consumer contracts**

1. This Article applies to a contract the object of which is the supply of goods or services to a person ("the consumer") for a purpose which can be regarded as being outside his trade or profession, or a contract for the provision of credit for that object.

2. Notwithstanding the provisions of Article 3, a choice of law made by the parties shall not have the result of depriving the consumer of the protection afforded to him by the mandatory rules of the law of the country in which he has his habitual residence:

— if in that country the conclusion of the contract was preceded by a specific invitation addressed to him or by advertising, and he had taken in that country all the steps necessary on his part for the conclusion of the contract, or

— if the other party or his agent received the consumer's order in that country, or

— if the contract is for the sale of goods and the consumer travelled from that country to another country and there gave his order, provided that the consumer's journey was arranged by the seller for the purpose of inducing the consumer to buy.

3. Notwithstanding the provisions of Article 4, a contract to which this Article applies shall, in the absence of choice in accordance with Article 3, be governed by the law of the country in which the consumer has his habitual residence if it is entered into in the circumstances described in paragraph 2 of this Article.

4. This Article shall not apply to:

(a) a contract of carriage;

(b) a contract for the supply of services where the services are to be supplied to the consumer exclusively in a country other than that in which he has his habitual residence.

5. Notwithstanding the provisions of paragraph 4, this Article shall apply to a contract which, for an inclusive price, provides for a combination of travel and accommodation.

Article 11   **Incapacity**

In a contract concluded between persons who are in the same country, a natural person who would have capacity under the law of that country may invoke his incapacity resulting from another law only if the other party to the contract was aware of this incapacity at the time of the conclusion of the contract or was not aware thereof as a result of negligence.

Courts and Legal Services Act 1990
(1990, c. 41)

8   Powers of Court of Appeal to award damages

(1) In this section "case" means any case where the Court of Appeal has power to order a new trial on the ground that damages awarded by a jury are excessive or inadequate.

(2) Rules of court may provide for the Court of Appeal, in such classes of case as may be specified in the rules, to have power, in place of ordering a new trial, to substitute for the sum awarded by the jury such sum as appears to the court to be proper.

34   The Authorised Conveyancing Practitioners Board

. . .

44   Compensation scheme

(1) The Board may, with the approval of the [Secretary of State], make rules establishing a scheme for compensating persons who have suffered loss in consequence of dishonesty on the part of the authorised practitioners or their employees.

(2) The rules may, in particular—

(a) provide for the establishment and functioning of an independent body (whether corporate or unincorporate) to administer the scheme and, subject to the rules, determine and regulate any matter relating to its operation;

(b) establish a fund out of which compensation is to be paid;

(c) provide for the levying of contributions from authorised practitioners and otherwise for financing the scheme and for the payment of contributions and other money into the fund;

(d) specify the terms and conditions on which, and the extent to which, compensation is to be payable and any circumstances in which the right to compensation is to be excluded or modified; and

(e) contain incidental and supplementary provisions.

61   Right of barrister to enter into contract for the provision of his services

(1) Any rule of law which prevents a barrister from entering into a contract for the provision of his services as a barrister is hereby abolished.

(2) Nothing in subsection (1) prevents the General Council of the Bar from making rules (however described) which prohibit barristers from entering into contracts or restrict their right to do so.

69   Exemption from liability for damages etc.

(1) Neither the [Secretary of State] nor any of the designated judges shall be liable in damages for anything done or omitted in the discharge or purported discharge of any of their functions under this Part.

(2) For the purposes of the law of defamation, the publication by the [Secretary of State] a designated judge or the [OFT] of any advice or reasons given by or to [it] in the exercise of functions under this Part shall be absolutely privileged.

Environmental Protection Act 1990
(1990, c. 43)

PART II   WASTE ON LAND

33   Prohibition on unauthorised or harmful deposit, treatment or disposal etc. of waste

. . .

34   Duty of care etc. as respects waste

(1) Subject to subsection (2) below, it shall be the duty of any person who imports, produces, carries, keeps, treats or disposes of controlled waste or, as a broker, has control of such waste, to take all such measures applicable to him in that capacity as are reasonable in the circumstances—

(a)   to prevent any contravention by any other person of section 33 above;

[(aa)   to prevent any contravention by any person of regulation 9 of the Pollution Prevention and Control (England and Wales) [*Sc: Scotland*] Regulations 2000 or of a condition of a permit granted under regulation 10 [*Sc: 7*] of those Regulations;]

(b)   to prevent the escape of the waste from his control or that of any other person;

(c)   on the transfer of the waste, to secure—

    (i)   that the transfer is only to an authorised person or to a person for authorised transport purposes; and

    (ii)   that there is transferred such a written description of the waste as will enable other persons to avoid a contravention of that section [or any condition of a permit granted under regulation 10 of those Regulations] and to comply with the duty under this subsection as respects the escape of waste.

(2) The duty imposed by subsection (1) above does not apply to an occupier of domestic property as respects the household waste produced on the property.[1]

[*(2) An occupier of domestic property—*

    (a) shall, as respects the household waste produced on the property, take reasonable care to secure that any transfer of waste is only to an authorised person or to a person for authorised transport purposes, and

    (b) shall not otherwise be subject to the duty imposed by subsection (1) above.][1]

(6) Any person who fails to comply with the duty imposed by subsection (1) above or with any requirement imposed under subsection (5) above shall be liable—

    (a) on summary conviction, to a fine not exceeding the statutory maximum; and

    (b) on conviction on indictment, to a fine.

(7) The Secretary of State shall, after consultation with such persons or bodies as appear to him representative of the interests concerned, prepare and issue a code of practice for the purpose of providing to persons practical guidance on how to discharge the duty imposed on them by subsection (1) above.

[1. *The italicized version of subsection (2) applies to Scotland.*]

[58B   Litigation funding agreements

(1) A litigation funding agreement which satisfies all of the conditions applicable to it by virtue of this section shall not be unenforceable by reason only of its being a litigation funding agreement.]

70   Power to deal with cause of imminent danger of serious pollution etc

(1) Where, in the case of any article or substance found by him on any premises which he has power to enter, an inspector has reasonable cause to believe that, in the circumstances in which he finds it, the article or substance is a cause of imminent danger of serious pollution of the environment or serious harm to human health, he may seize it and cause it to be rendered harmless (whether by destruction or otherwise).

73   Appeals and other provisions relating to legal proceedings and civil liability

(6) Where any damage is caused by waste which has been deposited in or on land, any person who deposited it, or knowingly caused or knowingly permitted it to be deposited, in either case so as to commit an offence under section 33(1) or 63(2) above, is liable for the damage except where the damage—

    (a) was due wholly to the fault of the person who suffered it; or

    (b) was suffered by a person who voluntarily accepted the risk of the damage being caused;

but without prejudice to any liability arising otherwise than under this subsection.

(7) The matters which may be proved by way of defence under section 33(7) above may be proved also by way of defence to an action brought under subsection (6) above.

(8) In subsection (6) above—

"damage" includes the death of, or injury to, any person (including any disease and any impairment of physical or mental condition); and "fault" has the same meaning as in the Law Reform (Contributory Negligence) Act 1945.

(9) For the purposes of the following enactments—

    (a) the Fatal Accidents Act 1976;

    (b) the Law Reform (Contributory Negligence) Act 1945; and

    (c) the Limitation Act 1980;

and for the purposes of any action of damages in Scotland arising out of the death of, or personal injury to, any person, any damage for which a person is liable under subsection (6) above shall be treated as due to his fault.

[PART IIA   CONTAMINATED LAND

78A   Preliminary

(2) "Contaminated land" is any land which appears to the local authority in whose area it is situated to be in such a condition, by reason of substances in, on or under the land, that—

    (a) significant harm is being caused or there is a significant possibility of such harm being caused; or

    (b) [pollution of controlled waters is being caused or there is a significant possibility of such pollution being caused];

and, in determining whether any land appears to be such land, a local authority shall, subject to subsection (5) below, act in accordance with guidance issued by the Secretary of State in accordance with section 78YA below with respect to the manner in which that determination is to be made.

(3) A "special site" is any contaminated land—

    (a) which has been designated as such a site by virtue of section 78C(7) or 78D(6) below; and

    (b) whose designation as such has not been terminated by the appropriate Agency under section 78Q(4) below.

(4) "Harm" means harm to the health of living organisms or other interference with the ecological systems of which they form part and, in the case of man, includes harm to his property.

(5) The questions—

    (a) what harm [or pollution of controlled waters] is to be regarded as "significant",

    (b) whether the possibility of significant harm [or pollution of controlled waters] being caused is "significant",

    [...]

shall be determined in accordance with guidance issued for the purpose by the Secretary of State in accordance with section 78YA below.

(6) Without prejudice to the guidance that may be issued under subsection (5) above, guidance under paragraph (a) of that subsection may make provision for different degrees of importance to be assigned to, or for the disregard of,—

    (a) different descriptions of living organisms or ecological systems [, or of poisonous, noxious or polluting matter or solid waste matter];

    (b) different descriptions of places [or controlled water, or different degrees of pollution]; or

    (c) different descriptions of harm to health or property, or other interference;

and guidance under paragraph (b) of that subsection may make provision for different degrees of possibility to be regarded as "significant" (or as not being "significant") in relation to different descriptions of significant harm [or of significant pollution].

(7) "Remediation" means—

    (a) the doing of anything for the purpose of assessing the condition of—

        (i)   the contaminated land in question;

        (ii) any controlled waters affected by that land; or

        (iii) any land adjoining or adjacent to that land;

(b) the doing of any works, the carrying out of any operations or the taking of any steps in relation to any such land or waters for the purpose—
    (i) of preventing or minimising, or remedying or mitigating the effects of, any significant harm, or any [significant] pollution of controlled waters, by reason of which the contaminated land is such land; or
    (ii) of restoring the land or waters to their former state; or
(c) the making of subsequent inspections from time to time for the purpose of keeping under review the condition of the land or waters;
and cognate expressions shall be construed accordingly.

(8) Controlled waters are "affected by" contaminated land if (and only if) it appears to the enforcing authority that the contaminated land in question is, for the purposes of subsection (2) above, in such a condition, by reason of substances in, on or under the land, that [significant pollution of those waters is being caused or there is a significant possibility of such pollution being caused].

(9) The following expressions have the meaning respectively assigned to them—
"the appropriate Agency" means—
    (a) in relation to England and Wales, the Environment Agency;
    (b) in relation to Scotland, the Scottish Environment Protection Agency;
"appropriate person" means any person who is an appropriate person, determined in accordance with section 78F below, to bear responsibility for any thing which is to be done by way of remediation in any particular case;
"charging notice" has the meaning given by section 78P(3)(b) below;
"controlled waters"—
    (a) in relation to England and Wales, has the same meaning as in Part III of the Water Resources Act 1991[except that "ground waters" does not include waters contained in underground strata but above the saturation zone]; and
    (b) in relation to Scotland, has the same meaning as in section 30A of the Control of Pollution Act 1974;
"creditor" has the same meaning as in the Conveyancing and Feudal Reform (Scotland) Act 1970;
"enforcing authority" means—
    (a) in relation to a special site, the appropriate Agency;
    (b) in relation to contaminated land other than a special site, the local authority in whose area the land is situated;
"heritable security" has the same meaning as in the Conveyancing and Feudal Reform (Scotland) Act 1970;
"local authority" in relation to England and Wales means—
    (a) any unitary authority;
    (b) any district council, so far as it is not a unitary authority;
    (c) the Common Council of the City of London and, as respects the Temples, the Sub-Treasurer of the Inner Temple and the Under-Treasurer of the Middle Temple respectively;
and in relation to Scotland means a council for an area constituted under section 2 of the Local Goverment etc. (Scotland) Act 1994;
"notice" means notice in writing;
"notification" means notification in writing;
"owner", in relation to any land in England and Wales, means a person (other than a mortgagee not in possession) who, whether in his own right or as trustee for any other person, is entitled to receive the rack rent of the land, or, where the land is not let at a rack rent, would be so entitled if it were so let;
"owner", in relation to any land in Scotland, means a person (other than a creditor in a heritable security not in possession of the security subjects) for the time being entitled to receive or who would, if the land were let, be entitled to receive, the rents of the land in connection with which the word is used and includes a trustee, factor, guardian or curator

and in the case of public or municipal land includes the persons to whom the management of the land is entrusted;

"pollution of controlled waters" means the entry into controlled waters of any poisonous,noxious or polluting matter or any solid waste matter;

"prescribed" means prescribed by regulations;

"regulations" means regulations made by the Secretary of State;

"remediation declaration" has the meaning given by section 78H(6) below;

"remediation notice" has the meaning given by section 78E(1) below;

"remediation statement" has the meaning given by section 78H(7) below;

"required to be designated as a special site" shall be construed in accordance with section 78C(8) below;

"substance" means any natural or artificial substance, whether in solid or liquid form or in the form of a gas or vapour;

"unitary authority" means—

(a) the council of a county, so far as it is the council of an area for which there are no district councils;

(b) the council of any district comprised in an area for which there is no county council;

(c) the council of a London borough;

(d) the council of a county borough in Wales.]

[78B   Identification of contaminated land

(1) Every local authority shall cause its area to be inspected from time to time for the purpose—

(a) of identifying contaminated land; and

(b) of enabling the authority to decide whether any such land is land which is required to be designated as a special site.

(2) In performing its functions under subsection (1) above a local authority shall act in accordance with any guidance issued for the purpose by the Secretary of State in accorance with section 78YA below.

(3) If a local authority identifies any contaminated land in its area, it shall give notice of that fact to—

(a) the appropriate Agency;

(b) the owner of the land;

(c) any person who appears to the authority to be in occupation of the whole or any part of the land; and

(d) each person who appears to the authority to be an appropriate person;

and any notice given under this subsection shall state by virtue of which of paragraphs (a) to (d) above it is given.

(4) If, at any time after a local authority has given any person a notice pursuant to subsection (3)(d) above in respect of any land, it appears to the enforcing authority that another person is an appropriate person, the enforcing authority shall give notice to that other person—

(a) of the fact that the local authority has identified the land in question as contaminated land; and

(b) that he appears to the enforcing authority to be an appropriate person.]

[78C   Identification and designation of special sites

(1) If at any time it appears to a local authority that any contaminated land in its area might be land which is required to be designated as a special site, the authority—

(a) shall decide whether or not the land is land which is required to be so designated; and

(b) if the authority decides that the land is land which is required to be so designated, shall give notice of that decision to the relevant persons.

(2) For the purposes of this section, "the relevant persons" at any time in the case of any land are the persons who at that time fall within paragraphs (a) to (d) below, that is to say—

(a) the appropriate Agency;

(b) the owner of the land;

(c) any person who appears to the local authority concerned to be in occupation of the whole or any part of the land; and

(d) each person who appears to that authority to be an appropriate person.

(3) Before making a decision under paragraph (a) of subsection (1) above in any particular case, a local authority shall request the advice of the appropriate Agency, and in making its decision shall have regard to any advice given by that Agency in response to the request.

(4) If at any time the appropriate Agency considers that any contaminated land is land which is required to be designated as a special site, that Agency may give notice of that fact to the local authority in whose area the land is situated.

(5) Where notice under subsection (4) above is given to a local authority, the authority shall decide whether the land in question—

(a) is land which is required to be designated as a special site or

(b) is not land which is required to be so designated, and shall give notice of that decision to the relevant persons.

(10) Without prejudice to the generality of his power to prescribe any description of land for the purposes of subsection (8) above, the Secretary of State, in deciding whether to prescribe a particular description of contaminated land for those purposes, may, in particular, have regard to—

(a) whether land of the description in question appears to him to be land which is likely to be in such a condition, by reason of substances in, on or under the land that—

(i)   serious harm would or might be caused, or

(ii) serious pollution of controlled waters would [or might be caused]; or

(b) whether the appropriate Agency is likely to have expertise in dealing with the kind of significant harm, or [significant] pollution of controlled waters, by reason of which land of the description in question is contaminated land.]

[78D   Referral of special site decisions to the Secretary of State

(1) In any case where—

(a) a local authority gives notice of a decision to the appropriate Agency pursuant to subsection (1)(b) or (5)(b) of section 78C above, but

(b) before the expiration of the period of twenty-one days beginning with the day on which that notice is so given, that Agency gives the local authority notice that it disagrees with the decision, together with a statement of its reasons for disagreeing,

the authority shall refer the decision to the Secretary of State and shall send to him a statement of its reasons for reaching the decision.

(3) Where a local authority refers a decision to the Secretary of State under subsection (1) above, it shall give notice of that fact to the relevant persons.

(4) Where a decision of a local authority is referred to the Secretary of State under subsection (1) above, he—

(a) may confirm or reverse the decision with respect to the whole or any part of the land to which it relates; and

(b) shall give notice of his decision on the referral—

(i)   to the relevant persons; and

(ii) to the local authority.]

[78E   Duty of enforcing authority to require remediation of contaminated land etc.

(1) In any case where—

(a) any land has been designated as a special site by virtue of section 78C(7) or 78D(6) above, or

    (b) a local authority has identified any contaminated land (other than a special site) in its area,

the enforcing authority shall, in accordance with such procedure as may be prescribed and subject to the following provisions of this Part, serve on each person who is an appropriate person a notice (in this Part referred to as a "remediation notice") specifying what that person is to do by way of remediation and the periods within which he is required to do each of the things so specified.

    (2) Different remediation notices requiring the doing of different things by way of remediation may be served on different persons in consequence of the presence of different substances in, on or under any land or waters.

    (3) Where two or more persons are appropriate persons in relation to any particular thing which is to be done by way of remediation, the remediation notice served on each of them shall state the proportion, determined under section 78F(7) below, of the cost of doing that thing which each of them respectively is liable to bear.

    (4) The only things by way of remediation which the enforcing authority may do, or require to be done, under or by virtue of this Part are things which it considers reasonable, having regard to—

        (a) the cost which is likely to be involved; and

        (b) the seriousness of the harm, or of the pollution of controlled waters, in question.

    (5) In determining for any purpose of this Part—

        (a) what is to be done (whether by an appropriate person, the enforcing authority or any other person) by way of remediation in any particular case,

        (b) the standard to which any land is, or waters are, to be remediated pursuant to the notice, or

        (c) what is, or is not, to be regarded as reasonable for the purposes of subsection (4) above,

the enforcing authority shall have regard to any guidance issued for the purposes by the Secretary of State.]

[78F Determination of the appropriate person to bear responsibility for remediation

    (1) This section has effect for the purpose of determining who is the appropriate person to bear responsibility for any particular thing which the enforcing authority determines is to be done by way of remediation in any particular case.

    (2) Subject to the following provisions of this section, any person, or any of the persons, who caused or knowingly permitted the substances, or any of the substances, by reason of which the contaminated land in question is such land to be in, on or under that land is an appropriate person.

    (3) A person shall only be an appropriate person by virtue of subsection (2) above in relation to things which are to be done by way of remediation which are to any extent referable to substances which he caused or knowingly permitted to be present in, on or under the contaminated land in question.

    (4) If no person has, after reasonable inquiry, been found who is by virtue of subsection (2) above an appropriate person to bear responsibility for the things which are to be done by way of remediation, the owner or occupier for the time being of the contaminated land in question is an appropriate person.

    (5) If, in consequence of subsection (3) above, there are things which are to be done by way of remediation in relation to which no person has, after reasonable inquiry, been found who is an appropriate person by virtue of subsection (2) above, the owner or occupier for the time being of the contaminated land in question is an appropriate person in relation to those things.

    (6) Where two or more persons would, apart from this subsection, be appropriate persons in relation to any particular thing which is to be done by way of remediation, the enforcing authority shall determine in accordance with guidance issued for the purpose by the Secretary of State whether any, and if so which, of them is to be treated as not being an appropriate person in relation to that thing.

(7) Where two or more persons are appropriate persons in relation to any particular thing which is to be done by way of remediation, they shall be liable to bear the cost of doing that thing in proportions determined by the enforcing authority in accordance with guidance issued for the purpose by the Secretary of State.

(8) Any guidance issued for the purposes of subsection (6) or (7) above shall be issued in accordance with section 78YA below.

(9) A person who has caused or knowingly permitted any substance ("substance A") to be in, on or under any land shall also be taken for the purposes of this section to have caused or knowingly permitted there to be in, on or under that land any substance which is there as a result of a chemical reaction or biological process affecting substance A.

(10) A thing which is to be done by way of remediation may be regarded for the purposes of this Part as referable to the presence of any substance notwithstanding that the thing in question would not have to be done—

    (a) in consequence only of the presence of that substance in any quantity; or

    (b) in consequence only of the quantity of that substance which any particular person caused, or knowingly permitted to be present.]

[78G   Grant of, and compensation for, rights of entry etc.

(1) A remediation notice may require an appropriate person to do things by way of remediation, notwithstanding that he is not entitled to do those things.

(2) Any person whose consent is required before any thing required by a remediation notice may be done shall grant, or join in granting, such rights in relation to any of the relevant land or waters as will enable the appropriate person to comply with any requirements imposed by the remediation notice.

(3) Before serving a remediation notice, the enforcing authority shall reasonably endeavour to consult every person who appears to the authority—

    (a) to be the owner or occupier of any of the relevant land or waters, and

    (b) to be a person who might be required by subsection (2) above to grant, or join in granting, any rights,

concerning the rights which that person may be so required to grant.

(4) Subsection (3) above shall not preclude the service of a remediation notice in any case where it appears to the enforcing authority that the contaminated land in question is in such a condition, by reason of substances in, on or under the land, that there is imminent danger of serious harm, or serious pollution of controlled waters, being caused.

(5) A person who grants, or joins in granting, any rights pursuant to subsection (2) above shall be entitled on making an application within such period as may be prescribed and in such manner as may be prescribed to such person as may be prescribed, to be paid by the appropriate person compensation of such amount as may be determined in such manner as may be prescribed.

(6) Without prejudice to the generality of the regulations that may be made by virtue of subsection (5) above, regulations by virtue of that subsection may make such provision in relation to compensation under this section as may be made by regulations by virtue of subsection (4) of section 35A above in relation to compensation under that section.

(7) In this section, "relevant land or waters" means—

    (a) the contaminated land in question;

    (b) any controlled waters affected by that land; or

    (c) any land adjoining or adjacent to the land or those waters.]

[78H   Restrictions and prohibitions on serving remediation notices
. . .]

[78J   Restrictions on liability relating to the pollution of controlled waters

(1) This section applies where any land is contaminated land by virtue of paragraph (b) of subsection (2) of section 78A above (whether or not the land is also contaminated land by virtue of paragraph (a) of that subsection).

(2) Where this section applies, no remediation notice given in consequence of the land in question being contaminated land shall require a person who is an appropriate person by

virtue of section 78F(4) and (5) above to do anything by way of remediation to that or any other land, or any waters, which he could not have been required to do by such a notice had paragraph (b) of section 78A(2) above (and all other references to pollution of controlled waters) been omitted from this Part.

(3) If, in a case where this section applies, a person permits, has permitted, or might permit, water from an abandoned mine or part of a mine—

    (a) to enter any controlled waters, or

    (b) to reach a place from which it is or, as the case may be, was likely, in the opinion of the enforcing authority, to enter such waters,

no remediation notice shall require him in consequence to do anything by way of remediation (whether to the contaminated land in question or to any other land or waters) which he could not have been required to do by such a notice had paragraph (b) of section 78A(2) above (and all other references to pollution of controlled waters) been omitted from this Part.

(4) Subsection (3) above shall not apply to the owner or former operator of any mine or part of a mine if the mine or part in question became abandoned after 31st December 1999. . . .]

[78K   Liability in respect of contaminating substances which escape to other land

(1) A person who has caused or knowingly permitted any substances to be in, on or under any land shall also be taken for the purposes of this Part to have caused or, as the case may be, knowingly permitted those substances to be in, on or under any other land to which they appear to have escaped.

(2) Subsections (3) and (4) below apply in any case where it appears that any substances are or have been in, on or under any land (in this section referred to as "land") as a result of their escape, whether directly or indirectly, from other land in, on or under which a person caused or knowingly permitted them to be.

(3) Where this subsection applies, no remediation notice shall require a person—

    (a) who is the owner or occupier of land A, and

    (b) who has not caused or knowingly permitted the substances in question to be in, on or under that land,

to do anything by way of remediation to any land or waters (other than land or waters of which he is the owner or occupier) in consequence of land A appearing to be in such a condition, by reason of the presence of those substances in, on or under it, that significant harm [, or significant pollution of controlled waters,] is being caused, or there is a significant possibility of such harm [or pollution] being caused, or that pollution of controlled waters is being, or is likely to be caused.

(4) Where this subsection applies, no remediation notice shall require a person—

    (a) who is the owner or occupier of land A, and

    (b) who has not caused or knowingly permitted the substances in question to be in, on or under that land,

to do anything by way of remediation in consequence of any further land in, on or under which those substances or any of them appear to be or to have been present as a result of their escape from land ("land B") appearing to be in such a condition, by reason of the presence of those substances in, on or under it, that significant harm [, or significant pollution of controlled waters,] is being caused, or there is a significant possibility of such harm [or pollution] being caused, or that pollution of controlled waters is being, or is likely to be caused, unless he is also the owner or occupier of land B.

(5) In any case where—

    (a) a person ("person A") has caused or knowingly permitted any substances to be in, on, or under any land,

    (b) another person ("person B") who has not caused or knowingly permitted those substances to be in, on or under that land becomes the owner or occupier of that land, and

(c) the substances, or any of the substances, mentioned in paragraph (a) above
appear to have escaped to other land,

no remediation notice shall require person B to do anything by way of remediation to that other land in consequence of the apparent acts or omissions of person A, except to the extent that person B caused or knowingly permitted the escape.

(6) Nothing in subsection (3), (4) or (5) above prevents the enforcing authority from doing anything by way of remediation under section 78N below which it could have done apart from that subsection, but the authoirty shall not be entitled under section 78P below to recover from any person any part of the cost incurred by the authority in doing by way of remediation anything which it is precluded by subsection (3), (4) or (5) above from requiring that person to do.

(7) in this section, "appear" means appear to the enforcing authority, and cognate expressions shall be construed accordingly.]

[78L   Appeals against remediation notices

(1) A person on whom a remediation notice is served may, within the period of twenty-one days beginning with the day on which the notice is served, appeal against the notice—

   [(a) if it was served by a local authority in England, or served by the Environment
        Agency in relation to land in England, to the Secretary of State;
   (b) if it was served by a local authority in Wales, or served by the Environment
        Agency in relation to land in Wales, to the National Assembly for Wales;]

and in the following provisions of this section "the appellate authority" means [the Secretary of State, or the National Assembly for Wales as the case may be].

(2) On any appeal under subsection (1) above the appellate authority—

   (a) shall quash the notice, if it is satisfied that there is a material defect in the notice;
        but
   (b) subject to that, may confirm the remediation notice, with or without modifica
        tion, or quash it.

. . .]

[78M   Offences of not complying with a remediation notice

(1) If a person on whom an enforcing authority serves a remediation notice fails, without reasonable excuse, to comply with any of the requirements of the notice, he shall be guilty of an offence.

. . .]

[78N   Powers of the enforcing authority to carry out remediation

(1) Where this section applies, the enforcing authority shall itself have power, in a case falling within paragraph (a) or (b) of section 78E(1) above, to do what is appropriate by way of remediation to the relevant land or waters.

. . .]

[78P   Recovery of, and security for, the cost of remediation by the enforcing authority

(1) Where, by virtue of section 78N(3)(a), (c), (e) or (f) above, the enforcing authority does any particular thing by way of remediation, it shall be entitled, subject to sections 78J(7) and 78K(6) above, to recover the reasonable cost incurred in doing it from the appropriate person or, if there are two or more appropriate persons in relation to the thing in question, from those persons in proportions determined pursuant to section 78F(7) above.

(2) In deciding whether to recover the cost, and, if so, how much of the cost, which it is entitled to recover under subsection (1) above, the enforcing authority shall have regard—

   (a) to any hardship which the recovery may cause to the person from whom the cost
        is recoverable; and

(b) to any guidance issued by the Secretary of State for the purposes of this subsection.
(3) Subsection (4) below shall apply in any case where—
    (a) any cost is recoverable under subsection (1) above from a person—
        (i) who is the owner of any premises which consist of or include the contaminated land in question; and
        (ii) who caused or knowingly permitted the substances, or any of the substances, by reason of which the land is contaminated and to be in, on or under the land; and
    (b) the enforcing authority serves a notice under this subsection (in this Part referred to as a "charging notice") on that person.
(4) Where this subsection applies—
    (a) the cost shall carry interest, at such reasonable rate as the enforcing authority may determine, from the date of service of the notice until the whole amount is paid; and
    (b) subject to the following provisions of this section, the cost and accrued interest shall be a charge on the premises mentioned in subsection (3)(a)(i) above.

. . .

(12) Where any cost is a charge on premises under this section, the enforcing authority may by order declare the cost to be payable with interest by instalments within the specified period until the whole amount is paid.
. . .]

[78Q   Special sites
. . .]

[78R   Registers
(1) Every enforcing authority shall maintain a register containing prescribed particulars of or relating to—
    (a) remediation notices served by that authority;
    (b) appeals against any such remediation notices;
    (c) remediation statements or remediation declarations prepared and published under section 78H above;
    (d) in relation to an enforcing authority in England and Wales, appeals against charging notices served by that authority;
    (e) notices under subsection (1)(b) or (5)(a) of section 78C above which have effect by virtue of subsection (7) of that section as the designation of any land as a special site;
    (f) notices under subsection (4)(b) or section 78D above which have effect by virtue of subsection (6) of that section as the designation of any land as a special site;
    (g) notices given by or to the enforcing authority under section 78Q(4) above terminating the designation of any land as a special site;
    (h) notifications given to that authority by persons—
        (i) on whom a remediation notice has been served, or
        (ii) who are or were required by virtue of section 78H(8)(a) above to prepare and publish a remediation statement,
    of what they claim has been done by them by way of remediation;
    (j) notifications given to that authority by owners or occupiers of land—
        (i) in respect of which a remidiation notice has been served, or
        (ii) in respect of which a remediation statement has been prepared and published,
    of what they claim has been done on the land in question by way of remediation;
    (k) convictions for such offences under section 78M above as may be prescribed;
    (l) such other matters relating to contaminated land as may be prescribed;
but that duty is subject to section 78S and 78T below.]

[78S   Exclusion from registers of information affecting national security
(1) No information shall be included in a register maintained under section 78R above if and so long as, in the opinion of the Secretary of State, the inclusion in the register of that

information, or information of that description, would be contrary to the interests of national security.]

[78T   Exclusion from registers of certain confidential information

(1) No information relating to the affairs of any individual or business shall be included in a register maintained under section 78R above, without the consent of that individual or the person for the time being carrying on that business, if and so long as the information—

(a) is, in relation to him, commercially confidential; and

(b) is not required to be included in the register in pursuance of directions under subsection (7) below:

but information is not commercially confidential for the purposes of this section unless it is determined under this section to be so by the enforcing authority or, on appeal, by the Secretary of State.

(8) Information excluded from a register shall be treated as ceasing to be commercially confidential for the purposes of this section at the expiry of the period of four years beginning with the date of the determination by virtue of which it was excluded; but the person who furnished it may apply to the authority for the information to remain excluded from the register on the ground that it is still commercially confidential and the authority shall determine whether or not that is the case.

(10) Information is, for the purposes of any determination under this section, commercially confidential, in relation to any individual or person, if its being contained in the register would prejudice to an unreasonable degree the commercial interests of that individual or person.

(11) For the purposes of subsection (10) above, there shall be disregarded any prejudice to the commercial interests of any individual or person so far as relating only to the value of the contaminated land in question or otherwise to the ownership or occupation of that land.]

[78YC   This Part and radioactivity

Except as provided by regulations, nothing in this Part applies in relation to harm, or pollution of controlled waters, so far as attributable, to any radioactivity possessed by any substance; but regulations may—

(a) provide for prescribed provisions of this Part to have effect with such modifications as the Secretary of State considers appropriate for the purpose of dealing with harm, or pollution of controlled waters, so far as attributable to any radioactivity possessed by any substances; or

(b) make such modifications of the Radioactive Substances Act 1993 or any other Act as the Secretary of State considers appropriate.]

PART III   STATUTORY NUISANCES AND CLEAN AIR

79   Statutory nuisances and inspections therefor

(1) [Subject to subsections (2) to (6A) below], the following matters constitute "statutory nuisances" for the purposes of this Part, that is to say—

(a) any premises in such a state as to be prejudicial to health or a nuisance;

(b) smoke emitted from premises so as to be prejudicial to health or a nuisance;

(c) fumes or gases emitted from premises so as to be prejudicial to health or a nuisance;

(d) any dust, steam, smell or other effluvia arising on industrial, trade or business premises and being prejudicial to health or a nuisance;

(e) any accumulation or deposit which is prejudicial to health or a nuisance;

(f) any animal kept in such a place or manner as to be prejudicial to health or a nuisance;

[(fa) any insects emanating from relevant industrial, trade or business premises and being prejudicial to health or a nuisance;]

[(fb) artificial light emitted from premises so as to be prejudicial to health or a nuisance;]

    (g) noise emitted from premises so as to be prejudicial to health or a nuisance;

[(ga) noise that is prejudicial to health or a nuisance and is emitted from or caused by a vehicle, machinery or equipment in a street;]

    (h) any other matter declared by any enactment to be a statutory nuisance;

and it shall be the duty of every local authority to cause its area to be inspected from time to time to detect any statutory nuisances which ought to be dealt with under section 80 below [or sections 80 and 80A below] and, where a complaint of a statutory nuisance is made to it by a person living within its area, to take such steps as are reasonably practicable to investigate the complaint.

(3) Subsection (1)(b) above does not apply to—

    (i) smoke emitted from a chimney of a private dwelling within a smoke control area

    (ii) dark smoke emitted from a chimney of a building or a chimney serving the furnace of a boiler or industrial plant attached to a building or for the time being fixed to or installed on any land,

    (iii) smoke emitted from a railway locomotive steam engine, or

    (iv) dark smoke emitted otherwise than as mentioned above from industrial or trade premises.

(4) Subsection (1)(c) above does not apply in relation to premises other than private dwellings.

(5) Subsection (1)(d) above does not apply to steam emitted from a railway locomotive engine.

[(5A) Subsection (1)(fa) does not apply to insects that are wild animals included in Schedule 5 to the Wildlife and Countryside Act 1981 (animals which are protected), unless they are included in respect of section 9(5) of that Act only.]

[(5B) Subsection (1)(fb) does not apply to artificial light emitted from—

    (a) an airport;

    (b) harbour premises;

    (c) railway premises, not being relevant separate railway premises;

    (d) tramway premises;

    (e) a bus station and any associated facilities;

    (f) a public service vehicle operating centre;

    (g) a goods vehicle operating centre;

    (h) a lighthouse;

    (i) a prison.]

(6) Subsection (1)(g) above does not apply to noise caused by aircraft other than model aircraft.

[(6A) Subsection (1)(ga) above does not apply to noise made—

    (a) by traffic,

    (b) by any naval, military or air force of the Crown or by a visiting force (as defined in subsection (2) above), or

    (c) by a political demonstration or a demonstration supporting or opposing a cause or campaign.]

(7) In this Part—

["appropriate person" means—

    (a) in relation to England, the Secretary of State;

    (b) in relation to Wales, the National Assembly for Wales;]

["equipment" includes a musical instrument;]

"noise" includes vibration;

["person responsible"—

    (a) in relation to a statutory nuisance, means the person to whose act, default or sufferance the nuisance is attributable;

(b) in relation to a vehicle, includes the person in whose name the vehicle is for the time being registered under the Vehicles Excise and Registration Act 1994 and any other person who is for the time being the driver of the vehicle;

(c) in relation to machinery or equipment, includes any person who is for the time being the operator of the machinery or equipment;]

"prejudicial to health" means injurious, or likely to cause injury, to health;

"premises" includes land and, subject to subsection (12) below, any vessel;

"private dwelling" means any building, or part of a building, used or intended to be used, as a dwelling;

"smoke" includes soot, ash, grit and gritty particles emitted in smoke;

["street" means a highway and any other road, footway, square or court that is for the time being open to the public;]

and any expressions used in this section and in the Clean Air Act 1956 or the Clean Air Act 1968 have the same meaning in this section as in that Act and section 34(2) of the Clean Air Act 1956 shall apply for the interpretation of the expression "dark smoke" and the operation of this Part in relation to it.

[(7A) Railway premises are relevant separate railway premises if—

(a) they are situated within—

(i) premises used as a museum or other place of cultural, scientific or historical interest, or

(ii) premises used for the purposes of a funfair or other entertainment, recreation or amusement, and

(b) they are not associated with any other railway premises.

(7B) For the purposes of subsection (7A)—

(a) a network situated as described in subsection (7A)(a) is associated with other railway premises if it is connected to another network (not being a network situated as described in subsection (7A)(a));

(b) track that is situated as described in subsection (7A)(a) but is not part of a network is associated with other railway premises if it is connected to track that forms part of a network (not being a network situated as described in subsection (7A)(a));

(c) a station or light maintenance depot situated as described in subsection (7A)(a) is associated with other railway premises if it is used in connection with the provision of railway services other than services provided wholly within the premises where it is situated.

In this subsection "light maintenance depot", "network", "railway services", "station" and "track" have the same meaning as in Part 1 of the Railways Act 1993.]

[(7C) In this Part "relevant industrial, trade or business premises" means premises that are industrial, trade or business premises as defined in subsection (7), but excluding—

(a) land used as arable, grazing, meadow or pasture land,

(b) land used as osier land, reed beds or woodland,

(c) land used for market gardens, nursery grounds or orchards,

(d) land forming part of an agricultural unit, not being land falling within any of paragraphs (a) to (c), where the land is of a description prescribed by regulations made by the appropriate person, and

(e) land included in a site of special scientific interest (as defined in section 52(1) of the Wildlife and Countryside Act 1981),

and excluding land covered by, and the waters of, any river or watercourse, that is neither a sewer nor a drain, or any lake or pond.

(7D) For the purposes of subsection (7C)—

"agricultural" has the same meaning as in section 109 of the Agriculture Act 1947;

"agricultural unit" means land which is occupied as a unit for agricultural purposes;

"drain" has the same meaning as in the Water Resources Act 1991;

"lake or pond" has the same meaning as in section 104 of that Act;
"sewer" has the same meaning as in that Act.]

80 Summary proceedings for statutory nuisances

(1) [Subject to subsection (2A)] Where a local authority is satisfied that a statutory nuisance exists, or is likely to occur or recur, in the area of the authority, the local authority shall serve a notice ("an abatement notice") imposing all or any of the following requirements—

  (a) requiring the abatement of the nuisance or prohibiting or restricting its occurrence or recurrence;

  (b) requiring the execution of such works, and the taking of such other steps, as may be necessary for any of those purposes,

and the notice shall specify the time or times within which the requirements of the notice are to be complied with.

(2) [Subject to section 80A(1) below, the abatement notice] shall be served—

  (a) except in a case falling within paragraph (b) or (c) below, on the person responsible for the nuisance;

  (b) where the nuisance arises from any defect of a structural character, on the owner of the premises;

  (c) where the person responsible for the nuisance cannot be found or the nuisance has not yet occurred, on the owner or occupier of the premises.

[(2A) Where a local authority is satisfied that a statutory nuisance falling within paragraph (g) of section 79(1) above exists, or is likely to occur or recur, in the area of the authority, the authority shall—

  (a) serve an abatement notice in respect of the nuisance in accordance with subsections (1) and (2) above; or

  (b) take such other steps as it thinks appropriate for the purpose of persuading the appropriate person to abate the nuisance or prohibit or restrict its occurrence or recurrence.

(2B) If a local authority has taken steps under subsection (2A)(b) above and either of the conditions in subsection (2C) below is satisfied, the authority shall serve an abatement notice in respect of the nuisance.

(2C) The conditions are—

  (a) that the authority is satisfied at any time before the end of the relevant period that the steps taken will not be successful in persuading the appropriate person to abate the nuisance or prohibit or restrict its occurrence or recurrence;

  (b) that the authority is satisfied at the end of the relevant period that the nuisance continues to exist, or continues to be likely to occur or recur, in the area of the authority.

(2D) The relevant period is the period of seven days starting with the day on which the authority was first satisfied that the nuisance existed, or was likely to occur or recur.

(2E) The appropriate person is the person on whom the authority would otherwise be required under subsection (2A)(a) above to serve an abatement notice in respect of the nuisance.]

(3) [A person served with an abatement notice] may appeal against the notice to a magistrates' court within the period of twenty-one days beginning with the date on which he was served with the notice.

(4) If a person on whom an abatement notice is served, without reasonable excuse, contravenes or fails to comply with any requirement or prohibition imposed by the notice, he shall be guilty of an offence.

(5) Except in a case falling within subsection (6) below, a person who commits an offence under subsection (4) above shall be liable on summary conviction to a fine not exceeding level 5 on the standard scale together with a further fine of an amount equal to one-tenth of that level for each day on which the offence continues after the conviction.

(6) A person who commits an offence under subsection (4) above on industrial, trade or business premises shall be liable on summary conviction to a fine not exceeding £20,000.[1]
[1. "£40,000" was substituted for "£20,000" for Scotland by the Anti-Social Behaviour etc (Scotland) Act 2004 (asp 8), s. 66, Sched. 2, para. 4.]

(7) Subject to subsection (8) below, in any proceedings for an offence under subsection (4) above in respect of a statutory nuisance it shall be a defence to prove that the best practicable means were used to prevent, or to counteract the effects of, the nuisance.

(8) The defence under subsection (7) above is not available—

    (a)   in the case of a nuisance falling within paragraph (a), (d), (e), (f)[, (fa)] or (g) of section 79(1) above except where the nuisance arises on industrial, trade or business premises;

    [(aza)   in the case of a nuisance falling within paragraph (fb) of section 79(1) above except where—

        (i)   the artificial light is emitted from industrial, trade or business premises, or

        (ii)   the artificial light (not being light to which sub-paragraph (i) applies) is emitted by lights used for the purpose only of illuminating an outdoor relevant sports facility;]

    [(aa)   in the case of a nuisance falling within paragraph (ga) o section 79(1) above except where the noise is emitted from or caused by a vehicle, machinery or equipment being used for industrial, trade or business purposes;]

    (b)   in the case of a nuisance falling within paragraph (b) of section 79(1) above except where the smoke is emitted from a chimney; and

    (c)   in the case of a nuisance falling within paragraph (c) or (h) of section 79(1) above.

[(8A) For the purposes of subsection (8)(aza) a relevant sports facility is an area, with or without structures, that is used when participating in a relevant sport, but does not include such an area comprised in domestic premises.

(8B) For the purposes of subsection (8A) "relevant sport" means a sport that is designated for those purposes by order made by the Secretary of State, in relation to England, or the National Assembly for Wales, in relation to Wales.

A sport may be so designated by reference to its appearing in a list maintained by a body specified in the order.

(8C) In subsection (8A) "domestic premises" means—

    (a) premises used wholly or mainly as a private dwelling, or

    (b) land or other premises belonging to, or enjoyed with, premises so used.]

(9) In proceedings for an offence under subsection (4) above in respect of a statutory nuisance falling within paragraph (g) [or (ga)] of section 79(1) above where the offence consists in contravening requirements imposed by virtue of subsection (1)(a) above it shall be a defence to prove—

    (a) that the alleged offence was covered by a notice served under section 60 or a consent given under section 61 or 65 of the Control of Pollution Act 1974 (construction sites, etc); or

    (b) where the alleged offence was committed at a time when the premises were subject to a notice under section 66 of that Act (noise reduction notice), that the level of noise emitted from the premises at that time was not such as to a con-stitute a contravention of the notice under that section; or

    (c) where the alleged offence was committed at a time when the premises were not subject to a notice under section 66 of that Act, and when a level fixed under section 67 of that Act (new buildings liable to abatement order) applied to the premises, that the level of noise emitted from the premises at that time did not exceed that level.

(10) Paragraphs (b) and (c) of subsection (9) above apply whether or not the relevant notice was subject to appeal at the time when the offence was alleged to have been committed.

[80A   Abatement notice in respect of noise in street

(1) In the case of a statutory nuisance within section 79(1)(ga) above that—

(a) has not yet occurred, or

(b) arises from noise emitted from or caused by an unattended vehicle or unattended machinery or equipment,

the abatement notice shall be served in accordance with subsection (2) below.

(2) The notice shall be served—

(a) where the person responsible for the vehicle, machinery or equipment can be found, on that person;

(b) where that person cannot be found or where the local authority determines that this paragraph should apply, by fixing the notice to the vehicle, machinery or equipment.

(3) Where—

(a) an abatement notice is served in accordance with subsection (2)(b) above by virtue of a determination of the local authority, and

(b) the person responsible for the vehicle, machinery or equipment can be found and served with a copy of the notice within an hour of the notice being fixed to the vehicle, machinery or equipment, a copy of the notice shall be served on that person accordingly.]

82   Summary proceedings by person aggrieved by statutory nuisances

(1) A magistrates' court may act under this section on a complaint made by any person on the ground that he is aggrieved by the existence of a statutory nuisance.

(2) If the magistrates' court is satisfied that the alleged nuisance exists, or that although abated it is likely to recur on the same premises [or, in the case of a nuisance within section 79(1)(ga) above, in the same street], the court shall make an order for either or both of the following purposes—

(a) requiring the defendant to abate the nuisance, within a time specified in the order, and to execute any work necessary for that purpose;

(b) prohibiting a recurrence of the nuisance, and requiring the defendant, within a time specified in the order, to execute any works necessary to prevent the recurrence, and may also impose on the defendant a fine not exceeding level 5 on the standard scale.

(3) If the magistrates' court is satisfied that the alleged nuisance exists and is such as, in the opinion of the court, to render premises unfit for human habitation, an order under subsection (2) above may prohibit the use of the premises for human habitation until the premises are, to the satisfaction of the court, rendered fit for that purpose.

(4) Proceedings for an order under subsection (2) above shall be brought—

(a) except in a case falling within [paragraph (b), (c) or (d) below], against the person responsible for the nuisance;

(b) where the nuisance arises from any defect of a structural character, against the owner of the premises;

(c) where the person responsible for the nuisance cannot be found, against the owner or occupier of the premises.

[(d) in the case of a statutory nuisance within section 79(1)(ga) above caused by noise emitted from or caused by an unattended vehicle or unattended machinery or equipment, against the person responsible for the vehicle, machinery or equipment.]

(5) [Subject to subsection (5A) below, where] more than one person is responsible for a statutory nuisance, subsections (1) to (4) above shall apply to each of those persons whether or not what any one of them is responsible for would by itself amount to a nuisance.

[(5A) In relation to a statutory nuisance within section 79(1)(ga) above for which more than one person is responsible (whether or not what any one of those persons is responsible for would by itself amount to such a nuisance), subsection (4)(a) above shall apply with the substitution of "each person responsible for the nuisance who can be found" for "the person responsible for the nuisance".

(5B) In relation to a statutory nuisance within section 79(1)(ga) above caused by noise emitted from or caused by an unattended vehicle or unattended machinery or equipment for which more than one person is responsible, subsection (4)(d) above shall apply with the substitution of "any person" for "the person".]

(6) Before instituting proceedings for an order under subsection (2) above against any person, the person aggrieved by the nuisance shall give to that person such notice in writing of his intention to bring the proceedings as is applicable to proceedings in respect of a nuisance of that description and the notice shall specify the matter complained of.

(7) The notice of the bringing of proceedings in respect of a statutory nuisance required by subsection (6) above which is applicable is—

    (a) in the case of a nuisance falling within paragraph (g) [or (ga)] of section 79(1) above, not less than three days' notice; and

    (b) in the case of a nuisance of any other description, not less than twenty-one days' notice;

but the Secretary of State may, by order, provide that this subsection shall have effect as if such period as is specified in the order were the minimum period of notice applicable to any description of statutory nuisance specified in the order.

(8) A person who, without reasonable excuse, contravenes any requirement or prohibition imposed by an order under subsection (2) above shall be guilty of an offence and liable on summary conviction to a fine not exceeding level 5 on the standard scale together with a further fine of an amount equal to one-tenth of that level for each day on which the offence continues after the conviction.

(9) Subject to subsection (1) below, in any proceedings for an offence under subsection (8) above in respect of a statutory nuisance it shall be a defence to prove that the best practicable means were used to prevent, or to counteract the effects of, the nuisance.

(10) The defence under subsection (9) above is not available—

    (a)   in the case of a nuisance falling within paragraph (a), (d), (e), (f)[, (fa)] or (g) of section 79(1) above except where the nuisance arises on industrial, trade or business premises;

    [(aza) in the case of a nuisance falling within paragraph (fb) of section 79(1) above except where—

        (i) the artificial light is emitted from industrial, trade or business premises, or

        (ii) the artificial light (not being light to which sub-paragraph (i) applies) is emitted by lights used for the purpose only of illuminating an outdoor relevant sports facility;]

    [(aa) in the case of a nuisance falling within paragraph (ga) of section 79(1) above except where the noise is emitted from or caused by a vehicle, machinery or equipment being used for industrial, trade or business purposes;]

    (b)   in the case of a nuisance falling within paragraph (b) of section 79(1) above except where the smoke is emitted from a chimney; and

    (c)   in the case of a nuisance falling within paragraph (c) or (h) or section 79(1) above; and

    (d)   in the case of a nuisance which is such as to render the premises unfit for human habitation.

[(10A) For the purposes of subsection (10)(aza) "relevant sports facility" has the same meaning as it has for the purposes of section 80(8)(aza).]

(11) If a person is convicted of an offence under subsection (8) above, a magistrates' court may, after giving the local authority in whose area the nuisance has occurred an opportunity of being heard, direct the authority to do anything which the person convicted was required to do by the order to which the conviction relates.

(12) Where on the hearing of proceedings for an order under subsection (2) above it is proved that the alleged nuisance existed at the date of the making of the complaint, then, whether or not at the date of the hearing it still exists or is likely to recur, the court shall order the defendant (or defendants in such proportions as appears fair and reasonable) to pay to the person bringing the proceedings such amount as the court considers reasonably sufficient to compensate him for any expenses properly incurred by him in the proceedings.

(13) If it appears to the magistrates' court that neither the person responsible for the nuisance nor the owner or occupier of the premises [or (as the case may be) the person responsible for the vehicle, machinery or equipment] can be found the court may, after giving the local authority in whose area the nuisance has occurred an opportunity of being heard, direct the authority to do anything which the court would have ordered that person to do.

Food Safety Act 1990
(1990, c. 16)

44 Protection of officers acting in good faith

(1) An officer of a food authority is not personally liable in respect of any act done by him—

(a) in the execution or purported execution of this Act; and

(b) within the scope of his employment,

if he did that act in the honest belief that his duty under this Act required or entitled him to do it.

(2) Nothing in subsection (1) above shall be construed as relieving any food authority from any liability in respect of the acts of their officers.

(3) Where an action has been brought against an officer of a food authority in respect of an act done by him—

(a) in the execution or purported execution of this Act; but

(b) outside the scope of his employment,

the authority may indemnify him against the whole or a part of any damages which he has been ordered to pay or any costs which he may have incurred if they are satisfied that he honestly believed that the act complained of was within the scope of his employment.

Human Fertilisation and Embryology Act 1990
(1990, c. 37)

27 Meaning of "mother"

(1) The woman who is carrying or has carried a child as a result of the placing in her of an embryo or of sperm and eggs, and no other woman, is to be treated as the mother of the child.

28 Meaning of "father"

. . .

29 Effect of sections 27 and 28

. . .

35 Disclosure in interests of justice: congenital disabilities, etc.

(1) Where for the purpose of instituting proceedings under section 1 of the Congenital Disabilities (Civil Liability) Act 1976 (civil liability to child born disabled) it is necessary to identify a person who would or might be the parent of a child but for sections 27 to 29 of this Act, the court may, on the application of the child, make an order requiring the Authority to

disclose any information contained in the register kept in pursuance of section 31 of this Act identifying that person.

National Health Service and Community Care Act 1990
(1990, c. 19)

4 NHS contracts

(1) In this Act the expression "NHS contract" means an arrangement under which one health service body ("the acquirer") arranges for the provision to it by another health service body ("the provider") of goods or services which it reasonably requires for the purposes of its functions.

(3) Whether or not an arrangement which constitutes an NHS contract would, apart from this subsection, be a contract in law, it shall not be regarded for any purpose as giving rise to contractual rights or liabilities, but if any dispute arises with respect to such an arrangement, either party may refer the matter to the Secretary of State for determination under the following provisions of this section.

(4) If, in the course of negotiations intending to lead to an arrangement which will be an NHS contract, it appears to a health service body—

  (a) that the terms proposed by another health service body are unfair by reason that the other is seeking to take advantage of its position as the only, or the only practicable, provider of the goods or services concerned or by reason of any other unequal bargaining position as between the prospective parties to the proposed arrangement, or

  (b) that for any other reason arising out of the relative bargaining position of the prospective parties any of the terms of the proposed arrangement cannot be agreed,

that health service body may refer the terms of the proposed arrangement to the Secretary of State for determination under the following provisions of this section.

(5) Where a reference is made to the Secretary of State under subsection (3) or subsection (4) above, the Secretary of State may determine the matter himself or, if he considers it appropriate, appoint a person to consider and determine it in accordance with regulations.

(6) By his determination of a reference under subsection (4) above, the Secretary of State or, as the case may be, the person appointed under subsection (5) above may specify terms to be included in the proposed arrangement and may direct that it be proceeded [...].

(7) A determination of a reference under subsection (3) above may contain such directions (including directions as to payment) as the Secretary of State or, as the case may be, person appointed under subsection (5) above considers appropriate to resolve the matter in dispute; [...].

(8) Without prejudice to the generality of his powers on a reference under subsection (3) above, the Secretary of State or, as the case may be, the person appointed under subsection (5) above may by his determination in relation to an arrangement constituting an NHS contract vary the terms of the arrangement or bring it to an end; and where an arrangement is so varied or brought to an end—

  (a) subject to paragraph (b) below, the variation or termination shall be treated as being effected by agreement between the parties; and

  (b) the directions included in the determination by virtue of subsection (7) above may contain such provisions as the Secretary of State or, as the case may be, the person appointed under subsection (5) above considers appropriate in order satisfactorily to give effect to the variation or to bring the arrangement to an end.

Child Support Act 1991
(1991, c. 48)

9   Agreements about maintenance

(1) In this section "maintenance agreement" means any agreement for the making, or for securing the making, of periodical payments by way of maintenance, or in Scotland aliment, to or for the benefit of any child.

(2) Nothing in this Act shall be taken to prevent any person from entering into a maintenance agreement.

(3) The existence of a maintenance agreement shall not prevent any party to the agreement, or any other person, from applying for a maintenance assessment with respect to any child to or for whose benefit periodical payments are to be made or secured under the agreement.

(4) Where any agreement contains a provision which purports to restrict the right of any person to apply for a maintenance assessment, that provision shall be void.

(5) Where section 8 would prevent any court from making a maintenance order in relation to a child and an absent parent of his, no court shall exercise any power that it has to vary any agreement so as—

    (a) to insert a provision requiring that absent parent to make or secure the making of periodical payments by way of maintenance, or in Scotland aliment, to or for the benefit of that child; or

    (b) to increase the amount payable under such a provision.

Water Industry Act 1991
(1991, c. 56)

209   Civil liability of undertakers for escapes of water etc

(1) Where an escape of water, however caused, from a pipe vested in a water undertaker causes loss or damage, the undertaker shall be liable, except as otherwise provided in this section, for the loss or damage.

(2) A water undertaker shall not incur any liability under subsection (1) above if the escape was due wholly to the fault of the person who sustained the loss or damage or of any servant, agent or contractor of his.

(3) A water undertaker shall not incur any liability under subsection (1) above in respect of any loss or damage for which the undertaker would not be liable apart from that sub-section and which is sustained—

    (a) by [the Environment Agency], a relevant undertaker or any statutory undertakers, within the meaning of section 336(1) of the Town and Country Planning Act 1990;

    (b) by any public gas supplier within the meaning of Part I of the Gas Act 1986 or the holder of a licence under section 6(1) of the Electricity Act 1989;

    (c) by any highway authority; or

    (d) by any person on whom a right to compensation is conferred by section 82 of the New Roads and Street Works Act 1991.

(4) The Law Reform (Contributory Negligence) Act 1945, the Fatal Accidents Act 1976 and the Limitation Act 1980 shall apply in relation to any loss or damage for which a water undertaker is liable under this section, but which is not due to the undertaker's fault, as if it were due to its fault.

(5) Nothing in subsection (1) above affects any entitlement which a water undertaker may have to recover contribution under the Civil Liability (Contribution) Act 1978; and for the purposes of that Act, any loss for which a water undertaker is liable under that subsection shall be treated as if it were damage.

(6) Where a water undertaker is liable under any enactment or agreement passed or made before April 1, 1982, to make any payment in respect of any loss or damage the undertaker shall not incur liability under subsection (1) above in respect of the same loss or damage.

(7) In this section "fault" has the same meaning as in the Law Reform (Contributory Negligence) Act 1945.

Water Resources Act 1991
(1991, c. 57)

161   Anti-pollution works and operations

(1) [Subject to subsections (1A) and (2) below,] where it appears to the Authority that any poisonous, noxious or polluting matter or any solid waste matter is likely to enter, or to be or to have been present in, any controlled waters, the Authority shall be entitled to carry out the following works and operations, that is to say—

    (a) in a case where the matter appears likely to enter any controlled waters, works and operations for the purpose of preventing it from doing so; or

    (b) in a case where the matter appears to be or to have been present in any controlled waters, works and operations for the purpose—

        (i) of removing or disposing of the matter;

        (ii) of remedying or mitigating any pollution caused by its presence in the waters; or

        (iii) so far as it is reasonably practicable to do so, of restoring the waters, including any fiora and fauna dependent on the aquatic environment of the waters, to their state immediately before the matter became present in the waters.

[(1A) Without prejudice to the power of the Agency to carry out investigations under subsection (1) above, the power conferred by that subsection to carry out works and operations shall only be exercisable in a case where—

    (a) the Agency considers it necessary to carry out forthwith any works or operations falling within paragraph (a) or (b) of that subsection; or

    (b) it appears to the Agency, after reasonable inquiry, that no person can be found on whom to serve a works notice under section 161A below.]

(2) Nothing in subsection (1) above shall entitle the Authority to impede or prevent the making of any discharge in pursuance of a consent given under Chapter II of Part III of this Act.

(3) Where the Authority carries out any such works or operations as are mentioned in subsection (1) above, it shall, subject to subsection (4) below, be entitled to recover the expenses reasonably incurred in doing so from any person who, as the case may be—

    (a) caused or knowingly permitted the matter in question to be present at the place from which it was likely, in the opinion of the Authority, to enter any controlled waters; or

    (b) caused or knowingly permitted the matter in question to be present in any controlled waters.

(4) No such expenses shall be recoverable from a person for any works or operations in respect of water from an abandoned mine which that person permitted to reach such a place as is mentioned in subsection (3) above or to enter any controlled waters.

(5) Nothing in this section—

    (a) derogates from any right of action or other remedy (whether civil or criminal) in proceedings instituted otherwise than under this section; or

    (b) affects any restriction imposed by or under any other enactment, whether public, local or private.

[161A   Notices requiring persons to carry out anti-pollution works and operations

(1) Subject to the following provisions of this section, where it appears to the Agency that any poisonous, noxious or polluting matter or any solid waste matter is likely to enter, or to be or to have been present in, any controlled waters, the Agency shall be entitled to serve a works notice on any person who, as the case may be,—

    (a) caused or knowingly permitted the matter in question to be present at the place from which it is likely, in the opinion of the Agency, to enter any controlled waters; or

    (b) caused or knowingly permitted the matter in question to be present in any controlled waters.

(2) For the purposes of this section, a "works notice" is a notice requiring the person on whom it is served to carry out such of the following works or operations as may be specified in the notice, that is to say—

    (a) in a case where the matter in question appears likely to enter any controlled waters, works or operations for the purpose of preventing it from doing so; or

    (b) in a case where the matter appears to be or to have been present in any controlled waters, works or operations for the purpose—

        (i)   of removing or disposing of the matter;

        (ii) of remedying or mitigating any pollution caused by its presence in the waters; or

        (iii) so far as it is reasonably practicable to do so, of restoring the waters, including any fiora and fauna dependent on the aquatic environment of the waters, to their state immediately before the matter became present in the waters.

(3) A works notice—

    (a) must specify the periods within which the person on whom it is served is required to do each of the things specified in the notice; and

    (b) is without prejudice to the powers of the Agency by virtue of section 161(1A)(a) above.

(4) Before serving a works notice on any person, the Agency shall reasonably endeavour to consult that person concerning the works or operations which are to be specified in the notice.

(11) Where the Agency—

    (a) carries out any such investigations as are mentioned in section 161(1) above,

    (b) (b)serves a works notice on a person in connection with the matter to which the investigations relate,

it shall (unless the notice is quashed or withdrawn) be entitled to recover the costs or expenses reasonably incurred in carrying out those investigations from that person.]

[161B   Grant of, and compensation for, rights of entry etc.

. . .]

[161D   Consequences of not complying with a works notice

(1) If a person on whom the Agency serves a works notice fails to comply with any of the requirements of the notice, he shall be guilty of an offence.]

208   Civil liability of the Authority for escapes of water etc.

(1) Where an escape of water, however caused, from a pipe vested in the Authority causes loss or damage, the Authority shall be liable, except as otherwise provided in this section, for the loss or damage.

(2) The Authority shall not incur any liability under subsection (1) above if the escape was due wholly to the fault of the person who sustained the loss or damage or of any servant, agent or contractor of his.

(3) The Authority shall not incur any liability under subsection (1) above in respect of any loss or damage for which the Authority would not be liable apart from that subsection

and which is sustained—

(a) by any water undertaker or sewerage undertaker or by any statutory undertakers, within the meaning of section 336(1) of the Town and Country Planning Act 1990;

(b) by any public gas supplier within the meaning of Part I of the Gas Act 1986 or the holder of a licence under section 6(1) of the Electricity Act 1989;

(c) by any highway authority; or

(d) by any person on whom a right to compensation is conferred by section 82 of the New Roads and Street Works Act 1991.

(4) The Law Reform (Contributory Negligence) Act 1945, the Fatal Accidents Act 1976 and the Limitation Act 1980 shall apply in relation to any loss or damage for which the Authority is liable under this section, but which is not due to the Authority's fault, as if it were due to its fault.

(5) Nothing in subsection (1) above affects any entitlement which the Authority may have to recover contribution under the Civil Liability (Contribution) Act 1978; and for the purposes of that Act, any loss for which the Authority is liable under that subsection shall be treated as if it were damage.

(6) Where the Authority is liable under any enactment or agreement passed or made before April 1, 1982, to make any payment in respect of any loss or damage the Authority shall not incur liability under subsection (1) above in respect of the same loss or damage.

(7) In this section "fault" has the same meaning as in the Law Reform (Contributory Negligence) Act 1945.

221   General interpretation

(1) In this Act, except in so far as the context otherwise requires—

...

"the Authority" means the National Rivers Authority...

["the Agency" means the Environment Agency;]...

Access to Neighbouring Land Act 1992
(1992, c. 23)

1   Access orders

(1) A person—

(a) who, for the purpose of carrying out works to any land (the "dominant land"), desires to enter upon any adjoining or adjacent land (the "servient land"), and

(b) who needs, but does not have, the consent of some other person to that entry, may make an application to the court for an order under this section ("an access order") against that other person.

(2) On an application under this section, the court shall make an access order if, and only if, it is satisfied—

(a) that the works are reasonably necessary for the preservation of the whole or any part of the dominant land; and

(b) that they cannot be carried out, or would be substantially more difficult to carry out, without entry upon the servient land;

but this subsection is subject to subsection (3) below.

(3) The court shall not make an access order in any case where it is satisfied that, were it to make such an order—

(a) the respondent or any other person would suffer interference with, or disturbance of, his use or enjoyment of the servient land, or

(b) the respondent, or any other person (whether of full age or capacity or not) in occupation of the whole or any part of the servient land, would suffer hardship, to such a degree by reason of the entry (notwithstanding any requirement of this Act or any term or condition that may be imposed under it) that it would be unreasonable to make the order.

(4) Where the court is satisfied on an application under this section that it is reasonably necessary to carry out any basic preservation works to the dominant land, those works shall be taken for the purposes of this Act to be reasonably necessary for the preservation of the land; and in this subsection "basic preservation works" means any of the following, that is to say—

    (a) the maintenance, repair or renewal of any part of a building or other structure comprised in, or situate on, the dominant land;

    (b) the clearance, repair or renewal of any drain, sewer, pipe or cable so comprised or situate;

    (c) the treatment, cutting back, felling, removal or replacement of any hedge, tree, shrub or other growing thing which is so comprised and which is, or is in danger of becoming, damaged, diseased, dangerous, insecurely rooted or dead;

    (d) the filling in, or clearance, of any ditch so comprised;

but this subsection is without prejudice to the generality of the works which may, apart from it, be regarded by the court as reasonably necessary for the preservation of any land.

(5) If the court considers it fair and reasonable in all the circumstances of the case, works may be regarded for the purposes of this Act as being reasonably necessary for the preservation of any land (or, for the purposes of subsection (4) above, as being basic preservation works which it is reasonably necessary to carry out to any land) notwithstanding that the works incidentally involve—

    (a) the making of some alteration, adjustment or improvement to the land, or

    (b) the demolition of the whole or any part of a building or structure comprised in or situate upon the land.

(6) Where any works are reasonably necessary for the preservation of the whole or any part of the dominant land, the doing to the dominant land of anything which is requisite for, incidental to, or consequential on, the carrying out of those works shall be treated for the purposes of this Act as the carrying out of works which are reasonably necessary for the preservation of that land; and references in this Act to works, or to the carrying out of works, shall be construed accordingly.

(7) Without prejudice to the generality of subsection (6) above, if it is reasonably necessary for a person to inspect the dominant land—

    (a) for the purpose of ascertaining whether any works may be reasonably necessary for the preservation of the whole or any part of that land,

    (b) for the purpose of making any map or plan, or ascertaining the course of any drain, sewer, pipe or cable, in preparation for, or otherwise in connection with, the carrying out of works which are so reasonably necessary, or

    (c) otherwise in connection with the carrying out of any such works,

the making of such an inspection shall be taken for the purposes of this Act to be the carrying out to the dominant land of works which are reasonably necessary for the preservation of that land; and references in this Act to works, or to the carrying out of works, shall be construed accordingly.

2 Terms and conditions of access orders

(1) An access order shall specify—

    (a) the works to the dominant land that may be carried out by entering upon the servient land in pursuance of the order;

    (b) the particular area of servient land that may be entered upon by virtue of the order for the purpose of carrying out those works to the dominant land; and

    (c) the date on which, or the period during which, the land may be so entered upon;

and in the following provisions of this Act any reference to the servient land is a reference to the area specified in the order in pursuance of paragraph (b) above.

(2) An access order may impose upon the applicant or the respondent such terms and conditions as appear to the court to be reasonably necessary for the purpose of avoiding or restricting—

(a) any loss, damage, or injury which might otherwise be caused to the respondent or any other person by reason of the entry authorised by the order; or

(b) any inconvenience or loss of privacy that might otherwise be so caused to the respondent or any other person.

(3) Without prejudice to the generality of subsection (2) above, the terms and conditions which may be imposed under that subsection include provisions with respect to—

(a) the manner in which the specified works are to be carried out;

(b) the days on which, and the hours between which, the work involved may be executed;

(c) the persons who may undertake the carrying out of the specified works or enter upon the servient land under or by virtue of the order;

(d) the taking of any such precautions by the applicant as may be specified in the order.

(4) An access order may also impose terms and conditions—

(a) requiring the applicant to pay, or to secure that such person connected with him as may be specified in the order pays, compensation for—

(i) any loss, damage or injury, or

(ii) any substantial loss of privacy or other substantial inconvenience,

which will, or might, be caused to the respondent or any other person by reason of the entry authorised by the order;

(b) requiring the applicant to secure that he, or such person connected with him as may be specified in the order, is insured against any such risks as may be so specified;

(c) requiring such a record to be made of the condition of the servient land, or of such part of it as may be so specified, as the court may consider expedient with a view to facilitating the determination of any question that may arise concerning damage to that land.

(5) An access order may include provision requiring the applicant to pay the respondent such sum by way of consideration for the privilege of entering the servient land in pursuance of the order as appears to the court to be fair and reasonable having regard to all the circumstances of the case, including in particular—

(a) the likely financial advantage of the order to the applicant and any persons connected with him; and

(b) the degree of inconvenience likely to be caused to the respondent or any other person by the entry;

but no payment shall be ordered under this subsection if and to the extent that the works which the applicant desires to carry out by means of the entry are works to residential land.

(6) For the purposes of subsection (5)(a) above, the likely financial advantage of an access order to the applicant and any persons connected with him shall in all cases be taken to be a sum of money equal to the greater of the following amounts, that is to say—

(a) the amount (if any) by which so much of any likely increase in the value of any land—

(i) which consists of or includes the dominant land, and

(ii) which is owned or occupied by the same person as the dominant land,

as may reasonably be regarded as attributable to the carrying out of the specified works exceeds the likely cost of carrying out those works with the benefit of the access order; and

(b) the difference (if it would have been possible to carry out the specified works without entering upon the servient land) between—

(i) the likely cost of carrying out those works without entering upon the servient land; and

(ii) the likely cost of carrying them out with the benefit of the access order.

(7) For the purposes of subsection (5) above, "residential land" means so much of any land as consists of—

    (a) a dwelling or part of a dwelling;

    (b) a garden, yard, private garage or outbuilding which is used and enjoyed wholly or mainly with a dwelling; or

    (c) in the case of a building which includes one or more dwellings, any part of the building which is used and enjoyed wholly or mainly with those dwellings or any of them.

(8) The persons who are to be regarded for the purposes of this section as "connected with" the applicant are—

    (a) the owner of any estate or interest in, or right over, the whole or any part of the dominant land;

    (b) the occupier of the whole or any part of the dominant land; and

    (c) any person whom the applicant may authorise under section 3(7) below to exercise the power of entry conferred by the access order.

(9) The court may make provision—

    (a) for the reimbursement by the applicant of any expenses reasonably incurred by the respondent in connection with the application which are not otherwise recoverable as costs;

    (b) for the giving of security by the applicant for any sum that might become payable to the respondent or any other person by virtue of this section or section 3 below.

3   Effect of access order

(1) An access order requires the respondent, so far as he has power to do so, to permit the applicant or any of his associates to do anything which the applicant or associate is authorised or required to do under or by virtue of the order or this section.

(2) Except as otherwise provided by or under this Act, an access order authorises the applicant or any of his associates, without the consent of the respondent,—

    (a) to enter upon the servient land for the purpose of carrying out the specified works;

    (b) to bring on to that land, leave there during the period permitted by the order and, before the end of that period, remove, such materials, plant and equipment as are reasonably necessary for the carrying out of those works; and

    (c) to bring on to that land any waste arising from the carrying out of those works, if it is reasonably necessary to do so in the course of removing it from the dominant land; but nothing in this Act or in any access order shall authorise the applicant or any of his associates to leave anything in, on or over the servient land (otherwise than in discharge of their duty to make good that land) after their entry for the purpose of carrying out works to the dominant land ceases to be authorised under or by virtue of the order.

(3) An access order requires the applicant—

    (a) to secure that any waste arising from the carrying out of the specified works is removed from the servient land forthwith;

    (b) to secure that, before the entry ceases to be authorised under or by virtue of the order, the servient land is, so far as reasonably practicable, made good; and

    (c) to indemnify the respondent against any damage which may be caused to the servient land or any goods by the applicant or any of his associates which would not have been so caused had the order not been made;

but this subsection is subject to subsections (4) and (5) below.

(4) In making an access order, the court may vary or exclude, in whole or in part,—

    (a) any authorisation that would otherwise be conferred by subsection 2(b) or (c) above; or

    (b) any requirement that would otherwise be imposed by subsection (3) above.

(5) Without prejudice to the generality of subsection (4) above, if the court is satisfied that it is reasonably necessary for any such waste as may arise from the carrying out of the specified works to be left on the servient land for some period before removal, the access order may, in place of subsection (3)(a) above, include provision—

(a) authorising the waste to be left on that land for such period as may be permitted by the order; and

(b) requiring the applicant to secure that the waste is removed before the end of that period.

(6) Where the applicant or any of his associates is authorised or required under or by virtue of an access order or this section to enter, or do any other thing, upon the servient land, he shall not (as respects that access order) be taken to be a trespasser from the beginning on account of his, or any other person's, subsequent conduct.

(7) For the purposes of this section, the applicant's "associates" are such number of persons (whether or not servants or agents of his) whom he may reasonably authorise under this subsection to exercise the power of entry conferred by the access order as may be reasonably necessary for carrying out the specified works.

4 Persons bound by access order, unidentified persons and bar on contracting out

(1) In addition to the respondent, an access order shall, subject to the provisions of the Land Charges Act 1972 and the [Land Registration Act 2002], be binding on—

(a) any of his successors in title to the servient land; and

(b) any person who has an estate or interest in, or right over, the whole or any part of the servient land which was created after the making of the order and who derives his title to that estate, interest or right under the respondent;

and references to the respondent shall be construed accordingly.

(2) If and to the extent that the court considers it just and equitable to allow him to do so, a person on whom an access order becomes binding by virtue of subsection (1)(a) or (b) above shall be entitled, as respects anything falling to be done after the order becomes binding on him, to enforce the order or any of its terms or conditions as if he were the respondent, and references to the respondent shall be construed accordingly.

(3) Rules of court may—

(a) provide a procedure which may be followed where the applicant does not know, and cannot reasonably ascertain, the name of any person whom he desires to make respondent to the application; and

(b) make provision enabling such an applicant to make such a person respondent by description instead of by name;

and in this subsection "applicant" includes a person who proposes to make an application for an access order.

(4) Any agreement, whenever made, shall be void if and to the extent that it would, apart from this subsection, prevent a person from applying for an access order or restrict his right to do so.

6 Variation of orders and damages for breach

(1) Where an access order or an order under this subsection has been made, the court may, on the application of any party to the proceedings in which the order was made or of any other person on whom the order is binding—

(a) discharge or vary the order or any of its terms or conditions;

(b) suspend any of its terms or conditions; or

(c) revive any term or condition suspended under paragraph (b) above; and in the application of subsections (1) and (2) of section 4 above in relation to an access order, any order under this subsection which relates to the access order shall be treated for the purposes of those subsections as included in the access order.

(2) If any person contravenes or fails to comply with any requirement, term or condition imposed upon him by or under this Act, the court may, without prejudice to any other

remedy available, make an order for the payment of damages by him to any other person affected by the contravention or failure who makes an application for relief under this subsection.

Carriage of Goods by Sea Act 1992
(1992, c. 50)

1 Shipping documents etc. to which Act applies

(1) This Act applies to the following documents, that is to say—
  (a) any bill of lading;
  (b) any sea waybill; and
  (c) any ship's delivery order.

(2) References in this Act to a bill of lading—
  (a) do not include references to a document which is incapable of transfer either by indorsement or, as a bearer bill, by delivery without indorsement; but
  (b) subject to that, do include references to a received for shipment bill of lading.

(3) References in this Act to a sea waybill are references to any document which is not a bill of lading but—
  (a) is such a receipt for goods as contains or evidences a contract for the carriage of goods by sea; and
  (b) identifies the person to whom delivery of the goods is to be made by the carrier in accordance with that contract.

(4) References in this Act to a ship's delivery order are references to any document which is neither a bill of lading nor a sea waybill but contains an undertaking which—
  (a) is given under or for the purposes of a contract for the carriage by sea of the goods to which the document relates, or of goods which include those goods; and
  (b) is an undertaking by the carrier to a person identified in the document to deliver the goods to which the document relates to that person.

(5) The Secretary of State may by regulations make provision for the application of this Act to cases where [an electronic communications network] or any other information technology is used for effecting transactions corresponding to—
  (a) the issue of a document to which this Act applies;
  (b) the indorsement, delivery or other transfer of such a document; or
  (c) the doing of anything else in relation to such a document.

(6) Regulations under subsection (5) above may—
  (a) make such modifications of the following provisions of this Act as the Secretary of State considers appropriate in connection with the application of this Act to any case mentioned in that subsection; and
  (b) contain supplemental, incidental, consequential and transitional provision; and the power to make regulations under that subsection shall be exercisable by statutory instrument subject to annulment in pursuance of a resolution of either House of Parliament.

2 Rights under shipping documents

(1) Subject to the following provisions of this section, a person who becomes—
  (a) the lawful holder of a bill of lading;
  (b) the person who (without being an original party to the contract of carriage) is the person to whom delivery of the goods to which a sea waybill relates is to be made by the carrier in accordance with that contract; or
  (c) the person to whom delivery of the goods to which a ship's delivery order relates is to be made in accordance with the undertaking contained in the order,

shall (by virtue of becoming the holder of the bill or, as the case may be, the person to whom delivery is to be made) have transferred to and vested in him all rights of suit under the contract of carriage as if he had been a party to that contract.

(2) Where, when a person becomes the lawful holder of a bill of lading, possession of the bill no longer gives a right (as against the carrier) to possession of the goods to which the bill relates, that person shall not have any rights transferred to him by virtue of subsection (1) above unless he becomes the holder of the bill—

> (a) by virtue of a transaction effected in pursuance of any contractual or other arrangements made before the time when such a right to possession ceased to attach to possession of the bill; or
>
> (b) as a result of the rejection to that person by another person of goods or documents delivered to the other person in pursuance of any such arrangements.

(3) The rights vested in any person by virtue of the operation of subsection (1) above in relation to a ship's delivery order—

> (a) shall be so vested subject to the terms of the order; and
>
> (b) where the goods to which the order relates form a part only of the goods to which the contract of carriage relates, shall be confined to rights in respect of the goods to which the order relates.

(4) Where, in the case of any document to which this Act applies—

> (a) a person with any interest or right in or in relation to goods to which the document relates sustains loss or damage in consequence of a breach of the contract of carriage; but
>
> (b) subsection (1) above operates in relation to that document so that rights of suit in respect of that breach are vested in another person,

the other person shall be entitled to exercise those rights for the benefit of the person who sustained the loss or damage to the same extent as they could have been exercised if they had been vested in the person for whose benefit they are exercised.

(5) Where rights are transferred by virtue of the operation of subsection (1) above in relation to any document, the transfer for which that subsection provides shall extinguish any entitlement to those rights which derives—

> (a) where that document is a bill of lading, from a person's having been an original party to the contract of carriage; or
>
> (b) in the case of any document to which this Act applies, from the previous operation of that subsection in relation to that document;

but the operation of that subsection shall be without prejudice to any rights which derive from a person's having been an original party to the contract contained in, or evidenced by, a sea waybill and, in relation to a ship's delivery order, shall be without prejudice to any rights deriving otherwise than from the previous operation of that subsection in relation to that order.

3 Liabilities under shipping documents

(1) Where subsection (1) of section 2 of this Act operates in relation to any document to which this Act applies and the person in whom rights are vested by virtue of that subsection—

> (a) takes or demands delivery from the carrier of any of the goods to which the document relates;
>
> (b) makes a claim under the contract of carriage against the carrier in respect of any of those goods; or
>
> (c) is a person who, at a time before those rights were vested in him, took or demanded delivery from the carrier of any of those goods,

that person shall (by virtue of taking or demanding delivery or making the claim or, in a case falling within paragraph (c) above, of having the rights vested in him) become subject to the same liabilities under that contract as if he had been a party to that contract.

(2) Where the goods to which a ship's delivery order relates form a part only of the goods to which the contract of carriage relates, the liabilities to which any person is subject by virtue of the operation of this section in relation to that order shall exclude liabilities in respect of any goods to which the order does not relate.

(3) This section, so far as it imposes liabilities under any contract on any person, shall be without prejudice to the liabilities under the contract of any person as an original party to the contract.

4 Representations in bills of lading

A bill of lading which—

(a) represents goods to have been shipped on board a vessel or to have been received for shipment on board a vessel; and

(b) has been signed by the master of the vessel or by a person who was not the master but had the express, implied or apparent authority of the carrier to sign bills of lading,

shall, in favour of a person who has become the lawful holder of the bill, be conclusive evidence against the carrier of the shipment of the goods or, as the case may be, of their receipt for shipment.

5 Interpretation etc.

(1) In this Act—

"bill of lading", "sea waybill" and "ship's delivery order" shall be construed in accordance with section 1 above;

"the contract of carriage"—

(a) in relation to a bill of lading or sea waybill, means the contract contained in or evidenced by that bill or waybill; and

(b) in relation to a ship's delivery order, means the contract under or for the purposes of which the undertaking contained in the order is given;

"holder", in relation to a bill of lading, shall be construed in accordance with subsection (2) below;

"information technology" includes any computer or other technology by means of which information or other matter may be recorded or communicated without being reduced to documentary form; [. . .].

(2) References in this Act to the holder of a bill of lading are references to any of the following persons, that is to say—

(a) a person with possession of the bill who, by virtue of being the person identified in the bill, is the consignee of the goods to which the bill relates;

(b) a person with possession of the bill as a result of the completion, by delivery of the bill, of any indorsement of the bill or, in the case of a bearer bill, of any other transfer of the bill;

(c) a person with possession of the bill as a result of any transaction by virtue of which he would have become a holder falling within paragraph (a) or (b) above had not the transaction been effected at a time when possession of the bill no longer gave a right (as against the carrier) to possession of the goods to which the bill relates;

and a person shall be regarded for the purposes of this Act as having become the lawful holder of a bill of lading wherever he has become the holder of the bill in good faith.

(3) References in this Act to a person's being identified in a document include references to his being identified by a description which allows for the identity of the person in question to be varied, in accordance with the terms of the document, after its issue; and the reference in section 1(3)(b) of this Act to a document's identifying a person shall be construed accordingly.

(4) Without prejudice to sections 2(2) and 4 above, nothing in this Act shall preclude its operation in relation to a case where the goods to which a document relates—

(a) cease to exist after the issue of the document; or

(b) cannot be identified (whether because they are mixed with other goods or for any other reason);

and references in this Act to the goods to which a document relates shall be construed accordingly.

(5) The preceding provisions of this Act shall have effect without prejudice to the application, in relation to any case, of the rules (the Hague-Visby Rules) which for the time being have the force of law by virtue of section 1 of the Carriage of Goods by Sea Act 1971.

Social Security Contributions and Benefits Act 1992
(1992, c. 4)

94   Right to industrial injuries benefit

(1) Industrial injuries benefit shall be payable where an employed earner suffers personal injury caused after 4 July 1948 by accident arising out of and in the course of his employment, being employed earner's employment.

(3) For the purposes of industrial injuries benefit an accident arising in the course of an employed earner's employment shall be taken, in the absence of evidence to the contrary, also to have arisen out of that employment.

97   Accidents in course of illegal employments

(1) Subsection (2) below has effect in any case where—

(a) a claim is made for industrial injuries benefit in respect of an accident, or of a prescribed disease or injury; or

(b) an application is made under [section 29 of the Social Security Act 1998] for a declaration that an accident was an industrial accident, or for a corresponding declaration as to a prescribed disease or injury.

(2) The Secretary of State may direct that the relevant employment shall, in relation to that accident, disease or injury, be treated as having been employed earner's employment notwithstanding that by reason of a contravention of, or non-compliance with, some provision contained in or having effect under an enactment passed for the protection of employed persons or any class of employed persons, either—

(a) the contract purporting to govern the employment was void; or

(b) the employed person was not lawfully employed in the relevant employment at the time when, or in the place where, the accident happened or the disease or injury was contracted or received.

(3) In subsection (2) above "relevant employment" means—

(a) in relation to an accident, the employment out of and in the course of which the accident arises; and

(b) in relation to a prescribed disease or injury, the employment to the nature of which the disease or injury is due.

98   Earner acting in breach of regulations, etc.

An accident shall be taken to arise out of and in the course of an employed earner's employment, notwithstanding that he is at the time of the accident acting in contravention of any statutory or other regulations applicable to his employment, or of any orders given by or on behalf of his employer, or that he is acting without instructions from his employer, if—

(a) the accident would have been taken so to have arisen had the act not been done in contravention of any such regulations or orders, or without such instructions, as the case may be; and

(b) the act is done for the purposes of and in connection with the employer's trade or business.

100   Accidents happening while meeting emergency
An accident happening to an employed earner in or about any premises at which he is for the time being employed for the purposes of his employer's trade or business shall be taken to arise out of and in the course of his employment if it happens while he is taking steps, on an actual or supposed emergency at those premises, to rescue, succour or protect persons who are, or are thought to be or possibly to be, injured or imperilled, or to avert or minimise serious damage to property.

101   Accident caused by another's misconduct etc.
An accident happening after 19 December 1961 shall be treated for the purposes of industrial injuries benefit, where it would not apart from this section be so treated, as arising out of an employed earner's employment if—
> (a) the accident arises in the course of the employment; and
> (b) the accident either is caused—
>> (i)   by another person's misconduct, skylarking or negligence, or
>> (ii) by steps taken in consequence of any such misconduct, skylarking or negligence, or
>> (iii) by the behaviour or presence of an animal (including a bird, fish or insect), or is caused by or consists in the employed earner being struck by any object or by lightning; and
> (c) the employed earner did not directly or indirectly induce or contribute to the happening of the accident by his conduct outside the employment or by any act not incidental to the employment.

174   References to Acts
In this Act—
> "the Administration Act" means the Social Security Administration Act 1992;

Trade Union and Labour Relations (Consolidation) Act 1992
(1992, c. 52)

1   Meaning of "trade union"
In this Act a "trade union" means an organisation (whether temporary or permanent)—
> (a) which consists wholly or mainly of workers of one or more descriptions and whose principal purposes include the regulation of relations between workers of that description or those descriptions and employers or employers' associations; or . . .

5   Meaning of "independent trade union"
In this Act an "independent trade union" means a trade union which—
> (a) is not under the domination or control of an employer or group of employers or of one or more employers' associations, and
> (b) is not liable to interference by an employer or any such group or association (arising out of the provision of financial or material support or by any other means whatsoever) tending towards such control;

and references to "independence", in relation to a trade union, shall be construed accordingly.

10   Quasi-corporate status of trade unions
> (1) A trade union is not a body corporate but—
>> (a) it is capable of making contracts;
>> (b) it is capable of suing and being sued in its own name, whether in proceedings relating to property or founded on contract or tort or any other cause of action; and

(c) proceedings for an offence alleged to have been committed by it or on its behalf may be brought against it in its own name.

11 Exclusion of common law rules as to restraint of trade

(1) The purposes of a trade union are not, by reason only that they are in restraint of trade, unlawful so as—

(a) to make any member of the trade union liable to criminal proceedings for conspiracy or otherwise, or

(b) to make any agreement or trust void or voidable.

(2) No rule of a trade union is unlawful or unenforceable by reason only that it is in restraint of trade.

15 Prohibition on use of funds to indemnify unlawful conduct

(1) It is unlawful for property of a trade union to be applied in or towards—

(a) the payment for an individual of a penalty which has been or may be imposed on him for an offence or for contempt of court,

(b) the securing of any such payment, or

(c) the provision of anything for indemnifying an individual in respect of such a penalty.

(2) Where any property of a trade union is so applied for the benefit of an individual on whom a penalty has been or may be imposed, then—

(a) in the case of a payment, an amount equal to the payment is recoverable by the union from him, and

(b) in any other case, he is liable to account to the union for the value of the property applied.

(3) If a trade union fails to bring or continue proceedings which it is entitled to bring by virtue of subsection (2), a member of the union who claims that the failure is unreasonable may apply to the court on that ground for an order authorising him to bring or continue the proceedings on the union's behalf and at the union's expense.

(4) In this section "penalty", in relation to an offence, includes an order to pay compensation and an order for the forfeiture of any property; and references to the imposition of a penalty for an offence shall be construed accordingly.

(6) This section does not affect—

(a) any other enactment, any rule of law or any provision of the rules of a trade union which makes it unlawful for the property of a trade union to be applied in a particular way; or

(b) any other remedy available to a trade union, the trustees of its property or any of its members in respect of an unlawful application of the union's property.

20 Liability of trade union in certain proceedings in tort

(1) Where proceedings in tort are brought against a trade union—

(a) on the ground that an act—

(i) induces another person to break a contract or interferes or induces another person to interfere with its performance, or

(ii) consists in threatening that a contract (whether one to which the union is a party or not) will be broken or its performance interfered with, or that the union will induce another person to break a contract or interfere with its performance, or

(b) in respect of an agreement or combination by two or more persons to do or to procure the doing of an act which, if it were done without any such agreement or combination, would be actionable in tort on such a ground,

then, for the purpose of determining in those proceedings whether the union is liable in respect of the act in question, that act shall be taken to have been done by the union if, but only if, it is to be taken to have been authorised or endorsed by the trade union in accordance with the following provisions.

(5) Where for the purposes of any proceedings an act is by virtue of this section taken to have been done by a trade union, nothing in this section shall affect the liability of any other person, in those or any other proceedings, in respect of that act.

(6) In proceedings arising out of an act which is by virtue of this section taken to have been done by a trade union, the power of the court to grant an injunction or interdict includes power to require the union to take such steps as the court considers appropriate for ensuring—

(a) that there is no, or no further, inducement of persons to take part or to continue to take part in industrial action, and

(b) that no person engages in any conduct after the granting of the injunction or interdict by virtue of having been induced before it was granted to take part or to continue to take part in industrial action.

The provisions of subsections (2) to (4) above apply in relation to proceedings for failure to comply with any such injunction or interdict as they apply in relation to the original proceedings.

22   Limit on damages awarded against trade unions in actions in tort

(1) This section applies to any proceedings in tort brought against a trade union, except—

(a) proceedings for personal injury as a result of negligence, nuisance or breach of duty;

(b) proceedings for breach of duty in connection with the ownership, occupation, possession, control or use of property;

(c) proceedings brought by virtue of Part I of the Consumer Protection Act 1987 (product liability).

In any proceedings in tort to which this section applies the amount which may [be] awarded against the union by way of damages shall not exceed the following limit—

Number of members of union	*Maximum award of damages*
Less than 5,000	£10,000
5,000 or more but less than 25,000	£50,000
25,000 or more but less than 100,000	£125,000
100,000 or more	£250,000

(3) The Secretary of State may by order amend subsection (2) so as to vary any of the sums specified . . .

113   Recovery of sums paid in case of fraud

(1) Where the Commissioner grants an application to a person who for the purposes of the application—

(a) has made a statement which he knew to be false in a material particular, or

(b) has recklessly made a statement which was false in a material particular,

he is entitled to recover from that person any sums paid by him to that person, or to any other person, by way of assistance.

(2) This does not affect the power of the Commissioner to enter into any agreement he thinks fit as to the terms on which assistance is provided.

127   Corporate or quasi-corporate status of employers' associations

(1) An employers' association may be either a body corporate or an unincorporated association.

(2) Where an employers' association is unincorporated—

(a) it is capable of making contracts;

(b) it is capable of suing and being sued in its own name, whether in proceedings relating to property or founded on contract or tort or any other cause of action; and

(c) proceedings for an offence alleged to have been committed by it or on its behalf may be brought against it in its own name.

128   Exclusion of common law rules as to restraint of trade

(1) The purposes of an unincorporated employers' association and, so far as they relate to the regulation of relations between employers and workers or trade unions, the purposes of an employers' association which is a body corporate are not, by reason only that they are in restraint of trade, unlawful so as—

    (a) to make any member of the association liable to criminal proceedings for conspiracy or otherwise, or

    (b) to make any agreement or trust void or voidable.

(2) No rule of an unincorporated employers' association or, so far as it relates to the regulation of relations between employers and workers or trade unions, of an employers' association which is a body corporate, is unlawful or unenforceable by reason only that it is in restraint of trade.

137   Refusal of employment on grounds related to union membership

(1) It is unlawful to refuse a person employment—

    (a) because he is, or is not, a member of a trade union, or

    (b) because he is unwilling to accept a requirement—

        (i) to take steps to become or cease to be, or to remain or not to become, a member of a trade union, or

        (ii) to make payments or suffer deductions in the event of his not being a member of a trade union.

(2) A person who is thus unlawfully refused employment has a right of complaint to an industrial tribunal.

138   Refusal of service of employment agency on grounds related to union membership

(1) It is unlawful for an employment agency to refuse a person any of its services—

    (a) because he is, or is not, a member of a trade union, or

    (b) because he is unwilling to accept a requirement to take steps to become or cease to be, or to remain or not to become, a member of a trade union.

(2) A person who is thus unlawfully refused any service of an employment agency has a right of complaint to an industrial tribunal.

140   Remedies

(1) Where the industrial tribunal finds that a complaint under section 137 or 138 is well-founded, it shall make a declaration to that effect and may make such of the following as it considers just and equitable—

    (a) an order requiring the respondent to pay compensation to the complainant of such amount as the tribunal may determine;

    (b) a recommendation that the respondent take within a specified period action appearing to the tribunal to be practicable for the purpose of obviating or reducing the adverse effect on the complainant of any conduct to which the complaint relates.

(2) Compensation shall be assessed on the same basis as damages for breach of statutory duty and may include compensation for injury to feelings.

(3) If the respondent fails without reasonable justification to comply with a recommendation to take action, the tribunal may increase its award of compensation or, if it has not made such an award, make one.

(4) The total amount of compensation shall not exceed the limit for the time being imposed by [section 124(1) of the Employment Rights Act 1996] (limit on compensation for unfair dismissal).

142   Awards against third parties

(1) If in proceedings on a complaint under section 137 or 138 either the complainant or the respondent claims that the respondent was induced to act in the manner complained of by pressure which a trade union or other person exercised on him by calling, organising, procuring or financing a strike or other industrial action, or by threatening to do so, the complainant or the respondent may request the industrial tribunal to direct that the person who he claims exercised the pressure be joined or sisted as a party to the proceedings.

(3) Where a person has been so joined or sisted as a party to the proceedings and the tribunal—

(a) finds that the complaint is well-founded,

(b) makes an award of compensation, and

(c) also finds that the claim in subsection (1) above is well-founded,

it may order that the compensation shall be paid by the person joined instead of by the respondent, or partly by that person and partly by the respondent, as the tribunal may consider just and equitable in the circumstances.

143   Interpretation and other supplementary provisions

(4) The remedy of a person for conduct which is unlawful by virtue of section 137 or 138 is by way of a complaint to an industrial tribunal in accordance with this Part, and not otherwise.

No other legal liability arises by reason that conduct is unlawful by virtue of either of those sections.

144   Union membership requirement in contract for goods or services void

A term or condition of a contract for the supply of goods or services is void in so far as it purports to require that the whole, or some part, of the work done for the purposes of the contract is done only by persons who are, or are not, members of trade unions or of a particular trade union.

145   Refusal to deal on union membership grounds prohibited

(1) A person shall not refuse to deal with a supplier or prospective supplier of goods or services on union membership grounds.

"Refuse to deal" and "union membership grounds" shall be construed as follows.

(2) A person refuses to deal with a person if, where he maintains (in whatever form) a list of approved suppliers of goods or services, or of persons from whom tenders for the supply of goods or services may be invited, he fails to include the name of that person in that list.

He does so on union membership grounds if the grounds, or one of the grounds, for failing to include his name is that if that person were to enter into a contract with him for the supply of goods or services, work to be done for the purposes of the contract would, or would be likely to, be done by persons who were, or who were not, members of trade unions or of a particular trade union.

(3) A person refuses to deal with a person if, in relation to a proposed contract for the supply of goods or services—

(a) he excludes that person from the group of persons from whom tenders for the supply of the goods or services are invited, or

(b) he fails to permit that person to submit such a tender, or

(c) he otherwise determines not to enter into a contract with that person for the supply of the goods or services.

He does so on union membership grounds if the ground, or one of the grounds, on which he does so is that if the proposed contract were entered into with that person, work to be done for the purposes of the contract would, or would be likely to, be done by persons who were, or who were not, members of trade unions or of a particular trade union.

(4) A person refuses to deal with a person if he terminates a contract with him for the supply of goods or services.

He does so on union membership grounds if the ground, or one of the grounds, on which he does so is that work done, or to be done, for the purposes of the contract has been, or is likely to be, done by persons who are or are not members of trade unions or of a particular trade union.

(5) The obligation to comply with this section is a duty owed to the person with whom there is a refusal to deal and to any other person who may be adversely affected by its contravention; and a breach of the duty is actionable accordingly (subject to the defences and other incidents applying to actions for breach of statutory duty).

[145A   Inducements relating to union membership or activities

(1) A worker has the right not to have an offer made to him by his employer for the sole or main purpose of inducing the worker—

  (a) not to be or seek to become a member of an independent trade union,

  (b) not to take part, at an appropriate time, in the activities of an independent trade union,

  (c) not to make use, at an appropriate time, of trade union services, or

  (d) to be or become a member of any trade union or of a particular trade union or one of a number of particular trade unions.

(5) A worker or former worker may present a complaint to an employment tribunal on the ground that his employer has made him an offer in contravention of this section.]

[145B   Inducements relating to collective bargaining

(1) A worker who is a member of an independent trade union which is recognised, or seeking to be recognised, by his employer has the right not to have an offer made to him by his employer if—

  (a) acceptance of the offer, together with other workers' acceptance of offers which the employer also makes to them, would have the prohibited result, and

  (b) the employer's sole or main purpose in making the offers is to achieve that result.

(2) The prohibited result is that the workers' terms of employment, or any of those terms, will not (or will no longer) be determined by collective agreement negotiated by or on behalf of the union.

(3) It is immaterial for the purposes of subsection (1) whether the offers are made to the workers simultaneously.

(5) A worker or former worker may present a complaint to an employment tribunal on the ground that his employer has made him an offer in contravention of this section.]

[145D   Consideration of complaint

(1) On a complaint under section 145A it shall be for the employer to show what was his sole or main purpose in making the offer.

(2) On a complaint under section 145B it shall be for the employer to show what was his sole or main purpose in making the offers.

(3) On complaint under section 145A or 145B, in determining any question whether the employer made the offer (or offers) or the purpose for which he did so, no account shall be taken of any pressure which was exercised on him by calling, organising, procuring or financing a strike or other industrial action, or by threatening to do so; and that question shall be determined as if no such pressure had been exercised.

(4) In determining whether an employer's sole or main purpose in making offers was the purpose mentioned in section 145B(1), the matters taken into account must include any evidence—

  (a) that when the offers were made the employer had recently changed or sought to change, or did not wish to use, arrangements agreed with the union for collective bargaining,

  (b) that when the offers were made the employer did not wish to enter into arrangements proposed by the union for collective bargaining, or

(c) that the offers were made only to particular workers, and were made for the sole or main purpose of rewarding those particular workers for their high level of performance or of retaining them because of their special value to the employer.]

[145E   Remedies

(1) Subsections (2) and (3) apply where the employment tribunal finds that a complaint under section 145A or 145B is well-founded.

(2) The tribunal—

(a) shall make a declaration to that effect, and

(b) shall make an award to be paid by the employer to the complainant in respect of the offer complained of.

(3) The amount of the award shall be £2,500 (subject to any adjustment of the award that may fall to be made under Part 3 of the Employment Act 2002).

(4) Where an offer made in contravention of section 145A or 145B is accepted—

(a) if the acceptance results in the worker's agreeing to vary his terms of employment, the employer cannot enforce the agreement to vary, or recover any sum paid or other asset transferred by him under the agreement to vary;

(b) if as a result of the acceptance the worker's terms of employment are varied, nothing in section 145A or 145B makes the variation unenforceable by either party.

(6) In ascertaining any amount of compensation under section 149, no reduction shall be made on the ground—

(a) that the complainant caused or contributed to his loss, or the act or failure complained of, by accepting or not accepting an offer made in contravention of section 145A or 145B, or

(b) that the complainant has received or is entitled to an award under this section.]

166   Consequences of failure to comply with order

(1) If on the application of an employee an industrial tribunal is satis?ed that the employer has not complied with the terms of an order for the reinstatement or re-engagement of the employee under section 163(4) or [(5)], the tribunal shall—

(a) make an order for the continuation of the employee's contract of employment, and

(b) order the employer to pay the employee such compensation as the tribunal considers just and equitable in all the circumstances having regard—

(i) to the infringement of the employee's right to be reinstated or re-engaged in pursuance of the order, and

(ii) to any loss suffered by the employee in consequence of the noncompliance.

(2) Section 164 applies to an order under subsection (1)(a) as in relation to an order under section 163.

(3) If on the application of an employee an industrial tribunal is satisfied that the employer has not complied with the terms of an order for the continuation of a contract of employment, the following provisions apply.

(4) If the non-compliance consists of a failure to pay an amount by way of pay specified in the order, the tribunal shall determine the amount owed by the employer on the date of the determination.

If on that date the tribunal also determines the employee's complaint that he has been unfairly dismissed, it shall specify that amount separately from any other sum awarded to the employee.

(5) In any other case, the tribunal shall order the employer to pay the employee such compensation as the tribunal considers just and equitable in all the circumstances having regard to any loss suffered by the employee in consequence of the non-compliance.

167   Interpretation and other supplementary provisions

(1) [Part X of the Employment Rights Act 1996] (unfair dismissal) has effect subject to the provisions of sections 152 to 166 above.

(2) Those sections shall be construed as one with that Part; and in those sections—

"complaint of unfair dismissal" means a complaint under [section 111 of the Employment Rights Act 1996];

"award of compensation for unfair dismissal" means an award of compensation for unfair dismissal under [section 112(4) or 117(3)(a)] of that Act; and

"order for reinstatement or re-engagement" means an order for reinstatement or re-engagement under [section 113] of that Act.

(3) Nothing in those sections shall be construed as conferring a right to complain of unfair dismissal from employment of a description to which that Part does not otherwise apply.

178   Collective agreements and collective bargaining

(1) In this Act "collective agreement" means any agreement or arrangement made by or on behalf of one or more trade unions and one or more employers or employers' associations and relating to one or more of the matters specified below; and "collective bargaining" means negotiations relating to or connected with one or more of those matters.

(2) The matters referred to above are—

(a) terms and conditions of employment, or the physical conditions in which any workers are required to work;

(b) engagement or non-engagement, or termination or suspension of employment or the duties of employment, of one or more workers;

(c) allocation of work or the duties of employment between workers or groups of workers;

(d) matters of discipline;

(e) a worker's membership or non-membership of a trade union;

(f) facilities for officials of trade unions; and

(g) machinery for negotiation or consultation, and other procedures, relating to any of the above matters, including the recognition by employers or employers' associations of the right of a trade union to represent workers in such negotiation or consultation or in the carrying out of such procedures.

179   Whether agreement intended to be a legally enforceable contract

(1) A collective agreement shall be conclusively presumed not to have been intended by the parties to be a legally enforceable contract unless the agreement—

(a) is in writing, and

(b) contains a provision which (however expressed) states that the parties intend that the agreement shall be a legally enforceable contract.

(2) A collective agreement which does satisfy those conditions shall be conclusively presumed to have been intended by the parties to be a legally enforceable contract.

(3) If a collective agreement is in writing and contains a provision which (however expressed) states that the parties intend that one or more parts of the agreement specified in that provision, but not the whole of the agreement, shall be a legally enforceable contract, then—

(a) the specified part or parts shall be conclusively presumed to have been intended by the parties to be a legally enforceable contract, and

(b) the remainder of the agreement shall be conclusively presumed not to have been intended by the parties to be such a contract.

(4) A part of a collective agreement which by virtue of subsection (3)(b) is not a legally enforceable contract may be referred to for the purpose of interpreting a part of the agreement which is such a contract.

180   Effect of provisions restricting right to take industrial action

(1) Any terms of a collective agreement which prohibit or restrict the right of workers to engage in a strike or other industrial action, or have the effect of prohibiting or restricting that right, shall not form part of any contract between a worker and the person for whom he works unless the following conditions are met.

(2) The conditions are that the collective agreement—

   (a) is in writing,

   (b) contains a provision expressly stating that those terms shall or may be incorpo-
       rated in such a contract,

   (c) is reasonably accessible at his place of work to the worker to whom it applies and
       is available for him to consult during working hours, and

   (d) is one where each trade union which is a party to the agreement is an indepen-
       dent trade union;

and that the contract with the worker expressly or impliedly incorporates those terms in the contract.

(3) The above provisions have effect notwithstanding anything in section 179 and notwithstanding any provision to the contrary in any agreement (including a collective agreement or a contract with any worker).

186   Recognition requirement in contract for goods or services void

A term or condition of a contract for the supply of goods or services is void in so far as it purports to require a party to the contract—

   (a) to recognise one or more trade unions (whether or not named in the contract) for
       the purpose of negotiating on behalf of workers, or any class of worker, employed
       by him, or

   (b) to negotiate or consult with, or with an official of, one or more trade unions
       (whether or not so named).

187   Refusal to deal on grounds of union exclusion prohibited

(1) A person shall not refuse to deal with a supplier or prospective supplier of goods or services if the ground or one of the grounds for his action is that the person against whom it is taken does not, or is not likely to—

   (a) recognise one or more trade unions for the purpose of negotiating on behalf of
       workers, or any class of worker, employed by him, or

   (b) negotiate or consult with, or with an official of, one or more trade unions.

(2) A person refuses to deal with a person if—

   (a) where he maintains (in whatever form) a list of approved suppliers of goods or
       services, or of persons from whom tenders for the supply of goods or services may
       be invited, he fails to include the name of that person in that list; or

   (b) in relation to a proposed contract for the supply of goods or services—

       (i)   he excludes that person from the group of persons from whom tenders for
              the supply of the goods or services are invited, or

       (ii)   he fails to permit that person to submit such a tender; or

       [(iii)] he otherwise determines not to enter into a contract with that person for
              the supply of the goods or services. [or]

   [(c) he terminates a contract with that person for the supply of goods or services.]

(3) The obligation to comply with this section is a duty owed to the person with whom there is a refusal to deal and to any other person who may be adversely affected by its contravention; and a breach of the duty is actionable accordingly (subject to the defences and other incidents applying to actions for breach of statutory duty).

219   Protection from certain tort liabilities

(1) An act done by a person in contemplation or furtherance of a trade dispute is not actionable in tort on the ground only—

(a) that it induces another person to break a contract or interferes or induces another person to interfere with its performance, or

(b) that it consists in his threatening that a contract (whether one to which he is a party or not) will be broken or its performance interfered with, or that he will induce another person to break a contract or interfere with its performance.

(2) An agreement or combination by two or more persons to do or procure the doing of an act in contemplation or furtherance of a trade dispute is not actionable in tort if the act is one which if done without any such agreement or combination would not be actionable in tort.

(3) Nothing in subsections (1) and (2) prevents an act done in the course of picketing from being actionable in tort unless it is done in the course of attendance declared lawful by section 220 (peaceful picketing).

(4) Subsections (1) and (2) have effect subject to sections 222 to 225 (action excluded from protection) [and to sections 226 (requirement of ballot before action by trade union) and 234A (requirement of notice to employer of industrial action); and in those sections "not protected" means excluded from the protection afforded by this section or, where the expression is used with reference to a particular person, excluded from that protection as respects that person.]

220 Peaceful picketing

(1) It is lawful for a person in contemplation or furtherance of a trade dispute to attend—

(a) at or near his own place of work, or

(b) if he is an official of a trade union, at or near the place of work of a member of the union whom he is accompanying and whom he represents,

for the purpose only of peacefully obtaining or communicating information, or peacefully persuading any person to work or abstain from working.

(2) If a person works or normally works—

(a) otherwise than at any one place, or

(b) at a place the location of which is such that attendance there for a purpose mentioned in subsection (1) is impracticable,

his place of work for the purposes of that subsection shall be any premises of his employer from which he works or from which his work is administered.

221 Restrictions on grant of injunctions and interdicts

(1) Where—

(a) an application for an injunction or interdict is made to a court in the absence of the party against whom it is sought or any representative of his, and

(b) he claims, or in the opinion of the court would be likely to claim, that he acted in contemplation or furtherance of a trade dispute,

the court shall not grant the injunction or interdict unless satisfied that all steps which in the circumstances were reasonable have been taken with a view to securing that notice of the application and an opportunity of being heard with respect to the application have been given to him.

(2) Where—

(a) an application for an interlocutory injunction is made to a court pending the trial of an action, and

(b) the party against whom it is sought claims that he acted in contemplation or furtherance of a trade dispute,

the court shall, in exercising its discretion whether or not to grant the injunction, have regard to the likelihood of that party's succeeding at the trial of the action in establishing any matter which would afford a defence to the action under section 219 (protection from certain tort liabilities) or section 220 (peaceful picketing).

This subsection does not extend to Scotland.

222   Action to enforce trade union membership

(1) An act is not protected if the reason, or one of the reasons, for which it is done is the fact or belief that a particular employer—

(a) is employing, has employed or might employ a person who is not a member of a trade union, or

(b) is failing, has failed or might fail to discriminate against such a person.

(2) For the purposes of subsection (1)(b) an employer discriminates against a person if, but only if, he ensures that his conduct in relation to—

(a) persons, or persons of any description, employed by him, or who apply to be, or are, considered by him for employment, or

(b) that provision of employment for such persons, is different, in some or all cases, according to whether or not they are members of a trade union, and is more favourable to those who are.

(3) An act is not protected if it constitutes, or is one of a number of acts which together constitute, an inducement or attempted inducement of a person—

(a) to incorporate in a contract to which that person is a party, or a proposed contract to which he intends to be a party, a term or condition which is or would be void by virtue of section 144 (union membership requirement in contract for goods or services), or

(b) to contravene section 145 (refusal to deal with person on grounds relating to union membership).

224   Secondary action

(1) An Act is not protected if one of the facts relied on for the purpose of establishing liability is that there has been secondary action which is not lawful picketing.

(2) There is secondary action in relation to a trade dispute when, and only when, a person—

(a) induces another to break a contract of employment or interferes or induces another to interfere with its performance, or

(b) threatens that a contract of employment under which he or another is employed will be broken or its performance interfered with, or that he will induce another to break a contract of employment or to interfere with its performance,

and the employer under the contract of employment is not the employer party to the dispute.

(3) Lawful picketing means acts done in the course of such attendance as is declared lawful by section 220 (peaceful picketing)—

(a) by a worker employed (or, in the case of a worker not in employment, last employed) by the employer party to the dispute, or

(b) by a trade union official whose attendance is lawful by virtue of subsection (1)(b) of that section.

(4) For the purposes of this section an employer shall not be treated as party to a dispute between another employer and workers of that employer; and where more than one employer is in dispute with his workers, the dispute between each employer and his workers shall be treated as a separate dispute.

In this subsection "worker" has the same meaning as in section 244 (meaning of "trade dispute").

(5) An act in contemplation or furtherance of a trade dispute which is primary action in relation to that dispute may not be relied on as secondary action in relation to another trade dispute.

Primary action means such action as is mentioned in paragraph (a) or (b) of subsection (2) where the employer under the contract of employment is the employer party to the dispute.

(6) In this section "contract of employment" includes any contract under which one person personally does work or performs services for another, and related expressions shall be construed accordingly.

225   Pressure to impose union recognition requirement

(1) An act is not protected if it constitutes, or is one of a number of acts which together constitute, an inducement or attempted inducement of a person—

(a) to incorporate in a contract to which that person is a party, or a proposed contract to which he intends to be a party, a term or condition which is or would be void by virtue of section 186 (recognition requirement in contract for goods or services), or

(b) to contravene section 187 (refusal to deal with person on grounds of union exclusion).

(2) An act is not protected if—

(a) it interferes with the supply (whether or not under a contract) of goods or services, or can reasonably be expected to have that effect, and

(b) one of the facts relied upon for the purpose of establishing liability is that a person has—

(i) induced another to break a contract of employment or interfered or induced another to interfere with its performance, or

(ii) threatened that a contract of employment under which he or another is employed will be broken or its performance interfered with, or that he will induce another to break a contract of employment or to interfere with its performance, and

(c) the reason, or one of the reasons, for doing the act is the fact or belief that the supplier (not being the employer under the contract of employment mentioned in paragraph (b)) does not, or might not—

(i) recognise one or more trade unions for the purpose of negotiating on behalf of workers, or any class of worker, employed by him, or

(ii) negotiate or consult with, or with an official of, one or more trade unions.

226   Requirement of ballot before action by trade union

(1) An act done by a trade union to induce a person to take part, or continue to take part, in industrial action—

[(a) is not protected unless the industrial action has the support of a ballot, and

(a) where section 226A falls to be complied with in relation to the person's employer, is not protected as respects the employer unless the trade union has complied with section 226A in relation to him.]

236   No compulsion to work

No court shall, whether by way of—

(a) an order for specific performance or specific implement of a contract of employment, or

(b) an injunction or interdict restraining a breach or threatened breach of such a contract,

compel an employee to do any work or attend at any place for the doing of any work.

237   Dismissal of those taking part in unofficial industrial action

(1) An employee has no right to complain of unfair dismissal if at the time of dismissal he was taking part in an unofficial strike or other unofficial industrial action.

(2) A strike or other industrial action is unofficial in relation to an employee unless—

(a) he is a member of a trade union and the action is authorised or endorsed by that union, or

(b) he is not a member of a trade union but there are among those taking part in the industrial action members of a trade union by which the action has been authorised or endorsed.

Provided that, a strike or other industrial action shall not be regarded as unofficial if none of those taking part in it are members of a trade union.

240   Breach of contract involving injury to persons or property

(1) A person commits an offence who wilfully and maliciously breaks a contract of service or hiring, knowing or having reasonable cause to believe that the probable consequences of his so doing, either alone or in combination with others, will be—

   (a) to endanger human life or cause serious bodily injury, or
   (b) to expose valuable property, whether real or personal, to destruction or serious injury.

(2) Subsection (1) applies equally whether the offence is committed from malice conceived against the person endangered or injured or, as the case may be, the owner of the property destroyed or injured, or otherwise.

(4) This section does not apply to seamen.

241   Intimidation or annoyance by violence or otherwise

(1) A person commits an offence who, with a view to compelling another person to abstain from doing or to do any act which that person has a legal right to do or abstain from doing, wrongfully and without legal authority—

   (a) uses violence to or intimidates that person or his [spouse or civil partner] or children, or injures his property,
   (b) persistently follows that person about from place to place,
   (c) hides any tools, clothes or other property owned or used by that person, or deprives him of or hinders him in the use thereof,
   (d) watches or besets the house or other place where that person resides, works, carries on business or happens to be, or the approach to any such house or place, or
   (e) follows that person with two or more other persons in a disorderly manner in or through any street or road.

244   Meaning of "trade dispute" in Part V

(1) In this Part a "trade dispute" means a dispute between workers and their employer which relates wholly or mainly to one or more of the following—

   (a) terms and conditions of employment, or the physical conditions in which any workers are required to work;
   (b) engagement or non-engagement, or termination or suspension of employment or the duties of employment, of one or more workers;
   (c) allocation of work or the duties of employment between workers or groups of workers;
   (d) matters of discipline;
   (e) a worker's membership or non-membership of a trade union;
   (f) facilities for officials of trade unions; and
   (g) machinery for negotiation or consultation, and other procedures, relating to any of the above matters, including the recognition by employers or employers' associations of the right of a trade union to represent workers in such negotiation or consultation or in the carrying out of such procedures.

245   Crown employees and contracts

Where a person holds any office or employment under the Crown on terms which do not constitute a contract of employment between that person and the Crown, those terms shall nevertheless be deemed to constitute such a contract for the purposes of—

   (a) the law relating to liability in tort of a person who commits an act which—
      (i) induces another person to break a contract, interferes with the performance of a contract or induces another person to interfere with its performance, or
      (ii) consists in a threat that a contract will be broken or its performance interfered with, or that any person will be induced to break a contract or interfere with its performance, and

(b) the provisions of this or any other Act which refer (whether in relation to contracts generally or only in relation to contracts of employment) to such an act.

273 Crown employment

(1) The provisions of this Act have effect (except as mentioned below) in relation to Crown employment and persons in Crown employment as in relation to other employment and other workers or employees.

(5) Sections 137 to 143 (rights in relation to trade union membership: access to employment) apply in relation to Crown employment otherwise than under a contract only where the terms of employment correspond to those of a contract of employment.

288 Restriction on contracting out

(1) Any provision in an agreement (whether a contract of employment or not) is void in so far as it purports—

(a) to exclude or limit the operation of any provision of this Act, or
(b) to preclude a person from bringing—
  (i) proceedings before an [employment tribunal] or the Central Arbitration Committee under any provision of this Act, [. . .].

[(2A) Subsection (1) does not apply to an agreement to refrain from instituting or continuing any proceedings, other than excepted proceedings, specified in subsection 1(b) of that section before an industrial tribunal if the conditions regulating compromise agreements under this Act are satisfied in relation to the agreement.

(2B) The conditions regulating compromise agreements under this Act are that—

(a) the agreement must be in writing;
(b) the agreement must relate to the particular [proceedings];
(c) the complainant must have received [advice from a relevant independent adviser] as to the terms and effect of the proposed agreement and in particular its effect on his ability to pursue his rights before an industrial tribunal;
(d) there must be in force, when the adviser gives the advice, a [contract of insurance, or an indemnity provided for members of a profession or professional body] covering the risk of a claim by the complainant in respect of loss arising in consequence of the advice;
(e) the agreement must identify the adviser; and
(f) the agreement must state that the conditions regulating compromise agreements under this Act are satisfied.]

Railways Act 1993
(1993, c. 43)

122 Statutory authority as a defence to actions in nuisance etc.

(1) Subject to the following provisions of this section—

(a) any person shall have authority—
  (i) to use, or to cause or permit any agent or independent contractor of his to use, rolling stock on any track, or
  (ii) to use, or to cause or permit any agent or independent contractor of his to use, any land comprised in a network, station or light maintenance depot for or in connection with the provision of network services, station services in light maintenance services, and
(b) any person who is the owner or occupier of any land shall have authority to authorise, consent to or acquiesce in—
  (i) the use by another of rolling stock on any track comprised in that land, or

         (ii) the use by another of that land for or in connection with the provision of network services, station services or light maintenance services,

if and so long as the qualifying conditions are satisfied in the particular case.

    (3) The authority conferred by this section is conferred only for the purpose of providing a defence of statutory authority—

      (a) in England and Wales—

         (i) in any proceedings, whether civil or criminal, in nuisance; or

        (ii) in any civil proceedings, other than proceedings for breach of statutory duty, in respect of the escape of things from land;

    (4) Nothing in this section shall be construed as excluding a defence of statutory authority otherwise available under or by virtue of any enactment.

Criminal Justice and Public Order Act 1994
(1994, c. 33)

60   Powers to stop and search in anticipation of violence

[(1) If a police officer of or above the rank of inspector reasonably believes—

      (a) that incidents involving serious violence may take place in any locality in his police area, and that it is expedient to give an authorisation under this section to prevent their occurrence, or

      (b) that persons are carrying dangerous instruments or offensive weapons in any locality in his police area without good reason,

he may give an authorisation that the powers conferred by this section shall be exercisable at any place within that locality for a specified period not exceeding twenty four hours.]

    [(4A) This section also confers on any constable in uniform power—

      (a) to require any person to remove any item which the constable reasonably believes that person is wearing wholly or mainly for the purpose of concealing his identity;

      (b) to seize any item which the constable reasonably believes any person intends to wear wholly or mainly for that purpose.]

    (5) A constable may, in the exercise of [the powers conferred by subsection (4) above], stop any person or vehicle and make any search he thinks fit whether or not he has any grounds for suspecting that the person or vehicle is carrying weapons or articles of that kind.

    (6) If in the course of a search under this section a constable discovers a dangerous instrument or an article which he has reasonable grounds for suspecting to be an offensive weapon, he may seize it.

61   Power to remove trespassers on land

    (1) If the senior police officer present at the scene reasonably believes that two or more persons are trespassing on land and are present there with the common purpose of residing there for any period, that reasonable steps have been taken by or on behalf of the occupier to ask them to leave and—

      (a) that any of those persons has caused damage to the land or to property on the land or used threatening, abusive or insulting words or behaviour towards the occupier, a member of his family or an employee or agent of his, or

      (b) that those persons have between them six or more vehicles on the land, he may direct those persons, or any of them, to leave the land and to remove any vehicles or other property they have with them on the land.

    (2) Where the persons in question are reasonably believed by the senior police officer to be persons who were not originally trespassers but have become trespassers on the land, the officer must reasonably believe that the other conditions specified in subsection (1) are

satisfied after those persons became trespassers before he can exercise the power conferred by that subsection.

(4) If a person knowing that a direction under subsection (1) above has been given which applies to him—

    (a) fails to leave the land as soon as reasonably practicable, or

    (b) having left again enters the land as a trespasser within the period of three months beginning with the day on which the direction was given, he commits an offence

    . . .

62 Supplementary powers of seizure

(1) If a direction has been given under section 61 and a constable reasonably suspects that any person to whom the direction applies has, without reasonable excuse—

    (a) failed to remove any vehicle on the land which appears to the constable to belong to him or to be in his possession or under his control; or

    (b) entered the land as a trespasser with a vehicle within the period of three months beginning with the day on which the direction was given,

the constable may seize and remove that vehicle.

[62A Power to remove trespassers: alternative site available

(1) If the senior police officer present at a scene reasonably believes that the conditions in subsection (2) are satisfied in relation to a person and land, he may direct the person—

    (a) to leave the land;

    (b) to remove any vehicle and other property he has with him on the land.

(2) The conditions are—

    (a) that the person and one or more others ("the trespassers") are trespassing on the land;

    (b) that the trespassers have between them at least one vehicle on the land;

    (c) that the trespassers are present on the land with the common purpose of residing there for any period;

    (d) if it appears to the officer that the person has one or more caravans in his possession or under his control on the land, that there is a suitable pitch on a relevant caravan site for that caravan or each of those caravans;

    (e) that the occupier of the land or a person acting on his behalf has asked the police to remove the trespassers from the land.]

[62C Failure to comply with direction under section 62A: seizure

(1) This section applies if a direction has been given under section 62A(1) and a constable reasonably suspects that a person to whom the direction applies has, without reasonable excuse—

    (a) failed to remove any vehicle on the relevant land which appears to the constable to belong to him or to be in his possession or under his control; or

    (b) entered any land in the area of the relevant local authority as a trespasser with a vehicle before the end of the relevant period with the intention of residing there.

(2) The relevant period is the period of 3 months starting with the day on which the direction is given.

(3) The constable may seize and remove the vehicle.]

63 Powers to remove persons attending or preparing for a rave

(1) This section applies to a gathering on land in the open air of [20] or more persons (whether or not trespassers) at which amplified music is played during the night (with or without intermissions) and is such as, by reason of its loudness and duration and the time at which it is played, is likely to cause serious distress to the inhabitants of the locality; and for this purpose—

    (a) such a gathering continues during intermissions in the music and where the gathering extends over several days, throughout the period during which amplified music is played at night (with or without intermissions); and

(b) "music" includes sounds wholly or predominantly characterised by the emission of a succession of repetitive beats.

[(1A) This section also applies to a gathering if—

(a) it is a gathering on land of 20 or more persons who are trespassing on the land; and

(b) it would be a gathering of a kind mentioned in subsection (1) above if it took place on land in the open air.]

(2) If, as respects any land [. . .], a police officer of at least the rank of superintendent reasonably believes that—

(a) two or more persons are making preparations for the holding there of a gathering to which this section applies,

(b) ten or more persons are waiting for such a gathering to begin there, or

(c) ten or more persons are attending such a gathering which is in progress,

he may give a direction that those persons and any other persons who come to prepare or wait for or to attend the gathering are to leave the land and remove any vehicles or other property which they have with them on the land.

(6) If a person knowing that a direction has been given which applies to him—

(a) fails to leave the land as soon as reasonably practicable, or

(b) having left again enters the land within the period of 7 days beginning with the day on which the direction was given,

he commits an offence . . .

64 Supplementary powers of entry and seizure

(4) If a direction has been given under section 63 and a constable reasonably suspects that any person to whom the direction applies has, without reasonable excuse—

(a) failed to remove any vehicle or sound equipment on the land which appears to the constable to belong to him or to be in his possession or under his control; or

(b) entered the land as a trespasser with a vehicle or sound equipment within the period of 7 days beginning with the day on which the direction was given,

the constable may seize and remove that vehicle or sound equipment.

65 Raves: power to stop persons from proceeding

(1) If a constable in uniform reasonably believes that a person is on his way to a gathering to which section 63 applies in relation to which a direction under section 63(2) is in force, he may, subject to subsections (2) and (3) below—

(a) stop that person, and

(b) direct him not to proceed in the direction of the gathering.

(2) The power conferred by subsection (1) above may only be exercised at a place within 5 miles of the boundary of the site of the gathering.

66 Power of court to forfeit sound equipment

(1) Where a person is convicted of an offence under section 63 in relation to a gathering to which that section applies and the court is satisfied that any sound equipment which has been seized from him under section 64(4), or which was in his possession or under his control at the relevant time, has been used at the gathering the court may make an order for forfeiture under this subsection in respect of that property.

(2) The court may make an order under subsection (1) above whether or not it also deals with the offender in respect of the offence in any other way and without regard to any restrictions on forfeiture in any enactment.

(3) In considering whether to make an order under subsection (1) above in respect of any property a court shall have regard—

(a) to the value of the property; and

(b) to the likely financial and other effects on the offender of the making of the order (taken together with any other order that the court contemplates making).

(4) An order under subsection (1) above shall operate to deprive the offender of his rights, if any, in the property to which it relates, and the property shall (if not already in their possession) be taken into the possession of the police.

(5) Except in a case to which subsection (6) below applies, where any property has been forfeited under subsection (1) above, a magistrates' court may, on application by a claimant of the property, other than the offender from whom it was forfeited under subsection (1) above, make an order for delivery of the property to the applicant if it appears to the court that he is the owner of the property.

(7) No application shall be made under subsection (5), or by virtue of subsection (6), above by any claimant of the property after the expiration of 6 months from the date on which an order under subsection (1) above was made in respect of the property.

(8) No such application shall succeed unless the claimant satisfies the court either that he had not consented to the offender having possession of the property or that he did not know, and had no reason to suspect, that the property was likely to be used at a gathering to which section 63 applies.

68   Offence of aggravated trespass

(1) A person commits the offence of aggravated trespass if he trespasses on land [. . .] and, in relation to any lawful activity which persons are engaging in or are about to engage in on that or adjoining land [. . .], does there anything which is intended by him to have the effect—

> (a) of intimidating those persons or any of them so as to deter them or any of them from engaging in that activity,
> (b) of obstructing that activity, or
> (c) of disrupting that activity.

[(1A) The reference in subsection (1) above to trespass includes, in Scotland, the exercise of access rights (within the meaning of the Land Reform (Scotland) Act 2003 (asp 2) up to the point when they cease to be exercisable by virtue of the commission of the offence under that subsection.]

(2) Activity on any occasion on the part of a person or persons on land is "lawful" for the purposes of this section if he or they may engage in the activity on the land on that occasion without committing an offence or trespassing on the land.

69   Powers to remove persons committing or participating in aggravated trespass

(1) If the senior police officer present at the scene reasonably believes—

> (a) that a person is committing, has committed or intends to commit the offence of aggravated trespass on land [. . .]; or
> (b) that two or more persons are trespassing on land [. . .] and are present there with the common purpose of intimidating persons so as to deter them from engaging in a lawful activity or of obstructing or disrupting a lawful activity,

he may direct that person or (as the case may be) those persons (or any of them) to leave the land.

(2) A direction under subsection (1) above, if not communicated to the persons referred to in subsection (1) by the police officer giving the direction, may be communicated to them by any constable at the scene.

(3) If a person knowing that a direction under subsection (1) above has been given which applies to him—

> (a) fails to leave the land as soon as practicable, or
> (b) having left again enters the land as a trespasser within the period of [51 weeks] beginning with the day on which the direction was given, he commits an offence.

Value Added Tax Act 1994
(1994, c. 23)

80   [**Credit for, or repayment of, overstated or overpaid VAT**]

[(1) Where a person—

(a) has accounted to the Commissioners for VAT for a prescribed accounting period (whenever ended), and

(b) in doing so, has brought into account as output tax an amount that was not output tax due,

the Commissioners shall be liable to credit the person with that amount.

(1A) Where the Commissioners—

(a) have assessed a person to VAT for a prescribed accounting period (whenever ended), and

(b) in doing so, have brought into account as output tax an amount that was not output tax due,

they shall be liable to credit the person with that amount.

(1B) Where a person has for a prescribed accounting period (whenever ended) paid to the Commissioners an amount by way of VAT that was not VAT due to them, otherwise than as a result of—

(a) an amount that was not output tax due being brought into account as output tax, or

(b) an amount of input tax allowable under section 26 not being brought into account,

the Commissioners shall be liable to repay to that person the amount so paid.]

(2) The Commissioners shall only be liable to [credit or] repay an amount under this section on a claim being made for the purpose.

[(2A) Where—

(a) as a result of a claim under this section by virtue of subsection (1) or (1A) above an amount falls to be credited to a person, and

(b) after setting any sums against it under or by virtue of this Act, some or all of that amount remains to his credit,

the Commissioners shall be liable to pay (or repay) to him so much of that amount as so remains.]

(3) It shall be a defence, in relation to a claim [under this section by virtue of subsection (1) or (1A) above, that the crediting] of an amount would unjustly enrich the claimant.]

[(3A) Subsection (3B) below applies for the purposes of subsection (3) above where—

(a) an amount would (apart from subsection (3) above) fall to be credited under subsection (1) or (1A) above to any person ("the taxpayer"), and

(b) the whole or a part of the amount brought into account as mentioned in paragraph (b) of that subsection has, for practical purposes, been borne by a person other than the taxpayer.]

(3B) Where, in a case to which this subsection applies, loss or damage has been or may be incurred by the taxpayer as a result of mistaken assumptions made in his case about the operation of any VAT provisions, that loss or damage shall be disregarded, except to the extent of the quantified amount, in the making of any determination—

(a) of whether or to what extent the [crediting] of an amount to the taxpayer would enrich him; or

(b) of whether or to what extent any enrichment of the taxpayer would be unjust.

(3C) In subsection (3B) above—

"the quantified amount" means the amount (if any) which is shown by the taxpayer to constitute the amount that would appropriately compensate him for loss or damage shown by him to have resulted, for any business carried on by him, from the making of the mistaken assumptions; and

"VAT provisions" means the provisions of—
> (a) any enactment, subordinate legislation or Community legislation (whether or not still in force) which relates to VAT or to any matter connected with VAT; or
> (b) any notice published by the Commissioners under or for the purposes of any such enactment or subordinate legislation.]

[(4) The Commissioners shall not be liable on a claim under this section—
> (a) to credit an amount to a person under subsection (1) or (1A) above, or
> (b) to repay an amount to a person under subsection (1B) above,

if the claim is made more than 3 years after the relevant date.

(4ZA) The relevant date is—
> (a) in the case of a claim by virtue of subsection (1) above, the end of the prescribed accounting period mentioned in that subsection, unless paragraph (b) below applies;
> (b) in the case of a claim by virtue of subsection (1) above in respect of an erroneous voluntary disclosure, the end of the prescribed accounting period in which the disclosure was made;
> (c) in the case of a claim by virtue of subsection (1A) above in respect of an assessment issued on the basis of an erroneous voluntary disclosure, the end of the prescribed accounting period in which the disclosure was made;
> (d) in the case of a claim by virtue of subsection (1A) above in any other case, the end of the prescribed accounting period in which the assessment was made;
> (e) in the case of a claim by virtue of subsection (1B) above, the date on which the payment was made.

In the case of a person who has ceased to be registered under this Act, any reference in paragraphs (b) to (d) above to a prescribed accounting period includes a reference to a period that would have been a prescribed accounting period had the person continued to be registered under this Act.

(4ZB) For the purposes of this section the cases where there is an erroneous voluntary disclosure are those cases where—
> (a) a person discloses to the Commissioners that he has not brought into account for a prescribed accounting period (whenever ended) an amount of output tax due for the period;
> (b) the disclosure is made in a later prescribed accounting period (whenever ended); and
> (c) some or all of the amount is not output tax due.]

[(4A) Where—
> (a) an amount has been credited under subsection (1) or (1A) above to any person at any time on or after 26th May 2005, and
> (b) the amount so credited exceeded the amount which the Commissioners were liable at that time to credit to that person,

the Commissioners may, to the best of their judgement, assess the excess credited to that person and notify it to him.]

(4C) Subsections (2) to (8) of section 78A apply in the case of an assessment under subsection (4A) above as they apply in the case of an assessment under section 78A(1).]

(6) A claim under this section shall be made in such form and manner and shall be supported by such documentary evidence as the Commissioners prescribe by regulations; and regulations under this subsection may make different provision for different cases.

[(7) Except as provided by this section, the Commissioners shall not be liable to repay an amount accounted for or paid to them by way of VAT that was not VAT due to them.]

[80A   Arrangements for reimbursing customers

(1) The Commissioners may by regulations make provision for reimbursement arrangements made by any person to be disregarded for the purposes of section 80(3) except where the arrangements—

> (a) contain such provision as may be required by the regulations; and
> (b) are supported by such undertakings to comply with the provisions of the arrangements as may be required by the regulations to be given to the Commissioners.

(2) In this section "reimbursement arrangements" means any arrangements for the purposes of a claim under section 80 which—

> (a) are made by any person for the purpose of securing that he is not unjustly enriched by the [crediting] of any amount in pursuance of the claim; and
> (b) provide for the reimbursement of persons who have for practical purposes borne the whole or any part of [the amount bought into account as mentioned in paragraph (b) of subsection (1) or (1A) of that section].

(3) Without prejudice to the generality of subsection (1) above, the provision that may be required by regulations under this section to be contained in reimbursement arrangements includes—

> (a) provision requiring a reimbursement for which the arrangements provide to be made within such period after the [crediting of that amount] to which it relates as may be specified in the regulations;
> [(b)provision for cases where an amount is credited but an equal amount is not reimbursed in accordance with the arrangements;]
> (c) provision requiring interest paid by the Commissioners on any amount [paid (or repaid)] by them to be treated in the same way as that amount for the purposes of any requirement under the arrangements to make reimbursement or to repay the Commissioners;
> (d) provision requiring such records relating to the carrying out of the arrangements as may be described in the regulations to be kept and produced to the Commissioners, or to an officer of theirs.

(4) Regulations under this section may impose obligations on such persons as may be specified in the regulations—

> (a) [to make the repayments, or give the notifications, to the Commissioners that they are required to make or give] in pursuance of any provisions contained in any reimbursement arrangements by virtue of subsection (3)(b) or (c) above;
> (b) to comply with any requirements contained in any such arrangements by virtue of subsection (3)(d) above.

(5) Regulations under this section may make provision for the form and manner in which, and the times at which, undertakings are to be given to the Commissioners in accordance with the regulations; and any such provision may allow for those matters to be determined by the Commissioners in accordance with the regulations.

(6) Regulations under this section may—

> (a) contain any such incidental, supplementary, consequential or transitional provision as appears to the Commissioners to be necessary or expedient; and
> (b) make different provision for different circumstances.

(7) Regulations under this section may have effect (irrespective of when the claim for [credit] was made) for the purposes of [the crediting of any amount] by the Commissioners after the time when the regulations are made; and, accordingly, such regulations may apply to arrangements made before that time.]

Criminal Injuries Compensation Act 1995
(1995, c. 53)

1   The Criminal Injuries Compensation Scheme

(1) The Secretary of State shall make arrangements for the payment of compensation to, or in respect of, persons who have sustained one or more criminal injuries.

(2) Any such arrangements shall include the making of a scheme providing, in particular, for—

    (a) the circumstances in which awards may be made; and

    (b) the categories of person to whom awards may be made.

(3) The scheme shall be known as the Criminal Injuries Compensation Scheme.

(4) In this Act—

"adjudicator" means a person appointed by the Secretary of State [or the Scottish Ministers] under section 5(1)(b);

"award" means an award of compensation made in accordance with the provisions of the Scheme;

"claim officer" means a person appointed by the Secretary of State under section 3(4)(b);

"compensation" means compensation payable under an award;

"criminal injury", "loss of earnings" and "special expenses" have such meaning as may be specified;

"the Scheme" means the Criminal Injuries Compensation Scheme;

"Scheme manager" means a person appointed by the Secretary of State to have overall responsibility for managing the provisions of the Scheme (other than those to which section 5(2) applies); and

"specified" means specified by the Scheme.

2   Basis on which compensation is to be calculated

(1) The amount of compensation payable under an award shall be determined in accordance with the provisions of the Scheme.

(2) Provision shall be made for—

    (a) a standard amount of compensation, determined by reference to the nature of the injury;

    (b) in such cases as may be specified, an additional amount of compensation calculated with respect to loss of earnings;

    (c) in such cases as may be specified, an additional amount of compensation calculated with respect to special expenses; and

    (d) in cases of fatal injury, such additional amounts as may be specified or otherwise determined in accordance with the Scheme.

(3) Provision shall be made for the standard amount to be determined—

    (a) in accordance with a table ("the Tariff") prepared by the Secretary of State as part of the Scheme and such other provisions of the Scheme as may be relevant; or

    (b) where no provision is made in the Tariff with respect to the injury in question, in accordance with such provisions of the Scheme as may be relevant.

(4) The Tariff shall show, in respect of each description of injury mentioned in the Tariff, the standard amount of compensation payable in respect of that description of injury.

(5) An injury may be described in the Tariff in such a way, including by reference to the nature of the injury, its severity or the circumstances in which it was sustained, as the Secretary of State considers appropriate.

(6) The Secretary of State may at any time alter the Tariff—

    (a) by adding to the descriptions of injury mentioned there;

    (b) by removing a description of injury;

    (c) by increasing or reducing the amount shown as the standard amount of compensation payable in respect of a particular description of injury; or

    (d) in such other way as he considers appropriate.

(7) The Scheme may—

    (a) provide for amounts of compensation not to exceed such maximum amounts as may be specified;

    (b) include such transitional provision with respect to any alteration of its provisions relating to compensation as the Secretary of State considers appropriate.

3   Claims and awards

(1) The Scheme may, in particular, include provision—

(a) as to the circumstances in which an award may be withheld or the amount of compensation reduced;

(b) for an award to be made subject to conditions;

(c) for the whole or any part of any compensation to be repayable in specified circumstances;

(d) for compensation to be held subject to trusts, in such cases as may be determined in accordance with the Scheme;

(e) requiring claims under the Scheme to be made within such periods as may be specified by the Scheme; and

(f) imposing other time limits.

(2) Where, in accordance with any provision of the Scheme, it falls to one person to satisfy another as to any matter, the standard of proof required shall be that applicable in civil proceedings.

(3) Where, in accordance with any provision of the Scheme made by virtue of subsection (1)(c), any amount falls to be repaid it shall be recoverable as a debt due to the Crown.

(4) The Scheme shall include provision for claims for compensation to be determined and awards and payments of compensation to be made—

(a) if a Scheme manager has been appointed, by persons appointed for the purpose by the Scheme manager; but

(b) otherwise by persons ("claims officers") appointed for the purpose by the Secretary of State.

(5) A claims officer—

(a) shall be appointed on such terms and conditions as the Secretary of State considers appropriate; but

(b) shall not be regarded as having been appointed to exercise functions of the Secretary of State or to act on his behalf.

(6) No decision taken by a claims officer shall be regarded as having been taken by, or on behalf of, the Secretary of State.

(7) If a Scheme manager has been appointed—

(a) he shall not be regarded as exercising functions of the Secretary of State or as acting on his behalf; and

(b) no decision taken by him or by any person appointed by him shall be regarded as having been taken by, or on behalf of, the Secretary of State.

7   Inalienability of awards

(1) Every assignment (or, in Scotland, assignation) of, or charge on, an award and every agreement to assign or charge an award shall be void.

(2) On the bankruptcy of a person in whose favour an award is made (or, in Scotland, on the sequestration of such a person's estate), the award shall not pass to any trustee or other person acting on behalf of his creditors.

[7A   Recovery of compensation from offenders: general

(1) The Secretary of State may, by regulations made by statutory instrument, make provision for the recovery from an appropriate person of an amount equal to all or part of the compensation paid in respect of a criminal injury.

(2) An appropriate person is a person who has been convicted of an offence in respect of the criminal injury.

(3) The amount recoverable from a person under the regulations must be determined by reference only to the extent to which the criminal injury is directly attributable to an offence of which he has been convicted.

(4) The regulations may confer functions in respect of recovery on—
  (a) claims officers;
  (b) if a Scheme manager has been appointed, persons appointed by the Scheme manager under section 3(4)(a).

(5) The regulations may not authorise the recovery of an amount in respect of compensation from a person to the extent that the compensation has been repaid in accordance with the Scheme.]

[7B Recovery notices

(1) If, under regulations made under section 7A(1), an amount has been determined as recoverable from a person, he must be given a notice (a "recovery notice") in accordance with the regulations which—
  (a) requires him to pay that amount, and
  (b) contains the information mentioned in subsection (2).

(2) The information is—
  (a) the reasons for the determination that an amount is recoverable from the person;
  (b) the basis on which the amount has been determined;
  (c) the way in which and the date before which the amount is required to be paid;
  (d) the means by which the amount may be recovered if it is not paid in accordance with the notice;
  (e) the grounds on which and the procedure by means of which he may seek a review if he objects to—
    (i) the determination that an amount is recoverable from him;
    (ii) the amount determined as recoverable from him.

(3) The Secretary of State may by order made by statutory instrument amend subsection (2) by—
  (a) adding information;
  (b) omitting information;
  (c) changing the description of information.]

[7C Review of recovery determinations

(1) Regulations under section 7A(1) shall include provision for the review, in such circumstances as may be prescribed by the regulations, of—
  (a) a determination that an amount is recoverable from a person;
  (b) the amount determined as recoverable from a person.

(2) A person from whom an amount has been determined as recoverable under the regulations may seek such a review only on the grounds—
  (a) that he has not been convicted of an offence to which the injury is directly attributable;
  (b) that the compensation paid was not determined in accordance with the Scheme;
  (c) that the amount determined as recoverable from him was not determined in accordance with the regulations.

(3) Any such review must be conducted by a person other than the person who made the determination under review.

(4) The person conducting any such review may—
  (a) set aside the determination that the amount is recoverable;
  (b) reduce the amount determined as recoverable;
  (c) increase the amount determined as recoverable;
  (d) determine to take no action under paragraphs (a) to (c).

(5) But the person conducting any such review may increase the amount determined as recoverable if (but only if) it appears to that person that the interests of justice require the amount to be increased.]

[7D Recovery proceedings

(1) An amount determined as recoverable from a person under regulations under section 7A(1) is recoverable from him as a debt due to the Crown if (but only if)—

(a) he has been given a recovery notice in accordance with the regulations which complies with the requirements of section 7B, and

(b) he has failed to pay the amount in accordance with the notice.

(2) In any proceedings for the recovery of the amount from a person, it is a defence for the person to show—

(a) that he has not been convicted of an offence to which the injury is directly attributable;

(b) that the compensation paid was not determined in accordance with the Scheme; or

(c) that the amount determined as recoverable from him was not determined in accordance with regulations under section 7A.

(3) In any such proceedings, except for the purposes of subsection (2)(b), no question may be raised or finding made as to the amount that was, or ought to have been, the subject of an award.

(4) For the purposes of section 9 of the Limitation Act 1980 (time limit for actions for sums recoverable by statute to run from date on which cause of action accrued) the cause of action to recover that amount shall be taken to have accrued—

(a) on the date on which the compensation was paid; or

(b) if later, on the date on which a person from whom an amount is sought to be recovered was convicted of an offence to which the injury is directly attributable.

(5) If that person is convicted of more than one such offence and the convictions are made on different dates, the reference in subsection (4)(b) to the date on which he was convicted of such an offence shall be taken to be a reference to the earlier or earliest (as the case may be) of the dates on which he was convicted of such an offence.]

9 Financial provisions

(1) The Secretary of State may pay such remuneration, allowances or gratuities to or in respect of claims officers and other persons appointed by him under this Act (other than adjudicators) as he considers appropriate.

(2) The Secretary of State may pay, or make such payments towards the provision of, such remuneration, pensions, allowances or gratuities to or in respect of adjudicators, as he considers appropriate.

(3) The Secretary of State may make such payments by way of compensation for loss of office to any adjudicator who is removed from office under section 5(7), as he considers appropriate.

(4) Sums required for the payment of compensation in accordance with the Scheme shall be provided by the Secretary of State out of money provided by Parliament.

(5) Where a Scheme manager has been appointed, the Secretary of State may make such payments to him, in respect of the discharge of his functions in relation to the Scheme, as the Secretary of State considers appropriate.

(6) Any expenses incurred by the Secretary of State under this Act shall be paid out of money provided by Parliament.

[(6A) Any expenses incurred by the Secretary of State under subsection (6) above as regards Scotland shall be reimbursed to the Secretary of State by the Scottish Minister.]

(7) Any sums received by the Secretary of State under any provision of the Scheme made by virtue of section 3(1)(c)[, or by virtue of regulations made under section 7A(1),] shall be paid by him into the Consolidated Fund.

Disability Discrimination Act 1995
(1995, c. 50)

25   Enforcement, remedies and procedure

(1) A claim by any person that another person—

    (a) has discriminated against him in a way which is unlawful under this Part; or

    (b) is by virtue of section 57 or 58 to be treated as having discriminated against him in such a way,

may be made the subject of civil proceedings in the same way as any other claim in tort or (in Scotland) in reparation for breach of statutory duty.

(2) For the avoidance of doubt it is hereby declared that damages in respect of discrimination in a way which is unlawful under this Part may include compensation for injury to feelings whether or not they include compensation under any other head.

(5) The remedies available in such proceedings are those which are available in the High Court or (as the case may be) the Court of Session.

[28V   Enforcement, remedies and procedure

(1) A claim by a person—

    (a) that a responsible body has discriminated against him in a way which is unlawful under this Chapter,

    (b) that a responsible body is by virtue of section 57 or 58 to be treated as having discriminated against him in such a way, or

    (c) that a person is by virtue of section 57 to be treated as having discriminated against him in such a way,

may be made the subject of civil proceedings in the same way as any other claim in tort or (in Scotland) in reparation for breach of statutory duty.

(2) For the avoidance of doubt it is hereby declared that damages in respect of discrimination in a way which is unlawful under this Chapter may include compensation for injury to feelings whether or not they include compensation under any other head.]

Landlord and Tenant (Covenants) Act 1995
(1995, c. 30)

3   Transmission of benefit and burden of covenants

(1) The benefit and burden of all landlord and tenant covenants of a tenancy—

    (a) shall be annexed and incident to the whole, and to each and every part, of the premises demised by the tenancy and of the reversion in them, and

    (b) shall in accordance with this section pass on an assignment of the whole or any part of those premises or of the reversion in them.

(2) Where the assignment is by the tenant under the tenancy, then as from the assignment the assignee—

    (a) becomes bound by the tenant covenants of the tenancy except to the extent that—

        (i)   immediately before the assignment they did not bind the assignor, or

        (ii) they fall to be complied with in relation to any demised premises not comprised in the assignment; and

    (b) becomes entitled to the benefit of the landlord covenants of the tenancy except to the extent that they fall to be complied with in relation to any such premises.

(3) Where the assignment is by the landlord under the tenancy, then as from the assignment the assignee—

    (a) becomes bound by the landlord covenants of the tenancy except to the extent that—

(i) immediately before the assignment they did not bind the assignor, or

(ii) they fall to be complied with in relation to any demised premises not comprised in the assignment; and

(b) becomes entitled to the benefit of the tenant covenants of the tenancy except to the extent that they fall to be complied with in relation to any such premises.

(4) In determining for the purposes of subsection (2) or (3) whether any covenant bound the assignor immediately before the assignment, any waiver or release of the covenant (in whatever terms) is expressed to be personal to the assignor shall be disregarded.

(5) Any landlord or tenant covenant of a tenancy which is restrictive of the user of land shall, as well as being capable of enforcement against an assignee, be capable of being enforced against any other person who is the owner or occupier of any demised premises to which the covenant relates, even though there is no express provision in the tenancy to that effect.

(6) Nothing in this section shall operate—

(a) in the case of a covenant which (in whatever terms) is expressed to be personal to any person, to make the covenant enforceable by or (as the case may be) against any other person; or

(b) to make a covenant enforceable against any person if, apart from this section, it would not be enforceable against him by reason of its not having been registered under the [Land Registration Act 2002] or the Land Charges Act 1972.

(7) To the extent that there remains in force any rule of law by virtue of which the burden of a covenant whose subject matter is not in existence at the time when it is made does not run with the land affected unless the covenantor covenants on behalf of himself and his assigns, that rule of law is hereby abolished in relation to tenancies.

4 Transmission of rights of re-entry

The benefit of a landlord's right of a re-entry under a tenancy—

(a) shall be annexed and incident to the whole, and to each and every part, of the reversion in the premises demised by the tenancy, and

(b) shall pass on an assignment of the whole or any part of the reversion in those premises.

5 Tenant released from covenants on assignment of tenancy

(1) This section applies where a tenant assigns premises demised to him under a tenancy.

(2) If the tenant assigns the whole of the premises demised to him, he—

(a) is released from the tenant covenants of the tenancy, and

(b) ceases to be entitled to the benefit of the landlord covenants of the tenancy, as from the assignment.

(3) If the tenant assigns part only of the premises demised to him, then as from the assignment he—

(a) is released from the tenant covenants of the tenancy, and

(b) ceases to be entitled to the benefit of the landlord covenants of the tenancy, only to the extent that those covenants fall to be complied with in relation to that part of the demised premises.

(4) This section applies as mentioned in subsection (1) whether or not the tenant is tenant of the whole of the premises comprised in the tenancy.

6 Landlord may be released from covenants on assignment of reversion

. . .

7 Former landlord may be released from covenants on assignment of reversion

. . .

9   Apportionment of liability under covenants binding both assignor and assignee of tenancy or reversion

(1) This section applies where—

(a) a tenant assigns part only of the premises demised to him by a tenancy;

(b) after the assignment both the tenant and his assignee are to be bound by a non-attributable tenant covenant of the tenancy; and

(c) the tenant and his assignee agree that as from the assignment liability under the covenant is to be apportioned between them in such manner as is specified in the agreement.

(2) This section also applies where—

(a) a landlord assigns the reversion in part only of the premises of which he is the landlord under a tenancy;

(b) after the assignment both the landlord and his assignee are to be bound by a non-attributable landlord covenant of the tenancy; and

(c) the landlord and his assignee agree that as from the assignment liability under the covenant is to be apportioned between them in such manner as is specified in the agreement.

(3) Any such agreement as is mentioned in subsection (1) or (2) may apportion liability in such a way that a party to the agreement is exonerated from all liability under a covenant.

(4) In any case falling within subsection (1) or (2) the parties to the agreement may apply for the apportionment to become binding on the appropriate person in accordance with section 10.

(5) In any such case the parties to the agreement may also apply for the apportionment to become binding on any person (other than the appropriate person) who is for the time being entitled to enforce the covenant in question; and section 10 shall apply in relation to such an application as it applies in relation to an application made with respect to the appropriate person.

(6) For the purposes of this section a covenant is, in relation to an assignment, a "non-attributable" covenant if it does not fall to be complied with in relation to any premises comprised in the assignment.

(7) In this section "the appropriate person" means either—

(a) the landlord of the entire premises referred to in subsection (1)(a) (or, if different parts of those premises are held under the tenancy by different landlords, each of those landlords), or

(b) the tenant of the entire premises referred to in subsection (2)(a) (or, if different parts of those premises are held under the tenancy by different tenants, each of those tenants),

depending on whether the agreement in question falls within subsection (1) or subsection (2).

10   Procedure for making apportionment bind other party to lease

(1) For the purposes of section 9 the parties to an agreement falling within subsection (1) or (2) of that section apply for an apportionment to become binding on the appropriate person if, either before or within the period of four weeks beginning with the date of the assignment in question, they serve on that person a notice informing him of—

(a) the proposed assignment or (as the case may be) the fact that the assignment has taken place;

(b) the prescribed particulars of the agreement; and

(c) their request that the apportionment should become binding on him.

(2) Where an application for an apportionment to become binding has been made in accordance with subsection (1), the apportionment becomes binding on the appropriate person if—

(a) he does not, within the period of four weeks beginning with the day on which the notice is served under subsection (1), serve on the parties to the agreement a notice in writing objecting to the apportionment becoming binding on him, or

(b) he does so serve such a notice but the court, on the application of the parties to the agreement, makes a declaration that it is reasonable for the apportionment to become binding on him, or

(c) he serves on the parties to the agreement a notice in writing consenting to the apportionment becoming binding on him and, if he has previously served a notice objecting thereto, stating that the notice is withdrawn.

(3) Where any apportionment becomes binding in accordance with this section, this shall be regarded as occurring at the time when the assignment in question takes place,

(4) In this section—

"the appropriate persons" has the same meaning as in section 9;

"the court" means a county court;

"prescribed" means prescribed by virtue of section 27.

11   Assignments in breach of covenant or by operation of law

(1) This section provides for the operation of sections 5 to 10 in relation to assignments in breach of a covenant of a tenancy or assignments by operation of law ("excluded assignment").

(2) In the case of an excluded assignment subsection (2) or (3) of section 5—

(a) shall not have the effect mentioned in the subsection in relation to the tenant as from that assignment, but

(b) shall have that effect as from the next assignment (if any) of the premises asigned by him which is not an excluded assignment.

(3) In the case of an excluded assignment subsection (2) or (3) of section 6 or 7—

(a) shall not enable the landlord or former landlord to apply for such a release as is mentioned in that subsection as from that assignment, but

(b) shall apply on the next assignment (if any) of the reversion assigned by the landlord which is not an excluded assignment so as to enable the landlord or former landlord to apply for any such release as from that subsequent assignment.

. . .

13   Covenants binding two or more persons

(1) Where in consequence of this Act two or more persons are bound by the same covenant, they are so bound both jointly and severally.

(2) Subject to section 24(2), where by virtue of this Act—

(a) two or more persons are bound jointly and severally by the same covenant, and

(b) any of the persons so bound is released from the covenant, the release does not extend to any other of those persons.

(3) For the purpose of providing for contribution between persons who, by virtue of this Act, are bound jointly and severally by a covenant, the Civil Liability (Contribution) Act 1978 shall have effect as if—

(a) liability to a person under a covenant were liability in respect of damage suffered by that person;

(b) references to damage accordingly include a breach of a covenant of a tenancy; and

(c) section 7(2) of that Act were omitted.

23   Effects of becoming subject to liability under, or entitled to benefit of, covenant etc.

(1) Where as a result of an assignment a person becomes by virtue of this Act, bound by or entitled to the benefit of a covenant, he shall not by virtue of this Act have any liability or rights under the covenant in relation to any time falling before the assignment.

(2) Subsection (1) does not preclude any such rights being expressly assigned to the person in question.

(3) Where as a result of an assignment a person becomes, by virtue of this Act, entitled to a right of re-entry contained in a tenancy, that right shall be exercisable in relation to any breach of a covenant of the tenancy occurring before the assignment as in relation to one occurring thereafter, unless by reason of any waiver or release it was not so exercisable immediately before the assignment.

24   Effects of release from liability under, or loss of benefit of, covenant

(1) Any release of a person from a covenant by virtue of this Act does not affect any liability of his arising from a breach of the covenant occurring before the release.

(2) Where—

(a) by virtue of this Act a tenant is released from a tenant covenant of a tenancy, and

(b) immediately before the release another person is bound by a covenant of the tenancy imposing any liability or penalty in the event of a failure to comply with that tenant covenant,

then, as from the release of the tenant, that other person is released from the covenant mentioned in paragraph (b) to the same extent as the tenant is released from that tenant covenant.

(3) Where a person bound by a landlord or tenant covenant of a tenancy—

(a) assigns the whole or part of his interest in the premises demised by the tenancy, but

(b) is not released by virtue of this Act from the covenant (with the result that sub-section (1) does not apply),

the assignment does not affect any liability of his arising from a breach of the covenant occurring before the assignment.

(4) Where by virtue of this Act a person ceases to be entitled to the benefit of a covenant, this does not affect any rights of his arising from a breach of the covenant occurring before he ceases to be so entitled.

25   Agreement void if it restricts operation of the Act

(1) Any agreement relating to a tenancy is void to the extent that—

(a) it would apart from this section have effect to exclude, modify or otherwise frustrate the operation of any provision of this Act, or

(b) it provides for—

(i)   the termination or surrender of the tenancy, or

(ii)   the imposition on the tenant of any penalty, disability or liability, in the event of the operation of any provision of this Act, or

(c) it provides for any of the matters referred to in paragraph (b)(i) or (ii) and does so (whether expressly or otherwise) in connection with, or in consequence of, the operation of any provision of this Act.

(2) To the extent that an agreement relating to a tenancy constitutes a covenant (whe-ther absolute or qualified) against the assignment, or parting with the possession, of the premises demised by the tenancy or any part of them—

(a) the agreement is not void by virtue of subsection (1) by reason only of the fact that as such the covenant prohibits or restricts any such assignment or parting with possession; but

(b) paragraph (a) above does not otherwise affect the operation of that subsection in relation to the agreement (and in particular does not preclude its application to the agreement to the extent that it purports to regulate the giving of, or the making of any application for, consent to any such assignment or parting with possession).

(3) In accordance with section 16(1) nothing in this section applies to any agreement to the extent that it is an authorised guarantee agreement; but (without prejudice to the

generality of subsection (1) above) an agreement is void to the extent that it is one falling within section 16(4)(a) or (b).

(4) This section applies to an agreement relating to a tenancy whether or not the agreement is—

(a) contained in the instrument creating the tenancy; or

(b) made before the creation of the tenancy.

Merchant Shipping Act 1995
(1995, c. 21)

92   Duty of ship to assist the other in case of collision

In every case of collision between two ships, it shall be the duty of the master of each ship, if and so far as he can do so without danger to his own ship, crew and passengers (if any)—

(a) to render to the other ship, its master, crew and passengers (if any) such assistance as may be practicable, and may be necessary to save them from any danger caused by the collision, and to stay by the other ship until he has ascertained that it has no need of further assistance; and

(b) to give to the master of the other ship the name of his own ship and also the names of the ports from which it comes and to which it is bound.

(2) The duties imposed on the master of a ship by subsection (1) above apply to the masters of United Kingdom ships and to the masters of foreign ships when in United Kingdom waters.

(3) The failure of the master of a ship to comply with the provisions of this section shall not raise any presumption of law that the collision was caused by his wrongful act, neglect, or default.

(4) If the master fails without reasonable excuse to comply with this section, he shall—

(a) in the case of a failure to comply with subsection (1)(a) above, be liable—

(i) on summary conviction, to a fine not exceeding £50,000 or imprisonment for a term not exceeding six months or both;

(ii) on conviction on indictment, to a fine or imprisonment for a term not exceeding two years or both; and

(b) in the case of a failure to comply with subsection (1)(b) above, be liable—

(i) on summary conviction, to a fine not exceeding the statutory maximum;

(ii) on conviction on indictment, to a fine;

and in either case if he is a certified officer, an inquiry into his conduct may be held, and his certificate cancelled or suspended.

93   Duty to assist ships, etc. in distress

(1) The master of a ship, on receiving at sea a signal of distress [from an aircraft] or information from any source that [an] aircraft is in distress, shall proceed with all speed to the assistance of the persons in distress (informing them if possible that he is doing so) unless he is unable, or in the special circumstances of the case considers it unreasonable or unnecessary, to do so, or unless he is released from this duty under subsection (4) or (5) below.

234   Power to pass over adjoining land

(1) In circumstances where this section applies by virtue of section 231 in relation to any vessel, all persons may, subject to subsections (3) and (4) below, for the purpose of—

(a) rendering assistance to the vessel,

(b) saving the lives of shipwrecked persons, or

(c) saving the cargo or equipment of the vessel,

pass and repass over any adjoining land without being subject to interruption by the owner or occupier and deposit on the land any cargo or other article recovered from the vessel.

(2) The right of passage conferred by subsection (1) above is a right of passage with or without vehicles.

(3) No right of passage is conferred by subsection (1) above where there is some public road equally convenient.

(4) The rights conferred by subsection (1) above shall be so exercised as to do as little damage as possible.

(5) Any damage sustained by an owner or occupier of land in consequence of the exercise of the right conferred by this section shall be a charge on the vessel, cargo or articles in respect of or by which the damage is caused.

(6) Any amount payable in respect of such damage shall, in case of dispute, be determined and shall, in default of payment, be recoverable in the same manner as the amount of salvage is determined and recoverable under this Part.

(7) If the owner or occupier of any land—

    (a) impedes or hinders any person in the exercise of the rights conferred by this section;

    (b) impedes or hinders the deposit on the land of any cargo or other article recovered from the vessel; or

    (c) prevents or attempts to prevent any cargo or other article recovered from the vessel from remaining deposited on the land for a reasonable time until it can be removed to a safe place of public deposit;

he shall be liable, on summary conviction, to a fine not exceeding level 3 on the standard scale.

Arbitration Act 1996
(1996, c. 23)

8 Whether agreement discharged by death of a party

(1) Unless otherwise agreed by the parties, an arbitration agreement is not discharged by the death of a party and may be enforced by or against the personal representatives of that party.

(2) Subsection (1) does not affect the operation of any enactment or rule of law by virtue of which a substantive right or obligation is extinguished by death.

29 Immunity of arbitrator

(1) An arbitrator is not liable for anything done or omitted in the discharge or purported discharge of his functions as arbitrator unless the act or omission is shown to have been in bad faith.

40 General duty of parties

(1) The parties shall do all things necessary for the proper and expeditious conduct of the arbitral proceedings.

74 Immunity of arbitral institutions, etc.

(1) An arbitral or other institution or person designated or requested by the parties to appoint or nominate an arbitrator is not liable for anything done or omitted in the discharge or purported discharge of that function unless the act or omission is shown to have been in bad faith.

(2) An arbitral or other institution or person by whom an arbitrator is appointed or nominated is not liable, by reason of having appointed or nominated him, for anything done or omitted by the arbitrator (or his employees or agents) in the discharge or purported discharge of his functions as arbitrator.

(3) The above provisions apply to an employee or agent of an arbitral or other institution or person as they apply to the institution or person himself.

87   Effectiveness of agreement to exclude court's jurisdiction

(1) In the case of a domestic arbitration agreement any agreement to exclude the jurisdiction of the court under—

(a) section 45 (determination of preliminary point of law), or

(b) section 69 (challenging the award: appeal on point of law),

is not effective unless entered into after the commencement of the arbitral proceedings in which the question arises or the award is made.

89   Application of unfair terms regulations to consumer arbitration agreements

(1) The following sections extend the application of the Unfair Terms in Consumer Contracts Regulations 1994 in relation to a term which constitutes an arbitration agreement.

For this purpose "arbitration agreement" means an agreement to submit to arbitration present or future disputes or differences (whether or not contractual).

90   Regulations apply where consumer is a legal person

The Regulations apply where the consumer is a legal person as they apply where the consumer is a natural person.

91   Arbitration agreement unfair where modest amount sought

(1) A term which constitutes an arbitration agreement is unfair for the purposes of the Regulations so far as it relates to a claim for a pecuniary remedy which does not exceed the amount specified by order for the purposes of this section.

Broadcasting Act 1996
(1996, c. 55)

99   Contract for exclusive right to televise listed event to be void

(1) Any contract entered into after the commencement of this section under which a television programme provider acquires rights to televise the whole or any part of a [Group A listed event] live for reception in the United Kingdom, or in any area of the United Kingdom, shall be void so far as it purports, in relation to the whole or any part of the event or in relation to reception in the United Kingdom or any area of the United Kingdom, to grant those rights exclusively to any one television programme provider.

107   Preparation by [OFCOM] of code relating to avoidance of unjust or unfair treatment or interference with privacy

(1) It shall be the duty of the [OFCOM] to draw up, and from time to time review, a code giving guidance as to principles to be observed, and practices to be followed, in connection with the avoidance of—

(a) unjust or unfair treatment in programmes to which this section applies, or

(b) unwarranted infringement of privacy in, or in connection with the obtaining of material included in, such programmes.

[*Communications Act 2003, s. 405(1): "... 'OFCOM' means the Office of Communications ...".*]

121   Certain statements etc. protected by qualified privilege for purposes of defamation

(1) For the purposes of the law relating to defamation—

(a) publication of any statement in the course of the consideration by the BSC of, and their adjudication on, a fairness complaint,

(b) publication by [OFCOM] of directions under section 119(1) relating to a fairness complaint, or

(c) publication of a report of [OFCOM], so far as the report relates to fairness complaints,

is privileged unless the publication is shown to be made with malice.

(2) Nothing in subsection (1) shall be construed as limiting any privilege subsisting apart from that subsection.

Damages Act 1996
(1996, c. 48)

1   Assumed rate of return on investment of damages

(1) In determining the return to be expected from the investment of a sum awarded as general damages for future pecuniary loss in an action for personal injury the court shall, subject to and in accordance with rules of court made for the purposes of this section, take into account such rate of return as may from time to time be prescribed by an order made by the Lord Chancellor.

(2) Subsection (1) above shall not however prevent the court taking a different rate of return into account if any party to the proceedings shows that it is more appropriate in the case in question.

(3) An order under subsection (1) above may prescribe different rates of return for different classes of case.

(4) Before making an order under subsection (1) above the Lord Chancellor shall consult the Government Actuary and the Treasury; and any order under that subsection shall be made by statutory instrument subject to annulment in pursuance of a resolution of either House of Parliament.

[(5) In the application of this section to Scotland—
   (a) for the reference to the Lord Chancellor in subsections (1) and (4) there is substituted a reference to the Scottish Ministers; and
   (b) in subsection (4)—
      (i) "and the Treasury" is omitted; and
      (ii) for "either House of Parliament" there is substituted "the Scottish Parliament".]

[**2   Periodical payments**

(1) A court awarding damages for future pecuniary loss in respect of personal injury—
   (a) may order that the damages are wholly or partly to take the form of periodical payments, and
   (b) shall consider whether to make that order.

(2) A court awarding other damages in respect of personal injury may, if the parties consent, order that the damages are wholly or partly to take the form of periodical payments.

(3) A court may not make an order for periodical payments unless satisfied that the continuity of payment under the order is reasonably secure.

(4) For the purpose of subsection (3) the continuity of payment under an order is reasonably secure if—
   (a) it is protected by a guarantee given under section 6 of or the Schedule to this Act,
   (b) it is protected by a scheme under section 213 of the Financial Services and Markets Act 2000 (compensation) (whether or not as modified by section 4 of this Act), or
   (c) the source of payment is a government or health service body.

(5) An order for periodical payments may include provision—
   (a) requiring the party responsible for the payments to use a method (selected or to be selected by him) under which the continuity of payment is reasonably secure by virtue of subsection (4);
   (b) about how the payments are to be made, if not by a method under which the continuity of payment is reasonably secure by virtue of subsection (4);
   (c) requiring the party responsible for the payments to take specified action to secure continuity of payment, where continuity is not reasonably secure by virtue of subsection (4);

(d) enabling a party to apply for a variation of provision included under paragraph (b), or (c).

(6) Where a person has a right to receive payments under an order for periodical payments, or where an arrangement is entered into in satisfaction of an order which gives a person a right to receive periodical payments, that person's right under the order or arrangement may not be assigned or charged without the approval of the court which made the order; and—

(a) a court shall not approve an assignment or charge unless satisfied that special circumstances make it necessary, and

(b) a purported assignment or charge, or agreement to assign or charge, is void unless approved by the court.

(7) Where an order is made for periodical payments, an alteration of the method by which the payments are made shall be treated as a breach of the order (whether or not the method was specified under subsection (5)(b)) unless—

(a) the court which made the order declares its satisfaction that the continuity of payment under the new method is reasonably secure,

(b) the new method is protected by a guarantee given under section 6 of or the Schedule to this Act,

(c) the new method is protected by a scheme under section 213 of the Financial Services and Markets Act 2000 (compensation) (whether or not as modified by section 4 of this Act), or

(d) the source of payment under the new method is a government or health service body.

(8) An order for periodical payments shall be treated as providing for the amount of payments to vary by reference to the retail prices index (within the meaning of section 833(2) of the Income and Corporation Taxes Act 1988) at such times, and in such a manner, as may be determined by or in accordance with Civil Procedure Rules.

(9) But an order for periodical payments may include provision—

(a) disapplying subsection (8), or

(b) modifying the effect of subsection (8).]

[**2A   Periodical payments: supplementary**

(1) Civil Procedure Rules may require a court to take specified matters into account in considering—

(a) whether to order periodical payments;

(b) the security of the continuity of payment;

(c) whether to approve an assignment or charge.

(2) For the purposes of section 2(4)(c) and (7)(d) "government or health service body" means a body designated as a government body or a health service body by order made by the Lord Chancellor.

(3) An order under subsection (2)—

(a) shall be made by statutory instrument, and

(b) shall be subject to annulment in pursuance of a resolution of either House of Parliament.

(4) Section 2(6) is without prejudice to a person's power to assign a right to the scheme manager established under section 212 of the Financial Services and Markets Act 2000.

(5) In section 2 "damages" includes an interim payment which a court orders a defendant to make to a claimant.

(6) In the application of this section to Northern Ireland—

(a) a reference to Civil Procedure Rules shall be taken as a reference to rules of court, and

(b) a reference to a claimant shall be taken as a reference to a plaintiff.

(7) Section 2 is without prejudice to any power exercisable apart from that section.]

[2B   Variation of orders and settlements

(1) The Lord Chancellor may by order enable a court which has made an order for periodical payments to vary the order in specified circumstances (otherwise than in accordance with section 2(5)(d)).

(2) The Lord Chancellor may by order enable a court in specified circumstances to vary the terms on which a claim or action for damages for personal injury is settled by agreement between the parties if the agreement—

(a) provides for periodical payments, and

(b) expressly permits a party to apply to a court for variation in those circumstances.

(3) An order under this section may make provision—

(a) which operates wholly or partly by reference to a condition or other term of the court's order or of the agreement;

(b) about the nature of an order which may be made by a court on a variation;

(c) about the matters to be taken into account on considering variation;

(d) of a kind that could be made by Civil Procedure Rules or, in relation to Northern Ireland, rules of court (and which may be expressed to be with or without prejudice to the power to make those rules).

(4) An order under this section may apply (with or without modification) or amend an enactment about provisional or further damages.

(5) An order under this section shall be subject to any order under section 1 of the Courts and Legal Services Act 1990 (allocation between High Court and county courts).

(6) An order under this section—

(a) shall be made by statutory instrument,

(b) may not be made unless the Lord Chancellor has consulted such persons as he thinks appropriate,

(c) may not be made unless a draft has been laid before and approved by resolution of each House of Parliament, and

(d) may include transitional, consequential or incidental provision.

(7) In subsection (4)—

"provisional damages" means damages awarded by virtue of subsection (2)(a) of section 32A of the Supreme Court Act 1981 or section 51 of the County Courts Act 1984 (or, in relation to Northern Ireland, paragraph 10(2)(a) of Schedule 6 to the Administration of Justice Act 1982), and

"further damages" means damages awarded by virtue of subsection (2)(b) of either of those sections (or, in relation to Northern Ireland, paragraph 10(2)(b) of Schedule 6 to the Administration of Justice Act 1982).]

3   Provisional damages and fatal accident claims

(1) This section applies where a person—

(a) is awarded provisional damages; and

(b) subsequently dies as a result of the act or omission which gave rise to the cause of action for which the damages were awarded.

(2) The award of the provisional damages shall not operate as a bar to an action in respect of that person's death under the Fatal Accidents Act 1976.

(3) Such part (if any) of—

(a) the provisional damages; and

(b) any further damages awarded to the person in question before his death,

as was intended to compensate him for pecuniary loss in a period which in the event falls after his death, shall be taken into account in assessing the amount of any loss of support suffered by the person or persons for whose benefit the action under the Fatal Accidents Act 1976 is brought.

(4) No award of further damages made in respect of that person after his death shall include any amount for loss of income in respect of any period after his death.

(5) In this section "provisional damages" means damages awarded by virtue of subsection (2)(a) of section 32A of the [Senior Courts Act 1981] or section 51 of the County Courts Act 1984 and "further damages" means damages awarded by virtue of subsection (2)(b) of either of those sections.

(6) Subsection (2) above applies whether the award of provisional damages was before or after the coming into force of that subsection; and subsections (3) and (4) apply to any award of damages under the 1976 Act or, as the case may be, further damages after the coming into force of those subsections.

(7) In the application of this section to Northern Ireland—

(a) for references to the Fatal Accidents Act 1976 there shall be substituted references to the Fatal Accidents (Northern Ireland) Order 1977;

(b) for the reference to subsection (2)(a) and (b) of section 32A of the [Senior Courts Act 1981] and section 51 of the County Courts Act 1984 there shall be substituted a reference to paragraph 10(2)(a) and (b) of Schedule 6 to the Administration of Justice Act 1982.

[4   Enhanced protection for periodical payments

(1) Subsection (2) applies where—

(a) a person has a right to receive periodical payments, and

(b) his right is protected by a scheme under section 213 of the Financial Services and Markets Act 2000 (compensation), but only as to part of the payments.

(2) The protection provided by the scheme shall extend by virtue of this section to the whole of the payments.

(3) Subsection (4) applies where—

(a) one person ("the claimant") has a right to receive periodical payments from another person ("the defendant"),

(b) a third person ("the insurer") is required by or in pursuance of an arrangement entered into with the defendant (whether or not together with other persons and whether before or after the creation of the claimant's right) to make payments in satisfaction of the claimant's right or for the purpose of enabling it to be satisfied, and

(c) the claimant's right to receive the payments would be wholly or partly protected by a scheme under section 213 of the Financial Services and Markets Act 2000 if it arose from an arrangement of the same kind as that mentioned in paragraph (b) but made between the claimant and the insurer.

(4) For the purposes of the scheme under section 213 of that Act—

(a) the claimant shall be treated as having a right to receive the payments from the insurer under an arrangement of the same kind as that mentioned in subsection (3)(b),

(b) the protection under the scheme in respect of those payments shall extend by virtue of this section to the whole of the payments, and

(c) no person other than the claimant shall be entitled to protection under the scheme in respect of the payments.

(5) In this section "periodical payments" means periodical payments made pursuant to—

(a) an order of a court in so far as it is made in reliance on section 2 above (including an order as varied), or

(b) an agreement in so far as it settles a claim or action for damages in respect of personal injury (including an agreement as varied).

(6) In subsection (5)(b) the reference to an agreement in so far as it settles a claim or action for damages in respect of personal injury includes a reference to an undertaking given by the Motor Insurers' Bureau (being the company of that name incorporated on 14th June 1946 under the Companies Act 1929), or an Article 75 insurer under the Bureau's Articles of Association, in relation to a claim or action in respect of personal injury.]

6   Guarantees for public sector settlements

(1) This section applies where—

(a) a claim or action for damages for personal injury is settled [on terms whereby the damages are to consist wholly or partly of periodical payments]; or

(b) a court awarding damages for personal injury makes an order incorporating such terms.

(2) If it appears to a Minister of the Crown that the payments are to be made by a body in relation to which he has, by virtue of this section, power to do so, he may guarantee the payments to be made under the agreement or order.

(3) The bodies in relation to which a Minister may give such a guarantee shall, subject to subsection (4) below, be such bodies as are designated in relation to the relevant government department by guidelines agreed upon between that department and the Treasury.

(4) A guarantee purporting to be given by a Minister under this section shall not be invalidated by any failure on his part to act in accordance with such guidelines as are mentioned in subsection (3) above.

(5) A guarantee under this section shall be given on such terms as the Minister concerned may determine but those terms shall in every case require the body in question to reimburse the Minister, with interest, for any sums paid by him in fulfilment of the guarantee.

(6) Any sums required by a Minister for fulfilling a guarantee under this section shall be defrayed out of money provided by Parliament and any sums received by him by way of reimbursement or interest shall be paid into the Consolidated Fund.

(7) A Minister who has given one or more guarantees under this section shall, as soon as possible after the end of each financial year, lay before each House of Parliament a statement showing what liabilities are outstanding in respect of the guarantees in that year, what sums have been paid in that year in fulfilment of the guarantees and what sums (including interest) have been recovered in that year in respect of the guarantees or are still owing.

(8) In this section "government department" means any department of Her Majesty's government in the United Kingdom and for the purposes of this section a government department is a relevant department in relation to a Minister if he has responsibilities in respect of that department.

[(8A) In the application of subsection (3) above to Scotland, for the words from "guidelines" to the end there shall be substituted "the Minister".]

[(8B) In the application of this section to Scotland, "relevant government department" shall be read as if it was a reference to any part of the Scottish Administration and subsection (8) shall cease to have effect.]

(9) The Schedule to this Act has effect for conferring corresponding powers on Northern Ireland departments.

7   Interpretation

(1) Subject to subsection (2) below, in this Act "personal injury" includes any disease and any impairment of a person's physical or mental condition and references to a claim or action for personal injury include references to such a claim or action brought by virtue of the Law Reform (Miscellaneous Provisions) Act 1934 and to a claim or action brought by virtue of the Fatal Accidents Act 1976.

(2) In the application of this Act to Scotland "personal injury" has the meaning given by section 10(1) of the Damages (Scotland) Act 1976.

(3) In the application of subsection (1) above to Northern Ireland for the references to the Law Reform (Miscellaneous Provisions) Act 1934 and to the Fatal Accidents Act 1976 there shall be substituted respectively references to the Law Reform (Miscellaneous Provisions) Act (Northern Ireland) 1937 and the Fatal Accidents (Northern Ireland) Order 1977.

8   Short title, extent and commencement

(2) Section 3 does not extend to Scotland but, subject to that, this Act extends to the whole of the United Kingdom.

Defamation Act 1996
(1996, c. 31)

Responsibility for publication

1   Responsibility for publication

(1) In defamation proceedings a person has a defence if he shows that—

(a) he was not the author, editor or publisher of the statement complained of,

(b) he took reasonable care in relation to its publication, and

(c) he did not know, and had no reason to believe, that what he did caused or contributed to the publication of a defamatory statement.

(2) For this purpose "author", "editor" and "publisher" have the following meanings, which are further explained in subsection (3)—

"author" means the originator of the statement, but does not include a person who did not intend that his statement be published at all;

"editor" means a person having editorial or equivalent responsibility for the content of the statement or the decision to publish it; and

"publisher" means a commercial publisher, that is, a person whose business is issuing material to the public, or a section of the public, who issues material containing the statement in the course of that business.

(3) A person shall not be considered the author, editor or publisher of a statement if he is only involved—

(a) in printing, producing, distributing or selling printed material containing the statement;

(b) in processing, making copies of, distributing, exhibiting or selling a film or sound recording (as defined in Part I of the Copyright, Designs and Patents Act 1988) containing the statement;

(c) in processing, making copies of, distributing or selling any electronic medium in or on which the statement is recorded, or in operating or providing any equipment, system or service by means of which the statement is retrieved, copied, distributed or made available in electronic form;

(d) as the broadcaster of a live programme containing the statement in circumstances in which he has no effective control over the maker of the statement;

(e) as the operator of or provider of access to a communications system by means of which the statement is transmitted, or made available, by a person over whom he has no effective control.

In a case not within paragraphs (a) to (e) the court may have regard to those provisions by way of analogy in deciding whether a person is to be considered the author, editor or publisher of a statement.

(4) Employees or agents of an author, editor or publisher are in the same position as their employer or principal to the extent that they are responsible for the content of the statement or the decision to publish it.

(5) In determining for the purposes of this section whether a person took reasonable care, or had reason to believe that what he did caused or contributed to the publication of a defamatory statement, regard shall be had to—

(a) the extent of his responsibility for the content of the statement or the decision to publish it,

(b) the nature or circumstances of the publication, and

(c) the previous conduct or character of the author, editor or publisher.

(6) This section does not apply to any cause of action which arose before the section came into force.

2   Offer to make amends

(1) A person who has published a statement alleged to be defamatory of another may offer to make amends under this section.

(2) The offer may be in relation to the statement generally or in relation to a specific defamatory meaning which the person making the offer accepts that the statement conveys ("a qualified offer").

(3) An offer to make amends—

(a) must be in writing,

(b) must be expressed to be an offer to make amends under section 2 of the Defamation Act 1996, and

(c) must state whether it is a qualified offer and, if so, set out the defamatory meaning in relation to which it is made.

(4) An offer to make amends under this section is an offer—

(a) to make a suitable correction of the statement complained of and a sufficient apology to the aggrieved party,

(b) to publish the correction and apology in a manner that is reasonable and practicable in the circumstances, and

(c) to pay the aggrieved party such compensation (if any), and such costs, as may be agreed or determined to be payable.

The fact that the offer is accompanied by an offer to take specific steps does not affect the fact that an offer to make amends under this section is an offer to do all the things mentioned in paragraphs (a) to (c).

(5) An offer to make amends under this section may not be made by a person after serving a defence in defamation proceedings brought against him by the aggrieved party in respect of the publication in question.

(6) An offer to make amends under this section may be withdrawan before it is accepted; and a renewal of an offer which has been withdrawn shall be treated as a new offer.

3   Accepting an offer to make amends

(1) If an offer to make amends under section 2 is accepted by the aggrieved party, the following provisions apply.

(2) The party accepting the offer may not bring or continue defamation proceedings in respect of the publication concerned against the person making the offer, but he is entitled to enforce the offer to make amends, as follows.

(3) If the parties agree on the steps to be taken in fulfilment of the offer, the aggrieved party may apply to the court for an order that the other party fulfil his offer by taking the steps agreed.

(4) If the parties do not agree on the steps to be taken by way of correction, apology and publication, the party who made the offer may take such steps as he thinks appropriate, and may in particular—

(a) make the correction and apology by a statement in open court in terms approved by the court, and

(b) give an undertaking to the court as to the manner of their publication.

(5) If the parties do not agree on the amount to be paid by way of compensation, it shall be determined by the court on the same principles as damages in defamation proceedings.

The court shall take account of any steps taken in fulfilment of the offer and (so far as not agreed between the parties) of the suitability of the correction, the sufficiency of the apology and whether the manner of their publication was reasonable in the circumstances, and may reduce or increase the amount of compensation accordingly.

(6) If the parties do not agree on the amount to be paid by way of costs, it shall be determined by the court on the same principles as costs awarded in court proceedings.

(7) The acceptance of an offer by one person to make amends does not affect any cause of action against another person in respect of the same publication, subject as follows.

(8) In England and Wales or Northern Ireland, for the purposes of the Civil Liability (Contribution) Act 1978—

(a) the amount of compensation paid under the offer shall be treated as paid in bona fide settlement or compromise of the claim; and

(b) where another person is liable in respect of the same damage (whether jointly or otherwise), the person whose offer to make amends was accepted is not required to pay by virtue of any contribution under section 1 of that Act a greater amount than the amount of the compensation payable in pursuance of the offer.

(9) In Scotland—

(a) subsection (2) of section 3 of the Law Reform (Miscellaneous Provisions) (Scotland) Act 1940 (right of one joint wrongdoer as respects another to recover contribution towards damages) applies in relation to compensation paid under an offer to make amends as it applies in relation to damages in an action to which that section applies; and

(b) where another person is liable in respect of the same damage (whether jointly or otherwise), the person whose offer to make amends was accepted is not required to pay by virtue of any contribution under section 3(2) of that Act a greater amount than the amount of compensation payable in pursuance of the offer.

(10) Proceedings under this section shall be heard and determined without a jury.

4 Failure to accept offer to make amends

(1) If an offer to make amends under section 2, duly made and not withdrawn, is not accepted by the aggrieved party, the following provisions apply.

(2) The fact that the offer was made is a defence (subject to subsection (3)) to defamation proceedings in respect of the publication in question by that party against the person making the offer.

A qualified offer is only a defence in respect of the meaning to which the offer related.

(3) There is no such defence if the person by whom the offer was made knew or had reason to believe that the statement complained of—

(a) referred to the aggrieved party or was likely to be understood as referring to him, and

(b) was both false and defamatory of that party;

but it shall be presumed until the contrary is shown that he did not know and had no reason to believe that was the case.

(4) The person who made the offer need not rely on it by way of defence, but if he does he may not rely on any other defence.

If the offer was a qualified offer, this applies only in respect of the meaning to which the offer related.

(5) The offer may be relied on in mitigation of damages whether or not it was relied on as a defence.

The meaning of a statement

7 Ruling on the meaning of a statement

In defamation proceedings the court shall not be asked to rule whether a statement is arguably capable, as opposed to capable, of bearing a particular meaning or meanings attributed to it.

Summary disposal of claim

8 Summary disposal of claim

(1) In defamation proceedings the court may dispose summarily of the plaintiffs claim in accordance with the following provisions.

(2) The court may dismiss the plaintiff's claim if it appears to the court that it has no realistic prospect of success and there is no reason why it should be tried.

(3) The court may give judgment for the plaintiff and grant him summary relief (see section 9) if it appears to the court that there is no defence to the claim which has a realistic prospect of success, and that there is no other reason why the claim should be tried.

Unless the plaintiff asks for summary relief, the court shall not act under this subsection unless it is satisfied that summary relief will adequately compensate him for the wrong he has suffered.

(4) In considering whether a claim should be tried the court shall have regard to—

(a) whether all the persons who are or might be defendants in repect of the publication complained of are before the court;

(b) whether summary disposal of the claim against another defendant would be inappropriate;

(c) the extent to which there is a conflict of evidence;

(d) the seriousness of the alleged wrong (as regards the content of the statement and the extent of publication); and

(e) whether it is justifiable in the circumstances to proceed to a full trial.

(5) Proceedings under this section shall be heard and determined without a jury.

9 Meaning of summary relief

(1) For the purposes of section 8 (summary disposal of claim) "'summary relief" means such of the following as may be appropriate—

(a) a declaration that the statement was false and defamatory of the plaintiff;

(b) an order that the defendant publish or cause to be published a suitable correction and apology;

(c) damages not exceeding £10,000 or such other amount as may be prescribed by order of the Lord Chancellor;

(d) an order restraining the defendant from publishing or further publishing the matter complained of.

(2) The content of any correction and apology, and the time, manner, form and place of publication, shall be for the parties to agree.

If they cannot agree on the content, the court may direct the defendant to publish or cause to be published a summary of the court's judgment agreed by the parties or settled by the court in accordance with rules of court.

If they cannot agree on the time, manner, form or place of publication, the court may direct the defendant to take such reasonable and practicable steps as the court considers appropriate.

[(2A) The Lord Chancellor must consult the Lord Chief Justice of England and Wales before making any order under subsection (1)(c) in relation to England and Wales.

(2B) The Lord Chancellor must consult the Lord Chief Justice of Northern Ireland before making any order under subsection (1)(c) in relation to Northern Ireland.

(2C) The Lord Chief Justice may nominate a judicial office holder (as defined in section 109(4) of the Constitutional Reform Act 2005) to exercise his functions under this section.

(2D) The Lord Chief Justice of Northern Ireland may nominate any of the following to exercise his functions under this section—

(a) the holder of one of the offices listed in Schedule 1 to the Justice (Northern Ireland) Act 2002;

(b) a Lord Justice of Appeal (as defined in section 88 of that Act).]

(3) Any order under subsection (1)(c) shall be made by statutory instrument which shall be subject to annulment in pursuance of a resolution of either House of Parliament.

10　Summary disposal: rules of court

(1) Provision may be made by rules of court as to the summary disposal of the plaintiff's claim in defamation proceedings.

(2) Without prejudice to the generality of that power, provision may be made—

(a) authorising a party to apply for summary disposal at any stage of the proceedings;

(b) authorising the court at any stage of the proceedings—

(i)　to treat any application, pleading or other step in the proceedings as an application for summary disposal, or

(ii)　to make an order for summary disposal without any such application;

(c) as to the time for serving pleadings or taking any other step in the proceedings in a case where there are proceedings for summary disposal;

(d) requiring the parties to identify any question of law or construction which the court is to be asked to determine in the proceedings;

(e) as to the nature of any hearing on the question of summary disposal, and in particular—

(i)　authorising the court to order affidavits or witness statements to be prepared for use as evidence at the hearing, and

(ii)　requiring the leave of the court for the calling of oral evidence, or the introduction of new evidence, at the hearing;

(f)　authorising the court to require a defendant to elect, at or before the hearing, whether or not to make an offer to make amends under section 2.

Evidence concerning proceedings in Parliament

13　Evidence concerning proceedings in Parliament

(1) Where the conduct of a person in or in relation to proceedings in Parliament is in issue in defamation proceedings, he may waive for the purposes of those proceedings, so far as concerns him, the protection of any enactment or rule of law which prevents proceedings in Parliament being impeached or questioned in any court or place out of Parliament.

(2) Where a person waives that protection—

(a) any such enactment or rule of law shall not apply to prevent evidence being given, questions being asked or statements, submissions, comments or findings being made about his conduct, and

(b) none of those things shall be regarded as infringing the privilege of either House of Parliament.

(3) The waiver by one person of that protection does not affect its operation in relation to another person who has not waived it.

(4) Nothing in this section affects any enactment or rule of law so far as it protects a person (including a person who has waived the protection referred to above) from legal liability for words spoken or things done in the course of, or for the purposes of or incidental to, any proceedings in Parliament.

(5) Without prejudice to the generality of subsection (4), that subsection applies to—

(a) the giving of evidence before either House or a committee;

(b) the presentation or submission of a document to either House or a committee;

(c) the preparation of a document for the purposes of or incidental to the transacting of any such business;

(d) the formulation, making or publication of a document, including a report, by or pursuant to an order of either House or a committee; and

(e) any communication with the Parliamentary Commissioner for Standards or any person having functions in connection with the registration of Members' interests.

In this subsection "a committee" means a committee of either House or a joint committee of both Houses of Parliament.

Statutory privilege

14   Reports of court proceedings absolutely privileged

(1) A fair and accurate report of proceedings in public before a court to which this section applies, if published contemporaneously with the proceedings, is absolutely privileged.

(2) A report of proceedings which by an order of the court, or as a consequence of any statutory provision, is required to be postponed shall be treated as published contemporaneously if it is published as soon as practicable after publication is permitted.

(3) This section applies to—

(a) any court in the United Kingdom,

(b) the European Court of Justice or any court attached to that court,

(c) the European Court of Human Rights, and

(d) any international criminal tribunal established by the Security Council of the United Nations or by an international agreement to which the United Kingdom is a party.

In paragraph (a) "court" includes any tribunal or body exercising the judicial power of the State.

15   Reports, etc. protected by qualified privilege

(1) The publication of any report or other statement mentioned in Schedule 1 to this Act is privileged unless the publication is shown to be made with malice, subject as follows.

(2) In defamation proceedings in respect of the publication of a report or other statement mentioned in Part II of that Schedule, there is no defence under this section if the plaintiff shows that the defendant—

(a) was requested by him to publish in a suitable manner a reasonable letter or statement by way of explanation or contradiction, and

(b) refused or neglected to do so.

For this purpose "in a suitable manner" means in the same manner as the publication complained of or in a manner that is adequate and reasonable in the circumstances.

(3) This section does not apply to the publication to the public, or a section of the public, of matter which is not of public concern and the publication of which is not for the public benefit.

(4) Nothing in this section shall be construed—

(a) as protecting the publication of matter the publication of which is prohibited by law, or

(b) as limiting or abridging any privilege subsisting apart from this section.

Supplementary provisions

17   Interpretation

(1) In this Act—

"publication" and "publish", in relation to a statement, have the meaning they have for the purposes of the law of defamation generally, but "publisher" is specially defined for the purposes of section 1;

"statement" means words, pictures, visual images, gestures or any other method of signifying meaning; and

"statutory provision" means—

(a) a provision contained in an Act or in subordinate legislation within the meaning of the Interpretation Act 1978

[(aa) a provision contained in an Act of the Scottish Parliament or in an instrument made under such an Act,], or

(b) a statutory provision within the meaning given by section 1(f) of the Interpretation Act (Northern Ireland) 1954.

20   Short title and saving

(2) Nothing in this Act affects the law relating to criminal libel.

SCHEDULES

Section 15   SCHEDULE 1

QUALIFIED PRIVILEGE

PART I   STATEMENTS HAVING QUALIFIED PRIVILEGEWITHOUT EXPLANATION OR CONTRADICTION

1. A fair and accurate report of proceedings in public of a legislature anywhere in the world.

2. A fair and accurate report of proceedings in public before a court anywhere in the world.

3. A fair and accurate report of proceedings in public of a person appointed to hold a public inquiry by a government or legislature anywhere in the world.

4. A fair and accurate report of proceedings in public anywhere in the world of an international organisation or an international conference.

5. A fair and accurate copy of or extract from any register or other document required by law to be open to public inspection.

6. A notice or advertisement published by or on the authority of a court, or of a judge or officer of a court, anywhere in the world.

7. A fair and accurate copy of or extract from matter published by or on the authority of a government or legislature anywhere in the world.

8. A fair and accurate copy of or extract from matter published anywhere in the world by an international organisation or an international conference.

PART II   STATEMENTS PRIVILEGED SUBJECT TO EXPLANATION OR CONTRADICTION

9.—(1) A fair and accurate copy of or extract from a notice or other matter issued for the information of the public by or on behalf of—

(a) a legislature in any member State or the European Parliament;

(b) the government of any member State, or any authority performing governmental functions in any member State or part of a member State, or the European Commission;

(c) an international organisation or international conference.

(2) In this paragraph "governmental functions" includes police functions.

10. A fair and accurate copy of or extract from a document made available by a court in any member State or the European Court of Justice (or any court attached to that court), or by a judge or officer of any such court.

11.—(1) A fair and accurate report of proceedings at any public meeting or sitting in the United Kingdom of—

(a) a local authority [, local authority committee or in the case of a local authority which are operating executive arrangements the executive of that authority or a committee of that executive];

(b) a justice or justices of the peace acting otherwise than as a court exercising judicial authority;

(c) a commission, tribunal, committee or person appointed for the purposes of any inquiry by any statutory provision, by Her Majesty or by a Minister of the Crown [a member of the Scottish Executive] or a Northern Ireland Department;

(d) a person appointed by a local authority to hold a local inquiry in pursuance of any statutory provision;

(e) any other tribunal, board, committee or body constituted by or under, and exercising functions under, any statutory provision.

[(1A) In the case of a local authority which are operating executive arrangements, a fair and accurate record of any decision made by any member of the executive where that record is required to be made and available for public inspection by virtue of section 22 of the Local Government Act 2000 or of any provision in regulations made under that section.]

(2) [In sub-paragraphs (1)(a) and (1A)—

"executive" and "executive arrangements" have the same meaning as in Part II of the Local Government Act 2000;]

"local authority" means—

(a) in relation to England and Wales, a principal council within the meaning of the Local Government Act 1972, any body falling within any paragraph of section 100J(1) of that Act or an authority or body to which the Public Bodies (Admission to Meetings) Act 1960 applies,

(b) in relation to Scotland, a council constituted under section 2 of the Local Government etc. (Scotland) Act 1994 or an authority or body to which the Public Bodies (Admission to Meetings) Act 1960 applies,

(c) in relation to Northern Ireland, any authority or body to which sections 23 to 27 of the Local Government Act (Northern Ireland) 1972 apply; and

"local authority committee" means any committee of a local authority or of local authorities, and includes—

(a) any committee or sub-committee in relation to which sections 100A to 100D of the Local Government Act 1972 apply by virtue of section 100E of that Act (whether or not also by virtue of section 100J of that Act), and

(b) any committee or sub-committee in relation to which sections 50A to 50D of the Local Government (Scotland) Act 1973 apply by virtue of section 50E of that Act.

(3) A fair and accurate report of any corresponding proceedings in any of the Channel Islands or the Isle of Man or in another member State.

12.—(1) A fair and accurate report of proceedings at any public meeting held in a member State. .

(2) In this paragraph a "public meeting" means a meeting bona fide and lawfully held for a lawful purpose and for the furtherance or discussion of a matter of public concern, whether admission to the meeting is general or restricted.

13.—(1) A fair and accurate report of proceedings at a general meeting of a UK public company.

(2) A fair and accurate copy of or extract from any document circulated to members of a UK public company—

(a) by or with the authority of the board of directors of the company,

(b) by the auditors of the company, or

(c) by any member of the company in pursuance of a right conferred by any statutory provision.

(3) A fair and accurate copy or extract from any document circulated to members of a UK public company which relates to the appointment, resignation, retirement or dismissal of directors of the company.

(4) In this paragraph "UK public company" means—

(a) a public company within the meaning of section 1(3) of the Companies Act 1985 or Article 12(3) of the Companies (Northern Ireland) Order 1986, or

(b) a body corporate incorporated by or registered under any other statutory provision, or by Royal Charter, or formed in pursuance of letters patent.

(5) A fair and accurate report of proceedings at any corresponding meeting of, or copy of or extract from any corresponding document circulated to members of, a public

company formed under the law of any of the Channel Islands or the Isle of Man or of another member State.

14. A fair and accurate report of any finding or decision of any of the following descriptions of association, formed in the United Kingdom or another member State, or of any committee or governing body of such an association—

    (a) an association formed for the purpose of promoting or encouraging the exercise of or interest in any art, science, religion or learning, and empowered by its constitution to exercise control over or adjudicate on matters of interest or concern to the association, or the actions or conduct of any person subject to such control or adjudication;

    (b) an association formed for the purpose of promoting or safeguarding the interests of any trade, business, industry or profession, or of the persons carrying on or engaged in any trade, business, industry or profession, and empowered by its constitution to exercise control over or adjudicate upon matters connected with that trade, business, industry or profession, or the actions or conduct of those persons;

    (c) an association formed for the purpose of promoting or safeguarding the interests of a game, sport or pastime to the playing or exercise of which members of the public are invited or admitted, and empowered by its constitution to exercise control over or adjudicate upon persons connected with or taking part in the game, sport or pastime;

    (d) an association formed for the purpose of promoting charitable objects or other objects beneficial to the community and empowered by its constitution to exercise control over or to adjudicate on matters of interest or concern to the association, or the actions or conduct of any person subject to such control or adjudication.

15.—(1) A fair and accurate report of, or copy of or extract from, any adjudication, report, statement or notice issued by a body, officer or other person designated for the purposes of this paragraph—

    (a) for England and Wales or Northern Ireland, by order of the Lord Chancellor, and

    (b) for Scotland, by order of the Secretary of State.

(2) An order under this paragraph shall be made by statutory instrument which shall be subject to annulment in pursuance of a resolution of either House of Parliament.

PART III SUPPLEMENTARY PROVISIONS

16.—(1) In this Schedule—

"court" includes any tribunal or body exercising the judicial power of the State;

"international conference" means a conference attended by representatives of two or more governments;

"international organisation" means an organisation of which two or more governments are members, and includes any committee or other subordinate body of such an organisation; and

"legislature" includes a local legislature.

(2) References in this Schedule to a member State include any European dependent territory of a member State.

(3) In paragraphs 2 and 6 "court" includes—

    (a) the European Court of Justice (or any court attached to that court) and the Court of Auditors of the European Communities,

    (b) the European Court of Human Rights,

    (c) any international criminal tribunal established by the Security Council of the United Nations or by an international agreement to which the United Kingdom is a party, and

    (d) the International Court of Justice and any other judicial or arbitral tribunal deciding matters in dispute between States.

(4) In paragraphs 1, 3 and 7 "legislature" includes the European Parliament.

17.—(1) Provision may be made by order identifying—

  (a) for the purposes of paragraph 11, the corresponding proceedings referred to in sub-paragraph (3);

  (b) for the purposes of paragraph 13, the corresponding meetings and documents referred to in sub-paragraph (5).

(2) An order under this paragraph may be made—

  (a) for England and Wales or Northern Ireland, by the Lord Chancellor, and

  (b) for Scotland, by the Secretary of State.

(3) An order under this paragraph shall be made by statutory instrument which shall be subject to annulment in pursuance of a resolution of either House of Parliament.

Education Act 1996
(1996, c. 56)

206 Control of contracts

(1) Where the procedure for acquisition of grant-maintained status is pending in relation to any school, this section applies to any contract which, if the proposals for acquisition of grant-maintained status were implemented, would or might bind the governing body incorporated under Chapter II.

(2) Except with the appropriate consent, a local authority shall not enter into a contract to which this section applies.

(3) In the case of a contract entered into after the proposals have been approved by the Secretary of State, "the appropriate consent" is that of the new governing body.

(4) In relation to any other contract, "the appropriate consent" is—

  (a) the consent of the existing governing body, and

  (b) if (on the assumption set out in subsection (1)) the contract will require the governing body incorporated under Chapter II to make payments amounting in aggregate to £15,000 or more, the consent of the Secretary of State.

(5) Any consent for the purposes of this section may be given either in respect of a particular contract or in respect of contracts of any class or description and either unconditionally or subject to conditions.

(6) A contract shall not be void by reason only that it has been entered into in contravention of this section and (subject to section 207) a person entering into a contract with a local authority or governing body shall not be concerned to enquire whether any consent required by this section has been given or any conditions of such a consent have been complied with.

(7) Where there is an obligation under a contract to which this section applies to provide any benefit other than money, subsection (4)(b) shall apply as if the obligation were to pay a sum of money corresponding to the value of the benefit to the recipient.

521 Examination of pupils for cleanliness

(1) A local education authority may by directions in writing authorise a medical officer of theirs to have the persons and clothing of pupils in attendance at relevant schools examined whenever in his opinion such examinations are necessary in the interests of cleanliness.

(3) An examination under this section shall be made by a person authorised by the authority to make such examinations; and, if the examination is of a girl, it shall not be made by a man unless he is a registered medical practitioner.

522 Compulsory cleansing of a pupil

(1) If, on an examination under section 521, the person or clothing of a pupil is found to be infested with vermin or in a foul condition, any officer of the local education authority

may serve a notice on the pupil's parent requiring him to cause the pupil's person and clothing to be cleansed.

(2) The notice shall inform the parent that, unless within the period specified in the notice the pupil's person and clothing are cleansed to the satisfaction of such person as is specified in the notice, the cleansing will be carried out under arrangements made by the authority.

(3) The period so specified shall not be less than 24 hours from the service of the notice.

(4) If, on a report being made to him by the specified person at the end of the specified period, a medical officer of the authority is not satisfied that the pupil's person and clothing have been properly cleansed, he may by order direct that they shall be cleansed under arrangements made by the authority under section 523.

(5) An order made under subsection (4) shall be sufficient to authorise any officer of the authority—

(a) to cause the pupil's person and clothing to be cleansed in accordance with arrangements made by the authority under section 523, and

(b) for that purpose to convey the pupil to, and detain him at, any premises provided in accordance with such arrangements.

523   Arrangements for cleansing of pupils

(1) A local education authority shall make arrangements for securing that the person or clothing of any pupil required to be cleansed under section 522 may be cleansed (whether at the request of a parent or in pursuance of an order under section 522(4)) at suitable premises, by suitable persons and with suitable appliances.

(2) Where the council of a district in the area of the authority are entitled to the use of any premises or appliances for cleansing the person or clothing of persons infested with vermin, the authority may require the council to permit the authority to use those premises or appliances for such purposes upon such terms as may be determined—

(a) by agreement between the authority and the council, or

(b) in default of such agreement, by the Secretary of State.

(3) Subsection (2) does not apply in relation to Wales.

(4) A girl may be cleansed under arrangements under this section only by a registered medical practitioner or by a woman authorised for the purpose by the authority.

[548   No right to give corporal punishment

(1) Corporal punishment given by, or on the authority of, a member of staff to a child—

(a) for whom education is provided at any school, or

(b) for whom education is provided, otherwise than at school, under any arrangements made by a local education authority, or

(c) for whom specified nursery education is provided otherwise than at school, cannot be justified in any proceedings on the ground that it was given in pursuance of a right exercisable by the member of staff by virtue of his position as such.

(2) Subsection (1) applies to corporal punishment so given to a child at any time, whether at the school or other place at which education is provided for the child, or elsewhere.

(3) The following provisions have effect for the purposes of this section.

(4) Any reference to giving corporal punishment to a child is to doing anything for the purpose of punishing that child (whether or not there are other reasons for doing it) which, apart from any justification, would constitute battery.

(5) However, corporal punishment shall not be taken to be given to a child by virtue of anything done for reasons that include averting—

(a) an immediate danger of personal injury to, or

(b) an immediate danger to the property of,

any person (including the child himself).

(6) "Member of staff", in relation to the child concerned, means—

(a) any person who works as a teacher at the school or other place at which education is provided for the child, or

(b) any other person who (whether in connection with the provision of education for the child or otherwise)—
   (i) works at that school or place, or—
   (ii) otherwise provides his services there (whether or not for payment), and has lawful control or charge of the child.

(7) "Child" (except in subsection (8)) means a person under the age of 18.

(8) "Specified nursery education" means full-time or part-time education suitable for children who have not attained compulsory school age which is provided—
   (a) by a local education authority; or
   (b) by any other person—
      (i) who is (or is to be) in receipt of financial assistance given by such an authority and whose provision of nursery education is taken into account by the authority in formulating proposals for the purposes of section 120(2)(a) of the School Standards and Framework Act 1998, or [..]

[550A Power of members of staff to restrain pupils

(1) A member of the staff of a school may use, in relation to any pupil at the school, such force as is reasonable in the circumstances for the purpose of preventing the pupil from doing (or continuing to do) any of the following, namely—
   (a) committing any offence,
   (b) causing personal injury to, or damage to the property of, any person (including the pupil himself), or
   (c) engaging in any behaviour prejudicial to the maintenance of good order and discipline at the school or among any of its pupils, whether that behaviour occurs during a teaching session or otherwise.

(2) Subsection (1) applies where a member of the staff of a school is—
   (a) on the premises of the school, or
   (b) elsewhere at a time when, as a member of its staff, he has lawful control or charge of the pupil concerned;
but it does not authorise anything to be done in relation to a pupil which constitutes the giving of corporal punishment within the meaning of section 548.

(3) Subsection (1) shall not be taken to prevent any person from relying on any defence available to him otherwise than by virtue of this section.

(4) In this section—
"member of the staff", in relation to a school, means any teacher who works at the school and any other person who, with the authority of the head teacher, has lawful control or charge of pupils at the school;
"offence" includes anything that would be an offence but for the operation of any presumption that a person under a particular age is incapable of committing an offence.]

[550B Detention outside school hours lawful despite absence of parental consent

(1) Where a pupil to whom this section applies is required on disciplinary grounds to spend a period of time in detention at his school after the end of any school session, his detention shall not be rendered unlawful by virtue of the absence of his parent's consent to it if the conditions set out in subsection (3) are satisfied.

(2) This section applies to any pupil who has not attained the age of 18 and is attending—
   (a) a school maintained by a local education authority;
   [...]
   (b) a city technology college [, city college for the technology of the arts or Academy].

(3) The conditions referred to in subsection (1) are as follows—
   (a) the head teacher of the school must have previously determined, and have—
      (i) made generally known within the school, and

(ii) taken steps to bring to the attention of the parent of every person who is for the time being a registered pupil there,

that the detention of pupils after the end of a school session is one of the measures that may be taken with a view to regulating the conduct of pupils;

(b) the detention must be imposed by the head teacher or by another teacher at the school specifically or generally authorised by him for the purpose;

(c) the detention must be reasonable in all the circumstances; and

(d) the pupil's parent must have been given at least 24 hours' notice in writing that the detention was due to take place.

(4) In determining for the purposes of subsection (3)(c) whether a pupil's detention is reasonable, the following matters in particular shall be taken into account—

(a) whether the detention constitutes a proportionate punishment in the circumstances of the case; and

(b) any special circumstances relevant to its imposition on the pupil which are known to the person imposing it (or of which he ought reasonably to be aware) including in particular—

(i)   the pupil's age,

(ii) any special educational needs he may have,

(iii) any religious requirements affecting him, and

(iv) where arrangements have to be made for him to travel from the school to his home, whether suitable alternative arrangements can reasonably be made by his parent.]

Housing Act 1996
(1996, c. 52)

[**153A   Anti-social behaviour injunction**

(1) This section applies to conduct—

(a) which is capable of causing nuisance or annoyance to any person, and

(b) which directly or indirectly relates to or affects the housing management functions of a relevant landlord.

(2) The court on the application of a relevant landlord may grant an injunction (an anti-social behaviour injunction) if each of the following two conditions is satisfied.

(3) The first condition is that the person against whom the injunction is sought is engaging, has engaged or threatens to engage in conduct to which this section applies.

(4) The second condition is that the conduct is capable of causing nuisance or annoyance to any of the following—

(a) a person with a right (of whatever description) to reside in or occupy housing accommodation owned or managed by the relevant landlord;

(b) a person with a right (of whatever description) to reside in or occupy other housing accommodation in the neighbourhood of housing accommodation mentioned in paragraph (a);

(c) a person engaged in lawful activity in or in the neighbourhood of housing accommodation mentioned in paragraph (a);

(d) a person employed (whether or not by the relevant landlord) in connection with the exercise of the relevant landlord's housing management functions.

(5) It is immaterial where conduct to which this section applies occurs.

(6) An anti-social behaviour injunction prohibits the person in respect of whom it is granted from engaging in conduct to which this section applies.]

[**153B   Injunction against unlawful use of premises**

(1) This section applies to conduct which consists of or involves using or threatening to use housing accommodation owned or managed by a relevant landlord for an unlawful purpose.

(2) The court on the application of the relevant landlord may grant an injunction prohibiting the person in respect of whom the injunction is granted from engaging in conduct to which this section applies.]

[153C   Injunctions: exclusion order and power of arrest

(1) This section applies if the court grants an injunction under subsection (2) of section 153A or 153B and it thinks that either of the following paragraphs applies—
  (a) the conduct consists of or includes the use or threatened use of violence;
  (b) there is a significant risk of harm to a person mentioned in section 153A(4).

(2) The court may include in the injunction a provision prohibiting the person in respect of whom it is granted from entering or being in—
  (a) any premises specified in the injunction;
  (b) any area specified in the injunction.

(3) The court may attach a power of arrest to any provision of the injunction.]

[153D   Injunction against breach of tenancy agreement

(1) This section applies if a relevant landlord applies for an injunction against a tenant in respect of the breach or anticipated breach of a tenancy agreement on the grounds that the tenant—
  (a) is engaging or threatening to engage in conduct that is capable of causing nuisance or annoyance to any person, or
  (b) is allowing, inciting or encouraging any other person to engage or threaten to engage in such conduct.

(2) The court may proceed under subsection (3) or (4) if it is satisfied—
  (a) that the conduct includes the use or threatened use of violence, or
  (b) that there is a significant risk of harm to any person.

(3) The court may include in the injunction a provision prohibiting the person in respect of whom it is granted from entering or being in—
  (a) any premises specified in the injunction;
  (b) any area specified in the injunction.

(4) The court may attach a power of arrest to any provision of the injunction.

(5) Tenancy agreement includes any agreement for the occupation of residential accommodation owned or managed by a relevant landlord.]

Noise Act 1996
(1996, c. 37)

[1   Application of sections 2 to 9
Sections 2 to 9 apply to the area of every local authority in England and Wales.]

2   Investigation of complaints of noise [. . .] at night

[(1) A local authority in England and Wales may, if they receive a complaint of the kind mentioned in subsection (2), arrange for an officer of the authority to take reasonable steps to investigate the complaint.]

(2) The kind of complaint referred to is one made by any individual present in a dwelling during night hours (referred to in this Act as "the complainant's dwelling") that excessive noise is being emitted).
  [(a)] another dwelling (referred to in this group of sections as "the offending dwelling") [,or
  (b) any premises in respect of which a premises licence or a temporary event notice has effect (referred to in this group of sections as "the offending premises")].

(3) A complaint under subsection (2) may be made by any means.

(4) If an officer of the authority is satisfied, in consequence of an investigation under subsection (1), that—

    (a) noise is being emitted from the offending dwelling [or the offending premises] during night hours, and

    (b) the noise, if it were measured from within the complainant's dwelling, would or might exceed the permitted level,

he may serve a notice about the noise under section 3.

(5) For the purposes of subsection (4), it is for the officer of the authority dealing with the particular case—

    (a) to decide whether any noise, if it were measured from within the complainant's dwelling, would or might exceed the permitted level, and

    (b) for the purposes of that decision, to decide whether to assess the noise from within or outside the complainant's dwelling and whether or not to use any device for measuring the noise.

(6) In this group of sections, "night hours" means the period beginning with 11 p.m. and ending with the following 7 a.m.

(7) Where a local authority receive a complaint under subsection (2) and the offending dwelling is[, or the offending premises are,] within the area of another local authority, the first local authority may act under this group of sections as if the offending dwelling [or the offending premises] were within their area, [. . .].

["premises licence" has the same meaning as in the Licensing Act 2003 (c. 17);

"temporary event notice" has the same meaning as in the Licensing Act 2003 (and is to be treated as having effect in accordance with section 171(6) of that Act).]

3   Warning notices

(1) A notice under this section (referred to in this Act as "a warning notice") must—

    (a) state that an officer of the authority considers—

        (i) that noise is being emitted from the offending dwelling [or the offending premises] during night hours, and

        (ii) that the noise exceeds, or may exceed, the permitted level, as measured from within the complainant's dwelling, and

    [(b) give warning—

        (i) in a case where the complaint is in respect of a dwelling, that any person who is responsible for noise which is emitted from the offending dwelling in the period specified in the notice and which exceeds the permitted level, as measured from within the complainant's dwelling, may be guilty of an offence;

        (ii) in a case where the complaint is in respect of other premises, that the responsible person in relation to the offending premises may be guilty of an offence if noise which exceeds the permitted level, as measured from within the complainant's dwelling, is emitted from the premises in the period specified in the notice.]

. . .

(5) For the purposes of this group of sections, a person is responsible for noise emitted from a dwelling if he is a person to whose act, default or sufferance the emission of the noise is wholly or partly attributable.

4   Offence where noise [from a dwelling] exceeds permitted level after service of notice

(1) If a warning notice has been served in respect of noise emitted from a dwelling, any person who is responsible for noise which—

    (a) is emitted from the dwelling in the period specified in the notice, and

    (b) exceeds the permitted level, as measured from within the complainant's dwelling,

is guilty of an offence.

(2) It is a defence for a person charged with an offence under this section to show that there was a reasonable excuse for the act, default or sufferance in question.

5 Permitted level of noise

(1) For the purposes of this group of sections, [the appropriate person] may by directions in writing determine the maximum level of noise (referred to in this group of sections as "the permitted level") which may be emitted during night hours from any dwelling [or other premises].

(2) The permitted level is to be a level applicable to noise as measured from within any other dwelling in the vicinity by an approved device used in accordance with any conditions subject to which the approval was given.

10 Powers of entry and seizure etc.

(1) The power conferred by subsection (2) may be exercised where an officer of a local authority has reason to believe that—

(a) a warning notice has been served in respect of noise emitted from a dwelling [or other premises], and

(b) at any time in the period specified in the notice, noise emitted from the dwelling [or other premises] has exceeded the permitted level, as measured from within the complainant's dwelling.

(2) An officer of a local authority, or a person authorised by the authority for the purpose, may enter the dwelling [or other premises] from which the noise in question is being or has been emitted and may seize and remove any equipment which it appears to him is being or has been used in the emission of the noise.

(3) A person exercising the power conferred by subsection (2) must produce his authority, if he is required to do so.

(4) If it is shown to a justice of the peace on sworn information in writing that—

(a) a warning notice has been served in respect of noise emitted from a dwelling [or other premises],

(b) at any time in the period specified in the notice, noise emitted from the dwelling [or other premises] has exceeded the permitted level, as measured from within the complainant's dwelling, and

(c) entry of an officer of the local authority, or of a person authorised by the authority for the purpose, to the dwelling [or other premises] has been refused, or such a refusal is apprehended, or a request by an officer of the authority, or of such a person, for admission would defeat the object of the entry,

the justice may by warrant under his hand authorise the local authority, by any of their officers or any person authorised by them for the purpose, to enter the [dwelling or other] premises, if need be by force.

(5) A person who enters any premises under subsection (2), or by virtue of a warrant issued under subsection (4), may take with him such other persons and such equipment as may be necessary; and if, when he leaves, the premises are unoccupied, must leave them as effectively secured against trespassers as he found them.

(6) A warrant issued under subsection (4) continues in force until the purpose for which the entry is required has been satisfied.

(7) The power of a local authority under section 81(3) of the Environmental Protection Act 1990 to abate any matter, where that matter is a statutory nuisance by virtue of section 79(1)(g) of that Act (noise emitted from premises so as to be prejudicial to health or a nuisance), includes power to seize and remove any equipment which it appears to the authority is being or has been used in the emission of the noise in question.

(8) A person who wilfully obstructs any person exercising any powers conferred under subsection (2) or by virtue of subsection (7) is liable, on summary conviction, to a fine not exceeding level 3 on the standard scale.

(9) The Schedule to this Act (which makes further provision in relation to anything seized and removed by virtue of this section) has effect.

12 Protection from personal liability

(1) A member of a local authority or an officer or other person authorised by a local authority is not personally liable in respect of any act done by him or by the local authority or any such person if the act was done in good faith for the purpose of executing powers conferred by, or by virtue, of this Act.

Section 10   SCHEDULE

POWERS IN RELATION TO SEIZED EQUIPMENT

Introductory

1. In this Schedule—
    (a) a "noise offence" means—
        (i) in relation to equipment seized under section 10(2) of this Act, an offence under section 4 of this Act, and
        (ii) in relation to equipment seized under section 81(3) of the Environmental Protection Act 1990 (as extended by section 10(7) of this Act), an offence under section 80(4) of that Act in respect of a statutory nuisance falling within section 79(1)(g) of that Act,
    (b) "seized equipment" means equipment seized in the exercise of the power of seizure and removal conferred by section 10(2) of this Act or section 81(3) of the Environment Protection Act 1990 (as so extended),
    (c) "related equipment", in relation to any conviction of or proceedings for a noise offence, means seized equipment used or alleged to have been used in the commission of the offence,
    (d) "responsible local authority", in relation to seized equipment, means the local authority by or on whose behalf the equipment was seized.

Retention

2.—(1) Any seized equipment may be retained—
    (a) during the period of twenty-eight days beginning with the seizure, or
    (b) if it is related equipment in proceedings for a noise offence instituted within that period against any person, until—
        (i) he is sentenced or otherwise dealt with for the offence or acquitted of the offence, or
        (ii) the proceedings are discontinued.
(2) Sub-paragraph (1) does not authorise the retention of seized equipment if—
    (a) a person has been given a fixed penalty notice under section 8 of this Act in respect of any noise,
    (b) the equipment was seized because of its use in the emission of the noise in respect of which the fixed penalty notice was given, and
    (c) that person has paid the fixed penalty before the end of the period allowed for its payment.

Forfeiture

3.—(1) Where a person is convicted of a noise offence the court may make an order ("a forfeiture order") for forfeiture of any related equipment.

(2) The court may make a forfeiture order whether or not it also deals with the offender in respect of the offence in any other way and without regard to any restrictions on forfeiture in any equipment.

(3) In considering whether to make a forfeiture order in respect of any equipment a court must have regard—

   (a) to the value of the equipment, and

   (b) to the likely financial and other effects on the offender of the making of the order (taken together with any other order that the court contemplates making).

(4) A forfeiture order operates to deprive the offender of any rights in the equipment to which it relates.

Consequences of forfeiture

4.—(1) Where any equipment has been forfeited under paragraph 3, a magistrates' court may, on application by a claimant of the equipment (other than the person in whose case the forfeiture order was made) make an order for delivery of the equipment to the applicant if it appears to the court that he is the owner of the equipment.

(2) No application may be made under sub-paragraph (1) by any claimant of the equipment after the expiry of the period of six months beginning with the date on which a forfeiture order was made in respect of the equipment.

(3) Such an application cannot succeed unless the claimant satisfies the court—

   (a) that he had not consented to the offender having possession of the equipment, or

   (b) that he did not know, and had no reason to suspect, that the equipment was likely to be used in the commission of a noise offence.

(4) Where the responsible local authority is of the opinion that the person in whose case the forfeiture order was made is not the owner of the equipment, it must take reasonable steps to bring to the attention of persons who may be entitled to do so their right to make an application under sub-paragraph (1).

(5) An order under sub-paragraph (1) does not affect the right of any person to take, within the period of six months beginning with the date of the order, proceedings for the recovery of the equipment from the person in possession of it in pursuance of the order, but the right ceases on the expiry of that period.

(6) If on the expiry of the period of six months beginning with the date on which a forfeiture order was made in respect of the equipment no order has been made under sub-paragraph (1), the responsible local authority may dispose of the equipment.

Return etc. of seized equipment

5. If in proceedings for a noise offence no order for forfeiture of related equipment is made, the court (whether or not a person is convicted of the offence) may give such directions as to the return, retention or disposal of the equipment by the responsible local authority as it thinks fit.

6.—(1) Where in the case of any seized equipment no proceedings in which it is related equipment are begun within the period mentioned in paragraph 2(1)(a)—

   (a) the responsible local authority must return the equipment to any person who—

      (i) appears to them to be the owner of the equipment, and

      (ii) makes a claim for the return of the equipment within the period mentioned in sub-paragraph (2), and

   (b) if no such person makes such a claim within that period, the responsible local authority may dispose of the equipment.

(2) The period referred to in sub-paragraph (1)(a)(ii) is the period of six months beginning with the expiry of the period mentioned in paragraph 2(1)(a).

(3) The responsible local authority must take reasonable steps to bring to the attention of persons who may be entitled to do so their right to make such a claim.

(4) Subject to sub-paragraph (6), the responsible local authority is not required to return any seized equipment under sub-paragraph (1)(a) until the person making the claim has paid any such reasonable charges for the seizure, removal and retention of the equipment as the authority may demand.

(5) If—
  (a) equipment is sold in pursuance of—
      (i)   paragraph 4(6),
      (ii) directions under paragraph 5, or
      (iii) this paragraph, and
  (b) before the expiration of the period of one year beginning with the date on which the equipment is sold any person satisfies the responsible local authority that at the time of its sale he was the owner of the equipment,

the authority is to pay him any sum by which any proceeds of sale exceed any such reasonable charges for the seizure, removal or retention of the equipment as the authority may demand.

(6) The responsible local authority cannot demand charges from any person under subparagraph (4) or (5) who they are satisfied did not know, and had no reason to suspect, that the equipment was likely to be used in the emission of noise exceeding the level determined under section 5.

Party Wall etc. Act 1996
(1996, c. 40)

7 Compensation etc.

(1) A building owner shall not exercise any right conferred on him by this Act in such a manner or at such time as to cause unnecessary inconvenience to any adjoining owner or to any adjoining occupier.

(2) The building owner shall compensate any adjoining owner and any adjoining occupier for any loss or damage which may result to any of them by reason of any work executed in pursuance of this Act.

(3) Where a building owner in exercising any right conferred on him by this Act lays open any part of the adjoining land or building he shall at his own expense make and maintain so long as may be necessary a proper hoarding, shoring or fans or temporary construction for the protection of the adjoining land or building and the security of any adjoining occupier.

(4) Nothing in this Act shall authorise the building owner to place special foundations on land of an adjoining owner without his previous consent in writing.

8 Rights of entry

(1) A building owner, his servants, agents and workmen may during usual working hours enter and remain on any land or premises for the purpose of executing any work in pursuance of this Act and may remove any furniture or fittings or take any other action necessary for that purpose.

(2) If the premises are closed, the building owner, his agents and workmen may, if accompanied by a constable or other police officer, break open any fences or doors in order to enter the premises.

(3) No land or premises may be entered by any person under subsection (1) unless the building owner serves on the owner and the occupier of the land or premises—
  (a) in case of emergency, such notice of the intention to enter as may be reasonably practicable;
  (b) in any other case, such notice of the intention to enter as complies with sub-section (4).

(4) Notice complies with this subsection if it is served in a period of not less than fourteen days ending with the day of the proposed entry.

Police Act 1996
(1996, c. 16)

88 Liability for wrongful acts of constables

(1) The chief officer of police for a police area shall be liable in respect of [any unlawful conduct of] constables under his direction and control in the performance or purported performance of their functions in like manner as a master is liable in respect of [any unlawful conduct of] his servants in the course of their employment, and accordingly shall [, in the case of a tort,] be treated for all purposes as a joint tortfeasor.

(2) There shall be paid out of the police fund—

   (a) any damages or costs awarded against the chief officer of police in any proceedings brought against him by virtue of this section and any costs incurred by him in any such procceedings so far as not recovered by him in the proceedings; and

   (b) any sum required in connection with the settlement of any claim made against the chief officer of police by virtue of this section, if the settlement is approved by the police authority.

(3) Any proceedings in respect of a claim made by virtue of this section shall be brought against the chief officer of police for the time being or, in the case of a vacancy in that office, against the person for the time being performing the functions of the chief officer of police; and references in subsections (1) and (2) to the chief officer of police shall be construed accordingly.

(4) A police authority may, in such cases and to such extent as appear to it to be appropriate, pay out of the police fund—

   (a) any damages or costs awarded against a person to whom this subsection applies in proceedings for [any unlawful conduct of] that person,

   (b) any costs incurred and not recovered by such a person in such proceedings, and

   (c) any sum required in connection with the settlement of a claim that has or might have given rise to such proceedings.

[(6) This section shall have effect where an international joint investigation team has been formed under the leadership of a constable who is a member of a police force as if—

   (a) any unlawful conduct, in the performance or purported performance of his functions as such, of any member of that team who is neither a constable nor an employee of the police authority were unlawful conduct of a constable under the direction and control of the chief officer of police of that force; and

   (b) subsection (4) applied, in the case of the police authority maintaining that force, to every member of that team to whom it would not apply apart from this subsection.

(7) In this section "international joint investigation team" means any investigation team formed in accordance with—

   (a) any framework decision on joint investigation teams adopted under Article 34 of the Treaty on European Union;

   (b) the Convention on Mutual Assistance in Criminal Matters between the Member States of the European Union, and the Protocol to that Convention, established in accordance with that Article of that Treaty; or

   (c) any international agreement to which the United Kingdom is a party and which is specified for the purposes of this section in an order made by the Secretary of State.]

Contract (Scotland) Act 1997
(1997, c. 34)

1   Extrinsic evidence of additional contract term etc.

(1) Where a document appears (or two or more documents appear) to comprise all the express terms of a contract or unilateral voluntary obligation, it shall be presumed, unless the contrary is proved, that the document does (or the documents do) comprise all the express terms of the contract or unilateral voluntary obligation.

(2) Extrinsic oral or documentary evidence shall be admissible to prove, for the purposes of subsection (1) above, that the contract or unilateral voluntary obligation includes additional express terms (whether or not written terms).

(3) Notwithstanding the foregoing provisions of this section, where one of the terms in the document (or in the documents) is to the effect that the document does (or the documents do) comprise all the express terms of the contract or unilateral voluntary obligation, that term shall be conclusive in the matter.

(4) This section is without prejudice to any enactment which makes provision as respects the constitution, or formalities of execution, of a contract or unilateral voluntary obligation.

2   Supersession

(1) Where a deed is executed in implement, or purportedly in implement, of a contract, an unimplemented, or otherwise unfulfilled, term of the contract shall not be taken to be superseded by virtue only of that execution or of the delivery and acceptance of the deed.

(2) Subsection (1) above is without prejudice to any agreement which the parties to a contract may reach (whether or not an agreement incorporated into the contract) as to supersession of the contract.

3   Damages for breach of contract of sale

Any rule of law which precludes the buyer in a contract of sale of property from obtaining damages for breach of that contract by the seller unless the buyer rejects the property and rescinds the contract shall cease to have effect.

4   Short title, extent etc.

(4) This Act extends to Scotland only.

Justices of the Peace Act 1997
(1997, c. 25)

51   Immunity for acts within jurisdiction

[(1)] No action shall lie against any justice of the peace or justices' clerk in respect of any act or omission of his—

    (a) in the execution of his duty—
        (i)   as such a justice; or
        (ii) as such a clerk exercising, by virtue of any statutory provision, any of the functions of a single justice; and
    (b) with respect to any matter within his jurisdiction.

52   Immunity for certain acts beyond jurisdiction

[(1)] An action shall lie against any justice of the peace or justices' clerk in respect of any act or omission of his—

    (a) in the purported execution of his duty—
        (i)   as such a justice; or
        (ii) as such a clerk exercising, by virtue of any statutory provision, any of the functions of a single justice; but

(b) with respect to a matter which is not within his jurisdiction, if, but only if, it is proved that he acted in bad faith.

Local Government (Contracts) Act 1997
(1997, c. 65)

Contracts for provision of assets or services

1 Functions to include power to enter into contracts

(1) Every statutory provision conferring or imposing a function on a local authority confers power on the local authority to enter into a contract with another person for the provision or making available of assets or services, or both, (whether or not together with goods), for the purposes of, or in connection with, the discharge of the function by the local authority.

(2) Where—

(a) a local authority enters into a contract such as is mentioned in subsection (1) ("the provision contract") under any statutory provision, and

(b) in connection with the provision contract, a person ("the financier") makes a loan to, or provides any other form of finance for, a party to the provision contract other than the local authority,

the statutory provision also confers power on the local authority to enter into a contract with the financier, or any insurer of or trustee for the financier, in connection with the provision contract.

(4) In this Act "assets" means assets of any description (whether tangible or intangible), including (in particular) land, buildings, roads, works, plant, machinery, vehicles, vessels, apparatus, equipment and computer software.

Certified contracts

2 Certified contracts to be *intra vires*

(1) Where a local authority has entered into a contract, the contract shall, if it is a certified contract, have effect (and be deemed always to have had effect) as if the local authority had had power to enter into it (and had exercised that power properly in entering into it).

(2) For the purposes of this Act a contract entered into by a local authority is a certified contract if (and, subject to subsections (3) and (4), only if) the certification requirements have been satisfied by the local authority with respect to the contract and they were so satisfied before the end of the certification period.

(3) A contract entered into by a local authority shall be treated as a certified contract during the certification period if the contract provides that the certification requirements are intended to be satisfied by the local authority with respect to the contract before the end of that period.

(4) Where a local authority has entered into a contract which is a certified contract ("the existing contract") and the existing contract is replaced by a contract entered into by it with a person or persons not identical with the person or persons with whom it entered into the existing contract, the replacement contract is also a certified contract if—

(a) the period for which it operates or is intended to operate ends at the same time as the period for which the existing contract was to operate, and

(b) apart from that, its provisions are the same as those of the existing contract.

(5) In this Act "the certification period", in relation to a contract entered into by a local authority, means the period of six weeks beginning with the day on which the local authority entered into the contract.

(6) Subsection (1) is subject to section 5 (special provisions about judicial reviews and audit reviews).

(7) The application of subsection (1) in relation to a contract entered into by a local authority does not affect any claim for damages made by a person who is not (and has never been) a party to the contract in respect of a breach by the local authority of any duty to do, or not to do, something before entering into the contract (including, in particular, any such duty imposed by a statutory provision for giving effect to any Community obligation relating to public procurement or by section 17(1) of the Local Government Act 1988).

3   The certification requirements

(1) In this Act "the certification requirements", in relation to a contract entered into by a local authority, means the requirements specified in subsections (2) to (4).

(2) The requirement specified in this subsection is that the local authority must have issued a certificate (whether before or after the contract is entered into)—

    (a) including details of the period for which the contract operates or is to operate,

    (b) describing the purpose of the contract,

    (c) containing a statement that the contract is or is to be a contract falling within section 4(3) or (4),

    (d) stating that the local authority had or has power to enter into the contract and specifying the statutory provision, or each of the statutory provisions, conferring the power,

    (e) stating that a copy of the certificate has been or is to be given to each person to whom a copy is required to be given by regulations,

    (f) dealing in a manner prescribed by regulations with any matters required by regulations to be dealt with in certificates under this section, and

    (g) confirming that the local authority has complied with or is to comply with any requirement imposed by regulations with respect to the issue of certificates under this section.

(3) The requirement specified in this subsection is that the local authority must have secured that the certificate is signed by any person who is required by regulations to sign it.

(4) The requirement specified in this subsection is that the local authority must have obtained consent to the issue of a certificate under this section from each of the persons with whom the local authority has entered, or is to enter, into the contract.

4   Certified contracts: supplementary

(1) Where the certification requirements have been satisfied in relation to a contract by a local authority, the certificate which has been issued shall have effect (and be deemed always to have had effect) as if the local authority had had power to issue it (and had exercised that power properly in issuing it); and a certificate which has been so issued is not invalidated by reason that anything in the certificate is inaccurate or untrue.

(2) Where the certification requirements have been satisfied in relation to a contract by a local authority within section 1(3)(a) or (d), the local authority shall secure that throughout the period for which the contract operates—

    (a) a copy of the certificate which has been issued is open to inspection by members of the public at all reasonable times without payment, and

    (b) members of the public are afforded facilities for obtaining copies of that certificate on payment of a reasonable fee.

(3) A contract entered into by a local authority falls within this subsection if—

    (a) it is entered into with another person for the provision or making available of services (whether or not together with assets or goods) for the purposes of, or in connection with, the discharge by the local authority of any of its functions, and

    (b) it operates, or is intended to operate, for a period of at least five years.

(4) A contract entered into by a local authority falls within this subsection if it is entered into, in connection with a contract falling within subsection (3), with—

(a) a person who, in connection with that contract, makes a loan to, or provides any other form of finance for, a party to that contract other than the local authority, or

(b) any insurer of or trustee for such a person.

6 Relevant discharge terms

(1) No determination or order made in relation to a certified contract on—

(a) an application for judicial review, or

(b) an audit review,

shall affect the enforceability of any relevant discharge terms relating to the contract.

(2) In this section and section 7 "relevant discharge terms", in relation to a contract entered into by a local authority, means terms—

(a) which have been agreed by the local authority and any person with whom the local authority entered into the contract,

(b) which either form part of the contract or constitute or form part of another agreement entered into by them not later than the day on which the contract was entered into, and

(c) which provide for a consequence mentioned in subsection (3) to ensue in the event of the making of a determination or order in relation to the contract on an application for judicial review or an audit review.

(3) Those consequences are—

(a) the payment of compensatory damages (measured by reference to loss incurred or loss of profits or to any other circumstances) by one of the parties to the other,

(b) the adjustment between the parties of rights and liabilities relating to any assets or goods provided or made available under the contract, or

(c) both of those things.

(4) Where a local authority has agreed relevant discharge terms with any person with whom it has entered into a contract and the contract is a certified contract, the relevant discharge terms shall have effect (and be deemed always to have had effect) as if the local authority had had power to agree them (and had exercised that power properly in agreeing them).

7 Absence of relevant discharge terms

(1) Subsection (2) applies where—

(a) the result of a determination or order made by a court on an application for judicial review or an audit review is that a certified contract does not have effect, and

(b) there are no relevant discharge terms having effect between the local authority and a person who is a party to the contract.

(2) That person shall be entitled to be paid by the local authority such sums (if any) as he would have been entitled to be paid by the local authority if the contract—

(a) had had effect until the time when the determination or order was made, but

(b) had been terminated at that time by acceptance by him of a repudiatory breach by the local authority.

(3) For the purposes of this section the circumstances in which there are no relevant discharge terms having effect between the local authority and a person who is a party to the contract include (as well as circumstances in which no such terms have been agreed) circumstances in which the result of a determination or order of a court, made (despite section 6(4)) on an application for judicial review or an audit review, is that such terms do not have effect.

Protection from Harassment Act 1997
(1997, c. 40)

1   Prohibition of harassment

(1) A person must not pursue a course of conduct—
  (a) which amounts to harassment of another, and
  (b) which he knows or ought to know amounts to harassment of the other.

[(1A) A person must not pursue a course of conduct—
  (a) which involves harassment of two or more persons, and
  (b) which he knows or ought to know involves harassment of those persons, and
  (c) by which he intends to persuade any person (whether or not one of those mentioned above)—
      (i)   not to do something that he is entitled or required to do, or
      (ii) to do something that he is not under any obligation to do.]

(2) For the purposes of this section, the person whose course of conduct is in question ought to know that it amounts to [or involves] harassment of another if a reasonable person in possession of the same information would think the course of conduct amounted to [or involved] harassment of the other.

(3) Subsection (1) [or (1A)] does not apply to a course of conduct if the person who pursued it shows—
  (a) that it was pursued for the purpose of presenting or detecting crime,
  (b) that it was pursued under any enactment or rule of law or to comply with any condition or requirement imposed by any person under any enactment, or
  (c) that in the particular circumstances the pursuit of the course of conduct was reasonable.

2   Offence of harassment

(1) A person who pursues a course of conduct in breach of [section 1 or (1A)] is guilty of an offence.

3   Civil remedy

(1) An actual or apprehended breach of [section 1(1)] may be the subject of a claim in civil proceedings by the person who is or may be the victim of the course of conduct in question.

(2) On such a claim, damages may be awarded for (among other things) any anxiety caused by the harassment and any financial loss resulting from the harassment.

(3) Where—
  (a) in such proceedings the High Court or a county court grants an injunction for the purpose of restraining the defendant from pursuing any conduct which amounts to harassment, and
  (b) the plaintiff considers that the defendant has done anything which he is prohibited from doing by the injunction,
the plaintiff may apply for the issue of a warrant for the arrest of the defendant.

. . .

(5) The judge or district judge to whom an application under subsection (3) is made may only issue a warrant if—
  (a) the application is substantiated on oath, and
  (b) the judge or district judge has reasonable grounds for believing that the defendant has done anything which he is prohibited from doing by the injunction.

(6) Where—
  (a) the High Court or a county court grants an injunction for the purpose mentioned in subsection (3)(a), and
  (b) without reasonable excuse the defendant does anything which he is prohibited from doing by the injunction,
he is guilty of an offence.

[3A Injunctions to protect persons from harassment within section 1(1A)

(1) This section applies where there is an actual or apprehended breach of section 1(1A) by any person ("the relevant person").

(2) In such a case—

(a) any person who is or may be a victim of the course of conduct in question, or

(b) any person who is or may be a person falling within section 1(1A)(c),

may apply to the High Court or a county court for an injunction restraining the relevant person from pursuing any conduct which amounts to harassment in relation to any person or persons mentioned or described in the injunction.]

4 Putting people in fear of violence

(1) A person whose course of conduct causes another to fear, on at least two occasions, that violence will be used against him is guilty of an offence if he knows or ought to know that his course of conduct will cause the other so to fear on each of those occasions.

(2) For the purposes of this section, the person whose course of conduct is in question ought to know that it will cause another to fear that violence will be used against him on any occasion if a reasonable person in possession of the same information would think the course of conduct would cause the other so to fear on that occasion.

(3) It is a defence for a person charged with an offence under this section to show that—

(a) his course of conduct was pursued for the purpose of preventing or detecting crime,

(b) his course of conduct was pursued under any enactment or rule of law or to comply with any condition or requirement imposed by any person under any enactment, or

(c) the pursuit of his course of conduct was reasonable for the protection of himself or another or for the protection of his or another's property.

5 Restraining orders

(1) A court sentencing or otherwise dealing with a person ("the defendant") convicted of an offence under section 2 or 4 may (as well as sentencing him or dealing with him in any other way) make an order under this section.

(2) The order may, for the purpose of protecting the victim [or victims] of the offence, or any other person mentioned in the order, from further conduct which—

(a) amounts to harassment, or

(b) will cause a fear of violence,

prohibit the defendant from doing anything described in the order.

. . .

(5) If without reasonable excuse the defendant does anything which he is prohibited from doing by an order under this section, he is guilty of an offence.

7 Interpretation of this group of sections

(1) This section applies for the interpretation of sections 1 to 5.

(2) References to harassing a person include alarming the person or causing the person distress.

[(3) A "course of conduct" must involve—

(a) in the case of conduct in relation to a single person (see section 1(1)), conduct on at least two occasions in relation to that person, or

(b) in the case of conduct in relation to two or more persons (see section 1(1A)), conduct on at least one occasion in relation to each of those persons.]

[(3A) A person's conduct on any occasion shall be taken, if aided, abetted, counselled or procured by another—

(a) to be conduct on that occasion of the other (as well as conduct of the person whose conduct it is); and

(b) to be conduct in relation to which the other's knowledge and purpose, and what he ought to have known, are the same as they were in relation to what was contemplated or reasonably foreseeable at the time of the aiding, abetting, counselling or procuring.]

(4) "Conduct" includes speech.

[(5) References to a person, in the context of the harassment of a person, are references to a person who is an individual.]

12 National security, etc.

(1) If the Secretary of State certifies that in his opinion anything done by a specified person on a specified occasion related to—

(a) national security,

(b) the economic well-being of the United Kingdom, or

(c) the prevention or detection of serious crime,

and was done on behalf of the Crown, the certificate is conclusive evidence that this Act does not apply to any conduct of that person on that occasion.

Social Security (Recovery of Benefits) Act 1997
(1997, c. 27)

1   Cases in which this Act applies

(1) This Act applies in cases where—

(a) a person makes a payment (whether on his own behalf or not) to or in respect of any other person in consequence of any accident, injury or disease suffered by the other, and

(b) any listed benefits have been, or are likely to be, paid to or for the other during the relevant period in respect of the accident, injury or disease.

(2) The reference above to a payment in consequence of any accident, injury or disease is to a payment made—

(a) by or on behalf of a person who is, or is alleged to be, liable to any extent in respect of the accident, injury or disease, or

(b) in pursuance of a compensation scheme for motor accidents;

but does not include a payment mentioned in Part I of Schedule 1.

(3) Subsection (1)(a) applies to a payment made—

(a) voluntarily, or in pursuance of a court order or an agreement, or otherwise, and

(b) in the United Kingdom or elsewhere.

(4) In a case where this Act applies—

(a) the "injured person" is the person who suffered the accident, injury or disease,

(b) the "compensation payment" is the payment within subsection (1)(a), and

(c) "recoverable benefit" is any listed benefit which has been or is likely to be paid as mentioned in subsection (1)(b).

2   Compensation payments to which this Act applies

This Act applies in relation to compensation payments made on or after the day on which this section comes into force, unless they are made in pursuance of a court order or agreement made before that day.

3   "The relevant period"

(1) In relation to a person ("the claimant") who has suffered any accident, injury or disease, "the relevant period" has the meaning given by the following subsections.

(2) Subject to subsection (4), if it is a case of accident or injury, the relevant period is the period of five years immediately following the day on which the accident or injury in question occurred.

(3) Subject to subsection (4), if it is a case of disease, the relevant period is the period of five years beginning with the date on which the claimant first claims a listed benefit in consequence of the disease.

(4) If at any time before the end of the period referred to in subsection (2) or (3)—

    (a) a person makes a compensation payment in final discharge of any claim made by or in respect of the claimant and arising out of the accident, injury or disease, or

    (b) an agreement is made under which an earlier compensation payment is treated as having been made in final discharge of any such claim,

the relevant period ends at that time.

4   Applications for certificates of recoverable benefits

(1) Before a person ("the compensator") makes a compensation payment he must apply to the Secretary of State for a certificate of recoverable benefits.

. . .

5   Information contained in certificates

(1) A certificate of recoverable benefits must specify, for each recoverable benefit—

    (a) the amount which has been or is likely to have been paid on or before a specified date, and

    (b) if the benefit is paid or likely to be paid after the specified date, the rate and period for which, and the intervals at which, it is or is likely to be so paid.

(2) In a case where the relevant period has ended before the day on which the Secretary of State receives the application for the certificate, the date specified in the certificate for the purposes of subsection (1) must be the day on which the relevant period ended.

(3) In any other case, the date specified for those purposes must not be earlier than the day on which the Secretary of State received the application.

(4) The Secretary of State may estimate, in such manner as he thinks fit, any of the amounts, rates or periods specified in the certificate.

(5) Where the Secretary of State issues a certificate of recoverable benefits, he must provide the information contained in the certificate to—

    (a) the person who appears to him to be the injured person, or

    (b) any person who he thinks will receive a compensation payment in respect of the injured person.

(6) A person to whom a certificate of recoverable benefits is issued or who is provided with information under subsection (5) is entitled to particulars of the manner in which any amount, rate or period specified in the certificate has been determined, if he applies to the Secretary of State for those particulars.

6   Liability to pay Secretary of State amount of benefits

(1) A person who makes a compensation payment in any case is liable to pay to the Secretary of State an amount equal to the total amount of the recoverable benefits.

(2) The liability referred to in subsection (1) arises immediately before the compensation payment or, if there is more than one, the first of them is made.

(3) No amount becomes payable under this section before the end of the period of 14 days following the day on which the liability arises.

(4) Subject to subsection (3), an amount becomes payable under this section at the end of the period of 14 days beginning with the day on which a certificate of recoverable benefits is first issued showing that the amount of recoverable benefit to which it relates has been or is likely to have been paid before a specified date.

7   Recovery of payments due under section 6

(1) This section applies where a person has made a compensation payment but—

    (a) has not applied for a certificate of recoverable benefits, or

    (b) has not made a payment to the Secretary of State under section 6 before the end of the period allowed under that section.

  (2) The Secretary of State may—

    (a) issue the person who made the compensation payment with a certificate of recoverable benefits, if none has been issued, or

    (b) issue him with a copy of the certificate of recoverable benefits or (if more than one has been issued) the most recent one,

and (in either case) issue him with a demand that payment of any amount due under section 6 be made immediately.

  (3) The Secretary of State may, in accordance with subsections (4) and (5), recover the amount for which a demand for payment is made under subsection (2) from the person who made the compensation payment.

  (4) If the person who made the compensation payment resides or carries on business in England and Wales and a county court so orders, any amount recoverable under subsection (3) is recoverable by execution issued from the county court or otherwise as if it were payable under an order of that court.

  (5) If the person who made the payment resides or carries on business in Scotland, any amount recoverable under subsection (3) may be enforced in like manner as an extract registered decree arbitral bearing a warrant for execution issued by the sheriff court of any sheriffdom in Scotland.

  (6) A document bearing a certificate which—

    (a) is signed by a person authorised to do so by the Secretary of State, and

    (b) states that the document, apart from the certificate, is a record of the amount recoverable under subsection (3),

is conclusive evidence that that amount is so recoverable.

  (7) A certificate under subsection (6) purporting to be signed by a person authorised to do so by the Secretary of State is to be treated as so signed unless the contrary is proved.

8 Reduction of compensation payment

  (1) This section applies in a case where, in relation to any head of compensation listed in column 1 of Schedule 2—

    (a) any of the compensation payment is attributable to the head, and

    (b) any recoverable benefit is shown against that head in column 2 of the Schedule.

  (2) In such a case, any claim of a person to receive the compensation payment is to be treated for all purposes as discharged if—

    (a) he is paid the amount (if any) of the compensation payment calculated in accordance with this section, and

    (b) if the amount of the compensation payment so calculated is nil, he is given a statement saying so by the person who (apart from this section) would have paid the gross amount of the compensation payment.

  (3) For each head of compensation listed in column 1 of the Schedule for which paragraphs (a) and (b) of subsection (1) are met, so much of the gross amount of the compensation payment as is attributable to that head is to be reduced (to nil, if necessary) by deducting the amount of the recoverable benefit or, as the case may be, the aggregate amount of the recoverable benefits shown against it.

  (4) Subsection (3) is to have effect as if a requirement to reduce a payment by deducting an amount which exceeds the payment were a requirement to reduce that payment to nil.

  (5) The amount of the compensation payment calculated in accordance with this section is—

    (a) the gross amount of the compensation payment,

less

    (b) the sum of the reductions made under subsection (3),

(and, accordingly, the amount may be nil).

9   Section 8: supplementary

(1) A person who makes a compensation payment calculated in accordance with section 8 must inform the person to whom the payment is made—

(a) that the payment has been so calculated, and

(b) of the date for payment by reference to which the calculation has been made.

(2) If the amount of a compensation payment calculated in accordance with section 8 is nil, a person giving a statement saying so is to be treated for the purposes of this Act as making a payment within section 1(1)(a) on the day on which he gives the statement.

(3) Where a person—

(a) makes a compensation payment calculated in accordance with section 8, and

(b) if the amount of the compensation payment so calculated is nil, gives a statement saying so,

he is to be treated, for the purpose of determining any rights and liabilities in respect of contribution or indemnity, as having paid the gross amount of the compensation payment.

(4) For the purposes of this Act—

(a) the gross amount of the compensation payment is the amount of the compensation payment apart from section 8, and

(b) the amount of any recoverable benefit is the amount determined in accordance with the certificate of recoverable benefits.

10   Review of certificates of recoverable benefits

[(1) Any certificate of recoverable benefits may be reviewed by the Secretary of State—

(a) either within the prescribed period or in prescribed cases or circumstances; and

(b) either on an application made for the purpose or on his own initiative.]

(2) On a review under this section the Secretary of State may either—

(a) confirm the certificate, or

(b) (subject to subsection (3)) issue a fresh certificate containing such variations as he considers appropriate, [or

(c) revoke the certificate.].

(3) The Secretary of State may not vary the certificate so as to increase the total amount of the recoverable benefits unless it appears to him that the variation is required as a result of the person who applied for the certificate supplying him with incorrect or insufficient information.

11   Appeals against certificates of recoverable benefits

(1) An appeal against a certificate of recoverable benefits may be made on the ground—

(a) that any amount, rate or period specified in the certificate is incorrect, or

(b) that listed benefits which have been, or are likely to be, paid otherwise than in respect of the accident, injury or disease in question have been brought into account [or

(c) that listed benefits which have not been, and are not likely to be, paid to the injured person during the relevant period have been brought into account, or

(d) that the payment on the basis of which the certificate was issued is not a payment within section 1(1)(a)].

(2) An appeal under this section may be made by—

(a) the person who applied for the certificate of recoverable benefits, or

[(aa) (in a case where that certificate was issued under section 7(2)(a)) the person to whom it was so issued, or]

(b) (in a case where the amount of the compensation payment has been calculated under section 8) the injured person or other person to whom the payment is made.

(3) No appeal may be made under this section until—

(a) the claim giving rise to the compensation payment has been finally disposed of, and

(b) the liability under section 6 has been discharged.

(4) For the purposes of subsection (3)(a), if an award of damages in respect of a claim has been made under or by virtue of—

(a) section 32A(2)(a) of [the Senior Courts Act 1981],

(b) section 12(2)(a) of the Administration of Justice Act 1982, or

(c) section 51(2)(a) of the County Courts Act 1984,

(orders for provisional damages in personal injury cases), the claim is to be treated as having been finally disposed of.

(5) Regulations may make provision—

(a) as to the manner in which, and the time within which, appeals under this section may be made,

(b) as to the procedure to be followed where such an appeal is made, and

(c) for the purpose of enabling any such appeal to be treated as an application for review under section 10.

12   Reference of questions to medical appeal tribunal

(1) The Secretary of State must refer an appeal under section 11 to an appeal tribunal.]

(3) In determining [any appeal under section 11], the tribunal must take into account any decision of a court relating to the same, or any similar, issue arising in connection with the accident, injury or disease in question.

(4) On [an appeal under section 11 an appeal tribunal] may either—

(a) confirm the amounts, rates and periods specified in the certificate of recoverable benefits, or

(b) specify any variations which are to be made on the issue of a fresh certificate under subsection (5) [or

(c) declare that the certificate of recoverable benefits is to be revoked.].

(5) When the Secretary of State has received [the decision of the tribunal on the appeal under section 11, he must in accordance with that decision] either—

(a) confirm the certificate against which the appeal was brought, or

(b) issue a fresh certificate [or

(c) revoke the certificate.].

(7) Regulations [. . .] may (among other things) provide for the non-disclosure of medical advice or medical evidence given or submitted following a reference under subsection (1).

13   Appeal to Social Security Commissioner

(1) An appeal may be made to a Commissioner against any decision of [an appeal tribunal] under section 12 on the ground that the decision was erroneous in point of law.

(2) An appeal under this section may be made by—

(a) the Secretary of State,

(b) the person who applied for the certificate of recoverable benefits, [. . .]

[(bb) (in a case where that certificate was issued under section 7(2)(a)) the person to whom it was so issued, or]

(c) (in a case where the amount of the compensation payment has been calculated in accordance with section 8) the injured person or other person to whom the payment is made.

14   Reviews and appeals: supplementary

(1) This section applies in cases where a fresh certificate of recoverable benefits is issued as a result of a review under section 10 or an appeal under section 11.

(2) If—

(a) a person has made one or more payments to the Secretary of State under section 6, and

(b) in consequence of the review or appeal, it appears that the total amount paid is more than the amount that ought to have been paid,

regulations may provide for the Secretary of State to pay the difference to that person, or to the person to whom the compensation payment is made, or partly to one and partly to the other.

(3) If—
- (a) a person has made one or more payments to the Secretary of State under section 6, and
- (b) in consequence of the review or appeal, it appears that the total amount paid is less than the amount that ought to have been paid,

regulations may provide for that person to pay the difference to the Secretary of State.

(4) Regulations under this section may provide—
- (a) for the re-calculation in accordance with section 8 of the amount of any compensation payment,
- (b) for giving credit for amounts already paid, and
- (c) for the payment by any person of any balance or the recovery from any person of any excess,

and may provide for any matter by modifying this Act.

15   Court orders

(1) This section applies where a court makes an order for a compensation payment to be made in any case, unless the order is made with the consent of the injured person and the person by whom the payment is to be made.

(2) The court must, in the case of each head of compensation listed in column 1 of Schedule 2 to which any of the compensation payment is attributable, specify in the order the amount of the compensation payment which is attributable to that head.

16   Payments into court

(1) Regulations may make provision (including provision modifying this Act) for any case in which a payment into court is made.

(2) The regulations may (among other things) provide—
- (a) for the making of a payment into court to be treated in prescribed circumstances as the making of a compensation payment,
- (b) for application for, and issue of, certificates of recoverable benefits, and
- (c) for the relevant period to be treated as ending on a date determined in accordance with the regulations.

(3) Rules of court may make provision governing practice and procedure in such cases.

(4) This section does not extend to Scotland.

17   Benefits irrelevant to assessment of damages

In assessing damages in respect of any accident, injury or disease, the amount of any listed benefits paid or likely to be paid is to be disregarded.

18   Lump sum and periodical payments

(1) Regulations may make provision (including provision modifying this Act) for any case in which two or more compensation payments in the form of lump sums are made by the same person to or in respect of the injured person in consequence of the same accident, injury or disease.

(2) The regulations may (among other things) provide—
- (a) for the re-calculation in accordance with section 8 of the amount of any compensation payment,
- (b) for giving credit for amounts already paid, and
- (c) for the payment by any person of any balance or the recovery from any person of any excess.

(3) For the purposes of subsection (2), the regulations may provide for the gross amounts of the compensation payments to be aggregated and for—
- (a) the aggregate amount to be taken to be the gross amount of the compensation payment for the purposes of section 8,
- (b) so much of the aggregate amount as is attributable to a head of compensation listed in column 1 of Schedule 2 to be taken to be the part of the gross amount which is attributable to that head;

and for the amount of any recoverable benefit shown against any head in column 2 of that Schedule to be taken to be the amount determined in accordance with the most recent certificate of recoverable benefits.

(4) Regulations may make provision (including provision modifying this Act) for any case in which, in final settlement of the injured person's claim, an agreement is entered into for the making of—

(a) periodical compensation payments (whether of an income or capital nature), or

(b) periodical compensation payments and lump sum compensation payments.

(5) Regulations made by virtue of subsection (4) may (among other things) provide—

(a) for the relevant period to be treated as ending at a prescribed time,

(b) for the person who is to make the payments under the agreement to be treated for the purposes of this Act as if he had made a single compensation payment on a prescribed date.

(6) A periodical payment may be a compensation payment for the purposes of this section even though it is a small payment (as defined in Part II of Schedule 1).

19 Payments by more than one person

(1) Regulations may make provision (including provision modifying this Act) for any case in which two or more persons ("the compensators") make compensation payments to or in respect of the same injured person in consequence of the same accident, injury or disease.

(2) In such a case, the sum of the liabilities of the compensators under section 6 is not to exceed the total amount of the recoverable benefits, and the regulations may provide for determining the respective liabilities under that section of each of the compensators.

(3) The regulations may (among other things) provide in the case of each compensator—

(a) for determining or re-determining the part of the recoverable benefits which may be taken into account in his case,

(b) for calculating or re-calculating in accordance with section 8 the amount of any compensation payment,

(c) for giving credit for amounts already paid, and

(d) for the payment by any person of any balance or the recovery from any person of any excess.

20 Amounts overpaid under section 6

(1) Regulations may make provision (including provision modifying this Act) for cases where a person has paid to the Secretary of State under section 6 any amount ("the amount of the overpayment") which he was not liable to pay.

(2) The regulations may provide—

(a) for the Secretary of State to pay the amount of the overpayment to that person, or to the person to whom the compensation payment is made, or partly to one and partly to the other, or

(b) for the receipt by the Secretary of State of the amount of the overpayment to be treated as the recovery of that amount.

(3) Regulations made by virtue of subsection (2)(b) are to have effect in spite of anything in section 71 of the Social Security Administration Act 1992 (overpayments—general).

(4) The regulations may also (among other things) provide—

(a) for the re-calculation in accordance with section 8 of the amount of any compensation payment,

(b) for giving credit for amounts already paid, and

(c) for the payment by any person of any balance or the recovery from any person of any excess.

(5) This section does not apply in a case where section 14 applies.

21 Compensation payments to be disregarded

(1) If, when a compensation payment is made, the first and second conditions are met, the payment is to be disregarded for the purposes of sections 6 and 8.

(2) The first condition is that the person making the payment—

    (a) has made an application for a certificate of recoverable benefits which complies with subsection (3), and

    (b) has in his possession a written acknowledgement of the receipt of his application.

(3) An application complies with this subsection if it—

    (a) accurately states the prescribed particulars relating to the injured person and the accident, injury or disease in question, and

    (b) specifies the name and address of the person to whom the certificate is to be sent.

(4) The second condition is that the Secretary of State has not sent the certificate to the person, at the address, specified in the application, before the end of the period allowed under section 4.

(5) In any case where—

    (a) by virtue of subsection (1), a compensation payment is disregarded for the purposes of sections 6 and 8, but

    (b) the person who made the compensation payment nevertheless makes a payment to the Secretary of State for which (but for subsection (1)) he would be liable under section 6,

subsection (1) is to cease to apply in relation to the compensation payment.

(6) If, in the opinion of the Secretary of State, circumstances have arisen which adversely affect normal methods of communication—

    (a) he may by order provide that subsection (1) is not to apply during a specified period not exceeding three months, and

    (b) he may continue any such order in force for further periods not exceeding three months at a time.

22 Liability of insurers

(1) If a compensation payment is made in a case where—

    (a) a person is liable to any extent in respect of the accident, injury or disease, and

    (b) the liability is covered to any extent by a policy of insurance,

the policy is also to be treated as covering any liability of that person under section 6.

(2) Liability imposed on the insurer by subsection (1) cannot be excluded or restricted.

(3) For that purpose excluding or restricting liability includes—

    (a) making the liability or its enforcement subject to restrictive or onerous conditions,

    (b) excluding or restricting any right or remedy in respect of the liability, or subjecting a person to any prejudice in consequence of his pursuing any such right or remedy, or

    (c) excluding or restricting rules of evidence or procedure.

(4) Regulations may in prescribed cases limit the amount of the liability imposed on the insurer by subsection (1).

(5) This section applies to policies of insurance issued before (as well as those issued after) its coming into force.

(6) References in this section to policies of insurance and their issue include references to contracts of insurance and their making.

23 Provision of information

(1) Where compensation is sought in respect of any accident, injury or disease suffered by any person ("the injured person"), the following persons must give the Secretary of State the prescribed information about the injured person—

    (a) anyone who is, or is alleged to be, liable in respect of the accident, injury or disease, and

    (b) anyone acting on behalf of such a person.

(2) A person who receives or claims a listed benefit which is or is likely to be paid in respect of an accident, injury or disease suffered by him, must give the Secretary of State the prescribed information about the accident, injury or disease.

(3) Where a person who has received a listed benefit dies, the duty in subsection (2) is imposed on his personal representative.

(4) Any person who makes a payment (whether on his own behalf or not)—

(a) in consequence of, or

(b) which is referable to any costs (in Scotland, expenses) incurred by reason of, any accident, injury or disease, or any damage to property, must, if the Secretary of State requests him in writing to do so, give the Secretary of State such particulars relating to the size and composition of the payment as are specified in the request.

(5) The employer of a person who suffers or has suffered an accident, injury or disease, and anyone who has been the employer of such a person at any time during the relevant period, must give the Secretary of State the prescribed information about the payment of statutory sick pay in respect of that person.

(6) In subsection (5) "employer" has the same meaning as it has in Part XI of the Social Security Contributions and Benefits Act 1992.

(7) A person who is required to give information under this section must do so in the prescribed manner, at the prescribed place and within the prescribed time.

(8) Section 1 does not apply in relation to this section.

24 Power to amend Schedule 2

(1) The Secretary of State may by regulations amend Schedule 2.

(2) A statutory instrument which contains such regulations shall not be made unless a draft of the instrument has been laid before and approved by resolution of each House of Parliament.

28 The Crown

This Act applies to the Crown.

29 General interpretation

In this Act—

["appeal tribunal" means an appeal tribunal constituted under Chapter I of Part I of the Social Security Act 1998;]

"benefit" means any benefit under the Social Security Contributions and Benefits Act 1992, a jobseeker's allowance or mobility allowance,

["Commissioner" has the same meaning as in Chapter II of Part I of the Social Security Act 1998 (see section 39);]

"compensation scheme for motor accidents" means any scheme or arrangement under which funds are available for the payment of compensation in respect of motor accidents caused, or alleged to have been caused, by uninsured or unidentified persons,

"listed benefit" means a benefit listed in column 2 of Schedule 2,

"payment" means payment in money or money's worth, and related expressions are to be interpreted accordingly,

"prescribed" means prescribed by regulations, and

"regulations" means regulations made by the Secretary of State.

30 Regulations and orders

(1) Any power under this Act to make regulations or an order is exercisable by statutory instrument.

(2) A statutory instrument containing regulations or an order under this Act (other than regulations under section 24 or an order under section 34) shall be subject to annulment in pursuance of a resolution of either House of Parliament.

(3) Regulations under section 20, under section 24 amending the list of benefits in column 2 of Schedule 2 or under paragraph 9 of Schedule 1 may not be made without the consent of the Treasury.

(4) Subsections (4), (5), (6) and (9) of section 189 of the Social Security Administration Act 1992 (regulations and orders—general) apply for the purposes of this Act as they apply for the purposes of that.

31   Financial arrangements

(1) There are to be paid out of the National Insurance Fund any expenses of the Secretary of State in making payments under section 14 or 20 to the extent that he estimates that those payments relate to sums paid out of that Fund.

(2) There are to be paid out of money provided by Parliament—

    (a) any expenses of the Secretary of State in making payments under section 14 or 20 to the extent that he estimates that those payments relate to sums paid out of the Consolidated Fund, and

    (b) (subject to subsection (1)) any other expenses of the Secretary of State incurred in consequence of this Act.

(3) Any sums paid to the Secretary of State under section 6 or 14 are to be paid—

    (a) into the Consolidated Fund, to the extent that the Secretary of State estimates that the sums relate to payments out of money provided by Parliament, and

    (b) into the National Insurance Fund, to the extent that he estimates that they relate to payments out of that Fund.

32   Power to make transitional, consequential etc. provisions

(1) Regulations may make such transitional and consequential provisions, and such savings, as the Secretary of State considers necessary or expedient in preparation for, in connection with, or in consequence of—

    (a) the coming into force of any provision of this Act, or

    (b) the operation of any enactment repealed or amended by a provision of this Act during any period when the repeal or amendment is not wholly in force.

(2) Regulations under this section may (among other things) provide—

    (a) for compensation payments in relation to which, by virtue of section 2, this Act does not apply to be treated as payments in relation to which this Act applies,

    (b) for compensation payments in relation to which, by virtue of section 2, this Act applies to be treated as payments in relation to which this Act does not apply, and

    (c) for the modification of any enactment contained in this Act or referred to in subsection (1)(b) in its application to any compensation payment.

SCHEDULES

Section 1   ## SCHEDULE 1

COMPENSATION PAYMENTS

PART I   EXEMPTED PAYMENTS

1. Any small payment (defined in Part II of this Schedule).

2. Any payment made to or for the injured person under [section 130 of the Powers of Criminal Courts (Sentencing) Act 2000] or section 249 of the Criminal Procedure (Scotland) Act 1995 (compensation orders against convicted persons).

3. Any payment made in the exercise of a discretion out of property held subject to a trust in a case where no more than 50 per cent. by value of the capital contributed to the trust was directly or indirectly provided by persons who are, or are alleged to be, liable in respect of—

    (a) the accident, injury or disease suffered by the injured person, or

    (b) the same or any connected accident, injury or disease suffered by another.

4. Any payment made out of property held for the purposes of any prescribed trust (whether the payment also falls within paragraph 3 or not).

5. [(1)] Any payment made to the injured person by an [insurer] under the terms of any contract of insurance entered into between the injured person and the company before—

    (a) the date on which the injured person first claims a listed benefit in consequence of the disease in question, or

    (b) the occurrence of the accident or injury in question.

6. Any redundancy payment falling to be taken into account in the assessment of damages in respect of an accident, injury or disease.

7. So much of any payment as is referable to costs.

8. Any prescribed payment.

PART II   POWER TO DISREGARD SMALL PAYMENTS

9.—(1) Regulations may make provision for compensation payments to be disregarded for the purposes of sections 6 and 8 in prescribed cases where the amount of the compensation payment, or the aggregate amount of two or more connected compensation payments, does not exceed the prescribed sum.

(2) A compensation payment disregarded by virtue of this paragraph is referred to in paragraph 1 as a "small payment".

(3) For the purposes of this paragraph—

    (a) two or more compensation payments are "connected" if each is made to or in respect of the same injured person and in respect of the same accident, injury or disease, and

    (b) any reference to a compensation payment is a reference to a payment which would be such a payment apart from paragraph 1.

Section 8   SCHEDULE 2

CALCULATION OF COMPENSATION PAYMENT

(1) *Head of compensation*	(2) *Benefit*
1. Compensation for earnings lost during the relevant period	[…]
	Disablement pension payable under section 103 of the 1992 Act
	Incapacity benefit
	Income support
	Invalidity pension and allowance
	Jobseeker's allowance
	Reduced earnings allowance
	Severe disablement allowance
	Sickness benefit
	Statutory sick pay

Unemployability supplement
Unemployment benefit

2. Compensation for cost of care incurred during the relevant period	Attendance allowance
	Care component of disability living allowance
	Disablement pension increase payable under section 104 or 105 of the 1992 Act
3. Compensation for loss of mobility during Mobility allowance the relevant period	Mobility allowance
	Mobility component of disability living allowance

Notes

1.—(1) References to incapacity benefit, invalidity pension and allowance, severe disablement allowance, sickness benefit and unemployment benefit also include any income support paid with each of those benefits on the same instrument of payment or paid concurrently with each of those benefits by means of an instrument for benefit payment.

(2) For the purpose of this Note, income support includes personal expenses addition, special transitional additions and transitional addition as defined in the Income Support (Transitional) Regulations 1987.

2. Any reference to statutory sick pay —

(a) includes only 80 per cent. of payments made between 6 April 1991 and 5 April 1994, and

(b) does not include payments made on or after 6 April 1994.

3. In this Schedule "the 1992 Act" means the Social Security Contributions and Benefits Act 1992.

Competition Act 1998
(1998, c. 41)

2 Agreements etc. preventing, restricting or distorting competition

(1) Subject to section 3, agreements between undertakings, decisions by associations of undertakings or concerted practices which—

(a) may affect trade within the United Kingdom, and

(b) have as their object or effect the prevention, restriction or distortion of competition within the United Kingdom,

are prohibited unless they are exempt in accordance with the provisions of this Part.

(2) Subsection (1) applies, in particular, to agreements, decisions or practices which—

(a) directly or indirectly fix purchase or selling prices or any other trading conditions;

(b) limit or control production, markets, technical development or investment;

(c) share markets or sources of supply;

(d) apply dissimilar conditions to equivalent transactions with other trading parties, thereby placing them at a competitive disadvantage;

(e) make the conclusion of contracts subject to acceptance by the other parties of supplementary obligations which, by their nature or according to commercial usage, have no connection with the subject of such contracts.

(3) Subsection (1) applies only if the agreement, decision or practice is, or is intended to be, implemented in the United Kingdom.

(4) Any agreement or decision which is prohibited by subsection (1) is void.

57 Defamation

For the purposes of the law relating to defamation, absolute privilege attaches to any advice, guidance, notice or direction given, or decision made, by the [OFT] in the exercise of any of [its] functions under this Part.

Crime and Disorder Act 1998
(1998, c. 37)

[13A   Parental compensation orders

(1) A magistrates' court may make an order under this section (a "parental compensation order") if on the application of a local authority it is satisfied, on the civil standard of proof—

(a) that the condition mentioned in subsection (2) below is fulfilled with respect to a child under the age of 10; and

(b) that it would be desirable to make the order in the interests of preventing a repetition of the behaviour in question.

(2) The condition is that the child has taken, or caused loss of or damage to, property in the course of—

(a) committing an act which, if he had been aged 10 or over, would have constituted an offence; or

(b) acting in a manner that caused or was likely to cause harassment, alarm or distress to one or more persons not of the same household as himself.

(3) A parental compensation order is an order which requires any person specified in the order who is a parent or guardian of the child (other than a local authority) to pay compensation of an amount specified in the order to any person or persons specified in the order who is, or are, affected by the taking of the property or its loss or damage.

(4) The amount of compensation specified may not exceed £5,000 in all.

(5) The Secretary of State may by order amend subsection (4) above so as to substitute a different amount.

(6) For the purposes of collection and enforcement, a parental compensation order is to be treated as if it were a sum adjudged to be paid on the conviction by the magistrates' court which made the order of the person or persons specified in the order as liable to pay the compensation.]

[13B   Parental compensation orders: the compensation

(1) When specifying the amount of compensation for the purposes of section 13A(3) above, the magistrates' court shall take into account—

(a) the value of the property taken or damaged, or whose loss was caused, by the child;

(b) any further loss which flowed from the taking of or damage to the property, or from its loss;

(c) whether the child, or any parent or guardian of his, has already paid any compensation for the property (and if so, how much);

(d) whether the child, or any parent or guardian of his, has already made any reparation (and if so, what it consisted of);

(e) the means of those to be specified in the order as liable to pay the compensation, so far as the court can ascertain them;

(f) whether there was any lack of care on the part of the person affected by the taking of the property or its loss or damage which made it easier for the child to take or damage the property or to cause its loss.

(2) If property taken is recovered before compensation is ordered to be paid in respect of it—

(a) the court shall not order any such compensation to be payable in respect of it if it is not damaged;

(b) if it is damaged, the damage shall be treated for the purposes of making a parental compensation order as having been caused by the child, regardless of how it was caused and who caused it.

(3) The court shall specify in the order how and by when the compensation is to be paid (for example, it may specify that the compensation is to be paid by instalments, and specify the date by which each instalment must be paid).

(4) For the purpose of ascertaining the means of the parent or guardian, the court may, before specifying the amount of compensation, order him to provide the court, within such period as it may specify in the order, such a statement of his financial circumstances as the court may require.

(5) A person who without reasonable excuse fails to comply with an order under subsection (4) above is guilty of an offence and is liable on summary conviction to a fine not exceeding level 3 on the standard scale.]

[13C   Parental compensation orders: supplemental

(1) Before deciding whether or not to make a parental compensation order in favour of any person, the magistrates' court shall take into account the views of that person about whether a parental compensation order should be made in his favour.

(2) Before making a parental compensation order, the magistrates' court shall obtain and consider information about the child's family circumstances and the likely effect of the order on those circumstances.]

[13E   Effect of parental compensation order on subsequent award of damages in civil proceedings

(1) This section has effect where—
  (a) a parental compensation order has been made in favour of any person in respect of any taking or loss of property or damage to it; and
  (b) a claim by him in civil proceedings for damages in respect of the taking, loss or damage is then to be determined.

(2) The damages in the civil proceedings shall be assessed without regard to the parental compensation order, but the claimant may recover only an amount equal to the aggregate of the following—
  (a) any amount by which they exceed the compensation; and
  (b) a sum equal to any portion of the compensation which he fails to recover.

(3) The claimant may not enforce the judgment, so far as it relates to such a sum as is mentioned in subsection (2)(b) above, without the permission of the court.]

Data Protection Act 1998
(1998, c. 29)

10   Right to prevent processing likely to cause damage or distress

(1) Subject to subsection (2), an individual is entitled at any time by notice in writing to a data controller to require the data controller at the end of such period as is reasonable in the circumstances to cease, or not to begin, processing, or processing for a specified purpose or in a specified manner, any personal data in respect of which he is the data subject, on the ground that, for specified reasons—
  (a) the processing of those data or their processing for that purpose or in that manner is causing or is likely to cause substantial damage or substantial distress to him or to another, and
  (b) that damage or distress is or would be unwarranted.

(2) Subsection (1) does not apply—
  (a) in a case where any of the conditions in paragraphs 1 to 4 of Schedule 2 is met, or
  (b) on such other cases as may be prescribed by the Secretary of State by order.

(3) The data controller must within twenty-one days of receiving a notice under subsection (1) ("the data subject notice") give the individual who gave it a written notice—
  (a) stating that he has complied or intends to comply with the data subject notice, or

(b) stating his reasons for regarding the data subject notice as to any extent unjustified and the extent (if any) to which he has complied or intends to comply with it.

(4) If a court is satisfied, on the application of any person who has given a notice under subsection (1) which appears to the court to be justified (or to be justified to any extent), that the data controller in question has failed to comply with the notice, the court may order him to take such steps for complying with the notice (or for complying with it to that extent) as the court thinks fit.

(5) The failure by a data subject to exercise the right conferred by subsection (1) or section 11(1) does not affect any other right conferred on him by this Part.

13   Compensation for failure to comply with certain requirements

(1) An individual who suffers damage by reason of any contravention by a data controller of any of the requirements of this Act is entitled to compensation from the data controller for that damage.

(2) An individual who suffers distress by reason of any contravention by a data controller of any of the requirements of this Act is entitled to compensation from the data controller for that distress if—

(a) the individual also suffers damage by reason of the contravention, or
(b) the contravention relates to the processing of personal data for the special purposes.

(3) On proceedings brought against a person by virtue of this section it is a defence to prove that he had taken such care as in all the circumstances was reasonably required to comply with the requirement concerned.

57   Avoidance of certain contractual terms relating to health records

(1) Any term or condition of a contract is void in so far as it purports to require an individual—

(a) to supply any other person with a record to which this section applies, or with a copy of such a record or a part of such a record, or
(b) to produce to any other person such a record, copy or part.

(2) This section applies to any record which—

(a) has been or is to be obtained by a data subject in the exercise of the right conferred by section 7, and
(b) consists of the information contained in any health record as defined by section 68(2).

Human Rights Act 1998
(1998, c. 42)

Introduction

1   The Convention Rights

(1) In this Act "the Convention rights" means the rights and fundamental freedoms set out in—

(a) Articles 2 to 12 and 14 of the Convention,
(b) Articles 1 to 3 of the First Protocol, and
(c) [Article 1 of the Thirteenth Protocol],

as read with Articles 16 to 18 of the Convention.

(2) Those Articles are to have effect for the purposes of this Act subject to any designated derogation or reservation (as to which see sections 14 and 15).

(3) The Articles are set out in Schedule 1.

(4) The Secretary of State may by order make such amendments to this Act as he considers appropriate to refiect the effect, in relation to the United Kingdom, of a protocol.

(5) In subsection (4) "protocol" means a protocol to the Convention—

(a) which the United Kingdom has ratified; or

(b) which the United Kingdom has signed with a view to ratification.

(6) No amendment may be made by an order under subsection (4) so as to come into force before the protocol concerned is in force in relation to the United Kingdom.

2   Interpretation of Convention rights

(1) A court or tribunal determining a question which has arisen in connection with a Convention right must take into account any—

(a) judgment, decision, declaration or advisory opinion of the European Court of Human Rights,

(b) opinion of the Commission given in a report adopted under Article 31 of the Convention,

(c) decision of the Commission in connection with Article 26 or 27(2) of the Convention, or

(d) decision of the Committee of Ministers taken under Article 46 of the Convention, whenever made or given, so far as, in the opinion of the court or tribunal, it is relevant to the proceedings in which that question has arisen.

(2) Evidence of any judgment, decision, declaration or opinion of which account may have to be taken under this section is to be given in proceedings before any court or tribunal in such manner as may be provided by rules.

(3) In this section "rules" means rules of court or, in the case of proceedings before a tribunal, rules made for the purposes of this section—

(a) by [. . .] the Secretary of State, in relation to any proceedings outside Scotland;

(b) by the Secretary of State, in relation to proceedings in Scotland; or

(c) by a Northern Ireland department, in relation to proceedings before a tribunal in Northern Ireland—

(i)   which deals with transferred matters; and

(ii) for which no rules made under paragraph (a) are in force.

Legislation

3   Interpretation of legislation

(1) So far as it is possible to do so, primary legislation and subordinate legislation must be read and given effect in a way which is compatible with the Convention rights.

(2) This section—

(a) applies to primary legislation and subordinate legislation whenever enacted;

(b) does not affect the validity, continuing operation or enforcement of any incompatible primary legislation; and

(c) does not affect the validity, continuing operation or enforcement of any incompatible subordinate legislation if (disregarding any possibility of revocation) primary legislation prevents removal of the incompatibility.

4   Declaration of incompatibility

(1) Subsection (2) applies in any proceedings in which a court determines whether a provision of primary legislation is compatible with a Convention right.

(2) If the court is satisfied that the provision is incompatible with a Convention right, it may make a declaration of that incompatibility.

(3) Subsection (4) applies in any proceedings in which a court determines whether a provision of subordinate legislation, made in the exercise of a power conferred by primary legislation, is compatible with a Convention right.

(4) If the court is satisfied—

    (a) that the provision is incompatible with a Convention right, and

    (b) that (disregarding any possibility of revocation) the primary legislation concerned prevents removal of the incompatibility,

it may make a declaration of that incompatibility.

(5) In this section "court" means—

    (a) the House of Lords;[1]

    (b) the Judicial Committee of the Privy Council;

    (c) the Courts-Martial Appeal Court;

    (d) in Scotland, the High Court of Justiciary sitting otherwise than as a trial court or the Court of Session;

    (e) in England and Wales or Northern Ireland, the High Court or the Court of Appeal

    [(f) the Court of Protection, in any matter being dealt with by the President of the Family Division, the Vice-Chanceller or a puisne judge of the High Court.].

(6) A declaration under this section ("a declaration of incompatibility")—

    (a) does not affect the validity, continuing operation or enforcement of the provision in respect of which it is given; and

    (b) is not binding on the parties to the proceedings in which it is made.

[1. Para. (a) will be "[(a) the Supreme Court]" when the Constitutional Reform Act 2005, Sched. 9, para. 66(1) is brought into force.]

5   Right of Crown to intervene

(1) Where a court is considering whether to make a declaration of incompatibility, the Crown is entitled to notice in accordance with rules of court.

(2) In any case to which subsection (1) applies—

    (a) a Minister of the Crown (or a person nominated by him),

    (b) a member of the Scottish Executive,

    (c) a Northern Ireland Minister,

    (d) a Northern Ireland department,

is entitled, on giving notice in accordance with rules of court, to be joined as a party to the proceedings.

(3) Notice under subsection (2) may be given at any time during the proceedings.

(4) A person who has been made a party to criminal proceedings (other than in Scotland) as the result of a notice under subsection (2) may, with leave, appeal to the House of Lords[1] against any declaration of incompatibility made in the proceedings.

(5) In subsection (4)—

"criminal proceedings" includes all proceedings before the Courts-Martial Appeal Court; and

"leave" means leave granted by the court making the declaration of incompatibility or by the House of Lords.[1]

[1. "Supreme Court" will be substituted for "House of Lords" when the Constitutional Reform Act 2005, Sched. 9, para. 66(3) is brought into force.]

Public authorities

6   Acts of public authorities

(1) It is unlawful for a public authority to act in a way which is incompatible with a Convention right.

(2) Subsection (1) does not apply to an act if—

    (a) as the result of one or more provisions of primary legislation, the authority could not have acted differently; or

    (b) in the case of one or more provisions of, or made under, primary legislation which cannot be read or given effect in a way which is compatible with the Convention rights, the authority was acting so as to give effect to or enforce those provisions.

(3) In this section "public authority" includes—
    (a) a court or tribunal, and
    (b) any person certain of whose functions are functions of a public nature,
but does not include either House of Parliament or a person exercising functions in connection with proceedings in Parliament.
[...]
(5) In relation to a particular act, a person is not a public authority by virtue only of subsection (3)(b) if the nature of the act is private.
(6) "An act" includes a failure to act but does not include a failure to—
    (a) introduce in, or lay before, Parliament a proposal for legislation; or
    (b) make any primary legislation or remedial order.

7 Proceedings

(1) A person who claims that a public authority has acted (or proposes to act) in a way which is made unlawful by section 6(1) may—
    (a) bring proceedings against the authority under this Act in the appropriate court or tribunal, or
    (b) rely on the Convention right or rights concerned in any legal proceedings,
but only if he is (or would be) a victim of the unlawful act.
(2) In subsection (1)(a) "appropriate court or tribunal" means such court or tribunal as may be determined in accordance with rules; and proceedings against an authority include a counterclaim or similar proceedings.
(3) If the proceedings are brought on an application for judicial review, the applicant is to be taken to have a sufficient interest in relation to the unlawful act only if he is, or would be, a victim of that act.
(4) If the proceedings are made by way of a petition for judicial review in Scotland, the applicant shall be taken to have title and interest to sue in relation to the unlawful act only if he is, or would be, a victim of that act.
(5) Proceedings under subsection (1)(a) must be brought before the end of—
    (a) the period of one year beginning with the date on which the act complained of took place; or
    (b) such longer period as the court or tribunal considers equitable having regard to all the circumstances,
but that is subject to any rule imposing a stricter time limit in relation to the procedure in question.
(6) In subsection (1)(b) "legal proceedings" includes—
    (a) proceedings brought by or at the instigation of a public authority; and
    (b) an appeal against the decision of a court or tribunal.
(7) For the purposes of this section, a person is a victim of an unlawful act only if he would be a victim for the purposes of Article 34 of the Convention if proceedings were brought in the European Court of Human Rights in respect of that act.
(8) Nothing in this Act creates a criminal offence.
(9) In this section "rules" means—
    (a) in relation to proceedings before a court or tribunal outside Scotland, rules made by [...] the Secretary of State for the purposes of this section or rules of court,
    (b) in relation to proceedings before a court or tribunal in Scotland, rules made by the Secretary of State for those purposes,
    (c) in relation to proceedings before a tribunal in Northern Ireland—
        (i)   which deals with transferred matters; and
        (ii) for which no rules made under paragraph (a) are in force,
        rules made by a Northern Ireland department for those purposes,
and includes provision made by order under section 1 of the Courts and Legal Services Act 1990.

(10) In making rules, regard must be had to section 9.

(11) The Minister who has power to make rules in relation to a particular tribunal may, to the extent he considers it necessary to ensure that the tribunal can provide an appropriate remedy in relation to an act (or proposed act) of a public authority which is (or would be) unlawful as a result of section 6(1), by order add to—

(a) the relief or remedies which the tribunal may grant; or

(b) the grounds on which it may grant any of them.

(12) An order made under subsection (11) may contain such incidental, supplemental, consequential or transitional provision as the Minister making it considers appropriate.

(13) "The Minister" includes the Northern Ireland department concerned.

8 Judicial remedies

(1) In relation to any act (or proposed act) of a public authority which the court finds is (or would be) unlawful, it may grant such relief or remedy, or make such order, within its powers as it considers just and appropriate.

(2) But damages may be awarded only by a court which has power to award damages, or to order the payment of compensation, in civil proceedings.

(3) No award of damages is to be made unless, taking account of all the circumstances of the case, including—

(a) any other relief or remedy granted, or order made, in relation to the act in question (by that or any other court), and

(b) the consequences of any decision (of that or any other court) in respect of that act,

the court is satisfied that the award is necessary to afford just satisfaction to the person in whose favour it is made.

(4) In determining—

(a) whether to award damages, or

(b) the amount of an award,

the court must take into account the principles applied by the European Court of Human Rights in relation to the award of compensation under Article 41 of the Convention.

(5) A public authority against which damages are awarded is to be treated—

(a) in Scotland, for the purposes of section 3 of the Law Reform (Miscellaneous Provisions) (Scotland) Act 1940 as if the award were made in an action of damages in which the authority has been found liable in respect of loss or damage to the person to whom the award is made;

(b) for the purposes of the Civil Liability (Contribution) Act 1978 as liable in respect of damage suffered by the person to whom the award is made.

(6) In this section—

"court" includes a tribunal;

"damages" means damages for an unlawful act of a public authority; and

"unlawful" means unlawful under section 6(1).

9 Judicial acts

(1) Proceedings under section 7(1)(a) in respect of a judicial act may be brought only—

(a) by exercising a right of appeal;

(b) on an application (in Scotland a petition) for judicial review; or

(c) in such other forum as may be prescribed by rules.

(2) That does not affect any rule of law which prevents a court from being the subject of judicial review.

(3) In proceedings under this Act in respect of a judicial act done in good faith, damages may not be awarded otherwise than to compensate a person to the extent required by Article 5(5) of the Convention.

(4) An award of damages permitted by subsection (3) is to be made against the Crown; but no award may be made unless the appropriate person, if not a party to the proceedings, is joined.

(5) In this section—

"appropriate person" means the Minister responsible for the court concerned, or a person or government department nominated by him;

"court" includes a tribunal;

"judge" includes a member of a tribunal, a justice of the peace and a clerk or other officer entitled to exercise the jurisdiction of a court;

"judicial act" means a judicial act of a court and includes an act done on the instructions, or on behalf, of a judge; and

"rules" has the same meaning as in section 7(9).

Remedial action

10 Power to take remedial action

(1) This section applies if—

    (a) a provision of legislation has been declared under section 4 to be incompatible with a Convention right and, if an appeal lies—

        (i) all persons who may appeal have stated in writing that they do not intend to do so;

        (ii) the time for bringing an appeal has expired and no appeal has been brought within that time; or

        (iii) an appeal brought within that time has been determined or abandoned; or

    (b) it appears to a Minister of the Crown or Her Majesty in Council that, having regard to a finding of the European Court of Human Rights made after the coming into force of this section in proceedings against the United Kingdom, a provision of legislation is incompatible with an obligation of the United Kingdom arising from the Convention.

(2) If a Minister of the Crown considers that there are compelling reasons for proceeding under this section, he may by order make such amendments to the legislation as he considers necessary to remove the incompatibility.

(3) If, in the case of subordinate legislation, a Minister of the Crown considers—

    (a) that it is necessary to amend the primary legislation under which the subordinate legislation in question was made, in order to enable the incompatibility to be removed, and

    (b) that there are compelling reasons for proceeding under this section,

he may by order make such amendments to the primary legislation as he considers necessary.

(4) This section also applies where the provision in question is in subordinate legislation and has been quashed, or declared invalid, by reason of incompatibility with a Convention right and the Minister proposes to proceed under paragraph 2(b) of Schedule 2.

(5) If the legislation is an Order in Council, the power conferred by subsection (2) or (3) is exercisable by Her Majesty in Council.

(6) In this section "legislation" does not include a Measure of the Church Assembly or of the General Synod of the Church of England.

(7) Schedule 2 makes further provision about remedial orders.

Other rights and proceedings

11 Safeguard for existing human rights

A person's reliance on a Convention right does not restrict—

    (a) any other right or freedom conferred on him by or under any law having effect in any part of the United Kingdom; or

    (b) his right to make any claim or bring any proceedings which he could make or bring apart from sections 7 to 9.

12 Freedom of expression

(1) This section applies if a court is considering whether to grant any relief which, if granted, might affect the exercise of the Convention right to freedom of expression.

(2) If the person against whom the application for relief is made ("the respondent") is neither present nor represented, no such relief is to be granted unless the court is satisfied—

    (a) that the applicant has taken all practicable steps to notify the respondent; or

    (b) that there are compelling reasons why the respondent should not be notified.

    (3) No such relief is to be granted so as to restrain publication before trial unless the court is satisfied that the applicant is likely to establish that publication should not be allowed.

    (4) The court must have particular regard to the importance of the Convention right to freedom of expression and, where the proceedings relate to material which the respondent claims, or which appears to the court, to be journalistic, literary or artistic material (or to conduct connected with such material), to—

    (a) the extent to which—

       (i) the material has, or is about to, become available to the public; or

       (ii) it is, or would be, in the public interest for the material to be published;

    (b) any relevant privacy code.

    (5) In this section—

"court" includes a tribunal; and

"relief" includes any remedy or order (other than in criminal proceedings).

13   Freedom of thought, conscience and religion

    (1) If a court's determination of any question arising under this Act might affect the exercise by a religious organisation (itself or its members collectively) of the Convention right to freedom of thought, conscience and religion, it must have particular regard to the importance of that right.

    (2) In this section "court" includes a tribunal.

Derogations and reservations

[*ss 14–17*]

Judges of the European Court of Human Rights

[*s 18*]

Parliamentary procedure

19   Statements of compatibility

    (1) A Minister of the Crown in charge of a Bill in either House of Parliament must, before Second Reading of the Bill—

    (a) make a statement to the effect that in his view the provisions of the Bill are compatible with the Convention rights ("a statement of compatibility"); or

    (b) make a statement to the effect that although he is unable to make a statement of compatibility the government nevertheless wishes the House to proceed with the Bill.

    (2) The statement must be in writing and be published in such manner as the Minister making it considers appropriate.

Supplemental

21   Interpretation, etc.

    (1) In this Act—

"amend" includes repeal and apply (with or without modifications);

"the appropriate Minister" means the Minister of the Crown having charge of the appropriate authorised government department (within the meaning of the Crown Proceedings Act 1947);

"the Commission" means the European Commission of Human Rights;

"the Convention" means the Convention for the Protection of Human Rights and Fundamental Freedoms, agreed by the Council of Europe at Rome on 4th November 1950 as it has effect for the time being in relation to the United Kingdom;

"declaration of incompatibility" means a declaration under section 4;

"Minister of the Crown" has the same meaning as in the Ministers of the Crown Act 1975;

"Northern Ireland Minister" includes the First Minister and the deputy First Minister in Northern Ireland;

"primary legislation" means any—

(a) public general Act;

(b) local and personal Act;

(c) private Act;

(d) Measure of the Church Assembly;

(e) Measure of the General Synod of the Church of England;

(f) Order in Council—

    (i) made in exercise of Her Majesty's Royal Prerogative;

    (ii) made under section 38(1)(a) of the Northern Ireland Constitution Act 1973 or the corresponding provision of the Northern Ireland Act 1998; or

    (iii) amending an Act of a kind mentioned in paragraph (a), (b) or (c);

and includes an order or other instrument made under primary legislation (otherwise than by the National Assembly for Wales, a member of the Scottish Executive, a Northern Ireland Minister or a Northern Ireland department) to the extent to which it operates to bring one or more provisions of that legislation into force or amends any primary legislation;

"the First Protocol" means the protocol to the Convention agreed at Paris on 20th March 1952;

"the Eleventh Protocol" means the protocol to the Convention (restructuring the control machinery established by the Convention) agreed at Strasbourg on 11th May 1994;

["the Thirteenth Protocol" means the protocol to the Convention (concerning the abolition of the death penalty in all circumstances) agreed at Vilnius on 3rd May 2002;]

"remedial order" means an order under section 10;

"subordinate legislation" means any—

(a) Order in Council other than one—

    (i) made in exercise of Her Majesty's Royal Prerogative;

    (ii) made under section 38(1)(a) of the Northern Ireland Constitution Act 1973 or the corresponding provision of the Northern Ireland Act 1998; or

    (iii) amending an Act of a kind mentioned in the definition of primary legislation;

(b) Act of the Scottish Parliament;

(c) Act of the Parliament of Northern Ireland;

(d) Measure of the Assembly established under section 1 of the Northern Ireland Assembly Act 1973;

(e) Act of the Northern Ireland Assembly;

(f) order, rules, regulations, scheme, warrant, byelaw or other instrument made under primary legislation (except to the extent to which it operates to bring one or more provisions of that legislation into force or amends any primary legislation);

(g) order, rules, regulations, scheme, warrant, byelaw or other instrument made under legislation mentioned in paragraph (b), (c), (d) or (e) or made under an Order in Council applying only to Northern Ireland;

(h) order, rules, regulations, scheme, warrant, byelaw or other instrument made by a member of the Scottish Executive, a Northern Ireland Minister or a Northern Ireland department in exercise of prerogative or other executive functions of Her Majesty which are exercisable by such a person on behalf of Her Majesty;

"transferred matters" has the same meaning as in the Northern Ireland Act 1998; and

"tribunal" means any tribunal in which legal proceedings may be brought.

(2) The references in paragraphs (b) and (c) of section 2(1) to Articles are to Articles of the Convention as they had effect immediately before the coming into force of the Eleventh Protocol.

(3) The reference in paragraph (d) of section 2(1) to Article 46 includes a reference to Articles 32 and 54 of the Convention as they had effect immediately before the coming into force of the Eleventh Protocol.

(4) The references in section 2(1) to a report or decision of the Commission or a decision of the Committee of Ministers include references to a report or decision made as provided by paragraphs 3, 4 and 6 of Article 5 of the Eleventh Protocol (transitional provisions).

(5) Any liability under the Army Act 1955, the Air Force Act 1955 or the Naval Discipline Act 1957 to suffer death for an offence is replaced by a liability to imprisonment for life or any less punishment authorised by those Acts; and those Acts shall accordingly have effect with the necessary modifications.

22   Short title, commencement, application and extent
   (5) This Act binds the Crown.
   (6) This Act extends to Northern Ireland.

Section 1(3)   SCHEDULE 1   THE ARTICLES

                        PART I   THE CONVENTION
                         RIGHTS AND FREEDOMS

Article 2   Right to life
   1. Everyone's right to life shall be protected by law. No one shall be deprived of his life intentionally save in the execution of a sentence of a court following his conviction of a crime for which this penalty is provided by law.
   2. Deprivation of life shall not be regarded as inficted in contravention of this Article when it results from the use of force which is no more than absolutely necessary:
      (a) in defence of any person from unlawful violence;
      (b) in order to effect a lawful arrest or to prevent the escape of a person lawfully detained;
      (c) in action lawfully taken for the purpose of quelling a riot or insurrection.

Article 3   Prohibition of torture
No one shall be subjected to torture or to inhuman or degrading treatment or punishment.

Article 4   Prohibition of slavery and forced labour
   1. No one shall be held in slavery or servitude.
   2. No one shall be required to perform forced or compulsory labour.
   3. For the purpose of this Article the term "forced or compulsory labour" shall not include:
      (a) any work required to be done in the ordinary course of detention imposed according to the provisions of Article 5 of this Convention or during conditional release from such detention;
      (b) any service of a military character or, in case of conscientious objectors in countries where they are recognised, service exacted instead of compulsory military service;
      (c) any service exacted in case of an emergency or calamity threatening the life or well-being of the community;
      (d) any work or service which forms part of normal civic obligations.

Article 5   Right to liberty and security
   1. Everyone has the right to liberty and security of person. No one shall be deprived of his liberty save in the following cases and in accordance with a procedure prescribed by law:

(a) the lawful detention of a person after conviction by a competent court;

(b) the lawful arrest or detention of a person for non-compliance with the lawful order of a court or in order to secure the fulfilment of any obligation prescribed by law;

(c) the lawful arrest or detention of a person effected for the purpose of bringing him before the competent legal authority on reasonable suspicion of having committed an offence or when it is reasonably considered necessary to prevent his committing an offence or fleeing after having done so;

(d) the detention of a minor by lawful order for the purpose of educational supervision or his lawful detention for the purpose of bringing him before the competent legal authority.

(e) the lawful detention of persons for the prevention of the spreading of infectious diseases, of persons of unsound mind, alcoholics or drug addicts or vagrants;

(f) the lawful arrest or detention of a person to prevent his effecting an unauthorised entry into the country or of a person against whom action is being taken with a view to deportation or extradition.

2. Everyone who is arrested shall be informed promptly, in a language which he understands, of the reasons for his arrest and of any charge against him.

3. Everyone arrested or detained in accordance with the provisions of paragraph 1(c) of this Article shall be brought promptly before a judge or other officer authorised by law to exercise judicial power and shall be entitled to trial within a reasonable time or to release pending trial. Release may be conditioned by guarantees to appear for trial.

4. Everyone who is deprived of his liberty by arrest or detention shall be entitled to take proceedings by which the lawfulness of his detention shall be decided speedily by a court and his release ordered if the detention is not lawful.

5. Everyone who has been the victim of arrest or detention in contravention of the provisions of this Article shall have an enforceable right to compensation.

Article 6   Right to a fair trial

1. In the determination of his civil rights and obligations or of any criminal charge against him, everyone is entitled to a fair and public hearing within a reasonable time by an independent and impartial tribunal established by law. Judgment shall be pronounced publicly but the press and public may be excluded from all or part of the trial in the interest of morals, public order or national security in a democratic society, where the interests of juveniles or the protection of the private life of the parties so require, or to the extent strictly necessary in the opinion of the court in special circumstances where publicity would prejudice the interests of justice.

2. Everyone charged with a criminal offence shall be presumed innocent until proved guilty according to law.

3. Everyone charged with a criminal offence has the following minimum rights:

(a) to be informed promptly, in a language which he understands and in detail, of the nature and cause of the accusation against him;

(b) to have adequate time and facilities for the preparation of his defence;

(c) to defend himself in person or through legal assistance of his own choosing or, if he has not sufficient means to pay for legal assistance, to be given it free when the interests of justice so require;

(d) to examine or have examined witnesses against him and to obtain the attendance and examination of witnesses on his behalf under the same conditions as witnesses against him;

(e) to have the free assistance of an interpreter if he cannot understand or speak the language used in court.

Article 7   No punishment without law

1. No one shall be held guilty of any criminal offence on account of any act or omission which did not constitute a criminal offence under national or international law at the time

when it was committed. Nor shall a heavier penalty be imposed than the one that was applicable at the time the criminal offence was committed.

2. This Article shall not prejudice the trial and punishment of any person for any act or omission which, at the time when it was committed, was criminal according to the general principles of law recognised by civilised nations.

Article 8   Right to respect for private and family life

1. Everyone has the right to respect for his private and family life, his home and his correspondence.

2. There shall be no interference by a public authority with the exercise of this right except such as is in accordance with the law and is necessary in a democratic society in the interests of national security, public safety or the economic well-being of the country, for the prevention of disorder or crime, for the protection of health or morals, or for the protection of the rights and freedoms of others.

Article 9   Freedom of thought, conscience and religion

1. Everyone has the right to freedom of thought, conscience and religion; this right includes freedom to change his religion or belief and freedom, either alone or in community with others and in public or private, to manifest his religion or belief, in worship, teaching, practice and observance.

2. Freedom to manifest one's religion or beliefs shall be subject only to such limitations as are prescribed by law and are necessary in a democratic society in the interests of public safety, for the protection of public order, health or morals, or for the protection of the rights and freedoms of others.

Article 10   Freedom of expression

1. Everyone has the right to freedom of expression. This right shall include freedom to hold opinions and to receive and impart information and ideas without interference by public authority and regardless of frontiers. This Article shall not prevent States from requiring the licensing of broadcasting, television or cinema enterprises.

2. The exercise of these freedoms, since it carries with it duties and responsibilities, may be subject to such formalities, conditions, restrictions or penalties as are prescribed by law and are necessary in a democratic society, in the interests of national security, territorial integrity or public safety, for the prevention of disorder or crime, for the protection of health or morals, for the protection of the reputation or rights of others, for preventing the disclosure of information received in confidence, or for maintaining the authority and impartiality of the judiciary.

Article 11   Freedom of assembly and association

1. Everyone has the right to freedom of peaceful assembly and to freedom of association with others, including the right to form and to join trade unions for the protection of his interests.

2. No restrictions shall be placed on the exercise of these rights other than such as are prescribed by law and are necessary in a democratic society in the interests of national security or public safety, for the prevention of disorder or crime, for the protection of health or morals or for the protection of the rights and freedoms of others. This Article shall not prevent the imposition of lawful restrictions on the exercise of these rights by members of the armed forces, of the police or of the administration of the State.

Article 12   Right to marry

Men and women of marriageable age have the right to marry and to found a family, according to the national laws governing the exercise of this right.

Article 14   Prohibition of discrimination

The enjoyment of the rights and freedoms set forth in this Convention shall be secured without discrimination on any ground such as sex, race, colour, language, religion, political or other opinion, national or social origin, association with a national minority, property, birth or other status.

Article 16 Restrictions on political activity of aliens
Nothing in Articles 10, 11 and 14 shall be regarded as preventing the High Contracting Parties from imposing restrictions on the political activity of aliens.

Article 17 Prohibition of abuse of rights
Nothing in this Convention may be interpreted as implying for any State, group or person any right to engage in any activity or perform any act aimed at the destruction of any of the rights and freedoms set forth herein or at their limitation to a greater extent than is provided for in the Convention.

Article 18 Limitation on use of restrictions on rights
The restrictions permitted under this Convention to the said rights and freedoms shall not be applied for any purpose other than those for which they have been prescribed.

PART II   THE FIRST PROTOCOL

Article 1 Protection of property
Every natural or legal person is entitled to the peaceful enjoyment of his possessions. No one shall be deprived of his possessions except in the public interest and subject to the conditions provided for by law and by the general principles of international law. The preceding pro-visions shall not, however, in any way impair the right of a State to enforce such laws as it deems necessary to control the use of property in accordance with the general interest or to secure the payment of taxes or other contributions or penalties.

Article 2 Right to education
No person shall be denied the right to education. In the exercise of any functions which it assumes in relation to education and to teaching, the State shall respect the right of parents to ensure such education and teaching in conformity with their own religious and philo-sophical convictions.

Article 3 Right to free elections
The High Contracting Parties undertake to hold free elections at reasonable intervals by secret ballot, under conditions which will ensure the free expression of the opinion of the people in the choice of the legislature.

[PART III   ARTICLE 1 OF THE THIRTEENTH PROTOCOL

Abolition   of the death penalty
The death penalty shall be abolished. No one shall be condemned to such penalty or executed.]

Late Payment of Commercial Debts (Interest) Act 1998
(1998, c. 20)

PART I   STATUTORY INTEREST ON QUALIFYING DEBTS

1 Statutory interest
    (1) It is an implied term in a contract to which this Act applies that any qualifying debt created by the contract carries simple interest subject to and in accordance with this Part.

(2) Interest carried under that implied term (in this Act referred to as "statutory interest") shall be treated, for the purposes of any rule of law or enactment (other than this Act) relating to interest on debts, in the same way as interest carried under an express contract term.

(3) This Part has effect subject to Part II (which in certain circumstances permits contract terms to oust or vary the right to statutory interest that would otherwise be conferred by virtue of the term implied by subsection (1)).

2 Contracts to which Act applies

(1) This Act applies to a contract for the supply of goods or services where the purchaser and the supplier are each acting in the course of a business, other than an excepted contract.

(2) In this Act "contract for the supply of goods or services" means—

(a) a contract of sale of goods; or

(b) a contract (other than a contract of sale of goods) by which a person does any, or any combination, of the things mentioned in subsection (3) for a consideration that is (or includes) a money consideration.

(3) Those things are—

(a) transferring or agreeing to transfer to another the property in goods;

(b) bailing or agreeing to bail goods to another by way of hire or, in Scotland, hiring or agreeing to hire goods to another; and

(c) agreeing to carry out a service.

(4) For the avoidance of doubt a contract of service or apprenticeship is not a contract for the supply of goods or services.

(5) The following are excepted contracts—

(a) a consumer credit agreement;

(b) a contract intended to operate by way of mortgage, pledge, charge or other security; and

[...]

(7) In this section—

"business" includes a profession and the activities of any government department or local or public authority;

"consumer credit agreement" has the same meaning as in the Consumer Credit Act 1974;

"contract of sale of goods" and "goods" have the same meaning as in the Sale of Goods Act 1979;

["government department" includes any part of the Scottish Administration;]

"property in goods" means the general property in them and not merely a special property.

3 Qualifying debts

(1) A debt created by virtue of an obligation under a contract to which this Act applies to pay the whole or any part of the contract price is a "qualifying debt" for the purposes of this Act, unless (when created) the whole of the debt is prevented from carrying statutory interest by this section.

(2) A debt does not carry statutory interest if or to the extent that it consists of a sum to which a right to interest or to charge interest applies by virtue of any enactment (other than section 1 of this Act).

This subsection does not prevent a sum from carrying statutory interest by reason of the fact that a court, arbitrator or arbiter would, apart from this Act, have power to award interest on it.

(3) A debt does not carry (and shall be treated as never having carried) statutory interest if or to the extent that a right to demand interest on it, which exists by virtue of any rule of law, is exercised.

[...]

4   Period for which statutory interest runs

(1) Statutory interest runs in relation to a qualifying debt in accordance with this section (unless section 5 applies).

(2) Statutory interest starts to run on the day after the relevant day for the debt, at the rate prevailing under section 6 at the end of the relevant day.

(3) Where the supplier and the purchaser agree a date for payment of the debt (that is, the day on which the debt is to be created by the contract), that is the relevant day unless the debt relates to an obligation to make an advance payment.

A date so agreed may be a fixed one or may depend on the happening of an event or the failure of an event to happen.

(4) Where the debt relates to an obligation to make an advance payment, the relevant day is the day on which the debt is treated by section 11 as having been created.

(5) In any other case, the relevant day is the last day of the period of 30 days beginning with—

> (a) the day on which the obligation of the supplier to which the debt relates is performed; or
>
> (b) the day on which the purchaser has notice of the amount of the debt or (where the amountis unascertained) the sum which the supplier claims is the amount of the debt, whichever is the later.

(6) Where the debt is created by virtue of an obligation to pay a sum due in respect of a period of hire of goods, subsection (5)(a) has effect as if it referred to the last day of that period.

(7) Statutory interest ceases to run when the interest would cease to run if it were carried under an express contract term.

(8) In this section "advance payment" has the same meaning as in section 11.

5   Remission of statutory interest

(1) This section applies where, by reason of any conduct of the supplier, the interests of justice require that statutory interest should be remitted in whole or part in respect of a period for which it would otherwise run in relation to a qualifying debt.

(2) If the interests of justice require that the supplier should receive no statutory interest for a period, statutory interest shall not run for that period.

(3) If the interests of justice require that the supplier should receive statutory interest at a reduced rate for a period, statutory interest shall run at such rate as meets the justice of the case for that period.

(4) Remission of statutory interest under this section may be required—

> (a) by reason of conduct at any time (whether before or after the time at which the debt is created); and
>
> (b) for the whole period for which statutory interest would otherwise run or for one or more parts of that period.

(5) In this section "conduct" includes any act or omission.

[5A   Compensation arising out of late payment

(1) Once statutory interest begins to run in relation to a qualifying debt, the supplier shall be entitled to a fixed sum (in addition to the statutory interest on the debt).

(2) That sum shall be—

> (a) for a debt less than £1,000, the sum of £40;
>
> (b) for a debt of £1,000 or more, but less than £10,000, the sum of £70;
>
> (c) for a debt of £10,000 or more, the sum of £100.

(3) The obligation to pay an additional fixed sum under this section in respect of a qualifying debt shall be treated as part of the term implied by section 1(1) in the contract creating the debt.]

6   Rate of statutory interest

(1) The Secretary of State shall by order made with the consent of the Treasury set the rate of statutory interest by prescribing—

    (a) a formula for calculating the rate of statutory interest; or

    (b) the rate of statutory interest.

(2) Before making such an order the Secretary of State shall, among other things, consider the extent to which it may be desirable to set the rate so as to—

    (a) protect suppliers whose financial position makes them particularly vulnerable if their qualifying debts are paid late; and

    (b) deter generally the late payment of qualifying debts.

PART II   CONTRACT TERMS RELATING TO LATE PAYMENT OF QUALIFYING DEBTS

7   Purpose of Part II

(1) This Part deals with the extent to which the parties to a contract to which this Act applies may by reference to contract terms oust or vary the right to statutory interest that would otherwise apply when a qualifying debt created by the contract (in this Part referred to as "the debt") is not paid.

(2) This Part applies to contract terms agreed before the debt is created; after that time the parties are free to agree terms dealing with the debt.

(3) This Part has effect without prejudice to any other ground which may affect the validity of a contract term.

8   Circumstances where statutory interest may be ousted or varied

(1) Any contract terms are void to the extent that they purport to exclude the right to statutory interest in relation to the debt, unless there is a substantial contractual remedy for late payment of the debt.

(2) Where the parties agree a contractual remedy for late payment of the debt that is a substantial remedy, statutory interest is not carried by the debt (unless they agree otherwise).

(3) The parties may not agree to vary the right to statutory interest in relation to the debt unless either the right to statutory interest as varied or the overall remedy for late payment of the debt is a substantial remedy.

(4) Any contract terms are void to the extent that they purport to—

    (a) confer a contractual right to interest that is not a substantial remedy for late payment of the debt, or

    (b) vary the right to statutory interest so as to provide for a right to statutory interest that is not a substantial remedy for late payment of the debt,

unless the overall remedy for late payment of the debt is a substantial remedy.

(5) Subject to this section, the parties are free to agree contract terms which deal with the consequences of late payment of the debt.

9   Meaning of "substantial remedy"

(1) A remedy for the late payment of the debt shall be regarded as a substantial remedy unless—

    (a) the remedy is insufficient either for the purpose of compensating the supplier for late payment or for deterring late payment; and

    (b) it would not be fair or reasonable to allow the remedy to be relied on to oust or (as the case may be) to vary the right to statutory interest that would otherwise apply in relation to the debt.

(2) In determining whether a remedy is not a substantial remedy, regard shall be had to all the relevant circumstances at the time the terms in question are agreed.

(3) In determining whether subsection (1)(b) applies, regard shall be had (without prejudice to the generality of subsection (2)) to the following matters—

(a) the benefits of commercial certainty;
(b) the strength of the bargaining positions of the parties relative to each other;
(c) whether the term was imposed by one party to the detriment of the other (whether by the use of standard terms or otherwise); and
(d) whether the supplier received an inducement to agree to the term.

10 Interpretation of Part II

(1) In this Part—

"contract term" means a term of the contract creating the debt or any other contract term binding the parties (or either of them);

"contractual remedy" means a contractual right to interest or any contractual remedy other than interest;

"contractual right to interest" includes a reference to a contractual right to charge interest;

"overall remedy", in relation to the late payment of the debt, means any combination of a contractual right to interest, a varied right to statutory interest or a contractual remedy other than interest;

"substantial remedy" shall be construed in accordance with section 9.

(2) In this Part a reference (however worded) to contract terms which vary the right to statutory interest is a reference to terms altering in any way the effect of Part I in relation to the debt (for example by postponing the time at which interest starts to run or by imposing conditions on the right to interest).

(3) In this Part a reference to late payment of the debt is a reference to late payment of the sum due when the debt is created (excluding any part of that sum which is prevented from carrying statutory interest by section 3).

PART III   GENERAL AND SUPPLEMENTARY

11 Treatment of advance payments of the contract price

(1) A qualifying debt created by virtue of an obligation to make an advance payment shall be treated for the purposes of this Act as if it was created on the day mentioned in subsection (3), (4) or (5) (as the case may be).

(2) In this section "advance payment" means a payment falling due before the obligation of the supplier to which the whole contract price relates ("the supplier's obligation") is performed, other than a payment of a part of the contract price that is due in respect of any part performance of that obligation and payable on or after the day on which that part performance is completed.

(3) Where the advance payment is the whole contract price, the debt shall be treated as created on the day on which the supplier's obligation is performed.

(4) Where the advance payment is a part of the contract price, but the sum is not due in respect of any part performance of the supplier's obligation, the debt shall be treated as created on the day on which the supplier's obligation is performed.

(5) Where the advance payment is a part of the contract price due in respect of any part performance of the supplier's obligation, but is payable before that part performance is completed, the debt shall be treated as created on the day on which the relevant part performance is completed.

(6) Where the debt is created by virtue of an obligation to pay a sum due in respect of a period of hire of goods, this section has effect as if—

(a) references to the day on which the supplier's obligation is performed were references to the last day of that period; and
(b) references to part performance of that obligation were references to part of that period.

(7) For the purposes of this section an obligation to pay the whole outstanding balance of the contract price shall be regarded as an obligation to pay the whole contract price and not as an obligation to pay a part of the contract price.

13   Assignments, etc.

(1) The operation of this Act in relation to a qualifying debt is not affected by—

    (a) any change in the identity of the parties to the contract creating the debt; or

    (b) the passing of the right to be paid the debt, or the duty to pay it (in whole or in part) to a person other than the person who is the original creditor or the original debtor when the debt is created.

(2) Any reference in this Act to the supplier or the purchaser is a reference to the person who is for the time being the supplier or the purchaser or, in relation to a time after the debt in question has been created, the person who is for the time being the creditor or the debtor, as the case may be.

(3) Where the right to be paid part of a debt passes to a person other than the person who is the original creditor when the debt is created, any reference in this Act to a debt shall be construed as (or, if the context so requires, as including) a reference to part of a debt.

(4) A reference in this section to the identity of the parties to a contract changing, or to a right or duty passing, is a reference to it changing or passing by assignment or assignation, by operation of law or otherwise.

14   Contract terms relating to the date for payment of the contract price

(1) This section applies to any contract term which purports to have the effect of postponing the time at which a qualifying debt would otherwise be created by a contract to which this Act applies.

(2) Sections 3(2)(b) and 17(1)(b) of the Unfair Contract Terms Act 1977 (no reliance to be placed on certain contract terms) shall apply in cases where such a contract term is not contained in written standard terms of the purchaser as well as in cases where the term is contained in such standard terms.

(3) In this section "contract term" has the same meaning as in section 10(1).

15   Orders and regulations

(1) Any power to make an order or regulations under this Act is exercisable by statutory instrument.

(2) Any statutory instrument containing an order or regulations under this Act, other than an order under section 17(2), shall be subject to annulment in pursuance of a resolution of either House of Parliament.

16   Interpretation

(1) In this Act—

"contract for the supply of goods or services" has the meaning given in section 2(2);

"contract price" means the price in a contract of sale of goods or the money consideration referred to in section 2(2)(b) in any other contract for the supply of goods or services;

"purchaser" means (subject to section 13(2)) the buyer in a contract of sale or the person who contracts with the supplier in any other contract for the supply of goods or services;

"qualifying debt" means a debt falling within section 3(1);

"statutory interest" means interest carried by virtue of the term implied by section 1(1); and

"supplier" means (subject to section 13(2)) the seller in a contract of sale of goods or the person who does one or more of the things mentioned in section 2(3) in any other contract for the supply of goods or services.

(2) In this Act any reference (however worded) to an agreement or to contract terms includes a reference to both express and implied terms (including terms established by a course of dealing or by such usage as binds the parties).

17 Short title, commencement and extent
(5) This Act extends to Northern Ireland.

National Minimum Wage Act 1998
(1998, c. 39)

1 Workers to be paid at least the national minimum wage
(1) A person who qualifies for the national minimum wage shall be remunerated by his employer in respect of his work in any pay reference period at a rate which is not less than the national minimum wage.

Scotland Act 1998
(1998, c. 46)

1 The Scottish Parliament
(1) There shall be a Scottish Parliament.

41 Defamatory statements
(1) For the purposes of the law of defamation—
    (a) any statement made in proceedings of the Parliament, and
    (b) the publication under the authority of the Parliament of any statement,
shall be absolutely privileged.
(2) In subsection (1), "statement" has the same meaning as in the Defamation Act 1996.

99 Rights and liabilities of the Crown in different capacities
(1) Rights and liabilities may arise between the Crown in right of Her Majesty's Government in the United Kingdom and the Crown in right of the Scottish Administration by virtue of a contract, by operation of law or by virtue of an enactment as they may arise between subjects.
(2) Property and liabilities may be transferred between the Crown in one of those capacities and the Crown in the other capacity as they may be transferred between subjects; and they may together create, vary or extinguish any property or liability as subjects may.
(3) Proceedings in respect of—
    (a) any property or liabilities to which the Crown in one of those capacities is entitled or subject under subsection (1) or (2), or
    (b) the exercise of, or failure to exercise, any function exercisable by an office-holder of the Crown in one of those capacities,
may be instituted by the Crown in either capacity; and the Crown in the other capacity may be a separate party in the proceedings.
(4) This section applies to a unilateral obligation as it applies to a contract.

Contracts (Rights of Third Parties) Act 1999
(1999, c. 31)

1 Right of third party to enforce contractual term
(1) Subject to the provisions of this Act, a person who is not a party to a contract (a "third party") may in his own right enforce a term of the contract if—

(a) the contract expressly provides that he may, or

(b) subject to subsection (2), the term purports to confer a benefit on him.

(2) Subsection (1)(b) does not apply if on a proper construction of the contract it appears that the parties did not intend the term to be enforceable by the third party.

(3) The third party must be expressly identified in the contract by name, as a member of a class or as answering a particular description but need not be in existence when the contract is entered into.

(4) This section does not confer a right on a third party to enforce a term of a contract otherwise than subject to and in accordance with any other relevant terms of the contract.

(5) For the purpose of exercising his right to enforce a term of the contract, there shall be available to the third party any remedy that would have been available to him in an action for breach of contract if he had been a party to the contract (and the rules relating to damages, injunctions, specific performance and other relief shall apply accordingly).

(6) Where a term of a contract excludes or limits liability in relation to any matter references in this Act to the third party enforcing the term shall be construed as references to his availing himself of the exclusion or limitation.

(7) In this Act, in relation to a term of a contract which is enforceable by a third party—

"the promisor" means the party to the contract against whom the term is enforceable by the third party, and

"the promisee" means the party to the contract by whom the term is enforceable against the promisor.

2   Variation and rescission of contract

(1) Subject to the provisions of this section, where a third party has a right under section 1 to enforce a term of the contract, the parties to the contract may not, by agreement, rescind the contract, or vary it in such a way as to extinguish or alter his entitlement under that right, without his consent if—

(a) the third party has communicated his assent to the term to the promisor,

(b) the promisor is aware that the third party has relied on the term, or

(c) the promisor can reasonably be expected to have foreseen that the third party would rely on the term and the third party has in fact relied on it.

(2) The assent referred to in subsection (1)(a)—

(a) may be by words or conduct, and

(b) if sent to the promisor by post or other means, shall not be regarded as communicated to the promisor until received by him.

(3) Subsection (1) is subject to any express term of the contract under which—

(a) the parties to the contract may by agreement rescind or vary the contract without the consent of the third party, or

(b) the consent of the third party is required in circumstances specified in the contract instead of those set out in subsection (1)(a) to (c).

(4) Where the consent of a third party is required under subsection (1) or (3), the court or arbitral tribunal may, on the application of the parties to the contract, dispense with his consent if satisfied—

(a) that his consent cannot be obtained because his whereabouts cannot reasonably be ascertained, or

(b) that he is mentally incapable of giving his consent.

(5) The court or arbitral tribunal may, on the application of the parties to a contract, dispense with any consent that may be required under subsection (1)(c) if satisfied that it cannot reasonably be ascertained whether or not the third party has in fact relied on the term.

(6) If the court or arbitral tribunal dispenses with a third party's consent, it may impose such conditions as it thinks fit, including a condition requiring the payment of compensation to the third party.

(7) The jurisdiction conferred on the court by subsections (4) to (6) is exercisable by both the High Court and a county court.

3   Defences etc. available to promisor

(1) Subsections (2) to (5) apply where, in reliance on section 1, proceedings for the enforcement of a term of a contract are brought by a third party.

(2) The promisor shall have available to him by way of defence or set-off any matter that—

   (a) arises from or in connection with the contract and is relevant to the term, and
   (b) would have been available to him by way of defence or set-off if the proceedings had been brought by the promisee.

(3) The promisor shall also have available to him by way of defence or set-off any matter if—

   (a) an express term of the contract provides for it to be available to him in proceedings brought by the third party, and
   (b) it would have been available to him by way of defence or set-off if the proceedings had been brought by the promisee.

(4) The promisor shall also have available to him—

   (a) by way of defence or set-off any matter, and
   (b) by way of counterclaim any matter not arising from the contract, that would have been available to him by way of defence or set-off or, as the case maybe, by way of counterclaim against the third party if the third party had been a party to the contract.

(5) Subsections (2) and (4) are subject to any express term of the contract as to the matters that are not to be available to the promisor by way of defence, set-off or counterclaim.

(6) Where in any proceedings brought against him a third party seeks in reliance on section 1 to enforce a term of a contract (including, in particular, a term purporting to exclude or limit liability), he may not do so if he could not have done so (whether by reason of any particular circumstances relating to him or otherwise) had he been a party to the contract.

4   Enforcement of contract by promisee

Section 1 does not affect any right of the promisee to enforce any term of the contract.

5   Protection of promisor from double liability

Where under section 1 a term of a contract is enforceable by a third party, and the promisee has recovered from the promisor a sum in respect of—

   (a) the third party's loss in respect of the term, or
   (b) the expense to the promisee of making good to the third party the default of the promisor,

then, in any proceedings brought in reliance on that section by the third party, the court or arbitral tribunal shall reduce any award to the third party to such extent as it thinks appropriate to take account of the sum recovered by the promisee.

6   Exceptions

(1) Section 1 confers no rights on a third party in the case of a contract on a bill of exchange, promissory note or other negotiable instrument.

(2) Section 1 confers no rights on a third party in the case of any contract binding on a company and its members under section 14 of the Companies Act 1985.

[(2A) Section 1 confers no rights on a third party in the case of any incorporation document of a limited liability partnership or any limited liability partnership agreement as defined in the Limited Liability Partnerships Regulations 2001 (S.I. No. 2001/1090).]

(3) Section 1 confers no right on a third party to enforce—

(a) any term of a contract of employment against an employee,

(b) any term of a worker's contract against a worker (including a home worker), or

(c) any term of a relevant contract against an agency worker.

(4) In subsection (3)—

(a) "contract of employment", "employee", "worker's contract", and "worker" have the meaning given by section 54 of the National Minimum Wage Act 1998,

(b) "home worker" has the meaning given by section 35(2) of that Act,

(c) "agency worker" has the same meaning as in section 34(1) of that Act, and

(d) "relevant contract" means a contract entered into, in a case where section 34 of that Act applies, by the agency worker as respects work falling within subsection (1)(a) of that section.

(5) Section 1 confers no rights on a third party in the case of—

(a) a contract for the carriage of goods by sea, or

(b) a contract for the carriage of goods by rail or road, or for the carriage of cargo by air, which is subject to the rules of the appropriate international transport convention,

except that a third party may in reliance on that section avail himself of an exclusion or limitation of liability in such a contract.

(6) In subsection (5) "contract for the carriage of goods by sea" means a contract of carriage—

(a) contained in or evidenced by a bill of lading, sea waybill or a corresponding electronic transaction, or

(b) under or for the purposes of which there is given an undertaking which is contained in a ship's delivery order or a corresponding electronic transaction.

(7) For the purposes of subsection (6)—

(a) "bill of lading", "sea waybill" and "ship's delivery order" have the same meaning as in the Carriage of Goods by Sea Act 1992, and

(b) a corresponding electronic transaction is a transaction within section 1(5) of that Act which corresponds to the issue, indorsement, delivery or transfer of a bill of lading, sea waybill or ship's delivery order.

(8) In subsection (5) "the appropriate international transport convention" means—

(a) in relation to a contract for the carriage of goods by rail, the Convention which has the force of law in the United Kingdom under [regulation 3 of the Railways (Convention on International Carriage by Rail) Regulations 2005],

(b) in relation to a contract for the carriage of goods by road, the Convention which has the force of law in the United Kingdom under section 1 of the Carriage of Goods by Road Act 1965, and

(c) in relation to a contract for the carriage of cargo by air—

(i) the Convention which has the force of law in the United Kingdom under section 1 of the Carriage by Air Act 1961, or

(ii) the Convention which has the force of law under section 1 of the Carriage by Air (Supplementary Provisions) Act 1962, or

(iii) either of the amended Conventions set out in Part B of Schedule 2 or 3 to the Carriage by Air Acts (Application of Provisions) Order 1967.

7 Supplementary provisions relating to third party

(1) Section 1 does not affect any right or remedy of a third party that exists or is available apart from this Act.

(2) Section 2(2) of the Unfair Contract Terms Act 1977 (restriction on exclusion etc. of liability for negligence) shall not apply where the negligence consists of the breach of an

obligation arising from a term of a contract and the person seeking to enforce it is a third party acting in reliance on section 1.

(3) In sections 5 and 8 of the Limitation Act 1980 the references to an action founded on a simple contract and an action upon a specialty shall respectively include references to an action brought in reliance on section 1 relating to a simple contract and an action brought in reliance on that section relating to a specialty.

(4) A third party shall not, by virtue of section 1(5) or 3(4) or (6), be treated as a party to the contract for the purposes of any other Act (or any instrument made under any other Act).

8   Arbitration provisions

(1) Where—

   (a) a right under section 1 to enforce a term ("the substantive term") is subject to a term providing for the submission of disputes to arbitration ("the arbitration agreement"), and

   (b) the arbitration agreement is an agreement in writing for the purposes of Part I of the Arbitration Act 1996,

the third party shall be treated for the purposes of that Act as a party to the arbitration agreement as regards disputes between himself and the promisor relating to the enforcement of the substantive term by the third party.

(2) Where—

   (a) a third party has a right under section 1 to enforce a term providing for one or more descriptions of dispute between the third party and the promisor to be submitted to arbitration ("the arbitration agreement"),

   (b) the arbitration agreement is an agreement in writing for the purposes of Part I of the Arbitration Act 1996, and

   (c) the third party does not fall to be treated under subsection (1) as a party to the arbitration agreement,

the third party shall, if he exercises the right, be treated for the purposes of that Act as a party to the arbitration agreement in relation to the matter with respect to which the right is exercised, and be treated as having been so immediately before the exercise of the right.

9   Northern Ireland

(1) In its application to Northern Ireland, this Act has effect with the modifications specified in subsections (2) and (3).

(2) In section 6(2), for "section 14 of the Companies Act 1985" there is substituted "Article 25 of the Companies (Northern Ireland) Order 1986".

(3) In section 7, for subsection (3) there is substituted—

"(3) In Articles 4(a) and 15 of the Limitation (Northern Ireland) Order 1989, the references to an action founded on a simple contract and an action upon an instrument under seal shall respectively include references to an action brought in reliance on section 1 relating to a simple contract and an action brought in reliance on that section relating to a contract under seal.".

10   Short title, commencement and extent

(1) This Act may be cited as the Contracts (Rights of Third Parties) Act 1999.

(2) This Act comes into force on the day on which it is passed but, subject to subsection (3), does not apply in relation to a contract entered into before the end of the period of six months beginning with that day.

(3) The restriction in subsection (2) does not apply in relation to a contract which—

   (a) is entered into on or after the day on which this Act is passed, and

   (b) expressly provides for the application of this Act.

(4) This Act extends as follows—

   (a) section 9 extends to Northern Ireland only;

   (b) the remaining provisions extend to England and Wales and Northern Ireland only.

EXPLANATORY NOTES

1. These explanatory notes . . . have been prepared by the Lord Chancellor's Department in order to assist the reader in understanding the Act. They do not form part of the Act and have not been endorsed by Parliament.

Section 3:   Defences etc. available to promisor

15. *Section 3* enables the promisor, in a claim by the third party, to rely on any defence or set-off arising out of the contract and relevant to the term being enforced, which would have been available to him had the claim been by the promisee. He may also rely on any defence or set-off, or make any counterclaim, where this would have been possible had the third party been a party to the contract.

16. *Subsection (2)* can be illustrated as follows—

(I) a third party can no more enforce a void, discharged or unenforceable contract than a promisee could;

(II) P1 (the promisor) and P2 (the promisee) contract that P2 will sell goods to P1, who will pay the contract price to P3 (the third party). In breach of contract, P2 delivers goods that are not of the standard contracted for. In an action for the price by P3 (just as in an action for the price by P2) P1 is entitled to reduce or extinguish the price by reason of the damages for breach of contract.

17. *Subsection (3)* can be illustrated as follows—
P1 and P2 contract that P1 will pay P3 if P2 transfers his car to P1. P2 owes P1 money under a wholly unrelated contract. P1 and P2 agree to an express term in the contract which provides that P1 can raise against a claim by P3 any matter which would have given P1 a defence or set-off to a claim by P2.

18. *Subsection (4)* makes it clear that the promisor also has available any defence or setoff, and any counterclaim not arising from the contract, which is specific to the third party. It can be illustrated as follows.

(I) P1 contracts with P2 to pay P3 £1000. P3 already owes P1 £600. P1 has a set-off to P3's claim so that P1 is only bound to pay P3 £400.

(II) P3 induced P1 to enter into the contract with P2 by misrepresentation, but P2 has no actual or constructive notice of that misrepresentation. P1 may have a defence (or a counterclaim for damages) against P3 which would not have been available had the action been brought by P2.

19. *Subsection (5)* makes subsections (2) and (4) subject to any express term of the contract which narrows the defences or set-offs available under section 3(2) or narrows the defences, set-offs or counterclaims available under section 3(4). For example—

(I) in relation to subsection (2), P2 agrees with P1 to purchase a painting, the painting to be delivered to P3, who is expressly given a right to enforce the delivery obligation. P2 owes P1 considerable sums for other art works purchased. P2 wishes to ensure that P3's right is not affected. P1 and P2 expressly agree that P1 may not raise against P3 defences and set-offs that would have been available to P1 in an action by P2.

(II) in relation to subsection (4), P1 agrees with P2 to pay £5000 to P3 if P2 will transfer a number of cases of wine to P1. P3 is in dispute with P1 over a prior contract and P1 alleges that P3 owes P1 money. P2 is concerned that P1 may seek to withhold part of the £5000 payable to P3 by raising a set-off or counterclaim against P3 in relation to the prior contract. Consequently P1 and P2 include an express term that P1 may raise no defences, set-offs or counterclaims of any nature whatever against a claim by P3 to enforce P1's obligation to pay the £5000.

20. *Subsection (6)* ensures that an analogous approach to that set out in subsections (2) to (5) applies where the proceedings are brought against the third party and he seeks to avail himself of, for example, an exclusion section.

Welfare Reform and Pensions Act 1999
(1999, c. 30)

68 Certain overpayments of benefit not to be recoverable

(1) An overpayment to which this section applies shall not be recoverable from the payee, whether by the Secretary of State or a local authority, under any provision made by or under Part III of the Administration Act (overpayments and adjustments of benefit).

(2) This section applies to an overpayment if—

(a) it is in respect of a qualifying benefit;

(b) it is referable to a decision given on a review that there has been an alteration in the relevant person's condition, being a decision to which effect is required to be given as from a date earlier than that on which it was given;

(c) the decision was given before 1 June 1999; and

(d) the overpayment is not excluded by virtue of subsection (6).

(3) In subsection (2)(b) the reference to a decision on a review that there has been an alteration in the relevant person's condition is a reference to a decision so given that that person's physical or mental condition either was at the time when the original decision was given, or has subsequently become, different from that on which that decision was based, with the result—

(a) that he did not at that time, or (as the case may be) has subsequently ceased to, meet any of the conditions contained in the following provisions of the Contributions and Benefits Act, namely—

(i)   section 64 (attendance allowance),

(ii) section 72(1) or (2) (care component of disability living allowance), and

(iii) section 73(1) or (2) (mobility component of that allowance); or

(b) that he was at that time, or (as the case may be) has subsequently become, capable of work in accordance with regulations made under section 171C(2) of that Act (the all work test).

(4) For the purposes of this section "qualifying benefit" means—

(a) attendance allowance;

(b) disability living allowance;

(c) any benefit awarded wholly or partly by reason of a person being (or being treated as being) in receipt of a component (at any rate) of disability living allowance or in receipt of attendance allowance;

(d) incapacity benefit;

(e) any benefit (other than incapacity benefit) awarded wholly or partly by reason of a person being (or being treated as being) incapable of work; or

(f) any benefit awarded wholly or partly by reason of a person being (or being treated as being) in receipt of any benefit falling within paragraph (c), (d) or (e).

(5) For the purposes of this section—

(a) "review" means a review taking place by virtue of section 25(1)(a) or (b), 30(2)(a) or (b) or 35(1)(a) or (b) of the Administration Act;

(b) "the relevant person", in relation to a review, means the person to whose entitlement to a qualifying benefit or to whose incapacity for work the review related; and

(c) "the original decision", in relation to a review, means the decision as to any such entitlement or incapacity to which the review related.

(6) An overpayment is excluded by virtue of this subsection if (before or after the passing of this Act)—

(a) the payee has agreed to pay a penalty in respect of the overpayment under section 115A of the Administration Act,

(b) the payee has been convicted of any offence (under section 111A or 112(1) or (1A) of that Act or otherwise) in connection with the overpayment, or

(c) proceedings have been instituted against the payee for such an offence and the proceedings have not been determined or abandoned.

(7) Nothing in this section applies to an overpayment to the extent that it was recovered from the payee (by any means) before 26 February 1999.

(8) In this section—

"benefit" includes any amount included in—

    (a) the applicable amount in relation to an income-related benefit (as defined by section 135(1) of the Contributions and Benefits Act), or

    (b) the applicable amount in relation to a jobseeker's allowance (as defined by section 4(5) of the Jobseekers Act 1995);

"income-related benefit" has the meaning given by section 123(1) of the Contributions and Benefits Act;

"overpayment" means an amount of benefit paid in excess of entitlement;

"the payee", in relation to an overpayment, means the person to whom the amount was paid.

91 Short title, general interpretation and Scottish devolution

(2) In this Act—

"the Administration Act" means the Social Security Administration Act 1992; . . .

Countryside and Rights of Way Act 2000
(2000, c. 37)

1 Principal definitions for Part I

(1) In this Part "access land" means any land which—

    (a) is shown as open country on a map in conclusive form issued by the appropriate countryside body for the purposes of this Part,

    (b) is shown on such a map as registered common land,

    (c) is registered common land in any area outside Inner London for which no such map relating to registered common land has been issued,

    (d) is situated more than 600 metres above sea level in any area for which no such map relating to open country has been issued, or

    (e) is dedicated for the purposes of this Part under section 16,

but does not (in any of those cases) include excepted land or land which is treated by section 15(1) as being accessible to the public apart from this Act.

2 Rights of public in relation to access land

(1) Any person is entitled by virtue of this subsection to enter and remain on any access land for the purposes of open-air recreation, if and so long as—

    (a) he does so without breaking or damaging any wall, fence, hedge, stile or gate, and

    (b) he observes the general restrictions in Schedule 2 and any other restrictions imposed in relation to the land under Chapter II.

(2) Subsection (1) has effect subject to subsections (3) and (4) and to the provisions of Chapter II.

(3) Subsection (1) does not entitle a person to enter or be on any land, or do anything on any land, in contravention of any prohibition contained in or having effect under any enactment, other than an enactment contained in a local or private Act.

(4) If a person becomes a trespasser on any access land by failing to comply with—

    (a) subsection (1)(a),

    (b) the general restrictions in Schedule 2, or

    (c) any other restrictions imposed in relation to the land under Chapter II, he may not, within 72 hours after leaving that land, exercise his right under subsection (1) to enter that land again or to enter other land in the same ownership.

12 Effect of right of access on rights and liabilities of owners

(1) The operation of section 2(1) in relation to any access land does not increase the liability, under any enactment not contained in this Act or under any rule of law, of a person interested in the access land or any adjoining land in respect of the state of the land or of things done or omitted to be done on the land.

(2) Any restriction arising under a covenant or otherwise as to the use of any access land shall have effect subject to the provisions of this Part, and any liability of a person interested in any access land in respect of such a restriction is limited accordingly.

(3) For the purposes of any enactment or rule of law as to the circumstances in which the dedication of a highway or the grant of an easement may be presumed, or may be established by prescription, the use by the public or by any person of a way across land in the exercise of the right conferred by section 2(1) is to be disregarded.

(4) The use of any land by the inhabitants of any locality for the purposes of open-air recreation in the exercise of the right conferred by section 2(1) is to be disregarded in determining whether the land has become a town or village green.

Electronic Communications Act 2000
(2000, c. 7)

7 Electronic signatures and related certificates

(1) In any legal proceedings—

    (a) an electronic signature incorporated into or logically associated with a particular electronic communication or particular electronic data, and

    (b) the certification by any person of such a signature,

shall each be admissible in evidence in relation to any question as to the authenticity of the communication or data or as to the integrity of the communication or data.

(2) For the purposes of this section an electronic signature is so much of anything in electronic form as—

    (a) is incorporated into or otherwise logically associated with any electronic communication or electronic data; and

    (b) purports to be so incorporated or associated for the purpose of being used in establishing the authenticity of the communication or data, the integrity of the communication or data, or both.

(3) For the purposes of this section an electronic signature incorporated into or associated with a particular electronic communication or particular electronic data is certified by any person if that person (whether before or after the making of the communication) has made a statement confirming that—

    (a) the signature,

    (b) a means of producing, communicating or verifying the signature, or

    (c) a procedure applied to the signature,

is (either alone or in combination with other factors) a valid means of establishing the authenticity of the communication or data, the integrity of the communication or data, or both.

8 Power to modify legislation

(1) Subject to subsection (3), the appropriate Minister may by order made by statutory instrument modify the provisions of—

    (a) any enactment or subordinate legislation, or

    (b) any scheme, licence, authorisation or approval issued, granted or given by or under any enactment or subordinate legislation,

in such manner as he may think fit for the purpose of authorising or facilitating the use of electronic communications or electronic storage (instead of other forms of communication or storage) for any purpose mentioned in subsection (2).

Finance Act 2000
(2000, c. 17)

Section 30   SCHEDULE 6

CLIMATE CHANGE LEVY

142 *Adjustment of contracts*

(1) Sub-paragraph (2) applies in the case of a contract for the supply of a taxable commodity if—

    (a) the contract is entered into before 1 April 2001 (whether before or after the passing of this Act) or at a time when supplies such as are provided for by the contract are not taxable supplies, but

    (b) supplies falling to be made under the contract will be, or become or will become, taxable supplies.

(2) The supplier of the commodity may unilaterally vary the contract by adjusting the price chargeable for any supply made under the contract if he does so for the purpose of passing on, to the person liable to pay for the supply, the burden (or any part of the burden) of the levy for which the supplier is liable to account on the supply.

(3) Sub-paragraph (4) applies in the case of a contract for the supply of a taxable commodity if it provides (whether as a result of a variation under sub-paragraph (2) or otherwise) for the passing on, to the person liable to pay for the supply, of the burden (or any part of the burden) of any levy for which the supplier is liable to account on the supply.

(4) The supplier of the commodity may unilaterally vary the contract by adjusting the price chargeable for any supply made under the contract if he does so for the purpose of giving effect (to any extent) to—

    (a) any change in the rate at which levy is charged on the supply;

    (b) levy ceasing to be chargeable on the supply.

(5) The powers conferred by this paragraph are in addition to any contractual powers.

Financial Services and Markets Act 2000
(2000, c. 8)

19 The general prohibition

(1) No person may carry on a regulated activity in the United Kingdom, or purport to do so, unless he is—

    (a) an authorised person; or

    (b) an exempt person.

(2) The prohibition is referred to in this Act as the general prohibition.

26 Agreements made by unauthorised persons

(1) An agreement made by a person in the course of carrying on a regulated activity in contravention of the general prohibition is unenforceable against the other party.

(2) The other party is entitled to recover—

    (a) any money or other property paid or transferred by him under the agreement; and

    (b) compensation for any loss sustained by him as a result of having parted with it.

(3) "Agreement" means an agreement—

    (a) made after this section comes into force; and

    (b) the making or performance of which constitutes, or is part of, the regulated activity in question.

(4) This section does not apply if the regulated activity is accepting deposits.

27 Agreements made through unauthorised persons

(1) An agreement made by an authorised person ("the provider")—

    (a) in the course of carrying on a regulated activity (not in contravention of the general prohibition), but

    (b) in consequence of something said or done by another person ("the third party") in the course of a regulated activity carried on by the third party in contravention of the general prohibition,

is unenforceable against the other party.

(2) The other party is entitled to recover—

    (a) any money or other property paid or transferred by him under the agreement; and

    (b) compensation for any loss sustained by him as a result of having parted with it.

(3) "Agreement" means an agreement—

    (a) made after this section comes into force; and

    (b) the making or performance of which constitutes, or is part of, the regulated activity in question carried on by the provider.

(4) This section does not apply if the regulated activity is accepting deposits.

28 Agreements made unenforceable by section 26 or 27

(1) This section applies to an agreement which is unenforceable because of section 26 or 27.

(2) The amount of compensation recoverable as a result of that section is—

    (a) the amount agreed by the parties; or

    (b) on the application of either party, the amount determined by the court.

(3) If the court is satisfied that it is just and equitable in the circumstances of the case, it may allow—

    (a) the agreement to be enforced; or

    (b) money and property paid or transferred under the agreement to be retained.

(4) In considering whether to allow the agreement to be enforced or (as the case may be) the money or property paid or transferred under the agreement to be retained the court must—

    (a) if the case arises as a result of section 26, have regard to the issue mentioned in subsection (5); or

    (b) if the case arises as a result of section 27, have regard to the issue mentioned in subsection (6).

(5) The issue is whether the person carrying on the regulated activity concerned reasonably believed that he was not contravening the general prohibition by making the agreement.

(6) The issue is whether the provider knew that the third party was (in carrying on the regulated activity) contravening the general prohibition.

(7) If the person against whom the agreement is unenforceable—

    (a) elects not to perform the agreement, or

    (b) as a result of this section, recovers money paid or other property transferred by him under the agreement,

he must repay any money and return any other property received by him under the agreement.

(8) If property transferred under the agreement has passed to a third party, a reference in section 26 or 27 or this section to that property is to be read as a reference to its value at the time of its transfer under the agreement.

(9) The commission of an authorisation offence does not make the agreement concerned illegal or invalid to any greater extent than is provided by section 26 or 27.

29 Accepting deposits in breach of general prohibition

(1) This section applies to an agreement between a person ("the depositor") and another person ("the deposit-taker") made in the course of the carrying on by the deposit-taker of accepting deposits in contravention of the general prohibition.

(2) If the depositor is not entitled under the agreement to recover without delay any money deposited by him, he may apply to the court for an order directing the deposit-taker to return the money to him.

(3) The court need not make such an order if it is satisfied that it would not be just and equitable for the money deposited to be returned, having regard to the issue mentioned in subsection (4).

(4) The issue is whether the deposit-taker reasonably believed that he was not contravening the general prohibition by making the agreement.

(5) "Agreement" means an agreement—

(a) made after this section comes into force; and

(b) the making or performance of which constitutes, or is part of, accepting deposits.

30   Enforceability of agreements resulting from unlawful communications

(1) In this section—

"unlawful communication" means a communication in relation to which there has been a contravention of section 21(1);

"controlled agreement" means an agreement the making or performance of which by either party constitutes a controlled activity for the purposes of that section; and

"controlled investment" has the same meaning as in section 21.

(2) If in consequence of an unlawful communication a person enters as a customer into a controlled agreement, it is unenforceable against him and he is entitled to recover—

(a) any money or other property paid or transferred by him under the agreement; and

(b) compensation for any loss sustained by him as a result of having parted with it.

(3) If in consequence of an unlawful communication a person exercises any rights conferred by a controlled investment, no obligation to which he is subject as a result of exercising them is enforceable against him and he is entitled to recover—

(a) any money or other property paid or transferred by him under the obligation; and

(b) compensation for any loss sustained by him as a result of having parted with it.

(4) But the court may allow—

(a) the agreement or obligation to be enforced, or

(b) money or property paid or transferred under the agreement or obligation to be retained,

if it is satisfied that it is just and equitable in the circumstances of the case.

(5) In considering whether to allow the agreement or obligation to be enforced or (as the case may be) the money or property paid or transferred under the agreement to be retained the court must have regard to the issues mentioned in subsections (6) and (7).

(6) If the applicant made the unlawful communication, the issue is whether he reasonably believed that he was not making such a communication.

(7) If the applicant did not make the unlawful communication, the issue is whether he knew that the agreement was entered into in consequence of such a communication.

(8) "Applicant" means the person seeking to enforce the agreement or obligation or retain the money or property paid or transferred.

(9) Any reference to making a communication includes causing a communication to be made.

(10) The amount of compensation recoverable as a result of subsection (2) or (3) is—

(a) the amount agreed between the parties; or

(b) on the application of either party, the amount determined by the court.

(11) If a person elects not to perform an agreement or an obligation which (by virtue of subsection (2) or (3)) is unenforceable against him, he must repay any money and return any other property received by him under the agreement.

(12) If (by virtue of subsection (2) or (3)) a person recovers money paid or property transferred by him under an agreement or obligation, he must repay any money and return any other property received by him as a result of exercising the rights in question.

(13) If any property required to be returned under this section has passed to a third party, references to that property are to be read as references to its value at the time of its receipt by the person required to return it.

71 Actions for damages

(1) A contravention of section 56(6) or 59(1) or (2) is actionable at the suit of a private person who suffers loss as a result of the contravention, subject to the defences and other incidents applying to actions for breach of statutory duty.

(2) In prescribed cases, a contravention of that kind which would be actionable at the suit of a private person is actionable at the suit of a person who is not a private person, subject to the defences and other incidents applying to actions for breach of statutory duty.

(3) "Private person" has such meaning as may be prescribed.

80 General duty of disclosure in listing particulars

(1) Listing particulars submitted to the competent authority under section 79 must contain all such information as investors and their professional advisers would reasonably require, and reasonably expect to find there, for the purpose of making an informed assessment of—

    (a) the assets and liabilities, financial position, profits and losses, and prospects of the issuer of the securities; and

    (b) the rights attaching to the securities.

81 Supplementary listing particulars

. . .

90 [Compensation for false or misleading statements or omissions]

(1) Any person responsible for listing particulars is liable to pay compensation to a person who has—

    (a) acquired securities to which the particulars apply; and

    (b) suffered loss in respect of them as a result of—

        (i) any untrue or misleading statement in the particulars; or

        (ii) the omission from the particulars of any matter required to be included by section 80 or 81.

(2) Subsection (1) is subject to exemptions provided by Schedule 10.

(3) If listing particulars are required to include information about the absence of a particular matter, the omission from the particulars of that information is to be treated as a statement in the listing particulars that there is no such matter.

(4) Any person who fails to comply with section 81 is liable to pay compensation to any person who has—

    (a) acquired securities of the kind in question; and

    (b) suffered loss in respect of them as a result of the failure.

(5) Subsection (4) is subject to exemptions provided by Schedule 10.

(6) This section does not affect any liability which may be incurred apart from this section.

(7) References in this section to the acquisition by a person of securities include references to his contracting to acquire them or any interest in them.

(8) No person shall, by reason of being a promoter of a company or otherwise, incur any liability for failing to disclose information which he would not be required to disclose in listing particulars in respect of a company's securities—

    (a) if he were responsible for those particulars; or

    (b) if he is responsible for them, which he is entitled to omit by virtue of section 82.

(9) The reference in subsection (8) to a person incurring liability includes a reference to any other person being entitled as against that person to be granted any civil remedy or to rescind or repudiate an agreement.

[(12) A person is not to be subject to civil liability solely on the basis of a summary in a prospectus unless the summary is misleading, inaccurate or inconsistent when read with the rest of the prospectus; and, in this subsection, a summary includes any translation of it.]

102   Exemption from liability in damages

(1) Neither the competent authority nor any person who is, or is acting as, a member, officer or member of staff of the competent authority is to be liable in damages for anything done or omitted in the discharge, or purported discharge, of the authority's functions.

(2) Subsection (1) does not apply—

    (a) if the act or omission is shown to have been in bad faith; or

    (b) so as to prevent an award of damages made in respect of an act or omission on the ground that the act or omission was unlawful as a result of section 6(1) of the Human Rights Act 1998.

131   Effect on transactions

The imposition of a penalty under this Part does not make any transaction void or unenforceable.

139   Miscellaneous ancillary matters

(1) Rules relating to the handling of money held by an authorised person in specified circumstances ("clients' money") may—

    (a) make provision which results in that clients' money being held on trust in accordance with the rules;

    (b) treat two or more accounts as a single account for specified purposes (which may include the distribution of money held in the accounts);

    (c) authorise the retention by the authorised person of interest accuring on the clients' money; and

    (d) make provision as to the distribution of such interest which is not to be retained by him.

(2) An institution with which an account is kept in pursuance of rules relating to the handling of clients' money does not incur any liability as constructive trustee if money is wrongfully paid from the account, unless the institution permits the payment—

    (a) with knowledge that it is wrongful; or

    (b) having deliberately failed to make enquiries in circumstances in which a reasonable and honest person would have done so.

(3) In the application of subsection (1) to Scotland, the reference to money being held on trust is to be read as a reference to its being held as agent for the person who is entitled to call for it to be paid over to him or to be paid on his direction or to have it otherwise credited to him.

(4) Rules may—

    (a) confer rights on persons to rescind agreements with, or withdraw offers to, authorised persons within a specified period; and

    (b) make provision, in respect of authorised persons and persons exercising those rights, for the restitution of property and the making or recovery of payments where those rights are exercised.

(5) "Rules" means general rules.

(6) "Specified" means specified in the rules.

150   Actions for damages

(1) A contravention by an authorised person of a rule is actionable at the suit of a private person who suffers loss as a result of the contravention, subject to the defences and other incidents applying to actions for breach of statutory duty.

213   The compensation scheme

(1) The Authority must by rules establish a scheme for compensating persons in cases where relevant persons are unable, or are likely to be unable, to satisfy claims against them.

(2) The rules are to be known as the Financial Services Compensation Scheme (but are referred to in this Act as "the compensation scheme").

(3) The compensation scheme must, in particular, provide for the scheme manager—

   (a) to assess and pay compensation, in accordance with the scheme, to claimants in respect of claims made in connection with regulated activities carried on (whether or not with permission) by relevant persons; and

   (b) to have power to impose levies on authorised persons, or any class of authorised person, for the purpose of meeting its expenses (including in particular expenses incurred, or expected to be incurred, in paying compensation, borrowing or insuring risks).

(4) The compensation scheme may provide for the scheme manager to have power to impose levies on authorised persons, or any class of authorised person, for the purpose of recovering the cost (whenever incurred) of establishing the scheme.

(5) In making any provision of the scheme by virtue of subsection (3)(b), the Authority must take account of the desirability of ensuring that the amount of the levies imposed on a particular class of authorised person reflects, so far as practicable, the amount of the claims made, or likely to be made, in respect of that class of person.

(6) An amount payable to the scheme manager as a result of any provision of the scheme made by virtue of subsection (3)(b) or (4) may be recovered as a debt due to the scheme manager.

222   Statutory immunity

(1) Neither the scheme manager nor any person who is, or is acting as, its board member, officer or member of staff is to be liable in damages for anything done or omitted in the discharge, or purported discharge, of the scheme manager's functions.

(2) Subsection (1) does not apply—

   (a) if the act or omission is shown to have been in bad faith; or

   (b) so as to prevent an award of damages made in respect of an act or omission on the ground that the act or omission was unlawful as a result of section 6(1) of the Human Rights Act 1998.

291   Liability in relation to recognised body's regulatory functions

(1) A recognised body and its officers and staff are not to be liable in damages for anything done or omitted in the discharge of the recognised body's regulatory functions unless it is shown that the act or omission was in bad faith.

(2) But subsection (1) does not prevent an award of damages made in respect of an act or omission on the ground that the act or omission was unlawful as a result of section 6(1) of the Human Rights Act 1998.

380   Injunctions

(3) If, on the application of the authority or the Secretary of State, the court is satisfied that any person may have—

   (a) contravened a relevant requirement, or

   (b) been knowingly concerned in the contravention of such a requirement,

it may make an order restraining (or in Scotland an interdict prohibiting) him from disposing of, or otherwise dealing with, any assets of his which it is satisfied he is reasonably likely to dispose of or otherwise deal with.

381   Injunctions in cases of market abuse

(3) Subsection (4) applies if, on the application of the Authority, the court is satisfied that any person—

(a) may be engaged in market abuse; or

(b) may have been engaged in market abuse.

(4) The court make an order restraining (or in Scotland an interdict prohibiting) the person concerned from disposing of, or otherwise dealing with, any assets of his which it is satisfied that he is reasonably likely to dispose of, or otherwise deal with.

382   Restitution orders

(1) The court may, on the application of the Authority or the Secretary of State, make an order under subsection (2) if it is satisfied that a person has contravened a relevant requirement, or been knowingly concerned in the contravention of such a requirement, and—

(a) that profits have accrued to him as a result of the contravention; or

(b) that one or more persons have suffered loss or been otherwise adversely affected as a result of the contravention.

(2) The court may order the person concerned to pay to the Authority such sum as appears to the court to be just having regard—

(a) in a case within paragraph (a) of subsection (1), to the profits appearing to the court to have accrued;

(b) in a case within paragraph (b) of that subsection, to the extent of the loss or other adverse effect;

(c) in a case within both of those paragraphs, to the profits appearing to the court to have accrued and to the extent of the loss or other adverse effect.

(3) Any amount paid to the Authority in pursuance of an order under subsection (2) must be paid by it to such qualifying person or distributed by it among such qualifying persons as the court may direct.

(4) On an application under subsection (1) the court may require the person concerned to supply it with such accounts or other information as it may require for any one or more of the following purposes—

(a) establishing whether any and, if so, what profits have accrued to him as mentioned in paragraph (a) of that subsection;

(b) establishing whether any person or persons have suffered any loss or adverse effect as mentioned in paragraph (b) of that subsection and, if so, the extent of that loss or adverse effect; and

(c) determining how any amounts are to be paid or distributed under subsection (3).

(5) The court may require any accounts or other information supplied under subsection (4) to be verified in such manner as it may direct.

(6) The jurisdiction conferred by this section is exercisable by the High Court and the Court of Session.

(7) Nothing in this section affects the right of any person other than the Authority or the Secretary of State to bring proceedings in respect of the matters to which this section applies.

(8) "Qualifying person" means a person appearing to the court to be someone—

(a) to whom the profits mentioned in subsection (1)(a) are attributable; or

(b) who has suffered the loss or adverse effect mentioned in subsection (1)(b).

(9) "Relevant requirement"—

(a) in relation to an application by the Authority, means a requirement—

(i)   which is imposed by or under this Act; or

(ii) which is imposed by or under any other Act and whose contravention constitutes an offence which the Authority has power to prosecute under this Act;

(b) in relation to an application by the Secretary of State, means a requirement which is imposed by or under this Act and whose contravention constitutes an offence which the Secretary of State has power to prosecute under this Act.

(10) In the application of subsection (9) to Scotland—

    (a) in paragraph (a)(ii) for "which the Authority has power to prosecute under this Act" substitute "mentioned in paragraph (a) or (b) of section 402(1); and

    (b) in paragraph (b) omit "which the Secretary of State has power to prosecute under this Act".

383 Restitution orders in cases of market abuse

(1) The court may, on the application of the Authority, make an order under subsection (4) if it is satisfied that a person ("the person concerned")—

    (a) has engaged in market abuse, or

    (b) by taking or refraining from taking any action has required or encouraged another person or persons to engage in behaviour which, if engaged in by the person concerned, would amount to market abuse,

and the condition mentioned in subsection (2) is fulfilled.

(2) The condition is—

    (a) that profits have accrued to the person concerned as a result; or

    (b) that one or more persons have suffered loss or been otherwise adversely affected as a result.

(3) But the court may not make an order under subsection (4) if it is satisfied that—

    (a) the person concerned believed, on reasonable grounds, that his behaviour did not fall within paragraph (a) or (b) of subsection (1); or

    (b) he took all reasonable precautions and exercised all due diligence to avoid behaving in a way which fell within paragraph (a) or (b) of subsection (1).

(4) The court may order the person concerned to pay to the Authority such sum as appears to the court to be just having regard—

    (a) in a case within paragraph (a) of subsection (2), to the profits appearing to the court to have accrued;

    (b) in a case within paragraph (b) of that subsection, to the extent of the loss or other adverse effect;

    (c) in a case within both of those paragraphs, to the profits appearing to the court to have accrued and to the extent of the loss or other adverse effect.

(5) Any amount paid to the Authority in pursuance of an order under subsection (4) must be paid by it to such qualifying person or distributed by it among such qualifying persons as the court may direct.

(6) On an application under subsection (1) the court may require the person concerned to supply it with such accounts or other information as it may require for any one or more of the following purposes—

    (a) establishing whether any and, if so, what profits have accrued to him as mentioned in subsection (2)(a);

    (b) establishing whether any person or persons have suffered any loss or adverse effect as mentioned in subsection (2)(b) and, if so, the extent of that loss or adverse effect; and

    (c) determining how any amounts are to be paid or distributed under subsection (5).

(7) The court may require any accounts or other information supplied under subsection (6) to be verified in such manner as it may direct.

(8) The jurisdiction conferred by this section is exercisable by the High Court and the Court of Session.

(9) Nothing in this section affects the right of any person other than the Authority to bring proceedings in respect of the matters to which this section applies.

(10) "Qualifying person" means a person appearing to the court to be someone—

    (a) to whom the profits mentioned in paragraph (a) of subsection (2) are attributable; or

    (b) who has suffered the loss or adverse effect mentioned in paragraph (b) of that subsection.

384 Power of Authority to require restitution

(1) The Authority may exercise the power in subsection (5) if it is satisfied that an authorised person ("the person concerned") has contravened a relevant requirement, or been knowingly concerned in the contravention of such a requirement, and—

(a) that profits have accrued to him as a result of the contravention; or

(b) that one or more persons have suffered loss or been otherwise adversely affected as a result of the contravention.

(2) The Authority may exercise the power in subsection (5) if it is satisfied that a person ("the person concerned")—

(a) has engaged in market abuse, or

(b) by taking or refraining from taking any action has required or encouraged another person or persons to engage in behaviour which, if engaged in by the person concerned, would amount to market abuse,

and the condition mentioned in subsection (3) is fulfilled.

(3) The condition is—

(a) that profits have accrued to the person concerned as a result of the market abuse; or

(b) that one or more persons have suffered loss or been otherwise adversely affected as a result of the market abuse.

(4) But the Authority may not exercise that power as a result of subsection (2) if, having considered any representations made to it in response to a warning notice, there are reasonable grounds for it to be satisfied that—

(a) the person concerned believed, on reasonable grounds, that his behaviour did not fall within paragraph (a) or (b) of that subsection; or

(b) he took all reasonable precautions and exercised all due diligence to avoid behaving in a way which fell within paragraph (a) or (b) of that sub-section.

(5) The power referred to in subsections (1) and (2) is a power to require the person concerned, in accordance with such arrangements as the Authority considers appropriate, to pay to the appropriate person or distribute among the appropriate persons such amount as appears to the Authority to be just having regard—

(a) in a case within paragraph (a) of subsection (1) or (3), to the profits appearing to the Authority to have accrued;

(b) in a case within paragraph (b) of subsection (1) or (3), to the extent of the loss or other adverse effect;

(c) in a case within paragraphs (a) and (b) of subsection (1) or (3), to the profits appearing to the Authority to have accrued and to the extent of the loss or other adverse effect.

(6) "Appropriate person" means a person appearing to the Authority to be someone—

(a) to whom the profits mentioned in paragraph (a) of subsection (1) or (3) are attributable; or

(b) who has suffered the loss or adverse effect mentioned in paragraph (b) of sub-section (1) or (3).

(7) "Relevant requirement" means—

(a) a requirement imposed by or under this Act; and

(b) a requirement which is imposed by or under any other Act and whose contra-vention constitutes an offence in relation to which this Act confers power to prosecute on the Authority.

(8) In the application of subsection (7) to Scotland, in paragraph (b) for "in relation to which this Act confers power to prosecute on the Authority" substitute "mentioned in paragraph (a) or (b) of section 402(1)".

385 Warning notices
(1) If the Authority proposes to exercise the power under section 384(5) in relation to a person, it must give him a warning notice.
(2) A warning notice under this section must specify the amount which the Authority proposes to require the person concerned to pay or distribute as mentioned in section 384(5).

386 Decision notices
(1) If the Authority decides to exercise the power under section 384(5), it must give a decision notice to the person in relation to whom the power is exercised.
(2) The decision notice must—
    (a) state the amount that he is to pay or distribute as mentioned in section 384(5);
    (b) identify the person or persons to whom that amount is to be paid or among whom that amount is to be distributed; and
    (c) state the arrangements in accordance with which the payment or distribution is to be made.
(3) If the Authority decides to exercise the power under section 384(5), the person in relation to whom it is exercised may refer the matter to the Tribunal.

Freedom of Information Act 2000
(2000, c. 36)

38 Health and safety
(1) Information is exempt information if its disclosure under this Act would, or would be likely to—
    (a) endanger the physical or mental health of any individual, or
    (b) endanger the safety of any individual.
(2) The duty to confirm or deny does not arise if, or to the extent that, compliance with section 1(1)(a) would, or would be likely to, have either of the effects mentioned in subsection (1).

56 No action against public authority
(1) This Act does not confer any right of action in civil proceedings in respect of any failure to comply with any duty imposed by or under this Act.

79 Defamation
Where any information communicated by a public authority to a person ("the applicant") under section 1 was supplied to the public authority by a third person, the publication to the applicant of any defamatory matter contained in the information shall be privileged unless the publication is shown to have been made with malice.

Learning and Skills Act 2000
(2000, c. 21)

72 Defamation
(1) For the purposes of the law of defamation a report published under a provision of, or made as a result of, this Part is privileged unless its publication is shown to have been made with malice.
(2) Nothing in subsection (1) limits any privilege subsisting apart from that subsection.

88 Defamation
(1) For the purposes of the law of defamation, any report under this Part is privileged unless its publication is shown to have been made with malice.
(2) Nothing in subsection (1) limits any privilege subsisting apart from that subsection.

Local Government Act 2000
(2000, c. 22)

74   Law of defamation

For the purposes of the law of defamation, any statement (whether written or oral) made by [the Public Services Ombudsman for Wales] in connection with the exercise of his functions under this Part shall be absolutely privileged.

92   Payments in cases of maladministration etc.

(1) Where a relevant authority consider—

    (a) that action taken by or on behalf of the authority in the exercise of their functions amounts to, or may amount to, maladministration, and

    (b) that a person has been, or may have been, adversely affected by that action, the authority may, if they think appropriate, make a payment to, or provide some other benefit for, that person.

(3) In this section—

"action" includes failure to act, ...

Postal Services Act 2000
(2000, c. 26)

89   Schemes as to terms and conditions for provision of a universal postal service

. . .

90   Exclusion of liability

(1) No proceedings in tort shall lie or, in Scotland, be competent against a universal service provider in respect of loss or damage suffered by any person in connection with the provision of a universal postal service because of—

    (a) anything done or omitted to be done in relation to any postal packet in the course of transmission by post, or

    (b) any omission to carry out arrangements for the collection of anything to be conveyed by post.

(2) No officer, servant, employee, agent or sub-contractor of a universal service provider shall be subject, except at the suit or instance of the provider, to any civil liability for—

    (a) any loss or damage in the case of which liability of the provider is excluded by subsection (1), or

    (b) any loss of, or damage to, an inland packet to which section 91 applies.

(3) No person engaged in or about the conveyance of postal packets and no officer, servant, employee, agent or sub-contractor of any such person shall be subject, except at the suit or instance of the universal service provider concerned, to any civil liability for—

    (a) any loss or damage in the case of which liability of the provider is excluded by subsection (1), or

    (b) any loss of, or damage to, an inland packet to which section 91 applies.

(4) In the application of subsection (1) to Scotland, the reference to proceedings in tort shall be construed in the same way as in section 43(b) of the Crown Proceedings Act 1947.

(5) This section is subject to section 91.

91   Limited liability for registered inland packets

(1) Proceedings shall lie or, in Scotland, be competent against a universal service provider under this section, but not otherwise, in respect of relevant loss of, or relevant damage to, an

inland packet in respect of which the universal service provider accepts liability under this section in pursuance of a scheme made under section 89.

(2) The references in subsection (1) to relevant loss or damage are to loss or damage so far as it is due to any wrongful act of, or any neglect or default by, an officer, servant, employee, agent or sub-contractor of the universal service provider while performing or purporting to perform in that capacity his functions in relation to the receipt, conveyance, delivery or other dealing with the packet.

(3) No proceedings shall lie or, in Scotland, be competent under this section in relation to a packet unless they are begun within the period of twelve months starting with the day on which the packet was posted.

Powers of Criminal Courts (Sentencing) Act 2000
(2000, c. 6)

73   Reparation orders

(1) Where a child or young person (that is to say, any person aged under 18) is convicted of an offence other than one for which the sentence is fixed by law, the court by or before which he is convicted may make an order requiring him to make reparation specified in the order—

(a) to a person or persons so specified; or

(b) to the community at large;

and any person so specified must be a person identified by the court as a victim of the offence or a person otherwise affected by it.

(3) In this section and section 74 below "make reparation", in relation to an offender, means make reparation for the offence otherwise than by the payment of compensation; and the requirements that may be specified in a reparation order are subject to section 74(1) to (3).

130   Compensation orders against convicted persons

(1) A court by or before which a person is convicted of an offence, instead of or in addition to dealing with him in any other way, may, on application or otherwise, make an order (in this Act referred to as a "compensation order") requiring him—

(a) to pay compensation for any personal injury, loss or damage resulting from that offence or any other offence which is taken into consideration by the court in determining sentence; or

(b) to make payments for funeral expenses or bereavement in respect of a death resulting from any such offence, other than a death due to an accident arising out of the presence of a motor vehicle on a road;

but this is subject to the following provisions of this section and to section 131 below.

(2) Where the person is convicted of an offence the sentence for which is fixed by law or falls to be imposed under section [110(2) or 111(2) above, section 51A(2) of the Firearms Act 1968 or section 225, 226, 227 or 228 of the Criminal Justice Act 2003,] subsection (1) above shall have effect as if the words "instead of or" were omitted.

(3) A court shall give reasons, on passing sentence, if it does not make a compensation order in a case where this section empowers it to do so.

(4) Compensation under subsection (1) above shall be of such amount as the court considers appropriate, having regard to any evidence and to any representations that are made by or on behalf of the accused or the prosecutor.

(5) In the case of an offence under the Theft Act 1968, where the property in question is recovered, any damage to the property occurring while it was out of the owner's possession

shall be treated for the purposes of subsection (1) above as having resulted from the offence, however and by whomever the damage was caused.

(6) A compensation order may only be made in respect of injury, loss or damage (other than loss suffered by a person's dependants in consequence of his death) which was due to an accident arising out of the presence of a motor vehicle on a road, if

(a) it is in respect of damage which is treated by subsection (5) above as resulting from an offence under the Theft Act 1968; or

(b) it is in respect of injury, loss or damage as respects which—

(i) the offender is uninsured in relation to the use of the vehicle; and

(ii) compensation is not payable under any arrangements to which the Secretary of State is a party.

(7) Where a compensation order is made in respect of injury, loss or damage due to an accident arising out of the presence of a motor vehicle on a road, the amount to be paid may include an amount representing the whole or part of any loss of or reduction in preferential rates of insurance attributable to the accident.

(8) A vehicle the use of which is exempted from insurance by section 144 of the Road Traffic Act 1988 is not uninsured for the purposes of subsection (6) above.

(9) A compensation order in respect of funeral expenses may be made for the benefit of anyone who incurred the expenses.

(10) A compensation order in respect of bereavement may be made only for the benefit of a person for whose benefit a claim for damages for bereavement could be made under section 1A of the Fatal Accidents Act 1976; and the amount of compensation in respect of bereavement shall not exceed the amount for the time being specified in section 1A(3) of that Act.

(11) In determining whether to make a compensation order against any person, and in determining the amount to be paid by any person under such an order, the court shall have regard to his means so far as they appear or are known to the court.

(12) Where the court considers—

(a) that it would be appropriate both to impose a fine and to make a compensation order, but

(b) that the offender has insufficient means to pay both an appropriate fine and appropriate compensation,

the court shall give preference to compensation (though it may impose a fine as well).

131 Limit on amount payable under compensation order of magistrates' court
. . .

132 Compensation orders: appeals etc.
. . .

133 Review of compensation orders
. . .

134 Effect of compensation order on subsequent award of damages in civil proceedings

(1) This section shall have effect where a compensation order, or a service compensation order or award, has been made in favour of any person in respect of any injury, loss or damage and a claim by him in civil proceedings for damages in respect of the injury, loss or damage subsequently falls to be determined.

(2) The damages in the civil proceedings shall be assessed without regard to the order or award, but the plaintiff may only recover an amount equal to the aggregate of the following—

(a) any amount by which they exceed the compensation; and

(b) a sum equal to any portion of the compensation which he fails to recover,

and may not enforce the judgment, so far as it relates to a sum such as is mentioned in paragraph (b) above, without the leave of the court.

(3) In this section a "service compensation order or award" means—

(a) an order requiring the payment of compensation under paragraph 11 of Schedule 5A to the Army Act 1955, of Schedule 5A to the Air Force Act 1955 or of Schedule 4A to the Naval Discipline Act 1957; or

(b) an award of stoppages payable by way of compensation under any of those Acts.

137 Power to order parent or guardian to pay fine, costs or [compensation or surcharge]

(1) Where—

(a) a child or young person (that is to say, any person aged under 18) is convicted of any offence for the commission of which a fine or costs may be imposed or a compensation order may be made, and

(b) the court is of the opinion that the case would best be met by the imposition of a fine or costs or the making of such an order, whether with or without any other punishment, the court shall order that the fine, compensation or costs awarded be paid by the parent or guardian of the child or young person instead of by the child or young person himself, unless the court is satisfied—

(i) that the parent or guardian cannot be found; or

(ii) that it would be unreasonable to make an order for payment, having regard to the circumstances of the case.

[(1A) Where but for this subsection a court would order a child or young person to pay a surcharge under section 161A of the Criminal Justice Act 2003, the court shall order that the surcharge be paid by the parent or guardian of the child or young person instead of by the child or young person himself, unless the court is satisfied—

(a) that the parent or guardian cannot be found; or

(b) that it would be unreasonable to make an order for payment, having regard to the circumstances of the case.]

(2) Where but for this subsection a court would impose a fine on a child or young person under—

[...]

(b) paragraph 2(1)(a) of Schedule 5 to this Act (breach of attendance centre order or attendance centre rules),

(c) paragraph 2(2)(a) of Schedule 7 to this Act (breach of supervision order),

(d) paragraph 2(2)(a) of Schedule 8 to this Act (breach of action plan order or reparation order),

(e) section 104(3)(b) above (breach of requirements of supervision under a detention and training order), or

(f) section 4(3)(b) of the Criminal Justice and Public Order Act 1994 (breach of requirements of supervision under a secure training order),

the court shall order that the fine be paid by the parent or guardian of the child or young person instead of by the child or young person himself, unless the court is satisfied—

(i) that the parent or guardian cannot be found; or

(ii) that it would be unreasonable to make an order for payment, having regard to the circumstances of the case.

(3) In the case of a young person aged 16 or over, [subsections (1) to (2)] above shall have effect as if, instead of imposing a duty, they conferred a power to make such an order as is mentioned in those subsections.

(4) Subject to subsection (5) below, no order shall be made under this section without giving the parent or guardian an opportunity of being heard.

(5) An order under this section may be made against a parent or guardian who, having been required to attend, has failed to do so.

(6) A parent or guardian may appeal to the Crown Court against an order under this section made by a magistrates' court.

(7) A parent or guardian may appeal to the Court of Appeal against an order under this section made by the Crown Court, as if he had been convicted on indictment and the order were a sentence passed on his conviction.

(8) In relation to a child or young person for whom a local authority have parental responsibility and who—

(a) is in their care, or

(b) is provided with accommodation by them in the exercise of any functions (in particular those under the Children Act 1989) which [are their social services functions within the meaning of]¹ the Local Authority Social Services Act 1970,

references in this section to his parent or guardian shall be construed as references to that authority.

(9) In subsection (8) above "local authority" and "parental responsibility" have the same meanings as in the Children Act 1989.

138 Fixing of fine[, compensation or surcharge] to be paid by parent or guardian

. . .

143 Powers to deprive offender of property used etc. for purposes of crime

(1) Where a person is convicted of an offence and the court by or before which he is convicted is satisfied that any property which has been lawfully seized from him, or which was in his possession or under his control at the time when he was apprehended for the offence or when a summons in respect of it was issued—

(a) has been used for the purpose of committing, or facilitating the commission of, any offence, or

(b) was intended by him to be used for that purpose,

the court may (subject to subsection (5) below) make an order under this section in respect of that property.

(2) Where a person is convicted of an offence and the offence, or an offence which the court has taken into consideration in determining his sentence, consists of unlawful possession of property which—

(a) has been lawfully seized from him, or

(b) was in his possession or under his control at the time when he was apprehended for the offence of which he has been convicted or when a summons in respect of that offence was issued,

the court may (subject to subsection (5) below) make an order under this section in respect of that property.

(3) An order under this section shall operate to deprive the offender of his rights, if any, in the property to which it relates, and the property shall (if not already in their possession) be taken into the possession of the police.

145 Application of proceeds of forfeited property

(1) Where a court makes an order under section 143 above in a case where—

(a) the offender has been convicted of an offence which has resulted in a person suffering personal injury, loss or damage, or

(b) any such offence is taken into consideration by the court in determining sentence,

the court may also make an order that any proceeds which arise from the disposal of the property and which do not exceed a sum specified by the court shall be paid to that person.

(2) The court may make an order under this section only if it is satisfied that but for the inadequacy of the offender's means it would have made a compensation order under which the offender would have been required to pay compensation of an amount not less than the specified amount.

148 Restitution orders

(1) This section applies where goods have been stolen, and either—

(a) a person is convicted of any offence with reference to the theft (whether or not the stealing is the gist of his offence); or

(b) a person is convicted of any other offence, but such an offence as is mentioned in paragraph (a) above is taken into consideration in determining his sentence.

(2) Where this section applies, the court by or before which the offender is convicted may on the conviction (whether or not the passing of sentence is in other respects deferred) exercise any of the following powers—

(a) the court may order anyone having possession or control of the stolen goods to restore them to any person entitled to recover them from him; or

(b) on the application of a person entitled to recover from the person convicted any other goods directly or indirectly representing the stolen goods (as being the proceeds of any disposal or realisation of the whole or part of them or of goods so representing them), the court may order those other goods to be delivered or transferred to the applicant; or

(c) the court may order that a sum not exceeding the value of the stolen goods shall be paid, out of any money of the person convicted which was taken out of his possession on his apprehension, to any person who, if those goods were in the possession of the person convicted, would be entitled to recover them from him;

and in this subsection "the stolen goods" means the goods referred to in subsection (1) above.

(3) Where the court has power on a person's conviction to make an order against him both under paragraph (b) and under paragraph (c) of subsection (2) above with reference to the stealing of the same goods, the court may make orders under both paragraphs provided that the person in whose favour the orders are made does not thereby recover more than the value of those goods.

(4) Where the court on a person's conviction makes an order under subsection (2)(a) above for the restoration of any goods, and it appears to the court that the person convicted—

(a) has sold the goods to a person acting in good faith, or

(b) has borrowed money on the security of them from a person so acting,

the court may order that there shall be paid to the purchaser or lender, out of any money of the person convicted which was taken out of his possession on his apprehension, a sum not exceeding the amount paid for the purchase by the purchaser or, as the case may be, the amount owed to the lender in respect of the loan.

(5) The court shall not exercise the powers conferred by this section unless in the opinion of the court the relevant facts sufficiently appear from evidence given at the trial or the available documents, together with admissions made by or on behalf of any person in connection with any proposed exercise of the powers.

(6) In subsection (5) above "the available documents" means—

(a) any written statements or admissions which were made for use, and would have been admissible, as evidence at the trial; and

[(b) such documents as were served on the offender in pursuance of regulations made under paragraph 1 of Schedule 3 to the Crime and Disorder Act 1998.]

(7) Any order under this section shall be treated as an order for the restitution of property within the meaning of section 30 of the Criminal Appeal Act 1968 (which relates to the effect on such orders of appeals).

(8) Subject to subsection (9) below, references in this section to stealing shall be construed in accordance with section 1(1) of the Theft Act 1968 (read with the provisions of that Act relating to the construction of section 1(1)).

(9) Subsections (1) and (4) of section 24 of that Act (interpretation of certain provisions) shall also apply in relation to this section as they apply in relation to the provisions of that Act relating to goods which have been stolen.

(10) In this section and section 149 below, "goods", except in so far as the context otherwise requires, includes money and every other description of property (within the meaning of the Theft Act 1968) except land, and includes things severed from the land by stealing.

(11) An order may be made under this section in respect of money owed by the Crown.

149   Restitution orders: supplementary

(1) The following provisions of this section shall have effect with respect to section 148 above.

(2) The powers conferred by subsections (2)(c) and (4) of that section shall be exercisable without any application being made in that behalf or on the application of any person appearing to the court to be interested in the property concerned.

Regulation of Investigatory Powers Act 2000
(2000, c. 23)

1   Unlawful interception

(3) Any interception of a communication which is carried out at any place in the United Kingdom by, or with the express or implied consent of, a person having the right to control the operation or the use of a private telecommunication system shall be actionable at the suit or instance of the sender or recipient, or intended recipient, of the communication if it is without lawful authority and is either—

> (a) an interception of that communication in the course of its transmission by means of that private system; or
>
> (b) an interception of that communication in the course of its transmission, by means of a public telecommunication system, to or from apparatus comprised in that private telecommunication system.

Terrorism Act 2000
(2000, c. 11)

Section 23   SCHEDULE 4

FORFEITURE ORDERS

Compensation

9.— (1) This paragraph applies where a restraint order is discharged under [paragraph 6(4)(a)].

(2) This paragraph also applies where a forfeiture order or a restraint order is made in or in relation to proceedings for an offence under any of sections 15 to 18 which—

> (a) do not result in conviction for an offence under any of those sections,
>
> (b) result in conviction for an offence under any of those sections in respect of which the person convicted is subsequently pardoned by Her Majesty, or
>
> (c) result in conviction for an offence under any of those sections which is subsequently quashed.

(3) A person who had an interest in any property which was subject to the order may apply to the High Court for compensation.

(4) The High Court may order compensation to be paid to the applicant if satisfied—

    (a) that there was a serious default on the part of a person concerned in the investigation or prosecution of the offence,

    (b) that the person in default was or was acting as a member of a police force, or was a member of the Crown Prosecution Service or was acting on behalf of the Service,

    (c) that the applicant has suffered loss in consequence of anything done in relation to the property by or in pursuance of the forfeiture order or restraint order, and

    (d) that, having regard to all the circumstances, it is appropriate to order compensation to be paid.

(5) The High Court shall not order compensation to be paid where it appears to it that proceedings for the offence would have been instituted even if the serious default had not occurred.

(6) Compensation payable under this paragraph shall be paid—

    (a) where the person in default was or was acting as a member of a police force, out of the police fund out of which the expenses of that police force are met, and

    (b) where the person in default was a member of the Crown Prosecution Service, or was acting on behalf of the Service, by the Director of Public Prosecutions.

10.— (1) This paragraph applies where—

    (a) a forfeiture order or a restraint order is made in or in relation to proceedings for an offence under any of sections 15 to 18, and

    (b) the proceedings result in a conviction which is subsequently quashed on an appeal under section 7(2) or (5).

(2) A person who had an interest in any property which was subject to the order may apply to the High Court for compensation.

(3) The High Court may order compensation to be paid to the applicant if satisfied—

    (a) that the applicant has suffered loss in consequence of anything done in relation to the property by or in pursuance of the forfeiture order or restraint order, and

    (b) that, having regard to all the circumstances, it is appropriate to order compensation to be paid.

(4) Compensation payable under this paragraph shall be paid by the Secretary of State.

Section 98   **SCHEDULE 12**

COMPENSATION

Right to compensation

1.— (1) This paragraph applies where under Part VII of this Act—

    (a) real or personal property is taken, occupied, destroyed or damaged, or

    (b) any other act is done which interferes with private rights of property.

(2) Where this paragraph applies in respect of an act taken in relation to any property or rights the Secretary of State shall pay compensation to any person who—

    (a) has an estate or interest in the property or is entitled to the rights, and

    (b) suffers loss or damage as a result of the act.

2. No compensation shall be payable unless an application is made to the Secretary of State in such manner as he may specify.

Trustee Act 2000
(2000, c. 29)

1 The duty of care

2. Whenever the duty under this subsection applies to a trustee, he must exercise such care and skill as is reasonable in the circumstances, having regard in particular—

    (a) to any special knowledge or experience that he has or holds himself out as having, and

    (b) if he acts as trustee in the course of a business or profession, to any special knowledge or experience that it is reasonable to expect of a person acting in the course of that kind of business or profession.

(2) In this Act the duty under subsection (1) is called "the duty of care".

3 Application of duty of care

Schedule 1 makes provision about when the duty of care applies to a trustee.

23 Liability for agents, nominees and custodians etc

(1) A trustee is not liable for any act or default of the agent, nominee or custodian unless he has failed to comply with the duty of care applicable to him, under paragraph 3 of Schedule 1—

    (a) when entering into the arrangements under which the person acts as agent, nominee or custodian, or

    (b) when carrying out his duties under section 22.

(2) If a trustee has agreed a term under which the agent, nominee or custodian is permitted to appoint a substitute, the trustee is not liable for any act or default of the substitute unless he has failed to comply with the duty of care applicable to him, under paragraph 3 of Schedule 1—

    (a) when agreeing that term, or

    (b) when carrying out his duties under section 22 in so far as they relate to the use of the substitute.

Section 2   SCHEDULE 1

APPLICATION OF DUTY OF CARE

1   Investment

The duty of care applies to a trustee—

    (a) when exercising the general power of investment or any other power of investment, however conferred;

    (b) when carrying out a duty to which he is subject under section 4 or 5 (duties relating to the exercise of a power of investment or to the review of investments).

2   Acquisition of land

The duty of care applies to a trustee—

    (a) when exercising the power under section 8 to acquire land;

    (b) when exercising any other power to acquire land, however conferred;

    (c) when exercising any power in relation to land acquired under a power mentioned in sub-paragraph (a) or (b).

3   Agents, nominees and custodians

(1) The duty of care applies to a trustee—

    (a) when entering into arrangements under which a person is authorised under section 11 to exercise functions as an agent;

(b) when entering into arrangements under which a person is appointed under section 16 to act as a nominee;

(c) when entering into arrangements under which a person is appointed under section 17 or 18 to act as a custodian;

(d) when entering into arrangements under which, under any other power, however conferred, a person is authorised to exercise ftmctions as an agent or is appointed to act as a nominee or custodian;

(e) when carrying out his duties under section 22 (review of agent, nominee or custodian, etc.).

(2) For the purposes of sub-paragraph (1), entering into arrangements under which a person is authorised to exercise functions or is appointed to act as a nominee or custodian includes, in particular—

(a) selecting the person who is to act,

(b) determining any terms on which he is to act, and

(c) if the person is being authorised to exercise asset management functions, the preparation of a policy statement under section 15.

4   Compounding of liabilities

The duty of care applies to a trustee—

(a) when exercising the power under section 15 of the Trustee Act 1925 to do any of the things referred to in that section;

(b) when exercising any corresponding power, however conferred.

5   Insurance

The duty of care applies to a trustee—

(a) when exercising the power under section 19 of the Trustee Act 1925 to insure property;

(b) when exercising any corresponding power, however conferred.

6   Reversionary interests, valuations and audit

The duty of care applies to a trustee—

(a) when exercising the power under section 22(1) or (3) of the Trustee Act 1925 to do any of the things referred to there;

(b) when exercising any corresponding power, however conferred.

7   Exclusion of duty of care

The duty of care does not apply if or in so far as it appears from the trust instrument that the duty is not meant to apply.

Enterprise Act 2002

(2002, c. 40)

1   The Office of Fair Trading

(1) There shall be a body corporate to be known as the Office of Fair Trading (in this Act referred to as "the OFT").

108   Defamation

For the purposes of the law relating to defamation, absolute privilege attaches to any advice, guidance, notice or direction given, or decision or report made, by the OFT, [OFCOM,] the Commission or the Secretary of State in the exercise of any of their functions under this Part [ss 22–130].

173   Defamation: Part 4 [ss 131–184]

For the purposes of the law relating to defamation, absolute privilege attaches to any advice, guidance, notice or direction given, or decision or report made, by the OFT, by the Secretary of State, by the appropriate Minister (other than the Secretary of State acting alone) or by the Commission in the exercise of any of their functions under this Part.

Land Registration Act 2002
(2002, c. 9)

8 Liability for making good void transfers etc.

If a legal estate is retransferred, regranted or recreated because of a failure to comply with the requirement of registration, the transferee, grantee or, as the case may be, the mortgagor—

    (a) is liable to the other party for all the proper costs of and incidental to the retransfer, regrant or recreation of the legal estate, and

    (b) is liable to indemnify the other party in respect of any other liability reasonably incurred by him because of the failure to comply with the requirement of registration.

Police Reform Act 2002
(2002, c. 30)

PART 4   POLICE POWERS ETC.
CHAPTER 1   EXERCISE OF POLICE POWERS ETC. BY CIVILIANS

38 Police powers for police authority employees

    (1) The chief officer of police of any police force may designate any person who—

        (a) is employed by the police authority maintaining that force, and

        (b) is under the direction and control of that chief officer,

as an officer of one or more of the descriptions specified in subsection (2).

    (2) The description of officers are as follows—

        (a) community support officer;

        (b) investigating officer,

        (c) detention officer,

        (d) escort officer

        [(e) staff custody officer.].

    (3) A Director General may designate any person who—

        (a) is an employee of his Service Authority, and

        (b) is under the direction and control of that Director General,

        as an investigating officer.

    (4) A chief officer of police or a Director General shall not designate a person under this section unless he is satisfied that that person—

        (a) is a suitable person to carry out the functions for the purposes of which he is designated;

        (b) is capable of effectively carrying out those functions; and

        (c) has received adequate training in the carrying out of those functions and in the exercise and performance of the powers and duties to be conferred on him by virtue of the designation.

    (5) A person designated under this section shall have the powers and duties conferred or imposed on him by the designation.

    (6) Powers and duties may be conferred or imposed on a designated person by means only of the application to him by his designation of provisions of the applicable Part of

Schedule 4 that are to apply to the designated person; and for this purpose the applicable Part of that Schedule is—

 (a) in the case of a person designated as a community support officer, Part 1;

 (b) in the case of a person designated as an investigating officer, Part 2;

 (c) in the case of a person designated as a detention officer, Part 3; and

 (d) in the case of a person designated as an escort officer, Part 4

 [(e) in the case of a person designated as a staff custody officer, Part 4A.].

(7) An employee of a police authority or of a Service Authority authorised or required to do anything by virtue of a designation under this section—

 (a) shall not be authorised or required by virtue of that designation to engage in any conduct otherwise than in the course of that employment; and

 (b) shall be so authorised or required subject to such restrictions and conditions (if any) as may be specified in his designation.

(8) Where any power exercisable by any person in reliance on his designation under this section is a power which, in the case of its exercise by a constable, includes or is supplemented by a power to use reasonable force, any person exercising that power in reliance on that designation shall have the same entitlement as a constable to use reasonable force.

(9) Where any power exercisable by any person in reliance on his designation under this section includes power to use force to enter any premises, that power shall not be exercisable by that person except—

 (a) in the company, and under the supervision, of a constable; or

 (b) for the purpose of saving life or limb or preventing serious damage to property.

Proceeds of Crime Act 2002
(2002, c. 29)

PART 1   ASSETS RECOVERY AGENCY

1   The Agency and its Director

(1) There shall be an Assets Recovery Agency (referred to in this Act as the Agency).

(2) The Secretary of State must appoint a Director of the Agency (referred to in this Act as the Director).

2   Director's functions: general

(1) The Director must exercise his functions in the way which he considers is best calculated to contribute to the reduction of crime.

PART 2   CONFISCATION: ENGLAND AND WALES

Confiscation orders

6   Making of order

(1) The Crown Court must proceed under this section if the following two conditions are satisfied.

(2) The first condition is that a defendant falls within any of the following paragraphs—

 (a) he is convicted of an offence or offences in proceedings before the Crown Court;

 (b) he is committed to the Crown Court for sentence in respect of an offence or offences under [section 3, 3A, 3B, 3C, 4, 4A or 6] of the Sentencing Act;

(c) he is committed to the Crown Court in respect of an offence or offences under section 70 below (committal with a view to a confiscation order being considered).

(3) The second condition is that—

(a) the prosecutor or the Director asks the court to proceed under this section, or

(b) the court believes it is appropriate for it to do so.

(4) The court must proceed as follows—

(a) it must decide whether the defendant has a criminal lifestyle;

(b) if it decides that he has a criminal lifestyle it must decide whether he has benefited from his general criminal conduct;

(c) if it decides that he does not have a criminal lifestyle it must decide whether he has benefited from his particular criminal conduct.

(5) If the court decides under subsection (4)(b) or (c) that the defendant has benefited from the conduct referred to it must—

(a) decide the recoverable amount, and

(b) make an order (a confiscation order) requiring him to pay that amount.

(6) But the court must treat the duty in subsection (5) as a power if it believes that any victim of the conduct has at any time started or intends to start proceedings against the defendant in respect of loss, injury or damage sustained in connection with the conduct.

(7) The court must decide any question arising under subsection (4) or (5) on a balance of probabilities.

(8) The first condition is not satisfied if the defendant absconds (but section 27 may apply).

(9) References in this Part to the offence (or offences) concerned are to the offence (or offences) mentioned in subsection (2).

7 Recoverable amount

(1) The recoverable amount for the purposes of section 6 is an amount equal to the defendant's benefit from the conduct concerned.

(2) But if the defendant shows that the available amount is less than that benefit the recoverable amount is—

(a) the available amount, or

(b) a nominal amount, if the available amount is nil.

(3) But if section 6(6) applies the recoverable amount is such amount as—

(a) the court believes is just, but

(b) does not exceed the amount found under subsection (1) or (2) (as the case may be).

(4) In calculating the defendant's benefit from the conduct concerned for the purposes of subsection (1), any property in respect of which—

(a) a recovery order is in force under section 266, or

(b) a forfeiture order is in force under section 298(2),

must be ignored.

(5) If the court decides the available amount, it must include in the confiscation order a statement of its findings as to the matters relevant for deciding that amount.

8 Defendant's benefit

(1) If the court is proceeding under section 6 this section applies for the purpose of—

(a) deciding whether the defendant has benefited from conduct, and

(b) deciding his benefit from the conduct.

(2) The court must—

(a) take account of conduct occurring up to the time it makes its decision;

(b) take account of property obtained up to that time.

(3) Subsection (4) applies if—

(a) the conduct concerned is general criminal conduct,

(b) a confiscation order mentioned in subsection (5) has at an earlier time been made against the defendant, and

(c) his benefit for the purposes of that order was benefit from his general criminal conduct.

(4) His benefit found at the time the last confiscation order mentioned in subsection (3)(c) was made against him must be taken for the purposes of this section to be his benefit from his general criminal conduct at that time.

(5) If the conduct concerned is general criminal conduct the court must deduct the aggregate of the following amounts—

(a) the amount ordered to be paid under each confiscation order previously made against the defendant;

(b) the amount ordered to be paid under each confiscation order previously made against him under any of the provisions listed in subsection (7).

(6) But subsection (5) does not apply to an amount which has been taken into account for the purposes of a deduction under that subsection on any earlier occasion.

(7) These are the provisions—

(a) the Drug Trafficking Offences Act 1986 (c. 32);

(b) Part 1 of the Criminal Justice (Scotland) Act 1987 (c. 41);

(c) Part 6 of the Criminal Justice Act 1988 (c. 33);

(d) the Criminal Justice (Confiscation) (Northern Ireland) Order 1990 (S.I. 1990/2588 (N.I. 17));

(e) Part 1 of the Drug Trafficking Act 1994 (c. 37);

(f) Part 1 of the Proceeds of Crime (Scotland) Act 1995 (c. 43);

(g) the Proceeds of Crime (Northern Ireland) Order 1996 (S.I. 1996/1299 (N.I. 9));

(h) Part 3 or 4 of this Act.

(8) The reference to general criminal conduct in the case of a confiscation order made under any of the provisions listed in subsection (7) is a reference to conduct in respect of which a court is required or entitled to make one or more assumptions for the purpose of assessing a person's benefit from the conduct.

9 Available amount

(1) For the purposes of deciding the recoverable amount, the available amount is the aggregate of—

(a) the total of the values (at the time the confiscation order is made) of all the free property then held by the defendant minus the total amount payable in pursuance of obligations which then have priority, and

(b) the total of the values (at that time) of all tainted gifts.

(2) An obligation has priority if it is an obligation of the defendant—

(a) to pay an amount due in respect of a fine or other order of a court which was imposed or made on conviction of an offence and at any time before the time the confiscation order is made, or

(b) to pay a sum which would be included among the preferential debts if the defendant's bankruptcy had commenced on the date of the confiscation order or his winding up had been ordered on that date.

(3) "Preferential debts" has the meaning given by section 386 of the Insolvency Act 1986 (c. 45).

76 Conduct and benefit

...

(4) A person benefits from conduct if he obtains property as a result of or in connection with the conduct.

(5) If a person obtains a pecuniary advantage as a result of or in connection with conduct, he is to be taken to obtain as a result of or in connection with the conduct a sum of money equal to the value of the pecuniary advantage.

(6) References to property or a pecuniary advantage obtained in connection with conduct include references to property or a pecuniary advantage obtained both in that connection and some other.

(7) If a person benefits from conduct his benefit is the value of the property obtained.

PART 5   CIVIL RECOVERY OF THE PROCEEDS ETC. OF UNLAWFUL CONDUCT

CHAPTER 1   INTRODUCTORY

240 General purpose of this Part

(1) This Part has effect for the purposes of—

  (a) enabling the enforcement authority to recover, in civil proceedings before the High Court or Court of Session, property which is, or represents, property obtained through unlawful conduct,

  (b) enabling cash which is, or represents, property obtained through unlawful conduct, or which is intended to be used in unlawful conduct, to be forfeited in civil proceedings before a magistrates' court or (in Scotland) the sheriff.

(2) The powers conferred by this Part are exercisable in relation to any property (including cash) whether or not any proceedings have been brought for an offence in connection with the property.

241 "Unlawful conduct"

(1) Conduct occurring in any part of the United Kingdom is unlawful conduct if it is unlawful under the criminal law of that part.

(2) Conduct which—

  (a) occurs in a country [or territory] outside the United Kingdom and is unlawful under the criminal law [applying in that country or territory], and

  (b) if it occurred in a part of the United Kingdom, would be unlawful under the criminal law of that part,

is also unlawful conduct.

(3) The court or sheriff must decide on a balance of probabilities whether it is proved—

  (a) that any matters alleged to constitute unlawful conduct have occurred, or

  (b) that any person intended to use any cash in unlawful conduct.

242 "Property obtained through unlawful conduct"

(1) A person obtains property through unlawful conduct (whether his own conduct or another's) if he obtains property by or in return for the conduct.

(2) In deciding whether any property was obtained through unlawful conduct—

  (a) it is immaterial whether or not any money, goods or services were provided in order to put the person in question in a position to carry out the conduct,

  (b) it is not necessary to show that the conduct was of a particular kind if it is shown that the property was obtained through conduct of one of a number of kinds, each of which would have been unlawful conduct.

CHAPTER 2   CIVIL RECOVERY IN THE HIGH COURT OR COURT OF SESSION

Proceedings for recovery orders

243   Proceedings for recovery orders in England and Wales or Northern Ireland

(1) Proceedings for a recovery order may be taken by the enforcement authority in the High Court against any person who the authority thinks holds recoverable property.

(2) The enforcement authority must serve the claim form—

(a) on the respondent, and

(b) unless the court dispenses with service, on any other person who the authority thinks holds any associated property which the authority wishes to be subject to a recovery order,

wherever domiciled, resident or present.

Vesting and realisation of recoverable property

266   Recovery orders

(1) If in proceedings under this Chapter the court is satisfied that any property is recoverable, the court must make a recovery order.

(2) The recovery order must vest the recoverable property in the trustee for civil recovery.

(3) But the court may not make in a recovery order—

(a) any provision in respect of any recoverable property if each of the conditions in subsection (4) or (as the case may be) (5) is met and it would not be just and equitable to do so, or

(b) any provision which is incompatible with any of the Convention rights (within the meaning of the Human Rights Act 1998 (c. 42)).

(4) In relation to a court in England and Wales or Northern Ireland, the conditions referred to in subsection (3)(a) are that—

(a) the respondent obtained the recoverable property in good faith,

(b) he took steps after obtaining the property which he would not have taken if he had not obtained it or he took steps before obtaining the property which he would not have taken if he had not believed he was going to obtain it,

(c) when he took the steps, he had no notice the property was recoverable,

(d) if a recovery order were made in respect of the property, it would, by reason of the steps, be detrimental to him.

(5) In relation to a court in Scotland, the conditions referred to in subsection (3)(a) are that—

(a) the respondent obtained the recoverable property in good faith,

(b) he took steps after obtaining the property which he would not have taken if he had not obtained it or he took steps before obtaining the property which he would not have taken if he had not believed he was going to obtain it,

(c) when he took the steps, he had no reasonable grounds for believing that the property was recoverable,

(d) if a recovery order were made in respect of the property, it would, by reason of the steps, be detrimental to him.

(6) In deciding whether it would be just and equitable to make the provision in the recovery order where the conditions in subsection (4) or (as the case may be) (5) are met, the court must have regard to—

(a) the degree of detriment that would be suffered by the respondent if the provision were made,

(b) the enforcement authority's interest in receiving the realised proceeds of the recoverable property.

(7) A recovery order may sever any property.

(8) A recovery order may impose conditions as to the manner in which the trustee for civil recovery may deal with any property vested by the order for the purpose of realising it.

[(8A) A recovery order made by a court in England and Wales or Northern Ireland may provide for payment under section 280 of reasonable legal expenses that a person has reasonably incurred, or may reasonably incur, in respect of—

(a) the proceedings under this Part in which the order is made, or

(b) any related proceedings under this Part.

(8B) If regulations under section 286B apply to an item of expenditure, a sum in respect of the item is not payable under section 280 in pursuance of provision under subsection (8A) unless—

(a) the enforcement authority agrees to its payment, or

(b) the court has assessed the amount allowed by the regulations in respect of that item and the sum is paid in respect of the assessed amount.]

(9) This section is subject to sections 270 to 278.

267 Functions of the trustee for civil recovery

(1) The trustee for civil recovery is a person appointed by the court to give effect to a recovery order.

(2) The enforcement authority must nominate a suitably qualified person for appointment as the trustee.

(3) The functions of the trustee are—

(a) to secure the detention, custody or preservation of any property vested in him by the recovery order,

(b) in the case of property other than money, to realise the value of the property for the benefit of the enforcement authority, and

(c) to perform any other functions conferred on him by virtue of this Chapter.

CHAPTER 4   GENERAL

Recoverable property

304 Property obtained through unlawful conduct

(1) Property obtained through unlawful conduct is recoverable property.

(2) But if property obtained through unlawful conduct has been disposed of (since it was so obtained), it is recoverable property only if it is held by a person into whose hands it may be followed.

(3) Recoverable property obtained through unlawful conduct may be followed into the hands of a person obtaining it on a disposal by—

(a) the person who through the conduct obtained the property, or

(b) a person into whose hands it may (by virtue of this subsection) be followed.

305 Tracing property, etc.

(1) Where property obtained through unlawful conduct ("the original property") is or has been recoverable, property which represents the original property is also recoverable property.

(2) If a person enters into a transaction by which—

(a) he disposes of recoverable property, whether the original property or property which (by virtue of this Chapter) represents the original property, and

(b) he obtains other property in place of it,

the other property represents the original property.

(3) If a person disposes of recoverable property which represents the original property, the property may be followed into the hands of the person who obtains it (and it continues to represent the original property).

306 Mixing property

(1) Subsection (2) applies if a person's recoverable property is mixed with other property (whether his property or another's).

(2) The portion of the mixed property which is attributable to the recoverable property represents the property obtained through unlawful conduct.

(3) Recoverable property is mixed with other property if (for example) it is used—

(a) to increase funds held in a bank account,

(b) in part payment for the acquisition of an asset,

(c) for the restoration or improvement of land,

(d) by a person holding a leasehold interest in the property to acquire the freehold.

307 Recoverable property: accruing profits

(1) This section applies where a person who has recoverable property obtains further property consisting of profits accruing in respect of the recoverable property.

(2) The further property is to be treated as representing the property obtained through unlawful conduct.

308 General exceptions

(1) If—

(a) a person disposes of recoverable property, and

(b) the person who obtains it on the disposal does so in good faith, for value and without notice that it was recoverable property,

the property may not be followed into that person's hands and, accordingly, it ceases to be recoverable.

(2) If recoverable property is vested, forfeited or otherwise disposed of in pursuance of powers conferred by virtue of this Part, it ceases to be recoverable.

(3) If—

(a) in pursuance of a judgment in civil proceedings (whether in the United Kingdom or elsewhere), the defendant makes a payment to the claimant or the claimant otherwise obtains property from the defendant,

(b) the claimant's claim is based on the defendant's unlawful conduct, and

(c) apart from this subsection, the sum received, or the property obtained, by the claimant would be recoverable property,

the property ceases to be recoverable.

In relation to Scotland, "claimant" and "defendant" are to be read as "pursuer" and "defender".

(4) If—

(a) a payment is made to a person in pursuance of a compensation order under Article 14 of the Criminal Justice (Northern Ireland) Order 1994 (S.I. 1994/2795 (N.I. 15)), section 249 of the Criminal Procedure (Scotland) Act 1995 (c. 46) or section 130 of the Powers of Criminal Courts (Sentencing) Act 2000 (c. 6), and

(b) apart from this subsection, the sum received would be recoverable property,

the property ceases to be recoverable.

(5) If—

(a) a payment is made to a person in pursuance of a restitution order under section 27 of the Theft Act (Northern Ireland) 1969 (c. 16 (N.I.)) or section 148(2) of the Powers of Criminal Courts (Sentencing) Act 2000 or a person otherwise obtains any property in pursuance of such an order, and

(b) apart from this subsection, the sum received, or the property obtained, would be recoverable property,

the property ceases to be recoverable.

(6) If—

    (a) in pursuance of an order made by the court under section 382(3) or 383(5) of the Financial Services and Markets Act 2000 (c. 8) (restitution orders), an amount is paid to or distributed among any persons in accordance with the court's directions, and

    (b) apart from this subsection, the sum received by them would be recoverable property,

the property ceases to be recoverable.

(7) If—

    (a) in pursuance of a requirement of the Financial Services Authority under section 384(5) of the Financial Services and Markets Act 2000 (power of authority to require restitution), an amount is paid to or distributed among any persons, and

    (b) apart from this subsection, the sum received by them would be recoverable property,

the property ceases to be recoverable.

(8) Property is not recoverable while a restraint order applies to it, that is—

    (a) an order under section 41, 120 or 190, or

    (b) an order under any corresponding provision of an enactment mentioned in section 8(7)(a) to (g).

(9) Property is not recoverable if it has been taken into account in deciding the amount of a person's benefit from criminal conduct for the purpose of making a confiscation order, that is—

    (a) an order under section 6, 92 or 156, or

    (b) an order under a corresponding provision of an enactment mentioned in section 8(7)(a) to (g),

and, in relation to an order mentioned in paragraph (b), the reference to the amount of a person's benefit from criminal conduct is to be read as a reference to the corresponding amount under the enactment in question.

(10) Where—

    (a) a person enters into a transaction to which section 305(2) applies, and

    (b) the disposal is one to which subsection (1) or (2) applies,

this section does not affect the recoverability (by virtue of section 305(2)) of any property obtained on the transaction in place of the property disposed of.

309   Other exemptions

. . .

310   Granting interests

(1) If a person grants an interest in his recoverable property, the question whether the interest is also recoverable is to be determined in the same manner as it is on any other disposal of recoverable property.

(2) Accordingly, on his granting an interest in the property ("the property in question")—

    (a) where the property in question is property obtained through unlawful conduct, the interest is also to be treated as obtained through that conduct,

    (b) where the property in question represents in his hands property obtained through unlawful conduct, the interest is also to be treated as representing in his hands the property so obtained.

Interpretation

314   Obtaining and disposing of property

(1) References to a person disposing of his property include a reference—

    (a) to his disposing of a part of it, or

(b) to his granting an interest in it,

(or to both); and references to the property disposed of are to any property obtained on the disposal.

(2) A person who makes a payment to another is to be treated as making a disposal of his property to the other, whatever form the payment takes.

(3) Where a person's property passes to another under a will or intestacy or by operation of law, it is to be treated as disposed of by him to the other.

(4) A person is only to be treated as having obtained his property for value in a case where he gave unexecuted consideration if the consideration has become executed consideration.

316 General interpretation

(1) In this Part—

. . .

dealing" with property includes disposing of it, taking possession of it or removing it from the United Kingdom,

"enforcement authority"—

    (a) in relation to England and Wales and Northern Ireland, means the Director,

    (b) in relation to Scotland, means the Scottish Ministers,

. . .

"property obtained through unlawful conduct" has the meaning given by section 242,

"recoverable property" is to be read in accordance with sections 304 to 310,

"recovery order" means an order made under section 266,

. . .

"unlawful conduct" has the meaning given by section 241,

"value" means market value.

(2) The following provisions apply for the purposes of this Part.

(3) For the purpose of deciding whether or not property was recoverable at any time (including times before commencement), it is to be assumed that this Part was in force at that and any other relevant time.

(4) Property is all property wherever situated and includes—

    (a) money,

    (b) all forms of property, real or personal, heritable or moveable,

    (c) things in action and other intangible or incorporeal property.

(5) Any reference to a person's property (whether expressed as a reference to the property he holds or otherwise) is to be read as follows.

(6) In relation to land, it is a reference to any interest which he holds in the land.

(7) In relation to property other than land, it is a reference—

    (a) to the property (if it belongs to him), or

    (b) to any other interest which he holds in the property.

. . .

Anti-social Behaviour Act 2003

(2003, c. 38)

PART 1   PREMISES WHERE DRUGS USED UNLAWFULLY

9 Exemption from liability for certain damages

(1) A constable is not liable for relevant damages in respect of anything done or omitted to be done by him in the performance or purported performance of his functions under this Part.

(2) A chief officer of police is not liable for relevant damages in respect of anything done or omitted to be done by a constable under his direction or control in the performance or purported performance of the constable's functions under this Part.

(3) Subsections (1) and (2) do not apply—

(a) if the act or omission is shown to have been in bad faith;

(b) so as to prevent an award of damages made in respect of an act or omission on the ground that the act or omission was unlawful by virtue of section 6(1) of the Human Rights Act 1998 (c. 42).

(4) This section does not affect any other exemption from liability for damages (whether at common law or otherwise).

(5) Relevant damages are damages in proceedings for judicial review or for the tort of negligence or misfeasance in public duty.

10 Compensation

(1) This section applies to any person who incurs financial loss in consequence of—

(a) the issue of a closure notice, or

(b) a closure order having effect.

(3) An application under this section must not be entertained unless it is made not later than the end of the period of three months starting with whichever is the later of—

(a) the day the court decides not to make a closure order,

(b) the day the Crown Court dismisses an appeal against a decision not to make a closure order;

(c) the day a closure order ceases to have effect.

(4) On an application under this section the court may order the payment of compensation out of central funds if it is satisfied—

(a) that the person had no connection with the use of the premises as mentioned in section 1(1),

(b) if the person is the owner or occupier of the premises, that he took reasonable steps to prevent the use,

(c) that the person has incurred financial loss as mentioned in subsection (1), and

(d) having regard to all the circumstances it is appropriate to order payment of compensation in respect of that loss.

(5) Central funds has the same meaning as in enactments providing for the payment of costs.

19 Parenting contracts in cases of exclusion from school or truancy

(1) This section applies where a pupil has been excluded on disciplinary grounds from a relevant school for a fixed period or permanently.

(2) This section also applies where a child of compulsory school age has failed to attend regularly at

[(a) a relevant school at which he is a registered pupil,

(b) any place at which education is provided for him in the circumstances mentioned in subsection (1) of section 444ZA of the Education Act 1996, and

(c) any place at which he is required to attend in the circumstances mentioned in subsection (2) of that section.]

(3) A local education authority or the governing body of a relevant school may enter into a parenting contract with a parent of the pupil or child.

(4) A parenting contract is a document which contains—

(a) a statement by the parent that he agrees to comply with such requirements as may be specified in the document for such period as may be so specified, and

(b) a statement by the local education authority or governing body that it agrees to provide support to the parent for the purpose of complying with those requirements.

(5) The requirements mentioned in subsection (4) may include (in particular) a requirement to attend a counselling or guidance programme.

(6) The purpose of the requirements mentioned in subsection (4)—

    (a) in a case falling within subsection (1), is to improve the behaviour of the pupil,

    (b) in a case falling within subsection (2), is to ensure that the child attends regularly at the relevant school at which he is a registered pupil.

(7) A parenting contract must be signed by the parent and signed on behalf of the local education authority or governing body.

(8) A parenting contract does not create any obligations in respect of whose breach any liability arises in contract or in tort.

(9) Local education authorities and governing bodies of relevant schools must, in carrying out their functions in relation to parenting contracts, have regard to any guidance which is issued by the appropriate person from time to time for that purpose.

25 Parenting contracts in respect of criminal conduct and anti-social behaviour

(1) This section applies where a child or young person has been referred to a youth offending team.

(2) The youth offending team may enter into a parenting contract with a parent of the child or young person if a member of that team has reason to believe that the child or young person has engaged, or is likely to engage, in criminal conduct or anti-social behaviour.

(3) A parenting contract is a document which contains—

    (a) a statement by the parent that he agrees to comply with such requirements as may be specified in the document for such period as may be so specified, and

    (b) a statement by the youth offending team that it agrees to provide support to the parent for the purpose of complying with those requirements.

(4) The requirements mentioned in subsection (3)(a) may include (in particular) a requirement to attend a counselling or guidance programme.

(5) The purpose of the requirements mentioned in subsection (3)(a) is to prevent the child or young person from engaging in criminal conduct or anti-social behaviour or further criminal conduct or further anti-social behaviour.

(6) A parenting contract must be signed by the parent and signed on behalf of the youth offending team.

(7) A parenting contract does not create any obligations in respect of whose breach any liability arises in contract or in tort.

(8) Youth offending teams must, in carrying out their functions in relation to parenting contracts, have regard to any guidance which is issued by the Secretary of State from time to time for that purpose.

PART 4   DISPERSAL OF GROUPS ETC.

30 Dispersal of groups and removal of persons under 16 to their place of residence

(1) This section applies where a relevant officer has reasonable grounds for believing—

    (a) that any members of the public have been intimidated, harassed, alarmed or distressed as a result of the presence or behaviour of groups of two or more persons in public places in any locality in his police area (the "relevant locality"), and

    (b) that anti-social behaviour is a significant and persistent problem in the relevant locality.

(2) The relevant officer may give an authorisation that the powers conferred on a constable in uniform by subsections (3) to (6) are to be exercisable for a period specified in the authorisation which does not exceed 6 months.

(3) Subsection (4) applies if a constable in uniform has reasonable grounds for believing that the presence or behaviour of a group of two or more persons in any public place in the relevant locality has resulted, or is likely to result, in any members of the public being intimidated, harassed, alarmed or distressed.

(4) The constable may give one or more of the following directions, namely—

    (a) a direction requiring the persons in the group to disperse (either immediately or by such time as he may specify and in such way as he may specify),

    (b) a direction requiring any of those persons whose place of residence is not within the relevant locality to leave the relevant locality or any part of the relevant locality (either immediately or by such time as he may specify and in such way as he may specify), and

    (c) a direction prohibiting any of those persons whose place of residence is not within the relevant locality from returning to the relevant locality or any part of the relevant locality for such period (not exceeding 24 hours) from the giving of the direction as he may specify;

but this subsection is subject to subsection (5).

(5) A direction under subsection (4) may not be given in respect of a group of persons—

    (a) who are engaged in conduct which is lawful under section 220 of the Trade Union and Labour Relations (Consolidation) Act 1992, or

    (b) who are taking part in a public procession of the kind mentioned in section 11(1) of the Public Order Act 1986 in respect of which—

        (i)   written notice has been given in accordance with section 11 of that Act, or

        (ii) such notice is not required to be given as provided by subsections (1) and (2) of that section.

(6) If, between the hours of 9 pm and 6 am, a constable in uniform finds a person in any public place in the relevant locality who he has reasonable grounds for believing—

    (a) is under the age of 16, and

    (b) is not under the effective control of a parent or a responsible person aged 18 or over,

he may remove the person to the person's place of residence unless he has reasonable grounds for believing that the person would, if removed to that place, be likely to suffer significant harm.

(7) In this section any reference to the presence or behaviour of a group of persons is to be read as including a reference to the presence or behaviour of any one or more of the persons in the group.

36 Interpretation

In this Part—

    "anti-social behaviour" means behaviour by a person which causes or is likely to cause harassment, alarm or distress to one or more other persons not of the same household as the person,

    . . .

    "public place" means—

    (a) any highway, and

    (b) any place to which at the material time the public or any section of the public has access, on payment or otherwise, as of right or by virtue of express or implied permission,

    . . .

PART 6   THE ENVIRONMENT

40 Closure of noisy premises

(1) The chief executive officer of the relevant local authority may make a closure order in relation to premises to which this section applies if he reasonably believes that—

    (a) a public nuisance is being caused by noise coming from the premises, and

    (b) the closure of the premises is necessary to prevent that nuisance.

(2) This section applies to premises if—
(a) a premises licence has effect in respect of them, or
(b) a temporary event notice has effect in respect of them.

(3) In this section "closure order" means an order which requires specified premises to be kept closed during a specified period which—
(a) does not exceed 24 hours, and
(b) begins when a manager of the premises receives written notice of the order.

(4) A person commits an offence if without reasonable excuse he permits premises to be open in contravention of a closure order.

(5) A person guilty of an offence under this section shall be liable on summary conviction to—
(a) imprisonment for a term not exceeding [51 weeks],
(b) a fine not exceeding £20,000, or
(c) both.

52 Exemption from liability in relation to [defacement removal notices]

(1) None of the persons mentioned in subsection (2) is to have any liability to any person responsible for the relevant surface for damages or otherwise (whether at common law or otherwise) arising out of anything done or omitted to be done in the exercise or purported exercise of—
(a) the power under subsection (4) of section 48 (including as provided for in sub-section (5) of that section), or
(b) the power under subsection (8) of that section.

(2) Those persons are—
(a) in the case of the power mentioned in subsection (1)(a)—
(i) the local authority and any employee of the authority, and
(ii) any person authorised by the authority under section 48(4) and the employer or any employee of that person, and
(b) in the case of the power mentioned in subsection (1)(b), the local authority and any employee of the authority.

(3) Subsection (1) does not apply—
(a) if the act or omission is shown to have been in bad faith;
(b) to liability arising out of a failure to exercise due care and attention;
(c) so as to prevent an award of damages made in respect of an act or omission on the ground that the act or omission was unlawful by virtue of section 6(1) of the Human Rights Act 1998 (c. 42).

(4) This section does not affect any other exemption from liability (whether at common law or otherwise).

(5) Section 48(11) is to apply for the purposes of this section as it applies for the purposes of that section.

PART 8   HIGH HEDGES

65 Complaints to which this Part applies

(1) This Part applies to a complaint which—
(a) is made for the purposes of this Part by an owner or occupier of a domestic property; and
(b) alleges that his reasonable enjoyment of that property is being adversely affected by the height of a high hedge situated on land owned or occupied by another person.

(2) This Part also applies to a complaint which—
(a) is made for the purposes of this Part by an owner of a domestic property that is for the time being unoccupied, and

(b) alleges that the reasonable enjoyment of that property by a prospective occupier of that property would be adversely affected by the height of a high hedge situated on land owned or occupied by another person,

as it applies to a complaint falling within subsection (1).

(4) This Part does not apply to complaints about the effect of the roots of a high hedge.

66 High hedges

(1) In this Part "high hedge" means so much of a barrier to light or access as—

(a) is formed wholly or predominantly by a line of two or more evergreens; and

(b) rises to a height of more than two metres above ground level.

(2) For the purposes of subsection (1) a line of evergreens is not to be regarded as forming a barrier to light or access if the existence of gaps significantly affects its overall effect as such a barrier at heights of more than two metres above ground level.

(3) A reference in this Part to a person's reasonable enjoyment of domestic property includes a reference to his reasonable enjoyment of a part of the property.

68 Procedure for dealing with complaints

(1) This section has effect where a complaint to which this Part applies—

(a) is made to the relevant authority; and

(b) is accompanied by such fee (if any) as the authority may determine.

(2) If the authority consider—

(a) that the complainant has not taken all reasonable steps to resolve the matters complained of without proceeding by way of such a complaint to the authority, or

(b) that the complaint is frivolous or vexatious,

the authority may decide that the complaint should not be proceeded with.

(3) If the authority do not so decide, they must decide—

(a) whether the height of the high hedge specified in the complaint is adversely affecting the complainant's reasonable enjoyment of the domestic property so specified; and

(b) if so, what action (if any) should be taken in relation to that hedge, in pursuance of a remedial notice under section 69, with a view to remedying the adverse effect or preventing its recurrence.

(4) If the authority decide under subsection (3) that action should be taken as mentioned in paragraph (b) of that subsection, they must as soon as is reasonably practicable—

(a) issue a remedial notice under section 69 implementing their decision;

(b) send a copy of that notice to the following persons, namely—

(i) every complainant; and

(ii) every owner and every occupier of the neighbouring land; and

(c) notify each of those persons of the reasons for their decision.

(5) If the authority—

(a) decide that the complaint should not be proceeded with, or

(b) decide either or both of the issues specified in subsection (3) otherwise than in the complainant's favour,

they must as soon as is reasonably practicable notify the appropriate person or persons of any such decision and of their reasons for it.

69 Remedial notices

(1) For the purposes of this Part a remedial notice is a notice—

(a) issued by the relevant authority in respect of a complaint to which this Part applies; and

(b) stating the matters mentioned in subsection (2).

(2) Those matters are—

(a) that a complaint has been made to the authority under this Part about a high hedge specified in the notice which is situated on land so specified;

 (b) that the authority have decided that the height of that hedge is adversely affecting the complainant's reasonable enjoyment of the domestic property specified in the notice;

 (c) the initial action that must be taken in relation to that hedge before the end of the compliance period;

 (d) any preventative action that they consider must be taken in relation to that hedge at times following the end of that period while the hedge remains on the land; and

 (e) the consequences under sections 75 and 77 of a failure to comply with the notice.

(3) The action specified in a remedial notice is not to require or involve—

 (a) a reduction in the height of the hedge to less than two metres above ground level; or

 (b) the removal of the hedge.

(6) "The compliance period" in the case of a remedial notice is such reasonable period as is specified in the notice for the purposes of subsection (2)(c) as the period within which the action so specified is to be taken; and that period shall begin with the operative date of the notice.

(8) While a remedial notice has effect, the notice—

 (a) shall be a local land charge; and

 (b) shall be binding on every person who is for the time being an owner or occupier of the land specified in the notice as the land where the hedge in question is situated.

(9) In this Part—

"initial action" means remedial action or preventative action, or both;

"remedial action" means action to remedy the adverse effect of the height of the hedge on the complainant's reasonable enjoyment of the domestic property in respect of which the complaint was made; and

"preventative action" means action to prevent the recurrence of the adverse effect.

71 Appeals against remedial notices and other decisions of relevant authorities

(1) Where the relevant authority—

 (a) issue a remedial notice,

 (b) withdraw such a notice, or

 (c) waive or relax the requirements of such a notice,

each of the persons falling within subsection (2) may appeal to the appeal authority against the issue or withdrawal of the notice or (as the case may be) the waiver or relaxation of its requirements.

(2) Those persons are—

 (a) every person who is a complainant in relation to the complaint by reference to which the notice was given; and

 (b) every person who is an owner or occupier of the neighbouring land.

75 Offences

(1) Where—

 (a) a remedial notice requires the taking of any action, and

 (b) that action is not taken in accordance with that notice within the compliance period or (as the case may be) by the subsequent time by which it is required to be taken,

every person who, at a relevant time, is an owner or occupier of the neighbouring land is guilty of an offence and shall be liable, on summary conviction, to a fine not exceeding level 3 on the standard scale.

(3) In proceedings against a person for an offence under subsection (1) it shall be a defence for him to show that he did everything he could be expected to do to secure compliance with the notice.

(4) In any such proceedings against a person, it shall also be a defence for him to show, in a case in which he—

(a) is not a person to whom a copy of the remedial notice was sent in accordance with a provision of this Part, and

(b) is not assumed under subsection (5) to have had knowledge of the notice at the time of the alleged offence,

that he was not aware of the existence of the notice at that time.

(5) A person shall be assumed to have had knowledge of a remedial notice at any time if at that time—

(a) he was an owner of the neighbouring land; and

(b) the notice was at that time registered as a local land charge.

(6) Section 198 of the Law of Property Act 1925 (c. 20) (constructive notice) shall be disregarded for the purposes of this section.

(7) Where a person is convicted of an offence under subsection (1) and it appears to the court—

(a) that a failure to comply with the remedial notice is continuing, and

(b) that it is within that person's power to secure compliance with the notice,

the court may, in addition to or instead of imposing a punishment, order him to take the steps specified in the order for securing compliance with the notice.

(8) An order under subsection (7) must require those steps to be taken within such reasonable period as may be fixed by the order.

(9) Where a person fails without reasonable excuse to comply with an order under subsection (7) he is guilty of an offence and shall be liable, on summary conviction, to a fine not exceeding level 3 on the standard scale.

76 Power to require occupier to permit action to be taken by owner

Section 289 of the Public Health Act 1936 (c. 49) (power of court to require occupier to permit work to be done by owner) shall apply with any necessary modifications for the purpose of giving an owner of land to which a remedial notice relates the right, as against all other persons interested in the land, to comply with the notice.

77 Action by relevant authority

(1) This section applies where—

(a) a remedial notice requires the taking of any action; and

(b) that action is not taken in accordance with that notice within the compliance period or (as the case may be) after the end of that period when it is required to be taken by the notice.

(2) Where this section applies—

(a) a person authorised by the relevant authority may enter the neighbouring land and take the required action; and

(b) the relevant authority may recover any expenses reasonably incurred by that person in doing so from any person who is an owner or occupier of the land.

(3) Expenses recoverable under this section shall be a local land charge and binding on successive owners of the land and on successive occupiers of it.

(4) Where expenses are recoverable under this section from two or more persons, those persons shall be jointly and severally liable for the expenses.

(5) A person shall not enter land in the exercise of a power conferred by this section unless at least 7 days' notice of the intended entry has been given to every occupier of the land.

(6) A person authorised under this section to enter land—

(a) shall, if so required, produce evidence of his authority before entering; and

(b) shall produce such evidence if required to do so at any time while he remains on the land.

(7) A person who enters land in the exercise of a power conferred by this section may—

(a) use a vehicle to enter the land;

    (b) take with him such other persons as may be necessary;

    (c) take with him equipment and materials needed for the purpose of taking the required action.

(8) If, in the exercise of a power conferred by this section, a person enters land which is unoccupied or from which all of the persons occupying the land are temporarily absent, he must on his departure leave it as effectively secured against unauthorised entry as he found it.

(9) A person who wilfully obstructs a person acting in the exercise of powers under this section to enter land and take action on that land is guilty of an offence and shall be liable, on summary conviction, to a fine not exceeding level 3 on the standard scale.

Communications Act 2003
(2003, c. 21)

104 Civil liability for breach of conditions or enforcement notification

    (1) The obligation of a person to comply with—

        (a) the conditions set under section 45 which apply to him,

        (b) requirements imposed on him by an enforcement notification under section 95, and

        (c) the conditions imposed by a direction under section 98 or 100,

shall be a duty owed to every person who may be affected by a contravention of the condition or requirement.

    (2) Where a duty is owed by virtue of this section to a person—

        (a) a breach of the duty that causes that person to sustain loss or damage, and

        (b) an act which—

            (i) by inducing a breach of the duty or interfering with its performance, causes that person to sustain loss or damage, and

            (ii) is done wholly or partly for achieving that result,

shall be actionable at the suit or instance of that person.

    (3) In proceedings brought against a person by virtue of subsection (2)(a) it shall be a defence for that person to show that he took all reasonable steps and exercised all due diligence to avoid contravening the condition or requirement in question.

    (4) The consent of OFCOM is required for the bringing of proceedings by virtue of subsection (1)(a).

    (5) Where OFCOM give a consent for the purposes of subsection (4) subject to conditions relating to the conduct of the proceedings, the proceedings are not to be carried on by that person except in compliance with those conditions.

405 General interpretation

    (1) In this Act, except so far as the context otherwise requires . . .

"OFCOM" means the Office of Communications; . . .

Courts Act 2003
(2003, c. 39)

31 Immunity for acts within jurisdiction

    (1) No action lies against a justice of the peace in respect of what he does or omits to do—

        (a) in the execution of his duty as a justice of the peace, and

        (b) in relation to a matter within his jurisdiction.

(2) No action lies against a justices' clerk or an assistant clerk in respect of what he does or omits to do—

    (a) in the execution of his duty as a justices' clerk or assistant clerk exercising, by virtue of an enactment, a function of a single justice of the peace, and

    (b) in relation to a matter within his jurisdiction.

32   Immunity for certain acts beyond jurisdiction

(1) An action lies against a justice of the peace in respect of what he does or omits to do—

    (a) in the purported execution of his duty as a justice of the peace, but

    (b) in relation to a matter not within his jurisdiction, if, but only if, it is proved that he acted in bad faith.

(2) An action lies against a justices' clerk or an assistant clerk in respect of what he does or omits to do—

    (a) in the purported execution of his duty as a justices' clerk or assistant clerk exercising, by virtue of an enactment, a function of a single justice of the peace, but

    (b) in relation to a matter not within his jurisdiction, if, but only if, it is proved that he acted in bad faith.

35   Indemnity

(1) "Indemnifiable amounts", in relation to a justice of the peace, justices' clerk or assistant clerk, means—

    (a) costs which he reasonably incurs in or in connection with proceedings in respect of anything done or omitted to be done in the exercise (or purported exercise) of his duty as a justice of the peace, justices' clerk or assistant clerk,

    (b) costs which he reasonably incurs in taking steps to dispute a claim which might be made in such proceedings,

    (c) damages awarded against him or costs ordered to be paid by him in such proceedings, or

    (d) sums payable by him in connection with a reasonable settlement of such proceedings or such a claim.

(2) Indemnifiable amounts relate to criminal matters if the duty mentioned in subsection (1)(a) relates to criminal matters.

(3) The Lord Chancellor must indemnify a justice of the peace, justices' clerk or assistant clerk in respect of—

    (a) indemnifiable amounts which relate to criminal matters, unless it is proved, in respect of the matters giving rise to the proceedings or claim, that he acted in bad faith, and

    (b) other indemnifiable amounts if, in respect of the matters giving rise to the proceedings or claim, he acted reasonably and in good faith.

(4) The Lord Chancellor may indemnify a justice of the peace, justices' clerk or assistant clerk in respect of other indemnifiable amounts unless it is proved, in respect of the matters giving rise to the proceedings or claim, that he acted in bad faith.

(5) Any question whether, or to what extent, a person is to be indemnified under this section is to be determined by the Lord Chancellor.

Criminal Justice Act 2003

(2003, c. 44)

329   Civil proceedings for trespass to the person brought by offender

(1) This section applies where—

    (a) a person ("the claimant") claims that another person ("the defendant") did an act amounting to trespass to the claimant's person, and

(b) the claimant has been convicted in the United Kingdom of an imprisonable offence committed on the same occasion as that on which the act is alleged to have been done.

(2) Civil proceedings relating to the claim may be brought only with the permission of the court.

(3) The court may give permission for the proceedings to be brought only if there is evidence that either—

(a) the condition in subsection (5) is not met, or

(b) in all the circumstances, the defendant's act was grossly disproportionate.

(4) If the court gives permission and the proceedings are brought, it is a defence for the defendant to prove both—

(a) that the condition in subsection (5) is met, and

(b) that, in all the circumstances, his act was not grossly disproportionate.

(5) The condition referred to in subsection (3)(a) and (4)(a) is that the defendant did the act only because—

(a) he believed that the claimant—

(i)   was about to commit an offence,

(ii) was in the course of committing an offence, or

(iii) had committed an offence immediately beforehand; and

(b) he believed that the act was necessary to—

(i)   defend himself or another person,

(ii) protect or recover property,

(iii) prevent the commission or continuation of an offence, or

(iv) apprehend, or secure the conviction, of the claimant after he had committed an offence;

or was necessary to assist in achieving any of those things.

(6) Subsection (4) is without prejudice to any other defence.

(8) In this section—

(a) the reference to trespass to the person is a reference to—

(i)   assault,

(ii) battery, or

(iii) false imprisonment;

(b) references to a defendant's belief are to his honest belief, whether or not the belief was also reasonable;

(c) "court" means the High Court or a county court; and

(d) "imprisonable offence" means an offence which, in the case of a person aged 18 or over, is punishable by imprisonment.

Health and Social Care (Community Health and Standards) Act 2003

(2003, c. 43)

PART 3   RECOVERY OF NHS CHARGES

NHS charges

150   Liability to pay NHS charges

(1) This section applies if—

(a) a person makes a compensation payment to or in respect of any other person (the "injured person") in consequence of any injury, whether physical or psychological, suffered by the injured person, and

    (b) the injured person has—

        (i)   received NHS treatment at a health service hospital as a result of the injury,

        (ii) been provided with NHS ambulance services as a result of the injury for the purpose of taking him to a health service hospital for NHS treatment (unless he was dead on arrival at that hospital), or

        (iii) received treatment as mentioned in sub-paragraph (i) and been provided with ambulance services as mentioned in sub-paragraph (ii).

    (2) The person making the compensation payment is liable to pay the relevant NHS charges—

    (a) in respect of—

        (i)   the treatment, in so far as received at a hospital in England or Wales,

        (ii) the ambulance services, in so far as provided to take the injured person to such a hospital,

to the Secretary of State,

    (b) in respect of—

        (i)   the treatment, in so far as received at a hospital in Scotland,

        (ii) the ambulance services, in so far as provided to take the injured person to such a hospital,

to the Scottish Ministers.

    (3) "Compensation payment" means a payment, including a payment in money's worth, made—

    (a) by or on behalf of a person who is, or is alleged to be, liable to any extent in respect of the injury, or

    (b) in pursuance of a compensation scheme for motor accidents,

but does not include a payment mentioned in Schedule 10.

    (4) Subsection (1)(a) applies—

    (a) to a payment made—

        (i)   voluntarily, or in pursuance of a court order or an agreement, or otherwise, and

        (ii) in the United Kingdom or elsewhere, and

    (b) if more than one payment is made, to each payment.

    (5) "Injury" does not include any disease.

    (6) Nothing in subsection (5) prevents this Part from applying to—

    (a) treatment received as a result of any disease suffered by the injured person, or

    (b) ambulance services provided as a result of any disease suffered by him,

if the disease in question is attributable to the injury suffered by the injured person (and accordingly that treatment is received or those services are provided as a result of the injury).

    (7) "NHS treatment" means any treatment (including any examination of the injured person) other than—

    (a) treatment provided by virtue of section 18A(4) or 65 of the 1977 Act, section 57 of, or paragraph 14 of Schedule 7A to, the 1978 Act or paragraph 14 of Schedule 2 to the National Health Service and Community Care Act 1990 (c. 19) (accommodation and services for private patients),

    (b) other treatment provided by an NHS foundation trust in pursuance of an undertaking to pay in respect of the treatment given by or on behalf of the injured person,

    (c) treatment provided at a health service hospital by virtue of section 72 of the 1977 Act or section 64 of the 1978 Act (permission for use of national health service accommodation or facilities in private practice), or . . .

    (11) "Compensation scheme for motor accidents" means any scheme or arrangement under which funds are available for the payment of compensation in respect of motor accidents caused, or alleged to have been caused, by uninsured or unidentified persons.

    (14) For the purpose of this Part, it is irrelevant whether a compensation payment is made with or without an admission of liability.

Certificates of NHS charges

151 Applications for certificates of NHS charges

(1) Before a person makes a compensation payment in consequence of any injury suffered by an injured person, he may apply for a certificate to the Secretary of State, the Scottish Ministers or both, according to whether he believes the relevant NHS charges payable by him (if any) would be due to the Secretary of State, the Scottish Ministers or both.

153 Information contained in certificates

(1) A certificate must specify the amount (or amounts) for which the person to whom it is issued is liable under section 150 (2).

(2) The amount (or amounts) to be specified is (or are) to be that (or those) set out in, or determined in accordance with, regulations, reduced if applicable in accordance with subsection (3) or regulations under subsection (10).

(3) If a certificate relates to a claim made by or on behalf of an injured person—

    (a) in respect of which a court in England and Wales or Scotland has ordered a reduction of damages in accordance with section 1 of the Law Reform (Contributory Negligence) Act 1945,

    (b) in respect of which a court in Northern Ireland has ordered a reduction of damages in accordance with section 2 of the Law Reform (Miscellaneous Provisions) Act (Northern Ireland) 1948,

    (c) in respect of which a court in a country other than England and Wales, Scotland or Northern Ireland has ordered a reduction of damages under any provision of the law of that country which appears to the Secretary of State or the Scottish Ministers (as the case may be) to correspond to section 1 of the Law Reform (Contributory Negligence) Act 1945,

    (d) in respect of which an officer of a court in England and Wales or Northern Ireland has entered or sealed an agreed judgement or order which specifies—

        (i) that the damages are to be reduced to reflect the injured person's share in the responsibility for the injury in question, and

        (ii) the amount or proportion by which they are to be so reduced,

    (e) in the case of which the parties to any resulting action before a court in Scotland have executed a joint minute which specifies—

        (i) that the action has been settled extra-judicially, and

        (ii) the matters mentioned in paragraph (d)(i) and (ii),

    (f) in respect of which a document has been made under any provision of the law of a country other than England and Wales, Scotland or Northern Ireland—

        (i) which appears to the Secretary of State to correspond to an agreed judgement or order entered or sealed by an officer of a court in England and Wales, and

        (ii) which specifies the matters mentioned in paragraph (d)(i) and (ii), or

    (g) in the case of which a document has been made under any provision of the law of a country other than England and Wales, Scotland or Northern Ireland—

        (i) which appears to the Scottish Ministers to correspond to a joint minute executed by the parties to a resulting action before a court in Scotland specifying that the action has been settled extra-judicially, and

        (ii) which specifies the matters mentioned in paragraph (d)(i) and (ii),

the amount (or amounts) specified in the certificate is (or are) to be that (or those) which would be so specified apart from this subsection, reduced by the same proportion as the reduction of damages.

(4) If a certificate relates to an injured person who has not received NHS treatment at a health service hospital or been provided with NHS ambulance services as a result of the injury, it must indicate that no amount is payable to the Secretary of State or the Scottish Ministers (as the case may be) by reference to that certificate.

155 Recovery of NHS charges

(1) This section applies if a person has made a compensation payment and either—

(a) subsection (7) of section 151 applies but he has not applied for a certificate as required by that subsection, or

(b) he has not made payment, in full, of any amount due under section 150(2) by the end of the period allowed under section 154.

(2) The Secretary of State, the Scottish Ministers or both, according to the circumstances of the case, may—

(a) in a case within subsection (1)(a), issue the person who made the compensation payment with a certificate, and

(b) in a case within subsection (1)(b), issue him with a copy of the certificate or (if more than one has been issued) the most recent one,

and, in either case, issue him with a demand that payment of any amount due under section 150(2) be made immediately.

(6) The Secretary of State or the Scottish Ministers may recover the amount for which a demand for payment is made under subsection (2) from the person who made the compensation payment.

Payments to hospitals or ambulance trusts

162 Payment of NHS charges to hospitals or ambulance trusts

(1) If the Secretary of State receives or the Scottish Ministers receive a payment of relevant NHS charges under section 150(2)—

(a) if the payment relates only to NHS treatment received at a health service hospital, he or they must pay the amount received to the responsible body of the health service hospital,

(b) if the payment relates only to the provision of NHS ambulance services, he or they must pay the amount received to the relevant ambulance trust,

(c) if the payment relates to NHS treatment received at more than one health service hospital, he or they must divide the amount received among the responsible bodies of the hospitals concerned in such manner as he considers or they consider appropriate,

(d) if the payment relates to NHS treatment received at one or more health service hospitals and the provision of NHS ambulance services, he or they must divide the amount received among the responsible body or bodies of the hospital or hospitals and any relevant ambulance trusts concerned in such manner as he considers or they consider appropriate.

(2) Subsection (1) does not apply to any amount received by the Secretary of State or the Scottish Ministers under section 150(2) which he is or they are required to repay in accordance with regulations under section 153(2).

(4) Any amounts received under this section by the responsible bodies of the health service hospitals concerned must be used for the purposes of providing goods and services for the benefit of patients receiving NHS treatment at those hospitals.

(5) Any amounts received under this section by the relevant ambulance trusts concerned must be used for the purposes of NHS ambulance services.

Miscellaneous and general

163 Regulations governing lump sums, periodical payments etc.

(1) Regulations may make provision (including provision modifying this Part)—

(a) for cases to which section 150(2) applies in which two or more compensation payments in the form of lump sums are made by the same person in respect of the same injury,

(b) for cases to which section 150(2) applies in which an agreement is entered into for the making of—

    (i) eriodical compensation payments (whether of an income or capital nature), or

    (ii) periodical compensation payments and lump sum compensation payments,

(c) for cases in which the compensation payment to which section 150(2) applies is an interim payment of damages which a court orders to be repaid.

(2) Regulations made by virtue of subsection (1)(a) may (among other things) provide—

    (a) for giving credit for amounts already paid, and

    (b) for the payment by any person of any balance or the recovery from any person of any excess.

(3) Regulations may make provision modifying the application of this Part in relation to cases in which a payment into court is made and, in particular, may provide—

    (a) for the making of a payment into court to be treated in prescribed circumstances as the making of a compensation payment,

    (b) for application for, and issue of, certificates.

164 Liability of insurers

(1) If a compensation payment is made in a case where—

    (a) a person is liable to any extent in respect of the injury, and

    (b) the liability is covered to any extent by a policy of insurance,

the policy is also to be treated as covering any liability of that person under section 150(2).

(2) Liability imposed on the insurer by subsection (1) cannot be excluded or restricted.

(3) For that purpose excluding or restricting liability includes—

    (a) making the liability or its enforcement subject to restrictive or onerous conditions,

    (b) excluding or restricting any right or remedy in respect of the liability, or subjecting a person to any prejudice in consequence of his pursuing any such right or remedy, or

    (c) excluding or restricting rules of evidence or procedure.

(4) Regulations may in prescribed cases limit the amount of the liability imposed on the insurer by subsection (1).

(5) This section applies in relation to policies of insurance issued before (as well as those issued after) the date on which it comes into force.

(6) References in this section to policies of insurance and their issue include references to contracts of insurance and their making.

165 Power to apply Part 3 to treatment at non-health service hospitals

. . .

166 The Crown

This Part binds the Crown.

Licensing Act 2003
(2003, c. 17)

170 Exemption of police from liability for damages

(1) A constable is not liable for relevant damages in respect of any act or omission of his in the performance or purported performance of his functions in relation to a closure order or any extension of it.

(2) A chief officer of police is not liable for relevant damages in respect of any act or omission of a constable under his direction or control in the performance or purported performance of a function of the constable's in relation to a closure order or any extension of it.

(3) But neither subsection (1) nor (2) applies—

    (a) if the act or omission is shown to have been in bad faith, or

    (b) so as to prevent an award of damages in respect of an act or omission on the grounds that the act or omission was unlawful as a result of section 6(1) of the Human Rights Act 1998 (c. 42) (incompatibility of act or omission with Convention rights).

    (4) This section does not affect any other exemption from liability for damages (whether at common law or otherwise).

    (5) In this section, "relevant damages" means damages awarded in proceedings for judicial review, the tort of negligence or misfeasance in public office.

Local Government Act 2003
(2003, c. 26)

6   Protection of lenders

A person lending money to a local authority shall not be bound to enquire whether the authority has power to borrow the money and shall not be prejudiced by the absence of any such power.

Civil Partnership Act 2004
(2004, c. 33)

1   Civil partnership

    (1) A civil partnership is a relationship between two people of the same sex ("civil partners")—

    (a) which is formed when they register as civil partners of each other—

      (i) in England or Wales (under Part 2),

      (ii) in Scotland (under Part 3),

      (iii) in Northern Ireland (under Part 4), or

      (iv) outside the United Kingdom under an Order in Council made under Chapter 1 of Part 5 (registration at British consulates etc. or by armed forces personnel), or

    (b) which they are treated under Chapter 2 of Part 5 as having formed (at the time determined under that Chapter) by virtue of having registered an overseas relationship.

69   Actions in tort between civil partners

    (1) This section applies if an action in tort is brought by one civil partner against the other during the subsistence of the civil partnership.

    (2) The court may stay the proceedings if it appears—

    (a) that no substantial benefit would accrue to either civil partner from the continuation of the proceedings, or

    (b) that the question or questions in issue could more conveniently be disposed of on an application under section 66.

    (3) Without prejudice to subsection (2)(b), the court may in such an action—

    (a) exercise any power which could be exercised on an application under section 66, or

    (b) give such directions as it thinks fit for the disposal under that section of any question arising in the proceedings.

73   Civil partnership agreements unenforceable

    (1) A civil partnership agreement does not under the law of England and Wales have effect as a contract giving rise to legal rights.

(2) No action lies in England and Wales for breach of a civil partnership agreement, whatever the law applicable to the agreement.

(3) In this section and section 74 "civil partnership agreement" means an agreement between two people—

    (a) to register as civil partners of each other—

        (i) in England and Wales (under this Part),

        (ii) in Scotland (under Part 3),

        (iii) in Northern Ireland (under Part 4), or

        (iv) outside the United Kingdom under an Order in Council made under Chapter 1 of Part 5 (registration at British consulates etc. or by armed forces personnel), or

    (b) to enter into an overseas relationship.

(4) This section applies in relation to civil partnership agreements whether entered into before or after this section comes into force, but does not affect any action commenced before it comes into force.

Companies (Audit, Investigations and Community Enterprise) Act 2004
(2004, c. 27)

16 Grants to bodies concerned with accounting standards etc.

. . .

18 Exemption from liability

(1) Where a grant has been paid by the Secretary of State to a body under section 16, this section prevents any liability in damages arising in respect of certain acts or omissions occurring during the period of 12 months beginning with the date on which the grant was paid.

(2) In this section—

"the exemption period" means the period of 12 months mentioned in subsection (1);

"a relevant body" means the body mentioned in that subsection or a body carrying on any subsidiary activities of that body (within the meaning of section 16);

"section 16(2) activities" means activities concerned with any of the matters set out in section 16(2).

(3) Neither a relevant body, nor any person who is (or is acting as) a member, officer or member of staff of a relevant body, is to be liable in damages for anything done, or omitted to be done, during the exemption period for the purposes of or in connection with—

    (a) the carrying on of any section 16(2) activities of the body, or

    (b) the purported carrying on of any such activities.

(4) Subsection (3) does not apply—

    (a) if the act or omission is shown to have been in bad faith; or

    (b) so as to prevent an award of damages in respect of the act or omission on the grounds that it was unlawful as a result of section 6(1) of the Human Rights Act 1998 (c. 42) (acts of public authorities incompatible with Convention rights).

Finance Act 2004
(2004, c. 12)

320 Exclusion of extended limitation period in England, Wales and Northern Ireland

(1) Section 32(1)(c) of the Limitation Act 1980 (c. 58) or, in Northern Ireland, Article 71(1)(c) of the Limitation (Northern Ireland) Order 1989 (S.I. 1989/1339 (N.I. 11)) (extended period for bringing an action in case of mistake) does not apply in relation to a mistake of law

relating to a taxation matter under the care and management of the Commissioners of Inland Revenue.

This subsection has effect in relation to actions brought on or after 8th September 2003.

(2) For the purposes of—

(a) section 35(5)(a) of the Limitation Act 1980 or, in Northern Ireland, Article 73(4)(a) of the Limitation (Northern Ireland) Order 1989 (circumstances in which time-barred claim may be brought in course of existing action), and

(b) rules of court or county court rules having effect for the purposes of those provisions,

as they apply to claims in respect of mistakes of the kind mentioned in subsection (1), a new claim shall not be regarded as arising out of the same facts, or substantially the same facts, if it is brought in respect of a different payment, transaction, period or other matter.

This subsection has effect in relation to claims made on or after 20th November 2003.

(3) If before the passing of this Act—

(a) an action is brought in relation to which a defence of limitation would have been available if subsection (1) had been in force, or

(b) a claim is made on or after 20th November 2003 that by virtue of section 35(1)(b) of the Limitation Act 1980 (c. 58) or, in Northern Ireland, Article 73(1)(b) of the Limitation (Northern Ireland) Order 1989 (S.I. 1989/1339 (N.I. 11)) is treated as an action brought before 8th September 2003 and that claim would not have been allowed if subsections (1) and (2) above had been in force,

the action (or so much of it as relates to a cause of action in respect of which a defence of limitation would have been available or, as the case may be, a claim would not have been allowed) shall be deemed to be discontinued on the passing of this Act and any payment made by the Commissioners in or towards meeting their liability in the action (or so much of the action as so relates) may be recovered by them (with interest from the date of the payment).

(4) Nothing in this section affects a claim made before 20th November 2003 that by virtue of section 35(1)(b) of the Limitation Act 1980 or, in Northern Ireland, Article 73(1)(b) of the Limitation (Northern Ireland) Order 1989 is treated as an action brought before 8th September 2003.

(5) For the purposes of this section a claim is treated as made before 20th November 2003 if—

(a) the Commissioners have before that date consented in writing to the making of the claim; or

(b) immediately before that date—

(i) the consent of the Commissioners has been sought and has not been refused, or

(ii) an application to the court for permission to make the claim has been made and has not been refused.

(6) The provisions of this section apply to any action or claim for relief from the consequences of a mistake of law, whether expressed to be brought on the ground of mistake or on some other ground (such as unlawful demand or ultra vires act).

(7) This section shall be construed as one with the Limitation Act 1980 or, in Northern Ireland, the Limitation (Northern Ireland) Order 1989.

321 Exclusion of extended prescriptive period in Scotland

. . .

Fire and Rescue Services Act 2004
(2004, c. 21)

11 Power to respond to other eventualities

(1) A fire and rescue authority may take any action it considers appropriate—

(a) in response to an event or situation of a kind mentioned in subsection (2);

(b) for the purpose of enabling action to be taken in response to such an event or situation.

(2) The event or situation is one that causes or is likely to cause—

(a) one or more individuals to die, be injured or become ill;

(b) harm to the environment (including the life and health of plants and animals).

(3) The power conferred by subsection (1) includes power to secure the provision of equipment.

(4) The power conferred by subsection (1) may be exercised by an authority outside as well as within the authority's area.

19 Charging

(1) The Secretary of State may by order authorise a fire and rescue authority to charge a person of a specified description for any action of a specified description taken by the authority.

(2) An order under subsection (1) may authorise charging for extinguishing fires, or protecting life and property in the event of fires, only in respect of fires which are at sea or under the sea.

(3) An order under subsection (1) may not authorise charging for emergency medical assistance.

(4) The power in subsection (1) includes power to authorise a charge to be imposed on, or recovered from, a person other than the person in respect of whom action is taken by the authority.

40 Emergency supply by water undertaker

(1) If a fire and rescue authority requests a water undertaker to provide a supply and pressure of water for the purposes of extinguishing a fire that is greater than the undertaker would otherwise provide, the undertaker must take all necessary steps in order to do so.

(2) For the purposes of complying with its obligation under subsection (1) a water under taker may shut off the water from the mains and pipes in any area.

44 Powers of fire-fighters etc in an emergency etc

(1) An employee of a fire and rescue authority who is authorised in writing by the authority for the purposes of this section may do anything he reasonably believes to be necessary—

(a) if he reasonably believes a fire to have broken out or to be about to break out, for the purpose of extinguishing or preventing the fire or protecting life or property;

(b) if he reasonably believes a road traffic accident to have occurred, for the purpose of rescuing people or protecting them from serious harm;

(c) if he reasonably believes an emergency of another kind to have occurred, for the purpose of discharging any function conferred on the fire and rescue authority in relation to the emergency;

(d) for the purpose of preventing or limiting damage to property resulting from action taken as mentioned in paragraph (a), (b) or (c).

(2) In particular, an employee of a fire and rescue authority who is authorised as mentioned in subsection (1) may under that subsection—

(a) enter premises or a place, by force if necessary, without the consent of the owner or occupier of the premises or place;

(b) move or break into a vehicle without the consent of its owner;

(c) close a highway;

(d) stop and regulate traffic;

(e) restrict the access of persons to premises or a place.

(3) A person commits an offence if without reasonable excuse he obstructs or interferes with an employee of a fire and rescue authority taking action authorised under this section.

45   Obtaining information and investigating fires

(1) An authorised officer may at any reasonable time enter premises—

    (a) for the purpose of obtaining information needed for the discharge of a fire and rescue authority's functions under section 7, 8 or 9, or

    (b) if there has been a fire in the premises, for the purpose of investigating what caused the fire or why it progressed as it did.

(2) In this section and section 46, "authorised officer" means an employee of a fire and rescue authority who is authorised in writing by the authority for the purposes of this section.

(3) An authorised officer may not under subsection (1)—

    (a) enter premises by force, or

    (b) demand admission as of right to premises occupied as a private dwelling unless 24 hours' notice in writing has first been given to the occupier of the dwelling.

(4) An authorised officer may not under subsection (1)(b) enter as of right premises in which there has been a fire if—

    (a) the premises are unoccupied, and

    (b) the premises were occupied as a private dwelling immediately before the fire, unless 24 hours' notice in writing has first been given to the person who was the occupier of the dwelling immediately before the fire.

(5) An authorised officer may apply to a justice of the peace if—

    (a) he considers it necessary to enter premises for the purposes of subsection (1), but

    (b) he is unable to do so, or considers that he is likely to be unable to do so, otherwise than by force.

(6) If on an application under subsection (5) a justice is satisfied that—

    (a) it is necessary for the officer to enter the premises for the purposes of subsection (1), and

    (b) he is unable to do so, or is likely to be unable to do so, otherwise than by force,

he may issue a warrant authorising the officer to enter the premises by force at any reasonable time.

(7) An authorised officer may also apply to a justice of the peace if he considers it necessary to enter a dwelling for the purposes of subsection (1) without giving notice as required by subsection (3)(b) or (4).

(8) If on an application under subsection (7) a justice is satisfied that it is necessary for the authorised officer to enter the dwelling for the purposes of subsection (1) without giving notice as required by subsection (3)(b) or (4), the justice may issue a warrant authorising the officer to enter the premises at any time (by force if necessary).

(9) An authorised officer exercising a power of entry under this section must, if so required, produce evidence of his authorisation under subsection (2), and any warrant under subsection (6) or (8)—

    (a) before entering the premises, or

    (b) at any time before leaving the premises.

46   Supplementary powers

(1) If an authorised officer exercises a power of entry under section 45(1)(a), he may—

    (a) take with him any other persons, and any equipment, that he considers necessary;

    (b) require any person present on the premises to provide him with any facilities, information, documents or records, or other assistance, that he may reasonably request.

(2) If an authorised officer exercises a power of entry under section 45(1)(b) he may—

    (a) take with him any other persons, and any equipment, that he considers necessary;

    (b) inspect and copy any documents or records on the premises or remove them from the premises;

    (c) carry out any inspections, measurements and tests in relation to the premises, or to an article or substance found on the premises, that he considers necessary;

    (d) take samples of an article or substance found on the premises, but not so as to destroy it or damage it unless it is necessary to do so for the purpose of the investigation;

    (e) dismantle an article found on the premises, but not so as to destroy it or damage it unless it is necessary to do so for the purpose of the investigation;

    (f) take possession of an article or substance found on the premises and detain it for as long as is necessary for any of these purposes—

        (i) to examine it and do anything he has power to do under paragraph (c) or (e);

        (ii) to ensure that it is not tampered with before his examination of it is completed;

        (iii) to ensure that it is available for use as evidence in proceedings for an offence relevant to the investigation;

    (g) require a person present on the premises to provide him with any facilities, information, documents or records, or other assistance, that he may reasonably request.

  (3) If an authorised officer exercises the power in subsection (2)(d) he must—

    (a) leave a notice at the premises (either with a responsible person or if that is impracticable fixed in a prominent position) giving particulars of the article or substance and stating that he has taken a sample of it, and

    (b) if it is practicable to do so, give to a responsible person at the premises a portion of the sample marked in a manner sufficient to identify it.

  (4) If an authorised officer exercises the power in subsection (2)(f) he must leave a notice at the premises (either with a responsible person or if that is impracticable fixed in a prominent position) giving particulars of the article or substance and stating that he has taken possession of it.

  (5) If in the exercise of any power under section 45 or this section an authorised officer enters premises which are unoccupied, or from which the occupier is temporarily absent, he must on his departure leave the premises as effectively secured against unauthorised entry as he found them.

  (6) A person commits an offence if without reasonable excuse—

    (a) he obstructs the exercise of any power under section 45 or this section, or

    (b) he fails to comply with any requirement under subsection (1)(b) or (2)(g).

  (7) A person guilty of an offence under subsection (6) is liable on summary conviction to a fine not exceeding level 3 on the standard scale.

58 Meaning of "emergency"

In this Act "emergency" means an event or situation that causes or is likely to cause—

    (a) one or more individuals to die, be seriously injured or become seriously ill, or

    (b) serious harm to the environment (including the life and health of plants and animals).

Higher Education Act 2004
(2004, c. 8)

17 Privilege in relation to law of defamation

  (1) For the purposes of the law of defamation, any proceedings relating to the review under the scheme of a qualifying complaint are to be treated as if they were proceedings before a court.

  (2) For those purposes, absolute privilege attaches to the publication of—

    (a) any decision or recommendation made under the scheme by a person responsible for reviewing a qualifying complaint, and

(b) any report under paragraph 6 or 7 of Schedule 3.

(3) In this section "the scheme" means the scheme for the review of qualifying complaints provided by the designated operator.

Housing Act 2004
(2004, c. 34)

73 Other consequences of operating unlicensed HMOs: rent repayment orders

(3) No rule of law relating to the validity or enforceability of contracts in circumstances involving illegality is to affect the validity or enforceability of—

(a) any provision requiring the payment of rent or the making of any other periodical payment in connection with any tenancy or licence of a part of an unlicensed HMO, or

(b) any other provision of such a tenancy or licence.

(4) But amounts paid in respect of rent or other periodical payments payable in connection with such a tenancy or licence may be recovered in accordance with subsection (5) and section 74.

(5) If—

(a) an application in respect of an HMO is made to a residential property tribunal by the local housing authority or an occupier of a part of the HMO, and

(b) the tribunal is satisfied as to the matters mentioned in subsection (6) or (8),

the tribunal may make an order (a "rent repayment order") requiring the appropriate person to pay to the applicant such amount in respect of the housing benefit paid as mentioned in subsection (6)(b), or (as the case may be) the periodical payments paid as mentioned in subsection (8)(b), as is specified in the order (see section 74(2) to (8)).

77 Meaning of "HMO"

In this Part—

(a) "HMO" means a house in multiple occupation as defined by sections 254 to 259 . . .

Pensions Act 2004
(2004, c. 35)

16 Restitution

(1) If, on the application of the Regulator, the court is satisfied that there has been a misuse or misappropriation of any of the assets of an occupational or personal pension scheme, it may order any person involved to take such steps as the court may direct for restoring the parties to the position in which they were before the misuse or misappropriation occurred.

(2) For this purpose a person is "involved" if he appears to the court to have been knowingly concerned in the misuse or misappropriation of the assets.

18 Pension liberation: interpretation

(2) Money is to be taken to have been liberated from a pension scheme if—

(a) the money directly or indirectly represents an amount that, in respect of accrued rights of a member of a pension scheme, has been transferred out of the scheme in pursuance of—

(i) a relevant statutory provision, or

(ii) a provision of the applicable rules, other than a relevant statutory provision,

> (b) the trustees or managers of the scheme transferred the amount out of the scheme on the basis that a third party ("the liberator") would secure that the amount was used in an authorised way,
>
> (c) the amount has not been used in an authorised way, and
>
> (d) the liberator has not secured, and is not likely to secure, that the amount will be used in an authorised way.

19   Pension liberation: court's power to order restitution

(1) This section applies where money has been liberated from a pension scheme.

(2) In this section "recoverable property" means (subject to subsection (3))—

> (a) the money or any of it, or
>
> (b) property (of any kind and wherever situated) that, directly or indirectly, represents any of the money.

(3) Where a person acquires the beneficial interest in recoverable property in good faith, for value and without notice that the property is, or (as the case may be) represents, money liberated from a pension scheme—

> (a) the property ceases to be recoverable property, and
>
> (b) no property that subsequently represents it is recoverable property.

(4) The court, on the application of the Regulator, may make such order as the court thinks just and convenient for the purpose of securing that recoverable property, or money representing its value or proceeds of its sale, is transferred—

> (a) towards a pension scheme,
>
> (b) towards an annuity or insurance policy, or
>
> (c) to the liberated member.

(5) An order under subsection (4) may (in particular) direct a person who holds recoverable property, or has any degree of control over recoverable property, to take steps for the purpose mentioned in that subsection.

20   Pension liberation: restraining orders

(1) The Regulator may make a restraining order in relation to an account with a deposit-taker if—

> (a) it is satisfied that the account contains money which has been liberated from a pension scheme,
>
> (b) it is satisfied that the account is held by or on behalf of—
>
> > (i) the liberator, or
> >
> > (ii) a person who has to, or in practice is likely to, ensure that the account is operated in accordance with the liberator's directions, and
>
> (c) the order is made pending consideration being given to the making of one or more repatriation orders in relation to the account under section 21.

(2) A restraining order is an order directing that no credit or debit of any amount may be made to the account concerned ("the restrained account") during the period for which the order has effect.

(3) A restraining order must—

> (a) specify the name of the deposit-taker in respect of which it is made,
>
> (b) identify the account in respect of which it is made, and
>
> (c) contain such other information as may be prescribed.

(9) Where a restraining order has effect, the deposit-taker must return to the payer any money credited to the restrained account in breach of the order.

21   Pension liberation: repatriation orders

(1) Subsections (2) and (3) apply where—

> (a) a restraining order has effect, and
>
> (b) the Regulator is satisfied that the restrained account contains an amount of money liberated from a pension scheme.

(2) The Regulator may by order—

   (a) direct the deposit-taker concerned to pay from the account a sum not exceeding that amount—

     (i)   towards a pension scheme,

     (ii) towards an annuity or insurance policy, or

     (iii) to the liberated member, and

   (b) where it makes an order under paragraph (a)(i), direct the trustees or managers of the scheme to apply the sum, in such manner as the Regulator may direct, for the purpose of providing benefits under the scheme to or in respect of the liberated member.

(3) If it appears to the Regulator, on taking an overall view of transactions taking place before the restraining order was made, that there are two or more individuals each of whom is a person who is or may be the liberated member in relation to some of the money, the Regulator may determine the sums to be paid from the restrained account under subsection (2) on any basis that appears to the Regulator to be just and reasonable.

52   Restoration orders where transactions at an undervalue

(1) This section applies in relation to an occupational pension scheme other than—

   (a) a money purchase scheme, or

   (b) a prescribed scheme or a scheme of a prescribed description.

(2) The Regulator may make a restoration order in respect of a transaction involving assets of the scheme if—

   (a) a relevant event has occurred in relation to the employer in relation to the scheme, and

   (b) the transaction is a transaction at an undervalue entered into with a person at a time which—

     (i)   is on or after 27th April 2004, but

     (ii) is not more than two years before the occurrence of the relevant event in relation to the employer.

(3) A restoration order in respect of a transaction involving assets of a scheme is such an order as the Regulator thinks fit for restoring the position to what it would have been if the transaction had not been entered into.

(4) For the purposes of this section a relevant event occurs in relation to the employer in relation to a scheme if and when on or after the appointed day—

   (a) an insolvency event occurs in relation to the employer, or

   (b) the trustees or managers of the scheme make an application under subsection (1) of section 129 or receive a notice from the Board of the Pension Protection Fund under subsection (5)(a) of that section (applications and notifications prior to the Board assuming responsibility for a scheme).

(6) For the purposes of this section and section 53, a transaction involving assets of a scheme is a transaction at an undervalue entered into with a person ("P") if the trustees or managers of the scheme or appropriate persons in relation to the scheme—

   (a) make a gift to P or otherwise enter into a transaction with P on terms that provide for no consideration to be provided towards the scheme, or

   (b) enter into a transaction with P for a consideration the value of which, in money or money's worth, is significantly less than the value, in money or money's worth, of the consideration provided by or on behalf of the trustees or managers of the scheme.

(9) The provisions of this section apply without prejudice to the availability of any other remedy, even in relation to a transaction where the trustees or managers of the scheme or appropriate persons in question had no power to enter into the transaction.

53   Restoration orders: supplementary

(3) A restoration order is of no effect to the extent that it prejudices any interest in property which was acquired in good faith and for value or any interest deriving from such an interest.

(4) Nothing in subsection (3) prevents a restoration order requiring a person to pay a sum of money if the person received a benefit as a result of the transaction otherwise than in good faith and for value.

(5) Where a person has acquired an interest in property from a person or has received a benefit as a result of the transaction and—

(a) he is one of the trustees or managers or appropriate persons who entered into the transaction as mentioned in subsection (6) of section 52, or

(b) at the time of the acquisition or receipt—

(i)   he has notice of the fact that the transaction was a transaction at an undervalue,

(ii)   he is a trustee or manager, or the employer, in relation to the scheme, or

(iii)   he is connected with, or an associate of, any of the persons mentioned in paragraph (a) or (b)(ii),

then, unless the contrary is shown, it is to be presumed for the purposes of subsections (3) and (4) that the interest was acquired or the benefit was received otherwise than in good faith.

54   Content and effect of a restoration order

(3) Where the restoration order imposes an obligation on a person ("A") to transfer or pay a sum of money to a person specified in the order ("B"), the sum is to be treated as a debt due from A to B.

(6) Where, by virtue of subsection (5), any amount is transferred or paid to the Board in respect of a debt due by virtue of a restoration order, the Board must pay the amount to the trustees or managers of the scheme.

256   No indemnification for fines or civil penalties

(1) No amount may be paid out of the assets of an occupational or personal pension scheme for the purpose of reimbursing, or providing for the reimbursement of, any trustee or manager of the scheme in respect of—

(a) a fine imposed by way of penalty for an offence of which he is convicted, or

(b) a penalty which he is required to pay under or by virtue of section 10 of the Pensions Act 1995 (c. 26) or section 168(4) of the Pension Schemes Act 1993 (c. 48) (civil penalties).

(2) For the purposes of subsection (1), providing for the reimbursement of a trustee or manager in respect of a fine or penalty includes (among other things) providing for the payment of premiums in respect of a policy of insurance where the risk is or includes the imposition of such a fine or the requirement to pay such a penalty.

Traffic Management Act 2004
(2004, c. 18)

72   Civil penalties for road traffic contraventions

(1) The appropriate national authority may make provision by regulations for or in connection with—

(a) the imposition of penalty charges in respect of road traffic contraventions that—

(i)   are subject to civil enforcement (see section 73), and

(ii)   are committed in an area that is a civil enforcement area for contraventions of that description (see section 74), and

(b) the payment of such penalty charges.

(3) The regulations shall include provision in respect of any description of conduct for which a penalty charge may be imposed—

(a) prohibiting criminal proceedings or the issuing of a fixed penalty notice in respect of conduct of that description, or

(b) securing that a penalty charge is not required to be paid, or is refunded, where the conduct is the subject of criminal proceedings or of a fixed penalty notice.

73 Contraventions subject to civil enforcement

(1) Schedule 7 specifies the road traffic contraventions that are subject to civil enforcement.

(2) These are—

(a) parking contraventions (see Part 1 of the Schedule);

(b) bus lane contraventions (see Part 2 of the Schedule);

(c) London lorry ban contraventions (see Part 3 of the Schedule);

(d) moving traffic contraventions (see Part 4 of the Schedule).

76 Civil enforcement officers

(1) A local authority may provide for the enforcement of road traffic contraventions for which it is the enforcement authority by individuals to be known as civil enforcement officers.

(2) A civil enforcement officer must be—

(a) an individual employed by the authority, or

(b) where the authority have made arrangements with any person for the purposes of this section, an individual employed by that person to act as a civil enforcement officer.

(3) Civil enforcement officers—

(a) when exercising specified functions must wear such uniform as may be determined by the enforcement authority in accordance with guidelines issued by the appropriate national authority, and

(b) must not exercise any of those functions when not in uniform.

Clean Neighbourhoods and Environment Act 2005
(2005, c. 16)

Nuisance parking offences

3 Exposing vehicles for sale on a road

(1) A person is guilty of an offence if at any time—

(a) he leaves two or more motor vehicles parked within 500 metres of each other on a road or roads where they are exposed or advertised for sale, or

(b) he causes two or more motor vehicles to be so left.

(2) A person is not to be convicted of an offence under subsection (1) if he proves to the satisfaction of the court that he was not acting for the purposes of a business of selling motor vehicles.

4 Repairing vehicles on a road

(1) A person who carries out restricted works on a motor vehicle on a road is guilty of an offence, subject as follows.

(2) For the purposes of this section "restricted works" means—

(a) works for the repair, maintenance, servicing, improvement or dismantling of a motor vehicle or of any part of or accessory to a motor vehicle;

(b) works for the installation, replacement or renewal of any such part or accessory.

(3) A person is not to be convicted of an offence under this section in relation to any works if he proves to the satisfaction of the court that the works were not carried out—

(a) in the course of, or for the purposes of, a business of carrying out restricted works; or

(b) for gain or reward.

(4) Subsection (3) does not apply where the carrying out of the works gave reasonable cause for annoyance to persons in the vicinity.

(5) A person is also not to be convicted of an offence under this section in relation to any works if he proves to the satisfaction of the court that the works carried out were works of repair which—

(a) arose from an accident or breakdown in circumstances where repairs on the spot or elsewhere on the road were necessary; and

(b) were carried out within 72 hours of the accident or breakdown or were within that period authorised to be carried out at a later time by the local authority for the area.

Gambling Act 2005
(2005, c. 19)

335 Enforceability of gambling contracts

(1) The fact that a contract relates to gambling shall not prevent its enforcement.

(2) Subsection (1) is without prejudice to any rule of law preventing the enforcement of a contract on the grounds of unlawfulness (other than a rule relating specifically to gambling).

336 Power of Gambling Commission to void bet

(1) The Commission may make an order under this subsection in relation to a bet accepted by or through the holder of—

(a) a general betting operating licence,

(b) a pool betting operating licence, or

(c) a betting intermediary operating licence.

(2) Where the Commission makes an order under subsection (1) in relation to a bet—

(a) any contract or other arrangement in relation to the bet is void, and

(b) any money paid in relation to the bet (whether by way of stake, winnings, commission or otherwise) shall be repaid to the person who paid it, and repayment may be enforced as a debt due to that person.

(3) The Commission may make an order under subsection (1) in relation to a bet only if satisfied that the bet was substantially unfair.

(4) In considering whether a bet was unfair the Commission shall, in particular, take account of any of the following that applies—

(a) the fact that either party to the bet supplied insufficient, false or misleading information in connection with it,

(b) the fact that either party to the bet believed or ought to have believed that a race, competition or other event or process to which the bet related was or would be conducted in contravention of industry rules,

(c) the fact that either party to the bet believed or ought to have believed that an offence under section 42 had been or was likely to be committed in respect of anything to which the bet related, and

(d) the fact that either party to the bet was convicted of an offence under section 42 in relation to the bet.

(5) An order under subsection (1) may be made in relation to a bet only during the period of six months beginning with the day on which the result of the bet is determined.

(6) But subsection (5) shall not apply to an order made taking account of the fact that a party to the bet was convicted of an offence under section 42 in relation to it.

337 Section 336: supplementary

(1) Where the Commission makes an order under section 336(1) in relation to a bet a party to the bet or to any contract or other arrangement in relation to the bet may appeal to the Gambling Appeals Tribunal; and the following provisions of Part 7 shall have effect (with any necessary modifications) in relation to an appeal under this section as they have effect in relation to an appeal under that Part—

(a) section 142,

(b) section 143,

(c) section 144,

(d) section 145,

(e) section 146,

(f) section 147, and

(g) section 149.

(2) The Commission may make an order under section 336(1) in relation to the whole, or any part or aspect of, a betting transaction.

(3) An order under section 336(1) may make incidental provision; in particular, an order may make provision about—

(a) the consequences of the order for bets connected with the bet which becomes void under the order;

(b) the consequences of the order for other parts or aspects of a betting transaction one part or aspect of which becomes void under the order.

(4) For the purposes of considering whether to make an order under section 336(1) in respect of a bet the Commission—

(a) may require a person by or through whom the bet is made or accepted to provide information or documents in relation to it, and

(b) may take into account information received from any other person.

(5) A person commits an offence if without reasonable excuse he fails to comply with a requirement under subsection (4).

(6) A person guilty of an offence under subsection (5) shall be liable on summary conviction to a fine not exceeding level 2 on the standard scale.

(7) In section 336(4)(b) "industry rules" means rules established by an organisation having, by virtue of an agreement, instrument or enactment, responsibility for the conduct of races, competitions or other events or processes.

338 Interim moratorium

(1) Where the Commission has reason to suspect that it may wish to make an order under section 336(1) in relation to a bet, the Commission may make an order under this subsection in relation to the bet.

(2) While an order under subsection (1) has effect in relation to a bet, an obligation to pay money in relation to the bet (whether by way of stake, winnings, commission or otherwise) shall have no effect.

(3) An order under subsection (1) shall have effect for the period of 14 days beginning with the day on which the order is made (subject to extension under subsection (4) and without prejudice to the making of a new order).

Inquiries Act 2005

(2005, c. 12)

37 Immunity from suit

(1) No action lies against—

(a) a member of an inquiry panel,

(b) an assessor, counsel or solicitor to an inquiry, or

(c) a person engaged to provide assistance to an inquiry,

in respect of any act done or omission made in the execution of his duty as such, or any act done or omission made in good faith in the purported execution of his duty as such.

(2) Subsection (1) applies only to acts done or omissions made during the course of the inquiry, otherwise than during any period of suspension (within the meaning of section 13).

(3) For the purposes of the law of defamation, the same privilege attaches to—

(a) any statement made in or for the purposes of proceedings before an inquiry (including the report and any interim report of the inquiry), and

(b) reports of proceedings before an inquiry,

as would be the case if those proceedings were proceedings before a court in the relevant part of the United Kingdom.

Mental Capacity Act 2005
(2005, c. 9)

PART 1   PERSONS WHO LACK CAPACITY

The principles

1   The principles

(1) The following principles apply for the purposes of this Act.

(2) A person must be assumed to have capacity unless it is established that he lacks capacity.

(3) A person is not to be treated as unable to make a decision unless all practicable steps to help him to do so have been taken without success.

(4) A person is not to be treated as unable to make a decision merely because he makes an unwise decision.

(5) An act done, or decision made, under this Act for or on behalf of a person who lacks capacity must be done, or made, in his best interests.

(6) Before the act is done, or the decision is made, regard must be had to whether the purpose for which it is needed can be as effectively achieved in a way that is less restrictive of the person's rights and freedom of action.

Preliminary

2   People who lack capacity

(1) For the purposes of this Act, a person lacks capacity in relation to a matter if at the material time he is unable to make a decision for himself in relation to the matter because of an impairment of, or a disturbance in the functioning of, the mind or brain.

(2) It does not matter whether the impairment or disturbance is permanent or temporary.

(3) A lack of capacity cannot be established merely by reference to—

(a) a person's age or appearance, or

(b) a condition of his, or an aspect of his behaviour, which might lead others to make unjustified assumptions about his capacity.

(4) In proceedings under this Act or any other enactment, any question whether a person lacks capacity within the meaning of this Act must be decided on the balance of probabilities.

(5) No power which a person ("D") may exercise under this Act—

(a) in relation to a person who lacks capacity, or

(b) where D reasonably thinks that a person lacks capacity,

is exercisable in relation to a person under 16.

(6) Subsection (5) is subject to section 18(3).

3 Inability to make decisions

(1) For the purposes of section 2, a person is unable to make a decision for himself if he is unable—

    (a) to understand the information relevant to the decision,

    (b) to retain that information,

    (c) to use or weigh that information as part of the process of making the decision, or

    (d) to communicate his decision (whether by talking, using sign language or any other means).

(2) A person is not to be regarded as unable to understand the information relevant to a decision if he is able to understand an explanation of it given to him in a way that is appropriate to his circumstances (using simple language, visual aids or any other means).

(3) The fact that a person is able to retain the information relevant to a decision for a short period only does not prevent him from being regarded as able to make the decision.

(4) The information relevant to a decision includes information about the reasonably foreseeable consequences of—

    (a) deciding one way or another, or

    (b) failing to make the decision.

4 Best interests

(1) In determining for the purposes of this Act what is in a person's best interests, the person making the determination must not make it merely on the basis of—

    (a) the person's age or appearance, or

    (b) a condition of his, or an aspect of his behaviour, which might lead others to make unjustified assumptions about what might be in his best interests.

(2) The person making the determination must consider all the relevant circumstances and, in particular, take the following steps.

(3) He must consider—

    (a) whether it is likely that the person will at some time have capacity in relation to the matter in question, and

    (b) if it appears likely that he will, when that is likely to be.

(4) He must, so far as reasonably practicable, permit and encourage the person to participate, or to improve his ability to participate, as fully as possible in any act done for him and any decision affecting him.

(5) Where the determination relates to life-sustaining treatment he must not, in considering whether the treatment is in the best interests of the person concerned, be motivated by a desire to bring about his death.

(6) He must consider, so far as is reasonably ascertainable—

    (a) the person's past and present wishes and feelings (and, in particular, any relevant written statement made by him when he had capacity),

    (b) the beliefs and values that would be likely to influence his decision if he had capacity, and

    (c) the other factors that he would be likely to consider if he were able to do so.

(7) He must take into account, if it is practicable and appropriate to consult them, the views of—

    (a) anyone named by the person as someone to be consulted on the matter in question or on matters of that kind,

    (b) anyone engaged in caring for the person or interested in his welfare,

    (c) any donee of a lasting power of attorney granted by the person, and

    (d) any deputy appointed for the person by the court,

as to what would be in the person's best interests and, in particular, as to the matters mentioned in subsection (6).

(8) The duties imposed by subsections (1) to (7) also apply in relation to the exercise of any powers which—

(a) are exercisable under a lasting power of attorney, or

(b) are exercisable by a person under this Act where he reasonably believes that another person lacks capacity.

(9) In the case of an act done, or a decision made, by a person other than the court, there is sufficient compliance with this section if (having complied with the requirements of subsections (1) to (7)) he reasonably believes that what he does or decides is in the best interests of the person concerned.

(10) "Life-sustaining treatment" means treatment which in the view of a person providing health care for the person concerned is necessary to sustain life.

(11) "Relevant circumstances" are those—

(a) of which the person making the determination is aware, and

(b) which it would be reasonable to regard as relevant.

5 Acts in connection with care or treatment

(1) If a person ("D") does an act in connection with the care or treatment of another person ("P"), the act is one to which this section applies if—

(a) before doing the act, D takes reasonable steps to establish whether P lacks capacity in relation to the matter in question, and

(b) when doing the act, D reasonably believes—

    (i) that P lacks capacity in relation to the matter, and

    (ii) that it will be in P's best interests for the act to be done.

(2) D does not incur any liability in relation to the act that he would not have incurred if P—

(a) had had capacity to consent in relation to the matter, and

(b) had consented to D's doing the act.

(3) Nothing in this section excludes a person's civil liability for loss or damage, or his criminal liability, resulting from his negligence in doing the act.

(4) Nothing in this section affects the operation of sections 24 to 26 (advance decisions to refuse treatment).

6 Section 5 acts: limitations

(1) If D does an act that is intended to restrain P, it is not an act to which section 5 applies unless two further conditions are satisfied.

(2) The first condition is that D reasonably believes that it is necessary to do the act in order to prevent harm to P.

(3) The second is that the act is a proportionate response to—

(a) the likelihood of P's suffering harm, and

(b) the seriousness of that harm.

(4) For the purposes of this section D restrains P if he—

(a) uses, or threatens to use, force to secure the doing of an act which P resists, or

(b) restricts P's liberty of movement, whether or not P resists.

(5) But D does more than merely restrain P if he deprives P of his liberty within the meaning of Article 5(1) of the Human Rights Convention (whether or not D is a public authority).

(6) Section 5 does not authorise a person to do an act which conflicts with a decision made, within the scope of his authority and in accordance with this Part, by—

(a) a donee of a lasting power of attorney granted by P, or

(b) a deputy appointed for P by the court.

(7) But nothing in subsection (6) stops a person—

(a) providing life-sustaining treatment, or

(b) doing any act which he reasonably believes to be necessary to prevent a serious deterioration in P's condition,

while a decision as respects any relevant issue is sought from the court.

7   Payment for necessary goods and services

(1) If necessary goods or services are supplied to a person who lacks capacity to contract for the supply, he must pay a reasonable price for them.

(2) "Necessary" means suitable to a person's condition in life and to his actual requirements at the time when the goods or services are supplied.

8   Expenditure

(1) If an act to which section 5 applies involves expenditure, it is lawful for D—

    (a) to pledge P's credit for the purpose of the expenditure, and

    (b) to apply money in P's possession for meeting the expenditure.

(2) If the expenditure is borne for P by D, it is lawful for D—

    (a) to reimburse himself out of money in P's possession, or

    (b) to be otherwise indemnified by P.

(3) Subsections (1) and (2) do not affect any power under which (apart from those subsections) a person—

    (a) has lawful control of P's money or other property, and

    (b) has power to spend money for P's benefit.

Lasting powers of attorney

9   Lasting powers of attorney

(1) A lasting power of attorney is a power of attorney under which the donor ("P") confers on the donee (or donees) authority to make decisions about all or any of the following—

    (a) P's personal welfare or specified matters concerning P's personal welfare, and

    (b) P's property and affairs or specified matters concerning P's property and affairs,

and which includes authority to make such decisions in circumstances where P no longer has capacity.

(2) A lasting power of attorney is not created unless—

    (a) section 10 is complied with,

    (b) an instrument conferring authority of the kind mentioned in subsection (1) is made and registered in accordance with Schedule 1, and

    (c) at the time when P executes the instrument, P has reached 18 and has capacity to execute it.

10   Appointment of donees

(1) A donee of a lasting power of attorney must be—

    (a) an individual who has reached 18, or

    (b) if the power relates only to P's property and affairs, either such an individual or a trust corporation.

(2) An individual who is bankrupt may not be appointed as donee of a lasting power of attorney in relation to P's property and affairs.

11   Lasting powers of attorney: restrictions

(1) A lasting power of attorney does not authorise the donee (or, if more than one, any of them) to do an act that is intended to restrain P, unless three conditions are satisfied.

(2) The first condition is that P lacks, or the donee reasonably believes that P lacks, capacity in relation to the matter in question.

(3) The second is that the donee reasonably believes that it is necessary to do the act in order to prevent harm to P.

(4) The third is that the act is a proportionate response to—

    (a) the likelihood of P's suffering harm, and

    (b) the seriousness of that harm.

(5) For the purposes of this section, the donee restrains P if he—

    (a) uses, or threatens to use, force to secure the doing of an act which P resists, or

    (b) restricts P's liberty of movement, whether or not P resists,

or if he authorises another person to do any of those things.

(6) But the donee does more than merely restrain P if he deprives P of his liberty within the meaning of Article 5(1) of the Human Rights Convention.

(7) Where a lasting power of attorney authorises the donee (or, if more than one, any of them) to make decisions about P's personal welfare, the authority—

    (a) does not extend to making such decisions in circumstances other than those where P lacks, or the donee reasonably believes that P lacks, capacity,

    (b) is subject to sections 24 to 26 (advance decisions to refuse treatment), and

    (c) extends to giving or refusing consent to the carrying out or continuation of a treatment by a person providing Health care for P.

(8) But subsection (7)(c)—

    (a) does not authorise the giving or refusing of consent to the carrying out or continuation of life-sustaining treatment, unless the instrument contains express provision to that effect, and

    (b) is subject to any conditions or restrictions in the instrument.

16   Powers to make decisions and appoint deputies: general

(1) This section applies if a person ("P") lacks capacity in relation to a matter or matters concerning—

    (a) P's personal welfare, or

    (b) P's property and affairs.

(2) The court may—

    (a) by making an order, make the decision or decisions on P's behalf in relation to the matter or matters, or

    (b) appoint a person (a "deputy") to make decisions on P's behalf in relation to the matter or matters.

(3) The powers of the court under this section are subject to the provisions of this Act and, in particular, to sections 1 (the principles) and 4 (best interests).

17   Section 16 powers: personal welfare

(1) The powers under section 16 as respects P's personal welfare extend in particular to—

    . . .

    (d) giving or refusing consent to the carrying out or continuation of a treatment by a person providing health care for P; . . .

18   Section 16 powers: property and affairs

(1) The powers under section 16 as respects P's property and affairs extend in particular to—

    (a) the control and management of P's property;

    (b) the sale, exchange, charging, gift or other disposition of P's property;

    (c) the acquisition of property in P's name or on P's behalf;

    (d) the carrying on, on P's behalf, of any profession, trade or business;

    (e) the taking of a decision which will have the effect of dissolving a partnership of which P is a member;

    (f) the carrying out of any contract entered into by P;

    (g) the discharge of P's debts and of any of P's obligations, whether legally enforceable or not;

    (h) the settlement of any of P's property, whether for P's benefit or for the benefit of others;

    (i) the execution for P of a will;

    (j) the exercise of any power (including a power to consent) vested in P whether
       beneficially or as trustee or otherwise;
    (k) the conduct of legal proceedings in P's name or on P's behalf.
  (3) The powers under section 16 as respects any other matter relating to P's property
and affairs may be exercised even though P has not reached 16, if the court considers it
likely that P will still lack capacity to make decisions in respect of that matter when he
reaches 18.
  (4) Schedule 2 supplements the provisions of this section.

19   Appointment of deputies

  (6) A deputy is to be treated as P's agent in relation to anything done or decided by him
within the scope of his appointment and in accordance with this Part.
  (7) The deputy is entitled—
    (a) to be reimbursed out of P's property for his reasonable expenses in discharging his
       functions, and
    (b) if the court so directs when appointing him, to remuneration out of P's property
       for discharging them.

20   Restrictions on deputies

  (5) A deputy may not refuse consent to the carrying out or continuation of life-sustaining treatment in relation to P.
  (6) The authority conferred on a deputy is subject to the provisions of this Act and, in
particular, sections 1 (the principles) and 4 (best interests).
  (7) A deputy may not do an act that is intended to restrain P unless four conditions are
satisfied.
  (8) The first condition is that, in doing the act, the deputy is acting within the scope of an
authority expressly conferred on him by the court.
  (9) The second is that P lacks, or the deputy reasonably believes that P lacks, capacity in
relation to the matter in question.
  (10) The third is that the deputy reasonably believes that it is necessary to do the act in
order to prevent harm to P.
  (11) The fourth is that the act is a proportionate response to—
    (a) the likelihood of P's suffering harm, or
    (b) the seriousness of that harm.
  (12) For the purposes of this section, a deputy restrains P if he—
    (a) uses, or threatens to use, force to secure the doing of an act which P resists, or
    (b) restricts P's liberty of movement, whether or not P resists,
or if he authorises another person to do any of those things.
  (13) But a deputy does more than merely restrain P if he deprives P of his liberty within
the meaning of Article 5(1) of the Human Rights Convention (whether or not the deputy is a
public authority).

Advance decisions to refuse treatment

24   Advance decisions to refuse treatment: general

  (1) "Advance decision" means a decision made by a person ("P"), after he has reached 18
and when he has capacity to do so, that if—
    (a) at a later time and in such circumstances as he may specify, a specified treatment
       is proposed to be carried out or continued by a person providing health care for
       him, and
    (b) at that time he lacks capacity to consent to the carrying out or continuation of the
       treatment,
the specified treatment is not to be carried out or continued.
  (2) For the purposes of subsection (1)(a), a decision may be regarded as specifying a
treatment or circumstances even though expressed in layman's terms.

(3) P may withdraw or alter an advance decision at any time when he has capacity to do so.

(4) A withdrawal (including a partial withdrawal) need not be in writing.

(5) An alteration of an advance decision need not be in writing (unless section 25(5) applies in relation to the decision resulting from the alteration).

25   Validity and applicability of advance decisions

(1) An advance decision does not affect the liability which a person may incur for carrying out or continuing a treatment in relation to P unless the decision is at the material time—

    (a) valid, and

    (b) applicable to the treatment.

(2) An advance decision is not valid if P—

    (a) has withdrawn the decision at a time when he had capacity to do so,

    (b) has, under a lasting power of attorney created after the advance decision was made, conferred authority on the donee (or, if more than one, any of them) to give or refuse consent to the treatment to which the advance decision relates, or

    (c) has done anything else clearly inconsistent with the advance decision remaining his fixed decision.

(3) An advance decision is not applicable to the treatment in question if at the material time P has capacity to give or refuse consent to it.

(4) An advance decision is not applicable to the treatment in question if—

    (a) that treatment is not the treatment specified in the advance decision,

    (b) any circumstances specified in the advance decision are absent, or

    (c) there are reasonable grounds for believing that circumstances exist which P did not anticipate at the time of the advance decision and which would have affected his decision had he anticipated them.

(5) An advance decision is not applicable to life-sustaining treatment unless—

    (a) the decision is verified by a statement by P to the effect that it is to apply to that treatment even if life is at risk, and

    (b) the decision and statement comply with subsection (6).

(6) A decision or statement complies with this subsection only if—

    (a) it is in writing,

    (b) it is signed by P or by another person in P's presence and by P's direction,

    (c) the signature is made or acknowledged by P in the presence of a witness, and

    (d) the witness signs it, or acknowledges his signature, in P's presence.

(7) The existence of any lasting power of attorney other than one of a description mentioned in subsection (2)(b) does not prevent the advance decision from being regarded as valid and applicable.

26   Effect of advance decisions

(1) If P has made an advance decision which is—

    (a) valid, and

    (b) applicable to a treatment,

the decision has effect as if he had made it, and had had capacity to make it, at the time when the question arises whether the treatment should be carried out or continued.

(2) A person does not incur liability for carrying out or continuing the treatment unless, at the time, he is satisfied that an advance decision exists which is valid and applicable to the treatment.

(3) A person does not incur liability for the consequences of withholding or withdrawing a treatment from P if, at the time, he reasonably believes that an advance decision exists which is valid and applicable to the treatment.

(4) The court may make a declaration as to whether an advance decision—

    (a) exists;

    (b) is valid;

    (c) is applicable to a treatment.

(5) Nothing in an apparent advance decision stops a person—

    (a) providing life-sustaining treatment, or

    (b) doing any act he reasonably believes to be necessary to prevent a serious deterioration in P's condition,

while a decision as respects any relevant issue is sought from the court.

Excluded decisions

27   Family relationships etc.

(1) Nothing in this Act permits a decision on any of the following matters to be made on behalf of a person—

    ...

    (b) consenting to have sexual relations, ...

28   Mental Health Act matters

(1) Nothing in this Act authorises anyone—

    (a) to give a patient medical treatment for mental disorder, or

    (b) to consent to a patient's being given medical treatment for mental disorder,

if, at the time when it is proposed to treat the patient, his treatment is regulated by Part 4 of the Mental Health Act.

Research

30   Research

(1) Intrusive research carried out on, or in relation to, a person who lacks capacity to consent to it is unlawful unless it is carried out—

    (a) as part of a research project which is for the time being approved by the appropriate body for the purposes of this Act in accordance with section 31, and

    (b) in accordance with sections 32 and 33.

(2) Research is intrusive if it is of a kind that would be unlawful if it was carried out—

    (a) on or in relation to a person who had capacity to consent to it, but

    (b) without his consent.

(3) A clinical trial which is subject to the provisions of clinical trials regulations is not to be treated as research for the purposes of this section.

(4) "Appropriate body", in relation to a research project, means the person, committee or other body specified in regulations made by the appropriate authority as the appropriate body in relation to a project of the kind in question.

(5) "Clinical trials regulations" means—

    (a) the Medicines for Human Use (Clinical Trials) Regulations 2004 (S.I. 2004/1031) and any other regulations replacing those regulations or amending them, and

    (b) any other regulations relating to clinical trials and designated by the Secretary of State as clinical trials regulations for the purposes of this section.

(6) In this section, section 32 and section 34, "appropriate authority" means—

    (a) in relation to the carrying out of research in England, the Secretary of State, and

    (b) in relation to the carrying out of research in Wales, the National Assembly for Wales.

31   Requirements for approval

(1) The appropriate body may not approve a research project for the purposes of this Act unless satisfied that the following requirements will be met in relation to research carried out

as part of the project on, or in relation to, a person who lacks capacity to consent to taking part in the project ("P").

(2) The research must be connected with—

(a) an impairing condition affecting P, or

(b) its treatment.

(3) "Impairing condition" means a condition which is (or may be) attributable to, or which causes or contributes to (or may cause or contribute to), the impairment of, or disturbance in the functioning of, the mind or brain.

(4) There must be reasonable grounds for believing that research of comparable effectiveness cannot be carried out if the project has to be confined to, or relate only to, persons who have capacity to consent to taking part in it.

(5) The research must—

(a) have the potential to benefit P without imposing on P a burden that is disproportionate to the potential benefit to P, or

(b) be intended to provide knowledge of the causes or treatment of, or of the care of persons affected by, the same or a similar condition.

(6) If the research falls within paragraph (b) of subsection (5) but not within paragraph (a), there must be reasonable grounds for believing—

(a) that the risk to P from taking part in the project is likely to be negligible, and

(b) that anything done to, or in relation to, P will not—

(i) interfere with P's freedom of action or privacy in a significant way, or

(ii) be unduly invasive or restrictive.

(7) There must be reasonable arrangements in place for ensuring that the requirements of sections 32 and 33 will be met.

32 Consulting carers etc.

(1) This section applies if a person ("R")—

(a) is conducting an approved research project, and

(b) wishes to carry out research, as part of the project, on or in relation to a person ("P") who lacks capacity to consent to taking part in the project.

(2) R must take reasonable steps to identify a person who—

(a) otherwise than in a professional capacity or for remuneration, is engaged in caring for P or is interested in P's welfare, and

(b) is prepared to be consulted by R under this section.

(3) If R is unable to identify such a person he must, in accordance with guidance issued by the appropriate authority, nominate a person who—

(a) is prepared to be consulted by R under this section, but

(b) has no connection with the project.

(4) R must provide the person identified under subsection (2), or nominated under subsection (3), with information about the project and ask him—

(a) for advice as to whether P should take part in the project, and

(b) what, in his opinion, P's wishes and feelings about taking part in the project would be likely to be if P had capacity in relation to the matter.

(5) If, at any time, the person consulted advises R that in his opinion P's wishes and feelings would be likely to lead him to decline to take part in the project (or to wish to withdraw from it) if he had capacity in relation to the matter, R must ensure—

(a) if P is not already taking part in the project, that he does not take part in it;

(b) if P is taking part in the project, that he is withdrawn from it.

(6) But subsection (5)(b) does not require treatment that P has been receiving as part of the project to be discontinued if R has reasonable grounds for believing that there would be a significant risk to P's health if it were discontinued.

(7) The fact that a person is the donee of a lasting power of attorney given by P, or is P's deputy, does not prevent him from being the person consulted under this section.

(8) Subsection (9) applies if treatment is being, or is about to be, provided for P as a matter of urgency and R considers that, having regard to the nature of the research and of the particular circumstances of the case—

    (a) it is also necessary to take action for the purposes of the research as a matter of urgency, but

    (b) it is not reasonably practicable to consult under the previous provisions of this section.

(9) R may take the action if—

    (a) he has the agreement of a registered medical practitioner who is not involved in the organisation or conduct of the research project, or

    (b) where it is not reasonably practicable in the time available to obtain that agreement, he acts in accordance with a procedure approved by the appropriate body at the time when the research project was approved under section 31.

(10) But R may not continue to act in reliance on subsection (9) if he has reasonable grounds for believing that it is no longer necessary to take the action as a matter of urgency.

33 Additional safeguards

(1) This section applies in relation to a person who is taking part in an approved research project even though he lacks capacity to consent to taking part.

(2) Nothing may be done to, or in relation to, him in the course of the research—

    (a) to which he appears to object (whether by showing signs of resistance or otherwise) except where what is being done is intended to protect him from harm or to reduce or prevent pain or discomfort, or

    (b) which would be contrary to—

        (i) an advance decision of his which has effect, or

        (ii) any other form of statement made by him and not subsequently withdrawn, of which R is aware.

(3) The interests of the person must be assumed to outweigh those of science and society.

(4) If he indicates (in any way) that he wishes to be withdrawn from the project he must be withdrawn without delay.

(5) P must be withdrawn from the project, without delay, if at any time the person conducting the research has reasonable grounds for believing that one or more of the requirements set out in section 31(2) to (7) is no longer met in relation to research being carried out on, or in relation to, P.

(6) But neither subsection (4) nor subsection (5) requires treatment that P has been receiving as part of the project to be discontinued if R has reasonable grounds for believing that there would be a significant risk to P's health if it were discontinued.

34 Loss of capacity during research project

(1) This section applies where a person ("P")—

    (a) has consented to take part in a research project begun before the commencement of section 30, but

    (b) before the conclusion of the project, loses capacity to consent to continue to take part in it.

(2) The appropriate authority may by regulations provide that, despite P's loss of capacity, research of a prescribed kind may be carried out on, or in relation to, P if—

    (a) the project satisfies prescribed requirements,

    (b) any information or material relating to P which is used in the research is of a prescribed description and was obtained before P's loss of capacity, and

    (c) the person conducting the project takes in relation to P such steps as may be prescribed for the purpose of protecting him.

(3) The regulations may, in particular,—

    (a) make provision about when, for the purposes of the regulations, a project is to be treated as having begun;

(b) include provision similar to any made by section 31, 32 or 33.

Independent mental capacity advocate service

35   Appointment of independent mental capacity advocates

(1) The appropriate authority must make such arrangements as it considers reasonable to enable persons ("independent mental capacity advocates") to be available to represent and support persons to whom acts or decisions proposed under sections 37, 38 and 39 relate.

36   Functions of independent mental capacity advocates

(1) The appropriate authority may make regulations as to the functions of independent mental capacity advocates.

37   Provision of serious medical treatment by NHS body

(1) This section applies if an NHS body—
   (a) is proposing to provide, or secure the provision of, serious medical treatment for a person ("P") who lacks capacity to consent to the treatment, and
   (b) is satisfied that there is no person, other than one engaged in providing care or treatment for P in a professional capacity or for remuneration, whom it would be appropriate to consult in determining what would be in P's best interests.

(2) But this section does not apply if P's treatment is regulated by Part 4 of the Mental Health Act.

(3) Before the treatment is provided, the NHS body must instruct an independent mental capacity advocate to represent P.

(4) If the treatment needs to be provided as a matter of urgency, it may be provided even though the NHS body has not been able to comply with subsection (3).

(5) The NHS body must, in providing or securing the provision of treatment for P, take into account any information given, or submissions made, by the independent mental capacity advocate.

(6) "Serious medical treatment" means treatment which involves providing, withholding or withdrawing treatment of a kind prescribed by regulations made by the appropriate authority.

Miscellaneous and supplementary

42   Codes of practice

(1) The Lord Chancellor must prepare and issue one or more codes of practice—
   (a) for the guidance of persons assessing whether a person has capacity in relation to any matter,
   (b) for the guidance of persons acting in connection with the care or treatment of another person (see section 5),
   (c) for the guidance of donees of lasting powers of attorney,
   (d) for the guidance of deputies appointed by the court,
   (e) for the guidance of persons carrying out research in reliance on any provision made by or under this Act (and otherwise with respect to sections 30 to 34),
   (f) for the guidance of independent mental capacity advocates,
   (g) with respect to the provisions of sections 24 to 26 (advance decisions and apparent advance decisions), and
   (h) with respect to such other matters concerned with this Act as he thinks fit.

(4) It is the duty of a person to have regard to any relevant code if he is acting in relation to a person who lacks capacity and is doing so in one or more of the following ways—
   (a) as the donee of a lasting power of attorney,
   (b) as a deputy appointed by the court,

(c) as a person carrying out research in reliance on any provision made by or under this Act (see sections 30 to 34),

(d) as an independent mental capacity advocate,

(e) in a professional capacity,

(f) for remuneration.

(5) If it appears to a court or tribunal conducting any criminal or civil proceedings that—

(a) a provision of a code, or

(b) a failure to comply with a code,

is relevant to a question arising in the proceedings, the provision or failure must be taken into account in deciding the question.

Railways Act 2005
(2005, c. 14)

44 Exclusion of liability for breach of statutory duty

(1) Subject to section 57 of the 1993 Act (validity and effect of final and provisional orders under section 55 of that Act), the obligations specified in subsection (2) shall not give rise to any form of duty or liability enforceable by civil proceedings for breach of statutory duty.

(2) Those obligations are—

(a) any obligation of a person under section 22(8) not to discontinue a railway passenger service;

(b) any obligation of a person under section 26(8) not to discontinue the operation of a network or part of a network;

(c) any obligation of a person under section 29(8) not to discontinue the use of a station or part of a station;

(d) any obligation of a person to comply with a requirement imposed under section 33(2);

(e) any obligation of a person to comply with conditions to which he has agreed under section 34(5);

(f) any obligation of a person under section 37(2) not to discontinue an experimental passenger service;

(g) any obligation of the Secretary of State or the Scottish Ministers under this Part to secure the provision of a railway passenger service, network or station or of a part of a network or station.

Serious Organised Crime and Police Act 2005
(2005, c. 15)

145 Interference with contractual relationships so as to harm animal research organisation

(1) A person (A) commits an offence if, with the intention of harming an animal research organisation, he—

(a) does a relevant act, or

(b) threatens that he or somebody else will do a relevant act,

in circumstances in which that act or threat is intended or likely to cause a second person (B) to take any of the steps in subsection (2).

(2) The steps are—

(a) not to perform any contractual obligation owed by B to a third person (C) (whether or not such non-performance amounts to a breach of contract);

(b) to terminate any contract B has with C;

(c) not to enter into a contract with C.

(3) For the purposes of this section, a "relevant act" is—

(a) an act amounting to a criminal offence, or

(b) a tortious act causing B to suffer loss or damage of any description;

but paragraph (b) does not include an act which is actionable on the ground only that it induces another person to break a contract with B.

(4) For the purposes of this section, "contract" includes any other arrangement (and "contractual" is to be read accordingly).

(5) For the purposes of this section, to "harm" an animal research organisation means—

(a) to cause the organisation to suffer loss or damage of any description, or

(b) to prevent or hinder the carrying out by the organisation of any of its activities.

(6) This section does not apply to any act done wholly or mainly in contemplation or furtherance of a trade dispute.

(7) In subsection (6) "trade dispute" has the same meaning as in Part 4 of the Trade Union and Labour Relations (Consolidation) Act 1992 (c. 52), except that section 218 of that Act shall be read as if—

(a) it made provision corresponding to section 244(4) of that Act, and

(b) in subsection (5), the definition of "worker" included any person falling within paragraph (b) of the definition of "worker" in section 244(5).

Equality Act 2006
(2006, c. 3)

PART 2 DISCRIMINATION ON GROUNDS OF RELIGION OR BELIEF

46 Goods, facilities and services

(1) It is unlawful for a person ("A") concerned with the provision to the public or a section of the public of goods, facilities or services to discriminate against a person ("B") who seeks to obtain or use those goods, facilities or services—

(a) by refusing to provide B with goods, facilities or services,

(b) by refusing to provide B with goods, facilities or services of a quality which is the same as or similar to the quality of goods, facilities or services that A normally provides to—

(i) the public, or

(ii) a section of the public to which B belongs,

(c) by refusing to provide B with goods, facilities or services in a manner which is the same as or similar to that in which A normally provides goods, facilities or services to—

(i) the public, or

(ii) a section of the public to which B belongs, or

(d) by refusing to provide B with goods, facilities or services on terms which are the same as or similar to the terms on which A normally provides goods, facilities or services to—

(i) the public, or

(ii) a section of the public to which B belongs.

(2) Subsection (1) applies, in particular, to—

(a) access to and use of a place which the public are permitted to enter,

(b) accommodation in a hotel, boarding house or similar establishment,

(c) facilities by way of banking or insurance or for grants, loans, credit or finance,

(d) facilities for entertainment, recreation or refreshment,

(e) facilities for transport or travel, and

(f) the services of a profession or trade.

(3) Where a skill is commonly exercised in different ways in relation to or for the purposes of different religions or beliefs, a person who normally exercises it in relation to or for the purpose of a religion or belief does not contravene subsection (1) by—

(a) insisting on exercising the skill in the way in which he exercises it in relation to or for the purposes of that religion or belief, or

(b) if he reasonably considers it impracticable to exercise the skill in that way in relation to or for the purposes of another religion or belief, refusing to exercise it in relation to or for the purposes of that other religion or belief.

(4) Subsection (1)—

(a) does not apply in relation to the provision of goods, facilities or services by a person exercising a public function, and

(b) does not apply to discrimination in relation to the provision of goods, facilities or services if discrimination in relation to that provision—

(i) is unlawful by virtue of another provision of this Part or by virtue of a provision of the Employment Equality (Religion or Belief) Regulations

(ii) would be unlawful by virtue of another provision of this Part or of those regulations but for an express exception.

(5) For the purposes of subsection (1) it is immaterial whether or not a person charges for the provision of goods, facilities or services.

47 Premises

(1) It is unlawful for a person to discriminate against another—

(a) in the terms on which he offers to dispose of premises to him,

(b) by refusing to dispose of premises to him, or

(c) in connection with a list of persons requiring premises.

(2) It is unlawful for a person managing premises to discriminate against an occupier—

(a) in the manner in which he provides access to a benefit or facility,

(b) by refusing access to a benefit or facility,

(c) by evicting him, or

(d) by subjecting him to another detriment.

(3) It is unlawful for a person to discriminate against another by refusing permission for the disposal of premises to him.

(4) This section applies only to premises in Great Britain.

48 Section 47: exceptions

. . .

57 Organisations relating to religion or belief

(1) This section applies to an organisation the purpose of which is—

(a) to practice a religion or belief,

(b) to advance a religion or belief,

(c) to teach the practice or principles of a religion or belief,

(d) to enable persons of a religion or belief to receive any benefit, or to engage in any activity, within the framework of that religion or belief, or

(e) to improve relations, or maintain good relations, between persons of different religions or beliefs.

(2) But this section does not apply to an organisation whose sole or main purpose is commercial.

(3) Nothing in this Part shall make it unlawful for an organisation to which this section applies or anyone acting on behalf of or under the auspices of an organisation to which this section applies—

(a) to restrict membership of the organisation,

    (b) to restrict participation in activities undertaken by the organisation or on its behalf or under its auspices,

    (c) to restrict the provision of goods, facilities or services in the course of activities undertaken by the organisation or on its behalf or under its auspices, or

    (d) to restrict the use or disposal of premises owned or controlled by the organisation.

(4) Nothing in this Part shall make it unlawful for a minister—

    (a) to restrict participation in activities carried on in the performance of his functions in connection with or in respect of an organisation to which this section relates, or

    (b) to restrict the provision of goods, facilities or services in the course of activities carried on in the performance of his functions in connection with or in respect of an organisation to which this section relates.

(5) But subsections (3) and (4) permit a restriction only if imposed—

    (a) by reason of or on the grounds of the purpose of the organisation, or

    (b) in order to avoid causing offence, on grounds of the religion or belief to which the organisation relates, to persons of that religion or belief.

66   Claim of unlawful action

(1) A claim that a person has done anything that is unlawful by virtue of this Part may be brought in a county court (in England and Wales) or in the sheriff court (in Scotland) by way of proceedings in tort (or reparation) for breach of statutory duty.

(5) In proceedings under this section, if the claimant (or pursuer) proves facts from which the court could conclude, in the absence of a reasonable alternative explanation, that an act which is unlawful by virtue of this Part has been committed, the court shall assume that the act was unlawful unless the respondent (or defender) proves that it was not.

68   Remedies

(1) This section applies to proceedings under section 66.

(2) A court may, in addition to any remedy available to it in proceedings for tort, grant any remedy that the High Court could grant in proceedings for judicial review.

(3) A court may not award damages in proceedings in respect of an act that is unlawful by virtue of section 45(3) if the respondent proves that there was no intention to treat the claimant unfavourably on grounds of religion or belief.

(4) A court may award damages by way of compensation for injury to feelings (whether or not other damages are also awarded).

72   Validity and revision of contracts

(1) A term of a contract is void where—

    (a) its inclusion renders the making of the contract unlawful by virtue of this Part,

    (b) it is included in furtherance of an act which is unlawful by virtue of this Part, or

    (c) it provides for the doing of an act which would be unlawful by virtue of this Part.

(2) Subsection (1) does not apply to a term the inclusion of which constitutes, or is in furtherance of, or provides for, unlawful discrimination against a party to the contract; but the term shall be unenforceable against that party.

(3) A term in a contract which purports to exclude or limit a provision of this Part is unenforceable by a person in whose favour the term would operate apart from this subsection.

(4) Subsection (3) does not apply to a contract settling a claim under section 66.

(5) On the application of a person interested in a contract to which subsection (1) applies, a county court or sheriff court may make an order for removing or modifying a term made unenforceable by that subsection; but an order shall not be made unless all persons affected—

    (a) have been given notice of the application (except where notice is dispensed with in accordance with rules of court), and

    (b) have been afforded an opportunity to make representations to the court.

(6) An order under subsection (5) may include provision in respect of a period before the making of the order.

74 Employers' and principals' liability

(1) Anything done by a person in the course of his employment shall be treated for the purposes of this Part as done by the employer as well as by the person.

(2) Anything done by a person as agent for another shall be treated for the purposes of this Part as done by the principal as well as by the agent.

(3) It is immaterial for the purposes of this section whether an employer or principal knows about or approves of an act.

(4) In proceedings under this Part against a person in respect of an act alleged to have been done by his employee it shall be a defence for the employer to provide that he took such steps as were reasonably practicable to prevent the employee—

    (a) from doing the act, or

    (b) from doing acts of that kind in the course of his employment.

Proposed Statutes

(Draft) Contributory Negligence Bill
(Law Com. No. 219)

A Bill to provide for reducing the damages recoverable for breach of a contractual duty to take reasonable care or exercise reasonable skill in cases where the claimant's failure to take reasonable care has contributed to the damage suffered by him.   [1993]

1   Contributory negligence in claims for breach of contract

(1) Where by virtue of an express or implied term of a contract a party is under a duty to take reasonable care or exercise reasonable skill or both in the performance of the contract and the party to whom that duty is owed suffers damage as the result—

(a) partly of a breach of that duty; and

(b) partly of his own failure to take reasonable care for the protection of himself or his interests,

the damages recoverable by that party on a claim in respect of the damage shall be reduced to such extent as the court thinks just and equitable having regard to the claimant's share in the responsibility for the damage.

(2) Subsection (1) above does not apply if the parties have agreed (in whatever terms and whether expressly or by implication) that the damages for breach of the contract are not to be reduced as there mentioned, for example by specifying a sum payable in the event of breach and constituting liquidated damages.

(3) Where subsection (1) above applies the court, in deciding whether and, if so, to what extent the damages recoverable by the claimant are to be reduced—

(a) shall disregard anything done or omitted by him before the contract was entered into; but

(b) shall have regard to the nature of the contract and the mutual obligations of the parties,

and in other respects shall apply the like principles as those applicable under section 1(1) of the Law Reform (Contributory Negligence) Act 1945.

(4) Where the damages recoverable by any person are reduced by virtue of subsection (1) above the court shall and and record what the damages would have been without the reduction.

(5) In subsection (1) above references to the party by or to whom the duty under the contract is owed include references to any person subject to, or entitled to the performance of, that duty by virtue of assignment or otherwise.

(6) In this section "the court" means, in relation to any claim, the court or arbitrator by whom the claim falls to be determined and "damage" includes loss of life and personal injury.

2   Consequential amendments

(1) In section 4(3) of the Crown Proceedings Act 1947 (Crown bound by Law Reform (Contributory Negligence) Act 1945) after "1945" there shall be inserted "and the Contributory Negligence Act 1993".

(2) In section 5 of the Fatal Accidents Act 1976 (reduction of damages under that Act if Law Reform (Contributory Negligence) Act 1945 would have reduced the damages recoverable in an action brought for the benefit of the deceased's estate) there shall be added at the end "and likewise if the damages in an action so brought would be reduced under section 1(1) of the Contributory Negligence Act 1993".

(3) In section 2(3)(b) of the Civil Liability (Contribution) Act 1978 (limit on liability of contributor) after "the Law Reform (Contributory Negligence) Act 1945" there shall be inserted, " the Contributory Negligence Act 1993".

3 Short title, commencement, saving and extent

(1) This Act may be cited as the Contributory Negligence Act 1993.

(2) This Act comes into force at the end of the period of two months beginning with the day on which it is passed.

(3) This Act does not apply to any contract entered into before the coming into force of this Act.

(4) This Act does not extend to Scotland or Northern Ireland.

(Draft) Restitution (Mistakes of Law) Bill
(Law Com. No. 227)

An Act to make provision in relation to claims made in any proceedings for restitution in respect of acts done under mistake.   [1994]

1 Claims to which Act applies

(1) In this Act "mistake claim" means a claim made in any proceedings for restitution of a sum in respect of an act done under mistake.

(2) In this Act "act" includes anything which may found a claim for restitution, that is to say, the making of a payment, the conferring of a non-pecuniary benefit or the doing of work.

2 Abrogation of mistake of law rule

The classification of a mistake as a mistake of law or as a mistake of fact shall not of itself be material to the determination of a mistake claim; and no such claim shall be denied on the ground that the alleged mistake is a mistake of law.

3 Effect on mistake claim of judicial change in the law

(1) An act done in accordance with a settled view of the law shall not be regarded as founding a mistake claim by reason only that a subsequent decision of a court or tribunal departs from that view.

(2) A view of the law may be regarded for the purposes of this section as having been settled at any time notwithstanding that it was not held unanimously or had not been the subject of a decision by a court or tribunal.

4 Savings

(1) This Act does not affect any mistake claim (whenever made) in respect of an act done before the date on which this Act comes into force.

(2) Without prejudice to the generality of subsection (1), nothing in this Act shall be taken to affect any question as to the existence or operation before that date of any rule whereby a mistake claim would be denied by reason of the alleged mistake being a mistake of law.

(3) An enactment which has the effect of excluding or restricting the right to bring a mistake claim in any particular circumstances shall have the same effect on any right to bring a mistake claim in those circumstances that may arise by virtue of section 2.

(4) In subsection (3) "enactment" includes an enactment comprised in subordinate legislation within the meaning of the Interpretation Act 1978.

5 Short title, commencement and extent
(1) This Act may be cited as the Restitution (Mistakes of Law) Act 1994.
(2) This Act shall come into force on such day as the Lord Chancellor may appoint by order made by statutory instrument.
(3) This Act extends to England and Wales only.

(Draft) Damages Bill
(Law Com. No. 247)

An Act to amend certain rules, and to clarify certain rules, of the law of damages.   [1997]

PART I   PUNITIVE DAMAGES

Introduction

1 Introduction
(1) This Part amends certain rules, and clarifies certain rules, relating to punitive damages.
(2) Punitive damages are damages which were commonly called exemplary before the passing of this Act.

Main provisions

2 The court's functions
If liability in respect of a cause of action is established a decision whether punitive damages should be awarded, or what their amount should be, must not be left to a jury.

3 Availability of punitive damages
(1) Punitive damages may be awarded only if permitted by this section.
(2) Punitive damages may be awarded only if they are claimed.
(3) Punitive damages may be awarded in respect of any tort or any equitable wrong.
(4) Punitive damages may be awarded in respect of any wrong arising under an Act if—
    (a) a person may recover compensation or damages in respect of the wrong, and
    (b) an award of punitive damages would be consistent with the policy of that Act.
(5) If a tort or an equitable wrong arises under an Act, subsection (4) applies to it and subsection (3) does not.
(6) Punitive damages may be awarded only if the defendant's conduct shows a deliberate and outrageous disregard of the plaintiff's rights.
(7) Punitive damages may be awarded only if the court believes that—
    (a) the defendant's conduct is such that the court should punish him for it, and
    (b) the other remedies available are inadequate to do that.
(8) Punitive damages may be awarded whether or not another remedy is granted.
(9) The fact that the defendant's conduct falls outside the following categories is not a ground for refusing to award punitive damages—
    (a) oppressive, arbitrary or unconstitutional conduct by a servant of the government;
    (b) conduct calculated to make a profit which might exceed compensation payable to the plaintiff.
(10) The court may regard deterring the defendant and others from similar conduct as an object of punishment.

4   Other sanctions

(1) In deciding whether to award punitive damages the court must have regard to the principle that they must not usually be awarded if, at any time before the decision falls to be made, the defendant has been convicted of an offence involving the conduct concerned.

(2) In deciding whether to award punitive damages the court must take account of any sanction imposed in respect of the conduct concerned as a result of action (such as an employer's disciplinary proceedings) not involving conviction of an offence.

(3) In applying subsection (1) the court must ignore section 1C of the Powers of Criminal Courts Act 1973 (which provides that a conviction discharging an offender absolutely or conditionally is not deemed a conviction for certain purposes).

5   Amount of punitive damages

(1) In deciding the amount of punitive damages the court must have regard to these principles—
   (a) the amount must not exceed the minimum needed to punish the defendant for his conduct;
   (b) the amount must be proportionate to the gravity of the defendant's conduct.

(2) In deciding the amount of punitive damages the court must take account of these matters—
   (a) the defendant's state of mind;
   (b) the nature of the rights infringed by the defendant;
   (c) the nature and extent of any loss or harm the defendant caused or intended to cause by his conduct;
   (d) the nature and extent of any benefit the defendant derived or intended to derive from his conduct;
   (e) any other matter the court considers relevant (except the defendant's means, which are dealt with in section 6).

(3) The court may regard deterring the defendant and others from similar conduct as an object of punishment.

6   The defendant's means

(1) If the court decides to award punitive damages it must indicate the amount it has in mind to award irrespective of the defendant's means.

(2) If the defendant shows that he does not have the means to discharge an award of that amount without undue hardship, the court must take account of his means in deciding the amount of punitive damages to award.

(3) If an amount awarded as punitive damages would have been more but for subsection (2) the court must record what the amount awarded would have been but for that subsection.

(4) The defendant's means include anything falling to be paid under a contract of insurance against the risk of an award of punitive damages.

Multiple parties

7   More than one person wronged

(1) This section applies if conduct constitutes, or is alleged to constitute, torts or other wrongs against two or more persons (the persons wronged).

(2) In deciding whether to award punitive damages or the amount of punitive damages to award (whether to one or more of the persons wronged)—
   (a) the court must take account of any settlement or compromise by any persons of a claim in respect of the conduct, but
   (b) the court may not take account of any such settlement or compromise unless the defendant consents to it doing so.

(3) If the court awards punitive damages to two or more of the persons wronged the aggregate amount awarded must be such that, while it takes account of the fact that more

than one party is awarded punitive damages, it does not punish the defendant excessively.

(4) If the court awards punitive damages to one or more of the persons wronged no later claim may be made for punitive damages as regards the conduct.

8   More than one wrongdoer

(1) Any liability of two or more persons in respect of punitive damages is several (and not joint or joint and several).

(2) Subsection (1) has effect subject to the law relating to—
    (a) vicarious liability;
    (b) the liability of a partner for the conduct of another partner.

(3) If the liability of two or more persons in respect of punitive damages is several no contribution in respect of the damages may be recovered by any of them from any other under section 1 of the Civil Liability (Contribution) Act 1978.

Other provisions

9   Insurance against punitive damages

(1) It is not contrary to public policy for the risk of an award of punitive damages to be the subject of a contract of insurance.

(2) No provision of an Act or of subordinate legislation must be taken to require the risk of an award of punitive damages to be the subject of a contract of insurance.

10   Standard of proof

If it is sought to establish a matter relating to the question whether punitive damages should be awarded, or to the question of their amount, the civil (not the criminal) standard of proof must be satisfied.

11   Vicarious liability

(1) A person may be vicariously liable to pay punitive damages in respect of another's conduct.

(2) In a case where, if punitive damages were to be awarded, a person would be vicariously liable to pay them in respect of another's conduct—
    (a) references to the defendant in sections 3 to 5 are to that other;
    (b) section 5(2)(e) applies as if "defendant's means, which are dealt with in section 6" read "means of the person vicariously liable or the person in respect of whose conduct he is vicariously liable".

(3) If the court decides to award punitive damages and a person is vicariously liable to pay them in respect of another's conduct, references to the defendant and his means in section 6 are to the person vicariously liable and his means.

PART II   CERTAIN OTHER DAMAGES

12   Restitutionary damages for outrageous conduct

(1) Restitutionary damages may be awarded if—
    (a) a tort or an equitable wrong is committed, and
    (b) the defendant's conduct shows a deliberate and outrageous disregard of the plaintiff's rights.

(2) Restitutionary damages may be awarded if a wrong arising under an Act is committed and each of these conditions is fulfilled—
    (a) a person may recover compensation or damages in respect of the wrong,
    (b) an award of restitutionary damages would be consistent with the policy of that Act, and
    (c) the defendant's conduct shows a deliberate and outrageous disregard of the plaintiff's rights.

(3) If a tort or an equitable wrong arises under an Act, subsection (2) applies to it and subsection (1) does not.

(4) If—

    (a) it falls to be decided whether subsection (1)(b) or (2)(c) is satisfied in relation to a plaintiff, and

    (b) punitive damages are claimed in the same proceedings (whether by that plaintiff or not),

the decision whether subsection (1)(b) or (2)(c) is satisfied must not be left to a jury.

(5) Subsections (1) and (2) do not prejudice any power to award restitutionary damages in other cases.

13 Certain damages for mental distress

(1) This section applies to damages which were commonly called aggravated before the passing of this Act and which—

    (a) are awarded against a person in respect of his motive or exceptional conduct, but

    (b) are not punitive damages or restitutionary damages.

(2) Damages to which this section applies may be awarded only to compensate for mental distress and must not be intended to punish.

PART III   MISCELLANEOUS AND GENERAL

Miscellaneous

14 Amendment of other legislation

(1) Section 1 of the Law Reform (Miscellaneous Provisions) Act 1934 (effect of death on certain causes of action) is amended as mentioned in subsections (2) and (3).

(2) Subsection (2)(a)(i) (damages recoverable for benefit of estate not to include exemplary damages) is repealed.

(3) After subsection (2) insert—

"(2A) Where a cause of action survives against the estate of a deceased person under this section, any damages recoverable against the estate may not include punitive damages.

(2B) Where a cause of action survives for the benefit of the estate of a deceased person under this section, any damages recoverable for the benefit of the estate may include punitive damages.

(2C) References in subsections (2A) and (2B) of this section to punitive damages are to damages to which Part I of the Damages Act 1997 relates."

(4) In section 13(2) of the Reserve and Auxiliary Forces (Protection of Civil Interests) Act 1951 (in certain proceedings the court may take account of the defendant's conduct with a view, if the court thinks fit, to awarding exemplary damages)—

    (a) for "exemplary" substitute "punitive";

    (b) at the end insert; " and the reference here to punitive damages is to damages to which Part I of the Damages Act 1997 relates".

(5) In the Copyright, Designs and Patents Act 1988, sections 97(2), 191J(2) and 229(3) (power to award additional damages for infringement of copyright, performer's property rights or design right) are repealed in consequence of section 3(4) of this Act.

General

15 Interpretation

(1) For the purposes of this Act this section interprets the following expressions (here listed alphabetically)—

    (a) Act;

    (b) conduct;

    (c) equitable wrong;

    (d) punitive damages;

    (e) restitutionary damages;

    (f) subordinate legislation.

(2) "Act" includes a local and personal or private Act.

(3) A reference to conduct includes a reference to omissions; and a reference to a person's conduct includes a reference to his conduct subsequent to that giving rise to the cause of action concerned.

(4) Each of the following is an equitable wrong—

    (a) a breach of fiduciary duty;

    (b) breach of confidence;

    (c) procuring or assisting a breach of fiduciary duty.

(5) References to punitive damages are to be construed in accordance with section 1(2).

(6) Restitutionary damages are damages designed to remove a benefit derived by a person from his tort or other wrong.

(7) "Subordinate legislation" means Orders in Council, orders, rules, regulations, schemes, warrants, byelaws and other instruments made under any Act.

16 Commencement

(1) Nothing in this Act affects a cause of action accruing before such day as the Lord Chancellor may appoint by order made by statutory instrument.

(2) Different days may be appointed for different provisions or for different purposes.

(3) An order under this section may include such supplementary, incidental, consequential or transitional provisions as appear to the Lord Chancellor to be necessary or expedient.

17 Extent

This Act extends to England and Wales only.

18 Citation

This Act may be cited as the Damages Act 1997.

(Draft) Negligence (Psychiatric Illness) Bill
(Law Com. No. 249)

An Act to amend and clarify the law relating to liability in negligence for psychiatric illness.

[1998]

New duties of care

1 Close tie: duty of care

(1) Subsection (2) imposes a duty of care for the purposes of the tort of negligence, and that subsection has effect subject to (and only to) subsections (3) to (6).

(2) A person (the defendant) owes a duty to take reasonable care to avoid causing another person (the plaintiff) to suffer a recognisable psychiatric illness as a result of the death, injury or imperilment of a third person (the immediate victim) if it is reasonably foreseeable that the defendant's act or omission might cause the plaintiff to suffer such an illness.

(3) The defendant must be taken not to have owed the duty unless—

    (a) his act or omission caused the death, injury or imperilment of the immediate victim, and

    (b) the plaintiff and the immediate victim had a close tie of love and affection immediately before the act or omission occurred or immediately before the onset of the plaintiff's illness (or both).

(4) The duty is not imposed if the court is satisfied that its imposition would not be just and reasonable—

(a) because of any factor by virtue of which the defendant owed no duty of care to the immediate victim,

(b) because the immediate victim voluntarily accepted the risk that the defendant's act or omission might cause his death, injury or imperilment, or

(c) because the plaintiff was involved in conduct which is illegal or contrary to public policy.

(5) The duty is not imposed if the plaintiff—

(a) voluntarily accepted the risk of suffering the illness, or

(b) excluded the duty.

(6) The duty is not imposed if a provision which is contained in or made under another enactment, or which has the force of law by virtue of another enactment, regulates the defendant's duty to the plaintiff as regards the act or omission in place of the common law rules of the tort of negligence.

2   Close tie: duty of care if defendant is victim

(1) Subsection (2) imposes a duty of care for the purposes of the tort of negligence, and that subsection has effect subject to (and only to) subsections (3) to (6).

(2) A person (the defendant) owes a duty to take reasonable care to avoid causing another person (the plaintiff) to suffer a recognisable psychiatric illness as a result of the death, injury or imperilment of the defendant if it is reasonably foreseeable that the defendant's act or omission might cause the plaintiff to suffer such an illness.

(3) The defendant must be taken not to have owed the duty unless—

(a) his act or omission caused his death, injury or imperilment, and

(b) the plaintiff and the defendant had a close tie of love and affection immediately before the act or omission occurred or immediately before the onset of the plaintiff's illness (or both).

(4) The duty is not imposed if the court is satisfied that its imposition would not be just and reasonable—

(a) because the defendant chose to cause his death, injury or imperilment, or

(b) because the plaintiff was involved in conduct which is illegal or contrary to public policy.

(5) The duty is not imposed if the plaintiff—

(a) voluntarily accepted the risk of suffering the illness, or

(b) excluded the duty.

(6) The duty is not imposed if a provision which is contained in or made under another enactment, or which has the force of law by virtue of another enactment, regulates the defendant's duty to the plaintiff as regards the act or omission in place of the common law rules of the tort of negligence.

3   Meaning of close tie

(1) Subsections (2) to (5) have effect to determine whether for the purposes of section 1 the plaintiff and the immediate victim had a close tie of love and affection at a particular time.

(2) If at the time concerned the plaintiff fell within any of the categories listed in subsection (4) he and the immediate victim must be conclusively taken to have had a close tie of love and affection at that time.

(3) Otherwise it is for the plaintiff to show that he and the immediate victim had a close tie of love and affection at the time concerned.

(4) The categories are—
  (a) the immediate victim's spouse;
  (b) either parent of the immediate victim;
  (c) any child of the immediate victim;
  (d) any brother or sister of the immediate victim;
  (e) the immediate victim's cohabitant.

(5) The plaintiff was the immediate victim's cohabitant at the time concerned if and only if—
  (a) though not married to each other, they lived together as man and wife for a period of at least two years immediately before the time concerned, or
  (b) though of the same gender, they had a relationship equivalent to that described in paragraph (a) for such a period.

(6) Subsections (2) to (5) also have effect to determine whether for the purposes of section 2 the plaintiff and the defendant had a close tie of love and affection at a particular time, reading references in those subsections to the immediate victim as references to the defendant.

Common law duty of care

4 Close tie: abolition of common law duty

The common law duty of care under the tort of negligence is abolished to the extent that (apart from this section)—
  (a) it would arise in respect of a recognisable psychiatric illness suffered by a person (A) as a result of the death, injury or imperilment of another (B),
  (b) it would depend on the existence of a close tie of love and affection between A and B, and
  (c) it would be imposed on the person (whether B or a third person) causing the death, injury or imperilment.

5 Removal of certain restrictions

(1) This section amends and clarifies the law relating to a claim which—
  (a) is founded on the common law duty of care under the tort of negligence, and
  (b) is made in respect of a recognisable psychiatric illness.

(2) It is not a condition of the claim's success that the illness was induced by a shock.

(3) The court may allow the claim even if the illness results from the defendant causing his own death, injury or imperilment.

General

6 Commencement

(1) Sections 1 to 4 apply if the act or omission causing the death, injury or imperilment occurs on or after the appointed day.

(2) Section 5 applies if the defendant's act or omission occurs on or after the appointed day.

(3) The appointed day is such day as the Lord Chancellor appoints for the purposes of this Act by order made by statutory instrument.

7 Extent

This Act extends to England and Wales only.

8 Citation

This Act may be cited as the Negligence (Psychiatric Illness) Act 1998.

(Draft) Damages (Role of Jury) Bill
(Law Com. No. 257)

A Bill to make provision about the role of the jury in relation to damages.   [1999]

1   Damages: role of jury

(1) In any action, other than an action for libel or slander, a decision about the amount of damages to be awarded as compensation for any recoverable loss must not be left to a jury.

(2) To the extent that an action for libel or slander is an action for personal injury, a decision about the amount of damages to be awarded as compensation for any recoverable loss must not be left to a jury.

(3) In any action, a decision whether to award punitive or restitutionary damages, or about the amount of such damages, must not be left to a jury.

(4) In subsections (1) and (2), the reference to a decision about the amount of damages to be awarded as compensation does not include a decision under section 1 of the Law Reform (Contributory Negligence) Act 1945 (apportionment of liability in case of contributory negligence) about the extent to which damages are to be reduced.

(5) In section 1(6) of that Act (under which, if a case is tried with a jury, the jury must determine the total damages recoverable if the claimant had not been at fault and the extent to which those damages are to be reduced) for the words from "determine" to the end there is substituted—

"(a) in relation to any damages whose amount is left to them for decision, determine—

(i)   the amount which would have been recoverable if the claimant had not been at fault, and

(ii) the extent to which the damages are to be reduced;

(b) in relation to any damages to be awarded as compensation whose amount is not left to them for decision, determine the extent to which the damages which would have been recoverable if the claimant had not been at fault are to be reduced."

(6) In this section—

"personal injury" includes any disease and any impairment of a person's physical or mental condition;

"restitutionary damages" means damages designed to remove a benefit derived by a person from his tort or other wrong."

2   Short title, commencement and extent

(1) This Act may be cited as the Damages (Role of Jury) Act 1999.

(2) This Act comes into force on such day as the Lord Chancellor may by order made by statutory instrument appoint.

(3) Nothing in this Act affects a cause of action accruing before the day on which this Act comes into force.

(4) This Act extends to England and Wales only.

(Draft) Penalty Clauses (Scotland) Bill
(Scot. Law Com. No. 171)

A Bill to make new provision for Scotland as respects the enforceability of penalty clauses in con-tracts and in unilateral voluntary obligations; and for connected purposes.   [1999]

1   Enforceability of penalty clauses

(1) A penalty clause in a contract is unenforceable in a particular case if the penalty which the clause provides for is manifestly excessive (whether or not having regard to any loss suffered) in that case.

(2) Any rule of law whereby such a clause is unenforceable if it is not founded in a pre-estimate of damages shall cease to have effect.

(3) In subsection (1) above—"penalty" means a penalty of any kind whatsoever (including, without prejudice to that generality, a forfeiture or an obligation to transfer); and "penalty clause"—

(a) does not include a clause of irritancy of a lease of land; but

(b) means any other clause, in whatever form, the substance of which is that a penalty is incurred in the event of breach of, or early termination of, the contract or failure to do, or to do in a particular way, something provided for in the contract.

(4) In determining, for the purposes of subsection (1) above, whether a penalty is manifestly excessive all circumstances which appear relevant shall be taken into account; and without prejudice to the generality of this subsection such circumstances may include circumstances arising after the contract is entered into.

2   Onus of proof

The onus of proving that a penalty is manifestly excessive shall lie on the party so contending.

3   Purported evasion

Where a term of a contract would (but for this section) have the effect of excluding or restricting the application of a provision of this Act in respect of that or any other contract, the term shall be void.

4   Power to modify a penalty

(1) Where a court determines that a penalty provided for in a contract is manifestly excessive in a particular case then on application it may, if it thinks fit, modify the penalty in that case so as to make the penalty clause enforceable in the case.

(2) In subsection (1) above, the reference to modifying a penalty shall be construed as including a reference to imposing a condition as respects the penalty.

(3) Subsection (1) above applies to a tribunal or arbiter as it applies to a court (provided that the tribunal or arbiter has power to adjudicate on the enforceability of the penalty).

5   Application of Act to unilateral voluntary obligations

This Act applies to unilateral voluntary obligations as it applies to contracts.

6   Short title, commencement and extent

(1) This Act may be cited as the Penalty Clauses (Scotland) Act 1999.

(2) This Act shall come into force at the end of that period of three months which begins with the day on which the Act is passed.

(3) This Act applies only as respects a penalty clause agreed to on or after the date on which the Act comes into force.

(4) This Act extends to Scotland only.

(Draft) Damages for Personal Injury (Gratuitous Services) Bill
(Law Com. No. 262)

A Bill to amend the law relating to damages in respect of the gratuitous provision of services in personal injury cases.

[1999]

1   Damages for gratuitous provision of services by defendant

In an action for personal injury, no rule of law is to be treated as preventing damages from being recovered in respect of the gratuitous provision of services for the injured person by an individual merely because he is the defendant.

2   Duty to account for damages for past gratuitous services

(1) This section applies to damages awarded in an action for personal injury which are awarded in respect of services which have been gratuitously provided for the injured person by an individual.

(2) If damages to which this section applies are recovered, the person by whom they are recovered shall be under an obligation to account for them to the individual who provided the services.

3   Interpretation

(1) In this Act "personal injury" includes any disease and any impairment of a person's physical or mental condition.

(2) References in this Act to the provision of services for an injured person include, in particular—

   (a) providing him with nursing care,

   (b) visiting him in hospital, and

   (c) carrying out any task that he would have carried out as part of running or maintaining the home or supporting his domestic or family life if he had not suffered the injury.

(3) For the purposes of this Act, an individual provides services gratuitously if he provides them—

   (a) without having any contractual right to payment in respect of their provision, and

   (b) otherwise than in the course of a business, profession or vocation.

4   Commencement and extent

(1) This Act shall come into force at the end of the period of two months beginning with the day on which it is passed.

(2) Nothing in this Act affects a cause of action accruing before the day on which this Act comes into force.

(3) This Act extends to England and Wales only.

5   Short title

This Act may be cited as the Damages for Personal Injury (Gratuitous Services) Act 1999.

(Draft) Fatal Accidents Bill
(Law Com. No. 263)

A Bill to amend the Fatal Accidents Act 1976; and for connected purposes.   [1999]

1   Extension of category of "dependants"

(1) Section 1 of the 1976 Act (right of action for wrongful act causing death) shall be amended as follows.

(2) In subsection (3) (persons who may benefit from action for damages), there shall be inserted at the end—

   "(h) any person not falling within any of paragraphs (a) to (g) above who was being wholly or partly maintained by the deceased immediately before the death or who would, but for the death, have been so maintained at a time beginning after the death."

(3) At the end of the section there shall be inserted—

"(7) For the purposes of this Act a person shall be treated as being wholly or partly maintained by another person if the other person, otherwise than for full valuable consideration, was making a substantial contribution in money or money's worth towards his reasonable needs."

2   Bereavement damages

For section 1A of the 1976 Act there shall be substituted—

"1A Bereavement damages.

(1) An action under this Act may consist of or include a claim for damages for bereavement.

(2) A claim for damages for bereavement shall be for the benefit of—

    (a) the wife or husband of the deceased;

    (b) any person who has lived with the deceased as husband and wife for a period of at least two years immediately before the death;

    (c) any person of the same gender as the deceased who has lived with the deceased for such a period in a relationship equivalent to that described in paragraph (b) above;

    (d) any person who, immediately before the death, was engaged to be married to the deceased;

    (e) any parent of the deceased;

    (f) any child of the deceased; and

    (g) any brother or sister of the deceased.

(3) Subject to subsection (4) below, the sum to be awarded as damages for bereavement shall comprise the standard amount in respect of each claimant (subject to any reduction in respect of contributory negligence on the part of the claimant or the deceased).

(4) If, in a case where there are more than three claimants, the sum under subsection (3) above exceeds the maximum permitted amount, the sum to be awarded as damages for bereavement shall be that amount.

(5) For the purposes of this section—

    (a) the standard amount is £10,000, and

    (b) the maximum permitted amount is £30,000,

subject, in each case, to adjustment to take account of changes in the retail prices index during the period beginning with the passing of the Fatal Accidents Act 1999 and ending with the date on which the damages are awarded.

(6) Where damages for bereavement are awarded in respect of two or more claimants, any amount recovered shall (subject to any deduction in respect of costs not recovered from the defendant) be divided among the claimants in the proportions which the amounts in respect of each under subsection (3) above bear to the total amount under that subsection.

(7) In the case of damages for bereavement, an award of interest under section 35A of the Supreme Court Act 1981 or section 69 of the County Courts Act 1984 (powers of High Court and county court to award interest on damages) shall be—

    (a) for the period beginning with the date on which the action is brought and ending with the date on which the damages are awarded, and

    (b) at the same rate for the time being applicable to damages for non-pecuniary loss in an action for personal injury.

(8) For the purposes of subsection (2)(d) above a person shall only be taken to have been engaged to be married to the deceased if the court is satisfied that the engagement was evidenced—

    (a) in writing;

    (b) by the gift of an engagement ring by one party to the engagement to the other in contemplation of their marriage; or

    (c) by a ceremony entered into by the parties in the presence of one or more other persons assembled for the purpose of witnessing the ceremony.

(9) In subsection (5) above 'retail prices index' means the general index of retail prices (for all items) published by the Office for National Statistics or anything published by that Office as a substitute when that index is not published.

(10) In this section 'claimant' means a person for whose benefit the claim for damages for bereavement is brought."

3   Treatment of gratuitous provision of services to dependant

(1) In section 3 of the 1976 Act (assessment of damages other than bereavement damages), after subsection (1) there shall be inserted—

"(1A) The court may treat the injury to a dependant resulting from the death as including the loss to an individual of gratuitously providing services for the dependant which the deceased would have provided but for his death.

(1B) The court shall not refuse to exercise the power conferred by subsection (1A) above merely because the individual is the defendant.

(1C) The reference in subsection (1A) above to providing services for the dependant includes, in particular—

(a) providing him with care, and

(b) carrying out any task as part of running or maintaining the home or supporting his domestic or family life.

(1D) For the purposes of subsection (1A) above an individual provides services gratuitously if he provides them—

(a) without having any contractual right to payment in respect of their provision, and

(b) otherwise than in the course of a business, profession or vocation."

(2) After section 4 of that Act there shall be inserted—

"4A   Duty to account for damages for past gratuitous services.

(1) If a dependant, or his personal representative, recovers damages which consist of or include damages awarded by virtue of section 3(1A) above, he shall he under an obligation to account for so much of the damages so awarded as relates to the provision of services before the date of the award.

(2) The obligation under subsection (1) above is owed to the individual by whom the services were provided."

4   Assessment of damages: marriage of dependants etc.

After section 3 of the 1976 Act there shall be inserted—

"3A   Assessment of damages: marriage of dependants etc.

(1) In assessing damages in an action under this Act, no account shall he taken of the following possibilities—

(a) where the deceased was married immediately before the death, the possibility that his marriage might have broken down; or

(b) where immediately before the death the deceased was living with another person as husband and wife or, if of the same gender, in an equivalent relationship, the possibility that the deceased might have ceased to so live with the other.

(2) Subsection (1)(a) above shall not apply if immediately before the death—

(a) the parties to the marriage were not living in the same household; or

(b) one of the parties to the marriage was petitioning for a decree of divorce, separation or nullity.

(3) In assessing the damages payable to a dependant in an action under this Act, there shall be taken into account (together with any other matter that appears to the court to be relevant to the action) the fact that since the death the dependant, or a person whose personal circumstances are relevant to the injury to the dependant—

(a) has married or re-married; or

(b) has entered into a relevant relationship.

(4) In assessing the damages payable to a dependant in an action under this Act, there shall not be taken into account the prospects of the dependant, or a person whose personal circumstances are relevant to the injury to the dependant—

 (a) marrying or re-marrying; or

 (b) entering into a relevant relationship.

(5) Subsection (4)(a) above shall not apply if the dependant, or person, is engaged to be married.

(6) For the purposes of subsection (5) above a person shall only he taken to be engaged to be married if the court is satisfied that the engagement is evidenced—

 (a) in writing;

 (b) by the gift of an engagement ring by one party to the engagement to the other in contemplation of their marriage; or

 (c) by a ceremony entered into by the parties in the presence of one or more other persons assembled for the purpose of witnessing the ceremony.

(7) For the purposes of this section a dependant, or a person whose personal circumstances are relevant to the injury to a dependant, enters into a relevant relationship if the dependant or person—

 (a) lives with another person as husband and wife or, if of the same gender, in an equivalent relationship; and

 (b) is wholly or partly maintained by the other person."

5   Assessment of damages: disregard of certain benefits

For section 4 of the 1976 Act there shall be substituted—

"4   Assessment of damages: disregard of certain benefits.

(1) In assessing damages in an action under this Act, no deduction shall be made in respect of—

 (a) any insurance money or private pension which has been or will or may be paid as a result of the death of the deceased,

 (b) any gift of money or other property which has been or will or may be made as a result of the death of the deceased, or

 (c) any benefit which has or will or may accrue to any person from the deceased's estate.

(2) Subsection (1) above shall not apply if, or to the extent that, it appears to the court that—

 (a) there is a correspondence between the benefit concerned and particular loss claimed in the action in respect of a dependant, and

 (b) the correspondence is such that in effect the loss is not suffered or is compensated for.

(3) In this section—

 'insurance money' includes a return of premiums;

 'pension' includes a return of contributions and any payment of a lump sum in respect of a person's employment;

 'private', in relation to pension, means arising otherwise than under the enactments relating to social security (including those in force in Northern Ireland)."

6   Minor and consequential amendments and repeals

(1) The 1976 Act shall be amended as set out in subsections (2) to (5) below.

(2) In section 1, in subsection (2) (which provides for the action for damages to be for the benefit of the dependants of the deceased), for "section 1A(2)" there shall be substituted "section 1A".

(3) In that section, in subsection (3), for paragraph (b) there shall be substituted—

 "(a) any person who has lived with the deceased as husband and wife for a period of at least two years immediately before the death;".

(4) In that section, in subsection (6) (construction of references to injury), for "Act" there shall be substituted "section".

(5) In section 3—

(a) subsection (3) (which prevents the re-marriage or prospects of remarriage of the deceased's widow from being takcn into account in assessing damages); and

(b) subsection (4) (which requires the fact that a person with whom the deceased was living as husband or wife had no right to financial support to be taken into account in assessing damages);

are hereby repealed.

7   Short title etc.

(1) This Act may be cited as the Fatal Accidents Act 1999.

(2) In this Act "the 1976 Act" means the Fatal Accidents Act 1976.

(3) This Act shall come into force at the end of the period of two months beginning with the date on which it is passed.

(4) Sections 1 to 5 above and section 6(1) to (5) above shall not apply to any cause of action arising on a death before this Act comes into force.

(5) Section 6(6) and (7) above shall not apply in relation to any death before this Act comes into force.

(6) This Act extends to England and Wales only.

APPENDIX B   FATAL ACCIDENTS ACT 1976 AMENDED IN ACCORDANCE WITH OUR DRAFT BILL

[Amendments in italics.]

1   Right of action for wrongful act causing death

(1) If death is caused by any wrongful act, neglect or default which is such as would (if death had not ensued) have entitled the person injured to maintain an action and recover damages in respect thereof, the person who would have been liable if death had not ensued shall be liable to an action for damages, notwithstanding the death of the person injured.

(2) Subject to *section 1A* below, every such action shall be for the benefit of the dependants of the person ("the deceased") whose death has been so caused.

(3) In this Act "dependant" means—

(a) the wife or husband or former wife or husband of the deceased;

(b) *any person who has lived with the deceased as husband and wife for a period of at least two years immediately before the death;*

(c) any parent or other ascendant of the deceased.

(d) any person who was treated by the deceased as his parent;

(e) any child or other descendant of the deceased;

(f) any person (not being a child of the deceased) who, in the case of any marriage to which the deceased was at any time a party, was treated by the deceased as a child of the family in relation to that marriage;

(g) any person who is, or is the issue of, a brother, sister, uncle or aunt of the deceased;

(h) *any person not falling within any of paragraphs (a) to (g) above who was being wholly or partly maintained by the deceased immediately before the death or who would, but for the death, have been so maintained at a time beginning after the death.*

(4) The reference to the former wife or husband of the deceased in subsection (3)(a) above includes a reference to a person whose marriage to the deceased has been annulled or declared void as well as a person whose marriage to the deceased has been dissolved.

(5) In deducing any relationship for the purposes of subsection (3) above—

(a) any relationship of affinity shall be treated as a relationship by consanguinity, any relationship of the half blood as a relationship of the whole blood, and the stepchild of any person as his child, and

(b) an illegitimate person shall be treated as the legitimate child of his mother and reputed father.

(6) Any reference in this *section* to injury includes any disease and any impairment of a person's physical or mental condition.

(7) For the purposes of this Act a person shall be treated as being wholly or partly maintained by another person if the other person, otherwise than for full valuable consideration, was making a substantial contribution in money or money's worth towards his reasonable needs.

1A   Bereavement

(1) An action under this Act may consist of or include a claim for damages for bereavement.

(2) A claim for damages for bereavement shall be for the benefit of—

(a) *the wife or husband of the deceased;*

(b) *any person who has lived with the deceased as husband and wife for a period of at least two years immediately before the death;*

(c) *any person of the same gender as the deceased who has lived with the deceased for such a period in a relationship equivalent to that described in paragraph (b) above;*

(d) *any person who, immediately before the death, was engaged to be married to the deceased;*

(e) *any parent of the deceased;*

(f) *any child of the deceased; and*

(g) *any brother or sister of the deceased.*

(3) Subject to subsection (4) below, the sum to be awarded as damages for bereavement shall comprise the standard amount in respect of each claimant (subject to any reduction in respect of contributory negligence on the part of the claimant or the deceased).

(4) If, in a case where there are more than three claimants, the sum under subsection (3) above exceeds the maximum permitted amount, the sum to be awarded as damages for bereavement shall be that amount.

(5) For the purposes of this section—

(a) *the standard amount is £10,000, and*

(b) *the maximum permitted amount is £30,000,*

subject, in each case, to adjustment to take account of changes in the retail prices index during the period beginning with the passing of the Fatal Accidents Act 1999 and ending with the date on which the damages are awarded.

(6) Where damages for bereavement are awarded in respect of two or more claimants, any amount recovered shall (subject to any deduction in respect of costs not recovered from the defendant) be divided among the claimants in the proportions which the amounts in respect of each under subsection (3) above bear to the total amount under that subsection.

(7) In the case of damages for bereavement, an award of interest under section 35A of the Supreme Court Act 1981 or section 69 of the County Courts Act 1984 (powers of High Court and county court to award interest on damages) shall be—

(a) *for the period beginning with the date on which the action is brought and ending with the date on which the damages are awarded, and*

(b) *at the same rate for the time being applicable to damages for non-pecuniary loss in an action for personal injury.*

(8) For the purposes of subsection (2)(d) above a person shall only be taken to have been engaged to be married to the deceased if the court is satisfied that the engagement was evidenced—

(a) *in writing;*

(b) *by the gift of an engagement ring by one party to the engagement to the other in contemplation of their marriage; or*

(c) *by a ceremony entered into by the parties in the presence of one or more other persons assembled for the purpose of witnessing the ceremony.*

(9) In subsection (5) above "retail prices index" means the general index of retail prices (for all items) published by the Office for National Statistics or anything published by that Office as a substitute when that index is not published.

(10) In this section "claimant" means a person for whose benefit the claim for damages for bereavement is brought.

2   Persons entitled to bring the action

(1) The action shall be brought by and in the name of the executor or administrator of the deceased.

(2) If—

    (a) there is no executor or administrator of the deceased, or

    (b) no action is brought within six months after the death by and in the name of an executor or administrator of the deceased,63

the action may be brought by and in the name of all or any of the persons for whose benefit an executor or administrator could have brought it.

(3) Not more than one action shall lie for and in respect of the same subject matter of complaint.

(4) The plaintiff in the action shall be required to deliver to the defendant or his solicitor full particulars of the persons for whom and on whose behalf the action is brought and of the nature of the claim in respect of which damages are sought to be recovered.

3   Assessment of damages

(1) In the action such damages, other than damages for bereavement, may be awarded as are proportioned to the injury resulting from the death to the dependants respectively.

(1A) The court may treat the injury to a dependant resulting from the death as including the loss to an individual of gratuitously providing services for the dependant which the deceased would have provided but for his death.

(1B) The court shall not refuse to exercise the power conferred by subsection (1A) above merely because the individual is the defendant.

(1C) The reference in subsection (1A) above to providing services for the dependant includes, in particular—

    (a) providing him with care, and

    (b) carrying out any task as part of running or maintaining the home or supporting his domestic or family life.

(1D) For the purposes of subsection (1A) above an individual provides services gratuitously if he provides them—

    (a) without having any contractual right to payment in respect of their provision, and

    (b) otherwise than in the course of a business, profession or vocation.

(2) After deducting the costs not recovered from the defendant any amount recovered otherwise than as damages for bereavement shall be divided among the dependants in such shares as may be directed.

(3) ...

(4) ...

(5) If the dependants have incurred funeral expenses in respect of the deceased, damages may be awarded in respect of those expenses.

(6) Money paid into court in satisfaction of a cause of action under this Act may be in one sum without specifying any person's share.

3A   Assessment of damages: marriage of dependants etc.

(1) In assessing damages in an action under this Act, no account shall be taken of the following possibilities—

    (a) where the deceased was married immediately before the death, the possibility that his marriage might have broken down; or

    (b) where immediately before the death the deceased was living with another person as husband and wife or, if of the same gender, in an equivalent relationship, the possibility that the deceased might have ceased to so live with the other.

(2) Subsection (1)(a) above shall not apply if immediately before the death—

    (a) the parties to the marriage were not living in the same household; or

    (b) one of the parties to the marriage was petitioning for a decree of divorce, separation or nullity.

(3) In assessing the damages payable to a dependant in an action under this Act, there shall be taken into account (together with any other matter that appears to the court to be relevant to the action) the fact that since the death the dependant, or a person whose personal circumstances are relevant to the injury to the dependant—

    (a) has married or re-married; or

    (b) has entered into a relevant relationship.

(4) In assessing the damages payable to a dependant in an action under this Act, there shall not be taken into account the prospects of the dependant, or a person whose personal circumstances are relevant to the injury to the dependant—

    (a) marrying or re-marrying; or

    (b) entering into a relevant relationship.

(5) Subsection (4)(a) above shall not apply if the dependant, or person, is engaged to be married.

(6) For the purposes of subsection (5) above a person shall only be taken to be engaged to be married if the court is satisfied that the engagement is evidenced—

    (a) in writing;

    (b) by the gift of an engagement ring by one party to the engagement to the other in contemplation of their marriage; or

    (c) by a ceremony entered into by the parties in the presence of one or more other persons assembled for the purpose of witnessing the ceremony.

(7) For the purposes of this section a dependant, or a person whose personal circumstances are relevant to the injury to a dependant, enters into a relevant relationship if the dependant or person—

    (a) lives with another person as husband and wife or, if of the same gender, in an equivalent relationship; and

    (b) is wholly or partly maintained by the other person.

4   Assessment of damages: disregard of certain benefits

(1) In assessing damages in an action under this Act, no deduction shall be made in respect of—

    (a) any insurance money or private pension which has been or will or may be paid as a result of the death of the deceased,

    (b) any gift of money or other property which has been or will or may be made as a result of the death of the deceased, or

    (c) any benefit which has or will or may accrue to any person from the deceased's estate.

(2) Subsection (1) above shall not apply if, or to the extent that, it appears to the court that—

    (a) there is a correspondence between the benefit concerned and particular loss claimed in the action in respect of a dependant, and

    (b) the correspondence is such that in effect the loss is not suffered or is compensated for.

(3) In this section—

"insurance money" includes a return of premiums;

"pension" includes a return of contributions and any payment of a lump sum in respect of a person's employment;

"private", in relation to pension, means arising otherwise than under the enactments relating to social security (including those in force in Northern Ireland).

4A   Duty to account for damages for past gratuitous services

(1) If a dependant, or his personal representative, recovers damages which consist of or include damages awarded by virtue of section 3(1A) above, he shall be under an obligation to account for so much of the damages so awarded as relates to the provision of services before the date of the award.

(2) The obligation under subsection (1) above is owed to the individual by whom the services were provided.

5 Contributory negligence

Where any person dies as the result partly of his own fault and partly of the fault of any other person or persons, and accordingly if an action were brought for the benefit of the estate under the Law Reform (Miscellaneous Provisions) Act 1934 the damages recoverable would be reduced under section 1(1) of the Law Reform (Contributory Negligence) Act 1945, any damages recoverable in an action under this Act shall be reduced to a proportionate extent.

(Draft) Contract (Scotland) Bill
(Scot. Law Com. No. 174)

An Act of the Scottish Parliament to reform certain rules of law relating to rights arising on, and remedies for, breach of contract and unilateral voluntary obligation.   [1999]

1 Restriction of right to payment for unwanted performance

(1) Where—

    (a) a party to a contract or the beneficiary under a conditional unilateral voluntary obligation (the "performing party") is, before completion of performance, informed by another party to the contract or the person undertaking the obligation that performance is no longer required;

    (b) the performing party is able to proceed or continue with performance without the co-operation of that other party or that person; and

    (c) either—

        (i) the performing party can, without unreasonable effort or expense, secure a reasonable substitute transaction; or

        (ii) it is unreasonable for the performing party to proceed or continue with performance,

then the performing party is not entitled, on so proceeding or continuing, to recover the consideration due under the contract or benefit due under the obligation in respect of performance occurring after the performing party has been so informed.

(2) Subsection (1) above does not affect any right of the performing party to recover damages for breach of contract or conditional unilateral voluntary obligation.

2 Non-patrimonial loss recoverable on breach

(1) Non-patrimonial loss or harm is included within the heads of damages which may be awarded for breach of contract or for breach of a unilateral voluntary obligation—

(2) The following are examples of the kinds of loss or harm referred to in subsection (1) above: injury to feelings, loss of reputation, loss of amenity, loss of satisfaction in obtaining performance of the contract or obligation, grief and distress.

3 Damages where losses etc. caused also by party not in breach

(1) Where loss or harm is caused to a party to a contract or a beneficiary of a unilateral voluntary obligation—

    (a) partly by breach of the contract by another party to it or breach of the obligation by the person undertaking it; and

    (b) partly by an act or omission of the first mentioned party or the beneficiary, the damages recoverable in respect of the breach may be reduced proportionately to the extent that the loss or harm was caused by that act or omission.

(2) In considering whether to reduce damages under subsection (1) above and the extent to which loss or harm was caused by a person's act or omission, a court shall have regard to the whole circumstances of the case, including the conduct of both or all persons concerned.

4   Interim specific implement

It is competent for the Court of Session or the sheriff to order interim specific implement of a contractual or unilateral voluntary obligation.

5   Application, commencement and citation

(1) Section 1 of this Act applies as respects contracts and conditional unilateral voluntary obligations in respect of which the performing party is, after this Act comes into force, informed by another party to the contract or, as the case may be, the person undertaking the obligation that performance is not required.

(2) Sections 2 to 4 above apply for the purposes of proceedings begun after this Act comes into force.

(3) This Act (except this subsection and subsection (4) below) comes into force on the expiry of two months after it has received Royal Assent.

(4) This Act may be cited as the Contract (Scotland) Act 1999.

(Draft) Limitation Bill
(Law Com. No. 270)

A Bill to make provision about time limits on the making of civil claims; and for connected purposes.
[2001]

PART I   THE STANDARD LIMITATION PROVISIONS

The standard limitation defences

1   The standard limitation defences

(1) It is a defence to a civil claim that the claim was not made before the end of the period of three years from the date of knowledge of the claimant.

(2) It is also a defence to a civil claim that the claim was not made before the end of the period of ten years from the starting date in relation to the cause of action on which the claim is founded.

(3) Subsections (1) and (2) are subject to the following provisions of this Act.

(4) In this Act "civil claim" means a claim made in civil proceedings in which the claimant seeks—

    (a) a remedy for a wrong,

    (b) restitution, or

    (c) the enforcement of a right.

(5) The reference in subsection (4) to a claim made in civil proceedings includes a reference to—

    (a) a claim made in the course of such proceedings by way of set-off or counterclaim,

    (b) a claim so made involving the addition or substitution of a new cause of action, and

    (c) a claim so made involving the addition or substitution of a party.

(6) Where a civil claim is founded on more than one cause of action, this Act shall apply as if a separate civil claim were made in respect of each cause of action.

(7) In this Act—

"civil proceedings" includes any proceedings in a court of law, including an ecclesiastical court,

"claimant" includes a person who makes a claim by way of set-off or counterclaim,

"defendant" includes a person against whom a claim by way of set-off or counterclaim is made.

The date of knowledge

2 The date of knowledge

(1) Subject to the following provisions of this section and this Act, any reference in this Act to a person's date of knowledge is a reference to the date on which he first had knowledge of—

    (a) the facts which give rise to the cause of action,

    (b) the identity of the defendant, and

    (c) where injury, loss or damage has occurred or a benefit has been obtained, the fact that the injury, loss, damage or benefit is significant.

(2) Subject to subsections (3) and (4), in determining the date on which a person first had knowledge of the facts which give rise to a cause of action, there shall be disregarded the extent (if any) of his knowledge on any date of whether those facts would or would not, as a matter of law, give rise to a cause of action.

(3) In the case of a cause of action in respect of a breach of duty (whether in tort, in contract or otherwise) which involves a failure to give correct advice as to the law, subsection (1) shall have effect as if it also required knowledge to be had of the fact that correct advice had not been, or may not have been, given.

(4) In the case of a cause of action in respect of restitution based on a mistake of law, subsection (1) shall have effect as if it also required knowledge to be had of the fact that a mistake of law had been, or may have been, made.

(5) For the purposes of this section, a person ("A") shall be regarded as having knowledge of the fact that any injury, loss, damage or benefit is significant—

    (a) if he has knowledge of the full extent of the injury, loss, damage or benefit, or

    (b) if a reasonable person with A's knowledge of the extent of the injury, loss, damage or benefit would think, on the assumption that the defendant did not dispute liability and was able to satisfy a judgment, that a civil claim was worth making in respect of the injury, loss, damage or benefit.

The starting date

3 The starting date

(1) Subject to the following provisions of this section and this Act, any reference in this Act to the starting date is a reference to the date on which the cause of action accrued.

(2) Subject to the following provisions of this section and this Act, any reference in this Act to the starting date—

    (a) in the case of a cause of action in tort which does not accrue unless injury, loss or damage occurs, or

    (b) in the case of a cause of action in respect of breach of statutory duty,

is a reference to the date of occurrence of the act or omission which gives rise to the cause of action (whether the cause of action accrues on that date or on a later date).

(3) Where two or more acts or omissions give rise to a single cause of action falling within subsection (2)(a) or (b), the starting date shall be determined by reference to the last of those acts or omissions.

(4) Subsections (2) and (3) do not apply to a cause of action in respect of a breach of the duty imposed by section 1 of the Defective Premises Act 1972.

Constructive knowledge etc.

4 Constructive knowledge

(1) For the purposes of this Act, a person's knowledge includes knowledge which he might reasonably have been expected to acquire—

    (a) from facts observable or ascertainable by him, or

    (b) where he has acted unreasonably in not seeking appropriate expert advice, from facts ascertainable by him with the help of such advice.

(2) In determining for the purposes of this section—

    (a) the knowledge which a person might reasonably have been expected to acquire, or

    (b) whether a person has acted unreasonably in not seeking appropriate expert advice,

his circumstances and abilities (so far as relevant) shall be taken into account.

(3) For the purposes of this Act, a person shall be treated as having knowledge of a fact if an agent of his—

    (a) who is under a duty to communicate that fact to him, or

    (b) who has authority to take decisions about the cause of action concerned,

has actual knowledge of that fact; but except as so provided a person shall not treated as having knowledge of a fact merely because an agent of his has knowledge of the fact.

(4) For the purposes of this section, a person has authority to take decisions about a cause of action if he has authority—

    (a) to seek legal advice in connection with the making of a civil claim in respect of the cause of action, or

    (b) to take decisions about whether to make such a claim.

5 Corporate knowledge etc.

(1) For the purposes of this Act, a relevant body shall be treated as having knowledge of a fact—

    (a) if a qualifying individual has knowledge of that fact, or

    (b) if the relevant body is treated as having knowledge of that fact by virtue of section 4(3).

(2) In this section "relevant body" means—

    (a) a body corporate,

    (b) a corporation sole,

    (c) a partnership, or

    (d) a body of persons which does not fall within paragraph (a) or (c) but which is capable of suing and being sued in its own name.

(3) In this section "qualifying individual", in relation to a relevant body, means an individual—

    (a) who is an officer of the body or has authority on behalf of the body to take decisions about the cause of action concerned (or is one of a number of individuals who together have such authority), or

    (b) who is an employee of the body and is under a duty to communicate any fact relevant to the cause of action concerned to any other employee of the body or to an individual falling within paragraph (a),

but does not include an individual falling within subsection (4).

(4) An individual falls within this subsection if he is an individual—

    (a) against whom the cause of action concerned subsists, or

    (b) who has dishonestly concealed any fact relevant to the cause of action concerned from any other individual falling within subsection (3)(a) or (b).

(5) Sections 4(4) and 26(6) shall apply for the purposes of this section as they apply for the purposes of those sections.

(6) In this section "officer" includes a partner.

Application of s. 1(1) to particular cases

6 Joint claims

(1) Subject to the following provisions of this section, where a cause of action is vested in two or more persons jointly or jointly and severally, section 1(1) shall apply separately in relation to each of them.

(2) Where, by virtue of subsection (1), the defence under section 1(1) is available against one or more, but not all, of the persons mentioned in that subsection, it may not be raised against the other or others.

(3) Subsection (1) does not apply to—

(a) a cause of action vested in a partnership, or

(b) a cause of action vested in trustees or personal representatives.

(4) Where a cause of action is vested in trustees or personal representatives, the date of knowledge of the trustees or personal representatives shall be treated as falling on the same date as the earliest date of knowledge of any person who was a trustee or personal representative on that date.

7   Assignment

(1) This section applies where a civil claim in respect of a cause of action is made by a person to whom the cause of action has been assigned ("the assignee").

(2) It is a defence to a civil claim in respect of the cause of action made by the assignee that the assignment was made after the end of the limitation period under section 1(1) which would have applied to a civil claim in respect of the cause of action made by any person in whom the cause of action was vested before him.

(3) If the assignment was made after the limitation period mentioned in subsection (2) has begun to run but before it has ended, that limitation period shall apply to a civil claim in respect of the cause of action made by the assignee.

(4) If the assignment was made before the limitation period mentioned in subsection (2) has begun to run, the limitation period under section 1(1) which is to apply to a civil claim in respect of the cause of action made by the assignee shall be treated as running from the later of—

(a) the date of the assignment, and

(b) the date of knowledge of the assignee.

(5) For the purposes of this section, a cause of action is assigned by a person if he enters into any transaction the effect of which is to assign his right to make a civil claim in respect of the cause of action.

(6) In determining for the purposes of subsection (2) whether the limitation period under section 1(1) would have applied to a civil claim made by a person, his date of knowledge shall be disregarded if it falls after the cause of action ceased to be vested in him.

PART II   MODIFICATIONS OF THE STANDARD LIMITATION PROVISIONS FOR PARTICULAR CLAIMS ETC.

Consumer protection

8   Claims under Part I of the Consumer Protection Act 1987

(1) Section 1(2) does not apply to a civil claim under any provision of Part 1 of the Consumer Protection Act 1987 ("the 1987 Act").

(2) A civil claim under any provision of Part I of the 1987 Act may not be made after the end of the period of ten years from the relevant time, within the meaning of section 4 of that Act.

(3) Subsection (2) operates to extinguish any right to make the civil claim and does so—

(a) whether or not that right has accrued, and

(b) whether or not time under any other limitation period under this Act applicable to the claim has begun to run at the end of that ten year period.

(4) Nothing in the following provisions of this Act—

(a) shall operate to override or extend the limitation period under subsection (2), or

(b) shall affect the operation of subsection (3).

Personal injury claims, claims for the benefit of an estate and claims under the
Fatal Accidents Act 1976

9   Disapplication of section 1(2)
Section 1(2) does not apply to—
> (a) a civil claim if and to the extent that the remedy sought by the claimant is damages in respect of personal injury to him,
> (b) a civil claim made by virtue of section 1 of the Law Reform (Miscellaneous Provisions) Act 1934 if and to the extent that the remedy sought by the claimant is damages in respect of personal injury to the deceased, or
> (c) a civil claim under the Fatal Accidents Act 1976.

10   Application of section 1(1) to claims for the benefit of an estate
> (1) This section applies where a civil claim in respect of a cause of action is made by virtue of section 1 of the Law Reform (Miscellaneous Provisions) Act 1934 ("the 1934 Act claim").
> (2) It is a defence to the 1934 Act claim that the deceased died after the end of the limitation period under section 1(1) which would have applied to a civil claim in respect of the cause of action made by him.
> (3) If the deceased died before the end of the limitation period mentioned in subsection (2), the limitation period under section 1(1) which is to apply to the 1934 Act claim shall be treated as running from the later of—
>> (a) the date of the deceased's death, and
>> (b) the date of knowledge of the deceased's personal representatives.

11   Claims under the Fatal Accidents Act 1976: further provision
> (1) It is a defence to a civil claim under the Fatal Accidents Act Fatal Accidents 1976 ("the 1976 Act") that the person injured died when he could no longer maintain a civil claim for damages in respect of the injury.
> (2) In relation to a civil claim under the 1976 Act—
>> (a) the limitation period under section 1(1) shall be treated as running from the date of knowledge of the person for whose benefit the claim is made, and
>> (b) where there are two or more persons for whose benefit the claim is made, section 1(1) shall apply separately in relation to each of them.
> (3) Where, by virtue of subsection (2)(b), the defence under section 1(1) is available against one or more, but not all, of the persons mentioned in subsection (2)(b), it may not be raised against the other or others.
> (4) For the purposes of this section, the person injured shall be treated as having died when he could no longer maintain a civil claim for damages in respect of the injury if at the time of his death—
>> (a) a defence under this Act, or under any other enactment limiting the time within which proceedings may be taken, could have been raised in respect of such a claim, or
>> (b) he could no longer maintain such a claim for any other reason.
> (5) In determining for the purposes of this section whether the person injured died when he could no longer maintain a civil claim for damages in respect of the injury, no account shall be taken of the possibility of any defence under this Act which could have been raised in respect of such a claim being disapplied under section 12.

Court's discretionary power

12   Court's discretionary power in certain cases
> (1) This section applies where a defence under this Act is raised in respect of—
>> (a) a personal injury claim, or
>> (b) a civil claim under the Fatal Accidents Act 1976 ("the 1976 Act").

(2) The court may direct that the defence shall not apply in relation to the claim if it is satisfied, having regard to—

    (a) any hardship which would be caused to the defendant (or any person whom he represents) if such a direction were given, and

    (b) any hardship which would be caused to the claimant (or any person whom he represents) if such a direction were not given,

that it would [*sic*] unjust not to give such a direction.

(3) In acting under this section the court must take into account—

    (a) the length of, and reasons for, the delay on the part of the claimant,

    (b) the effect of the passage of time on the ability of the defendant to defend the claim,

    (c) the effect of the passage of time on the cogency of any evidence adduced or likely to be adduced by the claimant or defendant,

    (d) the conduct of the defendant after the cause of action arose, including the extent (if any) to which he responded to requests reasonably made by the claimant for information or inspection for the purpose of discovering facts which were or might be relevant to the claim,

    (e) the extent to which the claimant acted promptly and reasonably once he knew that he might be entitled to make the claim,

    (f) the steps, if any, taken by the claimant to obtain medical, legal or other expert advice and the nature of any expert advice he may have received,

    (g) any alternative remedy or compensation available to the claimant,

    (h) the strength of the claimant's case, and

    (i) any other relevant circumstances.

(4) In relation to a personal injury claim falling within subsection (8)(b), any reference in subsection (3)(a) or (d) to (f) to the claimant includes a reference to the deceased.

(5) In relation to a civil claim under the 1976 Act, any reference in subsection (3)(a) or (d) to (f) to the claimant includes a reference to the deceased; and subsection (3) shall have effect with such modifications as may be appropriate in consequence of this subsection.

(6) Where a civil claim under the 1976 Act is made by personal representatives, any reference in subsection (3) to the claimant includes a reference to the person for whose benefit the claim is made.

(7) Where the court gives a direction under this section disapplying the defence under 11(1), the person injured shall be treated for the purposes of section 1(1) of the 1976 Act as if he had died when he could have maintained an action for damages in respect of the injury.

(8) In this section "personal injury claim" means—

    (a) a civil claim if and to the extent that the remedy sought by the claimant is damages in respect of personal injury to him,

    (b) a civil claim made by virtue of section 1 of the Law Reform (Miscellaneous Provisions) Act 1934 if and to the extent that the remedy sought by the claimant is damages in respect of personal injury to the deceased.

Claims for a contribution

13 Claims for a contribution

(1) The starting date in relation to a cause of action under section 1 of the Civil Liability (Contribution) Act 1978 to recover contribution in respect of any damage from any person shall be determined in accordance with this section.

(2) If the person concerned is held liable in respect of the damage—

    (a) by a judgment given in any civil proceedings, or

    (b) by an award made on any arbitration,

the starting date shall be the date on which the judgment is given or, as the case may be, the date of the award.

(3) For the purposes of subsection (2) no account shall be taken of any judgment or award given or made on appeal in so far as it varies the amount of damages awarded against the person concerned.

(4) If, in a case not falling within subsection (2), the person concerned makes or agrees to make any payment to a person in compensation for that damage (whether he admits any liability in respect of the damage or not), the starting date shall be the earliest date on which the amount paid or to be paid by him is agreed between him (or his representative) and that person.

Conversion

14   Conversion

(1) Where—
   (a) a cause of action has accrued to a person in respect of a conversion of goods which was not a theft from that person, and
   (b) before that person recovers possession of the goods, a further conversion takes place,
the starting date in relation to the further conversion shall be treated as falling on the date on which the original conversion took place.

(2) Where a cause of action has accrued to a person in respect of a conversion of goods which was a theft from that person—
   (a) section 2(1) shall have effect in relation to the theft, and any conversion related to the theft, as if it also required knowledge to be had of the location of the goods, and
   (b) subject to subsection (3), section 1(2) shall not apply to the theft or any conversion related to the theft.

(3) Section 1(2) shall apply to—
   (a) the first conversion related to the theft which involves a person purchasing the goods in good faith, and
   (b) any subsequent conversion related to the theft;
and the starting date in relation to any conversion falling within paragraph (a) or (b) shall be treated as falling on the date on which the goods are purchased by the person mentioned in paragraph (a).

(4) Where—
   (a) a cause of action in respect of the conversion of goods has accrued to a person,
   (b) the limitation period under section 1(2) (if any) which applies to that or any further conversion has ended before a civil claim is made in respect of that or any further conversion, and
   (c) that person has not recovered possession of the goods before the end of that period,
the title of that person to the goods shall be extinguished.

(5) A conversion of goods shall be treated for the purposes of this section as related to a theft of those goods if it occurs after the theft but before the person from whom they were stolen recovers possession of the goods.

(6) In this section—
"goods" includes all chattels personal other than things in action and money,
"theft" includes—
   (a) any conduct outside England and Wales which would be theft if committed in England and Wales, and
   (b) obtaining any goods (in England and Wales or elsewhere) in the circumstances described in section 15(1) of the Theft Act 1968 (obtaining by deception) or by blackmail within the meaning of section 21 of that Act.

Mortgages

15 Mortgages

(1) This Act does not apply to a civil claim to redeem a mortgage.

(2) Section 1(1) does not apply to—

(a) a civil claim for a remedy under a mortgage of land, or

(b) a civil claim which does not fall within paragraph (a) but which is a claim to enforce an obligation secured by a mortgage of land.

(3) Where any limitation period under this Act which applies to a civil claim by a mortgagee in respect of a mortgage would, apart from this subsection, end—

(a) during any period in which a prior mortgagee is in possession of the property subject to the mortgage, or

(b) during the period of one year beginning with the date on which the prior mortgagee ceases to be in possession of the property,

it shall instead be treated as ending at the end of the period mentioned in paragraph (b).

(4) No limitation period under this Act which applies to a civil claim by a mortgagee in respect of a mortgage shall run during any period in which the property subject to the mortgage consists of or includes any future interest or any life policy which has not matured or been determined.

(5) No limitation period under this Act which applies to a civil claim to foreclose a mortgage shall run during any period in which the mortgagee is in possession of the property subject to the mortgage.

(6) Where the limitation period under section 1(2) which would apply to a civil claim by a mortgagee in respect of a mortgage has ended before any such claim is made, the interest of the mortgagee in the property which is subject to the mortgage shall be extinguished.

(7) Any reference in this section to a civil claim by a mortgagee in respect of a mortgage is a reference to—

(a) a civil claim by a mortgagee for a remedy under the mortgage, or

(b) a civil claim by a mortgagee which does not fall within paragraph (a) but which is a claim to enforce an obligation secured by the mortgage.

(8) Any reference in this section to a mortgage includes a reference to a charge, and any reference to a mortgagee shall be construed accordingly.

(9) Any reference in this section to a mortgage of land includes a reference to a mortgage of land and other property.

Land

16 Recovery of land

(1) Subsections (1) and (2) of section 1 do not apply to a civil claim to recover land.

(2) Subject to the following provisions of this section, a civil claim to recover land may not be made by a person after the end of the period of ten years from the earlier of—

(a) the date on which the right of action to recover the land first accrued to him, and

(b) if it first accrued to some person through whom he claims, the date on which it first accrued to that person.

(3) In its application to a civil claim by the Crown to recover foreshore, subsection (2) shall have effect as if the period referred to in it were sixty years not ten years.

(4) Where any right of action to recover land which has ceased to be foreshore accrued to the Crown when the land was foreshore, a civil claim by the Crown to recover the land may not be made after the end of the period of—

(a) sixty years from the date of accrual of the right of action, or

(b) ten years from the date on which the land ceased to be foreshore, whichever period ends first.

(5) No civil claim may be made to recover any estate or interest in land under an assurance taking effect after the right of action to recover the land had accrued to—

(a) the person by whom the assurance was made,

(b) some person through whom he claimed, or

(c) some person entitled to a preceding estate or interest,

unless the claim is made within the period in which the person by whom the assurance was made could have made such a claim.

(6) Where—

(a) any person is entitled to any estate or interest in land in possession and, while so entitled, is also entitled to any future estate or interest in that land, and

(b) his right of action to recover the estate or interest in possession is barred by this Act,

no civil claim may be made by that person, or by any person claiming through him, in respect of the future estate or interest, unless in the meantime possession of the land has been recovered by a person entitled to an intermediate estate or interest in the land.

(7) In this section "foreshore" means the shore and bed of the sea and of any tidal water, below the line of the medium high tide between the spring tides and the neap tides.

17   Recovery of land; supplementary

(1) Schedule 1 (which contains provisions for determining the date of accrual of rights of action to recover land) has effect.

(2) The provisions of this Act relating to civil claims to recover land shall apply to equitable interests in land as they apply to legal estates in land.

(3) Accordingly a right of action to recover land shall be treated for the purposes of this Act as accruing to a person entitled in possession to an equitable interest in the land in the like manner and circumstances, and on the same date, as it would accrue if his interest were a legal estate in the land (and any relevant provision of Schedule 1 shall apply in any such case accordingly).

(4) For the purposes of the provisions of this Act relating to civil claims to recover land, an administrator of the estate of a deceased person shall be treated as claiming as if there had been no interval of time between the death of the deceased person and the grant of the letters of administration.

(5) Where land is vested in the incumbent from time to time of a benefice as a spiritual corporation sole but the benefice is vacant, a civil claim to recover the land (or any part of it) may be made in the name of and on behalf of the corporation sole by the priest in charge of the benefice or the sequestrators of the benefice.

18   Extinction of title to land

(1) Subject to section 75 of the Land Registration Act 1925 and the following provisions of this section, where a civil claim to recover land is not made by a person before the end of the limitation period under section 16 which would apply to the claim, the title of that person to the land shall be extinguished.

(2) Where the limitation period under section 16 has expired for the making of a civil claim to recover land by a tenant for life or a statutory owner of settled land—

(a) his legal estate shall not be extinguished if and so long as the right of action to recover the land of any person entitled to a beneficial interest in the land either has not accrued or has not been barred by this Act, and

(b) the legal estate shall accordingly remain vested in the tenant for life or statutory owner and shall devolve in accordance with the Settled Land Act 1925;

but if and when every such right of action has been barred by this Act, his legal estate shall be extinguished.

(3) Where any land is held upon trust and the limitation period under section 16 has expired for the making of a civil claim to recover the land by the trustees, the estate of the trustees shall not be extinguished if and so long as the right of action to recover the land of any person entitled to a beneficial interest in the land either has not accrued or has not been

barred by this Act; but if and when every such right has been so barred the estate of the trustees shall be extinguished.

(4) Where—

(a) any settled land is vested in a statutory owner, or

(b) any land is held upon trust,

a civil claim to recover the land may be made by the statutory owner or trustees on behalf of any person entitled to a beneficial interest in possession in the land whose right of action to recover the land has not been barred by this Act, notwithstanding that the right of action to recover the land of the statutory owner or trustees would apart from this subsection have been barred by this Act.

19   Recovery of proceeds of the sale of land

Section 1(1) does not apply to a civil claim to recover proceeds of the sale of land.

20   Certain claims for compensation or indemnity

. . .

21   Cure of defective disentailing assurance

. . .

Trusts and charities

22   Trusts and charities

(1) No limitation period under this Act which applies to a civil claim by a beneficiary to recover trust property or the proceeds of trust property shall run against him during any period in which he is entitled to a future interest in the trust property.

(2) A cause of action to recover property held on a bare trust shall not accrue unless and until the trustee acts in breach of trust.

(3) This Act does not apply to a civil claim made by the Attorney General or the Charity Commissioners for England and Wales with respect to a charity or the property or affairs of a charity.

(4) A beneficiary under a trust as against whom a defence under this Act could have been raised may not derive any greater or other benefit from a judgment or order obtained by any other beneficiary under the trust than he could have obtained if he had made the civil claim and a defence under this Act had been raised.

(5) In this section "charity" has the same meaning as in the Charities Act 1993.

Insolvency and bankruptcy

23   Insolvency and bankruptcy

Schedule 2 (which makes provision as to the application of section 1(1) in the case of insolvency and bankruptcy) has effect.

Derivative claims

24   Derivative claims

(1) Where—

(a) a cause of action is vested in a body corporate or trade union, and

(b) a civil claim in respect of the cause of action is made on behalf of the body corporate or trade union by a member of it,

the limitation period under section 1(1) which is to apply to the claim shall be treated as running from the date of knowledge of the member.

(2) Where a civil claim falling within subsection (1) is made by two or more members, section 1(1) shall apply separately in relation to each of them.

(3) Where, by virtue of subsection (2), the defence under section 1(1) is available against one or more, but not all, of the persons mentioned in that subsection, it may not be raised against the other or others.

Certain new claims

25 Certain new claims

(1) Where—
- (a) a civil claim is made in the course of any civil proceedings,
- (b) the claim is by way of set-off or counterclaim by a party who has not previously made any claim in the proceedings, and
- (c) if the claim had been made when the proceedings were commenced, it would not have been made after the end of any applicable limitation period under this Act,

no defence under this Act may be raised in respect of the claim.

(2) Where—
- (a) a civil claim ("the new claim") is made in the course of any civil proceedings,
- (b) the new claim involves the addition or substitution of a new cause of action,
- (c) the new claim arises out of the same conduct, transaction or events as are already in issue in a civil claim previously made in the proceedings ("the existing claim"), and
- (d) the existing claim was not made after the end of any applicable limitation period under this Act or any other enactment,

no defence under this Act may be raised in respect of the new claim.

(3) Where—
- (a) a civil claim ("the new claim") is made in the course of any civil proceedings,
- (b) the new claim involves the addition or substitution of a new party,
- (c) the addition or substitution is necessary for the determination of a civil claim previously made in the proceedings ("the existing claim"), and
- (d) the existing claim was not made after the end of any applicable limitation period under this Act or any other enactment,

no defence under this Act may be raised in respect of the new claim.

(4) The addition or substitution of a new party is not necessary for the determination of a civil claim previously made in civil proceedings unless—
- (a) the new party is substituted for a party whose name was given in that claim in mistake for the new party's name, or
- (b) that claim cannot be maintained by or against an existing party unless the new party is joined or substituted as a party to that claim.

(5) Rules of court may make provision which allows a party to a civil claim to claim relief in a new capacity in respect of a new cause of action notwithstanding that he had no title to make that claim at the time when the claim was made.

(6) Subsection (5) shall not affect the power of rules of court to make provision which allows a party to a civil claim to claim relief in a new capacity without adding or substituting a new cause of action.

PART III GENERAL MODIFICATIONS OF THE STANDARD LIMITATION PROVISIONS ETC.

Concealment

26 Concealment

(1) This section applies where a person ("A") against whom a cause of action subsists (or an agent of his) has dishonestly concealed from a person ("B") in whom the cause of action is vested (or an agent of his) any fact relevant to the cause of action.

(2) In its application to a civil claim in respect of the cause of action made by B, or any person claiming through him, against A, or any person claiming through him, the limitation period under section 1(2) or 16 shall not run during the period beginning with the date on which the fact was first dishonestly concealed and ending with the earliest date on which B, or any person claiming through him, first had knowledge of the fact.

(3) In the case of the fresh cause of action which accrues by virtue of section 3(1) of the Latent Damage Act 1986 (accrual of cause of action to successive owners in respect of latent damage to property), a fact dishonestly concealed from the person in whom the original cause of action mentioned in that section was vested (or an agent of his) shall be treated for the purposes of subsection (1) as dishonestly concealed from the person in whom the fresh cause of action is vested.

(4) Where the starting date in relation to a cause of action falling within section 3(2)(a) or (b) falls before the date of accrual of the cause of action, the cause of action shall be treated for the purposes of subsection (1) as subsisting against A, and vested in B, from the starting date.

(5) Nothing in this section enables a civil claim—

    (a) to recover, or recover the value of, any property, or

    (b) to enforce any charge against, or set aside any transaction affecting, property, to be made against the purchaser (or any person claiming through him) in any case where the property has been purchased for valuable consideration by an innocent third party since the concealment took place.

(6) A person shall not be treated for the purposes of this section as concealing a fact from another person unless—

    (a) he is a party to, or is privy to, any action the effect of which is to prevent that other person from discovering the fact for some time, or

    (b) he fails to disclose the fact to that other person in breach of a duty to do so.

(7) The provisions of Part I of this Act which apply for determining the date on which a person first had knowledge of a fact shall also apply for the purposes of subsection (2).

(8) For the purposes of subsection (2), knowledge acquired by a person after a cause of action ceased to be vested in him shall be disregarded.

(9) A purchaser is an innocent third party for the purposes of this section if he was not a party to the concealment and did not at the time of the purchase have reason to believe that the concealment had taken place.

Acknowledgments and part payments

27 Acknowledgements and part payments

(1) Subject to the following provisions of this section, where—

    (a) a person ("A") against whom a cause of action subsists has acknowledged the cause of action or made a payment in respect of it,

    (b) the acknowledgment or payment was made to a person ("B") in whom the cause of action is vested, and

    (c) the acknowledgment or payment was made before any limitation period under this Act which would apply to a civil claim in respect of the cause of action made by B (or any successor of his) against A (or any successor of his) has ended,

any such limitation period which has begun to run before the date on which the acknowledgment or payment was made shall instead be treated as running from that date.

(2) Subject to subsections (4) and (5), where—

    (a) a cause of action subsists against two or more persons jointly or jointly and severally, and

    (b) an acknowledgment or payment under this section is made by one or more, but not all, of those persons,

this section shall not operate to extend any limitation period under this Act which applies to any such person who does not make the acknowledgment or payment (or any successor of his).

(3) Subject to subsection (4), where—

    (a) a cause of action is vested in two or more persons jointly or jointly and severally, and

    (b) an acknowledgment or payment under this section is made to one or more, but not all, of those persons,

this section shall not operate to extend any limitation period under this Act which applies to any such person to whom the acknowledgment or payment is not made (or any successor of his).

(4) Where—

    (a) a cause of action subsists against or is vested in, trustees or personal representatives, and

    (b) an acknowledgment or payment under this section is made by or (as the case may be) to one or more, but not all, of the trustees or personal representatives,

the acknowledgment or payment shall bind or (as the case may be) be treated as made to all of the trustees or personal representatives.

(5) An acknowledgment or payment under this section in respect of the title to any land, benefice or mortgaged personal property by any person in possession of it shall bind all of the persons in possession of it during the ensuing limitation period.

(6) Where this section extends the limitation period under section 1(2) which applies to a civil claim in respect of the original cause of action mentioned in section 3 of the Latent Damage Act 1986 (accrual of cause of action to successive owners in respect of latent damage to property)), it shall also extend the limitation period under section 1(2) which applies to a civil claim in respect of the fresh cause of action which accrues by virtue of that section.

(7) Where the starting date in relation to a cause of action falling within section 3(2)(a) or falls before the date of accrual of the cause of action, the cause of action shall be treated for the purposes of subsection (1) as subsisting against A, and vested in B, from the starting date; and subsection (2) to (4) and (11) and (12) shall be construed accordingly.

(8) To be effective for the purposes of this section an acknowledgment must be in writing.

(9) For the purposes of this section an acknowledgment or payment made by or to an agent of a person shall be treated as made by or to that person.

(10) A limitation period which has been extended under this section may be further extended under this section by further acknowledgments or payments.

(11) For the purposes of this section, a person acknowledges a cause of action if—

    (a) he acknowledges liability in respect of the cause of action, or

    (b) he acknowledges any right or title upon which the cause of action is based.

(12) For the purposes of this section, a person makes a payment in respect of a cause of action if he makes a payment the effect of which is to—

    (a) acknowledge liability in respect of the cause of action, or

    (b) acknowledge any right or title upon which the cause of action is based.

(13) Where there is a payment of a part of the rent or interest due at any time, this section shall not operate to extend any limitation period under this Act which applies to a civil claim to recover the remainder then due.

(14) Any payment of interest shall be treated for the purposes of this section as a payment in respect of a cause of action to recover the principal debt.

Special parties

28 Children

Where a cause of action is vested in a person who was under the age of 18 on the starting date in relation to the cause of action, any limitation period under this Act which would apply to a civil claim in respect of the cause of action made by him shall be treated as ending—

(a) at the end of the period of three years from the date on which he attains the age of 18, or

(b) at the end of the period when the limitation period would otherwise end, whichever is the later.

29 Persons under a disability

(1) This section applies where a cause of action has accrued to a person ("the relevant person") who is under a disability at any time after the date of accrual of the cause of action.

(2) Subject to the following provisions of this section, the limitation period under section 1(1), so far as applicable to a civil claim in respect of the cause of action made by the relevant person, shall not run during any period in which he is under a disability.

(3) Subsections (4) and (5) apply where—

(a) the remedy sought by the relevant person in the civil claim mentioned in subsection (2) is damages in respect of personal injury to him,

(b) the relevant person is under a disability at the end of the period of ten years from the later of the date of accrual of the cause of action and the date of the onset of disability ("the ten year period"),

(c) there is a person ("the responsible person") who has responsibility for the relevant person at the end of the ten year period,

(d) the responsible person is not the defendant to the claim, and

(e) whether by virtue of subsection (2) or otherwise, the limitation period under section 1(1) has not ended by the end of the ten year period.

(4) Subsection (2) shall not apply after the end of the ten year period.

(5) The limitation period under section 1(1) shall instead be treated as running from the earlier of the following dates—

(a) the date of knowledge of the responsible person,

(b) the date of knowledge of any person who subsequently has responsibility for the relevant person, and

(c) if the relevant person ceases to be under a disability after the end of the ten year period, the date of knowledge of the relevant person;

but if any such date of knowledge falls before the end of the ten year period, it shall be treated for the purposes of this subsection as falling on the date immediately following the end of the ten year period.

(6) A person is under a disability for the purposes of this section if—

(a) he is unable by reason of mental disability to make decisions on matters relating to the cause of action concerned, or

(b) he is unable to communicate such decisions because of mental disability or physical impairment.

(7) In subsection (6) "mental disability" means a disability or disorder of the mind or brain, whether permanent or temporary, which results in an impairment or disturbance of mental functioning.

(8) For the purposes of this section a person has responsibility for the relevant person if—

(a) he is a member of the relevant person's family who has attained the age of 18 and is responsible for the day to day care of the relevant person, or

(b) he is a person who is authorised under Part VII of the Mental Health Act 1983 to conduct proceedings in the name of the relevant person.

Restrictions on making claims

30 Restrictions on making claims

(1) No limitation period under this Act which applies to a civil claim made by a person shall run against that person during any period after the accrual of the cause of action in which he is prevented by any enactment (other than this Act) or any rule of law from making the claim.

(2) A person shall not be regarded for the purposes of this section as prevented from making a claim—

- (a) where the claim could have been made on his behalf by a litigation friend,
- (b) where he is prevented from making the claim by reason only of a contractual term, or
- (c) if leave is required to make the claim, unless and until he has taken all reasonable steps to obtain that leave.

PART IV MISCELLANEOUS AND SUPPLEMENTAL

Miscellaneous

31 Agreements

(1) Subject to the following provisions of this section, nothing in this Act prevents the making of an agreement the terms of which—

- (a) modify or disapply any of the provisions of this Act, or
- (b) make provision in place of any of the provisions of this Act.

(2) An agreement is unenforceable if and to the extent that its terms—

- (a) modify or disapply, or make provision in place of, section 8 or this section,
- (b) in the case of the limitation period under section 1(2) or an agreed limitation period to which subsection (5) applies, reduces the protection given to a claimant by section 26,
- (c) reduces the protection given to a claimant by section 28, or
- (d) in the case of the limitation period under section 1(1) or an agreed limitation period to which subsection (4) applies, reduces the protection given to a claimant by section 29.

(3) Where neither the Unfair Contract Terms Act 1977 nor the Unfair Terms in Consumer Contracts Regulations 1999 apply to any terms of an agreement falling within subsection (1)(a) or (b), those terms shall be of no effect except in so far as they satisfy the requirement of reasonableness as stated in section 11(1) of the Unfair Contract Terms Act 1977; but this subsection shall not apply to an agreement to compromise or settle litigation.

(4) Subject to subsection (7) and the terms of any agreement, the provisions of this Act shall apply to an agreed limitation period which runs from a date determined by reference to a person's actual or constructive knowledge as they apply to the limitation period under section 1(1); and any reference in any provision of this Act (other than this section) to a limitation period or defence—

- (a) under section 1(1), or
- (b) under this Act,

shall be construed accordingly.

(5) Subject to the terms of any agreement, the provisions of this Act shall apply to an agreed limitation period which runs from a date determined otherwise than by reference to a person's actual or constructive knowledge as they apply to the limitation period under section 1(2); and any reference in any provision of this Act (other than this section) to a limitation period or defence—

- (a) under section 1(2), or
- (b) under this Act,

shall be construed accordingly.

(6) Subject to subsection (7), section 29(1) and (2) shall apply to an agreed limitation period to which subsection (5) applies as if the reference in section 29(2) to the limitation period under section 1(1) were a reference to the agreed limitation period.

(7) Section 29 (whether it applies by virtue of subsection (4) or subsection (6)) shall not operate to extend an agreed limitation period beyond the period of ten years from the starting date in relation to the cause of action.

(8) Any reference in this section to an agreed limitation period is a reference to a limitation period for which provision is made by the terms of any agreement (whether those

terms modify any limitation period under this Act or provide for a limitation period in place of any limitation period under this Act).

32   Claims in repect of certain loans

(1) A cause of action to recover the debt under a qualifying loan shall not accrue unless and until a demand in writing for repayment of the debt is made by or on behalf of the creditor (or, where there are joint creditors, by or on behalf of any one or more of them).

(2) In this section "qualifying loan" means a contract of loan which—

(a) does not provide for repayment of the debt on or before a fixed or determinable date, and

(b) does not effectively (whether or not it purports to do so) make the obligation to repay the debt conditional on a demand for repayment made by or on behalf of the creditor or on any other matter,

but a contract of loan is not a qualifying loan if, in connection with taking the loan, the debtor enters into a collateral obligation to pay the amount of the debt or any part of it (as, for example, by delivering a promissory note as security for the debt) on terms which do not satisfy both of the conditions in paragraphs (a) and (b).

33   Family proceedings

. . .

34   Equitable jurisdiction and remedies

(1) This Act does not apply to a civil claim for the specific performance of a contract to grant or transfer an interest in property if the claimant—

(a) has acquired an interest in the property by virtue of the contract, and

(b) is in possession of the property.

(2) Nothing in this Act affects any equitable jurisdiction to refuse relief on the ground of delay, acquiescence or otherwise.

35   Crown application

(1) This Act binds the Crown.

(2) This Act does not apply to any civil claim by the Crown for the recovery of any tax or duty or interest on any tax or duty.

(3) For the purposes of this Act, a civil claim by petition of right shall be treated as made on the date on which the petition is presented.

36   Saving for other limitation enactments

Except as provided by Schedules 3 and 4, this Act does not apply—

(a) to any civil claim for which a limitation period is provided by any other enactment (whenever passed or made), or

(b) to any civil claim to which the Crown is a party and for which, if it were between subjects, a limitation period would be provided by any such other enactment.

37   Burden of proof

(1) Where a defence to a civil claim is raised under section 1(1), 7(2) or 10(2) or paragraph 6(2) of Schedule 2, it is for the claimant to prove that the claim was made before the end of the limitation period applicable to that defence.

(2) Where a defence to a civil claim is raised under any other provision of this Act, it is for the defendant to prove that the claim was not made before the end of the limitation period applicable to that defence.

Supplemental

38   Interpretation

(1) In this Act—

"civil claim" shall be construed in accordance with section 1(4) to (6), "civil proceedings" shall be construed in accordance with section 1(7),

"claimant" shall be construed in accordance with section 1(7),

"date of knowledge" shall be construed in accordance with sections 2, 6(4) and 14(2),

"defendant" shall be construed in accordance with section 1(7),

"enactment" includes an enactment comprised in subordinate legislation (within the meaning of the Interpretation Act 1978),

"land" includes corporeal hereditaments, tithes and rentcharges and any legal or equitable estate or interest therein, but except as so provided does not include any incorporeal hereditament,

"personal injury" includes any disease and any impairment of a person's physical or mental condition,

"personal representative" includes an executor who has not proved the will (whether or not he has renounced probate), but not anyone appointed only as a special personal representative in relation to settled land,

"rent" includes a rentcharge and a rent service,

"rentcharge" means any annuity or periodical sum of money charged upon or payable out of land, except a rent service or interest on a mortgage on land,

"settled land", "statutory owner" and "tenant for life" have the same meaning as in the Settled Land Act 1925,

"starting date" shall be construed in accordance with sections 3, 13 and 14,

"successor", in relation to a person in whom a cause of action is vested or against whom a cause of action subsists, means his personal representatives or any other person on whom his rights or, as the case may be, liabilities in relation to the cause of action devolve (whether on death or bankruptcy or the disposition of property or the determination of a limited estate or interest in settled property or otherwise),

"trust" and "trustee" have the same meaning as in the Trustee Act 1925.

(2) Subject to subsection (3)—

   (a) a person shall be treated for the purposes of this Act as claiming through another person if he became entitled by, through, under or by the act of that other person to the right claimed, and

   (b) any person whose estate or interest might have been barred by a person entitled to an entailed interest in possession shall be treated for the purposes of this Act as claiming through the person so entitled.

(3) A person becoming entitled to any estate or interest by virtue of a special power of appointment shall not be treated for the purposes of this Act as claiming through the appointor.

(4) Any reference in this Act to a right of action to recover land shall include a reference to a right to enter into possession of the land or, in the case of rentcharges and tithes, to distrain for arrears of rent or tithe; and any reference in this Act to the making of a civil claim to recover land shall include a reference to the making of such an entry or distress.

(5) Any reference in this Act to the possession of land shall, in the case of tithes and rentcharges, be construed as a reference to the receipt of the tithe or rent; and any reference in this Act to the date of dispossession or discontinuance of possession of land shall, in the case of rentcharges, be construed as a reference to the date of the last receipt of rent.

(6) In the provisions of this Act relating to civil claims to recover land, any reference to the Crown includes a reference to the Duke of Cornwall.

(7) For the purposes of this Act a cause of action upon a judgment shall be treated as accruing on the date on which the judgment became enforceable.

39 Amendments and repeals

(1) Schedule 3 (minor and consequential amendments) has effect.

(2) Subject to subsection (3), the repeals set out in Schedule 4 have effect.

(3) Notwithstanding the repeal by this Act of the Limitation Act 1980, section 38(2) to (6) of that Act shall continue to have effect for the purposes of section 3(4) of the Charitable Trusts (Validation) Act 1954.

40 Commencement

(1) This Act comes into force at the end of the period of one year beginning with the day on which it is passed.

(2) Subject to the following provisions of this section, this Act has effect in relation to causes of action accruing and things taking place before, as well as in relation to causes of action accruing and things taking place after, the commencement of this Act.

(3) Nothing in this Act—

(a) enables any civil claim to be made which was barred by the Limitation Act 1980 or any other enactment before the commencement of this Act,

(b) applies to any civil claim made in civil proceedings which were commenced before the commencement of this Act or the title to any property which is the subject of any such claim, or

(c) applies to any cause of action in respect of a contract under seal or executed as a deed where the contract was made before the commencement of this Act.

(4) Where—

(a) a cause of action has accrued before the commencement of this Act, and

(b) no provision was made by any enactment passed or made before the passing of this Act, or by any rule of equity, for a limitation period to apply to a civil claim in respect of the cause of action,

any limitation period under this Act which applies to a civil claim in respect of the cause of action shall, if it would otherwise end earlier, be treated as ending at the end of the period of six years beginning with the day on which this Act comes into force.

(5) Where—

(a) the starting date in relation to a cause of action falls before the commencement of this Act, and

(b) provision was made by any enactment passed or made before the passing of this Act, or by any rule of equity, for a limitation period to apply to a civil claim in respect of the cause of action,

any limitation period under this Act which applies to a civil claim in respect of the cause of action shall, if it would otherwise end earlier, be treated as ending at the end of the limitation period which would have applied to the claim if this Act had not been passed.

(6) In determining for the purposes of subsection (5) the limitation period which would have applied if this Act had not been passed—

(a) section 32(1)(b) of the Limitation Act 1980 (concealment) shall be disregarded, and

(b) section 32(1)(a) or (c) of that Act (fraud and mistake) shall not operate to extend the end of any limitation period under that Act beyond the end of the period of six years beginning with the day on which this Act comes into force.

(7) In determining for the purposes of this section whether a civil claim is barred by the Limitation Act 1980 or any other enactment, section 32A or 33 of that Act or any other enactment enabling a limitation period to be overridden shall be disregarded.

(8) For the purposes of this section, a right to a payment under section 1(1) of the Vaccine Damage Payments Act 1979 shall be treated as a cause of action and a claim for such a payment shall be treated as a civil claim in respect of the cause of action.

41 Citation and extent

(1) This Act may be cited as the Limitation Act 2001.

(2) This Act extends to England and Wales only.

(Draft) Interest on Debts and Damages Bill
(Law Com. No. 287)

Draft of a Bill to amend the powers of courts to award interest on debts and damages; and for connected purposes.   [2004]

1 Award of interest by High Court

For section 35A of the Supreme Court Act 1981 (c. 54) (power of High Court to award interest on debts and damages) substitute—

"*35A Power of High Court to award interest on debts and damages*

(1) Subsection (2) applies where, during proceedings in the High Court for the recovery of a debt, the defendant pays the whole debt to the claimant.

(2) The court may award simple or compound interest on some or all of the debt for some or all of the period—

(a) beginning on the date when the cause of action arose, and

(b) ending on the date of the payment.

(3) Subsections (4) and (5) apply where, in proceedings for the recovery of a debt or damages, the High Court gives judgment to any extent in favour of the claimant.

(4) In relation to an action for damages for personal injuries or death in which the court gives judgment for damages exceeding £200, it must, unless it thinks there are special reasons why it should not, award simple or compound interest on—

(a) some or all of the damages for which it gives judgment, and

(b) if any sum is paid in respect of damages during the proceedings, some or all of that sum,

for some or all of the relevant period.

(5) Otherwise, the court may award simple or compound interest on—

(a) some or all of the sum for which it gives judgment in respect of the debt or damages, and

(b) if any sum is paid in that respect during the proceedings, some or all of that sum,

for some or all of the relevant period.

(6) "Relevant period" means the period beginning on the date when the cause of action arose and ending—

(a) in relation to any sum for which the court gives judgment, on the date of the judgment, and

(b) in relation to any sum paid during the proceedings, on the date of the payment.

(7) This section is subject to rules of court.

35B Section 35A: rate of interest,&c.

(1) In relation to an action for damages for personal injuries, interest awarded under section 35A on damages for non-pecuniary loss runs for the period for which it is awarded at such rate (or rates) as the court specifies.

(2) Otherwise, subject to rules of court, interest awarded under section 35A runs for the period for which it is awarded—

(a) at such rate (or rates) as the Secretary of State may by order specify, or

(b) if the court decides there are good reasons for awarding interest at some other rate (or rates), at such rate (or rates) as the court specifies.

(3) An order under subsection (2)(a) must be made by statutory instrument, which is subject to annulment in pursuance of a resolution of either House of Parliament.

(4) Where interest is awarded under section 35A, rules of court may make provision as to—

(a) matters to which the court must have regard when deciding whether to award simple or compound interest;

(b) circumstances in which, or heads of damage on which, compound interest may not be awarded;

(c) the method of calculating any compound interest awarded (and, in particular, the rests to be used in the calculation);

(d) matters to which the court must have regard when making a decision under subsection (2)(b) above.

(5) The court may not award interest under section 35A on a debt for a period during which, for whatever reason, interest already runs on it.

(6) But where interest on a debt is statutory interest under the Late Payment of Commercial Debts (Interest) Act 1998—

(a) the court may, on the application of the claimant, award interest under section 35A for the period during which the statutory interest runs, and

(b) if it does so, the claimant is not entitled to statutory interest under that Act for that period.

(7) Interest awarded under section 35A in respect of damages may be simple in respect of one head of damage and compound in respect of another.

(8) Interest under section 35A—

(a) may be calculated at different rates in respect of different parts of the period for which it runs, but

(b) may not be simple in respect of one part of that period and compound in respect of another.

(9) In section 35A and this section—

"claimant" means the person seeking the debt or damages,

"defendant" means the person from whom the claimant seeks the debt or damages, and

"personal injuries" includes any disease and any impairment of a person's physical or mental condition.

(10) Nothing in section 35A or this section affects the damages recoverable for the dishonour of a bill of exchange."

4   Consequential amendments and repeals

(3) In section 1 of the Late Payment of Commercial Debts (Interest) Act 1998 (c. 20) (statutory interest), after subsection (2), insert—

"(2A) But that is subject to—

(a) section 35B(6) of the Supreme Court Act 1981 (power of High Court to award interest under section 35A instead of statutory interest), and

(b) section 69A(6) of the County Courts Act 1984 (power of county courts to award interest under section 69 instead of statutory interest)."

(Draft) Unfair Contract Terms Bill
(Law Com. No. 292; Scot. Law Com. No. 199)

A Bill to limit the exclusion or restriction of civil liability by contract terms or notices; to limit the effect of unfair terms in consumer and small business contracts; to make provision about the protection of the collective interests of consumers; and for connected purposes.   [2005]

PART 1   BUSINESS LIABILITY FOR NEGLIGENCE

1   Business liability for negligence

(1) Business liability for death or personal injury resulting from negligence cannot be excluded or restricted by a contract term or a notice.

(2) Business liability for other loss or damage resulting from negligence cannot be excluded or restricted by a contract term or a notice unless the term or notice is fair and reasonable.

(3) "Business liability" means liability arising from—
  (a) anything that was or should have been done for purposes related to a business, or
  (b) the occupation of premises used for purposes related to the occupier's business.
(4) The reference in subsection (3)(a) to anything done for purposes related to a business includes anything done by an employee of that business within the scope of his employment.
(5) "Negligence" means the breach of—
  (a) an obligation to take reasonable care or exercise reasonable skill in the performance of a contract where the obligation arises from an express or implied term of the contract,
  (b) a common law duty to take reasonable care or exercise reasonable skill,
  (c) the common duty of care imposed by the Occupiers' Liability Act 1957 (c. 31) or the Occupiers' Liability Act (Northern Ireland) 1957 (c. 25 NI), or
  (d) the duty of reasonable care imposed by section 2(1) of the Occupiers' Liability (Scotland) Act 1960 (c. 30).
(6) It does not matter—
  (a) whether a breach of obligation or duty was, or was not, inadvertent, or
  (b) whether liability for it arises directly or vicariously.

2   Exceptions to section 1
(1) Section 1 does not prevent an employee from excluding or restricting his liability for negligence to his employer.
(2) Section 1 does not apply to the business liability of an occupier of premises to a person who obtains access to the premises for recreational or educational purposes if—
  (a) that person suffers loss or damage because of the dangerous state of the premises, and
  (b) allowing that person access to those premises for those purposes is not within the purposes of the occupier's business.
(3) Subsection (2) does not extend to Scotland.

3   Voluntary acceptance of risk
The defence that a person voluntarily accepted a risk cannot be used against him just because he agreed to or knew about a contract term, or a notice, appearing to exclude or restrict business liability for negligence in the case in question.

PART 2   CONSUMER CONTRACTS

Contracts in general

4   Terms of no effect unless fair and reasonable
(1) If a term of a consumer contract is detrimental to the consumer, the business cannot rely on the term unless the term is fair and reasonable.
(2) But subsection (1) does not apply to a term which defines the main subject-matter of a consumer contract, if the definition is—
  (a) transparent, and
  (b) substantially the same as the definition the consumer reasonably expected.
(3) Nor does subsection (1) apply to a term in so far as it sets the price payable under a consumer contract, if the price is—
  (a) transparent,
  (b) payable in circumstances substantially the same as those the consumer reasonably expected, and
  (c) calculated in a way substantially the same as the way the consumer reasonably expected.

(4) Nor does subsection (1) apply to a term which—

    (a) is transparent, and

    (b) leads to substantially the same result as would be produced as a matter of law if the term were not included.

(5) The reference to the price payable under a consumer contract does not include any amount, payment of which would be incidental or ancillary to the main purpose of the contract.

(6) "Price" includes remuneration.

Sale or supply of goods

5   Sale or supply to consumer

(1) This section applies to a consumer contract for the sale or supply of goods to the consumer.

(2) In the case of a contract for the sale of the goods, the business cannot rely on a term of the contract to exclude or restrict liability arising under any of the following sections of the 1979 Act—

    (a) section 12 (implied term that seller entitled to sell),

    (b) section 13 (implied term that goods match description),

    (c) section 14 (implied term that goods satisfactory and fit for the purpose),

    (d) section 15 (implied term that goods match sample).

(3) In the case of a contract for the hire-purchase of the goods, the business cannot rely on a term of the contract to exclude or restrict liability arising under any of the following sections of the 1973 Act—

    (a) section 8 (implied term that supplier entitled to supply),

    (b) section 9 (implied term that goods match description),

    (c) section 10 (implied term that goods satisfactory and fit for the purpose),

    (d) section 11 (implied term that goods match sample).

(4) In the case of any other contract for the transfer of property in the goods, the business cannot rely on a term of the contract to exclude or restrict liability arising under any of the following sections of the 1982 Act—

    (a) section 2 or 11B (implied term that supplier entitled to supply),

    (b) section 3 or 11C (implied term that goods match description),

    (c) section 4 or 11D (implied term that goods satisfactory and fit for the purpose),

    (d) section 5 or 11E (implied term that goods match sample).

(5) In the case of a contract for the hire of the goods, the business cannot rely on a term of the contract to exclude or restrict liability arising under any of the following sections of the 1982 Act—

    (a) section 8 or 11I (implied term that goods match description),

    (b) section 9 or 11J (implied term that goods satisfactory and fit for the purpose),

    (c) section 10 or 11K (implied term that goods match sample).

(6) Subsection (2)(b) to (d) does not apply if the contract is—

    (a) for the sale of second-hand goods, and

    (b) made at a public auction which the consumer had the opportunity to attend in person.

6   Sale or supply to business

(1) This section applies to a consumer contract for the sale or supply of goods to the business.

(2) In the case of a contract for the sale of the goods, the consumer cannot rely on a term of the contract to exclude or restrict liability—

    (a) arising under section 12 of the 1979 Act (implied term that seller entitled to sell), or

(b) unless the term is fair and reasonable, arising under either of the following sections of that Act—
   (i)   section 13 (implied term that goods match description),
   (ii) section 15 (implied term that goods match sample).
(3) In the case of a contract for the hire-purchase of the goods, the consumer cannot rely on a term of the contract to exclude or restrict liability—
   (a) arising under section 8 of the 1973 Act (implied term that supplier entitled to supply), or
   (b) unless the term is fair and reasonable, arising under either of the following sections of that Act—
      (i)   section 9 (implied term that goods match description),
      (ii) section 11 (implied term that goods match sample).

Supplemental

7   Regulation and enforcement
Schedule 1 confers functions on the OFT and regulators in relation to—
   (a) consumer contract terms,
   (b) terms drawn up or proposed for use as consumer contract terms,
   (c) terms which a trade association recommends for use as consumer contract terms, and
   (d) notices relating to the rights conferred or duties imposed by consumer contracts.

8   Ambiguity
(1) If it is reasonable to read a written term of a consumer contract in two (or more) ways, the term is to be read in whichever of those ways it is reasonable to think the more (or the most) favourable to the consumer.
(2) This section does not apply in relation to proceedings under Schedule 1 (regulation and enforcement of consumer contract terms, etc.).

PART 3   NON-CONSUMER CONTRACTS

Business contracts

9   Written standard terms
(1) This section applies where one party to a business contract ("A") deals on the written standard terms of business of the other ("B").
(2) Unless the term is fair and reasonable, B cannot rely on any of those terms to exclude or restrict its liability to A for breach of the contract.
(3) Unless the term is fair and reasonable, B cannot rely on any of those terms to claim that it has the right—
   (a) to carry out its obligations under the contract in a way substantially different from the way in which A reasonably expected them to be carried out, or
   (b) not to carry out all or part of those obligations.

10   Sale or supply of goods
(1) In the case of a business contract for the sale of goods, the seller cannot rely on a term of the contract to exclude or restrict liability arising under section 12 of the 1979 Act (implied term that seller entitled to sell).
(2) In the case of a business contract for the hire-purchase of goods, the supplier cannot rely on a term of the contract to exclude or restrict liability arising under section 8 of the 1973 Act (implied term that supplier entitled to supply).
(3) In the case of any other business contract for the transfer of property in goods, the supplier cannot rely on a term of the contract to exclude or restrict liability arising under section 2 or 11B of the 1982 Act (implied term that supplier entitled to supply).

Small business contracts

11   Non-negotiated terms

(1) This section applies where there is a small business contract and—

    (a) the terms on which one party ("A") deals include a term which the other party ("B") put forward during the negotiation of the contract as one of its written standard terms of business,

    (b) the substance of the term was not, as a result of negotiation, changed in favour of A, and

    (c) at the time the contract is made, A is a small business.

(2) If that term is detrimental to A, B cannot rely on the term unless the term is fair and reasonable.

(3) But subsection (2) does not apply to a term which defines the main subject-matter of a small business contract, if the definition is—

    (a) transparent, and

    (b) substantially the same as the definition A reasonably expected.

(4) Nor does subsection (2) apply to a term in so far as it sets the price payable under a small business contract, if the price is—

    (a) transparent,

    (b) payable in circumstances substantially the same as those A reasonably expected, and

    (c) calculated in a way substantially the same as the way A reasonably expected.

(5) Nor does subsection (2) apply to a term which—

    (a) is transparent, and

    (b) leads to substantially the same result as would be produced as a matter of law if the term were not included.

(6) The reference to the price payable under a small business contract does not include any amount, payment of which would be incidental or ancillary to the main purpose of the contract.

(7) "Price" includes remuneration.

Employment contracts

12   Written standard terms

(1) This section applies in relation to an employment contract under which an individual ("the employee") is employed by a business on its written standard terms of employment.

(2) Unless the term is fair and reasonable, the business cannot rely on any of those terms to exclude or restrict its liability for breach of the contract.

(3) Unless the term is fair and reasonable, the business cannot rely on any of those terms to claim it has the right—

    (a) to carry out its obligations under the contract in a way substantially different from the way in which the employee reasonably expected them to be carried out, or

    (b) not to carry out all or part of those obligations.

Private contracts

13   Sale or supply of goods

(1) This section applies if neither party to a contract for the sale or supply of goods enters into it for purposes related to a business of his.

(2) In the case of a contract for the sale of the goods, the seller cannot rely on a term of the contract to exclude or restrict liability—

    (a) arising under section 12 of the 1979 Act (implied term that seller entitled to sell), or

(b) unless the term is fair and reasonable, arising under either of the following sections of that Act—
  (i) section 13 (implied term that goods match description),
  (ii) section 15 (implied term that goods match sample).

(3) In the case of a contract for the hire-purchase of the goods, the supplier cannot rely on a term of the contract to exclude or restrict liability—

(a) arising under section 8 of the 1973 Act (implied term that supplier entitled to supply), or

(b) unless the term is fair and reasonable, arising under either of the following sections of that Act—
  (i) section 9 (implied term that goods match description),
  (ii) section 11 (implied term that goods match sample).

PART 4   THE "FAIR AND REASONABLE" TEST

The test

14 The test

(1) Whether a contract term is fair and reasonable is to be determined by taking into account—

(a) the extent to which the term is transparent, and

(b) the substance and effect of the term, and all the circumstances existing at the time it was agreed.

(2) Whether a notice is fair and reasonable is to be determined by taking into account—

(a) the extent to which the notice is transparent, and

(b) the substance and effect of the notice, and all the circumstances existing at the time when the liability arose (or, but for the notice, would have arisen).

(3) "Transparent" means—

(a) expressed in reasonably plain language,

(b) legible,

(c) presented clearly, and

(d) readily available to any person likely to be affected by the contract term or notice in question.

(4) Matters relating to the substance and effect of a contract term, and to all the circumstances existing at the time it was agreed, include the following—

(a) the other terms of the contract,

(b) the terms of any other contract on which the contract depends,

(c) the balance of the parties' interests,

(d) the risks to the party adversely affected by the term,

(e) the possibility and probability of insurance,

(f) other ways in which the interests of the party adversely affected by the term might have been protected,

(g) the extent to which the term (whether alone or with others) differs from what would have been the case in its absence,

(h) the knowledge and understanding of the party adversely affected by the term,

(i) the strength of the parties' bargaining positions,

(j) the nature of the goods or services to which the contract relates.

(5) Subsection (4) applies, with any necessary modifications, in relation to a notice as it applies in relation to a contract term.

(6) Schedule 2 contains an indicative and non-exhaustive list of consumer contract terms and small business contract terms which may be regarded as not being fair and reasonable.

(7) The Secretary of State may by order amend Schedule 2 so as to add, modify or omit an entry.

Burden of proof

15   Business liability for negligence

It is for a person wishing to rely on a contract term or a notice which purports to exclude or restrict liability of the kind mentioned in section 1(2) (business liability for negligence other than in case of death or personal injury) to prove that the term or notice is fair and reasonable.

16   Consumer contracts

(1) If an issue is raised as to whether a term in a consumer contract is fair and reasonable, it is for the business to prove that it is.

(2) But in proceedings under Schedule 1 (regulation and enforcement of consumer contracts) it is for a person claiming that a term in a consumer contract, or a notice, is not fair and reasonable to prove that it is not.

(3) It is for a person wishing to rely on a contract not being a consumer contract to prove that it is not.

17   Business contracts

(1) It is for a person wishing to rely on a term of a business contract to prove that the term is fair and reasonable.

(2) But in relation to a term to which section 11(2) (non-negotiated terms in small business contracts) applies, it is for a person claiming that the term is not fair and reasonable to prove that it is not.

PART 5   CHOICE OF LAW

18   Consumer contracts

(1) Where a term of a consumer contract applies (or appears to apply) the law of somewhere outside the United Kingdom, this Act has effect in relation to the contract if—

(a) the consumer was living in the United Kingdom when the contract was made, and

(b) all the steps which the consumer had to take for the conclusion of the contract were taken there by him or on his behalf.

(2) Subsection (3) applies where—

(a) a consumer contract has a close connection with the territory of the member States, and

(b) subsection (1) does not apply.

(3) This Act has effect in relation to the contract unless, according to the law of the forum, the provisions of the law of a member State (other than the United Kingdom) which give effect to the Directive have effect in relation to the contract.

(4) A court is not, for the purposes of this section, to treat a consumer contract as having a close connection with the territory of the member States if—

(a) the contract provides for goods to be supplied, or services to be performed, outside the European Union, and

(b) all the steps which the consumer had to take for the conclusion of the contract were taken outside the European Union by him or on his behalf.

(5) Subsection (4) does not apply if it nevertheless appears to the court from all the circumstances of the case that the contract does have a close connection with the territory of the member States.

(6) "Territory of the member States" means the same as it does for the purposes of the Treaty establishing the European Community (and, for the avoidance of doubt, any reference in this section to the territory of the member States is to be read as including a part of that territory).

(7) "The Directive" means Council Directive 93/13/EEC on unfair terms in consumer contracts.

19 Business contracts

(1) Part 1 (business liability for negligence) does not apply to a business contract term, and sections 9 to 11 (business contracts) do not apply to a business contract, if—

    (a) the law applicable to the term, or contract, is the law of a part of the United Kingdom,

    (b) it is the applicable law only by the choice of the parties, and

    (c) were it not for that choice, the applicable law would be the law of somewhere outside the United Kingdom.

(2) This Act has effect in relation to a business contract despite a term of the contract which applies (or appears to apply) the law of somewhere outside the United Kingdom if the contract is in every other respect wholly connected with the United Kingdom.

20 Small business contracts

(1) This Act has effect in relation to a small business contract despite a term of the contract which applies (or appears to apply) the law of somewhere outside the United Kingdom if—

    (a) A had a place of business in the United Kingdom when the contract was made, and

    (b) either of the following conditions applies in relation to the contract.

(2) The first condition is that—

    (a) the making of the contract was preceded in the United Kingdom by an invitation addressed specifically to A, or by advertising, about the main subject-matter of the contract, and

    (b) all the steps which A had to take for the making of the contract were taken in the United Kingdom by A through A's place of business there or on A's behalf.

(3) The second is that A's order was received by B in the United Kingdom.

(4) "A" and "B" mean, respectively, the persons referred to as A and B in section 11.

PART 6   MISCELLANEOUS AND SUPPLEMENTARY

Miscellaneous

21 Unfairness issue raised by court

A court may, in proceedings before it, raise an issue about whether a contract term or a notice is fair and reasonable even if none of the parties to the proceedings has raised the issue or indicated that it intends to raise it.

22 Exceptions

Schedule 3 sets out types of contract, and of contract term, to which this Act does not apply or to which specified provisions of this Act do not apply.

23 Secondary contracts

(1) A term of a contract ("the secondary contract") which reduces the rights or remedies, or increases the obligations, of a person under another contract ("the main contract") is subject to the provisions of this Act that would apply to the term if it were in the main contract.

(2) It does not matter for the purposes of this section whether the parties to the secondary contract are the same as the parties to the main contract.

(3) This section does not apply if the secondary contract is a settlement of a claim arising under the main contract.

24 Effect of unfair term on contract

Where a contract term cannot be relied on by a person as a result of this Act, the contract continues, so far as practicable, to have effect in every other respect.

Interpretation, etc.

25 Preliminary

Sections 26 to 32 define or otherwise explain expressions for the purposes of this Act.

26 "Consumer contract" and "business contract"

(1) "Consumer contract" means a contract (other than one of employment) between—

    (a) an individual ("the consumer") who enters into it wholly or mainly for purposes unrelated to a business of his, and

    (b) a person ("the business") who enters into it wholly or mainly for purposes related to his business.

(2) "Business contract" means a contract between two persons, each of whom enters into it wholly or mainly for purposes related to his business.

27 "Small business"

(1) "Small business" means a person in whose business the number of employees does not exceed—

    (a) nine, or

    (b) where the Secretary of State specifies by order another number for the purposes of this section, that number.

(2) But a person is not a small business if adding the number of employees in his business to the number of employees in any other business of his, or in any business of an associated person, gives a total exceeding the number which for the time being applies for the purposes of subsection (1).

(3) A reference to the number of employees in a business is to the number calculated according to Schedule 4.

28 "Associated person"

(1) For the purposes of this Act, two persons are associated if—

    (a) one controls the other, or

    (b) both are controlled by the same person.

(2) A person ("A") controls a body corporate ("B") if A can secure that B's affairs are conducted according to A's wishes, directions or instructions.

(3) The reference in subsection (2) to wishes, directions or instructions does not include advice given in a professional capacity.

(4) Subsection (2) applies, with any necessary modifications, in relation to an unincorporated association (other than a partnership) as it applies in relation to a body corporate.

(5) A person controls a partnership if he has the right to a share of more than half the assets or income of the partnership.

(6) For the purposes of this section, one person does not control another just because he grants that other person a right to supply goods or services.

29 "Small business contract"

(1) "Small business contract" means a business contract—

    (a) to which at least one of the parties is, at the time the contract is made, a small business, and

    (b) which does not come within any of four exceptions.

(2) The first exception is that the price payable under the contract exceeds £500,000.

(3) The second is that—

    (a) the transaction provided for by the contract forms part of a larger transaction, or part of a scheme or arrangement, and

    (b) the total price payable in respect of the larger transaction, or the scheme or arrangement, exceeds £500,000.

(4) The third is that—

    (a) a person agrees to carry on a regulated activity under the contract, and

    (b) he is an authorised person or, in relation to that activity, an exempt person.

(5) The fourth is that the contract is a series contract.

(6) A contract is a series contract if—

    (a) the transaction provided for by the contract forms part of a series, and

    (b) during the period of two years ending with the date of the contract, the total price payable under contracts providing for transactions in the series exceeds £500,000.

(7) A contract is also a series contract if, at the time the contract was made, both parties intended that—

    (a) the transaction provided for by the contract would form part of a series, and

    (b) the total price payable under contracts providing for transactions in the series and made during any period of two years, would exceed £500,000.

(8) Where a contract is a series contract, every subsequent contract providing for a transaction in the series is a series contract.

(9) The Secretary of State may by order vary the amount specified in subsections (2), (3), (6) and (7).

(10) "Authorised person", "exempt person" and "regulated activity" have the same meaning as in the Financial Services and Markets Act 2000 (c. 8).

30 "Excluding or restricting liability"

(1) A reference to excluding or restricting a liability includes—

    (a) making a right or remedy in respect of the liability subject to a restrictive or onerous condition;

    (b) excluding or restricting a right or remedy in respect of the liability;

    (c) putting a person at a disadvantage if he pursues a right or remedy in respect of the liability;

    (d) excluding or restricting rules of evidence or procedure.

(2) A reference in Part 1 or section 5, 6, 10 or 13 to excluding or restricting a liability includes preventing an obligation or duty arising or limiting its extent.

(3) A written agreement to submit current or future differences to arbitration is not to be regarded as excluding or restricting the liability in question.

31 "Hire-purchase" and "hire"

(1) A reference to a contract for the hire-purchase of goods is to a hire-purchase agreement within the meaning of the Consumer Credit Act 1974 (c. 39).

(2) A reference to a contract for the hire of goods is to be read with the 1982 Act.

32 General interpretation

(1) In this Act—

"the 1973 Act" means the Supply of Goods (Implied Terms) Act 1973 (c. 13),

"the 1979 Act" means the Sale of Goods Act 1979 (c. 54),

"the 1982 Act" means the Supply of Goods and Services Act 1982 (c. 29),

"associated person" has the meaning given in section 28,

"business contract" has the meaning given in section 26(2),

"business liability" has the meaning given in section 1(3) and (4),

"consumer", in relation to a party to a consumer contract, has the meaning given by section 26(1)(a),

"consumer contract" has the meaning given in section 26(1),

"court" means—

    (a) in England and Wales and Northern Ireland, the High Court or a county court, and

    (b) in Scotland, the Court of Session or a sheriff,

and, except in Schedule 1, includes a tribunal, arbitrator or arbiter,

"enactment" includes—

    (a) a provision of, or of an instrument made under, an Act of the Scottish Parliament or Northern Ireland legislation, and

(b) a provision of subordinate legislation (within the meaning of the Interpretation Act 1978 (c. 30)),

"fair and reasonable", in relation to a contract term or a notice, has the meaning given in section 14,

"goods" has the same meaning as in the 1979 Act,

"injunction" includes interim injunction,

"interdict" includes interim interdict,

"negligence" has the meaning given in section 1(5),

"notice" includes an announcement, whether or not in writing, and any other communication,

"the OFT" means the Office of Fair Trading,

"personal injury" includes any disease and any impairment of physical or mental condition,

"public authority" has the same meaning as in section 6 of the Human Rights Act 1998 (c. 42),

"regulator" has the meaning given in paragraph 10 of Schedule 1,

"small business" has the meaning given in section 27,

"small business contract" has the meaning given in section 29,

"statutory" means conferred by an enactment,

"supplier", in relation to a contract for the hire-purchase of goods or a contract for the hire of goods, means the person by whom goods are bailed or (in Scotland) hired to another person under the contract, and

"transparent" has the meaning given in section 14(3).

(2) A reference to a business includes a profession and the activities of a public authority.

(3) A reference to excluding or restricting liability is to be read with section 30.

(4) A reference to a contract for the hire-purchase or hire of goods is to be read with section 31.

Final provisions

33 Orders

(1) Any power of the Secretary of State to make an order under this Act is exercisable by statutory instrument.

(2) A statutory instrument containing an order under this Act, other than one containing an order under section 35 (commencement), is subject to annulment in pursuance of a resolution of either House of Parliament.

34 Consequential amendments and repeals, etc.

(1) Schedule 5 contains minor and consequential amendments.

(2) Schedule 6 contains repeals and revocations.

35 Short title, commencement and extent

(1) This Act may be cited as the Unfair Contract Terms Act 2005.

(2) The preceding provisions come into force on such day as the Secretary of State may by order appoint.

(3) Different days may be appointed for different provisions.

(4) No provision of this Act applies in relation to a contract term agreed before the commencement of the provision (except in so far as the term has been varied after that commencement).

(5) An amendment, repeal or revocation contained in Schedule 5 or 6 has the same extent as the enactment to which it relates.

(6) This Act extends to Northern Ireland.

SCHEDULES

Section 7   SCHEDULE 1

CONSUMER CONTRACT TERMS, ETC.:
REGULATION AND ENFORCEMENT

1   *Cases where this Schedule applies*
    (1) This Schedule applies to a complaint about—
        (a) a consumer contract term,
        (b) a term drawn up or proposed for use as a consumer contract term, or
        (c) a term which a trade association recommends for use as a consumer contract
            term.
    (2) This Schedule also applies to a complaint about—
        (a) a notice relating to the rights conferred or duties imposed by a consumer contract
            on the parties, or
        (b) any other notice purporting to exclude or restrict liability for negligence.

2   *Consideration of complaints*
    (1) If the OFT receives a complaint to which this Schedule applies, it must consider the
complaint unless—
        (a) it thinks that the complaint is frivolous or vexatious,
        (b) it is notified by a regulator that that regulator intends to consider the
            complaint, or
        (c) in the case of a complaint under paragraph 1(2)(b), it thinks that sub-paragraph
            (2) applies in relation to the notice.
    (2) This sub-paragraph applies in relation to a notice which—
        (a) does not exclude or restrict business liability for negligence, or
        (b) excludes or restricts such liability only in relation to a person who, at the time
            when the liability arises, is acting for purposes related to a business.
    (3) If the regulator intends to consider a complaint to which this Schedule applies, it
must—
        (a) notify the OFT that it intends to consider the complaint, and
        (b) consider the complaint.

3   *Application for injunction or interdict*
    (1) The OFT (or a regulator) may apply for an injunction or interdict against such persons
as it considers appropriate if it thinks that the term or notice to which the complaint relates
comes within this paragraph.
    (2) A term or notice comes within this paragraph if it purports to exclude or restrict
liability of the kind mentioned in—
        (a) section 1(1) (business liability for death or personal injury resulting from negli-
            gence), or
        (b) section 5 (implied terms in supply of goods to consumer).
    (3) A term or notice also comes within this paragraph if it—
        (a) is drawn up for general use, and
        (b) is not fair and reasonable.
    (4) A term also comes within this paragraph if—
        (a) however it is expressed, it is in its effect a term of a kind which the
            business usually seeks to include in the kind of consumer contract in question,
            and
        (b) it is not fair and reasonable.

(5) A term which comes within paragraph 1(b) or (c) (but not within paragraph 1(a)) is to be treated for the purposes of section 14 (the "fair and reasonable" test) as if it were a contract term.

4   *Notification of application*
(1) If a regulator intends to make an application under paragraph 3—
(a) it must notify the OFT of its intention, and
(b) it may make the application only if this paragraph applies.
(2) This paragraph applies if—
(a) the period of 14 days beginning with the date of the notification to the OFT has ended, or
(b) before the end of that period, the OFT allows the regulator to make the application.
(3) Where the OFT (or a regulator), having considered a complaint to which this Schedule applies, decides not to make an application under paragraph 3 in response to the complaint, it must give its reasons to the person who made the complaint.

5   *Determination of application*
(1) On an application under paragraph 3, the court may grant an injunction or interdict on such conditions, and against such of the respondents, as it thinks appropriate.
(2) The injunction or interdict may include provision about—
(a) a term or notice to which the application relates;
(b) any consumer contract term, or any notice, of a similar kind or like effect.
(3) It is not a defence to show that, because of a rule of law, a term to which the application relates is not, or could not be, an enforceable contract term.
(4) If a regulator makes the application, it must notify the OFT of—
(a) the outcome of the application, and
(b) if an injunction or interdict is granted, the conditions on which, and the identity of any person against whom, it is granted.

6   *Undertakings*
(1) The OFT (or a regulator) may accept from a relevant person an undertaking that he will comply with such conditions about the use of specified terms or notices, or of terms or notices of a specified kind, as he and the OFT (or the regulator) may agree.
(2) If a regulator accepts an undertaking under this paragraph, it must notify the OFT of—
(a) the conditions on which the undertaking is accepted, and
(b) the identity of the person who gave it.
(3) "Relevant person", in relation to the OFT or a regulator, means a person against whom it has applied, or thinks it is entitled to apply, for an injunction or interdict under paragraph 3.
(4) "Specified", in relation to an undertaking, means specified in the undertaking.

7   *Power to obtain information*
(1) The OFT (or a regulator which is a public authority) may, for a purpose mentioned in sub-paragraph (2)(a) or (b), give notice to a person requiring him to provide it with specified information.
(2) The purposes are—
(a) to facilitate the exercise of the OFT's (or the regulator's) functions for the purposes of this Schedule,
(b) to find out whether a person has complied, or is complying, with—
(i) an injunction or interdict granted under paragraph 5 on an application by the OFT (or the regulator), or
(ii) an undertaking accepted by it under paragraph 6.
(3) The notice must—
(a) be in writing,

(b) specify the purpose for which the information is required, and

(c) specify how and when the notice is to be complied with.

(4) The notice may require the production of specified documents or documents of a specified description.

(5) The OFT (or the regulator) may take copies of any documents produced in compliance with the notice.

(6) The notice may be varied or revoked by a subsequent notice under this paragraph.

(7) The notice may not require a person to provide information or produce documents which he would be entitled to refuse to provide or produce—

(a) in proceedings in the High Court, on the grounds of legal professional privilege;

(b) in proceedings in the Court of Session, on the grounds of confidentiality of communication.

(8) "Specified", in relation to a notice under this paragraph, means specified in the notice.

8 *Notices under paragraph 7: enforcement*

(1) If the OFT (or the regulator) thinks that a person (a "defaulter") has failed, or is failing, to comply with a notice given under paragraph 7, it may apply to the court for an order under this paragraph (a "compliance order").

(2) If the court thinks that the defaulter has failed to comply with the notice, it may make a compliance order.

(3) A compliance order—

(a) must specify such things as the court thinks it reasonable for the defaulter to do to ensure compliance with the notice;

(b) must require the defaulter to do those things;

(c) may require the defaulter to pay some or all of the costs or expenses of the application for the order ("the application costs").

(4) If the defaulter is a company or association, the court may, when acting under sub-paragraph (3)(c), require payment of some or all of the application costs by an officer of the company or association whom the court thinks responsible for the failure.

(5) If a regulator applies for a compliance order, it must notify the OFT of—

(a) the outcome of the application, and

(b) if the order is made, the conditions on which, and the identity of any person against whom, it is made.

(6) "Officer"—

(a) in relation to a company, means a director, manager, secretary or other similar officer of the company,

(b) in relation to a partnership, means a partner,

(c) in relation to any other association, means an officer of the association or a member of its governing body.

9 *Publication, information and advice*

(1) The OFT must arrange to publish details of any—

(a) application it makes for an injunction or interdict under paragraph 3;

(b) injunction or interdict granted on an application by it under paragraph 3;

(c) injunction or interdict notified to it under paragraph 5(4)(b);

(d) undertaking it accepts under paragraph 6(1);

(e) undertaking notified to it under paragraph 6(2);

(f) application it makes for a compliance order under paragraph 8(1);

(g) compliance order made under paragraph 8(2);

(h) compliance order notified to it under paragraph 8(5)(b).

(2) Sub-paragraph (3) applies where a person tells the OFT about a term or notice and asks the OFT whether that term or notice, or one of a similar kind or like effect, is or has been the subject of an injunction, interdict or undertaking under this Schedule.

(3) The OFT must reply; and if it replies that the term or notice, or one of a similar kind or like effect, is or has been the subject of an injunction, interdict or undertaking under this

Schedule, the OFT must give the person—
  (a) a copy of the injunction or interdict or details of the undertaking, and
  (b) if the person giving the undertaking has agreed to amend the term or notice concerned, a copy of the amendments.

(4) The OFT may arrange to publish advice and information about the provisions of this Act.

(5) A reference to an injunction or interdict under this Schedule is to an injunction or interdict—
  (a) granted on an application by the OFT under paragraph 3, or
  (b) notified to it under paragraph 5(4)(b).

(6) A reference to an undertaking under this Schedule is to an undertaking—
  (a) accepted by the OFT under paragraph 6(1), or
  (b) notified to it under paragraph 6(2).

10 *Meaning of "regulator"*

(1) For the purposes of this Schedule, "regulator" means—
  (a) the Financial Services Authority,
  (b) the Office of Communications,
  (c) the Information Commissioner,
  (d) the Gas and Electricity Markets Authority,
  (e) the Water Services Regulation Authority,
  (f) the Office of Rail Regulation,
  (g) the Northern Ireland Authority for Energy Regulation,
  (h) the Department of Enterprise, Trade and Investment in Northern Ireland,
  (i) a local weights and measures authority in Great Britain, or
  (j) a body designated as a regulator under sub-paragraph (3).

(2) The Secretary of State may by order amend sub-paragraph (1) so as to add, modify or omit an entry.

(3) Where the Secretary of State thinks that a body which is not a public authority represents the interests of consumers (or consumers of a particular description), he may by order designate the body as a regulator.

(4) The Secretary of State may cancel the designation if he thinks that the body has failed, or is likely to fail, to comply with a duty imposed on it under this Act.

(5) The Secretary of State must publish (and may from time to time vary) other criteria to be applied by him in deciding whether to make or cancel a designation under this paragraph.

11 *The Financial Services Authority*

Any function that the Financial Services Authority has under this Act is to be regarded, for the purposes of the Financial Services and Markets Act 2000 (c. 8), as a function that it has under that Act.

Section 14(6)   SCHEDULE 2

CONTRACT TERMS WHICH MAY BE REGARDED AS NOT FAIR AND REASONABLE

PART 1   INTRODUCTION

1—(1) A term of a consumer contract or small business contract may be regarded as not being fair and reasonable if it—
  (a) has the object or effect of a term listed in Part 2, and
  (b) does not come within an exception mentioned in Part 3.

(2) In this Schedule—

- (a) in relation to a consumer contract, "A" means the consumer and "B" means the business, and
- (b) in relation to a small business contract, "A" and "B" mean, respectively, the persons referred to as A and B in section 11.

PART 2   LIST OF TERMS

2 A term excluding or restricting liability to A for breach of contract.

3 A term imposing obligations on A in circumstances where B's obligation to perform depends on the satisfaction of a condition wholly within B's control.

4 A term entitling B, if A exercises a right to cancel the contract or if B terminates the contract as a result of A's breach, to keep sums that A has paid, the amount of which is unreasonable.

5 A term requiring A, when in breach of contract, to pay B a sum significantly above the likely loss to B.

6 A term entitling B to cancel the contract without incurring liability, unless there is also a term entitling A to cancel it without incurring liability.

7 A term entitling B, if A exercises a right to cancel the contract, to keep sums A has paid in respect of services which B has yet to supply.

8 A term in a fixed-term contract or a contract of indefinite duration entitling B to terminate the contract without giving A reasonable advance notice (except in an urgent case).

9 A term—

- (a) providing for a contract of fixed duration to be renewed unless A indicates otherwise, and
- (b) requiring A to give that indication a disproportionately long time before the contract is due to expire.

10 A term binding A to terms with which A did not have an opportunity to become familiar before the contract was made.

11 A term entitling B, without a good reason which is specified in the contract, to vary the terms of the contract.

12 A term entitling B, without a good reason, to vary the characteristics of the goods or services concerned.

13 A term requiring A to pay whatever price is set for the goods at the time of delivery (including a case where the price is set by reference to a list price), unless there is also a term entitling A to cancel the contract if that price is higher than the price indicated to A when the contract was made.

14 A term entitling B to increase the price specified in the contract, unless there is also a term entitling A to cancel the contract if the business does increase the price.

15 A term giving B the exclusive right (and, accordingly, excluding any power of a court) to determine—

- (a) whether the goods or services supplied match the definition of them given in the contract, or
- (b) the meaning of any term in the contract.

16 A term excluding or restricting B's liability for statements or promises made by B's employees or agents, or making B's liability for statements or promises subject to formalities.

17 A term requiring A to carry out its obligations in full (in particular, to pay the whole of the price specified in the contract) in circumstances where B has failed to carry out its obligations in full.

18 A term entitling B to transfer its obligations without A's consent.

19 A term entitling B to transfer its rights in circumstances where A's position might be weakened as a result.

20 A term excluding or restricting A's right—
(a) to bring or defend any action or other legal proceedings, or
(b) to exercise other legal remedies.
21 A term restricting the evidence on which A may rely.

PART 3   EXCEPTIONS

22 *Financial services contracts*
(1) Sub-paragraph (2) applies where a term in a financial services contract of indefinite duration provides that B may terminate the contract—
(a) by giving A relatively short advance notice, or
(b) if B has a good reason for terminating the contract, without giving A any advance notice.
(2) Paragraph 8 (termination without reasonable notice) does not apply to the term if the contract also provides that B must immediately inform A of the termination.
(3) Sub-paragraph (4) applies where a term in a financial services contract of indefinite duration provides that B may vary the interest rate or other charges payable under it—
(a) by giving A relatively short advance notice, or
(b) if B has a good reason for making the variation, without giving A any advance notice.
(4) Paragraph 11 (variation without good reason) does not apply to a term if the contract also provides that—
(a) B must as soon as practicable inform A of the variation, and
(b) A may then cancel the contract, without incurring liability.
(5) "Financial services contract" means a contract for the supply by B of financial services to A.

23 *Contracts of indefinite duration*
Paragraph 11 (variation without good reason) does not apply to a term in a contract of indefinite duration if the contract also provides that—
(a) B must give reasonable notice of the variation, and
(b) A may then cancel the contract, without incurring liability.

24 *Contracts for sale of securities, foreign currency, etc.*
(1) None of the following paragraphs applies to a contract term if sub-paragraph (2) or (3) applies—
(a) paragraph 8 (termination without reasonable notice),
(b) paragraph 11 (variation without good reason),
(c) paragraph 13 (determination of price at time of delivery),
(d) paragraph 14 (increase in price).
(2) This sub-paragraph applies if the contract is for the transfer of securities, financial instruments or anything else, the price of which is linked to—
(a) fluctuations in prices quoted on a stock exchange, or
(b) a financial index or market rate that B does not control.
(3) This sub-paragraph applies if the contract is for the sale of foreign currency (and, for this purpose, that includes foreign currency in the form of traveller's cheques or international money orders).

25 *Price index clauses*
Neither paragraph 13 nor paragraph 14 (determination of price at time of delivery or increase in price) applies to a contract term if—
(a) the term provides for the price of the goods or services to be varied by reference to an index of prices, and
(b) the contract specifies how a change to the index is to affect the price.

Section 22   SCHEDULE 3

EXCEPTIONS

1 *Legal requirements*
  (1) This Act does not apply to a contract term—
      (a) required by an enactment or a rule of law,
      (b) required or authorised by a provision in an international convention to which the United Kingdom or the European Community is a party, or
      (c) required by, or incorporated as a result of a decision or ruling of, a competent authority acting in the exercise of its statutory jurisdiction or any of its functions.
  (2) Sub-paragraph 1(c) does not apply if the competent authority is itself a party to the contract.
  (3) "Competent authority" means a public authority other than a local authority.

2 *Settlements of claims*
  (1) This Act does not apply to a contract term in so far as it is, or forms part of—
      (a) a settlement of a claim in tort;
      (b) a discharge or indemnity given by a person in consideration of the receipt by him of compensation in settlement of any claim which he has.
  (2) In sub-paragraph (1)—
      (a) paragraph (a) does not extend to Scotland, and
      (b) paragraph (b) extends only to Scotland.

3 *Insurance*
The following sections do not apply to an insurance contract (including a contract to pay an annuity on human life)—
      (a) section 1 (exclusion of business liability for negligence),
      (b) section 9 (exclusion of liability for breach of business contract where one party deals on written standard terms of the other),
      (c) section 11 (non-negotiated terms in small business contracts),
      (d) section 12 (exclusion of employer's liability under employment contract).

4 *Land*
The following sections do not apply to a contract term in so far as it relates to the creation, transfer, variation or termination of an interest or real right in land—
      (a) section 1 (exclusion of business liability for negligence),
      (b) section 9 (exclusion of liability for breach of business contract where one party deals on written standard terms of the other),
      (c) section 11 (non-negotiated terms in small business contracts).

5 *Intellectual property*
Nor do those sections apply to a contract term in so far as it relates to the creation, transfer, variation or termination of a right or interest in any patent, trade mark, copyright or designright, registered design, technical or commercial information or other intellectual property.

6 *Company formation, etc.*
Nor do those sections apply to a contract term in so far as it relates to—
      (a) the formation or dissolution of a body corporate or unincorporated association (including a partnership),
      (b) its constitution, or
      (c) the rights and obligations of its members.

7   *Securities*

Nor do those sections apply to a contract term in so far as it relates to the creation or transfer of securities or of a right or interest in securities.

8   *International supply contracts*

The following provisions do not apply to a business contract for the supply of goods where the supply is to be made to a place outside the United Kingdom—

      (a) section 1(2) (business liability for negligence other than in case of death or personal injury),

      (b) sections 9 to 11 (unfair terms in business contracts),

      (c) sections 19 and 20 (choice of law in business contracts).

Shipping

9—(1) Section 1(2) does not apply to a shipping contract unless it is also a consumer contract.

    (2) Sections 9 and 11 do not apply to a shipping contract.

    (3) "Shipping contract" means—

      (a) a contract of marine salvage or towage,

      (b) a charterparty of a ship or hovercraft, or

      (c) a contract for the carriage of goods by ship or hovercraft.

10—(1) This paragraph applies where goods are carried by ship or hovercraft under a contract which—

      (a) specifies that as the means of transport for part of the journey, or

      (b) does not specify a means of transport but does not exclude that one.

    (2) Section 1(2) does not apply to the contract, unless it is also a consumer contract, in so far as it relates to the carriage of the goods by that means of transport.

    (3) Sections 9 and 11 do not apply to the contract in so far as it relates to the carriage of the goods by that means of transport.

Section 27   SCHEDULE 4

CALCULATING THE NUMBER OF EMPLOYEES IN A BUSINESS

1   *Introduction*

    (1) This Schedule sets out how to calculate the number of employees that a party to a business contract, or an associated person, has in its business.

    (2) "The business period" means a continuous period for which—

      (a) the party to the business contract has been carrying on the business to which the contract relates, or

      (b) an associated person has been carrying on business.

2   *Calculation for established business*

Where the business period is at least twelve months ending on the last day of the month immediately before the month including the contract date—

      (a) work out how many full-time employees there are in the business on the last day of each of the twelve months ending with the last complete month before the contract date,

      (b) add together the numbers for those twelve days, and

      (c) divide the total by twelve.

Calculation for new business

    3 Where the business period is at least one complete month ending on the last day of the month immediately before the month including the contract date (but paragraph 2 does not apply)—

    (a) work out how many full-time employees there are in the business on the last day of each complete month,

    (b) add together the numbers for those days, and

    (c) divide the total by the number of complete months.

4 Where the business period is less than one complete month, but more than one day, before the contract date—

    (a) work out how many full-time employees there are in the business on each day,

    (b) add together the numbers for those days, and

    (c) divide that total by the number of days.

5 Where the party to the contract enters into it on the first day on which it carries on the business to which the contract relates, or an associated person has been carrying on business for only one day, work out how many full-time employees there are in the business on the day in question.

6   *The number of full-time employees in a business*

(1) This paragraph sets out how to work out how many full-time employees there are in a business.

(2) An employee who works for at least 35 hours a week for a business counts as one full-time employee.

(3) An employee who works for under 35 hours a week for a business (a "part-time employee") counts as a fraction of one full-time employee, with the fraction being calculated as—

$$\frac{A}{B}$$

where A and B are defined as follows.

(4) A is the number of hours a week which the part-time employee works for the business.

(5) B is—

    (a) the number of hours a week which a full-time employee of the same description as the part-time employee works for the business, or

    (b) if there are no full-time employees of that description, 35 hours a week.

(6) The number of hours a week which an employee works for a business is—

    (a) the number of hours a week which he is contractually required to work for the business, or

    (b) if he ordinarily works for a longer period than that, or his contract does not specify for how many hours a week he is to work, the number of hours a week he ordinarily works for the business,

but does not include any meal break, or rest period, exceeding 15 minutes.

Interpretation

7 "Contract date", in relation to a business contract, means the date on which the contract is made.

8 "Employee"—

    (a) in relation to any business, means an individual who works in the business under a contract of employment or a contract for services;

    (b) in relation to a business carried on by a partnership (or other unincorporated association), includes a partner (or member);

    (c) in relation to a business carried on by only one individual, includes that individual.

Section 34(1)   SCHEDULE 5

MINOR AND CONSEQUENTIAL AMENDMENTS

Misrepresentation Act 1967 (c. 7)

1 In section 3 of the Misrepresentation Act 1967 (c. 7) (avoidance of provision excluding liability for misrepresentation), for the words from "that term" to the end, substitute "that

term is of no effect unless it is fair and reasonable for the purposes of the Unfair Contract Terms Act 2005 (and, accordingly, Part 4 of that Act applies in relation to the term)".

Misrepresentation Act (Northern Ireland) 1967 (c. 14 (NI))

2 In section 3 of the Misrepresentation Act (Northern Ireland) 1967 (c. 14 (NI)) (avoidance of provision excluding liability for misrepresentation), make the same substitution.

Supply of Goods (Implied Terms) Act 1973 (c. 13)

3 The Supply of Goods (Implied Terms) Act 1973 (c. 13) is amended as follows.

4 In section 10 (implied undertakings as to quality or fitness)—
   (a) in subsections (2D) and (2F), for the words from "the person" to "consumer contract", substitute "the agreement is a consumer contract under which the goods are bailed or hired to the consumer", and
   (b) omit subsection (8).

5 In section 11A (the title to which becomes "Modification of remedies for breach of statutory condition where bailee not consumer")—
   (a) in subsection (1), for "the person to whom the goods are bailed does not deal as consumer" substitute "the agreement is not a consumer contract under which the goods are bailed to the consumer",
   (b) for subsection (3)(b) substitute—
      "(b) that the agreement was not a consumer contract under which the goods were bailed to the consumer.", and
   (c) omit subsection (4).

6 In section 12A (remedies for breach of hire-purchase agreements in Scotland)—
   (a) in subsection (2), after "consumer contract" insert "under which the goods are hired to the consumer", and
   (b) for subsection (3) substitute—
      "(3) For the purposes of subsection (2), if the creditor wishes to rely on a hire-purchase contract not being a consumer contract under which goods are hired to the consumer, it is for the creditor to prove that it is not.".

7 In section 14(1) (special provision about conditional sale agreements), for the words from "where" to the end substitute "which is a consumer contract under which the buyer is the consumer.".

8 In section 15(1) (interpretation)—
   (a) for the definition of "business" substitute—
      " 'business' includes a profession and the activities of a public authority (within the meaning of the Human Rights Act 1998 (c. 42))", and
   (b) at the appropriate place insert—
      " 'consumer contract', and 'the consumer' in relation to a consumer contract, have the same meaning as in section 26 of the Unfair Contract Terms Act 2005;".

Sale of Goods Act 1979 (c. 54)

9 The Sale of Goods Act 1979 (c. 54) is amended as follows.

10 In section 14 (implied terms about quality or fitness), in subsections (2D) and (2F), for the words from "the buyer" to "consumer contract" substitute "the contract is a consumer contract under which the buyer is the consumer".

11 In section 15A (the title to which becomes "Modifications of remedies for breach of condition where buyer not consumer"), for "the buyer does not deal as consumer" substitute "the contract is not a consumer contract under which the buyer is the consumer".

12 In section 15B (remedies for breach of contract in Scotland), in subsection (2), after "consumer contract" insert "under which the buyer is the consumer".

13 In section 20 (passing of risk), in subsection (4), for the words from "In a case" to "is a consumer" substitute "Where there is a consumer contract under which the buyer is the consumer".

14 In section 30 (delivery of wrong quantity), in subsection (2A), for "A buyer who does not deal as consumer" substitute "Where the contract is not a consumer contract under which the buyer is the consumer, the buyer".

15 In section 32 (delivery to carrier), in subsection (4), for the words from "In a case" to "is a consumer," substitute "Where there is a consumer contract under which the buyer is the consumer,".

16 In section 35 (acceptance), in subsection (3), for the words from "the buyer deals" to "consumer contract" substitute "there is a consumer contract under which the buyer is the consumer".

17 In section 48A (additional rights of buyer in consumer cases), for subsection (1)(a) substitute—

"(a) there is a consumer contract under which the buyer is the consumer,".

18 In section 55(1) (exclusion by parties of implied contractual terms), for "the Unfair Contract Terms Act 1977" substitute "the Unfair Contract Terms Act 2005".

19 In section 61 (interpretation)—

(a) in subsection (1), for the definition of "consumer contract" substitute—

"'consumer contract' and, in relation to a consumer contract, 'the consumer' have the same meaning as in section 26 of the Unfair Contract Terms Act 2005", and

(b) for subsection (5A) substitute—

"(5A) For the purposes of this Act, if the seller wishes to rely on a contract for the sale of goods not being a consumer contract under which the buyer is the consumer, it is for the seller to prove that it is not.".

Supply of Goods and Services Act 1982 (c. 29)

20 The Supply of Goods and Services Act 1982 (c. 29) is amended as follows.

21 In section 4 (implied terms about quality or fitness in contract for transfer of goods), in subsections (2B) and (2D), for "the transferee deals as consumer" substitute "the contract is a consumer contract under which the transferee is the consumer".

22 In section 5A (the title to which becomes "Modification of remedies for breach of statutory condition where transferee not consumer"), in subsection (1), for "the transferee does not deal as consumer" substitute "the contract is not a consumer contract under which the transferee is the consumer".

23 In section 9 (implied terms about quality or fitness), in subsections (2B) and (2D), for "the bailee deals as consumer" substitute "the contract is a consumer contract under which the bailee is the consumer".

24 In section 10A (the title to which becomes "Modification of remedies for breach of statutory condition where bailee not consumer"), in subsection (1), for "the bailee does not deal as consumer" substitute "the contract is not a consumer contract under which the bailee is the consumer".

25 In section 11(1) (exclusion of implied terms, etc.), for "the 1977 Act" substitute "the 2005 Act".

26 In section 11D (implied terms about quality or fitness in contract for transfer of goods in Scotland), in subsections (3A) and (3C), after "consumer contract" insert "and the transferee is the consumer".

27 In section 11F (remedies for breach of contract in Scotland), omit subsection (3).

28 In section 11J (implied terms about quality or fitness in contract for hire of goods in Scotland), in subsections (3A) and (3C), after "consumer contract" insert "and the person to whom the goods are hired is the consumer".

29 In section 11L(1) (exclusion of implied terms, etc. in Scotland), for "the 1977 Act" substitute "the 2005 Act".

30 In section 11M (additional rights of transferee in consumer cases), for subsection (1)(a) substitute—

"(a) there is a consumer contract under which the transferee is the consumer,".

31 In section 16(1) (exclusion of implied terms, etc.), for "the 1977 Act" substitute "the 2005 Act".

32 In section 18 (general interpretation)—

(a) in subsection (1), at the appropriate place insert—

" 'consumer contract' and, in relation to a consumer contract, 'the consumer' have the same meaning as in section 26 of the 2005 Act;", and

(b) for subsection (4) substitute—

"(4) For those purposes, if the transferor wishes to rely on a contract for the transfer of goods not being a consumer contract under which the transferee is the consumer, it is for the transferor to prove that it is not.

(5) Subsection (4) also applies in relation to a contract for the hire of goods; and for that purpose—

(a) 'transferor' includes the bailor or supplier, and

(b) 'transferee' includes the bailee or person to whom the goods are hired."

33 In section 19 (interpretation: references to Acts)—

(a) omit the definition of "the 1977 Act" and the word "and" immediately following it, and

(b) at the end, insert "; and

'the 2005 Act' means the Unfair Contract Terms Act 2005".

Merchant Shipping Act 1995 (c. 21)

34 In section 184 of the Merchant Shipping Act 1995 (c. 21) (Orders in Council relating to carriage within the British Islands), omit subsection (2).

Arbitration Act 1996 (c. 23)

35 The Arbitration Act 1996 (c. 23) is amended as follows.

36 In section 89 (the cross-heading immediately above which becomes "Consumer and small business arbitration agreements" and the title to which becomes "Application of the Unfair Contract Terms Act 2005")—

(a) for subsections (1) and (2) substitute—

"(1) Sections 90 and 91 extend the application of sections 4 and 11 of the 2005 Act (detrimental terms in consumer and small business contracts) in relation to a term which constitutes an arbitration agreement.

(2) For that purpose—

'the 2005 Act' means the Unfair Contract Terms Act 2005, and 'arbitration agreement' means an agreement to submit to arbitration present or future disputes or differences (whether or not contractual).", and

(b) in subsection (3), for "Those sections" substitute "Sections 90 and 91".

37 For section 90 substitute—

"90   Application where consumer is a legal person

Section 4 of the 2005 Act applies where the consumer is a legal person as it applies where the consumer is a natural person.".

38 In section 91(1) (arbitration agreement unfair where modest amount sought) for "the Regulations" substitute "sections 4 and 11 of the 2005 Act".

Late Payment of Commercial Debts (Interest) Act 1998 (c. 20)

39 In section 14 of the Late Payment of Commercial Debts (Interest) Act 1998 (c. 20) (postponement of date for payment of contract price) in subsection (2), for "Sections 3(2)(b) and 17(1)(b) of the Unfair Contract Terms Act 1977" substitute "Section 9 of the Unfair Contract Terms Act 2005".

Contracts (Rights of Third Parties) Act 1999 (c. 31)

40 In section 7(2) of the Contracts (Rights of Third Parties) Act 1999 (c. 31) (disapplication of restriction on exclusion of liability for negligence) for "Section 2(2) of the Unfair Contract Terms Act 1977" substitute "Section 1(2) of the Unfair Contract Terms Act 2005".

Compensation Bill
[as brought from the House of Lords into the House of Commons]

A Bill to specify certain factors that may be taken into account by a court determining a claim in negligence or breach of statutory duty; and to make provision for the regulation of claims management services.

[27th March 2006]

PART 1   STANDARD OF CARE

1   Deterrent effect of potential liability

A court considering a claim in negligence or breach of statutory duty may, in determining whether the defendant should have taken particular steps to meet a standard of care (whether by taking precautions against a risk or otherwise), have regard to whether a requirement to take those steps might—

    (a) prevent a desirable activity from being undertaken at all, to a particular extent or in a particular way, or

    (b) discourage persons from undertaking functions in connection with a desirable activity.

2   Apologies, offers of treatment or other redress

An apology, an offer of treatment or other redress, shall not of itself amount to an admission of negligence or breach of statutory duty.

PART 2   CLAIMS MANAGEMENT SERVICES

3   Provision of regulated claims management services

    (1) A person may not provide regulated claims management services unless—

        (a) he is an authorised person,

        (b) he is an exempt person,

        (c) the requirement for authorisation has been waived in relation to him in accordance with regulations under section 8, or

        (d) he is an individual acting otherwise than in the course of a business.

    (2) In this Part—

        (a) "authorised person" means a person authorised by the Regulator under section 4(1)(a),

        (b) "claims management services" means advice or other services in relation to the making of a claim,

        (c) "claim" means a claim for compensation, restitution, repayment or any other remedy or relief in respect of loss or damage or in respect of an obligation, whether the claim is made or could be made—

            (i) by way of legal proceedings,

            (ii) in accordance with a scheme of regulation (whether voluntary or compulsory), or

            (iii) in pursuance of a voluntary undertaking,

(d) "exempt person" has the meaning given by section 5(5), and

(e) services are regulated if they are—

    (i)   of a kind prescribed by order of the Secretary of State, or

    (ii) provided in cases or circumstances of a kind prescribed by order of the Secretary of State.

(3) For the purposes of this section—

(a) a reference to the provision of services includes, in particular, a reference to—

    (i)   the provision of financial services or assistance,

    (ii)   the provision of services by way of or in relation to legal representation,

    (iii) referring or introducing one person to another, and

    (iv) making inquiries, and

(b) a person does not provide claims management services by reason only of giving, or preparing to give, evidence (whether or not expert evidence).

(4) For the purposes of subsection (1)(d) an individual acts in the course of a business if, in particular—

(a) he acts in the course of an employment, or

(b) he otherwise receives or hopes to receive money or money's worth as a result of his action.

4 The Regulator

(1) The Secretary of State may by order designate a person ("the Regulator")—

(a) to authorise persons to provide regulated claims management services,

(b) to regulate the conduct of authorised persons, and

(c) to exercise such other functions as are conferred on the Regulator by or under this Part.

(2) The Secretary of State may designate a person only if satisfied that the person—

(a) is competent to perform the functions of the Regulator,

(b) will make arrangements to avoid any conflict of interest between the person's functions as Regulator and any other functions, and

(c) will promote the interests of persons using regulated claims management services (including, in particular, by—

    (i)   setting and monitoring standards of competence and professional conduct for persons providing regulated claims management services,

    (ii)   promoting good practice by persons providing regulated claims management services, in particular in relation to the provision of information about charges and other matters to persons using or considering using the services,

    (iii) promoting practices likely to facilitate competition between different providers of regulated claims management services, and

    (iv) ensuring that arrangements are made for the protection of persons using regulated claims management services (including arrangements for the handling of complaints about the conduct of authorised persons)).

(3) If the Secretary of State thinks that no existing person (whether an individual or a body corporate or unincorporate) is suitable for designation under subsection (1), he may by order establish a person for the purpose of being designated.

(4) The Regulator shall—

(a) comply with any directions given to him by the Secretary of State;

(b) have regard to any guidance given to him by the Secretary of State;

(c) have regard to any code of practice issued to him by the Secretary of State;

(d) try to meet any targets set for him by the Secretary of State;

(e) provide the Secretary of State with any report or information requested (but this paragraph does not require or permit disclosure of information in contravention of any other enactment).

(5) The Secretary of State shall lay before Parliament any code of practice issued by him to the Regulator.

(6) The Secretary of State may pay grants to the Regulator (which may be on terms or conditions, including terms and conditions as to repayment with or without interest).

(7) A reference in this Part to the Regulator includes a reference to a person acting on behalf of the Regulator or with his authority.

(8) The Secretary of State may by order revoke a person's designation under subsection (1).

(9) While no person is designated under subsection (1) the Secretary of State shall exercise functions of the Regulator.

(10) The Secretary of State may by order transfer (whether for a period of time specified in the order or otherwise) a function of the Regulator to the Secretary of State.

5 Exemptions

(1) The Secretary of State may by order provide that section 3(1) shall not prevent the provision of regulated claims management services by a person who is a member of a specified body.

(2) The Secretary of State may by order provide that section 3(1) shall not prevent the provision of regulated claims management services—

(a) by a specified person or class of person,

(b) in specified circumstances, or

(c) by a specified person or class of person in specified circumstances.

(3) Provision by virtue of subsection (1) or (2) may be expressed to have effect subject to compliance with specified conditions.

(4) Section 3(1) shall not prevent the provision of regulated claims management services by a person who is established or appointed by virtue of an enactment.

(5) For the purposes of this Part a person is "exempt" if, or in so far as, section 3(1) does not, by virtue of this section, prevent him from providing regulated claims management services.

6 Enforcement: offence

(1) A person commits an offence if he contravenes section 3(1).

(2) A person who is guilty of an offence under subsection (1) shall be liable—

(a) on conviction on indictment—

(i) to imprisonment for a term not exceeding two years,

(ii) to a fine, or

(iii) to both, or

(b) on summary conviction—

(i) to imprisonment for a term not exceeding 51 weeks,

(ii) to a fine not exceeding level 5 on the standard scale, or

(iii) to both.

(3) Until the commencement of section 281(4) and (5) of the Criminal Justice Act 2003 (c. 44) (51 week maximum term of sentences) the reference in subsection (3)(b)(i) above to 51 weeks shall have effect as if it were a reference to six months.

7 Enforcement: the Regulator

(1) The Regulator may apply to the court for an injunction restraining a person from providing regulated claims management services if he is not—

(a) an authorised person,

(b) an exempt person, or

(c) the subject of a waiver in accordance with regulations under section 8.

(2) In subsection (1) "the court" means the High Court or a county court.

(3) The Regulator may—

(a) investigate whether an offence has been committed under this Part;

(b) institute criminal proceedings in respect of an offence under this Part.

(4) For the purpose of investigating whether an offence has been committed under this Part the Regulator may require the provision of information or documents.

(5) On an application by the Regulator a judge of the High Court, Circuit judge or justice of the peace may issue a warrant authorising the Regulator to enter and search premises on which a person conducts or is alleged to conduct regulated claims management business, for the purposes of investigating whether an offence has been committed under this Part.

(6) The Regulator may take copies of written or electronic records found on a search by virtue of subsection (5) for a purpose specified in subsection (3)(a) or (b).

(7) In subsections (4) to (6) a reference to the Regulator includes a reference to a person authorised by him in writing.

(8) The Secretary of State shall make regulations—

(a) specifying matters of which a judge or justice of the peace must be satisfied, or to which he must have regard, before issuing a warrant under subsection (5), and

(b) regulating the exercise of a power under or by virtue of subsection (4) or (5) (whether by restricting the circumstances in which a power may be exercised, by specifying conditions to be complied with in the exercise of a power, or otherwise).

8   Regulations

(1) The Secretary of State shall make regulations about—

(a) authorisations under section 4(1);

(b) the functions of the Regulator.

(2) The Schedule specifies particular provision that may be made by the regulations.

(3) Transitional provision of regulations under this section may, in particular, make provision about the extent to which functions under this Part or under the regulations may be exercised in respect of matters arising before the commencement of a provision made by or by virtue of this Part.

9   Obstructing the Regulator

(1) A person commits an offence if without reasonable excuse he obstructs the Regulator in the exercise of a power—

(a) under section 7(4) to (6), or

(b) by virtue of paragraph 14 of the Schedule.

(2) A person who is guilty of an offence under subsection (1) shall be liable on summary conviction to a fine not exceeding level 5 on the standard scale.

10   Pretending to be authorised, &c.

(1) A person commits an offence if he falsely holds himself out as being—

(a) an authorised person,

(b) an exempt person, or

(c) the subject of a waiver in accordance with regulations under section 8.

(2) A person commits an offence if—

(a) he offers to provide regulated claims management services, and

(b) provision by him of those services would constitute an offence under this Part.

(3) For the purposes of subsection (2) a person offers to provide services if he—

(a) makes an offer to a particular person or class of person,

(b) makes arrangements for an advertisement in which he offers to provide services, or

    (c) makes arrangements for an advertisement in which he is described or presented as competent to provide services.

  (4) A person who is guilty of an offence under subsection (1) or (2) shall be liable—

    (a) on conviction on indictment—

      (i) to imprisonment for a term not exceeding two years,

      (ii) to a fine, or

      (iii) to both, or

    (b) on summary conviction—

      (i) to imprisonment for a term not exceeding 51 weeks,

      (ii) to a fine not exceeding level 5 on the standard scale, or

      (iii) to both.

  (5) Where a person commits an offence under this section by causing material to be displayed or made accessible, he shall be treated as committing the offence on each day during any part of which the material is displayed or made accessible.

  (6) Until the commencement of section 281(4) and (5) of the Criminal Justice Act 2003 (c. 44) (51 week maximum term of sentences) the reference in subsection (4)(b)(i) above to 51 weeks shall have effect as if it were a reference to six months.

11 The Claims Management Services Tribunal

  (1) There shall be a tribunal to be known as the Claims Management Services Tribunal.

  (2) The Tribunal shall be constituted as follows—

    (a) members of the Financial Services and Markets Tribunal shall also be members of the Claims Management Services Tribunal,

    (b) the President of the Financial Services and Markets Tribunal shall also act as President of the Claims Management Services Tribunal,

    (c) the Deputy President of the Financial Services and Markets Tribunal shall also act as Deputy President of the Claims Management Services Tribunal, and

    (d) the panel of chairmen of the Financial Services and Markets Tribunal shall also be the panel of chairmen of the Claims Management Services Tribunal.

  (3) An appeal or reference to the Tribunal shall be heard by a member of the panel of chairmen—

    (a) selected in accordance with arrangements made by the President, and

    (b) sitting alone or, in accordance with those arrangements, with one or two members of the lay panel;

and a chairman who sits with one other member shall have a casting vote.

  (4) The Lord Chancellor may make rules about the proceedings of the Tribunal; and the rules—

    (a) shall include provision about timing of references and appeals,

    (b) shall include provision for the suspension of decisions of the Regulator while an appeal could be brought or is pending,

    (c) shall include provision about the making of interim orders,

    (d) shall enable the Tribunal to suspend or further suspend (wholly or partly) the effect of a decision of the Regulator,

    (e) shall permit the Regulator to apply for the termination of the suspension of a decision of his,

    (f) may include provision about evidence,

    (g) may include provision about any other matter of a kind for which rules under section 132 of the Financial Services and Markets Act 2000 (c. 8) (the Financial Services and Markets Tribunal) may make provision,

    (h) may include transitional, consequential or incidental provision,

    (i) may make provision generally or only for specified cases or circumstances,

(j) may make different provision for different cases or circumstances,

(k) shall be made by statutory instrument, and

(l) shall be subject to annulment in pursuance of a resolution of either House of Parliament.

(5) The following provisions of Schedule 13 to the Financial Services and Markets Act 2000 shall have effect, with any necessary modifications, in relation to the Claims Management Services Tribunal—

(a) paragraph 5 (remuneration and allowances),

(b) paragraph 6 (staff),

(c) paragraph 7(3) and (4) (composition),

(d) paragraph 8 (sittings),

(e) paragraph 10 (practice directions),

(f) paragraph 11 (evidence), and

(g) paragraph 12(1) to (3) (decisions).

(6) In Part 1 of Schedule 1 to the Tribunals and Inquiries Act 1992 (c. 53) (tribunals under supervision of Council) insert at the appropriate place—

| "Claims management services | The Claims Management Services Tribunal established by the Compensation Act 2006." |

12   Appeals and references to Tribunal

(1) A person may appeal to the Claims Management Services Tribunal if the Regulator—

(a) refuses the person's application for authorisation,

(b) grants the person authorisation on terms or subject to conditions,

(c) imposes conditions on the person's authorisation,

(d) suspends the person's authorisation, or

(e) cancels the person's authorisation.

(2) The Regulator may refer to the Tribunal (with or without findings of fact or recommendations)—

(a) a complaint about the professional conduct of an authorised person, or

(b) the question whether an authorised person has complied with a rule of professional conduct.

(3) On a reference or appeal under this section the Tribunal—

(a) may take any decision on an application for authorisation that the Regulator could have taken;

(b) may impose or remove conditions on a person's authorisation;

(c) may suspend a person's authorisation;

(d) may cancel a person's authorisation;

(e) may remit a matter to the Regulator;

(f) may not award costs.

(4) An authorised person may appeal to the Court of Appeal against a decision of the Tribunal.

13   Interpretation

In this Part—

"action" includes omission,

"authorised person" has the meaning given by section 3,

"claim" has the meaning given by section 3,

"claims management services" has the meaning given by section 3,

"exempt person" has the meaning given by section 5(5),

"regulated claims management services" shall be construed in accordance with section 3(2)(e), "specified", in relation to an order or regulations, means specified in the order or regulations, and

"the Regulator" means (subject to section 4(7)) the person designated under section 4(1) or, where no person is designated or in so far as is necessary having regard to any order under section 4(10), the Secretary of State.

14 Orders and regulations

(1) An order or regulations under this Part—

    (a) may make provision that applies generally or only in specified cases or circumstances,

    (b) may make different provision for different cases or circumstances, and

    (c) may include transitional, incidental or consequential provision.

(2) An order or regulations under this Part shall be made by statutory instrument.

(3) An order under section 3(2)(e)—

    (a) may not be made unless the Secretary of State has consulted—

        (i) the Office of Fair Trading, and

        (ii) such other persons as he thinks appropriate, and

    (b) may not be made unless a draft has been laid before and approved by resolution of each House of Parliament.

(4) An order under section 4 may not be made unless a draft has been laid before, and approved by resolution of, each House of Parliament.

(5) An order under section 4(3) may include provision—

    (a) for the appointment of members;

    (b) for funding;

    (c) for dissolution (which may include provision enabling the Secretary of State to make provision for the transfer of property, rights and liabilities).

(6) An order under section 5 shall be subject to annulment in pursuance of a resolution of either House of Parliament.

(7) Regulations under section 7 or 8 may not be made unless a draft has been laid before, and approved by resolution of, each House of Parliament.

PART 3   GENERAL

15 Commencement

(1) The preceding provisions of this Act, other than section 1, shall come into force in accordance with provision made by order of the Secretary of State.

(2) An order under subsection (1)—

    (a) may make provision generally or only for specified purposes,

    (b) may make different provision for different purposes,

    (c) may make transitional, consequential or incidental provision, and

    (d) shall be made by statutory instrument.

16 Extent

This Act shall extend to England and Wales only.

17 Short title

(1) This Act may be cited as the Compensation Act 2006.

(2) Nothing in this Act shall impose any charge on the people or on public funds, or vary the amount or incidence of or otherwise alter any such charge in any manner, or affect the assessment, levying, administration or application of any money raised by any such charge.

Section 8   **SCHEDULE**

CLAIMS MANAGEMENT REGULATIONS

Introduction

1 In this Schedule "regulations" means regulations under section 8.

2 Regulations made by virtue of a provision of this Schedule may confer a discretion on the Regulator.

Waiver of requirement for authorisation

3 (1) Regulations may permit the Regulator to waive the requirement for authorisation, as mentioned in section 3(1)(c), in specified cases or circumstances.

(2) Regulations by virtue of this sub-paragraph may permit waiver in relation to a person only—

   (a) if the Secretary of State intends to exempt the person under section 5, and

   (b) for a single period not exceeding six months.

(3) The regulations may, in particular, permit or require the Regulator to provide for waiver to be subject to a condition of a kind specified in the regulations.

Grant of authorisations

4 (1) Regulations shall prescribe the procedure for applying to the Regulator for authorisation.

(2) Regulations may, in particular, require the provision of information or documents relating to the applicant or to any person who appears to the Regulator to be connected with the applicant.

5 (1) Regulations shall require the Regulator not to grant an application for authorisation unless satisfied of the applicant's competence and suitability to provide regulated claims management services of the kind to which the application relates.

(2) For that purpose the Regulator shall apply such criteria, and have regard to such matters, as the regulations shall specify.

(3) Regulations by virtue of sub-paragraph (2) may, in particular—

   (a) refer to a provision of directions, guidance or a code given or issued under section 4(4);

   (b) relate to persons who are or are expected to be employed or engaged by, or otherwise connected with, the applicant;

   (c) relate to—

      (i)   criminal records;

      (ii)   proceedings in any court or tribunal;

      (iii) proceedings of a body exercising functions in relation to a trade or profession;

      (iv)   financial circumstances;

      (v)   management structure;

      (vi)   actual or proposed connections or arrangements with other persons;

      (vii) qualifications;

      (viii) actual or proposed arrangements for training;

      (ix)   arrangements for accounting;

      (x)   practice or proposed practice in relation to the provision of information about fees;

      (xi)   arrangements or proposed arrangements for holding clients' money;

      (xii) arrangements or proposed arrangements for insurance.

6 Regulations may—
- (a) provide for authorisation to be on specified terms or subject to compliance with specified conditions;
- (b) permit the Regulator to grant authorisation on terms or subject to conditions;
- (c) permit the Regulator to grant an application for authorisation only to a specified extent or only in relation to specified matters, cases or circumstances.

7 Regulations may—
- (a) enable the Regulator to charge—
  - (i) fees in connection with applications for, or the grant of, authorisation;
  - (ii) periodic fees for authorised persons;
- (b) specify the consequences of failure to pay fees;
- (c) permit the charging of different fees for different cases or circumstances (which may, in particular, be defined wholly or partly by reference to turnover or other criteria relating to an authorised person's business);
- (d) permit the waiver, reduction or repayment of fees in specified circumstances;
- (e) provide for the amount of fees to be prescribed or controlled by the Secretary of State;
- (f) make provision for the manner in which fees are to be accounted for;
- (g) make provision for the application of income from fees (which may, in respect of a time when the Secretary of State is exercising functions of the Regulator under section 4(9) or (10), include provision permitting or requiring payment into the Consolidated Fund).

Conduct of authorised persons

8 (1) Regulations shall require the Regulator to prescribe rules for the professional conduct of authorised persons.

(2) Regulations under sub-paragraph (1) shall include provision—
- (a) about the manner in which rules are to be prepared and published (which may, in particular, include provision requiring—
  - (i) consultation;
  - (ii) the submission of a draft to the Secretary of State for approval);
- (b) about the consequences of failure to comply with the rules (which may, in particular, include—
  - (i) provision for rules to be treated as conditions of authorisations;
  - (ii) provision enabling the Regulator to impose conditions on, suspend or cancel authorisations.

9 (1) Regulations shall enable the Regulator to issue one or more codes of practice about the professional conduct of authorised persons.

(2) Regulations under sub-paragraph (1) shall include provision—
- (a) about the manner in which a code is to be prepared and published (which may, in particular, include provision requiring—
  - (i) consultation;
  - (ii) the submission of a draft to the Secretary of State for approval);
- (b) about the consequences of failure to comply with a code (which may, in particular—
  - (i) provide for compliance with a code to be treated as a condition of authorisations;
  - (ii) enable the Regulator to impose conditions on, suspend or cancel authorisations).

10 (1) Regulations shall provide for the Regulator to investigate complaints about the professional conduct of an authorised person.

(2) Regulations under sub-paragraph (1) shall enable the Regulator to—

    (a) impose conditions on a person's authorisation;

    (b) suspend a person's authorisation;

    (c) cancel a person's authorisation.

11 (1) Regulations may require, or permit the Regulator to require, an authorised person to take out a policy of professional indemnity insurance in respect of his actions in the course of providing or purporting to provide regulated claims management services.

(2) Regulations under sub-paragraph (1) may, in particular—

    (a) make provision about the level or nature of insurance cover to be provided by the policy;

    (b) include provision about failure to comply (which may, in particular, provide for compliance to be treated as a condition of authorisations or enable the Regulator to impose conditions on, suspend or cancel authorisations).

12 (1) Regulations may require the Regulator to establish a scheme to compensate a client of an authorised person where—

    (a) money is paid to the authorised person in complete or partial satisfaction of the client's claim, and

    (b) the client is unable to obtain all or part of the money because the authorised person becomes insolvent or is otherwise unable or unwilling to pay.

(2) In particular, regulations may make provision—

    (a) about the purchase of bonds or other forms of insurance or indemnity;

    (b) about the funding of the scheme (which may include the application of part of fees charged in accordance with paragraph 7 and may not include payments, or other financial assistance, by a Minister of the Crown);

    (c) about procedure in connection with compensation (including criteria to be applied);

    (d) about the amount of compensation.

Enforcement

13 Regulations may permit or require the Regulator to take action of a specified kind for the purpose of assessing compliance with terms or conditions of authorisations.

14 (1) Regulations may enable the Regulator, for the purpose of investigating a complaint about the activities of an authorised person or for the purpose of assessing compliance with terms and conditions of an authorisation, to require the provision of information or documents.

(2) The Regulations may provide that on an application by the Regulator a judge of the High Court, Circuit judge or justice of the peace may issue a warrant authorising the Regulator to enter and search premises on which a person conducts or is alleged to conduct regulated claims management business, for the purpose of—

    (a) investigating a complaint about the activities of an authorised person, or

    (b) assessing compliance with terms and conditions of an authorisation.

(3) Regulations may enable the Regulator to take copies of written or electronic records found on a search by virtue of sub-paragraph (2) for a purpose specified in that subsection.

(4) Regulations may enable the Regulator to impose conditions on, suspend or cancel a person's authorisation if—

    (a) a requirement imposed by virtue of sub-paragraph (1) is not complied with, or

    (b) an attempt to exercise a power by virtue of sub-paragraph (2) or (3) is obstructed.

(5) In this paragraph a reference to the Regulator includes a reference to a person authorised by him in writing.

(6) Regulations shall—
    (a) specify matters of which a judge or justice of the peace must be satisfied, or to which he must have regard, before issuing a warrant under sub-paragraph (2),
    (b) regulate the exercise of a power under or by virtue of sub-paragraph (1), (2) or (3) (whether by restricting the circumstances in which a power may be exercised, by specifying conditions to be complied with in the exercise of a power, or otherwise).

15 Regulations may make provision about the exercise by the Regulator of a power under section 7.

PART III

....

Statutory Instruments

Consumer Transactions (Restrictions on Statements) Order 1976
(SI 1976, No. 1813)

3 A person shall not, in the course of a business—
- (a) display, at any place where consumer transactions are effected (whether wholly or partly), a notice containing a statement which purports to apply, in relation to consumer transactions effected there, a term which would—
  - [(i) be void by virtue of section 6 or 20 of the Unfair Contract Terms Act 1977]
  - (ii) be inconsistent with a warranty (in Scotland a stipulation) implied by section 4(1)(c) of the Trading Stamps Act 1964 or section 4(1)(c) of the Trading Stamps Act (Northern Ireland) 1965 both as amended by the Act of 1973,
  - if applied to some or all such consumer transactions;
- (b) publish or cause to be published any advertisement which is intended to induce persons to enter into consumer transactions and which contains a statement purporting to apply in relation to such consumer transactions such a term as is mentioned in paragraph (a)(i) or (ii), being a term which would be void by virtue of, or as the case may be, inconsistent with, the provisions so mentioned if applied to some or all of those transactions;
- (c) supply to a consumer pursuant to a consumer transaction goods bearing, or goods in a container bearing, a statement which is a term of that consumer transaction and which is void by virtue of, or inconsistent with, the said provisions, or if it were a term of that transaction, would be so void or inconsistent;
- (d) furnish to a consumer in connection with the carrying out of a consumer transaction or to a person likely, as a consumer, to enter into such a transaction, a document which includes a statement which is a term of that transaction and is void or inconsistent as aforesaid, or, if it were a term of that transaction or were to become a term of a prospective transaction, would be so void or inconsistent.

4 A person shall not in the course of a business—
- (i) supply to a consumer pursuant to a consumer transaction goods bearing, or goods in a container bearing, a statement about the rights that the consumer has against that person or about the obligations to the consumer accepted by that person in relation to the goods (whether legally enforceable or not), being rights or obligations that arise if the goods are defective or are not fit for a purpose or do not correspond with a description;
- (ii) furnish to a consumer in connection with the carrying out of a consumer transaction or to a person likely, as a consumer, to enter into such a transaction with him or through his agency a document containing a statement about such rights and obligations, unless there is in close proximity to any such statement another statement which is clear and conspicuous and to the effect that the first mentioned statement does not or will not affect the statutory rights of a consumer.

5.—(1) This Article applies to goods which are supplied in the course of a business by one person ("the supplier") to another where, at the time of the supply, the goods were intended by the supplier to be, or might reasonably be expected by him to be, the subject of a subsequent consumer transaction.

(2) A supplier shall not—

(a) supply goods to which this Article applies if the goods bear, or are in a container bearing, a statement which sets all or describes or limits obligations (whether legally enforceable or not) accepted or to be accepted by him in relation to the goods, or

(b) furnish a document in relation to the goods which contains such a statement, unless there is in close proximity to any such statement another statement which is clear and conspicuous and to the effect that the first mentioned statement does not or will not affect the statutory rights of a consumer.

(3) A person does not contravene paragraph (2) above—

(i) in a case to which sub-paragraph (a) of that paragraph applies, unless the goods have become the subject of a consumer transaction;

(ii) in a case to which sub-paragraph (b) applies unless the document has been furnished to a consumer in relation to goods which were the subject of a consumer transaction, or to a person likely to become a consumer pursuant to such a transaction; or

(iii) by virtue of any statement if before the date on which this Article comes into operation the document containing, or the goods or container bearing, the statement has ceased to be in his possession.

Transfer of Undertakings (Protection of Employment) Regulations 1981
(SI 1981, No. 1794)

5 Effect of relevant transfer on contracts of employment, etc.

(1) [Except where objection is made under paragraph (4A) below,] A relevant transfer shall not operate so as to terminate the contract of employment of any person employed by the transferor in the undertaking or part transferred but any such contract which would otherwise have been terminated by the transfer shall have effect after the transfer as if originally made between the person so employed and the transferee.

[(4A) Paragraphs (1) and (2) above shall not operate to transfer his contract of employment and the rights, powers, duties and liabilities under or in connection with it if the employee informs the transferor or the transferee that he objects to becoming employed by the transferee.

(4B) Where an employee so objects the transfer of the undertaking or part in which he is employed shall operate so as to terminate his contract of employment with the transferor but he shall not be treated, for any purpose, as having been dismissed by the transferor.]

Package Travel, Package Holidays and Package Tours Regulations 1992
(SI 1992, No. 3288)

2 Interpretation

(1) In these Regulations—

"brochure" means any brochure in which packages are offered for sale;

"contract" means the agreement linking the consumer to the organiser or to the retailer, or to both, as the case may be;

"the Directive" means Council Directive 90/314/EEC on package travel, package holidays and package tours;

"offer" includes an invitation to treat whether by means of advertising or otherwise, and cognate expressions shall be construed accordingly;

"organiser" means the person who, otherwise than occasionally, organises packages and sells or offers them for sale, whether directly or through a retailer;

"the other party to the contract" means the party, other than the consumer, to the contract, that is, the organiser or the retailer, or both, as the case may be;

"package" means the pre-arranged combination of at least two of the following components when sold or offered for sale at an inclusive price and when the service covers a period of more than twenty-four hours or includes overnight accommodation—

    (a) transport;

    (b) accommodation;

    (c) other tourist services not ancillary to transport or accommodation and accounting for a significant proportion of the package,

and

    (i) the submission of separate accounts for different components shall not cause the arrangements to be other than a package;

    (ii) the fact that a combination is arranged at the request of the consumer and in accordance with his specific instructions (whether modified or not) shall not of itself cause it to be treated as other than pre-arranged;

and

"retailer" means the person who sells or offers for sale the package put together by the organiser.

(2) In the definition of "contract" in paragraph (1) above, "consumer" means the person who takes or agrees to take the package ("the principal contractor") and elsewhere in these Regulations "consumer" means, as the context requires, the principal contractor, any person on whose behalf the principal contractor agrees to purchase the package ("the other beneficiaries") or any person to whom the principal contractor or any of the other beneficiaries transfers the package ("the transferee").

3   Application of Regulations

(1) These Regulations apply to packages sold or offered for sale in the territory of the United Kingdom.

4   Descriptive matter relating to packages must not be misleading

(1) No organiser or retailer shall supply to a consumer any descriptive matter concerning a package, the price of a package or any other conditions applying to the contract which contains any misleading information.

(2) If an organiser or retailer is in breach of paragraph (1) he shall be liable to compensate the consumer for any loss which the consumer suffers in consequence.

5   Requirements as to brochures

(1) Subject to paragraph (4) below, no organiser shall make available a brochure to a possible consumer unless it indicates in a legible, comprehensive and accurate manner the price and adequate information about the matters specified in Schedule 1 to these Regulations in respect of the packages offered for sale in the brochure to the extent that those matters are relevant to the packages so offered.

(2) Subject to paragraph (4) below, no retailer shall make available to a possible consumer a brochure which he knows or has reasonable cause to believe does not comply with the requirements of paragraph (1).

(3) An organiser who contravenes paragraph (1) of this regulation and a retailer who contravenes paragraph (2) thereof shall be guilty of an offence and liable—

    (a) on summary conviction, to a fine not exceeding level 5 on the standard scale;

    (b) on conviction on indictment, to a fine.

(4) Where a brochure was first made available to consumers generally before 31 December 1992 no liability shall arise under this regulation in respect of an identical brochure being made available to a consumer at any time.

6 Circumstances in which particulars in brochure are to be binding

(1) Subject to paragraphs (2) and (3) of this regulation, the particulars in the brochure (whether or not they are required by regulation 5(1) above to be included in the brochure) shall constitute implied warranties (or, as regards Scotland, implied terms) for the purposes of any contract to which the particulars relate.

(2) Paragraph (1) of this regulation does not apply—

(a) in relation to information required to be included by virtue of paragraph 9 of Schedule 1 to these Regulations; or

(b) where the brochure contains an express statement that changes may be made in the particulars contained in it before a contract is concluded and changes in the particulars so contained are clearly communicated to the consumer before a contract is concluded.

(3) Paragraph (1) of this regulation does not apply when the consumer and the other party to the contract agree after the contract has been made that the particulars in the brochure, or some of those particulars, should not form part of the contract.

7 Information to be provided before contract is concluded

(1) Before a contract is concluded, the other party to the contract shall provide the intending consumer with the information specified in paragraph (2) below in writing or in some other appropriate form.

(2) The information referred to in paragraph (1) is—

(a) general information about passport and visa requirements which apply to [nationals of the member State or States concerned] who purchase the package in question, including information about the length of time it is likely to take to obtain the appropriate passports and visas;

(b) information about health formalities required for the journey and the stay; and

(c) the arrangements for security for the money paid over and (where applicable) for the repatriation of the consumer in the event of insolvency.

(3) If the intending consumer is not provided with the information required by paragraph (1) in accordance with that paragraph the other party to the contract shall be guilty of an offence and liable—

(a) on summary conviction, to a fine not exceeding level 5 on the standard scale; and

(b) on conviction on indictment, to a fine.

8 Information to be provided in good time

(1) The other party to the contract shall in good time before the start of the journey provide the consumer with the information specified in paragraph (2) below in writing or in some other appropriate form.

(2) The information referred to in paragraph (1) is the following—

(a) the times and places of intermediate stops and transport connections and particulars of the place to be occupied by the traveller (for example, cabin or berth on ship, sleeper compartment on train);

(b) the name, address and telephone number—

(i) of the representative of the other party to the contract in the locality where the consumer is to stay,

or, if there is no such representative,

(ii) of an agency in that locality on whose assistance a consumer in difficulty would be able to call,

or, if there is no such representative or agency, a telephone number or other information which will enable the consumer to contact the other party to the contract during the stay; and

(c) in the case of a journey or stay abroad by a child under the age of 16 on the day when the journey or stay is due to start, information enabling direct contact to be made with the child or the person responsible at the place where he is to stay; and

(d) except where the consumer is required as a term of the contract to take out an insurance policy in order to cover the cost of cancellation by the consumer or the cost of assistance, including repatriation, in the event of accident or illness, information about an insurance policy which the consumer may, if he wishes, take out in respect of the risk of those costs being incurred.

(3) If the consumer is not provided with the information required by paragraph (1) in accordance with that paragraph the other party to the contract shall be guilty of an offence and liable—

(a) on summary conviction, to a fine not exceeding level 5 on the standard scale;

(b) on conviction on indictment, to a fine.

9   Contents and form of contract

(1) The other party to the contract shall ensure that—

(a) depending on the nature of the package being purchased, the contract contains at least the elements specified in Schedule 2 to these Regulations;

(b) subject to paragraph (2) below, all the terms of the contract are set out in writing or such other form as is comprehensible and accessible to the consumer and are communicated to the consumer before the contract is made; and

(c) a written copy of these terms is supplied to the consumer.

(2) Paragraph (1)(b) above does not apply when the interval between the time when the consumer approaches the other party to the contract with a view to entering it is impracticable to comply with the sub-paragraph.

(3) It is an implied condition (or, as regards Scotland, an implied term) of the contract that the other party to the contract complies with the provisions of paragraph (1).

10   Transfer of bookings

(1) In every contract there is an implied term that where the consumer is prevented from proceeding with the package the consumer may transfer his booking to a person who satisfies all the conditions applicable to the package, provided that the consumer gives reasonable notice to the other party to the contract of his intention to transfer before the date when departure is due to take place.

(2) Where a transfer is made in accordance with the implied term set out in paragraph (1) above, the transferor and the transferee shall be jointly and severally liable to the other party to the contract for payment of the price of the package (or, if part of the price has been paid, for payment of the balance) and for any additional costs arising from such transfer.

11   Price revision

(1) Any term in a contract to the effect that the prices laid down in the contract may be revised shall be void and of no effect unless the contract provides for the possibility of upward or downward revision and satisfies the conditions laid down in paragraph (2) below.

(2) The conditions mentioned in paragraph (1) are that—

(a) the contract states precisely how the revised price is to be calculated;

(b) the contract provides that price revisions are to be made solely to allow for variations in—

(i) transportation costs, including the cost of fuel,

(ii) dues, taxes or fees chargeable for services such as landing taxes or embarkation or disembarkation fees at ports and airports, or

(iii) the exchange rates applied to the particular package; and

(3) Notwithstanding any terms of a contract,

(i) no price increase may be made in a specified period which may not be less than 30 days before the departure date stipulated; and

(ii) as against an individual consumer liable under the contract, no price increase may be made in respect of variations which would produce an increase of less than 2 per cent, or such greater percentage as the contract may specify ("none-ligible variations") and that the non-eligible variations shall be left out of account in the calculation.

12 Significant alterations to essential terms

In every contract there are implied terms to the effect that—

(a) where the organiser is constrained before the departure to alter significantly an essential term of the contract, such as the price (so far as regulation 11 permits him to do so), he will notify the consumer as quickly as possible in order to enable him to take appropriate decisions and in particular to withdraw from the contract without penalty or to accept a rider to the contract specifying the alterations made and their impact on the price; and

(b) the consumer will inform the organiser or the retailer of his decision as soon as possible.

13 Withdrawal by consumer pursuant to regulation 12 and cancellation by organiser

(1) The terms set out in paragraphs (2) and (3) below are implied in every contract and apply where the consumer withdraws from the contract pursuant to the term in it implied by virtue of regulation 12(a), or where the organiser, for any reason other than the fault of the consumer, cancels the package before the agreed date of departure.

(2) The consumer is entitled—

(a) to take a substitute package of equivalent or superior quality if the other party to the contract is able to offer him such a substitute; or

(b) to take a substitute package of lower quality if the other party to the contract is able to offer him one and to recover from the organiser the difference in price between the price of the package purchased and that of the substitute package; or

(c) to have repaid to him as soon as possible all the monies paid by him under the contract.

(3) The consumer is entitled, if appropriate, to be compensated by the organiser for nonperformance of the contract except where—

(a) the package is cancelled because the number of persons who agree to take it is less than the minimum number required and the consumer is informed of the cancellation, in writing, within the period indicated in the description of the package; or

(b) the package is cancelled by reason of unusual and unforeseeable circumstances beyond the control of the party by whom this exception is pleaded, the consequences of which could not have been avoided even if all due care had been exercised.

(4) Overbooking shall not be regarded as a circumstance falling within the provisions of sub-paragraph (b) of paragraph (3) above.

14 Significant proportion of services not provided

(1) The terms set out in paragraphs (2) and (3) below are implied in every contract and apply where, after departure, a significant proportion of the services contracted for is not provided or the organiser becomes aware that he will be unable to procure a significant proportion of the services to be provided.

(2) The organiser will make suitable alternative arrangements, at no extra cost to the consumer, for the continuation of the package and will, where appropriate, compensate the consumer for the difference between the services to be supplied under the contract and those supplied.

(3) If it is impossible to make arrangements as described in paragraph (2), or these are not accepted by the consumer for good reasons, the organiser will, where appropriate, provide the consumer with equivalent transport back to the place of departure or to another place to which the consumer has agreed and will, where appropriate, compensate the consumer.

15 Liability of other party to the contract for proper performance of obligations under contract

(1) The other party to the contract is liable to the consumer for the proper performance of the obligations under the contract, irrespective of whether such obligations are to be performed by that other party or by other suppliers of services but this shall not affect any remedy or right of action which that other party may have against those other suppliers of services.

(2) The other party to the contract is liable to the consumer for any damage caused to him by the failure to perform the contract or the improper performance of the contract unless the failure or the improper performance is due neither to any fault of that other party nor to that of another supplier of services, because—

(a) the failures which occur in the performance of the contract are attributable to the consumer;

(b) such failures are attributable to a third party unconnected with the provision of the services contracted for, and are unforeseeable or unavoidable; or

(c) such failures are due to—

(i) unusual and unforeseeable circumstances beyond the control of the party by whom this exception is pleaded, the consequences of which could not have been avoided even if all due care had been exercised; or

(ii) an event which the other party to the contract or the supplier of services, even with all due care, could not foresee or forestall.

(3) In the case of damage arising from the non-performance or improper performance of the services involved in the package, the contract may provide for compensation to be limited in accordance with the international conventions which govern such services.

(4) In the case of damage other than personal injury resulting from the non- performance or improper performance of the services involved in the package, the contract may include a term limiting the amount of compensation which will be paid to the consumer, provided that the limitation is not unreasonable.

(5) Without prejudice to paragraph (3) and paragraph (4) above, liability under paragraphs (1) and (2) above cannot be excluded by any contractual term.

(6) The terms set out in paragraphs (7) and (8) below are implied in every contract.

(7) In the circumstances described in paragraph (2)(b) and (c) of this regulation, the other party to the contract will give prompt assistance to a consumer in difficulty.

(8) If the consumer complains about a defect in the performance of the contract, the other party to the contract, or his local representative, if there is one, will make prompt efforts to find appropriate solutions.

(9) The contract must clearly and explicitly oblige the consumer to communicate at the earliest opportunity, in writing or any other appropriate form, to the supplier of the services concerned and to the other party to the contract any failure which he perceives at the place where the services concerned are supplied.

23 Enforcement

Schedule 3 to these Regulations (which makes provision about the enforcement of regulations 5, 7, 8, 16 and 22 of these Regulations) shall have effect.

24 Due diligence defence

(1) Subject to the following provisions of this regulation, in proceedings against any person for an offence under regulation 5, 7, 8, 16 or 22 of these Regulations, it shall be a defence for that person to show that he took all reasonable steps and exercised all due diligence to avoid committing the offence.

(2) Where in any proceedings against any person for such an offence the defence provided by paragraph (1) above involves an allegation that the commission of the offence was due—

(a) to the act or default of another; or

(b) to reliance on the information given by another, that person shall not, without the leave of the court, be entitled to rely on the defence unless, not less than seven clear days before the hearing of the proceedings, or, in Scotland, the trial diet, he has served a notice under paragraph (3) below on the person bringing the proceedings.

(3) A notice under this paragraph shall give such information identifying or assisting in the identification of the person who committed the act or default or gave the information as is in the possession of the person serving the notice at the time he serves it.

(4) It is hereby declared that a person shall not be entitled to rely on the defence provided by paragraph (1) above by reason of his reliance on information supplied by another, unless he shows that it was reasonable in all the circumstances for him to have relied on the information, having regard in particular—

    (a) to the steps which he took, and those which might reasonably have been taken, for the purpose of verifying the information; and

    (b) to whether he had any reason to disbelieve the information.

25 Liability of persons other than principal offender

(1) Where the commission by any person of an offence under regulations 5, 7, 8, 16 or 22 of these Regulations is due to an act or default committed by some other person in the course of any business of his, the other person shall be guilty of the offence and may be proceeded against and punished by virtue of this paragraph whether or not proceedings are taken against the first-mentioned person.

(2) Where a body corporate is guilty of an offence under any of the provisions mentioned in paragraph (1) above (including where it is so guilty by virtue of the said paragraph (1)) in respect of any act or default which is shown to have been committed with the consent or connivance of, or to be attributable to any neglect on the part of, any director, manager, secretary or other similar officer of the body corporate or any person who was purporting to act in any such capacity he, as well as the body corporate, shall be guilty of that offence and shall be liable to be proceeded against and punished accordingly.

(3) Where the affairs of a body corporate are managed by its members, paragraph (2) above shall apply in relation to the acts and defaults of a member in connection with his functions of management as if he were a director of the body corporate.

(5) On proceedings for an offence under regulation 5 by virtue of paragraph (1) above committed by the making available of a brochure it shall be a defence for the person charged to prove that he is a person whose business it is to publish or arrange for the publication of brochures and that he received the brochure for publication in the ordinary course of business and did not know and had no reason to suspect that its publication would amount to an offence under these Regulations.

26 Prosecution time limit

(1) No proceedings for an offence under regulation 5, 7, 8, 16 or 22 of these Regulations or under paragraphs 5(3), 6 or 7 of Schedule 3 thereto shall be commenced after—

    (a) the end of the period of three years beginning within the date of the commission of the offence; or

    (b) the end of the period of one year beginning with the date of the discovery of the offence by the prosecutor,

whichever is the earlier.

(2) For the purposes of this regulation a certificate signed by or on behalf of the prosecutor and stating the date on which the offence was discovered by him shall be conclusive evidence of that fact; and a certificate stating that matter and purporting to be so signed shall be treated as so signed unless the contrary is proved.

27 Saving for civil consequences

No contract shall be void or unenforceable, and no right of action in civil proceedings in respect of any loss shall arise, by reason only of the commission of an offence under regulations 5, 7, 8, 16 or 22 of these Regulations.

28   Terms implied in contract

Where it is provided in these Regulations that a term (whether so described or whether described as a condition or warranty) is implied in the contract it is so implied irrespective of the law which governs the contract.

Regulation 5   SCHEDULE 1

INFORMATION TO BE INCLUDED (IN ADDITION TO THE PRICE) IN BROCHURES WHERE RELEVANT TO PACKAGES OFFERED

1. The destination and the means, characteristics and categories of transport used.

2. The type of accommodation, its location, category or degree of comfort and its main features and, where the accommodation is to be provided in a member State, its approval or tourist classification under the rules of that member State.

3. The meals which are included in the package.

4. The itinerary.

5. General information about passport and visa requirements which apply for [nationals of the member State or States in which the brochure is made available] and health formalities required for the journey and the stay.

6.Either the monetary amount or the percentage of the price which is to be paid on account and the timetable for payment of the balance.

7. Whether a minimum number of persons is required for the package to take place and, if so, the deadline for informing the consumer in the event of cancellation.

8. The arrangements (if any) which apply if consumers are delayed at the outward or homeward points of departure.

9. The arrangements for security for money paid over and for the repatriation of the consumer in the event of insolvency.

Regulation 9   SCHEDULE 2

ELEMENTS TO BE INCLUDED IN THE CONTRACT IF RELEVANTTO THE PARTICULAR PACKAGE

1. The travel destination(s) and, where periods of stay are involved, the relevant periods, with dates.

2. The means, characteristics and categories of transport to be used and the dates, times and points of departure and return.

3. Where the package includes accommodation, its location, its tourist category of degree of comfort, its main features and, where the accommodation is to be provided in a member State, its compliance with the rules of that member State.

4. The meals which are included in the package.

5. Whether a minimum number of persons is required for the package to take place and, if so, the deadline for informing the consumer in the event of cancellation.

6. The itinerary.

7. Visits, excursions or other services which are included in the total price agreed for the package.

8. The name and address of the organiser, the retailer and, where appropriate, the insurer.

9. The price of the package, if the price may be revised in accordance with the term which may be included in the contract under regulation 11, an indication of the possibility of such price revisions, and an indication of any dues, taxes or fees chargeable for certain

services (land— ——— —sembarkation fees at ports and airports and tourist taxes) where su—————————— 1 the package.

10. T.————————— 1ethod of payment.

11. Sp—————————— he consumer has communicated to the organiser or retailer whe:———————— which both have accepted.

12. The ;—————————— nsumer must make any complaint about the failure to perform o: ———————— ce of the contract.

Regulation 2————————— IEDULE 3

—————————— RCEMENT

1   Enforcement ———

(1) Every loc————————— prity in Great Britain shall be an enforcement authority for the————————— 16 and 22 of these Regulations ("the relevant regulations"), an————————— such authority to enforce those provisions within their area————

Employers' Liability (Compulsory Insurance) Regulations 1998
(SI 1998, No. 2573)

1   Citation, commencement and interpretation

(2) In these Regulations—

"the 1969 Act" means the Employers' Liability (Compulsory Insurance) Act 1969;

. . .

2   Prohibition of certain conditions in policies of insurance

(1) For the purposes of the 1969 Act, there is prohibited in any contract of insurance any condition which provides (in whatever terms) that no liability (either generally or in respect of a particular claim) shall arise under the policy, or that any such liability so arising shall cease, if—

(a) some specified thing is done or omitted to be done after the happening of the event giving rise to a claim under the policy,

(b) the policy holder does not take reasonable care to protect his employees against the risk of bodily injury or disease in the course of their employment;

(c) the policy holder fails to comply with the requirements of any enactment for the protection of employees against the risk of bodily injury or disease in the course of their employment; or

(d) the policy holder does not keep specified records or fails to provide the insurer with or make available to him information from such records.

(2) For the purposes of the 1969 Act there is also prohibited in a policy of insurance any condition which requires—

(a) a relevant employee to pay; or

(b) an insured employer to pay the relevant employee, the first amount of any claim or any aggregation of claims.

(3) Paragraphs (1) and (2) above do not prohibit for the purposes of the 1969 Act a condition in a policy of insurance which requires the employer to pay or contribute any sum to the insurer in respect of the satisfaction of any claim made under the contract of insurance by a relevant employee or any costs and expenses incurred in relation to any such claim.

3   Limit of amount of compulsory insurance

(1) Subject to paragraph (2) below, the amount for which an employer is required by the 1969 Act to insure and maintain insurance in respect of relevant employees under one or

more policies of insurance shall be, or shall in aggregate be not less than £5 million in respect of—

    (a) a claim relating to any one or more of those employees arising out of any one occurrence; and

    (b) any costs and expenses incurred in relation to any such claim.

Provision and Use of Work Equipment Regulations 1998
(SI 1998, No. 2306)

2   Interpretation

(1) In these Regulations, unless the context otherwise requires—

"the 1974 Act" means the Health and Safety at Work etc. Act 1974;

"employer" except in regulation 3(2) and (3) includes a person to whom the requirements imposed by the Regulations apply by virtue of regulation 3(3)(a) and (b);

"essential requirements" means requirements described in regulation 10(1);

"the Executive" means the Health and Safety Executive;

"inspection" in relation to an inspection under paragraph (1) or (2) of regulation 6—

    (a) means such visual or more rigorous inspection by a competent person as is appropriate for the purpose described in the paragraph;

    (b) where it is appropriate to carry out testing for the purpose, includes testing the nature and extent of which are appropriate for the purpose;

"power press" means a press or press brake for the working of metal by means of tools, or for die proving, which is power driven and which embodies a flywheel and clutch;

"thorough examination" in relation to a thorough examination under paragraph (1), (2), (3) or (4) of regulation 32—

    (a) means a thorough examination by a competent person;

    (b) includes testing the nature and extent of which are appropriate for the purpose described in the paragraph;

"use" in relation to work equipment means any activity involving work equipment and includes starting, stopping, programming, setting, transporting, repairing, modifying, maintaining, servicing and cleaning;

"work equipment" means any machinery, appliance, apparatus, tool or installation for use at work (whether exclusively or not);

and related expressions shall be construed accordingly.

4   Suitability of work equipment

(1) Every employer shall ensure that work equipment is so constructed or adapted as to be suitable for the purpose for which it is used or provided.

(2) In selecting work equipment, every employer shall have regard to the working conditions and to the risks to the health and safety of persons which exist in the premises or undertaking in which that work equipment is to be used and any additional risk posed by the use of that work equipment.

(3) Every employer shall ensure that work equipment is used only for operations for which, and under conditions for which, it is suitable.

(4) In this regulation "suitable"[—

    (a) subject to paragraph (b), means suitable in any respect which it is reasonably foreseeable will affect the health and safety of any person; . . .]

5   Maintenance

(1) Every employer shall ensure that work equipment is maintained in an efficient state, in efficient working order and in good repair.

(2) Every employer shall ensure that where any machinery has a maintenance log, the log is kept up to date.

6   Inspection

(1) Every employer shall ensure that, where the safety of work equipment depends on the installation conditions, it is inspected—

    (a) after installation and before being put into service for the first time; or

    (b) after assembly at a new site or in a new location, to ensure that it has been installed correctly and is safe to operate.

(2) Every employer shall ensure that work equipment exposed to conditions causing deterioration which is liable to result in dangerous situations is inspected—

    (a) at suitable intervals; and

    (b) each time that exceptional circumstances which are liable to jeopardise the safety of the work equipment have occurred,

to ensure that health and safety conditions are maintained and that any deterioration can be detected and remedied in good time.

(3) Every employer shall ensure that the result of an inspection made under this regulation is recorded and kept until the next inspection under this regulation is recorded.

(4) Every employer shall ensure that no work equipment—

    (a) leaves his undertaking; or

    (b) if obtained from the undertaking of another person, is used in his undertaking, unless it is accompanied by physical evidence that the last inspection required to be carried out under this regulation has been carried out.

7   Specific risks

(1) Where the use of work equipment is likely to involve a specific risk to health or safety, every employer shall ensure that—

    (a) the use of that work equipment is restricted to those persons given the task of using it; and

    (b) repairs, modifications, maintenance or servicing of that work equipment is restricted to those persons who have been specifically designated to perform operations of that description (whether or not also authorised to perform other operations).

(2) The employer shall ensure that the persons designated for the purposes of sub-paragraph (b) of paragraph (1) have received adequate training related to any operations in respect of which they have been so designated.

8   Information and instructions

(1) Every employer shall ensure that all persons who use work equipment have available to them adequate health and safety information and, where appropriate, written instructions pertaining to the use of the work equipment.

(2) Every employer shall ensure that any of his employees who supervises or manages the use of work equipment has available to him adequate health and safety information and, where appropriate, written instructions pertaining to the use of the work equipment.

(3) Without prejudice to the generality of paragraphs (1) or (2), the information and instructions required by either of those paragraphs shall include information and, where appropriate, written instructions on—

    (a) the conditions in which and the methods by which the work equipment may be used;

    (b) foreseeable abnormal situations and the action to be taken if such a situation were to occur; and

    (c) any conclusions to be drawn from experience in using the work equipment.

(4) Information and instructions required by this regulation shall be readily comprehensive to those concerned.

9   Training

(1) Every employer shall ensure that all persons who use work equipment have received adequate training for purposes of health and safety, including training in the methods which

may be adopted when using the work equipment, any risks which such use may entail and precautions to be taken.

(2) Every employer shall ensure that any of his employees who supervises or manages the use of work equipment has received adequate training for purposes of health and safety, including training in the methods which may be adopted when using the work equipment, any risks which such use may entail and precautions to be taken.

10 Conformity with Community requirements

(1) Every employer shall ensure that an item of work equipment has been designed and constructed in compliance with any essential requirements, that is to say requirements relating to its design or construction in any of the instruments listed in Schedule 1 (being instruments which give effect to Community directives concerning the safety of products).

(2) Where an essential requirement applied to the design or construction of an item of work equipment, the requirements of regulations 11 to 19 and 22 to 29 shall apply in respect of that item only to the extent that the essential requirement did not apply to it.

(3) This regulation applies to items of work equipment provided for use in the premises or undertaking of the employer for the first time after 31 December 1992.

11 Dangerous parts of machinery

(1) Every employer shall ensure that measures are taken in accordance with paragraph (2) which are effective—

    (a) to prevent access to any dangerous part of machinery or to any rotating stock-bar; or

    (b) to stop the movement of any dangerous part of machinery or rotating stock-bar before any part of a person enters a danger zone.

(2) The measures required by paragraph (1) shall consist of—

    (a) the provision of fixed guards enclosing every dangerous part or rotating stock-bar where and to the extent that it is practicable to do so, but where or to the extent that it is not, then

    (b) the provision of other guards or protection devices where and to the extent that it is practicable to do so, but where or to the extent that it is not, then

    (c) the provision of jigs, holders, push-sticks or similar protection appliances used in conjunction with the machinery where and to the extent that it is practicable to do so, but where or to the extent that it is not, then

    (d) the provision of information, instruction, training and supervision.

(3) All guards and protection devices provided under sub-paragraphs (a) or (b) of paragraphs (2) shall—

    (a) be suitable for the purpose for which they are provided;

    (b) be of good construction, sound material and adequate strength;

    (c) be maintained in an efficient state, in efficient working order and in good repair;

    (d) not give rise to any increased risk to health or safety;

    (e) not be easily bypassed or disabled;

    (f) be situated at sufficient distance from the danger zone;

    (g) not unduly restrict the view of the operating cycle of the machinery, where such a view is necessary;

    (h) be so constructed or adapted that they allow operations necessary to fit or replace parts and for maintenance work, restricting access so that it is allowed only to the area where the work is to be carried out and, if possible, without having to dismantle the guard or protection device.

(4) All protection appliances provided under sub-paragraph (c) of paragraph (2) shall comply with sub-paragraphs (a) to (d) and (g) of paragraph (3).

(5) In this regulation—

"danger zone" means any zone in or around machinery in which a person is exposed to a risk to health or safety from contact with a dangerous part of machinery or a rotating stock-bar;

"stock-bar" means any part of a stock-bar which projects beyond the head-stock of a lathe.

12   Protection against specified hazards

(1) Every employer shall take measures to ensure that the exposure of a person using work equipment to any risk to his health or safety from any hazard specified in paragraph (3) is either prevented, or, where that is not reasonably practicable, adequately controlled.

(2) The measures required by paragraph (1) shall—

(a) be measures other than the provision of personal protective equipment or of information, instruction, training and supervision, so far as is reasonably practicable; and

(b) include, where appropriate, measures to minimise the effects of the hazard as well as to reduce the likelihood of the hazard occurring.

(3) The hazards referred to in paragraph (1) are—

(a) any article or substance falling or being ejected from work equipment;

(b) rupture or disintegration of parts of work equipment;

(c) work equipment catching fire or overheating;

(d) the unintended or premature discharge of any article or of any gas, dust, liquid, vapour or other substance which, in each case, is produced, used or stored in the work equipment;

(e) the unintended or premature explosion of the work equipment or any article or substance produced, used or stored in it.

(4) For the purposes of this regulation "adequately" means adequately having regard only to the nature of the hazard and the nature and degree of exposure to the risk.

(5) This regulation shall not apply where any of the following Regulations apply in respect of any risk to a person's health or safety for which such Regulations require measures to be taken to prevent or control such risk, namely—

(a) the Ionising Radiations Regulations 1985;

(b) the Control of Asbestos at Work Regulations 1987;

(c) the Control of Substances Hazardous to Health Regulations 1994;

(d) [the Control of Noise at Work Regulations 2005];

(e) the Construction (Head Protection) Regulations 1989;

(f) the Control of Lead at Work Regulations 1998

[(g) the Control of Vibration at Work Regulations 2005].

13   High or very low temperature

Every employer shall ensure that work equipment, parts of work equipment and any article or substance produced, used or stored in work equipment which, in each case, is at a high or very low temperature shall have protection where appropriate so as to prevent injury to any person by burn, scald or sear.

14   Controls for starting or making a significant change in operating conditions

(1) Every employer shall ensure that, where appropriate, work equipment is provided with one or more controls for the purposes of—

(a) starting the work equipment (including re-starting after a stoppage for any reason); or

(b) controlling any change in the speed, pressure or other operating conditions of the work equipment where such conditions after the change result in risk to health and safety which is greater than or of a different nature from such risks before the change.

(2) Subject to paragraph (3), every employer shall ensure that, where a control is required by paragraph (1), it shall not be possible to perform any operation mentioned in sub-paragraph (a) or (b) of that paragraph except by a deliberate action on such control.

(3) Paragraph (1) shall not apply to re-starting or changing operating conditions as a result of the normal operating cycle of an automatic device.

15   Stop controls

(1) Every employer shall ensure that, where appropriate, work equipment is provided with one or more readily accessible controls the operation of which will bring the work equipment to a safe condition in a safe manner.

(2) Any control required by paragraph (1) shall bring the work equipment to a complete stop where necessary for reasons of health and safety.

(3) Any control required by paragraph (1) shall, if necessary for reasons of health and safety, switch off all sources of energy after stopping the functioning of the work equipment.

(4) Any control required by paragraph (1) shall operate in priority to any control which starts or changes the operating conditions of the work equipment.

16   Emergency stop controls

(1) Every employer shall ensure that, where appropriate, work equipment is provided with one or more readily accessible emergency stop controls unless it is not necessary by reason of the nature of the hazards and the time taken for the work equipment to come to a complete stop as a result of the action of any control provided by virtue of regulation 15(1).

(2) Any control required by paragraph (1) shall operate in priority to any control required by regulation 15(1).

17   Controls

(1) Every employer shall ensure that all controls for work equipment are clearly visible and identifiable, including by appropriate marking where necessary.

(2) Except where necessary, the employer shall ensure that no control for work equipment is in a position where any person operating the control is exposed to a risk to his health or safety.

(3) Every employer shall ensure where appropriate—

(a) that, so far as is reasonably practicable, the operator of any control is able to ensure from the position of that control that no person is in a place where he would be exposed to any risk to his health or safety as a result of the operation of that control, but where or to the extent that it is not reasonably practicable;

(b) that, so far as is reasonably practicable, systems of work are effective to ensure that, when work equipment is about to start, no person is in a place where he would be exposed to a risk to his health or safety as a result of the work equipment starting, but where neither of these is reasonably practicable;

(c) that an audible, visible or other suitable warning is given by virtue of regulation 24 whenever work equipment is about to start.

(4) Every employer shall take appropriate measures to ensure that any person who is in a place where he would be exposed to a risk to his health or safety as a result of the starting or stopping of work equipment has sufficient time and suitable means to avoid that risk.

18   Control systems

(1) Every employer shall—

(a) ensure, so far as is reasonably practicable, that all control systems of work equipment are safe; and

(b) are chosen making due allowance for the failures, faults and constraints to be expected in the planned circumstances of use.

(2) Without prejudice to the generality of paragraph (1), a control system shall not be safe unless—

(a) its operation does not create any increased risk to health or safety;

(b) it ensures, so far as is reasonably practicable, that any fault in or damage to any part of the control system or the loss of supply of any source of energy used by the work equipment cannot result in additional or increased risk to health or safety;

(c) it does not impede the operation of any control required by regulation 15 or 16.

19   Isolation from sources of energy

(1) Every employer shall ensure that where appropriate work equipment is provided, suitable means to isolate it from all its sources of energy.

(2) Without prejudice to the generality of paragraph (1), the means mentioned in that paragraph shall not be suitable unless they are clearly identifiable and readily accessible.

(3) Every employer shall take appropriate measures to ensure that re-connection of any energy source to work equipment does not expose any person using the work equipment to any risk to his health or safety.

20   Stability

Every employer shall ensure that work equipment or any part of work equipment is stabilised by clamping or otherwise where necessary for purposes of health or safety.

21   Lighting

Every employer shall ensure that suitable and sufficient lighting, which takes account of the operations to be carried out, is provided at any place where a person uses work equipment.

22   Maintenance operations

Every employer shall take appropriate measures to ensure that work equipment is so constructed or adapted that, so far as is reasonably practicable, maintenance operations which involve a risk to health or safety can be carried out while the work equipment is shut down, or in other cases—

(a) maintenance operations can be carried out without exposing the person carrying them out to a risk to his health or safety; or

(b) appropriate measures can be taken for the protection of any person carrying out maintenance operations which involve a risk to his health or safety.

23   Markings

Every employer shall ensure that work equipment is marked in a clearly visible manner with any marking appropriate for reasons of health and safety.

24   Warnings

(1) Every employer shall ensure that work equipment incorporates any warnings or warning devices which are appropriate for reasons of health and safety.

(2) Without prejudice to the generality of paragraph (1), warnings given by warning devices on work equipment shall not be appropriate unless they are unambiguous, easily perceived and easily understood.

Unfair Terms in Consumer Contracts Regulations 1999
(SI 1999, No. 2083)

3   Interpretation

(1) In these Regulations—

"the Community" means the European Community;

"consumer" means any natural person who, in contracts covered by these Regulations, is acting for purposes which are outside his trade, business or profession;

"court" in relation to England and Wales and Northern Ireland means a county court or the High Court, and in relation to Scotland, the Sheriff or the Court of Session;

"Director" means the Director General of Fair Trading;

"EEA Agreement" means the Agreement on the European Economic Area signed at Oporto on 2nd May 1992 as adjusted by the protocol signed at Brussels on 17th March 1993;

"Member State" means a State which is a contracting party to the EEA Agreement;

"notified" means notified in writing;

"qualifying body" means a person specified in Schedule 1;

"seller or supplier" means any natural or legal person who, in contracts covered by these Regulations, is acting for purposes relating to his trade, business or profession, whether publicly owned or privately owned;

"unfair terms" means the contractual terms referred to in regulation 5.

[(1A) The references—

    (a) in regulation 4(1) to a seller or a supplier, and

    (b) in regulation 8(1) to a seller or supplier,

include references to a distance supplier and to an intermediary.

(1B) In paragraph (1A) and regulation 5(6)—

"distance supplier" means—

    (a) a supplier under a distance contract within the meaning of the Financial Services (Distance Marketing) Regulations 2004, or

    (b) a supplier of unsolicited financial services within regulation 15 of those Regulations; and "intermediary" has the same meaning as in those Regulations.]

(2) In the application of these Regulations to Scotland for references to an "injunction" or an "interim injunction" there shall be substituted references to an "interdict" or "interim interdict" respectively.

4 Terms to which these Regulations apply

(1) These Regulations apply in relation to unfair terms in contracts concluded between a seller or a supplier and a consumer.

(2) These Regulations do not apply to contractual terms which reflect—

    (a) mandatory statutory or regulatory provisions (including such provisions under the law of any Member State or in Community legislation having effect in the United Kingdom without further enactment);

    (b) the provisions or principles of international conventions to which the Member States or the Community are party.

5 Unfair Terms

A contractual term which has not been individually negotiated shall be regarded as unfair if, contrary to the requirement of good faith, it causes a significant imbalance in the parties' rights and obligations arising under the contract, to the detriment of the consumer.

(2) A term shall always be regarded as not having been individually negotiated where it has been drafted in advance and the consumer has therefore not been able to influence the substance of the term.

(3) Notwithstanding that a specific term or certain aspects of it in a contract has been individually negotiated, these Regulations shall apply to the rest of a contract if an overall assessment of it indicates that it is a pre-formulated standard contract.

(4) It shall be for any seller or supplier who claims that a term was individually negotiated to show that it was.

(5) Schedule 2 to these Regulations contains an indicative and non-exhaustive list of the terms which may be regarded as unfair.

[(6) Any contractual term providing that a consumer bears the burden of proof in respect of showing whether a distance supplier or an intermediary complied with any or all of the obligations placed upon him resulting from the Directive and any rule or enactment implementing it shall always be regarded as unfair.

(7) In paragraph (6)—

"the Directive" means Directive 2002/65/EC of the European Parliament and of the Council of 23 September 2002 concerning the distance marketing of consumer financial services and amending Council Directive 90/619/EEC and Directives 97/7/EC and 98/27/EC; and

"rule" means a rule made by the Financial Services Authority under the Financial Services and Markets Act 2000 or by a designated professional body within the meaning of section 326(2) of that Act.]

6   Assessment of unfair terms

(1) Without prejudice to regulation 12, the unfairness of a contractual term shall be assessed, taking into account the nature of the goods or services for which the contract was concluded and by referring, at the time of conclusion of the contract, to all the circumstances attending the conclusion of the contract and to all the other terms of the contract or of another contract on which it is dependent.

(2) In so far as it is in plain intelligible language, the assessment of fairness of a term shall not relate—

(a) to the definition of the main subject matter of the contract, or

(b) to the adequacy of the price or remuneration, as against the goods or services supplied in exchange.

7   Written contracts

(1) A seller or supplier shall ensure that any written term of a contract is expressed in plain, intelligible language.

(2) If there is doubt about the meaning of a written term, the interpretation which is most favourable to the consumer shall prevail but this rule shall not apply in proceedings brought under regulation 12.

8   Effect of unfair term

(1) An unfair term in a contract concluded with a consumer by a seller or supplier shall not be binding on the consumer.

(2) The contract shall continue to bind the parties if it is capable of continuing in existence without the unfair term.

9   Choice of law clauses

These Regulations shall apply notwithstanding any contract term which applies or purports to apply the law of a non-Member State, if the contract has a close connection with the territory of the Member States.

10   Complaints—consideration by Director

(1) It shall be the duty of the Director to consider any complaint made to him that any contract term drawn up for general use is unfair, unless—

(a) the complaint appears to the Director to be frivolous or vexatious; or

(b) a qualifying body has notified the Director that it agrees to consider the complaint.

(2) The Director shall give reasons for his decision to apply or not to apply, as the case may be, for an injunction under regulation 12 in relation to any complaint which these Regulations require him to consider.

(3) In deciding whether or not to apply for an injunction in respect of a term which the Director considers to be unfair, he may, if he considers it appropriate to do so, have regard to any undertakings given to him by or on behalf of any person as to the continued use of such a term in contracts concluded with consumers.

11   Complaints—consideration by qualifying bodies

(1) If a qualifying body specified in Part One of Schedule 1 notifies the Director that it agrees to consider a complaint that any contract term drawn up for general use is unfair, it shall be under a duty to consider that complaint.

(2) Regulation 10(2) and (3) shall apply to a qualifying body which is under a duty to consider a complaint as they apply to the Director.

12   Injunctions to prevent continued use of unfair terms

(1) The Director or, subject to paragraph (2), any qualifying body may apply for an injunction (including an interim injunction) against any person appearing to the Director or that body to be using, or recommending use of, an unfair term drawn up for general use in contracts concluded with consumers.

(2) A qualifying body may apply for an injunction only where—

    (a) it has notified the Director of its intention to apply at least fourteen days before the date on which the application is made, beginning with the date on which the notification was given; or

    (b) the Director consents to the application being made within a shorter period.

(3) The court on an application under this regulation may grant an injunction on such terms as it thinks fit.

(4) An injunction may relate not only to use of a particular contract term drawn up for general use but to any similar term, or a term having like effect, used or recommended for use by any person.

13 Powers of the Director and qualifying bodies to obtain documents and information

(1) The Director may exercise the power conferred by this regulation for the purpose of—

    (a) facilitating his consideration of a complaint that a contract term drawn up for general use is unfair; or

    (b) ascertaining whether a person has complied with an undertaking or court order as to the continued use, or recommendation for use, of a term in contracts concluded with consumers.

(2) A qualifying body specified in Part One of Schedule 1 may exercise the power conferred by this regulation for the purpose of—

    (a) facilitating its consideration of a complaint that a contract term drawn up for general use is unfair; or

    (b) ascertaining whether a person has complied with—

        (i) an undertaking given to it or to the court following an application by that body, or

        (ii) a court order made on an application by that body,

as to the continued use, or recommendation for use, of a term in contracts concluded with consumers.

(3) The Director may require any person to supply to him, and a qualifying body specified in Part One of Schedule 1 may require any person to supply to it—

    (a) a copy of any document which that person has used or recommended for use, at the time the notice referred to in paragraph (4) below is given, as a pre-formulated standard contract in dealings with consumers;

    (b) information about the use, or recommendation for use, by that person of that document or any other such document in dealings with consumers.

(4) The power conferred by this regulation is to be exercised by a notice in writing which may—

    (a) specify the way in which and the time within which it is to be complied with; and

    (b) be varied or revoked by a subsequent notice.

(5) Nothing in this regulation compels a person to supply any document or information which he would be entitled to refuse to produce or give in civil proceedings before the court.

(6) If a person makes default in complying with a notice under this regulation, the court may, on the application of the Director or of the qualifying body, make such order as the court thinks fit for requiring the default to be made good, and any such order may provide that all the costs or expenses of and incidental to the application shall be borne by the person in default or by any officers of a company or other association who are responsible for its default.

14 Notification of undertakings and orders to Director

A qualifying body shall notify the Director—

    (a) of any undertaking given to it by or on behalf of any person as to the continued use of a term which that body considers to be unfair in contracts concluded with consumers;

(b) of the outcome of any application made by it under regulation 12, and of the terms of any undertaking given to, or order made by, the court;

(c) of the outcome of any application made by it to enforce a previous order of the court.

15   Publication, information and advice

(1) The Director shall arrange for the publication in such form and manner as he considers appropriate, of—

(a) details of any undertaking or order notified to him under regulation 14;

(b) details of any undertaking given to him by or on behalf of any person as to the continued use of a term which the Director considers to be unfair in contracts concluded with consumers;

(c) details of any application made by him under regulation 12, and of the terms of any undertaking given to, or order made by, the court;

(d) details of any application made by the Director to enforce a previous order of the court.

(2) The Director shall inform any person on request whether a particular term to which these Regulations apply has been—

(a) the subject of an undertaking given to the Director or notified to him by a qualifying body; or

(b) the subject of an order of the court made upon application by him or notified to him by a qualifying body;

and shall give that person details of the undertaking or a copy of the order, as the case may be, together with a copy of any amendments which the person giving the undertaking has agreed to make to the term in question.

(3) The Director may arrange for the dissemination in such form and manner as he considers appropriate of such information and advice concerning the operation of these Regulations as may appear to him to be expedient to give to the public and to all persons likely to be affected by these Regulations.

[16   The functions of the Financial Services Authority

The functions of the Financial Services Authority under these Regulations shall be treated as functions of the Financial Services Authority under the Financial Services and Markets Act 2000.]

Regulation 3   SCHEDULE 1

QUALIFYING BODIES

[PART ONE]

[1. The Information Commissioner.
2. The Gas and Electricity Markets Authority.
3. The Director General of Electricity Supply for Northern Ireland.
4. The Director General of Gas for Northern Ireland.
5. [The Office of Communications].
6. [The Water Services Regulation Authority].
7. The Rail Regulator.
8. Every weights and measures authority in Great Britain.
9. The Department of Enterprise, Trade and Investment in Northern Ireland.
10. The Financial Services Authority.]

PART TWO

11. Consumers' Association.

Regulation 5(5)   SCHEDULE 2

INDICATIVE AND NON-EXHAUSTIVE LIST OF TERMS
WHICH MAY BE REGARDED AS UNFAIR

1. Terms which have the object or effect of—
   (a) excluding or limiting the legal liability of a seller or supplier in the event of the death of a consumer or personal injury to the latter resulting from an act or omission of that seller or supplier;
   (b) inappropriately excluding or limiting the legal rights of the consumer vis-à-vis the seller or supplier or another party in the event of total or partial non-performance or inadequate performance by the seller or supplier of any of the contractual obligations, including the option of offsetting a debt owed to the seller or supplier against any claim which the consumer may have against him;
   (c) making an agreement binding on the consumer whereas provision of services by the seller or supplier is subject to a condition whose realisation depends on his own will alone;
   (d) permitting the seller or supplier to retain sums paid by the consumer where the latter decides not to conclude or perform the contract, without providing for the consumer to receive compensation of an equivalent amount from the seller or supplier where the latter is the party cancelling the contract;
   (e) requiring any consumer who fails to fulfil his obligation to pay a disproportionately high sum in compensation;
   (f) authorising the seller or supplier to dissolve the contract on a discretionary basis where the same facility is not granted to the consumer, or permitting the seller or supplier to retain the sums paid for services not yet supplied by him where it is the seller or supplier himself who dissolves the contract;
   (g) enabling the seller or supplier to terminate a contract of indeterminate duration without reasonable notice except where there are serious grounds for doing so;
   (h) automatically extending a contract of fixed duration where the consumer does not indicate otherwise, when the deadline fixed for the consumer to express his desire not to extend the contract is unreasonably early;
   (i) irrevocably binding the consumer to terms with which he had no real opportunity of becoming acquainted before the conclusion of the contract;
   (j) enabling the seller or supplier to alter the terms of the contract unilaterally without a valid reason which is specified in the contract;
   (k) enabling the seller or supplier to alter unilaterally without a valid reason any characteristics of the product or service to be provided;
   (l) providing for the price of goods to be determined at the time of delivery or allowing a seller of goods or supplier of services to increase their price without in both cases giving the consumer the corresponding right to cancel the contract if the final price is too high in relation to the price agreed when the contract was concluded;
   (m)giving the seller or supplier the right to determine whether the goods or services supplied are in conformity with the contract, or giving him the exclusive right to interpret any term of the contract;
   (n) limiting the seller's or supplier's obligation to respect commitments undertaken by his agents or making his commitments subject to compliance with a particular formality;
   (o) obliging the consumer to fulfil all his obligations where the seller or supplier does not perform his;
   (p) giving the seller or supplier the possibility of transferring his rights and obligations under the contract, where this may serve to reduce the guarantees for the consumer, without the latter's agreement;

(q) excluding or hindering the consumer's right to take legal action or exercise any other legal remedy, particularly by requiring the consumer to take disputes exclusively to arbitration not covered by legal provisions, unduly restricting the evidence available to him or imposing on him a burden of proof which, according to the applicable law, should lie with another party to the contract.

2. Scope of paragraphs 1(g), (j) and (l)

(a) Paragraph 1(g) is without hindrance to terms by which a supplier of financial services reserves the right to terminate unilaterally a contract of indeterminate duration without notice where there is a valid reason, provided that the supplier is required to inform the other contracting party or parties thereof immediately.

(b) Paragraph 1(j) is without hindrance to terms under which a supplier of financial services reserves the right to alter the rate of interest payable by the consumer or due to the latter, or the amount of other charges for financial services without notice where there is a valid reason, provided that the supplier is required to inform the other contracting party or parties thereof at the earliest opportunity and that the latter are free to dissolve the contract immediately.

Paragraph 1(j) is also without hindrance to terms under which a seller or supplier reserves the right to alter unilaterally the conditions of a contract of indeterminate duration, provided that he is required to inform the consumer with reasonable notice and that the consumer is free to dissolve the contract.

(c) Paragraphs 1(g), (j) and (l) do not apply to:

— transactions in transferable securities, financial instruments and other products or services where the price is linked to fluctuations in a stock exchange quotation or index or a financial market rate that the seller or supplier does not control;

— contracts for the purchase or sale of foreign currency, traveller's cheques or international money orders denominated in foreign currency;

(d) Paragraph 1(l) is without hindrance to price indexation clauses, where lawful, provided that the method by which prices vary is explicitly described.

Consumer Protection (Distance Selling) Regulations 2000
(SI 2000, No. 2334)

3 Interpretation

(1) In these Regulations—

["the 2000 Act" means the Financial Services and Markets Act 2000;

"appointed representative" has the same meaning as in section 39(2) of the 2000 Act;

"authorised person" has the same meaning as in section 31(2) of the 2000 Act;]

"breach" means contravention by a supplier of a prohibition in, or failure to comply with a requirement of, these Regulations;

"business" includes a trade or profession;

"consumer" means any natural person who, in contracts to which these Regulations apply, is acting for purposes which are outside his business;

"court" in relation to England and Wales and Northern Ireland means a county court or the High Court, and in relation to Scotland means the Sheriff Court or the Court of Session;

"credit" includes a cash loan and any other form of financial accommodation, and for this purpose "cash" includes money in any form;

"Director" means the Director General of Fair Trading;

"distance contract" means any contract concerning goods or services concluded between a supplier and a consumer under an organised distance sales or service provision scheme run by the supplier who, for the purpose of the contract, makes exclusive use of one or more means of distance communication up to and including the moment at which the contract is concluded;

"EEA Agreement" means the Agreement on the European Economic Area signed at Oporto on 2 May 1992 as adjusted by the Protocol signed at Brussels on 17 March 1993;

"enactment" includes an enactment comprised in, or in an instrument made under, an Act of the Scottish Parliament;

"enforcement authority" means the Director, every weights and measures authority in Great Britain, and the Department of Enterprise, Trade and Investment in Northern Ireland;

"excepted contract" means a contract such as is mentioned in regulation 5(1);

["financial service" means any service of a banking, credit, insurance, personal pension, investment or payment nature;]

"means of distance communication" means any means which, without the simultaneous physical presence of the supplier and the consumer, may be used for the conclusion of a contract between those parties; and an indicative list of such means is contained in Schedule 1;

"Member State" means a State which is a contracting party to the EEA Agreement;

"operator of a means of communication" means any public or private person whose business involves making one or more means of distance communication available to suppliers;

"period for performance" has the meaning given by regulation 19(2);

"personal credit agreement" has the meaning given by regulation 14(8);

["regulated activity" has the same meaning as in section 22 of the 2000 Act;]

"related credit agreement" has the meaning given by regulation 15(5);

"supplier" means any person who, in contracts to which these Regulations apply, is acting in his commercial or professional capacity; and

"working days" means all days other than Saturdays, Sundays and public holidays.

(2) In the application of these Regulations to Scotland, for references to an "injunction" or an "interim injunction" there shall be substituted references to an "interdict" or an "interim interdict" respectively.

4   Contracts to which these Regulations apply
These Regulations apply, subject to regulation 6, to distance contracts other than excepted contracts.

5   Excepted contracts
(1) The following are excepted contracts, namely any contract—
- (a) for sale or other disposition of an interest in land except for a rental agreement;
- (b) for the construction of a building where the contract also provides for a sale or other disposition of an interest in land on which the building is constructed, except for a rental agreement;
- (c) relating to financial services [. . .];
- (d) concluded by means of an automated vending machine or automated commercial premises;
- (e) concluded with a telecommunications operator through the use of a public payphone;
- (f) concluded at an auction.

(2) References in paragraph (1) to a rental agreement—
- (a) if the land is situated in England and Wales, are references to any agreement which does not have to be made in writing (whether or not in fact made in writing) because of section 2(5)(a) of the Law of Property (Miscellaneous Provisions) Act 1989;
- (b) if the land is situated in Scotland, are references to any agreement for the creation, transfer, variation or extinction of an interest in land, which does not have to be

made in writing (whether or not in fact made in writing) as provided for in section 1(2) and (7) of the Requirements of Writing (Scotland) Act 1995; and

(c) if the land is situated in Northern Ireland, are references to any agreement which is not one to which section II of the Statute of Frauds, (Ireland) 1695 applies.

(3) Paragraph (2) shall not be taken to mean that a rental agreement in respect of land situated outside the United Kingdom is not capable of being a distance contract to which these Regulations apply.

6   Contracts to which only part of these regulations apply

(1) Regulations 7 to 20 shall not apply to a contract which is a "timeshare agreement" within the meaning of the Timeshare Act 1992 and to which that Act applies.

(2) Regulations 7 to 19(1) shall not apply to—

(a) contracts for the supply of food, beverages or other goods intended for everyday consumption supplied to the consumer's residence or to his workplace by regular roundsmen; or

(b) contracts for the provision of accommodation, transport, catering or leisure services, where the supplier undertakes, when the contract is concluded, to provide these services on a specific date or within a specific period.

(3) Regulations 19(2) to (8) and 20 do not apply to a contract for a "package" within the meaning of the Package Travel, Package Holidays and Package Tours Regulations 1992 which is sold or offered for sale in the territory of the Member States.

[(4) Regulations 7 to 14, 17 to 20 and 25 do not apply to any contract which is made, and regulation 24 does not apply to any unsolicited services which are supplied, by an authorised person where the making or performance of that contract or the supply of those services, as the case may be, constitutes or is part of a regulated activity carried on by him.

(5) Regulations 7 to 9, 17 to 20 and 25 do not apply to any contract which is made, and regulation 24 does not apply to any unsolicited services which are supplied, by an appointed representative where the making or performance of that contract or the supply of those services, as the case may be, constitutes or is part of a regulated activity carried on by him.]

7   Information required prior to the conclusion of the contract

(1) Subject to paragraph (4), in good time prior to the conclusion of the contract the supplier shall—

(a) provide to the consumer the following information—

   (i)   the identity of the supplier and, where the contract requires payment in advance, the supplier's address;

   (ii)   a description of the main characteristics of the goods or services;

   (iii) the price of the goods or services including all taxes;

   (iv) delivery costs where appropriate;

   (v)   the arrangements for payment, delivery or performance;

   (vi) the existence of a right of cancellation except in the cases referred to in regulation 13;

   (vii) the cost of using the means of distance communication where it is calculated other than at the basic rate;

   (viii) the period for which the offer or the price remains valid; and

   (ix) where appropriate, the minimum duration of the contract, in the case of contracts for the supply of goods or services to be performed permanently or recurrently;

(b) inform the consumer if he proposes, in the event of the goods or services ordered by the consumer being unavailable, to provide substitute goods or services (as the case may be) of equivalent quality and price; and

(c) inform the consumer that the cost of returning any such substitute goods to the supplier in the event of cancellation by the consumer would be met by the supplier.

(2) The supplier shall ensure that the information required by paragraph (1) is provided in a clear and comprehensible manner appropriate to the means of distance communication used, with due regard in particular to the principles of good faith in commercial transactions and the principles governing the protection of those who are unable to give their consent such as minors.

(3) Subject to paragraph (4), the supplier shall ensure that his commercial purpose is made clear when providing the information required by paragraph (1).

(4) In the case of a telephone communication, the identity of the supplier and the commercial purpose of the call shall be made clear at the beginning of the conversation with the consumer.

8   Written and additional information

(1) Subject to regulation 9, the supplier shall provide to the consumer in writing, or in another durable medium which is available and accessible to the consumer, the information referred to in paragraph (2), either—

    (a) prior to the conclusion of the contract, or

    (b) thereafter, in good time and in any event—

        (i) during the performance of the contract, in the case of services; and

        (ii) at the latest at the time of delivery where goods not for delivery to third parties are concerned.

(2) The information required to be provided by paragraph (1) is—

    (a) the information set out in paragraphs (i) to (vi) of Regulation 7(1)(a);

    (b) information about the conditions and procedures for exercising the right to cancel under regulation 10, including—

        (i) where a term of the contract requires (or the supplier intends that it will require) that the consumer shall return the goods to the supplier in the event of cancellation, notification of that requirement; [. . .]

        (ii) information as to whether the consumer or the supplier would be responsible under these Regulations for the cost of returning any goods to the supplier, or the cost of his recovering them, if the consumer cancels the contract under regulation 10;

        (iii) in the case of a contract for the supply of services, information as to how the right to cancel may be affected by the consumer agreeing to performance of the services beginning before the end of the seven working day period referred to in regulation 12;]

    (c) the geographical address of the place of business of the supplier to which the consumer may address any complaints;

    (d) information about any after-sales services and guarantees; and

    (e) the conditions for exercising any contractual right to cancel the contract, where the contract is of an unspecified duration or a duration exceeding one year.

9   Services performed through the use of a means of distance communication

(1) Regulation 8 shall not apply to a contract for the supply of services which are performed through the use of a means of distance communication, where those services are supplied on only one occasion and are invoiced by the operator of the means of distance communication.

(2) But the supplier shall take all necessary steps to ensure that a consumer who is a party to a contract to which paragraph (1) applies is able to obtain the supplier's geographical address and the place of business to which the consumer may address any complaints.

10   Right to cancel

(1) Subject to regulation 13, if within the cancellation period set out in regulations 11 and 12, the consumer gives a notice of cancellation to the supplier, or any other person previously notified by the supplier to the consumer as a person to whom notice of cancellation may be given, the notice of cancellation shall operate to cancel the contract.

(2) Except as otherwise provided by these Regulations, the effect of a notice of cancellation is that the contract shall be treated as if it had not been made.

(3) For the purposes of these Regulations, a notice of cancellation is a notice in writing or in another durable medium available and accessible to the supplier (or to the other person to whom it is given) which, however expressed, indicates the intention of the consumer to cancel the contract.

(4) A notice of cancellation given under this regulation by a consumer to a supplier or other person is to be treated as having been properly given if the consumer—

    (a) leaves it at the address last known to the consumer and addressed to the supplier or other person by name (in which case it is to be taken to have been given on the day on which it was left);

    (b) sends it by post to the address last known to the consumer and addressed to the supplier or other person by name (in which case, it is to be taken to have been given on the day on which it was posted);

    (c) sends it by facsimile to the business facsimile number last known to the consumer (in which case it is to be taken to have been given on the day on which it is sent); or

    (d) sends it by electronic mail, to the business electronic mail address last known to the consumer (in which case it is to be taken to have been given on the day on which it is sent).

(5) Where a consumer gives a notice in accordance with paragraph (4)(a) or (b) to a supplier who is a body corporate or a partnership, the notice is to be treated as having been properly given if—

    (a) in the case of a body corporate, it is left at the address of, or sent to, the secretary or clerk of that body; or

    (b) in the case of a partnership, it is left with or sent to a partner or a person having control or management of the partnership business.

11 Cancellation period in the case of contracts for the supply of goods

(1) For the purposes of regulation 10, the cancellation period in the case of contracts for the supply of goods begins with the day on which the contract is concluded and ends as provided in paragraphs (2) to (5).

(2) Where the supplier complies with regulation 8, the cancellation period ends on the expiry of the period of seven working days beginning with the day after the day on which the consumer receives the goods.

(3) Where a supplier who has not complied with regulation 8 provides to the consumer the information referred to in regulation 8(2), and does so in writing or in another durable medium available and accessible to the consumer, within the period of three months beginning with the day after the day on which the consumer receives the goods, the cancellation period ends on the expiry of the period of seven working days beginning with the day after the day on which the consumer receives the information.

(4) Where neither paragraph (2) nor (3) applies, the cancellation period ends on the expiry of the period of three months and seven working days beginning with the day after the day on which the consumer receives the goods.

(5) In the case of contracts for goods for delivery to third parties, paragraphs (2) to (4) shall apply as if the consumer had received the goods on the day on which they were received by the third party.

12 Cancellation period in the case of contracts for the supply of services

(1) For the purposes of regulation 10, the cancellation period in the case of contracts for the supply of services begins with the day on which the contract is concluded and ends as provided in paragraphs (2) to (4).

(2) Where the supplier complies with regulation 8 on or before the day on which the contract is concluded, the cancellation period ends on the expiry of the period of seven working days beginning with the day after the day on which the contract is concluded.

(3) [Subject to paragraph (3A)] Where a supplier who has not complied with regulation 8 on or before the day on which the contract is concluded provides to the consumer the information referred to in regulation 8(2) [. . .], and does so in writing or in another durable medium available and accessible to the consumer, within the period of three months beginning with the day after the day on which the contract is concluded, the cancellation period ends on the expiry of the period of seven working days beginning with the day after the day on which the consumer receives the information.

[(3A) Where the performance of the contract has begun with the consumer's agreement before the expiry of the period of seven working days beginning with the day after the day on which the contract was concluded and the supplier has not complied with regulation 8 on or before the day on which performance began, but provides to the consumer the information referred to in regulation 8(2) in good time during the performance of the contract, the cancellation period ends—

    (a) on the expiry of the period of seven seven working days beginning with the day after the day on which the consumer receives the information; or

    (b) if the performance of the contract is completed before the expiry of the period referred to in sub-paragraph (a), on the day when the performance of the contract is completed.]

(4) Where [none of paragraphs (2) to (3A) applies], the cancellation period ends on the expiry of the period of three months and seven working days beginning with the day after the day on which the contract is concluded.

13 Exceptions to the right to cancel

(1) Unless the parties have agreed otherwise, the consumer will not have the right to cancel the contract by giving notice of cancellation pursuant to regulation 10 in respect of contracts—

    [(a) for the supply of services if the performance of the contract has begun with the consumer's agreement—

        (i) before the end of the cancellation period applicable under regulation 12(2); and

        (ii) after the supplier has provided the information referred to in regulation 8(2)];

    (b) for the supply of goods or services the price of which is dependent on fluctuations in the financial market which cannot be controlled by the supplier;

    (c) for the supply of goods made to the consumer's specifications or clearly personalised or which by reason of their nature cannot be returned or are liable to deteriorate or expire rapidly;

    (d) for the supply of audio or video recordings or computer software if they are unsealed by the consumer;

    (e) for the supply of newspapers, periodicals or magazines; or

    (f) for gaming, betting or lottery services.

14 Recovery of sums paid by or on behalf of the consumer on cancellation, and return of security

(1) On the cancellation of a contract under regulation 10, the supplier shall reimburse any sum paid by or on behalf of the consumer under or in relation to the contract to the person by whom it was made free of any charge, less any charge made in accordance with paragraph (5).

(2) The reference in paragraph (1) to any sum paid on behalf of the consumer includes any sum paid by a creditor who is not the same person as the supplier under a personal credit agreement with the consumer.

(3) The supplier shall make the reimbursement referred to in paragraph (1) as soon as possible and in any case within a period not exceeding 30 days beginning with the day on which the notice of cancellation was given.

(4) Where any security has been provided in relation to the contract, the security (so far as it is so provided) shall, on cancellation under regulation 10, be treated as never having had

effect and any property lodged with the supplier solely for the purposes of the security as so provided shall be returned by him forthwith.

(5) Subject to paragraphs (6) and (7), the supplier may make a charge, not exceeding the direct costs of recovering any goods supplied under the contract, where a term of the contract provides that the consumer must return any goods supplied if he cancels the contract under regulation 10 but the consumer does not comply with this provision or returns the goods at the expense of the supplier.

(6) Paragraph (5) shall not apply where—

(a) the consumer cancels in circumstances where he has the right to reject the goods under a term of the contract, including a term implied by virtue of any enactment, or

(b) the term requiring the consumer to return any goods supplied if he cancels the contract is an "unfair term" within the meaning of the Unfair Terms in Consumer Contracts Regulations 1999.

(7) Paragraph (5) shall not apply to the cost of recovering any goods which were supplied as substitutes for the goods ordered by the consumer.

(8) For the purposes of these Regulations, a personal credit agreement is an agreement between the consumer and any other person ("the creditor") by which the creditor provides the consumer with credit of any amount.

15   Automatic cancellation of a related credit agreement

(1) Where a notice of cancellation is given under regulation 10 which has the effect of cancelling the contract, the giving of the notice shall also have the effect of cancelling any related credit agreement.

(2) Where a related credit agreement is cancelled by virtue of paragraph (1), the supplier shall, if he is not the same person as the creditor under that agreement, forthwith on receipt of the notice of cancellation inform the creditor that the notice has been given.

(3) Where a related credit agreement is cancelled by virtue of paragraph (1)—

(a) any sum paid by or on behalf of the consumer under, or in relation to, the credit agreement which the supplier is not obliged to reimburse under regulation 14(1) shall be reimbursed, except for any sum which, if it had not already been paid, would have to be paid under subparagraph (b);

(b) the agreement shall continue in force so far as it relates to repayment of the credit and payment of interest, subject to regulation 16; and

(c) subject to subparagraph (b), the agreement shall cease to be enforceable.

(4) Where any security has been provided under a related credit agreement, the security, so far as it is so provided, shall be treated as never having had effect and any property lodged with the creditor solely for the purposes of the security as so provided shall be returned by him forthwith.

(5) For the purposes of this regulation and regulation 16, a "related credit agreement" means an agreement under which fixed sum credit which fully or partly covers the price under a contract cancelled under regulation 10 is granted—

(a) by the supplier, or

(b) by another person, under an arrangement between that person and the supplier.

(6) For the purposes of this regulation and regulation 16—

(a) "creditor" is a person who grants credit under a related credit agreement;

(b) "fixed sum credit" has the same meaning as in section 10 of the Consumer Credit Act 1974;

(c) "repayment" in relation to credit means repayment of money received by the consumer, and cognate expressions shall be construed accordingly; and

(d) "interest" means interest on money so received.

16   Repayment of credit and interest after cancellation of a related credit agreement

(1) This regulation applies following the cancellation of a related credit agreement by virtue of regulation 15(1).

(2) If the consumer repays the whole or a portion of the credit—

    (a) before the expiry of one month following the cancellation of the credit agreement, or

    (b) in the case of a credit repayable by instalments, before the date on which the first instalment is due,

no interest shall be payable on the amount repaid.

(3) If the whole of a credit repayable by instalments is not repaid on or before the date referred to in paragraph (2)(b), the consumer shall not be liable to repay any of the credit except on receipt of a request in writing, signed by the creditor, stating the amounts of the remaining instalments (recalculated by the creditor as nearly as may be in accordance with the agreement and without extending the repayment period), but excluding any sum other than principal and interest.

(4) Where any security has been provided under a related credit agreement the duty imposed on the consumer to repay credit and to pay interest shall not be enforceable before the creditor has discharged any duty imposed on him by regulation 15(4) to return any property lodged with him as security on cancellation.

17   Restoration of goods by consumer after cancellation

(1) This regulation applies where a contract is cancelled under regulation 10 after the consumer has acquired possession of any goods under the contract other than any goods mentioned in regulation 13(1)(b) to (e).

(2) The consumer shall be treated as having been under a duty throughout the period prior to cancellation—

    (a) to retain possession of the goods, and

    (b) to take reasonable care of them.

(3) On cancellation, the consumer shall be under a duty to restore the goods to the supplier in accordance with this regulation, and in the meanwhile to retain possession of the goods and take reasonable care of them.

(4) The consumer shall not be under any duty to deliver the goods except at his own premises and in pursuance of a request in writing, or in another durable medium available and accessible to the consumer, from the supplier and given to the consumer either before, or at the time when, the goods are collected from those premises.

(5) If the consumer—

    (a) delivers the goods (whether at his own premises or elsewhere) to any person to whom, under regulation 10(1), a notice of cancellation could have been given; or

    (b) sends the goods at his own expense to such a person,

he shall be discharged from any duty to retain possession of the goods or restore them to the supplier.

(6) Where the consumer delivers the goods in accordance with paragraph (5)(a), his obligation to take care of the goods shall cease; and if he sends the goods in accordance with paragraph (5)(b), he shall be under a duty to take reasonable care to see that they are received by the supplier and not damaged in transit, but in other respects his duty to take care of the goods shall cease when he sends them.

(7) Where, at any time during the period of 21 days beginning with the day notice of cancellation was given, the consumer receives such a request as is mentioned in paragraph (4), and unreasonably refuses or unreasonably fails to comply with it, his duty to retain possession and take reasonable care of the goods shall continue until he delivers or sends the goods as mentioned in paragraph (5), but if within that period he does not receive such a request his duty to take reasonable care of the goods shall cease at the end of that period.

(8) Where—

    (a) a term of the contract provides that if the consumer cancels the contract, he must return the goods to the supplier, and

    (b) the consumer is not otherwise entitled to reject the goods under the terms of the

    (c) contract or by virtue of any enactment,

paragraph (7) shall apply as if for the period of 21 days there were substituted the period of 6 months.

(9) Where any security has been provided in relation to the cancelled contract, the duty to restore goods imposed on the consumer by this regulation shall not be enforceable before the supplier has discharged any duty imposed on him by regulation 14(4) to return any property lodged with him as security on cancellation.

(10) Breach of a duty imposed by this regulation on a consumer is actionable as a breach of statutory duty.

18   Goods given in part-exchange

(1) This regulation applies on the cancellation of a contract under regulation 10 where the supplier agreed to take goods in part-exchange (the "part-exchange goods") and those goods have been delivered to him.

(2) Unless, before the end of the period of 10 days beginning with the date of cancellation, the part-exchange goods are returned to the consumer in a condition substantially as good as when they were delivered to the supplier, the consumer shall be entitled to recover from the supplier a sum equal to the part-exchange allowance.

(3) In this regulation the part-exchange allowance means the sum agreed as such in the cancelled contract, or if no such sum was agreed, such sum as it would have been reasonable to allow in respect of the part-exchange goods if no notice of cancellation had been served.

(4) Where the consumer recovers from the supplier a sum equal to the part-exchange allowance, the title of the consumer to the part-exchange goods shall vest in the supplier (if it has not already done so) on recovery of that sum.

19   Performance

(1) Unless the parties agree otherwise, the supplier shall perform the contract within a maximum of 30 days beginning with the day after the day the consumer sent his order to the supplier.

(2) Subject to paragraphs (7) and (8), where the supplier is unable to perform the contract because the goods or services ordered are not available, within the period for performance referred to in paragraph (1) or such other period as the parties agree ("the period for performance"), he shall—

(a) inform the consumer; and

(b) reimburse any sum paid by or on behalf of the consumer under or in relation to the contract to the person by whom it was made.

(3) The reference in paragraph (2)(b) to any sum paid on behalf of the consumer includes any sum paid by a creditor who is not the same person as the supplier under a personal credit agreement with the consumer.

(4) The supplier shall make the reimbursement referred to in paragraph (2)(b) as soon as possible and in any event within a period of 30 days beginning with the day after the day on which the period for performance expired.

(5) A contract which has not been performed within the period for performance shall be treated as if it had not been made, save for any rights or remedies which the consumer has under it as a result of the non-performance.

(6) Where any security has been provided in relation to the contract, the security (so far as it is so provided) shall, where the supplier is unable to perform the contract within the period for performance, be treated as never having had any effect and any property lodged with the supplier solely for the purposes of the security as so provided shall be returned by him forthwith.

(7) Where the supplier is unable to supply the goods or services ordered by the consumer, the supplier may perform the contract for the purposes of these Regulations by providing substitute goods or services (as the case may be) of equivalent quality and price provided that—

(a) this possibility was provided for in the contract;

(b) prior to the conclusion of the contract the supplier gave the consumer the information required by regulation 7(1)(b) and (c) in the manner required by regulation 7(2).

(8) In the case of outdoor leisure events which by their nature cannot be rescheduled, paragraph 2(b) shall not apply where the consumer and the supplier so agree.

20 Effect of non-performance on related credit agreement

Where a supplier is unable to perform the contract within the period for performance—

(a) regulations 15 and 16 shall apply to any related credit agreement as if the consumer had given a valid notice of cancellation under regulation 10 on the expiry of the period for performance; and

(b) the reference in regulation 15(3)(a) to regulation 14(1) shall be read, for the purposes of this regulation, as a reference to regulation 19(2).

21 Payment by card

(1) Subject to paragraph (4), the consumer shall be entitled to cancel a payment where fraudulent use has been made of his payment card in connection with a contract to which this regulation applies by another person not acting, or to be treated as acting, as his agent.

(2) Subject to paragraph (4), the consumer shall be entitled to be recredited, or to have all sums returned by the card issuer, in the event of fraudulent use of his payment card in connection with a contract to which this regulation applies by another person not acting, or to be treated as acting, as the consumer's agent.

(3) Where paragraphs (1) and (2) apply, in any proceedings if the consumer alleges that any use made of the payment card was not authorised by him it is for the card issuer to prove that the use was so authorised.

(4) Paragraphs (1) and (2) shall not apply to an agreement to which section 83(1) of the Consumer Credit Act 1974 applies.

(6) For the purposes of this regulation—

"card issuer" means the owner of the card; and

"payment card" includes credit cards, charge cards, debit cards and store cards.

24 Inertia selling

(1) Paragraph (2) and (3) apply if—

(a) unsolicited goods are sent to a person ("the recipient") with a view to his acquiring them;

(b) the recipient has no reasonable cause to believe that they were sent with a view to their being acquired for the purposes of a business; and

(c) the recipient has neither agreed to acquire nor agreed to return them.

(2) The recipient may, as between himself and the sender, use, deal with or dispose of the goods as if they were an unconditional gift to him.

(3) The rights of the sender to the goods are extinguished.

(4) A person who, not having reasonable cause to believe there is a right to payment, in the course of any business makes a demand for payment, or asserts a present or prospective right to payment, for what he knows are—

(a) unsolicited goods sent to another person with a view to his acquiring them for purposes other than those of his business, or

(b) unsolicited services supplied to another person for purposes other than those of his business,

is guilty of an offence and liable, on summary conviction, to a fine not exceeding level 4 on the standard scale.

(5) A person who, not having reasonable cause to believe there is a right to payment, in the course of any business and with a view to obtaining payment for what he knows are unsolicited goods sent or services supplied as mentioned in paragraph (4)—

(a) threatens to bring any legal proceedings, or

(b) places or causes to be placed the name of any person on a list of defaulters or debtors or threatens to do so, or

(c) invokes or causes to be invoked any other collection procedure or threatens to do so,

is guilty of an offence and liable, on summary conviction, to a fine not exceeding level 5 on the standard scale.

(6) In this regulation—

"acquire" includes hire;

"send" includes deliver;

"sender", in relation to any goods, includes—

(a) any person on whose behalf or with whose consent the goods are sent;

(b) any other person claiming through or under the sender or any person mentioned in paragraph (a); and

(c) any person who delivers the goods; and

"unsolicited" means, in relation to goods sent or services supplied to any person, that they are sent or supplied without any prior request made by or on behalf of the recipient.

(7) For the purposes of this regulation, an invoice or similar document which—

(a) states the amount of a payment, and

(b) fails to comply with the [the conditions set out in Part 2 of the Schedule to the Regulatory Reform (Unsolicited Goods and Services Act 1971) (Directory Entries and Demands for Payment) Order 2005] or, as the case may be [the requirements of regulations made under], Article 6 of the Unsolicited Goods and Services (Northern Ireland) Order 1976 applicable to it, is to be regarded as asserting a right to the payment.

(8) Section 3A of the Unsolicited Goods and Services Act 1971 applies for the purposes of this regulation in its application to England, Wales and Scotland as it applies for the purposes of that Act.

(9) Article 6 of the Unsolicited Goods and Services (Northern Ireland) Order 1976 applies for the purposes of this regulation in its application to Northern Ireland as it applies for the purposes of that Order.

(10) This regulation applies only to goods sent and services supplied after the date on which it comes into force.

25 No contracting-out

(1) A term contained in any contract to which these Regulations apply is void if, and to the extent that, it is inconsistent with a provision for the protection of the consumer contained in these Regulations.

(2) Where a provision of these Regulations specifies a duty or liability of the consumer in certain circumstances, a term contained in a contract to which these Regulations apply, other than a term to which paragraph (3) applies, is inconsistent with that provision if it purports to impose, directly or indirectly, an additional duty or liability on him in those circumstances.

(3) This paragraph applies to a term which requires the consumer to return any goods supplied to him under the contract if he cancels it under regulation 10.

(4) A term to which paragraph (3) applies shall, in the event of cancellation by the consumer under regulation 10, have effect only for the purposes of regulation 14(5) and 17(8).

(5) These Regulations shall apply notwithstanding any contract term which applies or purports to apply the law of a non-Member State if the contract has a close connection with the territory of a Member State.

26 Consideration of complaints

(1) It shall be the duty of an enforcement authority to consider any complaint made to it about a breach unless—

(a) the complaint appears to the authority to be frivolous or vexatious; or

(b) another enforcement authority has notified the Director that it agrees to consider the complaint.

(2) If an enforcement authority notifies the Director that it agrees to consider a complaint made to another enforcement authority, the first mentioned authority shall be under a duty to consider the complaint.

(3) An enforcement authority which is under a duty to consider a complaint shall give reasons for its decision to apply or not to apply, as the case may be, for an injunction under regulation 27.

(4) In deciding whether or not to apply for an injunction in respect of a breach an enforcement authority may, if it considers it appropriate to do so, have regard to any undertaking given to it or another enforcement authority by or on behalf of any person as to compliance with these Regulations.

27   Injunctions to secure compliance with these Regulations

(1) The Director or, subject to paragraph (2), any other enforcement authority may apply for an injunction (including an interim injunction) against any person who appears to the Director or that authority to be responsible for a breach.

(2) An enforcement authority other than the Director may apply for an injunction only where—

    (a) it has notified the Director of its intention to apply at least fourteen days before the date on which the application is to be made, beginning with the date on which the notification was given; or

    (b) the Director consents to the application being made within a shorter period.

(3) The court on an application under this regulation may grant an injunction on such terms as it thinks fit to secure compliance with these Regulations.

28   Notification of undertakings and orders to the Director

An enforcement authority other than the Director shall notify the Director—

    (a) of any undertaking given to it by or on behalf of any person who appears to it to be responsible for a breach;

    (b) of the outcome of any application made by it under regulation 27 and of the terms of any undertaking given to or order made by the court;

    (c) of the outcome of any application made by it to enforce a previous order of the court.

29   Publication, information and advice

(1) The Director shall arrange for the publication in such form and manner as he considers appropriate of—

    (a) details of any undertaking or order notified to him under regulation 28;

    (b) details of any undertaking given to him by or on behalf of any person as to compliance with these Regulations;

    (c) details of any application made by him under regulation 27, and of the terms of any undertaking given to, or order made by, the court;

    (d) details of any application made by the Director to enforce a previous order of the court.

(2) The Director may arrange for the dissemination in such form and manner as he considers appropriate of such information and advice concerning the operation of these Regulations as it may appear to him to be expedient to give to the public and to all persons likely to be affected by these Regulations.

Regulation 3   SCHEDULE 1

INDICATIVE LIST OF MEANS OF DISTANCECOMMUNICATION

1. Unaddressed printed matter.
2. Addressed printed matter.
3. Letter.
4. Press advertising with order form.
5. Catalogue.
6. Telephone with human intervention.
7. Telephone without human intervention (automatic calling machine, audiotext).
8. Radio.
9. Videophone (telephone with screen).

10. Videotext (microcomputer and television screen) with keyboard or touch screen.
11. Electronic mail.
12. Facsimile machine (fax).
13. Television (teleshopping).

Electronic Commerce (EC Directive) Regulations 2002
(SI 2002, No. 2013)

2   Interpretation

(1) In these Regulations and in the Schedule...

"consumer" means any natural person who is acting for purposes other than those of his trade, business or profession;...

"the Directive" means Directive 2000/31/EC of the European Parliament and of the Council of 8 June 2000 on certain legal aspects of information society services, in particular electronic commerce, in the Internal Market (Directive on electronic commerce);...

"information society services" (which is summarised in recital 17 of the Directive as covering "any service normally provided for remuneration, at a distance, by means of electronic equipment for the processing (including digital compression) and storage of data, and at the individual request of a recipient of a service") has the meaning set out in Article 2(a) of the Directive, (which refers to Article 1(2) of Directive 98/34/EC of the European Parliament and of the Council of 22 June 1998 laying down a procedure for the provision of information in the field of technical standards and regulations, as amended by Directive 98/48/EC of 20 July 1998);...

"recipient of the service" means any person who, for professional ends or otherwise, uses an information society service, in particular for the purposes of seeking information or making it accessible;...

"service provider" means any person providing an information society service;

"the Treaty" means the treaty establishing the European Community.

(3) Terms used in the Directive other than those in paragraph (1) above shall have the same meaning as in the Directive.

9   Information to be provided where contracts are concluded by electronic means

(1) Unless parties who are not consumers have agreed otherwise, where a contract is to be concluded by electronic means a service provider shall, prior to an order being placed by the recipient of a service, provide to that recipient in a clear, comprehensible and unambiguous manner the information set out in (a) to (d) below—

    (a) the different technical steps to follow to conclude the contract;

    (b) whether or not the concluded contract will be filed by the service provider and whether it will be accessible;

    (c) the technical means for identifying and correcting input errors prior to the placing of the order; and

    (d) the languages offered for the conclusion of the contract.

(2) Unless parties who are not consumers have agreed otherwise, a service provider shall indicate which relevant codes of conduct he subscribes to and give information on how those codes can be consulted electronically.

(3) Where the service provider provides terms and conditions applicable to the contract to the recipient, the service provider shall make them available to him in a way that allows him to store and reproduce them.

(4) The requirements of paragraphs (1) and (2) above shall not apply to contracts concluded exclusively by exchange of electronic mail or by equivalent individual communications.

10   Other information requirements

Regulations 6, 7, 8 and 9(1) have effect in addition to any other information requirements in legislation giving effect to Community law.

11   Placing of the order

(1) Unless parties who are not consumers have agreed otherwise, where the recipient of the service places his order through technological means, a service provider shall—

(a) acknowledge receipt of the order to the recipient of the service without undue delay and by electronic means; and

(b) make available to the recipient of the service appropriate, effective and accessible technical means allowing him to identify and correct input errors prior to the placing of the order.

(2) For the purposes of paragraph (1)(a) above—

(a) the order and the acknowledgement of receipt will be deemed to be received when the parties to whom they are addressed are able to access them; and

(b) the acknowledgement of receipt may take the form of the provision of the service paid for where that service is an information society service.

(3) The requirements of paragraph (1) above shall not apply to contracts concluded exclusively by exchange of electronic mail or by equivalent individual communications.

12   Meaning of the term "order"

Except in relation to regulation 9(1)(c) and regulation 11(1)(b) where "order" shall be the contractual offer, "order" may be but need not be the contractual offer for the purposes of regulations 9 and 11.

13   Liability of the service provider

The duties imposed by regulations 6, 7, 8, 9(1) and 11(1)(a) shall be enforceable, at the suit of any recipient of a service, by an action against the service provider for damages for breach of statutory duty.

14   Compliance with Regulation 9(3)

Where on request a service provider has failed to comply with the requirement in regulation 9(3), the recipient may seek an order from any court having jurisdiction in relation to the contract requiring that service provider to comply with that requirement.

15   Right to rescind contract

Where a person—

(a) has entered into a contract to which these Regulations apply, and

(b) the service provider has not made available means of allowing him to identify and correct input errors in compliance with regulation 11(1)(b),

he shall be entitled to rescind the contract unless any court having jurisdiction in relation to the contract in question orders otherwise on the application of the service provider

Electronic Signatures Regulations 2002
(SI 2002, No. 318)

2   Interpretation

"certificate" means an electronic attestation which links signature-verification data to a person and confirms the identity of that person;

"certification-service-provider" means a person who issues certificates or provides other services related to electronic signatures;

"qualified certificate" means a certificate which meets the requirements in Schedule 1 and is provided by a certification-service-provider who fulfils the requirements in Schedule 2;

3   Supervision of certification-service-providers

(1) It shall be the duty of the Secretary of State to keep under review the carrying on of activities of certification-service-providers who are established in the United Kingdom and who issue qualified certificates to the public and the persons by whom they are carried on with a view to her becoming aware of the identity of those persons and the circumstances relating to the carrying on of those activities.

(2) It shall also be the duty of the Secretary of State to establish and maintain a register of certification-service-providers who are established in the United Kingdom and who issue qualified certificates to the public.

(3) The Secretary of State shall record in the register the names and addresses of those certification-service-providers of whom she is aware who are established in the United Kingdom and who issue qualified certificates to the public.

(4) The Secretary of State shall publish the register in such manner as she considers appropriate.

(5) The Secretary of State shall have regard to evidence becoming available to her with respect to any course of conduct of a certification-service-provider who is established in the United Kingdom and who issues qualified certificates to the public and which appears to her to be conduct detrimental to the interests of those persons who use or rely on those certificates with a view to making any of this evidence as she considers expedient available to the public in such manner as she considers appropriate.

4   Liability of certification-service-providers

(1) Where—

    (a) a certification-service-provider either—

        (i)   issues a certificate as a qualified certificate to the public, or

        (ii) guarantees a qualified certificate to the public,

    (b) a person reasonably relies on that certificate for any of the following matters—

        (i)   the accuracy of any of the information contained in the qualified certificate at the time of issue,

        (ii) the inclusion in the qualified certificate of all the details referred to in Schedule 1,

        (iii) the holding by the signatory identified in the qualified certificate at the time of its issue of the signature-creation data corresponding to the signature-verification data given or identified in the certificate, or

        (iv) the ability of the signature-creation data and the signature-verification data to be used in a complementary manner in cases where the certification-serviceprovider generates them both,

    (c) that person suffers loss as a result of such reliance, and

    (d) the certification-service-provider would be liable in damages in respect of any extent of the loss—

        (i)   had a duty of care existed between him and the person referred to in sub-paragraph (b) above, and

        (ii) had the certification-service-provider been negligent,

then that certification-service-provider shall be so liable to the same extent notwithstanding that there is no proof that the certification-service-provider was negligent unless the certification-service-provider proves that he was not negligent.

(2) For the purposes of the certification-service-provider's liability under paragraph (1) above there shall be a duty of care between that certification-service-provider and the person referred to in paragraph (1)(b) above.

5   Data protection

(1) A certification-service-provider who issues a certificate to the public and to whom this paragraph applies in accordance with paragraph (6) below—

(a) shall not obtain personal data for the purpose of issuing or maintaining that certificate otherwise than directly from the data subject or after the explicit consent of the data subject, and

(b) shall not process the personal data referred to in sub-paragraph (a) above—

    (i) to a greater extent than is necessary for the purpose of issuing or maintaining that certificate, or

    (ii) to a greater extent than is necessary for any other purpose to which the data subject has explicitly consented,

unless the processing is necessary for compliance with any legal obligation, to which the certification-service-provider is subject, other than an obligation imposed by contract.

(2) The obligation to comply with paragraph (1) above shall be a duty owed to any data subject who may be affected by a contravention of paragraph (1).

(3) Where a duty is owed by virtue of paragraph (2) above to any data subject, any breach of that duty which causes that data subject to sustain loss or damage shall be actionable by him.

(4) Compliance with paragraph (1) above shall also be enforceable by civil proceedings brought by the Crown for an injunction or for an interdict or for any other appropriate relief or remedy.

(5) Paragraph (4) above shall not prejudice any right that a data subject may have by virtue of paragraph (3) above to bring civil proceedings for the contravention or apprehended contravention of paragraph (1) above.

Regulation 2   SCHEDULE 2

(Annex II to the directive)

REQUIREMENTS FOR CERTIFICATION-SERVICE-PROVIDERS ISSUING QUALIFIED CERTIFICATES

Certification-service-providers must:

(a) demonstrate the reliability necessary for providing certification services;

(b) ensure the operation of a prompt and secure directory and a secure and immediate revocation service;

(c) ensure that the date and time when a certificate is issued or revoked can be determined precisely;

(d) verify, by appropriate means in accordance with national law, the identity and, if applicable, any specific attributes of the person to which a qualified certificate is issued;

(e) employ personnel who possess the expert knowledge, experience, and qualifications necessary for the services provided, in particular competence at managerial level, expertise in electronic signature technology and familiarity with proper security procedures; they must also apply administrative and management procedures which are adequate and correspond to recognised standards;

(f) use trustworthy systems and products which are protected against modification and ensure the technical and cryptographic security of the process supported by them;

(g) take measures against forgery of certificates, and, in cases where the certification-service-provider generates signature-creation data, guarantee confidentiality during the process of generating such data;

(h) maintain sufficient financial resources to operate in conformity with the requirements laid down in the Directive, in particular to bear the risk of liability for damages, for example, by obtaining appropriate insurance;

(i) record all relevant information concerning a qualified certificate for an appropriate period of time, in particular for the purpose of providing evidence of certification for the purposes of legal proceedings. Such recording may be done electronically;

(j) not store or copy signature-creation data of the person to whom the certification-service-provider provided key management services;

(k) before entering into a contractual relationship with a person seeking a certificate to support his electronic signature inform that person by a durable means of communication of the precise terms and conditions regarding the use of the certificate, including any limitations on its use, the existence of a voluntary accreditation scheme and procedures for complaints and dispute settlement. Such information, which may be transmitted electronically, must be in writing and in readily understandable language. Relevant parts of this information must also be made available on request to third parties relying on the certificate;

(l) use trustworthy systems to store certificates in a verifiable form so that:
— only authorised persons can make entries and changes,
— information can be checked for authenticity,
— certificates are publicly available for retrieval in only those cases for which the certificate-holder's consent has been obtained, and
— any technical changes compromising these security requirements are apparent to the operator.

Late Payment of Commercial Debts Regulations 2002
(SI 2002, No. 1674)

3   Proceedings restraining use of grossly unfair terms

(1) In this regulation:

(a) "small and medium-sized enterprises" means those enterprises defined in Annex 1 to Commission Regulation (EC) No 70/2001 of 12th January 2001 on the application of Articles 87 and 88 of the EC Treaty to State aid to small and medium-sized enterprises;

(b) "representative body" means an organisation established to represent the collective interests of small and medium-sized enterprises in general or in a particular sector or area.

(2) This regulation applies where a person acting in the course of a business has written standard terms on which he enters (or intends to enter) as purchaser into contracts to which the Late Payment of Commercial Debts (Interest) Act 1998 applies which include a term purporting to oust or vary the right to statutory interest in relation to qualifying debts created by those contracts.

(3) If it appears to the High Court that in all or any circumstances the purported use of such a term in a relevant contract would be void under the Late Payment of Commercial Debts (Interest) Act 1998, the court on the application of a representative body may grant an injunction against that person restraining him in those circumstances from using the offending term, on such terms as the court may think fit.

(4) Only a representative body may apply to the High Court under this regulation.

Electronic Communications Code (Conditions and Restrictions) Regulations 2003
(SI 2003, No. 2553)

2   Interpretation

(2) In these Regulations—

"the Act" means the Communications Act 2003; . . .

"code operator" means a person in whose case the electronic communications code is applied by a direction under section 106(3)(a) of the Act;

16 Funds for meeting liabilities

(1) A code operator must—

    (a) ensure that sufficient funds are available to meet the specified liabilities which—

        (i) arise on or before the date on which a relevant event occurs, or

        (ii) may arise at any time during the liability period,

from the exercise of rights conferred upon the code operator by paragraph 9 of the electronic communications code;

Financial Services (Distance Marketing) Regulations 2004

(SI 2004, No. 2095)

15 Unsolicited services

(1) A person ("the recipient") who receives unsolicited financial services for purposes other than those of his business from another person who supplies those services in the course of his business, shall not thereby become subject to any obligation (to make payment, or otherwise).

(2) Where, in the course of any business—

    (a) unsolicited financial services are supplied for purposes other than those of the recipient's business, and

    (b) a person includes with the supply of those services a demand for payment, or an assertion of a present or prospective right to payment in respect of those services,

that person is guilty of an offence and liable, on summary conviction, to a fine not exceeding level 4 on the standard scale.

(3) A person who, not having reasonable cause to believe that there is a right to payment, in the course of any business and with a view to obtaining payment for what he knows are unsolicited financial services supplied as mentioned in paragraph (2)—

    (a) threatens to bring any legal proceedings,

    (b) places or causes to be placed the name of any person on a list of defaulters or debtors or threatens to do so, or

    (c) invokes or causes to be invoked any other collection procedure or threatens to do so,

is guilty of an offence and liable, on summary conviction, to a fine not exceeding level 5 on the standard scale.

(4) In this regulation, "unsolicited" means, in relation to financial services supplied to any person, that they are supplied without any prior request made by or on behalf of that person.

(5) For the purposes of this regulation, a person who sends to a recipient an invoice or similar document which—

    (a) states the amount of a payment, and

    (b) does not comply with the requirements, applicable to invoices and similar documents, of regulations made under section 3A of the Unsolicited Goods and Services Act 1971 (contents and form of notes of agreement, invoices and similar documents) or, as the case may be, article 6 of the Unsolicited Goods and Services (Northern Ireland) Order 1976 (contents and form of notes of agreement, invoices and similar documents),

is to be regarded as asserting a right to the payment.

(6) Section 3A of the Unsolicited Goods and Services Act 1971 applies for the purposes of this regulation in its application to England, Wales and Scotland as it applies for the purposes of that Act.

(7) Article 6 of the Unsolicited Goods and Services (Northern Ireland) Order 1976 applies for the purposes of this regulation in its application to Northern Ireland as it applies for the purposes of that Order.

(8) This regulation is without prejudice to any right a supplier may have at any time, by contract or otherwise, to renew a distance contract with a consumer without any request made by or on behalf of that consumer prior to the renewal of that contract.

Damages (Variation of Periodical Payments) Order 2005
(SI 2005, No. 841)

1 Citation, commencement, interpretation and extent
(2) In this Order—
   (a) "the Act" means the Damages Act 1996;
   (b) "agreement" means an agreement by parties to a claim or action for damages which settles the claim or action and which provides for periodical payments;
   (c) "damages" means damages for future pecuniary loss in respect of personal injury;
   (d) "defence society" means the Medical Defence Union or the Medical Protection Society;
   (e) "variable agreement" means an agreement which contains a provision referred to in Article 9(1);
   (f) "variable order" means an order for periodical payments which contains a provision referred to in Article 2.
(3) In the application of this Order to Northern Ireland—
   (a) "claimant" means plaintiff;
   (b) "permission" means leave;
   (c) "statements of case" means, in the High Court, the writ and pleadings and, in the county court, the civil bill and any notice of intention to defend, defence, notice for particulars, replies and counterclaim.
(4) This Order extends to England and Wales and Northern Ireland.
(5) This Order applies to proceedings begun on or after the date on which it comes into force.

2 Power to make variable orders
If there is proved or admitted to be a chance that at some definite or indefinite time in the future the claimant will—
   (a) as a result of the act or omission which gave rise to the cause of action, develop some serious disease or suffer some serious deterioration, or
   (b) enjoy some significant improvement in his physical or mental condition, where that condition had been adversely affected as a result of that act or omission,
the court may, on the application of a party, with the agreement of all the parties, or of its own initiative, provide in an order for periodical payments that it may be varied.

3 Defendant's financial resources
Unless—
   (a) the defendant is insured in respect of the claim,
   (b) the source of payment under the order for periodical payments is a government or health service body within the meaning of section 2A(2) of the Act,
   (c) the payment is guaranteed under section 6 of or the Schedule to the Act, or
   (d) the order is made by consent and the claimant is neither a child nor a patient within the meaning of Part VII of the Mental Health Act 1983 or of Part VIII of the Mental Health (Northern Ireland) Order 1986,
the court will take into account the defendant's likely future financial resources in considering whether to make a variable order.

4 Award of provisional damages
The court may make a variable order in addition to an order for an award of provisional damages made by virtue of section 32A of the [Senior Courts Act 1981] or section 51 of the

County Courts Act 1984 or, in relation to Northern Ireland, paragraph 10(2)(a) of Schedule 6 to the Administration of Justice Act 1982.

5 Contents of variable order

Where the court makes a variable order—

    (a) the damages must be assessed or agreed on the assumption that the disease, deterioration or improvement will not occur;

    (b) the order must specify the disease or type of deterioration or improvement;

    (c) the order may specify a period within which an application for it to be varied may be made;

    (d) the order may specify more than one disease or type of deterioration or improvement and may, in respect of each, specify a different period within which an application for it to be varied may be made;

    (e) the order must provide that a party must obtain the court's permission to apply for it to be varied, unless the court otherwise orders.

6 Applications to extend period for applying for permission to vary

Where a period is specified under Article 5(c) or (d)—

    (a) a party may make more than one application to extend the period, and such an application is not to be treated as an application to vary a variable order for the purposes of Article 7;

    (b) a party may not make an application for the variable order to be varied after the end of the period specified or such period as extended by the court.

7 Limit on number of applications to vary

A party may make only one application to vary a variable order in respect of each specified disease or type of deterioration or improvement.

8 Case file

    (1) Where the court makes a variable order, the case file documents must be preserved by the court until the end of the period or periods specified under Article 5(c) or (d) or of any extension of them or, if no such period was specified, until the death of the claimant.

    (2) The case file documents are, unless the court otherwise orders—

    (a) the judgment as entered;

    (b) the statements of case;

    (c) the schedule of expenses and losses;

    (d) a transcript of the judge's oral judgment;

    (e) all medical reports relied on;

    (f) a transcript of any parts of the claimant's own evidence which the judge considers necessary;

    (g) any subsequent orders.

    (3) A court officer must ensure that the case file documents are provided by the parties where necessary and filed on the court file.

    (4) Where a variable order has been made, the legal representatives of the parties and, if the parties are insured, their insurers, must also preserve their own case file until the end of the period or periods specified under Article 5(c) or (d) or of any extension of them or, if no such period was specified, until the death of the claimant.

9 Variable agreements

    (1) If there is agreed to be a chance that at some definite or indefinite time in the future the claimant will—

    (a) as a result of the act or omission which gave rise to the cause of action, develop some serious disease or suffer some serious deterioration, or

    (b) enjoy some significant improvement in his physical or mental condition, where that condition had been adversely affected as a result of that act or omission, the parties to an agreement may agree that a party to it may apply to the court subsequently for its terms to be varied.

(2) Where the parties agree to permit an application to vary the terms of an agreement, the agreement—

> (a) must expressly state that a party to it may apply to the court for its terms to be varied;
>
> (b) must specify the disease or type of deterioration or improvement;
>
> (c) may specify a period within which an application for it to be varied may be made;
>
> (d) may specify more than one disease or type of deterioration or improvement and may, in respect of each, specify a different period within which an application for it to be varied may be made.

(3) A party who is permitted by an agreement to apply for its terms to be varied must obtain the court's permission to apply for it to be varied.

10   Application for permission

(1) An application for permission to apply for a variable order or a variable agreement to be varied must be accompanied by evidence—

> (a) that the disease, deterioration or improvement specified in the order or agreement has occurred, and
>
> (b) that it has caused or is likely to cause an increase or decrease in the pecuniary loss suffered by the claimant.

(2) Where the applicant is the claimant and he knows that the defendant is insured in respect of the claim and the identity of the defendant's insurers, he must serve the application notice on the insurers as well as on the defendant.

(3) Where the applicant is the claimant and he knows that the defendant is a member of a defence society and the identity of the defence society, he must serve the application notice on the defence society as well as on the defendant.

(4) The respondent to the application may, within 28 days after service of the application, serve written representations on the applicant and, if he does, must file them with the court.

(5) The court will deal with the application without a hearing.

11   Refusal of permission

(1) Where permission is refused, the applicant may, within 14 days after service of the order, request the decision to be reconsidered at a hearing.

(2) No appeal lies from an order refusing permission after reconsideration.

12   Grant of permission

(1) Where permission is granted, the court will also give directions as to the application for the variation of the variable order or the variable agreement.

(2) Directions must include directions as to—

> (a) the date by which the application for variation must be served and filed;
>
> (b) the service and filing of evidence.

(3) No appeal lies from an order granting permission.

13   Order for variation

(1) On an application for the variation of a variable order or a variable agreement, if the court is satisfied—

> (a) that the disease, deterioration or improvement specified in the order or agreement has occurred, and
>
> (b) that it has caused or is likely to cause an increase or decrease in the pecuniary loss suffered by the claimant,

it may order—

> (i) the amount of annual payments to be varied, either from the date of the application for permission or from the date of the application to vary if the

order did not require the permission of the court for an application to vary, or from such later date as it may specify in the order;

(ii) how each payment is to be made during the year and at what intervals;

(iii) a lump sum to be paid in addition to the existing periodical payments.

(2) Section 2(3) to (9) of the Act applies to orders under this Order as it applies to orders for periodical payments.

14   Application of rules of court

In England and Wales, the Civil Procedure Rules 1998 and in Northern Ireland, rules of court apply to applications under this Order, except where this Order makes provision inconsistent with Civil Procedure Rules or rules of court.

General Product Safety Regulations 2005
(SI 2005, No. 1803)

PART 1   GENERAL

2.   Interpretation

In these Regulations:—

"the 1987 Act" means the Consumer Protection Act 1987;

"Community law" includes a law in any part of the United Kingdom which implements a Community obligation;

"contravention" includes a failure to comply and cognate expressions shall be construed accordingly;

"dangerous product" means a product other than a safe product;

"distributor" means a professional in the supply chain whose activity does not affect the safety properties of a product;

"enforcement authority" means the Secretary of State, any other Minister of the Crown in charge of a government department, any such department and any authority or council mentioned in regulation 10;

"general safety requirement" means the requirement that only safe products should be placed on the market;

"the GPS Directive" means Directive 2001/95/EC of the European Parliament and of the Council of 3 December 2001 on general product safety;

"magistrates' court" in relation to Northern Ireland, means a court of summary jurisdiction;

"Member State" means a member State, Norway, Iceland or Liechtenstein;

"notice" means a notice in writing;

"officer", in relation to an enforcement authority, means a person authorised in writing to assist the authority in carrying out its functions under or for the purposes of the enforcement of these Regulations and safety notices, except in relation to an enforcement authority which is a government department where it means an officer of that department;

"producer" means—

(a) the manufacturer of a product, when he is established in a Member State and any other person presenting himself as the manufacturer by affixing to the product his name, trade mark or other distinctive mark, or the person who reconditions the product;

(b) when the manufacturer is not established in a Member State—

(i) if he has a representative established in a Member State, the representative,

(ii) in any other case, the importer of the product from a state that is not a Member State into a Member State;

(c) other professionals in the supply chain, insofar as their activities may affect the safety properties of a product;

"product" means a product which is intended for consumers or likely, under reasonably foreseeable conditions, to be used by consumers even if not intended for them and which is supplied or made available, whether for consideration or not, in the course of a commercial activity and whether it is new, used or reconditioned and includes a product that is supplied or made available to consumers for their own use in the context of providing a service. "product" does not include equipment used by service providers themselves to supply a service to consumers, in particular equipment on which consumers ride or travel which is operated by a service provider;

"recall" means any measure aimed at achieving the return of a dangerous product that has already been supplied or made available to consumers;

"recall notice" means a notice under regulation 15;

"record" includes any book or document and any record in any form;

"requirement to mark" means a notice under regulation 12;

"requirement to warn" means a notice under regulation 13;

"safe product" means a product which, under normal or reasonably foreseeable conditions of use including duration and, where applicable, putting into service, installation and maintenance requirements, does not present any risk or only the minimum risks compatible with the product's use, considered to be acceptable and consistent with a high level of protection for the safety and health of persons. In determining the foregoing, the following shall be taken into account in particular—

    (a) the characteristics of the product, including its composition, packaging, instructions for assembly and, where applicable, instructions for installation and maintenance,

    (b) the effect of the product on other products, where it is reasonably foreseeable that it will be used with other products,

    (c) the presentation of the product, the labelling, any warnings and instructions for its use and disposal and any other indication or information regarding the product, and

    (d) the categories of consumers at risk when using the product, in particular children and the elderly.

The feasibility of obtaining higher levels of safety or the availability of other products presenting a lesser degree of risk shall not constitute grounds for considering a product to be a dangerous product;

"safety notice" means a suspension notice, a requirement to mark, a requirement to warn, a withdrawal notice or a recall notice;

"serious risk" means a serious risk, including one the effects of which are not immediate, requiring rapid intervention;

"supply" in relation to a product includes making it available, in the context of providing a service, for use by consumers;

"suspension notice" means a notice under regulation 11;

"withdrawal" means any measure aimed at preventing the distribution, display or offer of a dangerous product to a consumer;

"withdrawal notice" means a notice under regulation 14.

Application

3.—(1) Each provision of these Regulations applies to a product in so far as there are no specific provisions with the same objective in rules of Community law governing the safety of the product other than the GPS Directive.

(2) Where a product is subject to specific safety requirements imposed by rules of Community law other than the GPS Directive, these Regulations shall apply only to the aspects and risks or category of risks not covered by those requirements. This means that:

    (a) the definition of "safe product" and "dangerous product" in regulation 2 and regulations 5 and 6 shall not apply to such a product in so far as concerns the risks or category of risks covered by the specific rules, and

(b) the remainder of these Regulations shall apply except where there are specific provisions governing the aspects covered by those regulations with the same objective.

4. These Regulations do not apply to a second-hand product supplied as a product to be repaired or reconditioned prior to being used, provided the supplier clearly informs the person to whom he supplies the product to that effect.

PART 2   OBLIGATIONS OF PRODUCERS AND DISTRIBUTORS

5.   General safety requirement

(1) No producer shall place a product on the market unless the product is a safe product.

(2) No producer shall offer or agree to place a product on the market or expose or possess a product for placing on the market unless the product is a safe product.

(3) No producer shall offer or agree to supply a product or expose or possess a product for supply unless the product is a safe product.

(4) No producer shall supply a product unless the product is a safe product.

6.   Presumption of conformity

(1) Where, in the absence of specific provisions in rules of Community law governing the safety of a product, the product conforms to the specific rules of the law of part of the United Kingdom laying down the health and safety requirements which the product must satisfy in order to be marketed in the United Kingdom, the product shall be deemed safe so far as concerns the aspects covered by such rules.

(2) Where a product conforms to a voluntary national standard of the United Kingdom giving effect to a European standard the reference of which has been published in the Official Journal of the European Union in accordance with Article 4 of the GPS Directive, the product shall be presumed to be a safe product so far as concerns the risks and categories of risk covered by that national standard. The Secretary of State shall publish the reference number of such national standards in such manner as he considers appropriate.

(3) In circumstances other than those referred to in paragraphs (1) and (2), the conformity of a product to the general safety requirement shall be assessed taking into account—

(a) any voluntary national standard of the United Kingdom giving effect to a European standard, other than one referred to in paragraph (2),

(b) other national standards drawn up in the United Kingdom,

(c) recommendations of the European Commission setting guidelines on product safety assessment,

(d) product safety codes of good practice in the sector concerned,

(e) the state of the art and technology, and

(f) reasonable consumer expectations concerning safety.

(4) Conformity of a product with the criteria designed to ensure the general safety requirement is complied with, in particular the provisions mentioned in paragraphs (1) to (3), shall not bar an enforcement authority from exercising its powers under these Regulations in relation to that product where there is evidence that, despite such conformity, it is dangerous.

7.   Other obligations of producers

(1) Within the limits of his activities, a producer shall provide consumers with the relevant information to enable them—

(a) to assess the risks inherent in a product throughout the normal or reasonably foreseeable period of its use, where such risks are not immediately obvious without adequate warnings, and

(b) to take precautions against those risks.

(2) The presence of warnings does not exempt any person from compliance with the other requirements of these Regulations.

(3) Within the limits of his activities, a producer shall adopt measures commensurate with the characteristics of the products which he supplies to enable him to—

    (a) be informed of the risks which the products might pose, and

    (b) take appropriate action including, where necessary to avoid such risks, withdrawal, adequately and effectively warning consumers as to the risks or, as a last resort, recall.

(4) The measures referred to in paragraph (3) include—

    (a) except where it is not reasonable to do so, an indication by means of the product or its packaging of—

        (i) the name and address of the producer, and

        (ii) the product reference or where applicable the batch of products to which it belongs; and

    (b) where and to the extent that it is reasonable to do so—

        (i) sample testing of marketed products,

        (ii) investigating and if necessary keeping a register of complaints concerning the safety of the product, and

        (iii) keeping distributors informed of the results of such monitoring where a product presents a risk or may present a risk.

8.   Obligations of distributors

(1) A distributor shall act with due care in order to help ensure compliance with the applicable safety requirements and in particular he—

    (a) shall not expose or possess for supply or offer or agree to supply, or supply, a product to any person which he knows or should have presumed, on the basis of the information in his possession and as a professional, is a dangerous product; and

    (b) shall, within the limits of his activities, participate in monitoring the safety of a product placed on the market, in particular by—

        (i) passing on information on the risks posed by the product,

        (ii) keeping the documentation necessary for tracing the origin of the product,

        (iii) producing the documentation necessary for tracing the origin of the product, and cooperating in action taken by a producer or an enforcement authority to avoid the risks.

(2) Within the limits of his activities, a distributor shall take measures enabling him to cooperate efficiently in the action referred to in paragraph (1)(b)(iii).

9.   Obligations of producers and distributors

(1) Subject to paragraph (2), where a producer or a distributor knows that a product he has placed on the market or supplied poses risks to the consumer that are incompatible with the general safety requirement, he shall forthwith notify an enforcement authority in writing of that information and—

    (a) the action taken to prevent risk to the consumer; and

    (b) where the product is being or has been marketed or otherwise supplied to consumers outside the United Kingdom, of the identity of each Member State in which, to the best of his knowledge, it is being or has been so marketed or supplied.

(2) Paragraph (1) shall not apply—

    (a) in the case of a second-hand product supplied as an antique or as a product to be repaired or reconditioned prior to being used, provided the supplier clearly informed the person to whom he supplied the product to that effect,

    (b) in conditions concerning isolated circumstances or products.

(3) In the event of a serious risk the notification under paragraph (1) shall include the following—

   (a) information enabling a precise identification of the product or batch of products in question,

   (b) a full description of the risks that the product presents,

   (c) all available information relevant for tracing the product, and

   (d) a description of the action undertaken to prevent risks to the consumer.

(4) Within the limits of his activities, a person who is a producer or a distributor shall co-operate with an enforcement authority (at the enforcement authority's request) in action taken to avoid the risks posed by a product which he supplies or has supplied. Every enforcement authority shall maintain procedures for such co-operation, including procedures for dialogue with the producers and distributors concerned on issues related to product safety.

PART 3   ENFORCEMENT

10.   Enforcement

(1) It shall be the duty of every authority to which paragraph (4) applies to enforce within its area these Regulations and safety notices.

(2) An authority in England or Wales to which paragraph (4) applies shall have the power to investigate and prosecute for an alleged contravention of any provision imposed by or under these Regulations which was committed outside its area in any part of England and Wales.

(3) A district council in Northern Ireland shall have the power to investigate and prosecute for an alleged contravention of any provision imposed by or under these Regulations which was committed outside its area in any part of Northern Ireland.

(4) The authorities to which this paragraph applies are:

   (a) in England, a county council, district council, London Borough Council, the Common Council of the City of London in its capacity as a local authority and the Council of the Isles of Scilly,

   (b) in Wales, a county council or a county borough council,

   (c) in Scotland, a council constituted under section 2 of the Local Government etc. (Scotland) Act 1994,

   (d) in Northern Ireland any district council.

(5) An enforcement authority shall in enforcing these Regulations act in a manner proportionate to the seriousness of the risk and shall take due account of the precautionary principle. In this context, it shall encourage and promote voluntary action by producers and distributors. Notwithstanding the foregoing, an enforcement authority may take any action under these Regulations urgently and without first encouraging and promoting voluntary action if a product poses a serious risk.

11.   Suspension notices

(1) Where an enforcement authority has reasonable grounds for suspecting that a requirement of these Regulations has been contravened in relation to a product, the authority may, for the period needed to organise appropriate safety evaluations, checks and controls, serve a notice ("a suspension notice") prohibiting the person on whom it is served from doing any of the following things without the consent of the authority, that is to say—

   (a) placing the product on the market, offering to place it on the market, agreeing to place it on the market or exposing it for placing on the market, or

   (b) supplying the product, offering to supply it, agreeing to supply it or exposing it for supply.

(2) A suspension notice served by an enforcement authority in relation to a product may require the person on whom it is served to keep the authority informed of the whereabouts of any such product in which he has an interest.

(3) A consent given by the enforcement authority for the purposes of paragraph (1) may impose such conditions on the doing of anything for which the consent is required as the authority considers appropriate.

12. Requirements to mark

(1) Where an enforcement authority has reasonable grounds for believing that a product is a dangerous product in that it could pose risks in certain conditions, the authority may serve a notice ("a requirement to mark") requiring the person on whom the notice is served at his own expense to undertake either or both of the following, as specified in the notice—

    (a) to ensure that the product is marked in accordance with requirements specified in the notice with warnings as to the risks it may present,

    (b) to make the marketing of the product subject to prior conditions as specified in the notice so as to ensure the product is a safe product.

(2) The requirements referred to in paragraph (1)(a) shall be such as to ensure that the product is marked with a warning which is suitable, clearly worded and easily comprehensible.

13. Requirements to warn

Where an enforcement authority has reasonable grounds for believing that a product is a dangerous product in that it could pose risks for certain persons, the authority may serve a notice ("a requirement to warn") requiring the person on whom the notice is served at his own expense to undertake one or more of the following, as specified in the notice—

    (a) where and to the extent it is practicable to do so, to ensure that any person who could be subject to such risks and who has been supplied with the product be given warning of the risks in good time and in a form specified in the notice,

    (b) to publish a warning of the risks in such form and manner as is likely to bring those risks to the attention of any such person,

    (c) to ensure that the product carries a warning of the risks in a form specified in the notice.

14. Withdrawal notices

(1) Where an enforcement authority has reasonable grounds for believing that a product is a dangerous product, the authority may serve a notice ("a withdrawal notice") prohibiting the person on whom it is served from doing any of the following things without the consent of the authority, that is to say—

    (a) placing the product on the market, offering to place it on the market, agreeing to place it on the market or exposing it for placing on the market, or

    (b) supplying the product, offering to supply it, agreeing to supply it or exposing it for supply.

(2) A withdrawal notice may require the person on whom it is served to take action to alert consumers to the risks that the product presents.

(3) In relation to a product that is already on the market, a withdrawal notice may only be served by an enforcement authority where the action being undertaken by the producer or the distributor concerned in fulfilment of his obligations under these Regulations is unsatisfactory or insufficient to prevent the risks concerned to the health and safety of persons.

(4) Paragraph (3) shall not apply in the case of a product posing a serious risk requiring, in the view of the enforcement authority, urgent action.

(5) A withdrawal notice served by an enforcement authority in relation to a product may require the person on whom it is served to keep the authority informed of the whereabouts of any such product in which he has an interest.

(6) A consent given by the enforcement authority for the purposes of paragraph (1) may impose such conditions on the doing of anything for which the consent is required as the authority considers appropriate.

15. Recall notices

(1) Subject to paragraph (4), where an enforcement authority has reasonable grounds for believing that a product is a dangerous product and that it has already been supplied or made available to consumers, the authority may serve a notice ("a recall notice") requiring the person on whom it is served to use his reasonable endeavours to organise the return of the product from consumers to that person or to such other person as is specified in the notice.

(2) A recall notice may require—

(a) the recall to be effected in accordance with a code of practice applicable to the product concerned, or

(b) the recipient of the recall notice to—

(i) contact consumers who have purchased the product in order to inform them of the recall, where and to the extent it is practicable to do so,

(ii) publish a notice in such form and such manner as is likely to bring to the attention of purchasers of the product the risk the product poses and the fact of the recall, or

(iii) make arrangements for the collection or return of the product from consumers who have purchased it or for its disposal,

and may impose such additional requirements on the recipient of the notice as are reasonable and practicable with a view to achieving the return of the product from consumers to the person specified in the notice or its disposal.

(3) In determining what requirements to include in a recall notice, the enforcement authority shall take into consideration the need to encourage distributors, users and consumers to contribute to its implementation.

(4) A recall notice may only be issued by an enforcement authority where—

(a) other action which it may require under these Regulations would not suffice to prevent the risks concerned to the health and safety of persons,

(b) the action being undertaken by the producer or the distributor concerned in fulfilment of his obligations under these Regulations is unsatisfactory or insufficient to prevent the risks concerned to the health and safety of persons, and

(c) the authority has given not less than seven days notice to the person on whom the recall notice is to be served of its intention to serve such a notice and where that person has before the expiry of that period by notice required the authority to seek the advice of such person as the Institute determines on the questions of—

(i) whether the product is a dangerous product,

(ii) whether the issue of a recall notice is proportionate to the seriousness of the risk, and

the authority has taken account of such advice.

(5) Paragraphs (4)(b) and (c) shall not apply in the case of a product posing a serious risk requiring, in the view of the enforcement authority, urgent action.

(6) Where a person requires an enforcement authority to seek advice as referred to in paragraph (4)(c), that person shall be responsible for the fees, costs and expenses of the Institute and of the person appointed by the Institute to advise the authority.

(7) In paragraphs 4(c) and (6) "the Institute" means the charitable organisation with registered number 803725 and known as the Chartered Institute of Arbitrators.

(8) A recall notice served by an enforcement authority in relation to a product may require the person on whom it is served to keep the authority informed of the whereabouts of any such product to which the recall notice relates, so far as he is able to do so.

(9) Where the conditions in paragraph (1) for serving a recall notice are satisfied and either the enforcement authority has been unable to identify any person on whom to serve a recall notice, or the person on whom such a notice has been served has failed to comply with it, then the authority may itself take such action as could have been required by a recall notice.

(10) Where—

(a) an authority has complied with the requirements of paragraph (4); and

(b) the authority has exercised its powers under paragraph (9) to take action following the failure of the person on whom the recall notice has been served to comply with that notice,

then the authority may recover from the person on whom the notice was served summarily as a civil debt, any costs or expenses reasonably incurred by it in undertaking the action referred to in sub-paragraph (b).

(11) A civil debt recoverable under the preceding paragraph may be recovered—

(a) in England and Wales by way of complaint (as mentioned in section 58 of the Magistrates' Courts Act 1980,

(b) in Northern Ireland in proceedings under Article 62 of the Magistrate's Court (Northern Ireland) Order 1981.

16. Supplementary provisions relating to safety notices

(1) Whenever feasible, prior to serving a safety notice the authority shall give an opportunity to the person on whom the notice is to be served to submit his views to the authority. Where, due to the urgency of the situation, this is not feasible the person shall be given an opportunity to submit his views to the authority after service of the notice.

(2) A safety notice served by an enforcement authority in respect of a product shall—

(a) describe the product in a manner sufficient to identify it;

(b) state the reasons on which the notice is based;

(c) indicate the rights available to the recipient of the notice under these Regulations and (where applicable) the time limits applying to their exercise; and

(d) in the case of a suspension notice, state the period of time for which it applies.

(3) A safety notice shall have effect throughout the United Kingdom.

(4) Where an enforcement authority serves a suspension notice in respect of a product, the authority shall be liable to pay compensation to a person having an interest in the product in respect of any loss or damage suffered by reason of the notice if—

(a) there has been no contravention of any requirement of these Regulations in relation to the product; and

(b) the exercise by the authority of the power to serve the suspension notice was not attributable to any neglect or default by that person.

(5) Where an enforcement authority serves a withdrawal notice in respect of a product, the authority shall be liable to pay compensation to a person having an interest in the product in respect of any loss or damage suffered by reason of the notice if—

(a) the product was not a dangerous product; and

(b) the exercise by the authority of the power to serve the withdrawal notice was not attributable to any neglect or default by that person.

(6) Where an enforcement authority serves a recall notice in respect of a product, the authority shall be liable to pay compensation to the person on whom the notice was served in respect of any loss or damage suffered by reason of the notice if—

(a) the product was not a dangerous product; and

(b) the exercise by the authority of the power to serve the recall notice was not attributable to any neglect or default by that person.

(7) An enforcement authority may vary or revoke a safety notice which it has served provided that the notice is not made more restrictive for the person on whom it is served or more onerous for that person to comply with.

(8) Wherever feasible prior to varying a safety notice the authority shall give an opportunity to the person on whom the original notice was served to submit his views to the authority.

17. Appeals against safety notices

(1) A person on whom a safety notice has been served and a person having an interest in a product in respect of which a safety notice (other than a recall notice) has been served may, before the end of the period of 21 days beginning with the day on which the notice was served, apply for an order to vary or set aside the terms of the notice.

(2) On an application under paragraph (1) the court or the sheriff, as the case may be, shall make an order setting aside the notice only if satisfied that—

(a) in the case of a suspension notice, there has been no contravention in relation to the product of any requirement of these Regulations,

(b) in the case of a requirement to mark or a requirement to warn, the product is not a dangerous product,

(c) in the case of a withdrawal notice—

   (i) the product is not a dangerous product, or

   (ii) where applicable, regulation 14(3) has not been complied with by the enforcement authority concerned,

(d) in the case of a recall notice—

   (i) the product is not a dangerous product, or

   (ii) regulation 15(4) has not been complied with,

(e) in any case, the serving of the safety notice concerned was not proportionate to the seriousness of the risk.

(3) On an application concerning the period of time specified in a suspension notice as the period for which it applies, the court or the sheriff, as the case may be, may reduce the period to such period as it considers sufficient for organising appropriate safety evaluations, checks and controls.

(4) On an application to vary the terms of a notice, the court or the sheriff, as the case may be, may vary the requirements specified in the notice as it considers appropriate.

(5) A person on whom a recall notice has been served and who proposes to make an application under paragraph (1) in relation to the notice may, before the end of the period of seven days beginning with the day on which the notice was served, apply to the court or the sheriff for an order suspending the effect of the notice and the court or the sheriff may, in any case where it considers it appropriate to do so, make an order suspending the effect of the notice.

(6) If the court or the sheriff makes an order suspending the effect of a recall notice under paragraph (5) in the absence of the enforcement authority, the enforcement authority may apply for the revocation of such order.

(7) An order under paragraph (5) shall take effect from the time it is made until—

(a) it is revoked under paragraph (6),

(b) where no application is made under paragraph (1) in respect of the recall notice within the time specified in that paragraph, the expiration of that time,

(c) where such an application is made but is withdrawn or dismissed for want of prosecution, the date of dismissal or withdrawal of the application, or

(d) where such an application is made and is not withdrawn or dismissed for want of prosecution, the determination of the application.

(8) Subject to paragraph (6), in Scotland the sheriff's decision under paragraph (5) shall be final.

(9) An application under this regulation may be made—

(a) by way of complaint to any magistrates' court in which proceedings have been brought in England and Wales or Northern Ireland—

   (i) in respect of a contravention in relation to the product of a requirement imposed by or under these Regulations; or

   (ii) for the forfeiture of the product under regulation 18;

(b) where no such proceedings have been brought, by way of complaint to any magistrates' court; or

(c) in Scotland, by summary application to the sheriff.

(10) A person aggrieved by an order made pursuant to an application under paragraph (1) by a magistrates' court in England, Wales or Northern Ireland, or by a decision of such a court not to make such an order, may appeal against that order or decision—

(a) in England and Wales, to the Crown Court;

(b) in Northern Ireland, to the county court.

18. Forfeiture: England and Wales and Northern Ireland

(1) An enforcement authority in England and Wales or Northern Ireland may apply for an order for the forfeiture of a product on the grounds that the product is a dangerous product.

(2) An application under paragraph (1) may be made—

    (a) where proceedings have been brought in a magistrates' court for an offence in respect of a contravention in relation to the product of a requirement imposed by or under these Regulations, to that court,

    (b) where an application with respect to the product has been made to a magistrates' court under regulation 17 (appeals against safety notices) or 25 (appeals against detention of products and records) to that court, and

    (c) otherwise, by way of complaint to a magistrates' court.

(3) An enforcement authority making an application under paragraph (1) shall serve a copy of the application on any person appearing to it to be the owner of, or otherwise to have an interest in, the product to which the application relates, together with a notice giving him the opportunity to appear at the hearing of the application to show cause why the product should not be forfeited.

(4) A person on whom notice is served under paragraph (3) and any other person claiming to be the owner of, or otherwise to have an interest in, the product to which the application relates shall be entitled to appear at the hearing of the application and show cause why the product should not be forfeited.

(5) The court shall not make an order for the forfeiture of a product—

    (a) if any person on whom notice is served under paragraph (3) does not appear, unless service of the notice on that person is proved, or

    (b) if no notice under paragraph (3) has been served, unless the court is satisfied that in the circumstances it was reasonable not to serve notice on any person.

(6) The court may make an order for the forfeiture of a product only if it is satisfied that the product is a dangerous product.

(7) Any person aggrieved by an order made by a magistrates' court for the forfeiture of a product, or by a decision of such a court not to make such an order, may appeal against that order or decision—

    (a) in England and Wales, to the Crown Court;

    (b) in Northern Ireland, to the county court.

(8) An order for the forfeiture of a product shall not take effect until the later of—

    (i) the end of the period within which an appeal under paragraph (7) may be brought or within which an application under section 111 of the Magistrates' Courts Act 1980 or article 146 of the Magistrates' Courts (Northern Ireland) Order 1981 (statement of case) may be made, or

    (ii) if an appeal or an application is so made, when the appeal or application is determined or abandoned.

(9) Subject to the following paragraph, where a product is forfeited it shall be destroyed in accordance with such directions as the court may give.

(10) On making an order for forfeiture of a product a magistrates' court may, if it considers it appropriate to do so, direct that the product shall (instead of being destroyed) be delivered up to such person as the court may specify, on condition that the person—

    (a) does not supply the product to any person otherwise than as mentioned in paragraph (11), and

    (b) on condition, if the court considers it appropriate, that he complies with any order to pay costs or expenses (including any order under regulation 28) which has been made against him in the proceedings for the order for forfeiture.

(11) The supplies which may be permitted under the preceding paragraph are—

    (a) a supply to a person who carries on a business of buying products of the same description as the product concerned and repairing or reconditioning them,

(b) a supply to a person as scrap (that is to say, for the value of materials included in the product rather than for the value of the product itself),

(c) a supply to any person, provided that being so supplied the product is repaired by or on behalf of the person to whom the product was delivered up by direction of the court and that following such repair it is not a dangerous product.

19.   Forfeiture: Scotland

(1) In Scotland a sheriff may make an order for forfeiture of a product on the grounds that the product is a dangerous product—

(a) on an application by a procurator-fiscal made in the manner specified in section 134 of the Criminal Procedure (Scotland) Act 1995, or

(b) where a person is convicted of any offence in respect of a contravention in relation to the product of a requirement imposed by or under these Regulations, in addition to any other penalty which the sheriff may impose.

(2) The procurator-fiscal making an application under paragraph (1)(a) shall serve on any person appearing to him to be the owner of, or otherwise to have an interest in, the product to which the application relates a copy of the application, together with a notice giving him the opportunity to appear at the hearing of the application to show cause why the product should not be forfeited.

(3) Service under paragraph (2) shall be carried out, and such service may be proved, in the manner specified for citation of an accused in summary proceedings under the Criminal Procedure (Scotland) Act 1995.

(4) A person upon whom notice is served under paragraph (2) and any other person claiming to be the owner of, or otherwise to have an interest in, the product to which the application relates shall be entitled to appear at the hearing of the application to show cause why the product should not be forfeited.

(5) The sheriff shall not make an order following an application under paragraph (1)(a)—

(a) if any person on whom notice is served under paragraph (2) does not appear, unless service of the notice on that person is proved; or

(b) if no notice under paragraph (2) has been served, unless the sheriff is satisfied that in the circumstances it was reasonable not to serve notice on any person.

(6) The sheriff may make an order under this regulation only if he is satisfied that the product is a dangerous product.

(7) Where an order for the forfeiture of a product is made following an application by the procurator-fiscal under paragraph (1)(a), any person who appeared, or was entitled to appear to show cause why the product should not be forfeited may, within twenty-one days of the making of the order, appeal to the High Court by Bill of Suspension on the ground of an alleged miscarriage of justice; and section 182(5)(a) to (e) of the Criminal Procedure (Scotland) Act 1995 shall apply to an appeal under this paragraph as it applies to a stated case under Part X of that Act.

(8) An order following an application under paragraph (1)(a) shall not take effect—

(a) until the end of the period of twenty-one days beginning with the day after the day on which the order is made; or

(b) if an appeal is made under paragraph (7) within that period, until the appeal is determined or abandoned.

(9) An order under paragraph (1)(b) shall not take effect—

(a) until the end of the period within which an appeal against the order could be brought under the Criminal Procedure (Scotland) Act 1995; or

(b) if an appeal is made within that period, until the appeal is determined or abandoned.

(10) Subject to paragraph (11), a product forfeited under this regulation shall be destroyed in accordance with such directions as the sheriff may give.

(11) If he thinks fit, the sheriff may direct that the product be released to such person as he may specify, on condition that that person does not supply the product to any other person otherwise than as mentioned in paragraph (11) of regulation 18.

20. Offences

(1) A person who contravenes regulations 5 or 8(1)(a) shall be guilty of an offence and liable on conviction on indictment to imprisonment for a term not exceeding 12 months or to a fine not exceeding £20,000 or to both, or on summary conviction to imprisonment for a term not exceeding three months or to a fine not exceeding the statutory maximum or to both.

(2) A person who contravenes regulation 7(1), 7(3) (by failing to take any of the measures specified in regulation 7(4)), 8(1)(b)(i), (ii) or (iii) or 9(1) shall be guilty of an offence and liable on summary conviction to imprisonment for a term not exceeding three months or to a fine not exceeding level 5 on the standard scale or to both.

(3) A producer or distributor who does not give notice to an enforcement authority under regulation 9(1) in respect of a product he has placed on the market or supplied commits an offence where it is proved that he ought to have known that the product poses risks to consumers that are incompatible with the general safety requirement and he shall be liable on summary conviction to imprisonment for a term not exceeding three months or to a fine not exceeding level 5 on the standard scale or to both.

(4) A person who contravenes a safety notice shall be guilty of an offence and liable on conviction on indictment to imprisonment for a term not exceeding 12 months or to a fine not exceeding £20,000 or to both, or on summary conviction to imprisonment for a term not exceeding three months or to a fine not exceeding the statutory maximum or to both.

21. Test purchases

(1) An enforcement authority shall have power to organise appropriate checks on the safety properties of a product, on an adequate scale, up to the final stage of use or consumption and for that purpose may make a purchase of a product or authorise an officer of the authority to make a purchase of a product.

(2) Where a product purchased under paragraph (1) is submitted to a test and the test leads to—

(a) the bringing of proceedings for an offence in respect of a contravention in relation to the product of any requirement imposed by or under these Regulations or for the forfeiture of the product under regulation 18 or 19, or

(b) the serving of a safety notice in respect of the product, and

(c) the authority is requested to do so and it is practicable for the authority to comply with the request,

then the authority shall allow the person from whom the product was purchased, a person who is a party to the proceedings, on whom the notice was served or who has an interest in the product to which the notice relates, to have the product tested.

22. Powers of entry and search etc.

(1) An officer of an enforcement authority may at any reasonable hour and on production, if required, of his credentials exercise any of the powers conferred by the following provisions of this regulation.

(2) The officer may, for the purposes of ascertaining whether there has been a contravention of a requirement imposed by or under these Regulations, enter any premises other than premises occupied only as a person's residence and inspect any record or product.

(3) The officer may, for the purpose of ascertaining whether there has been a contravention of a requirement imposed by or under these Regulations, examine any procedure (including any arrangements for carrying out a test) connected with the production of a product.

(4) If the officer has reasonable grounds for suspecting that the product has not been placed on the market or supplied in the United Kingdom since it was manufactured or

imported he may for the purpose of ascertaining whether there has been a contravention in relation to the product of a requirement imposed by or under these Regulations—

    (a) require a person carrying on a commercial activity, or employed in connection with a commercial activity, to supply all necessary information relating to the activity, including by the production of records,

    (b) require any record which is stored in an electronic form and is accessible from the premises to be produced in a form—

      (i)   in which it can be taken away, and

      (ii) in which it is visible and legible.

    (c) for the purpose of ascertaining (by testing or otherwise) whether there has been any such contravention, seize and detain samples of the product,

    (d) take copies of, or of an entry in, any records produced by virtue of sub-paragraph (a).

  (5) If the officer has reasonable grounds for suspecting that there has been a contravention in relation to a product of a requirement imposed by or under these Regulations, he may—

    (a) for the purpose of ascertaining whether there has been any such contravention, require a person carrying on a commercial activity, or employed in connection with a commercial activity, to supply all necessary information relating to the activity, including by the production of records,

    (b) for the purpose of ascertaining whether there has been any such contravention, require any record which is stored in an electronic form and is accessible from the premises to be produced in a form—

      (i)   in which it can be taken away, and

      (ii) in which it is visible and legible,

    (c) for the purpose of ascertaining (by testing or otherwise) whether there has been any such contravention, seize and detain samples of the product,

    (d) take copies of, or of an entry in, any records produced by virtue of sub-paragraph (a).

  (6) The officer may seize and detain any products or records which he has reasonable grounds for believing may be required as evidence in proceedings for an offence in respect of a contravention of any requirement imposed by or under these Regulations.

  (7) If and to the extent that it is reasonably necessary to do so to prevent a contravention of any requirement imposed by or under these Regulations, the officer may, for the purpose of exercising his power under paragraphs (4) to (6) to seize products or records—

    (a) require any person having authority to do so to open any container or to open any vending machine; and

    (b) himself open or break open any such container or machine where a requirement made under sub-paragraph (a) in relation to the container or machine has not been complied with.

23. Provisions supplemental to regulation 22 and search warrants etc.

  (1) An officer seizing any products or records shall, before he leaves the premises, provide to the person from whom they were seized a written notice—

    (a) specifying the products (including the quantity thereof) and records seized,

    (b) stating the reasons for their seizure, and

    (c) explaining the right of appeal under regulation 25.

  (2) References in paragraph (1) and regulation 25 to the person from whom something has been seized, in relation to a case in which the power of seizure was exercisable by reason of the product having been found on any premises, are references to the occupier of the premises at the time of the seizure.

  (3) If a justice of the peace—

    (a) is satisfied by written information on oath that there are reasonable grounds for believing either—

      (i) that any products or records which an officer has power to inspect under regulation 22 are on any premises and that their inspection is likely to disclose evidence that there has been a contravention of any requirement imposed by or under these Regulations, or

      (ii) that such a contravention has taken place, is taking place or is about to take place on any premises, and

   (b) is also satisfied by such information either—

      (i) that admission to the premises has been or is likely to be refused and that notice of the intention to apply for a warrant under this paragraph has been given to the occupier, or

      (ii) that an application for admission, or the giving of such a notice, would defeat the object of the entry or that the premises are unoccupied or that the occupier is temporarily absent and it might defeat the object of the entry to await his return.

the justice may by warrant under his hand, which shall continue in force for a period of one month, authorise any officer of an enforcement authority to enter the premises, if need be by force.

   (4) An officer entering premises by virtue of regulation 22 or a warrant under paragraph (3) may take him such other persons and equipment as may appear to him necessary.

   (5) On leaving any premises which a person is authorised to enter by a warrant under paragraph (3), that person shall, if the premises are unoccupied or the occupier is temporarily absent—

   (a) leave the premises as effectively secured against trespassers as he found them,

   (b) attach a notice such as is mentioned in paragraph (1) in a prominent place at the premises.

   (6) Where a product seized by an officer of an enforcement authority under regulation 22 or 23 is submitted to a test, the authority shall inform the person mentioned in paragraph (1) of the result of the test and, if—

   (a) proceedings are brought for an offence in respect of a contravention in relation to the product of any requirement imposed by or under these Regulations or for the forfeiture of the product under regulation 18 or 19; or

   (b) a safety notice is served in respect of the product; and

   (c) the authority is requested to do so and it is practicable for him to comply with the request,

then the authority shall allow a person who is a party to the proceedings or, on whom the notice was served or who has an interest in the product to which the notice relates to have the product tested.

   (7) If a person who is not an officer of an enforcement authority purports to act as such under regulation 22 or under this regulation he shall be guilty of an offence and liable on summary conviction to a fine not exceeding level 5 on the standard scale.

   (8) In the application of this section to Scotland, the reference in paragraph (3) to a justice of the peace shall include a reference to a sheriff and the reference to written information on oath shall be construed as a reference to evidence on oath.

   (9) In the application of this section to Northern Ireland, the reference in paragraph (3) to a justice of the peace shall include a reference to a lay magistrate and the references to an information on oath shall be construed as a reference to a complaint on oath.

24. Obstruction of officers

   (1) A person who—

   (a) intentionally obstructs an officer of an enforcement authority who is acting in pursuance of any provision of regulations 22 or 23; or

   (b) intentionally fails to comply with a requirement made of him by an officer of an enforcement authority under any provision of those regulations; or

(c) without reasonable cause fails to give an officer of an enforcement authority who is so acting any other assistance or information which the officer may reasonably require of him for the purposes of the exercise of the officer's functions under any provision of those regulations,

shall be guilty of an offence and liable on summary conviction to a fine not exceeding level 5 on the standard scale.

(2) A person shall be guilty of an offence if, in giving any information which is required by him by virtue of paragraph (1)(c)—

(a) he makes a statement which he knows is false in a material particular; or

(b) he recklessly makes a statement which is false in a material particular.

(3) A person guilty of an offence under paragraph (2) shall be liable—

(a) on conviction on indictment, to a fine;

(b) on summary conviction, to a fine not exceeding the statutory maximum.

25. Appeals against detention of products and records

(1) A person referred to in regulation 23(1) may apply for an order requiring any product or record which is for the time being detained under regulation 22 or 23 by an enforcement authority or by an officer of such an authority to be released to him or to another person.

(2) An application under the preceding paragraph may be made—

(a) to any magistrates' court in which proceedings have been brought in England and Wales or Northern Ireland—

(i) for an offence in respect of a contravention in relation to the product of a requirement imposed by or under these Regulation, or

(ii) for the forfeiture of the product under regulation 18,

(b) where no such proceedings have been brought, by way of complaint to a magistrates' court;

(c) in Scotland, by summary application to the sheriff.

(3) On an application under paragraph (1) to a magistrates' court or to the sheriff, the court or the sheriff may make an order requiring a product or record to be released only if the court or sheriff is satisfied—

(a) that proceedings

(i) for an offence in respect of any contravention in relation to the product or, in the case of a record, the product to which the record relates, of any requirement imposed by or under these Regulations; or

(ii) for the forfeiture of the product or, in the case of a record, the product to which the record relate, under regulation 18 or 19,

have not been brought or, having been brought, have been concluded without the product being forfeited; and

(b) where no such proceedings have been brought, that more than six months have elapsed since the product or records was seized.

(4) In determining whether to make an order under this regulation requiring the release of a product or record the court or sheriff shall take all the circumstances into account including the results of any tests on the product which have been carried out by or on behalf of the enforcement authority and any statement made by the enforcement authority to the court or sheriff as to its intention to bring proceedings for an offence in respect of a contravention in relation to the product of any requirement imposed by or under these Regulations.

(5) Where—

(a) more than 12 months have elapsed since a product or records were seized and the enforcement authority has not commenced proceedings for an offence in respect of a contravention in relation to the product (or, in the case of records, the product to which the records relate) of any requirement imposed by or under these Regulations or for the forfeiture of the product under regulation 18 or 19, or

(b) an enforcement authority has brought proceedings for an offence as mentioned in sub-paragraph (a) and the proceedings were dismissed and all rights of appeal have been exercised or the time for appealing has expired,

the authority shall be under a duty to return the product or records detained under regulation 22 or 23 to the person from whom they were seized.

(6) Where the authority is satisfied that some other person has a better right to a product or record than the person from whom they were seized, the authority shall, instead of the duty in paragraph (5), be under a duty to return it to that other person or, as the case may be, to the person appearing to the authority to have the best right to the product or record in question.

(7) Where different persons claim to be entitled to the return of a product or record that is required to be returned under paragraph (5), then it may be retained for as long as it reasonably necessary for the determination in accordance with paragraph (6) of the person to whom it must be returned.

(8) A person aggrieved by an order made under this regulation by a magistrates' court in England and Wales or Northern Ireland, or by a decision of such a court not to make such an order, may appeal against that order or decision—

(a) in England and Wales, to the Crown Court;

(b) in Northern Ireland, to the county court;

and an order so made may contain such provision as appears to the court to be appropriate for delaying the coming into force of the order pending the making and determination of any appeal (including any application under section 111 of the Magistrates' Courts Act 1980 or article 146 of the Magistrates' Courts (Northern Ireland) Order 1981 (statement of case)).

26. Compensation for seizure and detention

Where an officer of an enforcement authority exercises any power under regulation 22 or 23 to seize and detain a product, the enforcement authority shall be liable to pay compensation to any person having an interest in the product in respect of any loss or damage caused by reason of the exercise of the power if—

(a) there has been no contravention in relation to the product of any requirement imposed by or under these Regulations, and

(b) the exercise of the power is not attributable to any neglect or default by that person.

27. Recovery of expenses of enforcement

(1) This regulation shall apply where a court—

(a) convicts a person of an offence in respect of a contravention in relation to a product of any requirement imposed by or under these Regulations, or

(b) makes an order under regulation 18 or 19 for the forfeiture of a product.

(2) The court may (in addition to any other order it may make as to costs or expenses) order the person convicted or, as the case may be, any person having an interest in the product to reimburse an enforcement authority for any expenditure which has been or may be incurred by that authority—

(a) in connection with any seizure or detention of the product by or on behalf of the authority, or

(b) in connection with any compliance by the authority with directions given by the court for the purposes of any order for the forfeiture of the product.

28. Power of Secretary of State to obtain information

(1) If the Secretary of State considers that, for the purposes of deciding whether to serve a safety notice, or to vary or revoke a safety notice which he has already served, he requires information or a sample of a product he may serve on a person a notice requiring him:

(a) to furnish to the Secretary of State, within a period specified in the notice, such information as is specified;

   (b) to produce such records as are specified in the notice at a time and place so specified (and to produce any such records which are stored in any electronic form in a form in which they are visible and legible) and to permit a person appointed by the Secretary of State for that purpose to take copies of the records at that time and place;

   (c) to produce such samples of a product as are specified in the notice at a time and place so specified.

(2) A person shall be guilty of an offence if he—

   (a) fails, without reasonable cause, to comply with a notice served on him under paragraph (1); or

   (b) in purporting to comply with a requirement which by virtue of paragraph (1)(a) or (b) is contained in such a notice—

      (i) furnishes information or records which he knows are false in a material particular, or

      (ii) recklessly furnishes information or records which are false in a material particular.

(3) A person guilty of an offence under paragraph (2) shall—

   (a) in the case of an offence under sub-paragraph (a) of that paragraph, be liable on summary conviction to a fine not exceeding level 5 on the standard scale; and

   (b) in the case of an offence under sub-paragraph (b) of that paragraph, be liable—

      (i) on conviction on indictment, to a fine;

      (ii) on summary conviction, to a fine not exceeding the statutory maximum.

29. Defence of due diligence

(1) Subject to the following provisions of this regulation, in proceedings against a person for an offence under these Regulations it shall be a defence for that person to show that he took all reasonable steps and exercised all due diligence to avoid committing the offence.

(2) Where in any proceedings against any person for such an offence the defence provided by paragraph (1) involves an allegation that the commission of the offence was due—

   (a) to the act or default of another, or

   (b) to reliance on information given by another,

that person shall not, without the leave of the court, be entitled to rely on the defence unless, not less than seven clear days before, in England, Wales and Northern Ireland, the hearing of the proceedings or, in Scotland, the trial diet, he has served a notice under paragraph (3) on the person bringing the proceedings.

(3) A notice under this paragraph shall give such information identifying or assisting in the identification of the person who—

   (a) committed the act or default, or

   (b) gave the information,

as is in the possession of the person serving the notice at the time he serves it.

(4) A person may not rely on the defence provided by paragraph (1) by reason of his reliance on information supplied by another, unless he shows that it was reasonable in all the circumstances to have relied on the information, having regard in particular—

   (a) to the steps which he took, and those which might reasonably have been taken, for the purpose of verifying the information; and

   (b) to whether he had any reason to disbelieve the information.

30. Defence in relation to antiques

. . .

31. Liability of person other than principal offender

(1) Where the commission by a person of an offence under these Regulations is due to an act or default committed by some other person in the course of a commercial activity of his, the other person shall be guilty of the offence and may be proceeded against and punished by virtue of this paragraph whether or not proceedings are taken against the first-mentioned person.

(2) Where a body corporate is guilty of an offence under these Regulations (including where it is so guilty by virtue of paragraph (1)) in respect of any act or default which is shown to have been committed with the consent or connivance of, or to be attributable to any neglect on the part of, any director, manager, secretary or other similar officer of the body corporate or any person who was purporting to act in any such capacity he, as well as the body corporate, shall be guilty of that offence and shall be liable to be proceeded against and punished accordingly.

(3) Where the affairs of a body corporate are managed by its members, paragraph (2) shall apply in relation to the acts and defaults of a member in connection with his functions of management as if he were a director of the body corporate.

(4) Where a Scottish partnership is guilty of an offence under these Regulations (including where it is so guilty by virtue of paragraph (1)) in respect of any act or default which is shown to have been committed with the consent or connivance of, or to be attributable to any neglect on the part of, a partner in the partnership, he, as well as the partnership, shall be guilty of that offence and shall be liable to be proceeded against and punished accordingly.

PART 4   MISCELLANEOUS

36. Market surveillance
In order to ensure a high level of consumer health and safety protection, enforcement authorities shall within the limits of their responsibility and to the extent of their ability undertake market surveillance of products employing appropriate means and procedures and co-operating with other enforcement authorities and competent authorities of other Member States which may include:
  (a) establishment, periodical updating and implementation of sectoral surveillance programmes by categories of products or risks and the monitoring of surveillance activities, findings and results,
  (b) follow-up and updating of scientific and technical knowledge concerning the safety of products,
  (c) the periodical review and assessment of the functioning of the control activities and their effectiveness and, if necessary revision of the surveillance approach and organisation put in place.

42. Civil proceedings
These Regulations shall not be construed as conferring any right of action in civil proceedings in respect of any loss or damage suffered in consequence of a contravention of these Regulations.

Regulatory Reform (Unsolicited Goods and Services Act 1971) (Directory Entries and Demands for Payment) Order 2005
(SI 2005, No. 55)

1   Citation, commencement, extent and interpretation
(2) This Order does not extend to Northern Ireland.

(3) Expressions used in this Order which are also used in the Unsolicited Goods and Services Act 1971 have the same meaning as in that Act.

3 Subordinate provisions

(1) The provisions of the Schedule are subordinate provisions for the purposes of section 4 of the Regulatory Reform Act 2001.

5 The Electronic Commerce (EC Directive) Regulations 2002

The Electronic Commerce (EC Directive) Regulations 2002 apply to—

(a) this Order; and

(b) any subordinate provisions order (within the meaning of section 4(4) of the Regulatory Reform Act 2001) made in respect of the Schedule to this Order.

Article 3   SCHEDULE

PART 1   PARTICULARS OF DIRECTORY OR PROPOSED DIRECTORY WHICH MUST BE GIVEN IN A NOTE

The particulars referred to in section 3(3) of the Unsolicited Goods and Services Act 1971 are:

(a) the amount of the charge;

(b) the name of the directory or proposed directory;

(c) the name of the person producing the directory;

(d) the geographic address at which that person is established;

(e) if the directory is to be available in printed form, the proposed date of publication of the directory or of the issue in which the entry is to be included;

(f) if the directory or the issue in which the entry is to be included is to be put on sale, the price at which it is to be offered for sale and the minimum number of copies which are to be available for sale;

(g) if the directory or the issue of the directory in which the entry is to be included is to be distributed free of charge (whether or not it is also to be put on sale), the minimum numbers of copies which are to be so distributed; and

(h) if the directory is or is to be made available in a form other than printed form, adequate details of how it may be accessed.

PART 2   CONDITIONS APPLYING TO INVOICE OR SIMILAR DOCUMENT WHICH DOES NOT ASSERT RIGHT TO PAYMENT

The conditions referred to in section 6(2) of the Unsolicited Goods and Services Act 1971 are that the invoice or similar document must:

(a) be clear, legible and comprehensible; and

(b) contain the following statement, displayed in uppercase lettering and in a manner that makes that statement readily apparent to a reasonable person reading that invoice or similar document—

"THIS IS NOT A DEMAND FOR PAYMENT THERE IS NO OBLIGATION TO PAY THIS IS NOT A BILL"

PART 3   INFORMATION REQUIRED IN WRITTEN NOTICE

The notice referred to in section 3B(1)(h)(i) of the Unsolicited Goods and Services Act 1971 must specify the following information:

(a) the fact that the earlier contract is to be renewed or extended;

(b) the commencement date of the new contract;

(c) the cost to the purchaser of the new contract; and

(d) the fact that the purchaser may, within 21 days, write to the person by whom the notice is given withdrawing his consent to the renewal or extension of the contract.

PART 4   INFORMATION TO BE GIVEN TO A PURCHASER

The following information must be given to the purchaser pursuant to section 3B(1)(i)(ii) of the Unsolicited Goods and Services Act 1971:

(a) the name of the relevant publisher; and

(b) the fact that, if the purchaser enters into the new contract:

    (i)   the other party to the new contract will be the relevant publisher; and

    (ii) the parties to the earlier contract and the new contract will be different.

Public Contracts Regulations 2006
(SI 2006, No. 5)

30. Criteria for the award of a public contract

(1) Subject to regulation 18(27) and to paragraphs (6) and (9) of this regulation, a contracting authority shall award a public contract on the basis of the offer which—

(a) is the most economically advantageous from the point of view of the contracting authority; or

(b) offers the lowest price.

(2) A contracting authority shall use criteria linked to the subject matter of the contract to determine that an offer is the most economically advantageous including quality, price, technical merit, aesthetic and functional characteristics, environmental characteristics, running costs, cost effectiveness, after sales service, technical assistance, delivery date and delivery period and period of completion.

(3) Where a contracting authority intends to award a public contract on the basis of the offer which is the most economically advantageous it shall state the weighting which it gives to each of the criteria chosen in the contract notice or in the contract documents or, in the case of a competitive dialogue procedure, in the descriptive document.

(6) If an offer for a public contract is abnormally low the contracting authority may reject that offer but only if it has—

(a) requested in writing an explanation of the offer or of those parts which it considers contribute to the offer being abnormally low;

(b) taken account of the evidence provided in response to a request in writing; and

(c) subsequently verified the offer or parts of the offer being abnormally low with the economic operator.

(10) In this regulation "offer" includes a bid by one part of a contracting authority to provide services, to carry out work or works or to make goods available to another part of the contracting authority when the former part is invited by the latter part to compete with the offers sought from other persons.

Transfer of Undertakings (Protection of Employment) Regulations 2006
(SI 2006, No. 246)

2. Interpretation

(1) In these Regulations—

"assigned" means assigned other than on a temporary basis;

"collective agreement", "collective bargaining" and "trade union" have the same meanings respectively as in the 1992 Act;

"contract of employment" means any agreement between an employee and his employer determining the terms and conditions of his employment;

references to "contractor" in regulation 3 shall include a sub-contractor;

"employee" means any individual who works for another person whether under a contract of service or apprenticeship or otherwise but does not include anyone who provides services under a contract for services and references to a person's employer shall be construed accordingly;

"insolvency practitioner" has the meaning given to the expression by Part XIII of the Insolvency Act 1986;

references to "organised grouping of employees" shall include a single employee;

"recognised" has the meaning given to the expression by section 178(3) of the 1992 Act;

"relevant transfer" means a transfer or a service provision change to which these Regulations apply in accordance with regulation 3 and "transferor" and "transferee" shall be construed accordingly and in the case of a service provision change falling within regulation 3(1)(b), "the transferor" means the person who carried out the activities prior to the service provision change and "the transferee" means the person who carries out the activities as a result of the service provision change;

"the 1992 Act" means the Trade Union and Labour Relations (Consolidation) Act 1992;

"the 1996 Act" means the Employment Rights Act 1996;

"the 1996 Tribunals Act" means the Employment Tribunals Act 1996;

"the 1981 Regulations" means the Transfer of Undertakings (Protection of Employment) Regulations 1981.

(2) For the purposes of these Regulations the representative of a trade union recognised by an employer is an official or other person authorised to carry on collective bargaining with that employer by that trade union.

(3) In the application of these Regulations to Northern Ireland the Regulations shall have effect as set out in Schedule 1.

3. A relevant transfer

(1) These Regulations apply to—

(a) a transfer of an undertaking, business or part of an undertaking or business situated immediately before the transfer in the United Kingdom to another person where there is a transfer of an economic entity which retains its identity;

(b) a service provision change, that is a situation in which—

(i) activities cease to be carried out by a person ("a client") on his own behalf and are carried out instead by another person on the client's behalf ("a contractor");

(ii) activities cease to be carried out by a contractor on a client's behalf (whether or not those activities had previously been carried out by the client on his own behalf) and are carried out instead by another person ("a subsequent contractor") on the client's behalf; or

(iii) activities cease to be carried out by a contractor or a subsequent contractor on a client's behalf (whether or not those activities had previously been carried out by the client on his own behalf) and are carried out instead by the client on his own behalf,

and in which the conditions set out in paragraph (3) are satisfied.

(2) In this regulation "economic entity" means an organised grouping of resources which has the objective of pursuing an economic activity, whether or not that activity is central or ancillary.

(3) The conditions referred to in paragraph (1)(b) are that—

(a) immediately before the service provision change—

     (i) there is an organised grouping of employees situated in Great Britain which has as its principal purpose the carrying out of the activities concerned on behalf of the client;

    (ii) the client intends that the activities will, following the service provision change, be carried out by the transferee other than in connection with a single specific event or task of short-term duration; and

  (b) the activities concerned do not consist wholly or mainly of the supply of goods for the client's use.

(4) Subject to paragraph (1), these Regulations apply to—

  (a) public and private undertakings engaged in economic activities whether or not they are operating for gain;

  (b) a transfer or service provision change howsoever effected notwithstanding—

     (i) that the transfer of an undertaking, business or part of an undertaking or business is governed or effected by the law of a country or territory outside the United Kingdom or that the service provision change is governed or effected by the law of a country or territory outside Great Britain;

    (ii) that the employment of persons employed in the undertaking, business or part transferred or, in the case of a service provision change, persons employed in the organised grouping of employees, is governed by any such law;

  (c) a transfer of an undertaking, business or part of an undertaking or business (which may also be a service provision change) where persons employed in the undertaking, business or part transferred ordinarily work outside the United Kingdom.

(5) An administrative reorganisation of public administrative authorities or the transfer of administrative functions between public administrative authorities is not a relevant transfer.

(6) A relevant transfer—

  (a) may be effected by a series of two or more transactions; and

  (b) may take place whether or not any property is transferred to the transferee by the transferor.

(7) Where, in consequence (whether directly or indirectly) of the transfer of an undertaking, business or part of an undertaking or business which was situated immediately before the transfer in the United Kingdom, a ship within the meaning of the Merchant Shipping Act 1995 registered in the United Kingdom ceases to be so registered, these Regulations shall not affect the right conferred by section 29 of that Act (right of seamen to be discharged when ship ceases to be registered in the United Kingdom) on a seaman employed in the ship.

4. Effect of relevant transfer on contracts of employment

(1) Except where objection is made under paragraph (7), a relevant transfer shall not operate so as to terminate the contract of employment of any person employed by the transferor and assigned to the organised grouping of resources or employees that is subject to the relevant transfer, which would otherwise be terminated by the transfer, but any such contract shall have effect after the transfer as if originally made between the person so employed and the transferee.

(2) Without prejudice to paragraph (1), but subject to paragraph (6), and regulations 8 and 15(9), on the completion of a relevant transfer—

  (a) all the transferor's rights, powers, duties and liabilities under or in connection with any such contract shall be transferred by virtue of this regulation to the transferee; and

  (b) any act or omission before the transfer is completed, of or in relation to the transferor in respect of that contract or a person assigned to that organised grouping of resources or employees, shall be deemed to have been an act or omission of or in relation to the transferee.

(3) Any reference in paragraph (1) to a person employed by the transferor and assigned to the organised grouping of resources or employees that is subject to a relevant transfer, is a reference to a person so employed immediately before the transfer, or who would have been so employed if he had not been dismissed in the circumstances described in regulation 7(1), including, where the transfer is effected by a series of two or more transactions, a person so employed and assigned or who would have been so employed and assigned immediately before any of those transactions.

(4) Subject to regulation 9, in respect of a contract of employment that is, or will be, transferred by paragraph (1), any purported variation of the contract shall be void if the sole or principal reason for the variation is—

    (a) the transfer itself; or

    (b) a reason connected with the transfer that is not an economic, technical or organisational reason entailing changes in the workforce.

(5) Paragraph (4) shall not prevent the employer and his employee, whose contract of employment is, or will be, transferred by paragraph (1), from agreeing a variation of that contract if the sole or principal reason for the variation is—

    (a) a reason connected with the transfer that is an economic, technical or organisational reason entailing changes in the workforce; or

    (b) a reason unconnected with the transfer.

(6) Paragraph (2) shall not transfer or otherwise affect the liability of any person to be prosecuted for, convicted of and sentenced for any offence.

(7) Paragraphs (1) and (2) shall not operate to transfer the contract of employment and the rights, powers, duties and liabilities under or in connection with it of an employee who informs the transferor or the transferee that he objects to becoming employed by the transferee.

(8) Subject to paragraphs (9) and (11), where an employee so objects, the relevant transfer shall operate so as to terminate his contract of employment with the transferor but he shall not be treated, for any purpose, as having been dismissed by the transferor.

(9) Subject to regulation 9, where a relevant transfer involves or would involve a substantial change in working conditions to the material detriment of a person whose contract of employment is or would be transferred under paragraph (1), such an employee may treat the contract of employment as having been terminated, and the employee shall be treated for any purpose as having been dismissed by the employer.

(10) No damages shall be payable by an employer as a result of a dismissal falling within paragraph (9) in respect of any failure by the employer to pay wages to an employee in respect of a notice period which the employee has failed to work.

(11) Paragraphs (1), (7), (8) and (9) are without prejudice to any right of an employee arising apart from these Regulations to terminate his contract of employment without notice in acceptance of a repudiatory breach of contract by his employer.

PART IV

···

EU Materials[*]

Treaty establishing the European Economic Community
(Treaty of Rome, 1957)
(Rome, 25 March 1957, revised)

Article 81 (ex Art. 85)

1. The following shall be prohibited as incompatible with the common market: all agreements between undertakings, decisions by associations of undertakings and concerted practices which may affect trade between Member States and which have as their object or effect the prevention, restriction or distortion of competition within the common market, and in particular those which:

(a) directly or indirectly fix purchase or selling prices or any other trading conditions;

(b) limit or control production, markets, technical development, or investment;

(c) share markets or sources of supply;

(d) apply dissimilar conditions to equivalent transactions with other trading parties, thereby placing them at a competitive disadvantage;

(e) make the conclusion of contracts subject to acceptance by the other parties of supplementary obligations which, by their nature or according to commercial usage, have no connection with the subject of such contracts.

2. Any agreements or decisions prohibited pursuant to this Article shall be automatically void.

3. The provisions of paragraph 1 may, however, be declared inapplicable in the case of:

— any agreement or category of agreements between undertakings;

— any decision or category of decisions by associations of undertakings;

— any concerted practice or category of concerted practices;

which contributes to improving the production or distribution of goods or to promoting technical or economic progress, while allowing consumers a fair share of the resulting benefit, and which does not:

(a) impose on the undertakings concerned restrictions which are not indispensable to the attainment of these objectives;

(b) afford such undertakings the possibility of eliminating competition in respect of a substantial part of the products in question.

Article 82 (ex Art. 86)

Any abuse by one or more undertakings of a dominant position within the common market or in a substantial part of it shall be prohibited as incompatible with the common market in so far as it may affect trade between Member States. Such abuse may, in particular, consist in:

(a) directly or indirectly imposing unfair purchase or selling prices or other unfair trading conditions;

---

[*] Materials to be found at and taken from http://europa.eu/index_en.htm and whose permission to reproduce them is gratefully acknowledged. Please note that 'only European Community official Documents printed in the Official Journal of the European Union are deemed authentic'.

    (b) limiting production, markets or technical development to the prejudice of consumers;

    (c) applying dissimilar conditions to equivalent transactions with other trading parties, thereby placing them at a competitive disadvantage;

    (d) making the conclusion of contracts subject to acceptance by the other parties of supplementary obligations which, by their nature or according to commercial usage, have no connection with the subject of such contracts.

Council Directive
of 25 July 1985

on the approximation of the laws, regulations and administrative provisions of the Member States concerning liability for defective products (85/374/EEC: L 210/29)

THE COUNCIL OF THE EUROPEAN COMMUNITIES,

Having regard to the Treaty establishing the European Economic Community, and in particular Article 100 thereof,

    Having regard to the proposal from the Commission,

    Having regard to the opinion of the European Parliament,

    Having regard to the opinion of the Economic and Social Committee,

    Whereas approximation of the laws of the Member States concerning the liability of the producer for damage caused by the defectiveness of his products is necessary because the existing divergences may distort competition and affect the movement of goods within the common market and entail a differing degree of protection of the consumer against damage caused by a defective product to his health or property;

    Whereas liability without fault on the part of the producer is the sole means of adequately solving the problem, peculiar to our age of increasing technicality, of a fair apportionment of the risks inherent in modern technological production;

    Whereas liability without fault should apply only to movables which have been industrially produced; whereas, as a result, it is appropriate to exclude liability for agricultural products and game, except where they have undergone a processing of an industrial nature which could cause a defect in these products; whereas the liability provided for in this Directive should also apply to movables which are used in the construction of immovables or are installed in immovables;

    Whereas protection of the consumer requires that all producers involved in the production process should be made liable, in so far as their finished product, component part or any raw material supplied by them was defective; whereas, for the same reason, liability should extend to importers of products into the Community and to persons who present themselves as producers by affixing their name, trade mark or other distinguishing feature or who supply a product the producer of which cannot be identified;

    Whereas, in situations where several persons are liable for the same damage, the protection of the consumer requires that the injured person should be able to claim full compensation for the damage from any one of them;

    Whereas, to protect the physical well-being and property of the consumer, the defectiveness of the product should be determined by reference not to its fitness for use but to the lack of the safety which the public at large is entitled to expect; whereas the safety is assessed by excluding any misuse of the product not reasonable under the circumstances;

Whereas a fair apportionment of risk between the injured person and the producer implies that the producer should be able to free himself from liability if he furnishes proof as to the existence of certain exonerating circumstances;

Whereas the protection of the consumer requires that the liability of the producer remains unaffected by acts or omissions of other persons having contributed to cause the damage; whereas, however, the contributory negligence of the injured person may be taken into account to reduce or disallow such liability;

Whereas the protection of the consumer, requires compensation for death and personal injury as well as compensation for damage to property; whereas the latter should nevertheless be limited to goods for private use or consumption and be subject to a deduction of a lower threshold of a fixed amount in order to avoid litigation in an excessive number of cases; whereas this Directive should not prejudice compensation for pain and suffering and other non-material damages payable, where appropriate, under the law applicable to the case;

Whereas a uniform period of limitation for the bringing of action for compensation is in the interests both of the injured person and of the producer;

Whereas products age in the course of time, higher safety standards are developed and the state of science and technology progresses; whereas, therefore, it would not be reasonable to make the producer liable for an unlimited period for the defectiveness of his product; whereas therefore, liability should expire after a reasonable length of time, without prejudice to claims pending at law;

Whereas, to achieve effective protection of consumers, no contractual derogation should be permitted as regards the liability of the producer in relation to the injured person;

Whereas under the legal systems of the Member States an injured party may have a claim for damages based on grounds of contractual liability or on grounds of non-contractual liability other than that provided for in this Directive; in so far as these provisions also serve to attain the objective of effective protection of consumers, they should remain unaffected by this Directive; whereas, in so far as effective protection of consumers in the sector of pharmaceutical products is already also attained in a Member State under a special liability system, claims based on this system should similarly remain possible;

Whereas, to the extent that liability for nuclear injury or damage is already covered in all Member States by adequate special rules, it has been possible to exclude damage of this type from the scope of this Directive;

Whereas, since the exclusion of primary agricultural products and game from the scope of this Directive may be felt, in certain Member States, in view of what is expected for the protection of consumers, to restrict unduly such protection, it should be possible for a Member State to extend liability to such products;

Whereas, for similar reasons, the possibility offered to a producer to free himself from liability if he proves that the state of scientific and technical knowledge at the time when he put the product into circulation was not such as to enable the existence of a defect to be discovered may be felt in certain Member States to restrict unduly the protection of the consumer; whereas it should therefore be possible for a Member State to maintain in its legislation or to provide by new legislation that this exonerating circumstance is not admitted; whereas, in the case of new legislation, making use of this derogation should, however, be subject to a Community stand-still procedure, in order to raise, if possible, the level of protection in a uniform manner throughout the Community;

Whereas, taking into account the legal traditions in most of the Member States, it is inappropriate to set any financial ceiling on the producer's liability without fault; whereas, in so far as there are, however, differing traditions, it seems possible to admit that a Member State may derogate from the principle of unlimited liability by providing a limit for the total liability of the producer for damage resulting from a death or personal injury and caused by identical items with the same defect, provided that this limit is established at a level sufficiently high to guarantee adequate protection of the consumer and the correct functioning of the common market;

Whereas the harmonization resulting from this cannot be total at the present stage, but opens the way towards greater harmonization; whereas it is therefore necessary that the Council receive at regular intervals, reports from the Commission on the application of this Directive, accompanied, as the case may be, by appropriate proposals;

Whereas it is particularly important in this respect that a re-examination be carried out of those parts of the Directive relating to the derogations open to the Member States, at the expiry of a period of sufficient length to gather practical experience on the effects of these derogations on the protection of consumers and on the functioning of the common market, HAS ADOPTED THIS DIRECTIVE:

Article 1
The producer shall be liable for damage caused by a defect in his product.

Article 2
For the purpose of this Directive "product" means all movables, with the exception of primary agricultural products and game, even though incorporated into another movable or into an immovable. "Primary agricultural products" means the products of the soil, of stock-farming and of fisheries, excluding products which have undergone initial processing. "Product" includes electricity.

Article 3
1. "Producer" means the manufacturer of a finished product, the producer of any raw material or the manufacturer of a component part and any person who, by putting his name, trade mark or other distinguishing feature on the product presents himself as its producer.

Without prejudice to the liability of the producer, any person who imports into the Community a product for sale, hire, leasing or any form of distribution in the course of his business shall be deemed to be a producer within the meaning of this Directive and shall be responsible as a producer.

3. Where the producer of the product cannot be identified, each supplier of the product shall be treated as its producer unless he informs the injured person, within a reasonable time, of the identity of the producer or of the person who supplied him with the product. The same shall apply, in the case of an imported product, if this product does not indicate the identity of the importer referred to in paragraph 2, even if the name of the producer is indicated.

Article 4
The injured person shall be required to prove the damage, the defect and the causal relationship between defect and damage.

Article 5
Where, as a result of the provisions of this Directive, two or more persons are liable for the same damage, they shall be liable jointly and severally, without prejudice to the provisions of national law concerning the rights of contribution or recourse.

Article 6
1. A product is defective when it does not provide the safety which a person is entitled to expect, taking all circumstances into account, including:
    (a) the presentation of the product;
    (b) the use to which it could reasonably be expected that the product would be put;
    (c) the time when the product was put into circulation.
2. A product shall not be considered defective for the sole reason that a better product is subsequently put into circulation.

Article 7
The producer shall not be liable as a result of this Directive if he proves:
    (a) that he did not put the product into circulation; or

(b) that, having regard to the circumstances, it is probable that the defect which caused the damage did not exist at the time when the product was put into circulation by him or that this defect came into being afterwards; or

(c) that the product was neither manufactured by him for sale or any form of distribution for economic purpose nor manufactured or distributed by him in the course of his business; or

(d) that the defect is due to compliance of the product with mandatory regulations issued by the public authorities; or

(e) that the state of scientific and technical knowledge at the time when he put the product into circulation was not such as to enable the existence of the defect to be discovered; or

(f) in the case of a manufacturer of a component, that the defect is attributable to the design of the product in which the component has been fitted or to the instructions given by the manufacturer of the product.

Article 8

1. Without prejudice to the provisions of national law concerning the right of contribution or recourse, the liability of the producer shall not be reduced when the damage is caused both by a defect in product and by the act or omission of a third party.

2. The liability of the producer may be reduced or disallowed when, having regard to all the circumstances, the damage is caused both by a defect in the product and by the fault of the injured person or any person for whom the injured person is responsible.

Article 9

For the purpose of Article 1, "damage" means:

(a) damage caused by death or by personal injuries;

(b) damage to, or destruction of, any item of property other than the defective product itself, with a lower threshold of 500 ECU, provided that the item of property:

   (i) is of a type ordinarily intended for private use or consumption, and

   (ii) was used by the injured person mainly for his own private use or consumption.

This Article shall be without prejudice to national provisions relating to non-material damage.

Article 10

1. Member States shall provide in their legislation that a limitation period of three years shall apply to proceedings for the recovery of damages as provided for in this Directive. The limitation period shall begin to run from the day on which the plaintiff became aware, or should reasonably have become aware, of the damage, the defect and the identity of the producer.

2. The laws of Member States regulating suspension or interruption of the limitation period shall not be affected by this Directive.

Article 11

Member States shall provide in their legislation that the rights conferred upon the injured person pursuant to this Directive shall be extinguished upon the expiry of a period of 10 years from the date on which the producer put into circulation the actual product which caused the damage, unless the injured person has in the meantime instituted proceedings against the producer.

Article 12

The liability of the producer arising from this Directive may not, in relation to the injured person, be limited or excluded by a provision limiting his liability or exempting him from liability.

Article 13

This Directive shall not affect any rights which an injured person may have according to the rules of the law of contractual or non-contractual liability or a special liability system existing at the moment when this Directive is notified.

Article 14

This Directive shall not apply to injury or damage arising from nuclear accidents and covered by international conventions ratified by the Member States.

Article 15

    1. Each Member State may:

        (a) by way of derogation from Article 2, provide in its legislation that within the meaning of Article 1 of this Directive "product" also means primary agricultural products and game;

        (b) by way of derogation from Article 7(e), maintain or, subject to the procedure set out in paragraph 2 of this Article, provide in this legislation that the producer shall be liable even if he proves that the state of scientific and technical knowledge at the time when he put the product into circulation was not such as to enable the existence of a defect to be discovered.

    2. A Member State wishing to introduce the measure specified in paragraph 1(b) shall communicate the text of the proposed measure to the Commission. The Commission shall inform the other Member States thereof.

    The Member State concerned shall hold the proposed measure in abeyance for nine months after the Commission is informed and provided that in the meantime the Commission has not submitted to the Council a proposal amending this Directive on the relevant matter. However, if within three months of receiving the said information, the Commission does not advise the Member State concerned that it intends submitting such a proposal to the Council, the Member State may take the proposed measure immediately.

    If the Commission does submit to the Council such a proposal amending this Directive within the aforementioned nine months, the Member State concerned shall hold the proposed measure in abeyance for a further period of 18 months from the date on which the proposal is submitted.

    3. Ten years after the date of notification of this Directive, the Commission shall submit to the Council a report on the effect that rulings by the courts as to the application of Article 7(e) and of paragraph 1(b) of this Article have on consumer protection and the functioning of the common market. In the light of this report the Council, acting on a proposal from the Commission and pursuant to the terms of Article 100 of the Treaty, shall decide whether to repeal Article 7(e).

Article 16

    1. Any Member State may provide that a producer's total liability for damage resulting from a death or personal injury and caused by identical items with the same defect shall be limited to an amount which may not be less than 70 million ECU.

    2. Ten years after the date of notification of this Directive, the Commission shall submit to the Council a report on the effect on consumer protection and the functioning of the common market of the implementation of the financial limit on liability by those Member States which have used the option provided for in paragraph 1. In the light of this report the Council, acting on a proposal from the Commission and pursuant to the terms of Article 100 of the Treaty, shall decide whether to repeal paragraph 1.

Article 17

This Directive shall not apply to products put into circulation before the date on which the provisions referred to in Article 19 enter into force.

Article 18

1. For the purposes of this Directive, the ECU shall be that defined by Regulation (EEC) No. 3180/78, as amended by Regulation (EEC) No. 2626/84. The equivalent in national currency shall initially be calculated at the rate obtaining on the date of adoption of this Directive.

2. Every five years the Council, acting on a proposal from the Commission, shall examine and, if need be, revise the amounts in this Directive, in the light of economic and monetary trends in the Community.

Article 19

1. Member States shall bring into force, not later than three years from the date of notification of this Directive, the laws, regulations and administrative provisions necessary to comply with this Directive. They shall forthwith inform the Commission thereof.

2. The procedure set out in Article 15(2) shall apply from the date of notification of this Directive.

Article 20

Member States shall communicate to the Commission the texts of the main provisions of national law which they subsequently adopt in the field governed by this Directive.

Article 21

Every five years the Commission shall present a report to the Council on the application of this Directive and, if necessary, shall submit appropriate proposals to it.

Article 22

This Directive is addressed to the Member States.
Done at Brussels, 25 July 1985.

Council Directive
of 5 April 1993
on unfair terms in consumer contracts
(93/13/EEC: L 95/29)

THE COUNCIL OF THE EUROPEAN COMMUNITIES,
Having regard to the Treaty establishing the European Economic Community, and in particular Article 100A thereof,

Having regard to the proposal from the Commission,

In cooperation with the European Parliament,

Having regard to the opinion of the Economic and Social Committee,

Whereas it is necessary to adopt measures with the aim of progressively establishing the internal market before 31 December 1992; whereas the internal market comprises an area without internal frontiers in which goods, persons, services and capital move freely;

Whereas the laws of Member States relating to the terms of contract between the seller of goods or supplier of services, on the one hand, and the consumer of them, on the other hand, show many disparities, with the result that the national markets for the sale of goods and services to consumers differ from each other and that distortions of competition may arise amongst the sellers and suppliers, notably when they sell and supply in other Member States;

Whereas, in particular, the laws of Member States relating to unfair terms in consumer contracts show marked divergences;

Whereas it is the responsibility of the Member States to ensure that contracts concluded with consumers do not contain unfair terms;

Whereas, generally speaking, consumers do not know the rules of law which, in Member States other than their own, govern contracts for the sale of goods or services; whereas this lack of awareness may deter them from direct transactions for the purchase of goods or services in another Member State;

Whereas, in order to facilitate the establishment of the internal market and to safeguard the citizen in his role as consumer when acquiring goods and services under contracts which are governed by the laws of Member States other than his own, it is essential to remove unfair terms from those contracts;

Whereas sellers of goods and suppliers of services will thereby be helped in their task of selling goods and supplying services, both at home and throughout the internal market; whereas competition will thus be stimulated, so contributing to increased choice for Community citizens as consumers;

Whereas the two Community programmes for a consumer protection and information policy underlined the importance of safeguarding consumers in the matter of unfair terms of contract; whereas this protection ought to be provided by laws and regulations which are either harmonised at Community level or adopted directly at that level;

Whereas in accordance with the principle laid down under the heading "Protection of the economic interests of the consumers", as stated in those programmes: "acquirers of goods and services should be protected against the abuse of power by the seller or supplier, in particular against one-sided standard contracts and the unfair exclusion of essential rights in contracts";

Whereas more effective protection of the consumer can be achieved by adopting uniform rules of law in the matter of unfair terms; whereas those rules should apply to all contracts concluded between sellers or suppliers and consumers; whereas as a result *inter alia* contracts relating to employment, contracts relating to succession rights, contracts relating to rights under family law and contracts relating to the incorporation and organisation of companies or partnership agreements must be excluded from this Directive;

Whereas the consumer must receive equal protection under contracts concluded by word of mouth and written contracts regardless, in the latter case, of whether the terms of the contract are contained in one or more documents;

Whereas, however, as they now stand, national laws allow only partial harmonisation to be envisaged; whereas, in particular, only contractual terms which have not been individually negotiated are covered by this Directive; whereas Member States should have the option, with due regard for the Treaty, to afford consumers a higher level of protection through national provisions that are more stringent than those of this Directive;

Whereas the statutory or regulatory provisions of the Member States which directly or indirectly determine the terms of consumer contracts are presumed not to contain unfair terms; whereas, therefore, it does not appear to be necessary to subject the terms which reflect mandatory statutory or regulatory provisions and the principles or provisions of international contraventions to which the Member States or the Community are party; whereas in that respect the wording "mandatory statutory or regulatory provisions" in Article 1(2) also covers rules which, according to the law, shall apply between the contracting parties provided that no other arrangements have been established;

Whereas Member States must however ensure that unfair terms are not included, particularly because this Directive also applies to trades, business or professions of a public nature;

Whereas it is necessary to fix in a general way the criteria for assessing the unfair character of contract terms;

Whereas the assessment, according to the general criteria chosen, of the unfair character of terms, in particular in sale or supply activities of a public nature providing collective services which take account of solidarity among users, must be supplemented by a means of making an overall evaluation of the different interests involved; whereas this constitutes the requirement of good faith; whereas, in making an assessment of good faith, particular regard shall be had to the strength of the bargaining positions of the parties, whether the consumer had an inducement to agree to the term and whether the goods or services were sold or supplied to the special order of the consumer; whereas the requirement of good faith may be satisfied by the seller or supplier where he deals fairly and equitably with the other party whose legitimate interests he has to take into account;

Whereas, for the purposes of this Directive, the annexed list of terms can be of indicative value only and, because of the cause of the minimal character of the Directive, the scope of these terms may be the subject of amplification or more restrictive editing by the Member States in their national laws;

Whereas the nature of goods or services should have an influence on assessing the unfairness of contractual terms;

Whereas, for the purposes of this Directive, assessment of unfair character shall not be made of terms which describe the main subject matter of the contract nor the quality/price ratio of the goods or services supplied; whereas the main subject matter of the contract and the price/ quality ratio may nevertheless be taken into account in assessing the fairness of other terms; whereas it follows, *inter alia,* that in insurance contracts, the terms which clearly define or circumscribe the insured risk and the insurer's liability shall not be subject to such assessment since these restrictions are taken into account in calculating the premium paid by the consumer;

Whereas contracts should be drafted in plain, intelligible language, the consumer should actually be given an opportunity to examine all the terms and, if in doubt, the interpretation most favourable to the consumer should prevail;

Whereas Member States should ensure that unfair terms are not used in contracts concluded with consumers by a seller or supplier and that if, nevertheless, such terms are so used, they will not bind the consumer, and the contract will continue to bind the parties upon those terms if it is capable of continuing in existence without the unfair provisions;

Whereas there is a risk that, in certain cases, the consumer may be deprived of protection under this Directive by designating the law of a non-Member country as the law applicable to the contract; whereas provisions should therefore be included in this Directive designed to avert this risk;

Whereas persons or organisations, if regarded under the law of a Member State as having a legitimate interest in the matter, must have facilities for initiating proceedings concerning terms of contract drawn up for general use in contracts concluded with consumers, and in particular unfair terms, either before a court or before an administrative authority competent to decide upon complaints or to initiate appropriate legal proceedings; whereas this possibility does not, however, entail prior verification of the general conditions obtaining in individual economic sectors;

Whereas the courts or administrative authorities of the Member States must have at their disposal adequate and effective means of preventing the continued application of unfair terms in consumer contracts,

HAS ADOPTED THIS DIRECTIVE:

Article 1

1. The purpose of this Directive is to approximate the laws, regulations and administrative provisions of the Member States relating to unfair terms in contracts concluded between a seller or supplier and a consumer.

2. The contractual terms which reflect mandatory statutory or regulatory provisions and the provisions or principles of international conventions to which the Member States or the Community are party, particularly in the transport area, shall not be subject to the provisions of this Directive.

Article 2

For the purposes of this Directive:

(a) "unfair terms" means the contractual terms defined in Article 3;

(b) "consumer" means any natural person who, in contracts covered by this Directive, is acting for purposes which are outside his trade, business or profession;

(c) "seller or supplier" means any natural or legal person who, in contracts covered by this Directive, is acting for purposes relating to his trade, business or profession, whether publicly owned or privately owned.

Article 3

1. A contractual term which has not been individually negotiated shall be regarded as unfair if, contrary to the requirement of good faith, it causes a significant imbalance in the parties' rights and obligations arising under the contract, to the detriment of the consumer.

2. A term shall always be regarded as not individually negotiated where it has been drafted in advance and the consumer has therefore not been able to influence the substance of the term, particularly in the context of a pre-formulated standard contract.

The fact that certain aspects of a term or one specific term have been individually negotiated shall not exclude the application of this Article to the rest of a contract if an overall assessment of the contract indicates that it is nevertheless a pre-formulated standard contract.

Where any seller or supplier claims that a standard term has been individually negotiated, the burden of proof in this respect shall be incumbent on him.

3. The Annex shall contain an indicative and non-exhaustive list of the terms which may be regarded as unfair.

Article 4

1. Without prejudice to Article 7, the unfairness of a contractual term shall be assessed, taking into account the nature of the goods or services for which the contract was concluded and by referring, at the time of conclusion of the contract, to all the circumstances attending the conclusion of the contract and to all the other terms of the contract or of another contract on which it is dependent.

2. Assessment of the unfair nature of the terms shall relate neither to the definition of the main subject matter of the contract nor to the adequacy of the price and remuneration, on the one hand, as against the services or goods supplies in exchange, on the other, in so far as these terms are in plain intelligible language.

Article 5

In the case of contracts where all or certain terms offered to the consumer are in writing, these terms must always be drafted in plain, intelligible language.

Where there is doubt about the meaning of a term, the interpretation most favourable to the consumer shall prevail. This rule on interpretation shall not apply in the context of the procedures laid down in Article 7(2).

Article 6

1. Member States shall lay down that unfair terms used in a contract concluded with a consumer by a seller or supplier shall, as provided for under their national law, not be binding on the consumer and that the contract shall continue to bind the parties upon those terms if it is capable of continuing in existence without the unfair terms.

2. Member States shall take the necessary measures to ensure that the consumer does not lose the protection granted by this Directive by virtue of the choice of the law of a non-Member country as the law applicable to the contract if the latter has a close connection with the territory of the Member States.

Article 7

1. Member States shall ensure that, in the interests of consumers and of competitors, adequate and effective means exist to prevent the continued use of unfair terms in contracts concluded with consumers by sellers or suppliers.

2. The means referred to in paragraph 1 shall include provisions whereby persons or organisations, having a legitimate interest under national law in protecting consumers, may take action according to the national law concerned before the courts or before competent

administrative bodies for a decision as to whether contractual terms drawn up for general use are unfair, so that they can apply appropriate and effective means to prevent the continued use of such terms.

3. With due regard for national laws, the legal remedies referred to in paragraph 2 may be directed separately or jointly against a number of sellers or suppliers from the same economic sector or their associations which use or recommend the use of the same general contractual terms or similar terms.

Article 8
Member States may adopt or retain the most stringent provisions compatible with the Treaty in the area covered by this Directive, to ensure a maximum degree of protection for the consumer.

Article 9
The Commission shall present a report to the European Parliament and to the Council concerning the application of this Directive five years at the latest after the date in Article 10(1).

Article 10
1. Member States shall bring into force the laws, regulations and administrative provisions necessary to comply with this Directive no later than 31 December 1994. They shall forthwith inform the Commission thereof.

These provisions shall be applicable to all contracts concluded after 31 December 1994.

2. When Member States adopt these measures, they shall contain a reference to this Directive or shall be accompanied by such reference on the occasion of their official publication. The methods of making such a reference shall be laid down by the Member States.

3. Member States shall communicate the main provisions of national law which they adopt in the field covered by this Directive to the Commission.

Article 11
This Directive is addressed to the Member States.

Done at Luxembourg, 5 April 1993.

ANNEX   TERMS REFERRED TO IN ARTICLE 3(3)

1   Terms which have the object or effect of:
  (a) excluding or limiting the legal liability of a seller or supplier in the event of the death of a consumer or personal injury to the latter resulting from an act or omission of that seller or supplier;
  (b) inappropriately excluding or limiting the legal rights of the consumer *vis-à-vis* the seller or supplier or another party in the event of total or partial non-performance or inadequate performance by the seller or supplier of any of the contractual obligations, including the option of offsetting a debt owed to the seller or supplier against any claim which the consumer may have against him;
  (c) making an agreement binding on the consumer whereas provision of services by the seller or supplier is subject to a condition whose realisation depends on his own will alone;
  (d) permitting the seller or supplier to retain sums paid by the consumer where the latter decides not to conclude or perform the contract, without providing for the consumer to receive compensation of an equivalent amount from the seller or supplier where the latter is the party cancelling the contract;
  (e) requiring any consumer who fails to fulfil his obligation to pay a disproportionately high sum in compensation;

(f) authorising the seller or supplier to dissolve the contract on a discretionary basis where the same facility is not granted to the consumer, or permitting the seller or supplier to retain the sums paid for services not yet supplied by him where it is the seller or supplier himself who dissolves the contract;

(g) enabling the seller or supplier to terminate a contract of indeterminate duration without reasonable notice except where there are serious grounds for doing so;

(h) automatically extending a contract of fixed duration where the consumer does not indicate otherwise, when the deadline fixed for the consumer to express this desire not to extend the contract is unreasonably early;

(i) irrevocably binding the consumer to terms with which he had no real opportunity of becoming acquainted before the conclusion of the contract;

(j) enabling the seller or supplier to alter the terms of the contract unilaterally without a valid reason which is specified in the contract;

(k) enabling the seller or supplier to alter unilaterally without a valid reason any characteristics of the product or service to be provided;

(l) providing for the price of goods to be determined at the time of delivery or allowing a seller of goods or supplier of services to increase their price without in both cases giving the consumer the corresponding right to cancel the contract if the final price is too high in relation to the price agreed when the contract was concluded;

(m) giving the seller or supplier the right to determine whether the goods or services supplied are in conformity with the contract, or giving him the exclusive right to interpret any term of the contract;

(n) limiting the seller's or supplier's obligation to respect commitments undertaken by his agents or making his commitments subject to compliance with a particular formality;

(o) obliging the consumer to fulfil all his obligations where the seller or supplier does not perform his;

(p) giving the seller or supplier the possibility of transferring his rights and obligations under the contract, where this may serve to reduce the guarantees for the consumer, without the latter's agreement;

(q) excluding or hindering the consumer's right to take legal action or exercise any other legal remedy, particularly by requiring the consumer to take disputes exclusively to arbitration not covered by legal provisions, unduly restricting the evidence available to him or imposing on him a burden of proof which, according to the applicable law, should lie with another party to the contract.

2 Scope of subparagraphs (g), (j) and (l)

(a) Subparagraph (g) is without hindrance to terms by which a supplier of financial services reserves the right to terminate unilaterally a contract of indeterminate duration without notice where there is a valid reason, provided that the supplier is required to inform the other contracting party or parties thereof immediately.

(b) Subparagraph (j) is without hindrance to terms under which a supplier of financial services reserves the right to alter the rate of interest payable by the consumer or due to the latter, or the amount of other charges for financial services without notice where there is a valid reason, provided that the supplier is required to inform the other contracting party or parties thereof at the earliest opportunity and that the latter are free to dissolve the contract immediately.

Subparagraph (j) is also without hindrance to terms under which a seller or supplier reserves the right to alter unilaterally the conditions of a contract of indeterminate duration, provided that he is required to inform the consumer with reasonable notice and that the consumer is free to dissolve the contract.

(c) Subparagraphs (g), (j) and (l) do not apply to:
  — transactions in transferable securities, financial instruments and other products or services where the price is linked to fluctuations in a stock exchange quotation or index or a financial market rate that the seller or supplier does not control;

(d) Subparagraph (l) is without hindrance to price-indexation clauses, where lawful, provided that the method by which prices vary is explicitly described.

Directive 2000/31/EC of the European Parliament and of the Council
of 8 June 2000

on certain legal aspects of information society services, in particular electronic commerce, in the Internal Market (Directive on electronic commerce)

CHAPTER II   PRINCIPLES

Section 3   Contracts concluded by electronic means

Article 9   Treatment of contracts

1. Member States shall ensure that their legal system allows contracts to be concluded by electronic means. Member States shall in particular ensure that the legal requirements applicable to the contractual process neither create obstacles for the use of electronic contracts nor result in such contracts being deprived of legal effectiveness and validity on account of their having been made by electronic means.

2. Member States may lay down that paragraph 1 shall not apply to all or certain contracts falling into one of the following categories:

  (a) contracts that create or transfer rights in real estate, except for rental rights;
  (b) contracts requiring by law the involvement of courts, public authorities or professions exercising public authority;
  (c) contracts of suretyship granted and on collateral securities furnished by persons acting for purposes outside their trade, business or profession;
  (d) contracts governed by family law or by the law of succession.

3. Member States shall indicate to the Commission the categories referred to in paragraph 2 to which they do not apply paragraph 1. Member States shall submit to the Commission every five years a report on the application of paragraph 2 explaining the reasons why they consider it necessary to maintain the category referred to in paragraph 2(b) to which they do not apply paragraph 1.

Article 10   Information to be provided

1. In addition to other information requirements established by Community law, Member States shall ensure, except when otherwise agreed by parties who are not consumers, that at least the following information is given by the service provider clearly, comprehensibly and unambiguously and prior to the order being placed by the recipient of the service:

  (a) the different technical steps to follow to conclude the contract;
  (b) whether or not the concluded contract will be filed by the service provider and whether it will be accessible;
  (c) the technical means for identifying and correcting input errors prior to the placing of the order;
  (d) the languages offered for the conclusion of the contract.

2. Member States shall ensure that, except when otherwise agreed by parties who are not consumers, the service provider indicates any relevant codes of conduct to which he subscribes and information on how those codes can be consulted electronically.

3. Contract terms and general conditions provided to the recipient must be made available in a way that allows him to store and reproduce them.

4. Paragraphs 1 and 2 shall not apply to contracts concluded exclusively by exchange of electronic mail or by equivalent individual communications.

Article 11   Placing of the order

1. Member States shall ensure, except when otherwise agreed by parties who are not consumers, that in cases where the recipient of the service places his order through technological means, the following principles apply:

— the service provider has to acknowledge the receipt of the recipient's order without undue delay and by electronic means,

— the order and the acknowledgement of receipt are deemed to be received when the parties to whom they are addressed are able to access them.

2. Member States shall ensure that, except when otherwise agreed by parties who are not consumers, the service provider makes available to the recipient of the service appropriate, effective and accessible technical means allowing him to identify and correct input errors, prior to the placing of the order.

3. Paragraph 1, first indent, and paragraph 2 shall not apply to contracts concluded exclusively by exchange of electronic mail or by equivalent individual communications.

Directive 2001/95/EC of the European Parliament and of the Council

of 3 December 2001
on general product safety

THE EUROPEAN PARLIAMENT AND THE COUNCIL OF THE EUROPEAN UNION,

Having regard to the Treaty establishing the European Community, and in particular Article 95 thereof,

Having regard to the proposal from the Commission,

Having regard to the opinion of the Economic and Social Committee,

Acting in accordance with the procedure referred to in Article 251 of the Treaty, in the light of the joint text approved by the Conciliation Committee on 2 August 2001,

Whereas:

(1) Under Article 16 of Council Directive 92/59/EEC of 29 June 1992 on general product safety, the Council was to decide, four years after the date set for the implementation of the said Directive, on the basis of a report of the Commission on the experience acquired, together with appropriate proposals, whether to adjust Directive 92/59/EEC. It is necessary to amend Directive 92/59/EEC in several respects, in order to complete, reinforce or clarify some of its provisions in the light of experience as well as new and relevant developments on consumer product safety, together with the changes made to the Treaty, especially in Articles 152 concerning public health and 153 concerning consumer protection, and in the light of the precautionary principle. Directive 92/59/EEC should therefore be recast in the interest of clarity. This recasting leaves the safety of services outside the scope of this Directive, since the Commission intends to identify the needs, possibilities and priorities for Community action on the safety of services and liability of service providers, with a view to presenting appropriate proposals.

(2) It is important to adopt measures with the aim of improving the functioning of the internal market, comprising an area without internal frontiers in which the free movement of goods, persons, services and capital is assured.

(3) In the absence of Community provisions, horizontal legislation of the Member States on product safety, imposing in particular a general obligation on economic operators to market only safe products, might differ in the level of protection afforded to consumers. Such

disparities, and the absence of horizontal legislation in some Member States, would be liable to create barriers to trade and distortion of competition within the internal market.

(4) In order to ensure a high level of consumer protection, the Community must contribute to protecting the health and safety of consumers. Horizontal Community legislation introducing a general product safety requirement, and containing provisions on the general obligations of producers and distributors, on the enforcement of Community product safety requirements and on rapid exchange of information and action at Community level in certain cases, should contribute to that aim.

(5) It is very difficult to adopt Community legislation for every product which exists or which may be developed; there is a need for a broad-based, legislative framework of a horizontal nature to deal with such products, and also to cover lacunae, in particular pending revision of the existing specific legislation, and to complement provisions in existing or forthcoming specific legislation, in particular with a view to ensuring a high level of protection of safety and health of consumers, as required by Article 95 of the Treaty.

(6) It is therefore necessary to establish at Community level a general safety requirement for any product placed on the market, or otherwise supplied or made available to consumers, intended for consumers, or likely to be used by consumers under reasonably foreseeable conditions even if not intended for them. In all these cases the products under consideration can pose risks for the health and safety of consumers which must be prevented. Certain secondhand goods should nevertheless be excluded by their very nature.

(7) This Directive should apply to products irrespective of the selling techniques, including distance and electronic selling.

(8) The safety of products should be assessed taking into account all the relevant aspects, in particular the categories of consumers which can be particularly vulnerable to the risks posed by the products under consideration, in particular children and the elderly.

(9) This Directive does not cover services, but in order to secure the attainment of the protection objectives in question, its provisions should also apply to products that are supplied or made available to consumers in the context of service provision for use by them. The safety of the equipment used by service providers themselves to supply a service to consumers does not come within the scope of this Directive since it has to be dealt within conjunction with the safety of the service provided. In particular, equipment on which consumers ride or travel which is operated by a service provider is excluded from the scope of this Directive.

(10) Products which are designed exclusively for professional use but have subsequently migrated to the consumer market should be subject to the requirements of this Directive because they can pose risks to consumer health and safety when used under reasonably foreseeable conditions.

(11) In the absence of more specific provisions, within the framework of Community legislation covering safety of the products concerned, all the provisions of this Directive should apply in order to ensure consumer health and safety.

(12) If specific Community legislation sets out safety requirements covering only certain risks or categories of risks, with regard to the products concerned the obligations of economic operators in respect of these risks are those determined by the provisions of the specific legislation, while the general safety requirement of this Directive should apply to the other risks.

(13) The provisions of this Directive relating to the other obligations of producers and distributors, the obligations and powers of the Member States, the exchanges of information and rapid intervention situations and dissemination of information and confidentiality apply in the case of products covered by specific rules of Community law, if those rules do not already contain such obligations.

(14) In order to facilitate the effective and consistent application of the general safety requirement of this Directive, it is important to establish European voluntary standards covering certain products and risks in such a way that a product which conforms to a national standard transposing a European standard is to be presumed to be in compliance with the said requirement.

(15) With regard to the aims of this Directive, European standards should be established by European standardisation bodies, under mandates set by the Commission assisted by appropriate Committees. In order to ensure that products in compliance with the standards fulfil the general safety requirement, the Commission assisted by a committee composed of representatives of the Member States, should fix the requirements that the standards must meet. These requirements should be included in the mandates to the standardisation bodies.

(16) In the absence of specific regulations and when the European standards established under mandates set by the Commission are not available or recourse is not made to such standards, the safety of products should be assessed taking into account in particular national standards transposing any other relevant European or international standards, Commission recommendations or national standards, international standards, codes of good practice, the state of the art and the safety which consumers may reasonably expect. In this context; the Commission's recommendations may facilitate the consistent and effective application of this Directive pending the introduction of European standards or as regards the risks and/or products for which such standards are deemed not to be possible or appropriate.

(17) Appropriate independent certification recognised by the competent authorities may facilitate proof of compliance with the applicable product safety criteria.

(18) It is appropriate to supplement the duty to observe the general safety requirement by other obligations on economic operators because action by such operators is necessary to prevent risks to consumers under certain circumstances.

(19) The additional obligations on producers should include the duty to adopt measures commensurate with the characteristics of the products, enabling them to be informed of the risks that these products may present, to supply consumers with information enabling them to assess and prevent risks, to warn consumers of the risks posed by dangerous products already supplied to them, to withdraw those products from the market and, as a last resort, to recall them when necessary, which may involve, depending on the provisions applicable in the Member States, an appropriate form of compensation, for example exchange or reimbursement.

(20) Distributors should help in ensuring compliance with the applicable safety requirements. The obligations placed on distributors apply in proportion to their respective responsibilities. In particular, it may prove impossible, in the context of charitable activities, to provide the competent authorities with information and documentation on possible risks and origin of the product in the case of isolated used objects provided by private individuals.

(21) Both producers and distributors should cooperate with the competent authorities in action aimed at preventing risks and inform them when they conclude that certain products supplied are dangerous. The conditions regarding the provision of such information should be set in this Directive to facilitate its effective application, while avoiding an excessive burden for economic operators and the authorities.

(22) In order to ensure the effective enforcement of the obligations incumbent on producers and distributors, the Member States should establish or designate authorities which are responsible for monitoring product safety and have powers to take appropriate measures, including the power to impose effective, proportionate and dissuasive penalties, and ensure appropriate coordination between the various designated authorities.

(23) It is necessary in particular for the appropriate measures to include the power for Member States to order or organise, immediately and efficiently, the withdrawal of dangerous products already placed on the market and as a last resort to order, coordinate or organise the recall from consumers of dangerous products already supplied to them. Those powers should be applied when producers and distributors fail to prevent risks to consumers in accordance with their obligations. Where necessary, the appropriate powers and procedures should be available to the authorities to decide and apply any necessary measures rapidly.

(24) The safety of consumers depends to a great extent on the active enforcement of Community product safety requirements. The Member States should, therefore, establish

systematic approaches to ensure the effectiveness of market surveillance and other enforcement activities and should ensure their openness to the public and interested parties.

(25) Collaboration between the enforcement authorities of the Member States is necessary in ensuring the attainment of the protection objectives of this Directive. It is, therefore, appropriate to promote the operation of a European network of the enforcement authorities of the Member States to facilitate, in a coordinated manner with other Community procedures, in particular the Community Rapid Information System (RAPEX), improved collaboration at operational level on market surveillance and other enforcement activities, in particular risk assessment, testing of products, exchange of expertise and scientific knowledge, execution of joint surveillance projects and tracing, withdrawing or recalling dangerous products.

(26) It is necessary, for the purpose of ensuring a consistent, high level of consumer health and safety protection and preserving the unity of the internal market, that the Commission be informed of any measure restricting the placing on the market of a product or requiring its withdrawal or recall from the market. Such measures should be taken in compliance with the provisions of the Treaty, and in particular Articles 28, 29 and 30 thereof.

(27) Effective supervision of product safety requires the setting-up at national and Community levels of a system of rapid exchange of information in situations of serious risk requiring rapid intervention in respect of the safety of a product. It is also appropriate in this Directive to set out detailed procedures for the operation of the system and to give the Commission, assisted by an advisory committee, power to adapt them.

(28) This Directive provides for the establishment of non-binding guidelines aimed at indicating simple and clear criteria and practical rules which may change, in particular for the purpose of allowing efficient notification of measures restricting the placing on the market of products in the cases referred to in this Directive, whilst taking into account the range of situations dealt with by Member States and economic operators. The guidelines should in particular include criteria for the application of the definition of serious risks in order to facilitate consistent implementation of the relevant provisions in case of such risks.

(29) It is primarily for Member States, in compliance with the Treaty and in particular with Articles 28, 29 and 30 thereof, to take appropriate measures with regard to dangerous products located within their territory.

(30) However, if the Member States differ as regards the approach to dealing with the risk posed by certain products, such differences could entail unacceptable disparities in consumer protection and constitute a barrier to intra-Community trade.

(31) It may be necessary to deal with serious product-safety problems requiring rapid intervention which affect or could affect, in the immediate future, all or a significant part of the Community and which, in view of the nature of the safety problem posed by the product, cannot be dealt with effectively in a manner commensurate with the degree of urgency, under the procedures laid down in the specific rules of Community law applicable to the products or category of products in question.

(32) It is therefore necessary to provide for an adequate mechanism allowing, as a last resort, for the adoption of measures applicable throughout the Community, in the form of a decision addressed to the Member States, to cope with situations created by products presenting a serious risk. Such a decision should entail a ban on the export of the product in question, unless in the case in point exceptional circumstances allow a partial ban or even no ban to be decided upon, particularly when a system of prior consent is established. In addition, the banning of exports should be examined with a view to preventing risks to the health and safety of consumers. Since such a decision is not directly applicable to economic operators, Member States should take all necessary measures for its implementation. Measures adopted under such a procedure are interim measures, save when they apply to individually identified products or batches of products. In order to ensure the appropriate assessment of the need for, and the best preparation of such measures, they should be taken by the Commission, assisted by a committee, in the light of consultations with the Member

States, and, if scientific questions are involved falling within the competence of a Community scientific committee, with the scientific committee competent for the risk concerned.

(33) The measures necessary for the implementation of this Directive should be adopted in accordance with Council Decision 1999/468/EC of 28 June 1999 laying down the procedures for the exercise of implementing powers conferred on the Commission.

(34) In order to facilitate effective and consistent application of this Directive, the various aspects of its application may need to be discussed within a committee.

(35) Public access to the information available to the authorities on product safety should be ensured. However, professional secrecy, as referred to in Article 287 of the Treaty, must be protected in a way which is compatible with the need to ensure the effectiveness of market surveillance activities and of protection measures.

(36) This Directive should not affect victims' rights within the meaning of Council Directive 85/374/EEC of 25 July 1985 on the approximation of the laws, regulations and administrative provisions of the Member States concerning liability for defective products.

(37) It is necessary for Member States to provide for appropriate means of redress before the competent courts in respect of measures taken by the competent authorities which restrict the placing on the market of a product or require its withdrawal or recall.

(38) In addition, the adoption of measures concerning imported products, like those concerning the banning of exports, with a view to preventing risks to the safety and health of consumers must comply with the Community's international obligations.

(39) The Commission should periodically examine the manner in which this Directive is applied and the results obtained, in particular in relation to the functioning of market surveillance systems, the rapid exchange of information and measures adopted at Community level, together with other issues relevant for consumer product safety in the Community, and submit regular reports to the European Parliament and the Council on the subject.

(40) This Directive should not affect the obligations of Member States concerning the deadline for transposition and application of Directive 92/59/EEC,
HAVE ADOPTED THIS DIRECTIVE:

CHAPTER I

Objective—Scope—Definitions

Article 1

1. The purpose of this Directive is to ensure that products placed on the market are safe.

2. This Directive shall apply to all the products defined in Article 2(a). Each of its provisions shall apply in so far as there are no specific provisions with the same objective in rules of Community law governing the safety of the products concerned. Where products are subject to specific safety requirements imposed by Community legislation, this Directive shall apply only to the aspects and risks or categories of risks not covered by those requirements. This means that:

    (a) Articles 2(b) and (c), 3 and 4 shall not apply to those products insofar as concerns the risks or categories of risks covered by the specific legislation;

    (b) Articles 5 to 18 shall apply except where there are specific provisions governing the aspects covered by the said Articles with the same objective.

Article 2

For the purposes of this Directive:

    (a) "product" shall mean any product—including in the context of providing a service—which is intended for consumers or likely, under reasonably foreseeable conditions, to be used by consumers even if not intended for them, and is supplied or made available, whether for consideration or not, in the course of a commercial activity, and whether new, used or reconditioned.

This definition shall not apply to second-hand products supplied as antiques or as products to be repaired or reconditioned prior to being used, provided that the supplier clearly informs the person to whom he supplies the product to that effect;

(b) "safe product" shall mean any product which, under normal or reasonably foreseeable conditions of use including duration and, where applicable, putting into service, installation and maintenance requirements, does not present any risk or only the minimum risks compatible with the product's use, considered to be acceptable and consistent with a high level of protection for the safety and health of persons, taking into account the following points in particular.

   (i) the characteristics of the product, including its composition, packaging, instructions for assembly and, where applicable, for installation and maintenance;

   (ii) the effect on other products, where it is reasonably foreseeable that it will be used with other products;

   (iii) the presentation of the product, the labelling, any warnings and instructions for its use and disposal and any other indication or information regarding the product;

   (iv) the categories of consumers at risk when using the product, in particular children and the elderly.

The feasibility of obtaining higher levels of safety or the availability of other products presenting a lesser degree of risk shall not constitute grounds for considering a product to be "dangerous";

(c) "dangerous product" shall mean any product which does not meet the definition of "safe product" in (b);

(d) "serious risk" shall mean any serious risk, including those the effects of which are not immediate, requiring rapid intervention by the public authorities;

(e) "producer" shall mean:

   (i) the manufacturer of the product, when he is established in the Community, and any other person presenting himself as the manufacturer by affixing to the product his name, trade mark or other distinctive mark, or the person who reconditions the product;

   (ii) the manufacturer's representative, when the manufacturer is not established in the Community or, if there is no representative established in the Community, the importer of the product;

   (iii) other professionals in the supply chain, insofar as their activities may affect the safety properties of a product;

(f) "distributor" shall mean any professional in the supply chain whose activity does not affect the safety properties of a product;

(g) "recall" shall mean any measure aimed at achieving the return of a dangerous product that has already been supplied or made available to consumers by the producer or distributor;

(h) "withdrawal" shall mean any measure aimed at preventing the distribution, display and offer of a product dangerous to the consumer.

CHAPTER II

General safety requirement, conformity assessment criteria and European standards

Article 3

1. Producers shall be obliged to place only safe products on the market.

2. A product shall be deemed safe, as far as the aspects covered by the relevant national legislation are concerned, when, in the absence of specific Community provisions governing the safety of the product in question, it conforms to the specific rules of

national law of the Member State in whose territory the product is marketed, such rules being drawn up in conformity with the Treaty, and in particular Articles 28 and 30 thereof, and laying down the health and safety requirements which the product must satisfy in order to be marketed.

A product shall be presumed safe as far as the risks and risk categories covered by relevant national standards are concerned when it conforms to voluntary national standards transposing European standards, the references of which have been published by the Commission in the Official Journal of the European Communities in accordance with Article 4. The Member States shall publish the references of such national standards.

3. In circumstances other than those referred to in paragraph 2, the conformity of a product to the general safety requirement shall be assessed by taking into account the following elements in particular, where they exist:

  (a) voluntary national standards transposing relevant European standards other than those referred to in paragraph 2;
  (b) the standards drawn up in the Member State in which the product is marketed;
  (c) Commission recommendations setting guidelines on product safety assessment;
  (d) product safety codes of good practice in force in the sector concerned;
  (e) the state of the art and technology;
  (f) reasonable consumer expectations concerning safety.

4. Conformity of a product with the criteria designed to ensure the general safety requirement, in particular the provisions mentioned in paragraphs 2 or 3, shall not bar the competent authorities of the Member States from taking appropriate measures to impose restrictions on its being placed on the market or to require its withdrawal from the market or recall where there is evidence that, despite such conformity, it is dangerous.

Article 4

1. For the purposes of this Directive, the European standards referred to in the second subparagraph of Article 3(2) shall be drawn up as follows:

  (a) the requirements intended to ensure that products which conform to these standards satisfy the general safety requirement shall be determined in accordance with the procedure laid down in Article 15(2);
  (b) on the basis of those requirements, the Commission shall, in accordance with Directive 98/34/EC of the European Parliament and of the Council of 22 June 1998 laying down a procedure for the provision of information in the field of technical standards and regulations and of rules on information society services call on the European standardisation bodies to draw up standards which satisfy these requirements;
  (c) on the basis of those mandates, the European standardisation bodies shall adopt the standards in accordance with the principles contained in the general guidelines for cooperation between the Commission and those bodies;
  (d) the Commission shall report every three years to the European Parliament and the Council, within the framework of the report referred to in Article 19(2), on its programmes for setting the requirements and the mandates for standardisation provided for in subparagraphs (a) and (b) above. This report will, in particular, include an analysis of the decisions taken regarding requirements and mandates for standardisation referred to in subparagraphs (a) and (b) and regarding the standards referred to in subparagraph (c). It will also include information on the products for which the Commission intends to set the requirements and the mandates in question, the product risks to be considered and the results of any preparatory work launched in this area.

2. The Commission shall publish in the Official Journal of the European Communities the references of the European standards adopted in this way and drawn up in accordance with the requirements referred to in paragraph 1.

If a standard adopted by the European standardisation bodies before the entry into force of this Directive ensures compliance with the general safety requirement, the Commission shall decide to publish its references in the Official Journal of the European Communities.

If a standard does not ensure compliance with the general safety requirement, the Commission shall withdraw reference to the standard from publication in whole or in part.

In the cases referred to in the second and third subparagraphs, the Commission shall, on its own initiative or at the request of a Member State, decide in accordance with the procedure laid down in Article 15(2) whether the standard in question meets the general safety requirement. The Commission shall decide to publish or withdraw after consulting the Committee established by Article 5 of Directive 98/34/EC. The Commission shall notify the Member States of its decision.

CHAPTER III

Other obligations of producers and obligations of distributors

Article 5

1. Within the limits of their respective activities, producers shall provide consumers with the relevant information to enable them to assess the risks inherent in a product throughout the normal or reasonably foreseeable period of its use, where such risks are not immediately obvious without adequate warnings, and to take precautions against those risks.

The presence of warnings does not exempt any person from compliance with the other requirements laid down in this Directive.

Within the limits of their respective activities, producers shall adopt measures commensurate with the characteristics of the products which they supply, enabling them to:

(a) be informed of risks which these products might pose;

(b) choose to take appropriate action including, if necessary to avoid these risks, withdrawal from the market, adequately and effectively warning consumers or recall from consumers.

The measures referred to in the third subparagraph shall include, for example:

(a) an indication, by means of the product or its packaging, of the identity and details of the producer and the product reference or, where applicable, the batch of products to which it belongs, except where not to give such indication is justified and

(b) in all cases where appropriate, the carrying out of sample testing of marketed products, investigating and, if necessary, keeping a register of complaints and keeping distributors informed of such monitoring.

Action such as that referred to in (b) of the third subparagraph shall be undertaken on a voluntary basis or at the request of the competent authorities in accordance with Article 8(1)(f). Recall shall take place as a last resort, where other measures would not suffice to prevent the risks involved, in instances where the producers consider it necessary or where they are obliged to do so further to a measure taken by the competent authority. It may be effected within the framework of codes of good practice on the matter in the Member State concerned, where such codes exist.

2. Distributors shall be required to act with due care to help to ensure compliance with the applicable safety requirements, in particular by not supplying products which they know or should have presumed, on the basis of the information in their possession and as professionals, do not comply with those requirements. Moreover, within the limits of their respective activities, they shall participate in monitoring the safety of products placed on the market, especially by passing on information on product risks, keeping and providing the documentation necessary for tracing the origin of products, and cooperating in the action taken by producers and competent authorities to avoid the risks. Within the limits of their respective activities they shall take measures enabling them to cooperate efficiently.

3. Where producers and distributors know or ought to know, on the basis of the information in their possession and as professionals, that a product that they have placed on the market poses risks to the consumer that are incompatible with the general safety requirement, they shall immediately inform the competent authorities of the Member States thereof under the conditions laid down in Annex I, giving details, in particular, of action taken to prevent risk to the consumer.

The Commission shall, in accordance with the procedure referred to in Article 15(3), adapt the specific requirements relating to the obligation to provide information laid down in Annex I.

4. Producers and distributors shall, within the limits of their respective activities, cooperate with the competent authorities, at the request of the latter, on action taken to avoid the risks posed by products which they supply or have supplied. The procedures for such cooperation, including procedures for dialogue with the producers and distributors concerned on issues related to product safety, shall be established by the competent authorities.

CHAPTER IV

Specific obligations and powers of the Member States

Article 6

1. Member States shall ensure that producers and distributors comply with their obligations under this Directive in such a way that products placed on the market are safe.

2. Member States shall establish or nominate authorities competent to monitor the compliance of products with the general safety requirements and arrange for such authorities to have and use the necessary powers to take the appropriate measures incumbent upon them under this Directive.

3. Member States shall define the tasks, powers, organisation and cooperation arrangements of the competent authorities. They shall keep the Commission informed, and the Commission shall pass on such information to the other Member States.

Article 7

Member States shall lay down the rules on penalties applicable to infringements of the national provisions adopted pursuant to this Directive and shall take all measures necessary to ensure that they are implemented. The penalties provided for shall be effective, proportionate and dissuasive. Member States shall notify those provisions to the Commission by 15 January 2004 and shall also notify it, without delay, of any amendment affecting them.

Article 8

1. For the purposes of this Directive, and in particular of Article 6 thereof, the competent authorities of the Member States shall be entitled to take, inter alia, the measures in (a) and in (b) to (f) below, where appropriate:

    (a) for any product:
        (i)   to organise, even after its being placed on the market as being safe, appropriate checks on its safety properties, on an adequate scale, up to the final stage of use or consumption;
        (ii) to require all necessary information from the parties concerned;
        (iii) to take samples of products and subject them to safety checks;
    (b) for any product that could pose risks in certain conditions:
        (i)   to require that it be marked with suitable, clearly worded and easily comprehensible warnings, in the official languages of the Member State in which the product is marketed, on the risks it may present;
        (ii) to make its marketing subject to prior conditions so as to make it safe;
    (c) for any product that could pose risks for certain persons: to order that they be given warning of the risk in good time and in an appropriate form, including the publication of special warnings;

(d) for any product that could be dangerous:

for the period needed for the various safety evaluations, checks and controls, temporarily to ban its supply, the offer to supply it or its display;

(e) for any dangerous product:

to ban its marketing and introduce the accompanying measures required to ensure the ban is complied with;

(f) for any dangerous product already on the market:

(i) to order or organise its actual and immediate withdrawal, and alert consumers to the risks it presents;

(ii) to order or coordinate or, if appropriate, to organise together with producers and distributors its recall from consumers and its destruction in suitable conditions.

2. When the competent authorities of the Member States take measures such as those provided for in paragraph 1, in particular those referred to in (d) to (f), they shall act in accordance with the Treaty, and in particular Articles 28 and 30 thereof, in such a way as to implement the measures in a manner proportional to the seriousness of the risk, and taking due account of the precautionary principle.

In this context, they shall encourage and promote voluntary action by producers and distributors, in accordance with the obligations incumbent on them under this Directive, and in particular Chapter III thereof, including where applicable by the development of codes of good practice.

If necessary, they shall organise or order the measures provided for in paragraph 1(f) if the action undertaken by the producers and distributors in fulfilment of their obligations is unsatisfactory or insufficient. Recall shall take place as a last resort. It may be effected within the framework of codes of good practice on the matter in the Member State concerned, where such codes exist.

3. In particular, the competent authorities shall have the power to take the necessary action to apply with due dispatch appropriate measures such as those mentioned in paragraph 1, (b) to (f), in the case of products posing a serious risk. These circumstances shall be determined by the Member States, assessing each individual case on its merits, taking into account the guidelines referred to in point 8 of Annex II.

4. The measures to be taken by the competent authorities under this Article shall be addressed, as appropriate, to:

(a) the producer;

(b) within the limits of their respective activities, distributors and in particular the party responsible for the first stage of distribution on the national market;

(c) any other person, where necessary, with a view to cooperation in action taken to avoid risks arising from a product.

Article 9

1. In order to ensure effective market surveillance, aimed at guaranteeing a high level of consumer health and safety protection, which entails cooperation between their competent authorities, Member States shall ensure that approaches employing appropriate means and procedures are put in place, which may include in particular:

(a) establishment, periodical updating and implementation of sectoral surveillance programmes by categories of products or risks and the monitoring of surveillance activities, findings and results;

(b) follow-up and updating of scientific and technical knowledge concerning the safety of products;

(c) periodical review and assessment of the functioning of the control activities and their effectiveness and, if necessary, revision of the surveillance approach and organisation put in place.

2. Member States shall ensure that consumers and other interested parties are given an opportunity to submit complaints to the competent authorities on product safety and on surveillance and control activities and that these complaints are followed up as appropriate. Member States shall actively inform consumers and other interested parties of the procedures established to that end.

Article 10

1. The Commission shall promote and take part in the operation in a European network of the authorities of the Member States competent for product safety, in particular in the form of administrative cooperation.

2. This network operation shall develop in a coordinated manner with the other existing Community procedures, particularly RAPEX. Its objective shall be, in particular, to facilitate:

(a) the exchange of information on risk assessment, dangerous products, test methods and results, recent scientific developments as well as other aspects relevant for control activities;

(b) the establishment and execution of joint surveillance and testing projects;

(c) the exchange of expertise and best practices and cooperation in training activities;

(d) improved cooperation at Community level with regard to the tracing, withdrawal and recall of dangerous products.

CHAPTER V

Exchanges of information and rapid intervention situations

Article 11

1. Where a Member State takes measures which restrict the placing on the market of products—or require their withdrawal or recall—such as those provided for in Article 8(1)(b) to (f), the Member State shall, to the extent that such notification is not required under Article 12 or any specific Community legislation, inform the Commission of the measures, specifying its reasons for adopting them. It shall also inform the Commission of any modification or lifting of such measures.

If the notifying Member State considers that the effects of the risk do not or cannot go beyond its territory, it shall notify the measures concerned insofar as they involve information likely to be of interest to Member States from the product safety standpoint, and in particular if they are in response to a new risk which has not yet been reported in other notifications.

In accordance with the procedure laid down in Article 15(3) of this Directive, the Commission shall, while ensuring the effectiveness and proper functioning of the system, adopt the guidelines referred to in point 8 of Annex II. These shall propose the content and standard form for the notifications provided for in this Article, and, in particular, shall provide precise criteria for determining the conditions for which notification is relevant for the purposes of the second subparagraph.

2. The Commission shall forward the notification to the other Member States, unless it concludes, after examination on the basis of the information contained in the notification, that the measure does not comply with Community law. In such a case, it shall immediately inform the Member State which initiated the action.

Article 12

1. Where a Member State adopts or decides to adopt, recommend or agree with producers and distributors, whether on a compulsory or voluntary basis, measures or actions to prevent, restrict or impose specific conditions on the possible marketing or use, within its own territory, of products by reason of a serious risk, it shall immediately notify the Commission thereof through RAPEX. It shall also inform the Commission without delay of modification or withdrawal of any such measure or action.

If the notifying Member State considers that the effects of the risk do not or cannot go beyond its territory, it shall follow the procedure laid down in Article 11, taking into account the relevant criteria proposed in the guidelines referred to in point 8 of Annex II.

Without prejudice to the first subparagraph, before deciding to adopt such measures or to take such action, Member States may pass on to the Commission any information in their possession regarding the existence of a serious risk.

In the case of a serious risk, they shall notify the Commission of the voluntary measures laid down in Article 5 of this Directive taken by producers and distributors.

2. On receiving such notifications, the Commission shall check whether they comply with this Article and with the requirements applicable to the functioning of RAPEX, and shall forward them to the other Member States, which, in turn, shall immediately inform the Commission of any measures adopted.

3. Detailed procedures for RAPEX are set out in Annex II. They shall be adapted by the Commission in accordance with the procedure referred to in Article 15(3).

4. Access to RAPEX shall be open to applicant countries, third countries or international organisations, within the framework of agreements between the Community and those countries or international organisations, according to arrangements defined in these agreements. Any such agreements shall be based on reciprocity and include provisions on confidentiality corresponding to those applicable in the Community.

Article 13

1. If the Commission becomes aware of a serious risk from certain products to the health and safety of consumers in various Member States, it may, after consulting the Member States, and, if scientific questions arise which fall within the competence of a Community Scientific Committee, the Scientific Committee competent to deal with the risk concerned, adopt a decision in the light of the result of those consultations, in accordance with the procedure laid down in Article 15(2), requiring Member States to take measures from among those listed in Article 8(1)(b) to (f) if, at one and the same time:

(a) it emerges from prior consultations with the Member States that they differ significantly on the approach adopted or to be adopted to deal with the risk; and

(b) the risk cannot be dealt with, in view of the nature of the safety issue posed by the product, in a manner compatible with the degree of urgency of the case, under other procedures laid down by the specific Community legislation applicable to the products concerned; and

(c) the risk can be eliminated effectively only by adopting appropriate measures applicable at Community level, in order to ensure a consistent and high level of protection of the health and safety of consumers and the proper functioning of the internal market.

2. The decisions referred to in paragraph 1 shall be valid for a period not exceeding one year and may be confirmed, under the same procedure, for additional periods none of which shall exceed one year.

However, decisions concerning specific, individually identified products or batches of products shall be valid without a time limit.

3. Export from the Community of dangerous products which have been the subject of a decision referred to in paragraph 1 shall be prohibited unless the decision provides otherwise.

4. Member States shall take all necessary measures to implement the decisions referred to in paragraph 1 within less than 20 days, unless a different period is specified in those decisions.

5. The competent authorities responsible for carrying out the measures referred to in paragraph 1 shall, within one month, give the parties concerned an opportunity to submit their views and shall inform the Commission accordingly.

CHAPTER VI

Committee procedures

Article 14

1. The measures necessary for the implementation of this Directive relating to the matters referred to below shall be adopted in accordance with the regulatory procedure provided for in Article 15(2):

    (a) the measures referred to in Article 4 concerning standards adopted by the European standardisation bodies;

    (b) the decisions referred to in Article 13 requiring Member States to take measures as listed in Article 8(1)(b) to (f).

2. The measures necessary for the implementation of this Directive in respect of all other matters shall be adopted in accordance with the advisory procedure provided for in Article 15(3).

Article 15

1. The Commission shall be assisted by a Committee.

2. Where reference is made to this paragraph, Articles 5 and 7 of Decision 1999/468/EC shall apply, having regard to the provisions of Article 8 thereof.

The period laid down in Article 5(6) of Decision 1999/468/EC shall be set at 15 days.

3. Where reference is made to this paragraph, Articles 3 and 7 of Decision 1999/468/EC shall apply, having regard to the provisions of Article 8 thereof.

4. The Committee shall adopt its rules of procedure.

CHAPTER VII

Final provisions

Article 16

1. Information available to the authorities of the Member States or the Commission relating to risks to consumer health and safety posed by products shall in general be available to the public, in accordance with the requirements of transparency and without prejudice to the restrictions required for monitoring and investigation activities. In particular the public shall have access to information on product identification, the nature of the risk and the measures taken.

However, Member States and the Commission shall take the steps necessary to ensure that their officials and agents are required not to disclose information obtained for the purposes of this Directive which, by its nature, is covered by professional secrecy in duly justified cases, except for information relating to the safety properties of products which must be made public if circumstances so require, in order to protect the health and safety of consumers.

2. Protection of professional secrecy shall not prevent the dissemination to the competent authorities of information relevant for ensuring the effectiveness of market monitoring and surveillance activities. The authorities receiving information covered by professional secrecy shall ensure its protection.

Article 17

This Directive shall be without prejudice to the application of Directive 85/374/EEC.

Article 18

1. Any measure adopted under this Directive and involving restrictions on the placing of a product on the market or requiring its withdrawal or recall must state the appropriate reasons on which it is based. It shall be notified as soon as possible to the party concerned and

shall indicate the remedies available under the provisions in force in the Member State in question and the time limits applying to such remedies.

The parties concerned shall, whenever feasible, be given an opportunity to submit their views before the adoption of the measure. If this has not been done in advance because of the urgency of the measures to be taken, they shall be given such opportunity in due course after the measure has been implemented.

Measures requiring the withdrawal of a product or its recall shall take into consideration the need to encourage distributors, users and consumers to contribute to the implementation of such measures.

2. Member States shall ensure that any measure taken by the competent authorities involving restrictions on the placing of a product on the market or requiring its withdrawal or recall can be challenged before the competent courts.

3. Any decision taken by virtue of this Directive and involving restrictions on the placing of a product on the market or requiring its withdrawal or its recall shall be without prejudice to assessment of the liability of the party concerned, in the light of the national criminal law applying in the case in question.

Article 19

1. The Commission may bring before the Committee referred to in Article 15 any matter concerning the application of this Directive and particularly those relating to market monitoring and surveillance activities.

2. Every three years, following 15 January 2004, the Commission shall submit a report on the implementation of this Directive to the European Parliament and the Council.

The report shall in particular include information on the safety of consumer products, in particular on improved traceability of products, the functioning of market surveillance, standardisation work, the functioning of RAPEX and Community measures taken on the basis of Article 13. To this end the Commission shall conduct assessments of the relevant issues, in particular the approaches, systems and practices put in place in the Member States, in the light of the requirements of this Directive and the other Community legislation relating to product safety. The Member States shall provide the Commission with all the necessary assistance and information for carrying out the assessments and preparing the reports.

Article 20

The Commission shall identify the needs, possibilities and priorities for Community action on the safety of services and submit to the European Parliament and the Council, before 1 January 2003, a report, accompanied by proposals on the subject as appropriate.

Article 21

1. Member States shall bring into force the laws, regulations and administrative provisions necessary in order to comply with this Directive with effect from 15 January 2004. They shall forthwith inform the Commission thereof.

When Member States adopt those measures, they shall contain a reference to this Directive or be accompanied by such reference on the occasion of their official publication. The methods of making such reference shall be laid down by Member States.

2. Member States shall communicate to the Commission the provisions of national law which they adopt in the field covered by this Directive.

Article 22

Directive 92/59/EEC is hereby repealed from 15 January 2004, without prejudice to the obligations of Member States concerning the deadlines for transposition and application of the said Directive as indicated in Annex III.

References to Directive 92/59/EEC shall be construed as references to this Directive and shall be read in accordance with the correlation table in Annex IV.

Directive 2005/29/EC of the European Parliament and of the Council

of 11 May 2005

concerning unfair business-to-consumer commercial practices in the internal market and amending Council Directive 84/450/EEC, Directives 97/7/EC, 98/27/EC and 2002/65/EC of the European Parliament and of the Council and Regulation (EC) No 2006/2004 of the European Parliament and of the Council ("Unfair Commercial Practices Directive") (Text with EEA relevance)

THE EUROPEAN PARLIAMENT AND THE COUNCIL OF THE EUROPEAN UNION,

. . .

Whereas:

(1) Article 153(1) and (3)(a) of the Treaty provides that the Community is to contribute to the attainment of a high level of consumer protection by the measures it adopts pursuant to Article 95 thereof.

(2) In accordance with Article 14(2) of the Treaty, the internal market comprises an area without internal frontiers in which the free movement of goods and services and freedom of establishment are ensured. The development of fair commercial practices within the area without internal frontiers is vital for the promotion of the development of cross-border activities.

(3) The laws of the Member States relating to unfair commercial practices show marked differences which can generate appreciable distortions of competition and obstacles to the smooth functioning of the internal market. In the field of advertising, Council Directive 84/450/EEC of 10 September 1984 concerning misleading and comparative advertising establishes minimum criteria for harmonising legislation on misleading advertising, but does not prevent the Member States from retaining or adopting measures which provide more extensive protection for consumers. As a result, Member States' provisions on misleading advertising diverge significantly.

(4) These disparities cause uncertainty as to which national rules apply to unfair commercial practices harming consumers' economic interests and create many barriers affecting business and consumers. These barriers increase the cost to business of exercising internal market freedoms, in particular when businesses wish to engage in cross border marketing, advertising campaigns and sales promotions. Such barriers also make consumers uncertain of their rights and undermine their confidence in the internal market.

(5) In the absence of uniform rules at Community level, obstacles to the free movement of services and goods across borders or the freedom of establishment could be justified in the light of the case-law of the Court of Justice of the European Communities as long as they seek to protect recognised public interest objectives and are proportionate to those objectives. In view of the Community's objectives, as set out in the provisions of the Treaty and in secondary Community law relating to freedom of movement, and in accordance with the Commission's policy on commercial communications as indicated in the Communication from the Commission entitled "The follow-up to the Green Paper on Commercial Communications in the Internal Market", such obstacles should be eliminated. These obstacles can only be eliminated by establishing uniform rules at Community level which establish a high level of consumer protection and by clarifying certain legal concepts at Community level to the extent necessary for the proper functioning of the internal market and to meet the requirement of legal certainty.

(6) This Directive therefore approximates the laws of the Member States on unfair commercial practices, including unfair advertising, which directly harm consumers' economic interests and thereby indirectly harm the economic interests of legitimate competitors. In line with the principle of proportionality, this Directive protects consumers from the

consequences of such unfair commercial practices where they are material but recognises that in some cases the impact on consumers may be negligible. It neither covers nor affects the national laws on unfair commercial practices which harm only competitors' economic interests or which relate to a transaction between traders; taking full account of the principle of subsidiarity, Member States will continue to be able to regulate such practices, in conformity with Community law, if they choose to do so. Nor does this Directive cover or affect the provisions of Directive 84/450/EEC on advertising which misleads business but which is not misleading for consumers and on comparative advertising. Further, this Directive does not affect accepted advertising and marketing practices, such as legitimate product placement, brand differentiation or the offering of incentives which may legitimately affect consumers' perceptions of products and influence their behaviour without impairing the consumer's ability to make an informed decision.

(7) This Directive addresses commercial practices directly related to influencing consumers' transactional decisions in relation to products. It does not address commercial practices carried out primarily for other purposes, including for example commercial communication aimed at investors, such as annual reports and corporate promotional literature. It does not address legal requirements related to taste and decency which vary widely among the Member States. Commercial practices such as, for example, commercial solicitation in the streets, may be undesirable in Member States for cultural reasons. Member States should accordingly be able to continue to ban commercial practices in their territory, in conformity with Community law, for reasons of taste and decency even where such practices do not limit consumers' freedom of choice. Full account should be taken of the context of the individual case concerned in applying this Directive, in particular the general clauses thereof.

(8) This Directive directly protects consumer economic interests from unfair business-to consumer commercial practices. Thereby, it also indirectly protects legitimate businesses from their competitors who do not play by the rules in this Directive and thus guarantees fair competition in fields coordinated by it. It is understood that there are other commercial practices which, although not harming consumers, may hurt competitors and business customers. The Commission should carefully examine the need for Community action in the field of unfair competition beyond the remit of this Directive and, if necessary, make a legislative proposal to cover these other aspects of unfair competition.

(9) This Directive is without prejudice to individual actions brought by those who have been harmed by an unfair commercial practice. It is also without prejudice to Community and national rules on contract law, on intellectual property rights, on the health and safety aspects of products, on conditions of establishment and authorisation regimes, including those rules which, in conformity with Community law, relate to gambling activities, and to Community competition rules and the national provisions implementing them. The Member States will thus be able to retain or introduce restrictions and prohibitions of commercial practices on grounds of the protection of the health and safety of consumers in their territory wherever the trader is based, for example in relation to alcohol, tobacco or pharmaceuticals. Financial services and immovable property, by reason of their complexity and inherent serious risks, necessitate detailed requirements, including positive obligations on traders. For this reason, in the field of financial services and immovable property, this Directive is without prejudice to the right of Member States to go beyond its provisions to protect the economic interests of consumers. It is not appropriate to regulate here the certification and indication of the standard of fineness of articles of precious metal.

(10) It is necessary to ensure that the relationship between this Directive and existing Community law is coherent, particularly where detailed provisions on unfair commercial practices apply to specific sectors. This Directive therefore amends Directive 84/450/EEC, Directive 97/7/EC of the European Parliament and of the Council of 20 May 1997 on the protection of consumers in respect of distance contracts, Directive 98/27/EC of the European Parliament and of the Council of 19 May 1998 on injunctions for the protection of consumers' interests and Directive 2002/65/EC of the European Parliament and of the Council of

23 September 2002 concerning the distance marketing of consumer financial services. This Directive accordingly applies only in so far as there are no specific Community law provisions regulating specific aspects of unfair commercial practices, such as information requirements and rules on the way the information is presented to the consumer. It provides protection for consumers where there is no specific sectoral legislation at Community level and prohibits traders from creating a false impression of the nature of products. This is particularly important for complex products with high levels of risk to consumers, such as certain financial services products. This Directive consequently complements the Community acquis, which is applicable to commercial practices harming consumers' economic interests.

(11) The high level of convergence achieved by the approximation of national provisions through this Directive creates a high common level of consumer protection. This Directive establishes a single general prohibition of those unfair commercial practices distorting consumers' economic behaviour. It also sets rules on aggressive commercial practices, which are currently not regulated at Community level.

(12) Harmonisation will considerably increase legal certainty for both consumers and business. Both consumers and business will be able to rely on a single regulatory framework based on clearly defined legal concepts regulating all aspects of unfair commercial practices across the EU. The effect will be to eliminate the barriers stemming from the fragmentation of the rules on unfair commercial practices harming consumer economic interests and to enable the internal market to be achieved in this area.

(13) In order to achieve the Community's objectives through the removal of internal market barriers, it is necessary to replace Member States' existing, divergent general clauses and legal principles. The single, common general prohibition established by this Directive therefore covers unfair commercial practices distorting consumers' economic behaviour. In order to support consumer confidence the general prohibition should apply equally to unfair commercial practices which occur outside any contractual relationship between a trader and a consumer or following the conclusion of a contract and during its execution. The general prohibition is elaborated by rules on the two types of commercial practices which are by far the most common, namely misleading commercial practices and aggressive commercial practices.

(14) It is desirable that misleading commercial practices cover those practices, including misleading advertising, which by deceiving the consumer prevent him from making an informed and thus efficient choice. In conformity with the laws and practices of Member States on misleading advertising, this Directive classifies misleading practices into misleading actions and misleading omissions. In respect of omissions, this Directive sets out a limited number of key items of information which the consumer needs to make an informed transactional decision. Such information will not have to be disclosed in all advertisements, but only where the trader makes an invitation to purchase, which is a concept clearly defined in this Directive. The full harmonisation approach adopted in this Directive does not preclude the Member States from specifying in national law the main characteristics of particular products such as, for example, collectors' items or electrical goods, the omission of which would be material when an invitation to purchase is made. It is not the intention of this Directive to reduce consumer choice by prohibiting the promotion of products which look similar to other products unless this similarity confuses consumers as to the commercial origin of the product and is therefore misleading. This Directive should be without prejudice to existing Community law which expressly affords Member States the choice between several regulatory options for the protection of consumers in the field of commercial practices. In particular, this Directive should be without prejudice to Article 13(3) of Directive 2002/58/EC of the European Parliament and of the Council of 12 July 2002 concerning the processing of personal data and the protection of privacy in the electronic communications sector.

(15) Where Community law sets out information requirements in relation to commercial communication, advertising and marketing that information is considered as material under this Directive. Member States will be able to retain or add information requirements relating to contract law and having contract law consequences where this is allowed by the

minimum clauses in the existing Community law instruments. A non-exhaustive list of such information requirements in the acquis is contained in Annex II. Given the full harmonisation introduced by this Directive only the information required in Community law is considered as material for the purpose of Article 7(5) thereof. Where Member States have introduced information requirements over and above what is specified in Community law, on the basis of minimum clauses, the omission of that extra information will not constitute a misleading omission under this Directive. By contrast Member States will be able, when allowed by the minimum clauses in Community law, to maintain or introduce more stringent provisions in conformity with Community law so as to ensure a higher level of protection of consumers' individual contractual rights.

(16) The provisions on aggressive commercial practices should cover those practices which significantly impair the consumer's freedom of choice. Those are practices using harassment, coercion, including the use of physical force, and undue influence.

(17) It is desirable that those commercial practices which are in all circumstances unfair be identified to provide greater legal certainty. Annex I therefore contains the full list of all such practices. These are the only commercial practices which can be deemed to be unfair without a case-by-case assessment against the provisions of Articles 5 to 9. The list may only be modified by revision of the Directive.

(18) It is appropriate to protect all consumers from unfair commercial practices; however the Court of Justice has found it necessary in adjudicating on advertising cases since the enactment of Directive 84/450/EEC to examine the effect on a notional, typical consumer. In line with the principle of proportionality, and to permit the effective application of the protections contained in it, this Directive takes as a benchmark the average consumer, who is reasonably well-informed and reasonably observant and circumspect, taking into account social, cultural and linguistic factors, as interpreted by the Court of Justice, but also contains provisions aimed at preventing the exploitation of consumers whose characteristics make them particularly vulnerable to unfair commercial practices. Where a commercial practice is specifically aimed at a particular group of consumers, such as children, it is desirable that the impact of the commercial practice be assessed from the perspective of the average member of that group. It is therefore appropriate to include in the list of practices which are in all circumstances unfair a provision which, without imposing an outright ban on advertising directed at children, protects them from direct exhortations to purchase. The average consumer test is not a statistical test. National courts and authorities will have to exercise their own faculty of judgement, having regard to the case-law of the Court of Justice, to determine the typical reaction of the average consumer in a given case.

(19) Where certain characteristics such as age, physical or mental infirmity or credulity make consumers particularly susceptible to a commercial practice or to the underlying product and the economic behaviour only of such consumers is likely to be distorted by the practice in a way that the trader can reasonably foresee, it is appropriate to ensure that they are adequately protected by assessing the practice from the perspective of the average member of that group.

(20) It is appropriate to provide a role for codes of conduct, which enable traders to apply the principles of this Directive effectively in specific economic fields. In sectors where there are specific mandatory requirements regulating the behaviour of traders, it is appropriate that these will also provide evidence as to the requirements of professional diligence in that sector. The control exercised by code owners at national or Community level to eliminate unfair commercial practices may avoid the need for recourse to administrative or judicial action and should therefore be encouraged. With the aim of pursuing a high level of consumer protection, consumers' organisations could be informed and involved in the drafting of codes of conduct.

(21) Persons or organisations regarded under national law as having a legitimate interest in the matter must have legal remedies for initiating proceedings against unfair commercial practices, either before a court or before an administrative authority which is competent to

decide upon complaints or to initiate appropriate legal proceedings. While it is for national law to determine the burden of proof, it is appropriate to enable courts and administrative authorities to require traders to produce evidence as to the accuracy of factual claims they have made.

(22) It is necessary that Member States lay down penalties for infringements of the provisions of this Directive and they must ensure that these are enforced. The penalties must be effective, proportionate and dissuasive.

(23) Since the objectives of this Directive, namely to eliminate the barriers to the functioning of the internal market represented by national laws on unfair commercial practices and to provide a high common level of consumer protection, by approximating the laws, regulations and administrative provisions of the Member States on unfair commercial practices, cannot be sufficiently achieved by the Member States and can therefore be better achieved at Community level, the Community may adopt measures, in accordance with the principle of subsidiarity as set out in Article 5 of the Treaty. In accordance with the principle of proportionality, as set out in that Article, this Directive does not go beyond what is necessary in order to eliminate the internal market barriers and achieve a high common level of consumer protection.

(24) It is appropriate to review this Directive to ensure that barriers to the internal market have been addressed and a high level of consumer protection achieved. The review could lead to a Commission proposal to amend this Directive, which may include a limited extension to the derogation in Article 3(5), and/or amendments to other consumer protection legislation reflecting the Commission's Consumer Policy Strategy commitment to review the existing acquis in order to achieve a high, common level of consumer protection.

(25) This Directive respects the fundamental rights and observes the principles recognised in particular by the Charter of Fundamental Rights of the European Union,
HAVE ADOPTED THIS DIRECTIVE:

CHAPTER 1   GENERAL PROVISIONS

Art. 1 Purpose
The purpose of this Directive is to contribute to the proper functioning of the internal market and achieve a high level of consumer protection by approximating the laws, regulations and administrative provisions of the Member States on unfair commercial practices harming consumers' economic interests.

Art. 2 Definitions
For the purposes of this Directive:
>   (a) "consumer" means any natural person who, in commercial practices covered by this Directive, is acting for purposes which are outside his trade, business, craft or profession;
>   (b) "trader" means any natural or legal person who, in commercial practices covered by this Directive, is acting for purposes relating to his trade, business, craft or profession and anyone acting in the name of or on behalf of a trader;
>   (c) "product" means any goods or service including immovable property, rights and obligations;
>   (d) "business-to-consumer commercial practices" (hereinafter also referred to as "commercial practices") means any act, omission, course of conduct or representation, commercial communication including advertising and marketing, by a trader, directly connected with the promotion, sale or supply of a product to consumers;
>   (e) "to materially distort the economic behaviour of consumers" means using a commercial practice to appreciably impair the consumer's ability to make an

informed decision, thereby causing the consumer to take a transactional decision that he would not have taken otherwise;

(f) "code of conduct" means an agreement or set of rules not imposed by law, regulation or administrative provision of a Member State which defines the behaviour of traders who undertake to be bound by the code in relation to one or more particular commercial practices or business sectors;

(g) "code owner" means any entity, including a trader or group of traders, which is responsible for the formulation and revision of a code of conduct and/or for monitoring compliance with the code by those who have undertaken to be bound by it;

(h) "professional diligence" means the standard of special skill and care which a trader may reasonably be expected to exercise towards consumers, commensurate with honest market practice and/or the general principle of good faith in the trader's field of activity;

(i) "invitation to purchase" means a commercial communication which indicates characteristics of the product and the price in a way appropriate to the means of the commercial communication used and thereby enables the consumer to make a purchase;

(j) "undue influence" means exploiting a position of power in relation to the consumer so as to apply pressure, even without using or threatening to use physical force, in a way which significantly limits the consumer's ability to make an informed decision;

(k) "transactional decision" means any decision taken by a consumer concerning whether, how and on what terms to purchase, make payment in whole or in part for, retain or dispose of a product or to exercise a contractual right in relation to the product, whether the consumer decides to act or to refrain from acting;

(l) "regulated profession" means a professional activity or a group of professional activities, access to which or the pursuit of which, or one of the modes of pursuing which, is conditional, directly or indirectly, upon possession of specific professional qualifications, pursuant to laws, regulations or administrative provisions.

Art. 3 Scope

1. This Directive shall apply to unfair business-to-consumer commercial practices, as laid down in Article 5, before, during and after a commercial transaction in relation to a product.

2. This Directive is without prejudice to contract law and, in particular, to the rules on the validity, formation or effect of a contract.

3. This Directive is without prejudice to Community or national rules relating to the health and safety aspects of products.

4. In the case of conflict between the provisions of this Directive and other Community rules regulating specific aspects of unfair commercial practices, the latter shall prevail and apply to those specific aspects.

5. For a period of six years from 27 June 2007, Member States shall be able to continue to apply national provisions within the field approximated by this Directive which are more restrictive or prescriptive than this Directive and which implement directives containing minimum harmonisation clauses. These measures must be essential to ensure that consumers are adequately protected against unfair commercial practices and must be proportionate to the attainment of this objective. The review referred to in Article 18 may, if considered appropriate, include a proposal to prolong this derogation for a further limited period.

6. Member States shall notify the Commission without delay of any national provisions applied on the basis of paragraph 5.

7. This Directive is without prejudice to the rules determining the jurisdiction of the courts.

8. This Directive is without prejudice to any conditions of establishment or of authorisation regimes, or to the deontological codes of conduct or other specific rules governing regulated professions in order to uphold high standards of integrity on the part of the professional, which Member States may, in conformity with Community law, impose on professionals.

9. In relation to "financial services", as defined in Directive 2002/65/EC, and immovable property, Member States may impose requirements which are more restrictive or prescriptive than this Directive in the field which it approximates.

10. This Directive shall not apply to the application of the laws, regulations and administrative provisions of Member States relating to the certification and indication of the standard of fineness of articles of precious metal.

Art. 4 Internal market
Member States shall neither restrict the freedom to provide services nor restrict the free movement of goods for reasons falling within the field approximated by this Directive.

CHAPTER 2   UNFAIR COMMERCIAL PRACTICES

Art. 5 Prohibition of unfair commercial practices
1. Unfair commercial practices shall be prohibited.
2. A commercial practice shall be unfair if:
    (a) it is contrary to the requirements of professional diligence, and
    (b) it materially distorts or is likely to materially distort the economic behaviour with regard to the product of the average consumer whom it reaches or to whom it is addressed, or of the average member of the group when a commercial practice is directed to a particular group of consumers.

3. Commercial practices which are likely to materially distort the economic behaviour only of a clearly identifiable group of consumers who are particularly vulnerable to the practice or the underlying product because of their mental or physical infirmity, age or credulity in a way which the trader could reasonably be expected to foresee, shall be assessed from the perspective of the average member of that group. This is without prejudice to the common and legitimate advertising practice of making exaggerated statements or statements which are not meant to be taken literally.

4. In particular, commercial practices shall be unfair which:
    (a) are misleading as set out in Articles 6 and 7, or
    (b) are aggressive as set out in Articles 8 and 9.

5. Annex I contains the list of those commercial practices which shall in all circumstances be regarded as unfair. The same single list shall apply in all Member States and may only be modified by revision of this Directive.

Section 1   Misleading commercial practices

Art. 6 Misleading actions
1. A commercial practice shall be regarded as misleading if it contains false information and is therefore untruthful or in any way, including overall presentation, deceives or is likely to deceive the average consumer, even if the information is factually correct, in relation to one or more of the following elements, and in either case causes or is likely to cause him to take a transactional decision that he would not have taken otherwise:
    (a) the existence or nature of the product;
    (b) the main characteristics of the product, such as its availability, benefits, risks, execution, composition, accessories, after-sale customer assistance and complaint handling, method and date of manufacture or provision, delivery, fitness for purpose, usage, quantity, specification, geographical or commercial origin or the

results to be expected from its use, or the results and material features of tests or checks carried out on the product;

(c) the extent of the trader's commitments, the motives for the commercial practice and the nature of the sales process, any statement or symbol in relation to direct or indirect sponsorship or approval of the trader or the product;

(d) the price or the manner in which the price is calculated, or the existence of a specific price advantage;

(e) the need for a service, part, replacement or repair;

(f) the nature, attributes and rights of the trader or his agent, such as his identity and assets, his qualifications, status, approval, affiliation or connection and ownership of industrial, commercial or intellectual property rights or his awards and distinctions;

(g) the consumer's rights, including the right to replacement or reimbursement under Directive 1999/44/EC of the European Parliament and of the Council of 25 May 1999 on certain aspects of the sale of consumer goods and associated guarantees, or the risks he may face.

2. A commercial practice shall also be regarded as misleading if, in its factual context, taking account of all its features and circumstances, it causes or is likely to cause the average consumer to take a transactional decision that he would not have taken otherwise, and it involves:

(a) any marketing of a product, including comparative advertising, which creates confusion with any products, trade marks, trade names or other distinguishing marks of a competitor;

(b) non-compliance by the trader with commitments contained in codes of conduct by which the trader has undertaken to be bound, where:

(i) the commitment is not aspirational but is firm and is capable of being verified, and

(ii) the trader indicates in a commercial practice that he is bound by the code.

Art. 7 Misleading omissions

1. A commercial practice shall be regarded as misleading if, in its factual context, taking account of all its features and circumstances and the limitations of the communication medium, it omits material information that the average consumer needs, according to the context, to take an informed transactional decision and thereby causes or is likely to cause the average consumer to take a transactional decision that he would not have taken otherwise.

2. It shall also be regarded as a misleading omission when, taking account of the matters described in paragraph 1, a trader hides or provides in an unclear, unintelligible, ambiguous or untimely manner such material information as referred to in that paragraph or fails to identify the commercial intent of the commercial practice if not already apparent from the context, and where, in either case, this causes or is likely to cause the average consumer to take a transactional decision that he would not have taken otherwise.

3. Where the medium used to communicate the commercial practice imposes limitations of space or time, these limitations and any measures taken by the trader to make the information available to consumers by other means shall be taken into account in deciding whether information has been omitted.

4. In the case of an invitation to purchase, the following information shall be regarded as material, if not already apparent from the context:

(a) the main characteristics of the product, to an extent appropriate to the medium and the product;

(b) the geographical address and the identity of the trader, such as his trading name and, where applicable, the geographical address and the identity of the trader on whose behalf he is acting;

    (c) the price inclusive of taxes, or where the nature of the product means that the price cannot reasonably be calculated in advance, the manner in which the price is calculated, as well as, where appropriate, all additional freight, delivery or postal charges or, where these charges cannot reasonably be calculated in advance, the fact that such additional charges may be payable;

    (d) the arrangements for payment, delivery, performance and the complaint handling policy, if they depart from the requirements of professional diligence;

    (e) for products and transactions involving a right of withdrawal or cancellation, the existence of such a right.

    5. Information requirements established by Community law in relation to commercial communication including advertising or marketing, a non-exhaustive list of which is contained in Annex II, shall be regarded as material.

Section 2   Aggressive commercial practices

Art. 8   Aggressive commercial practices

A commercial practice shall be regarded as aggressive if, in its factual context, taking account of all its features and circumstances, by harassment, coercion, including the use of physical force, or undue influence, it significantly impairs or is likely to significantly impair the average consumer's freedom of choice or conduct with regard to the product and thereby causes him or is likely to cause him to take a transactional decision that he would not have taken otherwise.

Art. 9   Use of harassment, coercion and undue influence

In determining whether a commercial practice uses harassment, coercion, including the use of physical force, or undue influence, account shall be taken of:

    (a) its timing, location, nature or persistence;

    (b) the use of threatening or abusive language or behaviour;

    (c) the exploitation by the trader of any specific misfortune or circumstance of such gravity as to impair the consumer's judgement, of which the trader is aware, to influence the consumer's decision with regard to the product;

    (d) any onerous or disproportionate non-contractual barriers imposed by the trader where a consumer wishes to exercise rights under the contract, including rights to terminate a contract or to switch to another product or another trader;

    (e) any threat to take any action that cannot legally be taken.

CHAPTER 3   CODES OF CONDUCT

Art. 10   Codes of conduct

This Directive does not exclude the control, which Member States may encourage, of unfair commercial practices by code owners and recourse to such bodies by the persons or organisations referred to in Article 11 if proceedings before such bodies are in addition to the court or administrative proceedings referred to in that Article.

    Recourse to such control bodies shall never be deemed the equivalent of foregoing a means of judicial or administrative recourse as provided for in Article 11.

CHAPTER 4   FINAL PROVISIONS

Art. 11   Enforcement

    1. Member States shall ensure that adequate and effective means exist to combat unfair commercial practices in order to enforce compliance with the provisions of this Directive in the interest of consumers.

Such means shall include legal provisions under which persons or organisations regarded under national law as having a legitimate interest in combating unfair commercial practices, including competitors, may:

   (a) take legal action against such unfair commercial practices; and/or
   (b) bring such unfair commercial practices before an administrative authority competent either to decide on complaints or to initiate appropriate legal proceedings.

It shall be for each Member State to decide which of these facilities shall be available and whether to enable the courts or administrative authorities to require prior recourse to other established means of dealing with complaints, including those referred to in Article 10. These facilities shall be available regardless of whether the consumers affected are in the territory of the Member State where the trader is located or in another Member State.

It shall be for each Member State to decide:

   (a) whether these legal facilities may be directed separately or jointly against a number of traders from the same economic sector; and
   (b) whether these legal facilities may be directed against a code owner where the relevant code promotes non-compliance with legal requirements.

2. Under the legal provisions referred to in paragraph 1, Member States shall confer upon the courts or administrative authorities powers enabling them, in cases where they deem such measures to be necessary taking into account all the interests involved and in particular the public interest:

   (a) to order the cessation of, or to institute appropriate legal proceedings for an order for the cessation of, unfair commercial practices, or
   (b) if the unfair commercial practice has not yet been carried out but is imminent, to order the prohibition of the practice, or to institute appropriate legal proceedings for an order for the prohibition of the practice,

even without proof of actual loss or damage or of intention or negligence on the part of the trader.

Member States shall also make provision for the measures referred to in the first sub-paragraph to be taken under an accelerated procedure:

   — either with interim effect, or
   — with definitive effect,

on the understanding that it is for each Member State to decide which of the two options to select.

Furthermore, Member States may confer upon the courts or administrative authorities powers enabling them, with a view to eliminating the continuing effects of unfair commercial practices the cessation of which has been ordered by a final decision:

   (a) to require publication of that decision in full or in part and in such form as they deem adequate,
   (b) to require in addition the publication of a corrective statement.

3. The administrative authorities referred to in paragraph 1 must:

   (a) be composed so as not to cast doubt on their impartiality;
   (b) have adequate powers, where they decide on complaints, to monitor and enforce the observance of their decisions effectively;
   (c) normally give reasons for their decisions.

Where the powers referred to in paragraph 2 are exercised exclusively by an administrative authority, reasons for its decisions shall always be given. Furthermore, in this case, provision must be made for procedures whereby improper or unreasonable exercise of its powers by the administrative authority or improper or unreasonable failure to exercise the said powers can be the subject of judicial review.

Art. 12   Courts and administrative authorities: substantiation of claims

Member States shall confer upon the courts or administrative authorities powers enabling them in the civil or administrative proceedings provided for in Article 11:

(a) to require the trader to furnish evidence as to the accuracy of factual claims in relation to a commercial practice if, taking into account the legitimate interest of the trader and any other party to the proceedings, such a requirement appears appropriate on the basis of the circumstances of the particular case; and

(b) to consider factual claims as inaccurate if the evidence demanded in accordance with (a) is not furnished or is deemed insufficient by the court or administrative authority.

Art. 13   Penalties

Member States shall lay down penalties for infringements of national provisions adopted in application of this Directive and shall take all necessary measures to ensure that these are enforced. These penalties must be effective, proportionate and dissuasive.

Art. 17   Information

Member States shall take appropriate measures to inform consumers of the national law transposing this Directive and shall, where appropriate, encourage traders and code owners to inform consumers of their codes of conduct.

ANNEX I

Commercial practices which are in all circumstances considered unfair

Misleading commercial practices

(1) Claiming to be a signatory to a code of conduct when the trader is not.

(2) Displaying a trust mark, quality mark or equivalent without having obtained the necessary authorisation.

(3) Claiming that a code of conduct has an endorsement from a public or other body which it does not have.

(4) Claiming that a trader (including his commercial practices) or a product has been approved, endorsed or authorised by a public or private body when he/it has not or making such a claim without complying with the terms of the approval, endorsement or authorisation.

(5) Making an invitation to purchase products at a specified price without disclosing the existence of any reasonable grounds the trader may have for believing that he will not be able to offer for supply or to procure another trader to supply, those products or equivalent products at that price for a period that is, and in quantities that are, reasonable having regard to the product, the scale of advertising of the product and the price offered (bait advertising).

(6) Making an invitation to purchase products at a specified price and then:

(a) refusing to show the advertised item to consumers, or

(b) refusing to take orders for it or deliver it within a reasonable time, or

(c) demonstrating a defective sample of it,

with the intention of promoting a different product (bait and switch).

(7) Falsely stating that a product will only be available for a very limited time, or that it will only be available on particular terms for a very limited time, in order to elicit an immediate decision and deprive consumers of sufficient opportunity or time to make an informed choice.

(8) Undertaking to provide after-sales service to consumers with whom the trader has communicated prior to a transaction in a language which is not an official language of the Member State where the trader is located and then making such service available only in another language without clearly disclosing this to the consumer before the consumer is committed to the transaction.

(9) Stating or otherwise creating the impression that a product can legally be sold when it cannot.

(10) Presenting rights given to consumers in law as a distinctive feature of the trader's offer.

(11) Using editorial content in the media to promote a product where a trader has paid for the promotion without making that clear in the content or by images or sounds clearly identifiable by the consumer (advertorial). This is without prejudice to Council Directive 89/552/EEC.

(12) Making a materially inaccurate claim concerning the nature and extent of the risk to the personal security of the consumer or his family if the consumer does not purchase the product.

(13) Promoting a product similar to a product made by a particular manufacturer in such a manner as deliberately to mislead the consumer into believing that the product is made by that same manufacturer when it is not.

(14) Establishing, operating or promoting a pyramid promotional scheme where a consumer gives consideration for the opportunity to receive compensation that is derived primarily from the introduction of other consumers into the scheme rather than from the sale or consumption of products.

(15) Claiming that the trader is about to cease trading or move premises when he is not.

(16) Claiming that products are able to facilitate winning in games of chance.

(17) Falsely claiming that a product is able to cure illnesses, dysfunction or malformations.

(18) Passing on materially inaccurate information on market conditions or on the possibility of finding the product with the intention of inducing the consumer to acquire the product at conditions less favourable than normal market conditions.

(19) Claiming in a commercial practice to offer a competition or prize promotion without awarding the prizes described or a reasonable equivalent.

(20) Describing a product as "gratis", "free", "without charge" or similar if the consumer has to pay anything other than the unavoidable cost of responding to the commercial practice and collecting or paying for delivery of the item.

(21) Including in marketing material an invoice or similar document seeking payment which gives the consumer the impression that he has already ordered the marketed product when he has not.

(22) Falsely claiming or creating the impression that the trader is not acting for purposes relating to his trade, business, craft or profession, or falsely representing oneself as a consumer.

(23) Creating the false impression that after-sales service in relation to a product is available in a Member State other than the one in which the product is sold.

Aggressive commercial practices

(24) Creating the impression that the consumer cannot leave the premises until a contract is formed.

(25) Conducting personal visits to the consumer's home ignoring the consumer's request to leave or not to return except in circumstances and to the extent justified, under national law, to enforce a contractual obligation.

(26) Making persistent and unwanted solicitations by telephone, fax, e-mail or other remote media except in circumstances and to the extent justified under national law to enforce a contractual obligation. This is without prejudice to Article 10 of Directive 97/7/EC and Directives 95/46/EC and 2002/58/EC.

(27) Requiring a consumer who wishes to claim on an insurance policy to produce documents which could not reasonably be considered relevant as to whether the claim was valid, or failing systematically to respond to pertinent correspondence, in order to dissuade a consumer from exercising his contractual rights.

(28) Including in an advertisement a direct exhortation to children to buy advertised products or persuade their parents or other adults to buy advertised products for them. This provision is without prejudice to Article 16 of Directive 89/552/EEC on television broadcasting.

(29) Demanding immediate or deferred payment for or the return or safekeeping of products supplied by the trader, but not solicited by the consumer except where the product is a substitute supplied in conformity with Article 7(3) of Directive 97/7/EC (inertia selling).

(30) Explicitly informing a consumer that if he does not buy the product or service, the trader's job or livelihood will be in jeopardy.

(31) Creating the false impression that the consumer has already won, will win, or will on doing a particular act win, a prize or other equivalent benefit, when in fact either:
— there is no prize or other equivalent benefit, or
— taking any action in relation to claiming the prize or other equivalent benefit is subject to the consumer paying money or incurring a cost.

PART V

....

Codes

The Principles of European Contract Law
3rd edition

[Permission is granted by the Commission on European Contract Law for unlimited reproduction for non-commercial purposes only of the text of the articles.]

[March 2003]

CHAPTER 12   GENERAL PROVISIONS

SECTION 1   SCOPE OF THE PRINCIPLES

Article 1.101   Application of the principles

(1) These Principles are intended to be applied as general rules of contract law in the European Union.

(2) These Principles will apply when the parties have agreed to incorporate them into their contract or that their contract is to be governed by them.

(3) These Principles may be applied when the parties:

(a) have agreed that their contract is to be governed by "general principles of law", the "lex mercatoria" or the like; or

(b) have not chosen any system or rules of law to govern their contract.

(4) These Principles may provide a solution to the issue raised where the system or rules of law applicable do not do so.

Article 1.102   Freedom of contract

(1) Parties are free to enter into a contract and to determine its contents, subject to the requirements of good faith and fair dealing, and the mandatory rules established by these Principles.

(2) The parties may exclude the application of any of the Principles or derogate from or vary their effects, except as otherwise provided by these Principles.

Article 1.103   Mandatory law

(1) Where the law otherwise applicable so allows, the parties may choose to have their contract governed by the Principles, with the effect that national mandatory rules are not applicable.

(2) Effect should nevertheless be given to those mandatory rules of national, supranational and international law which, according to the relevant rules of private international law, are applicable irrespective of the law governing the contract.

Article 1.104   Application to questions of consent

(1) The existence and validity of the agreement of the parties to adopt or incorporate these Principles shall be determined by these Principles.

(2) Nevertheless, a party may rely upon the law of the country in which it has its habitual residence to establish that it did not consent if it appears from the circumstances that it

would not be reasonable to determine the effect of the party's conduct in accordance with these Principles.

Article 1.105 **Usages and practices**

(1) The parties are bound by any usage to which they have agreed and by any practice they have established between themselves.

(2) The parties are bound by a usage which would be considered generally applicable by persons in the same situation as the parties, except where the application of such usage would be unreasonable.

Article 1.106 **Interpretation and supplementation**

(1) These Principles should be interpreted and developed in accordance with their purposes. In particular, regard should be had to the need to promote good faith and fair dealing, certainty in contractual relationships and uniformity of application.

(2) Issues within the scope of these Principles but not expressly settled by them are so far as possible to be settled in accordance with the ideas underlying the Principles. Failing this, the legal system applicable by virtue of the rules of private international law is to be applied.

Article 1.107 **Application of the principles by way of analogy**

These Principles apply with appropriate modifications to agreements to modify or end a contract, to unilateral promises and to other statements and conduct indicating intention.

SECTION 2 GENERAL DUTIES

Article 1.201 **Good faith and fair dealing**

(1) Each party must act in accordance with good faith and fair dealing.

(2) The parties may not exclude or limit this duty.

Article 1.202 **Duty to co-operate**

Each party owes to the other a duty to co-operate in order to give full effect to the contract.

SECTION 3 TERMINOLOGY AND OTHER PROVISIONS

Article 1.301 **Meaning of terms**

In these Principles, except where the context otherwise requires:

(1) "act" includes omission;

(2) "court" includes arbitral tribunal;

(3) an "intentional" act includes an act done recklessly;

(4) "non-performance" denotes any failure to perform an obligation under the contract, whether or not excused, and includes delayed performance, defective performance and failure to co-operate in order to give full effect to the contract;

(5) a matter is "material" if it is one which a reasonable person in the same situation as one party ought to have known would influence the other party in its decision whether to contract on the proposed terms or to contract at all;

(6) "written" statements include communications made by telegram, telex, telefax and electronic mail and other means of communication capable of providing a readable record of the statement on both sides

Article 1.302 **Reasonableness**

Under these Principles reasonableness is to be judged by what persons acting in good faith and in the same situation as the parties would consider to be reasonable. In particular, in assessing what is reasonable the nature and purpose of the contract, the circumstances of the case and the usages and practices of the trades or professions involved should be taken into account.

Article 1.303 Notice

(1) Any notice may be given by any means, whether in writing or otherwise, appropriate to the circumstances.

(2) Subject to paragraphs (4) and (5), any notice becomes effective when it reaches the addressee.

(3) A notice reaches the addressee when it is delivered to it or to its place of business or mailing address, or, if it does not have a place of business or mailing address, to its habitual residence.

(4) If one party gives notice to the other because of the other's non-performance or because such non-performance is reasonably anticipated by the first party, and the notice is properly dispatched or given, a delay or inaccuracy in the transmission of the notice or its failure to arrive does not prevent it from having effect. The notice shall have effect from the time at which it would have arrived in normal circumstances.

(5) A notice has no effect if a withdrawal of it reaches the addressee before or at the same time as the notice.

(6) In this Article, "notice" includes the communication of a promise, statement, offer, acceptance, demand, request or other declaration.

Article 1.304 **Computation of time**

(1) A period of time set by a party in a written document for the addressee to reply or take other action begins to run from the date stated as the date of the document. If no date is shown, the period begins to run from the moment the document reaches the addressee.

(2) Official holidays and official non-working days occurring during the period are included in calculating the period. However, if the last day of the period is an official holiday or official non-working day at the address of the addressee, or at the place where a prescribed act is to be performed, the period is extended until the first following working day in that place.

(3) Periods of time expressed in days, weeks, months or years shall begin at 00.00 on the next day and shall end at 24.00 on the last day of the period; but any reply that has to reach the party which set the period must arrive, or any other act which is to be done must be completed, by the normal close of business in the relevant place on the last day of the period.

Article 1.305 **Imputed knowledge and intention**

If any person who with a party's assent was involved in making a contract, or who was entrusted with performance by a party or who performed with its assent:

    (a) knew or foresaw a fact, or ought to have known or foreseen it; or

    (b) acted intentionally or with gross negligence, or not in accordance with good faith and fair dealing,

this knowledge, foresight or behaviour is imputed to the party itself.

CHAPTER 2   FORMATION

SECTION 1   GENERAL PROVISIONS

Article 2.101 **Conditions for the conclusion of a contract**

(1) A contract is concluded if:

    (a) the parties intend to be legally bound, and

    (b) they reach a sufficient agreement without any further requirement.

(2) A contract need not be concluded or evidenced in writing nor is it subject to any other requirement as to form. The contract may be proved by any means, including witnesses.

Article 2.102 **Intention**

The intention of a party to be legally bound by contract is to be determined from the party's statements or conduct as they were reasonably understood by the other party.

Article 2.103   Sufficient agreement

(1) There is sufficient agreement if the terms:

    (a) have been sufficiently defined by the parties so that the contract can be enforced, or

    (b) can be determined under these Principles.

(2) However, if one of the parties refuses to conclude a contract unless the parties have agreed on some specific matter, there is no contract unless agreement on that matter has been reached.

Article 2.104   Terms not individually negotiated

(1) Contract terms which have not been individually negotiated may be invoked against a party who did not know of them only if the party invoking them took reasonable steps to bring them to the other party's attention before or when the contract was concluded.

(2) Terms are not brought appropriately to a party's attention by a mere reference to them in a contract document, even if that party signs the document.

Article 2.105   Merger clause

(1) If a written contract contains an individually negotiated clause stating that the writing embodies all the terms of the contract (a merger clause), any prior statements, undertakings or agreements which are not embodied in the writing do not form part of the contract.

(2) If the merger clause is not individually negotiated it will only establish a presumption that the parties intended that their prior statements, undertakings or agreements were not to form part of the contract. This rule may not be excluded or restricted.

(3) The parties' prior statements may be used to interpret the contract. This rule may not be excluded or restricted except by an individually negotiated clause.

(4) A party may by its statements or conduct be precluded from asserting a merger clause to the extent that the other party has reasonably relied on them.

Article 2.106   Written modification only

(1) A clause in a written contract requiring any modification or ending by agreement to be made in writing establishes only a presumption that an agreement to modify or end the contract is not intended to be legally binding unless it is in writing.

(2) A party may by its statements or conduct be precluded from asserting such a clause to the extent that the other party has reasonably relied on them.

Article 2.107   Promises binding without acceptance

A promise which is intended to be legally binding without acceptance is binding.

SECTION 2   OFFER AND ACCEPTANCE

Article 2.201   Offer

(1) A proposal amounts to an offer if:

    (a) it is intended to result in a contract if the other party accepts it, and

    (b) it contains sufficiently definite terms to form a contract.

(2) An offer may be made to one or more specific persons or to the public.

(3) A proposal to supply goods or services at stated prices made by a professional supplier in a public advertisement or a catalogue, or by a display of goods, is presumed to be an offer to sell or supply at that price until the stock of goods, or the supplier's capacity to supply the service, is exhausted.

Article 2.202   Revocation of an offer

(1) An offer may be revoked if the revocation reaches the offeree before it has dispatched its acceptance or, in cases of acceptance by conduct, before the contract has been concluded under Article 2.205(2) or (3).

(2) An offer made to the public can be revoked by the same means as were used to make the offer.

(3) However, a revocation of an offer is ineffective if:

(a) the offer indicates that it is irrevocable; or

(b) it states a fixed time for its acceptance; or

(c) it was reasonable for the offeree to rely on the offer as being irrevocable and the offeree has acted in reliance on the offer.

Article 2.203   Rejection

When a rejection of an offer reaches the offeror, the offer lapses.

Article 2.204   Acceptance

(1) Any form of statement or conduct by the offeree is an acceptance if it indicates assent to the offer.

(2) Silence or inactivity does not in itself amount to acceptance.

Article 2.205   Time of conclusion of the contract

(1) If an acceptance has been dispatched by the offeree the contract is concluded when the acceptance reaches the offeror.

(2) In case of acceptance by conduct, the contract is concluded when notice of the conduct reaches the offeror.

(3) If by virtue of the offer, of practices which the parties have established between themselves, or of a usage, the offeree may accept the offer by performing an act without notice to the offeror, the contract is concluded when the performance of the act begins.

Article 2.206   Time limit for acceptance

(1) In order to be effective, acceptance of an offer must reach the offeror within the time fixed by it.

(2) If no time has been fixed by the offeror acceptance must reach it within a reasonable time.

(3) In the case of an acceptance by an act of performance under article 2.205(3), that act must be performed within the time for acceptance fixed by the offeror or, if no such time is fixed, within a reasonable time.

Article 2.207   Late acceptance

(1) A late acceptance is nonetheless effective as an acceptance if without delay the offeror informs the offeree that he treats it as such.

(2) If a letter or other writing containing a late acceptance shows that it has been sent in such circumstances that if its transmission had been normal it would have reached the offeror in due time, the late acceptance is effective as an acceptance unless, without delay, the offeror informs the offeree that it considers its offer as having lapsed.

Article 2.208   Modified acceptance

(1) A reply by the offeree which states or implies additional or different terms which would materially alter the terms of the offer is a rejection and a new offer.

(2) A reply which gives a definite assent to an offer operates as an acceptance even if it states or implies additional or different terms, provided these do not materially alter the terms of the offer. The additional or different terms then become part of the contract.

(3) However, such a reply will be treated as a rejection of the offer if:

(a) the offer expressly limits acceptance to the terms of the offer; or

(b) the offeror objects to the additional or different terms without delay; or

(c) the offeree makes its acceptance conditional upon the offeror's assent to the additional or different terms, and the assent does not reach the offeree within a reasonable time.

Article 2.209   Conflicting general conditions

(1) If the parties have reached agreement except that the offer and acceptance refer to conflicting general conditions of contract, a contract is nonetheless formed. The general conditions form part of the contract to the extent that they are common in substance.

(2) However, no contract is formed if one party:

    (a) has indicated in advance, explicitly, and not by way of general conditions, that it does not intend to be bound by a contract on the basis of paragraph (1); or

    (b) without delay, informs the other party that it does not intend to be bound by such contract.

(3) General conditions of contract are terms which have been formulated in advance for an indefinite number of contracts of a certain nature, and which have not been individually negotiated between the parties.

Article 2.210   Professional's written confirmation

If professionals have concluded a contract but have not embodied it in a final document, and one without delay sends the other a writing which purports to be a confirmation of the contract but which contains additional or different terms, such terms will become part of the contract unless:

    (a) the terms materially alter the terms of the contract, or

    (b) the addressee objects to them without delay.

Article 2.211   Contracts not concluded through offer and acceptance

The rules in this section apply with appropriate adaptations even though the process of conclusion of a contract cannot be analysed into offer and acceptance.

SECTION 3   LIABILITY FOR NEGOTIATIONS

Article 2.301   Negotiations contrary to good faith

(1) A party is free to negotiate and is not liable for failure to reach an agreement.

(2) However, a party who has negotiated or broken off negotiations contrary to good faith and fair dealing is liable for the losses caused to the other party.

(3) It is contrary to good faith and fair dealing, in particular, for a party to enter into or continue negotiations with no real intention of reaching an agreement with the other party.

Article 2.302   Breach of confidentiality

If confidential information is given by one party in the course of negotiations, the other party is under a duty not to disclose that information or use it for its own purposes whether or not a contract is subsequently concluded. The remedy for breach of this duty may include compensation for loss suffered and restitution of the benefit received by the other party.

CHAPTER 3   AUTHORITY OF AGENTS

SECTION 1   GENERAL PROVISIONS

Article 3.101   Scope of the chapter

(1) This Chapter governs the authority of an agent or other intermediary to bind its principal in relation to a contract with a third party.

(2) This Chapter does not govern an agent's authority bestowed by law or the authority of an agent appointed by a public or judicial authority.

(3) This Chapter does not govern the internal relationship between the agent or intermediary and its principal.

Article 3.102 **Categories of representation**

(1) Where an agent acts in the name of a principal, the rules on direct representation apply (Section 2). It is irrelevant whether the principal's identity is revealed at the time the agent acts or is to be revealed later.

(2) Where an intermediary acts on instructions and on behalf of, but not in the name of, a principal, or where the third party neither knows nor has reason to know that the intermediary acts as an agent, the rules on indirect representation apply (Section 3).

SECTION 2   DIRECT REPRESENTATION

Article 3.201 **Express, implied and apparent authority**

(1) The principal's grant of authority to an agent to act in its name may be express or may be implied from the circumstances.

(2) The agent has authority to perform all acts necessary in the circumstances to achieve the purposes for which the authority was granted.

(3) A person is to be treated as having granted authority to an apparent agent if the person's statements or conduct induce the third party reasonably and in good faith to believe that the apparent agent has been granted authority for the act performed by it.

Article 3.202 **Agent acting in exercise of its authority**

Where an agent is acting within its authority as defined by article 3.201, its acts bind the principal and the third party directly to each other. The agent itself is not bound to the third party.

Article 3.203 **Unidentified principal**

If an agent enters into a contract in the name of a principal whose identity is to be revealed later, but fails to reveal that identity within a reasonable time after a request by the third party, the agent itself is bound by the contract.

Article 3.204 **Agent acting without or outside its authority**

(1) Where a person acting as an agent acts without authority or outside the scope of its authority, its acts are not binding upon the principal and the third party.

(2) Failing ratification by the principal according to article 3.207, the agent is liable to pay the third party such damages as will place the third party in the same position as if the agent had acted with authority. This does not apply if the third party knew or could not have been unaware of the agent's lack of authority.

Article 3.205 **Conflict of interest**

(1) If a contract concluded by an agent involves the agent in a conflict of interest of which the third party knew or could not have been unaware, the principal may avoid the contract according to the provisions of articles 4.112 to 4.116.

(2) There is presumed to be a conflict of interest where:

    (a) the agent also acted as agent for the third party; or

    (b) the contract was with itself in its personal capacity.

(3) However, the principal may not avoid the contract:

    (a) if it had consented to, or could not have been unaware of, the agent's so acting; or

    (b) if the agent had disclosed the conflict of interest to it and it had not objected within a reasonable time.

Article 3.206 **Subagency**

An agent has implied authority to appoint a subagent to carry out tasks which are not of a personal character and which it is not reasonable to expect the agent to carry out itself. The rules of this Section apply to the subagency; acts of the subagent which are within its and the agent's authority bind the principal and the third party directly to each other.

Article 3.207   Ratification by principal

(1) Where a person acting as an agent acts without authority or outside its authority, the principal may ratify the agent's acts.

(2) Upon ratification, the agent's acts are considered as having been authorised, without prejudice to the rights of other persons.

Article 3.208   Third party's right with respect to confirmation of authority

Where the statements or conduct of the principal gave the third party reason to believe that an act performed by the agent was authorised, but the third party is in doubt about the authorisation, it may send a written confirmation to the principal or request ratification from it. If the principal does not object or answer the request without delay, the agent's act is treated as having been authorised.

Article 3.209   Duration of authority

(1) An agent's authority continues until the third party knows or ought to know that:
  (a) the agent's authority has been brought to an end by the principal, the agent, or both; or
  (b) the acts for which the authority had been granted have been completed, or the time for which it had been granted has expired; or
  (c) the agent has become insolvent or, where a natural person, has died or become incapacitated; or
  (d) the principal has become insolvent.

(2) The third party is considered to know that the agent's authority has been brought to an end under paragraph (1)(a) above if this has been communicated or publicised in the same manner in which the authority was originally communicated or publicised.

(3) However, the agent remains authorised for a reasonable time to perform those acts which are necessary to protect the interests of the principal or its successors.

SECTION 3   INDIRECT REPRESENTATION

Article 3.301   Intermediaries not acting in the name of a principal

(1) Where an intermediary acts:
  (a) on instructions and on behalf, but not in the name, of a principal, or
  (b) on instructions from a principal but the third party does not know and has no reason to know this,
the intermediary and the third party are bound to each other.

(2) The principal and the third party are bound to each other only under the conditions set out in Articles 3.302 to 3.304.

Article 3.302   Intermediary's insolvency or fundamental non-performance to principal

If the intermediary becomes insolvent, or if it commits a fundamental non-performance towards the principal, or if prior to the time for performance it is clear that there will be a fundamental non-performance:
  (a) on the principal's demand, the intermediary shall communicate the name and address of the third party to the principal; and
  (b) the principal may exercise against the third party the rights acquired on the principal's behalf by the intermediary, subject to any defences which the third party may set up against the intermediary.

Article 3.303   Intermediary's insolvency or fundamental non-performance to third party

If the intermediary becomes insolvent, or if it commits a fundamental non-performance towards the third party, or if prior to the time for performance it is clear that there will be a fundamental non-performance:

(a) on the third party's demand, the intermediary shall communicate the name and address of the principal to the third party; and

(b) the third party may exercise against the principal the rights which the third party has against the intermediary, subject to any defences which the intermediary may set up against the third party and those which the principal may set up against the intermediary.

CHAPTER 4   VALIDITY

Article 4.101   Matters not covered
This chapter does not deal with invalidity arising from illegality, immorality or lack of capacity.

Article 4.102   Initial impossibility
A contract is not invalid merely because at the time it was concluded performance of the obligation assumed was impossible, or because a party was not entitled to dispose of the assets to which the contract relates.

Article 4.103   Fundamental mistake as to facts or law
(1) A party may avoid a contract for mistake of fact or law existing when the contract was concluded if:
   (a) (i) the mistake was caused by information given by the other party; or
       (ii) the other party knew or ought to have known of the mistake and it was contrary to good faith and fair dealing to leave the mistaken party in error; or
       (iii) the other party made the same mistake,
           and
   (b) the other party knew or ought to have known that the mistaken party, had it known the truth, would not have entered the contract or would have done so only on fundamentally different terms.
(2) However a party may not avoid the contract if:
   (a) in the circumstances its mistake was inexcusable, or
   (b) the risk of the mistake was assumed, or in the circumstances should be borne, by it.

Article 4.104   Inaccuracies in communication
An inaccuracy in the expression or transmission of a statement is to be treated as a mistake of the person which made or sent the statement and Article 4.103 applies.

Article 4.105   Adaptation of contract
(1) If a party is entitled to avoid the contract for mistake but the other party indicates that it is willing to perform, or actually does perform, the contract as it was understood by the party entitled to avoid it, the contract is to be treated as if it had been concluded as the that [*sic*] party understood it. The other party must indicate its willingness to perform, or render such performance, promptly after being informed of the manner in which the party entitled to avoid it understood the contract and before that party acts in reliance on any notice of avoidance.

(2) After such indication or performance the right to avoid is lost and any earlier notice of avoidance is ineffective.

(3) Where both parties have made the same mistake, the court may at the request of either party bring the contract into accordance with what might reasonably have been agreed had the mistake not occurred.

Article 4.106   Incorrect information
A party who has concluded a contract relying on incorrect information given it by the other party may recover damages in accordance with Article 4.117(2) and (3) even if the information does not give rise to a fundamental mistake under Article 4.103, unless the party which gave the information had reason to believe that the information was correct.

Article 4.107 Fraud

(1) A party may avoid a contract when it has been led to conclude it by the other party's fraudulent representation, whether by words or conduct, or fraudulent non-disclosure of any information which in accordance with good faith and fair dealing it should have disclosed.

(2) A party's representation or non-disclosure is fraudulent if it was intended to deceive.

(3) In determining whether good faith and fair dealing required that a party disclose particular information, regard should be had to all the circumstances, including:

(a) whether the party had special expertise;

(b) the cost to it of acquiring the relevant information;

(c) whether the other party could reasonably acquire the information for itself; and

(d) the apparent importance of the information to the other party.

Article 4.108 Threats

A party may avoid a contract when it has been led to conclude it by the other party's imminent and serious threat of an act:

(a) which is wrongful in itself, or

(b) which it is wrongful to use as a means to obtain the conclusion of the contract, unless in the circumstances the first party had a reasonable alternative.

Article 4.109 Excessive benefit or unfair advantage

(1) A party may avoid a contract if, at the time of the conclusion of the contract:

(a) it was dependent on or had a relationship of trust with the other party, was in economic distress or had urgent needs, was improvident, ignorant, inexperienced or lacking in bargaining skill, and

(b) the other party knew or ought to have known of this and, given the circumstances and purpose of the contract, took advantage of the first party's situation in a way which was grossly unfair or took an excessive benefit.

(2) Upon the request of the party entitled to avoidance, a court may if it is appropriate adapt the contract in order to bring it into accordance with what might have been agreed had the requirements of good faith and fair dealing been followed.

(3) A court may similarly adapt the contract upon the request of a party receiving notice of avoidance for excessive benefit or unfair advantage, provided that this party informs the party which gave the notice promptly after receiving it and before that party has acted in reliance on it.

Article 4.110 Unfair terms not individually negotiated

(1) A party may avoid a term which has not been individually negotiated if, contrary to the requirements of good faith and fair dealing, it causes a significant imbalance in the parties' rights and obligations arising under the contract to the detriment of that party, taking into account the nature of the performance to be rendered under the contract, all the other terms of the contract and the circumstances at the time the contract was concluded.

(2) This Article does not apply to:

(a) a term which defines the main subject matter of the contract, provided the term is in plain and intelligible language; or to

(b) the adequacy in value of one party's obligations compared to the value of the obligations of the other party.

Article 4.111 Third persons

Where a third person for whose acts a party is responsible, or who with a party's assent is involved in the making of a contract:

(1) (a) causes a mistake by giving information, or knows of or ought to have known of a mistake,

(b) gives incorrect information,

(c) commits fraud,

(d) makes a threat, or

(e) takes excessive benefit or unfair advantage,

remedies under this Chapter will be available under the same conditions as if the behaviour or knowledge had been that of the party itself.

(2) Where any other third person:

(a) gives incorrect information,

(b) commits fraud,

(c) makes a threat, or

(d) takes excessive benefit or unfair advantage,

remedies under this Chapter will be available if the party knew or ought to have known of the relevant facts, or at the time of avoidance it has not acted in reliance on the contract.

Article 4.112   Notice of avoidance

Avoidance must be by notice to the other party.

Article 4.113   Time limits

(1) Notice of avoidance must be given within a reasonable time, with due regard to the circumstances, after the avoiding party knew or ought to have known of the relevant facts or became capable of acting freely.

(2) However, a party may avoid an individual term under Article 4.110 if it gives notice of avoidance within a reasonable time after the other party has invoked the term.

Article 4.114   Confirmation

If the party who is entitled to avoid a contract confirms it, expressly or impliedly, after it knows of the ground for avoidance, or becomes capable of acting freely, avoidance of the contract is excluded.

Article 4.115   Effect of avoidance

On avoidance either party may claim restitution of whatever it has supplied under the contract, provided it makes concurrent restitution of whatever it has received. If restitution cannot be made in kind for any reason, a reasonable sum must be paid for what has been received.

Article 4.116   Partial avoidance

If a ground of avoidance affects only particular terms of a contract, the effect of an avoidance is limited to those terms unless, giving due consideration to all the circumstances of the case, it is unreasonable to uphold the remaining contract.

Article 4.117   Damages

(1) A party who avoids a contract under this Chapter may recover from the other party damages so as to put the avoiding party as nearly as possible into the same position as if it had not concluded the contract, provided that the other party knew or ought to have known of the mistake, fraud, threat or taking of excessive benefit or unfair advantage.

(2) If a party has the right to avoid a contract under this Chapter, but does not exercise its right or has lost its right under the provisions of Articles 4.113 or 4.114, it may recover, subject to paragraph (1), damages limited to the loss caused to it by the mistake, fraud, threat or taking of excessive benefit or unfair advantage. The same measure of damages shall apply when the party was misled by incorrect information in the sense of Article 4.106.

(3) In other respects, the damages shall be in accordance with the relevant provisions of Chapter 9, Section 5, with appropriate adaptations.

Article 4.118   Exclusion or restriction of remedies

(1) Remedies for fraud, threats and excessive benefit or unfair advantage-taking, and the right to avoid an unfair term which has not been individually negotiated, cannot be excluded or restricted.

(2) Remedies for mistake and incorrect information may be excluded or restricted unless the exclusion or restriction is contrary to good faith and fair dealing.

Article 4.119 Remedies for non-performance

A party who is entitled to a remedy under this Chapter in circumstances which afford that party a remedy for non-performance may pursue either remedy.

CHAPTER 5   INTERPRETATION

Article 5.101 General rules of interpretation

(1) A contract is to be interpreted according to the common intention of the parties even if this differs from the literal meaning of the words.

(2) If it is established that one party intended the contract to have a particular meaning, and at the time of the conclusion of the contract the other party could not have been unaware of the first party's intention, the contract is to be interpreted in the way intended by the first party.

(3) If an intention cannot be established according to (1) or (2), the contract is to be interpreted according to the meaning that reasonable persons of the same kind as the parties would give to it in the same circumstances.

Article 5.102 Relevant circumstances

In interpreting the contract, regard shall be had, in particular, to:
- (a) the circumstances in which it was concluded, including the preliminary negotiations;
- (b) the conduct of the parties, even subsequent to the conclusion of the contract;
- (c) the nature and purpose of the contract;
- (d) the interpretation which has already been given to similar clauses by the parties and the practices they have established between themselves;
- (e) the meaning commonly given to terms and expressions in the branch of activity concerned and the interpretation similar clauses may already have received;
- (f) usages; and
- (g) good faith and fair dealing.

Article 5.103 Contra proferentem rule

Where there is doubt about the meaning of a contract term not individually negotiated, an interpretation of the term against the party who supplied it is to be preferred.

Article 5.104 Preference to negotiated terms

Terms which have been individually negotiated take preference over those which have not.

Article 5.105 Reference to contract as a whole

Terms are to be interpreted in the light of the whole contract in which they appear.

Article 5.106 Terms to be given effect

An interpretation which renders the terms of the contract lawful, or effective, is to be preferred to one which would not.

Article 5.107 Linguistic discrepancies

Where a contract is drawn up in two or more language versions none of which is stated to be authoritative, there is, in case of discrepancy between the versions, a preference for the interpretation according to the version in which the contract was originally drawn up.

CHAPTER 6   CONTENTS AND EFFECTS

Article 6.101 Statements giving rise to contractual obligations

(1) A statement made by one party before or when the contract is concluded is to be treated as giving rise to a contractual obligation if that is how the other party reasonably

understood it in the circumstances, taking into account:
- (a) the apparent importance of the statement to the other party;
- (b) whether the party was making the statement in the course of business; and
- (c) the relative expertise of the parties.

(2) If one of the parties is a professional supplier which gives information about the quality or use of services or goods or other property when marketing or advertising them or otherwise before the contract for them is concluded, the statement is to be treated as giving rise to a contractual obligation unless it is shown that the other party knew or could not have been unaware that the statement was incorrect.

(3) Such information and other undertakings given by a person advertising or marketing services, goods or other property for the professional supplier, or by a person in earlier links of the business chain, are to be treated as giving rise to a contractual obligation on the part of the professional supplier unless it did not know and had no reason to know of the information or undertaking.

Article 6.102   Implied terms
In addition to the express terms, a contract may contain implied terms which stem from
- (a) the intention of the parties,
- (b) the nature and purpose of the contract, and
- (c) good faith and fair dealing.

Article 6.103   Simulation
When the parties have concluded an apparent contract which was not intended to reflect their true agreement, as between the parties the true agreement prevails.

Article 6.104   Determination of price
Where the contract does not fix the price or the method of determining it, the parties are to be treated as having agreed on a reasonable price.

Article 6.105   Unilateral determination by a party
Where the price or any other contractual term is to be determined by one party and that party's determination is grossly unreasonable, then notwithstanding any provision to the contrary, a reasonable price or other term shall be substituted.

Article 6.106   Determination by a third person
(1) Where the price or any other contractual term is to be determined by a third person, and it cannot or will not do so, the parties are presumed to have empowered the court to appoint another person to determine it.

(2) If a price or other term fixed by a third person is grossly unreasonable, a reasonable price or term shall be substituted.

Article 6.107   Reference to a non-existent factor
Where the price or any other contractual term is to be determined by reference to a factor which does not exist or has ceased to exist or to be accessible, the nearest equivalent factor shall be substituted.

Article 6.108   Quality of performance
If the contract does not specify the quality, a party must tender performance of at least average quality.

Article 6.109   Contract for an indefinite period
A contract for an indefinite period may be ended by either party by giving notice of reasonable length.

Article 6.110   Stipulation in favour of a third party
(1) A third party may require performance of a contractual obligation when its right to do so has been expressly agreed upon between the promisor and the promisee, or when such

agreement is to be inferred from the purpose of the contract or the circumstances of the case. The third party need not be identified at the time the agreement is concluded.

(2) If the third party renounces the right to performance the right is treated as never having accrued to it.

(3) The promisee may by notice to the promisor deprive the third party of the right to performance unless:

(a) the third party has received notice from the promisee that the right has been made irrevocable, or

(b) the promisor or the promisee has received notice from the third party that the latter accepts the right.

Article 6.111   Change of circumstances

(1) A party is bound to fulfil its obligations even if performance has become more onerous, whether because the cost of performance has increased or because the value of the performance it receives has diminished.

(2) If, however, performance of the contract becomes excessively onerous because of a change of circumstances, the parties are bound to enter into negotiations with a view to adapting the contract or terminating it, provided that:

(a) the change of circumstances occurred after the time of conclusion of the contract,

(b) the possibility of a change of circumstances was not one which could reasonably have been taken into account at the time of conclusion of the contract, and

(c) the risk of the change of circumstances is not one which, according to the contract, the party affected should be required to bear.

(3) If the parties fail to reach agreement within a reasonable period, the court may:

(a) end the contract at a date and on terms to be determined by the court; or

(b) adapt the contract in order to distribute between the parties in a just and equitable manner the losses and gains resulting from the change of circumstances.

In either case, the court may award damages for the loss suffered through a party refusing to negotiate or breaking off negotiations contrary to good faith and fair dealing.

CHAPTER 7   PERFORMANCE

Article 7.101   Place of performance

(1) If the place of performance of a contractual obligation is not fixed by or determinable from the contract it shall be:

(a) in the case of an obligation to pay money, the creditor's place of business at the time of the conclusion of the contract;

(b) in the case of an obligation other than to pay money, the obligor's place of business at the time of the conclusion of the contract.

(2) If a party has more than one place of business, the place of business for the purpose of the preceding paragraph is that which has the closest relationship to the contract, having regard to the circumstances known to or contemplated by the parties at the time of conclusion of the contract.

(3) If a party does not have a place of business its habitual residence is to be treated as its place of business.

Article 7.102   Time of performance

A party has to effect its performance:

(1) if a time is fixed by or determinable from the contract, at that time;

(2) if a period of time is fixed by or determinable from the contract, at any time within that period unless the circumstances of the case indicate that the other party is to choose the time;

(3) in any other case, within a reasonable time after the conclusion of the contract.

Article 7.103   Early performance

(1) A party may decline a tender of performance made before it is due except where acceptance of the tender would not unreasonably prejudice its interests.

(2) A party's acceptance of early performance does not affect the time fixed for the performance of its own obligation.

Article 7.104   Order of performance

To the extent that the performances of the parties can be rendered simultaneously, the parties are bound to render them simultaneously unless the circumstances indicate otherwise.

Article 7.105   Alternative performance

(1) Where an obligation may be discharged by one of alternative performances, the choice belongstothe party which is to perform, unless the circumstances indicate otherwise.

(2) If the party which is to make the choice fails to do so by the time required by the contract, then:

    (a) if the delay in choosing is fundamental, the right to choose passes to the other party;

    (b) if the delay is not fundamental, the other party may give a notice fixing an additional period of reasonable length in which the party to choose must do so. If the latter fails to do so, the right to choose passes to the other party.

Article 7.106   Performance by a third person

(1) Except where the contract requires personal performance the creditor cannot refuse performance by a third person if:

    (a) the third person acts with the assent of the debtor; or

    (b) the third person has a legitimate interest in performance and the debtor has failed to perform or it is clear that it will not perform at the time performance is due.

(2) Performance by the third person in accordance with paragraph (1) discharges the debtor.

Article 7.107   Form of payment

(1) Payment of money due may be made in any form used in the ordinary course of business.

(2) A creditor which, pursuant to the contract or voluntarily, accepts a cheque or other order to pay or a promise to pay is presumed to do so only on condition that it will be honoured. The creditor may not enforce the original obligation to pay unless the order or promise is not honoured.

Article 7.108   Currency of payment

(1) The parties may agree that payment shall be made only in a specified currency.

(2) In the absence of such agreement, a sum of money expressed in a currency other than that of the place where payment is due may be paid in the currency of that place according to the rate of exchange prevailing there at the time when payment is due.

(3) If, in a case falling within the preceding paragraph, the debtor has not paid at the time when payment is due, the creditor may require payment in the currency of the place where payment is due according to the rate of exchange prevailing there either at the time when payment is due or at the time of actual payment.

Article 7.109   Appropriation of performance

(1) Where a party has to perform several obligations of the same nature and the performance tendered does not sufice to discharge all of the obligations, then subject to paragraph (4) the party may at the time of its performance declare to which obligation the performance is to be appropriated.

(2) If the performing party does not make such a declaration, the other party may within a reasonable time appropriate the performance to such obligation as it chooses. It shall inform

the performing party of the choice. However, any such appropriation to an obligation which:
>(a) is not yet due, or
>(b) is illegal, or
>(c) is disputed, is invalid.

(3) In the absence of an appropriation by either party, and subject to paragraph (4), the performance is appropriated to that obligation which satisfies one of the following criteria in the sequence indicated:
>(a) the obligation which is due or is the first to fall due;
>(b) the obligation for which the creditor has the least security;
>(c) the obligation which is the most burdensome for the debtor,
>(d) the obligation which has arisen first. If none of the preceding criteria applies, the performance is appropriated proportionately to all obligations.

(4) In the case of a monetary obligation, a payment by the debtor is to be appropriated, first, to expenses, secondly, to interest, and thirdly, to principal, unless the creditor makes a different appropriation.

Article 7.110   Property not accepted

(1) A party which is left in possession of tangible property other than money because of the other party's failure to accept or retake the property must take reasonable steps to protect and preserve the property.

(2) The party left in possession may discharge its duty to deliver or return:
>(a) by depositing the property on reasonable terms with a third person to be held to the order of the other party, and notifying the other party of this; or
>(b) by selling the property on reasonable terms after notice to the other party, and paying the net proceeds to that party.

(3) Where, however, the property is liable to rapid deterioration or its preservation is unreasonably expensive, the party must take reasonable steps to dispose of it. It may discharge its duty to deliver or return by paying the net proceeds to the other party.

(4) The party left in possession is entitled to be reimbursed or to retain out of the proceeds of sale any expenses reasonably incurred.

Article 7.111   Money not accepted

Where a party fails to accept money properly tendered by the other party, that party may after notice to the first party discharge its obligation to pay by depositing the money to the order of the first party in accordance with the law of the place where payment is due.

Article 7.112   Costs of performance

Each party shall bear the costs of performance of its obligations.

CHAPTER 8   NON-PERFORMANCE AND REMEDIES IN GENERAL

Article 8.101   Remedies available

(1) Whenever a party does not perform an obligation under the contract and the non-performance is not excused under Article 8.108, the aggrieved party may resort to any of the remedies set out in Chapter 9.

(2) Where a party's non-performance is excused under Article 8.108, the aggrieved party may resort to any of the remedies set out in Chapter 9 except claiming performance and damages.

(3) A party may not resort to any of the remedies set out in Chapter 9 to the extent that its own act caused the other party's non-performance.

Article 8.102   Cumulation of remedies

Remedies which are not incompatible may be cumulated. In particular, a party is not deprived of its right to damages by exercising its right to any other remedy.

Article 8.103   Fundamental non-performance

A non-performance of an obligation is fundamental to the contract if:

    (a) strict compliance with the obligation is of the essence of the contract; or

    (b) the non-performance substantially deprives the aggrieved party of what it was entitled to expect under the contract, unless the other party did not foresee and could not reasonably have foreseen that result; or

    (c) the non-performance is intentional and gives the aggrieved party reason to believe that it cannot rely on the other party's future performance.

Article 8.104   Cure by non-performing party

A party whose tender of performance is not accepted by the other party because it does not conform to the contract may make a new and conforming tender where the time for performance has not yet arrived or the delay would not be such as to constitute a fundamental nonperformance.

Article 8.105   Assurance of performance

(1) A party which reasonably believes that there will be a fundamental non-performance by the other party may demand adequate assurance of due performance and mean-while may withhold performance of its own obligations so long as such reasonable belief continues.

(2) Where this assurance is not provided within a reasonable time, the party demanding it may terminate the contract if it still reasonably believes that there will be a fundamental non-performance by the other party and gives notice of termination without delay.

Article 8.106   Notice fixing additional period for performance

(1) In any case of non-performance the aggrieved party may by notice to the other party allow an additional period of time for performance.

(2) During the additional period the aggrieved party may withhold performance of its own reciprocal obligations and may claim damages, but it may not resort to any other remedy. If it receives notice from the other party that the latter will not perform within that period, or if upon expiry of that period due performance has not been made, the aggrieved party may resort to any of the remedies that may be available under chapter 9.

(3) If in a case of delay in performance which is not fundamental the aggrieved party has given a notice fixing an additional period of time of reasonable length, it may terminate the contract at the end of the period of notice. The aggrieved party may in its notice provide that if the other party does not perform within the period fixed by the notice the contract shall terminate automatically. If the period stated is too short, the aggrieved party may terminate, or, as the case may be, the contract shall terminate automatically, only after a reasonable period from the time of the notice.

Article 8.107   Performance entrusted to another

A party who entrusts performance of the contract to another person remains responsible for performance.

Article 8.108   Excuse due to an impediment

(1) A party's non-performance is excused if it proves that it is due to an impediment beyond its control and that it could not reasonably have been expected to take the impediment into account at the time of the conclusion of the contract, or to have avoided or overcome the impediment or its consequences.

(2) Where the impediment is only temporary the excuse provided by this article has effect for the period during which the impediment exists. However, if the delay amounts to a fundamental non-performance, the creditor may treat it as such.

(3) The non-performing party must ensure that notice of the impediment and of its effect on its ability to perform is received by the other party within a reasonable time after the non-performing party knew or ought to have known of these circumstances. The other party is entitled to damages for any loss resulting from the non-receipt of such notice.

Article 8.109   Clause excluding or restricting remedies
Remedies for non-performance may be excluded or restricted unless it would be contrary to good faith and fair dealing to invoke the exclusion or restriction.

CHAPTER 9   PARTICULAR REMEDIES FOR NON-PERFORMANCE

SECTION 1   RIGHT TO PERFORMANCE

Article 9.101   Monetary obligations
(1) The creditor is entitled to recover money which is due.
(2) Where the creditor has not yet performed its obligation and it is clear that the debtor will be unwilling to receive performance, the creditor may nonetheless proceed with its performance and may recover any sum due under the contract unless:
    (a) it could have made a reasonable substitute transaction without significant effort or expense; or
    (b) performance would be unreasonable in the circumstances.

Article 9.102   Non-monetary obligations
(1) The aggrieved party is entitled to specific performance of an obligation other than one to pay money, including the remedying of a defective performance.
(2) Specific performance cannot, however, be obtained where:
    (a) performance would be unlawful or impossible; or
    (b) performance would cause the debtor unreasonable effort or expense; or
    (c) the performance consists in the provision of services or work of a personal character or depends upon a personal relationship, or
    (d) the aggrieved party may reasonably obtain performance from another source.
(3) The aggrieved party will lose the right to specific performance if it fails to seek it within a reasonable time after it has or ought to have become aware of the non-performance.

Article 9.103   Damages not precluded
The fact that a right to performance is excluded under this Section does not preclude a claim for damages.

SECTION 2   WITHHOLDING PERFORMANCE

Article 9.201   Right to withhold performance
(1) A party who is to perform simultaneously with or after the other party may withhold performance until the other has tendered performance or has performed. The first party may withhold the whole of its performance or a part of it as may be reasonable in the circumstances.
(2) A party may similarly withhold performance for as long as it is clear that there will be a non-performance by the other party when the other party's performance becomes due.

SECTION 3   TERMINATION OF THE CONTRACT

Article 9.301   Right to terminate the contract
(1) A party may terminate the contract if the other party's non-performance is fundamental.
(2) In the case of delay the aggrieved party may also terminate the contract under Article 8.106 (3).

Article 9.302   Contract to be performed in parts
If the contract is to be performed in separate parts and in relation to a part to which a counter-performance can be apportioned, there is a fundamental non-performance, the

aggrieved party may exercise its right to terminate under this Section in relation to the part concerned. It may terminate the contract as a whole only if the non-performance is fundamental to the contract as whole.

Article 9.303   Notice of termination

(1) A party's right to terminate the contract is to be exercised by notice to the other party.

(2) The aggrieved party loses its right to terminate the contract unless it gives notice within a reasonable time after it has or ought to have become aware of the non-performance.

(a) When performance has not been tendered by the time it was due, the aggrieved party need not give notice of termination before a tender has been made. If a tender is later made it loses its right to terminate if it does not give such notice within a reasonable time after it has or ought to have become aware of the tender.

(b) If, however, the aggrieved party knows or has reason to know that the other party still intends to tender within a reasonable time, and the aggrieved party unreasonably fails to notify the other party that it will not accept performance, it loses its right to terminate if the other party in fact tenders within a reasonable time.

(4) If a party is excused under Article 8.108 through an impediment which is total and permanent, the contract is terminated automatically and without notice at the time the impediment arises.

Article 9.304   Anticipatory non-performance

Where prior to the time for performance by a party it is clear that there will be a fundamental non-performance by it, the other party may terminate the contract.

Article 9.305   Effects of termination in general

(1) Termination of the contract releases both parties from their obligation to effect and to receive future performance, but, subject to Articles 9.306 to 9.308, does not affect the rights and liabilities that have accrued up to the time of termination.

(2) Termination does not affect any provision of the contract for the settlement of disputes or any other provision which is to operate even after termination.

Article 9.306   Property reduced in value

A party who terminates the contract may reject property previously received from the other party if its value to the first party has been fundamentally reduced as a result of the other party's non-performance.

Article 9.307   Recovery of money paid

On termination of the contract a party may recover money paid for a performance which it did not receive or which it properly rejected.

Article 9.308   Recovery of property

On termination of the contract a party which has supplied property which can be returned and for which it has not received payment or other counter-performance may recover the property.

Article 9.309   Recovery for performance that cannot be returned

On termination of the contract a party which has rendered a performance which cannot be returned and for which it has not received payment or other counter-performance may recover a reasonable amount for the value of the performance to the other party.

SECTION 4   PRICE REDUCTION

Article 9.401   Right to reduce price

(1) A party which accepts a tender of performance not conforming to the contract may reduce the price. This reduction shall be proportionate to the decrease in the value of the performance at the time this was tendered compared to the value which a conforming tender would have had at that time.

(2) A party which is entitled to reduce the price under the preceding paragraph and which has already paid a sum exceeding the reduced price may recover the excess from the other party.

(3) A party which reduces the price cannot also recover damages for reduction in the value of the performance but remains entitled to damages for any further loss it has suffered so far as these are recoverable under Section 5 of this Chapter.

SECTION 5   DAMAGES AND INTEREST

Article 9.501   Right to damages

(1) The aggrieved party is entitled to damages for loss caused by the other party's non-performance which is not excused under Article 8.108.

(2) The loss for which damages are recoverable includes:

    (a) non-pecuniary loss; and

    (b) future loss which is reasonably likely to occur.

Article 9.502   General measure of damages

The general measure of damages is such sum as will put the aggrieved party as nearly as possible into the position in which it would have been if the contract had been duly performed. Such damages cover the loss which the aggrieved party has suffered and the gain of which it has been deprived.

Article 9.503   Foreseeability

The non-performing party is liable only for loss which it foresaw or could reasonably have foreseen at the time of conclusion of the contract as a likely result of its non-performance, unless the non-performance was intentional or grossly negligent.

Article 9.504   Loss attributable to aggrieved party

The non-performing party is not liable for loss suffered by the aggrieved party to the extent that the aggrieved party contributed to the non-performance or its effects.

Article 9.505   Reduction of loss

(1) The non-performing party is not liable for loss suffered by the aggrieved party to the extent that the aggrieved party could have reduced the loss by taking reasonable steps.

(2) The aggrieved party is entitled to recover any expenses reasonably incurred in attempting to reduce the loss.

Article 9.506   Substitute transaction

Where the aggrieved party has terminated the contract and has made a substitute transaction within a reasonable time and in a reasonable manner, it may recover the difference between the contract price and the price of the substitute transaction as well as damages for any further loss so far as these are recoverable under this Section.

Article 9.507   Current price

Where the aggrieved party has terminated the contract and has not made a substitute transaction but there is a current price for the performance contracted for, it may recover the difference between the contract price and the price current at the time the contract is terminated as well as damages for any further loss so far as these are recoverable under this Section.

Article 9.508   Delay in payment of money

(1) If payment of a sum of money is delayed, the aggrieved party is entitled to interest on that sum from the time when payment is due to the time of payment at the average commercial bank short-term lending rate to prime borrowers prevailing for the contractual currency of payment at the place where payment is due.

(2) The aggrieved party may in addition recover damages for any further loss so far as these are recoverable under this Section.

Article 9.509   Agreed Payment for non-performance

(1) Where the contract provides that a party which fails to perform is to pay a specified sum to the aggrieved party for such non-performance, the aggrieved party shall be awarded that sum irrespective of its actual loss.

(2) However, despite any agreement to the contrary the specified sum may be reduced to a reasonable amount where it is grossly excessive in relation to the loss resulting from the non-performance and the other circumstances.

Article 9.510   Currency by which damages are to be measured

Damages are to be measured by the currency which most appropriately reflects the aggrieved party's loss.

CHAPTER 10   PLURALITY OF PARTIES

SECTION 1   PLURALITY OF DEBTORS

Article 10.101   Solidary, separate and communal obligations

(1) Obligations are solidary when all the debtors are bound to render one and the same performance and the creditor may require it from any one of them until full performance has been received.

(2) Obligations are separate when each debtor is bound to render only part of the performance and the creditor may require from each debtor only that debtor's part.

(3) An obligation is communal when all the debtors are bound to render the performance together and the creditor may require it only from all of them.

Article 10.102   When solidary obligations arise

(1) If several debtors are bound to render one and the same performance to a creditor under the same contract, they are solidarily liable, unless the contract or the law provides otherwise.

(2) Solidary obligations also arise where several persons are liable for the same damage.

(3) The fact that the debtors are not liable on the same terms does not prevent their obligations from being solidary.

Article 10.103   Liability under separate obligations

Debtors bound by separate obligations are liable in equal shares unless the contract or the law provides otherwise.

Article 10.104   Communal obligations: special rule when money claimed for non-performance

Notwithstanding Article 10.101(3), when money is claimed for non-performance of a communal obligation, the debtors are solidarily liable for payment to the creditor.

Article 10.105   Apportionment between solidary debtors

(1) As between themselves, solidary debtors are liable in equal shares unless the contract or the law provides otherwise.

(2) If two or more debtors are liable for the same damage under Article 10:102(2), their share of liability as between themselves is determined according to the law governing the event which gave rise to the liability.

Article 10.106   Recourse between solidary debtors

(1) A solidary debtor who has performed more than that debtor's share may claim the excess from any of the other debtors to the extent of each debtor's unperformed share, together with a share of any costs reasonably incurred.

(2) A solidary debtor to whom paragraph (1) applies may also, subject to any prior right and interest of the creditor, exercise the rights and actions of the creditor, including accessory securities, to recover the excess from any of the other debtors to the extent of each debtor's unperformed share.

(3) If a solidary debtor who has performed more than that debtor's share is unable, despite all reasonable efforts, to recover contribution from another solidary debtor, the share of the others, including the one who has performed, is increased proportionally.

Article 10.107   Performance, set-off and merger in solidary obligations

(1) Performance or set-off by a solidary debtor or set-off by the creditor against one solidary debtor discharges the other debtors in relation to the creditor to the extent of the performance or set-off.

(2) Merger of debts between a solidary debtor and the creditor discharges the other debtors only for the share of the debtor concerned.

Article 10.108   Release or settlement in solidary obligations

(1) When the creditor releases, or reaches a settlement with, one solidary debtor, the other debtors are discharged of liability for the share of that debtor.

(2) The debtors are totally discharged by the release or settlement if it so provides.

(3) As between solidary debtors, the debtor who is discharged from that debtor's share is discharged only to the extent of the share at the time of the discharge and not from any supplementary share for which that debtor may subsequently become liable under Article 10:106(3).

Article 10.109   Effect of judgment in solidary obligations

A decision by a court as to the liability to the creditor of one solidary debtor does not affect:

(a) the liability to the creditor of the other solidary debtors; or

(b) the rights of recourse between the solidary debtors under Article 10:106.

Article 10.110   Prescription in solidary obligations

Prescription of the creditor's right to performance ("claim") against one solidary debtor does not affect:

(a) the liability to the creditor of the other solidary debtors; or

(b) the rights of recourse between the solidary debtors under Article 10:106.

Article 10.111   Opposability of other defences in solidary obligations

(1) A solidary debtor may invoke against the creditor any defence which another solidary debtor can invoke, other than a defence personal to that other debtor. Invoking the defence has no effect with regard to the other solidary debtors.

(2) A debtor from whom contribution is claimed may invoke against the claimant any personal defence that that debtor could have invoked against the creditor.

SECTION 2   PLURALITY OF CREDITORS

Article 10.201   Solidary, separate and communal claims

(1) Claims are solidary when any of the creditors may require full performance from the debtor and when the debtor may render performance to any of the creditors.

(2) Claims are separate when the debtor owes each creditor only that creditor's share of the claim and each creditor may require performance only of that creditor's share.

(3) A claim is communal when the debtor must perform to all the creditors and any creditor may require performance only for the benefit of all.

Article 10.202   Apportionment of separate claims

Separate creditors are entitled to equal shares unless the contract or the law provides otherwise.

Article 10.203 Difficulties of executing a communal claim

If one of the creditors in a communal claim refuses, or is unable to receive, the performance, the debtor may discharge the obligation to perform by depositing the property or money with a third party according to Articles 7.110 or 7.111 of the Principles.

Article 10.204 Apportionment of solidary claims

(1) Solidary creditors are entitled to equal shares unless the contract or the law provides otherwise.

(2) A creditor who has received more than that creditor's share must transfer the excess to the other creditors to the extent of their respective shares.

Article 10.205 Regime of solidary claims

(1) A release granted to the debtor by one of the solidary creditors has no effect on the other solidary creditors.

(2) The rules of Articles 10.107, 10.109, 10.110 and 10.111(1) apply, with appropriate adaptations, to solidary claims.

CHAPTER 11   ASSIGNMENT OF CLAIMS

SECTION 1:   GENERAL PRINCIPLES

Article 11.101 Scope of chapter

(1) This Chapter applies to the assignment by agreement of a right to performance ("claim") under an existing or future contract.

(2) Except where otherwise stated or the context otherwise requires, this Chapter also applies to the assignment by agreement of other transferable claims.

(3) This Chapter does not apply:
  (a) to the transfer of a financial instrument or investment security where, under the law otherwise applicable, such transfer must be by entry in a register maintained by or for the issuer; or
  (b) to the transfer of a bill of exchange or other negotiable instrument or of a negotiable security or a document of title to goods where, under the law otherwise applicable, such transfer must be by delivery (with any necessary indorsement).

(4) In this Chapter "assignment" includes an assignment by way of security.

(5) This Chapter also applies, with appropriate adaptations, to the granting by agreement of a right in security over a claim otherwise than by assignment.

Article 11.102 Contractual claims generally assignable

(1) Subject to Articles 11.301 and 11.302, a party to a contract may assign a claim under it.

(2) A future claim arising under an existing or future contract may be assigned if at the time when it comes into existence, or at such other time as the parties agree, it can be identified as the claim to which the assignment relates.

Article 11.103 Partial assignment

A claim which is divisible may be assigned in part, but the assignor is liable to the debtor for any increased costs which the debtor thereby incurs.

Article 11.104 Form of Assignment

An assignment need not be in writing and is not subject to any other requirement as to form. It may be proved by any means, including witnesses.

SECTION 2 EFFECTS OF ASSIGNMENT AS BETWEEN ASSIGNOR AND ASSIGNEE

Article 11.201 Rights transferred to assignee

(1) The assignment of a claim transfers to the assignee:

(a) all the assignor's rights to performance in respect of the claim assigned; and

(b) all accessory rights securing such performance.

(2) Where the assignment of a claim under a contract is associated with the substitution of the assignee as debtor in respect of any obligation owed by the assignor under the same contract, this Article takes effect subject to Article 12.201.

Article 11.202 When assignment takes effect

(1) An assignment of an existing claim takes effect at the time of the agreement to assign or such later time as the assignor and assignee agree.

(2) An assignment of a future claim is dependent upon the assigned claim coming into existence but thereupon takes effect from the time of the agreement to assign or such later time as the assignor and assignee agree.

Article 11.203 Preservation of assignee's rights against assignor

An assignment is effective as between the assignor and assignee, and entitles the assignee to whatever the assignor receives from the debtor, even if it is ineffective against the debtor under Article 11.301 or 11.302.

Article 11.204 Undertakings by assignor

By assigning or purporting to assign a claim the assignor undertakes to the assignee that:

(a) at the time when the assignment is to take effect the following conditions will be satisfied except as otherwise disclosed to the assignee:

(i) the assignor has the right to assign the claim;

(ii) the claim exists and the assignee's rights are not affected by any defences or rights (including any right of set-off) which the debtor might have against the assignor; and

(iii) the claim is not subject to any prior assignment or right in security in favour of any other party or to any other encumbrance;

(b) the claim and any contract under which it arises will not be modified without the consent of the assignee unless the modification is provided for in the assignment agreement or is one which is made in good faith and is of a nature to which the assignee could not reasonably object; and

(c) the assignor will transfer to the assignee all transferable rights intended to secure performance which are not accessory rights.

SECTION 3 EFFECTS OF ASSIGNMENT AS BETWEEN ASSIGNEE AND DEBTOR

Article 11.301 Contractual prohibition of assignment

(1) An assignment which is prohibited by or is otherwise not in conformity with the contract under which the assigned claim arises is not effective against the debtor unless:

(a) the debtor has consented to it; or

(b) the assignee neither knew nor ought to have known of the non-conformity; or

(c) the assignment is made under a contract for the assignment of future rights to payment of money.

(2) Nothing in the preceding paragraph affects the assignor's liability for the non-conformity.

Article 11.302 Other ineffective assignments

An assignment to which the debtor has not consented is ineffective against the debtor so far as it relates to a performance which the debtor, by reason of the nature of the performance or the relationship of the debtor and the assignor, could not reasonably be required to render to anyone except the assignor.

Article 11.303 Effect on debtor's obligation

(1) Subject to Article 11.301, 11.302, 11.307 and 11.308, the debtor is bound to perform in favour of the assignee if and only if the debtor has received a notice in writing from the assignor or the assignee which reasonably identifies the claim which has been assigned and requires the debtor to give performance to the assignee.

(2) However, if such notice is given by the assignee, the debtor may within a reasonable time request the assignee to provide reliable evidence of the assignment, pending which the debtor may withhold performance.

(3) Where the debtor has acquired knowledge of the assignment otherwise than by a notice conforming to paragraph (1), the debtor may either withhold performance from or give performance to the assignee.

(4) Where the debtor gives performance to the assignor, the debtor is discharged if and only if the performance is given without knowledge of the assignment.

Article 11.304 Protection of debtor

A debtor who performs in favour of a person identified as assignee in a notice of assignment under Article 11:303 is discharged unless the debtor could not have been unaware that such person was not the person entitled to performance.

Article 11.305 Competing demands

A debtor who has received notice of two or more competing demands for performance may discharge liability by conforming to the law of the due place of performance, or, if the performances are due in different places, the law applicable to the claim.

Article 11.306 Place of performance

(1) Where the assigned claim relates to an obligation to pay money at a particular place, the assignee may require payment at any place within the same country or, if that country is a Member State of the European Union, at any place within the European Union, but the assignor is liable to the debtor for any increased costs which the debtor incurs by reason of any change in the place of performance.

(2) Where the assigned claim relates to a non-monetary obligation to be performed at a particular place, the assignee may not require performance at any other place.

Article 11.307 Defences and rights of set-off

(1) The debtor may set up against the assignee all substantive and procedural defences to the assigned claim which the debtor could have used against the assignor.

(2) The debtor may also assert against the assignee all rights of set-off which would have been available against the assignor under Chapter 13 in respect of any claim against the assignor:

    (a) existing at the time when a notice of assignment, whether or not conforming to Article 11.303(1), reaches the debtor; or

    (b) closely connected with the assigned claim.

Article 11.308 Unauthorised modification not binding on assignee

A modification of the claim made by agreement between the assignor and the debtor, without the consent of the assignee, after a notice of assignment, whether or not conforming to Article 11.303(1), reaches the debtor does not affect the rights of the assignee against the debtor unless the modification is provided for in the assignment agreement or is one which is made in good faith and is of a nature to which the assignee could not reasonably object.

SECTION 4   ORDER OF PRIORITY BETWEEN ASSIGNEE AND COMPETING CLAIMANTS

Article 11.401   Priorities

(1) Where there are successive assignments of the same claim, the assignee whose assignment is first notified to the debtor has priority over any earlier assignee if at the time of the later assignment the assignee under that assignment neither knew nor ought to have known of the earlier assignment.

(2) Subject to paragraph (1), the priority of successive assignments, whether of existing or future claims, is determined by the order in which they are made.

(3) The assignee's interest in the assigned claim has priority over the interest of a creditor of the assignor who attaches that claim, whether by judicial process or otherwise, after the time the assignment has taken effect under Article 11.202.

(4) In the event of the assignor's bankruptcy, the assignee's interest in the assigned claim has priority over the interest of the assignor's insolvency administrator and creditors, subject to any rules of the law applicable to the bankruptcy relating to:

(a) publicity required as a condition of such priority;

(b) the ranking of claims; or

(c) the avoidance or ineffectiveness of transactions in the bankruptcy proceedings.

CHAPTER 12   SUBSTITUTION OF NEW DEBTOR: TRANSFER OF CONTRACT

SECTION 1   SUBSTITUTION OF NEW DEBTOR

Article 12.101   Substitution: general rules

(1) A third person may undertake with the agreement of the debtor and the creditor to be substituted as debtor, with the effect that the original debtor is discharged.

(2) A creditor may agree in advance to a future substitution. In such a case the substitution takes effect only when the creditor is given notice by the new debtor of the agreement between the new and the original debtor.

Article 12.102   Effects of substitution on defences and securities

(1) The new debtor cannot invoke against the creditor any rights or defences arising from the relationship between the new debtor and the original debtor.

(2) The discharge of the original debtor also extends to any security of the original debtor given to the creditor for the performance of the obligation, unless the security is over an asset which is transferred to the new debtor as part of a transaction between the original and the new debtor.

(3) Upon discharge of the original debtor, a security granted by any person other than the new debtor for the performance of the obligation is released, unless that other person agrees that it should continue to be available to the creditor.

(4) The new debtor may invoke against the creditor all defences which the original debtor could have invoked against the creditor.

SECTION 2   TRANSFER OF CONTRACT

Article 12.201   Transfer of contract

(1) A party to a contract may agree with a third person that that person is to be substituted as the contracting party. In such a case the substitution takes effect only where, as a result of the other party's assent, the first party is discharged.

(2) To the extent that the substitution of the third person as a contracting party involves a transfer of rights to performance ("claims"), the provisions of Chapter 11 apply; to the extent that obligations are transferred, the provisions of Section 1 of this Chapter apply.

CHAPTER 13   SET-OFF

Article 13.101   Requirements for set-off
If two parties owe each other obligations of the same kind, either party may set off that party's right to performance ("claim") against the other party's claim, if and to the extent that, at the time of set-off, the first party:
  (a) is entitled to effect performance; and
  (b) may demand the other party's performance.

Article 13.102   Unascertained claims
  (1) A debtor may not set off a claim which is unascertained as to its existence or value unless the set-off will not prejudice the interests of the other party.
  (2) Where the claims of both parties arise from the same legal relationship it is presumed that the other party's interests will not be prejudiced.

Article 13.103   Foreign currency set-off
Where parties owe each other money in different currencies, each party may set off that party's claim against the other party's claim, unless the parties have agreed that the party declaring set-off is to pay exclusively in a specified currency.

Article 13.104   Notice of set-off
The right of set-off is exercised by notice to the other party.

Article 13.105   Plurality of claims and obligations
  (1) Where the party giving notice of set-off has two or more claims against the other party, the notice is effective only if it identifies the claim to which it relates.
  (2) Where the party giving notice of set-off has to perform two or more obligations towards the other party, the rules in Article 7.109 apply with appropriate adaptations.

Article 13.106   Effect of set-off
Set-off discharges the obligations, as far as they are coextensive, as from the time of notice.

Article 13.107   Exclusion of right of set-off
Set-off cannot be effected:
  (a) where it is excluded by agreement;
  (b) against a claim to the extent that that claim is not capable of attachment; and
  (c) against a claim arising from a deliberate wrongful act.

CHAPTER 14   PRESCRIPTION

SECTION 1   GENERAL PROVISION

Article 14.101   Claims subject to prescription
A right to performance of an obligation ("claim") is subject to prescription by the expiry of a period of time in accordance with these Principles.

SECTION 2   PERIODS OF PRESCRIPTION AND THEIR COMMENCEMENT

Article 14.201   General period
The general period of prescription is three years.

Article 14.202   Period for a claim established by legal proceedings

(1) The period of prescription for a claim established by judgment is ten years.

(2) The same applies to a claim established by an arbitral award or other instrument which is enforceable as if it were a judgment.

Article 14.203   Commencement

(1) The general period of prescription begins to run from the time when the debtor has to effect performance or, in the case of a right to damages, from the time of the act which gives rise to the claim.

(2) Where the debtor is under a continuing obligation to do or refrain from doing something, the general period of prescription begins to run with each breach of the obligation.

(3) The period of prescription set out in Article 14.202 begins to run from the time when the judgment or arbitral award obtains the effect of res judicata, or the other instrument becomes enforceable, though not before the debtor has to effect performance.

SECTION 3   EXTENSION OF PERIOD

Article 14.301   Suspension in case of ignorance

The running of the period of prescription is suspended as long as the creditor does not know of, and could not reasonably know of:

(a) the identity of the debtor; or

(b) the facts giving rise to the claim including, in the case of a right to damages, the type of damage.

Article 14.302   Suspension in case of judicial and other proceedings

(1) The running of the period of prescription is suspended from the time when judicial proceedings on the claim are begun.

(2) Suspension lasts until a decision has been made which has the effect of res judicata, or until the case has been otherwise disposed of.

(3) These provisions apply, with appropriate adaptations, to arbitration proceedings and to all other proceedings initiated with the aim of obtaining an instrument which is enforceable as if it were a judgment.

Article 14.303   Suspension in case of impediment beyond creditor's control

(1) The running of the period of prescription is suspended as long as the creditor is prevented from pursuing the claim by an impediment which is beyond the creditor's control and which the creditor could not reasonably have been expected to avoid or overcome.

(2) Paragraph (1) applies only if the impediment arises, or subsists, within the last six months of the prescription period.

Article 14.304   Postponement of expiry in case of negotiations

If the parties negotiate about the claim, or about circumstances from which a claim might arise, the period of prescription does not expire before one year has passed since the last communication made in the negotiations.

Article 14.305   Postonement of expiry in case of incapacity

(1) If a person subject to an incapacity is without a representative, the period of prescription of a claim held by or against that person does not expire before one year has passed after either the incapacity has ended or a representative has been appointed.

(2) The period of prescription of claims between a person subject to an incapacity and that person's representative does not expire before one year has passed after either the incapacity has ended or a new representative has been appointed.

Article 14.306   Postponement of expiry: deceased's estate
Where the creditor or debtor has died, the period of prescription of a claim held by or against the deceased's estate does not expire before one year has passed after the claim can be enforced by or against an heir, or by or against a representative of the estate.

Article 14.307   Maximum length of period
The period of prescription cannot be extended, by suspension of its running or postponement of its expiry under these Principles, to more than ten years or, in case of claims for personal injuries, to more than thirty years. This does not apply to suspension under Article 14.302.

SECTION 4   RENEWAL OF PERIODS

Article 14.401   Renewal by acknowledgement
   (1) If the debtor acknowledges the claim, vis-à-vis the creditor, by part payment, payment of interest, giving of security, or in any other manner, a new period of prescription begins to run.
   (2) The new period is the general period of prescription, regardless of whether the claim was originally subject to the general period of prescription or the ten year period under Article 14.202. In the latter case, however, this Article does not operate so as to shorten the ten year period.

Article 14.402   Renewal by attempted execution
The ten year period of prescription laid down in Article 14.202 begins to run again with each reasonable attempt at execution undertaken by the creditor.

SECTION 5   EFFECTS OF PRESCRIPTION

Article 14.501   General effect
   (1) After expiry of the period of prescription the debtor is entitled to refuse performance.
   (2) Whatever has been performed in order to discharge a claim may not be reclaimed merely because the period of prescription had expired.

Article 14.502   Effect on ancillary claims
The period of prescription for a right to payment of interest, and other claims of an ancillary nature, expires not later than the period for the principal claim.

Article 14.502   Effect on set-off
A claim in relation to which the period of prescription has expired may nonetheless be set off, unless the debtor has invoked prescription previously or does so within two months of notification of set-off.

SECTION 6   MODIFICATION BY AGREEMENT

Article 14.601   Agreements concerning prescription
   (1) The requirements for prescription may be modified by agreement between the parties, in particular by either shortening or lengthening the periods of prescription.
   (2) The period of prescription may not, however, be reduced to less than one year or extended to more than thirty years after the time of commencement set out in Article 14.203.

CHAPTER 15   ILLEGALITY

Article 15.101   Contracts contrary to fundamental principles
A contract is of no effect to the extent that it is contrary to principles recognised as fundamental in the laws of the Member States of the European Union.

Article 15.102   Contracts infringing mandatory rules

(1) Where a contract infringes a mandatory rule of law applicable under Article 1.103 of these Principles, the effects of that infringement upon the contract are the effects, if any, expressly prescribed by that mandatory rule.

(2) Where the mandatory rule does not expressly prescribe the effects of an infringement upon a contract, the contract may be declared to have full effect, to have some effect, to have no effect, or to be subject to modification.

(3) A decision reached under paragraph (2) must be an appropriate and proportional response to the infringement, having regard to all relevant circumstances, including:

    (a) the purpose of the rule which has been infringed;

    (b) the category of persons for whose protection the rule exists;

    (c) any sanction that may be imposed under the rule infringed;

    (d) the seriousness of the infringement;

    (e) whether the infringement was intentional; and

    (f) the closeness of the relationship between the infringement and the contract.

Article 15.103   Partial ineffectiveness

(1) If only part of a contract is rendered ineffective under Articles 15.101 or 15.102, the remaining part continues in effect unless, giving due consideration to all the circumstances of the case, it is unreasonable to uphold it.

(2) Articles 15.104 and 15.105 apply, with appropriate adaptations, to a case of partial ineffectiveness.

Article 15.104   Restitution

(1) When a contract is rendered ineffective under Articles 15.101 or 15.102, either party may claim restitution of whatever that party has supplied under the contract, provided that, where appropriate, concurrent restitution is made of whatever has been received.

(2) When considering whether to grant restitution under paragraph (1), and what con-current restitution, if any, would be appropriate, regard must be had to the factors referred to in Article 15.102(3).

(3) An award of restitution may be refused to a party who knew or ought to have known of the reason for the ineffectiveness.

(4) If restitution cannot be made in kind for any reason, a reasonable sum must be paid for what has been received.

Article 15.105   Damages

(1) A party to a contract which is rendered ineffective under Articles 15.101 or 15.102 may recover from the other party damages putting the first party as nearly as possible into the same position as if the contract had not been concluded, provided that the other party knew or ought to have known of the reason for the ineffectiveness.

(2) When considering whether to award damages under paragraph (1), regard must be had to the factors referred to in Article 15.102(3).

(3) An award of damages may be refused where the first party knew or ought to have known of the reason for the ineffectiveness.

CHAPTER 16   CONDITIONS

Article 16.101   Types of condition

A contractual obligation may be made conditional upon the occurrence of an uncertain future event, so that the obligation takes effect only if the event occurs (suspensive condition) or comes to an end if the event occurs (resolutive condition).

Article 16.102   Interference with conditions

(1) If fulfilment of a condition is prevented by a party, contrary to duties of good faith and fair dealing or co-operation, and if fulfilment would have operated to that party's disadvantage, the condition is deemed to be fulfilled.

(2) If fulfilment of a condition is brought about by a party, contrary to duties of good faith and fair dealing or co-operation, and if fulfilment operates to that party's advantage, the condition is deemed not to be fulfilled.

Article 16.102   Effect of condition

(1) Upon fulfilment of a suspensive condition, the relevant obligation takes effect unless the parties otherwise agree.

(2) Upon fulfilment of a resolutive condition, the relevant obligation comes to an end unless the parties otherwise agree.

CHAPTER 17   CAPITALISATION OF INTEREST

Article 17.101   When interest to be added to capital

(1) Interest payable according to Article 9.508(1) is added to the outstanding capital every 12 months.

(2) Paragraph (1) of this Article does not apply if the parties have provided for interest upon delay in payment.

Unidroit Principles for International Commercial Contracts 2004

[Reproduced from the Unidroit Principles of International Commercial Contracts, published by the International Institute for the Unification of Private Law (Unidroit), Rome, Italy, Copyright © Unidroit 2004, by permission of Unidroit. Readers are reminded that the official version of the Unidroit Principles of International Commercial Contracts 2004 contains not only the black-letter rules reproduced hereunder, but also detailed comments on each article and, where appropriate, illustrations. The volume may be ordered from UNIDROIT at www.unidroit.org. For an update of international case law and bibliography relating to the Principles see www.unilex.info.]

[2004]

PREAMBLE

(Purpose of the Principles)

These Principles set forth general rules for international commercial contracts.

They shall be applied when the parties have agreed that their contract be governed by them.[2]

They may be applied when the parties have agreed that their contract be governed by general principles of law, the *lex mercatoria* or the like.

They may provide a solution to an issue raised when it proves impossible to establish the relevant rule of the applicable law.

They may be used to interpret or supplement international uniform law instruments.

They may serve as a model for national and international legislators.

---

[2] Parties wishing to provide that their agreement be governed by the Principles might use the following words, adding any desired exceptions or modifications: "This contract shall be governed by the UNIDROIT Principles (2004) [except as to Articles...]". Parties wishing to provide in addition for the application of the law of a particular jurisdiction might use the following words: "This contract shall be governed by the UNIDROIT Principles (2004) [except as to Articles...], supplemented when necessary by the law of [jurisdiction X]".

CHAPTER 1   GENERAL PROVISIONS

1.1   Freedom of contract
The parties are free to enter into a contract and to determine its content.

1.2   No form required
Nothing in these Principles requires a contract to be concluded in or evidenced by writing. It may be proved by any means, including witnesses.

1.3   Binding character of contract
A contract validly entered into is binding upon the parties. It can only be modified or terminated in accordance with its terms or by agreement or as otherwise provided under these Principles.

1.4   Mandatory rules
Nothing in these Principles shall restrict the application of mandatory rules, whether of national, international, or supranational origin, which are applicable in accordance with the relevant rules of private international law.

1.5   Exclusion or modification by the parties
The parties may exclude the application of these Principles or derogate from or vary the effect of any of their provisions, except as otherwise provided in the Principles.

1.6   Interpretation and supplementation of the Principles
(1) In the interpretation of these Principles, regard is to be had to their international character and to their purposes including the need to promote uniformity in their application.

(2) Issues within the scope of these Principles but not expressly settled by them are as far as possible to be settled in accordance with their underlying general principles.

1.7   Good faith and fair dealing
(1) Each party must act in accordance with good faith and fair dealing in international trade.

(2) The parties may not exclude or limit this duty.

1.8   Inconsistent behaviour
A party cannot act inconsistently with an understanding it has caused the other party to have and upon which that other party reasonably has acted in reliance to its detriment.

1.9   Usages and practices
(1) The parties are bound by any usage to which they have agreed and by any practices which they have established between themselves.

(2) The parties are bound by a usage that is widely known to and regularly observed in international trade by parties in the particular trade concerned except where the application of such a usage would be unreasonable.

1.10   Notice
(1) Where notice is required it may be given by any means appropriate to the circumstances.

(2) A notice is effective when it reaches the person to whom it is given.

(3) For the purpose of paragraph (2) a notice "reaches" a person when given to the person orally or delivered at that person's place of business or mailing address.

(4) For the purpose of this article "notice" includes a declaration, demand, request or any other communication of intention.

1.11   Definitions
In these Principles
— "court" includes arbitration tribunal;

— where a party has more than one place of business the relevant "place of business" is that which has the closest relationship to the contract and its performance, having regard to the circumstances known to or contemplated by the parties at any time before or at the conclusion of the contract.

— "obligor" refers to the party who is to perform an obligation and "obligee" refers to the party who is entitled to performance of that obligation.

— "writing" means any mode of communication that preserves a record of the information contained therein and is capable of being reproduced in tangible form.

1.12 Computation of time set by parties

(1) Official holidays or non-business days occurring during a period set by parties for an act to be done are included in calculating the period.

(2) However, if the last day of the period is an official holiday or a non-business day at the place of business of the party to do the act, the period is extended until the first business day which follows, unless the circumstances indicate otherwise.

(3) The relevant time zone is that of the place of business of the party setting the time, unless the circumstances indicate otherwise.

CHAPTER 2   FORMATION AND AUTHORITY OF AGENTS

SECTION 1   FORMATION

2.1.1 Manner of formation

A contract may be concluded either by the acceptance of an offer or by conduct of the parties that is sufficient to show agreement.

2.1.2 Definition of offer

A proposal for concluding a contract constitutes an offer if it is sufficiently definite and indicates the intention of the offeror to be bound in case of acceptance.

2.1.3 Withdrawal of offer

(1) An offer becomes effective when it reaches the offeree.

(2) An offer, even if it is irrevocable, may be withdrawn if the withdrawal reaches the offeree before or at the same time as the offer.

2.1.4 Revocation of offer

(1) Until a contract is concluded an offer may be revoked if the revocation reaches the offeree before it has dispatched an acceptance.

(2) However, an offer cannot be revoked
   (a) if it indicates, whether by stating a fixed time for acceptance or otherwise, that it is irrevocable; or
   (b) if it was reasonable for the offeree to rely on the offer as being irrevocable and the offeree has acted in reliance on the offer.

2.1.5 Rejection of offer

An offer is terminated when a rejection reaches the offeror.

2.1.6 Mode of acceptance

(1) A statement made by or other conduct of the offeree indicating assent to an offer is an acceptance. Silence or inactivity does not in itself amount to acceptance.

(2) An acceptance of an offer becomes effective at the moment the indication of assent reaches the offeror.

(3) However, if, by virtue of the offer or as a result of practices which the parties have established between themselves or of usage, the offeree may indicate assent by performing an act without notice to the offeror, the acceptance is effective at the moment the act is performed.

2.1.7 Time of acceptance

An offer must be accepted within the time the offeror has fixed or, if no time is fixed, within a reasonable time having regard to the circumstances, including the rapidity of the means of communication employed by the offeror. An oral offer must be accepted immediately unless the circumstances indicate otherwise.

2.1.8 Acceptance within a fixed period of time

A period of acceptance fixed by the offeror begins to run from the time that the offer is dispatched. A time indicated in the offer is deemed to be the time of dispatch unless the circumstances indicate otherwise.

2.1.9 Late acceptance. Delay in acceptance

(1) A late acceptance is nevertheless effective as an acceptance if without undue delay the offeror so informs the offeree or gives a notice to that effect.

(2) If a communication containing a late acceptance shows that it has been sent in such circumstances that if its transmission had been normal it would have reached the offeror in due time, the late acceptance is effective as an acceptance unless, without undue delay, the offeror informs the offeree that it considers the offer as having lapsed.

2.1.10 Withdrawal of acceptance

An acceptance may be withdrawn if the withdrawal reaches the offeror before or at the same time as the acceptance would have become effective.

2.1.11 Modified acceptance

(1) A reply to an offer which purports to be an acceptance but contains additions, limitations or other modifications is a rejection of the offer and constitutes a counter-offer.

(2) However, a reply to an offer which purports to be an acceptance but contains additional or different terms which do not materially alter the terms of the offer constitutes an acceptance, unless the offeror, without undue delay, objects to the discrepancy. If the offeror does not object, the terms of the contract are the terms of the offer with the modifications contained in the acceptance.

2.1.12 Writings in confirmation

If a writing which is sent within a reasonable time after the conclusion of the contract and which purports to be a confirmation of the contract contains additional or different terms, such terms become part of the contract, unless they materially alter the contract or the recipient, without undue delay, objects to the discrepancy.

2.1.13 Conclusion of contract dependent on agreement on specific matters or in a particular form

Where in the course of negotiations one of the parties insists that the contract is not concluded until there is agreement on specific matters or in a particular form, no contract is concluded before agreement is reached on those matters or in that form.

2.1.14 Contract with terms deliberately left open

(1) If the parties intend to conclude a contract, the fact that they intentionally leave a term to be agreed upon in further negotiations or to be determined by a third person does not prevent a contract from coming into existence.

(2) The existence of the contract is not affected by the fact that subsequently

    (a) the parties reach no agreement on the term, or

    (b) the third person does not determine the term,

provided that there is an alternative means of rendering the term definite that is reasonable in the circumstances, having regard to the intention of the parties.

2.1.15 Negotiations in bad faith

(1) A party is free to negotiate and is not liable for failure to reach an agreement.

(2) However, a party who has negotiated or breaks off negotiations in bad faith is liable for the losses caused to the other party.

(3) It is bad faith, in particular, for a party to enter into or continue negotiations when intending not to make an agreement with the other party.

2.1.16 Duty of confidentiality

Where information is given as confidential by one party in the course of negotiations, the other party is under a duty not to disclose that information or to use it improperly for his own purposes, whether or not a contract is subsequently concluded. Where appropriate, the remedy for breach of that duty may include compensation based on the benefit received by the other party.

2.1.17 Merger clauses

A contract in writing which contains a clause indicating that the writing completely embodies the terms on which the parties have agreed cannot be contradicted or supplemented by evidence of prior statement or agreements. However, such statements or agreements may be used to interpret the writing.

2.1.18 Modification in particular form

A contract in writing which contains a clause requiring any modification or termination by agreement to be in a particular form may not be otherwise modified or terminated. However, a party may be precluded by its conduct from asserting such a clause to the extent that the other party has acted in reliance on that conduct Article 2.1.19.

2.1.19 Contracting under standard terms

(1) Where one party or both parties use standard terms in concluding a contract, the general rules on formation apply, subject to Articles 2.1.20–2.1.22.

(2) Standard terms are provisions which are prepared in advance for general and repeated use by one party and which are actually used without negotiation with the other party.

2.1.20 Surprising terms

(1) No term contained in standard terms which is of such a character that the other party could not reasonably have expected it, is effective unless it has been expressly accepted by that party.

(2) In determining whether a term is of such a character regard is to be had to its content, language and presentation.

2.1.21 Conflict between standard terms and non-standard terms

In the case of conflict between a standard term and a term which is not a standard term the latter prevails.

2.1.22 Battle of forms

Where both parties use standard terms and reach agreement except on those terms, a contract is concluded on the basis of the agreed terms and of any standard terms which are common in substance unless one party clearly indicates in advance, or later and without undue delay informs the other party, that it does not intend to be bound by such a contract.

SECTION 2   AUTHORITY OF AGENTS

2.2.1 Scope of the Section

(1) This Section governs the authority of a person, the agent, to affect the legal relations of another person, the principal, by or with respect to a contract with a third party, whether the agent acts in its own name or in that of the principal.

(2) It governs only the relations between the principal or the agent on the one hand, and the third party on the other.

(3) It does not govern an agent's authority conferred by law or the authority of an agent appointed by a public or judicial authority.

2.2.2 Establishment and scope of the authority of the agent

(1) The principal's grant of authority to an agent may be express or implied.

(2) The agent has authority to perform all acts necessary in the circumstances to achieve the purposes for which the authority was granted.

2.2.3 Agency disclosed

(1) Where an agent acts within the scope of its authority and the third party knew or ought to have known that the agent was acting as an agent, the acts of the agent shall directly affect the legal relations between the principal and the third party and no legal relation is created between the agent and the third party.

(2) However, the acts of the agent shall affect only the relations between the agent and the third party, where the agent with the consent of the principal undertakes to become the party to the contract.

2.2.4 Agency undisclosed

(1) Where an agent acts within the scope of its authority and the third party neither knew nor ought to have known that the agent was acting as an agent, the acts of the agent shall affect only the relations between the agent and the third party.

(2) However, where such an agent, when contracting with the third party on behalf of a business, represents itself to be the owner of that business, the third party, upon discovery of the real owner of the business, may exercise also against the latter the rights it has against the agent.

2.2.5 Agent acting without or exceeding its authority

(1) Where an agent acts without authority or exceeds its authority, its acts do not affect the legal reactions between the principal and the third party.

(2) However, where the principal causes the third party reasonably to believe that the agent has authority to act on behalf of the principal and that the agent is acting within the scope of that authority, the principal may not invoke against the third party the lack of authority of the agent.

2.2.6 Liability of agent acting without or exceeding its authority

(1) An agent that acts without authority or exceeds its authority is, failing ratification by the principal, liable for damages that will put the third party in the same position as if the agent had acted with authority and not exceeded its authority.

(2) However, the agent is not liable if the third party knew or ought to have known that the agent had no authority or was exceeding its authority.

2.2.7 Conflict of interests

(1) If a contract concluded by an agent involves the agent in a conflict of interests with the principal of which the third party knew or ought to have known, the principal may avoid the contract. The right to avoid is subject to Articles 3.12 and 3.14 to 3.17.

(2) However, the principal may not avoid the contract
  (a) if the principal had consented to, or knew or ought to have known, the agent's involvement in the conflict of interests; or
  (b) if the agent had disclosed the conflict of interests to the principal and it had not objected within a reasonable time.

2.2.8 Subagency

An agent has implied authority to appoint a subagent to perform acts which it is not reasonable to expect the agent to perform itself. The rules of this chapter apply to the subagency.

2.2.9   Ratification

(1) An act by an agent that acts without authority or exceeds its authority may be ratified by the principal. On ratification the act produces the same effects as if it had initially been carried out with authority.

(2) The third party may by notice to the principal specify a reasonable period of time for ratification. If the principal does not ratify within that period it can no longer do so.

(3) Where, at the time of the agent's act, the third party neither knew nor ought to have known of the lack of authority, it may, at any time before ratification, by notice to the principal indicate its refusal to become bound by a ratification.

2.2.10   Termination of authority

(1) Termination of authority is not effective in relation to the third party unless the third party knew or ought to have known of it.

(2) Notwithstanding the termination of its authority, an agent remains authorised to perform the acts that are necessary to prevent harm to the principal's interests.

CHAPTER 3   VALIDITY

3.1   Matters not covered

These Principles do not deal with invalidity arising from

    (a) lack of capacity;

    (b) immorality or illegality.

3.2   Validity of mere agreement

A contract is concluded, modified or terminated by the mere agreement of the parties, without any further requirement.

3.3   Initial impossibility

(1) The mere fact that at the time of the conclusion of the contract the performance of the obligation assumed was impossible shall not effect the validity of the contract.

(2) The mere fact that at the time of the conclusion of the contract a party was not entitled to dispose of the assets to which the contract relates, does not effect the validity of the contract.

3.4   Definition of mistake

Mistake is an erroneous assumption relating to facts or to law existing when the contract was concluded.

3.5   Relevant mistake

(1) A party may only avoid the contract for mistake if, when the contract was concluded, the mistake was of such importance that a reasonable person in the same situation as the party in error would only have contracted the contract on materially different terms or would not have contracted at all if the true state of affairs had been known, and

    (a) the other party made the same mistake, or caused the mistake, or knew or ought to have known of the mistake and it was contrary to reasonable commercial standards of fair dealing to leave the mistaken party in error; or

    (b) the other party had not at the time of avoidance acted in reliance on the contract.

(2) However, a party may not avoid the contract, if

    (a) it was grossly negligent in committing the mistake; or

    (b) the mistake relates to a matter in regard to which the risk of mistake was assumed or, having regard to the circumstances, should be borne by the mistaken party.

3.6   Error in expression or transmission

An error occurring in the expression or transmission of a declaration is considered to be a mistake of the person from whom the declaration emanated.

3.7   Remedies for non-performance

A party is not entitled to avoid the contract on the ground of mistake if the circumstances on which that party relies afford, or could have afforded, him a remedy for non-performance.

3.8   Fraud

A party may avoid the contract when it has been led to conclude the contract by the other party's fraudulent representation, including language or practices, or fraudulent nondisclosure of circumstances which, according to reasonable commercial standards of fair dealing, the latter party should have disclosed.

3.9   Threat

A party may avoid the contract whenhe has been led to conclude the contract by the other party's unjustified threat which, having regard to the circumstances, is so imminent and serious as to leave the first party no reasonable alternative. In particular, a threat is unjustified if the act or omission with which a party has been threatened is wrongful in itself, or it is wrongful to use it as a means to obtain the conclusion of the contract.

3.10   Gross disparity

(1) A party may avoid a contract or an individual term of it if, at the time of the conclusion of the contract, the contract or term unjustifiably gave the other party an excessive advantage. Regard is to be had, among other factors, to

(a) the fact that the other party has taken unfair advantage of the first party's dependence, economic distress or urgent needs, or of its improvidence, ignorance, inexperience or lack of bargaining skill; and

(b) the nature and purpose of the contract.

(2) Upon the request of the party entitled to avoidance, a court may adapt the contract or term in order to make it accord with reasonable commercial standards of fair dealing.

(3) A court may also adapt the contract or term upon the request of the party receiving notice of avoidance, provided that that party informs the other party of its request promptly after receiving such notice and before the other party has acted in reliance on it. The provisions of Article 3.13(2) apply accordingly.

3.11   Third persons

(1) Where fraud, threat, gross disparity or a party's mistake is imputable to, or is known or ought to be known by, a third person for whose acts the other party is responsible, the contract may be avoided under the same conditions as if the behaviour or knowledge had been that of the party itself.

(2) Where fraud, threat or gross disparity is imputable to a third person for whose acts the other party is not responsible, the contract may be avoided if that party knew or ought to have known of the fraud, threat or disparity, or has not at the time of avoidance acted in reliance on the contract.

3.12   Confirmation

If the party entitled to avoid the contract expressly or impliedly confirms the contract after the period of time for giving notice of avoidance has begun to run, avoidance of the contract is excluded.

3.13   Loss of right to avoid

(1) If a party is entitled to avoid the contract for mistake but the other party declares itself willing to perform or performs the contract as it was understood by the party entitled to avoidance, the contract is considered to have been concluded as the latter party understood it. The other party must make such a declaration or render such performance promptly after having been informed of the manner in which the party entitled to avoidance had understood the contract and before that party has acted in reliance on a notice of avoidance.

(2) After such a declaration or performance the right to avoidance is lost and any earlier notice of avoidance is ineffective.

3.14   Notice of avoidance
The right of a party to avoid the contract is exercised by notice to the other party.

3.15   Time limits
(1) Notice of avoidance shall be given within a reasonable time, having regard to the circumstances, after the avoiding party knew or could not have been unaware of the relevant facts or became capable of acting freely.

(2) Where an individual term of the contract may be avoided by a party under Article 3.10, the period of time for giving notice of avoidance begins to run when that term is asserted by the other party.

3.16   Partial avoidance
If a ground of avoidance affects only individual terms of the contract, the effect of avoidance is limited to those terms unless, having regard to the circumstances, it is unreasonable to uphold the remaining contract.

3.17   Retroactive effect of avoidance
(1) Avoidance takes effect retroactively.

(2) On avoidance either party may claim restitution of whatever it has supplied under the contract or the part of it avoided, provided that it concurrently makes restitution of whatever it has received under the contract or the part of it avoided or, if it cannot make restitution in kind, it must make an allowance for what it has received.

3.18   Damages
Irrespective of whether or not the contract has been avoided, the party who knew or ought to have known of the ground for avoidance is liable for damages so as to put the other party into the same position in which it would have been in if it had not concluded the contract.

3.19   Mandatory character of the provisions
The provisions of this Chapter are mandatory, except insofar as they relate to the binding force of mere agreement, initial impossibility or mistake.

3.20   Unilateral declarations
The provisions of this Chapter apply with appropriate adaptations to any communication of intention addressed by one party to the other.

CHAPTER 4   INTERPRETATION

4.1   Intention of the parties
(1) A contract shall be interpreted according to the common intention of the parties.

(2) If such an intention cannot be established, the contract shall be interpreted according to the meaning that reasonable persons of the same kind as the parties would give to it in the same circumstances.

4.2   Interpretation of statements and other conduct
(1) The statements and other conduct of a party shall be interpreted according to that party's intention if the other party knew or could not have been unaware of that intention.

(2) If the preceding paragraph is not applicable, such statements and other conduct shall be interpreted according to the meaning that a reasonable person of the same kind as the other party would give to it in the same circumstances.

4.3   Relevant circumstances
(1) In applying Articles 4.1 and 4.2, regard shall be had to all the circumstances, including
    (a) any preliminary negotiations between the parties;
    (b) any practices which the parties have established between themselves;

(c) any conduct of the parties subsequent to the conclusion of the contract;
(d) the nature and purpose of the contract;
(e) the meaning commonly given to terms and expressions in the trade concerned; and
(f) usages.

4.4 Reference to contract or statement as a whole

Terms and expressions shall be interpreted in the light of the whole contract or statement in which they appear.

4.5 All terms to be given effect

Contract terms shall be interpreted so as to give effect to all the terms rather than to deprive some of them of effect.

4.6 *Contra proferentem* rule

If contract terms supplied by one party are unclear, an interpretation against that party is preferred.

4.7 Linguistic discrepancies

Where a contract is drawn up in two or more language versions which are equally author-itative there is, in case of discrepancy between the versions, a preference for the interpreta-tion according to the version in which the contract was originally drawn up.

4.8 Supplying an omitted term

(1) Where the parties to a contract have not agreed with respect to a term which is important for a determination of their rights and duties, a term which is appropriate in the circumstances shall be supplied.

(2) In determining what is an appropriate term regard shall be had, among other factors, to
(a) the intention of the parties;
(b) the nature and purpose of the contract;
(c) good faith and fair dealing;
(d) reasonableness.

CHAPTER 5   CONTENT AND THIRD PARTY RIGHTS

SECTION 1   CONTENT

5.1.1 Express and implied obligations

The contractual obligations of the parties may be express or implied.

5.1.2 Implied obligations

Implied obligations stem from
(a) the nature and purpose of the contract;
(b) practices established between the parties and usages;
(c) good faith and fair dealing;
(d) reasonableness.

5.1.3 Co-operation between the parties

Each party shall co-operate with the other party, when such co-operation may reasonably be expected for the performance of that party's obligations.

5.1.4 Duty to achieve a specific result; duty of best efforts

(1) To the extent that an obligation of a party involves a duty to achieve a specific result, that party is bound to achieve that result.

(2) To the extent that an obligation of a party involves a duty of best efforts in the performance of an activity, that party is bound to make such efforts as would be made by a reasonable person of the same kind in the same circumstances.

5.1.5 Determination of kind of duty involved

In determining the extent to which an obligation of a party involves a duty of best efforts in the performance of an activity or a duty to achieve a specific result, regard shall be had, among other factors, to

(a) the way in which the obligation is expressed in the contract;

(b) the contractual price and other terms of the contract;

(c) the degree of risk normally involved in achieving the expected result;

(d) the ability of the other party to influence the performance of the obligation.

5.1.6 Determination of quality of performance

Where the quality of performance is neither fixed by, nor determinable from, the contract, a party is bound to render a performance of a quality that is reasonable and not less than average in the circumstances.

5.1.7 Price determination

(1) Where a contract does not fix or make provision for determining the price, the parties are considered, in the absence of any indication to the contrary, to have made reference to the price generally charged at the time of the conclusion of the contract for such performance under comparable circumstances in the trade concerned or, if no such price is available, to a reasonable price.

(2) Where the price is to be determined by one party and that determination is manifestly unreasonable, a reasonable price shall be substituted notwithstanding any contract term to the contrary.

(3) Where the price is to be fixed by a third person, and that person cannot or will not do so, the price shall be a reasonable price.

(4) Where the price is to be fixed by reference to factors which do not exist or have ceased to exist or to be accessible, the nearest equivalent factor shall be treated as a substitute.

5.1.8 Contract for an indefinite period

A contract for an indefinite period may be ended by either party by giving notice a reasonable time in advance.

5.1.9 Release by agreement

(1) An obligee may release its right by agreement with the obligor.

(2) An offer to release a right gratuitously shall be deemed accepted if the obligor does not reject the offer without delay after having become aware of it.

SECTION 2 THIRD PARTY RIGHTS

5.2.1 Contracts in favour of third parties

(1) Parties (the "promisor" and the "promisee") may confer by express or implied agreement a right on a third party (the "beneficiary").

(2) The existence and content of the beneficiary's right against the promisor are determined by the agreement of the parties and are subject to any conditions or other limitations under the agreement.

5.2.2 Third party identifiable

The beneficiary must be identifiable with adequate certainty by the contract but need not be in existence at the time the contract is made.

5.2.3 Exclusion and limitation clauses

The conferment of rights in the beneficiary includes the right to invoke a clause in the contract which excludes or limits the liability of the beneficiary.

5.2.4 Defences

The promisor may assert against the beneficiary all defences which the promisor could assert against the promisee.

5.2.5   Revocation

The contracting parties may modify or revoke the rights conferred by the contract on the beneficiary until the beneficiary has accepted them or reasonably acted in reliance on them.

5.2.6   Renunciation

The beneficiary may renounce a right conferred on it.

CHAPTER 6   PERFORMANCE

SECTION 1   PERFORMANCE IN GENERAL

6.1.1   Time of performance

A party must perform its obligations:

> (a) if a time is fixed by or determinable from the contract, at that time;
> (b) if a period of time is fixed by or determinable from the contract, at any time within that period unless circumstances indicate that the other party is to choose a time; or
> (c) in any other case, within a reasonable time after the conclusion of the contract.

6.1.2   Performance at one time or in instalments

In cases under Article 6.1.1(b) or (c), a party must perform its obligations at one time if that performance can be rendered at one time and the circumstances do not indicate otherwise.

6.1.3   Partial performance

(1) The obligee may reject an offer to perform in part at the time performance is due, whether or not such offer is coupled with an assurance as to the balance of the performance, unless the obligee has no legitimate interest in so doing.

(2) Additional expenses caused to the obligee by partial performance are to be borne by the obligor without prejudice to any other remedy.

6.1.4   Order of performance

(1) To the extent that the performances of the parties can be rendered simultaneously, the parties are bound to render them simultaneously unless the circumstances indicate otherwise

(2) To the extent that the performance of only one party requires a period of time, that party is bound to render its performance first, unless the circumstances indicate otherwise.

6.1.5   Earlier performance

(1) The obligee may reject an earlier performance unless it has no legitimate interest in so doing.

(2) Acceptance by a party of an earlier performance does not affect the time for the performance of its own obligation if that time has been fixed irrespective of the performance of the other party's obligations.

(3) Additional expenses caused to the obligee by earlier performance are to be borne by the obligor, without prejudice to any other remedy.

6.1.6   Place of performance

(1) If the place of performance is neither fixed by, nor determinable from, the contract, a party is to perform:

> (a) a monetary obligation, at the obligee's place of business;
> (b) any other obligation, at its own place of business.

(2) A party must bear any increase in the expenses incidental to performance which is caused by a change in its place of business subsequent to the conclusion of the contract.

6.1.7 Payment by cheque or other instrument

(1) Payment may be made in any form used in the ordinary course of business at the place for payment.

(2) However, an obligee who accepts, either by virtue of paragraph (1) or voluntarily, a cheque, an other order to pay or a promise to pay, is presumed to do so only on condition that it will be honoured.

6.1.8 Payment by funds transfer

(1) Unless the obligee has indicated a particular account, payment may be made by a transfer to any of the financial institutions in which the obligee has made it known that it has an account.

(2) In case of payment by a transfer the obligation of the obligor is discharged when the transfer to the obligee's financial institution becomes effective.

6.1.9 Currency of payment

(1) If a monetary obligation is expressed in a currency other than that of the place for payment, it may be paid by the obligor in the currency of the place for payment unless

(a) that currency is not freely convertible; or

(b) the parties have agreed that payment should be made only in the currency in which the monetary obligation is expressed.

(2) If it is impossible for the obligor to make payment in the currency in which the monetary obligation is expressed, the obligee may require payment in the currency of the place for payment, even in the case referred to in paragraph (1)(b).

(3) Payment in the currency of the place for payment is to be made according to the applicable rate of exchange prevailing there when payment is due.

(4) However, if the obligor has not paid at the time when payment is due, the obligee may require payment according to the applicable rate of exchange prevailing either when payment is due or at the time of actual payment.

6.1.10 Currency not expressed

Where a monetary obligation is not expressed in a particular currency, payment must be made in the currency of the place where payment is to be made.

6.1.11 Costs of performance

Each party shall bear the costs of performance of its obligations.

6.1.12 Imputation of payments

(1) An obligor owing several monetary obligations to the same obligee may specify at the time of payment the debt to which it intends the payment to be applied. However, the payment discharges first any expenses, then interests due and finally the principal.

(2) If the obligor makes no such specification, the obligee may, within a reasonable time after payment, declare to the obligor the obligation to which it imputes the payment, provided that the obligation is due and undisputed.

(3) In the absence of imputation under paragraphs (1) or (2), payment is imputed to that obligation which satisfies one of the following criteria in the order indicated:

(a) an obligation which is due or which is the first to fall due;

(b) an obligation for which the obligee has least security;

(c) the obligation which is the most burdensome for the obligor;

(d) the obligation which has arisen first.

If none of the preceding criteria applies, payment is imputed to all the obligations proportionally.

6.1.13 Imputation of non-monetary obligations

Article 6.1.12 applies with appropriate adaptions to the imputation of performances of nonmonetary obligations.

6.1.14 Application for public permission

Where the law of a State requires a public permission affecting the validity of the contract or its performance and neither that law nor the circumstances indicate otherwise

(a) if only one party has his place of business in that State, that party shall take the measures necessary to obtain the permission;

(b) in any other case the party whose performances requires permission shall take the necessary measures.

6.1.15 Procedure in applying for permission

(1) The party required to take the measures necessary to obtain the permission shall do so without undue delay and shall bear any expenses incurred.

(2) That party shall whenever appropriate give the other party notice of the grant or refusal of such permission without undue delay.

6.1.16 Permission neither granted nor refused

(1) If, notwithstanding the fact that the party responsible has taken all measures required, permission is neither granted nor refused within an agreed period or, where no period has been agreed, within a reasonable time from the conclusion of the contract, either party is entitled to terminate the contract.

(2) Where the permission affects some terms only, paragraph (1) does not apply if, having regard to the circumstances, it is reasonable to uphold the remaining contract even if the permission is refused.

6.1.17 Permission refused

(1) The refusal of a permission affecting the validity of the contract renders the contract void. If the refusal affects the validity of some terms only, only such terms are void if, having regard to the circumstances of the case, it is reasonable to uphold the remaining contract.

(2) Where the refusal of a permission renders the performance of the contract impossible in whole or in part, the rules on non-performance apply.

SECTION 2   HARDSHIP

6.2.1 Contract to be observed

Where the performance of a contract becomes more onerous for one of the parties, that party is nevertheless bound to perform its obligations subject to the following provisions on hardship.

6.2.2 Definition of hardship

There is hardship where the occurrence of events fundamentally alters the equilibrium of the contract either because the cost of a party's performance has increased or because the value of the performance a party receives has diminished, and

(a) the events occur or become known to the disadvantaged party after the conclusion of the contract;

(b) the events could not reasonably have been taken into account by the disadvantaged party at the time of the conclusion of the contract;

(c) the events are beyond the control of the disadvantaged party; and

(d) the risk of the events was not assumed by the disadvantaged party.

6.2.3 Effects of hardship

(1) In a case of hardship the disadvantaged party is entitled to request renegotiations. The request shall be made without undue delay and shall indicate the grounds on which it is based.

(2) The request for renegotiation does not in itself entitle the disadvantaged party to withhold performance.

(3) Upon failure to reach agreement within a reasonable time either party may resort to the court.

(4) If a court finds hardship it may, if reasonable,

    (a) terminate the contract at a date and on terms to be fixed; or

    (b) adapt the contract with a view to restoring its equilibrium.

CHAPTER 7   NON-PERFORMANCE

SECTION 1   NON-PERFORMANCE IN GENERAL

7.1.1   Non-performance defined

Non-performance is failure by a party to perform any of its obligations under the contract, including defective performance or late performance.

7.1.2   Interference by the other party

A party may not rely on the non-performance of the other party to the extent that such nonperformance was caused by the first party's act or omission or by another event as to which the first party bears the risk.

7.1.3   Withholding performance

(1) Where the parties are to perform simultaneously, either party may withhold performance until the other party tenders its performance.

(2) Where the parties are to perform consecutively, the party that is to perform later may withhold its performance until the first party has performed.

7.1.4   Cure by non-performing party

(1) The non-performing party may, at its own expense, cure any non-performance, provided that

    (a) without undue delay, it gives notice indicating the proposed manner and timing of the cure;

    (b) cure is appropriate in the circumstances;

    (c) the aggrieved party has no legitimate interest in refusing cure; and

    (d) cure is effected promptly.

(2) The right to cure is not precluded by notice of termination.

(3) Upon effective notice of cure, rights of the aggrieved party that are inconsistent with the non-performing party's performance are suspended until the time for cure has expired.

(4) The aggrieved party may withhold performance pending cure.

(5) Notwithstanding cure, the aggrieved party retains the right to claim damages for delay as well as for any harm caused or not prevented by the cure.

7.1.5   Additional period for performance

(1) In a case of non-performance the aggrieved party may by notice to the other party allow an additional period of time for performance.

(2) During the additional period the aggrieved party may withhold performance of its own reciprocal obligations and may claim damages but may not resort to any other remedy. If it receives notice from the other party that the latter will not perform within that period, or if upon expiry of that period due performance has not been made, the aggrieved party may resort to any of the remedies that may be available under this Chapter.

(3) Where in a case of delay in performance which is not fundamental the aggrieved party has given notice allowing an additional period of time of reasonable length, it may terminate the contract at the end of that period. If the additional period is not of reasonable length it shall be extended to a reasonable length. The aggrieved party may in its notice provide that if the other party fails to perform within the period allowed by the notice the contract shall automatically terminate.

(4) Paragraph (3) does not apply when the obligation which has not been performed is only a minor part of the non-performing party.

7.1.6   Exemption clauses

A term which limits or excludes one party's liability for non-performance or which permits one party to render performance substantially different from what the other party reasonably expected may not be invoked if it would be grossly unfair to do so, having regard to the purpose of the contract.

7.1.7   *Force majeure*

(1) Non-performance by a party is excused if that party proves that the non-performance was due to an impediment beyond its control and that it could not reasonably be expected to have taken the impediment into account at the time of the conclusion of the contract or to have avoided or overcome it or its consequences.

(2) When the impediment is only temporary, the excuse shall have effect for such period as is reasonable having regard to the effect of the impediment on performance of the contract.

(3) A party who fails to perform must give notice to the other party of the impediment and its effect on its ability to perform. If the notice is not received by the other party within a reasonable time after the party who fails to perform knew or ought to have known of the impediment, it is liable for damages resulting from such non-receipt;

(4) Nothing in this article prevents a party from exercising a right to terminate the contract or withhold performance or request interest on money due.

SECTION 2   RIGHT TO PERFORMANCE

7.2.1   Performance of monetary obligation

Where a party who is obliged to pay money does not do so, the other party may require payment.

7.2.2   Performance of non-monetary obligation

Where a party who owes an obligation other than one to pay money does not perform, the other party may require performance, unless

    (a) performance is impossible in law or in fact;

    (b) performance or, when relevant, enforcement is unreasonably burdensome or expensive;

    (c) the party entitled to performance may reasonably obtain performance from another source;

    (d) performance is of an exclusively personal character; or

    (e) the party entitled to performance does not require performance within a reasonable time after it has, or ought to have, become aware of the nonperformance.

7.2.3   Repair and replacement of defective performance

The right to performance includes in appropriate cases the right to require repair, replacement or other cure of a defective performance. The provisions of Articles 7.2.1 and 7.2.2 apply accordingly.

7.2.4   Judicial penalty

(1) Where the court orders a party to perform, it may also direct that this party pay a penalty if it does not comply with the order.

(2) The penalty shall be paid to the aggrieved party unless mandatory provisions of the law of the forum provide otherwise. Payment of the penalty to the aggrieved party does not exclude any claim for damages.

7.2.5 Change of remedy

(1) An aggrieved party who has required performance of a non-monetary obligation and who has not received performance within a period fixed or otherwise within a reasonable period of time may invoke any other remedy.

(2) Where the decision of a court for performance of a non-monetary obligation cannot be enforced, the aggrieved party may invoke any other remedy.

SECTION 3   TERMINATION

7.3.1 Right to terminate the contract

(1) A party may terminate the contract where the failure of the other party to perform an obligation under the contract amounts to a fundamental non-performance.

(2) In determining whether a failure to perform an obligation amounts to a fundamental non-performance regard shall be had, in particular, to whether

    (a) the non-performance substantially deprives the aggrieved party of what it was entitled to expect under the contract unless the other party did not foresee and could not reasonably have foreseen such result;

    (b) strict compliance with the obligation which has not been performed is of essence under the contract;

    (c) the non-performance is intentional or reckless;

    (d) the non-performance gives the aggrieved party reason to believe that it cannot rely on the other party's future performance;

    (e) the non-performing party will suffer disproportionate loss as a result of the preparation or performance if the contract is terminated.

(3) In the case of delay the aggrieved party may also terminate the contract if the other party fails to perform before the time allowed it under Article 7.1.5 has expired.

7.3.2 Notice of termination

(1) The right of a party to terminate the contract is to be exercised by notice to the other party.

(2) If performance has been offered late or otherwise does not conform to the contract the aggrieved party will lose its right to terminate the contract unless it gives notice to the other party within a reasonable time after it has or ought to have become aware of the offer or of the non-conforming performance.

7.3.3 Anticipatory non-performance

Where prior to the date for performance by one of the parties it is clear that there will be a fundamental non-performance by that party, the other party may terminate the contract.

7.3.4 Adequate assurance of due performance

A party who reasonably believes that there will be a fundamental non-performance by the other party may demand adequate assurance of due performance and may meanwhile withhold its own performance. Where this assurance is not provided within a reasonable time the party demanding it may terminate the contract.

7.3.5 Effects of termination in general

(1) Termination of the contract releases both parties from their obligation to effect and to receive future performance.

(2) Termination does not preclude a claim for damages for non-performance.

(3) Termination does not affect any provision in the contract for the settlement of disputes or any other term of the contract which is to operate even after termination.

7.3.6   Restitution

(1) On termination of the contract either party may claim restitution of whatever it has supplied, provided that such party concurrently makes restitution of whatever it has received. If restitution in kind is not possible or appropriate allowance should be made in money whenever reasonable.

(2) However, if performance of the contract has extended over a period of time and the contract is divisible, such restitution can only be claimed for the period after termination has taken effect.

SECTION 4   DAMAGES

7.4.1   Right to damages

Any non-performance gives the aggrieved party a right to damages either exclusively or in conjunction with any other remedies except where the non-performance is excused under these Principles.

7.4.2   Full compensation

(1) The aggrieved party is entitled to full compensation for harm as a result of the non-performance. Such harm includes both any loss which it suffered and any gain of which it was deprived, taking into account any gain to the aggrieved party resulting from its avoidance of cost or harm.

(2) Such harm may be non-pecuniary and includes, for instance, physical suffering or emotional distress.

7.4.3   Certainty of harm

(1) Compensation is due only for harm, including future harm, that is established with a reasonable degree of certainty.

(2) Compensation may be due for the loss of a chance in proportion to the probability of its occurrence.

(3) Where the amount of damages cannot be established with a sufficient degree of certainty, the assessment is at the discretion of the court.

7.4.4   Foreseeability of harm

The non-performing party is liable only for harm which it foresaw or could reasonably have foreseen at the time of the conclusion of the contract as being likely to result from its nonperformance.

7.4.5   Proof of harm in case of replacement transaction

Where the aggrieved party has terminated the contract and has made a replacement transaction within a reasonable time and in a reasonable manner it may recover the difference between the contract price and the price of the replacement transaction as well as damages for any further harm.

7.4.6   Proof of harm by current price

(1) Where the aggrieved party has terminated the contract and has not made a replacement transaction but there is a current price for the performance contracted for, it may recover the difference between the contract price and the price current at the time the contract is terminated as well as damages for any further harm.

(2) Current price is the price generally charged for goods delivered or services rendered in comparable circumstances at the place where the contract should have been performed or, if there is no current price at that place, the current price at such other place that appears reasonable to take as a reference.

7.4.7   Harm due in part to aggrieved party

Where the harm is due in part to an act or omission of the aggrieved party or to another event as to which that party bears the risk, the amount of damages shall be reduced to the extent these factors have contributed to the harm, having regard to the conduct of each of the parties.

7.4.8 Mitigation of harm

(1) The non-performing party is not liable for harm suffered by the aggrieved party to the extent that the harm could have been reduced by the latter party's taking reasonable steps.

(2) The aggrieved party is entitled to recover any expenses reasonably incurred in attempting to reduce the harm.

7.4.9 Interest for failure to pay money

(1) If a party does not pay a sum of money when it falls due the aggrieved party is entitled to interest upon that sum from the time when payment is due to the time of payment whether or not the non-payment is excused.

(2) The rate of interest shall be the average bank short-term lending rate to prime borrowers prevailing for the currency of payment at the place for payment, or where no such rate exists at that place, then the same rate in the State of the currency of payment. In the absence of such a rate at either place the rate of interest shall be the appropriate rate fixed by the law of the State of the currency of payment.

(3) The aggrieved party is entitled to additional damages if the non-payment caused it a greater harm.

7.4.10 Interest on damages

Unless otherwise agreed, interests on damages for non-performance of non-monetary obligations accrues as from the time of non-performance.

7.4.11 Manner of monetary redress

(1) Damages are to be paid in a lump sum. However, they may be payable in instalments when the nature of the harm makes this appropriate.

(2) Damages to be paid in instalments may be indexed.

7.4.12 Currency in which to assess damages

Damages are to be assessed either in the currency in which the monetary obligation was expressed or in the currency in which the harm was suffered, whichever is more appropriate.

7.4.13 Agreed payment for non-performance

(1) Where the contract provides that a party who does not perform is to pay a specified sum to the aggrieved party for such non-performance, the aggrieved party is entitled to that sum irrespective of its actual harm.

(2) However, notwithstanding any agreement to the contrary the specified sum may be reduced to a reasonable amount where it is grossly excessive in relation to the harm resulting from the non-performance and to the other circumstances.

CHAPTER 8   SET-OFF

8.1 Conditions of set-off

(1) Where two parties owe each other money or other performances of the same kind, either of them ("the first party") may set-off its obligation against that of its obligee ("the other party") if at the time of set-off

    (a) the first party is entitled to perform its obligation

    (b) the other party's obligation is ascertained as to its existence and amount and performance is due.

(2) If the obligations of both parties arise from the same contract, the first party may also set-off its obligation against an obligation of the other party which is not ascertained as to its existence or to its amount.

8.2   Foreign currency set-off

Where the obligations are to pay money in different currencies, the right of set-off may be exercised, provided that both currencies are freely convertible and the parties have not agreed that the first party shall pay only in a specified currency.

8.3   Set-off by notice

The right of set-off is exercised by notice to the other party.

8.4   Content of notice

(1) The notice must specify the obligations to which it relates

(2) If the notice does not specify the obligation against which set-off is exercised, the other party may, within a reasonable time, declare to the first party the obligation to which set-off relates, or, if no such declaration is made, the set-off will relate to all the obligations proportionally.

8.5   Effect of set-off

(1) Set-off discharges the obligations.

(2) If obligations differ in amount, set-off discharges the obligations up to the amount of the lesser obligation.

(3) Set-off takes effect as from the time of notice.

CHAPTER 9   ASSIGNMENT OF RIGHTS, TRANSFER OF OBLIGATIONS, ASSIGNMENT OF CONTRACTS

SECTION 1   ASSIGNMENT OF RIGHTS

9.1.1   Definitions

"Assignment of a right" means the transfer by agreement from one person (the "assignor") to another person (the "assignee"), including transfer by way of security, of the assignor's right to payment of a monetary sum or other performance from a third person ("the obligor").

9.1.2   Exclusions

This Section does not apply to transfers made under the special rules governing the transfers:

(a) of instruments such as negotiable instruments, documents of title or financial instruments, or

(b) of rights in the course of transferring a business.

9.1.3   Assignability of non-monetary rights

A right to non-monetary performance may be assigned only if the assignment does not render the obligation significantly more burdensome.

9.1.4   Partial assignment

(1) A right to payment of a monetary sum may be assigned partially.

(2) A right to other performance may be assigned partially only if it is divisible, and the assignment does not render the obligation significantly more burdensome.

9.1.5   Future rights

A future right is deemed to be transferred at the time of the agreement, provided the right, when it comes into existence, can be identified as the right to which the assignment relates.

9.1.6   Rights assigned without individual specification

A number of rights may be assigned without individual specification provided such rights can be identified as rights to which the assignment relates at the time of the assignment or when they come into existence.

9.1.7   Agreement between assignor and assignee sufficient

(1) A right is assigned by mere agreement between assignor and assignee, without notice to the obligor.

(2) The consent of the obligor is not required, unless the obligation, in the circumstances, is of an essentially personal character.

9.1.8 Obligor's additional costs

The obligor has a right to be compensated by the assignor or the assignee for any additional costs caused by the assignment.

9.1.9 Non-assignment clauses

(1) Assignment of a right to payment of a monetary sum is effective notwithstanding an agreement between the assignor and the obligor limiting or prohibiting such assignment. However, the assignor may be liable to the obligor for breach of contract.

(2) Assignment of a right to other performance is ineffective, if it is contrary to an agreement between the assignor and the obligor limiting or prohibiting the assignment. Nevertheless, the assignment is effective if the assignee, at the time of assignment, neither knew nor ought to have known of the agreement; the assignor may then be liable to the obligor for breach of contract.

9.1.10 Notice to the obligor

(1) Until receiving a notice of the assignment, from either the assignor or the assignee, the obligor is discharged by paying the assignor.

(2) After receiving such a notice, the obligor is discharged only by paying the assignee.

9.1.11 Successive assignments

If the same right has been assigned by the same assignor to two or more successive assignees, the obligor is discharged by paying according to the order in which the notices were received.

9.1.12 Adequate proof of assignment

(1) If notice of the assignment is given by the assignee, the obligor may request the assignee to provide within a reasonable time adequate proof that the assignment has been made.

(2) Until adequate proof is provided, the obligor may withhold payment.

(3) Unless adequate proof is provided, notice is not effective.

(4) Adequate proof includes, but is not limited to, any writing emanating from the assignor and indicating that the assignment has taken place.

9.1.13 Defences and rights of set-off

(1) The obligor may assert against the assignee all defences which the obligor could assert against the assignor.

(2) The obligor may exercise against the assignee any right of set-off available to the obligor against the assignor up to the time notice of assignment was received.

9.1.14 Rights related to the right assigned

Assignment of a right transfers to the assignee:

    (a) all the assignor's rights to payment or other performance under the contract in respect of the right assigned, and

    (b) all rights securing performance of the right assigned.

9.1.15 Assignor's undertakings

The assignor undertakes towards the assignee, except as otherwise disclosed to the assignee, that:

    (a) the assigned right exists at the time of the assignment, unless the right is a future right;

    (b) the assignor is entitled to assign the right;

    (c) the right has not been previously assigned to another assignee, and it is free from any right or claim from a third party;

    (d) the obligor does not have any defences;

(e) neither the obligor nor the assignor has given notice of set-off concerning the assigned right and will not give any such notice;

(f) the assignor will reimburse the assignee for any payment received from the obligor before notice of the assignment was given.

SECTION 2   TRANSFER OF OBLIGATIONS

9.2.1   Modes of transfer

An obligation to pay money or render other performance may be transferred from one person (the "original obligor") to another person (the "new obligor") either

(a) by an agreement between the original obligor and the new obligor subject to Article 9.2.3, or

(b) by an agreement between the obligee and the new obligor, by which the new obligor assumes the obligation.

9.2.2   Exclusion

This Section does not apply to transfers of obligations made under the special rules governing transfers of obligations in the course of transferring a business.

9.2.3   Requirement of obligee's consent to transfer

Transfer of an obligation by an agreement between the original and the new obligor requires the consent of the obligee.

9.2.4   Advance consent of obligee

(1) The obligee may give its consent in advance.

(2) The transfer of the obligation becomes effective when notice of the transfer is given to the obligee or when the obligee acknowledges it.

9.2.5   Discharge of original obligor

(1) The obligee may discharge the original obligor.

(2) The obligee may also retain the original obligor as an obligor in case the new obligor does not perform properly.

(3) Otherwise the original obligor remains as an obligor, jointly and severally with the new obligor.

9.2.6   Third party performance

(1) Without the obligee's consent, the obligor may contract with another person that this person will perform the obligation in place of the obligor, unless the obligation, in the circumstances, has an essentially personal character.

(2) The obligee retains its claim against the obligor.

9.2.7   Defences and rights of set-off

(1) The new obligor may assert against the obligee all defences which the original obligor could assert against the obligee.

(2) The new obligor may not exercise against the obligee any right of set-off available to the original obligor against the obligee.

9.2.8   Rights related to the obligation transferred

(1) The obligee may assert against the new obligor all its rights to payment or other performance under the contract in respect of the obligation transferred.

(2) If the original obligor is discharged under Article 9.2.5(1), a security granted by any person other than the new obligor for the performance of the obligation is discharged, unless that other person agrees that it should continue to be available to the obligee.

(3) Discharge of the original obligor also extends to any security of the original obligor given to the obligee for the performance of the obligation, unless the security is over an asset which is transferred as part of a transaction between the original and the new obligor.

SECTION 3   ASSIGNMENT OF CONTRACTS

9.3.1 Definitions
"Assignment of a contract" means the transfer by agreement from one person (the "assignor") to another person (the "assignee") of the assignor's rights and obligations arising out of a contract with another person (the "other party").

9.3.2 Exclusion
This Section does not apply to assignment of contracts made under the special rules governing transfers of contracts in the course of transferring a business.

9.3.3 Requirement of consent of the other party
Assignment of a contract requires the consent of the other party.

9.3.4 Advance consent of the other party
(1) The other party may give its consent in advance.
(2) The assignment of the contract becomes effective when notice of the assignment is given to the other party or when the other party acknowledges it.

9.3.5 Discharge of the assignor
(1) The other party may discharge the assignor.
(2) The other party may also retain the assignor as an obligor in case the assignee does not perform properly.
(3) Otherwise the assignor remains as the other party's obligor, jointly and severally with the assignee.

9.3.6 Defences and rights of set-off
(1) To the extent that assignment of a contract involves an assignment of rights, Article 9.1.13 applies accordingly.
(2) To the extent that assignment of a contract involves a transfer of obligations, Article 9.2.7 applies accordingly.

9.3.7 Rights transferred with the contract
(1) To the extent that assignment of a contract involves an assignment of rights, Article 9.1.14 applies accordingly.
(2) To the extent that assignment of a contract involves a transfer of obligations, Article 9.2.8 applies accordingly.

CHAPTER 10   LIMITATION PERIODS

10.1 Scope of the chapter
(1) The exercise of rights governed by these Principles is barred by expiration of a period of time, referred to as "limitation period", according to the rules of this chapter.
(2) This chapter does not govern the time within which one party is required under these Principles, as a condition for the acquisition or exercise of its right, to give notice to the other party or perform any act other than the institution of legal proceedings.

10.2 Limitation periods
(1) The general limitation period is three years beginning on the day after the day the obligee knows or ought to know the facts as a result of which the obligee's right can be exercised.
(2) In any event, the maximum limitation period is ten years beginning on the day after the day the right can be exercised.

10.3 Modification of limitation periods by the parties
(1) The parties may modify the limitation periods.

(2) However they may not

  (a) shorten the general limitation period to less than one year;

  (b) shorten the maximum limitation period to less than 4 years;

  (c) extend the maximum limitation period to more than 15 years.

10.4 New limitation period by acknowledgement
(1) Where the obligor, before the expiration of the general limitation period, acknowledges the right of the obligee, a new general limitation period begins on the day after the day of the acknowledgement.

(2) The maximum limitation period does not begin to run again, but may be exceeded by the beginning of a new general limitation period under Art. 10.2(1).

10.5 Suspension by judicial proceedings
(1) The running of the limitation period is suspended

  (a) when the obligee performs any act, by commencing judicial proceedings or in judicial proceedings already instituted, that is recognised by the law of the court as asserting the obligee's right against the obligor;

  (b) in the case of the obligor's insolvency when the obligee has asserted its rights in the insolvency proceedings; or

  (c) in the case of proceedings for dissolution of the entity which is the obligor when the obligee has asserted its rights in the dissolution proceedings.

(2) Suspension lasts until a final decision has been issued or until the proceedings have been otherwise terminated.

10.6 Suspension by arbitral proceedings
(1) The running of the limitation period is suspended when the obligee performs any act, by commencing arbitral proceedings or in arbitral proceedings already instituted, that is recognised by the law of the arbitral tribunal as asserting the obligee's right against the obligor. In the absence of regulations for arbitral proceedings or provisions determining the exact date of the commencement of arbitral proceedings, the proceedings are deemed to commence on the date on which a request that the right in dispute should be adjudicated reaches the obligor.

(2) Suspension lasts until the proceedings have been terminated by a binding decision of the arbitral tribunal or otherwise.

10.7 Alternative dispute resolution
The provisions of Arts. 10.5 and 10.6 apply with appropriate modifications to other proceedings whereby parties request a third person to assist them in their attempt to reach an amicable settlement of their dispute.

10.8 Suspension in case of force majeure, death or incapacity
(1) Where the obligee has been prevented by an impediment that is beyond its control and that it could neither avoid nor overcome, from causing a limitation period to cease to run under the preceding articles, the general limitation period is suspended so as not to expire before one year after the relevant impediment has ceased to exist.

(2) Where the impediment consists of the incapacity or death of the obligee or obligor, suspension ceases when a representative for the incapacitated or deceased party or its estate has been appointed or a successor inherited the respective party's position; the additional one year period under para. 1 applies respectively.

10.9 The effects of expiration of limitation period
(1) The expiration of the limitation period does not extinguish the right.

(2) For the expiration of the limitation period to have effect, the obligor must assert it as a defence.

(3) A right may still be relied on as a defence even though the expiration of the limitation period for that right has been asserted.

10.10   Exercise of set-off after expiration of the limitation period
The obligee may exercise the right of set-off until the obligor has asserted the expiration of the limitation period.

10.11   Restitution
Where there has been performance in order to discharge an obligation, there is no right of restitution merely because the period of limitation has expired.

Draft Rules on Unjustified Enrichment
(Scot. Law Com. D.P. No. 99, Appendix)

[1996]

1   General principle
A person who has been enriched at the expense of another person is bound, if the enrichment is unjustified, to redress the enrichment.

2   Enrichment
(1) A person is enriched if he acquires an economic benefit.

(2) A person acquires an economic benefit if his net worth is increased or is prevented from being decreased, and accordingly a person may be enriched, among other ways, by
> (a) acquiring money or other property
> (b) having value added to property
> (c) being freed, in whole or in part, from an obligation, or
> (d) being saved from a loss or expenditure

(3) A person is treated as acquiring an economic benefit under a void contract, or under a voidable contract which has been reduced, rescinded or otherwise set aside, or under a contract which has been terminated by frustration or rescission for breach or by some other means (apart from full performance) or under any other transaction or purported transaction which does not provide legal cause for the acquisition, if he would have acquired an economic benefit but for the fact that he gave consideration, and accordingly in such circumstances both parties to the transaction or purported transaction may be regarded as being enriched.

3   At the expense of another person
(1) The enrichment of one person is at the expense of another person if it is the direct result of
> (a) a payment, grant, transfer, incurring of liability, or rendering of services by the other person
>> (i)   to the enriched person
>> (ii) in fulfilment of an obligation of the enriched person
>> (iii) in adding value to the enriched person's property, or
>> (iv) in acquiring some other economic benefit for the enriched person, or
> (b) in any case not covered by paragraph (a), an interference with the patrimonial rights of the other person otherwise than by the operation of natural forces.

(2) A person interferes with the patrimonial rights of another person if, among other things, he
> (a) extinguishes those rights or acts in such a way that they are extinguished
> (b) disposes or purports to dispose of property belonging to that other person
> (c) uses property which that other person has the right to use to the exclusion of the interferer, or

(d) actively intercepts a benefit due to the other person but a person does not interfere with the patrimonial rights of another person merely because he breaches a contract between himself and the other person.

(3) A person who claims redress or any unjustified enrichment resulting from an interference with his patrimonial rights is treated for the purpose of any claims by or against third parties as thereby ratifying the interference.

(4) A person who purchases property in good faith from someone who is not the owner of the property is not treated as being enriched at the expense of the owner or of any former owner by reason only of any economic benefit derived by him from the purchase of the property; and the same rule applies to any other acquirer, in good faith and for value, of the right, or of what purports to be the right, to deal with the property or rights of another, and to anyone deriving title from such a purchaser or acquirer.

(5) Where a person (E) has been enriched indirectly as a result of performance by another person (C) under a contract between C and a third party (T), E's enrichment is not regarded as being at the expense of C, even if C is unable to recover under his contract with T.

(6) This rule is subject to rule 8 (which deals with certain exceptional cases where redress is due for indirect enrichment).

4   Unjustified

An enrichment is unjustified unless it is justified under rules 5 or 6.

5   Enrichment justified by legal cause

(1) An enrichment is justified if the enriched person is entitled to it by virtue of
   (a) an enactment
   (b) a rule of law
   (c) a court decree
   (d) a contract (whether or not the person claiming redress is a party) or unilateral voluntary obligation
   (e) a will or trust
   (f) a gift, or
   (g) some other legal cause.

(2) The reference to an enactment or rule of law in rule 5(1) is to an enactment or rule of law which confers rights directly and not to an enactment or rule of law in so far as it operates indirectly by regulating the effects of court decrees, contracts, wills, trusts, gifts or other legal causes.

(3) A purported or apparent legal cause does not justify an enrichment if it is void or if, being voidable, it has been reduced, rescinded or otherwise set aside.

(4) An acquisition of property is not a justified enrichment merely because legal title to the property has been acquired.

6   Enrichment justified by public policy

(1) An enrichment is justified if it is the result of
   (a) work or expenditure which was undertaken or incurred by the other person for his own benefit, or for the benefit of a third party or the public at large, which has incidentally conferred a benefit on the enriched person, and which was undertaken or incurred when the person knew or could reasonably have been expected to know that there would be a benefit to the enriched person and accepted, or could reasonably be supposed to have accepted, the risk that the enriched person would not pay for the benefit
   (b) the voluntary and deliberate conferring by the other person of a benefit on the enriched person, in the knowledge that it is not due and in acceptance of the risk that the enriched person may choose not to pay or do anything in return
   (c) a voluntary performance by the other person of an obligation which has prescribed, even if he erroneously believed that the obligation was still due, provided that any due counter-performance has been given

    (d) a voluntary performance by the other person of an obligation which is invalid for some formal reason only, even if he erroneously believed that the obligation was valid, provided that any due counter-performance has been given

or if there is some other consideration of public policy which requires it to be regarded as justified.

(2) For the purpose of rule 6(1)(a) "benefit", in relation to a person who has done work or provided services in tendering for a contract or in the anticipation of obtaining a contract, includes the benefit to the person of having, or improving, the chance of obtaining the contract.

7 Exceptions to rules 5 and 6

(1) Rule 5(1)(b) does not apply in so far as the enrichment is the result of any rule of law on the acquisition of property by accession or specification, or any analogous rule whereby one person may acquire another's property when it becomes attached to or mixed with his own.

(2) Rule 5(1)(d) does not apply in so far as the contract or obligation,

    (a) is unenforceable because of an enactment or rule of law (whether or not it is also illegal), unless allowing redress for the enrichment would contravene the policy underlying the enactment or rule of law.

    (b) has been terminated by rescission or frustration or some other means (apart from full performance) and the contract or obligation does not, expressly or impliedly, exclude redress in respect of the benefit in question.

(3) For the purpose of rule 7(2)(b) a contract which provides for performance in several parts or stages is presumed, unless the contract indicates the contrary, to exclude redress in so far as performance by one party under, and substantially in accordance with, the contract has been met by performance by the other party under, and substantially in accordance with, the contract.

(4) Rule 5(1)(f) does not apply where the gift

    (a) was made in error, whether of fact or law, or

    (b) was subject to a condition, which has been met, that it would be returned.

(5) Rule 6(1)(a) and (b) do not apply where the other person has, in circumstances where it was reasonable to do so,

    (a) paid a monetary debt due by the enriched person

    (b) fulfilled an alimentary obligation due by the enriched person

    (c) incurred expenditure or performed services necessary for preserving the life, health or welfare of the enriched person, or

    (d) incurred expenditure or performed services urgently necessary for preserving the property of the enriched person or preventing it from being dangerous.

8 Redress for indirect enrichment

(1) (a) Where a person (E) has acquired money or money's worth from a third party (T) by disposing or purporting to dispose of property belonging to another person (C), or by otherwise interfering with C's patrimonial rights, or by disposing of property acquired by him from C under a transaction voidable at C's instance, E's enrichment is treated, notwithstanding anything in the preceding rules, as being at the expense of C and as not being justified by any contract between himself and T.

    (b) Paragraph (a) does not apply if E was a purchaser in good faith of the property in question, or had otherwise acquired, in good faith and for value, the right, or what purported to be the right, to deal with the property or rights in question, or had derived title from such a purchaser or acquirer.

(2) Where a person (T) has been enriched at the expense of another person (C) and T has transferred to another person (E) any benefit arising out of the enrichment then, notwithstanding anything in the preceding rules, E is taken to be enriched at the expense of C and neither the transfer by T to E, nor any voluntary obligation underlying the transfer, justifies the enrichment if

> (a) T's enrichment at the expense of C was unjustified or was justified only by a transaction voidable at C's instance
>
> (b) C is unable to recover from T, or cannot reasonably be expected to attempt to recover from T, and
>
> (c) the acquisition by E from T was not in good faith and for value.

(3) Where a person (E) has been enriched by receiving a benefit from a trust estate or from the estate of a deceased person, the fact that E's enrichment is the result of a transfer from a trustee or executor does not prevent him from being liable to make redress to

> (a) a creditor of the estate to the extent that the creditor, because of the transfer to the beneficiary, has been unable to recover from the trustee or executor, or
>
> (b) a person (the true beneficiary) who is legally entitled to the benefit in question.

(4) Where a debtor pays the wrong person, that person is enriched at the expense of the true creditor in so far as the payment extinguishes the liability of the debtor to the true creditor.

(5) Nothing in these rules affects any procedural rule designed to avoid duplication of proceedings.

9   Redress due

(1) The redress due by an enriched person under these rules is such transfer of property or payment of money, or both, as is required to redress the enriched person's unjustified enrichment at the expense of the claimant.

(2) The redress due is assessed in accordance with the rules in the schedule in any case where those rules are applicable.

(3) Where the enriched person has been enriched at the expense of the claimant in more than one way, the rules in the schedule apply cumulatively unless there would be double redress in respect of the same enrichment.

(4) This rule is subject to the provisions of rule 10.

10   Court's powers to refuse or modify award

(1) Where, in an action for unjustified enrichment, it appears to the court that each party is bound to make redress to the other, the court may

> (a) refuse to grant decree against the defender until satisfied that the pursuer has made, or will make, the redress due by him, or
>
> (b) where both obligations are to pay money, set off one entitlement against the other and grant decree for the difference.

(2) Where, in an action for unjustified enrichment based on the passive receipt of a benefit by the enriched person, it appears to the court.

> (a) that the enriched person had no reasonable opportunity to refuse the benefit
>
> (b) that the enriched person would have refused the benefit if he had had such an opportunity
>
> (c) that the enriched person cannot, or cannot reasonably be expected to, convert the value of the benefit into money or money's worth, and
>
> (d) that it would be inequitable to make a full award the court may refuse or modify the award accordingly.

(3) Where, in an action for unjustified enrichment based on the defender's acquisition of the pursuer's property by accession or specification or any analogous rule, it appears to the court that the pursuer has acted in good faith and that, having regard to the respective values of the properties involved, the conduct of the parties and all other relevant factors, the most appropriate and equitable solution would be for the defender to be ordered to sell to the pursuer such property at such a price as would enable the pursuer to regain his property without prejudice to the defender, the court may grant decree accordingly.

(4) Notwithstanding anything in the preceding rules, a court deciding an action for unjustified enrichment may refuse to make an award, or may make a reduced award, or may grant decree subject to conditions, if it considers

(a) that the person enriched, where he did not know, and could not reasonably be expected to know, that redress was due, changed his position (whether by spending money, disposing of property, consuming property or its fruits, abandoning rights, failing to exercise rights in time, or otherwise) in reliance on his enrichment, and it would for that reason be inequitable to make a full award or grant decree unconditionally

(b) that the claimant was so culpable or negligent in causing the unjustified enrichment that it would be inequitable or contrary to public policy to make a full award or grant decree unconditionally

(c) that the claimant would be unjustly enriched if a full award were made or if decree were granted unconditionally, or

(d) that, for any other reason, it would be inequitable or contrary to public policy to make a full award or grant decree unconditionally.

11 Bars to proceedings

(1) (a) An action for unjustified enrichment cannot be brought under these rules if there is, or was,

    (i) a special statutory or contractual procedure for dealing with the situation giving rise to the enrichment or

    (ii) another legal remedy for the enrichment and if the claimant could reasonably have been expected to use that procedure or remedy.

(b) Paragraph (a) does not apply if the enactment or contract providing the other procedure or remedy indicates expressly or impliedly that it is intended to be in addition to any remedy available under the general law on unjustified enrichment.

(c) The availability of damages for loss does not preclude an action for redress of unjustified enrichment but, without prejudice to his right to claim damages for any consequential or other loss, the claimant cannot claim both redress of the other party's unjustified enrichment and damages for his corresponding loss.

(2) (a) A person who, before a court decision in proceedings to which he was not a party, has made a payment or transfer which was apparently due under the law as it was commonly supposed to be at that time cannot bring an action for unjustified enrichment in respect of that payment or transfer on the ground that the decision has shown that the law was not as it was commonly supposed to be and that the payment or transfer was accordingly not in fact due.

(b) In the preceding paragraph, "decision" in any case where a decision is affirmed or restored on appeal means the decision so affirmed or restored and not the decision affirming or restoring it.

(3) The bars mentioned in this rule are in addition to any bar resulting from the operation of the general law on personal bar.

12 Areas of law not affected

(1) These rules replace the existing Scottish common law on unjustified enrichment, including

    (a) the common law on restitution in so far as it is part of the law on unjustified enrichment

    (b) the common law on repetition and recompense, and

    (c) the *condictio indebiti*; the *condictio causa data causa non secuta*; the *condictio ob turpem vel iniustam causam*; the *condictio ob non causam*; the *condictio sine causa*; the *actio in quantum locupletior factus est*; and the *actio de in rem verso* in so far as they form part of the existing law.

(2) Nothing in these rules affects

    (a) any enacted law

  (b) the law on rights of relief of cautioners and co-obligants

  (c) the law on subrogation of insurers or those who have paid an indemnity

  (d) the law derived from the case of *Walker* v *Milne* (whereby loss suffered or expenditure incurred in the expectation of a contract may in certain circumstances be recovered)

  (e) the law on the rights of a defrauded person as against the creditors of the person who defrauded him

  (f) the law on the recovery by a person of the possession or control of his own property or of any other property to the possession or control of which he is entitled

  (g) the law on the special obligations of those in a fiduciary position

  (h) the law on general average or salvage

  (i) the law on *negotiorum gestio.*

13   Interpretation

(1) In these rules, and in the schedule where applicable,

  (a) "court decree" includes the decision of any tribunal, quasi-judicial body or arbiter having jurisdiction

  (b) "enactment" includes subordinate legislation

  (c) "gift" includes a gratuitous waiver, renunciation or discharge of a right

  (d) "he" means he, she or it; "him" means him, her or it; and "his" means his, hers or its

  (e) "patrimonial rights" include rights flowing from the ownership of property, rights to protect confidential information and other rights having an economic value but do not include purely personal rights, such as the rights to life, liberty, bodily integrity or reputation, and

  (f) "property" means property of any kind, corporeal or incorporeal, heritable or moveable.

(2) Any reference in these rules to a contract which has been terminated by rescission or frustration includes a reference to a contract which has been substantially terminated by rescission or frustration and a reference to a severable part of a contract which has been terminated by rescission or frustration.

SCHEDULE   REDRESS DUE

PART I

E acquires benefit directly from C

1. This part of the schedule applies where the enriched person (E) has been enriched by acquiring a benefit directly from the claimant (C).

2.—(1) Where the unjustified enrichment resulted from the acquisition of money by E from C, the redress due by E to C is the amount acquired, with interest from the time of acquisition.

(2) Where the unjustified enrichment resulted from the acquisition of other property by E from C, the redress due by E to C is

  (a) if the property is corporeal and can be returned in substantially the same condition as it was in at the time of the acquisition, the return of the property in that condition along with a sum of money to take account of any benefit derived by E from the ownership, use or possession of the property and interest on that sum where appropriate

  (b) if the property is corporeal and cannot be returned in substantially the same condition as it was in at the time of the acquisition, the amount which it would have been reasonable to expect E to pay C for the property at the time of its acquisition by E, with interest on that amount from the time of acquisition

(c) if the property is incorporeal, the return of the property where possible and, whether or not return is possible, a sum of money to take account of any benefit derived by E from the ownership of the property and interest on that sum where appropriate.

3. Where the unjustified enrichment resulted from the addition of value by C to E's property, the redress due by E to C is the amount which it would have been reasonable to expect E to pay C for his work or expenditure in adding that value, or the amount of value added (at the time when the addition was made), if less, with interest where appropriate.

4. Where the unjustified enrichment resulted from the discharge or reduction of any liability of E by means of a payment by C, the redress due by E to C is the amount paid, with interest from the date of payment.

5. Where the unjustified enrichment resulted from E's being saved a loss or expenditure by receiving C's services, the redress due by E to C is the amount which it would have been reasonable to expect E to pay for those services, or the amount of loss or expenditure saved, if less, with interest where appropriate.

6.—(1) Where the unjustified enrichment resulted from E's being saved a loss or expenditure by using or possessing C's property, the redress due by E to C is the amount which it would have been reasonable to expect E to pay for that use or possession, or the amount of loss or expenditure saved, if less, with interest where appropriate.

(2) Where the unjustified enrichment resulted from E's being saved a loss or expenditure by consuming C's property, the redress due by E to C is the amount which it would have been reasonable to expect E to pay for the property at the time of consumption, or the amount of loss or expenditure saved, if less, with interest where appropriate.

(3) Where the unjustified enrichment resulted from E's being saved a loss or expenditure by interfering with C's patrimonial rights in any other way, the redress due by E to C is the amount which it would have been reasonable to expect E to pay C, at the time of the interference, for permission to interfere with those rights in that way in the circumstances, or the amount of loss or expenditure saved, if less, with interest where appropriate.

7. Where the unjustified enrichment resulted from the acquisition of any other benefit by E from C, the redress due by E to C is the amount which it would have been reasonable to expect E to pay C for the benefit at the time or acquisition, or the amount of E's actual enrichment, if less, with interest where appropriate.

PART II

E acquires benefit from T at indirect expense of C

8. This part of the schedule applies where the enriched person (E) has been enriched indirectly at the expense of the claimant (C).

9. Where E has enriched himself by using or disposing of C's property, or otherwise interfering with C's patrimonial rights, in order to obtain money or money's worth from a third party (T) the redress due by E to C is the amount which it would have been reasonable for E to pay C at the time of the use, disposal or interference for permission to use or dispose of C's property or to interfere with his rights in that way, or the amount of E's actual enrichment attributable to the use, disposal or interference, if less, with interest where appropriate.

10. Where E has been indirectly enriched at the expense of C as a result of the transfer of a benefit from a third party (T) in the circumstances covered by rule 8(2) (transfer of benefit arising from unjustified enrichment to person taking otherwise than in good faith and for value) T is treated as if he had been acting as E's agent and accordingly the redress due by E to C is the same, and is due on the same conditions, as it would have been if E had acquired the benefit directly from C.

11. Where E has been indirectly enriched at the expense of C in the circumstances covered by rule 8(3) (transfers from trusts or executries) the redress due by E to C is

(1) where C is a creditor claiming under rule 8(3)(a) the amount of the debt due to C out of the estate or the amount of E's enrichment out of the estate, whichever is the less, with interest where appropriate.

(2) where C is a true beneficiary claiming under rule 8(3)(b), and the benefit due to him out of the estate and received by E was a special legacy, the transfer of the subject matter of the legacy along with a sum to take account of any benefit derived by E from its use or possession or, if the subject matter of the legacy cannot be transferred in substantially the same condition as it was in when acquired by E, an amount representing its value when acquired by E, with interest from that date.

(3) where C is a true beneficiary claiming under rule 8(3)(b), and the benefit due to him out of the estate and received by E was not a special legacy, the amount of the benefit due to C out of the estate or the amount of E's unjustified enrichment out of the estate, whichever is the less, with interest where appropriate.

PART III

General

12. Any reference in this schedule to the return of property includes a reference to a return by reconveyance or by any other means by which ownership can be restored to the other person.

13. For the purposes of paragraph 2(2) corporeal property acquired by the enriched person by accession or specification, or any analogous rule whereby one person may acquire another's property when it becomes attached to or mixed with his own, is treated as property which cannot be returned in substantially the same condition as it was in at the time of acquisition.

14. Where property is to be returned or transferred to the claimant by the enriched person under these rules, the expenses of the return or transfer are to be borne

(1) by the claimant if the enrichment was in good faith, or

(2) by the enriched person if the enrichment was in bad faith unless a court dealing with the claim orders otherwise.

15. In assessing what it would have been reasonable for E to pay C for any interference with C's rights or for permission to interfere with those rights regard may be had to any factors which would have made C reluctant or unwilling to permit the interference.

Principles of European Tort Law

[*These Principles were published by the European Group on Tort Law in May 2005, under the auspices of the European Centre of Tort and Insurance Law.*]

TITLE I   BASIC NORM

Chapter 1   Basic Norm

Art. 1:101   Basic norm

(1) A person to whom damage to another is legally attributed is liable to compensate that damage.

(2) Damage may be attributed in particular to the person

(a) whose conduct constituting fault has caused it; or

(b) whose abnormally dangerous activity has caused it; or

(c) whose auxiliary has caused it within the scope of his functions.

TITLE II   GENERAL CONDITIONS OF LIABILITY

Chapter 2   Damage

Art. 2:101   Recoverable damage

Damage requires material or immaterial harm to a legally protected interest.

Art. 2:102   Protected interests

(1) The scope of protection of an interest depends on its nature; the higher its value, the precision of its definition and its obviousness, the more extensive is its protection.

(2) Life, bodily or mental integrity, human dignity and liberty enjoy the most extensive protection.

(3) Extensive protection is granted to property rights, including those in intangible property.

(4) Protection of pure economic interests or contractual relationships may be more limited in scope. In such cases, due regard must be had especially to the proximity between the actor and the endangered person, or to the fact that the actor is aware of the fact that he will cause damage even though his interests are necessarily valued lower than those of the victim.

(5) The scope of protection may also be affected by the nature of liability, so that an interest may receive more extensive protection against intentional harm than in other cases.

(6) In determining the scope of protection, the interests of the actor, especially in liberty of action and in exercising his rights, as well as public interests also have to be taken into consideration.

Art. 2:103   Legitimacy of damage

Losses relating to activities or sources which are regarded as illegitimate cannot be recovered.

Art. 2:104   Preventive expenses

Expenses incurred to prevent threatened damage amount to recoverable damage in so far as reasonably incurred.

Art. 2:105   Proof of damage

Damage must be proved according to normal procedural standards. The court may estimate the extent of damage where proof of the exact amount would be too difficult or too costly.

Chapter 3   Causation

Section 1   Conditio sine qua non and qualifications

Art. 3:101   Conditio sine qua non

An activity or conduct (hereafter: activity) is a cause of the victim's damage if, in the absence of the activity, the damage would not have occurred.

Art. 3:102   Concurrent causes

In case of multiple activities, where each of them alone would have caused the damage at the same time, each activity is regarded as a cause of the victim's damage.

Art. 3:103   Alternative causes

(1) In case of multiple activities, where each of them alone would have been sufficient to cause the damage, but it remains uncertain which one in fact caused it, each activity is regarded as a cause to the extent corresponding to the likelihood that it may have caused the victim's damage.

(2) If, in case of multiple victims, it remains uncertain whether a particular victim's damage has been caused by an activity, while it is likely that it did not cause the damage of all victims, the activity is regarded as a cause of the damage suffered by all victims in proportion to the likelihood that it may have caused the damage of a particular victim.

Art. 3:104   Potential causes
(1) If an activity has definitely and irreversibly led the victim to suffer damage, a subsequent activity which alone would have caused the same damage is to be disregarded.

(2) A subsequent activity is nevertheless taken into consideration if it has led to additional or aggravated damage.

(3) If the first activity has caused continuing damage and the subsequent activity later on also would have caused it, both activities are regarded as a cause of that continuing damage from that time on.

Art. 3:105   Uncertain partial causation
In the case of multiple activities, when it is certain that none of them has caused the entire damage or any determinable part thereof, those that are likely to have [minimally] contributed to the damage are presumed to have caused equal shares thereof.

Art. 3:106   Uncertain causes within the victim's sphere
The victim has to bear his loss to the extent corresponding to the likelihood that it may have been caused by an activity, occurrence or other circumstance within his own sphere.

Section 2   Scope of Liability

Art. 3:201   Scope of Liability
Where an activity is a cause within the meaning of Section 1 of this Chapter, whether and to what extent damage may be attributed to a person depends on factors such as
    (a) the foreseeability of the damage to a reasonable person at the time of the activity, taking into account in particular the closeness in time or space between the damaging activity and its consequence, or the magnitude of the damage in relation to the normal consequences of such an activity;
    (b) the nature and the value of the protected interest (Article 2:102);
    (c) the basis of liability (Article 1:101);
    (d) the extent of the ordinary risks of life; and
    (e) the protective purpose of the rule that has been violated.

TITLE III   BASES OF LIABILITY

Chapter 4   Liability based on fault

Section 1   Conditions of liability based on fault

Art. 4:101   Fault
A person is liable on the basis of fault for intentional or negligent violation of the required standard of conduct.

Art. 4:102   Required standard of conduct
(1) The required standard of conduct is that of the reasonable person in the circumstances, and depends, in particular, on the nature and value of the protected interest involved, the dangerousness of the activity, the expertise to be expected of a person carrying it on, the foreseeability of the damage, the relationship of proximity or special reliance between those involved, as well as the availability and the costs of precautionary or alternative methods.

(2) The above standard may be adjusted when due to age, mental or physical disability or due to extraordinary circumstances the person cannot be expected to conform to it.

(3) Rules which prescribe or forbid certain conduct have to be considered when establishing the required standard of conduct.

Art. 4:103   Duty to protect others from damage

A duty to act positively to protect others from damage may exist if law so provides, or if the actor creates or controls a dangerous situation, or when there is a special relationship between parties or when the seriousness of the harm on the one side and the ease of avoiding the damage on the other side point towards such a duty.

Section 2   Reversal of the burden of proving fault

Art. 4:201   Reversal of the burden of proving fault in general

(1) The burden of proving fault may be reversed in light of the gravity of the danger presented by the activity.

(2) The gravity of the danger is determined according to the seriousness of possible damage in such cases as well as the likelihood that such damage might actually occur.

Art. 4:202   Enterprise Liability

(1) A person pursuing a lasting enterprise for economic or professional purposes who uses auxiliaries or technical equipment is liable for any harm caused by a defect of such enterprise or of its output unless he proves that he has conformed to the required standard of conduct.

(2) "Defect" is any deviation from standards that are reasonably to be expected from the enterprise or from its products or services.

Chapter 5   Strict liability

Art. 5:101   Abnormally dangerous activities

(1) A person who carries on an abnormally dangerous activity is strictly liable for damage characteristic to the risk presented by the activity and resulting from it.

(2) An activity is abnormally dangerous if
> (a) it creates a foreseeable and highly significant risk of damage even when all due care is exercised in its management and
> (b) it is not a matter of common usage.

(3) A risk of damage may be significant having regard to the seriousness or the likelihood of the damage.

(4) This Article does not apply to an activity which is specifically subjected to strict liability by any other provision of these Principles or any other national law or international convention.

Art. 5:102   Other strict liabilities

(1) National laws can provide for further categories of strict liability for dangerous activities even if the activity is not abnormally dangerous.

(2) Unless national law provides otherwise, additional categories of strict liability can be found by analogy to other sources of comparable risk of damage.

Chapter 6   Liability for others

Art. 6:101   Liability for minors or mentally disabled persons

A person in charge of another who is a minor or subject to mental disability is liable for damage caused by the other unless the person in charge shows that he has conformed to the required standard of conduct in supervision.

Art. 6:102   Liability for auxiliaries

(1) A person is liable for damage caused by his auxiliaries acting within the scope of their functions provided that they violated the required standard of conduct.

(2) An independent contractor is not regarded as an auxiliary for the purposes of this Article.

TITLE IV   DEFENCES

Chapter 7   Defences in general

Art. 7:101   Defences based on justifications

(1) Liability can be excluded if and to the extent that the actor acted legitimately

    (a) in defence of his own protected interest against an unlawful attack (self-defence),

    (b) under necessity,

    (c) because the help of the authorities could not be obtained in time (self-help),

    (d) with the consent of the victim, or where the latter has assumed the risk of being harmed, or

    (e) by virtue of lawful authority, such as a licence.

(2) Whether liability is excluded depends upon the weight of these justifications on the one hand and the conditions of liability on the other.

(3) In extraordinary cases, liability may instead be reduced.

Art. 7:102   Defences against strict liability

(1) Strict liability can be excluded or reduced if the injury was caused by an unforeseeable and irresistible

    (a) force of nature (force majeure), or

    (b) conduct of a third party.

(2) Whether strict liability is excluded or reduced, and if so, to what extent, depends upon the weight of the external influence on the one hand and the scope of liability (Article 3:201) on the other.

(3) When reduced according to paragraph (1)(b), strict liability and any liability of the third party are solidary in accordance with Article 9:101(1)(b).

Chapter 8   Contributory conduct or activity

Art. 8:101   Contributory conduct or activity of the victim

(1) Liability can be excluded or reduced to such extent as is considered just having regard to the victim's contributory fault and to any other matters which would be relevant to establish or reduce liability of the victim if he were the tortfeasor.

(2) Where damages are claimed with respect to the death of a person, his conduct or activity excludes or reduces liability according to para. 1.

(3) The contributory conduct or activity of an auxiliary of the victim excludes or reduces the damages recoverable by the latter according to para. 1.

TITLE V   MULTIPLE TORTFEASORS

Chapter 9   Multiple Tortfeasors

Art 9:101   Solidary and several liability: relation between victim and multiple tortfeasors

(1) Liability is solidary where the whole or a distinct part of the damage suffered by the victim is attributable to two or more persons. Liability is solidary where:

    (a) a person knowingly participates in or instigates or encourages wrongdoing by others which causes damage to the victim; or

    (b) one person's independent behaviour or activity causes damage to the victim and the same damage is also attributable to another person;

    (c) a person is responsible for damage caused by an auxiliary in circumstances where the auxiliary is also liable.

(2) Where persons are subject to solidary liability, the victim may claim full compensation from any one or more of them, provided that the victim may not recover more than the full amount of the damage suffered by him.

(3) Damage is the same damage for the purposes of paragraph (1)(b) above when there is no reasonable basis for attributing only part of it to each of a number of persons liable to the victim. For this purpose it is for the person asserting that the damage is not the same to show that it is not. Where there is such a basis, liability is several, that is to say, each person is liable to the victim only for the part of the damage attributable to him.

Art 9:102   Relation between persons subject to solidary liability

(1) A person subject to solidary liability may recover a contribution from any other person liable to the victim in respect of the same damage. This right is without prejudice to any contract between them determining the allocation of the loss or to any statutory provision or to any right to recover by reason of subrogation [cessio legis] or on the basis of unjust enrichment.

(2) Subject to paragraph (3) of this Article, the amount of the contribution shall be what is considered just in the light of the relative responsibility for the damage of the persons liable, having regard to their respective degrees of fault and to any other matters which are relevant to establish or reduce their liability. A contribution may amount to full indemnification. If it is not possible to determine the relative responsibility of the persons liable they are to be treated as equally responsible.

(3) Where a person is liable for damage done by an auxiliary under Article 9:101 he is to be treated as bearing the entire share of the responsibility attributable to the auxiliary for the purposes of contribution between him and any tortfeasor other than the auxiliary.

(4) The obligation to make contribution is several, that is to say, the person subject to it is liable only for his apportioned share of responsibility for the damage under this Article; but where it is not possible to enforce a judgment for contribution against one person liable his share is to be reallocated among the other persons liable in proportion to their responsibility.

TITLE VI   REMEDIES

Chapter 10   Damages

Section 1   Damages in general

Art. 10:101   Nature and purpose of damages

Damages are a money payment to compensate the victim, that is to say, to restore him, so far as money can, to the position he would have been in if the wrong complained of had not been committed. Damages also serve the aim of preventing harm.

Art. 10:102   Lump sum or periodical payments

Damages are awarded in a lump sum or as periodical payments as appropriate with particular regard to the interests of the victim.

Art. 10:103   Benefits gained through the damaging event

When determining the amount of damages benefits which the injured party gains through the damaging event are to be taken into account unless this cannot be reconciled with the purpose of the benefit.

Art. 10:104   Restoration in kind

Instead of damages, restoration in kind can be claimed by the injured party as far as it is possible and not too burdensome to the other party.

Section 2   Pecuniary damage

Art. 10:201   Nature and determination of pecuniary damage

Recoverable pecuniary damage is a diminution of the victim's patrimony caused by the damaging event. Such damage is generally determined as concretely as possible but it may be determined abstractly when appropriate, for example by reference to a market value.

Art. 10:202   Personal injury and death

(1) In the case of personal injury, which includes injury to bodily health and to mental health amounting to a recognised illness, pecuniary damage includes loss of income, impairment of earning capacity (even if unaccompanied by any loss of income) and reasonable expenses, such as the cost of medical care.

(2) In the case of death, persons such as family members whom the deceased maintained or would have maintained if death had not occurred are treated as having suffered recoverable damage to the extent of loss of that support.

Art. 10:203   Loss, destruction and damage of things

(1) Where a thing is lost, destroyed or damaged, the basic measure of damages is the value of the thing or the diminution in its value and for this purpose it is irrelevant whether the victim intends to replace or repair the thing. However, if the victim has replaced or repaired it (or will do so), he may recover the higher expenditure thereby incurred if it is reasonable to do so.

(2) Damages may also be awarded for loss of use of the thing, including consequential losses such as loss of business.

Section 3   Non-pecuniary damage

Art. 10:301   Non-pecuniary damage

(1) Considering the scope of its protection (Article 2:102), the violation of an interest may justify compensation of non-pecuniary damage. This is the case in particular where the victim has suffered personal injury; or injury to human dignity, liberty, or other personality rights. Non-pecuniary damage can also be the subject of compensation for persons having a close relationship with a victim suffering a fatal or very serious non-fatal injury.

(2) In general, in the assessment of such damages, all circumstances of the case, including the gravity, duration and consequences of the grievance, have to be taken into account. The degree of the tortfeasor's fault is to be taken into account only where it significantly contributes to the grievance of the victim.

(3) In cases of personal injury, non-pecuniary damage corresponds to the suffering of the victim and the impairment of his bodily or mental health. In assessing damages (including damages for persons having a close relationship to deceased or seriously injured victims) similar sums should be awarded for objectively similar losses.

Section 4   Reduction of damages

Art. 10:401   Reduction of damages

In an exceptional case, if in light of the financial situation of the parties full compensation would be an oppressive burden to the defendant, damages may be reduced. In deciding whether to do so, the basis of liability (Article 1:101), the scope of protection of the interest (Article 2:102) and the magnitude of the damage have to be taken into account in particular.

INDEX